SOCIAL PSYCHOLOGY

SOCIAL PSYCHOLOGY

3rd Edition

Eliot R. Smith

Indiana University, Bloomington

Diane M. Mackie

University of California, Santa Barbara

Psychology Press
Taylor & Francis Group
HOVE AND NEW YORK

Published in 2007 by
Psychology Press
Taylor & Francis Group
711 Third Avenue
New York, NY 10017
www.psypress.com

Published in Great Britain by
Psychology Press
Taylor & Francis Group
27 Church Road
Hove, East Sussex
BN3 2FA
www.psypress.com

Psychology Press is an imprint of the Taylor & Francis Group, an informa business

British Library Cataloguing in Publication Data
A catalogue record for this book is available from the British Library

Library of Congress Cataloging-in-Publication Data
Smith, Eliot R.
    Social psychology / Eliot R. Smith & Diane M. Mackie.—3rd ed.
        p. cm.
    Includes bibliographical references and index.
    1. Social psychology. I. Mackie, Diane M. II. Title.

    HM1033.S55 2006
    302—dc22   2006030037

ISBN10: 1–84169–408–8 (hbk)
ISBN10: 1–84169–409–6 (pbk)
ISBN13: 978–1–84169–408–5 (hbk)
ISBN13: 978–1–84169–409–2 (pbk)

Cover design by Sandra Heath
Typeset in India by Newgen Imaging Systems (P) Ltd.

About the Authors

Eliot Smith is Professor of Psychological and Brain Sciences at Indiana University, Bloomington and holds a Special Chair in the Department of Social Psychology at the Free University, Amsterdam, Netherlands. His research interests range widely, including person perception, prejudice and intergroup relations, political and social opinions, and situated and embodied cognition. He has published more than 100 scientific articles and chapters on these and other topics, and his work has been supported by research grants from the National Institute of Mental Health and the National Science Foundation. Professor Smith earned his B.A. and Ph.D. at Harvard University, and before moving to Bloomington held positions at the University of California, Riverside and at Purdue University. Besides this textbook, he has authored two books, *Beliefs about Inequality* (with James Kluegel) and *Research Methods in Social Relations* (6th ed., with Charles Judd and Louise Kidder), as well as editing *Beyond Prejudice: Differentiated Reactions to Social Groups* (with Diane Mackie). Among his professional honors are the Gordon Allport Intergroup Relations award in 1998, the Thomas M. Ostrom Award for contributions to social cognition in 2004, and the Society of Social and Personality Psychology's Theoretical Innovation Prize in 2005. He has been chair of a grant review committee at the National Institute of Mental Health, Associate Editor of *Journal of Personality and Social Psychology*, and most recently Editor of *Personality and Social Psychology Review*, the field's premier outlet for new theoretical developments. These positions have given him tremendous appreciation for the best work in every area of social psychology. Professor Smith is married to Pamela Grenfell Smith, a poet and storyteller. They take great joy in their grown-up children, who share their passions for world music, science fiction, and good cooking, but the big deal for them is their astonishingly accomplished first grandchild, Griffin James Hassett.

Diane M. Mackie is Professor of Psychology and Communication at the University of California, Santa Barbara, where she has been honored with a Distinguished Teaching Award and listed as one of "Ten Terrific Teachers" by UCSB students. Professor Mackie grew up in New Zealand, received her B.A. and M.A. at the University of Auckland, New Zealand, and then worked as a researcher at the University of Geneva, Switzerland. She received her Ph.D. in Social Psychology from Princeton University in 1984. These opportunities to become steeped in both European and North American traditions of social psychology are reflected in her interests in integrating different perspectives and approaches both in her research and in this textbook. The author of more than 100 articles, chapters, and books on persuasion, social influence, group interaction, and intergroup relations, Professor Mackie is also co-editor of *Affect, Cognition, and Stereotyping: Interactive Processes in Group Perception* (with David Hamilton) as well as *Beyond Prejudice: Differentiated Reactions to Social Groups* (with Eliot Smith). Reflecting her broad interests, Professor Mackie has served as Associate Editor for *Personality and Social Psychology Review*, *Group Processes and Intergroup Relations*, and *Personality and Social Psychology Bulletin*, as well as on the editorial boards of almost all of the major social psychological journals. Both the National Science Foundation and the National Institutes of Health have funded her research. A fellow of the Association for Psychological Science, Society for Personality and Social Psychology, and Society for the Psychological Study of Social Issues, Professor Mackie includes among her professional honors receiving the Western Psychological Association's Outstanding Researcher Award in 1992, being named the Rocky Mountain Psychological Association's Psi Chi Distinguished Lecturer in 2000, and winning the Gordon Allport Intergroup Relations Award in 1998. However by far her greatest (and busiest) honor is being Mom to a terrific 10-year-old sax playing shooting guard, Alex, and a sensational 7-year-old artist and soccer star, Nico.

*To Our Children
Miranda Hassett,
Thomas Smith, Alex Mackie,
and
Nico Mackie*

Contents in Brief

Social Psychology in Applied Settings

This brief index provides a ready reference to major application sections integrated within the chapters. Other shorter discussions of applied topics also appear throughout the book.

Contents

3 Perceiving Individuals 57

4 The Self 95

Preface

"No wise fish would go anywhere without a porpoise" claims *Alice in Wonderland*'s Mock Turtle. "Why, if a fish came to ME, and told me he was going on a journey, I should say 'With what porpoise?' " Had the Mock Turtle asked us our purpose in undertaking this textbook writing journey, the answer would have been simple. We wanted to convey to an undergraduate audience some of our excitement about and appreciation for the richness and variety of human social behavior, by presenting social psychology in a conceptually integrated way. Both of us have felt frustration at textbooks that portray social behavior as a list of interesting but unrelated phenomena explained by numerous never-to-be-heard-from-again theories. We have felt disappointment when laboratory studies are presented in isolation from "real world" settings—the courtroom, school, supermarket, or hospital—where real applications take place. And we have been concerned that the very special nature of social psychology as the interface between the individual and the social world becomes lost in treatments that emphasize one of these aspects over the other.

Our purpose, then, has been integration. Our goal is to present both social behavior and the science that studies it in a conceptually and thematically integrated way. We want to show students not just the wonderfully diverse *what* of social behavior, but the impressively orderly and organized *how* and *why* of it. Our pursuit of these goals is reflected in three ways of weaving together the content of this book.

Three Types of Integration

INTEGRATION OF DIVERSE TOPICS THROUGH UNIFYING PRINCIPLES. Eight basic principles that apply to social behavior emerge and re-emerge in the text. The two most fundamental ones are that people construct their social reality and that social influence pervades social life. Simply put, people help define their social environments at the same time their social environments influence them. In addition, we structure our discussion of people's interaction with their social world by introducing three overarching motivational principles and three processing principles that direct and determine thoughts, feelings, and actions. The powerful effects of these principles give coherence to our descriptions of research findings and theoretical approaches in every area of social psychology. By focusing on these core ideas, students can enhance their conceptual understanding of social psychology and can take away from the course knowledge that is applicable to their everyday lives.

INTEGRATION OF THE SOCIAL AND THE COGNITIVE. Our discipline was founded—indeed broke away from its parent field of psychology—on the idea that people's behavior depends on their perceptions and interpretations of social situations. Recent research in social cognition has started to spell out in detail how these cognitive processes operate. But social psychologists are also aware that social motives, interpersonal relationships, and emotional attachments to group membership guide and direct everything people do. The intertwining of social processes with cognitive processes is the essential tension of human social behavior, and we have made it a central theme of our textbook. The theme is reflected in the social and cognitive nature of the unifying principles. It is reflected again in the research data we describe: we have made a special effort to bring together the contributions of both North American and European social psychologists, who have emphasized somewhat different aspects of the cognitive/social interface. Finally, it is mirrored in our special focus on cultural, ethnic, and national similarities and differences in social behavior.

INTEGRATION OF BASIC SCIENCE AND APPLICATIONS. Historically, social psychology has focused simultaneously on advancing theory and addressing important social problems. In our book we stress that the same underlying processes of social perception, social influence, and social relations operate in the experimental laboratory, field research, and people's everyday lives. In each chapter we describe the practical implications of the theory and research being discussed. We do so with examples such as:

- A discussion of polygraph usage next to a section on nonverbal cues to deception.

- An overview of jury decision-making in the chapter on group influence.

- A discussion of how members of socially devalued groups handle negative evaluations in the workplace, as part of the presentation of the effects of group membership.

- An account of subliminal advertising following the description of persuasion and counterargument.

These applications should stimulate students to think about the breadth and generality of the underlying processes, reinforcing the idea that ours is an integrated field.

In formulating and pursuing these integrative goals we have been inspired by the example set by Krech and Crutchfield's famous 1948 social psychology text. Despite the huge differences between the social psychology of their day and ours, their approach and ours are similar in several key ways. Most fundamentally, Krech and Crutchfield also aimed at a systematic, integrated treatment. They stressed the linkages between basic and applied research: "The basic guiding principle has been that a theoretically sound social psychology is also a practically valid and immediately useful social psychology" (p. vii). Finally, they emphasized the role of both social and cognitive processes in social behavior, drawing particularly on what was the most active area of cognitive psychology in their time: the study of perception. The ideas presented in the Krech and Crutchfield text had a profound influence on those who taught us social psychology and who instilled in us in turn a passion for combining, intertwining, and integrating the social and the cognitive.

The impetus for an integrated treatment of social psychology is the same today as it was two generations ago. There is an esthetic pleasure in showing students how the diverse findings of our field fit together in an intellectually coherent way. As people who care deeply about our field, we take pride in demonstrating social psychology's growth as a science and the accumulation of knowledge about social behavior. The integrative enterprise also reveals the existence of a number of fascinating yet underresearched areas. For example, huge amounts of research have examined the processes by which attitudes affect behavior. Though the effect of *norms* on behavior is equally great—and arguably greater, only a scattering of existing studies address the processes by which norms have this effect.

However, the most important benefits of integration are pedagogical: showing students social psychology as an integrated whole, rather than as a list of topics that happen to share a label, makes our field both *easier to understand* and *more applicable*. As the same few principles emerge again and again in diverse topic areas, these ideas serve as a coherent organizing framework for particular findings and theories. Many studies of science education support the integrated approach. Science is most effectively taught to students of all ages not by cramming them full of "facts" but by stressing integrative themes, presenting findings in their context, and showing theories together with their applications (Tobias, 1990; Celis, 1993). Thus, all students should find our text enjoyable and understandable. We believe that our approach will enable them to do well in the course and also to take away ideas that will help them to understand themselves and others better throughout their lives.

Organization of the Text

After two chapters that introduce the field of social psychology and the conceptual basis of its research methods, the remaining chapters are organized into three broad topic areas that build one on another: social perception, social influence, and social relations. Within each of these areas are four chapters.

In terms of the book's integrative principles, the material on social perception (Chapters 3–6) naturally emphasizes the role of cognitive processes, but it continually reinforces the idea that all cognition is socially influenced—even such basic and personal ideas as what we think about the self. The section on social influence (Chapters 7–10) naturally focuses on the role of social processes, but it stresses that the effects of social processes are also mediated through cognitive processes—for example, the amount of effort people devote to processing persuasive arguments. Finally, the section on social relations (Chapters 11–14) illustrates the ways that social and cognitive processes are inextricably intertwined as they influence the ways we get to know and like other people, cooperate in groups, and harm or help others. The book ends with a brief Epilogue that summarizes the major themes and reflects on some of their interrelationships and applications.

Although this organization seems to us to enhance the thematic presentation of concepts and topics, the integrated nature of the material allows instructors considerable flexibility in organizing the course. The instructors' manual suggests several different teaching sequences that emphasize different approaches to the material—without surrendering the advantages of integration. For example, those who wish to focus on the "social" before the "psychology" will find that the social influence section can easily precede the social perception chapters.

In keeping with our integrated approach, there are no separate chapters on "law," "business," or "education." Instead of relegating these interesting topics to a "back of the bus" position, we have integrated applications of social psychological theories and research results throughout the book. In this way, we hope to reinforce and strengthen the idea that exactly the same processes studied by researchers in their labs operate in applied settings to produce socially significant effects. Further, we operate with a broad definition of what is "applied," considering not only major societal institutions like law and business, but also such topics as personal relationships and divorce, media violence and aggression, social support and health, cooperation in solving environmental problems, "choking under pressure" in sports, conflicts in international relations, and the effectiveness of advertising. Text sections focusing on such applied topics are flagged by blue boxes before their headings. For the convenience of instructors who wish to devote lecture time specifically to summing up the implications of social psychology for one or more applied areas, and for students with a special interest in a particular area, a topical index to applications is on page ix.

Features to Enhance Learning

Our text has a number of special features to aid the student's learning.

FOCUS ON PRINCIPLES. The emergence and re-emergence of the basic principles are noted by the repetition of key words or phrases designed to activate and re-activate these concepts in students' minds. To further the idea that the same principles recur again and again, we provide margin references to related points in other chapters. These references direct students who are interested in conceptual parallels between different topics to look either forward or back in the text to find them, citing specific pages.

INTEGRATIVE REFLECTIONS. The end of the narrative of each chapter is devoted to *Concluding Comments*, our reflections on some larger issues raised by the chapter, on interrelations among chapters, or on special aspects of the way the principles play themselves out in the chapter. In these sections we step back a bit from the details of a particular topic, and place it in its larger context, both in theoretical terms and in its relation to everyday life.

ORGANIZATIONAL FEATURES. Each chapter opens with an outline of the chapter's main headings, followed by an introduction to the key problems and topics to be discussed. In addition, each major section within the chapter begins with a short preview to give the reader an idea of what is coming. Such advance organizers provide a simple structure that helps students understand material as they read it for the first time. For example, by identifying the main ideas of the section, the preview allows students to focus their initial reading on grasping those ideas rather than becoming sidetracked by details.

GRAPHICAL FEATURES. In line with our emphasis on the principles that underlie the diversity of behavior, explanations are often supplemented by graphical flow-charts, representations of key processes that demonstrate how and why such behavior arises. Results from key studies are also shown in the form of easy-to-understand bar charts.

OTHER FEATURES. A running glossary defines the most significant terms and concepts on the pages on which they occur. All entries are repeated in a cumulative glossary at the end of the book for convenient reference. Finally, the end of each chapter also features a verbal summary that includes the key terms, for review and reference.

Supplements that Accompany the Text

The *Resources for Teaching Social Psychology, 3rd Edition* CD-ROM includes the *Instructor's Manual*, written by Angela Lipsitz of Northern Kentucky University (and reviewed for this new edition by Holly Carvalho). This provides extended outlines, lecture suggestions, discussion topics, classroom demonstrations, handouts, and lists of audiovisual materials for each chapter of the text. To help develop student appreciation of the integrated approach to social behavior, this manual includes extended coverage of how the basic principles are manifest in each chapter, and how each chapter builds on and develops themes from earlier chapters. There are also suggestions for teaching the material in different sequences, and for using the text to provide an extended focus on specific areas of application. In addition, the manual suggests several ways in which the issues of differences within and between cultures discussed throughout the text might be highlighted.

The CD-ROM also includes a test bank of multiple-choice questions prepared by Marielle Stel and Raymond Smeets of Leiden University. Questions emphasize concept acquisition, understanding of underlying processes and principles, integration of material within a chapter, and application of chapter material to everyday situations, as well as assessing factual knowledge. Psychology Press provides both a printed test bank and a computerized test-generation system that use these questions as a data base.

A full chapter-by-chapter PowerPoint lecture course written by Eliot Smith and Diane Mackie is also included on the CD-ROM. Lecture slides are highlighted with a color-coded key to illustrate themes, key terms, and applied issues.

The *SocSLP* (Social Psychology Student Learning Program), written by Marielle Stel and Raymond Smeets of Leiden University, is a unique online resource for students. Each chapter from *Social Psychology 3rd edition* is condensed into a summary version, providing an effective set of revision notes with page cross-references to this textbook. These online chapters also provide an integrative framework for other interactive multimedia materials in the *SocSLP* including interactive exercises, active reference links to journal articles, revision question test banks, case studies, research activities, chapter overviews in flow chart format, and links to related web sites.

All supplements that accompany the text are also available in Dutch.

Acknowledgments

As the Mock Turtle no doubt knew, it takes more than just a porpoise to allow wise fish to complete a journey. We owe thanks to many, many people who have helped us not just to make the journey but to become wise fish. First, our friends, students, and colleagues over the years have provided advice and social support—Chris Agnew, Jim Blascovich, Don Carlston, Heather Claypool, Nancy Collins, Riki Conrey, Alice Eagly, Amber Garcia, Patricia Garcia-Prieto, Dave Hamilton, Ed Hirt, Heejung Kim, Janice Kelly, Zoe Kinias, Stan Klein, Angie Maitner, Brenda Major, Dan Miller, Wes Moons, Devon Ray, Missy Ryan, BJ Rydell, Charlie Seger, Sarah Queller, David Sherman, Jim Sherman, Zak Tormala, and Duane Wegener were particularly important to us. The many undergraduate students who participated in classroom tests of various drafts of the manuscript were also extremely helpful to us—even their occasional puzzled looks provided useful feedback. The all-engrossing process of writing a book always becomes an imposition on family, friends, and companions. We are grateful to Pamela Smith, Thomas Smith, Alex Mackie, and Nico Mackie for putting up with us and giving us perspective on our work. We promise to be in a better mood from now on, to talk about something else every once in a while, and to stop trying to use them as examples in the book.

We have been lucky indeed to have worked with the many dedicated and talented people at Psychology Press. We began with the conviction that a textbook taking an integrated approach to social psychology could be written. We thank J. George Owen, good friend and incomparable next-door neighbor, for encouraging us in this process and Gün Semin for steering us toward Psychology Press.

Many of our colleagues and friends generously gave their time to review portions of this text. We are particularly grateful to those who have used the previous editions in their classrooms over the years, and for the comments, suggestions, and encouragement that they have passed along to us. Christopher Agnew and Frederica Conrey were especially helpful in the process of revising specific chapters for the third edition. To all those who reviewed various portions of the manuscript, and whose insightful comments have often gently shaped and smoothed the ideas we present here, our heartfelt thanks:

Christopher R. Agnew, *Purdue University*
John Bargh, *Yale University*
Mark Bennett, *University of Dundee*
Leonard Berkowitz, *University of Wisconsin-Madison*
Hart Blanton, *University of North Carolina, Chapel Hill*
William Michael Brown, *Rutgers University*

Russell Clark, *University of North Texas*
Frederica Conrey, *Indiana University, Bloomington*
John F. Dovidio, *University of Connecticut*
Klaus Fiedler, *University of Heidelberg*
Jens Förster, *International University Bremen*
Michael Furr, *Wake Forest University*
Roger Giner-Sorolla, *The University of Kent at Canterbury*
Rosanna E. Guadagno, *University of Alabama*
P.J. Henry, *DePaul University*
Hubert J.M. Hermans, *Radboud University of Nijmegen*
Guido Hertel, *University of Wuerzburg*
Jolanda Jetten, *University of Exeter*
Shinobu Kitayama, *University of Michigan*
Barbara Krahé, *University of Potsdam*
Joachim Krueger, *Brown University*
Tom Postmes, *University of Exeter*
Fabio Sani, *University of Dundee*
Karl E. Scheibe, *Wesleyan University*
Steven J. Scher, *Eastern Illinois University*
Norbert Schwarz, *University of Michigan*
Gün R. Semin, *Free University, Amsterdam*
Steve Stroessner, *Columbia University*
David Trafimow, *New Mexico State University*
Annette Thomson, *Open University, and University of Glasgow, Crichton Campus*
Mark Van Vugt, *University of Kent at Canterbury*
Eva Walther, *University of Heidelberg*
Duane T. Wegener, *Purdue University*

Finally, we would like to thank each other for the many benefits of co-authorship. Through our collaboration on each section and sometimes each sentence of the text, we believe we have accomplished a sort of integration through teamwork. We learned to respect and admire each other's different strengths and talents, to appreciate each other's different views of the field, and to blame each other when deadlines were missed! We also became much better friends in the process.

To The Student

As you begin your study of social psychology, you may be wondering what this field is all about, and how it relates to your own personal experiences. You are in for a treat, because it is a fascinating field that has much to do with you. Our goal in writing this book is to convey some of the excitement and satisfaction that comes with understanding more about your own and others' social behavior.

One of the reasons that social psychology is so fascinating is that the limitless variety of social behavior we see around us every day can be understood as effects of a few basic principles. Rather than asking you to memorize a large number of un-related ideas, we have tried to write a book that makes those basic principles easy for you to *see*, *understand*, *remember*, and *apply* in your own life. We have sought to accomplish this by

- Clearly *identifying* the most basic principles so that you can distinguish them from the many interesting (but less important) facts, studies, and comments.

- *Illustrating* the way the basic principles apply to a wide range of situations, including research studies and people's everyday lives.

In our years of studying and teaching, we have found that certain ways of approaching written material can greatly facilitate learning. Based on that experience, we have included a number of features in each chapter to assist you. The basic premise underlying these features is that *effective studying and learning is an active process*. You won't get much out of this or any other textbook if you try to rush through a whole chapter rapidly and passively, the way you might approach a mystery novel. You should divide up the chapter into chunks, read each chunk more than once, and reflect on what you have read. Here are some suggestions on how to do that.

- Start by reading the chapter title and looking at the outline of headings. Read the chapter introduction. Browse through the photos, cartoons, figures, and tables. This process will give you a general overview of the chapter's content.

- Every chapter contains several major sections. Work on one section at a time, paying particular attention to the *previews* (brief shaded sections that follow major headings), a unique feature that offers a capsule survey of the information that follows. By giving you an idea of what is coming, the previews make it easier to understand the material the first time you read it. The previews will tell you the main ideas of the section, to help you avoid getting bogged down in details or mistaking a subsidiary point for the key idea.

- Keep alert for appearances of the basic principles. By focusing on these core ideas, you will be able to build an integrated and coherent picture of social psychology's research findings and theories. To remind you of the basic principles, we use the same key words or phrases whenever an example of their operation arises.

- Follow up on the *margin references* whenever they interest you or when you are not sure you remember an idea or argument. This feature is designed to remind you of related points elsewhere in the book and to point out similarities or parallels between chapters, helping you to link new material to what you already know.

- The important terms and concepts of the field are presented in **boldface** and are defined in the margin of the page on which they appear. Psychologists use technical terms for precision in writing. Don't try to memorize their definitions on first reading; it is more important first to understand the gist of what you are reading. You will find it helpful, however, to learn these terms on second reading and to review them when studying for an exam. An alphabetical glossary of terms and definitions can be found at the back of the book.

• After you have finished studying each of the chapter's main sections, read the concluding comments and the summary. If anything in the summary seems unfamiliar or unclear, reread the relevant section of the text.

Finally, we urge you to enjoy yourself. Think about what you are reading and what it means for your own life, and for society at large. Ask questions about what you read, and pose your own questions about what issues need to be thought about next by social psychologists—perhaps by you! We think social psychology is fascinating. We hope that what you learn here will convince you of that too.

How To Use This Book

This new edition of *Social Psychology* has been thoughtfully designed to present textbook material in a user-friendly manner. Eliot Smith and Diane Mackie have provided a fascinating mix of broad concepts and specific examples. Our challenge as the publisher is to present them to you in a clean, easy-to-read format that draws attention to important information but does not distract from the important framework the authors have created. These pages illustrate some of the most important features that should be utilized when teaching or reading this book.

Theme tables at the end of each chapter summarize the most important applications of the basic principles

of our individual abilities, preferences, and talents enables us to choose the partners, pastimes, and professions that suit us best. It lets us know where we fit in the social world and provides a starting point in any attempt at change or improvement. But psychologists know that it is not enough to "know thyself." Self-esteem is equally central in our lives. Viewing the self as both good and in control—even in exaggerated ways—protects our emotional and physical well-being as we cope with inconsistencies, failures, and stress. Whenever we think about the self, we are faced with two, sometimes conflicting, motives: enhancing the self and accurately evaluating the self.

The dual needs for accurate self-knowledge and positive self-esteem play themselves out in a variety of ways that were discussed throughout this chapter. Sometimes we seek accurate assessments of the self; at other times we engage in biased searches or interpretations to come up with self-enhancing information. Sometimes we compare ourselves with similar others and sometimes with others who are worse off than we are. Sometimes we choose our behaviors to accurately reflect the person we believe we are, but at other times we try to create a positive impression of ourselves. Even the ways we defend ourselves against such threats as negative feedback, obvious shortcomings, and large and small stressors provoke the same dilemma. The warm glow of positive thinking infuses us with strength to clear life's many hurdles, but escaping into a fantasy world of self-enhancement can just as easily set us up for a fall. Taking negative feedback at face value can help us to deal constructively with, and possibly to overcome, our failures and shortcomings. But it can also be painful.

Does this mean we are caught in a no-win situation, forced to make trade-offs between reality and illusion, happiness and depression? Are our choices limited to being eternal optimists, happy but out of touch, or hard realists, on top of the facts but miserable because of it? Fortunately, we have other options. The recipe for a healthy sense of self calls for both accurate self-knowledge and protective self-enhancement, in just the right amounts at just the right times. Weighing these ingredients may be the most important aspect of constructing and maintaining the self. The correct measure of self-enhancement keeps our spirits high and our body healthy, while a judicious amount of self-assessment keeps our goals realistic and our efforts focused in the best direction. A good dollop of self-evaluation tells us what we need to do, a splash of self-enhancement gives us the courage to do it.

CHAPTER 4 THEMES

- **Construction of Reality**
  We construct an impression of the self, based on a multitude of cues.

- **Pervasiveness of Social Influence**
  Our perceptions of other people and their reactions to us pervasively influence our self-concept and self-esteem.

- **Striving for Mastery**
  Perceiving that we control our environment helps mental well-being and physical health.

- **Valuing Me and Mine**
  Self-enhancing biases shape our self-concept and elevate self-esteem.

- **Conservatism**
  Once formed, the self-concept is resistant to change and well defended against threats.

- **Accessibility**
  The self-concept and self-esteem depend on information and experiences that come readily to mind.

SUMMARY

Constructing the Self-Concept: What We Know About Ourselves. People construct the **self-concept** in much the same way that they form impressions of others, using similar types of information and similar interpretive processes. People often infer their own characteristics from their observed behaviors, as **self-perception theory** notes. They also use thoughts and feelings and other people's reactions to form opinions about themselves. Finally, **social comparison theory** describes how people compare themselves to others to learn what characteristics make them unique.

Despite the general similarity of the ways people learn about themselves and others, self-knowledge is richer and more detailed than knowledge about others. People can observe themselves in more situations and have better access to private

Chapter summaries recall the major points stressed in the text, and synthesize specific concepts into larger themes

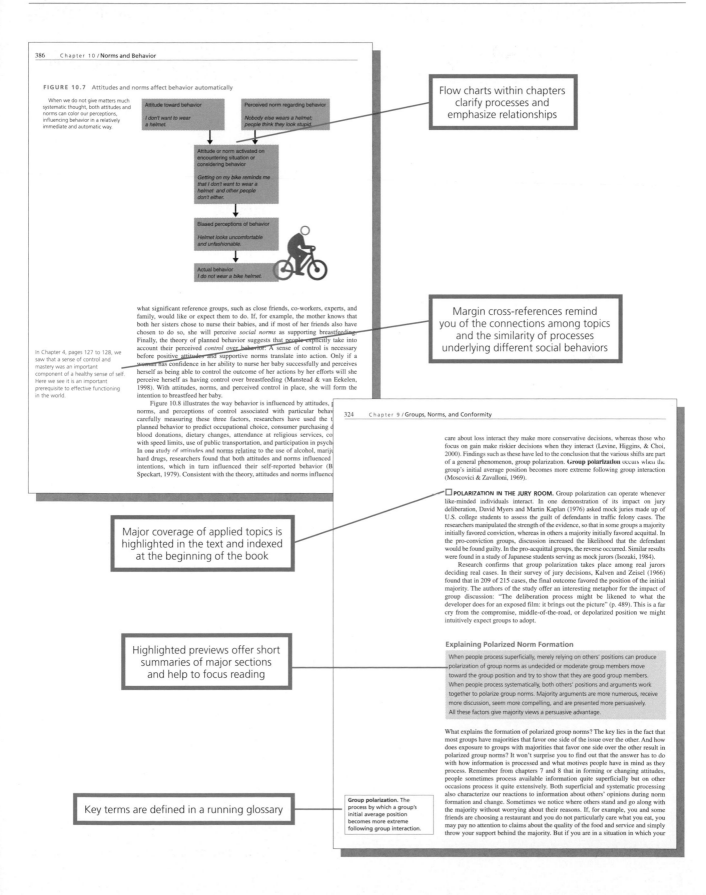

386   Chapter 10 / Norms and Behavior

FIGURE 10.7   Attitudes and norms affect behavior automatically

When we do not give matters much systematic thought, both attitudes and norms can color our perceptions, influencing behavior in a relatively immediate and automatic way.

Attitude toward behavior

I don't want to wear a helmet.

Perceived norm regarding behavior

Nobody else wears a helmet; people think they look stupid.

Attitude or norm activated on encountering situation or considering behavior

Getting on my bike reminds me that I don't want to wear a helmet and other people don't either.

Biased perceptions of behavior

Helmet looks uncomfortable and unfashionable.

Actual behavior

I do not wear a bike helmet.

Flow charts within chapters clarify processes and emphasize relationships

what significant reference groups, such as close friends, co-workers, experts, and family, would like or expect them to do. If, for example, the mother knows that both her sisters chose to nurse their babies, and if most of her friends also have chosen to do so, she will perceive *social norms* as supporting breastfeeding. Finally, the theory of planned behavior suggests that people explicitly take into account their perceived *control* over behavior. A sense of control is necessary before positive attitudes and supportive norms translate into action. Only if a woman has confidence in her ability to nurse her baby successfully and perceives herself as being able to control the outcome of her actions by her efforts will she perceive herself as having control over breastfeeding (Manstead & van Eekelen, 1998). With attitudes, norms, and perceived control in place, she will form the intention to breastfeed her baby.

In Chapter 4, pages 127 to 128, we saw that a sense of control and mastery was an important component of a healthy sense of self. Here we see it is an important prerequisite to effective functioning in the world.

Figure 10.8 illustrates the way behavior is influenced by attitudes, norms, and perceptions of control associated with particular behavior. By carefully measuring these three factors, researchers have used the theory of planned behavior to predict occupational choice, consumer purchasing decisions, blood donations, dietary changes, attendance at religious services, compliance with speed limits, use of public transportation, and participation in psychotherapy. In one study of attitudes and norms relating to the use of alcohol, marijuana, and hard drugs, researchers found that both attitudes and norms influenced intentions, which in turn influenced their self-reported behavior (Bentler & Speckart, 1979). Consistent with the theory, attitudes and norms influenced

Margin cross-references remind you of the connections among topics and the similarity of processes underlying different social behaviors

324   Chapter 9 / Groups, Norms, and Conformity

care about loss interact they make more conservative decisions, whereas those who focus on gain make riskier decisions when they interact (Levine, Higgins, & Choi, 2000). Findings such as these have led to the conclusion that the various shifts are part of a general phenomenon, group polarization. **Group polarization** occurs when the group's initial average position becomes more extreme following group interaction (Moscovici & Zavalloni, 1969).

☐ **POLARIZATION IN THE JURY ROOM.** Group polarization can operate whenever like-minded individuals interact. In one demonstration of its impact on jury deliberation, David Myers and Martin Kaplan (1976) asked mock juries made up of U.S. college students to assess the guilt of defendants in traffic felony cases. The researchers manipulated the strength of the evidence, so that in some groups a majority initially favored conviction, whereas in others a majority initially favored acquittal. In the pro-conviction groups, discussion increased the likelihood that the defendant would be found guilty. In the pro-acquittal groups, the reverse occurred. Similar results were found in a study of Japanese students serving as mock jurors (Isozaki, 1984).

Research confirms that group polarization takes place among real jurors deciding real cases. In their survey of jury decisions, Kalven and Zeisel (1966) found that in 209 of 215 cases, the final outcome favored the position of the initial majority. The authors of the study offer an interesting metaphor for the impact of group discussion: "The deliberation process might be likened to what the developer does for an exposed film: it brings out the picture" (p. 489). This is a far cry from the compromise, middle-of-the-road, or depolarized position we might intuitively expect groups to adopt.

Explaining Polarized Norm Formation

When people process superficially, merely relying on others' positions can produce polarization of group norms as undecided or moderate group members move toward the group position and try to show that they are good group members. When people process systematically, both others' positions and arguments work together to polarize group norms. Majority arguments are more numerous, receive more discussion, seem more compelling, and are presented more persuasively. All these factors give majority views a persuasive advantage.

What explains the formation of polarized group norms? The key lies in the fact that most groups have majorities that favor one side of the issue over the other. And how does exposure to groups with majorities that favor one side over the other result in polarized group norms? It won't surprise you to find out that the answer has to do with how information is processed and what motives people have in mind as they process. Remember from chapters 7 and 8 that in forming or changing attitudes, people sometimes process available information quite superficially but on other occasions process it quite extensively. Both superficial and systematic processing also characterize our reactions to information about others' opinions during norm formation and change. Sometimes we notice where others stand and go along with the majority without worrying about their reasons. If, for example, you and some friends are choosing a restaurant and you do not particularly care what you eat, you may pay no attention to claims about the quality of the food and service and simply throw your support behind the majority. But if you are in a situation in which your

Major coverage of applied topics is highlighted in the text and indexed at the beginning of the book

Highlighted previews offer short summaries of major sections and help to focus reading

Group polarization. The process by which a group's initial average position becomes more extreme following group interaction.

Key terms are defined in a running glossary

1

What Is Social Psychology?

I n the fall of 1951, Princeton University's undefeated football team played Dartmouth College in a particularly hard-fought game. The teams were long-term rivals, and the game started rough and went downhill from there. Penalties punctuated the game, and fights left players on both sides with serious injuries before Princeton finally won. One month later, two social psychologists asked Princeton and Dartmouth undergraduates to view a film of the game (Hastorf & Cantril, 1954). The responses were astonishing. Princeton fans and Dartmouth supporters reported seeing events so differently that they might have been watching different games. Princeton students saw a constant barrage of Dartmouth violence and poor sportsmanship, with Princeton players occasionally retaliating in self-defense. Dartmouth students rated the teams as equally aggressive but saw their battered team's infractions as understandable responses to brutal Princeton attacks. One Dartmouth alumnus who watched the film saw so few Dartmouth violations that he concluded he must have been sent an edited copy of the film.

Perhaps these findings are not really so astonishing if you consider that fans of opposing teams hardly ever agree on the impartiality of the umpiring. Similarly, partisan observers of political debates almost always proclaim their own candidate "the winner," and proud parents at the school music contest often disagree with the judges' decision. Yet consider the profound questions that these findings raise. If the world is objectively "out there" for all to see, how can observers reach such different conclusions about what seems to be the same event? Why do we so often end up seeing exactly what we expected to see, and how then can we decide what "really" happened? Can the same innocent feelings of belonging that make us see our team, our candidate, or our child in such positive terms also produce biased judgments, unfair decisions, and unequal treatment of others?

Thirty years after Hastorf and Cantril's study, researchers at Vanderbilt University asked two groups of students to consider the difficult issue of whether convicted criminals should be given probation as an alternative to imprisonment (Axsom, Yates, & Chaiken, 1987). One group of students had a special reason to be concerned with the issue: They had been led to believe that the probation policy might soon be introduced in their area. For the other group, the issue was merely academic—the policy was not being considered for their community. The researchers told the students that, to help them make up their minds, they would hear a tape of a local candidate speaking in favor of the issue at a political rally. What the students were not told was that the researchers had actually prepared four quite different tapes. On one tape, the candidate put forward compelling evidence in support of probation while an enthusiastic audience warmly applauded his words. On a second, the same effective presentation elicited scattered hisses, boos, and heckling from the audience. A third tape had the candidate giving rambling, specious, and disjointed arguments, which were met with enthusiastic applause from the audience. And on the fourth tape, the weak arguments were greeted by boos and hissing.

When the researchers polled the students whose interest in the probation issue was merely academic, the impact of the audience's taped response was clear. Students in this group who heard either of the tapes on which the audience greeted the candidate's position with enthusiasm adopted the position themselves, and those who heard the tapes on which the audience voiced disdain rejected the candidate's position. A completely different pattern of responses emerged among students who expected the issue to affect their community. These students focused on the content of the speech. They were swayed if they heard the candidate give cogent arguments but remained unpersuaded if the arguments were weak—regardless of the applause or hisses of the taped audience. Why were the reactions of other people so compelling to some students and so unimportant to others? Why did some participants "go with the flow" while others considered the issues carefully? Did some students care less than others about being right, or were all of the students trying to take different paths to the "truth?"

Like the Vanderbilt students, we are all bombarded daily by attempts to persuade us: advertising campaigns, paid political messages, even the cajoling of friends and family. Consider the last time you were persuaded by one of these attempts. What approach was used by the person who persuaded you? Did that person present you with the hard facts, or did he or she play on your emotions? If you were told that "everyone else" had already joined the parade, would you be more likely to go along or more likely to rebel? Or would it depend on the issue?

Questions like those raised by these studies lure social psychologists into their labs every day in search of reliable answers. Social psychology offers a special perspective on human behavior, because the social aspects of human behavior—the ways that people's thoughts and actions are affected by other people—can be both powerful and puzzling. Our goal in this book is to give you some insight into how people act, and why they act the way they do, by introducing you to some of the many questions social psychologists ask about social behavior, the ways they go about answering those questions, and the answers they have found. We know that you will find these questions intriguing and hope that the often surprising conclusions will make you want to delve more deeply into these compelling issues.

Our first step will be to provide a definition of social psychology: to chart out the territory we will be covering and to give you a glimpse of what makes the terrain so fascinating. We next describe how social psychology developed its special perspective on human behavior. Like other fields of human inquiry, contemporary social psychology is a product of its own history and of the history of the societies in which it developed. With a quick survey of the past behind us, we then map out the territory ahead. The final part of the chapter provides a sneak preview of the material we cover in the rest of this book. To help you find your way with confidence, we point out some signposts and landmarks to look for along the route.

A Definition of Social Psychology

Social psychology is the scientific study of the effects of social and cognitive processes on the way individuals perceive, influence, and relate to others. Notice that social psychology is defined as a science, that social psychologists are as keenly interested in underlying social and cognitive processes as they are in overt behavior, and that the central concern of social psychology is how people understand and interact with others. Let us consider each of these components in turn.

The Scientific Study . . .

Social psychologists, like other scientists, gather knowledge systematically, by means of scientific methods. These methods help to produce knowledge that is less subject to the biases and distortions that often characterize common-sense knowledge.

This shaded text is a brief preview of the section that follows. For advice on how you can use it to improve your efficiency in studying the text, turn back to the "To the Student" section in the Preface.

Of course, you have been studying social behavior all your life. Everyone uses common sense and "street smarts" to make sense of the social world they inhabit because we all want to make good friends, reach mutually satisfying decisions, raise children properly, hire the best personnel, and live in peace and security rather than in conflict and fear. How does the social psychologist's approach differ from our everyday approaches? The answer is found in methods, not goals (Fletcher & Haig, 1990). Although scientific researchers and common-sense observers share many goals—both wish to understand, predict, and influence people's thoughts and behavior—their methods for achieving those goals differ greatly.

As common-sense observers, people often reach conclusions about social behavior based on their own or others' experiences. Therefore common-sense knowledge is sometimes inconsistent, even contradictory. You may have heard, for example, that "opposites attract," and also the reverse, that "birds of a feather flock together." As scientists, on the other hand, social psychologists study social behavior systematically, seeking to avoid the misconceptions and distortions that so often afflict our common-sense knowledge. Of course, even scientific knowledge is not infallible. The history of science shows that many conclusions proposed as scientific truths are eventually overturned by new observations or new insights. But as you will see in Chapter 2, scientific conclusions are sounder and more resistant to challenge than common-sense knowledge because they are based on systematic methods of gathering information and are constructed with an awareness of the possibility of error.

. . . of the Effects of Social and Cognitive Processes . . .

The presence of other people, the knowledge and opinions they pass on to us, and our feelings about the groups to which we belong all deeply influence us through social processes, whether we are with other people or alone. Our perceptions, memories, emotions, and motives also exert a pervasive influence on us through cognitive processes. Effects of social and cognitive processes are not separate; they are inextricably intertwined.

Social psychology. The scientific study of the effects of social and cognitive processes on the way individuals perceive, influence, and relate to others.

A first date, a classroom presentation, a job interview, a problem-solving session with co-workers: What do these situations have in common? Each is a situation in

Social processes. The ways in which other people influence people's understanding of the world and guide their actions.

Cognitive processes. The ways in which people's memories, perceptions, thoughts, emotions, and motives influence their understanding of the world and guide their actions.

which others observe us or interact with us, influencing our thoughts, feelings, and behavior. We try to make a good impression, to live up to the standards of the people we care about, to cooperate or compete with others as appropriate. These examples show the operation of social processes. **Social processes** are the ways in which our thoughts, feelings, and actions are influenced by the people around us, the groups to which we belong, our personal relationships, the teachings of our parents and culture, and the pressures we experience from others.

Cognitive processes, on the other hand, are the ways in which our memories, perceptions, thoughts, emotions, and motives guide our understanding of the world and our actions. Note that emotion and motivation are intrinsic parts of every cognitive process, just as are memory and thought. Modern social psychology rejects the misleading opposition—dating back to ancient Greek philosophers—between pure, rational thought and irrational emotions. Cognitive processes affect every aspect of our lives, because the content of our thoughts, the goals toward which we strive, and the feelings we have about people and activities—all the ways we act and react in the social world—are based on what we believe the world is like.

Though we have defined them separately, in reality social and cognitive processes are inextricably intertwined. To illustrate their intimate connections, consider these two points.

First, social processes affect us even when others are not physically present: We are social creatures even when alone. Faced with an important decision, we often stop to think about the possible reactions of absent friends, relatives, or fellow group members, and these thoughts can also influence us. Even during many of our most private activities—studying, practicing a musical instrument, exercising, or showering—we are motivated by our concern for what others think of us. Think about the last time you rode an elevator in which you were the only passenger. We bet you stood facing the doors, just as you would have if other people had been physically present. Because our group memberships become part of who we are, they influence us even when other group members are absent. Whether other supporters are present or not, we rise to the defense of our party's political platform and feel elated about our college team's victory. We react in this way because our party or our college has become a basic part of our identity. In cases like these, by considering the group in the individual, social psychologists examine how people are affected by their knowledge of what is expected of them, that is, by their knowledge about the beliefs, attitudes, and actions that are considered appropriate for members of their group.

■ **Group influence far from the group.** These Egyptian soccer players are celebrating a goal scored in a 1999 World Cup match in America. Although engaged in a sporting competition, and far away from their homeland, they so thoroughly accept their Muslim faith that they stop and pray after the goal. For all of us, beliefs, attitudes, and practices endorsed by the groups to which we belong strongly affect our thoughts, feelings, and actions. This is true even when we are far away from other group members.

Second, the social processes that affect us even when others are physically present depend on how we interpret those others and their actions, and therefore on the operation of cognitive processes. The impact of other people's arguments or comments in a group discussion depends on how we think and feel about their statements: Is the argument strong and compelling, or shaky and questionable? Does a particular comment indicate that the other person has thought seriously about the issue or is the comment ill considered or even offensive? By studying the individual in the group, researchers gain insights into how people are affected by others who are physically present, whether they offer friendly hugs or scornful glares, provide trustworthy information or try to deceive, lead by example or wait for someone to follow. But in all these cases, the way others affect us depends on our own thoughts and feelings.

Whether we are alone or together with others, then, both social and cognitive processes operate together to affect everything we think, feel, and do.

. . . on the Way Individuals Perceive, Influence, and Relate to Others

Social psychology focuses on the effects of social and cognitive processes on the way individuals perceive, influence, and relate to others. Understanding these processes can help us comprehend why people act the way they do, and it may also help solve important social problems.

Social psychology seeks to understand the social behavior of individuals, a focus that distinguishes it from sociology, political science, and other social sciences. The cognitive and social processes we have just described affect individuals as they perceive, influence, and relate to others. Consequently, these processes shape all forms of social behavior, including some that are significant concerns in today's world. Here are some examples of social behaviors that are important concerns and some questions social psychologists might ask about them.

- *Why do many marriages end in divorce?* A social psychologist might study divorce as an outcome of the social and cognitive processes of conflict in marriages. The research might focus on questions like the following: How do couples interpret events that put the relationship under stress? What alternatives to the relationship do they believe they have? What types of actions in the course of an argument determine whether one partner storms angrily out of the house or allow the couple to kiss and make up after a fight? Whereas sociologists might study the effects of unemployment on divorce rates in a society, social psychologists might instead examine the ways that being unemployed causes conflict and divorce, by affecting how the partners think about their relationship or how they try to influence one another.

- *How do door-to-door salespeople sell products?* Have you ever found yourself, as a salesperson departed from your door, holding an item that you never wanted and wondering how you were manipulated into purchasing it? A social psychologist would be interested in knowing the social and cognitive processes that induced you to buy. For example, how can a sales pitch expertly play on the consumer's needs, desires, or feelings of guilt or obligation? In contrast, an economist might study whether newspaper advertisements or door-to-door sales techniques produce more total sales.

- *What causes outbreaks of ethnic violence?* An historian or journalist might document the unique events that sparked a particular conflict. To the social psychologist, however, intergroup hostility stems from fundamental aspects of the ways people think about and interact with members of different groups. These include both people's competition for concrete resources (like jobs and political clout) and people's attitudes, emotions, and actions toward their own and other social groups. Social psychologists would ask whether the ways people categorize individuals into groups, the stereotypes they form about others, their preferences for people "just like them," or their feelings of power or powerlessness contribute to intergroup hostility.

Thus, social psychology seeks an understanding of the reasons people act the way they do in social situations. Such an understanding helps us explain events in our own lives: that disastrous first date, the successful job interview, the loneliness of being the new kid on the block, the hesitation we feel before making a major decision. It also helps us comprehend the factors that contribute to the complex events of our times: crime and violence, ethnic unrest and civil war, the spread of the AIDS epidemic, the destruction of the global environment. And if we understand how people are influenced by social and cognitive processes, we can begin developing solutions for such pressing social problems. For example, knowing that stereotypes and prejudice about members of other religious groups may have contributed to violent conflict in the Middle East or Northern Ireland suggests that changing those beliefs might help to prevent recurrences. In fact, social-psychological research has been instrumental in exposing workplace discrimination (Fiske, Bersoff, Borgida, Deaux, & Heilman, 1991) and investigating why innocent people sometimes confess to crimes they did not commit (Kassin & Gudjonnson, 2004). It has suggested policies to lessen the impact of violence and explicit sex in the media on young people (Anderson, Berkowitz and others, 2003) and to improve classroom environments for minorities and women (Steele, 1992). It has also been influential in finding ways to change perceptions of the risks of AIDS (Fisher & Fisher, 1992) and in developing programs to reduce international tensions (Lindskold, 1986). Thus the social-psychological perspective invites us not only to understand but also to act on that understanding.

Historical Trends and Current Themes in Social Psychology

How did social psychology come to develop its particular point of view? Like any field of knowledge, social psychology is a product of its past. The current focus of its research reflects historical events of the 20th century, changing societal concerns, and developments in other scientific fields, as well as changes in the techniques social psychologists have used in their research. This brief survey of the field's history will place the field in context and serve as a partial explanation for where social psychology stands today.

Social Psychology Becomes an Empirical Science

Soon after the emergence of scientific psychology in the late 19th century, researchers began considering questions about social influences on human thought and action.

From the time of the ancient Greeks, the study of the human condition was considered to be the domain of philosophy. Like social psychologists today, early philosophers recognized the impact that other people can have on individual behavior. Plato, for example, speculated about the "crowd mind," arguing that even the wisest individuals, if assembled into a crowd, might be transformed into an irrational mob. Through the ages, philosophers continued to theorize about the workings of the human mind—and they still do—but the development of social psychology had to await the emergence of its parent discipline, the science of psychology. This new field was born in the late 19th century, when a few researchers in Germany, impressed by laboratory methods being used by physiologists, began to employ experimental techniques to understand mental processes like sensation, memory, and judgment.

The experimental investigation of social-psychological issues began soon afterward, as researchers in North America, Britain, and France began the task of systematically measuring how behavior is influenced by the presence of others. A study published in 1898 by an American researcher, Norman Triplett, is sometimes cited as the first research study in social psychology (G. W. Allport, 1954a). Triplett, having noticed that swimmers and cyclists performed better when competing against their rivals than when practicing by themselves, wondered whether the presence of other people has a generally beneficial effect on performance. To find out, he asked schoolchildren to wind fishing line onto reels as quickly as possible, with and without others present. Sure enough, the children's performance improved in the presence of others. This interesting finding, however, appeared to contradict a conclusion that Max Ringelmann, a French agricultural engineer, had reached in an even earlier study conducted in the 1880s. Ringelmann found that when people worked together to pull on a rope or push on a cart, they put less effort into the task than when they worked alone (Ringelmann, 1913). The study of group effects on performance still continues today, and we now know that Ringelmann's and Triplett's results are not necessarily inconsistent. As you will see in Chapter 12, the presence of others often facilitates performance when individual contributions are easily identified, but it reduces performance when people are "lost in a crowd."

For the first social psychologists, this puzzle was just one among many questions about how people influence one another. Early researchers also tackled questions about how facial expressions and body movements reveal people's feelings, how people conform to the suggestions of others, and the role that experimenters might play in influencing the outcomes of research (Haines & Vaughan, 1979). The first two textbooks bearing the name *Social Psychology* appeared in 1908. One of these, by psychologist William McDougall, argued that all social behavior stems from innate tendencies or instincts, an idea that was popular throughout psychology at the time. The other, by sociologist E. A. Ross, took up the theme that was soon to become social psychology's central concern: that people are heavily influenced by others, whether those others are physically present or not.

Social Psychology Splits From General Psychology Over What Causes Behavior

Throughout much of the 20th century, North American psychology was dominated by behaviorism, but social psychologists maintained an emphasis on the important effects of thoughts and feelings on behavior.

Although it arrived on the coattails of general psychology, social psychology soon developed an identity distinct from that of its parent discipline. Early in the 20th century, North American psychology as a whole became dominated by the behaviorist viewpoint. This perspective, exemplified by the work of John B. Watson and

B. F. Skinner, denied the scientific validity of explanations for behavior that invoke mental events like thoughts, feelings, and emotions. For radical behaviorists, a legitimate science of human activity could be based only on the study of observable behavior as influenced by observable environmental stimuli.

Most social psychologists, however, resisted the behaviorist view that thoughts and feelings had no place in scientific explanations. They accepted the behaviorists' argument that the ultimate goal of science is to explain behavior, but their studies showed that behavior could not be explained without taking into account people's thoughts and feelings. Social psychologists learned that individuals often hold divergent views of, and react in different ways to, the same object or idea, be it a football game, a political candidate, or capitalism. Such findings could be explained only by differences in individuals' attitudes, personality traits, impressions of others, group identifications, and emotions (F. H. Allport, 1924). Behaviorists were certainly right in their belief that external stimuli can influence behavior. However, social psychologists maintained that the effect of any stimulus depends on how individuals and groups interpret it. Right from the start, then, social psychology was distinctive in its conviction that understanding and measuring people's perceptions, beliefs, and feelings is essential to understanding their overt behavior (E. E. Jones, 1985).

The Rise of Nazism Shapes the Development of Social Psychology

In the 1930s and 1940s, many European social psychologists fled to North America, where they had a major influence on the field's direction. Significant questions generated by the rise of Nazism and the Second World War shaped research interests during this period.

It has been said that the one person who has had the most impact on the development of social psychology in North America is Adolf Hitler (Cartwright, 1979). Ironic though this observation is, it contains important elements of truth. In fact, both the events that precipitated the Second World War and the war itself had a dramatic and lasting impact on social psychology.

As Nazi domination spread across Europe in the 1930s, a number of psychologists fled their homelands to continue distinguished scientific careers in North America. One result was that the major growth in social psychology was concentrated in North America for the next few decades. In addition, this influx of European researchers consolidated social psychology's special emphasis on how people interpret the world and how they are influenced by others. Most European researchers were trained not in the behaviorist tradition that was prominent in North America but in Gestalt theory, which took for granted the role cognitive processes play in our interpretations of the social world. Around the same time, researchers became increasingly impressed by anthropologists' accounts of the pervasiveness of cultural influences on people's thoughts and behavior. It fell to social psychologists to identify the mechanisms by which such influences occurred, and they soon developed techniques to perform realistic studies of complex social influences in the laboratory. Muzafer Sherif's (1936) elegant experiments, for example, showed that a social group can influence even a person's perception and interpretation of physical reality, as you will see in Chapter 9 of this text.

But the war's effect on social psychology went beyond bringing a new group of skilled researchers to North America. Revelations of Nazi genocide led a horrified world to ask questions about the roots of prejudice (Adorno, Frenkel-Brunswik,

Levinson, & Sanford, 1950). How could people feel and act on such murderous hatred for Jews, Gypsies, homosexuals, and members of other groups? These questions still resonate today as the world contemplates ethnic conflicts in Rwanda, Iraq, Sri Lanka, and the Middle East, and "gay bashing" on the streets of North American cities.

Conditions created by the Second World War also drew social psychologists into the search for solutions to immediate practical problems. With food in short supply and rationing in full swing, the U.S. government asked social psychologists how to convince civilians to change their eating habits: to eat less steak and more kidneys and liver, to drink more milk, and to feed their babies cod-liver oil and orange juice (K. Lewin, 1947). Social psychologists were also called on to help the military maintain troop morale, improve the performance of aircraft and tank crews (Stouffer, 1949), and teach troops to resist enemy propaganda—and even to brush their teeth regularly (Hovland, Janis, & Kelley, 1953).

Social psychologists fell to applied research with a will, realizing that they would be able to develop and test general theories of behavior even as they solved practical problems. As we will see in Chapter 10, Kurt Lewin (1947) found that active participation in discussion groups, by establishing behavior in a social context, was more effective in changing what women fed their families than passive listening to lectures on the topic. Lewin's findings are still successfully applied in support groups like Weight Watchers, Overeaters Anonymous, and many other organizations. Samuel Stouffer's (1949) research on American soldiers' morale showed that it depended more on the soldiers' interpretations of how they were doing compared to other enlisted men than on how well they were actually doing. Satisfaction with the rate of promotion, for example, was sometimes lower in units with higher-than-average promotion rates. Stouffer suggested that in these units the soldiers' expectations of promotion were high, setting them up for disappointment if others were promoted but they were not. The importance of comparisons with others and the ways comparisons can lead to feelings of relative deprivation are still important topics in current social-psychological research. And, though we may be amused by Carl Hovland's assignment of devising ways to persuade GIs to brush their teeth regularly, current theories of persuasion build on his original demonstration

■ **Social influences on scientific concerns.** This German photograph from 1938 shows an advertisement for a special edition of *Der Stürmer* with the headline "Jews Are Criminals." Many of the social psychologists who fled Nazi-dominated Europe were horrified at the Nazis' success in swaying the public mind against the Jews. These concerns triggered lifelong efforts to understand the roots of prejudice, the causes of obedience, the power of propaganda, and other social issues.

that persuasion depends on who delivers the message, who receives the message, and how the message is processed (Hovland and others, 1953).

During this crucial period of research and theory building, the work of one social psychologist in particular embodied the themes that characterized the young discipline. Kurt Lewin, one of the scientists who had fled Hitler, held that all behavior depends on the individual's *life space,* which he defined as a subjective map of the individual's current goals and his or her social environment (K. Lewin, 1936). Perhaps you can see how Lewin's ideas sum up two of social psychology's enduring themes: that people's subjective interpretation of reality is the key determinant of their beliefs and behaviors, and that social influences structure those interpretations and behaviors. Lewin's work also reflected the close link between research aimed at understanding the underlying social and cognitive causes of behavior and research aimed at solving important social problems, a link that will receive considerable attention throughout this book. Lewin had a gift for conducting research that combined the testing of theories with the solving of problems. As he put it, "There is nothing so practical as a good theory" (K. Lewin, 1951, p. 169).

Growth and Integration

During the 1950s and 1960s, social psychology grew and flourished, moving toward an integrated theoretical understanding of social and cognitive processes and toward further applications of social-psychological theory to important applied problems.

Both basic and applied social psychology flourished during the prosperous 1950s and 1960s. Backed by expanding university enrollments and generous government grants, researchers addressed a great variety of topics central to understanding social behavior. Research contributions during this period laid the foundations of what we now know about self-esteem, prejudice and stereotyping, conformity, persuasion and attitude change, impression formation, interpersonal attraction and intimate relationships, and intergroup relations, all still key topics within social psychology today.

During the same period, as Europe recovered and rebuilt from the destruction of the war, social psychologists in several countries there developed theoretical and research approaches to a wide range of topics, particularly those involving group memberships, influence within groups, and the often competitive relationships between groups (Doise, 1978; Moscovici, 1980; Tajfel, 1978). By the 1970s, social psychology on both sides of the Atlantic had developed a set of reliable and repeatable findings, which is a mark of scientific maturity. The time was ripe for both internal integration, the melding of various specific topic areas into broader explanations of behavior, and external integration, increasing attention to neighboring scientific fields and to significant social concerns. And so the movement toward integration began.

INTEGRATION OF COGNITIVE AND SOCIAL PROCESSES. The study of cognitive processes became a natural framework for integration both within and outside social psychology. As the tight grip of behaviorism on North American psychology was finally broken, a cognitive revolution got under way in the 1960s (Neisser, 1967). Cognitive themes and theories swiftly gained attention in experimental, developmental, personality, and even clinical psychology. Of course, the cognitive revolution was no revolution for social psychology. Cognitive themes such as the importance of people's interpretations in shaping their reactions to events were familiar to social psychologists because their foundations had been laid decades earlier in Allport's, Sherif's, and Lewin's work in the 1930s and in Stouffer's and Hovland's studies in the 1940s. Concepts such as attitudes, norms, and beliefs, already common currency in social psychology, began to be applied to new areas of study: personal relationships, aggression and altruism, stereotyping and discrimination. These applications were greatly facilitated during the 1970s and 1980s by the adoption of research techniques that had been found to be valuable by cognitive psychologists studying perception and memory. Thus, theoretical concerns and proven experimental methods converged as researchers in many areas of social psychology focused on the study of cognitive processes (E. E. Jones, 1985).

Concern with cognitive processes is only one side of the coin, however. Social psychologists have always been aware that social processes, including personal and group relationships and social influence, also impinge on everything people do. True, our behavior is a function of our perceptions and interpretations and our attitudes and beliefs, but those factors in turn are fundamentally shaped by our relationships to others, our thoughts about their reactions, and the group memberships that help us define who we are (Markus, Kitayama, & Heiman, 1996). Scientific understanding of the way social and cognitive processes work together to mold all social behavior has benefited from the increasing integration of North American social psychology with European social psychology, where the impact of social group memberships has long been a dominant theme. Today, researchers in all domains of social psychology are weaving together the effects of cognitive and social processes to provide explanations of people's experience and behavior.

INTEGRATION OF BASIC SCIENCE AND SOCIAL PROBLEMS. Can technological advancement by itself offer solutions to such global threats as resource depletion, environmental pollution, war and ethnic conflict, and overpopulation? Many people believe the answer to that question is no. Instead, solving such massive problems requires profound changes in human behavior.

Social psychologists are attacking these and other crucial social problems, and this attack will require their best theoretical efforts. In this regard, social psychologists are lucky. Scientists in many other fields have to choose whether they will work on purely theoretical issues or apply their theoretical knowledge to practical problems. A materials scientist, for example, may seek to understand the nature of the molecular bonds that produce stronger materials, but it is the engineer who will use the new materials to design an improved wind-turbine blade. Social psychologists do not have to make this kind of choice. It is difficult to think of a single area of social-psychological research that does not have some application to significant social issues. Whether social psychologists are looking at close relationships or divorce, altruism or aggression, attitude change or the effectiveness of advertising, intergroup conflict or its resolution, they simultaneously address the basic theoretical questions that spur pure scientific curiosity and the important phenomena that affect our daily lives.

Traditionally, many psychologists have thought of basic and applied research as distinct, even opposite, areas, with applied research taking a back seat to basic research. This stance is foreign to contemporary social psychology. Because virtually all social-psychological research is relevant to significant social issues, it is simultaneously basic and applied. The same underlying social and cognitive processes operate wherever people perceive, influence, and interact with each other, both inside the research laboratory and outside it, in schools, factories, courtrooms, playgrounds, boardrooms, and neighborhoods. For this reason, as we describe theories and research areas throughout this text, we will also discuss their applied implications. As you will see, talented researchers are studying social-psychological processes in many applied settings, with a particular focus on major issues relevant to health, education, law, the environment, and business. We have created special section headings to help you locate discussions of particularly important applications to areas such as the following:

- *Health.* Good health is just a matter of good diet, regular exercise, and lucky genes, right? Wrong. The emotions we experience, the amount of stress we encounter from daily hassles, our ability to find love and acceptance in close relationships, and even the way we feel about ourselves can influence our bodies as well as our minds. When public health officials promote exercise and fight drug abuse, when hospitals allow patients more control over their treatments, and when support groups speed recovery from illness, addiction, and grief, social-psychological processes are playing a part in producing sound minds in sound bodies.

- *Education.* As teachers teach and students learn, more is being communicated than just Spanish and geography. Teachers' expectations can shape their pupils' self-esteem, self-confidence, and even their actual performance. Classroom activities can encourage competition or cooperation and can eliminate or exacerbate ethnic and gender stereotypes. No wonder that for some the classroom is an open field of opportunity, whereas for others it is a minefield of adversity and disappointment.

- *Law.* How do the police extract confessions? Do lie detectors really work? Is a defendant in suit and tie more credible than one in prison fatigues? How might leading questions and inadmissible evidence influence a juror's thinking? Does the minority opinion of a dissenting juror ever sway jury verdicts? From crime to conviction, social-psychological processes are at work as police enforce laws, juries weigh evidence, and societies try to distribute justice.

- *Environment.* Japanese commuters buy whiffs of oxygen from coin-operated machines in subways, yields of Atlantic fisheries decline, and American motorists waste hours in traffic jams. These human dimensions of environmental change are among those motivating social psychologists to discover how individuals can be encouraged to conserve energy or to recycle used materials. Others are working hard to determine the ways groups can be convinced to cooperate in harvesting renewable resources instead of overexploiting and destroying them.

- *Business.* From advertising to sales techniques to the pitfalls of managerial decision making, social-psychological processes are the gears that drive the wheels of business. Consider, for example, the way effective leadership can mold diverse individuals into a smoothly functioning work team, while ineffective leadership generates only conflict, dissatisfaction, and low productivity.

In social psychology, the everyday world is not just a place to test discoveries made during laboratory research. Instead, social psychologists regard issues that are important outside the laboratory—ethnic conflict, the AIDS epidemic, crime and aggression, declining productivity, global interdependence—as both a source of theoretical ideas and a target for solutions (J. Rodin, 1985).

How the Approach of This Book Reflects an Integrative Perspective

Not surprisingly, given the way social psychology has developed, our conception of social psychology is an integrated one. In this text we share with you our view of social psychology as a field that integrates not only the cognitive and the social but also basic theory and applied research. We believe that all the diversity and richness of human social behavior can be understood in terms of a few fundamental social-psychological processes. These processes flow from eight principles: two fundamental axioms, three motivational principles, and three processing principles.

As we describe specific topics like attraction, aggression, altruism, and attitude change, we will show you how all these forms of social behavior flow from the interaction of these same fundamental principles. At the same time, seeing these principles at work in different settings, producing apparently different forms of social behavior, will enhance your understanding of their meanings and implications. Here we give you just a quick introduction to these basic principles and the processes that flow from them.

Two Fundamental Axioms of Social Psychology

> Two fundamental axioms of social psychology are that people construct their own reality and that social influence is pervasive.

Two fundamental axioms, or most important principles, integrate all the topics in this text. The first is that people construct their own reality. The second is that social influence pervades all social life.

CONSTRUCTION OF REALITY. At first glance, studying social behavior may seem to be an exercise in the obvious. As we go through our daily routines, we trust that we are seeing the world around us as it is—that an objective reality exists "out there" for all to see. When we join friends to watch a ball game or to eat dinner in a restaurant, we assume that we all see the same game and hear the same enjoyable dinner-time conversation. When we meet someone new, we quickly form an impression of what he or she "is like." And when we see someone raise a fist, furrow a brow, or slump in a chair, we know what the behavior means because "actions speak louder than words." Because we assume that our impressions are accurate and true, we usually expect anyone else who meets the same person, goes on the same date, or sees the same action to share those impressions.

Every now and then, however, we are forced to think twice. Discovering how different the reactions of others can be to the "same" social event overturns our usual lack of awareness of the extent to which we construct our own reality. Try reminiscing with one of your parents about what happened on your first day of school, and you may discover that your memories of the details of that milestone in your lives are quite different. Or, like the Princeton and Dartmouth sports fans, compare your recollection of an important game with the view of the opposing team's fans and see if you agree about what happened. At such times we discover that we do not, in fact, share the same experience. A fist can be raised in intimidation or triumph, and a furrowed brow can indicate depression or concentration. What is real for each of us is a **construction of reality**, shaped in part by cognitive processes (the way our minds work) and in part by social processes (influence from others who are actually present or whose presence we imagine).

Cognitive processes operate as we piece together fragments of information, draw inferences from them, and try to weave them into a coherent whole. We may hear a speaker deliver a series of arguments, note the audience's response, draw inferences about how others feel, and decide whether the message is worth our close consideration. In this sense, a person's view of the world is certainly in the eye—or the ear—of the beholder.

Construction of reality. The axiom that each person's view of reality is a construction, shaped both by cognitive processes (the ways our minds work) and by social processes (influence from others either actually present or imagined).

■ **Who is this woman?** Is Hillary Rodham Clinton a calculating manipulator or a victim of nasty gossip? A cutthroat political climber or a cookie-baking mom? Or is she none of these? The answer depends on who is doing the perceiving—conservative detractors, the liberal media, her family, or Clinton herself. What seems real to us is socially constructed and, like beauty, is in the eye of the beholder.

Social processes enable us to influence and be influenced by the views of others as we pursue agreement about the nature of reality. Within the groups that are important to us, agreement is our standard for interpreting and responding to events. For example, most members of Western societies enjoy kissing, although the meaning of the kiss varies, depending on whom we kiss and how. But when the Thonga of southeast Africa first saw Europeans kissing, they were disgusted by what they regarded as "eating each other's saliva and dirt" (Hyde, 1979, p. 18). Whether we are Thonga cattle herders or German university students, we tune in to others' interpretations—our parents' views about kisses or the cheers or boos of an audience listening to a speech—and we use those interpretations as the basis for our own responses. In this sense, a person's view of the world is at least in part a reflection of what is seen in the eyes of others.

PERVASIVENESS OF SOCIAL INFLUENCE. We could probably all agree that other people influence our public behavior and that our actions in turn can influence what others say and do. Having supporters at our back gives us a bit more courage to speak out; face-to-face confrontations with detractors may frighten us into silence.

Recall, however, that we said earlier that others can influence us even when we are alone. The **pervasiveness of social influence** means that other people influence all of our thoughts, feelings, and behavior, whether those others are physically present or not. Our thoughts about others' reactions and our identification with social groups mold our innermost perceptions, thoughts, feelings, motives, and even our sense of self. Do you proudly think of yourself as a fan of the Amsterdam Ajax soccer team, a member of your temple, a citizen of Canada? Our allegiances may be small scale, such as membership in families, teams, and committees, or large scale, including affiliations based on race, ethnicity, religion, gender, or the society and culture in which we live. But whether the group is large or small, our membership in it provides a frame and a filter through which we view social events. The Dartmouth–Princeton game had a particular meaning for students from each school and a quite different meaning for people who felt no allegiance to either team. Even among those on the same side, the game meant different things to the team members and their fans.

We sometimes experience social influence as social pressure, as when we encounter an aggressive salesperson or are berated for holding out on an otherwise unanimous jury. But social influence is most profound when it is least evident: when it shapes our most fundamental assumptions and beliefs about the world without our realizing it. The reactions of the Princeton and Dartmouth fans were certainly shaped and biased by their school allegiances, but were the fans aware of that influence? Probably not. We would not expect anyone to think, "I'd better interpret that tackle as vicious because my friends will reject me if I don't." Social influences have surrounded us since infancy, and it is therefore no surprise that we usually are unaware of their impact. Does the fish know it swims in water? Sometimes it takes a shift in perspective to make us aware of the impact of social influence. Such shifts are familiar to all of us: A rebellious teenager becomes a

Pervasiveness of social influence. The axiom that other people influence all of an individual's thoughts, feelings, and behavior, whether those others are physically present or not.

parent and imposes a curfew on his own teenagers; a die-hard Braves fan moves from Atlanta to Toronto and eventually joins with her new co-workers to support the Blue Jays. Even then, such changes often seem so natural that we attribute them not to social influence but to simple reality, for example, the self-evident fact that the Blue Jays are just the best team. Throughout this text, you will see evidence of the powerful effect social influence has in molding the reality we construct for ourselves—and therefore our thoughts, feelings, and actions—whether we are together with others or alone with our thoughts.

Three Motivational Principles

As they construct reality and influence and are influenced by others, people have three basic motives: to strive for mastery, to seek connectedness with others, and to value themselves and others connected to them.

As individuals and groups construct reality while influencing and being influenced by others, they direct their thoughts, feelings, and behaviors toward three important goals.

PEOPLE STRIVE FOR MASTERY. Mastery refers to understanding ourselves and the world around us and applying that understanding to help us control outcomes in our lives. Each of us **strives for mastery**: We seek to understand and predict events in the social world in order to obtain many types of rewards. Achieving mastery is an important incentive in our attempt to form and hold accurate opinions and beliefs about the world, because accurate beliefs can guide us to effective and satisfying actions. For example, if you want the last available part-time job at the campus bookstore, forming an accurate impression of the manager's needs and knowing yourself well enough to give a convincing account of your qualifications may help you get the job. Similarly, insightfully diagnosing business problems and successfully understanding students' and faculty members' needs may help you keep such a job. In many everyday decisions, individuals and groups choose to act in ways that appear likely to lead to the most rewarding results, guided by the most reliable and accurate information we can muster.

PEOPLE SEEK CONNECTEDNESS. In **seeking connectedness**, each person attempts to create and maintain feelings of mutual support, liking, and acceptance from those they care about and value. For members of groups in conflict, such as Israelis and Palestinians, actions that benefit their group often seem even more important than civil peace and an end to conflict. Apparently, conforming to group standards, even standards that have destructive consequences for people outside the group, fulfills a need for belonging and connectedness. But the consequences are not always destructive. This same fundamental motive cements the relationships that bring joy and meaning to our lives, linking us to our teammates, families, friends, and lovers.

PEOPLE VALUE ME AND MINE. The motivational principle of **valuing me and mine** means that we are motivated to see ourselves and anything or anyone connected to us, such as our families, teams, nations, or even possessions, in a positive light. Even people with life-threatening illnesses can maintain a positive view of themselves by comparing themselves with others who are even worse off. Our

Striving for mastery. The motivational principle that people seek to understand and predict events in the social world in order to obtain rewards.

Seeking connectedness. The motivational principle that people seek support, liking, and acceptance from the people and groups they care about and value.

Valuing me and mine. The motivational principle that people desire to see themselves, and other people and groups connected to themselves, in a positive light.

biased views of those who are connected to us often explain why members of different groups see the same events in very different ways. A Princeton fan may view the Dartmouth quarterback's broken leg as an accident—unfortunate, but part of the game of football and certainly not something that reflects badly on the Princeton team. A Dartmouth supporter might blame the injury on a viciously dirty tackle, clear evidence that the Princeton team is incapable of good sportsmanship. Little wonder that these fans came away from the game with very different views of it, views that emphasized the positive characteristics of their own teams and let them feel good about themselves.

Three Processing Principles

The operation of social and cognitive processes is described by three processing principles: Established views are slow to change, accessible information has the most impact, and processing is sometimes superficial but at other times goes into great depth.

In seeking rewards and connectedness and in valuing me and mine, people and groups gather and interpret information about the world in which they live. Three principles describe the cognitive and social processes that operate as we construct a picture of reality, influence other people, and are influenced by them.

CONSERVATISM: ESTABLISHED VIEWS ARE SLOW TO CHANGE. Conservatism is the principle that individuals' and groups' views of the world are slow to change and prone to perpetuate themselves. The Princeton supporters, convinced that their Tigers were the better team, interpreted what they saw through the filter of their beliefs. Their selective perceptions thus supported their views of reality, as did the influence of their group, the equally biased fans around them. Examples of conservatism are almost endless: the first impressions we form of job applicants, the stereotypes we harbor about other groups, or preferences we nurture for the brand of peanut butter Mom always bought. But in all these cases and more, the principle is the same: established knowledge tends to perpetuate itself. In the chapters to come you will see why prior beliefs, expectations, and preferences are so hard to change, and you will become more aware of the consequences of their resiliency. You will also appreciate the enormous amount of effort needed to budge them at all.

ACCESSIBILITY: ACCESSIBLE INFORMATION HAS THE MOST IMPACT. From football games to political debates, every social situation provides an incredibly rich array of information—so rich that we could not consider all its details. Consequently, we are likely to consider, remember, and use only a tiny fraction of the potentially relevant information when we make judgments or decisions. **Accessibility** is the principle that whatever information is most readily available to us usually has the most impact on our thoughts, feelings, and behavior. In many situations, what comes most easily to mind is what we were already thinking. So, to return to the football example, Dartmouth stalwarts used their conviction that their team is good as a basis for their judgments of what happened. In other situations, we base our judgments on the information that is most easily noticed and interpreted. For many of the students who listened to the probation speech without

Conservatism. The processing principle that individuals' and groups' views of the world are slow to change and prone to perpetuate themselves.

Accessibility. The processing principle that the information that is most readily available generally has the most impact on thoughts, feelings, and behavior.

expecting to be personally affected, enthusiastic applause or disapproving whistles were the most noticeable and had the most impact on their judgments.

SUPERFICIALITY VERSUS DEPTH: PEOPLE CAN PROCESS SUPERFICIALLY OR IN DEPTH. Much of the time, people seem to operate on automatic, putting little effort into forming a superficial picture of reality and relying heavily on whatever information is most accessible. But sometimes, particularly when we notice that events fail to match our expectations or when our important goals are threatened, we take the time and trouble to process information more extensively. These are examples of the principle of **superficiality versus depth**. Confronted with an opposing point of view—one that clearly contradicted their own—students who cared about probation reconsidered their positions. They reviewed the arguments and based their opinions on the content of the speeches rather than on the circumstances of their presentation. Disagreement or rejection challenges not only our sense of mastery and understanding but also our feelings of connectedness, triggering anxiety and uncertainty. Threats to any of our important goals may motivate us to consider information in more depth and to think hard about our own beliefs and actions.

The interrelationships among the eight basic principles of social psychology are summarized in Figure 1.1.

> **Superficiality versus depth.**
> The processing principle that people ordinarily put little effort into dealing with information, but at times are motivated to consider information in more depth.

FIGURE 1.1 Interrelations among the eight basic principles of social psychology

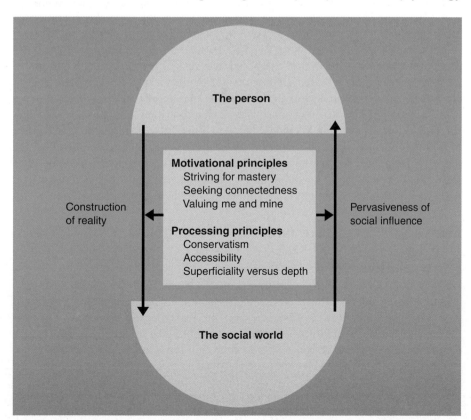

- Two fundamental axioms link the individual person to the social world. Each person constructs his or her own picture of social reality, which then guides all thoughts, feelings, and actions. At the same time, the pervasiveness of social influence also affects the person's thoughts, feelings, and behavior. Three motivational principles and three processing principles determine both the nature of the constructed reality and the nature of the social influence.

Common Processes, Diverse Behaviors

In combination, these eight principles account for all types of social behavior, including thoughts and actions that are useful and valuable as well as those that are misleading and destructive.

In combination, then, these eight principles account for all types of social behavior. This includes not only desirable outcomes such as accurate decisions, successful social interactions, and harmonious relationships between groups, but also more problematic and negative forms of behavior. As our examples demonstrate, exactly the same processes that produce useful and valuable outcomes in some situations produce misleading and destructive outcomes in others. Our ability to construct reality allows us to see our world as a coherent and meaningful place, but it also opens the door to bias and misinterpretation. Social influences sometimes provide us with safety in numbers, but they also may lead us like lambs to the slaughter. The drive for connectedness and the value we place on me and mine can give us the warm glow of belonging, but it can also prompt us to reject, devalue, and exclude others not in our chosen circle. Basing decisions on accessible information often produces extremely efficient decision making but sometimes leads to bad decisions. Even when we contemplate information as thoughtfully as possible, we are not always guaranteed an accurate decision. Sometimes the very act of thinking about things can slant our interpretations and introduce mistakes without our being aware of the problem.

Human behavior is not always as simple as it seems, but neither is it impenetrable to scientific inquiry or impossible to understand systematically. In fact, although social behavior is incredibly diverse, this diversity results from the operation of these same few processes. Thus, as you move from chapter to chapter in this text, watch for these principles at work. We offer some help by calling attention to the principles and general themes of the book. In addition, we make special efforts to present theories and research findings as interrelated sets of ideas by placing cross-references to related ideas in the margins. We know that disconnected items of information are hard to remember and do not contribute much to a real under-standing of social behavior. We would like you to see this text as an integrated story of (a) the fundamental social and cognitive processes that operate as human beings perceive, influence, and interact with others, and (b) the way social psychologists learn about these processes, both in the laboratory and in the world of everyday life. It is a fascinating story, and we hope you will learn much about yourself and others as you follow it through the text.

Plan of the Book

The first two chapters of this text are an introduction to social psychology, covering the "Why?" and the "How?" of our science. The remainder of the book explores the "What?" of social psychology—the topic areas that make up the discipline. In this chapter we have tried to convey *why* social psychologists ask the questions they do. Chapter 2 tells more about how they seek answers.

- *Asking and Answering Research Questions.* Have we convinced you already that people's interpretive processes and social surroundings may bias what they know? Scientists are no exception. Chapter 2 describes the logical checks and balances built into the structure of science that help researchers guard against subjectivity and bias.

Chapters 3 through 14 explore what social psychologists study. Following our definition of social psychology, we deal in turn with how individuals perceive others (Chapters 3–6), influence others (Chapters 7–10), and relate to others (Chapters 11–14).

Chapters 3 through 6 focus on *social perception,* the way we come to know and understand the basic elements of our social world: individuals and social groups.

- *Perceiving Individuals.* From fleeting impressions of passing strangers to the intimate familiarity of our best friend, Chapter 3 deals with knowing and understanding other people.

- *The Self.* What person is probably most important, most near and dear to each of us? Chapter 4 describes how we understand the self.

- *Perceiving Groups.* In Chapter 5, we investigate the beliefs and feelings people develop about social groups like working women, Russians, schoolteachers, or Muslims.

- *Social Identity.* Chapter 6 brings these topics together in a discussion of how we come to see ourselves as members of a social group, and how a group can become part of the self.

Social influence is the impact each of us has on others, and it is the topic of Chapters 7 through 10. Each of us is constantly influencing and being influenced by others. Others affect us whether they are in our face, like an aggressive salesperson, or on our minds even when we are alone.

- *Attitudes and Attitude Change.* Advertisements aim at our pocketbooks, political campaigns play on our fears, debates appeal to our reason. Do they change our minds? If so, how? Chapter 7 gives some answers to questions like these.

- *Attitudes and Behavior.* In the right circumstances, attitudes both reflect and guide behaviors. Chapter 8 tells a tale of the mutual influence of attitudes and behaviors.

- *Groups, Norms, and Conformity.* A different kind of mutual influence is the focus of Chapter 9. Here we examine how groups reach agreement and why that agreement has such compelling effects on group members.

- *Norms and Behavior.* Chapter 10 describes the effects of groups on what people do, not just on what they think. Bringing all the chapters of this section together, we describe how attitudes and group influences combine to affect behavior.

In the final four chapters we concentrate on *social relations,* the bonds that link us one to another, as individuals and as groups. Whether we are bound by attraction or cooperation, or shackled by aggression and conflict, our relations with others can pull us together or drive us apart.

- *Liking and Loving.* Chapter 11 takes a close look at feelings of attraction to other people and the formation and development of close and loving relationships. We also review what social psychology can tell us about why relationships flourish or wither.

- *Interaction in Groups.* Small groups—management committees, paramedic teams, juries, and others—do most of society's work. Chapter 12's topic is how we interact with others in small groups, and how groups work to accomplish shared tasks.

- *Aggression and Conflict.* Who can watch the evening news without being struck by the many conflicts that pit person against person or group against group? In Chapter 13 we analyze the path of such conflicts: how they can arise, escalate, and, sometimes, be resolved.

- *Helping and Cooperation.* Dramatic incidents of selfless heroism or more commonplace acts of cooperation that benefit others: Why do they occur? Chapter 14 examines the conditions under which we help other people and our reasons for doing so.

The text ends with an epilogue, a brief concluding comment that summarizes the major themes and reflects on some of their interrelationships and applications.

As you read this book, we invite you to join us in seeing social-psychological principles at work in people's actions and interactions. Seeing events around you in this framework is the first and most essential step toward becoming a social psychologist and having the fun of doing research that advances our knowledge of how social-psychological principles work and of applying the principles to real and important problems. But you do not have to do research to use your new knowledge to understand why your friends act as they do, how other people influence you, or what accounts for group conflicts around the world. We hope you will come to appreciate both the usefulness and the excitement of social psychology.

SUMMARY

 A Definition of Social Psychology. Social psychology is the scientific study of the effects of social and cognitive processes on the way individuals perceive, influence, and relate to others. Like other scientists, social psychologists gather knowledge systematically by means of scientific methods. These methods help produce knowledge that is less subject to the biases and distortions that often characterize common-sense knowledge.

The physical presence of other people, the knowledge and opinions that they pass on to us, and our feelings about the groups to which we belong all deeply influence us through **social processes**, whether we are with other people or alone. Our perceptions, memories, emotions, and motives also influence us through **cognitive processes**. Effects of social and cognitive processes are not separate; they are inextricably intertwined.

All types of social behavior, including individuals' perceptions of, influence on, and relationships with others, reflect the operation of social and cognitive processes. Understanding these processes can help us comprehend why people act the way they do, and it may also help solve important social problems.

Historical Trends and Current Themes in Social Psychology. Social psychology emerged soon after the beginning of scientific psychology in the late 19th century, when researchers began considering questions about social influences on human thought and action. Through much of the 20th century, North American psychology was dominated by behaviorism, but social psychologists maintained an emphasis on the important effects of thoughts and feelings on behavior.

In the 1930s and 1940s, many European social psychologists fled to North America, where they had a major influence on the field's direction. Throughout this period, significant questions inspired by the rise of Nazism and the Second World War shaped research interests.

During the 1950s and 1960s, social psychology grew and flourished, moving toward an integrated theoretical understanding of social and cognitive processes and toward further applications of social-psychological theory to important applied problems.

How the Approach of This Book Reflects an Integrative Perspective. Social psychology is a field that integrates not only the cognitive and the social but also basic theory and applied research. All the diversity and richness of human social behavior can be understood in terms of eight basic principles. Two fundamental axioms of social psychology are that people **construct their own reality** and that **social influence is pervasive**. Three motivational principles are that, as they construct reality and influence and are influenced by others, people **strive for mastery**, or understanding and control of their environment; **seek connectedness** with others; and **value me and mine**. People's thoughts and actions are also influenced by three processing principles. One is **conservatism**: Established views are slow to change. Another is **accessibility**: Easily accessed information has the most impact. The final principle is **superficiality versus depth**: People can process superficially or in depth. In combination, these eight principles account for all types of social behavior, including thoughts and actions that are useful and valuable as well as those that are misleading and destructive.

Plan of the Book. This text has four main sections. Chapters 1 and 2 introduce social psychology and its typical research methods. Chapters 3 through 6 focus on social perception, the ways that people interpret and understand other people, themselves, and social groups. Chapters 7 through 10 deal with social influence, the ways that people and groups affect each other as they interact and communicate. Chapters 11 through 14 describe the social relations that lead people to form relationships, work together in groups, and help and hurt each other.

2

Asking and Answering Research Questions

Imagine winning the state lottery. Or receiving a promotion after only 5 months in your new position. Or getting a would-be buyer to meet your price on the sale of your used car. How do you think you would react to these events? Most people would anticipate being very happy. Now imagine finding out that you have a life-threatening illness, that you have stayed in the same job for years and still have little hope of advancement, or that you got much less for your used car than you had hoped for. You probably would predict that you would be quite unhappy about these alternatives. It might surprise you to learn that social-psychological research has shown that these intuitively obvious conclusions are not always true. Lottery winners are soon no happier than the rest of us (Brickman, Coates, & Janoff-Bulman, 1978). Those receiving rapid promotions are often more dissatisfied than people with less chance of advancement (Stouffer, Suchman, DeVinney, Star, & Williams, 1949). Patients with serious illnesses often show remarkably good spirits (J. V. Wood, Taylor, & Lichtman, 1985). And the money actually gained or lost in negotiation with others has little to do with people's satisfaction about the outcome (Loewenstein, Thompson, & Bazerman, 1989).

Most people find these research findings pretty surprising. Common sense tells us that good outcomes make people feel happy, contented, and satisfied, and that negative events or failures make us unhappy. But conclusions based on scientific research are not always the same as those we reach using everyday common sense or intuition. And when those conclusions differ, which should you trust: research findings or common sense? Are research findings really more dependable, trustworthy, or accurate than our everyday understanding of social behavior?

These kinds of questions are at the heart of this chapter. Social psychology is an *empirical science*, meaning that its theories and conclusions about social behavior rest on the results of research. Like other scientists, most social psychologists believe that scientific research methods produce answers that are more likely to be trustworthy and unbiased than those we arrive at through everyday common sense, hunches, and intuitions. Why? It is not that scientists are perfectly objective logicians like *Star Trek*'s Mr. Spock or Commander Data. On the contrary, scientists are human, too, and they are just as vulnerable as anyone else to preconceptions, prejudices, and wishful thinking. But this is exactly why scientific methods are so important. Most people are unaware of the biases in their everyday thinking and knowledge, and they therefore fail to guard against them. Because scientists know that biases can distort their reasoning and their findings, they use research methods specifically designed to counter such slips in thinking.

Most of this chapter is dedicated to describing the lengths to which social psychologists go to try to keep their research free from bias and error. Their goal is to reach general conclusions about human social behavior that are as trustworthy as possible. Understanding the practical and logical steps researchers take to reach this goal will help you grasp *why* social psychologists do the sorts of research you will read about in this book. It will also help you to judge which research findings should be taken seriously and when research you read about in magazines or on the web falls short of its goal.

But good science is about more than just producing trustworthy and general results. Social-psychological research is a human enterprise, in which people are both the investigators and the investigated. This situation inevitably raises issues of values and ethics. How should research participants be treated? Are there research questions that should not be pursued? Should the results of research be made known to everyone, no matter how they will use those results? No researcher can ignore these questions, and neither should any consumer of social-psychological research. As you read this chapter and the rest of this text, you may wish to reflect on the values implicit in social psychologists' work and on how your own values guide your reactions to the topics and results that we will discuss. Clarifying ethical and value stands about research issues is just as important to good science as carefully following the rules of the scientific method.

A Note to the Student on How to Use This Chapter

Research methods can seem dry and abstract, compared to the richness and excitement of the substance of social psychology. Although some familiarity with research methods is essential for understanding how social psychologists reach their conclusions about people's social behavior, instructors may use this chapter in different ways. Some may assign this chapter early in the course, corresponding to its place in the book. Others may ask you to read this chapter after two or three substantive chapters, so that your knowledge of some meaningful and important studies can serve as background for deeper understanding of research methods. Other instructors may not assign this chapter at all, preferring to describe research methods in lectures or handouts.

Whatever your instructor's approach, we add one piece of advice. Through the book, as you read about particular studies, you may wonder what justifies the research conclusions, or feel concerned about the well-being of participants in the study. When issues like these arise in your mind, it is a good idea to turn back to this chapter as a resource to help you think about the issues. So if you question a study's conclusion that violence in the media can *cause* people to become more aggressive, you might want to look at the section on experimental designs and the strength of causal inferences on pages 34–35. Or if you wonder how a study using North American college students as participants can shed light on the reactions of other kinds of people or people in other cultures, see the section on the generalizability of research on pages 37–40. These examples illustrate some ways this chapter can serve as a resource for understanding how and why research is conducted, throughout the entire course.

Research Questions and the Role of Theory

Origins of Research Questions

> Research questions are provoked by curiosity about why people act the way they do. In turn, this curiosity often reflects concern about important social problems.

Research is almost always provoked by curiosity: the researcher's desire to know the answer to some question about events, ideas, and people. Some questions are provoked by unexpectedly negative or positive events. Well-publicized events such as the brutality of ethnic warfare in the Sudan and the global outpouring of aid for Asian tsunami victims provoke questions about hatred and altruism. The shocking acts of suicide bombers who give their lives to kill their group's perceived enemies cause social psychologists, like other observers, to ask what motivates these individuals. And the way rescuers work together to help victims of earthquakes, floods, hurricanes, and fires stimulates researchers' curiosity about processes leading to cooperation. But research ideas also stem from questioning the mundane and the accepted—the everyday events that affect the lives of all of us. Why do women still earn less than men performing the same jobs? How good are people at judging others' characters? How can city managers convince more motorists to carpool? Is breaking up really hard to do, even if you are the breaker-upper rather than the broken-up-with?

Part of what makes a person choose to become a social psychologist is a healthy store of curiosity about why people act the way they do. Notice, however, that many of these questions go beyond mere curiosity. Many social psychologists try to explain and solve social problems that have a major impact on many people's lives: racial prejudice, gender discrimination, depletion of environmental resources, violence, unhealthy lifestyles, and depression. And although individual events and people may provoke their research questions, social psychologists do not strive merely to understand *specific* events or *specific* individuals. They seek instead to discover general principles that explain the behavior of many people in many situations. From those principles will flow an understanding of why behavior occurs and under what conditions.

What Is a Scientific Theory?

> Social psychologists seek to develop scientific theories to explain social behavior. A scientific theory is a statement about the causal relationships among abstract constructs. It is a statement that holds for specified types of people, times, and settings.

To conduct their research, social psychologists have to translate specific questions about individuals and events into general statements about social behavior. Consider, for example, some of the research referred to at the beginning of this chapter. One study interviewed women diagnosed with breast cancer and noted whether they compared themselves to others who were adjusting better or worse to the disease (J. V. Wood and others, 1985). In another study, business school students engaged in a mock negotiation with an opponent, then learned that the opponent was happy or sad about the outcome (Loewenstein and others, 1989). What was the point of these exercises? Were the researchers concerned only about the behavior of particular cancer patients, or about specific students involved in one set of negotiations? Not at all. The real goal of these studies was not to gauge the reactions of particular individuals in particular situations but rather to test a general social-psychological theory about human behavior. In fact, all the research referred to in the introduction to the chapter was testing some aspect of *social comparison theory*, the idea that people evaluate their abilities, opinions, and outcomes by comparing themselves to others (Festinger, 1954). All of our judgments about ourselves, as slow or smart, right or wrong, winners or losers, are affected by our comparisons of our own abilities, attitudes, and outcomes to those of others.

Theories provide general explanations for social behavior. More formally, a **scientific theory** satisfies three requirements:

- It is a statement about constructs.

- It describes causal relations.

- It is general in scope.

Let us look more closely at each part of this definition.

1. *Theories are about constructs.* **Constructs** are abstract concepts like "anxiety," "aggression," or "self-esteem." "The knowledge of others' attitudes" and "the evaluation of one's own attitudes" are two constructs that feature in social comparison theory. Each of these constructs is abstract, in that it cannot be directly observed. You cannot see knowledge or touch an evaluation.

2. *Theories describe causal relations.* Theories describe causal relations among constructs, stating that a change in one construct (the cause) produces a corresponding change in another construct (the effect). Social comparison theory is a theory about cause and effect: Our knowledge of other people's outcomes, performances, or opinions causes changes in how we evaluate our own outcomes, performances, or opinions.

   Because theories offer reasons to explain why events occur, they are very powerful. If we know that one state or event causes another, we can take practical steps, known as interventions, to change behavior or solve problems. The knowledge that people evaluate their own abilities and attitudes by reference to those of other people, for example, could have a variety of practical applications. A city might decide to saturate the community with posters featuring the names and photos of city residents who form carpools. Social comparison theory would predict that knowing that their neighbors are committed to carpooling might cause other residents to decide to share rides. Similarly, medical personnel who work with patients

---

Information gleaned from comparison to others has a major impact on what people think and how they feel about themselves, as described in Chapter 4, pages 99 and 110 to 112.

Scientific theory. A statement that satisfies three requirements: It is about constructs; it describes causal relations; and it is general in scope, although the range of generality differs for different theories.

Constructs. Abstract and general concepts that are used in theories and that are not directly observable.

with treatable forms of cancer might encourage those patients to compare themselves with other people who have more serious forms of the disease. Such a comparison might help them to cope better with their illness. Both of these strategies are made possible by research showing that comparisons between our own experiences and those of other people actually cause us to feel and act in certain ways.

3. *Theories are general in scope.* Theories are intended to be general in scope, applying to many people in different settings and times. However, the range of applicability may vary from one theory to another. Social comparison theory, for example, is intended to be a broadly applicable statement about how all people evaluate many aspects of their life. And, indeed, judging one's own experience in the context of what happens to others does appear to be a general human characteristic, although reactions to the comparison may differ in different cultures (Moghaddam, Taylor, & Wright, 1993).

Other theories, however, have a more limited scope. Perhaps they pertain only to males, or only to people raised in some Asian cultures. The more generally applicable a theory is, the more useful it is because it will hold for many different kinds of people in many different situations and at many different times. Currently, however, little is known about just how broadly many social-psychological theories can be applied (M. H. Bond, 1988; Markus, Kitayama, & Heiman, 1996). This important issue of the generality of theories is explored in more detail later in this chapter.

Testing Theories: From Theory to Research

Theories are not worth much unless they are tested, and so the ultimate goal of research is to test theories. This testing allows social psychologists to assess whether a theory offers a good explanation of human behavior. Theories can be evaluated only on the basis of valid research: research that is trustworthy because the researcher has taken pains to exclude bias and error. How can researchers be sure their research is valid and can provide evidence for or against theories? It turns out that valid research is guided by the three properties of theories just described (T. D. Cook & Campbell, 1979; Judd, Smith, & Kidder, 1991).

1. Because theories deal with constructs—abstract concepts—researchers have to be sure the specific observations they make in their studies are in fact relevant to those constructs. For example, researchers studying how social comparisons affect cancer patients' adjustment to their illness must have some way to accurately measure the patients' adjustment.

2. Because theories describe causal relations, researchers have to be sure they know the causes of any changes in behavior they find in their studies Research must allow the conclusion that the cancer patients' successful adjustment is due to the social comparisons they make, rather than to some other, extraneous cause.

3. Because theories are general in scope, researchers have to be sure they have learned something about how people in general, not just a few individuals, think, feel, and act. Conclusions about effects of social comparisons on patients' adjustment would be most valuable if they held for those with

many types of disease (not just cancer), and to patients who are treated at home as well as in hospitals, for example.

Research that meets these three criteria is said to have *construct validity, internal validity,* and *external validity.* As we shall see, all three of these criteria are essential links in the logical chain by which research supports theory. Although decisions about every aspect of research may have implications for all three forms of validity, construct validity has the most to do with the way constructs are measured, internal validity with the design of a study, and external validity with the populations and settings used in the research.

Construct Validity and Approaches to Measurement

To provide a valid test of a theory, research must have construct validity, which means that the independent and dependent variables used in the research must correspond to the intended theoretical constructs. Construct validity is endangered if participants behave in ways they think are socially desirable. Researchers ensure construct validity by measuring independent and dependent variables in many different ways.

The researcher's first task is to make sure that the research has good **construct validity**, meaning that the events that occur in the research setting actually correspond to the theoretical constructs under investigation. This is not always an easy task.

Remember that cause and effect constructs are abstract concepts (like anxiety or social comparison) that are not directly observable. Their presence or absence has to be inferred through observable variables (factors on which people can vary). Variables that are considered to be causal factors are called **independent variables**. Variables representing effects are called **dependent variables**, because they depend on the causal or independent variable.

An example can help clarify these terms. Let's consider a theory called *realistic conflict theory.* This theory states that hostility between social groups is caused by direct competition for limited resources. Researchers have tried to study the abstract construct of "competition for limited resources," for example, by measuring people's belief that their department and another department are pitted against each other for a share of an organizational budget. The theory suggests that this belief (the study's independent variable) will cause another construct, "hostility between social groups," to increase. To measure this construct, researchers have looked at dependent variables such as negative stereotypes, insults, refusal to help, and acts of aggression that rival groups direct toward each other. If the concrete independent and dependent variables used in the research correspond to the intended theoretical constructs, the researchers will be able to draw valid conclusions about those constructs.

Construct validity has two parts. First, independent and dependent variables must correspond to the intended construct, and second, they must not correspond to other constructs. As you will see in the pages that follow, much of the ingenuity in social-psychological research goes into selecting and refining ways to measure important theoretical constructs without measuring other, unintended constructs.

Construct validity. The extent to which the independent and dependent variables used in research correspond to the theoretical constructs under investigation.

Independent variable. A concrete manipulation or measurement of a construct that is thought to influence other constructs.

Dependent variable. A concrete measurement of a construct that is thought to be influenced by other constructs.

■ **The Rattlers and the Eagles.** These archival photographs show two groups of boys who participated in Muzafer Sherif's famous study testing realistic conflict theory, to be described in Chapter 13. On the left, the boys compete in a tug of war, an activity that corresponds to the construct of competition for limited resources because only the winning group received prizes. On the right, the boys cooperate to solve a problem with the water tank. This activity reflects the theoretical construct of cooperation for common goals, which the study found can reduce intergroup conflict.

THREATS TO CONSTRUCT VALIDITY. Unfortunately, ensuring construct validity is a pretty tall order. A common problem is that a variable may be affected by other influences besides the construct that it is intended to measure. Suppose researchers tried to measure intergroup hostility by asking workers in the organization how much they liked members of the competing department. Workers might be unwilling to admit that they hate their co-workers, so their ratings might not honestly reflect their feelings of hostility. This threat to construct validity is called **social desirability response bias**: people's tendency to act in ways that make them look good (M. J. Rosenberg, 1969). Consider another example. A researcher wishing to measure the construct of conscientiousness might ask the following questions: Are you a punctual person? Do you keep your promises? Do you carry your share of responsibilities in group projects? The problem is that most people's responses to such questions would reflect both their appraisal of their conscientiousness and their tendency to say good things about themselves. The researcher might think she is measuring conscientiousness, but in fact she also would be measuring people's desire to look good. Social psychologists must be constantly on guard against the threat of social desirability as well as other biases in their measurements. This is particularly true when researchers are interested in attitudes or behaviors that might meet with some social disapproval, such as stereotyping, prejudice, aggression, or unusual opinions or lifestyles.

ENSURING CONSTRUCT VALIDITY. Researchers take great pains to avoid compromising the construct validity of their studies. They do so by choosing their measurements very carefully and by using multiple measures.

1. *Using the best measure for the purpose.* Researchers try hard to choose measurement techniques that tap the construct under investigation but minimize other influences. Measures used in research fall into a few distinct categories, each with its own strengths and weaknesses.

> **Social desirability response bias.** People's tendency to act in ways that they believe others find acceptable and approve of.

Sally Forth

© KING FEATURES SYNDICATE. Reprinted with permission.

Self-report measures, which rely on asking the individual about his or her thoughts, feelings, or behaviors, are probably the best available source of information about beliefs, attitudes, and intentions. But they are also particularly susceptible to social desirability biases, especially if the topic is a sensitive one. Thus, asking people overt questions about their racial prejudice might not produce answers with high construct validity (Dunton & Fazio, 1997).

A researcher studying racial prejudice might decide, therefore, that a better technique for his particular study would be to use *observational measures:* to directly watch and record people's behavior. The researcher could watch, for example, how close a participant stood or sat next to a person of another race and whether people participating in intergroup interactions displayed relaxed smiles or nervous fidgeting. Observational measures often have good construct validity, particularly when participants are unaware of being observed. Of course, if the research setting is public or if participants know they are being observed, social desirability biases could still undermine construct validity.

Performance measures are most appropriate for some research goals. Performance measures ask participants to perform some task as well as they can, for example, by answering questions as rapidly and accurately as possible or by recalling as much as they can about information presented earlier. A performance measure of prejudice might require participants to read a complicated description of a character's successes and failures and then to recall everything they could from the story. If participants recalled mostly successes when they believed the character was White but mostly failures if the same character was described as Hispanic, the researcher might conclude that the participants were prejudiced against Hispanics. Because people usually just try to perform as well as they can on such tasks, social desirability tends to be less of a problem than it is with self-report or observational measures.

Like any good carpenter or chef, a social psychology researcher must choose the right measurement tool for the job at hand. Measures that prove to be particularly precise and effective ways of assessing constructs often become quite popular in research, as ones with less construct validity fall by the wayside. But even the best available measure might not by itself guarantee construct validity.

2. *Using multiple measures.* Because different kinds of measures have different strengths, the best way a researcher can ensure construct validity is to use multiple measures.

The use of multiple measures increases researchers' confidence in their findings. To understand why, imagine you wanted to be sure your boss was in a good mood before you asked for time off. You check her expression for a smile and conclude she probably is feeling fine. Because you really are not sure, however, you ask a co-worker, who reports that the supervisor has been quite amicable. Still, you decide to see if she chooses to work out during her lunch hour—usually a good sign of an upbeat mood. Each of these very different means of gathering information has its own unique problems, but the accumulated evidence all points to the fact that your boss is feeling pretty chipper. You can see how your conviction that you were actually reading the supervisor's mood accurately would grow with each converging piece of evidence, even though no single piece of evidence could be conclusive in itself. When different measures produce the same results it works the same way: Researchers can be reasonably confident that they are measuring the intended construct and nothing else.

Now imagine for a moment that you are part of a research team trying to test the impact of positive or negative mood on helping. How could you assess the dependent variable construct, helping? You can probably think of a number of different possibilities. You might ask people about their intentions to help. Alternatively, you could count the number of spilled papers they retrieve or tally the dollars they donate to a worthy cause. A third possibility is to time how long it takes the research participants to come to another person's aid. These are diverse measures of willingness to help. Which should you use? Your best choice might be "all of the above." By using so many diverse measures of willingness to help, researchers increase the likelihood that the construct of helping will be adequately measured.

Internal Validity and Types of Research Design

> To provide a valid test of a theory, research must allow observers to conclude that changes in the independent variable actually caused changes in the dependent variable. If both the independent and dependent variables are measured, the research may lack internal validity because many other unknown factors could affect the research results. Random assignment of participants to groups followed by manipulation of independent variables allow the researcher to draw stronger conclusions about cause and effect.

A good test of a theory provides solid evidence about cause and effect. Research has high **internal validity** if the researcher can confidently conclude that a change in the independent variable *caused* a change in the dependent variable. Whether or not such a conclusion can be drawn depends primarily on a study's *research design*, which specifies how research participants will be selected and treated. Some types of research designs offer a higher level of internal validity than do others.

THREATS TO INTERNAL VALIDITY. The major threat to internal validity is that factors other than changes in the independent variable may be present and may

> **Internal validity.** The extent to which it can be concluded that changes in the independent variable actually caused changes in the dependent variable in a research study.

be causing the observed changes in the dependent variable. Eliminating all such alternative factors is often very difficult, as you will see in the following example.

The *contact hypothesis* is a theory that states that casual, friendly contact with members of a different ethnic group increases liking for that group (G. W. Allport, 1954b). One obvious way of testing this idea involves investigating the impact of important, naturally occurring forms of contact, such as a person's everyday encounters with different groups in the neighborhood, on liking for various groups. Rudolf Kalin and J. W. Berry (1982) did just that, using data from a public opinion survey. The survey asked what Canadians thought of English-speaking and French-speaking Canadians, Canadian Native Americans, and Canadians of German, Jewish, Italian, and Ukrainian descent. Kalin and Berry compared the survey data with information from the Canadian Census to establish which ethnic groups lived in the same neighborhoods as the various survey respondents. Their results showed that people who lived in areas with a relatively high percentage of a particular group liked that group more than did people who lived far away from members of the group. This study is an example of a **nonexperimental research** design, a design in which researchers simply measure both the independent variable (in this case, neighborhood ethnic composition) and the dependent variable (people's opinions of groups).

Unfortunately, nonexperimental designs are vulnerable to many threats to internal validity. For example, measurement of the independent variable in this survey does allow researchers to identify participants who live near many French-speaking Canadians and participants who do not. However, the nonexperimental design cannot rule out the possibility that these two groups of participants may differ in many other unknown ways. As a result, even if the groups differ in their general favorability toward French-speaking Canadians, researchers cannot confidently state the cause of that difference. Although highly favorable responses may be due to the causal impact of frequent contact with the group in the participants' neighborhood, other factors besides increased contact could also be the cause. In fact, you can probably think of several alternative explanations. For example, rather than contact causing the liking, liking may cause the contact. That is, people who hold more positive views of a group might choose to move into or remain in areas in which many members of that group live. Another explanation may be that people who live in a particular neighborhood share other personal characteristics, such as a particular type of social background, that influence both where the people live and how they feel about ethnic diversity.

In a nonexperimental design it is always possible that people who differ on the intended independent variable may also differ in other unintended ways. Each additional difference offers an alternative explanation for any results researchers find. And each alternative explanation for differences in the dependent variable threatens the internal validity of the research.

The conditions under which intergroup contact can undermine prejudice and help resolve intergroup conflict are described in Chapter 5, pages 178 to 181, and Chapter 13, pages 511 to 513.

Nonexperimental research. A research design in which both the independent and dependent variables are measured.

■ **Yes, but is it internally valid?** Many nonexperimental studies find that children exposed to violent television or video games are more aggressive than those who are not. Unfortunately, these designs lack internal validity. Their results cannot tell us whether what the children are watching causes aggression, or whether aggressive children prefer such video games and television programs. To establish the causal role of TV and video game violence, social psychologists have turned to experimental research designs with high internal validity, as discussed in Chapter 13.

ENSURING INTERNAL VALIDITY. Given the vast number of differences that characterize humankind, is it possible to set up a research design that ensures that groups of people can be expected to differ only in the way the researcher intends? Amazingly, the answer is yes. This feat can be accomplished by using an **experimental research** design. Two aspects of experimental design are crucial for internal validity: First, participants are *randomly assigned* to experimental groups (sometimes called *conditions*). Random assignment of the participants in a study is distinct from random selection of participants from some larger set of people, a topic that we will discuss later in this chapter. Second, after the random assignment takes place, the independent variable is *manipulated* (or intentionally varied) rather than simply measured. Here is how these two processes work.

First, researchers divide participants into groups that are equivalent. To do so, they use a technique similar to a lottery or a flip of a coin to assign participants to different groups. **Random assignment** gives every person who is a participant in an experiment exactly the same chance of ending up in any given experimental group. Random assignment of participants ensures that the groups are approximately equivalent in every way. Suppose you started out with 20 people, 10 men and 10 women, and randomly divided them into two groups by flipping a coin for each person. Would it be likely that all of the women would end up in one group and all the men in the other? It could happen, but it is extremely unlikely; in fact, this outcome would occur less often than once in 500,000 times. Because the coin has the same chance of landing head-up each time it is flipped, every person has an equal chance of being assigned to the "heads" group. In the end, each group will probably have a roughly even number of males and females. The same logic applies not just to gender but to all attributes of the individuals who are being assigned: their age, eye color, friendliness, shoe size, and even other characteristics the researcher would not think of or could not measure. So, on the average, random assignment creates groups that are approximately equivalent to one another before the manipulation is applied.

This sets the stage for the second important step in an experimental design: The researcher now manipulates, or intentionally varies, the independent variable so that participants in the different conditions are exposed to different treatments. Because the groups were expected to be equivalent to begin with, this procedure creates groups that differ only in terms of the independent variable. Finally, the researcher measures the dependent variable. Now it is reasonable to conclude that any observed differences in the dependent variable were caused by the independent variable, simply because no other differences between the groups are expected to exist. Of course, manipulations as well as measures must have good construct validity for an experiment to be meaningful. That is, a good manipulation (like a good measure) must successfully cause changes in the desired theoretical construct, but not in other, unintended constructs.

Donna Desforges and her associates (1991) used an experimental design when they set out to test the contact hypothesis. These researchers randomly assigned some participants, U.S. college students, to work cooperatively with a person described as a former mental patient. (The "patient" was actually a *confederate*, a research assistant playing a specific role in the study.) Other participants simply sat in the same room with the person. The students who interacted with the individual came to hold more positive beliefs about former mental patients than did the students who simply worked in the same room. We can be confident that the interaction caused this difference because the groups of students who received these two treatments were created by random assignment and therefore can be expected to be equivalent in every other way.

Experimental research. A research design in which researchers randomly assign participants to different groups and manipulate one or more independent variables.

Random assignment. The procedure of assigning participants to different experimental groups so that every participant has exactly the same chance as every other participant of being in any given group.

EXPERIMENTAL VERSUS NONEXPERIMENTAL RESEARCH DESIGNS. A researcher who wishes to test a theory may choose either an experimental or a nonexperimental design. In general, experimental designs offer higher internal validity and therefore permit stronger tests of the causal relations between constructs. If a nonexperimental study shows that the dependent variable and independent variable go together, that result is consistent with a causal theory. For example, Kalin and Berry's (1982) finding that people who lived in ethnically diverse neighborhoods are lower in ethnic prejudice is certainly consistent with the contact hypothesis. The result does not provide strong support for the theory, however, because factors other than the independent variable could also be causing the observed pattern of results. Experimental designs provide stronger tests of theory because the combination of random assignment and manipulation of the independent variable rules out virtually all alternative explanations.

Why, then, would a researcher ever use a nonexperimental design? The reasons are quite straightforward. First, some theoretically important independent variables, like gender, ethnicity, or area of residence, obviously cannot be intentionally varied. Thus, Kalin and Berry could not practically have assigned people to live in neighborhoods near or far from members of other ethnic groups. Second, for ethical reasons, researchers must not manipulate variables like participants' relationships with their marriage partner, or their feelings of depression, or the degree of their ethnic prejudice. And, finally, other research manipulations just cannot be as powerful as the variation in constructs found in everyday life. For example, no experimental study of the effects of television watching on aggression could faithfully reproduce the accumulated effect of watching 4 or more hours of television every day for a period of 10 or 20 years. For all these reasons, nonexperimental designs are sometimes the most appropriate. Table 2.1 summarizes the advantages and disadvantages of experimental and nonexperimental designs.

External Validity and Research Populations and Settings

To provide a valid test of a theory, research must have external validity, meaning that its results can be generalized to other people, settings, and times. Some theories apply to many different kinds of people and places, whereas others apply more narrowly. When a theory is intended to apply to a particular population and setting, external validity is ensured by conducting studies using that population and setting. When a theory is intended to apply generally *across* different people, places, and times, external validity is ensured by conducting repeated tests of the theory in diverse populations, settings, and cultures.

TABLE 2.1. Advantages and Disadvantages of Nonexperimental and Experimental Designs

Type of validity	Nonexperimental design	Experimental design
Internal validity	*Low*, because the lack of random assignment and manipulation means that alternative explanations for results may be possible.	*High*, because random assignment and manipulation allow alternative causal explanations to be ruled out.
Construct validity	*High*, if powerful effects of real-life variables—including those that cannot practically or ethically be manipulated—can be studied in their natural contexts.	*Low*, when practical or ethical constraints render manipulations weak or artificial. *High*, when manipulations can adequately vary theoretically important constructs.

A single research study is usually conducted with a single type of participant at a single time and in a single location. Research has **external validity** if its results can be assumed to generalize, that is, to hold for other types of participants, other times, or other places relevant to the theory.

The results of the study by Desforges and her associates (1991), for example, offer support for the contact hypothesis. But you might wonder whether these results would be found *only* if the participants were North American college students, or *only* if the contact group was former mental patients. One of the important functions of research is to determine just how broadly theories generalize. Recall from the earlier discussion in this chapter that the more generalizable a theory is, the more powerful it is because it explains the behavior of many different people in many different situations. But not all theories claim to hold true for all people in all places (T. D. Cook & Campbell, 1979; Kruglanski, 1975): Some research aims at generalizing to specific people in specific places. Most of the research you will read about in this text, however, seeks to generalize more broadly *across* various kinds of people, places, and times.

GENERALIZING *TO* VERSUS GENERALIZING *ACROSS* PEOPLE AND PLACES. In some research, a specific target population and setting is the researcher's primary interest. Applied research, where the goal is to use scientific findings to solve immediate practical problems, often falls into this category. For example, researchers have long known that when people have a sense of control over their situation they cope better with stress. A physician might wonder whether an increased sense of control could help seriously ill patients cope better when they are hospitalized. A study that attempts to answer this question has a specific and relevant population and setting. Only people hospitalized with serious illnesses can be used as participants if the goal is to answer this particular research question. In fact, as a result of such studies, giving hospitalized patients some control over their situation is now a widely used technique for helping them deal with stressful medical procedures (Pranulis, Dabbs, & Johnson, 1975).

Most research you will read about in this text does not attempt to generalize to a single, specific target population or setting. Instead, as you will see, the research goal is usually a broader sort of generalization across various factors. One way to think about this goal is to ask the questions: Does the research have implications for many types of people in various places at more than one time period? Does the research apply, for example, to women as well as men? To Israelis and Koreans, as well as North Americans? To people living in the year 2020 as well as those living today? A typical study is conducted with a limited number of participants of a particular type—usually college students—in one location at one point in time. Few people would be interested in research results that applied only to those participants at that time and place. The key question therefore becomes: Exactly what aspects of the research conclusions will successfully generalize?

Let us return to the example of the North American college students who engaged in a cooperative learning task in the laboratory with a person they believed was a former mental patient. Those students came to hold more favorable beliefs about one group, former mental patients (Desforges and others, 1991). What generalization can be drawn from this finding, assuming it passes the tests of construct validity and internal validity? One could ask whether exactly the same finding would be obtained among Ethiopian college students, among Israeli sixth graders, and among adults in Papua-New Guinea. But social-psychological researchers rarely study participant populations as diverse as these; indeed, the

> **External validity.** The extent to which research results can be generalized to other appropriate people, times, and settings.

very concept of a "former mental patient" would be meaningless to some of these groups. The reason is that this is not precisely the right question to ask about generalizability. Whether the study's *specific findings* can be directly generalized is not the crucial issue.

What is the appropriate generalization? To answer that question, we need to recall the fundamental reason why a study like that of Desforges and her associates is conducted. That study was not aimed at generalizing to some target population or setting. Nor was it intended to reveal some modestly interesting fact about people's opinions of former mental patients, that is, about the specific dependent variable used in the study. Instead, the goal was to test a theory regarding causal relations among abstract constructs. In this case, the theory states that under specific conditions, friendly interaction with individual group members often causes positive changes in people's attitudes and beliefs about the group. This theoretical level defines the generalization that is expected. So we would not expect all kinds of people all around the world to hold the same views about former mental patients. We would, however, expect to find that similar processes of belief and attitude change are caused by friendly interaction with group members, and that is what the great majority of studies on the topic show (Pettigrew & Tropp, 2006).

Recall that we emphasized in Chapter 1 that you should seek to learn general principles about social psychology rather than a long list of findings of specific studies. In exactly the same way, researchers hope that the underlying principles, rather than the details of the findings, will generalize from one population and setting to other appropriate ones. Figure 2.1 illustrates this idea: The results of a

FIGURE 2.1   Research results generalize through theories

■ Most studies are conducted to test theories. The theory may then make predictions that apply to different people and places. The results of a particular study are not generalized *directly*, but they have implications for other people, times, and places to the extent that the results support a valid and general theory.

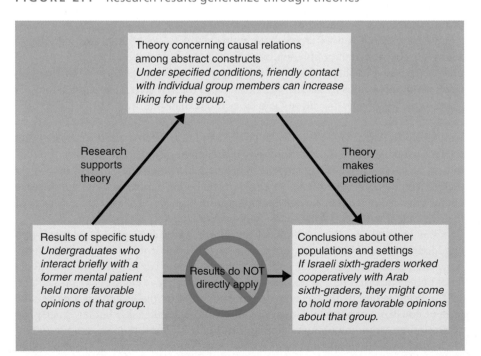

study are not applied directly to another population or setting but are used to support a general theory, which in turn has implications for other people and places (Mook, 1980).

EXTERNAL VALIDITY AND RESEARCH PARTICIPANTS. Recall that if research has external validity, its results can be assumed to hold for other types of participants, other times, or other places relevant to the theory. The first major threat to such generalizations thus involves the types of *people* studied. One problem is the use of participants who are unrepresentative of all the people to whom a theory is intended to apply. College students differ in many ways from the average person (Jaffe, 2005). For example, compared with the general population, they tend to be younger and more intelligent; they probably have less stable close relationships; they are still involved in forming new roles and images of themselves; and they are less likely to have experienced serious illness, divorce, or parenthood. Can researchers assume that *all* research findings obtained with college student participants will generalize to all other types of people? Of course not.

As we have said, however, researchers ordinarily do not wish to generalize specific findings. Their usual goal is to generalize a broader conclusion about underlying causal processes. So one would not expect, for example, to find that the issues responsible for arguments and conflict were the same for both college dating couples and older married couples. Nevertheless, the effect of arguments on the partners' satisfaction with their relationships might be similar for both kinds of couples. Or, to use another example, students may not have as many well-developed social roles as older people, but the process by which students form their views of themselves and the effects of those views on behavior may be the same for many groups of diverse people. Thus, generalizing about causal explanations is more justifiable than generalizing about the content of thoughts and behavior.

The social-psychological processes that are most likely to operate in similar ways among diverse groups of people are the most basic processes. Research has shown that these include the ways people respond to social influence from others, use the most accessible information, and seek mastery over their environment and connectedness with other people. As you will see in later chapters, these are the sorts of processes many social psychologists have investigated, often using college students as participants because they are easily accessible. Still, the only way to be really sure that research conclusions generalize is to repeat the research with different types of participants because, as you will see, sometimes even conclusions about processes cannot be generalized (Jaffe, 2005).

CULTURES AND EXTERNAL VALIDITY. People who have traveled in a country other than their own can testify that patterns of social behavior differ, and anthropologists' scientific observations confirm this conclusion. Since social psychology remains largely a Western phenomenon, do the research conclusions of social psychologists generalize across the world's societies and cultures? Once again, the answer is, "It depends." We can answer this question only by examining the specific set of research conclusions that we expect to generalize. Consider the observation that people tend to have certain expectations, or stereotypes, about what other social groups are like. Though the stereotypes that French and Australian citizens (for example) have of the English will probably be very different, the way the two groups of people develop those stereotypes and how they use them are likely to be

If you are interested in how and why people form stereotypes, why they are so resistant to change, and what can be done to overcome that resistance, look at Chapter 5, where these topics are covered.

very similar. Culture strongly dictates the content of people's thoughts and actions. The processes by which that content is developed and used, however, are more likely to be generalizable.

Sometimes both content and processes can differ for members of different cultures. For example, members of Western cultures are particularly likely to think of themselves as separate from other people and to define themselves in terms of their uniqueness. For this reason, such cultures are often termed *individualist* or *independent*. In *collectivist* or *interdependent* cultures like Japan and many other Eastern nations, people tend to think of themselves as linked to others, and they define themselves in terms of their relationships to others (Markus, Kitayama, & Heiman, 1996). The different content of their self-concepts leads to several differences in the ways members of different cultures process information about the self, respond to social conflict and disagreement, and experience emotions. Any theory on these topics that has been formulated and tested in only one type of culture may not generalize to members of other cultures.

EXTERNAL VALIDITY AND LABORATORY RESEARCH. As noted earlier, the representativeness of participants and the influences of cultures are two factors that can limit generalizability. A third major factor is the setting or place in which the research is conducted. Each research setting, whether in the laboratory or outside it, has advantages and disadvantages that arise from its particular characteristics.

Most social-psychological research is conducted in the laboratory because the researcher can control this setting. In the laboratory, the researcher can randomly assign participants to different conditions, manipulate independent variables while keeping other factors constant, and measure dependent variables with high construct validity. The chief virtue of the laboratory setting is that experimental designs with high internal validity are most easily implemented there.

But the lab also has a down side. One disadvantage is the short time span of most studies, which usually last no more than a few hours. Another is the somewhat artificial quality of many laboratory manipulations and measures. A researcher may, for example, ask participants to donate to another student the points they earn in the experiment and then count those points and use them as a measure of the concept of helping. You might wonder how well such measures correspond to nonlaboratory examples of helping, like volunteering 3 hours a week at the church food pantry.

Another potential weakness of the laboratory for external validity is that participants probably pay much more attention to the information provided in the laboratory than they would in some other context. In laboratory research on persuasion, for example, participants read persuasive messages and their attitudes are measured. Different kinds of messages can then be shown to be more or less effective. But outside the laboratory people do not go around reading every persuasive communication they see! Do you read every political poster on every lawn in your neighborhood? Or every ad for cold medicine in your bus or subway car? In everyday life outside the lab, the effectiveness of any persuasive message depends crucially on its ability to attract your attention. Thus, when different processes operate in laboratory and nonlaboratory settings, theories supported by findings from the laboratory may not apply to nonlaboratory settings.

A final disadvantage of laboratory settings is that participating in research may itself elicit special motives. When people are aware that they are being

■ **Ensuring construct validity by getting real.** To ensure that participants' reactions to manipulations are not contaminated by their beliefs about how they should act in a laboratory setting, social psychologists sometimes stage incidents in public to gauge people's natural reactions. Here a man pretends to verbally abuse and threaten another. How might you react if you came upon this scene?

studied, they may start to wonder, "What are they trying to get at here?" and their perceptions of the purpose of the research (whether the perceptions are accurate or wildly off base) may then affect their behaviors. Behaviors that are based on the participant's perceptions of the research purpose are said to be influenced by **demand characteristics**. Demand characteristics threaten construct validity because elements of the experiment other than the intended construct—the participants' impressions of what the researcher wants or expects—may affect the participants' behavior (Orne, 1962; Rosenthal, 1969). When research takes place in a strange and novel environment like the laboratory, people are remarkably sensitive to subtle cues that tell them how they are expected to act. This effect was clearly demonstrated in a study in which participants were asked to judge the degree of success or failure shown in a series of photographed faces (Rosenthal & Fode, 1963). One group of participants was guided through the study by a researcher who had been led to believe that the photos represented "successful" faces. The second group worked with a researcher led to believe that the same photos showed faces of "failure." Both researchers followed identical procedures and gave their participants identically worded instructions. Though participants were told nothing about the photos, they could pick up clues about the expected responses from the researchers' subtle nonverbal behaviors. In each group, the participants' evaluations of the photos corresponded exactly to the researcher's expectations. Because their responses reflected not only the intended construct (perceptions of the photos) but also demand characteristics (the responses the researcher seemed to expect), this study demonstrates how construct validity can be compromised.

To counteract demand characteristics, researchers often exercise extra precautions with members of the research team who will have contact with participants. These team members are prevented from knowing the responses that are expected from any particular participant. This precaution is taken so that the team members cannot subtly and unintentionally communicate those expectations to the participant. In addition, as you will see later in this chapter, researchers often attempt to conceal the true purpose of their research from participants and, in some cases, may even mislead participants about the purpose. Despite all these precautions, any research that takes place in the laboratory always has to be carefully scrutinized for the potential impact of demand characteristics.

EXTERNAL VALIDITY AND NONLABORATORY RESEARCH. The strengths and weaknesses of *field research*—research that takes place outside the laboratory—complement those of laboratory research. Field researchers can study the long-term effects of such variables as relationship development or public health campaigns. They can measure concrete, powerful variables. For example, instead of counting the points students donate in experiments, they can count donations of blood as a measure of helping. Field researchers can also study the effects of an earthquake prediction, an alarming event that could not ethically or practically be reproduced in a laboratory. Thus, field research often has good construct validity: The variables used in the research correspond to the intended theoretical constructs. And if random assignment and manipulation of independent variables can be implemented in the field, the use of an experimental design can also provide good internal validity. That means that the researcher can confidently conclude that the manipulations of the independent variables caused the change in the dependent variables. However, for practical reasons,

Demand characteristics. Cues in a research setting that lead participants to make inferences about what researchers expect or desire and that therefore bias how the participants act.

■ **Cultural differences: When can research findings be generalized?** These Chinese workers are participating in a corporate-sponsored exercise program. Their notion of "working out" differs greatly from what someone from a Western culture would envision. Social psychologists—aware that not all research findings generalize across cultures—have started to explore cultural effects on many scientific theories. These new findings are discussed throughout this book.

carrying out experiments outside the laboratory is often very difficult. As a result, most field studies are nonexperimental in design.

Field research, whether experimental or nonexperimental, can have high external validity if it avoids triggering the special processes, such as demand characteristics or concern for social desirability, that often occur in the laboratory setting. However, you should not make the mistake of assuming that research conducted in field settings always has more external validity than laboratory research. Diverse field settings, such as hospitals, airport departure lounges, and office cafeterias, also have particular characteristics that influence people's thoughts, motives, and actions in specific ways. Research conducted in one of these settings may or may not generalize to another, just as laboratory research may or may not generalize to a field setting.

ENSURING EXTERNAL VALIDITY. The keys to achieving external validity, then, depend on the underlying research purpose.

1. *If the goal is to generalize to some specific target population and setting, the participants and setting must be representative of the target.* For example, if the goal is to see how assembly-line workers respond to changes in a supervisor's behavior, a study of assembly-line workers in their factory would be the most useful and appropriate.

2. *If the goal is to generalize across people, places, and times, the best way to do so is to repeat the research in multiple settings and with multiple populations, including people from different cultures.* Most of the research you will read about in this text is concerned with generalizing across people and places. Ultimately, as social psychology adopts a more integrative perspective and becomes less bound by Western culture, two important consequences will follow. Cultural variables, such as East–West differences in self-conceptions, will be incorporated into theories so that cultural differences in social behavior can be explained rather than merely described. In addition, more research will be performed in diverse cultural settings, so that such broadly integrative theories can be developed and tested. Indeed, social psychology is currently moving in these directions (Nisbett, 2003; Markus, Kitayama, & Heiman, 1996; Moghaddam and others, 1993). Throughout this book, we will report the results of cross-cultural research whenever it throws new light on our understanding of the social and cognitive processes that influence human behavior.

Construct, internal, and external validity pertain to different aspects of the research process, are threatened by different factors, and are ensured by different types of strategies. Table 2.2 summarizes the most important characteristics of the three types of validity.

TABLE 2.2. Properties of Theories and Corresponding Characteristics of the Three Forms of Research Validity

Property of theory	Corresponding type of validity	Threats to validity	Relevant aspects of research	Ideal research characteristics
A theory deals with abstract constructs.	Construct validity: Observable variables used in research match the theoretical constructs.	Participants may respond in socially desirable ways or act in accordance with perceived demands.	Measures and manipulations	Multiple measures; multiple manipulations
A theory proposes causal relations among constructs.	Internal validity: Relationship among observable variables is due to postulated causal process.	Alternative causal explanations may be possible.	Designs	Experimental designs
A theory is general in scope, although the range varies across theories.	External validity: Research results can be obtained with many types of people, times, and settings.	Findings may apply to only limited types of people, times, or settings.	Populations and settings	Multiple replications

Evaluating Theories: The Bottom Line

Theories become generally accepted if the results of multiple valid studies show them to be superior to rival theories. Sometimes theories that seem to compete are in fact complementary explanations of events. Social-psychological research cannot help but be influenced by researchers' personal beliefs and cultural values. However, the rigorous use of research methods is our best hope for excluding the biases and errors that characterize everyday thinking.

Theories about social behavior ultimately stand or fall on the basis of how well they are supported by the results of valid research. As shown in Figure 2.2, the process involves a logical chain in which all three types of validity play a part. And just as a chain can be no stronger than its weakest link, each type of validity is crucial if research is to provide support for a theory.

Of course, no theory ultimately stands or falls on the basis of a single study. The results of any one study might have been influenced by simple mistakes by the researcher, the use of particular manipulations or measures, poor internal validity, special characteristics of the participants, or even chance variation. Indeed, researchers' attempts to increase one form of validity (for example, internal validity) often decrease other forms (external or construct validity). Kalin and Berry's (1982) survey testing the contact hypothesis in the field had high construct and external validity, as it measured long-term and powerful intergroup contact in the general population. But, as we pointed out earlier, that study had low internal validity because many differences other than degree of contact might explain the results. In contrast, the test of the same theory in a laboratory setting by Desforges and others (1991) had high internal validity because participants were randomly assigned

■ To test a theory, researchers must follow a logical chain. Only if the research has high construct validity, strong internal validity, and good external validity can the theory be supported with confidence. Any weak link breaks the inferential chain.

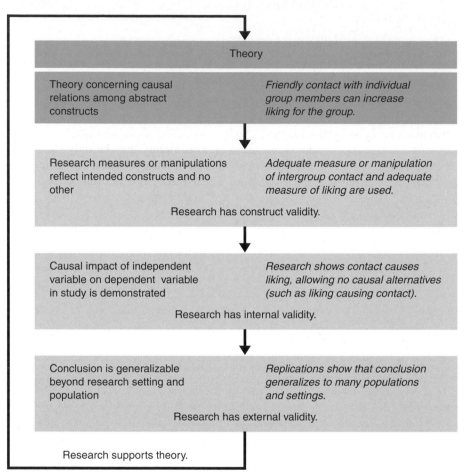

FIGURE 2.2   The role of research validity in supporting theory

to different levels of contact. But that study, in turn, had questionable construct and external validity, given the artificial nature of the laboratory cooperative learning task.

THE IMPORTANCE OF REPLICATION. Because no single study can be fully convincing by itself, researchers seek to **replicate**, or reproduce, the results of prior research. Indeed, scientists are required to report the procedures and methods used in their studies so that other researchers can repeat the research. The most important replications produce the same results by using different manipulations of the theoretical constructs in studies carried out in different settings with different participant populations.

Because replications provide such convincing support for theories, social psychologists often compare the results of different tests of the same theory. They perform these comparisons using *meta-analysis,* a systematic technique for locating relevant studies and summarizing their results (H. Cooper, 1990; Rosenthal, 1991). Meta-analysis allows researchers to examine the generality of results across replications conducted by different researchers using diverse methods, settings, and

Replication. Conducting new studies in an effort to provide evidence for the same theoretically predicted relations found in prior research.

participant populations. When many such studies all produce similar results, they provide stronger evidence for or against theories. Thus, for example, because studies as different as Kalin and Berry's (1982) survey and Desforges and her associates' (1991) laboratory tests show the same result, we can have greater confidence that intergroup contact does indeed increase liking. Because replication is so important, you will often see more than one study or the results of a meta-analysis cited to support conclusions reported in this text.

COMPETITION WITH OTHER THEORIES. The theories that social psychologists propose to explain social events or processes sometimes compete with and contradict each other. Eventually, one theory may stand out among all the others as being more consistent with replicated research findings. This victory may be only temporary, however. Research in social psychology, like that in other sciences, is ongoing, and any day some psychologist may propose a new theory that is even better able to explain the set of research findings. For this reason, scientists avoid applying the term *proven* to a theory. At best, a theory is *generally accepted,* a phrase that points to the importance of social consensus—the judgment made by the community of scientists.

In some cases, theories that first compete to explain research findings turn out to provide complementary explanations of events. Consider, for example, the competition that took place in the 1960s and 1970s between two theories that seemed to explain why attitudes often change to reflect people's behavior. In a series of studies, participants were assigned the task of writing an essay supporting a position they initially opposed. Researchers demonstrated that after the participants wrote the essay, their attitudes often became more similar to the view they had advocated in their writing (Goethals, Cooper, & Nacify, 1979; Linder, Cooper, & Jones, 1967). To explain these changes, one group of social psychologists, those who supported *cognitive dissonance theory,* argued that when people choose to act inconsistently (such as writing an essay they disagree with), the inconsistency creates psychological tension. The tension can be resolved, they proposed, if attitudes change to become consistent with behavior (moving toward the stand taken in the essay). In contrast, proponents of *self-perception theory* suggested that such changes occurred merely because people observed their own behavior and inferred their attitudes from their

Peanuts

behavior. "I agreed to write the supportive essay, therefore I suppose I must have a supportive attitude."

Although researchers conducted many studies and compared the predictions of the two theories, they were not able to settle the controversy. Cognitive dissonance theory and self-perception theory were each supported by some results, and neither theory gained general acceptance at the expense of the other. Finally, researchers Russell Fazio, Mark Zanna, and Joel Cooper (1977) noticed an interesting difference between the two sets of findings. Most successful tests of self-perception theory occurred when people behaved in ways not too inconsistent with their original attitudes. But the successful tests of cognitive dissonance theory seemed to be those in which people were induced to act in a way that directly opposed their initial convictions. This observation led Fazio, Zanna, and Cooper to suggest that the two theories offer a complementary understanding of the effect of behavior on attitudes. Perhaps self-perception processes operate to change attitudes when behavior is mildly different from initial attitudes. Cognitive dissonance processes, on the other hand, might kick in when behavior is so divergent from original attitudes that the discrepancy is upsetting. Further research confirmed their suggestions. Thus, two theories that started out as seeming competitors now work together to provide a better understanding of the interplay between action and attitudes, as you will see in Chapter 8.

GETTING THE BIAS OUT. Perhaps you can see now why scientists prefer to believe well-supported theories, even if they sometimes conflict with common sense. Research methods are designed to exclude many biases and errors by maintaining concern with all three forms of validity.

1. *Concern for construct validity*—making sure that observable events are good measures of general constructs—helps researchers avoid incorrect interpretations of specific events. Consider, for example, a conversation in which a New Yorker has trouble communicating with a person from the deep South. New Yorkers tend to speak faster than people from other areas of the United States, particularly those from the South, and they leave shorter pauses between "turns" in the conversation (Tannen, 1990). If the New Yorker interprets the difficulty of conversing with a Southerner as a sign that the Southerner is a bit slow-witted, rather than as an effect of different group standards for speech, an error of construct validity has affected this common-sense interpretation.

2. *Concern for internal validity*—being certain that one event causes another—makes it less likely that researchers will fall into the everyday trap of failing to consider alternative explanations. For example, if you see a man fidgeting nervously while waiting to be called in for a job interview, you might assume that he is basically an anxious person. That assumption, however, does not consider the fact that anyone waiting for an important interview is likely to feel nervous. Research needs to exclude such alternative explanations for behavior before citing the behavior as good evidence for or against a theory.

3. *Concern for external validity*—being sure an observation can be generalized—makes it clear why we should not base conclusions about human nature on our own limited and usually unrepresentative experience. A Southerner visiting Manhattan may be brushed aside by a rude New

In fact, people often jump quickly to the conclusion that behavior reflects personality, without looking for alternate explanations. You'll find out why in Chapter 3, pages 70 to 72.

Yorker who grabs the only available taxi during a downpour. If the Southerner concludes that all New Yorkers are rude, an error in external validity has been made. Such a broad generalization is hardly justified on the basis of one obnoxious individual.

But you should not assume that scientists always successfully achieve their objective of excluding bias and error from their research methods. On the contrary, the scientific enterprise is full of judgment calls that open the door to such influences as researchers' personal attitudes and beliefs, cultural beliefs, educational background, scientific training, or religious, moral, and political views. Scientists, after all, are human beings and are no more able than anyone else to stand outside their culture and society and evaluate theories with a pure, detached rationality (Gould, 1978). Thus, they tend to prefer theories that are consistent with their culture's generally accepted beliefs and values. For example, the 1935 *Handbook of Social Psychology* contained chapters on the "negro," the "red man," the "white man," and the "yellow man." The contents reflected the unquestioned assumptions of that time—assumptions that most people today would regard as offensively racist and sexist.

Feminist psychologists have pointed out some cultural assumptions about women and men that have crept unnoticed into scientific practice (Hare-Mustin & Marecek, 1988; McGrath, Kelly, & Rhodes, 1993; Peplau & Conrad, 1989; C. W. Sherif, 1979). For example, in some areas of research, such as the study of achievement motivation, the conclusions have been based almost entirely on responses of male participants. Although deciding to limit the participant pool to males may have allowed the researchers to avoid some complexities, other unwanted consequences may have resulted. For example, unique aspects of women's behavior may never be discovered if results from men are assumed to generalize to all humans. And even if such differences are discovered, they may be inappropriately interpreted as mere deviations from the male "standard" rather than legitimate parts of the human standard (Denmark, Russo, Frieze, & Sechzer, 1988).

Nevertheless, their fundamental reliance on research findings has often enabled social psychologists to expose and overturn generally accepted myths and falsehoods. For example, many social psychologists participated in preparing a statement presented to the U.S. Supreme Court in the 1954 *Brown v. Board of Education* case. Challenging the prevailing acceptance of "separate but equal" education for Whites and Blacks, the statement summarized research evidence showing that racially segregated schools could never be equal. That statement contributed to the Court's landmark decision to overturn legally enforced school segregation (Klineberg, 1986). Science is a human enterprise with no guarantees of objectivity. Nevertheless, its research techniques are the best ways yet devised to limit the effects of bias.

The Role of Ethics and Values in Research

Social psychology is both similar to and different from other scientific disciplines. Like all scientists, psychologists have responsibilities to the scientific community. Scientists must not falsify or misrepresent their procedures or data. They must avoid personal attacks in scientific controversies, while engaging in full, no-holds-barred debates on theoretical and empirical issues. And they must allocate credit fairly for scientific work. They must not plagiarize other scholars' work, and in publications, they must give credit to all who earned it by working on the research project. Good science depends on the integrity of each researcher, and serious violations of these rules of conduct are not tolerated.

But social psychology shares with the other social and behavioral sciences a special element. Recall that the statement was made earlier in the chapter that in social psychology, humans are both the investigators and the investigated. In social-psychological research, there are people filling out questionnaires as well as devising them, people exposed to independent variables as well as manipulating them, and people in front of the camera as well as at the controls. The inherently people-packed nature of social-psychological research means that researchers often must grapple not only with research problems and scientific responsibility but also with issues of values and ethics. When designing and conducting studies that might provide answers to questions about human behavior, researchers must always ask whether the end justifies the means. Do the research results justify the experiences of the research participants? And when the results are in hand, another question must be answered. If those findings can easily be applied to society as a whole, will the results of research be used in a socially responsible way? The issues of fairness to research participants and of social responsibility are a special part of social psychologists' scientific training (*Ethical Principles*, 1992).

Being Fair to Participants

Researchers seek to treat their participants fairly, often ensuring that participants know what they will experience in the study and agree to it in advance. However, to avoid biases when sensitive topics are investigated, researchers sometimes deceive participants about various aspects of the study. If deception is used, participants must be given information about research procedures and purposes at the conclusion of the study.

One of social psychology's best-known experiments began about 30 years ago when Philip Zimbardo of Stanford University signed up male volunteers between 17 and 30 years of age to participate for pay in a study of "prison life" (Haney, Banks, & Zimbardo, 1973; Zimbardo, Banks, Haney, & Jaffe, 1973). Some of the men were randomly assigned to be prison guards and others to be prisoners. Unexpectedly, the "prisoners" were taken into custody by real police officers, fingerprinted, and taken to the "prison," which had been set up, complete with barred cells, in the basement of the psychology building. Dressed in shapeless prison smocks and wearing ankle chains, the prisoners were at the mercy of any rules the "guards" cared to invent and enforce. As time passed, the cruelty and abusiveness of the guards and the passivity and dehumanization of the prisoners increased. The experiment soon went out of control: First one prisoner, then another, was released with depressive or psychotic symptoms. In the end, the entire experiment had to be terminated less than halfway through its planned duration.

Unexpected as they were, the results of the experiment led Zimbardo to conclude that the institutional roles of prisoner and guard caused the sometimes shocking behaviors in his prison. It was not the personalities of these initially normal, well-adjusted men that produced the results. The finding was no doubt important; perhaps, by extension, the same conclusion applies to what happens daily inside actual prison walls. But did the results justify the research participants' experiences, which were far more difficult and stressful than they had expected? When it became clear that the participants were given almost no details about the research project at the time they signed up, it appeared that the study violated a number of the special obligations psychologists have to their research participants.

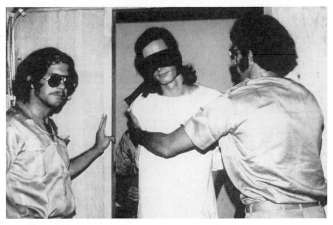

■ **Do research ends justify means?** In this photo of the Stanford prison experiment, a student assigned to the role of prisoner is handcuffed, blindfolded, and searched. Although these experiences caused considerable psychological distress, the results of the experiment provided important information about the sometimes frightening power of social roles and institutions. Such an experiment could not be conducted today. Yet the same questions about research remain: Can the social significance of results justify studies in which participants have unpleasant experiences? Can the same questions be asked in less potentially damaging ways? What do you think?

Primary among those obligations, of course, is to avoid harming participants. Potential harm can come from several different sources. Self-reports or observations may reveal things about participants that they would not wish to have publicly known. In most studies, this threat is routinely averted by keeping participants' responses completely anonymous and unidentifiable. Another source of harm is that people can be upset or distressed by their participation in research, as they were in the Zimbardo study. Participants may experience intense distress when they are involved in potentially doing harm, are required to make difficult decisions, or are placed in situations over which they have no control. They also may be upset by their own reactions to events, as the fake prison guards may have been when they realized how easily they had become brutal.

Research on topics as divergent as helping and stereotyping often causes distress when participants later realize that their actions were socially undesirable. This is a dilemma social psychologists face: They want their research to address many important issues, but in such research some participants may discover potentially damaging information about themselves or others. How, then, can researchers ethically proceed with their studies? The answer is by obtaining participants' **informed consent**, and social psychologists arrived at that answer partly in response to concern over studies like the Stanford prison project. Researchers must now help protect participants against the possibility of harm by telling participants they can withdraw from a study without penalty at any time. And they must give any volunteer enough information about the research to allow the person to make an informed decision about participating. "Without penalty" means that participants (often college students) cannot be coerced into participating, and any rewards resulting from participation, such as earning course credit, must be made available in alternative ways, such as through conducting library research. "Informed consent" does not mean participants are told everything about the research. They do not need to know the specific theory being tested, the rationale for the procedures, or other technical details. Participants must, however, be informed about and consent to the experiences they personally will undergo, such as filling out personality questionnaires, watching a videotape of erotic scenes, or participating in a group discussion. People who know they are free to participate

Informed consent. Consent voluntarily given by an individual who decides to participate in a study after being told what will be involved in participation.

and know what will happen to them if they do participate can freely choose to avoid any procedure they consider potentially harmful. How many of Zimbardo's participants do you think would have agreed to the experiment had they been informed in advance?

THE USE OF DECEPTION IN RESEARCH. Because of the importance of informed consent, ethical questions arise when researchers use *deception* to keep participants in the dark about various aspects of the research. Most instances of deception are relatively trivial. Participants are often told in advance what they will experience during the study (for example, watching a brief video clip and filling out a questionnaire) without being told the exact purpose of the study or the details of the procedure until their participation is complete.

In other cases, participants are actually misled about what will happen to them. Charles Hardy and Bibb Latané constructed an elaborate ruse to compare people's efforts on a task when they thought they were working alone versus their efforts in the presence of others. The researchers told participants the study concerned the effects of sensory deprivation on noise production. This explanation provided a rationale for having the participants wear earphones and blindfolds so that they had to rely on a researcher's word as to whether they were alone or with others. When told to yell and clap as loudly as they could, participants made less noise when they thought a second person was performing with them, compared to when they thought they were working alone (Hardy & Latané, 1986). Although deception was involved, its consequences were rather minor. But not all deception is this benign. In Stanley Milgram's famous study of obedience to authority, which we will discuss in detail in Chapter 10, participants were led to believe that they were giving increasingly strong electric shocks to another person. That individual cried out in pain, demanded that the procedure be stopped because he had a heart condition, and ultimately fell silent, suggesting that he might be unconscious or even dead. Of course, none of this was true, but because participants believed it, the entire experience was extremely stressful for them.

Why would social psychologists engage in such practices? The point of deception, whether trivial or consequential, is to combat demand characteristics and social desirability biases while gathering information about socially important topics. Think honestly about how you would act if a researcher told you, "This study concerns the effects of racial prejudice on reactions to requests for help," or "We are testing the ways failure at an important task can affect people's self-esteem." Perhaps you and everyone else would refuse to participate, and thus these topics could never be studied. Even if you did agree to participate, how could you prevent your knowledge of the topic from affecting your responses? Perhaps you might try, with the best of intentions, to help confirm the researcher's expectations. Or you might act in the most socially acceptable way you could think of. Either of these reactions, which are responses to factors other than the researcher's intended causal construct, would invalidate the research findings.

Most researchers argue that many social-psychological topics, such as helping, aggression, racial and gender prejudice, and conformity, are so sensitive that deception is often necessary to produce valid results. Yet the use of deception frequently makes it impossible to obtain truly informed consent, and it runs counter to most people's ideas about honest and fair treatment of others. Once again the question

This drop-off in individual effort often found in groups, called social loafing, *is discussed in detail in Chapter 12.*

arises: Does the end justify the means? Most researchers are willing to use deception as a last resort when they judge the research topic to be highly important and when no other alternatives are feasible. Even then, they try to keep deception to a minimum, and they inform participants of the deception as soon as possible through **debriefing**. Debriefing has several goals:

- The participant can raise questions and concerns about the research, and the researcher can address them.

- The researcher can fully explain any necessary deception.

- The researcher and participant can discuss the overall purpose and methods of the study, thereby enhancing the educational value of research participation.

- The researcher can detect and deal with any possible negative effects of the research.

Because most of its goals are important even for nondeceptive research, debriefing is now customary in most research. When deception is involved, however, debriefing is particularly important. If a participant is led to believe that he or she has failed at an important task, for example, the deception is carefully explained and every effort is made to ensure that participants leave the study feeling no worse than when they entered (L. Ross, Lepper, & Hubbard, 1975). In response to a heightened concern with ethical issues, the studies that social psychologists perform today usually have little potential for long-lasting harm. That was not always true of earlier studies. Consider the prison experiment again, for example. These researchers offered their participants extensive debriefing, but you may wonder whether any after-the-fact explanations could fully eliminate lasting ill effects of such powerful experiences (Baumrind, 1964; Milgram, 1964). Fortunately, most research shows that debriefing can provide deceived participants with more positive attitudes both about themselves and about research activities (Y. M. Epstein, Suedfeld, & Silverstein, 1973; S. S. Smith & Richardson, 1983; W. C. Thompson, Cohen, & Rosenhan, 1980). To do so, the debriefing must be thorough and professional, emphasize the importance of the research, and treat participants with respect.

When it comes to making difficult decisions about research ethics, a researcher is not forced to rely solely on his or her individual judgment. Since the mid-1970s, universities and other research institutions have established Institutional Review Boards. These committees, whose members include both scientists and members of the community, review and approve research plans before the research is conducted. They have the power to ask for changes in the plan or even to deny approval if they believe a study may harm participants. Despite some researchers' initial fear that the approval process would interfere with worthwhile research, it has worked smoothly in most instances. The greater ethical sensitivity that exists today, which was sparked largely by controversy over a few well-publicized studies like Zimbardo's, means that some types of study can probably no longer be performed. Take a moment to think about how you, as a member of a review board, would weigh the social and scientific importance of a study like Zimbardo's against the undoubted stress it would cause to participants.

Debriefing. Informing research participants—as soon as possible after the completion of their participation in research—about the purposes, procedures, and scientific value of the study, and discussing any questions participants may have.

Being Helpful to Society

Researchers have obligations as citizens and members of society to make choices about what topics to study and how their findings should be applied. Although social-psychological research cannot decide moral or ethical questions, valid research can provide relevant evidence to inform individual and societal decision making about such issues.

Like every individual, each scientist has his or her own conception of responsibility to society and to humanity. Social psychologists have long focused on major social issues like poverty, prejudice, pollution, and peace because we believe that our discipline can contribute to solving these problems. As you read this book you will see some of the results of this research.

Of course, psychologists often disagree about social and political issues. In the area of research, these differences often show up as disagreements over how science can best serve society. For instance, one researcher who studies persuasion may firmly believe that advertising offers major economic benefits by informing consumers about available products and services. Another researcher may believe just as firmly that advertising manipulates and exploits consumers, that it creates limitless desires for this year's model and encourages people to spend money on products they do not truly need. Given their differences, these two researchers would presumably also disagree on the appropriate application of social-psychological research on persuasion. The first might act as a consultant, assisting companies that want to use the research to make their advertising more effective. The second might instead use the same research findings to develop ways to teach children to resist the lure of ads for faddish toys. And a third researcher might take a middle ground, endorsing the use of knowledge of persuasion processes as legitimate in public health campaigns to encourage healthier lifestyles but opposing their use in selling consumer products. These three views represent disagreements about how science can best serve society.

In practice, every researcher must come to her or his own decisions about how research findings should be applied. Psychologists can refuse to participate in research they find morally objectionable and can encourage others to do the same. Many researchers, for example, question the benefit of conducting research designed to show gender or ethnic differences, especially in politically and legally sensitive areas like leadership potential or propensity to aggression.

Social psychology is an empirical science, and as such it is designed to answer empirical questions. The results of research will not answer questions of morality and ethics: whether abortion is right or wrong, whether or when aggression is justified, or how much our individual freedoms should be curtailed by a government's concern for the population as a whole. Such issues must be decided by every individual—scientist and nonscientist alike—through the democratic political process. But we can hope that this political process is informed by the results of valid scientific research where it is relevant. This is one role that social psychology can play in the larger society. Although research cannot tell us whether abortion is right or wrong, it can tell us who has abortions and why, how women make such difficult decisions, how they adjust to the experience, and whether it has effects on their later emotions, attitudes, and behaviors. These are all issues that may enter into individuals' moral judgments.

CONCLUDING COMMENTS

 Chapter 1 described how each of us, individually and as a member of social groups, constructs his or her own picture of reality. Scientists are no different from anybody else in this respect, even as they ply their trade. Relying on inference, deduction, and generalization, they draw on fragmentary, incomplete, and sometimes contradictory bits of research evidence to construct a coherent picture of reality. A scientific theory—a statement about unobservable causal relationships among abstract constructs—is intended to be such a picture.

Because scientific theories are invented rather than discovered, the scientific enterprise draws on its practitioners' creativity and imagination. The greatest contributions of Galileo, Newton, Darwin, and Einstein were not new data, but deep insights into new conceptions of reality that organized and explained existing evidence. On a more mundane level, creativity is also a crucial ingredient as scientists devise ways to test existing theories. A clever study, like a novel theory, is a product of creative imagination as well as disciplined hard work. As any social psychologist will tell you, this is one of the main reasons why doing research is fun.

Science is a human activity. Needless to say, then, it cannot be completely logical and unbiased. Just as scientists, like all humans, construct a version of reality based on bits and pieces of evidence, so are scientists, like all humans, subject to biases. Cultural values, political and religious views, and personal preferences may influence the problems that scientists choose to study or the theories they find congenial or abhorrent. Further, once a scientist creates or endorses a theory, it is likely to influence the way he or she evaluates research. A researcher may uncritically applaud some studies because their results support a "pet" theory, while dismissing less supportive studies as methodologically flawed or inadequately generalizable. Still, the standards and procedures of science, especially its public nature and its emphasis on the possibility of bias, limit the effects of such biases. And the danger of bias recedes even further when a number of studies conducted by scientists with diverse theoretical orientations in various places converge to support a theory.

This text now turns from "how we find out" to "what we know" about social behavior. However, the transition is not as drastic as you might think. As Chapter 1 pointed out, all of us, scientists and nonscientists alike, are constantly constructing theories to help explain what we experience. As you will see throughout this text, these processes are at work when people watch a football game, read a political advertisement, or deal with conflict in a relationship. One of the most important applications of these processes occurs when we get to know someone, when we form impressions of what others are "really like." Just as scientists try to explain "the facts" theoretically, we all gather information about others and try to make sense of it by forming a coherent impression. The information we gather and the

CHAPTER 2 THEMES

- **Construction of Reality**
  Scientific theories are developed to summarize and explain observed patterns of behavior.

- **Pervasiveness of Social Influence**
  Scientists are influenced not only by the rules and customs of science but also by personal and cultural values and goals.

- **Striving for Mastery**
  Scientists attempt to understand and predict nature.

way we put it together can have a dramatic impact on how we act and react to the others around us.

SUMMARY

 Research Questions and the Role of Theory. Research questions are provoked by curiosity about why people act the way they do. In turn, this curiosity often reflects concern about important social problems. Social psychologists seek to develop scientific theories to provide explanations for social behavior. A **scientific theory** is a statement about causal relationships among abstract, general **constructs**. It is a statement that holds for specified types of people, times, and settings.

Testing Theories: From Theory to Research. To provide a valid test of a theory, research must have three types of validity. **Construct validity** means that the **independent variables** and **dependent variables**—the concrete manipulations or measures used in the research—must correspond to the intended theoretical constructs. Construct validity is threatened by **social desirability response bias** if participants act in ways they think are socially desirable. Researchers ensure construct validity by manipulating and measuring independent and dependent variables in many different ways.

To provide a valid test of a theory, research must also have **internal validity** so that observers can conclude that changes in the independent variable actually caused changes in the dependent variable. In **nonexperimental research** designs in which both independent and dependent variables are measured, the research may lack internal validity because many other unknown causal factors could affect the research results. **Random assignment** of participants to groups, followed by manipulation of independent variables, defines **experimental research** designs. Experiments allow researchers to draw stronger conclusions about cause and effect.

Finally, research must have **external validity**, meaning that its results can be generalized to other people, settings, and times. Some theories apply to many different kinds of people and places, whereas others apply more narrowly. When a theory is intended to apply to a particular population and setting, external validity is ensured by conducting studies using that population and setting. When a theory is intended to apply more generally across different people, places, and times, external validity is ensured by conducting **replications**, repeated tests of the theory in diverse populations, settings, and cultures.

Theories become generally accepted if the results of multiple valid studies show them to be superior to rival theories. Sometimes theories that seem to compete are in fact complementary explanations of events. Social-psychological research cannot help but be influenced by researchers' personal beliefs and cultural values. However, striving to maximize all three forms of validity is our best hope for excluding the biases and errors that characterize everyday thinking.

The Role of Ethics and Values in Research. Researchers seek to treat their participants fairly, often ensuring that participants know what they will experience in the study and agree to it in advance, a procedure called **informed consent**. However, to avoid biases when sensitive topics are investigated, researchers sometimes deceive participants about various aspects of the study. If deception is used, participants must be given information about research procedures and purposes in a **debriefing** at the conclusion of the study.

Researchers have obligations as citizens and members of society to make choices about what topics to study and how their findings should be applied. Although social-psychological research cannot decide moral or ethical questions, valid research can provide relevant evidence to inform individual and societal decision making about such questions.

3

Perceiving Individuals

The summer before you entered college, perhaps you got in touch with your future roommate—many colleges are now giving students their roommates' email addresses to ease such interaction. As you exchanged mail or instant messages and made plans for furnishing your room, it is likely that you built up an impression of what the future roommate was like—whether a partier, a serious and studious person, or a committed social activist. Thinking back, how well did that impression match what you learned when you actually met your roommate? In fact, impressions formed on-line often turn out to be strikingly inaccurate when tested against real interaction, as many roommates and even people who fall in love over the internet can attest. One student confessed to some anxiety based on unsatisfying email exchanges with a future roommate, but was happily surprised when she met her, saying "She was nothing like I had pictured her" (Cohen, 2002). How can first impressions be so misleading?

On the other hand, our impressions of other people are not always wrong. As a student of social psychology, you are probably an interested observer of other people's behavior, and you probably believe that you do reasonably well at understanding other people and forming judgments about them. Indeed, research shows that in many situations, our impressions of other people can be quite accurate. For example, people can make fairly accurate judgments even about strangers, assessing their poise, warmth, and sociability after just a few minutes of observation (Ambady, Bernieri, & Richeson, 2000; Funder & Colvin, 1988).

What accounts for the puzzling mixture of accuracy and inaccuracy in our perceptions of other people? Why do we immediately like some people and dislike others on first meeting them, sometimes without even knowing the reasons? This chapter explores the ways that people construct, maintain, and change their impressions of others. First, we describe how people rely on general knowledge plus some convenient principles to form impressions of strangers. Surprisingly, these judgments are often quite accurate, at least accurate enough to let people move smoothly through most everyday social encounters.

Sometimes, however, we need to go beyond snap judgments to form detailed impressions of others. Employers must decide which job applicants are right for

■ **Different cues, different person?**
We are used to thinking of others as having fixed personalities and attributes. This doctor's physical appearance, body language, and behavior all contribute to the impression we form of her, as does the context in which we interact with her. It is likely that people meeting her in her favorite bar will have a different view of her as pictured below, than her coworkers do when they see her as pictured above.

> **Cognitive representation.** A body of knowledge that an individual has stored in memory.

their business needs, and teachers must decide which students know the material. And, of course, all of us like some people more than others, and these feelings affect us as we decide whom to befriend or work with. Does giving more thought to impressions increase their accuracy? Not necessarily, because, as this chapter explains, our motives and expectations can slant our judgments. Although Juliet may spend a lot of time thinking about Romeo, you probably would ask someone else if you wanted an impartial picture of his personality. As you will see, once our minds are made up, we find it hard to see, let alone accept, evidence that contradicts our views.

Of course, sometimes we have to face facts that are clearly inconsistent with our impressions. What happens then? Our discussion concludes with a description of the ways we can change impressions to accommodate contradictory evidence. How we handle inconsistency has important consequences for the accuracy of our impressions—and therefore for the success of our dealings with others.

Forming First Impressions: Cues, Interpretations, and Inferences

Try to answer a few questions about the people pictured in the photo on the right. Who would rather read the philosophical works of Jean-Paul Sartre than the latest Tom Clancy thriller? Who would prefer season tickets to the Metropolitan Opera, and who to the Oakland A's? Which person would *you* choose to get together with for lunch? You can probably answer such questions fairly readily and with some confidence. These are among the different aspects of an impression of another person. Impressions include many elements, including the person's behaviors and physical appearance (Carlston, 1994). However, the core elements are how much we like the person and our perceptions of what the person is "really like," including their underlying personality characteristics, personal goals, and values.

Our knowledge about people's characteristics and the ways they are related to one another is one type of **cognitive representation**, a term for a body of knowledge an individual has stored in his or her memory (E. R. Smith, 1998). We have cognitive representations of situations, people, and social groups. For example, our knowledge of what typically happens at a child's birthday party is a cognitive representation. Our impressions of specific individuals are cognitive representations, and so are our beliefs about members of particular occupations, nationalities, and ethnic groups. Because our stored knowledge influences virtually all of our social beliefs and behaviors, the effects of various types of cognitive representations are described throughout this text.

Why do we form impressions of situations, social groups, or individual people? The answer is that impressions guide our actions in ways that meet our needs for both concrete rewards and connectedness to other people. An impression that someone is generous might lead you to approach her (rather than someone else) for a loan until payday. An impression that someone else is smart might encourage you to choose that person as a study partner. And general positive or negative impressions—our liking for some people and distaste for others—influence our choices of companions to spend time with or share our personal thoughts and feelings with, and ultimately, what close relationships we form.

Thus, the impressions that we construct guide us along the paths of our social lives.

The Raw Materials of First Impressions

Perceptions of other people begin with visible cues, including the person's physical appearance, nonverbal communication, environment, and overt behavior. Familiarity also affects impressions, generally leading to increased liking. Cues that stand out and attract attention in the particular context in which they occur are particularly influential.

■ **Physical appearance offers many cues to people's personality and preferences**, but these cues are interpreted through our own prior beliefs. Which of these people would you predict listens to alternative rock music? Who do you think reads up on stock market trends? What impression might you form of the woman on the left?

The raw materials of first impressions are the way people look and how they act. However, these cues are informative only because we believe that appearance and behavior reflect personality characteristics, preferences, and lifestyles. This section focuses on the knowledge that guides our first impressions of others: the aspects of a person's appearance and behavior that call particular representations to mind, and the kinds of personal characteristics that are associated with those aspects of appearance and behavior.

IMPRESSIONS FROM PHYSICAL APPEARANCE. According to tennis star Andre Agassi, "Image is everything." It may not be everything to everyone, but physical appearance certainly influences our impressions of other people, as it probably influenced your reactions to the people in the photo above. After all, the way people look is usually our first and sometimes our only cue to what they are like, and impressions based on people's appearance can even alter our interpretations of what they say (Hassin & Trope, 2000). Our ideas about the meaning of physical appearance are endless. Blondes are sociable and fun-loving, but redheads are fiery and quick-tempered. People who wear glasses are scholarly and those with silvery hair are distinguished. People rely on many beliefs like these when they meet a stranger, even though most are unsupported by research. Still, some aspects of impressions based on appearance may be surprisingly accurate (Zebrowitz & Collins, 1997).

Physical beauty, particularly a beautiful face, calls up a variety of positive expectations. Apparently people assume that "what is beautiful is good" (Dion, Berscheid, & Walster, 1972) or, as the German poet and philosopher Johann Schiller wrote over a century ago: "Physical beauty is the sign of an interior beauty, a spiritual and moral beauty" (1882). We expect highly attractive people to be more interesting, warm, outgoing, and socially skilled than less attractive people (Eagly & Makhijani, 1991; Feingold, 1992b).

For these reasons, physical appearance is an important element in people's attraction to strangers. In a classic study, Elaine Walster and her colleagues (Walster, Aronson, Abrahams, & Rottman, 1966) randomly paired college men and women for an evening of talking and dancing. The researchers unobtrusively rated each student's attractiveness and social skills, and they also obtained their grades and their scores on intelligence and personality tests. After the evening ended, the researchers asked the students how satisfied they were with their dates. The partner's physical attractiveness was by far the most important influence on both men's and women's satisfaction. It also strongly influenced the likelihood that the men would contact their partners to seek another date. None of the other variables measured in this study—intelligence, social skills, or personality differences—had a similar influence on liking for the partner.

Well, you may say, physical attractiveness may be important to college students in a dating context, but does it have more general effects? The answer is yes. When elementary school teachers in one study were shown information about some children, including their photos, the teachers rated the more attractive youngsters as possessing more intelligence and academic potential (Clifford, 1975). Physically attractive men tend to gain status in their social groups (Anderson, John, Keltner, & Kring, 2001). More attractive defendants have lower bail set in misdemeanor cases (Downs & Lyons, 1991), and if they are convicted, they receive lighter prison sentences (Stewart, 1985). Apparently justice is not blind, after all! Even young children prefer their physically attractive peers, while regarding unattractive youngsters as unfriendly and aggressive (Dion & Berscheid, 1974). And these tendencies transcend any specific culture, for people from different cultures generally agree in judgments of attractiveness and in the traits they associate with it (Dion, 2002). Clearly, physical beauty has a pervasive influence on our perceptions and evaluations of other people, even when dating and romance are not at issue.

Beauty is not the only physical characteristic that influences perceptions of other people. Certain patterns of facial features can also function this way. Some people have *baby-faced* features: large, round eyes, high eyebrows, and a small chin. In studies conducted in both the United States and Korea, Diane Berry and Leslie McArthur found that baby-faced adult males were viewed as more naive, honest, kind, and warm than males of more mature facial appearance (Berry & McArthur, 1985; McArthur & Berry, 1987). Because of these perceptions, baby-faced adults are more likely to be chosen as dates by people who like to dominate others, but are less likely to be recommended for jobs that require mature characteristics like competence or leadership ability (Zebrowitz, Tenenbaum, & Goldstein, 1991). A fascinating study by Alexander Todorov and his colleagues (Todorov, Mandisodza, Goren, & Hall, 2005) showed that impressions of competence based on facial appearance even influence voting patterns. The researchers showed college students facial photos of the two major-party candidates from U.S. House and Senate races in distant states, and asked the students (who did not recognize any of the candidates) to choose which one appeared more competent. Amazingly, the candidates chosen by the students as appearing more competent were more likely to actually win their elections! Although the voters in those elections had access to much more information about the candidates, including such important matters as their party affiliations, issue positions, and experience, the results of this study suggest that simple impressions based on physical appearance also contribute to voting choices.

☐ **PHYSICAL APPEARANCE IN THE WORKPLACE.** Liking based on physical appearance can have an impact on our everyday work lives. One researcher found that newly hired professional men taller than 6 feet 2 inches received starting salaries 10% higher than those given to men under 6 feet (Knapp, 1978). And a study by economists found that that in both the United States and Canada, workers with below-average looks earned as much as 10% less than their average-looking counterparts, while those with above-average looks earned about 5% more than average (Hamermesh & Biddle, 1993). These findings were generally similar across different occupations, rather than being limited to jobs (like those in sales or customer service) where good looks might naturally help attract customers.

Attractiveness may be a mixed blessing for women in the workplace, however. One study asked people to evaluate a fictitious assistant vice president of a corporation on the basis of a photo. Some of them saw a photo of an attractive male; others saw a less attractive male. Still other research participants saw an attractive or an unattractive female. The participants rated the attractive male as higher in ability than the unattractive one, but the reverse was true for female (Heilman & Stopeck, 1985). According to the researchers, participants suspected that an attractive woman might have been promoted because of her appearance rather than her ability.

IMPRESSIONS FROM NONVERBAL COMMUNICATION. Did your mother tell you that the proper way to greet people was to "stand up straight, look them in the eye, smile, and shake hands firmly"? If so, she knew how much information is communicated by facial expressions, eye contact, and body language. In general, people who readily express their feelings nonverbally are liked more than less expressive individuals (Friedman, Riggio, & Casella, 1988). Specific aspects of nonverbal behavior are important for impression formation as well. Members of Western cultures tend to like people who orient their bodies toward us—facing us directly, leaning toward us, nodding while we speak—and we believe that they like us (Mehrabian, 1972). We also tend to like people who look at us with dilated pupils, which are generally a sign of interest and attention (Niedenthal & Cantor, 1986). Voices can also convey much information. In one study, students listened to the recorded voice of a person reading a fixed text, and then tried to judge which of two same-sex photos was the person they had just heard. Surprisingly, they were over 75% accurate in this task (Krauss, Freyberg, & Morsella, 2002).

Body language offers a special insight into people's moods and emotions (Ekman, Friesen, & Ellsworth, 1972). In such diverse cultures as those of Germany, Hong Kong, Japan, Turkey, and the United States, people express sadness and happiness, fear and anger, surprise and disgust with similar bodily postures and facial expressions, and they interpret them in similar ways (Ekman and others, 1987). When shown videotapes of actors portraying emotions as described in a Hindu treatise on dance written 2000 years ago, American students were just as accurate as Hindus from India in identifying 10 emotions (Hejmadi, Davidson, & Rozin, 2000). Based on such findings, researchers concluded that emotional expression is a kind of universal language. However, recent findings show that despite some general agreement, interpretations of emotional expressions often differ between Western and non-Western cultures, particularly for the emotions of surprise, sadness, and disgust (Markus, Kitayama, & Heiman, 1996; Russell, 1994).

As we will see in Chapter 4, the very basis of emotions—whether they arise from a person's private feelings or from a network of social relationships—also differs from one culture to another.

DETECTION OF DECEPTION. Have you ever wondered how people can be gullible enough to lose their savings to a con artist who has told them some outrageous lie? Or how an instructor could believe some far-fetched excuse spun by one of your classmates? Perhaps you told yourself that you could never be so easily deceived. Maybe not, but detecting lies is not always easy.

Paul Ekman and Wallace Friesen (1974) suggest that liars often give themselves away with nonverbal cues, but those cues are not the ones we usually watch for. Most people look for evidence of deception in a liar's face or words, when in fact these are what the liar can easily control (DePaulo, Lassiter, & Stone, 1982; Ekman & Friesen,

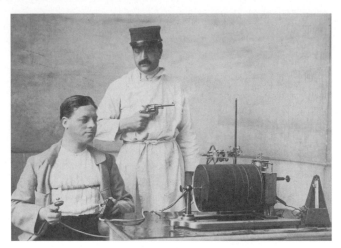

■ **William M. Marston** invented the first lie detector in 1915, claiming he could reveal verbal deception by observing levels of systolic blood pressure. This picture, taken in the same year, shows a prisoner undergoing psychological testing with a primitive polygraph, as a guard stands behind him with a pistol! Given its questionable reliability, and the fact that most of us do not have such an instrument at our disposal, what clues might you ordinarily look for to gauge whether someone is telling the truth?

1974). The best cues are a quivering or high-pitched tone of voice or restless movements of the hands and feet. People who pay attention to those cues are relatively successful at detecting deception, and accuracy can be equally as high across cultures and languages as within a culture (Bond & Atoum, 2000).

The fact that people tend to use the wrong cues in assessing truthfulness may also account for a seemingly paradoxical finding: In some circumstances, the less information people receive, the better they are at detecting deception. For example, people can detect deception better when they see only the speaker's body on videotape than when they see both the body and face. Focusing on the easily controlled face apparently leads them astray (Zuckerman, DePaulo, & Rosenthal, 1981). Similarly, people who observe someone speaking usually pay most attention to the speaker's words and consequently are relatively poor at detecting the body's hints at deception. One study found that research participants who are distracted by a difficult cognitive task, which prevents them from giving full attention to the speaker's words, are better at detecting deception than participants without any distraction (Gilbert & Krull, 1988).

□ **LIE DETECTION IN THE LEGAL SYSTEM.** Given the difficulty of detecting deception, perhaps it is not surprising that some people have looked for more mechanical means of exposing dishonesty. The "lie detector" that you may have read about in newspaper stories about crime investigations is a *polygraph*, a device that measures signs of physiological arousal, such as rapid breathing, increased heart rate, and sweating, as the test taker answers questions. Because people cannot completely control these responses, they are assumed to reveal the extra stress and effort of lying. However, current research evidence suggests that polygraph examinations are not precise enough to warrant their widespread use. In one study, for example, polygraph examiners correctly detected 75% of guilty suspects, but they also declared guilty 37% of those who were actually innocent (Lykken, 1985; Saxe, Dougherty, & Cross, 1985).

Nevertheless, polygraph tests continue to be widely used. Much of their apparent effectiveness may derive from superstitions about the device rather than from its inherent accuracy. Some criminal suspects who anticipate that their lies will be detected may decide to confess when confronted with a polygraph examination (Lykken, 1985). Similarly, some dishonest job seekers may avoid employers who use the polygraph to screen applicants.

IMPRESSIONS FROM FAMILIARITY. Most of us tend to develop positive feelings about the people we encounter frequently in our everyday lives (Festinger, Schachter, & Back, 1950; Zajonc, 1968). Of course, such encounters may lead to an acquaintanceship or even friendship, as we will discuss in Chapter 11. But even when little or no interaction takes place, mere exposure to another person increases liking. Richard Moreland and Scott Beach (1992) demonstrated this effect when they arranged for four women to attend varying numbers of sessions of a large college lecture course. The women sat quietly and took notes without interacting with any of the students. At the end of the semester, students in the course viewed slides of the women and answered questions about their impressions of them. The students thought the women they had seen more often were more interesting, attractive, warm, and intelligent than the women who had attended fewer class sessions. The students also thought they would like the more familiar women better and would enjoy spending time with them. As you can see, familiarity alone can be one basis for developing a positive impression and feelings of liking for another person.

IMPRESSIONS FROM ENVIRONMENTS. The environments that people construct and inhabit contain many clues to their personality, behaviors, and values. For example, your dorm room might feature a poster of Martin Luther King or a large collection of science-fiction books; your work area might be well organized or messy. Can observers form impressions of you from these types of cues? To answer this question, Samuel Gosling and his colleagues (Gosling, Ko, Mannarelli, & Morris, 2002) had a number of observers enter bedrooms in apartments or college dorms (with the occupants' permission, of course!) and look around, then rate their impressions of the person who lived there. The observers never met the occupants, and photos and any references to the occupant's name were covered up. The observers' ratings based on the rooms were quite accurate, when compared to the occupants' ratings of themselves and ratings made by friends who knew them well. Remarkably, similar levels of accuracy were obtained in another study in which observers looked at single-person offices or cubicles in a bank, a real estate agency, and other businesses—even though office decor is much more restricted than that in a bedroom. Because we select and create physical environments that both reflect and reinforce who we are, observers can learn a lot about us from those environments.

IMPRESSIONS FROM BEHAVIOR. Physical appearance and environmental cues may be helpful, but the most genuinely useful resource for developing an impression of another person is the individual's behavior (Gilbert, 1998). If you know that someone donates hours of free time working in a local food bank, you may reasonably conclude that the person is caring, altruistic, and philanthropic. If you find out that someone stole money from a cash register at work, you can probably assume that he or she is dishonest. Like these examples, many behaviors are strongly linked to particular personality traits. Indeed, people are often advised to judge others by their deeds, not by their appearance or their words. The processes by which people draw inferences from others' behaviors will be described in detail shortly.

WHICH CUES CAPTURE ATTENTION? Imagine sitting in the cafeteria idly watching those around you. What cues might attract your attention? You might notice that one person makes loud and nasty comments to the clerk at the cash register, that another drinks three cups of coffee in quick succession, and that a third towers over all the other people in the room. Characteristics that are different stand out, and this is true for all kinds of characteristics, including behaviors such as making rude comments or physical cues like tallness. Or suppose you learn that someone has two hobbies: playing tennis and keeping snakes as pets. You will probably find the person's unusual taste in pets more revealing than the more commonplace athletic interests. If you were going to buy this person a book as a gift, would you be more likely to choose one on snakes or one on tennis? Research suggests you'd go for herpetology (Nelson & Miller, 1995).

In cases like this, what makes a characteristic stand out is its rarity or uniqueness. **Salience** refers to a cue's ability to attract attention in its context. Of course, a

Salience. The ability of a cue to attract attention in its context.

FIGURE 3.1   Salient cues dominate impressions

■ Our impression of the same individual may differ greatly from one situation to another because attributes that stand out in one context may go unnoticed in another. An attribute that is salient in its context may give rise to inferences that become part of our first impression of a person.

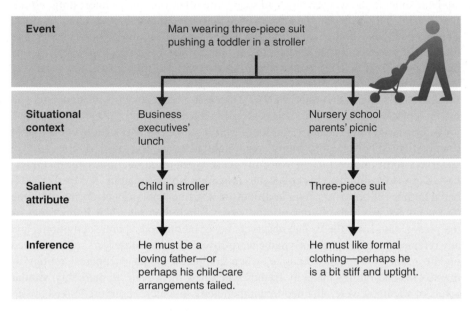

Event	Man wearing three-piece suit pushing a toddler in a stroller	
Situational context	Business executives' lunch	Nursery school parents' picnic
Salient attribute	Child in stroller	Three-piece suit
Inference	He must be a loving father—or perhaps his child-care arrangements failed.	He must like formal clothing—perhaps he is a bit stiff and uptight.

Unusual and salient characteristics not only make a difference in our impressions of others, but also help us define ourselves, as you will see in Chapter 4, page 107.

cue that is unusual or unexpected in one context may be quite normal in another, as Figure 3.1 shows. The person who towered over everyone might be salient in the cafeteria but not on the basketball court, surrounded by equally tall team members. Thus, attributes that stand out in one context may be quite normal in another. When we have information about a person's physical appearance, their nonverbal communication, and some of their behavior, those aspects that are salient are likely to grab our attention and provide the basis for first impressions.

Interpreting Cues

Cues have no meaning in themselves. Instead, they are interpreted in the light of our stored knowledge about people, behaviors, traits, and social situations. Stored knowledge that is linked to the cue itself or is easy to bring to mind is most likely to be used in interpreting cues.

We seem to leap effortlessly from the cues of appearance, body language, and behavior to liking or disliking a person, and to conclusions about his or her inner characteristics. Yet none of the cues we use in perceiving people have much meaning in themselves. No behavior, appearance, gesture, or expression indicates a person's inner qualities *directly*. Instead, even our first impressions rely on rapid but seemingly effortless cognitive processes (Chun, Spiegel, & Kruglanski, 2002; Gilbert, 1998). These processes operate spontaneously even when we are not specifically trying to make sense of another individual, that is, even when we are processing superficially rather than devoting a lot of thought to the issue.

The first step in processing is interpreting the cues themselves: deciding whether a wrinkled brow reflects menace or puzzlement, or whether a lie is an act of deceit or of loyalty. Two crucial kinds of stored knowledge help us make these decisions: the associations we have already learned, and the thoughts that are currently in our mind.

THE ROLE OF ASSOCIATIONS IN INTERPRETATION. On learning that someone was caught stealing money from the cash register at the local convenience store, most people would immediately conclude that the person is dishonest. Why do we jump to that conclusion? The answer has to do with the strong link that exists between two cognitive representations. Our concept of stealing money is **associated**, or linked, to our knowledge about the trait of dishonesty. When we think about stealing, the associated trait of dishonesty is *activated*, or brought to mind. To understand why association is important, imagine a child's toy box containing a jumble of all kinds of toys, among them a paddle connected by a string to a rubber ball. If you pull the paddle out of the box (think of this as hearing about the behavior of stealing) you can be sure the ball (the associated trait of dishonesty) will soon follow.

Associations can arise from *similarity in meanings* between two cognitive representations, like the similarity between the act of stealing and the concept of dishonesty. However, even unrelated ideas can become associated if they are repeatedly *thought about together*. Thus, Lennon and McCartney, cops and robbers, and Windows and Microsoft have become associated concepts for most of us. Of course, these learned connections depend on the culture that surrounds us. Suppose a co-worker expresses agreement when you voice objections to his new plans, but then goes ahead with the plans anyway. A North American might decide that the co-worker is insincere, but in Japan the same behavior, agreeing with criticism, is regarded as simple politeness. As this example suggests, members of different cultures have different associations and therefore arrive at different interpretations for the same behavior (Markus and others, 1996).

Once we form an association, it links the two cognitive representations just as the string links the paddle to the ball. If either of the linked representations comes to mind, the other will usually come to mind also. Because of these patterns of stored associations, some cues are easier to interpret than others. For example, the act of turning in money that was found in a lonely spot with no witnesses is so closely connected with our idea of honesty that we would be hard pressed to interpret the behavior in any other way. Similarly, superior performance in the decathlon immediately conjures up the idea of athleticism. In cases like these, people spontaneously think of the associated trait when they comprehend a behavior, even if they are not specifically trying to form an impression of the person (Uleman, Hon, Roman, & Moskowitz, 1996). For example, in one study participants examined photos of people together with written descriptions of behaviors that strongly implied a trait. Even if instructed simply to familiarize themselves with these materials rather than to form impressions of the pictured individuals, the participants formed associations linking the traits with the people (Carlston & Skowronski, 1994).

THE ROLE OF ACCESSIBILITY IN INTERPRETATION. The meaning of a behavior is not always so clear. Imagine discovering that someone you know had shared test answers with a classmate. How would you interpret that behavior? The act of sharing could reflect either helpfulness or dishonesty, and you might have difficulty choosing one interpretation over the other. In such cases, we tend to rely on relevant information we currently have in mind. The **accessibility** of knowledge—the ease and speed with which it comes to mind and is used—exerts a powerful influence on the interpretaton of behavior or other cues. Going back to our toybox metaphor,

Accessibility. The processing principle that individuals' and groups' views of the world are slow to change and prone to perpetuate themselves.

Association. A link between two or more cognitive representations.

■ **In Western culture**, a host may be concerned or even offended if a guest leaves uneaten food on their plate. Was the meal unsatisfactory? Paradoxically, in Japan an empty plate signals a desire for more food and implies that the portion was inadequate. This may well be deemed as an insult to the host. Accessible knowledge influences the way in which any action is interpreted, and thus cultural ideas about appropriate behavior change the interpretation of the action.

An important source of expectations about other people is their social group memberships (age, gender, ethnicity, occupation, and the like). The powerful effects of such expectations will be discussed in detail in Chapter 5.

accessible toys are those near the top of the pile, whereas the less accessible ones are buried near the bottom.

The more accessible the knowledge, the more likely it is to come to mind automatically, without our consciously trying to retrieve it, and the more likely it is to guide our interpretation of cues (Ford & Thompson, 2000; Higgins, 1996). Thus, someone whose ideas about helpfulness are highly accessible may interpret the act of sharing answers as a helpful act. Another person, perhaps an instructor for whom the concept of academic dishonesty is more accessible, might see the same behavior as dishonest—a quite different interpretation. Among the factors that influence the accessibility of knowledge are concurrent activation by other sources, and recent and frequent past activation.

ACCESSIBILITY FROM CONCURRENT ACTIVATION OF KNOWLEDGE. Whatever thoughts are in our mind when we are forming an impression may activate cognitive representations, making them highly accessible and likely to affect our interpretations. For instance, generally positive or negative information may be made accessible by our current moods. Thus, moods have a well-documented impact on how we react to others. People in a happy and cheerful mood see both their own and others' behavior through rose-colored glasses, evaluating all behavior more positively than do people in neutral moods (Isen, 1987; Williamson & Clark, 1989). Economists have been surprised to learn that moods can even affect the stock market: markets tend to rise on sunny days and to fall on gloomy days (Hulbert, 2001). Presumably, investors are more upbeat about the future when fine weather puts them in a positive mood.

Our expectations also act as accessible knowledge that can powerfully influence our interpretations of behaviors or other information. In a classic demonstration of the effects of expectations, Harold Kelley (1950) arranged for a guest instructor to conduct 20-minute discussions in psychology courses. Before the guest's appearance, the students were given background information about the guest instructor. Though they were unaware of it, different students were given different background information. Some students learned that the guest instructor was "a very warm person, industrious, critical, practical, and determined." Others were informed that he was "a rather cold person, industrious, critical, practical, and determined." All students then had an extensive opportunity to observe the instructor's actual behavior during the discussion. When the students later rated his personality, the results clearly demonstrated the effects of expectation. Students who expected the instructor to be warm rated him as more considerate, informal, sociable, popular, good-natured, humorous, and humane than did those who expected a colder individual.

The effects of expectations on social perception are pervasive (Harris, 1991; Rosenthal, 1985). Supporters of opposing candidates in presidential debates expect that their own candidate will show statesmanlike behavior and leadership potential and will win the debate. And when the debate is over, each group of supporters is usually sure that they saw just that (Kinder & Sears, 1985). And because doctors and staff in psychiatric hospitals expect their patients to display disturbed behavior, one study found that they were unable to detect perfectly normal people who had themselves admitted to a hospital under a ruse (Rosenhan, 1973).

We often form expectations based on the situation in which a behavior occurs, which we then use to help interpret the behavior. Look at the photo on the next page, for example. Is the man expressing grim determination or anger? Yaacov Trope (1986) found that people answer such questions in different ways, depending on what they know about the situation. Trope showed students photos of people wearing ambiguous facial expressions together with information about the context. The same expression looked grief-stricken to students who were told the photographed person was attending a funeral, but was interpreted as tearful laughter by those who thought the person was at a comedy performance. Indeed, situational information can override even relatively unambiguous facial expressions when people interpret others' emotions (Carroll & Russell, 1996).

■ **Emotional expressions** are some of the easiest signals for humans to understand. But before you come to a firm conclusion, turn the page.

ACCESSIBILITY FROM RECENT ACTIVATION. A toy that a child has recently used can be found near the top of the toy chest. Similarly, a cognitive representation that has recently been brought to mind also remains accessible for a time (Wyer & Srull, 1989). Therefore, anything that brings an idea to mind—even coincidental, irrelevant events—can make it accessible and influence our interpretations of behavior. Imagine walking down the street with a friend and noticing in passing a movie poster featuring Clint Eastwood in an aggressive pose holding a handgun. Could the poster increase the accessibility of your cognitive representations related to hostility and aggression? If so, might it influence your interpretations, leading you to see hostility in an ambiguous remark made by your friend when none was intended?

The answer to both of these questions is yes. To demonstrate this effect, Tory Higgins and his colleagues (Higgins, Rholes, & Jones, 1977) asked students to memorize several words. One group memorized words related to the positive trait *adventurous*, while another group learned words related to the negative trait *reckless*. This procedure was intended to activate stored knowledge about one or the other of these two traits, thereby making that knowledge accessible for a time. Then, in what students thought was an unrelated experiment, they read a description of Donald, who had climbed Mount McKinley, gone white-water kayaking, and driven in a demolition derby. Later, the two groups were asked to describe Donald's activities. Their descriptions showed that the first group of students, for whom *adventurous* was accessible, saw Donald's behavior as daring, whereas those who had focused on words relating to *reckless* saw his behavior as foolhardy and rash. Correspondingly, the "adventurous" students evaluated Donald more positively than the "reckless" group.

Higgins and his colleagues (1977) wondered whether this effect would occur if any positive or negative word was made accessible. They used the same procedure with traits like *obedient* or *disrespectful*, but activating these traits had no effect on people's interpretations of Donald because they were not applicable to his behaviors. People use cognitive representations that are both accessible and applicable when they interpret incoming information.

Activating a cognitive representation to increase its accessibility and make it more likely to be used is called **priming**. The effects of priming can be long-lasting and rather subtle. Concepts that have been primed can remain accessible and influence later interpretations for as long as 24 hours (Srull & Wyer, 1980). Their impact does not even depend on people's awareness of the activation! To demonstrate this, John Bargh and Paula Pietromonaco (1982) showed some participants neutral words, while others saw words related to the trait of hostility. Then both groups read a description of a character's ambiguous behaviors. When the groups' responses were compared, those primed with the hostility-related words interpreted the behaviors as more hostile and aggressive. The interesting twist is that the presentation of the priming words was so brief—a mere flash on a computer screen—that the participants could not say what the words were. Even when people are unable to identify a word consciously, encountering the word can still make cognitive representations accessible and influence the interpretation of later information. Other similar studies have

Priming. The activation of a cognitive representation to increase its accessibility and thus the likelihood that it will be used.

Chapter 7, especially pages 262 to 265, will discuss the thought-provoking possibility that our attitudes might similarly be influenced without our awareness.

confirmed this remarkable finding (Draine & Greenwald, 1998; Niedenthal, 1990). So even if you just glimpse the Clint Eastwood poster out of the corner of your eye without consciously registering it, it might make you interpret someone's behaviors as aggressive.

ACCESSIBILITY FROM FREQUENT ACTIVATION: CHRONIC ACCESSIBILITY. What toys are usually found lying at the top of the toy box? The ones that get dragged out and played with every day. The same is true of thoughts. The frequent use of a cognitive representation over days, months, or years can make it *chronically accessible* (Bargh, Bond, Lombardi, & Tota, 1986; Higgins, 1996a). When this happens, people repeatedly use the same concepts in interpreting others' behavior. For example, intelligence might always be important in one person's judgments, whereas friendliness or helpfulness might matter more to someone else. In fact, people can more easily recognize information relevant to their "favorite" traits and can remember it better than unrelated information (Bargh & Thein, 1985; Higgins, King, & Mavin, 1982). Imagine, for instance, that you observed someone performing many behaviors: greeting friends, going to a party, studying in the library, and working at a part-time job. If friendliness is chronically accessible for you, you would be more likely to notice and later remember the first two of these behaviors. Another observer for whom intelligence is a chronically accessible concept would more easily notice and remember the time the person spent in the library.

■ **The social context of interpretation**. Even our understanding of emotional expression is influenced by the social context. Now that you know that Andy Roddick is celebrating his win at the 2003 U.S. Open, his look is not one of anger or bitterness, but of victory.

☐ **ACCESSIBILITY AND SEXISM IN A JOB INTERVIEW.** Television and print advertisements often use sex to sell products like beer and automobiles, implicitly promising the intended male consumers that attractive women will flock around them if they purchase the correct product. Do such ads make thoughts about women as sex objects more accessible? Might this priming even affect the way men treat women they meet? Laurie Rudman and Eugene Borgida (1995) showed one group of male students a series of TV commercials that the researchers felt portrayed women as sex objects, while another group saw commercials for similar products (such as beer or cars) that lacked sexist imagery. The students then were asked, as a favor to the experimenter, to interview a female student (actually a confederate) for a job assisting the research project. The students who had viewed the sexist ads (compared to the nonsexist ones) sat closer to the interviewee and asked her more personal and inappropriate questions. After the interview, they recalled more about her physical appearance, but less about the information she had revealed in the interview. They also rated her as more friendly, but as less competent in terms of her potential job duties! Finally, the interviewee, who did not know which priming video each man had viewed, rated how much she felt the interviewer had been looking at her body and how sexually motivated he was. These ratings were also higher for the men who had watched the sexist commercials. It seems that the concept of viewing women as sex objects can be primed, affecting men's

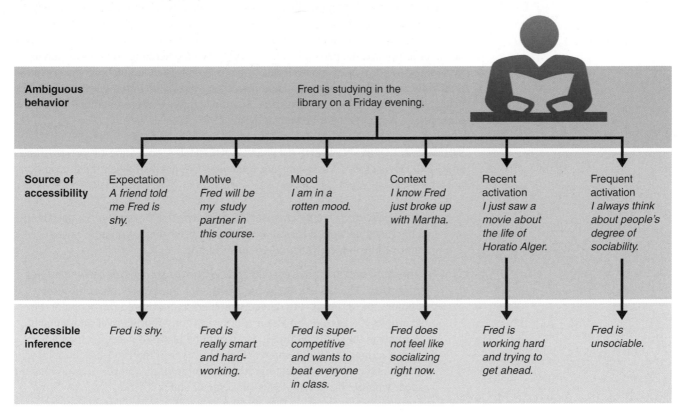

FIGURE 3.2 Accessibility shapes inferences about behavior

■ The same behavior can give rise to a variety of inferences, depending on what cognitive representations are accessible for the observer. Expectations, motives, and moods are just some of the many factors that can influence accessibility.

judgments and behavior toward real women over whom they may hold power. It is worth pondering the fact that in this study, these effects were produced by typical, everyday TV commercials, not extreme or pornographic materials.

As you have seen in the last several pages, accessibility has many sources, and it works in many ways to alter the interpretation of a given behavior, as summarized in Figure 3.2. In fact, as you will see throughout this book, the principle of accessibility has implications for many of our thoughts and actions, not only for our impressions of others.

Characterizing the Behaving Person: Correspondent Inferences

People often assume that others have inner qualities that correspond to their observable behaviors. This assumption is frequently made even when external factors could have influenced the behaviors.

Sometimes off-the-cuff interpretations shaped by associations and accessible cognitive representations are enough for us. If we never expect to interact with a person again, we may not go beyond interpreting their looks or their behaviors. Sometimes circumstances require us to take a second step: using the behavior to decide what the person is really like. Does a menacing expression reveal a dangerous person? Does deceitful behavior imply that the person is untrustworthy? Characterizing someone as having a personality trait that corresponds to his or her behavior is called making a **correspondent inference**. When a correspondent inference follows the initial interpretation of a behavior, it completes a *first impression*, an initial cognitive representation of what the other person is like (Gilbert, Pelham, & Krull, 1988; Trope, 1986).

WHEN IS A CORRESPONDENT INFERENCE JUSTIFIED? According to Edward Jones and Keith Davis (1965), correspondent inferences are justified when three conditions hold true:

- *The individual freely chooses to perform the behavior.* No one should conclude that a child forced to write a pleasant thank-you note for an unloved birthday gift actually feels grateful.

- *The behavior has few effects that distinguish it from other courses of action.* The fewer effects that a behavior shares with other possible choices, the easier it is to decide which effect motivated the behavior. For example, if a person chooses a college in sunny Florida over an identical campus in the chilly Midwest, we would be justified in seeing the choice as reflecting a love of warm weather. However, if the Florida school also has a better reputation, that muddies the inferential waters—it is no longer clear whether the person loves sunshine or status.

- *The behavior is unexpected rather than expected or typical.* When it is not fashionable to be patriotic, one can reasonably assume that neighbors who fly their country's flag outside their home feel strongly about the issue. The unexpectedness of the behavior increases our confidence in the leap from behavior to a trait inference.

THE CORRESPONDENCE BIAS: PEOPLE ARE WHAT THEY DO. In a study designed to test these ideas about correspondent inferences, Edward Jones and Victor Harris (1967) found some unexpected results. Each participant in the study read an essay favoring or opposing Fidel Castro's communist regime in Cuba. Some were told that the writer of the essay had freely chosen what position to take. When asked to guess the writer's real opinion, these participants naturally assumed that it mirrored the position taken in the essay.

Other participants learned that the writer was given no choice: The position had been assigned. You might expect these individuals to realize that a required essay, like a dictated thank-you note, carries no information whatsoever about the writer's actual opinion. But they did not. Instead, like those who thought the essay writer had a choice, the second group of participants concluded that the writer actually held the views expressed in the essay, as Figure 3.3 shows. In other words, they made an unjustified correspondent inference when they inferred that the writer's opinion corresponded with the writer's behavior.

Our tendency to draw correspondent inferences even when they are not justified, for example, when other possible causes of the behavior exist, is known as the **correspondence bias**. Another term for the correspondence bias is *fundamental attribution*

Correspondent inference. The process of characterizing someone as having a personality trait that corresponds to his or her observed behavior.

Correspondence bias. The tendency to infer an actor's personal characteristics from observed behaviors, even when the inference is unjustified because other possible causes of the behavior exist.

FIGURE 3.3   The correspondence bias: People are what they do

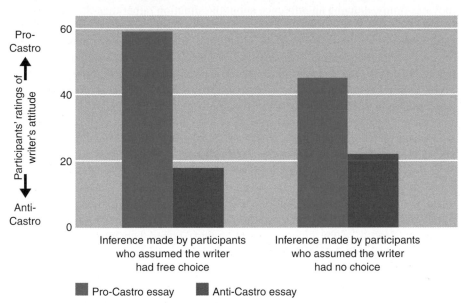

■ Participants who read an essay and thought the writer had freely chosen the position were likely to infer that the writer's true position corresponded to that advocated in the essay (left bars). However, they were nearly as likely to make the same inference when they knew that the writer had no choice about the position (right). People often leap to the conclusion that behaviors reflect inner characteristics, when situational forces are truly responsible. (Based on Jones & Harris, 1967.)

error (Ross, 1977). The correspondence bias has been demonstrated repeatedly, both inside and outside the social psychology laboratory (Gilbert, 1998; Jones, 1990b). People tend to assume that the behaviors they observe must reflect the actors' inner characteristics even though other aspects of the situation could explain those behaviors.

☐ **CORRESPONDENCE BIAS IN THE WORKPLACE.** The correspondence bias has serious implications for fairness in the workplace. If others see us as having personal characteristics that fit with our behaviors, impressions of us can be shaped by behaviors we are instructed to perform (Ross, Amabile, & Steinmetz, 1977). Consider the results of a study in which groups of five participants were assigned in an obviously random way to two "manager" and three "clerk" positions (Humphrey, 1985). For a couple of hours, the managers made decisions, read documents, dictated letters to customers, and performed other varied and challenging tasks. Meanwhile the clerks filed papers, alphabetized cards, and filled out forms in triplicate, with little opportunity to make decisions or display initiative. When the participants rated each other at the end of the study, they did not recognize that the randomly assigned roles conveyed no information about their personal characteristics or abilities. Managers and clerks alike believed that managers were assertive and decisive, with real leadership potential. Even the clerks predicted that managers would be more successful than clerks in their real-life future careers.

When the correspondence bias occurs, roles make the person. Given this bias, how likely is it that even a highly competent secretary will ever be seen as having what it takes to be an effective manager?

LIMITS ON THE CORRESPONDENCE BIAS. Despite its power and pervasiveness, the correspondence bias does not inevitably affect our impressions of other people. Consider the following situation: You are waiting in line at a movie theater to see the latest comedy hit. As the audience from the previous showing streams out of the theater, you notice someone grinning broadly and chuckling. The correspondence

It is the correspondence bias—our belief that people's acts reflect their inner qualities rather than situational pressures—that makes some of the most central and important research results in social psychology so unexpected and therefore compelling. For example, it is this bias that makes it seem paradoxical that perfectly ordinary people often follow orders to carry out actions that injure innocent victims (Chapter 10, pages 369 to 379).

bias would suggest that you should see him as a jolly person—but do you think that is what you would do? You would more likely take his reactions as evidence that the movie is funny, drawing an inference about the situation rather than the person. This is what Douglas Krull (1993) found. As in this example, when people are specifically motivated to find out about the situation, the correspondence bias is reduced or reversed. Perhaps in the Jones and Harris (1967) study, the correspondence bias emerged because the research participants generally assumed that they were supposed to draw conclusions about the person (the writer's true attitude toward Castro) rather than the situation (being instructed to write an essay).

Culture also sets limits on the correspondence bias. In Western cultures, individuals are seen as independent and autonomous, responsible for their own thoughts, feelings, and actions (Markus, and others, 1996; Nisbett, 1987). Thus, Western observers naturally tend to assume that people's inner dispositions cause their behaviors, leading to the correspondence bias. In non-Western cultures, particularly in Asia, people are assumed to be interdependent with, rather than independent from, their groups (P. B. Smith & Bond, 1993). Thoughts, emotions, and actions are more often assumed to be caused by aspects of the group or social context rather than by factors within an autonomous individual. Therefore Asians, compared to Westerners, consider a wider range of causal alternatives—including situational as well as personal factors—when explaining behaviors (Choi, Dalal, Kim-Prieto, & Park, 2003). And as a result, in Asian cultures the correspondence bias is somewhat less prevalent (Fiske, Kitayama, Markus, & Nisbett, 1998). When observers pay attention to potential situational causes of a behavior, they are less likely to immediately leap to an inference that the actor possesses the corresponding trait (Trope & Gaunt, 2000).

Though our snap judgments about other people seem to just "come to us," in reality we actively construct them, though without effort, intention, or even much ability to control their emergence. The construction follows the steps summarized in Figure 3.4, proceeding from initial cues to correspondent inferences.

FIGURE 3.4   The processes involved in constructing a first impression

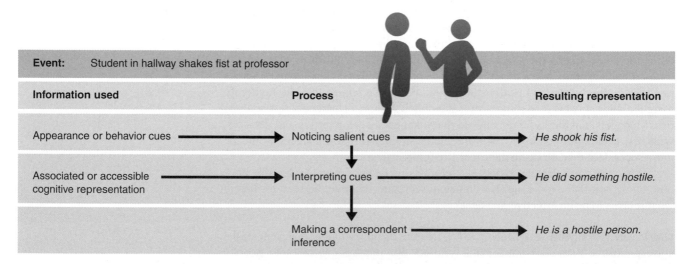

■ Although forming a first impression seems immediate and effortless, it involves processes of noticing salient cues, interpreting them, and making correspondent inferences about the person's characteristics.

Beyond First Impressions: Systematic Processing

Think back to the last time someone paid you a particularly outrageous compliment. Did you buy it? Perhaps you took the compliment at face value and, drawing a correspondent inference, decided that the person had a particularly high opinion of you. Probably, however, you were not quite so naive. Astute observers know that people say and do things for many reasons: the desire to flatter others, the demands of social situations, or the wish to receive something in return. Because we know that actions do not always reflect the inner person, we sometimes try to avoid the correspondence bias, correcting our first impressions by considering other possible causes of behaviors (Gilbert and others, 1988).

Initial impressions formed with minimal effort and thought on the basis of just one or two obvious attributes—such as impressions based on the assumption that inner characteristics correspond directly to observed behavior—are one example of **superficial processing**. But sometimes a quick glance at another person does not tell us all we want to know. Then we may think more deeply and take more information into account—a process termed **systematic processing**. We do this in the hope of forming a more adequate impression, although as we will see this hope is not always realized.

Processing systematically requires two ingredients. One is *motivation*: Only when people have some reason to form a deeper or more complex impression will they generally expend the effort to go beyond superficial processing. The second ingredient is the *ability* to process thoroughly: adequate time to think, freedom from distractions, and so on. When both motivation and ability to process are in the mix, systematic processing is likely to result. And as we will see throughout this book, this is true not only when people are forming impressions of others. In many different areas of life—when we are reading advertisements and thinking about buying a new product, or when we are interacting with a member of a stereotyped group—the extent to which people think systematically can be crucial in determining the outcomes.

Causal Attributions

To go beyond a first impression, people must engage in more extensive thought, particularly to explain others' behaviors. People are likely to consider potential causes that are generally accessible, salient in context, or suggested by the pattern of available information. Cultural learning also influences attributions.

In the process of person perception, the systematic processing that people perform when they are willing and able includes making **causal attributions**: judgments about the cause of a behavior or an event. In fact, making inferences about the causes of people's behaviors is central to our perception of other people, for example, when we try to interpret an unexpected compliment by thinking about whether it reflects the speaker's true opinion or an effort at flattery. We draw on many types of information as we think about others' actions and attempt to understand why they have occurred.

ATTRIBUTIONS TO ACCESSIBLE CAUSES. The more accessible a potential cause, the more likely it is to be taken as an explanation of behavior. Thus, William Rholes

Superficial processing. Relying on accessible information to make inferences or judgments, while expending little effort in processing.

Systematic processing. Giving thorough, effortful consideration to a wide range of information relevant to a judgment.

Causal attribution. A judgment about the cause of a behavior or other event.

and John Pryor (1982) reasoned, priming should influence people's causal attributions, just as it can affect their initial interpretations of behaviors. To test their hypothesis, the researchers first exposed students to words like *aviator* or *rug*, to make those concepts more accessible in memory. They then asked the students to explain hypothetical events, such as "The pilot liked the carpet." Those who had been primed with *aviator* attributed the behavior to the actor, while those who had seen *rug* attributed the behavior to the stimulus object. More accessible causes are more likely to be seen as responsible for an event.

ATTRIBUTIONS TO SALIENT CAUSES. The more noticeable or attention-getting a potential cause is, the more likely it is to be used to explain behavior. And what is noticeable can depend literally on the perceiver's point of view. To demonstrate the impact of salience on attribution, Shelley Taylor and Susan Fiske (1975) arranged an experiment in which six students watched a two-person conversation from different viewing positions, as Figure 3.5 shows. When questioned about what they had seen, the students attributed a greater causal role to the person they were directly watching. They gave that person higher ratings for dominating the conversation and dictating its tone and outcome.

Salient features—whether they are people we are focusing on, bright colors, moving images, loud voices, or any other outstanding feature—can draw our attention, thereby turning a potential cause into the probable cause (McArthur & Post, 1977; Robinson & McArthur, 1982). Salience has these effects not only when people make quick, relatively unthinking judgments, but even when they make an effort to think carefully and be accurate (E. R. Smith & Miller, 1979). Salient causes are given more weight even when they are situational factors, as well as causes within the individual (Trope & Gaunt, 2000).

FIGURE 3.5   Salient causes dominate impressions

■ In this study, two people held a conversation as six others watched. The observers were seated so two could most easily see participant *A*, two faced participant *B*, and two could see both participants equally well. The results? The observers attributed a greater causal role to the participant they were directly watching than to the other participant. (Adapted from Taylor & Fiske, 1975, copyright © 1975 by the American Psychological Association. Adapted with permission.)

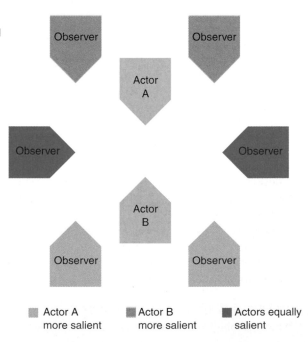

■ Actor A more salient   ■ Actor B more salient   ■ Actors equally salient

Consider the implications of these findings for courtroom proceedings. Imagine jurors watching a videotape of a suspect confessing while being interrogated by police. Was the confession voluntary (attributable to the suspect) or was it coerced by pressure from the detectives? Salience can affect observers' answers to this question When observers view a confession with the video camera focused on the suspect, rather than from a viewpoint focused mainly on the interrogating detective, they judge the confession to be more voluntary and less coerced (Lassiter, Geers, Munhall, Handley, & Beers, 2001). Is it any wonder that police agencies that are videotaping interrogations almost always focus the camera on the suspect?

ATTRIBUTIONS BASED ON COVARIATION INFORMATION. Knowledge stored in the mind—cognitive representations that are activated by associations, accessibility, or salience—does not always provide ready answers to causal questions. Observing a behavior, such as a graduate student flattering a professor (as graduate students do from time to time) may not immediately bring any particular causal attribution to mind. In such situations, people can try to ascertain the cause of the event by collecting *covariation information*, information about potential causal factors that are present when the event occurs and absent when it does not.

Harold Kelley (1967) considered three major categories of possible causes of a social event like flattery. First, he suggested, the behavior might be explained by something about the actor. Thus, the graduate student might be insecure about his standing in the department and might respond by flattering all professors frequently. Second, the behavior might be due to something about the stimulus or target of the behavior. Perhaps this professor is known to be susceptible to flattery. Third, the behavior might be caused by something about the particular situation or circumstances. Perhaps the graduate student plans to ask this professor for a letter of recommendation later in the day.

How do people decide which kind of attribution to make? Kelley (1967) argued that people look for a potential cause that is present when the behavior occurs and is absent when the behavior is absent. Therefore, an observer would seek out information about whether the student flatters other people (termed *distinctiveness* information), about whether other people flatter the professor (*consensus* information), and about whether the student flatters the professor in other circumstances (*consistency* information).

You can probably guess some of the predictions that derive from Kelley's reasoning. Assume the professor, like a social magnet, seems to draw flattery from everyone, including this rather reserved student who rarely flatters anyone. In that case, most people would conclude that something about the professor is causing the flattery, as can be seen in Table 3.1. But perhaps that is not the case. Perhaps the student flatters lots of people, most other people do not flatter the professor, and the student flatters her every time they meet. In that case, there is probably something special about the graduate student that explains the flattery. Given these pieces of information, people would attribute the behavior to the actor. As a third possibility, maybe the flattery occurred only today but did not occur last week, and few people in the history of the department have ever flattered this professor, who in fact is quite an unpleasant person. In this final case, most people would see the graduate student's behavior as due to some particular situation or circumstance (McArthur, 1972). Perhaps the student is, after all, about to request a letter of recommendation.

CULTURAL DIFFERENCES IN ATTRIBUTIONS. People from different cultures learn to consider different types of causes for many behaviors. When Joan Miller (1984)

TABLE 3.1. Information About the Presence or Absence of Potential Causes Influences Attributions

Event *The graduate student flatters a professor*

	Situation A	Situation B	Situation C
Consensus	High *Almost everyone flatters this professor.*	Low *Almost nobody flatters this professor.*	Low *Almost nobody flatters this professor.*
Distinctiveness	High *The graduate student does not flatter anyone else.*	Low *The graduate student flatters almost everyone.*	High *The graduate student does not flatter anyone else.*
Consistency	High *The graduate student flatters this professor almost all the time.*	High *The graduate student flatters this professor almost all the time.*	Low *The graduate student does not flatter this professor on most occasions.*
	↓	↓	↓
Attribution	*Something about the professor (stimulus)*	*Something about the graduate student (person)*	*Something about the particular time or situation (circumstances)*

looked at the way children and adults from the United States and India explained behaviors, she found striking cultural differences. Only adults from the United States were likely to attribute behavior to the actor's general personality traits. For example, adult Americans explained examples of cheating and dishonesty on the basis of the actor's general traits, like competitiveness or selfishness. Adults from India and children from both countries placed more emphasis on other characteristics of the actor, such as his or her roles and social relationships. Cheating might be explained by the fact that the actor was unemployed and needed money, or that he had a history of conflict with his victim. The American children used more trait-based explanations with increasing age, however, suggesting that they learned this pattern from their culture over time. In another study, Morris and Peng (1994) described a murder case to Americans and Chinese and asked them to explain the event. The Americans tended to say things like, "He was a psycho." In contrast, Chinese perceivers did not attribute the event to causes within the actor, but located the cause in the social relationships between the murderer, his victim, and the larger social context.

These attributional differences reflect the fact that, as we noted earlier, different cultures incorporate quite different assumptions about the basic nature of human beings. In Western cultures, people are seen as independent and autonomous, responsible for their own actions. Many non-Western cultures, in contrast, portray individuals as interdependent with their groups and social contexts, rather than as separate from them (Markus and others, 1996). As a result, a larger number of potential causes of behavior, including causes outside the individual, must be considered (Choi and others, 2003). The explanations that people from different cultures provide for behaviors mirror such differences in their basic conceptions of people.

Using Attributions to Correct First Impressions

When external factors appear to have caused behavior, people may attempt to correct an initial inference about the actor's characteristics. This correction takes time and cognitive effort, however, so it often does not occur.

Attributional thinking may lead us to revise our initial correspondent inferences; that is, we may become less confident that the actor's inner characteristics correspond to his or her behavior. This process is termed *discounting*, which refers to reducing a belief in one potential cause of behavior, such as the flatterer's true opinion, because there is another viable cause, his need for a favor (Kelley, 1972). When you see your classmates sweating and biting their fingernails as they await the calculus exam, the associated trait of anxiety immediately springs to mind. Processing superficially, you may go on to draw a correspondent inference—to form a first impression that the students are nervous people. However, if you think more systematically about the circumstances in which the behavior is occurring—the looming examination—you might take a third step and correct your initial impression by discounting, concluding that the nail biters may not be such nervous Nellies after all.

This third step seems so logical and sensible that one might wonder why people so often fall prey to the correspondence bias, even when situational causes are quite obvious. The answer lies in the fact that the first two steps, labeling the behavior and characterizing the person, are relatively easy, and frequently occur automatically, without any conscious effort. In contrast, the third step, using causal reasoning to correct the impression, is difficult unless a situational cause is quite salient or accessible (Gilbert, 1991; Trope & Gaunt, 2000). Causal reasoning usually takes time and effort and, as we all can testify, things that take more time and effort often do not get done at all.

Daniel Gilbert and his colleagues (1988) have demonstrated that extra effort is required to discount an initial impression. In their experiment, students watched a videotaped interview of an obviously nervous woman, with the sound turned off. The topics she was supposed to be discussing were displayed as subtitles on the TV screen. One group of students believed the interview centered on such highly personal, anxiety-provoking topics as "My sexual fantasies" or "My most embarrassing moment." Another group thought she was discussing innocuous matters like "My favorite vacation." After seeing the interview, all students were asked to rate how anxious a person the woman was in general. A correspondent inference would suggest that because the woman showed signs of nervousness, she must be a nervous type. However, the researchers reasoned, those who knew of a situational cause for her anxiety—the personal topics—should engage in discounting. And, indeed, their ratings of her general level of anxiety were lower than those of the students who thought the topics were mundane.

Two additional groups of students in the experiment went through exactly the same procedure with one exception: The researchers required these students to memorize the topics the woman was supposed to be discussing. Gilbert and his colleagues predicted that this distracting activity would leave them with insufficient cognitive resources to engage in effortful discounting. As expected, the distracted students

People in cultures like the United States tend to think of others in terms of their traits, and those in more interdependent cultures, such as India, emphasize roles and social relationships. This difference is also evident when people think about themselves, as you will see in Chapter 4, especially pages 104 to 107.

FIGURE 3.6   Correcting impressions is hard work

■ Participants who could focus their attention on their judgments rated a woman as a less anxious person when they knew she was discussing sensitive topics (left). In contrast, participants who were distracted by an additional task failed to discount (right). Those who believed the topics were sensitive assigned approximately the same ratings as those assigned by participants who believed the topics were innocuous. (Based on Gilbert and others, 1988.)

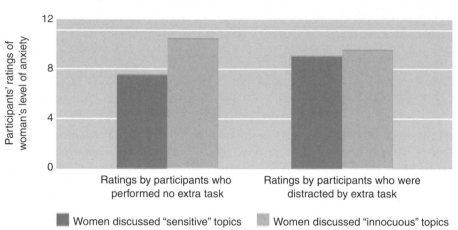

Women discussed "sensitive" topics   Women discussed "innocuous" topics

failed to discount their initial impressions. That is, they rated the woman as an anxious type even though they successfully memorized the anxiety-provoking topics (see Figure 3.6). Apparently, because the memory task absorbed some of their cognitive resources, they never went back to change their initial correspondent inferences, even though the role of situational factors, the anxiety-producing topics, was quite obvious. As this study shows, unless we are willing and able to process information systematically, the principle of conservatism applies: We stick with our first impressions.

All the typical demands of everyday interaction—trying to remember other people's names and faces, planning what we want to say, or working to create a good impression—also require considerable cognitive capacity. Thus, interaction itself may limit our ability to form accurate impressions of the people with whom we interact, leaving our impressions very much at the mercy of the behaviors we happen to see people perform first.

Putting It All Together: Forming Complex Impressions

One person's impression of another individual usually includes several characteristics. People may infer additional traits based on their knowledge or observations of the individual. The multiple components of an impression may become linked as people attempt to infer causal connections among them. Overall evaluations, too, are usually constructed by integrating multiple aspects of an impression.

Our everyday encounters with other people are likely to reveal more about them than just a single characteristic. How, then, do we develop coherent overall impressions? Imagine being introduced to Paul at a city council meeting. As you chat, you find that in addition to his involvement in city politics, Paul sells salad dressing and popcorn, acts in movies, contributes to newspaper advertisements for political causes, writes to his congressional representative regularly, and drives race cars. How would you put together all this information into an overall impression of Paul? We form our overall impressions by integrating multiple characteristics, whether they are traits or evaluations of the person.

INTEGRATING TRAIT INFORMATION. We usually expect certain traits to go together. Knowing that an acquaintance is generous, for example, often leads us to expect that he will be warm as well. These patterns of associations among traits, called *implicit personality theories* (Schneider, 1973), can guide the development and elaboration of complex impressions of others. For example, if you conclude that Paul is daring because he drives race cars, you might immediately conclude that he also is reckless or dominating because most people associate these traits with the trait daring (Rosenberg, Nelson, & Vivekananthan, 1968). In general, people seem to think that most positive traits are related to each other and that negative traits form another distinct group. When people rely on their implicit personality theories, they may infer that a person has many positive qualities on the basis of a single good one, and they may expect a lot of negative characteristics if they learn about one bad quality. Learning that someone is pessimistic, most people would expect him or her to also be irritable, cold, vain, and finicky. The fact that trait associations are structured in this way illustrates the central role of evaluation in our thinking about other people.

The general patterns of implicit personality theories are widely shared within a culture, but an individual may also make certain idiosyncratic trait inferences, depending on his or her own experiences (E. R. Smith & Zárate, 1992). For example, suppose you have a friend who is both exceptionally clumsy and quite reliable. If you meet someone else who is clumsy you might infer that this person is also reliable (Andersen & Cole, 1990; Lewicki, 1985). These two traits would be associated for you because they are both included in your cognitive representation of your friend, even though they are not connected in most people's implicit personality theories. In addition, you would probably like the person because of his or her resemblance to your friend (Andersen & Baum, 1994).

As we observe or infer more and more characteristics of an individual, we try to organize what we know and create an overall impression that is a complex and interlinked whole. For example, if you notice that several behaviors have similar trait implications, you may think about them together. This reflection, in turn, may cause the behaviors to become associated in your mind. For example, you may realize that Paul's behaviors of attending the council meeting, supporting the political ad campaigns, and writing letters to his congressional representative all reflect political activism. David Hamilton and his colleagues (Hamilton, Katz, & Leirer, 1980) suggest that behaviors that represent the same trait are linked into associated clusters in memory as people mentally organize their impressions of others. Supporting this idea, these researchers found that when people were asked to recall behaviors of a person they had earlier read about, they often recalled a number of behaviors reflecting the same trait in sequence, followed by behaviors linked to a different trait, and so on.

We may also make sense of a person's diverse behaviors and traits by creating causal links among them (Park, 1986; Prentice, 1990). You may know, for example, that a star athlete is quick-tempered. You might assume that she has a burning competitive drive that causes both her athletic successes and her outbursts of temper. These processes of inferring additional traits and linking multiple traits and behaviors into an integrated whole thus allow us to build impressions that are unified and coherent, not just lists of seemingly unrelated characteristics.

INTEGRATING EVALUATIONS. Most of the people we meet in everyday life are neither saints nor axe murderers, but have some positive and some negative characteristics. How do we put together our admiration for someone's artistic talents, positive feelings about their attractive appearance, and dismay at their occasional rude behavior into an overall evaluation? We could simply average the evaluations and conclude that overall, two positives and one negative lead to a mildly positive impression. However, we tend to give negative information more weight than positive information when we integrate impressions in this way, a pattern termed a *negativity effect* (Baumeister, Bratslavsky, Finkenauer, & Vohs, 2001; Skowronski & Carlston, 1989). We do this partly because negative information is generally surprising and unexpected—after all, more people are generally polite than rude. Therefore, the negative information seems more extreme and informative than comparable positive information. In addition, negative aspects of an object can sometimes "contaminate" or spoil positive aspects (Rozin & Royzman, 2001)—just imagine finding a fly in your bowl of delicious soup. Rarely if ever does a single positive item have the power to reverse our evaluation of a generally negative object.

Particularly when we are thinking carefully and systematically about another person, we may go beyond simply averaging our evaluations of their characteristics. We try to construct a more meaningful type of integration, just as we integrate traits into a complex and causally linked overall impression. In this case the first information we learn may be used as a basis for interpreting and evaluating other information. If we first learn that the person is an artist, for instance, when we notice the occasional rudeness, it may become just an aspect of "the artistic temperament," perhaps even acquiring a neutral or positive evaluation. As this example suggests, evaluations of traits or other personal characteristics are not fixed and constant, but depend on the total impression of the person (Hamilton & Zanna, 1974).

The Accuracy of Considered Impressions

Even considered impressions may not be completely accurate. When people devote extra thought to forming an impression, biases may still limit their accuracy, and the extra efforts may only confirm an existing positive or negative view. Unless people are aware of such biases in social perception, they are unlikely to try to correct them.

When we go beyond a first impression, both making attributions and integrating multiple behaviors and traits require considerable thought. What might motivate the expenditure of all this cognitive effort? And will the extra effort guarantee that considered impressions are unbiased, valid conceptions of what the person is really like?

MOTIVATION TO BE ACCURATE. Accuracy is one of the strongest motivations for working hard on forming an impression. Suppose you have a new acquaintance, Tom, and you are sure your friend will like him. You realize that your friend might hold you responsible if you bring Tom along to a party and he turns out to be rude or boring. If it is important to be accurate because you will be held accountable, you will probably make an extra effort to gather information (Kruglanski & Freund, 1983). This effort sometimes allows us to overcome the effects of an initial expectation (Neuberg, 1989a).

We can also be particularly motivated to form accurate perceptions of people when we will have to work with them (Flink & Park, 1991; Srull & Brand, 1983). In one study, students learned that they would shortly meet a man who had previously been hospitalized for schizophrenia. Some of the students were told they would simply meet him, but others believed that they would work cooperatively with him on a joint task (Neuberg & Fiske, 1987). The students then received an information sheet describing the man's personal background, hobbies, and so on. Those who expected to cooperate with him spent more time reading about his personal characteristics, and used that additional information in forming their impressions. In contrast, the others spent less time reading about the man's attributes and formed an impression that was based almost entirely on the schizophrenia diagnosis.

Suspicion about someone's motives may also cause us to think before leaping to a correspondent inference, as Steven Fein (1996) demonstrated. Students read a speech on a controversial issue that was supposedly the work of an applicant for a summer internship. One group of students were told that the writer had been assigned the position without having any choice. Like the participants who read essays about Castro in the original Jones and Harris (1967) study, this group fell prey to the correspondence bias: they inferred that the writer privately held the position espoused in the speech. In contrast, another group was told that the writer had freely chosen the side of the issue supported by the speech, and that the views given in the speech matched the position of the professor who would be evaluating the writer's application. Apparently inferring that the applicant might have been trying to curry favor, the students drew no inferences about the writer's personal position. Suspicion of ulterior motives evidently motivates people to think hard about the causes of behavior, which reduces their susceptibility to the correspondence bias.

■ **Your impression of your new co-worker** may be biased by your preconceived ideas that he or she will be a valuable contributor to your team or that he or she may be a rival for a much-desired promotion.

MOTIVES BESIDES ACCURACY. When people devote extra efforts to processing information about others, it is not always in the service of accuracy. One study showed that when perceiving another person accurately might create interpersonal problems, people may be motivated to avoid accuracy. Jeffry Simpson and his colleagues (Simpson, Ickes, & Blackstone, 1995) had members of dating couples evaluate photographs of highly attractive opposite-sex individuals and then attempt to guess each other's thoughts and feelings about the task. When the situation posed a threat to the couple's relationship (for example, when the relationship was insecure), these guesses were relatively inaccurate. Accuracy is not always the primary goal of person perception!

At times our judgments are inaccurate because our hopes and desires guide our search for and our interpretation of facts (Kruglanski & Freund, 1983; Kunda, 1990). In one study, for example, students evaluated the trivia knowledge of a man whom they expected to be either their competitor or their partner in a contest. All students had watched him answer a few practice questions correctly. Those who expected to be the man's future partners rated his trivia ability higher than did those who expected to compete with him (Klein & Kunda, 1992).

As these studies show, our approach to perceiving other people or the world in general is sometimes like that of an attorney constructing the best possible case for a client (Baumeister & Newman, 1994). Rather than conducting an unbiased search with accuracy as the only goal, we hunt for evidence that supports our preferred conclusion. And because behavior is often ambiguous, we often find just what we are seeking. If the trivia player is to be our partner, we focus on how much knowledge his answers displayed; if we will have to compete with him, we instead emphasize how easy the practice questions were. When our search succeeds, we remain unaware of the biases in the search process and we blissfully forget that, had we searched with different goals, we might have unearthed a very different body of evidence.

AWARENESS OF BIAS AS A MOTIVE. Most of the time we remain blind to our biases, accepting the world we perceive at face value. We think that what we see is what actually is, because we are so good at constructing a coherent representation of reality (Gilbert, 1998). And we ordinarily get along well enough relying on our construction of reality (Fiske, 1993). But sometimes, perhaps when we compare notes with another person who sees things differently, we realize that our views may be biased. Awareness of bias may motivate us to devote extra effort to thinking about other people (Lombardi, Higgins, & Bargh, 1987; Strack, Schwarz, Bless, Kubler, & Wanke, 1989). Have you ever had a friend give a glowing description of someone you regarded as narrow-minded, hostile, and uncouth? Disagreement often motivates us to think hard to determine the truth, or at least to convince ourselves that other people's interpretations and judgments, not our own, are biased. If disagreement never surfaces, however, we may feel quite satisfied with the impressions we form. We operate on the motto "If it ain't broke, don't fix it," and we generally do not even try to correct our impressions.

Even when awareness of a potential bias makes us try to correct our impressions, a lack of time or cognitive resources may undermine our best intentions and leave us unable to make the correction (Martin, Seta, & Crelia, 1990). Only when both motivation and cognitive ability are available will we attempt to counteract potential biases. At that point, our attempted correction will depend on our beliefs about the nature and direction of the bias (Wegener & Petty, 1995). For example, suppose you meet someone on a brightly sunny spring day when your boss has just given you a big raise. If you are aware that you are in a terrific mood and believe that it might bias your impression in a positive direction, you will probably attempt to correct your impression of the person by making it more negative—trying to cancel out the assumed bias (Wegener & Petty, 2001). The net result of this process may be a more accurate judgment, but only if your theory about the direction and size of the bias is relatively correct.

Figure 3.7 summarizes all the processes involved in impression formation, from noticing cues to interpreting them, inferring traits, and integrating multiple traits to form an overall impression. What is surprising is how little aware we usually are of all this processing. Our impressions of others seem to be formed immediately, rarely requiring much thought. But in fact, this sense of immediacy actually reflects the unobtrusive efficiency with which our interpretive processes construct our picture of reality.

The Impact of Impressions: Using, Defending, and Changing Impressions

Once we have formed an impression of another person, whether it is a snap judgment or a thoughtful construction, and whether it is biased or accurate, we use it to guide our decisions and social interactions. Thus, once we have concluded that the next-door neighbor is a generous fellow, we trust that our interpretation represents objective reality. And even if these impressions are biased, they take on reality as we act on them.

FIGURE 3.7   From snap judgments to complex impressions

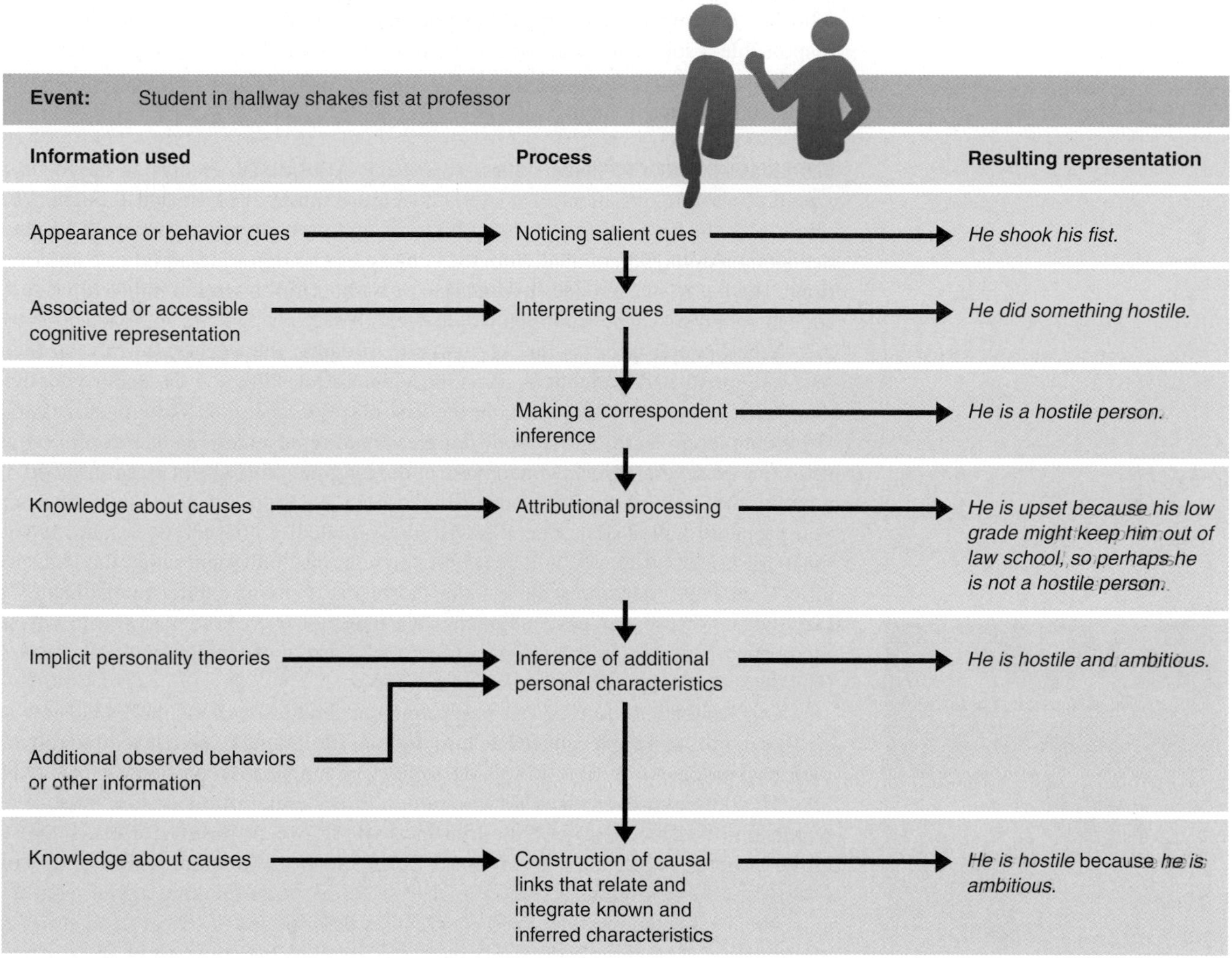

Event:	Student in hallway shakes fist at professor	
Information used	**Process**	**Resulting representation**
Appearance or behavior cues	Noticing salient cues	*He shook his fist.*
Associated or accessible cognitive representation	Interpreting cues	*He did something hostile.*
	Making a correspondent inference	*He is a hostile person.*
Knowledge about causes	Attributional processing	*He is upset because his low grade might keep him out of law school, so perhaps he is not a hostile person.*
Implicit personality theories Additional observed behaviors or other information	Inference of additional personal characteristics	*He is hostile and ambitious.*
Knowledge about causes	Construction of causal links that relate and integrate known and inferred characteristics	*He is hostile because he is ambitious.*

Impressions and Judgments

Once an impression is formed, it becomes a basis for decisions and behaviors. Sometimes decisions about others rest on simple, superficial processing; at other times people engage in extensive processing, attempting to put together the implications of all relevant information.

Imagine that you need to find several housemates. As you interview a few candidates, you may develop complex, well-articulated impressions of each of them. Whom should you pick? What aspects of your impressions will influence your decision? Sometimes only a single aspect of an impression really matters. If the only thing you care about is a compatible lifestyle (similar tastes in music, similar preferences for late hours), the happy-go-lucky night person may seem to be your best bet. If a shared interest in animal rights is your most important criterion, you certainly will not choose the woman in the fur coat. Often, however, more than one aspect of your impression seems important. You want someone you like, who has a compatible lifestyle, but you also want that person to be financially responsible—someone who will not stick you with bills for unpaid rent and telephone calls each month. How do we make judgments about others on the basis of our impressions of them?

SUPERFICIAL PROCESSING: USING A SINGLE ATTRIBUTE. Decisions based on a single accessible or salient characteristic require minimal effort and thought. You might pick the best-looking person who turns up to see your apartment or base your decision on some other equally obvious characteristic, ignoring all other considerations. Having to make a decision quickly or without full attention might force such superficial processing even if you would prefer a more systematic approach.

When people process quickly and superficially, they generally rely on their past judgments and evaluations of an individual, rather than on the underlying evidence that led to those judgments in the first place (Carlston & Skowronski, 1986). For example, on learning that your congressional representative takes conservative positions on several issues, you may form the judgment that she is a conservative. If a new issue, such as capital punishment, becomes a topic for political discussion, you probably will assume that she will take an equally conservative stand. If you make this assumption, you will be relying on your past judgment rather than on specific statements the representative may have made about capital punishment. In fact, when we use our past judgments we may not even bother to retrieve from memory or reconsider the specific facts on which those judgments were based (Hastie & Park, 1986; Sherman & Klein, 1994).

Our tendency to rely on our past judgments and evaluations makes us slow to change our thinking and can lead us into trouble. For example, people tend to rely on their past judgments even if those judgments were made in circumstances that create bias. If a doting mother asked for an opinion of her rather ordinary son, most of us would find it difficult to describe him in anything except positive terms. Interestingly, giving such a slanted description may affect our private impressions of the son (Higgins, 1998a; Higgins & McCann, 1984). Rather than thinking again about the evidence, people tend to draw on their previous descriptions of others—forgetting or ignoring the fact that these descriptions were shaped by the demands of an audience.

SYSTEMATIC PROCESSING: INTEGRATING MULTIPLE FACTORS. When we apply for jobs or loans, we all hope that those evaluating the application will process it with conscientiousness and depth, taking account of more than one of our characteristics. As noted earlier, when people know their decisions matter and when accuracy is extremely important to them, they often do carry out such systematic processing (Neuberg, 1989a; Neuberg & Fiske, 1987). One way of combining multiple factors is termed the *algebraic* approach. It is similar to the way an "ideal" consumer decides which appliance or automobile to buy: examining the *Consumer Reports* table of each brand's advantages and disadvantages and weighting each feature according to its importance for the particular decision (Anderson, 1981). For example, if you are considering someone as a potential date, you might assess the person in terms of a variety of individual qualities, some similar to and some different from those you would consider for a potential study partner.

Alternatively, people may integrate multiple items of information in a less mechanical way. Instead of evaluating each attribute independently, people may

■ **Tell us her story**. Is this young woman a vegetarian? Is she a college fine-arts major? When people process superficially they may draw conclusions like these based on easily accessible stereotypes linked to physical appearance. If we were processing systematically, we might also take into consideration other relevant information, such as the fact that these characteristics are relatively rare in the population.

attempt to fit the information together into a meaningful whole. In this integration process, one item may subtly change the meaning of others (Asch, 1946; Asch & Zukier, 1984). For example, suppose one person is described as intelligent and cold, and another as intelligent and warm. The very meaning of intelligent seems to differ in these two descriptions, connoting something like "calculating" or "sly" when combined with cold, but taking on the meaning of "wise" in the context of warm. When people use this *configural* approach to evaluate a person's multiple attributes, their overall judgment may depend on the particular way they combine the attributes. As mentioned earlier in this chapter, integrating multiple characteristics often involves causal reasoning, as when we infer that coldness leads people to use their intelligence in self-centered ways, making them seem calculating.

Defending Impressions

Impressions tend to resist change, partly because an initial impression can alter the interpretation of later information. As a result, impressions may even survive the discrediting of the information on which they were based. Impressions shape overt interaction as well as judgments. They often lead people to seek consistent information or even to elicit confirming actions from others.

Once formed, our impressions of others can influence both our private judgments about those individuals and our interactions with them. As we obtain further information, we may slant our interpretations to maintain our impressions unchanged. And as we treat people in ways that reflect our existing impressions and expectations, we may produce in them the very behavior we expect to see. The principle of conservatism can be seen clearly here: Once formed, our beliefs about other people are slow to change, in part because they tend to maintain themselves.

IMPRESSIONS SHAPE INTERPRETATIONS. Suppose you are watching the quiz show *The Weakest Link*. One contestant gives quick correct answers early in the show but cools off as the questions continue. Another contestant starts out with a series of wrong answers and then improves. By the first commercial break, they have an equal number of right and wrong answers. Which contestant seems more intelligent to you? If you are like most people, you will give the edge to the one who started strongly (Jones, Rock, Shaver, Goethals, & Ward, 1968). Our initial impressions can set up an expectation that shapes our interpretations of later information—letting the early information have a greater impact, in what is called a *primacy effect* (Asch, 1946).

In an illustration of the lasting effects of initial impressions, Bernadette Park (1986) arranged for small groups of strangers to meet together repeatedly over 7-week period. After the first meeting, and periodically after that, participants wrote descriptions of one another. Week after week, first impressions dominated these profiles. The characteristics noted after the very first meeting turned up repeatedly, even though the first impressions were based on little information. Apparently initial impressions biased the participants' interpretations of later behavior. So when you meet new people, putting your best foot forward right from the start is much easier than trying to change opinions once you have put your foot in it.

IMPRESSIONS RESIST REBUTTAL. Because our impressions can shape the interpretation of later information, their effects can persist even if the initial impression is discovered to be false. This distortion is called the *perseverance bias* (Lord, Lepper,

■ **First impressions are lasting impressions**. Arnold Schwarzenegger was elected as governor of California in 2003. But despite his success as a politician, for many people he is inextricably linked with his character in *The Terminator*. In fact he has acquired the nickname of 'The Governator'!

& Preston, 1984). To investigate this bias, Lee Ross and his colleagues (1975) arranged for female students to observe others performing a decision-making task. Some observers received false feedback that made it appear that the decision maker performed quite well, getting 24 of 25 items correct. Others learned that the decision maker performed poorly, with only 10 correct items. The experimenter then revealed that the feedback had been randomly determined and had no relation to the decision maker's actual performance. However, even after the observers learned of this deception, their ratings of the decision makers' ability and their predictions of future performance still showed the effects of the now-discredited feedback. For example, observers who initially thought a decision maker had succeeded predicted that she would get an average of 19 items correct on a future trial; conversely, observers who initially saw failure predicted only 14.5 for the same decision maker. As this experiment shows, once beliefs have influenced our interpretation of other information, it is difficult to undo their effects completely if we later learn the beliefs are false (Gilbert, Krull, & Malone, 1990; Gilbert & Osborne, 1989). No wonder that it is notoriously difficult to counteract rumors after they get started (Rosnow & Fine, 1976).

The most effective way to reduce or eliminate the perseverance bias is to explicitly consider the opposite possibility (Lord, Lepper, & Preston, 1984). Learning that the supposed 24 of 25 score was false had little effect on the observers in Ross's study. However, considering the possibility that the individual might have actually performed quite poorly could have reduced the bias.

☐ **PERSEVERANCE IN THE COURTROOM.** When legally inadmissible evidence is introduced in courtroom proceedings, it can be stricken from the official trial record. The judge may even instruct jurors to disregard it. Unfortunately, jurors cannot wipe the information from their minds as easily as the court reporter can expunge the record. In fact, research has found that inadmissible evidence does influence jurors' deliberations and verdicts (Thompson, Fong, & Rosenhan, 1981). The same is true of discredited evidence. In one mock-trial study, for example, one group of participants saw minimal evidence against the defendant, and only 18% voted for conviction. A second group saw the same evidence plus an eyewitness identification of the defendant; in that group, 72% voted for conviction. A third group, after receiving all this information, learned that the eyewitness was legally blind and was not wearing his glasses at the time he claimed to have seen the defendant. This discrediting information had virtually no impact, however, reducing the conviction rate only to 68% (Loftus, 1974). The perseverance bias means that, as in this example, information may have effects that persist even after the information is found to be false.

SELECTIVELY SEEKING IMPRESSION-CONSISTENT BEHAVIOR. Most of us are somewhat inconsistent in our behaviors—for instance, we may act shy at some times and outgoing at others. What would happen if someone expected you to be outgoing and attempted to test that belief? He or she might ask you leading questions about occasions when you were outgoing, for example, when you were the center of attention at a large party or particularly enjoyed a social gathering (Snyder & Swann, 1978). As you recounted such instances, the questioner's initial hypothesis would seem to be confirmed. But was it? If the questions had focused on the times you felt shy and avoided other people, you would have been able to report on those equally well. Any hypothesis about another person could probably be confirmed if tested in this way.

Actually, people do not always ask biased or leading questions to test their beliefs about others. Given a choice, they often prefer questions that are diagnostic—that is, questions whose answers will provide information about the truth or falsity of the hypothesis (Trope, Bassok, & Alon, 1984). For example, a diagnostic question to assess whether someone is outgoing could take the following form: "Would you rather attend a large party or have a quiet get-together with one or two close friends?" Unlike the earlier example, this question would not necessarily produce a false confirmation of an initial hypothesis. However, coming up with properly diagnostic questions is often difficult unless the questioner is aware of alternatives to the given hypothesis (Higgins & Bargh, 1987; Hodgins & Zuckerman, 1993). As we have already seen, a strategy of "considering the opposite"— thinking about the possibility that the person might be quiet and retiring rather than outgoing—can reduce biases (Trope & Mackie, 1987).

CREATING IMPRESSION-CONSISTENT BEHAVIOR: THE SELF-FULFILLING PROPHECY.
Suppose you believe, for whatever reason, that people from the southern United States tend to be gracious and friendly. When you meet a Southerner, you will probably act warmly, and the person will naturally reciprocate. You will probably end up liking the person, just as you thought you would. Of course, the outcome might be quite different if your initial expectation was that Southerners would be hostile and unfriendly. As this example demonstrates, we do more than just ask other people about their behaviors. Our initial impressions may actually *create* corresponding behaviors (Synder, Tanke, & Berscheid, 1977; Zebrowitz, Hall, Murphy, & Rhodes, 2002). When a person's expectation about another causes that person to act in ways that confirm the expectation, the process is called a **self-fulfilling prophecy** (Darley & Fazio, 1980; Merton, 1948). Figure 3.8 portrays an example of this process.

Of course, if people were aware of their influence on others, they might try to discount that influence to improve the accuracy of their impressions. However, people sometimes fail to recognize even their clear and overt influences on others. To demonstrate this point, researchers set up an interview situation in which interviewers and interviewees read questions and answers from fixed scripts (Gilbert & Jones, 1986). The questions concerned politics; the prepared answers reflected a conservative or liberal viewpoint. The interviewer read each question and then pushed a "Liberal" or "Conservative" button, as specified by the script, to signal which answer the interviewee should read. Of course, by pushing the buttons, the interviewers themselves controlled the answers they heard. But did they recognize their own influence? No. They rated the interviewees as conservative when most of their answers were conservative, and liberal when most answers were liberal. It is surprisingly difficult for people to recognize the effects of their own actions on others, and without such awareness we cannot correct our impressions to improve their validity.

> **Self-fulfilling prophecy.** The process by which one person's expectations about another become reality by eliciting behaviors that confirm the expectations.

FIGURE 3.8   Expectations create confirmation: The self-fulfilling prophecy

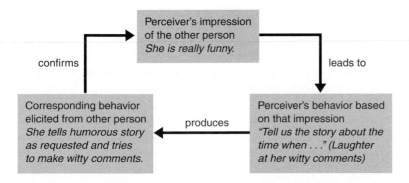

■ Once we have formed an impression of another person, our expectations often lead us to behave in ways that elicit expectation-confirming behaviors.

☐ **SELF-FULFILLING PROPHECY IN THE CLASSROOM AND THE WORKPLACE.**
Self-fulfilling prophecies can operate anywhere: at home, on the job, and in the classroom. In studies pioneered by Robert Rosenthal and his colleagues, researchers gave schoolteachers the names of some pupils in their classes who were expected to "bloom" intellectually over the next few months (Rosenthal, 1985; Rosenthal & Jacobson, 1968). Actually, the students had been selected at random. Later in the school year all the students were tested. Multiple studies using this technique have shown that children identified as "bloomers" tend to perform better than their classmates—on objective tests, not just in the teachers' own estimation. The teachers' high expectations for these children are somehow translated into actual achievement over the course of a few months. The reason may be that teachers give students more attention and more challenging assignments when they expect them to perform at a high level (Cooper & Good, 1983). These types of teacher behaviors improve students' performance. Similar processes operate in the workplace, where supervisors' impressions shape subordinates' actual performance (Kierein & Gold, 2000; McNatt, 2000), an effect that is particularly strong when the worker's initial performance level is low.

LIMITS ON THE SELF-FULFILLING PROPHECY. How vulnerable are we to the effects of other people's expectations, particularly those of people such as teachers or employers, who have some power over us? To some extent, the answer to that question is determined by our self-views, our awareness of the views others have of us, and our social motives in the situation.

When the person being perceived has strong views about him- or herself, the self-fulfilling effects of a perceiver's expectations become weaker. William Swann and Robin Ely (1984) demonstrated this fact in an ingenious experiment in which they created a conflict between a perceiver's expectations and the other person's own self-views. The researchers paired previously unacquainted female students, selecting one as a target and the other as a perceiver. Some of the targets were self-described introverts and others were extroverts. Some of each group had great confidence in their self-knowledge, whereas others were less confident. The perceiver in each pair was led to have the opposite expectation about the target; for some, the expectation was held with great confidence and for others, with some tentativeness. Perceivers interviewed the targets three times, and then both women's impressions were assessed. Whose views exerted the most force? Most of the time, those of the target: Perceivers usually changed their original impression to match the target's self-views. The effects of the self-fulfilling prophecy emerged only when the target initially had been uncertain about her self-views and the perceiver confidently believed the reverse. In such cases, the self-fulfilling prophecy influenced both the target's overt behavior and her self-views.

Self-fulfilling prophecies can also be foiled when targets are aware of the perceivers' expectations. If you met someone who expected you to be uncertain and naive, would you make a special effort to show your independence and sophistication? Many people would react just this way. Indeed, research shows that people who are aware of others' unfavorable expectations about them often succeed in disconfirming those expectations (Hilton & Darley, 1985).

Third, self-fulfilling prophecies are weaker when the targets are motivated to convey accurate impressions, rather than trying to make the interaction go smoothly and pleasantly (Snyder & Haugen, 1995). This finding suggests that when targets confirm perceivers' expectations, it is often out of their general desire for social acceptance and connectedness.

Thus, the self-fulfilling prophecy does not affect everyone equally. Like the schoolchildren in Rosenthal's studies, some people—those who are uncertain about their self-views, are unaware of others' beliefs, or want to make interactions run smoothly—are especially vulnerable to shaping by others' expectations.

Dealing With Inconsistent Information

People sometimes encounter information that is clearly inconsistent with an impression. They may attempt to explain it away in various ways, or they may take it into account and assume that the other person has changed. Most of the time, however, impressions of others' personal characteristics are stable and difficult to change.

Consider the many mental tricks you may use to sustain your impression of another person. Believing that Albert is intelligent, you notice only his ground-breaking discoveries in science. When his behavior is ambiguous, you interpret it as being smart rather than stupid. Sometimes you seek out evidence of his intelligence, questioning him about his latest ideas on relativity rather than about the times he forgot where he parked his car. You may even create the opportunity for Albert to be smart by giving him his own lab, a supply of freshly sharpened pencils, a supercomputer, and all the coffee he can drink. Then, one day, Albert does something so remarkably stupid—so unambiguously inconsistent with your belief—that there can be no denying it. How would you handle this conflict? You could explain away this inconsistency, defending your original impression to the death. Or you could take account of the information in ways that make your impression of Albert more accurate.

RECONCILING INCONSISTENCIES. When we encounter inconsistent and contradictory information about someone, it challenges two central social motives. Our sense of mastery and understanding is threatened by the unexpected information, and our ability to maintain a relationship or social interaction with the person may also be thrown into doubt. Inconsistent information is therefore generally unwelcome (Olson, Roese, & Zanna, 1996). This is why we often prefer to gloss over and ignore it, continuing to process superficially rather than paying attention to the inconsistency. However, important inconsistencies are likely to trigger systematic processing, when people have adequate time to devote to the task (Hamilton, Driscoll, & Worth, 1989; Srull, Lichtenstein, & Rothbart, 1985).

How would you react, for example, if one friend told you that a classmate is kind and another friend said that the same person is hostile? When people in one study were presented with such contradictory trait descriptions and asked to describe their impressions in their own words, they creatively integrated the seemingly inconsistent traits (Asch & Zukier, 1984). They decided, for example, that the person was hostile to most people but kind to family members, or that the person masked a hostile disposition with an appearance of kindness.

When people make the effort to reconcile inconsistent and contradictory information, it has several effects on cognitive processing and memory.

1. *People spend more time thinking about unexpected behaviors than about expected ones.* For example, if you read that your liberal state senator is fighting for a conservative position such as a reduction in the minimum wage for young workers, you might pay extra attention, although you might quickly pass over more expected news of his support of several liberal causes (Belmore & Hubbard, 1987).

2. *People try to explain unexpected behaviors—to make sense of them.* Thus, you might begin to wonder why the senator supports reducing the minimum wage. Perhaps you will decide that he supports this measure because it will provide more jobs for the poor and disadvantaged, whose cause he generally favors. As we noted earlier, people are more likely to make causal attributions about unexpected events than about events that are normal and expected (Hastie, 1984).

3. *Extra processing improves people's ability to recall inconsistent behaviors.* The special attributional processing that we give to inconsistent behaviors may help us remember them better than the behaviors consistent with our expectations (Hastie & Kumar, 1979; Srull, 1981). In fact, any behaviors that people explain can be better recalled at a later time, compared with behaviors that people read but do not explain (Hastie, 1984). This is true whether the behaviors are consistent or inconsistent with the person's expectations.

Even when people make an effort at reconciliation, their impressions of others do not always change. For example, in a study conducted in the Netherlands, inconsistent behaviors (such as negative behaviors performed by a generally well-liked person) had no effect on people's impressions (Vonk, 1995). One reason is that the extensive processing may be directed at explaining away the inconsistency. If unexpected behaviors can be attributed to situational factors, the initial impression can be maintained intact (Crocker, Hannah, & Weber, 1983). Thus, a battered woman might defend her impression that her abusive partner is basically a good person by attributing his occasional violence to external factors, such as the effects of alcohol or, sadly, even some behavior of her own.

INTEGRATING INCONSISTENCIES. Still, as you get to know someone well over a period of time, encounters with more and more potential inconsistencies should lead you to develop a more complex impression of the person. Jennifer Welbourne (2001) found that in these circumstances impressions do indeed become less consistent and also more complex and elaborated, featuring a larger number of causal links. The causal attributions may reflect the perceiver's attempts to interpret and reconcile inconsistencies, as we just discussed. Interestingly, the most complex impressions were not necessarily of those individuals the perceiver had known for the longest time, but of individuals who were encountered in a number of different contexts. If you only see someone in the classroom day after day, week after week, your impression may remain quite simple and consistent. It is when you also get to know them in the context of their family, performing in the community theater, and in their part-time job that impressions grow more multi-faceted and complex.

ALTERING IMPRESSIONS: IS FUNDAMENTAL CHANGE POSSIBLE? By now, you may be pretty pessimistic about the possibility of ever changing an established impression. Because so many processes tend to maintain our views, it is not surprising that even long weeks of interaction can leave people's initial impressions largely intact (Kenny, 1991; Park, 1986). Is fundamental change in impressions ever possible? Linda Silka's (1989) research offers some reason for optimism. Silka's participants read the life history of a young woman who appeared, at least on the surface, to change greatly. Lany Tyler was a high school cheerleader who, although she initially failed to win admission to college, eventually obtained a Ph.D. and became a Princeton University professor of history. Those asked to write about how Lany had changed had no trouble identifying examples, noting that she changed "from the stereotypical 'social butterfly' to an intellectually geared individual" (p. 126). This finding suggests that when people are actively looking for change in an individual, they are able to perceive it. Indeed, faced with inconsistent information for which no situational explanations are obvious, people often make sense of the behaviors by assuming that the person's beliefs, attitudes, motivation, or ability has changed (Allison, Mackie, Muller, & Worth, 1993; Silka, 1989).

Like many other aspects of person perception, perceptions of change differ for different perceivers, and in different cultures. Some people are generally ready to believe that an individual's personality or abilities have changed over time, while others seem to see these kinds of psychological attributes as fixed and unchanging (Dweck & Leggett, 1988). And Asians (compared to Westerners) are more likely to view people's behavior as changing with circumstances and social contexts. As we have said, this is one reason that in explaining behaviors Asians are less affected by the correspondence bias (Norenzayan & Nisbett, 2000). In fact, this tendency appears to be just one facet of a much more general readiness to perceive change among Asians. Li-Jun Ji and others (Ji, Nisbett, & Su, 2001) gave simple scenarios to American and Chinese college students. The scenarios described a situation and asked about the possibility that it would change to the reverse; for example, "Richard grew up in a poor family but he managed to go to college. How likely is it that he will become rich some day?" or "Two children are fighting in kindergarten. How likely is it that they will ever become lovers?" Across five varied scenarios, the Chinese rated the possibility of change higher than Americans. In another study, the researchers showed graphs that portrayed a change (for example, the worldwide death rate for cancer was shown as decreasing) and asked how likely it was that the trend would continue or reverse. Again, the Chinese saw a reversal of the current trend as more likely than did the Americans. The general emphasis on change in Asian cultures means that Asians may be more willing than Westerners to see people as changing in fundamental ways, or as simultaneously possessing opposite characteristics.

Even Americans can form such complex impressions in the right circumstances, however. Susan Babey and her colleagues (Babey, Queller, & Klein, 1998) gave students information about a person that changed over time—starting out with mostly intelligent behaviors but ending with mostly unintelligent ones. As expected, students who saw only the first part of the information formed a corresponding impression of the person as intelligent. Students who also saw the later, less intelligent behaviors revised this initial impression and concluded that the person was actually fairly stupid. However, the researchers found evidence that this new impression did not completely replace the original impression in the students' memory. Instead, both impressions seemed to be maintained simultaneously, though the more recently formed one was more accessible. People's actual behavior is complex and variable—even smart people do stupid things sometimes, after all—and our impressions can at least sometimes capture some of the multi-faceted nature of the people we observe and interact with.

CONCLUDING COMMENTS

As you reflect on the evidence presented in this chapter, you may conclude that biases in impressions are pretty hard to overcome. Most of the time that is true. We get a lot of mileage out of the simple general principle that behavior reflects personality. Yet we also know that human nature is more complicated than this rule would indicate. When accuracy is of the utmost importance, we attend fully, process carefully, and are rewarded with more accurate impressions of other people. But why are simple principles, with all their possibilities of bias, usually more than adequate for our needs?

First, in many cases, our needs for accuracy in day-to-day life are modest. Correspondent inferences work perfectly well if our encounters with people are limited to particular situations or roles. For example, your assumption that the office bookkeeper is a quiet and restrained person on the basis of his office demeanor will not create problems if the office is the only place the two of you interact—though you might be surprised to see how he acts at a wild party. We can ignore people's individual personalities and still interact successfully with them if their behaviors are governed largely by the power of social situations and roles.

Second, people's behavior in particular situations often accurately reflects their personalities because they choose to be in those situations. Suppose you watch someone telling jokes at a comedy try-out. Technically, it might be correct that her provocative, lively, and funny behaviors are called for by this situation. But since the would-be comedian *chose* the situation, it is probably reasonable to assume that she is a lively, funny person. Thus, a correspondent inference works just fine.

Third, correspondent inferences are often accurate because other people offer us accurate cues to their true nature, at least as they themselves perceive it. As you will see in the next chapter, being perceived accurately by others is rewarding, and being mis-perceived is frustrating and uncomfortable. So the lover of baroque music might wear a J. S. Bach T-shirt to let us know. Even if the cues a new acquaintance offers do not ring quite true, it is often wise to go along for the ride, accepting rather than challenging the person. Certainly the interaction will go more smoothly if we save the other's face.

Thus, people's tendency to take others' behaviors or observable cues at face value can grease the wheels of social interaction, and this tendency usually lets us get along quite well. Still, going beyond first impressions to seek greater accuracy in person perception is sometimes important. When choosing a housemate, we want to predict a variety of compatible behaviors accurately on the basis of a few items of background information and a brief conversation. Serving on a jury, we want to decide whether the defendant or the accuser is telling the truth.

In the final analysis, both accurate and inaccurate impressions flow from the same underlying *processes* that people use as they attempt to understand others. Therefore, it is these processes that social psychologists seek to understand. They include tapping our stored knowledge to make quick inferences about observed behaviors, thinking about the causes of behaviors or other events, integrating multiple items of information to make a decision and reconciling inconsistencies. People use these basic processes not only to understand other people, but also to understand other social objects. In the chapters that follow we will discuss how similar processes operate as we perceive and interpret ourselves (Chapter 4), our own and other social groups (Chapter 5), consumer products and social issues (Chapter 7), our loved ones (Chapter 11), even our enemies (Chapter 13). Nothing in the nature of these processes necessarily leads to either accurate or inaccurate judgments. Accuracy depends more on the circumstances in which the processes are applied: the amount of useful information available, the applicability of the person's knowledge, the amount of effort the person is willing and able to put in, and whether the goal is to be accurate or to form a particular impression. Our perceptions of *all* social objects—including other people—are not determined solely by their observable characteristics. Instead, they also reflect our own individuality and uniqueness as perceivers: our motives and biases, our cognitive limitations, and the content and accessibility of our pre-existing knowledge.

SUMMARY

 Forming First Impressions: Cues, Interpretations, and Inferences. Perceptions of other people begin with visible cues, including physical appearance, nonverbal communication, and overt behavior. Familiarity also affects impressions, generally leading to increased liking. Cues that are **salient**—that stand out and attract attention in the context in which they occur—are particularly influential.

These cues have no meaning in themselves, but are interpreted in the light of our existing knowledge or **cognitive representations** of people, behaviors, traits, and social situations. A representation that is **associated** with the cue itself or is **accessible** and easy to bring to mind is most likely to be used in interpreting cues. Accessibility can stem from the person's expectations, moods, or the situational context, or from recent activation (termed **priming**) or frequent activation of the representation.

When processing **superficially**, people often make **correspondent inferences**, assuming that others have inner qualities that correspond to their observable behaviors. In fact, people often make correspondent inferences even when situational causes actually account for behaviors, a pattern termed the **correspondence bias**.

Beyond First Impressions: Systematic Processing. To go beyond a first impression, people must engage in more **systematic** thought, particularly to make **causal attributions** for behavior. People usually consider potential causes that are associated with the behavior, generally accessible, salient in context, or suggested by the pattern of available information.

When external factors appear to have caused behavior, people may attempt to correct their initial correspondent inference about the actor's characteristics. This correction takes time and cognitive effort, however, so it often does not occur.

An impression of another person usually includes several characteristics. People may infer additional traits based on their knowledge or observations of the individual. The multiple components of an impression may become linked as people attempt to infer causal connections among them. Overall evaluations, too, are usually constructed by integrating multiple aspects of an impression.

Even considered impressions may not be completely accurate. When people devote extra thought to forming an impression, biases may still limit their accuracy, and the extra efforts may only confirm an existing positive or negative view. Unless people are aware of such biases in social perception, they are unlikely to try to correct them.

The Impact of Impressions: Using, Defending, and Changing Impressions. Once an impression is formed, it becomes a basis for judgments and behaviors. Sometimes decisions about others rest on simple, superficial processing; at other times, people engage in systematic processing, attempting to put together the implications of all relevant information.

Impressions tend to resist change, partly because an initial impression can alter the interpretation of later information. As a result, impressions may survive even the discrediting of the information on which they were based. Impressions shape overt interaction as well as judgments. They often lead people to seek consistent information or even to elicit confirming actions from others, creating a **self-fulfilling prophecy**.

Still, sometimes people encounter information that is clearly inconsistent with an impression. They may attempt to explain it away in various ways, or they may take it into account and assume that the other person has changed. Most of the time, however, people's impressions of others' personal characteristics are stable and difficult to change.

4

The Self

How do you rate your driving skills? Your honesty, social sensitivity, and leadership skills? Are you about average, below average, or above average on these personal qualities? It turns out that most people think of themselves as above average on a wide range of desirable characteristics like these (Larwood & Whittaker, 1977; Svenson, 1981; Weinstein, 1987), and perhaps you do too. But stop to think about it. When nearly one million high school students were surveyed in one study, 89% said they were above average in ability to get along with others—and they can't all be right. The same goes for the 70% who rated themselves above average on leadership, and the 60% who said the same thing about their athletic skills (College Board, 1976–77). This self-enhancing tendency has been termed the "Lake Wobegon effect," after the humorist Garrison Keillor's mythical town where "all the children are above average." How do people arrive at these inflated views of themselves, and then defend them in the face of inevitable negative evidence? How does our tendency to see ourselves in a highly positive light co-exist with our needs to perceive ourselves accurately?

Questions like these are important because what you think of yourself, how you feel about yourself, and the ways you choose to express yourself influence virtually all aspects of your life, including mental well-being as well as physical health. In this chapter we examine the processes that help us not only to learn accurately what we are like but also to protect and enhance that image we label "self."

What is this "self" anyway? Since ancient times philosophers have admonished: "Know thyself," for the self is *an object of knowledge.* You may be confident that you are shy or honest or intelligent or attractive. You may feel that, all things considered, you are a pretty decent human being. But how did you come to know these things about yourself? The first part of this chapter looks at the way we form our impressions of the self, how we come to know what we are like, and how we feel about ourselves. As you will see, the way we form impressions of the self is very similar to the way we perceive other people. However, we bring more biases to the process of self-perception. For most of us, although the self-portraits we paint are accurate in a general way, they are also colored by powerful motivational pressures to think well of ourselves.

Why do we need to know who we are? The reason is that self-knowledge is crucial in *directing and regulating our thoughts, feelings, and behaviors.* Self-knowledge lets us seek out situations that match our capabilities: Knowing ourselves to be good at tennis, we welcome the opportunity to compete on the court. Similarly, goals that are important in defining who we are direct our emotional responses to events. For example, valued accomplishments arouse pride and joy, while events that threaten or thwart us evoke the prick of fear or the sting of anger. And when we choose to coach Little League on the weekends or volunteer to lead tours through the art museum, our sense of self guides our behavior as we try to show others the kind of person we are. In the second section of the chapter we see the self in action, regulating and directing our interpretations and interactions with the social world.

In the final section of this chapter we consider what happens when our sense of self is challenged—when what happens is not what we planned, hoped for, or expected. Will juggling a career and parenthood, fighting rush-hour traffic, or struggling to make ends meet be too much for you? How do people cope with sudden illness, the loss of a job, a house once full of children becoming an "empty nest"? The last part of the chapter examines our attempts to cope with stresses, failures, and inconsistencies. As you will see, the way we defend ourselves against threats and disappointments influences not only our emotional well-being but also our physical health.

Constructing the Self-Concept: What We Know About Ourselves

Self-knowledge has two components: the self-concept, what we know about ourselves, and self-esteem, how we feel about ourselves. Although these parts of our self seem as familiar and comfortable as a favorite pair of jeans, both in fact are constantly developing and changing as our experiences, life circumstances, and social surroundings change. In fact, just as our impressions of other people are constructions based on a few available cues and our own general knowledge, self-knowledge is also actively constructed rather than simply or directly "known." Indeed, if complete self-understanding were easily attained, philosophers would not have to advise us to seek the self, therapists would not spend hours helping people get in touch with themselves, and bookstore self-help shelves would not be nearly so well stocked.

Sources of the Self-Concept

People construct the self-concept in much the same way that they form impressions of others, using similar types of information and similar interpretive processes. People often infer their own characteristics from their observed behaviors. They also use thoughts and feelings and other people's reactions to form opinions about themselves. Finally, people compare themselves to others to learn what characteristics make them unique.

The **self-concept** is the set of all an individual's beliefs about his or her personal qualities. We piece together our self-concept over time from our interpretations of many different kinds of information.

DRAWING INFERENCES FROM OUR BEHAVIOR. "How do I know what I think until I see what I say?" asked British author E. M. Forster. His tongue-in-cheek

Self-concept. All of an individual's knowledge about his or her personal qualities.

comment captures the key idea of Daryl Bem's (1967) **self-perception theory**: We can learn things about ourselves by observing our own behavior. When we contemplate our church attendance and conclude we are religious, or star in a community theater production and decide we are extroverted, self-perception processes are at work (Rhodewalt & Agustsdottir, 1986; Salancik & Conway, 1975). According to the theory, our overt behaviors are most important as a source of self-knowledge when we lack strong inner feelings that might tell us, for example, that we feel nearly sick with stage-fright every minute we are before an audience.

In addition, people are most likely to draw inferences about themselves from behaviors that they see themselves as having freely chosen. These behaviors are driven by *intrinsic motivation*: We are doing what we want to do rather than what we have to do. In contrast, when a behavior is performed as a means to some external end, it is governed by *extrinsic motivation*. Not only does such a behavior reveal less about our inner qualities, but we often lose pleasure in performing it (Deci, 1971; Harackiewicz, 1979).

■ **Practice for the mind as well as the body**. World-famous tenor Luciano Pavarotti during a break from one of his equally famous rehearsals, pictured here with Tracy Chapman. During rehearsal he prepares body and mind for demanding performances, not only singing those golden high notes but also visualizing an actual stage performance. Research has shown that visualizing in this way is an effective technique.

Ironically, providing external rewards often undermines intrinsic motivation, as Mark Lepper and his colleagues (Lepper, Greene, & Nisbett, 1973) have demonstrated. They introduced preschool children to an attractive new activity: drawing with colorful felt-tip markers. After drawing for a while, some children received a previously promised "Good Player" certificate, others unexpectedly received the same certificate, and still others received nothing. One to two weeks later, the markers were placed in the children's regular classroom. The amount of free time each child spent playing with the markers was recorded as a measure of their intrinsic motivation. The children who had not been rewarded and those who had received the unexpected reward retained their motivation, drawing for about 16% of the time. In contrast, children who expected and received an award used the markers for an average of only 8.6% of their free time.

The researchers explained their drop in motivation in terms of self-perception. Children who saw themselves drawing pictures when a reward had been promised must have concluded that they drew for the reward, not just for the pleasure of creating the picture. In contrast, drawing with no anticipation of reward allowed other youngsters to infer that the activity must be interesting and enjoyable. External rewards can undermine intrinsic motivation, particularly when they are perceived as bribes that externally control behavior, rather than as bonuses that demonstrate competence and mastery (Deci, 1975).

We do not actually have to carry out behaviors to engage in self-perception processes: Even imagined behaviors can do the trick. Take a moment to picture yourself doing various things to help preserve the environment, perhaps recycling aluminum cans or carpooling twice weekly. Do you now see yourself as a more environmentally aware person? Research suggests that imagining these behaviors might lead you to such a conclusion (C. A. Anderson & Godfrey, 1987). Of course, if you had been asked to imagine yourself taking 30-minute showers or keeping the thermostat at 80 degrees in winter, you might have come to the opposite conclusion about yourself.

Self-perception theory. The theory that people make inferences about their personal characteristics on the basis of their overt behaviors when internal cues are weak or ambiguous.

What explains these findings? Thinking about actual or imagined behavior increases the accessibility of related personal characteristics. Thus, you might imagine solving a puzzle and then reflect on your good spatial memory, recalling that you loved to play with puzzles as a child. As thoughts like these come to mind, they become the basis for a self-inference: "I am very good at solving puzzles." Seeing the self as possessing relevant traits may improve not only your confidence, persistence, and effort, but also your actual performance on the task (Campbell & Fairey, 1985). Athletes and sports psychologists have put such findings to work in training routines that incorporate imagery. For example, in one study, runners were divided into two groups. One group was given strength training on an exercise bicycle; the other was not. Some members of each group were also instructed to imagine themselves sprint-racing (Van Gyn, Wenger, & Gaul, 1990). Of course, sweating on the exercise cycles improved all the runners' performances, but those who also imagined themselves sprinting later obtained better race times than those who did not.

DRAWING INFERENCES FROM THOUGHTS AND FEELINGS. No one knows you as well as you know yourself, right? Perhaps this is because our most significant clues to self-knowledge are our private reactions to the world: our thoughts and feelings. Recall that self-perception theory states that people draw inferences from their own behaviors mostly when internal cues, such as thoughts and feelings, are weak. These cues can tell us more about ourselves than our overt behavior does, precisely because thoughts and feelings are less influenced by external pressures (Andersen & Ross, 1984). Attending your best friend's wedding may prompt you to act like the life and soul of the party, but your inner feelings of envy and loss tell you more about yourself. One study underlines the importance of thoughts and feelings for self-knowledge (Andersen, 1984). Some observers in the study heard participants talk about their thoughts and feelings in various everyday situations, while others heard participants describe only their behaviors in those situations. The observers then wrote down their impressions. Observers who listened to descriptions of thoughts and feelings formed impressions that matched the participants' own self-concept more accurately than the impressions recorded by observers who heard only about behaviors. This finding suggests that our thoughts and feelings can play a bigger role than behaviors in our inferences about what we are like.

EFFECTS OF OTHER PEOPLE'S REACTIONS. Other people's views of us also contribute to the development of the self-concept. In 1902, the sociologist Charles H. Cooley coined the phrase the "looking-glass self" to indicate that one source of our self-knowledge is other people's reactions to us. These reactions serve as a kind of mirror, reflecting our image so that we, too, can see it (Felson, 1989). Parents coo over us. Peers belittle us. Relatives note with pleasure that we remind them of devout Aunt Agatha. Reactions like these tell us we are cute, clumsy, or religious.

One study supported the concept of the looking-glass self when it compared the behaviors of three groups of schoolchildren. Teachers and others repeatedly told some of the children that they *were* tidy. Children in another group were repeatedly instructed that they *should be* tidy, and the third group was not told anything special. The researchers then observed how much litter each group spread around. The tidiest youngsters were those in the first group. Labeled as tidy, they behaved accordingly, reflecting their new self-concept (R. L. Miller, Brickman, & Bolen, 1975).

Like the self-fulfilling prophecy (discussed in Chapter 3), the looking-glass self involves an observer's reactions that influence someone else's behavior and self-concept (D. T. Miller & Turnbull, 1986). Chapter 3 noted that self-fulfilling prophecies mainly affect people who are uncertain of their actual self-concept, and the same is true with the looking-glass self. Thus, others' reactions have the largest effects on young children (as in the study just described) or others who lack firm self-concepts. For most adults, in contrast, self-views rely more on other types of evidence, such as comparisons with other people, and are only weakly related to the opinions of other people (Malloy & Albright, 1990; Shrauger & Schoeneman, 1979). Perhaps part of the reason for the weakness of these effects is that we are often unaware of what other people actually think about us (Kenny & DePaulo, 1993).

A real standout. People tend to describe themselves in terms of the characteristics that make them different from those around them. Thus, the little boy is probably quite conscious of his blonde hair, which distinguishes him from all of the members of his dark-haired family.

SOCIAL COMPARISON. If you, as a moderately skilled chess player, want to know how good you really are, your best approach is not to listen to what other people tell you about your playing skills, but to play a lot of games and see how many you win. This approach makes sense, because according to **social comparison theory**, the self-concept is often shaped by comparisons between ourselves and others. This theory was initially proposed by Leon Festinger (1954), who assumed that people want to evaluate themselves accurately and that they therefore seek out *similar* others for comparison. Thus, you will learn more by comparing your game with that of opponents with similar skills than by judging yourself against either Garry Kasparov or a rank beginner. In fact, multiple motives lead people to compare themselves to others (Suls, Martin, & Wheeler, 2002). These motives include not only the desire for accurate self-evaluations but also desires for empathy and connectedness, for inspiration from others' outstanding performances (Lockwood & Kunda, 1997), or for positive feelings about themselves from making comparisons to others who are worse off (Helgeson & Mickelson, 1995). These motives in turn will influence who we choose for comparisons.

By revealing what physical or social attributes distinguish us from familiar or similar others, social comparisons are important in allowing us to construct a sense of our own uniqueness. The attributes that distinguish us from most others often become defining features of the self. A left-hander is more likely to think of handedness, a personally distinguishing attribute, than is a right-handed person. Children writing self-descriptions are likely to mention characteristics, such as wearing glasses or being short, that mark them as unusual in their family or classroom (W. J. McGuire & McGuire, 1981; W. J. McGuire & Padawer-Singer, 1978). By summarizing the ways in which we differ from others, social comparison permits us to construct a self-concept that gives each of us a strong sense of being unique and distinctive.

Figure 4.1 shows the many sources of the self-concept. Note that social influences are pervasive even as we are constructing the self and learning what makes us unique.

Chapter 6 will deal with the aspects of self-knowledge, such as our membership in social groups, that we share in common with other people.

Social comparison theory. The theory that people learn about and evaluate their personal qualities by comparing themselves to others.

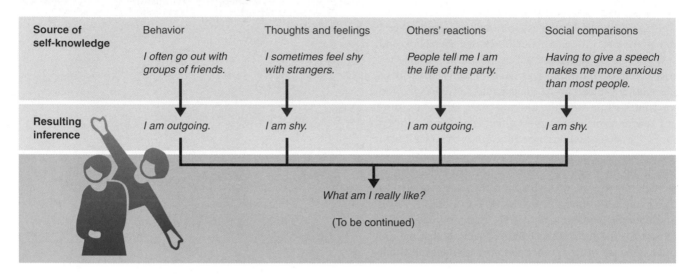

FIGURE 4.1   Sources of self-knowledge

■ Because no one is totally consistent all the time, multiple sources of information about ourselves may lead to potentially conflicting inferences, which will eventually have to be integrated.

Learning About Self and Others: The Same or Different?

Despite the general similarity between the ways people learn about themselves and about others, self-knowledge is richer and more detailed than knowledge about others. People can observe themselves in more situations and have better access to private thoughts and feelings. People also tend to explain their own and other people's behaviors differently, attributing their own actions to properties of the situation or the stimulus, while generally explaining others' actions by their personal characteristics. However, even people's explanations for their own behaviors may be inaccurate.

Most of the time, the cues we use to learn about ourselves are the same sorts of cues we use to learn about others. For instance, we draw inferences from our own behaviors, and we monitor other people's reactions to us. Our reliance on similar sorts of cues creates important similarities between our knowledge about the self and about others, but there are differences as well, particularly in the amount of knowledge we have and in the inferences we draw from it.

DIFFERENCES IN AMOUNT OF KNOWLEDGE. We usually have a greater quantity and variety of information about ourselves than we have about others. For example, we see ourselves in a wider range of situations and for more time than we observe anyone else. This fact probably explains why we view ourselves as quite variable and flexible, whereas we view other people as more set in their ways (T. L. Baxter & Goldberg, 1987). Asked to state whether they are serious or carefree, for example, most people will describe themselves and those they know well by saying, "In-between," or "It depends." But they freely characterize those they know less well as closer to the extremes (Prentice,

1990; Sande, Goethals, & Radloff, 1988). Interestingly, people seem to realize that observers are likely to see them as less variable and more consistent than the way they see themselves (Krueger, Ham, & Linford, 1996).

DIFFERENCES IN ATTRIBUTION. Because we have greater access to our own reactions, we are more aware of the impact people, places, and events have on us than of the impact they have on others. As a result, we may draw different inferences about the causes of behaviors. Recall for a moment the last time you became really angry and yelled at someone. Why did you act the way you did? Try to answer the same question about the last person who became irate at you. Why did he or she do that?

If you are like most people, you answered these similar questions in very different ways. In explaining your own aggressive actions, you probably pointed to external factors, perhaps saying that the person you became angry with had been really annoying and provocative. Answering the same question about someone else, you probably cited that person's personal characteristics: He or she is just an aggressive type who boils over easily. Why the difference? People tend to attribute their own choices to situational factors but to make *correspondent inferences*—assumptions that behavior reflects personality characteristics—for others. Such **actor–observer differences in attributions** for behavior have been found repeatedly (Gioia & Sims, 1985; E. E. Jones & Nisbett, 1972). You can find a small sample of these differences by reading a few letters to the personal-advice column in your local newspaper. Watch how people seeking advice tend to explain their own actions by citing external reasons, and to explain others' behaviors by describing those people's personal characteristics (Schoeneman & Rubanowitz, 1985).

■ **Actor–observer differences in attribution.** Golden State Warriors Mike Dunleavy collides with Washington Wizards Michael Ruffin who was called for an offensive foul. Washington Wizards' fans might have seen this as caused by the rough-and-tumble of intense competition but other observers, especially those supporting the Warriors, might attribute such an incident to the aggressive nature of the Wizards player.

Why do these actor–observer differences in attribution occur? There are several reasons.

1. *Whatever grabs our attention stands out.* When we witness another person's behavior, that person is salient: He or she is the focus of attention and stands out against the background (Heider, 1958; Storms, 1973). In contrast, when we act, we literally look out at the world, so the stimulus or trigger for our action is the salient factor. You see the snake in the grass as causing your sudden jump, whereas a passerby focuses mainly on your startle response and may conclude that you are an easily frightened person.

2. *Different sets of causal alternatives are considered for the self and for others.* When asked why something occurred, people consider alternative causes, but they consider different alternatives for the self and for others (Kahneman & Miller, 1986; McGill, 1989). For example, if someone asks you why you liked the latest John Grisham thriller, you will probably assume that the questioner means why you liked it *as compared to other books.* Obviously, then, it would be reasonable to cite the aspects of

> **Actor–observer differences in attribution.** The tendency to attribute our own behaviors to situational causes while seeing others' acts as due to their inner characteristics.

the novel that distinguish it from others. But if someone asks why a friend of yours liked the same book, you might assume that the questioner seeks to learn why this friend *among all other people* liked the book, and so you might cite some of your friend's unique personal characteristics (McGill, 1989). The difference in assumed comparisons for self and others produces very different answers (Wells & Gavanski, 1989).

3. *Actors usually explain their behaviors by their own beliefs and goals, while observers more often cite more remote causes of those beliefs or goals (Malle, 1999).* Thus, you might say you tried out for the track team because you wanted an activity that would help you stay fit (your goal) and believed you would be able to make the team. In contrast, a friend might explain your behavior by noting that one of your close relatives was overweight and died of heart disease: a potential cause that presumably contributed to your goal of keeping fit.

SIMILARITIES IN ACCURACY. Although we know more about ourselves than about others, that knowledge is not always sufficient to let us make more accurate judgments about ourselves than about others. In fact, being the leading authority on the topic does not guarantee that we are always aware of why we think, feel, and act the way we do (Nisbett & Wilson, 1977). Consider the efforts of 50 students who for 5 weeks kept diaries of their positive and negative moods and tried to identify the sources of those moods. They recorded many potential causes, such as whether the weather was sunny or wet and whether it was a Monday or a weekend day. Another group of students was simply asked to describe how these factors *generally* affect people's moods. Despite their efforts at self-analysis, the diary keepers' reports about the causes of their own moods were no more accurate than the blind guesses of people who did not know them (Wilson, Laser, & Stone, 1982). Apparently, all the participants relied on general causal theories, like the idea that rainy days and Mondays cause blue moods, even if they were explaining their own moods. Self-knowledge does not guarantee insight into our own unique actions and reactions: We use our general knowledge about human behavior to interpret ourselves as well as others.

Multiple Selves

> Because people see themselves in a wide range of situations and roles, self-knowledge is organized around multiple roles, activities, and relationships. People vary in the number and diversity of "selves" that they believe they possess.

As information about the self accumulates from all these different sources, we become aware that we have many different "selves." We begin to see that some of our behaviors, thoughts, and feelings depend on what we are doing and who our companions are (Markus & Wurf, 1987). For instance, most of us probably act and feel differently when we are working with our office mates—perhaps more responsibly and less playfully—than we do when we are with family and close friends. Social comparisons also vary from situation to situation. Someone who is one of the least polite people at work may be the most polite family member at home. Others' reactions also differ. Older relatives may view a 40-year-old physician as a youngster, but his co-workers may see him as a mature leader in the field of transplant surgery.

How do we deal with all this varying and potentially confusing information? We organize it according to our various roles, activities, and relationships

(Carver & Scheier, 1981; James, 1890; T. B. Rogers, 1981; Stryker, 1980). Thus, a woman might consider herself studious in academic situations, hard-working at the office, and fun-loving when relaxing with a group of friends. Each of these different *self-aspects* summarizes what she believes she is like in a particular domain, role, or activity. Other self-aspects may reflect additional roles and activities such as sister, lover, chess player, or jogger (Hoelter, 1985). Distinct self-aspects in our mental representation of the self are the inner reflection of the fact that we actually do think, feel, and behave differently when we are in different social roles, groups, and relationships.

Putting It All Together: Constructing a Coherent Self-Concept

People try to fit the diverse elements of the self-concept together in a way that seems coherent and stable. Coherence can be attained by making accessible only limited aspects of the self at any given time, by selectively remembering past acts, by explaining away inconsistencies, and by focusing on a few central traits.

Self-knowledge does not come to us in final form, neatly wrapped with ribbon and bow. Instead, the label warns: "Some assembly required." When we construct a self-concept from disparate pieces of self-knowledge derived from our multiple roles and social interactions, the pieces may not fit together very well. You may be an eager participant in one class but unmotivated in another. You may be a vociferous team leader but reserved off the field. Like the pieces of a Lego set, a person's self-aspects must be assembled into a coherent whole if the individual is to have a sense of unity and constancy. People use a number of strategies to construct this coherent sense of self (Baumeister, 1998).

COHERENCE THROUGH LIMITED ACCESSIBILITY. Imagine for a moment a house in which every room is furnished in a different style: a country kitchen, a southwestern bedroom, a stately traditional living room. If you stood in a central hallway viewing all the rooms at once, the house would truly be a hodgepodge. But if you stepped into one room and closed the door, the decor would be coherent and the ambience comfortable. We often deal with inconsistencies among the various parts of our self-concept in the same way: We relax comfortably in one role because other inconsistent roles are out of sight and out of mind.

What opens and closes the doorways between our several selves? The accessibility of different parts of our self-knowledge is the key. In one study, researchers asked biased questions to induce students to reflect on either their past introverted or extraverted behaviors (Fazio, Effrein, & Falender, 1981). Increasing the accessibility of a biased subset of the self-concept in this way not only caused the students to rate themselves as more introverted or extraverted (depending on their experimental condition), but even made them behave accordingly. As this experiment demonstrates, most people have different and even inconsistent bits of self-knowledge potentially available, but it is the self-knowledge that is currently accessible that will govern thoughts and behavior. Thus, for example, at work you may see yourself as logical, persistent, and authoritative, ignoring other traits (such as fun-loving or carefree) that characterize your leisure-time self. Different self-aspects will be accessible in work versus play situations, so you will rarely be uncomfortably aware of potential inconsistencies.

COHERENCE THROUGH SELECTIVE MEMORY. As people think about their past, they reconstruct an autobiography that integrates their various self-aspects and characteristics (Bruner, 1986; Gergen & Gergen, 1988). For example, people whose behavior has changed from shy to outgoing may retrieve a biased set of autobiographical memories in which they were always outgoing (M. Ross & Conway, 1986). Reconstruction may shape the basic materials drawn from memory in a way that suits the person's current goals (Conway & Pleydell-Pearce, 2000), as inconvenient or inconsistent bits of information are simply forgotten (Greenwald, 1980). This strategy gives the person a sense of self that feels coherent over time, even if it fails to accurately record the facts of personal history. Michael Ross (1989) speculates that adults' frequent reminiscences (particularly to their misbehaving children) about their own praiseworthy, responsible childhood may be a product of reconstruction. As a responsible adult, it is easy to misremember one's child self as having been equally responsible and to forget incidents of childish carelessness.

COHERENCE THROUGH ATTRIBUTION. Would it surprise you to learn that your co-workers find you rather changeable—quiet and deferential one moment but bossy and domineering the next? If you are like most people, it probably would. You might reply that of course you are deferential when the boss is around, but when she is not, somebody has to get things organized. We explain our behaviors as reasonable responses to situations, so we are unlikely to see variations in our behavior as significant signs of instability. As pointed out earlier, most people attribute their own behavior to circumstances, not to stable, general personality traits (E. E. Jones & Nisbett, 1972). This tactic enables us to interpret our inconsistent behavior as a result of inconsistent circumstances, not of our inconsistent selves.

COHERENCE THROUGH SELECTING A FEW KEY TRAITS. People also construct a unified and enduring sense of self by noting a few core attributes that they believe characterize them uniquely among people and consistently across situations. These important and distinctive personal characteristics form the *self-schema* (Markus, 1977). Once a particular characteristic is incorporated into the self-schema, people notice and process information about it very efficiently. For example, people whose self-schema includes a trait like helpful can answer questions like "Are you helpful?" more quickly than other individuals (Markus, 1977). People tend to see evidence for these core traits even in their most mundane behaviors, thereby reinforcing their sense of a stable and unitary self (Cantor & Kihlstrom, 1987). Thus, you might see confirmation for your view of yourself as helpful even in a trivial interaction like giving directions to a stranger on campus. And, as we will see, people are quick to reject feedback that is inconsistent with their self-schema, thereby increasing their sense of consistency even further (Markus, 1977; Swann & Hill, 1982).

As we saw earlier, different sources often provide mixed information about the self. But Figure 4.2 illustrates the several ways that people can construct a self-concept that is coherent and meaningful.

Cultural Differences in the Self-Concept

Cultures influence the type of self-concept that people construct. Members of Western, independent cultures stress the self-schema, traits that generally describe them across situations, while those in interdependent cultures emphasize their roles and relationships with others.

FIGURE 4.2   Reconciling inconsistancies: Forming a coherant self-concept

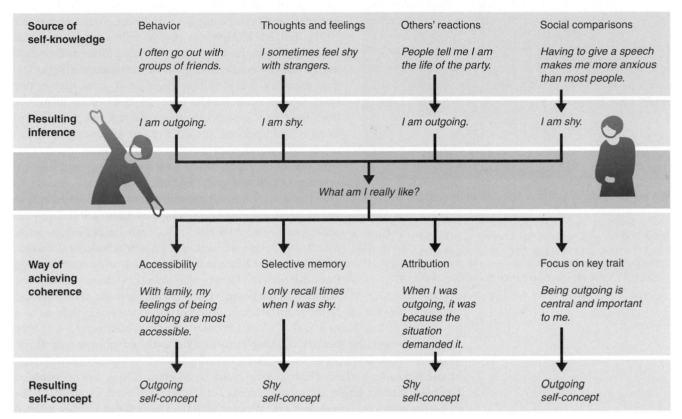

Source of self-knowledge	Behavior	Thoughts and feelings	Others' reactions	Social comparisons
	I often go out with groups of friends.	*I sometimes feel shy with strangers.*	*People tell me I am the life of the party.*	*Having to give a speech makes me more anxious than most people.*
Resulting inference	*I am outgoing.*	*I am shy.*	*I am outgoing.*	*I am shy.*

What am I really like?

Way of achieving coherence	Accessibility	Selective memory	Attribution	Focus on key trait
	With family, my feelings of being outgoing are most accessible.	*I only recall times when I was shy.*	*When I was outgoing, it was because the situation demanded it.*	*Being outgoing is central and important to me.*
Resulting self-concept	*Outgoing self-concept*	*Shy self-concept*	*Shy self-concept*	*Outgoing self-concept*

■ We have several ways to reconcile inconsistencies in the process of forming a stable and coherent self-concept. Different people select different strategies from among these alternatives.

Imagine two recalcitrant 4-year-olds, each steadfastly refusing to taste the carrots. "Just try them," coaxes one mother, "vegetables help you grow up big and strong. You want to be big and strong, don't you?" The other caregiver tries a different tactic: "Think of the farmer who grew the carrots so you could have them to eat. He will be so disappointed if you don't like them. Just a taste, to make the farmer happy!" Perhaps you recognize one or the other of these strategies. In fact, the first "you-oriented" approach is more often used by parents in cultures that emphasize individuality, whereas the second strategy reflects the "other-directed" concerns of community-oriented cultures. Do cultures with such different emphases also foster different conceptions of the self?

Although members of all cultures seek a coherent sense of the self, Hazel Markus and Shinobu Kitayama (1991; Markus, Kitayama, & VandenBos, 1996) suggest that different cultures offer diverse visions of what a self is like. In many of the countries of North America and Western Europe, people tend to see the self as independent, separate from other people, and revealed primarily in inner thoughts and feelings. North American students describing themselves tend to list general attributes that mark them as unique or distinctive individuals, such as "I am intelligent" or "I am musical"—the sort of characteristics that make up the self-schema.

In contrast, people in the *interdependent* cultures found in many parts of Asia, Africa, and South America tend to see the self as connected with others and revealed primarily in social roles and relationships, not in unique personal

■ **A match made by culture.** Many Western women may wonder at Masake Owado's choice of mate. The princess, shown here in an official wedding photo, gave up a brilliant diplomatic career and her legal existence as a person to marry Japan's Crown Prince Naruhito. From the point of view of Japanese culture with its valuing of connectedness to others and the greater good of the group, the choice may not have been so hard to understand.

characteristics. Chinese students are more likely than Westerners to define themselves in terms of relationships, roles, or attributes they share with others, such as "I am a daughter" or "I am Buddhist" (Trafimow, Triandis, & Goto, 1991). Indeed, a Japanese person will experience social connections and ties to others as the core of the self, even if those linkages conflict with his or her inner feelings. The importance of social surroundings is so great that in one study where Asian people were asked to recall memories from their own past, they often reported visualizing them from a "third person" perspective—as if looking at themselves from an observer's viewpoint. Americans, in contrast, typically report experiencing such memories from their own visual perspective (Cohen & Gunz, 2002).

Because relationships with others are so important in interdependent cultures, members of those cultures rely on self-aspects—their social roles and relationships with others—to define the self, not on self-schemata (Cousins, 1989; Markus & Kitayama, 1991). In one study demonstrating this difference, Cross and others (Cross, Kanagawa, Markus, & Kitayama, 1995) asked Japanese and American college students to describe themselves in different social contexts, such as in a professor's office, with a friend, or alone. American students were more likely than Japanese to describe themselves using general traits such as optimistic or warm. Moreover, their descriptions varied less across the different contexts than did those of the Japanese students (Kanagawa, Cross, & Markus, 2001). For example, a Japanese student might mention academic characteristics such as smart in the professor's office context, but not in other settings. As a result of this kind of variation of the self between different contexts, Asians may have self-concepts that incorporate more inconsistencies and even contradictions than Westerners do (Choi & Choi, 2002). Table 4.1 shows some of the contrasts between independent and interdependent cultural views of the self.

Across all cultures, though, there are similarities in self-knowledge. For one thing, Gardner and others (Gardner, Gabriel, & Lee, 1999) found that priming American students with an independent versus interdependent sense of self caused them to display the types of values and judgments characteristic of independent versus interdependent cultures. Thus, each of us has the capacity to think of ourselves in both of these ways, and our cultural surroundings or more transitory influences like priming can make one or the other more accessible.

Most important, in all cultures the primary function of the self-concept is the same. For people to survive and flourish, they must adapt successfully to their environment, particularly the social environment consisting of other people. The self-concept is a crucial aid in that adaptation. Knowing our unique configuration of personal talents and social ties allows us to choose goals that we can reasonably attain, avoid situations that make us miserable, and act in ways that play up our strong points while compensating for our shortcomings (Higgins, 1996b). The self-concept is most helpful in guiding our adaptation if it is accurate. If we held inflated ideas of our own capabilities, we might be tempted into situations that demanded more than we could produce, setting ourselves up for disappointment and failure. Accuracy is one important goal as we construct our self-knowledge, then, but as we will see, it is not the only goal.

TABLE 4.1. Some Differences Between Construction of the Self in Independent and Interdependent Cultures

Feature	Independent culture	Interdependent culture
Definition of the self	Unique individual, separate from social context	Connected with others in mesh of social roles and relationships
Structure of the self	Unitary and stable, constant across situations and relationships	Fluid and variable, changing from one situation or relationship to another
Important features	Internal, private self (abilities, thoughts, feelings, traits)	External, public self (statuses, roles, relationships)
Significant tasks	Being unique Expressing yourself Promoting your own goals Being direct (saying what's on your mind)	Belonging, fitting in Acting appropriately Promoting group goals Being indirect (reading others' minds)

Source: Adapted from "Culture and the self: Implications for cognition, emotion, and motivation," by H. Markus and S. Kitayama, *Psychological Review, 98,* p. 230. Copyright © 1991 by the American Psychological Association. Adapted with permission.

Constructing Self-Esteem: How We Feel About Ourselves

The self-concept is *what we think* about the self; **self-esteem**, the positive or negative evaluation of the self, is *how we feel* about it (E. E. Jones, 1990a). Self-esteem is reflected in people's agreement or disagreement with statements like: "I feel I'm a person of worth," or "On the whole, I am satisfied with myself" (M. Rosenberg, 1965). Why is self-esteem important? Our level of self-esteem plays a role in the crucial adaptive function of the self: It tells us from moment to moment and from year to year how we are doing in constructing a positively valued self that lets us function well, attaining concrete rewards and fostering connectedness with others.

Balancing Accurate Self-Knowledge and Self-Enhancement

Accurate self-knowledge regarding our capabilities and preferences is important for guiding us through our lives in ways that suit our needs and abilities. But accuracy is not the only consideration in evaluating the self: We are also greatly influenced by motivational pressures to think well of the self. These motivations color and bias many of our thoughts and feelings.

Self-esteem summarizes how we are doing at using our self-knowledge to navigate the social world and achieve our goals. To see how this works, consider that to successfully regulate anything, such as your financial life, it is important to keep track of your current standing, for example with a bank statement showing your balance at the end of each month. Like a bank statement that shows how well you are

Self-esteem. An individual's positive or negative evaluation of himself or herself.

managing your income and expenses, self-esteem is a signal of how well you are doing in successfully adapting to your own social world (Leary, Tambor, Terdal, & Downs, 1995). It tracks the net result of your successes and failures, achievements and difficulties, as well as your acclaim or rejection by important other people (Baldwin & Sinclair, 1996). But to serve its proper role in monitoring the self-regulation process, self-esteem should be a relatively accurate reflection of how you are doing. What use would be an inaccurate bank statement that showed you with thousands of dollars more than you really have? It would only encourage you to overspend and leave you with an empty account and a pile of bounced checks.

Yet here is a puzzle. Despite the clear value of accurate knowledge about how we are doing, people generally tend to inflate their own abilities and accomplishments, seeking to elevate their self-esteem. For example, consider the "Lake Wobegon" effect that we discussed at the beginning of this chapter. Pick a few traits—honesty, social sensitivity, and leadership, for example—and ask some people to rate themselves on each. You will probably find few people who rate themselves below average on any one (let alone on all) of these qualities (Larwood & Whittaker, 1977; Svenson, 1981; Weinstein, 1987). Of course, the vaguer the criteria for a characteristic, the easier it is for people to see themselves as above average. Thus, people are more likely to believe they are better than average in sensitivity, discipline, or sophistication than in punctuality, a trait easily measured against the clock (Dunning, Meyerowitz, & Holzberg, 1989). For the same reason, people are more likely to estimate that they are above average on dimensions of morality than on dimensions of intellectual performance (Allison, Messick, & Goethals, 1989).

People's high views of themselves even extend to things they own or are attached to in some way (Beggan, 1992). In fact, if you're like most people, you probably even prefer letters that occur in your name to other letters (Nuttin, 1987). This preference is related to other measures of self-esteem, suggesting that it is due to an automatic, nonconscious tendency to favorably evaluate ourselves and things linked with ourselves (Koole, Dijksterhuis, & van Knippenberg, 2001). Does our tendency to prefer letters in our own names have any implications beyond serving as evidence for an evaluative bias favoring the self? A remarkable series of studies by Brett Pelham and his colleagues (Pelham, Carvallo, & Jones, 2005) demonstrate that the bias may even shape some of the most important life decisions that people make. As people decide where to live, if they are affected by their preferences for letters in their own names, they would tend to end up living in cities or states whose names resemble their own. Consistent with this hypothesis, Pelham and colleagues find, women named Florence, Georgia, Louise, and Virginia are more likely to live in Florida, Georgia, Louisiana, and Virginia (respectively) than they would be by chance alone! The same principle applies when people choose occupations: if you are named Dennis, you might feel an unaccountable attraction toward the idea of becoming a dentist, a hypothesis also confirmed by the researchers. Dennis might even feel an extra dose of romantic attraction toward a woman named Denise—and indeed, state records show that people do indeed marry others who happen to share their first or last initial, at a rate higher than one would expect by chance.

These and other findings reflect our desire to view ourselves in a positive light. Thus, as we will see in the next few sections, our level of self-esteem often reflects compromises between accurate self-evaluation and unrealistic self-enhancement. Many types of events and experiences affect self-esteem, as we tally our successes and failures and compare ourselves to others. Though these types of information

Calvin and Hobbes by Bill Watterson

could allow us to form reasonably accurate assessments of how we stand, at the same time **self-enhancing biases** sneak into the processes of gathering and interpreting information (Kunda, 1990).

Evaluating Personal Experiences: Some Pain but Mainly Gain

Events that affect us positively or negatively influence our self-esteem, but we try in several ways to accumulate more positive than negative experiences.

Remember how happy you felt the first time you beat your regular opponent at tennis? And how your image of yourself plunged on the day you broke up with your first love? Experiences like these can raise or lower self-esteem at a moment's notice. However, self-enhancing biases can color the impact of our experiences on self-esteem. Almost without thinking about it, most of us stack the deck so that life produces more gain and less pain.

One obvious way we do this is to choose situations in which we can shine. One of the authors of this text is a member of two choirs and regularly chooses to sing in public; the other takes care to avoid embarrassment by putting a great distance between herself, choirs, and even occasional invitations to Karaoke nights. Most of us tend to abandon relationships that make us miserable, hobbies that we are unskilled at, and careers that do not allow us to flourish. Instead, our life choices often move us into domains that let us be all that we can be.

BIASED MEMORIES: RECALLING SUCCESSES. We not only select areas of life in which we can succeed, but also tend to remember our successes more than our failures. For one thing, we inflate our own contributions to joint efforts or projects. In part, this effect may stem from the unbiased workings of memory. It is easy to remember one's own contributions to a joint project; the hours others worked are naturally less vivid. However, people inflate their own contributions to a lesser extent when a project ends in failure (M. Ross & Sicoly, 1979). If overestimating were due only to superior memory for one's own actions, then the overestimate should occur to an equal extent when a project fails. Since it does not, we can

> **Self-enhancing bias.** Any tendency to gather or interpret information concerning the self in a way that leads to overly positive evaluations.

infer that the tendency stems at least in part from a self-enhancing motive to overestimate one's positive contributions.

Even when we try to retrieve memories of our past performances in an unbiased fashion, we tend to end up with a sample that is slanted in our favor. Memories that come to mind most easily are those associated with the outcome being considered (Kunda, 1990). So if you are gauging your career success, your past achievements will come to mind more readily than your failed opportunities. As a result, you would conclude you have been pretty successful. Of course, if you had searched instead for career failures, you might have found some of those, too.

Thus, as we try to pull together relevant evidence, most information we bring to the surface will probably suggest how good we are. In one demonstration of this self-enhancing bias in memory, students were led to believe that either extroversion or introversion was a desirable characteristic (Sanitioso, Kunda, & Fong, 1990). When the students then recalled relevant past behaviors, they described more memories of the sort they believed to be desirable. Success and failure do not have to be very important to bias our recall. People who were led to believe that tooth-brushing has negative effects on health remembered brushing their teeth less frequently in the past than others who thought brushing was a healthy practice (M. Ross, McFarland, & Fletcher, 1981).

For reasons like these, although our assessment of each individual experience may be largely accurate, most of us amass more positive experiences than negative ones, both in reality and in memory. On the other hand, the impact of those experiences is not the same for everyone. Recall that as we described above, people organize their self-knowledge around multiple self-aspects. People who have many and diverse self-aspects are said to have a high level of *self-complexity* (Linville, 1985). Because a given event, such as a career success, tends to directly impact only one or a few self-aspects (such as an employee self), it should have a more dramatic positive effect overall on a person with low self-complexity. This is because the uplifting effect of the event on mood and well-being will not be diluted by many other, unaffected self-aspects. This hypothesis has been confirmed by a meta-analysis summarizing over 70 studies on the issue (Rafaeli-Mor & Steinberg, 2002). However, the meta-analysis found that self-complexity does not generally alter the effects of negative events or failures, which seem to have about the same negative impact on people regardless of their level of self-complexity.

Social Comparisons: Better or Worse Than Others?

We also evaluate ourselves by making comparisons with others. These comparisons also are sometimes self-enhancing.

Self-esteem, like the self-concept, depends on social comparisons. Consider, for example, the plight of a young man who recently enrolled in one of our universities with a basketball scholarship. He is an athlete of above-average talent who is expected, in time, to make real contributions to the team. The problem is that his older brother, who played at the same school 2 years earlier, was a major star and is now beginning a career as a professional. It seems inevitable that the young man will be compared to his older brother.

How might these comparisons influence the player's self-esteem if his performance is not equal to his brother's? Abraham Tesser's (1988) model of *self-evaluation maintenance* suggests two possible reactions. They both depend on the *closeness* of the other person, for example, the fact that the star player was a brother rather than a cousin, and the *importance* or centrality of the attribute in question for the person's self-concept. Suppose the young man was planning to compete in track and field instead of basketball. Then he would be likely to feel good because of the reflected glory of his brother's impressive accomplishments. But if playing basketball is an important and central part of the younger brother's self-concept, disappointment stemming from the comparison could overwhelm his pleasure in his brother's success. In fact, being outperformed by a sibling or close friend may be even more painful than being beaten by a stranger, because the likelihood of social comparison is greater. Sometimes we want to bask in a loved one's reflected glory; at other times the glare of his or her achievement is just too painfully illuminating.

As this example illustrates, we cannot always choose whom to compare ourselves with (J. V. Wood, 1989). Most of us have probably had the unfortunate experience of performing in public, for example, at a track meet, speech contest, or piano recital, immediately after the local superstar turned in a superb performance. This kind of inescapable comparison can induce feelings of envy and resentment and can lower self-esteem (Salovey & Rodin, 1984; Tesser & Collins, 1988). However, forced comparisons can have positive as well as negative consequences. Consider the top three competitors in an Olympic event, all of whom are awarded medals. The silver medalist naturally compares him- or herself to the winner, and probably doesn't feel good about coming in second. However, for the bronze medalist, the most natural comparison is to the fourth-place competitor, who gets no medal at all! Based on these ideas about social comparison, Victoria Medvec and her colleagues (Medvec, Madey, & Gilovich, 1995) coded videotapes of the 1992 Summer Olympic Games. Indeed, they found that the facial expressions of the bronze medal winners—who had performed less well in absolute terms—were happier than those of the silver medal winners.

Chapter 6, pages 195 to 197, will discuss in more detail the ways in which connections with other people can help us feel good or bad about ourselves.

BIASED COMPARISONS: DEFINITELY BETTER THAN OTHERS. Social comparisons sometimes help us gain an accurate picture of our skills and abilities, but we often attempt to avoid comparisons that make us look bad. One common tactic we employ is establishing distance between ourselves and those who are successful. We do this by either downplaying our similarities to them or backing off from our relationships with them (Tesser, 1988). Another form of protection involves *downward comparisons*, which involve comparing ourselves with others who are less fortunate or less successful. For example, Bram Buunk and his colleagues (Buunk, Oldersma, & de Dreu, 2001) found that when people were asked to list aspects of their relationships that were "better than most people's," eliciting favorable social comparisons, they felt more positive about their relationships, compared to other people who just listed good aspects of their relationships without making social comparisons. Similarly, an average grade on the calculus final looks better in the light of the failing grades some students received. A not-so-exciting home life sure beats the misery experienced by recently divorced friends. In fact, people who learn that they have some positive attribute tend to underestimate the number of others who share the same

"Of course you're going to be depressed if you keep comparing yourself with successful people."

characteristic—a bias that fosters a sense of superiority (Goethals, Messick, & Allison, 1991).

Even when the situation is objectively pretty grim, it can help to know that life could be worse. Interviews with breast-cancer patients, for example, found that they compared themselves with others who were worse off: people whose disease was not responding to treatments, or those who lacked social support or contracted the disease at a comparatively young age (S. E. Taylor & Lobel, 1989). Buoyed by such comparisons, most cancer patients think they are better off than their peers (S. E. Taylor, Falke, Shoptaw, & Lichtman, 1986).

Why Self-Enhance?

Despite the value of accurate self-knowledge, self-enhancement occurs for two primary reasons. Some actions that appear self-enhancing are aimed at actual self-improvement, reflecting successful self-regulation. And high self-esteem can be an important resource that protects us against stress and threats to the self.

We noted earlier that successful dealings with the social world demand self-knowledge that is accurate and self-esteem that is an unbiased indicator of how we are doing. But if that is true, why are we so prone to biases that create and maintain positively biased views of ourselves? The answer has two parts.

First, some of the ways people strive for high self-esteem really amount to efforts at self-improvement. For example, you might work hard to learn to play a musical instrument to ensure that your public performances will be successful, earning you applause and boosted self-esteem. To return to our earlier analogy of self-esteem as a statement giving your bank balance, people may try to increase their income or reduce their spending as a way to increase their balance. In fact, this is simply an example of successful self-regulation, with self-esteem (or the bank balance) telling us how well we are doing in attaining our valued goals.

Second, self-esteem has value above and beyond its usefulness as an indicator of our level of success in our commerce with the world. People prefer to feel good about themselves—to value "me and mine." For example, high self-esteem is associated with generally positive emotions and a lower likelihood of depression (J. D. Campbell, Chew, & Scratchley, 1991; Tennen & Affleck, 1993). And, as we will see later in this chapter, high self-esteem not only feels good but has real positive effects on our lives, acting as a kind of resource that can buffer us from some of the blows of fortune. For both of these reasons, people often process information about the self in ways that favor a positive view. In other words, despite the clear usefulness of knowing one's bank balance accurately, we suspect that if people guessed how much they had in the bank on any given day, more estimates would be high than low. Despite these positive points, we will see later in the chapter that high self-esteem is not an unmixed blessing.

Thus, as Figure 4.3 summarizes, self-esteem reflects a compromise between the stern mirror of accurate self-assessment and some self-enhancing biases that give our image a positive tilt and a rosy glow. We often avoid situations in which we do not perform well, refuse to compare ourselves with more successful others, and fail to notice that we are not all that we could or should be. Even if our inadequacies become obvious, however, we are not without resources. Later in the chapter you will see that failures, inconsistencies, and shortcomings set off some of the self's best defense mechanisms.

FIGURE 4.3   Events, self-evaluation, and self-enhancement

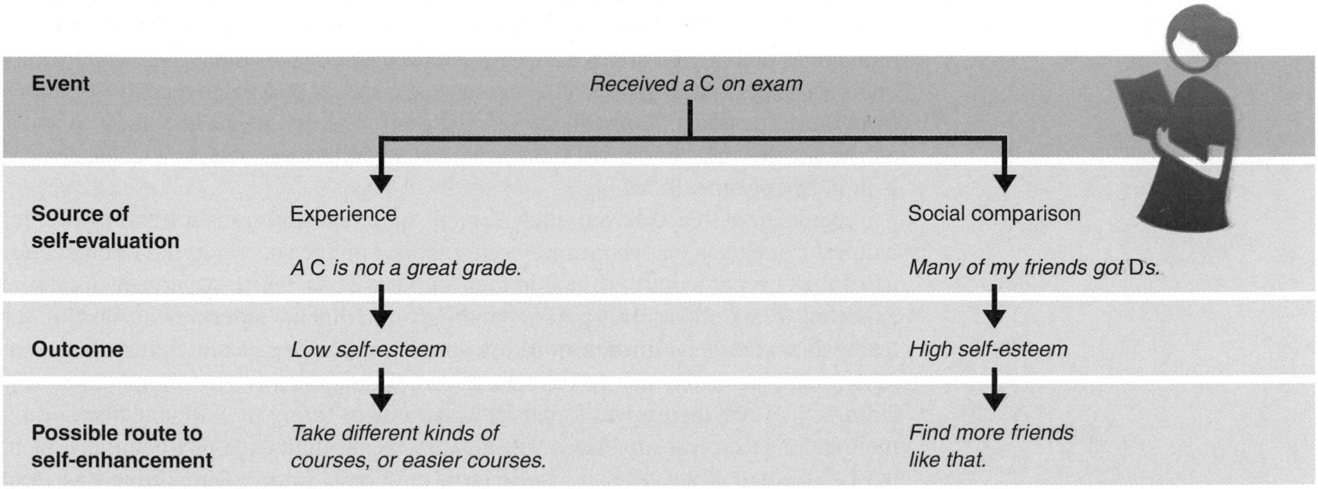

Event	Received a C on exam	
Source of self-evaluation	Experience	Social comparison
	A C is not a great grade.	Many of my friends got Ds.
Outcome	Low self-esteem	High self-esteem
Possible route to self-enhancement	Take different kinds of courses, or easier courses.	Find more friends like that.

Self-Esteem in Cultural Context

Like most other aspects of the self, self-enhancing biases operate somewhat differently in different cultures. Independent cultures emphasize positive individual characteristics as the source of self-esteem, while interdependent cultures stress connectedness to others. Despite these differences, self-esteem functions in all cultures to indicate how well we are meeting our most important motives for mastery and connectedness.

■ Many self-relevant events are neither intrinsically positive nor intrinsically negative. Instead, they must be interpreted and evaluated. The evaluation process may lead to increases or decreases in self-esteem, and it almost always leaves room for operation of self-enhancing biases.

Since so many aspects of the self differ between independent and interdependent cultures, you may be wondering whether biases related to self-esteem operate in the same way in all cultures. In fact, people from interdependent Asian cultures show intriguing differences from the patterns typically found in North America and Western Europe. Shinobu Kitayama and his colleagues (Kitayama, Markus, Matsumoto, & Norasakkunkit, 1997) observe that although self-enhancement is common among Americans, Japanese people and other Asians are less prone to this bias. For example, Japanese students (whether in Japan or studying in America) score lower on self-esteem questionnaires than American students do. Japanese people may even reverse the self-enhancing bias, showing a greater tendency to accept negative rather than positive information about the self (Kitayama, Takagi, & Matsumoto, 1995).

Does this mean that members of interdependent cultures are psychologically unhealthy? Kitayama and his colleagues (1997) argue otherwise. They propose that the sensitivity to negative information about the self that is found in interdependent cultures actually serves as a form of self-criticism, which is ultimately meant to improve one's actions and ability to fit in harmoniously with others. In North America and other independent cultures, the view of the self as autonomous and separate from others means that positive personal attributes are the fundamental source of personal worth. In this cultural setting, self-enhancement is natural. In contrast, in interdependent cultures, connectedness among individuals and groups is emphasized over personal autonomy. The value of the self is measured not by outstanding individual characteristics, but by adjustment to others' expectations and shared ideals. Thus in Japanese schools, it is common for classes to take time at the end of a day to reflect on the ways they have failed to meet class goals, either as individuals or as a group (Lewis, 1995). Such self-criticism is both a way of affirming one's acceptance of shared social standards and a way of seeking to remedy deviations from those standards. From this perspective, self-criticism is just as natural a way of enhancing the value of the self in interdependent cultures as overt self-enhancement is in independent cultures.

Another reason that self-enhancement may take different forms in different cultural contexts is that people may self-enhance on the specific types of characteristics that are particularly valued in their culture. Thus, North Americans might be expected to see themselves as outstandingly intelligent, independent, and fit for leadership—the very attributes that are valued in an independent culture (Kurman, 2001; Sedikides, Gaertner, & Toguchi, 2003). But members of more interdependent cultures may see themselves as particularly good at fitting in with others or suiting their actions to social situations. Self-enhancement might exist in all cultures, then, but be directed at whatever traits are most culturally valued. Supporting this idea, Japanese students show a preference for letters that are included in their own names—a relatively subtle and indirect measure of self-esteem—just as Americans do (Kitayama & Karasawa, 1997).

Despite such cultural variations, the function of self-esteem is the same for everyone. The ups and downs of self-esteem are not just meaningless fluctuations. Rather, self-esteem serves a crucial function as the self regulates our thoughts, feelings, and behavior: It signals how well we are doing in fulfilling our fundamental social motives for mastery of our environment and connectedness with others (Leary and others, 1995). People differ in their relative sensitivity to these two motives, with men's self-esteem more influenced by successes or failures involving mastery and women's self-esteem more affected by connectedness (Josephs, Markus, & Tafarodi, 1992). Cultural differences are important as well, as just described. For everyone, though, success and acceptance (that is, events that help us feel in control and connected to others) make us feel particularly good about ourselves, while failure, rejection, and loss can knock us to our knees. And, as you will see later, people with high and low self-esteem differ significantly in the ways they respond to and cope with all kinds of life experiences.

Effects of the Self: Processes of Self-Regulation

What is the fundamental purpose of having a self? The answer is that what we know about ourselves functions to regulate—to control and govern—many important aspects of our lives, including our thoughts, emotions and behavior.

The Self and Thoughts About Ourselves and Others

The self-concept, once formed, is relatively difficult to change. People avoid or actively reject information that is inconsistent with their established self-views. Self-knowledge also serves as a framework for perceiving other people and processing social information in general.

Once we have constructed a self-concept, the familiar principle of conservatism comes into operation, and we become much less open to new information about the self. A young child might begin to think of himself as tidy after noticing that he neatens up his room a few times, but once the self-concept is firmly established, people no longer have to make inferences from their behaviors to decide who they are (S. B. Klein & Loftus, 1993; Schell, Klein, & Babey, 1996). In fact, most of the time inconsistent behaviors have little impact on firmly established self-knowledge (Chaiken & Baldwin, 1981; Fazio and others, 1981). Other people's reactions also play less of a role after self-knowledge in a particular domain becomes entrenched (B. P. Allen, 1988). Feedback inconsistent with an established self-concept is avoided, distrusted, or resisted—even if it is flattering (Markus, 1977; Swann & Read, 1981). This function of the self is important in creating our sense of a stable personal identity, making us subjectively the same person when we awaken each morning. In fact, people with an unstable or fluctuating self-concept tend to have low self-esteem and high emotional reactivity to daily events (Campbell, 1990; Campbell & Lavallee, 1993), illustrating the value of having a secure and certain sense of self.

An established self-concept influences not only the way we think about ourselves but also the way we perceive and remember social information in general. For example, when we perceive other people we tend to notice and use information that is important in our own self-concept (Markus, Smith, & Moreland, 1985; Sedikides & Skowronski, 1993). So if you think of yourself as honest, you may be particularly likely to note other people's honest or dishonest behaviors, and to use that information in making judgments about them. The self-concept also affects memory. When we process information in relation to the self-concept, for example by making judgments about whether a series of traits describe the self or not, we remember those traits better than we do if we make other judgments, such as whether the traits are positive or negative (Symons & Johnson, 1997). The self-concept tells us what types of social information are particularly important to us, so it serves as an organizing framework for perceiving and remembering information about people in general.

The Self and Emotions: For Me or Against Me?

Emotions are sparked by interpretations of self-relevant events and their causes. Emotions signal the occurrence of significant events and motivate us to act in response, for example, to flee from danger. As they perform this self-regulation function, emotions involve the whole self, body and mind: They involve facial expressions, physiological responses, subjective feelings, and overt behaviors.

Emotions mark the most meaningful moments of our lives. Feelings like pride, anxiety, joy, fear, or anger signal that something important to the self is happening (Zajonc, 1998). Fear signals that a danger must be escaped; joy lets us know that a positive outcome should be celebrated. The intrusive quality of emotions forces us to pay attention to significant events, even as the positive or negative quality of the emotion indicates the nature of the event. Emotions also direct behavior toward a goal. For example, fear turns our efforts toward escaping from threat, and anger toward harming the target. Because of their intrusiveness, emotions often seem to "just happen" to us, but as we shall see, they actually depend on the perceiver's interpretation of both the self and the external world.

FIGURE 4.4   Appraisals dictate emotional reactions to events

Event	You are hungry; you open the refrigerator and find that it is empty.				
Situation	Your housemate was supposed to shop but did not.	Oops, you were supposed to shop but forgot to.	The food money has run out, and payday is next week.	Thank goodness, someone finished the cake. You would have eaten it.	Finally, all the food is eaten, so you can clean the refrigerator.
Appraisals	Negative event caused by other's controllable action	Negative event caused by own controllable action	Negative event caused by un-controllable action	Potential negative event failed to occur	Positive event has occurred
Emotion	Anger	Guilt	Sadness	Relief	Joy
Action tendency	Hurt other person (yell at roommate)	Want to disappear (quickly go to bed hungry)	Withdraw (do nothing)	Relax (forget about cake; read a book)	Feel excited (clean refrigerator)

■ Here are examples of different emotions and action tendencies arising from different appraisals of the same event—in this case, opening the refrigerator and finding that it is empty.

Appraisal. An individual's interpretation of a self-relevant event or situation that directs emotional responses and behavior.

HOW DO EMOTIONS ARISE? Emotions are complex and multifaceted and involve the entire self, body and mind. When you feel angry, your heart pounds and blood rushes to your face. You want to strike out at the target of your anger. You believe deeply that he or she injured you without cause. Thoughts, feelings, bodily reactions, and desires for action are tied together in patterns that characterize different emotions. Which of these many components is primary in *causing* the emotion? Psychologists have offered different answers to this question over the years. A century ago, William James (1884) argued that sensations from the skin and muscles were the chief causes of the experience of emotion. A generation ago, Stanley Schachter and Jerome Singer (1962) identified emotion as the product of physiological arousal plus a belief concerning its cause.

The prevailing view today is that emotions are caused by appraisals of a self-relevant object or event (Arnold, 1960; Frijda, 1986; Roseman, Spindel, & Jose, 1990; Tomaka, Blascovich, Kibler, & Ernst, 1997). An **appraisal** is an interpretation of an event, including both the causes of the event and how the event affects the self. Different appraisals of the same situation can produce different emotions, as is illustrated in Figure 4.4 for the everyday event of feeling hungry and finding the refrigerator empty. Two types of appraisals are particularly important in influencing emotions.

1. *Our appraisal of the event's positive or negative implications for the self.* Actions and events that we interpret as supportive of ourselves and our goals produce positive emotions such as joy, hope, and gratitude.

If you were trying to lose 10 pounds to fit into a new swimsuit but had just succumbed to the temptation of finishing off yesterday's chocolate cake, you might be relieved to find an empty refrigerator. But how would you feel if the shelves were empty because the food money had run out and your paycheck was not due for another 2 days? You probably would be both angry and frightened by this event. Actions and events that threaten, frustrate, or repel us evoke negative emotions like fear, anger, and disgust.

2. *Our appraisal of who or what caused or controlled the event.* Was someone to blame, or was the event beyond everyone's control? And did you bring about the event, or was someone else responsible? The emotions you feel and the actions you subsequently take will be quite different depending on your answer to those two questions. If the refrigerator is empty because you worked so many overtime hours that the stores closed before you could get to them, you will have one set of responses. But if your housemate failed to contribute his share of the grocery money and shopping chores, your feelings and actions will be quite different. Figure 4.4 shows how our appraisal of credit or blame affects emotions (Weiner, 1985).

Like all interpretations, appraisals are flexible, not cut and dried. As we saw in Chapter 3, many factors can influence how we appraise events, including the context, accessible thoughts, and transient moods. And, as always, other people's reactions play a large role in our appraisals. A toddler who trips over her feet may burst into either tears or giggles, depending on whether others gasp with concern or laugh. When other people seem to judge that a situation warrants calmness or dejection or goofy lightheartedness, we often follow suit (Schachter & Singer, 1962).

As these examples illustrate, we can be misled about the emotions we are feeling and about their causes. Our appraisals and the labels we apply to our own inner feelings are often based on salient cues: conspicuous features, people, or events that may or may not correspond to the true causes of our emotions (Reisenzein, 1983; Russell, 2003). In many cases, of course, the salient object that we identify as the cause of our emotion—the wasp buzzing around your head and threatening to sting, for example—is truly the cause of our fearful feelings. But in other cases the salient object may not be the real cause. You might believe you are angry with your child because of her annoying behavior, when the true cause of your anger is your run-in with your boss earlier in the day. An experiment by James Olson (1990) demonstrated this point by misleading participants about the cause of their anxiety. Everyone in the experiment expected to be exposed to "subliminal noise" as they were videotaped while delivering a speech. Some people were told the noise would arouse them physiologically, and others were told it would relax them. Although no noise was actually played, the participants' beliefs about it still influenced their emotions. Those who thought the noise would arouse them rated themselves as less anxious and made fewer speech errors than those who expected to be relaxed by the noise. Apparently those who expected arousal attributed their stage fright to the "noise," whereas those who expected relaxation had no such excuse.

Thus, like other aspects of self-knowledge, the emotions we experience and our beliefs about their causes actually reflect our interpretations. And, of course, culture can strongly affect the ways we interpret events and therefore the kinds of emotions we feel. Japanese people, for example, are more likely than Westerners to report feeling emotions like connectedness, indebtedness, and familiarity, which tie the self to important others (Markus & Kitayama, 1991; Mesquita, 2001). Despite such cultural differences, some researchers assume that at least a few "basic" emotions are common to all human cultures, although there is not full consensus on what these emotions are (Russell, 2003; Wierzbicka, 1994; Zajonc, 1998).

APPRAISALS, EMOTIONS, BODILY RESPONSES: ALL TOGETHER NOW. Our appraisals of events not only cause our emotions but also affect many aspects of our body and mind. People in many different cultures smile when they feel happy, frown when they feel sad, and wrinkle their brow when they feel angry (Ekman and others, 1987). Physiological systems come on line, revving us up or calming us down. We are motivated to act: to strike back in anger, escape in fear, or move closer in happiness. Some of these action tendencies, like attack and flight, appear to be universal and biologically determined. Other emotional behaviors are, of course, learned and differ from one culture to another (Frijda, Kuipers, & ter Schure, 1989; Markus & Kitayama, 1991).

Emotions also affect thinking, focusing us on the content of our appraisals. Thus, in the grip of extreme rage you may be totally focused on the thought of how your antagonist mistreated you and how he deserves to have his lights punched out (Keltner, Ellsworth, & Edwards, 1993; Tiedens & Linton, 2001). Strong emotions of any sort, positive or negative, can create intense arousal that limits people's ability to pay attention to other events (Easterbrook, 1959).

These components—appraisals, bodily responses, subjective feelings, and emotionally driven behavior—are frequently activated together. As a result, they become associated so that any one aspect can engage all the rest. If your heart is pounding, your face is contorted in a snarl, and your fists are tightly clenched, you are likely to feel anger, just as anger provokes those same responses. Because our inner feelings and outward expressions of emotion are linked, bodily signs of emotion often intensify emotional feelings (Adelmann & Zajonc, 1989; Ekman, 1992). Fritz Strack and his colleagues (Strack, Martin, & Stepper, 1988) ingeniously demonstrated this point by having participants write with a pen either clenched tightly between their teeth or held loosely between pursed lips. These maneuvers force expressions resembling a smile and a scowl, respectively, although participants were unaware of this fact. (Try it yourself.) The experimenters then asked both groups to assign ratings to a series of cartoons, telling how funny they were. The participants holding the pen between their teeth in a "smile" assigned higher ratings than did those holding the pen "scowlingly" between their lips.

If an emotional facial expression promotes emotional experience, it stands to reason that an inconsistent expression will reduce the intensity of the emotion. Have you ever been in a clutch situation and been terrified you might fail? Perhaps you were about to speak to a large audience. Did you take a couple of long deep breaths to calm yourself down or lock your face in a determined grin? If so, you were trying to take advantage of the way emotions often follow bodily expressions.

As Figure 4.5 shows, emotions tie together all aspects of body and soul, action and thought (De Rivera, 1977; Shaver, Schwartz, Kirson, & O'Connor, 1987).

The Self in Action: Regulating Behavior

Self-regulation involves comparing the self with internal standards. The outcomes of these comparisons can motivate us to behave in particular ways. Although our thoughts are turned outward most of the time, some events create heightened awareness of the self, including our internal standards and whether we measure up to them.

FIGURE 4.5   Components of emotions

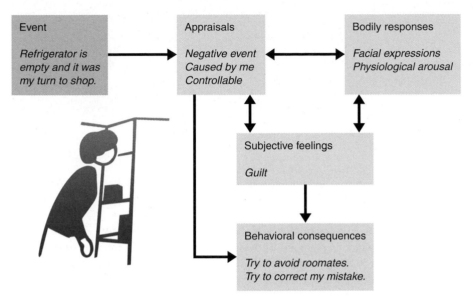

Event		Appraisals		Bodily responses
Refrigerator is empty and it was my turn to shop.	→	*Negative event Caused by me Controllable*	↔	*Facial expressions Physiological arousal*

Subjective feelings

Guilt

Behavioral consequences

*Try to avoid roomates.
Try to correct my mistake.*

■ When events are appraised as self-relevant, the resulting emotion has many components: cognitive appraisals, physiological responses, and subjective feelings. Each component can affect the others, and all may contribute to emotionally driven behaviors.

One of the most fundamental aspects of self-regulation involves the way self-knowledge motivates our behavior toward important goals or standards. This is because our self-knowledge includes not only conceptions of what we are currently like, but also significant personal standards toward which we strive. Tory Higgins (1987) calls these personal standards *self-guides*. Self-guides come in two flavors: the *ideal self* (the person we would like to be) and the *ought self* (the person we feel we should be; Higgins, 1987; Markus & Nurius, 1986). Ideal self-guides include the traits that help you match your aspirations; ought self-guides include those that help you meet your obligations. Self-guides are the part of the self-concept most closely and directly tied to the self-regulatory function (Higgins, 1996b).

According to Higgins's **self-discrepancy theory**, the difference between who we think we actually are and our self-guides influences our emotional well-being and ultimately our self-esteem (Strauman & Higgins, 1988). For example, a self-discrepancy could arise if you would ideally like to be slender and athletic, but think you actually are a corpulent couch potato. Ideal selves represent positive outcomes toward which people strive, termed *promotion goals* (Higgins, 1998b). Discrepancies from ideal selves produce feelings of disappointment, sadness, and dejection, but when people actually attain promotion goals, they feel joy or elation. The emotional consequences are different, however, if the discrepancy concerns an ought self, as Figure 4.6 shows. Ought selves generally involve negative outcomes that people try to avoid, or *prevention goals*: For example, you may feel that you ought to avoid divorce or being fired from a job. Discrepancies from an ought self, or failures to accomplish prevention goals, lead to emotions of anxiety and agitation. Accomplishing these goals produces feelings of relief and relaxation.

Notice that the very same goal, such as staying married, might represent an ideal for one person and an ought for another person. This is because it can be thought of as either a promotion goal ("maintaining a happy marriage") or a prevention goal ("avoiding marital conflict and divorce"). In terms of the emotional impact of failing to attain the goal, what matters is the way each individual thinks about it

Self-discrepancy theory. The theory that people evaluate themselves against internal "ideal" and "ought" standards, producing specific emotional consequences.

FIGURE 4.6   Summary of self-discrepancy theory

■ Discrepancies between the actual self and ideal or ought self-guides give rise to specific emotions. They also have long-term negative consequences that affect the body as well as the mind.

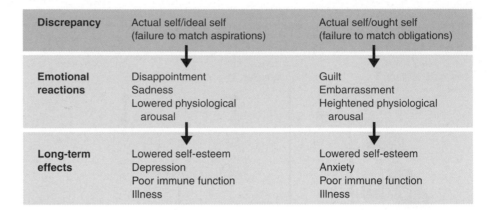

(Higgins, Shah, & Friedman, 1997). Not only do individuals within a culture differ in this way, but members of collectivist cultures tend to emphasize oughts and prevention goals, while members of individualist cultures generally focus more on ideals and promotion goals (Elliot, Chirkov, Kim, & Sheldon, 2001).

Behavioral strategies as well as emotional reactions depend on how people think about their goals. In one study, students were asked which of several strategies for friendship they would use. The choices included some strategies that involved seeking positive outcomes, such as being generous and supportive with friends, and some that involved avoiding negative outcomes, such as not losing contact with friends or not gossiping about them. Consistent with their general tendency to focus on promotion or prevention goals, those students who emphasized ideals chose more of the positive strategies, while those who emphasized oughts chose more of the negative ones (Higgins, Roney, Crowe, & Hymes, 1994).

NEGATIVE EFFECTS OF SELF-DISCREPANCIES. Self-discrepancies motivate us to meet our personal goals and standards, but at a price: awareness of the ways in which we fall short is painful! Self-discrepancies can in extreme cases trigger negative emotions that lead to a cycle of sadness and anxiety, lowered self-esteem, and even depression (Csikszentmihalyi & Figurski, 1982; Pyszczynski & Greenberg, 1987). Certain situations can exaggerate our awareness of discrepancies from our self-guides, and some people are generally highly aware of them.

1. *Self-focusing situations.* Do you know someone who hates being photographed or having his or her voice recorded? The reason may be that these situations focus our attention inward on ourselves. Thus, talking about ourselves, being scrutinized by an audience or a camera, even catching sight of ourselves in a mirror, can create **self-awareness**, directing our attention to our internal standards and heightening our awareness of whether we measure up to them. According to the theory of self-awareness, focusing attention on the self makes self-discrepancies obvious, which is why it is often unpleasant (Carver & Scheier, 1981; Duval & Wicklund, 1972). Research supports this proposition: People often report feeling relatively unhappy when thinking about themselves (Csikszentmihalyi & Figurski, 1982).

2. *Self-focusing individuals.* People differ in the tendency to devote attention to the self. Table 4.2 shows some examples of statements used to measure the

Self-awareness. A state of heightened awareness of the self, including the individual's internal standards and whether he or she measures up to them.

TABLE 4.2. Examples of Items Used to Measure Private Self-Consciousness

1. I'm always trying to figure myself out.
2. I reflect about myself a lot.
3. I never scrutinize myself.
4. I'm alert to changes in my mood.
5. I'm constantly examining my motives.

Note: A person who agrees with items like 1, 2, 4, and 5, and disagrees with item 3 and similar items is probably high in private self-consciousness. The actual scale contains many more than five items, so it can more accurately classify people as high or low in private self-consciousness.

Source: From "Public and private self-consciousness: Assessment and theory," by A. Fenigstein, M. F. Scheier, & A. H. Buss, *Journal of Consulting and Clinical Psychology, 43,* p. 524. Copyright © 1975 by the American Psychological Association. Reprinted with permission.

---

tendency to focus on one's own internal states and feelings. People like this are more likely to be aware of, and to try to cope with, any discrepancy between their actual self and their internalized standards (Carver & Scheier, 1981). Their increased awareness means that negative self-related information leads to stronger feelings of distress and sadness (Scheier & Carver, 1977).

Temptations and Other Threats to Self-Regulation

When situations offer us short-term benefits that detract from our longer-term goals, we can actively and effortfully choose strategies to overcome these temptations.

Every dieter knows what it is like to stroll past a batch of delicious doughnuts in a shop window; every student knows how it feels to be invited out for the evening by friends when a term paper is due the next day. Temptations like these are obvious threats to self-regulation, for they force us to choose between immediately appealing short-term benefits and the more abstract longer-term gains of sticking with our diets or our schoolwork. How do we deal with temptations? According to Yaacov Trope and Ayelet Fishbach (2000), several strategies can weaken the effects of temptations and allow us to better accomplish our long-term goals. We can self-administer penalties or rewards to encourage ourselves to stick with our goals. For example, a dieter may decide to buy himself a new CD every week he successfully resists off-limits snack foods. Or we can pay a non-refundable annual membership fee at the health club to encourage ourselves to stick with our exercise and fitness program. We can also try to think of the acts that contribute to our long-term goals in especially positive ways, linking them to our central values (such as being healthy and fit, or getting good grades and a good job on graduation). Note that this second strategy has the effect of turning those actions (dieting or studying) from things that we feel we *ought* to do into things we *want* to do. Trope and Fishbach (2000) as well as Berg and others (Berg, Janoff-Bulman, & Cotter, 2001) find that strategies like these do effectively help people resist short-term temptations and thereby meet their more enduring goals.

Even with strategies like these, self-regulation can be hard work. In fact, Roy Baumeister and his colleagues (Baumeister, Muraven, & Tice, 2000) liken self-regulation to exercising a muscle. At first the exercise may be easy, but with repetitions it becomes harder and harder. And after the muscle is fatigued, it may be difficult to use it for another purpose for some time until it recovers. Similarly, exerting self-control in one task (such as trying to suppress thoughts about a particular object, or having to wait in a room with a plate full of tempting cookies) weakens people's ability to exercise control in a completely different task, such as persisting in a difficult figure-drawing or anagram-solving task. The fact that self-regulation depletes some inner resource in this way may even account for the observation that people who are fatigued, under stress, or are low in regulatory resources for other reasons often turn to binge eating, alcohol consumption or other tempting behaviors that are damaging in the long run (Tice, Bratslavsky, & Baumeister, 2001).

Taking Account of Other People's Standards

Sometimes people act in ways that express their true inner selves. At other times, people are concerned with shaping others' opinions in order to gain power, influence, or approval. But even behaviors intended for others' consumption may end up influencing people's private views of themselves.

We follow not only our own self-standards, but also the desires and wants that other people have for us. Those standards can be brought to mind by specific people who represent them, as Mark Baldwin and his colleagues (Baldwin, Carrell, & Lopez, 1990) demonstrated. The researchers primed some research participants, who were Roman Catholic college students, by exposing them very briefly to a scowling photo of Pope John Paul II. As an experimental control, other participants saw a similarly grim-faced photo of social psychologist Robert Zajonc, whose unfamiliar face would not be associated with any particular standards for these students. When later asked to evaluate themselves, the practicing Catholics who had seen the photo of the Pope felt worse about themselves, whereas participants who saw Zajonc displayed no such effect.

But people do not always simply conform to others' standards for them. In fact, we shape our behaviors to try to affect other people in two very different ways. We can attempt to express and convey to others who we actually are, or we can select our behaviors to convey particular impressions that we believe others will value.

SELF-EXPRESSION: I AM WHAT I AM. When people engage in **self-expression**, they attempt to demonstrate their self-concept through their actions. Self-expression confirms and reinforces the individual's sense of self and also conveys it to other people. If you think of yourself as a committed supporter of animal welfare, you may see many of your behaviors—volunteering at the Humane Society or campaigning to stop unnecessary cosmetics testing—as expressions and affirmations of that self-concept. Research shows that, if given a choice, most people prefer to enter social situations that allow them to act in a way consistent with their self-concept (M. Snyder & Gangestad, 1982), and prefer relationship partners who agree with their own self-images (Swann, Hixon, & de la Ronde, 1992). Thus, an outgoing man may accept invitations to parties, and an organized woman may take a job that offers clearly structured tasks. As we will see later in this chapter, self-expression is so beneficial to us that it can even serve as a powerful coping strategy when we are under stress.

SELF-PRESENTATION: I AM WHAT YOU WANT ME TO BE. Sometimes we try to create a desirable impression, whether we believe the impression is accurate or not. Thus, another motive for choosing particular behaviors is **self-presentation**, trying to shape other people's impressions of us in order to gain power, influence, or

Self-expression. A motive for choosing behaviors that are intended to reflect and express the self-concept.

Self-presentation. A motive for choosing behaviors intended to create in observers a desired impression of the self.

approval (Jones & Pittman, 1982; Tedeschi, 1981). Most people care about conveying a positive impression to others. After all, attracting a desirable date or impressing a job interviewer can have a real impact on the course of our lives. Even in less crucial situations, we usually want to show the world a face it can like, admire, and respect. In fact, ingratiation, trying to convey the impression we are likable, and self-promotion, trying to convey an impression of competence, are two of the most common goals of social interaction (Arkin, 1981; Leary, 1995).

We all have had so much practice trying to win approval and respect that ingratiation and self-promotion should be easy. To be seen as likable, we go out of our way to help, to fit in with the other person's wishes, and to deliver charming compliments. To be seen as competent, we play up our strong points, mention our accomplishments, and display our knowledge. But self-presentation is fraught with potential pitfalls; taken too far, these qualities become blatant flattery or unseemly boasting. For advice on how to ingratiate yourself smoothly and subtly, look at Table 4.3. Illustrating the dangers of self-presentational efforts, in one study that took place in India, a hypothetical character who discussed a possible promotion with his boss in an ingratiating fashion was rated as both less likable and less competent than a character who did not try to ingratiate (Pandey & Singh, 1986). But notice that in this study the research participants were observing from the sidelines; they were not themselves the targets of ingratiation. In general, ingratiation has little effect on observers' liking for the ingratiator, but strong effects on the target (Gordon, 1996). It can be difficult to resist flattery aimed directly at you!

FROM SELF TO BEHAVIOR, AND BACK AGAIN. Self-presentation can amount to a sort of "trying a self on for size," perhaps acting in a way that is consistent with an ideal "wanna-be" self (Baumeister, 1982). Adolescents, for example, may experiment with such selves as "rebel," "intellectual," or "environmental activist." These experiments can have lasting effects because self-presenters often end up influencing themselves just as much as their audience. For example, when people

---

TABLE 4.3. The Self-Presenter's Handbook, Lesson 1: How to Make Others Like You Without Being Obvious

Don't let others notice that you are conforming to their opinions. (Or, if you are going to try to get in someone's good books, keep it credible.)
- Disagree on trivial issues, agree on important ones.
- Be wish-washy when you disagree, forceful when you agree.

Be modest (selectively).
- Make gentle fun of your standing on unimportant traits.
- Put yourself down in areas that don't make much difference.

Keep your need for others' approval under wraps.
- Don't conform or flatter someone in a situation where it is expected—for example, when talking to your boss just before annual raises are handed out.
- Use these tactics only when you really need to.
- Get others to do the self-presentation for you—for example, in letters of reference.

Bask in others' reflected glory if you can.
- Make casual references to connections with winners.
- Link yourself to losers only when it cannot be used against you.

Source: Adapted from *Interpersonal perception*, by E. E. Jones, 1990, San Francisco: Freeman, p. 184.

are instructed to present themselves as extraverted, they later give themselves higher ratings on that dimension (Gergen, 1965; Jones, Rhodewalt, Berglas, & Skelton, 1981; Schlenker, 1985). Interestingly, the presence of an audience is crucial in shaping effects of self-presentation. Schlenker and his colleagues (Schlenker, Dlugolecki, & Doherty, 1994) had participants prepare for an interaction in which they would present themselves in a certain way to other people, but then the interaction never took place. In contrast to participants who actually engaged in the self-presentation, these participants showed minimal change in their self-concepts. Just recalling past extraverted actions may be enough to alter the self-concept (C. A. Anderson & Godfrey, 1987), but making a self-presentation before an audience has stronger effects, illustrating the fundamentally interpersonal nature of the self. These studies show that even a single self-presentation has effects on the private self, but sorting out the portrayal from the self may be even more difficult as the performance becomes routine. We would do well to heed sociologist Erving Goffman's warning: Choose your self-presentations carefully, for what starts out as a mask may become your face (Goffman, 1959).

PERSONALITY DIFFERENCES IN BEHAVIOR: SELF-MONITORING. Although everyone engages in both self-expression and self-presentation, people show stable preferences for one or the other. This individual difference is called **self-monitoring** (M. Snyder, 1974). High self-monitors typically shape their behaviors to project the impression they think their current audience or situation demands. Low self-monitors behave in ways that express their internal attitudes and dispositions, and they therefore behave more consistently from audience to audience and situation to situation (Gangestad & Snyder, 2000). You might like to answer the questions in Table 4.4 to see whether you tend to be high or low in self-monitoring.

The importance of personality differences in self-monitoring was demonstrated by a study of people's reactions to success or failure at a rather peculiar task: portraying themselves as corrupt and immoral individuals (E. E. Jones, Brenner, & Knight, 1990). In a simulated job interview, each participant pretended to be an ambitious, selfish person who would be suitable for a "cutthroat position in a dog-eat-dog environment." Some participants learned that their act was convincing by overhearing comments like "He wouldn't mind selling his mother down the river." Others learned they had failed in their portrayals. High self-monitors felt better about themselves when they succeeded at the task, even though success meant

Self-monitoring. A personality characteristic defined as the degree to which people are sensitive to the demands of social situations and shape their behaviors accordingly.

TABLE 4.4. Examples of Items Used to Measure Self-Monitoring

1. I have considered being an entertainer.
2. In a group of people I am rarely the center of attention.
3. I have trouble changing my behavior to suit different people and different situations.
4. I guess I put on a show to impress or entertain people.
5. I may deceive people by being friendly when I really dislike them.

Note: People who agree with items 1, 4, and 5 and disagree with items 2 and 3 are probably high in self-monitoring. The actual scale contains many more than five items, so it can more accurately classify people as high or low in self-monitoring.

Source: From "The self-monitoring of expressive behavior," by M. Snyder, 1974, *Journal of Personality and Social Psychology, 30,* p. 531. Copyright © 1974 by the American Psychological Association. Reprinted with permission.

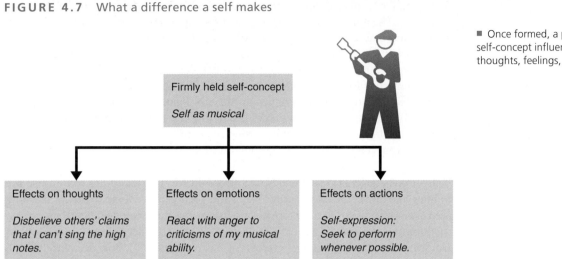

FIGURE 4.7   What a difference a self makes

Firmly held self-concept

Self as musical

■ Once formed, a person's self-concept influences his or her thoughts, feelings, and actions.

Effects on thoughts

Disbelieve others' claims that I can't sing the high notes.

Effects on emotions

React with anger to criticisms of my musical ability.

Effects on actions

Self-expression: Seek to perform whenever possible.

convincing others that they were corrupt. Apparently creating an "appropriate" impression was more important than being true to who they really were. In contrast, low self-monitors felt better about themselves after *failing* at this task. They prefer being seen as they truly are instead of successfully, even profitably, putting on a false face.

Once we have constructed a sense of self, we begin to use it to regulate many aspects of our lives. Our self-concept tends to resist change and to influence our thoughts, emotions, and behavior. Figure 4.7 summarizes some of the effects of the self.

Defending the Self: Coping With Stresses, Inconsistencies, and Failures

Our sense of self is our most valued possession, and we certainly treat it that way. We use it continually, as both a guide for action and an aid in interpreting others' reactions to us. We keep it polished and in good repair as we enhance our self-esteem and present our best face to others. And, as we shall see, we strive to defend our sense of self against all comers. When events set off our security alarms, we may respond in two different ways. We may attempt to deal with what set off the alarm, or we may try to change the way it makes us feel.

Threats to the Well-Being of the Self

When threatened by external events or negative feedback, people must defend their sense of who and what they are. Major failures and disasters obviously threaten the self, but so do inconsistent information and daily hassles and stresses. Threats to the self affect not only emotional well-being but also physical health. The most damaging threats are those we appraise as uncontrollable.

Anything that contradicts our sense of who we are and how we feel can cause us to question our impression of the self. Many types of events can pose significant threats. Failures—flubbing the driver's test, ending a marriage in divorce—expose us to negative feedback about who we are and what we do. Inconsistencies—illness in a usually healthy person, an empty nest for an at-home mom—provide us with information that contradicts who and what we thought we were. Awareness of our own mortality can be a powerful threat to the self (Solomon, Greenberg, & Pyszczynski, 2000). Events do not have to be negative to be inconsistent. Because they change our lives, even joyous occasions like getting married or becoming a parent also require difficult changes in the self-concept. Finally, stress also arises from daily events: the small but relentless grind-you-down frustrations and hassles of everyday life, the boredom of routine, the pressures of the rat-race. All these types of events call our sense of self into question.

EMOTIONAL AND PHYSICAL EFFECTS OF THREAT. Threats to the self arouse the gamut of negative emotions. Experiences like losing a loved one to illness or being fired from a job for poor performance activate the most intense emotions: terror, crushing depression. However, people with high self-esteem are at least in part protected from the negative effects of such events (Taylor, Kemeny, Reed, Bower, & Gruenwald, 2000). The protective effect is found even when the events are extreme, as George Bonnanno and his colleagues (Bonnanno, Field, Kovacevic, & Kaltman, 2002) found in a study of people affected by the brutal civil war in Bosnia. In contrast, when people's self-esteem is overinflated or unstable, the impact of negative events may be magnified (Kernis & Goldman, 2003). People with unrealistically inflated self-views, which may be especially unstable and highly vulnerable to negative information, are the most likely to turn to violence and aggression (Baumeister, Smart, & Boden, 1996; Bushman & Baumeister, 1998). Similarly, people whose self-concept is much higher than their friends' ratings of them—those who are most likely to have their lofty views challenged from time to time—tend to have poor social skills, and the negative effects on mental health may last for years (Colvin, Block, & Funder, 1995).

Threats to the self have effects beyond our emotions. Research over the past 20 years has convinced even the sometimes-skeptical medical community that such events also contribute to physical illness (Salovey, Rothman, & Rodin, 1998). Major setbacks adversely affect our health, but so do everyday minor hassles: arguing with a best friend, receiving a parking ticket, having to wait in line at the bank. Threats to the self bring us down, tick us off, and also alter our immune responses, nervous-system activity, and blood pressure—the kinds of physiological changes that contribute to illness (S. Cohen, Doyle, Skoner, & Fireman, 1995; O'Leary, 1990; J. Rodin & Salovey, 1989). For example, one study found that when people were reminded of significant self-discrepancies, levels of "natural killer" cell activity in their blood-stream decreased (Strauman, Lemieux, & Coe, 1993). These immune-system cells are important in defending the body against viral infections and cancers.

It is the negative emotions we experience in response to threats that put physical health at risk. People who habitually respond to failures, setbacks, and stresses with negative emotions are the most likely to suffer physically (Watson & Pennebaker, 1989). One of the best-known examples of this finding is the Type A behavior pattern, which is associated with risks of heart disease in both men and women (Booth-Kewley & Friedman, 1987; Thoresen & Low, 1990). The Type A pattern includes ambitiousness, competitiveness, rapid speech style, hostility, and anger, but not all of these characteristics are harmful to health. Anger and hostility appear to be the most important risk factors (Booth-Kewley & Friedman, 1987). People who react with rage to everyday annoyances, such as noticing that the person before them in the 10-items-or-less line at the supermarket has 11 items in the shopping cart, may be at greatest risk from heart disease (Angier, 1990a).

Several remarkable studies have now demonstrated that the effects of positive emotions endure across major portions of a lifetime. One study (Harker & Keltner, 2001) had observers rate the amount of positive emotion evident in women's college yearbook photos, and found that the ratings predicted positive outcomes in the women's marriages and their personal well-being, as much as 30 years after the photos were taken. Another study examined autobiographical statements written by Roman Catholic nuns when they entered their religious order at an average age of 22 years, early in the 1900s. Although all these nuns lived in quite similar objective circumstances, those whose youthful statements had more positive emotional content turned out to be longer-lived. The death rates of those with the most positive statements were 2.5 times lower than those showing the least positive emotion (Danner, Snowdon, & Friesen, 2001). These and other similar results (e.g., Martin and others, 2002) show that positive emotion is strongly associated with better health across many years or even decades.

THREAT AND APPRAISALS OF CONTROL. We must respond to frustrations, shortcomings, hassles, disasters, or any events we appraise as a threat. By far the most threatening events, however, are those we judge to be out of our control (Rodin & Salovey, 1989). Think about how the perception of control might affect some of your own responses. Do you feel more comfortable driving a car or riding in an airplane? Most people choose driving even though flying is as much as 10 times safer than driving, as measured in deaths per mile. Our deep-seated preference for control is one reason for this perverse response. When our basic motive to master our environment is called into question, a vital part of our sense of self is threatened. Feeling that events are beyond one's control increases the likelihood of many kinds of negative outcomes, including worker "burnout" and the perception of overcrowding in dormitories and prisons (Paulus, 1988; Pines, Aronson, & Kafry, 1981). For example, if you were assigned roommates in a dormitory suite, you would probably feel more crowded than if you roomed with the same number of individuals whom you had picked yourself. Not surprisingly, the anxiety and frustration that accompany lack of control take their toll on physical well-being. Uncontrollable stressful events are much more hazardous to health than controllable ones (Fleming, Baum, & Weiss, 1987; Kiecolt-Glaser & Glaser, 1988; Salovey and others, 1998).

☐ **CONTROL AND DEPRESSION.** Perhaps the most negative result of repeated experiences of lack of control is *learned helplessness* (Abramson, Seligman, & Teasdale, 1978; M. E. P. Seligman, 1975). Animals and humans that have endured uncontrollable outcomes often give up attempting to control their fate (M. E. P. Seligman & Maier, 1967). In one study in which people were exposed to inescapable bursts of noise, they later failed to protect themselves from noises they could easily have stopped (Hiroto, 1974). Learned helplessness can undermine people's efforts to master their situations. For example, people who work on insoluble problems or experience uncontrollable failures may give up trying, even in situations where their efforts might be of use. Part of the reason may be that repeated thoughts, such as "I can't do anything" or "My efforts are useless," and the associated sad and hopeless emotions interfere with the thought processes that would help people actually gain control (Sedek & Kofta, 1990).

Findings such as these have led researchers to argue that appraisals of events as uncontrollable contribute to *clinical depression*, a psychological disorder characterized

FIGURE 4.8   Attributions, learned helplessness, and depression

■ When a negative event is seen as due to a general and uncontrollable cause, people may give up and stop trying—a symptom of learned helplessness. Depression results when the cause of a negative event is seen not only as global and uncontrollable but also as internal.

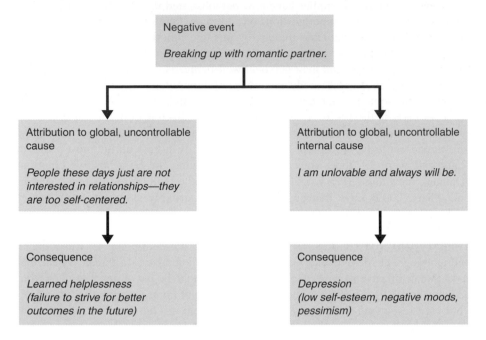

by negative moods, low self-esteem, pessimism, and a disruption of thinking, sleeping, eating, and activity patterns (Abramson and others, 1978). Figure 4.8 shows how the process works. A negative event or situation that occurs is appraised as both uncontrollable and laden with widespread implications for many areas of the person's life. The expectation of lack of control produces learned helplessness.

But learned helplessness is only part of depression. If global, enduring, uncontrollable events are also attributed to internal causes, that is, perceived to be "my fault," depression is the likely result (Abramson and others, 1978). For instance, in explaining the break-up of a romantic relationship, a person might conclude that he is now and always will be completely and totally unlovable. This explanation robs him of control in his present situation and of any hope of finding a future loving relationship. Research shows that people who use this *depressive attributional style* are more likely than others to become depressed when things go wrong in their lives (C. A. Anderson, Jennings, & Arnoult, 1988). The effects can last for years and can damage physical as well as mental health. Peterson and his colleagues (C. Peterson, Seligman, & Vaillant, 1988) examined interviews of men recorded when they were college students in the early 1940s, coding their attributions about negative events as depressive or not. The men were medically examined from time to time over the ensuing decades, with highly consistent results: The men who had explained negative events more pessimistically in their early 20s experienced poorer physical and mental health even into their 60s.

Defending Against Threat: Emotion-Focused Coping

To defend against threats, people sometimes try to manage their emotional responses to threat through escape, distraction, redefinition of an event's importance, or self-expression.

Though learned helplessness may keep people from doing anything about events that are appraised as threats to the self, people ordinarily respond with **coping strategies**, efforts to reduce the negative consequences produced by threatening events. In one common type of coping response, *emotion-focused coping*, people attempt to deal with the negative emotions associated with the event, perhaps by escaping or avoiding the threatening situation. Faced with family discord, for example, a person could ignore the problem or become immersed in some distracting hobby or activity. How do these strategies of emotion-focused coping work?

ESCAPING FROM THREAT: SHIPPING OUT. When events conspire to bring home our failures and shortcomings, a common first impulse is to ship out rather than shape up. After all, escape mercifully terminates the painful awareness of inadequacies (Gibbons & Wicklund, 1982). Experimental evidence bears out the idea that people who have fallen short of a personal standard will make a quick exit from the stressful situation—if they can. In one study, an experimenter told participants that they had scored very well or very poorly on a test of intelligence and creativity and then asked them to wait 5 minutes for a second experimenter. For half of the participants, the waiting room was equipped with a mirror and videocamera, both designed to induce self-awareness. Did the combination of embarrassing self-discrepancies (scoring poorly on the test) and self-awareness make escape look like the best option? Apparently so. The people who scored poorly and were told to wait in the specially equipped room left significantly sooner than did other participants (Duval & Wicklund, 1972).

Even as mundane a behavior as watching TV may be a way for some people to escape painful self-awareness through distraction. To test this idea, Sophia Moskalenko and Steven Heine (2003) also gave participants false feedback about their test performance, and then seated each one in front of a TV set to watch a videotape as the next part of the study. When the tape came on, showing nature scenes with a musical soundtrack, the experimenter exclaimed that this was the wrong tape and went supposedly to get the correct one, leaving the participant alone as the video played. The participants who had received failure feedback watched the tape much longer than those who thought they had succeeded. The researchers concluded that distraction through television viewing can effectively relieve the discomfort associated with painful failures or self-discrepancies. In contrast, successful participants had little wish to be distracted from their self-related thoughts!

Escape can take other forms as well. People drink, take drugs, and engage in "just for kicks" risky behavior for many reasons, but sometimes these activities are attempts at blotting out the self, eliminating the uncomfortable consequences of self-discrepancies (Baumeister, 1991). For example, Jay Hull (1981) found that people really can "drown their sorrows" with alcohol: Alcohol consumption temporarily reduces self-awareness.

DOWNPLAYING THREAT: ACCENTUATE THE POSITIVE, ELIMINATE THE NEGATIVE.
Besides escape through drinking or distraction, another way to manage the negative consequences of poor performances is to downplay their importance in comparison to other domains of life. Reaffirming and expressing the personal characteristics we see as most important and value most highly can help us cope with failure, uncertainty, and stress in other areas (Steele, 1988). Shelley Taylor (1983) found that breast-cancer patients who were facing the possibility of death often expressed and reaffirmed what they regarded as their most basic self-aspects.

> **Coping strategies.** Efforts undertaken to reduce negative consequences of self-threatening events.

Some individuals quit dead-end jobs, while others turned to writing poetry or reaffirmed significant relationships.

A similar process can affect anyone—not just those with life-threatening illnesses—when we are reminded of our own mortality. According to Terror Management Theory (Solomon and others, 2000), such a reminder leads us to cope by reaffirming our most basic cultural worldviews, such as religious beliefs or views about what is most important in life. These reaffirmations can often lead to positive, prosocial behaviors like helping similar others. But they also have a more negative side, generating intolerance and rejection for the deviant, the defiant, and the just "different"—anyone who fails to conform to the cultural worldview (Solomon and others, 2000).

Thus, when faced with irrefutable evidence of our couch-potato behavior and our selfish motives, we may downplay the importance of those topics, deciding that slimness and generosity are not all they are cracked up to be—compared to other areas of life. Research shows, for example, that the more highly skilled people are on dimensions like academic ability, social skills, or artistic ability, the more important they think those dimensions are; conversely, the less skilled, the less importance they attach to the dimensions (Pelham, 1991).

WORKING THROUGH THREAT: SELF-EXPRESSION. "Sometimes I wonder how all those who do not write, compose, or paint can manage to escape the madness, the melancholia, the panic fear which is inherent in the human situation." As novelist Graham Greene realized (1980, p. 285), self-expression helps people cope emotionally. Even such simple forms of self-expression as talking about the feelings produced by threatening events can help overcome some of their emotional and physical costs (Bulman & Wortman, 1977; Tait & Silver, 1989).

James Pennebaker (1997) has championed the idea that bringing to the surface deeply buried stressful events can help alleviate some of their negative effects. In one dramatic illustration of this idea, he and his colleagues asked some students to write about personally traumatic life events that they had never before discussed, and they asked others to write about trivial topics (Pennebaker, Kiecolt-Glaser, & Glaser, 1988). The students were assured that their names would not be connected to what they wrote. On the 4 successive days of the experiment, the first group dealt with extremely significant events in their lives, including such traumas as the sudden death of a sibling or childhood sexual abuse. Not surprisingly, they reported more negative emotions and more physical discomforts (headaches, muscle tension, pounding heart) at the time, compared with participants who wrote about unimportant topics. However, physiological measures showed that immune-system functioning was superior among students who wrote about traumas. This health benefit persisted for 6 weeks, during which these students visited the university health center less often than did the other participants. Other studies have replicated these powerful effects.

Of course, although these participants benefited in the long run, the immediate impact of writing about traumatic events was negative. Before agreeing to participate in this study, the students were warned that they might be asked to write about extremely upsetting events. In addition, researchers conducting studies of this type are always prepared to refer for counseling any participants who become overly distressed. Traumatic events do, of course, harm the victim in many ways, and merely thinking and writing about the event cannot remove all its negative effects. But writing about them can at least help reduce the costs of suppressing and inhibiting painful thoughts, and it is often the first step toward appraising negative events differently (Horowitz, 1987; Lepore, Ragan, & Jones, 2000). As you will see, reappraising events is one way to cope directly with problems.

WOMEN UNDER STRESS: TEND AND BEFRIEND. According to Shelley Taylor, women are more likely than men to cope emotionally with stress by nurturing themselves, their kin, and other people, and by creating and maintaining social networks of close others. Taylor has named this pattern "tend and befriend" (Taylor, Klein, Lewis, Grueneward, Gurung, & Updegraff, 2000). Men are instead more likely to display "fight or flight" responses when under stress. This sex difference is so stable and robust that of 26 studies examining people's tendency to affiliate with others under stress, 25 found that women were more likely than men to do so (Luckow, Reifman, & McIntosh, 1998). And although men are less likely to engage in them, "tend and befriend" actions help men as well as women deal emotionally with stress (Taylor, Klein, and others, 2000).

Attacking Threat Head-On: Problem-Focused Coping

Sometimes people respond to threats directly, attempting to reinterpret or remove the negative event or situation itself. Strategies include making excuses, seeking to take control, or directly attacking the problem.

Focusing on the emotional responses produced by threats to the self can help us to feel good about ourselves, but sometimes we prefer tackling events head on. For one thing, as we noted earlier, suppressing emotional feelings can be hard work (Baumeister and others, 2000). Illustrating this point, one study found that when students watched an emotionally evocative film under instructions to suppress their emotions, the effortful suppression actually reduced their ability to remember details from the film (Richards & Gross, 2000). Instead of trying to suppress emotional responses, the alternative strategy of *problem-focused coping* directs people's cognitive, emotional, and behavioral resources toward reinterpreting the event as nonthreatening (rather than just trying to manage emotional reactions to the threat), or toward physically removing the event.

MAKING EXCUSES: IT'S NOT MY FAULT. What happens when our worst fears are realized and we do fail a test, get caught out in a lie, or get pulled over for speeding on the expressway? Although we have all wished the earth would open up and swallow us in such circumstances, our usual recourse is to apologize, offer excuses, and try to pick up where we left off. Whenever an action ends in disaster and threatens our self-concept, a good excuse is worth its weight in gold.

Why are excuses so important? The answer has to do with *self-enhancing attributions* that distort people's explanations for successes and failures (Mullen & Riordan, 1988). Most people like to take credit for their successes and notable accomplishments and to attribute failure to external causes. A good grade on an exam reflects well on our intelligence and motivation, while a failing grade is surely due to poorly written test items, an emergency at home, a sudden bout of the flu, or even loud music playing down the hall (D. T. Miller & Ross, 1975).

SELF-HANDICAPPING. A good excuse can be even more valuable if it is lined up before the performance: If we do fail, our defense is already in place. Charles Snyder and his colleagues found that people often use disclaimers like shyness, anxiety, ill health, or disruptive events when they anticipate failing at an important task (C. R. Snyder & Higgins, 1988; C. R. Snyder, Smith, Augelli, & Ingram, 1985). Letting others think we are shy, sick, or under stress seems preferable to conveying the impression that we are unlikable or incompetent.

If verbal excuses help us save face, could the creation of actual barriers to successful performance do the same? Strange as it may seem, some people actually sabotage their own performances to provide excuses for subsequent failures. The strategy is called *self-handicapping* (Berglas & Jones, 1978). To see how and why self-handicapping might work, imagine that you have been bragging for months about your chicken curry, and now your friends are finally coming over for dinner. It suddenly occurs to you that your culinary skills may not quite match those you have advertised. Is there any way out? One possibility is self-handicapping: You could intentionally arrange to run out of a crucial ingredient for the curry. In attributional terms, self-handicapping is a no-lose proposition: Observers' impressions of your skill will be even more positive than they otherwise would be, regardless of the dinner's failure or success. If the curry is not so great, your reputation as a great cook will be saved as your friends blame the disaster on the missing ingredient rather than on your poor skills. If the dinner is wonderful anyway, your culinary expertise will appear even more impressive.

But remember, the attributional benefit of self-handicapping is purchased at the cost of lowering the real probability of good performance (Baumgardner & Brownlee, 1987). Edward Hirt and his colleagues discovered another potential cost, as well: observers—especially women—dislike those who self-handicap and rate them negatively on a wide range of traits (Hirt, McCrea, & Boris, 2003). The reason seems to be that women, more than men, value effort for itself, and have little respect for those who make excuses rather than trying hard in performance situations. All in all, these interpersonal costs mean that self-handicapping is usually counterproductive.

TAKING CONTROL OF THE PROBLEM. If external attributions usually help us to save face, what do you make of the following finding? In one survey of U.S. residents, people who regarded themselves as poor or economically struggling were questioned about their attributions for their situation and about their general emotional well-being. Poor people who believed they had had a fair chance to achieve felt more pride and joy and less guilt and disappointment about their lives than those who believed that external forces had held them back (E. R. Smith & Kluegel, 1982). That is, even when their outcomes are negative, people often feel better if they think they have control. Blaming external factors for failures might let you off the hook momentarily, but interpreting the forces that influence your life as *controllable* will put you back in charge for the long term. Feelings of control are so important that we attempt to exert control whenever we can (R. W. White, 1959), and they lead us to try harder and often perform better (Dweck, 1986). In fact, we often exaggerate the amount of control we possess, even in situations actually ruled by chance (Langer, 1975). For example, most people who play the state lottery prefer to pick their "lucky number," even though any number would have an equal chance of winning.

What gives people the feeling that they can control events in their lives? One crucial ingredient is their confidence in their ability to deal with a particular area, such as passing exams in psychology or successfully managing their social life. This confidence in our ability to produce the outcomes we desire is termed *self-efficacy* (Bandura, 1986). Self-efficacy is particularly strongly linked with the way people explain their failures: whether they explain them in terms of controllable or uncontrollable causes. If the bank bounces one of your checks for the third time this month and you explain it by saying, "Oh, I just can't keep a checkbook balanced; I'm no good at finance," you are pointing to your supposed lack of ability—an uncontrollable cause. If you blame the situation on your lack of effort or attention, you are pointing to a potentially controllable cause. Such an explanation for a failure should lead you to try harder to keep track of your deposits and withdrawals, which may result in fewer overdraft fees in the future.

☐ **CONTROL AND LIFE GOALS.** The issue of who is in control is central even when people set overall directions for their lives. Take a moment to contemplate your most important long-term objectives and goals. Do these aspirations reflect your own internally guided choices, or are they goals that other people have selected for you? Consistent with the general benefits of control, actions and goals that we choose for ourselves benefit us psychologically more than those that are externally imposed. Tim Kasser and Richard Ryan (1996) asked people to rate the importance they personally attached to several different life goals. These goals included some that the researchers classified as intrinsic or self-chosen, such as positive relationships with friends and family, community service, or health, as well as some goals the researchers viewed as involving external approval or rewards, such as financial success, fame, and physical attractiveness. The researchers also measured several forms of physical and psychological well-being, including physical symptoms and depression. Consistent results emerged in separate studies of undergraduate students and of adults from 18 to 79 years old. Those who attached more importance to the intrinsic goals tended to have better well-being and lower levels of depression and psychological distress, compared to those whose aspirations were classified as more extrinsic. It seems that striving for wealth, fame, and beauty is not a sure route to happiness. Instead, people whose most important goals reflect intrinsic values, goals involving such things as relatedness to others and community service, have the best life outcomes overall.

SOLVING THE PROBLEM: RISING TO THE CHALLENGE. The negative feelings aroused by failures, self-discrepancies, and stress can have positive motivational consequences. We do not always ship out; sometimes we decide to shape up. For example, the painful nature of self-discrepancies can motivate people to change themselves, to live up to their own ideals and self-guides. Self-awareness often makes people behave in ways consistent with their own personal values (Gibbons, 1978). Startled by being labeled as a couch potato, the former star athlete might decide to substitute an hour of lifting weights for an hour of watching TV reruns. When we can attribute bad outcomes to controllable factors, we can activate strategies designed to change our performance. If you decide that your low grade was due to a lack of preparation rather than an inability to understand the material, setting up a regular study time may help you prepare for the next exam well in advance. When people try to change, the support and encouragement of others—a spouse or a group of friends, for instance—is generally crucial (Heatherton & Nichols, 1994).

■ **Rising to the challenge.** Lance Armstrong (left) is shown here in the 16th stage of the Tour de France. For three years before his first Tour win in 1999, the Texan was diagnosed with testicular, brain and lung cancer and given less than a 50-50 chance of survival. Now, with a career boasting seven Tour de France wins between 1999 and 2005, he truely has demonstrated an incredible turnaround.

This fact underlines the social and interpersonal nature of the self: Whether we are trying to change our overt behavior, our self-esteem, or the way we think about ourselves, these changes depend on our social surroundings.

How to Cope?

The individual's resources as well as characteristics of the threatening situation dictate the best response to threats. No single type of response is always best, but many types of coping can help overcome the threat, preserve psychological well-being, and protect physical health.

As we have seen, there are many ways to cope with threats to the self. Both problem-focused and emotion-focused coping can improve psychological well-being and lessen the health damage caused by threatening events (F. Cohen, 1984; Kiecolt-Glaser, Fisher, & Ogrocki, 1987). But which type works better? The answer depends on who is being threatened—the individual and the resources she or he brings to the situation—and also on the nature of the threat, particularly its controllability.

SELF-ESTEEM AS A RESOURCE FOR COPING. People vary in the cognitive and emotional resources they have to aid in coping. Self-esteem is not only an indicator of how well we are meeting our fundamental social motives for mastery and connectedness, but also an important resource for coping with threats to the self. Those with high self-esteem roll out a formidable arsenal of weapons to defend against threats. For example, they fight negative feedback, setbacks, or stress with an aggressive use of self-enhancing biases and problem-focused coping (J. D. Brown, 1986; S. Epstein, 1992; Josephs, Larrick, Steele, & Nisbett, 1992). They compare themselves with others who are worse off and make self-enhancing attributions for their failures and shortcomings. A challenge to one aspect of the self-concept, such as interpersonal sensitivity, may be met with affirmation of another aspect: generosity, athletic prowess, or intellectual acumen (Steele, 1988). Finally, a strong sense of control lets people with high self-esteem tackle problems head-on. The successful use of this impressive array of self-enhancing biases and coping strategies restores and maintains high self-esteem so the whole cycle can begin again (S. E. Taylor & Brown, 1988). Like a reflection in a series of fun-house mirrors, high self-esteem leads to self-enhancement and successful coping, which restore high self-esteem, which triggers self-enhancement, and so on. No wonder, then, that people with high self-esteem have more stable levels of self-esteem and clearer self-concepts (J. D. Campbell, 1990), and also respond to threat with far fewer emotional and physical symptoms than do those with low self-esteem (J. D. Brown & Smart, 1991).

If you have ever interacted with someone who has low self-esteem, however, you may have noticed a completely different set of reactions. Rather than predicting that the rain clouds will be followed by spring flowers, people with low self-esteem seem resigned to permanent flood conditions. Indeed, depressed people and those with low self-esteem are much less likely to self-enhance than others (Alloy & Abramson, 1979; S. E. Taylor & Brown, 1988). They make downward comparisons less often, remember more negative things about themselves, and assume they have less control over events.

So it is clear that everyday decisions—whether to apply for graduate school, try out for the band, or ask a popular classmate for a date—are very different proposals

Calvin and Hobbes by Bill Watterson

for different individuals, depending on their level of self-esteem. Great rewards might follow from taking these actions, but individuals with low self-esteem may be unable to take the risk because they are highly sensitive to the possibility of failure and embarrassment (Leary, Barners, & Griebel, 1986). "To the person high in self-esteem . . . the world is an oyster bed of opportunities to enhance themselves, but to the person low in self-esteem, it is a minefield that can humiliate and depress" (Josephs, Larrick, and others, 1992, p. 35). The differences between the ways people with high or low self-esteem approach events can compound across a lifetime. affecting the ways we deal with daily threats and ultimately our physical health.

CONTROLLABILITY AND COPING. The best way to cope depends on the characteristics of the threat as well as on those of the threatened person. Depending on their appraisals of the threat and of their own resources, people can choose among many possible coping strategies, as Figure 4.9 shows. Every style of coping, however, has costs as well as benefits. The most important appraisal is of a threat's controllability. Controllable threats, those that one is confident in being able to handle, really represent *challenges* rather than threats (Blascovich & Tomaka, 1996). People's emotional responses to challenges are generally positive or only mildly negative, and physiological responses (including heart-rate changes, for instance) are geared toward successful mobilization and effective action. With challenges, problem-focused coping might work best, even if it increases immediate distress (S. M. Miller & Mangan, 1983). In contrast, when threats are appraised as uncontrollable, escape, distraction, and other forms of emotion-focused coping may be the only effective ways to deal with them (Folkman, 1984). Unlike challenges, threats elicit negative feelings and physiological responses that are ineffective and perhaps even health-damaging.

But the difference between a threat and a challenge is not so much in the event itself as in the way one looks at it. In one study Joe Tomaka and his colleagues (1997) gave

■ **On their own but out of control.** Crowded dormitory rooms are a reality in many colleges today, and crowding is a potent source of stress that can produce anxiety and physical illness, as well as low grades. But just as control can reduce the effects of many other sources of stress, control—in the form of choosing one's own roommates—reduces the effects of crowding.

FIGURE 4.9   Ways of coping and their effects

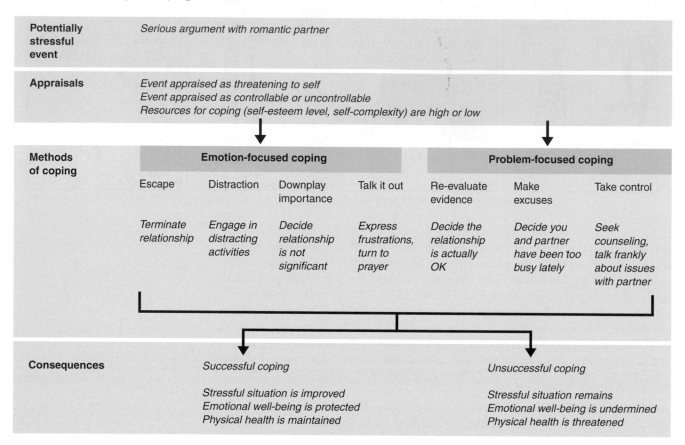

Potentially stressful event	*Serious argument with romantic partner*						
Appraisals	*Event appraised as threatening to self* *Event appraised as controllable or uncontrollable* *Resources for coping (self-esteem level, self-complexity) are high or low*						

Methods of coping	**Emotion-focused coping**				**Problem-focused coping**		
	Escape	Distraction	Downplay importance	Talk it out	Re-evaluate evidence	Make excuses	Take control
	Terminate relationship	*Engage in distracting activities*	*Decide relationship is not significant*	*Express frustrations, turn to prayer*	*Decide the relationship is actually OK*	*Decide you and partner have been too busy lately*	*Seek counseling, talk frankly about issues with partner*

Consequences	*Successful coping*	*Unsuccessful coping*
	Stressful situation is improved *Emotional well-being is protected* *Physical health is maintained*	*Stressful situation remains* *Emotional well-being is undermined* *Physical health is threatened*

■ Appraisals of a self-threatening event—particularly of its controllability—and of one's coping resources influence the selection of coping strategies. Successful or unsuccessful coping may influence emotional well-being and physical health—as well as affecting the concrete stressful situation itself.

Aid in fighting stress also comes from external sources. The presence of others who give support, advice, and assistance can help ward off the negative consequences of threat. We see how this happens in Chapter 11, pages, 417 to 419.

students a mental arithmetic task, introducing the task for some students by stressing the need for both speed and accuracy (making the task somewhat threatening) and for others by asking them to think of the task as "a challenge" and to think of themselves as "someone capable of meeting that challenge." This simple difference in instructions for the very same task elicited the physiological response patterns characteristic of threats versus challenges. Once again, as we have seen so many times in this chapter, the way people regard the stressful event is crucial.

CONCLUDING COMMENTS

We started the chapter by saying that one of the most important life tasks each of us faces is understanding both who we are and how we feel about ourselves. Philosophers have long admonished us to "know thyself," the first aspect of this important task. An accurate understanding of our individual abilities, preferences, and talents enables us to choose the partners, pastimes, and professions that suit us best. It lets us know where we fit in the social world and provides a starting point in any attempt at change or improvement. But psychologists know that it is not enough to "know thyself." Self-esteem is equally central in our lives. Viewing the self as both good and in control—even in exaggerated ways—protects our emotional and physical well-being as we cope with inconsistencies, failures, and stress. Whenever we think about the self, we are faced with two, sometimes conflicting, motives: enhancing the self and accurately evaluating the self.

The dual needs for accurate self-knowledge and positive self-esteem play themselves out in a variety of ways that were discussed throughout this chapter. Sometimes we seek accurate assessments of the self; at other times we engage in biased searches or interpretations to come up with self-enhancing information. Sometimes we compare ourselves with similar others and sometimes with others who are worse off than we are. Sometimes we choose our behaviors to accurately reflect the person we believe we are, but at other times we try to create a positive impression of ourselves. Even the ways we defend ourselves against such threats as negative feedback, obvious shortcomings, and large and small stressors provoke the same dilemma. The warm glow of positive thinking infuses us with strength to clear life's many hurdles, but escaping into a fantasy world of self-enhancement can just as easily set us up for a fall. Taking negative feedback at face value can help us to deal constructively with, and possibly to overcome, our failures and shortcomings. But it can also be painful.

Does this mean we are caught in a no-win situation, forced to make trade-offs between reality and illusion, happiness and depression? Are our choices limited to being eternal optimists, happy but out of touch, or hard realists, on top of the facts but miserable because of it? Fortunately, we have other options. The recipe for a healthy sense of self calls for both accurate self-knowledge and protective self-enhancement, in just the right amounts at just the right times. Weighing these ingredients may be the most important aspect of constructing and maintaining the self. The correct measure of self-enhancement keeps our spirits high and our body healthy, while a judicious amount of self-assessment keeps our goals realistic and our efforts focused in the best direction. A good dollop of self-evaluation tells us what we need to do, a splash of self-enhancement gives us the courage to do it.

CHAPTER 4 THEMES

- **Construction of Reality**
  We construct an impression of the self, based on a multitude of cues.

- **Pervasiveness of Social Influence**
  Our perceptions of other people and their reactions to us pervasively influence our self-concept and self-esteem.

- **Striving for Mastery**
  Perceiving that we control our environment helps mental well-being and physical health.

- **Valuing Me and Mine**
  Self-enhancing biases shape our self-concept and elevate self-esteem.

- **Conservatism**
  Once formed, the self-concept is resistant to change and well defended against threats.

- **Accessibility**
  The self-concept and self-esteem depend on information and experiences that come readily to mind.

S U M M A R Y

Constructing the Self-Concept: What We Know About Ourselves. People construct the **self-concept** in much the same way that they form impressions of others, using similar types of information and similar interpretive processes. People often infer their own characteristics from their observed behaviors, as **self-perception theory** notes. They also use thoughts and feelings and other people's reactions to form opinions about themselves. Finally, **social comparison theory** describes how people compare themselves to others to learn what characteristics make them unique.

Despite the general similarity of the ways people learn about themselves and others, self-knowledge is richer and more detailed than knowledge about others. People can observe themselves in more situations and have better access to private thoughts and feelings. People also tend to explain their own and other people's behaviors differently, producing **actor–observer differences in attribution**. They attribute their own actions to properties of the situation or the stimulus, while generally explaining others' actions by their personal characteristics. However, even people's explanations for their own behaviors may be inaccurate.

Because people see themselves in a wide range of situations and roles, self-knowledge is organized around multiple self-aspects representing roles, activities, and relationships.

People try to fit the diverse elements of the self-concept together in a way that seems coherent and stable. Coherence can be attained by making accessible only limited aspects of the self at any given time, by selectively remembering past acts, by explaining away inconsistencies, and by focusing on a few central traits. Cultures influence the ways in which people seek coherence. Members of Western, independent cultures stress the self-schema, traits that generally describe them across situations, while those in interdependent cultures emphasize their roles and relationships with others.

Constructing Self-Esteem: How We Feel About Ourselves. Accurate self-knowledge regarding our capabilities and preferences is important for guiding us through our lives in ways that suit our needs and abilities. But accuracy is not the only consideration in evaluating the self: **Self-esteem** is also greatly influenced by motivational pressures to think well of the self. These motivations color many of our thoughts and feelings about the self through **self-enhancing biases**.

Events that affect us positively or negatively influence our self-esteem, but we try in several ways to accumulate more positive than negative experiences. We also evaluate ourselves by making comparisons with others. These comparisons also are sometimes self-enhancing. Despite the value of accurate self-knowledge, self-enhancement occurs for two primary reasons. Some actions that appear self-enhancing are aimed at actual self-improvement, reflecting successful self-regulation. And high self-esteem can be an important resource that protects us against stress and threats to the self.

Like most other aspects of the self, self-enhancing biases operate somewhat differently in different cultures. Independent cultures emphasize positive individual characteristics as the source of self-esteem, while interdependent cultures stress connectedness to others. Despite these differences, self-esteem functions in all cultures to indicate how well we are meeting our most important motives for mastery and connectedness.

Effects of the Self: Processes of Self-Regulation. The self-concept, once formed, is relatively difficult to change. People avoid or actively reject information that is inconsistent with their established self-views. Self-knowledge also serves as a framework for perceiving other people and influences what types of social information we will remember.

The self regulates many aspects of our lives. Emotions are sparked by **appraisals** of self-relevant events and their causes or controllability. Emotions signal the occurrence of significant events and motivate us to act in response, for example, to flee from danger. As they perform this self-regulation function, emotions involve the whole self, body and mind: They activate facial expressions, physiological responses, subjective feelings, and overt behaviors.

Self-discrepancy theory describes how people compare the self with internal standards. The outcomes of these comparisons can motivate us to behave in particular ways. Although our thoughts are turned outward most of the time, some events create **self-awareness**, including our internal standards and whether we measure up to them. Focusing attention on the self makes self-discrepancies obvious. When situations offer us short-term benefits that detract from our longer-term goals and standards, we can actively and effortfully choose strategies to overcome these temptations.

The self also directs behavior. Sometimes people engage in **self-expression**, acting in ways that express their true inner selves. At other times, people are concerned with **self-presentation**, attempting to shape others' opinions in order to gain power, influence, or approval. The personality variable of **self-monitoring** reflects the degree to which people seek one or the other of these two general goals. But even behaviors intended for others' consumption may end up influencing people's private views of themselves.

Defending the Self: Coping with Stresses, Inconsistencies, and Failures. When threatened by external events or negative feedback, people must defend their sense of who and what they are. Major failures and disasters obviously threaten the self, but so do inconsistent information, daily hassles, and stresses. Threats to the self affect not only emotional well-being but also physical health. The most damaging threats are those we appraise as uncontrollable.

Faced with threats, people respond with **coping strategies**. Sometimes they try to manage their emotional responses to threat through escape, distraction, redefinition of an event's importance, or self-expression. At other times, people respond to threats directly, trying to reduce the negative consequences of self-threatening events. Possible strategies are making excuses, seeking to take control, or directly attacking the problem.

The individual's resources, including self-esteem, as well as characteristics of the threatening situation, dictate the best response to threats. No single type of response is always best, but many types of coping can help overcome the threat, preserve psychological well-being, and protect physical health.

5

Perceiving Groups

Through late 2001 and the first half of 2002, employers in the Boston and Chicago areas received a number of résumés in response to help-wanted ads they had placed in the newspapers for sales, clerical, and administrative jobs. Nothing surprising there—except that these were not submitted by ordinary job-seekers, but by a team of economists conducting a study. The résumés were drawn from a pool of over 100 showing generally equivalent qualifications, and different first names were randomly attached to each one. Some first names were male and some female, and some names were common among Whites and others among Blacks. Thus, one employer might have seen a particular job application under the name Kristen Jones, while another saw exactly the same application with the name Latonya Jones. Did the employers' evaluations of the applications depend on the apparent racial identity of the applicant? The answer is yes. Overall, applicants whose names sounded White were called for interviews 50% more often than those with Black-sounding names (Krueger, 2002). This astounding difference held for both male and female names, and in both Boston and Chicago. Additional analyses showed that for applicants with White names, those with stronger credentials (such as experience and awards) received more requests for interviews. But for apparently Black applicants, stronger credentials did not yield much benefit.

The evidence provided by this study, as well as other studies in which matched Black and White candidates are sent to apply in person for the same job, strongly suggests that some employers engage in racial discrimination. The term **discrimination** refers to positive or negative behavior directed toward a social group and its members. Of course, people are usually concerned with negative behaviors—with discrimination against a specific group—but discrimination against one group inevitably amounts to discrimination in favor of others. For example, the former South African system of apartheid—legally enforced segregation—victimized Blacks while preserving the power and wealth of the small White minority. Apartheid and many other forms of discrimination are illegal in the United States, but many people still find themselves ill-treated because of their group memberships. Physical attacks, vandalism, harassment, and threats against Jews, Blacks, Asian Americans, and gay men and lesbians have been widely reported in recent years, leading some

> **Discrimination.** Any positive or negative behavior that is directed toward a social group and its members.

communities to pass laws providing extra punishment for "hate crimes" (Garofalo, 1997; Green, Glaser, & Rich, 1998). Economic discrimination victimizes women and people of color when they try to purchase a used car, rent or purchase a home, or negotiate a salary (Abrams, 1991; Goldin, 1990; W. E. Schmidt, 1990). And, as many young Black men are well aware, their experiences with the criminal justice system differ substantially from those of most Whites (D. A. Bell, 1973; Silverstein, 1965).

Unfortunately, discrimination seems to be found everywhere around the globe. Turks and other foreigners living in Germany have been victims of verbal abuse, beatings, arson, and murder by neo-Nazis and teenage "skinheads" (Moseley, 1998). In Europe, Black soccer players—even major stars of their teams—are frequently subjected to racist chants (Vecsey, 2003). French Canadians feel oppressed by the English-speaking majority; Canadian Mohawk Indians feel oppressed by French Canadians. Tamils in Sri Lanka, women in Afghanistan, and Blacks in South Africa have little access to adequate schooling, health care, or political power.

What leads one group of people to victimize another? Religious thinkers, political leaders, social scientists, and others have searched for an answer to this important question. Social psychologists believe that the underlying processes leading to discrimination usually include **prejudice**, positive or negative evaluations of a social group and its members. Once again, people's concern is most often with negative reactions, which range all the way from mild dislike to blind hatred. As you will see in the first part of this chapter, prejudice is complex and multifaceted, and its roots can be traced to cognitive and social processes that guide our every interaction with groups. So many processes contribute to prejudice, in fact, that we will need two chapters (Chapters 5 and 6) to tell the whole story.

Prejudice can be "hot" or "cold." Virulent and emotional hatred for other groups, such as that espoused by the Nazis or the Ku Klux Klan, is easy to recognize. It shows itself in burning crosses, campaigns of "ethnic cleansing," pogroms, and massacres. Unfortunately, the very obviousness of this type of bigotry and hatred may blind us to a more insidious type of prejudice based on the calm assumption that certain groups just "do not have what it takes" and should therefore be excluded from desirable positions, wealth, or power. This quieter, cooler form of prejudice is at work when sports-team owners profit from the performance of Black athletes on the field but can never find a "qualified" Black for a managerial or front-office job. And it is present when a construction union maintains an all-male membership by keeping women out of apprenticeship programs, or when a real estate agent steers prospective home buyers who are Hispanic to particular neighborhoods. Such discriminatory actions are carried out calmly, routinely, and without any of the familiar overt signs of bigotry. But even though no hooded robes or swastika armbands are anywhere in sight, very real harm is suffered by those on the receiving end.

In this chapter we start with the very basis of prejudice: the way in which people divide the world into social groups. We then consider the **stereotypes**, or impressions that people form of groups by associating the groups with particular characteristics (Eagly & Mladinic, 1989; D. L. Hamilton, 1981). The sometimes biased and often sketchy impressions we form of groups can permeate our thinking and become a basis for both prejudice and discrimination. For example, many White Americans associate Blacks with characteristics like a lack of education and laziness. In the case of a Black job applicant, this stereotype may translate into prejudice (negative reactions to the information on the résumé) and discrimination (a failure to offer an interview).

Prejudice. A positive or negative evaluation of a social group and its members.

Stereotype. A cognitive representation or impression of a social group that people form by associating particular characteristics and emotions with the group.

Is it possible to eliminate the stereotypical thinking that contributes to prejudice? Will Black job-seekers ever have their credentials evaluated fairly, by the same standards as their White counterparts? The answer is a cautious but optimistic yes. Stereotypes can be changed, though it does not happen easily. Initial impressions of groups, like first impressions of individuals, tend to have lasting power. Established stereotypes often influence thoughts and actions in ways that make stereotypes resistant to modification. But as you will see in the final section of this chapter, the defenses protecting stereotypes from change can be breached under some conditions. Negative stereotypes can then be replaced by more favorable impressions, and prejudice can be replaced by more positive evaluations.

Targets of Prejudice: Social Groups

Any group that shares a socially meaningful common characteristic can be a target for prejudice. Different cultures emphasize different types of groups, but race, religion, gender, age, social status, and cultural background are important dividing lines in many societies.

Stereotypes, prejudice, discrimination: We have been talking about processes that depend on identifying people as members of social groups. But what is it that turns "people" into "members of social groups"? A **social group** is two or more people who share some common characteristic that is socially meaningful for themselves or for others (Shaw, 1976; Tajfel & Turner, 1979; J. C. Turner, 1981). The key phrase here is *socially meaningful*. People who share just any attribute, such as pedestrians who happen to be waiting in the same place to cross the same street, do not qualify as a social group (D. L. Hamilton & Sherman, 1996). Categories of people who share socially meaningful attributes—college students, Quakers, the "working poor," white-collar criminals, environmentalists—are groups, however. So are members of smaller groups who interact face-to-face while performing shared tasks (such as the cast of a play or members of a committee). People may assume that these smaller groups are even more "groupy" in terms of their similarities and shared values than are larger social categories (Lickel, Hamilton, & Sherman, 2001). So groups can be of many types. In fact, individuals who believe they share socially significant attributes are a group even if others do not think of them that way. Likewise, people who are seen by others as sharing meaningful similarities are a group even if they themselves do not hold that view. Recent immigrants who see themselves as blending into their new culture are often disappointed when their new compatriots think of them as "foreigners." Social groups exist very much in the eyes of their beholders.

Socially meaningful characteristics, of course, can change from time to time and from culture to culture. If several British and French men and women are discussing dating, they will probably think of themselves and each other primarily as members of the groups "men" or "women." If the topic shifts to the Euro currency, however, the implicit lines of group membership will probably shift as well. These people may now see themselves and each other as members of national groups that are affected differently by European economic union.

Even though rapid changes in perception of group membership are possible, each society and culture generally emphasizes particular group distinctions. In most North American and European countries today, discussion of stereotypes and prejudice is likely to make people think of "racial" groups. And because most research

Members of some groups have much more in common than shared features. Interaction and shared goals also affect group members' beliefs, feelings, and behaviors in important ways, as you will see in Chapters 9 and 12.

Social group. Two or more people who share some common characteristic that is socially meaningful for themselves or for others.

■ **Multiple group memberships.** Listening to the tour guide and snapping shots of landmarks, these people share the socially meaningful characteristics of "tourists." But several of them share memberships in other social groups. Thus, under different circumstances they could be categorized in terms of their family membership, age, ethnicity, or gender.

on these issues has been conducted in North America and Europe, it displays a strong focus on racial stereotypes and prejudice, particularly on Whites' perceptions and reactions to Blacks. Interestingly, though, the concept of "race" originated fairly recently (around the middle of the 19th century) to provide a pseudoscientific justification for socially determined differences in the treatment of different groups (Gould, 1981). Thus, race is largely a social concept with little, if any, biological meaning (Dobzhansky, 1973). For most of recorded history, not race but religion has been the characteristic that elicited the most prejudice and discrimination. This is still true today in many parts of the world (G. W. Allport, 1954b, p. xi). In Lebanon, for example, the characteristic that matters is whether a person is Muslim or Christian; in Northern Ireland, Catholic or Protestant identity is what counts. In still other places, cultural background is the trigger for prejudice. The Chinese, for example, have historically been prejudiced against the Japanese, the Japanese against the Koreans, and so on.

Social Categorization: Dividing the World into Social Groups

> People identify individuals as members of social groups because they share socially meaningful features. Social categorization is helpful because it allows people to deal with others efficiently and appropriately. However, social categorization also exaggerates similarities within groups and differences between groups, and hence it forms the basis for stereotyping.

"Doggie," says the 2-year-old, pointing to a horse. "Doggie," she says again as she spies a cat. This common mistake reflects an attempt at categorization, the process of recognizing individual objects as members of a category because they share certain features. Categorization is the process by which we group things or people, and it is an intrinsic part of the way we think about and try to understand the nonsocial world. In the same way, we divide the enormous number of individuals we meet into groups, lumping them together on the basis of their shared socially relevant features. Instead of individuals, they become men, women, Whites, Flemish, Jews, elderly persons, single mothers, or blue-collar workers. **Social categorization** occurs when people are perceived as members of social groups rather than unique individuals. Gender, ethnicity, and age are obvious bases for social categorization, but they are not the only attributes we use. Name tags, uniforms, or tools of the trade, for example, help us categorize people by occupation, whereas accent and speech dialect may identify an individual's nationality, regional background, or social class.

Why does social categorization occur? It is a useful, even essential tool—one that enables us to master our environment and function effectively in society (S. E. Taylor, 1981; Wilder, 1986). Think, for example, what you gain when you categorize the man standing by the library stacks as a librarian (Andersen & Klatsky, 1987; C. F. Bond & Brockett, 1987). First, you can infer that he will help you locate a book, check it out, and even keep the place quiet so you can study.

Social categorization. The process of identifying individual people as members of a social group because they share certain features that are typical of the group.

That is, knowing that this individual is a member of the group "librarians" tells you he has many characteristics shared by members of that group, even if they are not immediately obvious. Second, categorization allows you to ignore unimportant information. You can focus on what is relevant—his knowledge of books and where they are kept—without having to notice the color of his suit or wonder about his political leanings, food preferences, or lifestyle. Social categorization saves you the effort of having to deal with all the unique aspects of every individual you meet, when they are irrelevant to your interaction. Thus, categorization has a dual purpose: It provides useful information that cannot immediately be perceived, and it allows us to ignore unnecessary information (Bruner, 1957).

However, as victims of prejudice and discrimination know well, categorization has negative side effects. Social categorization makes all members of a group seem more similar to each other than they would be if they were not categorized (McGarty & Penny, 1988; Tajfel & Wilkes, 1963). This is true whether people sort others into groups on the basis of real differences or of arbitrary and trivial characteristics. The librarian who breeds cocker spaniels and the librarian who writes movie scripts seem more similar if we focus only on their shared group membership as librarians. Because of this increased similarity, people often overestimate group members' uniformity and overlook their diversity (G. W. Allport, 1954b; Brigham, 1971; Wilder, 1981). Thus, we go from a world in which some professors are forgetful to one in which all professors are absentminded, and we move beyond the news that a majority of the voters have cast their ballots for a right-wing Republican to the idea that the electorate is uniformly conservative (Allison & Messick, 1985).

Social categorization also exaggerates differences between groups. Thinking about Serena Williams and Andre Agassi as members of different gender or ethnic groups makes them seem more different than if we think of them both as world-champion tennis players. In fact, once we categorize people into groups, we become more aware of the characteristics that make one group different from another rather than of those that make them similar (Krueger & Rothbart, 1990). For example, in the United States, men are slightly more aggressive than women, yet impressions of gender groups vastly overestimate that small difference (C. L. Martin, 1987). These negative aspects of social categorization are presumably responsible for the fact that people who are most concerned with accurately categorizing others into groups also tend to be the most prejudiced against those groups (Blascovich, Wyer, Swart, & Kibler, 1997). Social categorization brings the world into sharper focus, but the exaggeration of similarities within groups and differences between groups is the price we pay for better resolution.

Forming Impressions of Groups: Establishing Stereotypes

There are many similarities between the ways we form impressions of individuals (as described in Chapter 3) and the ways we form impressions of groups. Yet there are also subtle differences that contribute to the special properties of group stereotypes (D. L. Hamilton & Sherman, 1996). To understand these special properties we must first answer two questions: What kinds of characteristics are included in stereotypes? What motivates people to form stereotypes?

The Content of Stereotypes

Many different kinds of characteristics are included in stereotypes, which can be positive or negative. Some stereotypes accurately reflect actual differences between groups, though in exaggerated form. Other stereotypes are completely inaccurate.

STEREOTYPES INCLUDE MANY TYPES OF CHARACTERISTICS. Walter Lippmann, a journalist who introduced the current meaning of the term stereotype in 1922, saw stereotypes as "pictures in the head," simplified mental images of what groups look like and what they do. Stereotypes often do incorporate physical appearance, typical interests and goals, preferred activities and occupations, and similar characteristics (Andersen & Klatzky, 1987; Brewer, 1988; Deaux & Lewis, 1983, 1984). Yet they usually go well beyond what groups look like or act like, to include the personality traits group members are believed to share and the positive or negative emotions or feelings group members arouse in others.

Early research on stereotypes found that college students held well-developed beliefs about the traits characterizing various ethnic groups (D. Katz & Braly, 1933). Considerable social pressure now exists against the public expression of such beliefs, but stereotypes have not disappeared. Do you have an image of what the "typical" college professor, accountant, or truck driver is like? Or, if you are an English Canadian, what is your view of French Canadians? Research suggests you may think of them as talkative, excitable, and proud (Gardner, Lalone, Nero, & Young, 1988), whereas French Canadians may describe you as educated, dominant, and ambitious (Aboud & Taylor, 1971). Russians view men of Caucasian nationalities—Georgians, Armenians, and others from the mountainous Caucasus region—as brazen, flashy, criminally inclined, and likely to accost respectable women in the street (Bohlen, 1992). According to a recent study of 300 U.S. communities, a majority of respondents believes that Blacks are less industrious, intelligent, and even patriotic than Whites, despite the dramatic overrepresentation of Blacks in the armed forces (*New York Times*, 1991).

Gender stereotypes are held even more strongly and confidently than ethnic stereotypes (Jackman & Senter, 1981). Most people describe women as sensitive, warm, dependent, and people-oriented, whereas men are considered dominant, independent, task-oriented, and aggressive (Ashmore, 1981; Spence, Deaux, & Helmreich, 1985). In fact, these gender stereotypes are found in similar forms among adults and children in North and South America, Asia, Africa, Europe, and Australia (J. E. Williams & Best, 1982).

Group stereotypes also incorporate the positive or negative emotions that group members arouse in others. For example, observers may regard members of one group with feelings of disgust and repulsion, a second group with fear and apprehension, and yet a third with respect and admiration (Fiske, Cuddy, Glick, & Xu, 2002; Mackie & Hamilton, 1993; E. R. Smith & Mackie, 2005). As a result, the first group may be labeled "disgusting," the second "hostile," and the third "admirable." As we will see shortly, our emotions can have important effects on our actual face-to-face interactions with members of stereotyped groups.

STEREOTYPES CAN BE EITHER POSITIVE OR NEGATIVE. As these examples make clear, stereotypes can include positive as well as negative characteristics (Rudman, 2005). You may wonder, though, why we should be concerned with positive beliefs about groups. After all, positive stereotypes may represent attributes, such as women's sensitivity, that group members themselves value and take pride in claiming. Still, even positive stereotypes can have negative consequences. Consider the belief, widespread among White American college students, that Asian Americans are straight-A students. One problem with that stereotype is its implication that everyone in the group is the same, and, as Chapter 4 showed, people generally prefer to be thought of in terms of their unique personal characteristics.

A second problem created by positive stereotypes is that they may set unrealizably high standards, so that an Asian-American student who gets average grades may be regarded as particularly dull (E. R. Smith & Ho, 1999). Finally, positive stereotypes may be part of an overall pattern of paternalistic attitudes toward a social group that actually reinforces the group's weakness and dependence. For example, a common set of beliefs about women includes the idea that they are pure and moral, delicate, and in need of men's protection. This pattern has been termed "benevolent sexism" (Glick & Fiske, 1996) because despite its apparent positive tone, people who hold this set of beliefs also tend to hold more hostile beliefs about women, such as that they attempt to manipulate men or are overly ready to claim discrimination. In fact, a study examining 19 nations shows that nations with higher average scores on benevolent sexism also tend to have more gender inequality, for example lower representation of women in powerful and well-paying jobs (Glick et al., 2000).

The psychological consequences of stereotyping are overestimated uniformity and rigid expectations, and the social translation of those consequences is prejudice and discrimination. This connection warrants our concern with stereotypes, regardless of whether they are positive or negative.

STEREOTYPES CAN BE ACCURATE OR INACCURATE. Perhaps even more important than whether stereotypes are positive or negative is the issue of whether they are accurate or inaccurate. No good yardstick is available for measuring the accuracy or inaccuracy of most stereotypes. There is no solid evidence, for example, on the relative frequency with which Georgian versus Russian men accost female passers-by. In addition, many concepts included in common stereotypes, for example, "clannish," "lazy," or "dirty," are so subjective as to be virtually meaningless.

Nevertheless, other aspects of stereotypes can be measured against "reality," and when they are, researchers find some to be accurate in direction if not in degree (Judd & Park, 2005; Jussim, 2005). This is not surprising since people often join together in clubs, political parties, professional associations, and other groups precisely because they share attitudes, feelings, and beliefs. This self-sorting process creates real group differences that may be reflected in stereotypes. Social customs also help create accurate stereotypes by prescribing what men and women, teenagers and retirees, and different racial groups can or should think, feel, and do. For example, as Table 5.1 shows, many gender stereotypes accurately describe the direction of differences that research has identified between men's behavior and women's behavior, although often in exaggerated form (Eagly, 1995; C. L. Martin, 1987). Similarly, Black and White college students' stereotypes of these two groups on attributes such as "dance well," "have high SAT math scores," and "self-centered" generally differ in the same direction as the group members' self-descriptions (C. S. Ryan, 1996).

Yet stereotypes can also be inaccurate. Consider an early study of Californians' stereotypes of Armenian Americans (LaPiere, 1936). The researcher compared official statistics on this small, segregated minority with popular stereotypes about

TABLE 5.1. Do Gender Stereotypes Reflect Actual Gender Differences? Results from Meta-Analyses

Gender stereotypes	Differences identified by research
Aggressiveness: (male) aggressive (female) soft-hearted	Men are more aggressive than women overall. The difference is larger for physical than for psychological aggression, and in situations in which aggression may be dangerous.
Influenceability: (male) independent (female) submissive, dependent	Women are more influenceable than men. The difference is larger for influence exerted by a group than for persuasive messages, and larger when the topic is regarded as "masculine."
Emotionality: (male) strong, tough (female) affectionate, anxious, emotional, sensitive, sentimental	Women are more nonverbally expressive and more nonverbally sensitive than men.
Leadership style: (male) autocratic, dominant (female) sensitive, emotional	As leaders, women are more democratic and men are more autocratic. The difference is larger in laboratory studies than in studies of leadership in real, ongoing organizations.

Sources: Stereotypes—J. E. Williams and Best (1982); Meta-analyses of research on gender differences—Eagly (1987), Eagly and Johnson (1990).

their behavior. Whereas Californians claimed that Armenians were constantly in trouble with the law, records showed that only about 1.5% had arrest records, compared with about 6% of the rest of the population. Similarly, Californians believed Armenians were more likely to be on welfare than working. In fact, only 1 of every 500 Armenians had applied for welfare, while the proportion for all Californians was five times higher. As another example, many people hold the stereotype that men are more effective leaders than are women. A recent meta-analysis of the research, in contrast, found no sex differences (or even small differences favoring women) in leadership effectiveness in business, educational, or government organizations (Eagly, Karau, & Makhijani, 1995).

Finally, there is one sense in which every stereotype is inaccurate: when it is viewed as applying to every member of a group. Not every French Canadian is talkative; not every woman is emotional; not every Asian American is a straight-A student. So it is an error for anyone to confidently assume that an individual member of a group possesses all of the group's stereotypic qualities.

But whatever their content—positive characteristics or negative ones, accurate descriptions or inaccurate distortions—stereotypes are a very real part of our daily lives. Each of us could reel off dozens of well-known stereotypes. Used-car dealers cannot be trusted; the French are great lovers. Nobel-winning physicist Leon Lederman, in advocating a TV series to humanize the image of physicists, said: "Scientists fall in love. But when was the last time you saw a physicist on TV galloping off into the sunset with a beautiful woman?" ("The Romance," 1995). Think about this for a moment. Did you notice Lederman's stereotypic assumption that a physicist is both male and heterosexual?

Why do people form and use stereotypes? Many different social motives have been suggested to account for them, including some people's need to resolve intense inner psychological conflicts as well as more everyday social and cognitive processes.

Seeking the Motives behind Stereotyping

Early theorists traced prejudice and extreme negative stereotypes to deep inner conflicts in a few disturbed individuals, rather than to more normal social motives such as mastery and connectedness.

Social psychologists' first systematic attempts to explain stereotypes and prejudice were triggered by the genocidal policies of the Nazis during the Third Reich (Ashmore & Del Boca, 1981). The unprecedented nature of Nazi prejudice and discrimination seemed to call for equally extreme explanations, and led to the idea that hatred of other groups is abnormal. Drawing on the work of Sigmund Freud, Theodor Adorno and his colleagues (Adorno, Frenkel-Brunswik, Levinson, & Sanford, 1950) argued that hatred for social groups, as well as the accompanying extreme negative stereotypes, has its roots in the inner conflicts of those with *authoritarian personalities*. These are people who cannot accept their own hostility, believe uncritically in the legitimacy of authority, and see their own inadequacies in others. The theorists argued that prejudice and rigid negative stereotypes against other groups serve to protect such individuals from an awareness of their painful inner conflicts and self-doubts. To understand Adorno's position, imagine, for example, an authoritarian athletic coach who doubts his own abilities but is not consciously aware of those feelings. His response to a lost game might be to see his players as clumsy and incompetent and to heap blame on them for their loss.

There is something psychologically satisfying about the authoritarian personality explanation of prejudice. We would like to see the mental and emotional deviance of certain individuals as responsible for prejudice, and the extreme stereotypes that accompany and justify that prejudice. These phenomena then become the exception rather than the rule, problems that *other* people have. Unfortunately, despite its appeal, this explanation does not stand up against the accumulated evidence (Altemeyer, 1981; Billig, 1976). Some individuals' extreme prejudice may in fact flow from deep inner conflicts (Esses, Haddock, & Zanna, 1993). However, as the examples cited at the beginning of the chapter suggest, prejudice and stereotypes seem to be the rule and not the exception. In fact, they are so pervasive that social psychologists have come to a more mundane, but also more consequential, conclusion: Prejudice and stereotypes most often grow out of the same social and cognitive processes that affect all aspects of our lives—such as our desires to understand our social environments and to connect with other people.

Motives for Forming Stereotypes: Mastery through Summarizing Personal Experiences

Stereotypes can be learned through personal experience with group members, but may still be biased because people pay attention to extremes or inaccurately perceive groups' characteristics. Social roles often shape group members' behaviors, but people attribute the behaviors to group members' inner characteristics. Emotions arising in interactions with group members can also become part of stereotypes. Finally, learning about groups can take place through media portrayals as well as firsthand experiences.

The world is getting smaller. Throughout Europe, boundaries between nations and peoples are becoming more permeable with increasing economic integration. Residents of Germany, France, and Italy are more often coming face to face with immigrants about whom they know little: Albanians, Mozambicans, Arabs, and Turks. Changes in U.S. immigration patterns have created a similar situation. The new family moving into the apartment across the hall might be Vietnamese Hmong, or the new sales representative joining your company might be from El Salvador.

As people encounter groups for the first time, their interactions with the newcomers can become the basis of stereotypes. In the absence of other information, idiosyncratic experiences with only one or two Hmong or Salvadorans are used to construct a personal stereotype of the group. And even if people interact with more than one member of an unfamiliar group with the genuine intention of forming an accurate, unbiased impression, the interactions themselves often generate exaggerated stereotypes (Rothbart, Dawes, & Park, 1984).

Surprisingly, encounters with individual group members can affect even well-established stereotypes. Henderson-King and Nisbett (1996) demonstrated such an effect by arranging for White students to observe a confederate, pretending to be another experimental participant, behave in a rude and hostile manner toward the experimenter. In some cases, the confederate was Black and in other cases White, while in a third condition no hostile interaction took place. The participants were then asked to conduct a mock interview of another student for a position of residence hall counselor. They were given a list of suggested questions and told that the interview could last up to 20 minutes. The student to be interviewed turned out to be Black. The participants who had previously seen another Black's negative behavior ended the interview much sooner (after an average of just 8 minutes) compared to those who had seen a White behaving in the same obnoxious fashion or who had seen no negative behavior at all (about 10½ minutes). Evidently, a single group member's negative acts can activate negative thoughts and feelings about the entire group, even when the group is familiar. Perhaps this same process is responsible for the finding that exposure to rap music expressing violent and anti-female sentiments, performed by Black artists, made students more negative toward Blacks in general (Rudman & Lee, 2002).

Fortunately, bringing to mind positively evaluated group members can make feelings about a group more positive as well. Galen Bodenhausen and his colleagues (Bodenhausen, Schwarz, Bless, & Waenke, 1995) demonstrated that when people have recently thought about well-liked Blacks (such as Bill Cosby or Oprah Winfrey), their opinions on issues related to Blacks' position in American society become more positive. Findings like these suggest that positive or negative impressions of individual group members form an important part of people's overall impressions of a group (E. R. Smith & Zárate, 1992).

But this fact raises a puzzle. Why do firsthand observations of individual group members—seemingly the most trustworthy form of information—often lead to stereotypes of their groups that are biased and exaggerated? There are several reasons.

PEOPLE NOTICE SOME MEMBERS MORE THAN OTHERS. Next time you are at a party, stand back a little and glance around the room. Whom are you most likely to notice, even in passing? The guest in the tuxedo, when everyone else is wearing blue jeans? Or the very tall woman standing over by the window? If these people stand out, it is because our attention is typically drawn to what is unusual, unexpected, or salient (L. Z. McArthur, 1981). For this reason, distinctive individuals can have a disproportionate impact on the formation of group stereotypes, as Myron Rothbart and his colleagues (Rothbart, Fulero, Jensen, Howard, & Birrel, 1978) demonstrated. One group of participants in their experiment read a list of the actions of 50 men, 10 of whom had committed nonviolent crimes. A second group of participants read the same list, but the criminal actions of the 10 men were violent and salient. The participants were later asked how many men from each group had committed crimes. Compared with those exposed to the nonviolent crimes, participants exposed to the violent crimes thought that more group members had committed crimes.

SOME INFORMATION ATTRACTS MORE ATTENTION THAN OTHER INFORMATION. Even if a few extremes stand out, why do our impressions of groups remain unchanged when we encounter other group members whose appearance or actions are quite ordinary? The answer is that biases in processing lead us to form an association between unusual or distinctive characteristics and rare or infrequently encountered groups. These processes can operate even if we have no prior stereotype of a group, so they can generate a stereotype more or less out of thin air.

Suppose you move to a new city and discover that the residents there classify themselves as Eastsiders or Westsiders, but you have no idea what characteristics are associated with these categories. As you read the "Police Blotter" column in the local newspaper, you notice that more Eastsiders than Westsiders are mentioned. Most members of each group are named for innocent reasons, such as reporting a mysteriously broken car window or having a cat stranded in a tree, but about a third of each group are named as crime suspects. What impressions would you form of the two groups?

According to David Hamilton and Robert Gifford (1976), you might overestimate the incidence of crime among the Westsiders, the smaller group. Your overestimate would illustrate the creation of an *illusory correlation*, a perceived association between two characteristics that are not actually related. In a demonstration of the illusory correlation, Hamilton and Gifford asked participants to read a series of sentences, each describing a desirable or undesirable behavior performed by a member of Group A or Group B. For both groups, more desirable behaviors were reported than undesirable ones: The ratio was about two positive behaviors for every negative one. Overall, participants saw more sentences about Group A than about Group B. When participants were asked their impressions of the groups, they liked Group B less. They had formed an illusory correlation by perceiving a link between the two relatively infrequent and distinctive characteristics: undesirable behavior, and membership in the group about which they had read less often.

What explains this surprising bias in our perceptions of groups? Researchers have found that when something occurs infrequently, it becomes distinctive and people pay attention to it. When one of the behavior descriptions involves two distinctive characteristics occurring together—a Group B member doing something antisocial—it really stands out. These behaviors may attract special attention when people encounter them (D. L. Hamilton & Sherman, 1989). Or they may have a disproportionate impact when people combine what they know into judgments about the groups (Fiedler, 1991; E. R. Smith, 1991). Either way, these doubly distinctive behaviors have the greatest impact on the impressions we form of groups. So suppose that people have only limited encounters with members of a group that is numerically small or segregated. Even if criminal acts are equally rare among members of a large group and those of the small group, observers may form an illusory correlation, judging the small group to be more criminal than the larger group.

SOCIAL ROLES TRIGGER CORRESPONDENCE BIASES. Regardless of how often we encounter a group, what we see the group doing has a big impact on our impressions. Yet even this kind of firsthand observation can lead to biased stereotypes when a group's social role shapes the behavior that can be observed. Consider a stereotype that the citizens of Moscow seem to have developed recently. In increasing numbers, farmers from the sunny lands of Azerbaijan, Georgia, Dagestan, and other regions of the Caucasus are setting up stalls in major Russian cities to sell fresh fruits, vegetables, chickens, and other goods that are scarce or unavailable in ordinary food stores. But far from welcoming this new source of food, Russians are turning against the Caucasians, resentful of their apparent prosperity and the high prices they charge. Russians have overturned Caucasians' stalls in the markets and scrawled slogans like "Russia for the Russians" on walls. One Russian woman commented, "In my view, frankly, they deserve to get beaten up. These southerners are so brazen that it gets to the point where an average Russian man can't take it anymore" (Bohlen, 1992).

This upsurge in prejudice based on stereotypes of the Caucasians as brazen and dishonest may involve social roles. Most Russians interact with Caucasians only in their role of produce vendor, and the Caucasians' behavior is constrained by that occupational role. Because the Russians remain largely oblivious to the effects that the role has on the farmers' behavior, they form a stereotype that reflects the characteristics of the role. Of course, Russian vegetable buyers are not unique in this regard. Most of us form our impressions of doctors by watching a doctor care for us or for a loved one, or of ministers or rabbis by watching one perform a religious ceremony. Our stereotypes of particular groups typically reflect the social roles occupied by those groups (D. T. Campbell, 1967; Eagly, 1987). Consider the following facts.

- In the Middle Ages, money handling was one of very few occupations open to Jews, who soon came to be seen as excelling in this occupation for reasons of personality, that is, because they were inherently "sharp" and "frugal." These same traits have been attributed to many other groups: the Chinese in Indonesia and Malaysia, Muslim merchants in eastern and southern Africa, Korean merchants in Black neighborhoods in the United States, and now produce sellers from the Caucasus in Russia. What do these wildly diverse groups have in common? They all fill the same "middleman" economic niche in their societies (Pettigrew, 1968). Apparently the role produces the assumed personality characteristics, rather than the other way around.

- In virtually every society, socioeconomically disadvantaged groups, regardless of their ethnicity, are seen as ignorant, lazy, loud, dirty, and carefree. In the United States this stereotype has been applied to a number of groups in the last century: first to poor Irish immigrants, then to the first wave of Italian immigrants, and more recently to Puerto Rican and Mexican Americans (Pettigrew, 1968; L. Ross & Nisbett, 1990). As the economic position of a group rises, stereotypes about them change and, like hand-me-down clothing, the lower-class stereotype is passed on to some new and less fortunate group.

- Stereotypes adapt rapidly as a group's roles change. Such changes are especially obvious in times of war or hardship, as we shall see in Chapter 13. As peace is replaced by war, the Germans become "Huns" and the Japanese

"Japs." And as war is replaced by peace, German ruthlessness becomes German efficiency, and Japanese cunning becomes Japanese ingenuity.

As all these facts suggest, stereotypes do not reflect what groups are actually like. Instead, they reflect the roles groups play in society relative to the perceiver (Fiske and others, 2002). The correspondence bias leads people to see behavior as reflecting others' inner dispositions, even if roles or situational contingencies truly cause the behavior. As can be seen in Figure 5.1, the outcome is the formation of a stereotype.

How and why people fall prey to the correspondence bias when making inferences was discussed in Chapter 3, pages 70 to 72.

SOCIAL ROLES AND GENDER STEREOTYPES. Males' and females' differing social roles also contribute to gender stereotypes (Eagly, 1987). (Look back at Table 5.1 for some examples.) The process works like this: Virtually all societies assign men and women to somewhat different roles and occupations (Wood & Eagly, 2002). In Western cultures, for example, men are more often employed outside the home, while women are more likely to be responsible for home and family. Employee roles demand the kinds of traits—task-orientation, assertiveness, rationality—that characterize the traditional male stereotype. In contrast, the role of homemaker requires those qualities—sensitivity, warmth, gentleness—that characterize the female stereotype (Eagly & Steffen, 1984). Thus, men and women tend to act in ways that are appropriate for their roles. And if observers note those differences and fail to make allowances for the effects of roles, they may conclude that men are by nature task oriented, and women interpersonally oriented.

A clever laboratory study by Curt Hoffman and Nancy Hurst (1990) demonstrated this process. Students read descriptions of fictitious groups of "Orinthians" and "Ackmians" who supposedly inhabit a distant planet. Most Orinthians were described as involved in child care, whereas Ackmians were mainly employed outside the home. All child-care workers (regardless of group membership) were described as typically nurturant, affectionate, and gentle, and all employees as

FIGURE 5.1 Social roles shape stereotypes

Social, cultural, economic, political, and historical factors create social roles.

↓

Social roles are assigned to groups.
Caucasian farmers sell produce in Russian cities.

↓

Group members perform role-appropriate behaviors.
Farmers charge as much as they can, and some become prosperous.

↓

Through correspondence bias, role-associated behaviors are attributed to personality characteristics.
These farmers are greedy and flashy people.

↓

Stereotype of group forms.
Caucasians are by nature greedy and flashy.

■ The roles allocated to a particular group influence group members' behavior. Based on that behavior, observers are likely to be influenced by the correspondence bias—ignoring the effects of the roles and attributing the behavior to the group members' personality characteristics. These characteristics then become part of the stereotype of the group.

typically competitive and ambitious. However, participants asked to guess these creatures' typical psychological characteristics attached traits to the groups rather than to the roles, and assumed that Orinthians (not child-care workers) were nurturant and Ackmians (not employees) were competitive (see Figure 5.2). That is, each group was seen as having psychological characteristics appropriate for the group's typical role. Once the stereotype was formed, participants applied it even to individual group members whose occupations clashed with the stereotype: they saw an employed Ackmian as more competitive and ambitious than an employed Orinthian. This finding suggests that the different typical social roles of men and women contribute to shaping earthly gender stereotypes. The effect is not inevitable, however. Mark Schaller and his colleagues (Schaller, Asp, Rosell, & Heim, 1996) found that people can be trained to avoid these inferential errors.

BETWEEN-GROUP INTERACTIONS GENERATE EMOTION. Roles are not the only things that shape and constrain people's interactions. Whenever people move outside their own group, they enter unknown social territory. This happens, for example, when people reside in a foreign country, rise from the blue-collar ranks to middle management, or encounter ethnic newcomers in their neighborhoods. Feelings of uncertainty and concern often arise when people interact with novel groups, and these feelings can influence the stereotypes people form.

Dutch adults described just these feelings when asked about their everyday dealings with Surinamers, Turks, and Moroccans, groups that recently have immigrated in large numbers to the Netherlands (Dijker, 1987). According to the respondents, interactions with these groups produced anxiety, and the interactions with Moroccans and Turks—the groups culturally most different from the

FIGURE 5.2   Roles and stereotypes on a distant planet

■ Participants viewed group members who performed their group's typical roles as possessing psychological characteristics appropriate for that role. They then generalized those characteristics to all group members. Thus, they saw an Ackmian engaged in child care as more assertive than an Orinthian city worker. (Based on Hoffman & Hurst, 1990.)

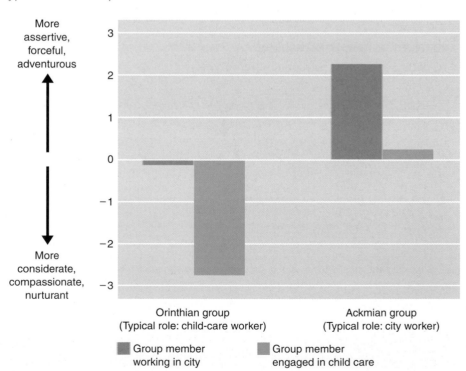

native-born Dutch—also provoked feelings of irritation. North American college students responded the same way when asked to imagine what emotions they might experience in a casual conversation with someone of a different race (Vanman & Miller, 1993). The most frequently reported emotion was irritation, followed closely by dislike, apprehension, and anxiety. Other research shows that the presence of another man they know to be homosexual can make heterosexual men nervous and uncomfortable (L. A. Jackson & Sullivan, 1989).

Why are interactions across group lines so often tinged with arousal and anxiety? In intergroup interactions, ignorance is not bliss. For example, Walter Stephan and Cookie Stephan (1985) found that the less Asian Americans and Whites in Hawaii knew about each other's groups, the more anxious and irritated they felt when they met. The same researchers obtained similar results when they investigated interactions between Latinos and Whites in New Mexico. Not knowing what to do or say and not knowing how another person will react usually creates awkwardness, frustration, and impatience. Yet, with only 51% of Whites working with members of other races and only 47% socializing with members of other races outside of work, ignorance and unfamiliarity continue to be the rule (*Newsweek*, 1991).

When even relatively benign cross-group interactions cause anxiety and irritation, imagine the strength of emotion that is generated when groups threaten one another, compete for scarce resources, and violate one another's values (Neuberg & Cottrell, 2002; Stephan & Renfro, 2002). In these circumstances, powerful emotions become associated with group encounters, and anxiety, irritation, and awkwardness are soon overwhelmed by fear, anger, frustration, and revulsion. The emotions provoked by uncomfortable intergroup encounters then become an integral part of a stereotype (Devos, Silver, Mackie, & Smith, 2002; Olson & Fazio, 2002; E. R. Smith, 1993). When interaction with a group is repeatedly accompanied by negative emotion, bad feelings are soon transferred to the group itself through the process of *classical conditioning* or *evaluative conditioning*. Evaluative conditioning occurs when a person or object that has been repeatedly paired with a particular emotion begins itself to elicit the emotion. After several uncomfortable interactions, the emotions arising from the encounter become associated with the group, so that seeing group members, hearing the group mentioned, or even thinking about the group will itself reactivate the emotion. An individual who repeatedly experiences disgust, fear, or hatred in interactions with group members eventually will view the group as *intrinsically* disgusting, threatening, or loathsome.

More of the factors that increase the emotional intensity of prejudice become obvious in Chapter 6, pages 206 to 209, and Chapter 13, pages 500 to 503.

Of course, being ill at ease is hardly the majority's prerogative. On the contrary, finding oneself on alien social territory is both a more common and a more negative experience for minority group members than for majority group members (Lord & Saenz, 1985). Anyone stands out in such circumstances, and the smaller the minority, the more its members stand out (Mullen, 1987), and therefore the greater their discomfort.

One potential benefit of school desegregation is that it provides an increased range of informal contexts in which members of different groups can meet with ease. Unfortunately, however, desegregated classrooms often empty out into resegregated cafeterias and playgrounds, where members of each group congregate to the exclusion of others (Schofield, 1978). Perhaps one reason for this voluntary self-segregation is people's desire to minimize the discomfort of being in different social surroundings: Being constantly on one's guard can take its toll. In recent years, historically Black colleges have experienced a surge in applications from Black students, including many of the nation's very best students who could attend

■ **Learning stereotypes from those you love.** Children can learn stereotypes and prejudice by imitating those they trust and by conforming to the norms of the groups they belong to. This can happen long before they understand the consequences of such beliefs.

any college they chose (Radin, 1992). The main reason seems to be the students' desire not to stand out as different, to be able to relax and focus on studies in an emotionally supportive environment.

LEARNING STEREOTYPES FROM THE MEDIA. People's experience with members of particular social groups comes not only from direct personal interactions: we also learn about others from art, literature, popular music, television, and film. Not surprisingly, media portrayals of groups often reflect stereotypes that are deeply ingrained in a culture (Jost & Hamilton, 2005). This pattern is found in today's rap music and other forms of confrontational art (Nields, 1991), but it also occurred in William Shakespeare's plays, written over 350 years ago. Othello is called "thick lips" because he is Black. Shylock is spat on because he is a Jew. Lady Macbeth wishes to be unsexed because women are weak. Richard III attributes his evil to his physical deformity, and King Lear is reviled because he is old.

Today's cultural medium of choice is television, of course. On an average day, North American children watch 3 hours of television, and during those hours children receive a mixed message. Prime-time entertainment television has, for example, reversed the traditional invisibility of people of color. *The Cosby Show*, which portrayed the family life of a Black doctor and lawyer and their children, ranked as the most popular show in the United States for more than 5 years. However, news and documentary programs send different messages. One study of Philadelphia local TV news found that in comparison to actual crime statistics, Blacks are overrepresented as crime suspects while Whites are more often portrayed as crime victims (Romer, Jamieson, & de Coteau, 1998). And Blacks remain nearly invisible in major national magazines, although they make up over 15% of all magazine readers. One study of advertisements appearing in 27 national magazines between 1988 and 1991 found that only about 3% of the models were Black, and most of those were depicted as athletes, musicians, or objects of charity (Rothenberg, 1991). In 2002, Halle Berry became the first Black woman to appear on the cover of *Cosmopolitan* magazine in over a decade (Carr, 2002).

How norms form, and why we generally go along with our group's norms, are considered in detail in Chapters 9 and 10.

Media portrayals of other groups are no better. The elderly are generally depicted in highly stereotypic terms as frail, unattractive, and useless (A. Williams & Giles, 1998). Asian Americans appear frequently in television ads (in over 8% of commercials, compared to their 3.6% of the U.S. population), but are usually cast in stereotypic ways. Consistent with the "work ethic" stereotype, Asian Americans are generally portrayed in business settings and only rarely in home or family settings (C. R. Taylor & Stern, 1997). Differences between Chinese, Japanese, and Koreans are minimized or ignored. Latinos fare equally poorly. Though they constitute 9% of the U.S. population, they were only 1% of characters portrayed in the 1992 TV season, and of these characters, 16% committed crimes, twice the percentage of other groups ("Study Shows," 1994). All in all, media stereotyping and underrepresentation send a strongly biased message.

☐ **GENDER STEREOTYPES AND THE MEDIA.** Media messages about women can be summed up in a single word: contradictory. On the one hand, television programming increasingly has portrayed women in realistic or counterstereotypic roles. Popular dramatic and comedy series often feature strong female characters who are competent, assertive, independent, and successful in their careers. However, during the commercial breaks a different type of message comes through. Analyses of French-language television ads in Quebec and radio ads in Australia replicate findings from the U.S.: Commercials typically reinforce gender stereotypes (Dalcourt, 1996; Hurtz & Durkin, 1997). For example, male voice-overs predominate when the voice of an "expert" is required. Men and women generally sell gender-stereotypic products: Men sell lawnmowers and computers, women sell shoes and toilet bowl cleaners. Photographs as well as ads offer different portrayals of men and women: examination of magazines in 12 countries revealed that men's faces were much more likely to be featured prominently than were women's faces (D. Archer, Iratani, Kimes, & Barrios, 1983; Nigra, Hill, Gelbein, & Clark, 1988). This difference may be due to the cultural concern with women's whole bodies, which are more likely to be shown than men's bodies. In addition, stereotypically male traits such as intelligence and rationality may be symbolized and reinforced by photos of the head (D. Archer and others, 1983). But children's cartoons probably represent the pinnacle of gender stereotypes. In the United States (T. L. Thompson & Zerbinos, 1995) and in Hong Kong (Chu & McIntyre, 1995), cartoons consistently show boys as active, rough, and often violent, while girls are shown as home-oriented, concerned with their appearance, and interested in boys.

Do biased media portrayals of men and women matter? Experimental studies suggest that the answer is yes. Florence Geis and her colleagues (Geis, Brown, Jennings, & Porter, 1984; Jennings, Geis, & Brown, 1980) showed college women one of two sets of television commercials. One set depicted men and women in traditional roles, with the woman playing an alluring and subordinate role. In the other set the roles were reversed, with the man shown as subordinate and seductive. The young women who watched the traditional commercials later expressed lower self-confidence, less independence, and fewer career aspirations than did those who watched the nontraditional commercials. Meta-analyses summarizing many studies support the conclusion that media content increases viewers' acceptance of gender stereotypes (Herrett-Skjellum & Allen, 1996). If media portrayals can subtly influence viewers' thinking about themselves as men and women, it is undoubtedly true that they become part of our thinking about members of other groups as well.

Motives for Forming Stereotypes: Connectedness to Others

Social learning contributes to stereotypes. Stereotypes and discriminatory behavior are often accepted and endorsed as right and proper by members of a particular group. Group members learn such stereotypes from family and peers. As stereotypes are communicated, they may become even stronger.

Stereotypes can be formed as summaries of our experiences with members of social groups, and as we have seen, whether those experiences are direct or through the media they can give rise to biased perceptions. But our desire to master the world by summarizing our concrete experiences is not the only motive behind the formation of stereotypes. Stereotypes also serve our desire to establish connections with similar others, when we adopt the same stereotypes that those others hold. For this reason, stereotypes often come to us ready-made and prepackaged, and we learn them in particular social, economic, cultural, religious, and political contexts (Stangor & Schaller, 1996).

LEARNING STEREOTYPES FROM OTHERS. Parents, teachers, and peers offer us our first lessons about group differences. By age 5, for example, most children have begun to develop clear-cut racial attitudes (Goodman, 1952; Rosenfield & Stephan, 1981). Parents and teachers do not have to teach hate explicitly, although they sometimes do. Children can pick up stereotypes and prejudice simply by observing and imitating their elders: listening to disparaging group labels or derogatory jokes that elicit approving laughter, following family rules against playing with those "other" children.

Parents' and teachers' words and deeds reflect **social norms**, generally accepted ways of thinking, feeling, or behaving that people in a group agree on and endorse as right and proper (Thibaut & Kelley, 1959). When stereotypes and prejudices are deeply embedded in the social norms of a culture, people learn them naturally as part of growing up (Crandall & Stangor, 2005). In fact, those who adhere most closely to their culture's social norms also show the most prejudice (Pettigrew, 1958). In a recent study students rated numerous groups (such as ethnic and religious groups, political groups, as well as other groups such as murderers and thieves) in terms of how socially acceptable it would be to hold negative views of the groups. They also rated their own personal views of the same groups. Answers to these two questions were almost perfectly related, suggesting that people's actual opinions of the groups were strongly driven by their perceptions of social norms—that is, by the acceptability of prejudice against each group (Crandall & Eshleman, 2003). A study by Stangor and others (Stangor, Sechrist, & Jost, 2001) also showed that learning about others' prejudiced opinions shapes perceptions of social norms, and in turn makes people more prejudiced themselves.

SOCIAL COMMUNICATION OF STEREOTYPES. Stereotypes may even become stronger through the process of social communication. When people form impressions of a group by being told about them secondhand, their impressions are more stereotypic than those of people who learn about the group through firsthand experience (Thompson, Judd, & Park, 2000). These secondhand impressions, once formed, remain highly stereotypic even after later direct experience with the group itself. Discussion of group members' behaviors among several people also tends to make their impressions more stereotypic (Brauer, Judd, & Jacquelin, 2001). Although stereotypes are sometimes communicated quite directly and explicitly, they can be conveyed more subtly as well. For example, racist or sexist jokes indicate that prejudiced attitudes toward the target group are socially acceptable, which tends to make those who hear the jokes more prejudiced themselves (Ford, 2000).

Motives for Forming Stereotypes: Justifying Inequalities

The stereotypes prevalent in a society often serve to justify existing social inequalities. They do so by portraying groups as deserving their social roles and positions on the basis of their own characteristics.

Social norms. Generally accepted ways of thinking, feeling, or behaving that people in a group agree on and endorse as right and proper.

Our direct or indirect experiences with members of other groups, and the beliefs and norms prevalent in our own groups, usually work together to reinforce each other and, ultimately, to reinforce the perception that members of different groups are naturally suited for the roles they play. Most cultures, for example, assign nurturing roles to women, so perceivers see women as "naturally" nurturing. As we have seen, this perception reflects the correspondence bias: People fail to realize that women's roles demand nurturing behaviors, and so they attribute the behaviors to women's personalities

(Eagly, 1987). The stereotype that women are "naturally" suited to nurturing is further strengthened as people learn what society teaches about women. This stereotype soon becomes the basis for an inference with even more serious consequences. The belief that women have the right stuff to care for others then becomes a justification for retaining them in that role: They have the perfect qualifications. Most stereotypes, like this example, justify groups' existing places and roles in society as right, natural, and inevitable (Jost & Banaji, 1994; Yzerbyt, Rocher, & Schadron, 1997).

Every society maintains inequalities that benefit some groups and hurt others. In Taiwan, people from mainland China who fled the Communists in 1949 still dominate native Taiwanese. Gaps in income and opportunity between men and women and between most Whites and people of color persist in the United States. As stereotypes reflecting these differences have developed, they have justified and rationalized the underlying inequalities (Pettigrew, 1980). For example, historically, women and people of color have often been viewed in ways that justified their treatment as childlike, unintelligent, and weak, and thus in need of direction and guidance (Hacker, 1951). And in fact, people who believe inequality is natural and right—views that are more often found among members of dominant groups, such as Whites and males—are particularly likely to be prejudiced against others (Pratto, Sidanius, Stallworth, & Malle, 1994).

Why do we slide so quickly down the slope from behavior to stereotype to justification of inequality? One reason may be the widespread belief that the world is just and that people therefore deserve what they get and get what they deserve. This *just-world belief* (Lerner, 1980) leads people to blame victims for their misfortunes. This effect was demonstrated by one study in which students watched a woman apparently receive painful electric shocks (Lerner & Simmons, 1966). Did they react with sympathy toward this unfortunate victim? On the contrary, most derogated the victim, concluding that she must have done something to deserve her suffering. Rape victims, victims of spouse abuse, and people with AIDS often suffer the same fate (Carli & Leonard, 1989; Hunter & Ross, 1991), as do those whose social roles confine them to subordinate positions. It is no surprise, then, that people who believe more strongly that the world is just also tend to be prejudiced against gays and other groups (Crandall & Cohen, 1994). It is comforting to believe that bad things happen only to bad people: that AIDS is a punishment for taking drugs or for a gay lifestyle, or that poor people are lazy and shiftless (Furnham & Gunter, 1984; R. Robinson & Bell, 1978). Believing that groups' positions in society are somehow deserved, fitting, or justified lets us off the hook morally, as Martin Luther King (1967) observed so astutely:

> *It seems to be a fact of life that human beings cannot continue to do wrong without eventually reaching out for some rationalization to clothe their acts in the garments of righteousness. And so, with the growth of slavery, men had to convince themselves that a system which was so economically profitable was morally justifiable. The attempt to give moral sanction to a profitable system gave birth to the doctrine of white supremacy.* (p. 72)

Bit by bit, our personal experiences and the influence of others help us construct a coherent impression of the social groups around us. As Figure 5.3 shows, the information we weave together is a product both of our own personal interactions and of the influence of others, and biases can enter into the process in several ways. And as we will see in Chapter 6, our own group memberships provide additional scope for stereotypes and biases in the ways we view others. For all these reasons

FIGURE 5.3   Multiple sources of stereotypes

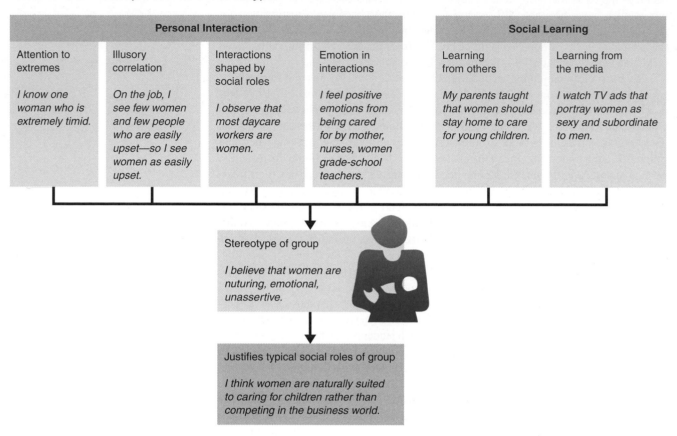

■ People's impressions of groups are formed by their personal interactions with group members and by what they learn from others. Multiple sources of information often converge to support a stereotype that justifies the social roles typically held by group members.

group impressions are rarely just neutral descriptions, but often have a strong evaluative tinge. When we think of men as aggressive, of immigrants as cliquish, or of Scots as thrifty, those terms have evaluative implications, whether positive or negative, mild or extreme. Moreover, stereotypes often incorporate emotions we associate with groups. We see some groups not only as hostile, stubborn, aggressive, and deviant but also as frightening, frustrating, threatening, and repulsive. Once these beliefs and feelings are firmly established, they take on a life of their own, provoking prejudiced judgments and directing discriminatory behavior.

Using Stereotypes: From Preconceptions to Prejudice

Stephen Carter, a professor at Yale Law School who is Black, described the following encounter at a conference.

A dapper, buttoned-down young white man glanced at my nametag, evidently ignored the name but noted the school, and said, "If you're at Yale, you must know this Carter fellow who wrote that article about thus-and-so." Well, yes, I admitted. I did know that Carter fellow slightly. An awkward pause ensued. And then the young man, realizing his error, apologized . . . . "Oh," he said, "you're Carter."
(Carter, 1991, p. 56)

The young man's assumptions about race and academic excellence had been embarrassingly revealed. As Carter notes, "Since this young man liked the article, its author could not, in his initial evaluation, have been a person of color. He had not even conceived of that possibility, or he would have glanced twice at my name tag" (p. 57).

Once a stereotype exists, it influences what people think and how they behave toward members of stereotyped groups. In fact, stereotype effects are so pervasive that they can even affect our judgments of inanimate objects! When computers are programmed to "talk" with synthesized male voices, people take their evaluations more seriously than if they use female voices; on matters related to relationships, people prefer advice given by a computer in a female voice. This is true even when people are specifically told that a male programmer created the software in the first place (Reeves & Nass, 1996). Stereotypes can have this impact whether we are making snap judgments of others quickly and with minimal thought—like the young man at the conference—or making considered judgments involving extensive processing of information.

Activation of Stereotypes

> Once established, a stereotype can be activated by obvious cues, use of group labels, or the presence of a group member, especially a minority in a social situation. Some stereotypes are learned so well and used so often that their content comes to mind automatically.

A stereotype can influence judgments or actions only if it comes to mind. Does this happen frequently? You bet it does! The very first thing we notice about other people is often their group memberships, and once a category is activated, the associated stereotype comes to mind as well. In fact, some categories seem so important that we use them to classify people even when they appear irrelevant to the social context. Consider the first thing most people ask the parents of a newborn: Is it a girl or a boy? In almost every social situation, perceivers note general categories like gender, race, and age (Brewer, 1988; Stangor, Lynch, Duan, & Glass, 1992).

WHAT ACTIVATES STEREOTYPES? The more obvious and salient the cues to category membership, the more likely it is that the category and its related stereotypes will come to mind. Indeed, women with a highly feminine physical appearance and dress are perceived as also having highly feminine natures (Deaux & Lewis, 1984; Forsyth, Schlenker, Leary, & McCown, 1985). The deliberate use of pejorative group labels, ethnic or sexist jokes, or slurs can bring stereotypes to a listener's mind at once (Ford, 2000; Greenberg & Pyszczynski, 1985).

A category often becomes particularly salient when only a single member of the group is present. Consider an increasingly common occurrence: A woman is

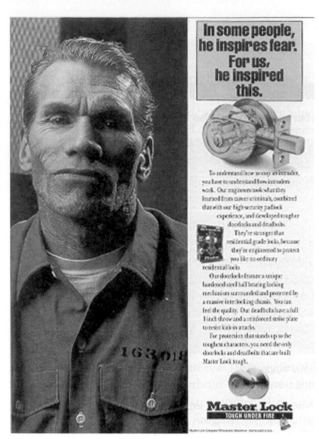

In some people,
he inspires fear.
For us,
he inspired
this.

To understand how wrong criminals,
you have to understand how intruders
work. Our engineers took what they
learned from career criminals, combined
that with our high-security padlock
experience, and developed tougher
doorlocks and deadbolts.

They're stronger than
residential grade locks, because
they're engineered to protect
you like no ordinary
residential lock.

Our doorlocks feature a unique
hardened steel ball bearing locking
mechanism surrounded and protected by
a massive interlocking chassis. You can
feel the quality. Our deadbolts have a full
1-inch throw and a reinforced strike plate
to resist kick-in attacks.

For protection that stands up to the
toughest characters, you need the only
doorlocks and deadbolts that are built
Master Lock tough.

Master Lock
TOUGH UNDER FIRE

■ **Stereotypes at work**. This model's "hardened criminal" appearance is calculated to activate stereotype-consistent information. If the image successfully instils fear in us and thus makes the need for protection salient, we may well be inspired to head for the hardware store, and the advertisement will have achieved its goal.

In Chapter 3, pages 67 to 68, we described evidence that words that could not be consciously read nevertheless could bring related beliefs to mind, without the perceiver's awareness.

hired as a member of a previously all-male work crew, or a single Latino student joins a class or seminar. Because of their salience, such solo appearances draw much more attention, and the extra attention usually leads to particularly stereotypic perceptions. A solo male seems more masculine and a solo female more feminine than they would in a more evenly split group (S. E. Taylor, 1981; S. E. Taylor, Fiske, Etcoff, & Ruderman, 1978). Field studies in work organizations have recorded the same effects (Kanter, 1977). "Token" integration of a workplace or other social setting—admitting a single member of a previously excluded group—can thus increase the likelihood of stereotyped thinking rather than decrease it.

STEREOTYPES CAN BE ACTIVATED AUTOMATICALLY. If reminders of group membership surround us, the ease with which race, gender, age, or other categories come to mind can set off a vicious cycle. The more often a category is used, the more accessible it becomes; the more accessible it is, the more it is used (Higgins, 1996a; Stangor and others, 1992). In fact, a stereotype sometimes becomes so well learned and so often used that its activation becomes automatic. Cues that relate to group membership can bring stereotypic information to mind, even if the perceiver does not consciously notice the group membership at all!

One recent study by Bernd Wittenbrink, Charles Judd, and Bernadette Park (2001) supports the view that stereotypes can be automatically activated. The researchers set out to determine whether a very brief exposure to the word BLACK or WHITE, so brief that the word was not consciously seen, could make words related to Black or White stereotypes more accessible, speeding responses to those stereotypic words. Their study involved a number of trials. On each trial, students saw XXXXX on a computer screen, followed by either a word or a nonsense letter string. Some of the words were related to Black or White stereotypes. Participants had to press one of two keys to indicate whether or not the letters on the screen spelled an English word. Unknown to the participants, on some trials the word BLACK or WHITE was also flashed on the screen before the XXXXX—so briefly that it could not be consciously registered. However, as studies we have already described show, such words can still act as a prime. Results showed that participants responded to negative Black stereotypic words (such as poor, dishonest, and violent) more quickly on trials where the word BLACK had been flashed as a prime. The same was true of positive White stereotypic words (such as intelligent, successful, and wealthy) on trials with WHITE primes. This effect was stronger for participants who had been identified (by separate questionnaires) as relatively high in anti-Black prejudice.

These results show that group labels automatically activate group stereotypes, at least among highly prejudiced participants. This process would increase those individuals' readiness to interpret ambiguous behaviors as related to the stereotypic traits. The automatic nature of this stereotype activation is demonstrated by the occurrence of the effect when the participants could not consciously read the prime words. Other studies have obtained similar results (Blair & Banaji, 1996; Lepore & Brown, 1997; Macrae, Bodenhausen, Milne, & Calvini, 1999).

FIGURE 5.4   Facial electromyography (EMG): An indirect measure of attitudes

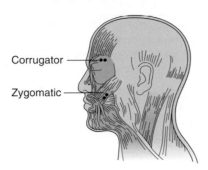

Corrugator

Zygomatic

■ When people react positively to an attitude object, activity in the zygomatic muscles increases, whereas negative responses are accompanied by increased activity in the corrugator muscles. Although this activity cannot be observed with the naked eye, it can be measured by electrodes placed at the indicated positions. (Adapted from Petty & Cacioppo, 1986, p. 42.)

FEELINGS ABOUT GROUPS CAN BE ACTIVATED AUTOMATICALLY. Can general positive or negative feelings about a group, as well as the specific trait information contained in stereotypes, also be activated automatically? One approach to this question involves physiological measurement (Cacioppo, Petty, Losch, & Kim, 1986). Facial electromyography (EMG) measures electrical activity in the facial muscles that create expressions such as smiles or frowns, as shown in Figure 5.4. Electrical activity can be measured even when changes in facial expressions are not visible, and evidence suggests that these measurements can accurately assess people's automatically activated positive or negative feelings about social groups (Vanman, Paul, Ito, & Miller, 1997). However, this approach requires specialized equipment, a carefully controlled environment, and extremely cooperative research participants.

Another approach to this question uses methods similar to the study by Wittenbrink and his colleagues (2001). Russell Fazio and his colleagues (Fazio, Jackson, Dunton, & Williams, 1995) used a priming technique in which participants saw images of Black or White faces on a computer screen, followed by words that were clearly positive or negative but unrelated to racial stereotypes (words like sunshine or disease). Their task was simply to press one of two keys as rapidly as possible to indicate whether the word is positive or negative. For most participants, responses to positive words were faster following a White person's face, and responses to negative words faster following a Black face (Fazio and others, 1995). These differences in response speed, which indicate the individual's relative evaluation of Blacks and Whites, are very difficult if not impossible for the person to control or conceal. Another technique, the Implicit Association Test (IAT), has also been used to measure people's automatic associations of social groups with positive or negative evaluations (Greenwald, McGhee, & Schwartz, 1998). The IAT is described in Figure 5.5. Although some researchers have raised questions about the interpretation of the IAT (Olson & Fazio, 2004), recent evidence largely supports its validity (Nosek, 2005).

Measuring Stereotypes and Prejudice

Stereotypes can be measured by asking plain questions or in more subtle ways that make it difficult for people to hide prejudiced feelings. However, people who reveal stereotypes or prejudice in subtle ways while overtly denying them may not be dishonest; they may actually hold conflicting views.

FIGURE 5.5   The Implicit Association Test

Sequence	Task Name / Instructions: For specific type of stimulus, press left or right response button	Examples of stimuli and correct responses
1	**Black-White Names** Black name - Left White name - Right	Meredith - Right Tashika - Left Betsy - Right
2	**Pleasant-Unpleasant Words** Pleasant word - Left Unpleasant word - Right	poison - Right gift - Left disaster - Right
3	**Initial Combined Task** Black name or pleasant word - Left White name or unpleasant word - Right	Peggy - Right evil - Right Ebony - Left miracle - Left
4	**Reversed Black-White Names** Black name - Right White name - Left	Courtney - Left Shereen - Right Tia - Right
5	**Reversed Combined Task** Black name or unpleasant word - Left White name or pleasant word - Right	peace - Left Latisha - Right filth - Right Nancy - Left

■ The Implicit Association Test (IAT; Greenwald, McGhee, & Schwartz, 1998) involves a series of tasks, performed in the indicated order. Each task involves making a response by pressing one of two buttons (labeled Left and Right in this figure) for each of a number of names or words presented on a computer screen. The computer records how long it takes to complete a fixed number of trials of each task. This figure shows the use of the IAT to measure people's evaluations of Blacks versus Whites as an example, but the same approach can be adapted to measure evaluations of any two groups.

The first two tasks (sequence numbers 1 and 2) are quite easy, and participants are able to respond rapidly. When responses to both names and words are required (as in the combined tasks 3 and 5), however, performance may be easy or difficult, depending on the way the responses go together. For most White participants, the combination shown as sequence number 3 (where Black names and pleasant words require the same response) is much more difficult than the combination in sequence number 5 (where White names and pleasant words are given the same response). By measuring how much longer it takes participants to complete the more difficult combination task compared to the other one, researchers are able to assess how strongly the participants associate the Black category with negative evaluations and the White category with positive ones. It is very difficult, if not impossible, for participants to intentionally alter their patterns of responses in order to conceal their evaluations of the categories.

To read more about the Implicit Association Test or to try it for yourself, visit the Project Implicit website, http://projectimplicit.net

We have just described some of the sophisticated techniques that researchers have used to demonstrate that stereotypes or prejudiced evaluations of social groups can be automatically activated, without people's intention or even awareness. As you may have realized, these techniques offer a means to measure people's stereotypes or prejudice. And indeed, the measurement of stereotypes and prejudice has been a continuing problem affecting research in this area. A generation or two ago, measuring stereotypes or prejudice was a relatively easy task: Researchers could just ask, and generally received honest answers because social norms were much more accepting of group-based biases (D. Katz & Braly, 1933). However, more recently, people have become less likely to endorse group stereotypes or to openly reveal prejudice against racial or other groups (Devine, 1989; Dovidio & Fazio, 1992). Does this mean that stereotyping and prejudice have actually declined over time? Or only that people are now less likely to be honest about such socially sensitive matters? Or, perhaps most intriguingly, that people still harbor group stereotypes or prejudices of which they are not consciously aware?

In fact, many people who deny harboring stereotypes or prejudice, apparently with great sincerity, nevertheless show telltale signs of these phenomena when tested with modern *implicit measures*. Implicit measures, like the priming measures just discussed, are based on some difficult-to-control aspect of people's performance, such as their response speed or accuracy, and do not rely on people's ability or willingness to report their beliefs or feelings (Fazio & Olson, 2003). The underlying question is how we should interpret this pattern. At first glance, it is tempting to assume that implicit measures offer a direct route to people's unchanging, "true" inner beliefs and feelings, in contrast to explicit self-report measures, which can be distorted by social desirability biases and other transitory effects. In this view, people who show prejudice on an implicit measure like the IAT yet deny it when asked are simply lying to make themselves look good (to others or to themselves). However tempting it may be, this view is not correct. Implicit measures of group prejudice are now known to be affected by many situational factors, including recent encounters with liked or disliked group members, and even the race of the experimenter who administers the tasks (Blair, 2002; Lowery, Hardin, & Sinclair, 2001). We have to conclude that implicit measures are not a direct "pipeline" to the person's true inner attitudes, free of distortions by situational or social factors.

A clear understanding of differences between self-reports and implicit measures begins with the assumption that at least some people are perfectly honest and sincere in saying they reject group stereotypes and prejudice. If implicit measures nevertheless show that they display subtle forms of prejudice, perhaps these individuals can be accused of lacking insight into what these sophisticated research techniques reveal about them, but not of dishonestly denying prejudices that they secretly realize they maintain. To get a personal sense of what this means, take the IAT yourself (at http://projectimplicit.net/) and see what you think! If you regard yourself as a generally unprejudiced person, you may, like your authors, be upset and perhaps even ashamed at the biases that the IAT may suggest you have. The common pattern of overt denials combined with subtle indications of the presence of stereotypes and prejudice may actually reflect the fact that many people have learned stereotypes from an early age—from parents, the media, the culture in general—despite honestly attempting to escape their influence (Devine, 1989). Unfortunately, as we will see shortly, their good intentions cannot always be carried out.

Thus, current research does not support the view that implicit measures give the "true" picture while self-report measures are systematically misleading. Instead, implicit and overt measures of stereotypes and prejudice simply measure different aspects of an individual's overall views of a social group. If this is the case, implicit and explicit stereotypes and prejudice should predict different sorts of consequences. And this is what actually occurs. Consider, for example, the finding by Jack Dovidio, Kerry Kawakami, and Samuel Gaertner (2002) that implicit measures of prejudice were related to White students' subtle nonverbal friendliness toward a Black confederate—a type of response that is relatively less controllable. In contrast, the students' levels of overtly reported racial prejudice were related to the positivity of their verbal statements toward the Black confederate, an aspect of their behavior that was more controllable. Similarly, Leslie Ashburn-Nardo and her colleagues (Ashburn-Wardo, Knowles, & Monteith, 2003) found that Black students' implicit preference for Whites versus Blacks, as measured by an IAT, influenced their choice to work with a White or Black partner for a challenging task. Thus, current researchers often use both implicit and explicit measures of stereotyping and prejudice in their studies, to produce the fullest possible picture of people's impressions and reactions to other groups.

Impact of Stereotypes on Judgments and Actions

Stereotypes can affect our interpretations of behaviors performed by members of groups, and also our actions toward them. In extreme cases, stereotypes may even affect life-or-death judgments. Stereotypes have greater effects when judgments must be made under time pressure, when emotions are intense, and when people hold positions of power.

Once activated, stereotypes or feelings about a group can serve as a basis for making judgments or guiding action toward a group. For one thing, stereotypes can cause us to focus on one group membership (whether an occupational, racial, or gender group) and therefore to ignore other, competing group memberships (Macrae, Bodenhausen, Milne, & Jetten, 1994). As a result, all members of the stereotyped group become just the same. Being treated as an anonymous, interchangeable group member is a common experience for victims of stereotyping and prejudice. Virtually every woman professor or business manager can tell stories about being mistaken for the secretary; many a male Hispanic homeowner can recall times when he was out working in his yard, and passersby assumed he was the hired gardener.

Stereotypes can change people's interpretations of behaviors performed by members of different groups. For example, suppose a man and a woman both succeed in some difficult task, such as selling $1,000,000 of residential real estate in a month. For an observer who has stereotypic ideas about gender differences in abilities, the success might be attributed to a man's great skills—but to the woman's luck (Deaux & Emswiller, 1974). Obviously, such attributions would lead to lower expectations that the woman (compared to the man) would continue her successful ways in the future.

Stereotypes can also affect more consequential judgments about others, as recent studies have compellingly demonstrated. Imagine a police officer, patrolling in a dangerous neighborhood. If a stranger suddenly appears on the street holding a metal object in his hand, the officer may have only moments to decide whether the object is a weapon or something perfectly innocent, like a cell phone. In a well-publicized event in February 1999, Amadou Diallo was

■ **Impact of stereotypes on judgments**. It's situations like this that illustrate just how wrong we might be if stereotypes bias our judgments. If you judged this woman, shown here at work as a firefighter, according to the stereotype usually associated with women, you might be in for a surprise!

shot to death in New York City in a hail of 41 police bullets. The officers thought he was holding a gun, but investigation showed that he had only his wallet in his hand. Diallo was Black; might racial stereotypes have influenced the police officers' judgments? According to research by Keith Payne (2001), the answer may be yes. In his study, Black or White faces were shown on a computer screen as primes, followed by a photo of either a handgun or a tool such as pliers or a screwdriver. The participants had to press one of two keys to indicate whether the object was a weapon or a tool. They identified guns faster, and in a second study actually misidentified tools as guns more often, when primed with a Black face rather than a White one. These results suggest that common stereotypes of Blacks as violent or crime-prone could have real implications for the way Black people are treated in threatening situations.

Another study by Joshua Correll and his colleagues (Correll, Park, Judd, & Wittenbrink, 2002) took the idea a step further. In their study, students were instructed to push a button to "shoot" if a person pictured on the computer screen held a gun, but to press a second, "don't shoot" button if the person was unarmed. The pictured person was sometimes White and sometimes Black, and some members of each group were shown holding guns. When the photo showed someone holding a gun, participants were substantially quicker to "pull the trigger" if the person was Black than if he was White. Even more thought-provoking was the result in a second study: when participants were forced to make decisions under great time pressure, unarmed Blacks were "shot" 16% of the time, compared to only 12% for unarmed Whites. Conversely, the students failed to shoot at an armed Black only 7% of the time, while they made such errors 12% of the time for armed Whites. A final study that recruited community members from bus stations and malls as participants replicated the results of the college student participants—and revealed that the bias was just as large and in the same direction for Black participants as for Whites.

You may be wondering whether these results apply to actual police officers. Correll and his associates (2002) are careful to note that their results say nothing about police officers' behavior, because they did not test any police in their studies. Moreover, intensive police training might lead to a reduction in this type of bias. Yet it is disturbing to think of even the possibility that common negative stereotypes about Blacks may have tragic real-world effects, when people make life-and-death decisions under extreme stress and time pressure, as the example of Amadou Diallo suggests.

LESS CAPACITY, MORE STEREOTYPING. Indeed, research shows that time pressure or other conditions that limit people's cognitive capacity generally increase the effects of stereotypes on their judgments. For example, people who must make quick decisions about others are more likely to rely on stereotypes than are those who can take their time (Freund, Kruglanski, & Shpitzajzen, 1985; Kruglanski & Freund, 1983). In one study, the less time people had, the more likely they were to rely on gender stereotypes in deciding among male and female job candidates (Bechtold, Naccarato, & Zanna, 1986). And in a study using the same priming method as Payne (2001), people's tendency to misidentify tools as weapons when primed by Black faces was magnified by time pressure (Payne, Lambert, & Jacoby, 2002).

Lack of time is not the only factor that can increase the impact of stereotypes. Sometimes information is just too complex to process adequately. In such circumstances, people may rely on stereotypes as their best bet for making the judgments, even if they have plenty of time and the consequences of their decisions are important. In one mock jury trial, for example, participants role-playing jurors based their decisions on their unfavorable stereotypes of the Latino defendant when the information relevant to making the judgment was complex. They did not show stereotypic biases when the information was presented in a simpler way (Bodenhausen & Lichtenstein, 1987).

Almost anything that diminishes an individual's cognitive capacity can also increase the impact of stereotypes on judgment. Are you a morning person or a night person? In either case, you probably realize that at certain times of day your thinking is not at its best. Galen Bodenhausen (1990) wondered whether time of day could have an impact on stereotyping. He used a questionnaire to measure whether participants were "morning types" or "evening types" and then assigned them randomly to experimental sessions that met at 9 a.m., 3 p.m., or 8 p.m. Their task was to read several items of evidence about a fictitious character named either Roberto Garcia or Robert Garner, who was accused of assault. After reading the evidence, participants were asked about Garcia/Garner's guilt. When people were scheduled for their worst times, they were more prone to rely on their stereotypic expectations that Latinos are aggressive and to assert that the Latino individual had committed the crime (see Figure 5.6). So morning people: Beware of stereotyping others after lunch. And night people: Watch what you think in the morning!

MORE EMOTION, MORE STEREOTYPING. If the impact of stereotypes is magnified when decision making is difficult, what happens when emotions like anxiety, irritation, or anger cloud our judgment? If you suspect that stereotyping will get worse, you are right (Mackie & Hamilton, 1993). By disrupting careful processing and short-circuiting attention, strong emotions increase our reliance on

FIGURE 5.6   Stereotyping by the clock?

■ At people's nonpreferred times of day, they were more likely to fall back on ethnic stereotyping. For morning people, the stereotype of Latinos as aggressive had its greatest effect on their judgments of guilt in the afternoon and evening. For night owls, the effect of the stereotype was greatest in the morning. (Based on Bodenhausen, 1990.)

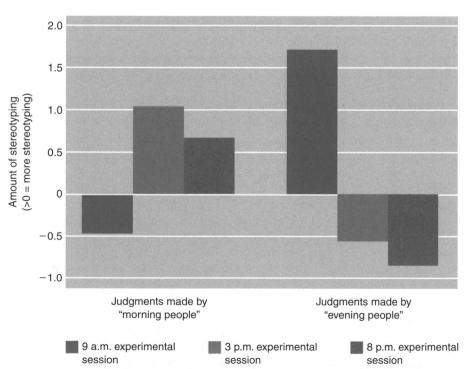

9 a.m. experimental session

3 p.m. experimental session

8 p.m. experimental session

stereotypes (Dijker, 1987; C. W. Stephan & Stephan, 1984). For example, fear, anxiety, and sadness increase the impact of stereotypic expectations on perceptions of individual group members (D. L. Hamilton, Stroessner, & Mackie, 1993; H.-S. Kim & Baron, 1988; Wilder & Shapiro, 1988), and they decrease recognition of differences among group members (Stroessner & Mackie, 1992). In one study of the effect of anger on stereotyping, students playing mock jurors were asked to decide the guilt or innocence of a defendant whom some believed to be a Latino and others thought was ethnically nondescript (Bodenhausen & Kramer, 1990, cited in Bodenhausen, 1993). Students who were made to feel angry by an experimental manipulation before reading the evidence were more likely to deliver a guilty verdict against the Latino defendant than against the other defendant. In contrast, those who were not angered treated the two defendants the same.

MORE POWER, MORE STEREOTYPING. Besides transitory factors like distraction or emotions, more permanent conditions such as people's positions of power also contribute to stereotyping. Suppose a Latino boss interacts with a subordinate who is a woman. Which of the two individuals is more likely to perceive the other in stereotypic ways? Probably the boss (Fiske, 1993). Power leads to stereotyping for two general reasons, as Stephanie Goodwin and her colleagues (Goodwin, Gubin, Fiske, & Yzerbyt, 2000) have demonstrated. First, the powerful have less need than the powerless to perceive others accurately; they can be cognitively lazy and simply apply stereotypes. Second, many stereotypes actively support the social position of the powerful and the broader system that gives groups differential access to power (Glick & Fiske, 2001; Jost & Banaji, 1994). For both these reasons, those in powerful positions may be in particular danger of stereotyping others—and it is sobering to recognize that powerful individuals are those whose biases are most likely to have real-world effects.

Trying to Overcome Stereotype Effects

People may try to overcome the effects of stereotypes by suppressing stereotypic thoughts, correcting for their impact on judgments, or exposing themselves to counterstereotypic information. However, all these tactics require motivation and cognitive capacity.

Evidently, we are often in danger of making stereotypic snap judgments because common and well-learned stereotypes can be activated automatically. This is especially true, as we have seen, when our processing capacity is limited, we are in a highly emotional state, or we are in a position of relative power. If the content of stereotypes comes to mind unbidden, and can influence our thoughts, feelings, and behaviors every time we encounter a group member, can people do anything to overcome stereotype effects?

Fortunately, the answer is yes. Even though negative stereotypic information may be activated whenever a particular category comes to mind—at the mere sight or sound of a group member—negative judgments about the group or its members are not inevitable. The activation of a category brings certain information to mind, but we do not have to rely on this information alone. Instead, people can make conscious efforts to avoid thinking of stereotypes, can revise and correct any judgments that they suspect may have been influenced by stereotypes, or can intentionally expose themselves to counterstereotypic information.

SUPPRESSING STEREOTYPIC THOUGHTS. Think back to the last time you had a conversation with a member of a group about which you had well-learned negative stereotypes. Naturally, during the conversation you probably worked hard to avoid expressing any stereotypic thoughts or feelings. However, your well-intentioned efforts at suppressing the stereotype might have had negative results later! This conclusion rests on fascinating research by Neil Macrae and his colleagues (1994). The British students who participated in this study were shown a photograph of a skinhead, a member of a social group linked to extremely negative stereotypes, and were asked to write a paragraph about a day in this person's life. Half were told to avoid using any stereotypes or preconceptions, while the other half were not given any special instructions. Those who were told to suppress the stereotype clearly were able to do so: Their paragraphs were less stereotypic than those written by the other participants. Next, the participants were told that they would meet the skinhead in person, and were taken into another room where a coat and other items (evidently belonging to the skinhead) were draped over a chair, making it appear that he had left the room momentarily. Participants selected a seat for themselves, and the distance from the skinhead's supposed seat was measured. Those who had earlier suppressed the negative skinhead stereotype now chose to sit farther away from the skinhead!

Other studies found similar results when people suppressed stereotypes on their own because they believed that using stereotypes was inappropriate, rather than because of an experimenter's instruction (Macrae, Bodenhausen, & Milne, 1998). Consistent with other research suggesting that once-suppressed thoughts often rebound and become even more accessible (Wegner, 1994), suppressing a stereotype may make its content more likely to influence our thoughts and feelings later. Suppressing stereotypes may not always be possible, either. Consider the studies by Payne and his colleagues (2002) on tool versus weapon judgments primed by Black or White faces, described earlier. Results in those studies were virtually identical for participants who were specifically instructed to avoid using race as for those who were instructed to use race in making their judgments. Thus suppressing or simply trying to avoid using stereotypes may not be the best approach to eliminating stereotype effects on our thoughts and judgments (Monteith, Sherman, & Devine, 1998).

CORRECTING STEREOTYPIC JUDGMENTS. A different approach involves correction rather than suppression. If we think that an unwanted stereotype may have influenced our thinking, we can try to correct for its effects, for example, by trying hard to be pleasant (Wegener & Petty, 1997). A half-century ago Gordon Allport (1958) quoted two college students writing anonymously about their feelings about groups:

> *Intellectually, I am firmly convinced that this prejudice against Italians is unjustified. And in my present behavior to Italian friends I try to lean over backwards to counteract the attitude. But it is remarkable how strong a hold it has on me.* (p. 310)

> *These prejudices make me feel narrow-minded and intolerant and therefore I try to be as pleasant as possible. I get so angry with myself for having such feelings, but somehow I do not seem to be able to quench them.* (p. 311)

Patricia Devine (1989) argues that these quotations capture exactly what most nonprejudiced people do. She believes that virtually everyone is affected by the negative content of early learned and deeply ingrained stereotypes, but that some people try to overcome their insidious consequences by correcting their judgments. Thus, being unprejudiced does not mean never having stereotypic thoughts or feelings, but rather acknowledging them and making a conscious effort to avoid being influenced by them. Like trying to break any bad habit, this work is not easy, for it requires people to wrestle with inner conflicts between the negative stereotypes they have learned and the nonprejudiced views they also hold (I. Katz & Hass, 1988).

When well-intentioned people try to correct judgments that they suspect may have been affected by stereotypes, they may even make overly positive judgments of stereotyped group members. This outcome was observed in studies by Kent Harber (1998). In these studies, White college students read essays that were intentionally filled with major stylistic flaws and content errors, and gave feedback to the supposed essay writers. When the participants believed the writer was a Black student, the feedback was more positive and supportive than when the writer was believed to be White. In cases like this, people may alter their judgments to avoid appearing prejudiced—not only to others, but even more important, to themselves. But this can have several negative effects. For one thing, withholding honest feedback on major flaws in students' work deprives the students of an opportunity to learn and improve. And in addition, intentionally correcting our judgments can take time and mental resources. The inability to make corrections is undoubtedly one reason that a lack of time and cognitive capacity leads to judgments that are more stereotypic, as we described earlier.

ACTIVATING COUNTERSTEREOTYPIC INFORMATION. Potentially even more effective than correction is a strategy of intentionally exposing oneself to counterstereotypic information. Irene Blair and her colleagues (Blair, Ma, & Lenton, 2001) asked people to self-generate counterstereotypical mental images. They used the stereotype that men are stronger than women, and instructed some participants to form a mental image of a strong woman. Different participants, of course, interpreted this idea differently, with some visualizing a body-builder type who is physically strong, while others thought of a grandmotherly woman who was a strong source of emotional support for her family. This imaging task reduced the strength of the stereotype of women as weak, according to an implicit measure (a version of the IAT), compared to participants who formed an irrelevant mental image. In a related approach, Kerry Kawakami and her associates (Kawakami, Dovidio, Moll, Hermsen, & Russin, 2000) investigated a strategy that could be called "just say no" to stereotypes. Participants went through a long series of trials in which they pressed a "no" button to stereotypical pairings of photos and words, and "yes" to counterstereotypical pairings. Like Blair's counterstereotypic mental imagery, this task also reduced implicit stereotypes, and the effect was long-lasting, observed for at least 24 hours.

Beyond Simple Activation: Effects of Stereotypes on Considered Judgments

Even when people make considered judgments, established stereotypes exert an effect. People tend to look for stereotype-confirming, not disconfirming, evidence and to interpret ambiguous information as stereotype-consistent. People may even elicit stereotype-consistent information from others by the way they interact with them.

We have seen that people often use stereotypes when they are in a hurry, when they make judgments without much thought, or when they are emotionally upset. Unfortunately, stereotypes also leave their mark even when people try to gather more information. Stereotypes often guide our decisions because we generally believe they are accurate—for two main reasons. First, when we learn information that appears consistent with our expectations, we will leap to the conclusion that those expectations were correct. And, as you will see, stereotypes can bias the information people process, producing apparent consistency. Second, confidence also flows from consensus. A stereotype that is socially shared—as most stereotypes are—boosts our confidence by letting us know that other people agree with our beliefs and react in the same way we do.

In many situations, of course, confidence in a stereotype is not enough. We need to see beyond group membership and consider personal characteristics, reactions, or emotions. For example, in choosing an employee, competency is more important than gender, and in choosing a friend, shared tastes and preferences are more important than race. So in some situations—when the judgment is important and when we choose to devote attention to the task—we may try to go beyond group stereotypes and collect further information about people as individuals (Fiske & Neuberg, 1990; M. L. Hoffman, 1986; M. J. Rodin, 1987). When we do this, stereotypic information is less likely to come to mind (Macrae, Bodenhausen, Milne, Thorn, & Castelli, 1997). Even when we collect additional information, however, stereotypes can subtly bias the way we see other people.

SEEKING EVIDENCE TO CONFIRM THE STEREOTYPE: JUST TELL ME WHERE TO LOOK. How do stereotypes distort our considered judgments about others? One source of bias is our stereotypic expectations: We tend to notice and remember what we expect to see. For one thing, when people are given both stereotypic and stereotype-inconsistent information about a person, they tend to spend more time reading and thinking about the stereotypic information (Neuberg & Fiske, 1987). If they are allowed to select what information they will receive, they are likely to ask for more stereotype-consistent information (L. Johnston & Macrae, 1994).

Stereotypic biases affect not only the information we seek out and attend to, but also what we remember. Recall from Chapter 3's discussion of person perception that when we are especially motivated to pay attention to an individual, we carefully process unexpected information and remember it particularly well (Hastie & Kumar, 1979). For example, suppose you have an impression of an individual as generally self-centered, but then observe the person volunteering four consecutive weekends to work on building a Habitat for Humanity house. As we described in Chapter 3, you are likely to think hard about this unexpected behavior, and you will probably remember it particularly well when you think about the person again. However, this special processing of unexpected behaviors is less likely to occur with groups (D. L. Hamilton & Sherman, 1996). That is, if you think of a group as self-centered but learn that a group member volunteered for Habitat, you are unlikely to devote the same kind of special processing to the inconsistent behavior or to remember it well. In fact, you may remember mostly stereotype-consistent information about the group (D. L. Hamilton & Rose, 1980; Rothbart, Evans, & Fulero, 1979). This memory bias means that once a stereotype is in place, people may falsely recall that the stereotype was confirmed in their actual encounters with group members. As D. L. Hamilton and Rose (1980) concluded, believing is seeing. When bias molds people's observations and memories so that they fit their

We discussed the conditions that lead people to go beyond their initial exceptations to consider others as individuals in Chapter 3, pages 80 to 82.

stereotypes, the stereotypes grow even stronger (Rothbart & John, 1985; Wilder & Shapiro, 1984).

INTERPRETING EVIDENCE TO FIT THE STEREOTYPE: WELL, IF YOU LOOK AT IT THAT WAY. The implications of a good deal of the information we gather are not immediately obvious. As a person on a lonely street at night reaches for an object in his pocket, who is to say whether he is pulling out a handgun or just a cell-phone or a pack of cigarettes? When information is ambiguous, activation of a stereotype influences our interpretation of the behavior (or of the individual performing the behavior), making it seem consistent with the stereotype (Darley & Gross, 1983).

In a study demonstrating this point, Andrew Sagar and Janet Schofield (1980) showed schoolchildren stick-figure drawings of children who were identified as Black or White, and described each stick-child's behavior. For example, a picture of two students sitting one behind the other in a classroom was accompanied by the following description: "Mark was sitting at his desk, working on his social studies assignment, when David started poking him in the back with the eraser end of his pencil. Mark just kept on working. David kept poking him for a while and then he finally stopped." When David was Black, the children saw his behavior as more mean and threatening than when he was White. Thus, the same behavior was interpreted differently depending on who the actor was and what stereotype his group membership evoked.

Stereotypes can similarly influence our interpretations of others' behavior in everyday situations, as an episode recounted to author Studs Terkel (1992) demonstrates. A White man described how his wife, driving down the street in a Black neighborhood, noticed that the people on the street corners were all gesturing at her forcefully. Frightened, she closed the car windows and drove very determinedly through the area. Only after several blocks did she discover that she was going the wrong way on a one-way street and that the pedestrians had merely been trying to help her. If stereotypes can bend our interpretation of behaviors in one direction or another, some group impressions may be almost impossible to counteract (Rothbart & Park, 1986).

COMPARING INFORMATION TO STEREOTYPIC STANDARDS: THAT LOOKS GOOD, FOR A GROUP MEMBER. At 5 feet 10 inches, Sarah is more likely to be called "tall" than Samuel, who is also 5 feet 10. This is just common sense; Sarah is indeed tall *for a woman*. But this example illustrates one additional way stereotypes can affect our judgments: by shifting our standards for judgments, at least on characteristics like "tall" or "smart" or "athletic" that involve a strong subjective element. Monica Biernat and Melvin Manis (1994) illustrated this effect when they had students judge essays on stereotypically "masculine" or "feminine" topics supposedly written by a woman or a man. Letter grades given to the essays revealed, as expected, that gender-congruent essays were evaluated more highly; for example, Joan's essay on eye makeup received a higher grade than the identical essay supposedly written by John. Yet the students' ratings of the essays on a subjective scale (for example, from "poor" to "excellent") showed no differences by the author's supposed gender. Evidently the students believed that John's essay on the feminine topic, while not as good as Joan's, was still "good" *for a man*. Group stereotypes (for example, that men would not be expected to know much about makeup) affect the standards used to assign such subjective ratings. Looking at this finding another way, it is interesting to realize that even when members of different groups are rated the same—as when the subjective scale was used in this study—stereotypes may still be operating, subtly affecting not only people's perceptions of group members but also the standards they use to make and express their judgments (Kobrynowicz & Biernat, 1997).

CONSTRAINING EVIDENCE TO FIT THE STEREOTYPE: THE SELF-FULFILLING PROPHECY. Not only do people seek out stereotype-consistent behavior, they may even elicit it. One of us observed just such a situation when he was in graduate school. Two of his fellow students who had co-authored a paper ran into the professor who had given them their assignment. The professor immediately engaged the male student co-author in conversation, spending several minutes complimenting him on the paper and discussing a few of its fine points. The woman student stood by, silently fuming. So did the observer, because he knew that the woman was by far the more talented student and suspected that three quarters of the work on the paper was hers. Yet the professor, stereotypically assuming that the male student was the primary author, was holding a conversation that reinforced his opinion that the male student could talk intelligently on the topic while the female student had nothing to say.

When stereotypes lead us to act in ways that produce the very behaviors that confirm our expectations, the stereotype becomes a *self-fulfilling prophecy*. Recall from Chapter 3 that when people interact with someone about whom they hold a particular expectation, they often induce that person to confirm the expectation (M. Snyder, Tanke, & Berscheid, 1977). Similarly, people's actions often elicit information that confirms and maintains their group stereotypes. When we ask women about their family and men about their job, our behavior produces responses that are likely to tell us what we already know. Alternatively, we may simply not bother to gather much specific information from people who are members of a stereotyped group. In one study, perceivers who held a stereotypic expectation about someone sought less information from them in an interview, asking fewer questions than when the target person was not described as a member of a stereotyped group (Trope & Thompson, 1997).

☐ **SELF-FULFILLING PROPHECIES IN SCHOOL AND AT WORK.** The self-fulfilling nature of stereotypes can set up a chain reaction in which not only the perceiver's beliefs but also the actual behavior of members of the stereotyped groups are affected (Word, Zanna, & Cooper, 1974). In the classroom, the consequences can be devastating. For this reason, researchers have intensively studied the effects of teachers' expectations on student performance. Expectations may be based on social categorizations like gender, race, or social class, or on personal characteristics like physical attractiveness (M. J. Harris, 1991). When teachers' expectations for students are high, they tend to treat them with more warmth, teach them more material, and give them more chances to contribute to discussions and answer questions in class. These differences translate directly into differences in student achievement (M. J. Harris & Rosenthal, 1985). Such findings make it clear why we should be concerned about studies like one showing that classroom teachers generally give more attention and encouragement to boys than to girls (Wellesley College Center for Research on Women, 1992). Another study undertaken in a New York City suburb indicated that teachers' expectations for Black children are consistently lower than for White children, regardless of the children's actual abilities (S. I. Ross & Jackson, 1991). And a recent review, though it argued that self-fulfilling prophecy effects in classrooms are generally small, acknowledged that they can have powerful effects on students from generally negatively stereotyped groups (Jussim & Harber, 2005).

Self-fulfilling prophecies operate in the workplace, too. An employer's preconceptions can predetermine the outcome of applications for job openings. For example, interviewers who believe that a particular candidate is not suitable for a position are likely to probe for negative information (Binning, Goldstein, Garcia, & Scatteregia, 1988), whereas those with positive preconceptions tend to spend time gaining and giving positive information (Phillips & Dipboye, 1989). In one study, White participants interviewed Black or White applicants. When dealing with Blacks, they conducted briefer interviews and sat farther away, causing the applicants to react in a less confident and effective manner (Word and others, 1974). Self-fulfilling prophecies also restrict the opportunities of employees already on the job. Employers can generate confirmations of their stereotypes in a number of subtle ways. A supervisor who regularly interrupts his female subordinates is clearly communicating to them that their contributions are unimportant, damaging their self-confidence. A boss who delegates responsibilities to his female staff but then checks up on every detail is not only advertising his distrust but also denying the women the opportunity to prove their competence.

No wonder then that group stereotypes, like other cognitive representations, tend to perpetuate themselves and to be slow to change. When people process superficially, stereotypes alone can dictate their judgments. When people process more extensively, stereotypes influence what they see and how they interpret it. Either way, the outcome is likely to be a judgment consistent with the stereotype, as Figure 5.7 demonstrates.

FIGURE 5.7   Stereotypes are self-perpetuating

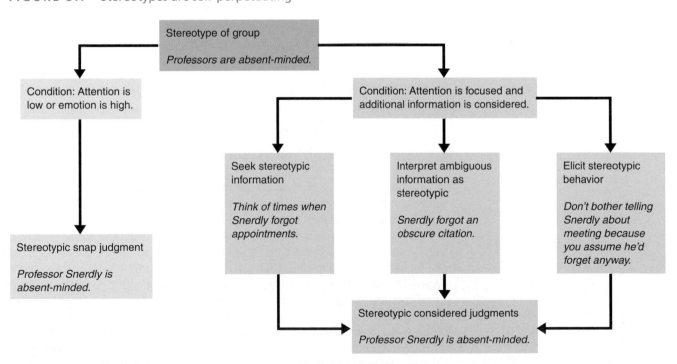

■ Whether people make snap judgments or attempt to process information more carefully, stereotypes shape their thoughts and actions. In most cases, the result seems to confirm and perpetuate the stereotype.

■ **Pursuing a dream to overcome a stereotype**. These Japanese athletes are taking part in the opening ceremony of the 2006 Turin Paralympics. The Paralympics are Olympic style, elite sporting events for athletes from six different disability groups. The games emphasize the participants' athletic achievements rather than their disability, and in so doing silently break the stereotype that those with disabilities would somehow be less fit to compete athletically. This also serves to reinforce the ethos that an individual should be judged first and foremost by his or her individual skills and expertise, rather than on group membership.

Changing Stereotypes: Overcoming Bias to Reduce Prejudice

Even though people sometimes selectively gather, interpret, and elicit information so that their stereotypes are confirmed, they may eventually have an experience that unambiguously contradicts their impression of a group. For example, a member of a group regarded as hostile and clannish may move into the neighborhood and turn out to be unobjectionable, even pleasant. Could getting to know likable individual group members change negative stereotypes of another group? Somehow, we like to think that stereotypes are born out of ignorance, so that simply learning more about a group will put them to rest.

That simple idea—that contact with individual members who violate the group stereotype should bring about its downfall—is the basis of one of the oldest and most researched theories of stereotype change. The **contact hypothesis** suggests that under certain conditions, direct contact between members of different groups can reduce intergroup stereotyping, prejudice, and discrimination (G. W. Allport, 1954a). When members of different groups socialize, perhaps they can exchange the kind of information that undermines stereotypic thinking. Getting to know group members on a one-to-one-basis should make it obvious that they do not fit the group stereotype. In the face of this inconsistent information, common sense says that the stereotype should change.

Barriers to Stereotype Change

> Even when people obtain information that is blatantly inconsistent with a stereotype, stereotypes may remain unchanged. This is because people can explain away the inconsistency, create a new category for exceptions to the rule, and see the behavior of unusual group members as being irrelevant to the group stereotype.

Unfortunately, reality is not as straightforward as common sense. Consider, for example, the high level of contact between men and women, police officers and gang members, Palestinians and Israelis. None of these contact situations has been a prejudice-reduction success story. The problem lies in the fact that contact in and of itself—even contact that contradicts a stereotype—may not undermine a stereotype (G. W. Allport, 1954a; Amir, 1969; W. G. Stephan, 1987). In fact, exposure to inconsistent information can trigger powerful mechanisms that protect established stereotypes from change.

EXPLAINING AWAY INCONSISTENT INFORMATION. Well-intentioned authors of uplifting stories for young people sometimes devise plots in which the hero holds a negative stereotype about Group X, meets an X, after some initial misunderstandings gets to know the X as a person, and finally decides the stereotype was wrong and Xs are as likable as anybody else. The idea that a

Contact hypothesis. The theory that certain types of direct contact between members of hostile groups will reduce stereotyping and prejudice.

stereotype can be changed by a single inconsistent experience, a process called *conversion* (Rothbart, 1981), is appealing. But the plot somehow seems contrived. Does true conversion occur so easily?

One barrier to stereotype change is the fact that when people even notice information that fails to fit their expectations, they often just explain it away. Information that is in some way discrepant often makes us look hard for its causes, and thus makes it likely that we will find some "special circumstances" to explain it. If we interpret friendly and positive behaviors performed by a member of a disliked group as just the result of special circumstances, we will not accept the behaviors as a reflection of the actor's true nature (Crocker, Hannah, & Weber, 1983; Gordon & Anderson, 1995). Similarly, women who succeed in a "man's world" are often viewed as highly motivated or very lucky, rather than as very able (Deaux & Emswiller, 1974; Heilman & Stopek, 1985). Encountering a few successful women, or individuals who violate other stereotypes, generally does not change observers' stereotypes.

COMPARTMENTALIZING INCONSISTENT INFORMATION. Even when inconsistent information is too plentiful to be explained away, people can still defend their stereotypes by resorting to specific **subtypes**: social categories that are narrower than broad groups like men or Latinos. For example, German students have different stereotypes for subtypes of women, such as "chick," housewife, career woman, and "woman's libber" (Eckes, 1994). Older people are also categorized into common subtypes such as respected elder statesman, sweet grandmother, and inactive senior citizen (Brewer, Dull, & Lui, 1981).

Although these differentiated categories permit the perceiver to formulate fine-grained expectations about different group members, they also protect stereotyped beliefs from change. If we place a group of people who are exceptions to the rule in a new category, the old rule can remain inviolate. Male executives who work along-side highly competent female colleagues can form a "career woman" subtype that allows them to maintain a more general belief that *most* women cannot succeed in business (Rothbart & John, 1985; Weber & Crocker, 1983). Similarly, we can maintain our view that outstanding physical feats are the province of the young if we compartmentalize stereotype-inconsistent older people in special subtypes. We merely create an exceptions-to-the-rule category for people like John Glenn, who at age 76 took another space trip 38 years after he became the first American to orbit the earth, or Johnny Kelly, who completed his 57th Boston marathon at age 83.

DIFFERENTIATING ATYPICAL GROUP MEMBERS: CONTRAST EFFECTS. Stereotype-inconsistent information can be defused in yet a third way. If we cannot explain away inconsistencies or create new subtypes, we may defend our stereotypes by seeing stereotype-disconfirming individuals as remarkable or exceptional people. When stereotypic expectations serve as a background against which individual group members are judged, people who do not behave as expected seem even more different, creating what is called a *contrast effect*. In one study, for example, researchers created stereotypes of patients in a mental hospital. They had college students read statements, supposedly written by the hospital's patients, that revealed the patients as either severely disturbed or only mildly disturbed (Manis, Nelson, & Shedler, 1988). The students then read statements by other patients who showed a moderate level of pathology. Because of the contrast with their expectations, those who had been led to expect severe disturbance judged these new patients to be only mildly ill, whereas those who expected only mild

Subtype. A narrower and more specific social group, such as housewife or feminist, that is included within a broad social group, like women.

disturbance thought the new patients were extremely ill. Similar processes probably explain why people's stereotypes of an employed woman are quite different from those for a "typical woman" and are very similar to their impression of an employed man. People apparently assume that employed women have actively chosen that role and that only the most ambitious and independent women—the ones most unlike the rest of their group—would so choose (Eagly & Steffen, 1984).

Through contrast effects, members who deviate from expectations for their group seem even more different from the rest of the group than they really are. As a result, perceivers can easily decide that these unusual people are not true group members at all: Their difference makes them exceptions to the rule. As such, they have little bearing on people's impressions of the group as a whole (Rasinski, Crocker, & Hastie, 1985; Rothbart & John, 1985).

Overcoming Stereotype Defenses: The Kind of Contact That Works

Effective contact has to provide stereotype-inconsistent information that is repeated (so that it cannot be explained away), that involves many group members (so that subtyping is prevented), and that comes from typical group members (so that contrast will not occur). Contact is especially effective when it involves the formation of actual friendships across group lines. Under these conditions, contact does reduce stereotypes and improve intergroup relations.

Positive and cooperative intergroup contact can not only change stereotypes, but also help resolve ongoing conflict between groups. Thus, we will return to the question of what kinds of contact are most effective when we consider intergroup conflict in Chapter 13, pages 509 to 513.

Given all the barriers to stereotype change, it might seem that contact between groups is not a very useful remedy for altering stereotypes and reducing prejudice. Yet across an incredibly wide range of situations, contact does have generally positive effects. A meta-analysis of literally hundreds of studies shows that people with more intergroup contact tend to be less prejudiced, whether the contact occurs in public housing units, schoolrooms, workplaces, or in shorter-term interactions (Pettigrew, 1998). What about the possibility that low prejudice produces contact rather than the reverse? Perhaps only people who were unprejudiced in the first place chose to be in situations where they would encounter members of other groups. The meta-analysis convincingly shows that this process, however plausible it is, cannot be responsible for the total effect. For example, contact that is forced rather than voluntary actually has stronger effects on reducing prejudice (Pettigrew, 1998). However, even though contact is generally helpful, some types of contact are more effective than others (S. W. Cook, 1985; Kenworthy, Turner, Hewstone, & Voci, 2005; W. G. Stephan, 1987). To allow the kind of information exchange that undermines stereotypic thinking and reduces prejudice, contact situations must expose people to information that cannot be explained away, subtyped, or contrasted.

REPEATED INCONSISTENCY: AN ANTIDOTE FOR "EXPLAINING AWAY." One counterstereotypic act can easily be explained away. The sales manager who expects inferior performances from women might attribute a woman sales rep's single week of outstanding sales just to extra effort or sheer luck. However, if the strong performance continues week after week, these attributions become harder to support (Kelley, 1967). When behavior remains stable over time and circumstances, attributions to the person are warranted. Thus, stereotype change requires counterstereotypic behaviors to be performed more than once or twice. Of course, this places a special burden on members of stereotyped groups. They cannot afford to perform poorly, even once, for fear that a failure will reinforce rather than change others' stereotypes (Steele, 1992).

WIDESPREAD INCONSISTENCY: AN ANTIDOTE FOR SUBTYPING. Even if the sales manager in the previous example changes his impression of that particular woman sales rep, he may still maintain his stereotype by simply compartmentalizing her as a member of a small subgroup of highly competent women. When behaviors are performed by just a few individual group members, perceivers may create a subtype to insulate their general stereotype from change. To illustrate how this defense can be overcome, Reneé Weber and Jennifer Crocker (1983) gave people information about many behaviors performed by members of a group. Some learned that just a few group members performed stereotype-inconsistent behaviors; the other members' actions were all in line with the stereotype. These participants did not change their overall stereotype of the group, presumably because they categorized the few inconsistent individuals into a new subtype (Johnston & Hewstone, 1992). In contrast, other participants who learned that the same number of inconsistent behaviors were spread out over a large number of group members were more likely to change their stereotype. In the latter case, the inconsistent individuals could not be considered a subtype: Too many group members had unusual, counterstereotypic features.

BEING TYPICAL AS WELL AS INCONSISTENT: AN ANTIDOTE FOR CONTRAST EFFECTS. People have other weapons besides subtypes to use in defense of their stereotypes. Recall that group members who violate the stereotype may simply be considered highly unusual individuals—so atypical that their characteristics have no impact on impressions of "typical" group members (Johnston & Hewstone, 1992). This defense can be overcome if individual stereotype violators provide strong and consistent reminders of their group membership. In one study, college students interacted with a confederate posing as a student from a rival college. The students initially disliked people from the other school, but this particular interaction was positive and friendly. The students' general beliefs about those attending the rival school, however, became more positive only if the confederate acted and dressed in ways perceived to be "typical" of the rival college (Wilder, 1984). If the confederate did not display such highly typical characteristics, the friendly interaction had no impact on students' general views about the other college.

This finding poses a dilemma for group members who wish to change others' negative stereotypes by being a positive example of their group. The very accomplishments and valued attributes that make you a *positive* example may make you less of an *example*, by making you less typical of the group in the eyes of an observer who holds negative stereotypes (Desforges and others, 1991; Rothbart & John, 1985). Indeed, any sort of extensive personal information about you, whether positive or negative, can make you seem less of a group member (Fein & Hilton, 1992). As others get to know you as an individual, they may fail to generalize their positive feelings about you to other members of your group. If your goal is stereotype change, therefore, you should repeatedly remind others of your group membership, so that they cannot treat you as an exception to the rule.

PERSONAL RELATIONSHIPS: COMBINING THE CONDITIONS THAT MAKE CONTACT EFFECTIVE. When interaction involves the right kind of contact—contact that blocks attribution, subtyping, and contrast effects—stereotypes can change. The key ingredient may be contact that encourages the development of a real personal relationship involving positive feelings and sharing of thoughts and feelings—in other words, a friendship—rather than a mere acquaintanceship (Pettigrew, 1998). Stephen Wright and his colleagues (S. C. Wright, Aron, McLaughlin-Volpe, & Ropp, 1997) set out to test this idea in a laboratory study, by first creating conflict between experimentally created groups and then trying friendly contact as a way of reducing it. College students were randomly assigned to two teams that then participated in a series of problem-solving and creativity competitions. Though this procedure alone often suffices to build conflict, as you will see in Chapter 13, the experimenters helped it along in various ways. For example, each team was asked to provide an evaluation of the other team's problem solutions, and the experimenters covertly edited these comments to make them more negative before delivering them to the other team. After steps like these had built up negative feelings between the groups, one member from each group was selected, ostensibly as part of an unrelated study, to participate in a dyadic getting-to-know-you task that established feelings of personal closeness. Finally, all members of both groups, after learning about the experimentally created friendship between these individual members, again rated both groups.

The results of this experimentally created contact were clear. The individual members who built up a close relationship with the opposite-group partner rated that group more positively. Perhaps of greater importance, the other group members did so as well! It seems that not only having a member of another group as a friend, but even knowing that someone else from your group has a member of the other group as a friend, is sufficient to reduce negative feelings about that group. This optimistic conclusion has been confirmed in additional studies (S. C. Wright and others, 1997).

Other laboratory research has demonstrated similar positive effects of intergroup contact. Donna Desforges and her associates (1991) set up a 1-hour laboratory session in which participants interacted with a confederate posing as a former mental patient, a member of a group about which the participants had negative stereotypes. The contact was structured to be cooperative in nature, and as a result friendship budded, and the students came to like their partners. They also developed improved attitudes toward former mental patients in general. Similarly, a brief, pleasant contact with a Hispanic college student sufficed to improve White students' attitudes toward that group, regardless of whether or not the Hispanic student fit common stereotypes of that group (Wolsko, Park, Judd, & Bachelor, 2003). In general, contact seems to be most effective in creating warm and positive feelings about another group, rather than in changing specific stereotypes of the group (Tropp & Pettigrew, 2005).

☐ **INTERGROUP CONTACT IN THE NEIGHBORHOOD.** Finding that friendly contact breaks down stereotypes in the controlled conditions of the laboratory is one thing, but can the right kind of contact break down prejudice in other settings, too? Several studies suggest that reductions in prejudice are associated with increased everyday contact.

The 1950s were a period of large-scale desegregation of public housing units in the United States, creating the conditions for research on the effects of living near members of other groups. Morton Deutsch and Mary Collins (1951) studied the responses of White families assigned to live alongside Black families as well as Whites living in all-White buildings. When the groups were compared, those living in desegregated housing, and particularly those who lived closest to Black families, had more positive feelings about Blacks. Such contact also dissolved stereotypes

Chapter 2, pages 41 to 42, describes why replication of findings inside and outside the laboratory increases researchers' confidence that contact of the right kind does in fact reduce prejudice.

about the previously unknown group. Two Canadian researchers obtained similar results when they matched national survey data on prejudice with census information on the racial composition of residential neighborhoods (Kalin & Berry, 1982). People felt relatively positive about the groups that lived nearby, suggesting again that informal, everyday contact reduces prejudice.

Finally, Thomas Pettigrew (1997) analyzed survey data from Britain, France, the Netherlands, and Germany. People were asked whether they had any friends who were members of racial groups with common negative stereotypes (such as Turkish immigrants in Germany or North Africans in France). Those with such friendships were also less prejudiced against the outgroup, to a greater extent than could be explained by the simple fact that less prejudiced individuals would be more likely to form such friendships in the first place. The effects of a cross-group friendship were not even limited to the specific group: A French person who had an Algerian friend became less predjudiced not only against Algerians, but against other groups as well (Pettigrew, 1997). In fact, heroic Gentiles who risked their lives rescuing Jews from the Nazis seem to have had more cross-group friendships in their own childhoods (Oliner & Oliner, 1988). Thus, the results of nonexperimental studies of contact and friendship in the neighborhood converge with experimental findings from the laboratory. Contact can reduce group prejudice and stereotyping, but it has to be the right kind of contact: contact that permits the development of friendships across group lines.

Before we review the bottom line for changing stereotypes, we should pause to consider for a moment whether all stereotypes ought to be changed. If you have a stereotype that neo-Nazis are evil, but meet a member of that group who smiles politely and acts pleasant, should this experience alter your stereotype? Many of us might say no. And a Frenchman may not want to change the stereotype that the French are good cooks, any more than a Marine would disavow his group's stereotype of toughness and bravery.

Many individuals, though, in keeping with today's social norms, have decided that they do not endorse or wish to use stereotypes of racial, gender, religious, or ethnic groups of the sort that were commonly accepted in past decades. In such cases changing stereotypes is possible, but not easy. Although many factors conspire to keep stereotypes in place, exposure to the right kinds of information can eventually beat down the defense mechanisms that protect stereotypes from change. Even when old stereotypes are activated, people can choose to counter them with nonprejudiced thoughts, feelings, and behaviors. Figure 5.8 shows both the factors that make stereotypes resistant to change and the factors that can finally overcome that resistance. Although it is sometimes difficult to find situations that have all the necessary ingredients working together, contact of the right type can break down negative stereotypes and engender warm feelings of friendship with particular individuals. When this kind of contact is extensive and sustained, those positive feelings can become generalized to the group as a whole, changing stereotypes and reducing prejudice.

CONCLUDING COMMENTS

One theme that has surfaced repeatedly in this book is that our social knowledge is slow to change and tends to perpetuate itself. Stereotypes offer perhaps the most dramatic illustration of this principle, for they perpetuate themselves in two different ways.

FIGURE 5.8   Possible fates of stereotype-inconsistent information

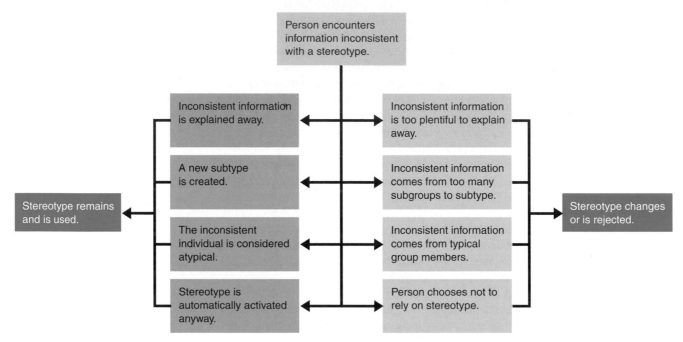

■ Inconsistent information will not always lead people to change or reject their stereotypes, because people have many ways to defend stereotypes against such information (shown on the left side of figure). However, these defenses can be overcome if the inconsistent information appears in the right patterns, or if the individual intentionally chooses not to rely on the stereotype (right side). In some circumstances, stereotypes can be changed.

First, within each individual, the effects of stereotypes mean that believing is seeing. Stereotypes color our perceptions so that unclear or ambiguous events are quickly interpreted in line with the stereotype. If we think politicians are self-serving, we might decide that any action they take is made only for its publicity value. When we read in the newspaper that our member of Congress donated $100 to the local orphanage, for example, we then conclude that the donation was meant to attract media attention. Even when we try to think hard and process carefully, stereotypes shape the information we seek out, remember, and use to make judgments. We might question the politician about foreign junkets rather than efforts on behalf of the district, or we might remember negative campaign tactics rather than sponsorship of important legislation. Even when inconsistent information comes our way, we are likely to defend our stereotypes by explaining away inconsistencies, forming subtypes, or contrasting a particular individual as a praiseworthy exception to the rule.

Of course, none of these self-fulfilling and defensive tendencies are intentional. No one consciously decides, "I want to maintain my biased and stereotypic view of politicians, so don't confuse me with the facts!" Instead, our stereotypes, like our other cognitive representations, constitute the picture of reality we have constructed for ourselves. And for this reason, their effects are below the level of our awareness. We don't try to defend and maintain our stereotypic beliefs, it just happens that way most of the time.

The pervasiveness and power of the self-fulfilling quality of stereotypes within each person's head is only half of the complete story: Stereotypes perpetuate themselves and resist change in society as well. As we have seen, stereotypes generally reflect the roles society allocates to members of the stereotyped group. If more women than men care for children, if members of one ethnic group tend to be small shopkeepers while most members of another group hold unrewarding jobs as menial laborers, those roles will become the raw material of stereotypes. People are likely to end up believing that women are nurturant, that the first ethnic group is greedy and grasping, and that the second group is lazy and dirty. Stereotypes track social roles both because the roles limit the behaviors that we observe individual group members performing, and because the culture and media generally foster the idea that personal characteristics fit roles. Thus the circle is closed. Because people believe groups are naturally suited for the roles they play, those beliefs become the justification for keeping the groups in those roles. Social change that would alter groups' roles is seen as a violation of the natural order of things, becoming morally wrong as well as impractical.

Thus stereotypes have self-fulfilling force not only in an individual's head but also in society. Because stereotypes operate on two levels, changing them will demand alterations not only in the way we think, but also in the way we live. We need to consciously reflect on the extent to which social roles and other external constraints determine not only other people's actions but also our own. Equally, we need to interact with members of all groups in more varied contexts, to see them in more diverse roles, and to work toward change in social inequalities that are reflected in and rationalized by stereotypes.

Could changes like these allow us to retain the benefits of social categorization while eliminating the costs of stereotypes? We would still perceive groups, but we would know each group for its positive and valued characteristics. Perhaps all groups would respect and value all other groups, a goal that is implicit in the concept of multiculturalism. Unfortunately, another factor stands in the way of developing a society in which all groups are equally valued and respected: We all show strong preferences for the groups to which we belong. In Chapter 6 we consider the consequences of this preference for the way we think about and act toward others and ourselves.

CHAPTER 5 THEMES

- **Construction of Reality**
  We construct impressions of social groups based on our interactions with group members and what we learn from others.

- **Pervasiveness of Social Influence**
  These interactions and the things we learn are shaped by society and culture.

- **Striving for Mastery**
  Stereotypes often reflect individuals' actual social experiences.

- **Conservatism**
  Stereotypes perpetuate themselves by shaping both the way we think and the way we act.

- **Superficiality Versus Depth**
  Stereotypes influence judgments made quickly with little thought and also judgments made by collecting further information.

SUMMARY

Discrimination, or treatment of individuals based on their group memberships, and **prejudice**, evaluations of individuals as group members, or evaluations of social groups, are significant problems in the world today. Both social and cognitive factors contribute to prejudice. One important source is people's **stereotypes**: positive or negative beliefs about a group's characteristics.

Any **social group** that shares a socially meaningful common characteristic can be a target for prejudice. Different cultures emphasize different types of groups, but race, religion, gender, age, social status, and cultural background are important dividing lines in many societies. People identify individuals as members of social groups because they share socially meaningful features. This process of **social categorization** is helpful because it allows people to deal with others efficiently and appropriately. However, it also exaggerates similarities within groups and differences between groups, and hence it forms the basis for stereotyping.

Forming Impressions of Groups: Establishing Stereotypes. Many different kinds of characteristics are included in stereotypes, which can be positive or negative. Some stereotypes accurately reflect actual differences between groups, though in exaggerated form. Other stereotypes are completely inaccurate.

Early theorists traced prejudice to deep inner conflicts in a few disturbed individuals, rather than to more normal social motives such as mastery and connectedness. Stereotypes can be learned through personal experience with group members, but may still be biased because people pay attention to extremes or inaccurately perceive groups' characteristics. Social roles often shape group members' behaviors, but people attribute the behaviors to group members' inner characteristics. The emotions generated by interaction with certain groups can also become part of stereotypes about those groups. Learning about groups can take place through media portrayals as well as firsthand experiences.

Social learning also contributes to stereotypes. Stereotypes and discrimination are often accepted and endorsed as right and proper by members of a particular group, becoming **social norms**. Group members then learn these beliefs and behaviors from family and peers. As stereotypes are communicated, they may become even stronger.

The stereotypes prevalent in a society often serve to justify existing social inequalities. They do so by portraying groups as deserving their social roles and positions on the basis of their own characteristics.

Using Stereotypes: From Preconceptions to Prejudice. Once established, a stereotype can be activated by obvious cues, use of group labels, or the presence of a group member, especially as a minority in a social situation. Some stereotypes are learned so well and used so often that their content comes to mind automatically.

The same research techniques that demonstrate stereotypes are automatically activated offer subtle ways to measure stereotypes and prejudice, which make it difficult for people to hide biases that they could readily conceal in answers to plain questions. However, people who reveal stereotypes or prejudice in subtle ways while overtly denying them may actually hold conflicting views rather than being dishonest.

Once activated, stereotypes can affect our interpretations of behaviors performed by members of groups, and also our actions toward them. In extreme cases, stereotypes may even affect life-or-death judgments. Stereotypes have greater effects when judgments must be made under time pressure, when emotions are intense, and when people hold positions of power.

People may try to overcome the effects of stereotypes by suppressing stereotypic thoughts, correcting for their impact on judgments, or exposing themselves to counterstereotypic information. However, all these tactics require motivation and cognitive capacity.

Even when people make considered judgments, established stereotypes exert an effect. People tend to look for stereotype-confirming, not disconfirming, evidence and to interpret ambiguous information as stereotype-consistent. People may even elicit stereotype-consistent information from others by the way they interact with them.

Changing Stereotypes: Overcoming Bias to Reduce Prejudice. Research on how stereotypes may be changed in society has focused on the **contact hypothesis**, the idea that under certain conditions, contact with members of a stereotyped group may reduce stereotyping and prejudice. But contact is not always sufficient. Even when people obtain information that is blatantly inconsistent with a stereotype, stereotypes may remain unchanged because people explain away the inconsistency, create a new **subtype** for exceptions to the rule, and see the behavior of unusual group members as irrelevant to the group stereotype.

To be effective, contact has to provide stereotype-inconsistent information that is repeated (so it cannot be explained away), that involves many group members (so subtyping is prevented), and that comes from typical group members (so contrast will not occur). Contact is especially effective when it involves the formation of actual friendships across group lines. Under these conditions, contact does reduce stereotypes and improve intergroup relations.

6

Social Identity

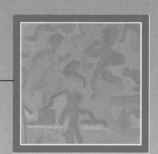

As part of your participation in a psychological experiment, you learn that you will be videotaped being interviewed about various social and academic aspects of your life as a student. The experimenter shows you a sample videotape, which turns out to show a student who appears almost incredibly successful: earning straight A's in premed courses, well dressed and attractive, full of self-confidence—yet still coming across as likable and not arrogant. Now you are given a questionnaire asking you to rate your own academic ability, social competence, and so on. With the superstar interview still echoing in your mind, wouldn't your ratings perhaps be a little below the top of the scale? In contrast, suppose you saw a real loser instead of the superstar. The same actor (for the interviews were staged, of course) portrayed a sloppily dressed, unmotivated individual who came across as socially awkward and not terribly intelligent. Wouldn't your self-ratings go up a bit in this case? Many studies similar to this have established that making social comparisons to another person's outstanding performance lowers people's self-ratings, while witnessing a poor performance raises them.

Marilynn Brewer and Joseph Weber (1994), though, added a new twist to their study when they also manipulated group membership. Before seeing the videotape, each participant took a bogus test classifying him or her into one of two personality types, one that was said to include 80% of college students and the other only 20%. The videotaped actor was also said to belong to one or the other group. Did group membership affect the outcomes of the social comparison? It certainly did. When the videotaped interviewee was a member of the larger group, social comparison had its typical effect: Participants felt bad if the performance was great and good if it was terrible, regardless of their own group membership. But consider what happened when the videotaped student belonged to the minority group:

- For a majority group participant, a videotape of a minority interviewee had no effect whatever on the participant's self-concept. It seems that majority group members simply do not compare themselves to minorities.

We described the effects of social comparison on the self in Chapter 4, pages 110 to 112.

• Even more striking, minority group participants who saw a minority interviewee reacted in the opposite way from the usual social comparison process. They felt good if their fellow group member gave a great performance, and bad if he or she looked terrible! Could it be that people in this
situation do not compare themselves as individuals against other individuals, but psychologically share in the positive or negative image the other
person's performance gives to their group?

As these findings show, being a member of a group influences many of our
thoughts, feelings, and actions. You may feel good or bad about yourself depending
on the specific groups that come to your mind. Being part of the Filipino
community or the swim team, being a woman or a member of any other group can
boost or lower self-esteem if we identify with the group. Group memberships are an
essential part of the self.

Group membership can confer tremendous benefits. Groups give us a sense of
belonging and worth, of being valued for who we are (Tajfel, 1972). As group
members, we can bask in the glow of achievements other than our own and feel at
home in a haven of similarity and understanding. A sense of group membership that
connects us to others is the basis for our participation in social life. It even protects our
mental well-being and physical health, as you will see in Chapter 11. Group membership supports our needs for mastery as well as connectedness. Our groups can offer us
support and confidence in our ways of understanding the world (Festinger, 1954;
Hogg & Abrams, 1993), a topic that will receive much more attention in Chapter 9.

The many benefits of group belonging come at a cost, however. Because our
groups are so important for defining the self, we need to see them as attractive,
valued, and successful. Unfortunately, valuing our own groups often entails preferring them over other groups. Regard, esteem, and liking for *in-groups*—groups to
which we belong—at times become coupled with disregard, derogation, and dislike
for *out-groups*. When this occurs, as sociologist William Graham Sumner (1906) said
long ago, "loyalty to the in-group . . . [and] hatred and contempt for outsiders . . .
all grow together" (p. 13). From school rivalries to ethnic prejudice to national
patriotism, both the exaltation of in-groups and the belittling of out-groups reflect
the importance of group membership for each of us.

These positive and negative sides of our group memberships will both be
explored throughout this chapter. The chapter first describes the way people come
to view social groups as aspects of the self: how we learn what group memberships
mean, and what factors conspire to make a particular membership significant at any
given time. The chapter then turns to the consequences of placing ourselves and
others in social categories. Once a group membership is activated, it affects the way
we see and respond to ourselves and others. Shared group membership tends to
make us view other in-group members as similar to ourselves and as likable, so we
try to treat them justly and fairly. But we often respond to out-group members with
indifference, active dislike, or even overt discrimination.

The chapter concludes with a discussion of the effects of belonging to a group
that others look down on. From playgrounds to boardrooms, being Muslim, speaking
with an accent, using a wheelchair, being gay or lesbian, or being on welfare can
provoke scorn, dislike, and avoidance. Such negative group identities can take their
toll on individuals and groups. But this outcome is not inevitable, and the chapter
concludes by describing how people resist the implications of a negative identity
and even work to change society's evaluation of their groups.

Categorizing Oneself as a Group Member

Some group memberships are so important that they become a basic part of our view of ourselves. Try asking a friend to take a piece of paper and write 10 different sentences beginning "I am . . . " When people perform this task they typically list some individual characteristics such as "I am outgoing" or "I am tall," but they also list group memberships: "I am a woman," "I am Taiwanese." In fact, most people list more group than individual characteristics (M. H. Kuhn & McPartland, 1954). The process of seeing oneself as a member of a group is known as **self-categorization** (J. C. Turner, Hogg, Oakes, Reicher, & Wetherell, 1987). Self-categorization is flexible and can readily shift (Mussweiler, Gabriel, & Bodenhausen, 2000). Depending on the social context, for example, sometimes you may see yourself as a Mexican-American, other times as a student, and still other times as a unique individual, with group memberships temporarily receding into the background. The term **social identity** refers to the way we feel about the group memberships that we share with others (M. Rosenberg, 1979; Tajfel, 1972). According to Henri Tajfel's **social identity theory**, people seek to derive positive self-esteem from their group memberships. Social identity turns "I" into "we"; it extends the self out beyond the skin to include other members of our groups—and, as we will see, it generally involves positive feelings about both ourselves, and others.

Although some group memberships are only fleetingly important—being part of the "white shirts" team in a lunch-hour basketball game, for example—most group memberships are stable and enduring. Membership in gender and ethnic groups lasts a lifetime. Being a member of the Duran or the Jackson family, or being Muslim, Roman Catholic, or Buddhist is just as long-lasting. How do we learn what characteristics are associated with our groups?

Learning About Our Groups

> People learn about the groups to which they belong in the same ways that they learn the characteristics of other groups: by observing other group members or from the culture.

To review the kinds of information on which we base impressions of groups, see Chapter 5, especially pages 149 to 157.

We learn about our own groups in the same ways that we learn stereotypes of other groups: Lessons come from parents, teachers, peers, and the media. However, our most important lessons generally come from fellow group members and what they do (Prentice & Miller, 2002). Consider your first job. What did it mean to become part of the team in the typing pool, on the factory floor, or in corporate headquarters? Did people joke around, or was the atmosphere pretty serious? Probably you figured out what it meant to be an employee in your company primarily—maybe only—by watching others. To illustrate the importance of interaction with group members, one study tracked sorority pledges' perceptions of their groups over an academic year and found that as they got to know them better, these women saw their groups in increasingly stereotypic terms—in other words, they learned the stereotypes (C. S. Ryan & Bogart, 1997).

In this way, what we and other group members do often becomes the basis for group stereotypes. But what we do generally depends on our cultural roles. In any society, members of a group may occupy particular roles that influence who they are. In the United States, for example, women are only 1% of automobile mechanics and carpenters and 8% of engineers, compared to 79% of cashiers, 84% of

Self-categorization. The process of seeing oneself as a member of a social group.

Social identity. Those aspects of the self-concept that derive from an individual's knowledge and feelings about the group memberships he or she shares with others.

Social identity theory. The theory that people's motivation to derive self-esteem from their group memberships is one driving force behind in-group bias.

elementary school teachers, and 93% of nurses (Wootton, 1997). Do a group's common roles and occupations influence group members' views of themselves? The answer is a qualified yes. People may not make direct inferences about their own characteristics on the basis of role-constrained behaviors as readily as observers do. Still, roles affect the individuals who hold them because as people enact their roles, they acquire role-related skills and develop tendencies to behave in certain ways. These skills and tendencies in turn make those behaviors, and correspondent self-inferences, more likely. A woman's experiences raising young children may leave her better able to interpret nonverbal behaviors or to comfort people when they are distressed. Or a man's past training in the use of aggression, perhaps in military service or organized sports, may leave him with the belief that aggressive behaviors are often effective. Thus, performing a role based on gender or on membership in some other group can shape our future behaviors and, ultimately, our self-knowledge (Eagly, 1987).

By turning to Chapter 4, pages 101 to 102, you can remind yourself of the reasons for this actor–observer difference in attributions.

Accessibility of Group Memberships

> Knowledge about group memberships may be activated by direct reminders, such as group labels; by the presence of out-group members; by being a minority; or by intergroup conflict. Group membership is particularly significant in some cultures and for some individuals, who tend to see the world in terms of that group membership.

No matter how extensive our knowledge about the characteristics of our groups, that knowledge will have little impact unless the group membership comes to mind. Imagine that you are a male Midwestern feminist, or a female Canadian conservative. Perhaps you are also musically talented, near-sighted, and love Cajun food. In what circumstances will your gender, politics, or other group memberships be more important than your individual attributes? And which group membership will matter? A variety of social and cognitive factors can conspire to make a particular group membership accessible. These range from temporary situational factors, to more enduring aspects of social structure or culture, to stable individual differences.

■ **Welcome to who you are.** As this young Native American boy at a Powwow dons the traditional headdress and face paintings, while watching his elders perform a traditional dance, he also learns what it means to be a member of his tribe. So it is with every group. As socialisation processes teach them history, traditions, and customs, young members absorb even deeper lessons: who they are and what their group stands for.

DIRECT REMINDERS OF MEMBERSHIP. If someone calls you "Reverend," or "nerd," or uses an ethnic slur, you are reminded directly though perhaps temporarily about your social identity. Honorary titles or pejorative labels bring group membership home in a hurry (Billig & Tajfel, 1973; Charters & Newcomb, 1958). Being offered a "senior citizen" discount at a restaurant or movie theater may be an unwelcome reminder of one's age (Stock, 1995). For this reason, some people in their 60s still pay the full admission price for a movie, refusing to take advantage of the discount! Often, however, the process is more subtle. Circumstances remind us of our similarities with others, and this activates knowledge of group membership. The mere presence of other in-group members can be a potent reminder (Doise & Sinclair, 1973; Wilder & Shapiro, 1991). Just hearing another New Zealand accent is enough to make one of the authors of this text "feel" like a New Zealander, and seeing someone in a Harvard T-shirt reminds the other author of his New England background. When group similarities are highlighted, as when a team wears uniforms or when members coordinate their actions for a common goal, membership and all it entails become even more accessible. This process is powerful enough to overcome alternative categorizations that might be important in other circumstances (Gaertner, Mann, Dovidio, Murrell, & Pomare, 1990).

So White and Surinamese soccer players join together on the Dutch national team, and Republicans and Democrats coordinate their talents on a town planning committee.

PRESENCE OF OUT-GROUP MEMBERS. The presence of out-group members can also be a forcible reminder of shared group membership, as demonstrated in a study conducted in Belgium. Two groups of Belgian university students were asked to write descriptions of typical students of Belgian and North African origin. For one group, the experimenter who made this request was a North African; for the other, the experimenter was Belgian. The responses of the students who wrote in the presence of an out-group member, the North African experimenter, revealed greater identification with their Belgian in-group (Marques, Yzerbyt, & Rijsman, 1988). Apparently, the presence of even a single out-group member is enough to increase our focus on in-group membership.

When outsiders are present, resourceful group members sometimes put their mouth where their membership is, using language to emphasize their identification with their group. For example, when French-speaking Canadians were confronted with English-speaking Canadians in one experiment, the French speakers either broadened their accents or switched to their native language altogether (Bourhis, Giles, Leyens, & Tajfel, 1978). Ethnic languages are important sources of social identity, as efforts by French speakers in Canada, Catalans in Spain, and Welsh nationalists in Britain to preserve their languages all attest.

BEING A MINORITY. If a few out-group members arriving on the scene can make in-group membership accessible, imagine the impact when they actually outnumber the in-group. In Chapter 4, we noted that people are more likely to think of themselves in terms of individual characteristics that are unusual or distinctive in their social group (W. J. McGuire & Padawer-Singer, 1978). The same principle operates at the group level: People are more likely to think of themselves in terms of their memberships in smaller groups than in larger ones (Brewer, 1991; Mullen, 1991; S. E. Taylor and others, 1978). The study by Brewer and Weber (1994) described at the beginning of this chapter illustrated this point, showing that members of a minority group were more likely than members of a majority to base their self-esteem on the performance of a fellow group member.

Consider the results obtained when William McGuire and his colleagues (W. J. McGuire, McGuire, & Winton, 1979) asked grade-school children to talk for 5 minutes about themselves and carefully coded these self-descriptions. As can be seen in Figure 6.1, the researchers found that boys and girls from households where their gender was in the minority were more likely to mention gender than were children from households where their gender made up the majority. Similarly, children whose ethnic group constituted a minority at school were more likely to mention their ethnicity in informal self-descriptions than were children who were part of the ethnic majority (W. J. McGuire, McGuire, Child, & Fujioka, 1978). Think about your friend's completions of the "I am . . . " sentences. Did your friend list group memberships that make him or her different from most other people?

CONFLICT OR RIVALRY. Although all of these transitory circumstances can make a social identity accessible, probably the most potent factor that brings group membership to mind is ongoing conflict or rivalry between groups (Doise & Weinberger, 1973; Ryen & Kahn, 1975). One experiment set up a discussion on a social issue, either between a male and a female participant who disagreed on the

You may recall a similar point from Chapter 5, pages 161 to 162: A solo member of a group tends to be perceived by observers in terms of that group membership.

■ **A unique car with unique owners?**
Sharing unusual characteristics can make those characteristics socially significant. Owners of the distinctive Volkswagen New Beetle have achieved group status: They find themselves honking at each other on the freeway and gathering in parking lots to discuss their cars.

Less flower. More power.

Drivers wanted. VW

Chapter 13 will describe the several vivid demonstrations of the effects of intergroup conflict on group identification, including the famed "Robbers Cave" study.

issue or between two men and two women, who disagreed along gender lines (Hogg & Turner, 1987). In the second condition, because the conflict was along group lines, participants identified more strongly with their groups, for example, by rating themselves as more typical of their sex. The importance of conflict also means that people identify more strongly with groups that they learn are targets of discrimination from the societal mainstream (Jetten, Branscombe, Schmitt, & Spears, 2001). Even a news report of rivalry can remind us of group loyalties. In one study, exposure to a campus newspaper headline like "Humanities, Science Majors at Odds Over Core Program" was enough to increase the accessibility of students' identity as scientists or humanists (V. Price, 1989). All in all, conflict is perhaps the most powerful factor in making a group membership accessible.

CULTURAL DIFFERENCES IN THE IMPORTANCE OF GROUP MEMBERSHIP. Group membership does not exist in a vacuum, of course, but has an importance that depends on the cultural context. Interdependent cultures, like most in Asia, South America, and Africa, foster and reinforce views of the self in group terms (Markus, Kitayama, & Heiman, 1996; Trafimow & Finlay, 2001). People from these cultures tend to see themselves as members of larger groups or categories—perhaps as workers at a particular plant, graduates of a certain school, or inhabitants of a

FIGURE 6.1   Being in the minority matters

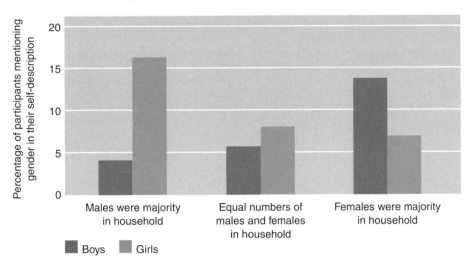

■ In this study, grade-school children spoke for five minutes in response to the instruction "Tell us about yourself." Notice that both boys and girls were more likely to mention their gender if their gender was a minority at home. (Based on W. J. McGuire and others, 1979.)

specific village. In such societies, family units are often multigenerational and employment relationships may last a lifetime.

In contrast, people who live in the United States, Canada, Northern Europe, and other individualistic cultures are encouraged to think of themselves in comparatively idiosyncratic terms, for example, as tall, dark, and handsome. They tend to value freedom, personal enjoyment, and the achievement of individual goals, while viewing group memberships as temporary and changeable (Bellah, Madsen, Sullivan, Tipton, & Swidler, 1985). Members of these societies have high divorce rates and often seem comfortable switching churches or employers. Thus, cultural differences can affect whether people think of themselves more often as individuals or as members of groups, and by so doing, they can create corresponding differences in social behavior (Markus & Kitayama, 1991). But as we will see throughout this chapter, even in individualistic cultures in which group memberships are seen as more fluid and less omnipresent, group memberships make a big difference to people's ways of thinking about themselves and those around them (Jetten, Postmes, & McAuliffe, 2002).

☐ **PERSONALITY DIFFERENCES IN GROUP MEMBERSHIP IMPORTANCE.** Every time you think of yourself as a group member—as, perhaps, a Texan, a psychologist, or a single mother—the mere thought increases the likelihood that you will think of yourself that way again. A group membership that is personally very significant—religious identification for a member of the clergy, party affiliation for a politician, or racial or ethnic group membership for a civil rights leader—will be frequently activated and highly accessible. This accessibility produces reliable differences in the way each of us habitually sees ourselves and others. For example, people for whom gender is chronically important and accessible have "male" or "female" as part of their self-schema (S. Bem, 1981). Accordingly, these individuals tend to perceive, and to react to, themselves and others in terms of gender rather than other social attributes (Frable, 1989). Similarly, people who are more racially prejudiced or more prone to use racial stereotypes seem more concerned with categorizing others by race (Blascovich and others, 1997; Zárate & Smith, 1990). Figure 6.2 summarizes all the factors that can make a social identity accessible.

To remind yourself of the consequences of having a particular trait as part of the self-schema, see Chapter 4, especially page 104.

FIGURE 6.2 Factors that make a social identity accessible

■ Many factors can increase the accessibility of a particular group membership. Not only obvious reminders, like group labels or intergroup conflict, but even relatively subtle factors like the presence of out-group members can activate our knowledge of group membership. A particular membership that is significant in the general culture or is personally important to an individual may be highly accessible virtually all the time.

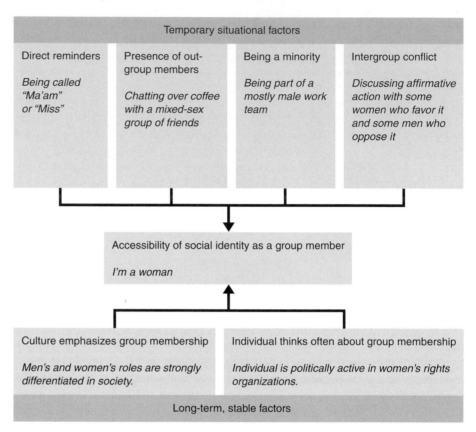

Me, You, and Them: Effects of Social Categorization

Does it really make a difference if we see ourselves as Belgians, Californians, socialists, or libertarians? It certainly does! When group memberships surface, they influence the way we see ourselves and others, making a huge difference in how we think, feel, and act. The reason is that group memberships not only help define our self and tell us who we are, but they also connect us to some people (fellow in-group members) at the same time as they divide us from others (out-group members). As we discuss these three effects of group memberships in turn, you will see that they are all interconnected.

"I" Becomes "We": Social Categorization and the Self

Activated knowledge about a group membership has multiple effects on people's self-concept and self-esteem. The group's typical characteristics become standards for members' behavior. Group memberships also influence people's moods and self-esteem as they feel bad about their groups' failures or good about their successes. Relatively small groups typically have the greatest effects.

SEEING ONSELF AS A GROUP MEMBER. Seeing oneself as a group member means that the group's typical characteristics become norms or standards for one's own behavior (J. C. Turner, Hogg, Oakes, Reicher, & Wetherell, 1987). As a result, people tend to think and act in group-typical ways. One experiment demonstrated this effect by having some students listen to a discussion in which one group presented pro-environmental attitudes. Some of the students were about to join the group voicing the positive attitudes, while others knew they would not be joining. The students who were going to join the group rated themselves as higher in environmental awareness than did the other students who heard the same discussion (Mackie, 1986). In other words, their own opinions moved toward the group's position. In another study, Dutch university students were presented with a comparison that was potentially threatening to their group; for example, psychology students were asked to compare their own group to physics students on intelligence (Spears, Doosje, & Ellemers, 1997). The way students responded to this threat depended on their initial level of identification with their group. Students who identified only weakly avoided the threat by dissociating themselves from the in-group. But students who strongly identified with their group tended to show group solidarity by rating themselves as highly typical of their group. As this result shows, factors that activate people's group identity—even social comparisons that are threatening to the group—can cause people to see themselves as typical group members.

The same process is responsible for the finding that when laboratory groups include men, women speak more tentatively than they do in all-female groups (Carli, 1990). The presence of men apparently makes the women's identity as females accessible, causing them to act in ways that they regard as typical of women, such as by avoiding assertive speech. In fact, gender group norms are generally highly valued, so acting in accordance with those norms tends to make people feel good about themselves (W. Wood, Christensen, Hebl, & Rothgerber, 1997).

☐ **ACCESSIBILITY OF GENDER IDENTITY IN THE CLASSROOM.** If group memberships can affect people's behavior in a situation as transient as a research discussion group, what is the likely long-term impact of highly accessible gender roles? College enrollment statistics suggest that they may influence women's and men's career and educational choices. In coeducational schools, men tend to major in the hard sciences and mathematics, and women in the humanities and fine arts. These majors are consistent with traditional stereotypes of men and women, which a mixed-sex environment renders more accessible. In contrast, compared with their counterparts in coeducational schools, women in women's colleges are more likely to major in science or math, and men in men's colleges, in the arts or humanities (E. R. Smith, 1977). Though many factors no doubt contribute to explaining outcomes like these, could the reduced salience of gender in single-sex schools reduce the impact of gender stereotypes on men's and women's choices of major?

LIKING OURSELVES: SOCIAL IDENTITY AND SELF-ESTEEM. We have all experienced it: We feel great when our team wins. When Brazil's soccer team won the 2002 World Cup championship, rebounding from a painful defeat in the

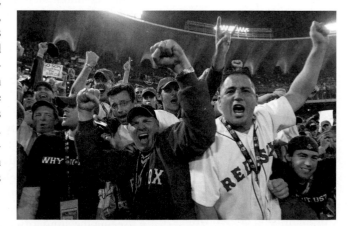

■ **Basking in reflected glory.** When we identify with a group, their emotional ups and downs become our own. Like these Boston Red Fox fans, we are not only happy to join in a victory celebration, we are happy *because* our team has won.

final game of the previous tournament 4 years earlier, hundreds of thousands of their fans poured into the streets for a frenzied celebration. Why? Because our groups are part of ourselves, when good things happen to our team, our school, or our city, we feel good—about life and about ourselves. Recall that in the experiment described at the outset of this chapter, the same process made members of a minority group feel good or bad depending on the performance of a fellow group member (Brewer & Weber, 1994).

Strivers for positive self-esteem that we are, we play up group memberships that make us feel good about ourselves (Mussweiler, Gabriel, & Bodenhausen, 2000; Tesser, 1988). Robert Cialdini and his co-workers (1976) investigated this tendency to **BIRG** (pronounced to rhyme with "surge"), or *bask in the reflected glory* of a positive group identification, by counting "in-group" clothing worn on school days following football games. At seven universities they found that students wore more school sweatshirts, baseball caps, scarves, and pins if the football team won than if it lost.

To test their hypothesis that links to a positive group membership serve to raise self-esteem, Cialdini and his colleagues (1976) gave students a brief general-knowledge test and temporarily raised or lowered their self-esteem by manipulating the results. Some randomly selected students were told falsely that they had performed poorly on the test, and others were told that they had done well. The students were then asked, seemingly incidentally, to describe the outcome of a recent game. In their descriptions, the students who thought they had failed the test were more likely to associate themselves with winning teams (referring to them as "we") and to dissociate themselves from losing teams (referring to them as "they"), than were students who believed they had done well and whose self-esteem was intact. Thus, people BIRG as a way of restoring positive self-regard, and they do so particularly when self-esteem is threatened.

SOCIAL IDENTITY AND EMOTIONS. Group memberships lead us to experience emotions on behalf of our groups, as well as affecting our self-esteem (E. R. Smith, 1993). In one study demonstrating this point, psychology students were told about another psychology student at a different university who had been treated unfairly by authorities. In one condition where the participants were subtly reminded of their common identity with the victim, they reported feeling less happy and more angry—despite the fact that they themselves remained totally unaffected by the events (Gordijn, Wigboldus, & Yzerbyt, 2001). People experience anger, fear, pride, guilt, or other emotions in response to events that affect their groups because identification with a group makes the group part of the self, giving the group emotional significance (Iyer, Leach, & Crosby, 2003; Mackie, Devos, & Smith, 2000).

BALANCING INDIVIDUALITY AND CONNECTEDNESS. As we saw in Chapter 4, people generally like to see themselves as unique individuals, distinct from others. Yet they are also motivated to seek connectedness and similarity with others. Can people balance these two seemingly incompatible needs? In fact, group membership can simultaneously satisfy both. Perceiving the differences between our group and other groups provides feelings of being unique and special, while seeing the similarity among members within our group can help us feel connected and similar (Brewer, 1991). Though individual and cultural differences influence the relative strengths of these opposing motives, the best balance for most people most of the time involves membership in relatively small groups. A group that is

You may recall from Chapter 4, pages 109 to 110, that, in the same way, people tend to play up the idiosyncratic characteristics they feel good about.

BIRG (bask in reflected glory). A way of boosting self-esteem by identifying oneself with the accomplishments or good qualities of fellow in-group members.

too small might not be an adequate basis for group pride, but in a group that is too large, the person might be too anonymous to attain much respect. One study confirmed this idea by showing that people's identification with small groups increased when experimental manipulations increased their desires *either* for connectedness or for uniqueness (Pickett, Bonner, & Coleman, 2002). Relatively small groups seem to provide the best balance between similarity and group identification on the one hand and uniqueness and recognition for one's individual qualities on the other (Brewer, 1991; Hornsey & Jetten, 2004).

Others Become "We": Social Categorization and the In-Group

When group membership is highly accessible, people see other in-group members as similar in their central group-linked characteristics. However, extensive personal interaction (when group membership is not activated) also provides knowledge about their unique and diverse personal characteristics. People like fellow in-group members and tend to treat them in fair, humane, and altruistic ways, seeing the other members as similar to themselves in their goals and interests.

An accessible group membership is not just an aspect of the individual self, like one's height or chess-playing ability. Instead, this aspect of social identity links the individual to others and therefore influences the way the person thinks, feels, and acts toward other in-group members.

PERCEIVING FELLOW IN-GROUP MEMBERS. When we think about fellow in-group members, what is uppermost in our minds? When group membership is accessible, we think mostly about the features we believe we share with the group, thereby causing us to see other in-group members as similar to ourselves (Chen & Kenrick, 2002; Gramzow, Gaertner, & Sedikides, 2001). In one demonstration of this effect, students were assigned to groups ostensibly on the basis of their artistic preferences. They were then asked to guess the extent to which other in-group members shared their own personal characteristics and preferences (V. L. Allen & Wilder, 1979). As expected, the students assumed that all members of the group would be very similar in art preferences. Surprisingly, they also thought that in-group members' interests, activities, and even personality traits would match their own. Anything that increases the accessibility of group membership—being a minority, engaging in competition, even just making judgments about another group, for example—further enhances this assumed similarity (Haslam, Oakes, Turner, & McGarty, 1995; Mussweiler & Bodenhausen, 2002; B. Simon, 1992).

Although a highly accessible shared group membership leads us to focus on our similarities with other in-group members, we also manage to learn quite a lot about other in-group members' personal qualities—the things that make them unique as individuals. This awareness of specific, personal attributes develops as we interact with other members in a variety of contexts and situations (J. C. Turner and others, 1987). It is particularly acute when personal rather than group identities are most salient, as when a group of close friends chat together over dinner.

Knowing about others' unique characteristics helps us to find our own place in the group. As Chapter 4 noted, we define our personal selves in terms of what makes us distinct from others (W. J. McGuire and others, 1978; Park & Rothbart, 1982). Among your fellow students, you may be the serious one, the conservationist, the lover of country music. Of course, to make these differentiations you have to pay attention to the personality, passions, and preferences of your fellow in-group members. In doing so, you learn a lot about them—so much that when group membership is not highly accessible, you are likely to see your group as quite diverse in characteristics not related to group membership (Park & Judd, 1990).

LIKING IN-GROUP MEMBERS: TO BE US IS TO BE LOVABLE. Because they share our attributes, fellow in-group members become part of "me and mine" and so we like them, usually much more than we like out-group members (Otten & Wentura, 2001). Asked to evaluate essays or creative solutions to problems, people treat their own group's work more generously than out-group products. They choose to interact with and to befriend members of their own rather than of another group (Brewer, 1979; Brewer & Silver, 1978). Even people assigned to groups on a trivial or random basis evaluate their own group as more positive and desirable than other groups, and the in-group bias is stronger yet when the groups are real and meaningful (Mullen, Brown, & Smith, 1992).

Indeed, the very concept "we" seems to have positive connotations, as compared with the concept "they" (Perdue, Dovidio, Gurtman, & Tyler, 1990). When people have seen nonsense syllables (like *xeh*) paired with the word *we*, they have more positive feelings about them, compared to syllables paired with the word *they*. Participants also respond more quickly to positive words that follow the prime "we" than to those that follow "they." This is true even when the prime words are flashed too quickly to be consciously read. Both of these findings suggest that the label "we" automatically activates positive associations that facilitate the recognition of other positive words. In a clever study of the consequences of these effects for intergroup behavior, students were asked to read a description of the task that they were to perform with other individuals. For one group of participants, this task was described as "something we all have to do our best on"; for other participants it was "something they have to do their best on." When asked to imagine the quality of the interaction and the likability of the other participants, those who had been exposed to the in-group pronouns had more positive expectations than those who had read out-group pronouns (Dovidio & Gaertner, 1993).

It may have occurred to you that attraction to other in-group members is somehow different from "ordinary" feelings of liking for another individual. After all, attraction usually depends on getting to know someone—on recognizing their desirable personal characteristics and your common interests. In contrast, attraction in group situations seems to depend merely on the knowledge of shared group membership (J. C. Turner, Sachdev, & Hogg, 1983). Indeed, people often prefer others who are typical members of an in-group even if those people would not be especially likable on the merits of their individual characteristics alone. This pattern has been observed in many types of groups, including work groups and the members of an Australian football team (Hogg, Cooper-Shaw, & Holzworth, 1993; Hogg & Hardie, 1991; Schmitt & Branscombe, 2001). In a sense, in-group members are liked not as individuals but as representatives of the liked group (Clement & Krueger, 1998).

GIVING IN-GROUP MEMBERS THE LANGUAGE ADVANTAGE. This special kind of liking for fellow in-group members influences the very language people use to describe others' actions (Maass, 1999). Anne Maass and her colleagues (Maass, Salvi, Arcuri, & Semin, 1989) prepared cartoon drawings depicting positive actions by in-group and out-group members. Asked to describe the actions, participants gave relatively concrete and specific descriptions of out-group behavior, whereas the in-group descriptions were more abstract and general. If an out-group member comforted a lost child on a crowded street, participants said "he talked to the child," or some similarly specific statement. The same action by an in-group member elicited "he helped" or "cared for the child." The researchers argue that the concreteness of the out-group descriptions implicitly casts the behaviors as ungeneralizable, one-of-a-kind instances, while the more abstract terms used for in-group actions emphasize their links to the actor's positive general characteristics, such as helpfulness or caring. Another study found that people answer questions about positive attributes of the in-group or negative attributes of the out-group on the basis of their general impressions of those groups. But when asked about negative in-group or positive out-group characteristics, the participants tried to recall specific behaviors from memory (J. W. Sherman, Klein, Laskey, & Wyer, 1998). Like the linguistic bias just described, this judgment strategy implicitly frames unexpected types of behaviors (such as negative acts by in-group members) as isolated, specific occurrences, that is, as exceptions to the rule rather than the general rule.

You might have noticed that the attributions we make about our groups are just like the self-enhancing attributions we make as individuals. To check the parallels for yourself, see Chapter 4, pages 131 to 132.

TREATING THE IN-GROUP RIGHT: JUSTICE AND ALTRUISM. If in-group members are lovable and similar to us, we will want to treat them as we ourselves would like to be treated. Indeed, people sometimes act in ways that seem to make no sense from the perspective of individual costs and benefits. Parents scrimp and save to leave an inheritance for their children. Soldiers sacrifice their lives for their comrades or their country. From the perspective of a social group, however, actions like these make a great deal of sense. Groups prosper when their members are willing to subordinate personal interests to the group and to help other members in times of need. This has been true since members of many early hunting societies shared the meat from large animals among the whole group (A. P. Fiske, 1992). When group memberships are uppermost in people's minds, they often act in these altruistic ways, showing more concern for treating others fairly than for getting the largest share of rewards (Tyler, Lind, Ohbuchi, Sugawara, & Huo, 1998; Wenzel, 2004).

When people see the world through the lens of their group memberships, what is best for the group blurs together with what is best for the individual. As "I" becomes "we," the distinction between self-interest and group interest vanishes (J. C. Turner and others, 1987). This merging of perceived individual and group interests constitutes the psychological basis for fair and altruistic behavior. Over a century ago, Charles Darwin (1871/1909) argued that morality derives originally "from the social instincts": Actions are judged good or bad "solely as they obviously affect the welfare of the tribe." When people think of themselves as members of a family, community, ethnic group, or nation, they *feel like* and *feel for* fellow in-group members. As a result, treating those others with fairness and compassion—indeed, treating others as they themselves would like to be treated—becomes easy, natural, and the right thing to do (Deutsch, 1973, 1990; Staub, 1978; Struch & Schwartz, 1989).

It is this unification of self-interest and group-interest that makes altruistic and self-sacrificing behavior possible, as we will see in Chapter 14. It is also the basis of effective functioning of small interacting groups, a topic discussed in detail in Chapter 12.

An accessible group membership makes other in-group members part of "me and mine." Shared group membership has dramatic effects on the way we think about, evaluate, and behave toward other members, as shown in Figure 6.3.

FIGURE 6.3   Social identity turns others into "we"

■ When a shared group membership is accessible, it has positive effects on the way we see, evaluate, and treat other group members.

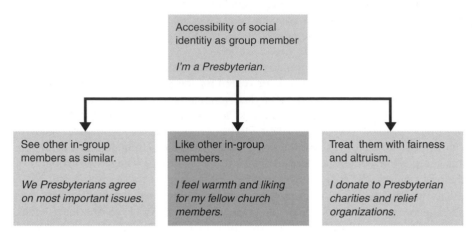

Accessibility of social identitiy as group member

I'm a Presbyterian.

See other in-group members as similar.

We Presbyterians agree on most important issues.

Like other in-group members.

I feel warmth and liking for my fellow church members.

Treat them with fairness and altruism.

I donate to Presbyterian charities and relief organizations.

Others Become "They": Social Categorization and the Out-Group

People see out-groups as uniform and homogeneous. People also dislike, devalue, and discriminate against out-group members, depending on the extent to which they are seen as threatening to the in-group. When the out-group is simply different, it elicits mild dislike. When the out-group is seen as outdoing the in-group, this more serious threat results in resentment, dislike, and overt discrimination. Out-groups that are seen as severe threats to the in-group elicit murderous hatred, discrimination, aggression, or moral exclusion.

The comedian Emo Phillips (cited in D. L. Hamilton & Mackie, 1990) describes a conversation with a suicidal man threatening to jump off a bridge:

> *I said, "Are you a Christian or a Jew?" He said, "A Christian." I said, "Me too. Protestant or Catholic?" He said, "Protestant." I said, "Me too. What franchise?" He says "Baptist." I said, "Me too. Northern Baptist or Southern Baptist?" He says, "Northern Baptist." I said, "Me too. Northern Conservative Baptist or Northern Liberal Baptist?" He says, "Northern Conservative Baptist." I said, "Me too. Northern Conservative Fundamentalist Baptist or Northern Conservative Reformed Baptist?" He says, "Northern Conservative Fundamentalist Baptist." I said, "Me too. Northern Conservative Fundamentalist Baptist, Great Lakes Region, or Northern Conservative Fundamentalist Baptist, Eastern Region?" He says, "Northern Conservative Fundamentalist Baptist, Great Lakes Region." I said, "Me too. Northern Conservative Fundamentalist Baptist, Great Lakes Region, Council of 1879 or Northern Conservative Fundamentalist Baptist, Great Lakes Region, Council of 1912?" He says, "Northern Conservative Fundamentalist Baptist, Great Lakes Region, Council of 1912." I said, "Die, heretic!" and I pushed him over.* (D. L. Hamilton & Mackie, 1990, p. 110)

Emo Phillips makes comic what more often is tragic: the tendency to hate and mistreat those who are not members of our in-group, regardless of how similar to us they may seem to outsiders. We have seen that people generally feel good about their own groups, and while this tendency may be benign, all too often bringing one group up in the world also means putting others down. Unfortunately, anthropological evidence suggests that hostility toward out-groups is common in intergroup relations. Throughout human history and in every human culture, esteem, consideration, and favoritism await in-group members, whereas disdain, discrimination, and domination are often the fate of those categorized as out-group members (LeVine & Campbell, 1972). What conditions encourage the transition from mild in-group favoritism to often violent out-group hostility? The process that culminates in these negative outcomes begins with a perception of out-group members as all alike: faceless people who lack individuality.

PERCEIVING THE OUT-GROUP AS HOMOGENEOUS: "THEY'RE ALL ALIKE!". A member of an Isla Vista, California, band explained, "Los Angeles bands are all homogeneous. Seattle bands all sound like Seattle bands. But Isla Vista music is more original. Bands here play all kinds of music!" (Lagerquist, 1992). You should have no difficulty finding other examples of this **out-group homogeneity effect**: the tendency to perceive out-group members as "all the same" compared to the relatively more diverse in-group. People of European origin typically see the widely diverse groups of Native Americans as "all the same" while finding great diversity and variety among those of European descent. Brothers in one fraternity find members of other houses just as they expected them, but do not think they themselves fit their own group's stereotype (Linville, Fisher, & Salorey, 1989; Mullen & Hu, 1989). Thus the tendency to see out-groups as relatively homogeneous is quite widespread. What accounts for this effect?

One obvious potential explanation involves numbers: We usually know more in-group members than out-group members, and we are therefore more aware of their diversity. The more students you know on your campus, for example, the better your chances are of coming across a wide variety of individuals, such as the vegetarian gourmet cook, the athlete majoring in engineering, and the antinuclear activist. No wonder the in-group seems more diverse than the students at another, less familiar college (Linville and others, 1989). But lack of familiarity with the out-group cannot be the whole story. In fact, even members of laboratory groups, meeting under carefully controlled conditions so that participants have equal information about their own and other groups, see their fellow group members as more varied than members of other groups (Judd & Park, 1988; Mackie, Sherman, & Worth, 1993). And in studies that follow the development of group impressions as people get to know each other by interacting over many weeks, increasing familiarity often makes people view groups as increasingly homogeneous (Oakes, Haslam, Morrison, & Grace, 1995). On the basis of studies like these, it is clear that familiarity alone cannot fully explain the out-group homogeneity effect.

Another important factor is the relatively constrained nature of typical interactions with out-group members. The very presence of an outsider may be enough to make the group close ranks and present a unified front. In fact, people's exposure to out-groups often takes place in settings where no individual interaction is even possible, for example, when students from a rival school attend a sports event en masse. In such settings, one can easily gain the impression that out-group members are pretty much all alike. In contrast, interactions with in-group members are likely to be relatively more varied, relaxed, and informal (Rothbart, Dawes, & Park, 1984).

Out-group homogeneity effect. The tendency to see the out-group as relatively more homogeneous and less diverse than the in-group.

Finally, as we stated earlier, people habitually focus on the personal character-istics that make them unique and different from others. Within the in-group, this means that we learn a lot about others' characteristics in the process of finding out what differentiates us from them. But we can feel unique and different from out-group members just by noting their group-defining characteristics, such as ethnic-ity, gender, nationality, or university affiliation (J. C. Turner and others, 1987). In a study demonstrating this effect, Bernadette Park and Myron Rothbart (1982) asked students to read brief newspaper stories about men and women. When they later were asked to recall as much as they could about the protagonists, they remembered more personal details, such as occupation, about same-sex than about opposite-sex individuals (see Figure 6.4).

Although these cognitive and social processes mean that out-groups are usually perceived as more homogeneous than in-groups, there are interesting excep-tions to the rule. When the in-group is a minority, it tends to be perceived as more homogeneous than the majority out-group, by outsiders and by its own members (R. Brown & Smith, 1989; B. Simon & Brown, 1987). But even this exception can be explained by the same processes outlined earlier. People who belong to a small minority may know even more members of the majority out-group than members of their own small in-group. They often see majority individuals in a wide variety of roles and situations, and they can expect to interact with them as frequently as with members of their own small group. And, if the majority commands more power and resources than the minority, minority group members may have to depend upon the majority and will have to be careful to treat individual majority group members in appropriate ways (Fiske, 1993a). For all these reasons, members of minority groups typically have strong reasons for recognizing the variability of the majority group, as well as of their own in-group.

Not only perceptions of variability, but actual variability of groups may also be affected by structural factors such as group power and numbers. Unequal power also tends to make members of the lower-power group act in more uniform and

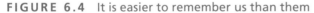

FIGURE 6.4   It is easier to remember us than them

■ In this study, men and women were asked to read a "newspaper story" and, at a later time, to recall information about the main characters. As you can see, men more easily recalled the occupations of male characters, whereas women more easily recalled female characters' occupations. (Based on Park & Rothbart, 1982.)

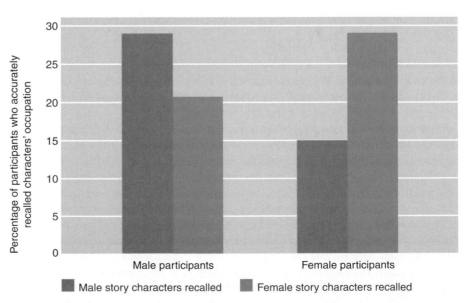

homogeneous ways (Guinote, Judd, & Brauer, 2002). And as we have already seen, group membership is more often on the minds of minorities than of majorities (Mullen, 1991). Its accessibility in turn causes people to see themselves as typical group members and to act accordingly (B. Simon & Hamilton, 1994). Thus, low power and minority status sometimes increase group members' actual, as well as perceived, uniformity of thoughts and actions.

☐ **OUT-GROUP HOMOGENEITY IN THE LEGAL SYSTEM.** The out-group homogeneity effect extends even to the perception of physical characteristics, and this can have destructive effects. People can recognize the faces of members of their own ethnic group more easily than the faces of members of other groups, an effect called the *cross-race identification bias* (Anthony, Copper, & Mullen, 1992; Bothwell, Brigham, & Malpass, 1989). Apparently, members of other groups "all look alike." In one study, Texas convenience store clerks were asked to identify three male customers—actually experimental confederates—who had stopped by to make a purchase earlier in the day. One confederate was Black, another was Mexican-American, and the third was Anglo-American. The shop clerks were also members of these three ethnic groups. As Figure 6.5 shows, the clerks made more accurate identifications of the customer belonging to their own group than they did of the customers from the other two groups (Platz & Hosch, 1988). As familiarity with a group grows, so too does identification accuracy (A. G. Goldstein & Chance, 1985). No wonder, then, that criminal defendants and their attorneys often question the accuracy of eyewitness identifications across ethnic group lines.

The tendency to see members of the out-group as all alike may in itself be relatively harmless, but it sets the stage for worse feelings and behavior. You need only look at any newspaper, turn on the television newscast, or flip back to the examples in Chapter 5 to see ample evidence that groups treat other groups badly, in

FIGURE 6.5 Inaccuracy in cross-ethnic identification

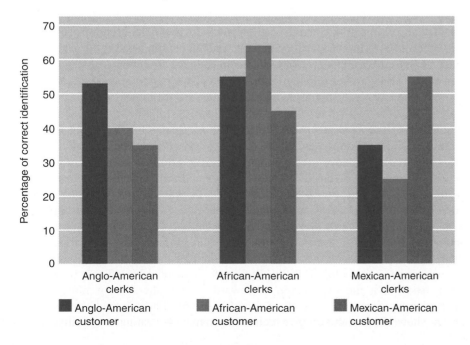

■ Convenience store clerks who were either Anglo-American, African-American, or Mexican-American tried to identify customers that researchers had sent to visit their store earlier. The three customers also belonged to one of the three ethnic groups. As shown here, clerks were best able to identify customers from their own group. (Based on Platz & Hosch, 1988.)

ways ranging from mild dislike and overt discrimination all the way to domination, exploitation, and massacre. As we will see, one important factor in the way out-groups are treated is how much threat they seem to pose to the in-group.

EFFECTS OF MERE CATEGORIZATION: DISCRIMINATION FAVORING THE IN-GROUP. For ethnic conflict in the Sudan or Iraq, or any of the other manifold examples of one group's maltreatment of another, multiple explanations can be offered. These include negative stereotypes, mutual ignorance and fear, unjust distribution of resources, and a history of conflict. However, perhaps the most sobering body of social-psychological research on the issue reaches a startling conclusion: Explanations like these are not always necessary. Discrimination can occur when a dividing line simply creates two groups, even in the absence of these common sources of antagonism.

In one of the experiments that initially demonstrated this point, a number of English boys aged 14 to 16 were assigned to Group X or Group W on the basis of a coin toss (Billig & Tajfel, 1973). The groups had no defining characteristics, and members did not know which other individuals were in each group. There was no basis for in-group or out-group stereotypes, and the groups had no history of conflict or antagonism—indeed, no history at all. For all these reasons, this situation was appropriately labeled a **minimal intergroup situation**. After being assigned to a group, each boy was given the opportunity to distribute rewards worth a small amount of money to two other individuals. For example, he might be asked to divide, in any way he wanted, 15 points between two other boys, who were identified only as "Member number 49 of the W group" and "Member number 72 of the X group."

The late European social psychologist Henri Tajfel devised this procedure as a baseline for further comparisons. He planned to go beyond merely categorizing participants into groups, and to add other ingredients, such as negative stereotypes or conflict over resources, one at a time until prejudice and discrimination developed. However, the results in the baseline situation confounded the researchers' expectations. Even in this minimal situation, the boys favored their own group: They awarded more points to members of their in-group than to boys in the out-group. They were not always blatantly unfair; for example, of the 15 points, boys awarded an average of 8.08 to the in-group and 6.92 to the out-group. However, the bias in favor of the in-group was consistent, and this finding was replicated in many other similar studies (Brewer, 1979; Mullen and others, 1992). Simple categorization into groups seems to be sufficient reason for people to dispense valued rewards in ways that favor in-group members over those who are "different."

DISCRIMINATION AND SOCIAL IDENTITY. What explains the favoritism found in minimal intergroup situations? Were people simply seeking material gain for the in-group? Tajfel was not so sure. His further explorations of behavior in minimal intergroup situations revealed a startling tendency: Participants often favor the in-group over the out-group *even when doing so costs the in-group in absolute terms*. For example, Tajfel gave some of his participants a choice between option A, which allocates 11 points to an in-group member and 7 to an out-group member, and option B, which gives 17 points to each. Many preferred option A, which gave the in-group an edge over the out-group, even though choosing A instead of B cost the in-group 6 points (Tajfel, Billig, Bundy, & Flament, 1971). These results and others show that the expectation of rewards is not the driving force behind intergroup discrimination (Gagnon & Bourhis, 1996). A host of studies of minimal groups showed that members give their own group higher ratings on positive traits,

Minimal intergroup situation. A research situation in which people are categorized, on an arbitrary or trivial basis, into groups that have no history, no conflicts of interest, and no stereotypes.

Cartoon © Jules Feiffer

evaluations of performance, and inferences of morality (Brewer, 1979). Apparently, group members want to make their groups better, stronger, and more lovable in any way available to them.

These findings led Tajfel to propose that just as we strive to view our individual selves positively, we also want to view our social identities in positive terms. This idea was the basis for *social identity theory*, which argues that people's motivation to derive positive self-esteem from their group memberships is one driving force behind in-group bias (Tajfel and others, 1971). Preferring the in-group over the out-group becomes a way of expressing regard for the in-group, and it is therefore a way of feeling good about oneself, of valuing me and mine (M. Rubin & Hewstone, 1998). Interestingly, studies show that people in minimal intergroup situations do not discriminate when allocating negative outcomes (like unpleasant blasts of noise) as they do when handing out praise or money (Otten & Mummendey, 2000). This finding again illustrates the distinction between in-group favoritism (which occurs even in minimal intergroup situations) and out-group hostility, which requires other ingredients such as direct intergroup conflict. Only when in-group preference is joined by threat or conflict do people shift from simply rewarding the in-group to actively punishing the out-group.

Group memberships have many benefits: They give us a sense of belonging and connectedness, as well as helping us to master and understand the world correctly. (We will discuss many of these benefits in more detail in Chapter 9.) However, enhancing self-esteem is indeed one of the most important effects of group membership, as social identity theory holds. The finding that people can increase their self-esteem by discriminating against out-groups has been repeatedly confirmed (Lemyre & Smith, 1985; Hewstone, Rubin, & Willis, 2002; M. Rubin & Hewstone, 1998). And people are particularly likely to choose this tactic when their self-esteem has recently suffered a blow. In a study by Steven Fein and Steven Spencer (1997), for example, some participants were given false negative feedback on a supposed intelligence test. They then read a detailed description about a young actor's struggles to begin a career in New York City. If the description of the actor implied that he was probably gay, participants who had been made to feel bad about themselves rated the actor in highly negative and stereotypic terms. The ratings were more positive if the actor was described as heterosexual, or if the participant had received no negative feedback. Other kinds of threat, like being reminded of their own mortality, can also increase people's tendency to express biased views of out-groups (Nelson, Moore, Olivetti, & Scott, 1997).

But in the minimal intergroup situation, what is the threat that might spur people to discriminate against the out-group? In fact, being categorized in one of two unknown groups constitutes a threat to most people. Consider the experimental situation from the participant's point of view. You are assigned to a totally meaning-less group and referred to by a code number rather than by name. Your only possible source of identity is the in-group/out-group distinction, and even the in-group cannot provide much of a positive identity because it is indistinguishable from the out-group. The results of one study demonstrated that this type of categorization can indeed be threatening. In the study, some participants were categorized as member 16 of an unknown "Red group," while others were assigned the personal code number 16 but were not categorized. Those assigned to an unknown group were found to have lower self-esteem than the other participants (Lemyre & Smith, 1985). The lost self-esteem was restored only by the opportunity to discriminate in favor of the in-group—to say, in effect, that the difference between the in-group and the out-group is that the in-group is better.

EFFECTS OF PERCEIVED DISADVANTAGE: LET'S COMPETE WITH THEM. Mild threats to a group can occur within the laboratory, but the often more severe threats in the outside world have the same effect of triggering intergroup discrimination. The effects differ, however, depending on the relative status positions of the groups (Ellemers & van Knippenberg, 1997; Bettencourt, Charlton, Dorr, & Hume, 2001). When higher-status groups are threatened, they tend to discriminate on dimensions that are centrally relevant to the group distinction. Thus, the economically successful tend to stereotype groups with lower economic standing as lazy, lacking ambition, and unintelligent—traits seen as quite relevant to economic position and success. In contrast, lower-status groups show more discrimination on other dimensions that are less directly relevant to status. So lower-class groups frequently evaluate themselves more favorably than higher-class out-groups on dimensions like friendliness, cooperativeness, or likability (Sachdev & Bourhis, 1991).

In general, unequal status amplifies intergroup discrimination. If groups perceive themselves as losing out to an out-group that is gaining in status, power, or prosperity, they often turn from mild dislike to stronger emotions (Fiske, 2002). Anger, resentment, and support for overt discrimination against the out-group are frequent outcomes. For example, Whites in the United States who regard their racial group as threatened by out-groups tend to oppose interracial marriage, affirmative action, school desegregation programs, and welfare spending (J. M. Jones, 1992; Sears & Allen, 1984).

EFFECTS OF EXTREME THREAT: THEY THREATEN US, SO LET'S ATTACK FIRST. One evening in October 1998, two men lured Matthew Shepard, a 21-year-old college student in Laramie, Wyoming, from a bar out to their pickup truck. Driving out of town, they beat Shepard severely, fracturing his skull with a blow from a pistol butt. Finally, they burned him, and left him tied to a fence in near-freezing temperatures. When a passerby found him 18 hours later he was rushed to a hospital, but he never regained consciousness and died several days later. The two attackers did not know Shepard personally, and they had no history of disagreement or conflict with him. Their only motive for this brutal crime was that Shepard was gay. What can explain this kind of hatred? Stereotypes can produce group prejudice, as we discussed in Chapter 5, and Shepard's attackers probably believed that gay men have a variety of negative characteristics. But can stereotypes fully account for such murderous hatred?

When prejudice turns from dislike to extreme hatred, it usually reflects the perception that what "they" stand for threatens everything that "we" stand for (Brewer, 2001). When people see such extreme threat, they usually respond in two interrelated ways. First, they exalt in-group symbols and values. Past or present group leaders, flags, slogans, and the group's historical accomplishments are glorified and cast in a totally positive light. Second, they derogate, hate, and attack the out-group they perceive as threatening. Thus, hatred for outsiders often arises in connection with the exaltation of in-group symbols, whether the hatred is directed against homosexuals, women, immigrants, or racial, ethnic, or religious groups (Kinder, 1986; Sears, 1988). Recall that in the minimal intergroup situation, preferences for the in-group are relatively mild, taking the form of favoring the in-group with good things but usually not giving the out-group an unfair share of punishments (Otten & Mummendey, 2000). However, extreme group threat ties together glorification of the in-group and hatred for the out-group into an ominous package (Branscombe & Wann, 1994).

One reason that in-group love and out-group hate become tied together is that people see their in-group norms and standards as applying beyond their own group, and use them to judge the out-group as well. Naturally, the out-group will fall short, and this failure then becomes a rationale for disliking or even mistreating the out-group (Mummendey & Wenzel, 1999). For example, when the former East and West Germany were reunited, many West Germans assumed that their own group's stereotypical characteristics (such as efficiency and productivity) were defining characteristics of Germans in general. As a consequence, they devalued the former East Germans (who saw themselves quite differently, as sincere and sociable) for failing to match these in-group-based standards. The negative views of the out-group arising from this process can be avoided when people hold a broader, more inclusive view of the higher-level group; for example, when they see that after reunification there is more than one way to be a German.

Thus, the exaltation of in-group values and symbols goes hand in hand with mistreatment of out-groups, precisely because in-group values are used to justify the mistreatment (Esses, Haddock, & Zanna, 1993; Sears, 1988). In the 18th and 19th centuries, for example, some Christian leaders cited biblical passages as evidence that slavery was divinely sanctioned (Swartley, 1983). Of course, many of their contemporaries posed the opposite argument, that slavery contradicted the basic message of the Bible. Apologists for slavery took such arguments as assaults on in-group values, as Albert Taylor Bledsoe did in his defense of slavery in 1860: "The history of interpretation furnishes no examples of more willful and violent perversions of the sacred text than are to be found in the

■ **Symbolic prejudice.** Some of the most virulent intergroup hatred arises from reverence for an in-group's cherished values when out-groups threaten those values. Here supporters of religious party Jamiat-e-Ulma-e-Islam express their rage at the publication of cartoons depicting the Prophet Mohammad (first printed in a Danish newspaper) by burning something of great symbolic significance, a U.S. flag. Images of Prophet Mohammed are strictly forbidden in Islam.

writings of the abolitionists. They seem to consider themselves above the scriptures . . . They put themselves above the law of God" (Swartley, 1983, p. 49). Today, some people are using similar arguments to oppose equal legal rights for homosexuals. When people perceive threats to their groups, esteem and reverence for in-group symbols are often accompanied by prejudice against out-groups—which is justified by reference to those very symbols.

Examples of prejudice and discrimination fueled by perceptions of extreme threat are easy to find. One took place when the Communist regime in the former Yugoslavia began to fail around 1990. People of Serbian descent felt themselves threatened by Croatians and Muslims, and under a strongly nationalist leader, Slobo-dan Milosevic, they launched military campaigns aimed at "ethnic cleansing," creating a new, larger homeland by killing members of other groups or driving them from their homes and lands. Similar patterns were found in the genocidal attacks in Rwanda launched in 1994 by Hutu extremists against Tutsi and moderate Hutus, and in the attacks beginning in 2003 by ethnically Arab militias against Black residents in the Darfur region of the Sudan. In all these cases, the victimized out-group was perceived, because of cultural, ethnic, or religious differences, as threatening the valued in-group's control of the government or other major societal symbols and institutions.

MORAL EXCLUSION. Groups that carry discrimination to its murderous extreme view out-groups as fundamentally inferior to the in-group—as subhuman and outside the domain in which the rules of morality apply (Opotow, 1990). History records numerous instances in which slaves, women, racial and religious minorities, and enemies of the nation or ruling power have been treated as fundamentally inferior to those who held power. This attitude allows us to suspend behaviors we usually consider both human and humane, such as helping others and treating them fairly and justly. These rules of justice and civility depend on seeing oneself and others as members of a larger community, and they therefore may not apply to out-group members (T. R. Tyler & Lind, 1990). When this perception is held by a powerful in-group, while members of relatively powerless groups are excluded from the scope of moral principles, the stage may be set for extreme intergroup oppression, massacre, or genocide (Opotow, 1990; Sachdev & Bourhis, 1991).

Moral exclusion can begin with symptoms that appear relatively benign, such as a belief in the in-group's moral superiority. The disease quickly spreads, however. In-group members may portray the out-group in subhuman terms, often by labeling them as vermin, barbarians, or even germs "infecting" the pure in-group, or by dismissing their ability to experience human sentiments like joy or grief (Paladino and others, 2002; Vaes, Paladino, Castelli, Leyens, & Giovanazzi, 2003). Destructive actions against the out-group may be rationalized by the idea that "they brought it on themselves" or by self-justifying comparisons with horrible atrocities committed by others. The actions may be given euphemistic and mislead-ing labels, like Hitler's genocidal "final solution" or the Serbian "ethnic cleansing." Finally, group members reject personal responsibility for hateful or destructive acts by appealing to the in-group's welfare as a source of higher moral authority. These aspects of moral exclusion often play a role in the dynamics of intergroup conflict, which we will discuss in Chapter 13.

People's reactions to out-groups usually stop short of virulent hatred and moral exclusion. Still, as shown in Figure 6.6, the reactions, though they range from mild to intense, are always negative. Moreover, prejudice and discrimination against out-groups are found in all cultures (LeVine & Campbell, 1972), and they may be even stronger in the interdependent cultures of Asia and Africa than in Western, independent

FIGURE 6.6 Social identity turns others into "them"

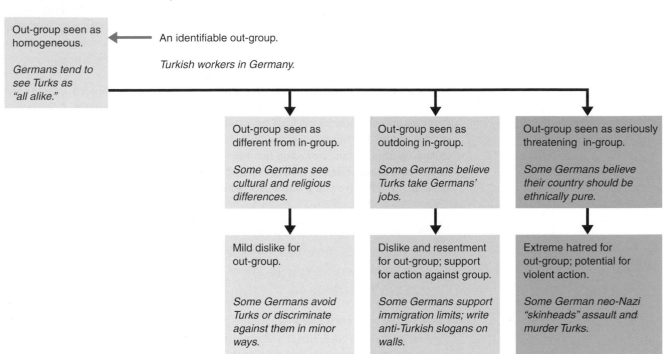

Out-group seen as homogeneous.

Germans tend to see Turks as "all alike."

An identifiable out-group.

Turkish workers in Germany.

Out-group seen as different from in-group.

Some Germans see cultural and religious differences.

Out-group seen as outdoing in-group.

Some Germans believe Turks take Germans' jobs.

Out-group seen as seriously threatening in-group.

Some Germans believe their country should be ethnically pure.

Mild dislike for out-group.

Some Germans avoid Turks or discriminate against them in minor ways.

Dislike and resentment for out-group; support for action against group.

Some Germans support immigration limits; write anti-Turkish slogans on walls.

Extreme hatred for out-group; potential for violent action.

Some German neo-Nazi "skinheads" assault and murder Turks.

■ Out-group members tend to be seen as "all alike." In addition, they are often disliked and victimized by discrimination, depending on the magnitude of threat they are seen as posing to the in-group. Negative reactions may range from mild dislike, due to the simple perception of difference, to extreme hatred or even genocide when the in-group's very existence is believed to be threatened.

cultures (Hsu, 1983; Moghaddam Taylor, & Wright, 1993). Dislike, distrust, and discrimination seem to be intrinsic parts of the way people respond to out-groups: When intergroup threats emerge, negative treatment of the outgroup is inextricably linked to the esteem and favor that in-groups enjoy.

When Group Memberships Are Negative

What are the costs of belonging to a group that is disliked, discriminated against, or excluded from the scope of moral principles? Members of these groups are likely to suffer from unequal economic opportunity, lack of access to quality education and medical care, and poor living conditions. In the United States, for example, the infant mortality rate for Blacks is more than twice the average for Whites; in fact, it is worse than the rate in Malaysia. Forty-three of every 100 Black children live in poverty, and nearly half of the murder victims in the United States are Black.

Group membership can impose other important costs as well, and the price is paid in decreased self-esteem and emotional well-being. If a group becomes part of the member's view of the self, the effects of belonging to a *stigmatized*, or negatively evaluated, group may be pervasive (Crocker, Major, & Steele, 1998). Brian Mullen and Joshua Smyth (2004) found that specific immigrant groups in the

United States that were more frequently targeted by negative ethnic slurs actually had higher suicide rates—a tragic reminder of the power of hateful speech in people's lives. Does being stigmatized inevitably drag down the individual, as this finding suggests? Or can the group become a source of pride for its members even when others look down on them? What kinds of strategies can people use, either as individuals or on behalf of an entire group, to escape or overcome their stigmatization? This part of the chapter will consider all these questions.

Stigmatization is not a problem just for members of small minority groups like homosexuals or Blacks. Most of us belong to one or more groups that society devalues and stigmatizes, at least in certain contexts—women, people of color, the elderly, recent immigrants, people with AIDS, the overweight, disabled people, the unemployed, the addicted; the list seems endless. If you cannot think of any negatively regarded groups that you belong to yourself, perhaps reading the questions in Table 6.1 will give you a sense of what others experience.

Effects of Stigmatized Group Memberships

> Negative stereotypes about the abilities of a group's members can become self-fulfilling, actually harming the members' performances. Belonging to a devalued group also poses a threat to self-esteem.

EFFECTS ON PERFORMANCE. Realizing that others think that your group does not have what it takes to perform well is a psychological burden in itself. However, recent research shows that this type of **stereotype threat** can actually act as a self-fulfilling prophecy, bringing about confirmation of the stereotype. To examine this

---

TABLE 6.1. Turning the Tables: Questions Implying that Group Membership is Abnormal and Devalued

1. What do you think caused your heterosexuality?
2. When and how did you decide you were a heterosexual?
3. Is it possible that heterosexuality is just a phase you may grow out of?
4. Is it possible your heterosexuality stems from a neurotic fear of others of the same sex?
5 If you've never slept with a person of the same sex, is it possible that all you need is a good same-sex lover?
6. To whom have you disclosed your heterosexual tendencies?
7. Why do heterosexuals feel compelled to seduce others into their lifestyle?
8. Why do you insist on flaunting your heterosexuality? Why can't you just be who you are and keep quiet about it?
9. Why do heterosexuals place so much emphasis on sex?
10. There seem to be very few happy heterosexuals. Techniques have been developed that might enable you to change. Have you considered aversion therapy?
11. Considering the menace of hunger and overpopulation, can the human race survive if everyone were heterosexual like yourself?
12. Despite social support of marriage, the divorce rate is still 50 percent. Why are there so few stable relationships among heterosexuals?

Note: This questionnaire has been used in sensitivity-training workshops to provoke discussion. Does it give you a sense of what it might feel like to belong to a group that most people dislike and regard as abnormal?

Source: From *Working It Out: The Newsletter for Gay and Lesbian Employment Issues.*

Stereotype threat. The fear of confirming others' negative stereotype of your group.

process, Claude Steele and Joshua Aronson (1995) used the common stereotype that Black Americans are unintelligent and academically untalented. They gave Black and White students a difficult test, telling some that it was highly related to intellectual ability and telling others that the test was "just a laboratory exercise." When the test was described as an unimportant exercise, or when the research participants were not asked to record their race on the experimental materials, Black students performed as well as White students (when appropriate statistical adjustments were made for the students' individual levels of academic preparation, as measured by their SAT scores). But in the condition that posed a stereotype threat—when the test was said to tap intellectual ability and the student's race was explicitly identified—Black students scored more poorly than Whites. Similar effects have been found with a different group with a different stereotype about performance: women, and the idea that women are less able than men at math (Spencer, 1994). Women perform worse than men when presented with very difficult math tests under standard instructions, but this difference vanishes if the participants are simply told that on "this particular test" research has found that there is no gender difference in performance! Stereotype threat harms performance even for members of generally high-status and nonstigmatized groups, like White males, in specific domains, such as "natural athletic ability," where negative stereotypes exist about them (Stone, 2002).

What accounts for these unsettling effects? Steele and his colleagues believe that the very knowledge that other people hold a negative stereotype about your group's performance can bring the stereotype to mind, even if you do not personally believe it. The result may be anxiety and reduced performance (Steele & Aronson, 1995). You may worry, for example, that any mistake you make will not only harm you personally, but will reflect negatively on your whole group, confirming the invidious stereotype in the minds of observers. Simone Young, one of the first women to conduct major symphony orchestras around the world, said: "Somehow, if a man gets in front of an orchestra and does a bad job, people say 'Well, we won't have him back again.' But if a woman fails, they say, 'See what happens when you have a woman conductor'" (Tommasini, 1996). Such worries about the impact of failure on the entire group may be the underlying reason that stereotype threat reduces people's ability to hold information in memory, which can harm performance on many types of task (Croizet and others, 2004; Schmader & Johns, 2003).

Interestingly, providing people with an external excuse for a potential poor performance can reduce stereotype threat and its effects on performance. When R. P. Brown and Josephs (1999) gave male and female students a difficult math test, the standard gender difference in performance emerged. However, if a faked computer problem eliminated the students' chance to do practice problems before taking the test, the women's performance improved. With an external excuse available for a possible poor performance, the women had no reason to fear that failure would confirm the gender stereotype. Because stereotype threat is not an issue for men in the area of math performance, the excuse had no effect on the men's test scores.

Another factor that can protect people from stereotype threat is the presence of role models who exemplify high performance by members of the stereotyped group. Thus, the presence of a female experimenter who is a math expert safeguards women's performance on a difficult test, although the same test elicits stereotype threat effects when the experimenter is male (Marx & Roman, 2002). Like the finding by Brewer and Weber (1994) described at the beginning of the chapter, this study points again to the fact that for members of minorities or stigmatized groups, other group members' performances are crucial ingredients for attaining success and mastery as well as positive self-esteem.

EFFECTS ON SELF-ESTEEM. However negative the effects on task performance, belonging to a socially devalued group can have effects on self-esteem that are more subtle, but perhaps ultimately even more severe. Because social group membership contributes so directly to individual self-identity, belonging to a negatively regarded group can take its toll on the individual. Kenneth Clark, a distinguished social psychologist whose research contributed to the 1954 U.S. Supreme Court decision mandating school desegregation, commented, "Human beings . . . whose daily experience tells them that almost nowhere in society are they respected and granted the ordinary dignity and courtesy accorded to others, will, as a matter of course, begin to doubt their self worth" (K. B. Clark, 1965, p. 64).

Clark was right to be worried, for feelings about group membership do have a major impact on the emotional and physical well-being of members of stigmatized groups (Twenge & Crocker, 2002). One group of researchers measured Black and White students' personal self-esteem, their feelings about their group memberships, and symptoms of depression (Luhtanen & Crocker, 1992). For Whites, low personal self-esteem was the key factor that increased the risk of depression. For Blacks, in contrast, not personal but *collective self-esteem*—positive or negative feelings about group membership—was more strongly related to depression (Luhtanen, Blaine, & Crocker, 1991). Writers like Malcolm X (1966) have eloquently described their struggles in coming to terms with their ethnic identity, integrating a socially stigmatized group membership into a positive overall sense of self. And negative feelings arising from group membership are not limited to socially disadvantaged groups. Even members of dominant groups like men, when reminded of their group's privileges and advantages over women, can have their self-esteem lowered by feelings of guilt (Branscombe, 1998; Doosje, Branscombe, Spears, & Manstead, 1998).

Wouldn't you expect that belonging to a group that many people look down on, despise, and discriminate against would bring *you* down? Then consider this puzzle: Individual members of many stigmatized groups, including Blacks, people with developmental disabilities, and people who are facially disfigured, have self-esteem that is just as high as that of individuals who are not members of these groups (Crocker & Major, 1989). Clearly, at least some members of negatively regarded groups can defend and enhance their self-esteem. How are they able to value themselves in a society that devalues their groups?

This is not the first time we have seen that feeling bad about oneself can produce symptoms of depression. Look back at Chapter 4, pages 127 to 128.

Defending Individual Self-Esteem

> Belonging to a group that is disliked and discriminated against by others can have a major impact on the individual. But this experience does not inevitably lead to lowered self-esteem, because people can attribute negative reactions to others' prejudice or compare themselves to fellow in-group members.

USING ATTRIBUTIONS TO ADVANTAGE. A Black person described a common dilemma to a White reporter:

> *If you go into a restaurant and get totally lousy service, you know it's for one reason. They do totally lousy service. I go into a restaurant and I get*

totally lousy service, I don't know why . . . Is it because we're black or is it because . . . it's a bad service person? (Duke & Morin, 1992)

When a member of a devalued group is treated badly, attributional ambiguity is created: The treatment might have been due to group membership. The same uncertainty arises in more significant form when group members are rejected for jobs, promotions, or bank loans. People in these situations are free to attribute others' behavior to prejudice against their group.

One clever experiment demonstrated that people often see another person's behavior as a response to a stigma, even when the stigma could not possibly have had any effect (Kleck & Strenta, 1980). Participants were made up to look as if they had a large and disfiguring facial scar, which they examined in a mirror before the experimenter applied "moisturizer." Without the participants' knowledge, the moisturizer they thought would "set their make-up" in fact removed the scar. Participants then spent several minutes with a second person to assess the effects of the disfigurement on social interaction. Those who falsely believed they were disfigured thought their scar had a tremendous effect on how they were treated, even though their partners were of course unaware of the stigma. People who permanently belong to stigmatized groups, like the Black restaurant patron, always have group membership accessible as a potential explanation for the way others treat them.

Attributing negative outcomes to others' prejudice against one's group instead of to one's personal failings can protect self-esteem against the negative psychological effects of failure (Crocker & Major, 1989; Crocker and others, 1998). Interestingly, making attributions to group-based prejudice appears to be uniquely effective, more than attributions to other external factors. To demonstrate this point, Christian Crandall and his colleagues put male students into a brief conversation with an attractive woman (Crandall, Tsang, Harvey, & Britt, 2000). Before the conversation, the men had to eat either a mint candy or an entire clove of raw garlic. When the woman (by prearrangement) gave them negative feedback after the interaction, the men who had eaten garlic naturally tended to attribute their rejection to their breath rather than, say, their lack of social skills. Strikingly, though, making these attributions did not elevate their self-esteem. Only when participants were able to attribute others' negative feedback to prejudice against a meaningful group, rather than to a purely individual characteristic like garlic breath, did such self-protective attributions actually elevate self-esteem.

Despite its potential benefits for self-esteem, attributing negative outcomes to prejudice against one's group, like many of the self-enhancing biases described in Chapter 4, also carries important costs. First, negative feedback is sometimes realistic, and discounting it can prevent accurate self-assessment and self-improvement. Second, the strategy may breed a sense of hopelessness and a loss of control: If one always expects to be treated primarily as a group member, no personal action will make any difference. Third, members of stigmatized groups who attribute their outcomes to others' prejudice may earn reputations as "complainers," leading to social rejection (Kaiser & Miller, 2001).

Finally, attributing other people's reactions to group membership can destroy trust in positive feedback. Are praise and promotions signs of respect and admiration for one's accomplishments, or are they due to sympathy, pity, and resigned affirmative action? Research suggests that members of stigmatized groups are likely to suspect the latter—to discount positive feedback and attribute honors and accomplishments to others' efforts to appear unprejudiced. Unfortunately, these cynical views are sometimes right. Leaning over backwards to avoid seeming prejudiced, people sometimes inflate their evaluations of members of disliked out-groups compared to their ratings of in-group members who turn in the same performance (Crocker, Voelkl, Testa, & Major, 1991).

Thus, belonging to a stigmatized group can be a buffer against the chill of negative feedback, but it also barricades you from the warm pleasure usually derived from positive feedback. Perhaps it is awareness of these costs that keeps some members of stigmatized groups from making attributions to others' prejudice unless the evidence is virtually unavoidable. As we will see shortly, even people who accurately view their group as a target of societal discrimination sometimes deny that they themselves have been affected.

☐ **ATTRIBUTIONAL AMBIGUITY IN THE WORKPLACE.** Not knowing how to interpret feedback can create serious workplace problems for people with disabilities, women, and other groups. For example, if a few wheelchair users are hired at a typical business, they draw more than their fair share of attention. Like members of other groups, they may feel that their every move is scrutinized and that their behavior reflects not only on themselves but on all people with disabilities (Pettigrew & Martin, 1987).

In some cases, an employee may suspect that he or she is a token, a single group member hired in order to avoid more thoroughgoing change. Consider the dilemma this suspicion creates: In these circumstances, people find it hard to trust feedback because outcomes seem to be determined by group membership. For example, women managers who believe they were hired because of their gender show lower organizational commitment and job satisfaction and higher role stress than women who believe they were hired for their abilities (Chacko, 1982).

In an experimental demonstration of this effect, one group of men and women were told that they were selected for a leadership role because they had scored well on leadership potential tests. Another group learned that they had been selected because the experimenter "needed more" of their gender in leadership positions (Heilman, Simon, & Repper, 1987). Later, the participants learned that they had either succeeded or failed on the leadership task. As can be seen in Figure 6.7, women

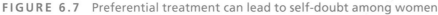

FIGURE 6.7   Preferential treatment can lead to self-doubt among women

■ Men or women were led to believe that they were chosen as leaders either on the basis of merit or through gender-based preferential treatment. They were then told that they either succeeded or failed on a leadership task. When male participants rated their own leadership ability, as the left bars show, their ratings were about equal in all conditions. However, women who thought that they had been chosen on the basis of gender doubted their own leadership ability—whether they had succeeded or failed. (Based on Heilman and others, 1987.)

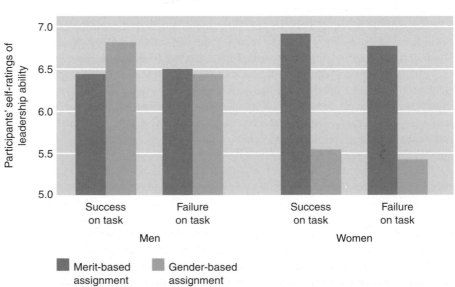

selected on the basis of gender rather than merit devalued their own leadership ability, regardless of whether they performed well or poorly as leaders. The women in this condition also reported less interest in persisting as leaders. In contrast, men did not show such self-doubts, whether they believed their selection reflected merit or gender-based preference. Members of groups that are typically devalued and discriminated against are the most at risk from attributional ambiguities involving performance feedback. Fortunately, these negative effects of group-based selection can be overcome when the role of merit (and not *solely* group membership) in the selection process is emphasized (Heilman, Battle, Keller, & Lee, 1998).

MAKING THE MOST OF INTRAGROUP COMPARISONS. Chapter 4 showed that social comparisons are an important source of self-evaluation. Thus, is it any wonder that a female middle manager in a large firm might choose to think of herself as "one of the highest-ranking women here at Acme Corporation" rather than to compare herself to the male members of top corporate management (Major, 1994)? This kind of in-group comparison is also typical of ethnic groups. One study found that Black schoolchildren who compared themselves mainly with other Blacks had higher self-esteem than those who compared themselves with White children (M. Rosenberg & Simmons, 1971). Intragroup comparisons not only boost self-esteem by showing us that we are better off than some others, they also remind us of in-group members who are doing particularly well—even if we are not. When given the opportunity to choose others for comparisons, schoolchildren from low-status groups in both New Zealand and the United States often name other in-group members who are high performers in the social, academic, or athletic domains (Aboud, 1976; Mackie, 1984). And recall that in the social comparison study cited at the beginning of this chapter, members of an artificial "minority group" got a boost from a fellow group member's good performance (Brewer & Weber, 1994); similar patterns are displayed by members of an actual minority group, African-American college students (Blanton, Crocker, & Miller, 2000).

WOMEN'S SELF-ESTEEM: WHAT'S SO SPECIAL ABOUT GENDER? We now have a partial solution to the puzzle posed earlier: Members of stigmatized groups, such as Blacks, can use several strategies to maintain levels of self-esteem equal to that of the dominant group, in this case, Whites. Still, another puzzle remains. Even though they also can use all of the strategies we have discussed, women seem to have lower self-esteem than men (Freiberg, 1991a; Major, Barr, Zubeck, & Babey, 1999). The gender gap in self-esteem initially arises in adolescence, when teachers and other adults often discourage girls from academic pursuits while giving boys more attention and more challenging assignments in class.

The self-esteem difference has real consequences: Girls are much more likely than boys to lower their career aspirations, feeling that they are "not smart enough" to fulfill their dreams (Freiberg, 1991a). These findings remind us that psychological strategies of self-esteem defense are

■ **Formulating self-esteem.** Young girls like these are as interested in science and math as their male peers. But by adolescence, differential treatment by adults may have begun to take its toll on self-esteem. Often reacting to a teacher's belief that they are not smart enough to do things they may have excelled at in elementary school, young women begin to doubt their own abilities. They may then see career choices in math or science as out of reach.

not always sufficient when teachers and other powerful people actually treat students from different groups differently. The findings also suggest that the same strategies may not work equally well for all groups (Frable, 1997). For example, in the United States, Blacks have higher self-esteem than Whites. But Hispanics, Asians, and Native Americans are lower than Whites (Twenge & Crocker, 2002). One reason that gender may be special is that gender roles are learned extremely early in life and are reinforced by parents and peers. As a result, both men and women usually place a high value on behaving in accordance with these roles and may see gender as a more central aspect of the self than other group memberships (S. T. Fiske & Stevens, 1993).

Individual Mobility: Escaping Negative Group Membership

If self-protective strategies are insufficient, people can attempt to escape from membership in a negatively regarded group. They can psychologically disidentify with the group, for example, by playing down group memberships that reflect badly on them or by regarding themselves as atypical group members. Another option is to dissociate, to escape physically, by "passing" or keeping group membership hidden "in the closet."

When strategies intended to buffer self-esteem against the implications of negative group membership prove ineffective, people may turn to more long-term solutions involving individual mobility, social creativity, or social change (Ellemers, Spears, & Doosje, 2002; Tajfel & Turner, 1979). **Individual mobility** is a strategy involving individual escape from membership in a negative group, either through disidentification (creating a psychological distance between oneself and the group) or through dissociation (physically escaping the group). Escape frees the individual from many of the costs of group membership and leaves the group's situation as a whole unchanged in the short run. Social creativity and social change strategies, in contrast, involve direct efforts to improve society's evaluation of the entire group. Note, however, that large amounts of individual mobility may also create social change over time. For example, as increasing numbers of women overcome stereotypes and discrimination to enter previously male-dominated occupations, their actions may, over time, alter societal stereotypes of women. Recall that the roles typically held by group members are often reflected in stereotypes of the group (Eagly, 1987).

DISIDENTIFICATION: PUTTING THE GROUP AT A PSYCHOLOGICAL DISTANCE. Individual mobility can be purely psychological, as when people *disidentify*, or minimize their personal connections to the group. One strategy is to avoid reminders of membership in a stigmatized group, as a laboratory study demonstrated (C. R. Snyder, Lassegard, & Ford, 1986). Students participated in a group problem-solving session and each group received success feedback, failure feedback, or no feedback at all. The experimenter then announced that they could take home team badges that advertised their group membership. Would team performance influence pride of membership? Apparently so. Over half of the members of groups that succeeded or received no feedback took badges home. But only 9% of those on a losing team welcomed the opportunity to announce their membership in it.

People can also disidentify from a group by publicly criticizing and devaluing an in-group member's poor performance. This reaction, termed *the black sheep*

Individual mobility. The strategy of individual escape, either physical or psychological, from a stigmatized group.

effect (Marques & Yzerbyt, 1988), makes it clear that the critic regards the poor performance as unrepresentative of the group. For example, imagine that you (a law student) have to evaluate speeches given by a fellow law student and by a philosophy student. If the law student's speech was third-rate, your self-categorization with him would put you in an uncomfortable situation. In these circumstances, you might be inclined to downgrade the in-group speaker, rating her even more negatively than an out-group member who performed equally poorly. By doing so, you will make it clear that this in-group member's performance is not representative of your group. Marques and Yzerbyt (1988) obtained exactly this pattern of results. People rated successful in-group members higher, and poorly performing in-group members lower, compared with out-group members. When the previously cheering fans turn to booing and hissing the home team's losses with even more enthusiasm, perhaps part of their motivation is to psychologically distance themselves from poor performance (Branscombe, Wann, Noel, & Coleman, 1993).

Yet a third way of disidentifying is to consider *oneself* to be an exception rather than a typical group member. For example, many women acknowledge that women in general are discriminated against but insist that discrimination does not affect them personally (Crosby, Pufall, Snyder, O'Connell, & Whalen, 1989; Ellemers, 2001). The same pattern of beliefs is found among many other groups, including French-speakers in Quebec and immigrants to Canada from Haiti and India (D. M. Taylor, Wright, Moghaddam, & Lalonde, 1990). Of course, there could be many reasons for this belief, and it is certainly possible that some individual group members are fortunate enough to escape discrimination personally. But the belief is held most often by those who identify least strongly with their groups, suggesting that the belief serves, at least in part, as a psychological distancing mechanism (H. J. Smith & Spears, 1996).

One study suggests that disidentification has a potential cost. Ferdman (1989) showed managers in an organization a videotaped interview with a Hispanic manager. Some saw an interview in which the individual discussed only personal, individuating information, with no explicit mention of his ethnicity. In another version of the interview the Hispanic man also described how important his group identity was to him and mentioned his participation in several Hispanic organizations. Those who watched the second version of the interview evaluated the man more positively, implying that people who play down their group memberships risk negative responses from others.

DISSOCIATION: PUTTING THE GROUP AT A PHYSICAL DISTANCE. Whereas disidentifying takes place in the mind, *dissociating* involves actual escape from a disadvantaged group or concealment of group membership. This form of individual mobility occurs, for example, when immigrants cast off their cultural and linguistic heritage and become indistinguishable members of a new nationality. Gays or lesbians who are "in the closet" are concealing their group membership. A related strategy of some historical importance is "passing," a pattern in which light-skinned individuals of African ancestry adopted a White identity, or American Jews adopted anglicized names and the customs of Gentile society (K. Lewin, 1948).

■ **"The critical and fundamental point is that ethnic background and/or composition should NOT make a difference. It does NOT make a difference to me. The bottom line is that I am an American . . . and proud of it!"** When Tiger Woods pounced on the professional golf circuit, winning the Masters at the young age of 21 and even getting his own Wheaties box, every aspect of him was suddenly in the spotlight, including his African-American/Asian heritage. As his quote illustrates, Woods wants to be admired for his individual talents and not merely in terms of his group memberships.

How successful is escape as a solution to membership in a negatively evaluated group? The answer seems to be that it is a mixed blessing. The individual does reap some personal benefits, such as freedom from discrimination, but for some, these benefits may be outweighed by the strategy's potential costs. New members of a group often suffer the isolation of not being thought quite the same as those "born to it." In addition, concealing group membership can be lonely and dangerous. The heartache of having to join in the laughter at antigay or racist jokes might be surpassed only by anxiety at being "outed." To deal with the problems of living with a concealed stigmatized identity, a recent study suggests that the potential anonymity provided by the internet can help. Results found that interactive discussions on newsgroups devoted to group support can be an important source of identity for those with concealable stigmatized group memberships (such as drug addiction or homosexuality). Comparing people who participate in such newsgroups with participants in similar support newsgroups for nonconcealable stigmas (such as stuttering or being overweight), Katelyn McKenna and John Bargh (1998) found that the newsgroups involving concealable characteristics were more important to the lives of their members and had greater impact on their member's emotions and behavior. In effect, participation in the newsgroup increased members' acceptance of their identity, replacing feelings of isolation and just being different.

Finally, those who conceal their group membership give up opportunities to influence others' thinking about their group. U.S. Representative Barney Frank kept his homosexuality secret when he was first elected to Congress. He recalls that when he lobbied his colleagues on gay issues, "They would say 'Ah, you're right. But you know, it's not that important.' The pain gay people felt was unknown. We were hiding it from them. How the hell are they supposed to know when we were making damn sure they didn't?" (Schmalz, 1992).

Disidentification and dissociation are not viable options for many group members. Instead of separating from the group, either psychologically or physically, group members can directly seek to change society's negative evaluation of their group.

Social Creativity: Redefining Group Membership as Positive

Sometimes group members attempt to change society's evaluation of their in-group, through redefining group characteristics in positive terms.

When individual escape is difficult, a group that is faced with a negative identity can introduce and emphasize alternative dimensions on which the in-group is superior. A group of French boys at a summer camp showed this kind of **social creativity** when they found themselves in a hut-building contest with another team that had better construction materials (Lemaine, 1974). Realizing their inability to construct a large and sturdy structure, they created an elaborate garden around their mediocre cabin and asked the judges to consider them the garden-building winners. By introducing a new dimension of competition, the group maintained its superiority and distinctiveness. Similarly, players on the last-place team in an ice hockey league cannot make a claim on skill and competitiveness, but they may be able to think of themselves as "cleaner" and more sportsmanlike than other teams. For one team, adopting this belief served to maintain the players'

Social creativity. The strategy of introducing and emphasizing new dimensions of social comparison, on which a negatively regarded group can see itself as superior.

self-esteem, even though it seemed to correspond very little with reality—observers and coaches viewed the last-place team as one of the "dirtiest" in the league (Lalonde, 1992). In studies involving both laboratory-created and real-life groups, Jackson and others (L. A. Jackson, Sullivan, Harnish, & Hodge, 1996) found that social creativity strategies were used more when the group boundaries were relatively fixed. When boundaries were permeable, individual mobility became a preferred strategy.

Some women show social creativity by accepting society's definition of femininity and seeking a positive group identity through its distinctive positive characteristics. For example, they may emphasize dimensions of achievement that they view as specifically feminine, such as nurturing or peacemaking (Branscombe, 1998). Along the same lines, a gay pride movement has emerged, with an emphasis on celebrating the accomplishments of gays and lesbians, particularly in artistic and cultural fields. "Black is beautiful!" was one group's statement that distinctive characteristics that have been derogated by the majority, such as skin color, language, or cultural heritage, can be redefined as a source of pride (Bourhis and others, 1978). These social creativity strategies, however, may not lead in any direct way to lasting changes in a group's position in society. For example, emphasizing women's positive qualities as nurturers or peacemakers may proclaim the value of feminine qualities and strengthen collective self-esteem, but it does not directly challenge social definitions of gender roles. It may even unintentionally provide rationales and justifications for the continued exclusion of women from positions of economic or political power. Direct challenges to such exclusion are the key to the third strategy, social change.

Social Change: Changing the Intergroup Context

Finally, group members may engage in direct intergroup conflict or struggle, or seek to overturn the in-group/out-group distinction altogether.

Strikes, protest marches, and struggles in the courts and legislatures to outlaw discrimination are familiar tactics of the civil rights movement in the United States. These tactics reflect a social change strategy of confronting and challenging the hierarchy of group domination. **Social change** refers to the strategy of improving the overall societal situation of a group held in low esteem. Social change is generally preferred by people who identify strongly with their group and who see individual mobility as impossible. Rather than changing only their personal situation, they wish to, and believe they can, change the way society regards their group as a whole (Ellemers, Spears, & Doosje, 2002; Tajfel & Turner, 1979). The main tactics employed by these determined group members are social competition and recategorization.

SOCIAL COMPETITION. Sometimes groups attempt to build in-group solidarity and oppose domination by the out-group, by taking direct action to improve the relative position, status, power, and resources of the in-group. When they do so, they are engaging in *social competition* by directly seeking to change the conditions that disadvantage them. This is the strategy that leads to in-group bias, when a group member gives the in-group an edge over the out-group by allocating his or her group more resources, evaluating in-group products more positively, and judging

Social change. The strategy of improving the overall societal situation of a stigmatized group.

the in-group to be morally and socially superior. Of course, what looks like opportunity for advancement to disadvantaged groups often appears as a threat to a dominant group. Earlier, we saw that favored groups respond with increased levels of prejudice and discrimination against out-groups when they see those groups as threats. Thus, social competition strategies are likely to provoke a backlash from powerful groups.

Groups engage in these strategies when they believe they can make a difference and improve their situation in concrete ways (Tajfel & Turner, 1979) or when their members strongly identify with the group (Ellemers and others, 2002; B. Simon and others, 1998). Collective actions to advance a group's interests are often most effective when group members stick together, emphasizing their homogeneity in attitudes and values (Doosje, Ellemers, & Spears, 1995; Simon & Brown, 1987).

Social competition strategies take many forms, including drives for self-sufficiency, autonomy, and separatism among racial or ethnic minorities such as French Canadians or Basques in Spain. Everywhere in society, lobbies and advocacy organizations seek social changes that will benefit particular groups. The American Association of Retired Persons and Gray Panthers mobilize efforts on behalf of seniors. Groups such as the Coalition of Citizens with Disabilities and Mainstream, Inc. lead "wheelchair rebellions." Radical gay and lesbian organizations such as Queer Nation actively combat gay bashing, antigay prejudice, and negative portrayals of homosexuals in the media while lobbying for open and equal opportunities for their group. Individuals as well as organizations can engage in social competition strategies, for example, by creating informal associations of group members aimed at community building and mutual support. Individuals can also speak out against stereotypes, prejudice, and discrimination whenever they encounter them: in ethnic slurs, sexist jokes, or "old boy" hiring practices in organizations.

RECATEGORIZATION: CHANGING THE DEFINITION OF IN-GROUP. Social change can also come through transcending group categorizations. In most business organizations, for example, there will be both male and female members among both the senior staff and the junior staff. Thus, some individuals who are out-group members on one dimension will be in-group members on another; the categorizations by professional status and gender cut across each other (Doise, 1978). What impact does this *cross-categorization* have on in-group bias? To find out, one experimenter set up groups in which out-group members on one dimension were in-group members on another dimension. When such a cross-categorization was introduced, intergroup discrimination against members of partially overlapping in-groups was greatly reduced (Vanbeselaere, 1991). This technique cannot completely wipe out discrimination, however. The male senior staffers may expand their in-group to include senior females or junior males, bestowing on them the many benefits of in-group membership. In this sense, cross-categorization also produces recategorization, but the female junior staff remain outside even the redrawn group boundaries. Another way of putting it is that cross-categorization redirects prejudice rather than reducing it: evaluations of double outgroup members may become more negative, even as evaluations of partially overlapping groups are improved (Mullen, Migdal, & Hewstone, 2001).

Another promising way to transcend group antipathies is to form new inclusive in-groups from which esteem and identity can be derived (S. Feshbach & Singer,

1957; Gaertner & Dovidio, 2000). Laboratory demonstrations using experimentally created minimal groups have confirmed that blurring boundaries can coalesce groups into one larger overarching structure, thereby reducing bias and discrimination (Nier and others, 2001). Samuel Gaertner and his colleagues (Gaertner, Mann, Murrell, & Dovidio, 1989) found, for example, that intergroup relations were improved when members of two subgroups were placed at alternating seats around a table and when they gave the joint group a new and separate name. However, creating new, inclusive in-groups does not necessarily mean denying the importance of the former group memberships (Condor & Brown, 1988).

"COLOR-BLINDNESS" OR VALUING GROUP DIFFERENCES? How many times have you heard someone say "I don't care if he's black, white, green, or purple—I'll judge him by his job performance!" Statements like these express a "color-blind" ideology, the idea that race should not affect the way people are treated, and should therefore be disregarded and even actively ignored (Schofield, 1986). This ideology fits well with the emphasis on individual achievement that prevails in independent cultures, so it has a strong appeal to many people. It may be an appropriate and desirable approach in organizations where job performance can be objectively measured and used to rank and reward people independent of their race or other group memberships.

Another reason that some advocate the color-blind approach is a concern that an emphasis on group differences may foster intergroup hostility and prejudice. The available evidence, however, does not support that fear. Studies by Christopher Wolsko and his colleagues (Wolsko, Park, Judd, & Wittenbrink, 2000) gave students a brief message emphasizing either a multicultural viewpoint (that groups differ and should be valued for their own unique contributions) or a color-blind viewpoint (that group differences are only skin-deep and all groups are essentially similar in the ways that matter). Those who received the color-blind message did indeed display weaker stereotypes of racial in-groups and out-groups, as one might expect. However, they did not evaluate out-groups any more positively than those who received the multicultural message. The researchers concluded that the color-blind perspective may succeed in distracting attention from group differences, but without necessarily leading to increased intergroup acceptance (Park & Judd, 2005). Similar findings were obtained in a study of Dutch schools that included significant minorities of Turkish children: in classrooms where teachers incorporated lessons about ethnic discrimination and cultural differences, the children evaluated the out-group more favorably (Kinket & Verkuyten, 1999). Although this study is nonexperimental and cannot establish causality, these results also cast doubt on the idea behind the color-blind approach, that acknowledging group differences will inevitably increase intergroup bias.

In addition, the color-blind ideology has important disadvantages. First, in schools and many other settings, including even the workplace, the values of getting to know about other cultures and learning to live and work alongside culturally different individuals are important, perhaps as important as individual task performance. Janet Schofield (1986) found that color-blind ideology impeded such learning, for example, by keeping schoolchildren and teachers from capitalizing on their cultural diversity to enrich their perspectives.

Second, color-blind ideology desensitizes members of a dominant group to the value placed on group membership by members of minority or disadvantaged groups. Charles Judd and his colleagues (Judd, Park, Ryan, Brauer, & Kraus, 1995)

These recategorization strategies are important weapons in the fight against intergroup conflict. We discuss their implications for reducing conflict in Chapter 13, pages 511 to 513.

found that many White Americans professed color-blindness, refusing with apparent sincerity even to acknowledge that Whites and Blacks differ in important ways. Yet the Blacks in the same study regarded their group membership as quite meaningful and important to them. From their perspective, color-blindness denies an important social identity and may even translate into a demand for assimilation, that is, for members of minority groups to adopt the values and customs of the dominant White group. Of course, this demand is unlikely to appeal to Blacks who value their own group membership. In fact, when Whites who see themselves as unprejudiced assert with all good intentions that group memberships are irrelevant and should be ignored, Blacks may regard this refusal to recognize and honor valued group differences as just the newest form of prejudice.

Clearly, a balance is required. Members of different groups can share common goals and work together, while simultaneously maintaining their own group memberships as sources of identity and esteem (Condor & Brown, 1988; Eller & Abrams, 2004). Despite its appeal, a color-blind ideology that denies both the reality and the value of group differences is not the answer to intergroup conflict and misunderstanding.

One Goal, Many Strategies

Those who most strongly identify with a group and see group boundaries as fixed tend to choose social change rather than individual mobility strategies. However, no single approach is always best for dealing with a negatively evaluated group membership, just as no single coping strategy is uniformly the best way to handle threats to the individual self.

As you can see in Figure 6.8, there is more than one way to cope with the threat to social identity posed by negative group memberships. No one way is always better or worse than others; like the strategies for coping with threats to the individual self that were described in Chapter 4, the effectiveness of each method depends on many factors. The size of a group, the resources its members control, the ease or difficulty of concealing or changing group membership, and the personal significance of group membership for each individual will all influence how people respond (Eberhard & Fiske, 1996; Ellemers and others, 2002). It is no surprise, then, that different groups tend to prefer distinct strategies for coping when others disdain and discriminate against them (Frable, 1997).

The two most important factors that affect people's choices among strategies are the strength of their group identification and their perceptions of the possibility of individual mobility (Tajfel & Turner, 1979; Wright, Taylor, & Moghaddam, 1990). The importance of group identification was illustrated in studies with Dutch university students conducted by Naomi Ellemers and her colleagues (Ellemers, Spears, & Doosje, 1997). Students who were led to identify strongly with a low-status group were less likely to seek individual mobility out of the group. They also perceived their group as homogeneous, a display of group solidarity that is associated with collective action such as social competition. The key role of the perceived possibility of individual mobility was underlined in studies showing that people prefer to seek individual mobility out of a disadvantaged group whenever they see that as possible (Wright and others, 1990). They do this

FIGURE 6.8 How can I value myself when others devalue my group?

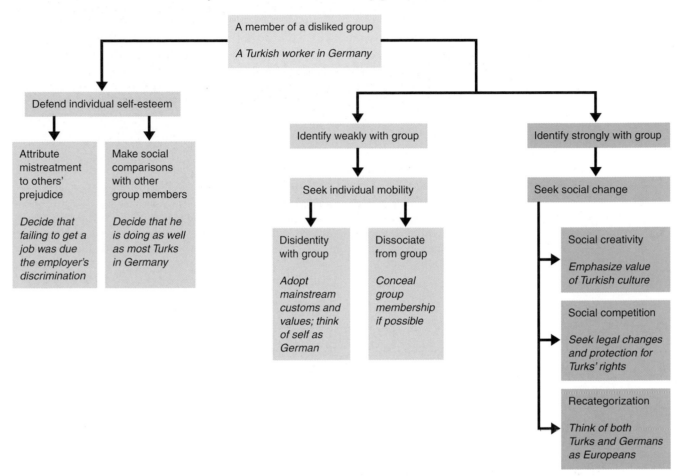

■ Members of groups that suffer dislike and discrimination try to defend their individual self-esteem. In addition, they may seek escape from their group through individual mobility or seek to improve the whole group's situation through social change, depending on the strength of their identification with the group.

even if they knew that only a trivial or token number of individuals would be permitted to escape from their original group. Only when the group members realized that absolutely no mobility was possible did they turn to more disruptive social competition strategies.

At times, multiple forces push and pull people in different directions. For example, many African Americans feel a fundamental tension between the desire to maintain in-group solidarity and the desire for individual advancement in White-dominated society. Deep, often emotional disagreements have sprung up between advocates of various strategies. It seems to some that "in order to be accepted by Whites they must give up everything that is Black; that if they played basketball before they now have to play golf" (L. Williams, 1991). Yet those who seek professional advancement sometimes "fear that if you are successful you will be too alienated from Black people," according to Cornel West, a Princeton University professor (Cary, 1992). The different strategies of individual mobility, social

TABLE 6.2. Three Types of Responses to a Likable Member of a Disliked Group

Response	*Knowing* a likable member of a disliked group	*Being* a likable member of a disliked group
See the individual as unrepresentative of the group; separate beliefs about the group from beliefs about the individual.	Exclude the individual from the group by seeing him or her as a special type of the general category (*subtyping*) or by seeing him or her as extremely different from typical category members (*contrasting*).	Remove the self from the group, either psychologically by down-playing group membership as an aspect of the self (*disidentification*) or physically by escaping from or concealing group membership (*dissociation*).
See the individual as representative of the group; use beliefs about the individual to modify beliefs about the group.	See the likable individual as a typical group member, improving the evaluation of the group (*stereotype change*).	Attempt to make society's evaluation of the group more positive (*social change*). Interpret the group and its history, culture, and other distinctive aspects in positive terms (*social creativity*) or struggle to change the group's generally low status and power in society (*social competition*).
Change the lines of social categorization.	Merge the out-group into a larger in-group.	Expand the in-group to include former out-groups.

creativity, and social change often contradict each other. Nevertheless, all aim at improving the group's situation and any one of them may be appropriate for a particular individual or group, given the unique social situation.

In thinking about the ways in which people cope with *being* a likable member of a devalued group, you may have noticed some similarities with the ways in which people deal with *meeting* a likable member of a disliked group (discussed in Chapter 5). These parallels, detailed in Table 6.2, are no accident. They reflect the fundamental principle that group memberships influence our thoughts and feelings about individual group members, whether the individual is someone else or the self.

CONCLUDING COMMENTS

 Social identity is central to every aspect of social behavior, just as this chapter occupies a central place in this text. The concept of social identity, as discussed in this chapter, makes clear how intertwined are people's knowledge about groups, their conceptions of themselves, and their impressions of others. Group memberships not only shape the ways we perceive our own and other groups, but also fundamentally affect the ways we perceive other individuals and ourself. Not only do we see ourselves in group terms and act in accordance with in-group standards and norms, but as in-groups become part of the self, we think about our groups in many of the same ways that we think about ourselves as individuals. For example, various biases lead us to value *me and mine*—to view not only ourselves but also our groups through rose-colored glasses.

Social identities anchor us in the social world by connecting us to other people—people we otherwise might have little reason to trust, to like, or even to know at all. Because relationships are encouraged and even made possible by our assumptions about what we have in common, group belonging and identification provide a truly social basis for thinking, feeling, and acting. Thus, understanding group membership is vital for understanding many aspects of social behavior. As you will see in later chapters, the effects of our groups on our beliefs, opinions, and behavior; on our close and loving relationships with other individuals; and on the ways we act in face-to-face groups all depend crucially on the ways we accept and identify with in-groups. No wonder, then, that we often feel lost and adrift when we lose important social identities, as when we are expelled or fired, or when our social identities are threatened, for example, when we experience discrimination and realize that others devalue our group. We may still be the individuals we always were, but important parts of our whole selves have been damaged or have disappeared because our place in the social world is lost or threatened.

Negative views of out-groups sprout from the same roots as people's positive views of themselves and their own kind. The biased stereotypes of groups that were discussed in Chapter 5 are only part of the underpinning of prejudice and discrimination. Disregard and maltreatment of others are supported by our social and psychological investment in our own groups as well. When group membership is most important, out-group members are only faceless outsiders; their individuality is of little concern to us. We see "them" as all the same and as totally different from us in their goals, values, and beliefs. As we will see, this way of thinking is an important basis for both aggression and intergroup conflict.

Perhaps understanding how group membership can contribute to hurtful and destructive human behavior will help provide solutions to some of these problems by redefining in-groups and out-groups. Whether the effects of social identity are good or bad, the fundamental fact remains that our sense of self extends beyond our skin to encompass some people and exclude others, with powerful implications for how we see and treat others and ourselves.

CHAPTER 6 THEMES

- **Construction of Reality**
  We construct the self using our knowledge about our social groups.

- **Pervasiveness of Social Influence**
  This construction process imports social influences into the very core of the self.

- **Seeking Connectedness**
  Group memberships that we share with others are rewarding.

- **Valuing Me and Mine**
  We positively value the groups to which we belong as well as our individual self.

SUMMARY

Categorizing Oneself as a Group Member. Group membership can turn into a **social identity** that links them with others, when the group becomes a significant part of a person's self-concept through the process of **self-categorization**. According to **social identity theory**, people seek to derive self-esteem from their in-group membership. People learn about the groups to which they belong in the same ways that they learn the characteristics of other groups: through observation of other group members or from the culture.

Knowledge about group memberships may be activated by direct reminders, such as group labels; by the presence of out-group members; by being a minority; or by intergroup conflict. Group membership is particularly significant in some cultures and for some individuals, who tend to see the world in terms of that group membership.

Me, You, and Them: Effects of Social Categorization. Activated knowledge about a group membership has multiple effects on people's self-concept and self-esteem. The group's typical characteristics become standards for members' behavior. Group membership also influences people's moods and self-esteem, as they feel bad about their group's failures or **BIRG** (bask in reflected glory) when their group succeeds. Relatively small groups typically have the greatest effects on their members' feelings.

When group membership is highly accessible, people see other in-group members as similar in their central group-linked characteristics. However, extensive personal interaction (when group membership is not salient) also provides knowledge about their unique and diverse personal characteristics. People like in-group members and tend to treat them in fair, humane, and altruistic ways because people see them as similar to themselves in their goals and interests.

In contrast, the **out-group homogeneity effect** causes people to see out-groups as uniform and homogeneous. People also dislike, devalue, and discriminate against out-group members, depending on the extent to which they are seen as threatening the in-group. When the out-group is simply different, it elicits mild dislike. This effect can be demonstrated even in the **minimal intergroup situation**, in which mere categorization results in mild discrimination against the out-group.

When the out-group is seen as outdoing the in-group, this more serious threat results in resentment, dislike, and overt discrimination. Out-groups that are seen as severe threats to the in-group elicit glorification of in-group values and symbols, which often goes hand in hand with murderous hatred, discrimination, aggression, or moral exclusion.

When Group Memberships Are Negative. Negative stereotypes about a group's ability can become self-fulfilling, actually harming the group members' performances when **stereotype threat** is present. In addition, belonging to a group that others dislike or discriminate against poses a threat to self-esteem. However, people can defend self-esteem by attributing negative reactions to others' prejudice or by making most of their social comparisons against fellow in-group members.

If these strategies are insufficient to protect individual self-esteem, people can use **individual mobility** strategies: attempting to escape their membership in a stigmatized group. They can psychologically disidentify with the group, for example, by playing down group membership or by regarding themselves as atypical group members. Another option is to dissociate: to escape physically, by "passing" or keeping group membership hidden "in the closet."

Sometimes group members adopt **social creativity** strategies, attempting to alter society's evaluation of their in-group by redefining group characteristics in positive terms. Finally, they may seek **social change** by engaging in direct intergroup conflict or struggle, or seeking to overturn the in-group/out-group distinction altogether. No one approach is always best for dealing with a negatively regarded group membership, just as no single coping strategy is uniformly the best way to handle threats to the individual self.

7

Attitudes and Attitude Change

What do the following events have in common? Golf professional Tiger Woods recommends Asahi Beverages in Japan and tennis star Anna Kournikova swears by Charles Schwab investment products. A dating service sends out ten thousand e-mails to singles in the United States and Canada, touting its ability to help them find their one true love. Religious groups seek converts on street corners, scientists dispute evidence for a well-established theory,[*] and friends argue over the best movie to see.

In all of these cases, a person or a group is trying to develop, strengthen, or change the attitudes of others. An **attitude** is any cognitive representation that summarizes our evaluation of an *attitude object*. Attitude objects may be the self, other people, things, actions, events, or ideas (W. J. McGuire, 1985; Zanna & Rempel, 1988). People can—and do—hold attitudes about just about anything. You may realize from this definition that we have already dealt with some attitudes in earlier chapters. Liking for others, discussed in Chapter 3, is an attitude about other individuals; self-esteem (Chapter 4) is an attitude about ourselves; and prejudice (Chapters 5 and 6) reflects attitudes toward our own and other groups. Although Chapters 7 and 8 focus on attitudes about objects, issues, events, ideas, and actions, what we say in these two chapters can also be applied to evaluations of ourselves, other people, and social groups. Because attitudes are so pervasive, the study of attitudes and *attitude change*—how attitudes form and how they can be modified—has been a central concern in social psychology since the discipline began. Both this chapter and the next focus on the development, maintenance, and change of attitudes and on the important impact attitudes have on what we think, feel, and do.

This chapter begins by asking what attitudes are and why we form them. Knowing the kind of information attitudes are based on gives us clues about how to develop, strengthen, or change attitudes through persuasion. **Persuasion** is the process by which attitudes are developed, strengthened, or changed by communication. As you will see, persuasive communications can be subtle or direct, funny or frightening, intriguingly innovative, or boringly repetitive. They may appeal to cold logic or

Attitude. A cognitive representation that summarizes an individual's evaluation of a particular person, group, thing, action, or idea.

Persuasion. The process of forming, strengthening, or changing attitudes by communication.

play on emotions. Some we find easy to resist, whereas others immediately push our persuasion buttons.

What makes some persuasive messages effective while others fail to change our minds? It won't surprise you to know that the answer lies in the way people process persuasive communications. As you will see in the second section of the chapter, how carefully we consider persuasive information determines what kinds of appeals are effective, for what kinds of people, under what kinds of conditions. Thinking carefully about persuasive appeals can be the difference between being at their mercy and resisting their appeals. As you will see in the final section of the chapter, despite the sophistication of many of the techniques used to influence us, whether we are persuaded or not is largely up to us.

Attitudes and Their Origins

Do you agree with laws that ban smoking on airplanes? Should more Eastern European countries be allowed to join the European Union? Do you think people should talk on their mobile phones while driving? Should women serve in military combat units? The answers people give to these kinds of questions reveal their attitudes, or evaluations of attitude objects. Attitudes can be favorable, neutral, or unfavorable, so attitudes are said to have a positive, neutral, or negative *direction*. Attitudes also differ in *intensity*, reflecting whether the evaluation is moderate or extreme. For researchers to be able to examine the fascinating properties of attitudes, they first need to measure them.

Measuring Attitudes

> Attitude researchers infer attitudes from how people react to attitude objects. Such reactions can range from subtle evaluative reactions of which people are unaware, to more direct expressions of support or opposition in word or deed. Attempts to assess these different reactions have demonstrated that implicit attitudes can sometimes differ from explicit attitudes.

Like other mental representations discussed in earlier chapters, attitudes can't be weighed, watched, or observed under microscopes. Social psychologists have to infer an attitude's direction and intensity on the basis of what people say or do. The most straightforward way to measure attitudes is to ask people to report their attitudes: to say what they think. Consumer surveys, political polls, and even our daily exchange of opinions with friends and family are forms of *self-reports*. Social psychologists usually get people to report their attitudes using attitude scales. An *attitude scale* is a series of questions that provides precise and reliable information about how strongly people agree or disagree with, favor or oppose, or like or dislike any attitude object (Dawes & Smith, 1985). Respondents choose among options that range from an extreme negative evaluation through a neutral point to an extreme positive evaluation, thus assessing intensity and direction. Researchers have to be quite careful constructing such scales. The attitudes that people report can be easily influenced by how such questions are worded. In the United States, for example, asking "Should students be allowed to pray in public schools?" might well yield different reponses than asking "Should students be forbidden to pray in public schools?" Expressed attitudes can also be influenced by the response alternatives people are given. For example, if asked to rate a particular politician on a scale from 0 to 10, many more people report a negative evaluation (using the numbers 0–4) than they do if asked to rate the same politician on a scale ranging from −5 to +5 (apparently no one wants to use those negative numbers). Researchers need to keep in mind that the words they use and the response options they offer can subtly change the attitudes people report (Schwarz, 1999).

Social psychologists also use *observations* of behavior to gauge attitudes. For example, they might infer attitude direction from whether people volunteer to stuff envelopes for a campaign to save the spotted owl, and intensity from how many envelopes they are willing to stuff (Deci, 1975; Wilson & Dunn, 1986). Many kinds of behaviors can tell researchers about attitudes: how close people approach to attitude objects, how often they choose or use them, how much they are willing to risk or spend for them, how much time or effort they expend to promote or obtain them, and whether people are willing to try to persuade another person in favor of or against a given attitude object.

Self-report techniques and observational measures are less useful when people hold unpopular attitudes that they may want to hide or deny (D. T. Campbell, 1963). When people suspect that their attitudes differ from what most other people think, or from what other people think is good, they are reluctant to express their true attitudes. Just as people might not want to admit that they have a negative attitude— a prejudice—against some social group, they typically don't like to admit that they favor underage drinking and unprotected sex, or that they think it's just fine to illegally download music and movies from the internet. Attitude researchers have developed a number of techniques to get around people's desire to hide what they really think.

Some self-report techniques guarantee anonymity, so participants can be honest because the opinions they express won't be linked to them. Other techniques increase the honesty of participants' answers by convincing them that their "real" physiological reactions about issues such as drug and alcohol use, for example, are being measured, even when that's not true (Quigley-Fernandez & Tedeschi, 1978; Wech, Lundstrom, & Moore, 1989). Here's how this technique works. Experimenters secretly find out the participant's attitude on one topic, perhaps from a previous attitude questionnaire. They then instruct the participant to try to trick the "attitude detection" machinery about that topic and show that the "equipment" can catch the participant in the lie. Convinced that their real attitudes can be detected, participants tend to tell the truth about other sensitive topics. Other techniques assess attitudes so subtly that participants aren't aware of revealing their opinions (Hammond, 1948; Vargas, von Hippel, & Petty, 2004). Supposed tests of obscure general knowledge ("Did U.S. President Bush gain an A or a C grade point average in his college studies?") often reflect attitudes (supporters of Mr. Bush might guess that he earned the higher grade, for example).

In their desire to know what people really think, researchers have also come up with techniques that reveal attitudes in ways that respondents cannot readily control. By measuring involuntary muscle activity, for example, facial electromyography (EMG) allows precise measurements of both the intensity and the direction of attitudes on such sensitive issues as alcohol abuse or pre-marital sex (Cacioppo & Petty, 1979; Cacioppo, Petty, Losch, & Kim, 1986). Measuring the time people take to make a particular response to an attitude object can tell researchers how people really see the object, regardless of what they say about it

■ **Tell us what you think.** Like this interviewer, most social psychologists measure attitudes using self-report techniques—a method that relies on people expressing the intensity and direction of their opinions openly and honestly.

The ways that subtle techniques such as facial EMG and the IAT are used to measure implicit attitudes about other groups—the potentially unpopular evaluations that people might want to hide or deny—were discussed in more detail in Chapter 5. To refresh your memory about how implicit and explicit measures of prejudice might differ, and what that means, see Chapter 5, pages 165 to 166.

(Greenwald, McGhee, & Schwartz, 1998). If an object is evaluated positively, for example, people may take longer to respond to it if it is seen with or associated to something negative.

Such subtle measurement techniques sometimes reveal that people's automatic evaluations of objects (called *implicit attitudes*) are different from the attitudes they overtly express about them (called *explicit attitudes*; Fazio & Olson, 2003). For example, almost everyone has implicitly negative attitudes toward spiders, even though many people suppress their automatic negative responses and say they feel just fine about spiders (de Jong, van den Hout, Rietbroek, & Huijding, 2003). So different versions of attitudes (one negative, one "just fine", for example) about the same object (spiders, for example) might routinely exist at the same time. If implicit and explicit attitudes differ, which is the "true" attitude? Are implicit attitudes (over which people have less conscious control) what people "really" think about attitude objects, while their explicit attitudes (over which they have more control) just reflect socially desirable responses? Recent research suggests that's not the case: implicit attitudes aren't pure measures of people's "true" evaluations, and explicit attitudes aren't always socially desirable distortions. We now know that just like explicit measures, implicit measures of attitudes change over time and are affected by the accessibility and importance of situational factors. In fact, implicit and explicit attitudes about the same attitude object seem to be more sensitive to different kinds of information (Wilson, Lindsey, & Schooler, 2000; Gawronski, Strack, & Bodenhausen, 2005). Implicit attitudes reflect the positive or negative associations that people have to an object—even if those are unwanted—whereas explicit attitudes are more likely to reflect the evaluations that people wish to endorse, whether they wish to do so for commendable reasons (overcoming phobias and prejudices) or for less commendable reasons like social desirability (Dasgupta & Greenwald, 2001; Karpinski & Hilton, 2001). So both implicit and explicit measures of attitudes have important things to tell us about how and why evaluations form and how and why they change, the topics of concern in this chapter. It turns out that implicit and explicit attitudes can also have different effects on behavior, a topic covered in the next chapter. By learning more about when and why implicit and explicit attitudes differ, social psychologists are learning much more about the causes and consequences of attitudes.

You might remember that implicit and explicit stereotypes and prejudices work in exactly the some way, see Chapter 5, pages 165 to 166.

Attitude Formation: Why and How?

People form attitudes because attitudes are useful. Attitudes help people master the environment and express important connections with others. Attitudes are assembled from three types of information: beliefs about the object's characteristics, feelings and emotions about the object, and information about past and current actions toward the object. Negative information and accessible information are weighted more heavily. Once an attitude forms, it becomes closely linked to the representation of the object.

Are you for or against democracy? How do you feel about your best friend? We expect that you can answer these questions without much thought. Many attitudes are so well established and so frequently used that people can express them and act on them without a second thought. But even familiar things that now elicit almost a knee-jerk evaluative response were once evaluated for the first time. Where do attitudes come from? Why do we construct attitudes toward almost every object in our social world? And how do we come to favor one idea and resist another, to like one object and dislike something else?

WHY ATTITUDES FORM. Forming attitudes comes naturally to humans. Research on brain activity shows that people evaluate almost everything they encounter and do so very quickly (Bargh, Chaiken, Raymond, & Hymes, 1996; De Houwer, Hendrickx, & Baeyens, 1997; Duckworth, Bargh, Garcia, & Chaiken, 2002). This is almost certainly because attitudes are so useful (Ajzen, 2001; D. Katz, 1960; Maio & Olson, 2000; M. B. Smith, Bruner, & White, 1956). First, attitudes help people master the environment. Holding an attitude toward chocolate ice cream, for example, helps us quickly summarize its pluses and minuses and how to deal with it. Attitudes help organize and simplify our experience, orienting us to the important characteristics of an attitude object so we can deal with it efficiently. What's important about chocolate ice cream? Our attitude tells us, for example, that it's the taste and the texture, not the smell or the packaging, that count: those are the features to focus on, the features that make the difference (Fazio, 2000). This focusing and simplifying role is called the *object appraisal function* or *knowledge function* of attitudes. Attitudes also steer us toward things that will help us achieve our goals and keep us away from things that will hurt us, serving an *instrumental* or *utilitarian function* (Ennis & Zanna, 2000). A positive attitude makes sure we approach chocolate ice cream on a regular basis; a negative attitude helps keep us away from it! Both the object appraisal or knowledge function, and the instrumental or utilitarian function of attitudes help us master the environment.

Second, attitudes are useful because they help us gain and maintain connectedness with others. People's impressions of others are influenced by the attitudes the others express (Shavitt & Nelson, 2000). So holding a particular attitude lets people express their true selves, affirm the groups they belong to, and show what they stand for. If being "a liberal" is crucial to who you are, for example, you may find it important to hold certain attitudes on the environment, immigration laws, and public schooling. This *social identity function* or *value-expressive function* of attitudes helps us define ourselves. At the same time, expressing the "right" views can smooth interactions and allow us to make a good impression (Chaiken, Giner-Sorolla, & Chen, 1996). When this *impression management function* is uppermost, people try to adopt and support the attitude that they think their audience also endorses (Nienhuis, Manstead & Spears, 2001). Both the social identity or value-expressive function and the impression management function of attitudes help us stay connected to others.

Many attitudes serve both mastery and connectedness functions, although not always to the same degree. Attitudes toward practical objects like a computer or electric drill or rain boots, for example, may serve an object appraisal or utilitarian function much more than they do a social identity one. Attitudes about religious practices, a cherished memento from childhood, or the animal rights movement, on the other hand, are probably more expressive of a person's identity (Shavitt, 1990). Because attitudes may serve different functions, we can form multiple attitudes about one and the same object (Tourangeau, Rasinski, Bradburn, & D'Andrade, 1989; Wilson and others, 2000). We may have a different attitude about our local club's cap, for example, when our team loses the soccer final (when the hat serves identity functions) than when the hat keeps off the sun on a hot day (serving a utilitarian function).

We encountered attitudes that serve the value-expressive or social identity function in Chapter 6, pages 207 to 208. Value-expressive attitudes are so centrally tied to our definitions of ourselves and our groups that any threat to them becomes a threat to the self and to the group.

CULTURAL DIFFERENCES IN ATTITUDE FUNCTION. Cultural differences also influence what functions attitudes serve, and thus why particular attitudes form. As we first pointed out in Chapter 3, independent cultures, like those found in North America, emphasize the individual. Individuals in these cultures see themselves as independent and tend to hold attitudes that allow them to show that they are distinct from others. Interdependent cultures, such as those found in Asia, on the other hand, are more concerned with group harmony and belongingness. Individuals in those countries see themselves in more interdependent terms and are more likely to hold attitudes that demonstrate similarity with their peers (Aaker & Schmitt, 2001). So it's not surprising that persuaders in different cultures make these different functions salient in their appeals. American ads emphasize rugged individualism, personal success, and independence with slogans like: "The art of being unique," or "You, only better" (Han & Shavitt, 1993). Japanese and Korean ads emphasize group benefits, interpersonal harmony, and family integrity with slogans like: "We have a way of bringing people together," and "Sharing is beautiful" (Aaker, Benet-Martinez, & Garolera, 2001; Han & Shavitt, 1993). These strategies work: Ads that emphasize functions that are consistent with cultural ideals are more persuasive (Aaker & Williams, 1998; Tak, Kaid, & Lee, 1997).

THE BUILDING BLOCKS OF ATTITUDE. As people encounter information about an attitude object (either by interacting with it, seeing it associated with other liked or disliked objects, or by hearing about it from friends, family, teachers, or the media), they build a mental representation of it. This representation can include cognitive, affective, and behavioral information associated with the object (Ostrom, 1969; Trafimow & Sheeran, 1998; Zanna & Rempel, 1988).

Because impressions of ourselves, others, and other groups discussed in earlier chapters are also attitudes, they too are based on cognitive, affective, and behavioral information. In Chapter 5, for example, we saw that what we think group members are like, how we feel about them, and our actions toward them could all contribute to prejudice.

1. *Cognitive information* is what people know about an attitude object—the facts and beliefs they have about it. Perhaps the high incidence of lung cancer among smokers has convinced you that cigarette smoking causes disease. This belief is cognitive information about this attitude object, cigarette smoking.

2. *Affective information* consists of how people feel about the object—the feelings and emotions the attitude object arouses. Experiencing nausea or anger when you are in a smoky closed area qualifies as affective information associated with cigarette smoking.

3. *Behavioral information* is knowledge about people's past, present, or future interactions with the attitude object. The fact that you do not smoke is behavioral information relevant to cigarette smoking.

Any of these types of information can contribute to an attitude. If your evaluation of a particular occupation reflects your beliefs about how much you can make in that profession, for example, your opinion is based on cognitive information. Many attitudes reflect mainly cognitive information about attitude objects (Fishbein & Ajzen, 1975), especially if that information comes from hearsay rather than direct experience (Millar & Millar, 1996; Tesser, 1993).

On the other hand, affective information has the edge in many attitudes (Abelson, Kinder, Peters, & Fiske, 1982; Edwards & von Hippel, 1995; Zajonc, 1980). There are several reasons why affective information can play such an important role in attitudes. We often get affective information first, before encountering cognitive information (as when we have a gut reaction to a new roommate before even getting to know what she is like). Affective inputs might simply overwhelm cognitions. Needles and blood often trigger strong negative emotional reactions that can determine attitudes toward donating blood, for example, regardless of supportive cognitions (Breckler & Wiggins, 1989). Many affective reactions to sensory information like tastes, smells, loud noises, or repugnant sights reflect an inborn preference for pleasure over pain. Because such reactions are hard wired as the result of evolutionary influences, it makes sense that they play a big role in determining attitudes. People also differ by temperament and disposition in ways that determine their attitudes. You may recognize yourself or some of your friends as having one of those sunny dispositions that typically have positive attitudes about most things most of the time, or as being one of those darker types who dislike most things most of the time (George, 1990). Both the inherited human preference for pleasure over pain and inherited individual differences in disposition and temperament probably help explain why some attitudes are linked to our genes (Tesser, 1993). That is why the attitudes of identical twins are more likely to be similar than the attitudes of nonidentical twins, even when the identical twins are reared apart (Waller, Kojetin, Bouchard, Lykken, & Tellegen, 1990).

Information about behavior can also dominate attitudes, particularly if that behavior is habitual. Donating to the Multiple Sclerosis Fund year after year, for example, is likely to have a powerful influence on attitudes toward the charity (Fazio & Zanna, 1981). Because of the varied and important influence that behavior can have on attitudes, we discuss this topic in much more detail in Chapter 8. Although attitudes can be based on just one type of information, most attitudes probably reflect a mixture of the building blocks (Breckler & Wiggins, 1989; Zanna & Rempel, 1988).

PUTTING IT ALL TOGETHER. How do evaluative summaries—attitudes—emerge from all the information that accumulates about attitude objects? Three principles hold. First, consistency is the name of the game. People typically form attitudes that are consistent with most of what they know, feel, and experience, as Figure 7.1 suggests. Having lots of positive information about an attitude object typically results in a positive attitude. Similarly, the presence of negative beliefs, feelings, or behaviors produces a negative attitude (Festinger, 1957; Heider, 1944; M. Rosenberg, 1956).

The second principle of attitude formation is that the bad outweighs the good. Negative information has an edge over positive information—it's preferentially encoded, weighted more heavily, and is harder to "cancel out" than positive information (Baumeister and others, 2001; Eiser, Fazio, Stafford, & Prescott, 2003; Ito, Larsen, Smith, & Cacioppo, 1998). The third principle is that accessible information—information that comes most easily to mind or that grabs our attention—dominates attitude judgments. People who have just been led to focus on conservative values like the importance of hard work, for example, have less favorable attitudes toward government spending on welfare programs than do people who have just been led to focus on government responsibility (Tourangeau & Rasinski, 1988). Information that is accessible because it is perceptually salient also exerts a strong effect on attitudes. We tend to prefer foods that have obvious smell or taste appeal, for example, rather than those who have hidden nutritional benefits. In the same way, accessible motives and goals can determine our attitudes. If you are buying a car for utilitarian reasons, one model's excellent fuel economy and sound maintenance record will be salient, and your attitude toward the car will be positive. On the other hand, if you think that what you drive reflects who you are, the same model's vinyl seats and plastic accessories will make your attitude toward it negative.

FIGURE 7.1   Attitude formation and measurement

■ If you learn that George Strait donates money to several charities, feel relaxed when you listen to his music, and know that you would drive over one hundred miles to see him in concert, you are likely to form a positive attitude toward the popular country singer. The attitude in turn will influence thoughts, feelings, and observable behaviors. Researchers draw on these effects to measure the underlying attitude.

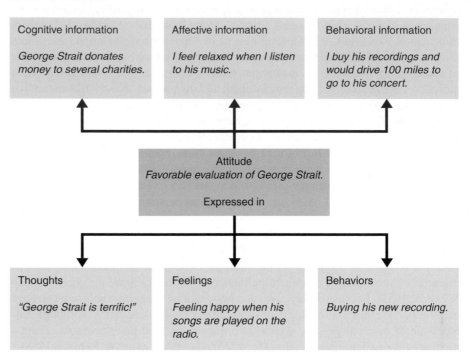

Cognitive information

George Strait donates money to several charities.

Affective information

I feel relaxed when I listen to his music.

Behavioral information

I buy his recordings and would drive 100 miles to go to his concert.

Attitude
Favorable evaluation of George Strait.

Expressed in

Thoughts

"George Strait is terrific!"

Feelings

Feeling happy when his songs are played on the radio.

Behaviors

Buying his new recording.

Typically, people do gather information more on one side of an issue than the other. If everyone in your home, club, and church group is politically conservative, for example, your day-to-day interactions will provide a one-sided view of the issues. In fact, many commentators have noted that in the United States, communities are becoming increasingly homogeneous, so that most people interact with a majority of people who share their opinions most of the time (Brooks, 2004). People are thus increasingly exposed to only one side or the other of a given issue. First reactions also make inconsistency less likely. After all, if your first early encounter with lima beans, bean sprouts, or guavas is largely negative, you probably avoid them from then on. This prevents you from gathering further information that might contradict your lopsidedly negative information base.

Of course, the different pieces of information that accumulate do not always imply a consistent evaluation of an attitude object and can't always be reconciled. Most people know arguments on both sides of major social issues, such as immigration control, the death penalty, and environmental management (Judd & Kulik, 1980). Having cognitions that are evaluatively inconsistent with feelings toward particular attitude objects is also a common experience. For example, you might think blood drives are an excellent idea at the same time that you feel nauseated at the sight of a hypodermic needle. Such *ambivalent* attitudes reflect both positive and negative reactions to the attitude object (I. Katz, 1981; Priester & Petty, 2001; M. M. Thompson & Zanna, 1995). For example, 51% of U.S. citizens report conflicted reactions toward abortion, with favorable views toward a women's right to choose in some circumstances but not others (Gallup Poll, 2002).

Thus, the direction and intensity of our attitudes reflects the number and importance of cognitive, affective, and behavioral pieces of information we accumulate about an attitude object and how we put those pieces together.

LINKING ATTITUDES TO THEIR OBJECTS. As soon as we form an evaluative summary or attitude about an attitude object, it becomes part of our cognitive representation of the object, as seen in Figure 7.2. This means that encountering objects typically brings attitudes associated with those objects immediately to mind as well (Bargh and others, 1996; Ito and others, 1998). The more often this joint activation of object and evaluation occurs, the closer and stronger the link between object and attitude becomes. This tight coupling has three important consequences. First, the stronger the link, the more automatically the attitude pops to mind whenever we encounter or think about the object (Fazio, 1986, 2001). For example, we don't come across just a spider, but a truly repulsive spider. In fact, we may not be able to think about the object without our attitude coming to mind, even if we wanted to. Second, the stronger the link, the more likely it is that our attitude will become a shorthand substitute for all the information we have about the object. When people ask you what you think of country singers the Dixie Chicks, your attitude tells you: "I like them," without your having to think about

FIGURE 7.2   Linking an attitude to the object

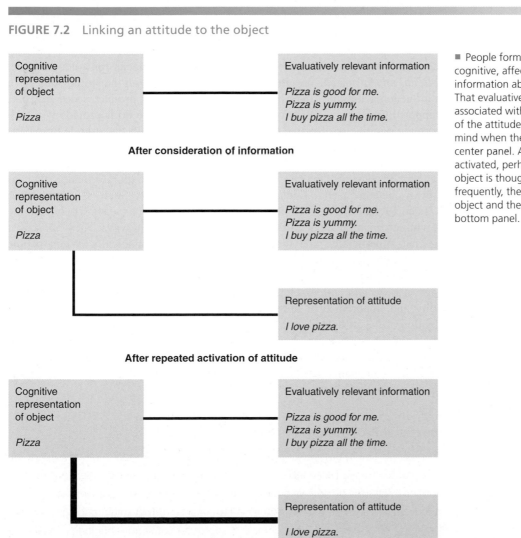

After consideration of information

After repeated activation of attitude

■ People form an attitude based on cognitive, affective, and behavioral information about an attitude object. That evaluative summary also becomes associated with the mental representation of the attitude object and can come to mind when the object is encountered, center panel. As the attitude is repeatedly activated, perhaps because the attitude object is thought about or encountered frequently, the link between the object and the attitude strengthens, bottom panel.

the cognitions, feelings, and behaviors that initially generated your reaction (Lingle & Ostrom, 1979). Third, the stronger the link, the less easily the attitude is moved around by new information. When an attitude is well established and immediately accessible, it is not as influenced by other information we encounter (Petty, Priester, & Wegener, 1994). People are more confident and certain about such strongly linked attitudes than about those that are less accessible (Holland, Verplanken, & Van Knippenberg, 2003).

Superficial and Systematic Routes to Persuasion: From Snap Judgments to Considered Opinions

We form attitudes because they are useful to us. But other people also find our attitudes useful. In the marketplace, political arena, or classroom—wherever you go—you will find people trying to influence you to develop new attitudes or change old ones. And if positive beliefs, feelings, or behaviors produce positive attitudes, and negative beliefs, feelings, and behaviors produce negative attitudes, the persuader's task should be quite straightforward. *Rational messages*, which focus on the attitude object's attributes, can provide cognitive building blocks for a new attitude. *Emotional appeals* can be designed to associate feelings with the attitude object, in turn influencing attitudes. To ensure that you will love their product, scorn drug use, or support immigration restrictions, all persuaders need to do is provide you with important cognitive or affective information consistent with the attitude they want you to develop. Right?

Actually, it's not that simple. Like the proverbial horse that can be led to water but cannot be convinced to drink, people can be provided with information but cannot always be convinced to think, or at least to think deeply. Shelly Chaiken (1980, 1987) and Richard Petty and John Cacioppo (1981, 1986) have shown that people deal with information about attitude objects in two different ways: They can scan it somewhat superficially, and they can consider it systematically. When people engage in *superficial processing*, they rely on accessible or salient information to make rather simple evaluative inferences about the attitude object. When people engage in *systematic processing*, they go beyond simple cues and also consider the validity and importance of attitude-relevant information and what it means for evaluation of the attitude object. Most of the time, we process information superficially. Sometimes something happens to make us also take more notice of attitude relevant evidence. As we shall see, both kinds of processing—superficial and systematic—can change attitudes, but they do so in very different ways and under different conditions.

These two types of processing should sound familiar, because superficial and systematic processing also come into play when we make judgments about other individuals (Chapter 3, pages 64 to 80) and about members of groups (Chapter 5, pages 166 to 176).

Superficial Processing: Persuasion Shortcuts

When people do not give persuasive communications much thought, various superficial aspects of the persuasive appeal can lead to attitude change. For example, people might be influenced by positive or negative objects or events associated with the attitude object, or by other feelings they are experiencing. They might also agree with messages from attractive, expert, or familiar sources or with familiar or long messages.

When you thumb absentmindedly through a magazine, you pay very little attention to the actual words in the ads. Nevertheless, despite the superficiality of your processing, information is getting through. Even at a glance, you may notice the beautiful people using a product, the amount of evidence that supports an advertising claim, or the irritating or appealing photos in an advertisement. An advertisement may evoke feelings of nostalgia, sentimentality, disgust, or fear. A persuasive setting—a store or a mall—may feature inviting smells and cheerful music or glaring lights and uncomfortable temperatures. Because such simple pieces of information are themselves associated with and activate positive or negative evaluations, they can act as **persuasion heuristics**. The presence or absence of a positive cue can make people like or dislike the attitude object without thinking about it in any depth (Chaiken, 1980, 1987). When people form attitudes based on persuasion heuristics rather than thinking about the attitude object itself, Petty and Cacioppo (1981, 1986) describe them as taking a *peripheral route to persuasion*. When people are processing superficially, a wide range of cues can influence their attitudes.

ATTITUDES BY ASSOCIATION. Some attitude objects, such as perfumes, baby products, and vacations, inevitably appeal to the emotions. Think of the pleasure associated with playing with a cute baby or lying on a sun-drenched beach. No wonder ads for baby products and vacations play on our emotions. But emotional appeals can also influence our attitudes about emotionally neutral products. The happily splashing baby can sell faucets as well as baby powder. Political candidates can reminisce about their childhoods to promote policy changes. And classical music can become theme songs for wines, airlines, and long-lasting batteries. Why do advertisers want babies, nostalgia, and well-loved music in their ads?

If positive events are repeatedly associated with an attitude object, the attitude object soon comes to elicit the feelings associated with those events. To demonstrate this effect, Michael Olson and Russell Fazio (2002) asked female students to watch a series of slides that included pairings of novel objects with clearly positive or negative words or images. A later test showed that these subtle associations had created attitudes: objects earlier paired with positive images or words were now seen as positive, and objects paired with negative images or words were seen as negative. This process is called *classical or evaluative conditioning* (Walther, 2002), and it is demonstrated in Figure 7.3. Evaluative conditioning probably explains the popularity of the business lunch and the fund-raising dinner. Associating a sales pitch or an appeal for a donation with good food may well increase its persuasiveness (Janis, Kaye, & Kirschner, 1965). Music can be used the same way. In one study that looked at the effect of popular music on attitudes, students in a management class watched what they believed to be an ad agency's pilot version of an advertisement for a ball-point pen (Gorn, 1982). The ad offered minimal information about the pen, but it was accompanied in one condition by popular rock-and-roll music and in the other by unpopular classical music. What happened when students were later allowed to choose a pen as a reward for their participation in the study? They were much more likely to choose the pen that had been accompanied by the popular rock-and-roll music. Adding positive associations to an attitude product can boost its evaluations—and its sales.

Evaluative conditioning is the backbone of the emotional appeal, or "soft sell." As one advertising expert put it: "It sets off the product as something pretty wonderful by draping around it as many pleasant associations as possible" (Martineau, 1957, pp. 13–14). Of course, persuasion professionals need to be careful that a positive

Evaluative conditioning can occur between any pairs of stimuli. We discussed the impact of evaluative conditioning on reactions to social groups in Chapter 5, page 155.

Persuasion heuristic. Association of a cue that is positively or negatively evaluated with the attitude object, allowing the attitude object to be evaluated quickly and without much thought.

FIGURE 7.3   Evaluative conditioning and attitude formation

■ Suppose that people encounter a neutral object associated with a stimulus that they evaluate positively or negatively. After this happens a few times, the feelings produced by the stimulus become associated with the object, resulting in the formation of an attitude.

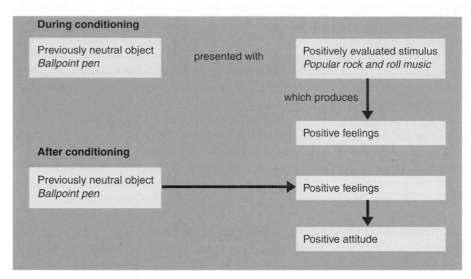

association in one culture translates when their campaign goes international. Baby food manufacturer Gerber, for example, has done well in the U.S. market by labeling their product with an adorable smiling baby. Using the same packaging in the African market was not a success: Because of the low literacy rate, products there are often labeled with a picture of their contents!

Of course, evaluative conditioning works the same way when negative events are associated with an attitude object. The clear waters and sandy beaches used to mean beauty and prosperity for the families who live along the coast of Thailand. After the devastation caused by tsunamis following a massive 2004 earthquake in the area, the sea is now associated with destruction and death. As one man put it: "We now look at the sea and see a cemetery." And during the 2000 United States presidential election, it became clear that the word RATS was flashed very briefly—for less than one-thirtieth of a second—during a television spot attacking part of the Democratic platform. Republicans denied any deliberate attempt at persuasion, claiming the brief insertion was accidental (Berke, 2000). Nevertheless, it would have made a fine textbook example of how to create a negative association through evaluative conditioning.

MOODS AS HEURISTIC CUES: IF I FEEL GOOD, I MUST LIKE IT. Frolicking babies and great music might not just make attitude objects seem good—they can make us feel good too. And these feelings can also influence our evaluations. When people rely on their current feelings to evaluate an attitude object, they are using the "How do I feel about it?" heuristic (Schwarz & Clore, 1988). Now if positive or negative feelings are actually elicited by the attitude object, as when being with a date makes you feel good or sky-diving makes you feel sick, it makes sense to rely on your current feelings to evaluate the date positively and the sky-diving negatively. But sometimes feelings that exist quite independently of an attitude object can get mixed up with the attitude object itself. Sometimes people just feel good, perhaps because the sun is shining, the music is upbeat, or they just received a compliment. Or they feel bad—maybe a friend is ill or they failed a test. In these circumstances, using the "How do I feel about it?" heuristic might lead people astray, making everything look good when they're feeling good and everything look bad when they're not. This does seem to happen. Students evaluate their lives more positively when interviewed on sunny, upbeat days than they do on rainy, downbeat days for example. Luckily, some gentle reminders of why they might be feeling that way are usually enough to make people realize that what they are feeling is not relevant and adjust their attitude appropriately (Albarracin & Kumkale, 2003). Like other heuristics, the "How do I feel about it?" cue is most powerful when people process only superficially.

THE FAMILIARITY HEURISTIC: FAMILIARITY MAKES THE HEART GROW FONDER.
There's nothing more comforting than the presence of old friends, repeated rituals, familiar surroundings. In fact, repeated exposure to a stimulus increases people's liking for it. Consider what happened, for example, when Robert Zajonc (1968) showed college students unfamiliar "Turkish words" like *saracik* and *dilikli* different numbers of times and asked them to pronounce the word. When they were later asked to guess how positive or negative each word was, people rated more positively the words they had seen more often. This **mere exposure effect**, the finding that people prefer things to which they have been more frequently exposed, is one of the most replicated findings in social psychology. This association between familiarity and goodness is so powerful that it operates even when people are unaware of whether or how often they have seen the stimulus before. In fact, the mere exposure effect is even stronger when people are unaware of how frequently they have been exposed to the stimuli (Bornstein, Leone, & Galley, 1987; Kunst-Wilson & Zajonc, 1980).

Recall from Chapter 3, pages 62 to 63, that frequent exposure to a person similarly increases liking for that person.

Perhaps because of the positive feelings associated with familiarity, familiar stimuli can also be more persuasive. People agree more with the views of others they have seen before than with sources they are seeing for the first time, even if the sources use the same arguments (Weisbuch, Mackie, & Garcia-Marques, 2003). People judge sentences that they have heard before (even in the context of a different task) to be more credible and valid (Arkes, Hackett, & Boehme, 1989). They misremember familiar statements as coming from credible sources (Fragale & Heath, 2004). They are more persuaded by a weak message that has been recently repeated than by one they are hearing for the first time (Garcia-Marques & Mackie, 2001; Claypool, Mackie, Garcia-Marques, McIntosh, & Udal, 2004). Even framing arguments in terms of familiar idioms and metaphors makes arguments more convincing than phrases conveying the same information in more literal form. In one study, for example, Daniel Howard (1997) presented college students with a message urging them to begin financial planning for retirement soon. The content of the persuasive message was summarized using either familiar phrases or more literal arguments. For example, some students received the advice: "Don't bury your head in the sand" and "Don't put all your eggs in one basket." Others were told: "Don't pretend a problem doesn't exist" and "Don't risk everything on a single venture." Use of the familiar phrases was more effective: Those hearing the more commonplace advice developed more positive attitudes toward financial planning. One important reason that familiarity might have these effects is that previously encountered information can be more easily processed (Reber, Schwarz, & Winkielman, 2004).

The persuasive effects of familiarity can create some unexpected outcomes. When you tell someone that something isn't true, familiarity effects might make them more likely to think it is true if they later hear it again. This is one of the

Mere exposure effect. People's tendency to prefer objects to which they have been more frequently exposed.

reasons that rumors are so hard to squash. Hearing the rumor again makes it seem more credible, but so too does hearing the rumor and hearing that it is not true (Allport & Lepkin, 1945). Ironically, consumer warnings on packages can become consumer recommendations for the same reasons. In one study, repeatedly telling older adults that a consumer claim was false helped them remember it as false in the short term, but after a three day delay, the oft-repeated claim was more likely to be remembered as true! The claim itself became more familiar and thus seemed more valid, but the contradictory evidence (But guess what—it's not true!) got lost (Skurnik, Yoon, Park & Schwarz, 2005).

THE ATTRACTIVENESS HEURISTIC: AGREEING WITH THOSE WE LIKE. If surrounding an attitude object with positive associations makes it seem more positive, no wonder advertisements often pair an attitude object with a popular or attractive figure. These communicators make no claim to expertise, so why does someone who turns our head also change our minds? Evaluative priming tells us that associating someone we like with the attitude object makes us think that it too is likable. No wonder that Roger Ailes (1988), adviser to both the Reagan and Bush U.S. presidential campaigns, calls likability a persuasive "magic bullet": "If you could master one element of personal communication that is more powerful than anything, it is the quality of being likable. If your audience likes you, they'll forgive just about everything else" (p. 81).

■ **The attractiveness heuristic.** Milk producers know that ads like this one featuring supermodel Naomi Campbell use the persuasive power of an attractive source to make magazine readers buy milk without having to think carefully about its benefits.

He seems to be right. Attractive people are well liked, and others are more likely to agree with them and think they're right (Byrne, 1971; Insko, 1981). No wonder then that attractive people are more likely to get their way. In one study attractive confederates were able to get many more people to agree to sign a petition than were less attractive ones (Chaiken, 1979). And surveys show that voters prefer candidates they find attractive (M. L. Patterson, Churchill, Burger, & Powell, 1992). So attractiveness serves as a persuasion cue: If David Beckham chooses Vodafone and Mia Hamm drinks Gatorade, consumers will want to buy those products too—at least that is what advertisers hope!

These aren't the only advantages that attractive people have over the rest of the population. See Chapter 3, page 59, and Chapter 11, pages 394 to 395.

When advertisers use attractive communicators, they usually make them the most prominent feature of the appeal. Does emphasizing a communicator's attractiveness increase our reliance on the attractiveness heuristic? Apparently so. Suzanne Pallak (1983) showed two groups of women the same article, which urged donations in support of the arts. One of the groups also saw a vivid color photo of an attractive man who had supposedly written the article. Others students saw only a blurred photocopy of the man's photograph. Although the arguments were exactly the same, women for whom the communicator's attractiveness was made salient were much more persuaded than were women for whom the man's appearance was not so obvious.

THE EXPERTISE HEURISTIC: AGREEING WITH THOSE WHO KNOW. "Life exists elsewhere in our galaxy!" Imagine that this sentence had caught your attention as you flipped through the television channels on a Sunday afternoon. You soon discover that the source of the intriguing statement is a talk-show guest, a farmer who claims he has been taken for multiple rides on a spaceship. Would you nod in agreement or snort with derision? Imagine now that you had heard this same claim from European Space Agency Director, Jean-Jacques Dordain, a member of the French Académie des Technologies and the National Air and Space Academy. Would your reaction be different?

Research suggests that it would. Because communicators with excellent credentials usually offer compelling arguments, people often associate them with opinions that should be respected: Experts know what they are talking about. On the basis of this association, the *expertise heuristic* leads people to accept the validity of a claim on the basis of who says it, not what is said (Hovland & Weiss, 1951; Sternthal, Dholakia, & Leavitt, 1978).

Why is a European Space Agency adminstrator an expert source while the space-traveling farmer is not? To be credible, communicators must be competent. *Competence* refers to proof of the communicator's accomplishment or status in a particular field. When an ad features Ronaldo in action on the soccer field, a robed judge banging a gavel in a wood-paneled courtroom, or a stethoscope-bedecked doctor writing prescriptions, its creators are hoping to capitalize on the expertise heuristic. One early demonstration of this simple association between occupation and competence compared the persuasive powers of a judge and a drug dealer (Kelman & Hovland, 1953). Participants were told that one or the other had recommended relatively lenient treatment of a juvenile delinquent. As you might expect, they found the judge more persuasive than the drug dealer.

Occupation is not the only cue that suggests competence. Research findings indicate that fast talkers also convey an image of expertise. As long as people can understand the gist of a message, the faster the message is delivered, the more objective, intelligent, and knowledgeable the communicator is seen to be (MacLachlan & Siegel, 1980). When they give quick confident replies to lawyers' questions, witnesses appear more credible and competent (Erickson, Lind, Johnson, & O'Barr, 1978). Rapid delivery also makes it harder for listeners to tell a strong appeal from a weak one (S. M. Smith & Shaffer, 1995). In fact, running television ads at 120% of their normal speed can increase the persuasiveness of weak commercials (D. L. Moore, Hausknecht, & Thamodaran, 1986). There are limits, however. If delivery is so rapid that the meaning of the message is lost, persuasion is undermined. And when listeners really care about the topic, they are less likely to let a fast talker influence their attitudes (S. M. Smith & Shaffer, 1995).

People expect expert communicators not only to know the facts but also to tell the truth (Eagly, Wood, & Chaiken, 1978). Thus, after competence, *trustworthiness* is the most important characteristic a credible communicator can have. That is why communicators sometimes earn persuasion points by presenting both sides of an issue; the strategy makes them seem well-informed and fair-minded (R. A. Jones & Brehm, 1970). Trustworthiness is also the goal when advertisers arrange for their audience to "sit in on" or "overhear" product testimonials and "slice of life" endorsements. If the communication seems to happen by accident, rather than being tailored specifically for the listener's ears, the casual observer is likely to think it is true and is easily persuaded (Walster & Festinger, 1962).

Of course, we are likely to be taken in by these ploys only if we are processing very minimally. If we devote even a little more attention to the communication, we might be prompted to ask why a particular source is advocating a particular position (Eagly, Chaiken, & Wood, 1981). Such *attributional processing* can undermine a communicator's apparent trustworthiness. Imagine, for example, that an advertisement for Sergio Tacchini sportswear featuring tennis star Martina Hingis prompts you to wonder why Hingis endorses the product. Does Hingis promote that brand because of the quality of the product? Could it be that this particular line of sportswear is so terrific that Hingis cannot help but recommend it? If the ad leads to the belief that the communicator's position reflects the stimulus object's actual qualities—deciding that Hingis endorses Tacchini because the clothes are so good—such a stimulus attribution produces persuasion (Eagly and others, 1978). If the advocate seems to have ulterior motives, however, people become suspicious. If they recognize that Hingis—like Venus Williams with Reebok, Patty Schnyder with Adidas, and Mirjana Lucic with Fila—is well paid for such an endorsement, they may find the ad less persuasive: Maybe it's the money talking, not the quality of the gear. Attributional processing may explain why people are particularly impressed when communicators seem to speak or act against their own best interests (Knight & Weiss, 1980). We would probably be persuaded if we learned that Martina Hingis owns stock in a competing sportswear company but feels compelled to recommend Sergio Tacchini because of its quality.

Attributional processing (processing concerned with discovering the causes for behavior) and the conditions that lead to stimulus attributions were discussed in Chapter 3, pages 73 to 77.

THE MESSAGE-LENGTH HEURISTIC: LENGTH EQUALS STRENGTH. If we are processing superficially, even the form of a persuasive appeal can help persuade us. Perhaps you have noticed over the years that longer campaign speeches seem more convincing than briefer ones. Such observations might produce a simple *message-length heuristic*: The longer the message, the more valid it appears to be. Ads that pointedly list "the 25 best reasons" to prefer a product are trying to invoke this heuristic. Table 7.1 describes another persuasion technique

---

TABLE 7.1. Length Equals Strength: The Ben Franklin Close

A *close* is a persuasive technique that "closes a deal." A salesperson using the Ben Franklin close would begin with a story like this:

> As you know, Ben Franklin has always been considered one of the wisest men America has ever had. Whenever he felt himself in a situation where he couldn't quite make up his mind, he felt pretty much as you do now. If it was the right thing, he wanted to be sure he did it. If it was the wrong thing, he wanted to be just as sure that he avoided it. Isn't that about the way you feel?

> So here's what he would do to arrive at a decision. He would take a clean sheet of paper and draw a line down the middle, like this. On one side of the line he would list all the reasons why he should make a "yes" decision and on the other side of the line he would list all the reasons against making this decision. When he was through, he would count the reasons that he was able to tally on each side, and his decision was made for him. Why don't we try it here and see what happens?

As the customer attempts to come up with reasons for buying the product, the salesperson helps suggest and list reasons. When it comes to producing reasons for the other side, however, the salesperson leaves the customer to work alone. Often it will be difficult for one person to generate more reasons than two people can. With the sheet of paper showing more reasons "for" than "against," the customer can be influenced by the message-length heuristic.

Source: Adapted with permission of Lexington Books, a division of Rowman & Littlefield Publishers, Inc., from J. Jacoby (1984). Some social psychological perspectives on closing. In J. Jacoby & C. S. Craig (Eds.), *Personal selling* (pp. 73–92). Copyright © 1984 by Lexington Books.

that encourages people to rely on the sheer number of arguments supporting a particular position.

Of course, quantity does not always mean quality, and the focus on numbers can blind us to the inadequacy of the reasoning. Imagine the following scenario. You are waiting in line at the photocopy machine when you are approached by someone wanting to cut ahead of you. Her request is relatively small: She wants to make only five copies. Would you find her simple request persuasive? About 60% of students waiting in line to use the copy machine at the City University of New York did (Langer, Blank, & Chanowitz, 1978). Now imagine that the would-be line cutter not only made the same request but also explained that she was in a rush. Would this legitimate argument in favor of letting her go ahead be even more persuasive? If you say yes, you agree with the New York students, 94% of whom agreed to the request when given a good reason.

These findings suggest that the quality of a message increases persuasiveness, but is that always the case? If people are processing superficially—relying on whether the request is long or not, for example—maybe anything that just *sounds like* an argument or reason will do. In fact, other people were approached by the woman with a request and an empty explanation that only sounded like a reason: "Excuse me, I have five pages. May I use the Xerox machine, because I have to make some copies?" Ninety-three percent of those approached this way agreed to let her go ahead! When people rely on the message-length heuristic, a longer message, no matter what it says, seems compelling (Petty & Cacioppo, 1984). As you will see later, however, when a request is substantial enough to provoke more extensive processing, for example, if the person had to make fifty copies instead of five, people will think more carefully about the reason.

Other superficial aspects of persuasive appeals can also act as heuristics. Many people are strong believers in the "you get what you pay for" heuristic: When items like perfume, wine, and jewelry are sold for higher prices, we think they are of better quality (McConnell, 1968; R. A. Peterson, 1977). And many people are particularly impressed by speeches or advertisements that contain numbers, graphs, or equations, perhaps because they convey an air of scientific objectivity (Chaiken, 1987). Perhaps this explains why political candidates often bring statistics when they take their platform to the people.

Much of the time, the associations that underlie persuasion heuristics allow us to effectively evaluate the attitude objects we encounter. Experts usually know what they are talking about, and a long message often yields more relevant information than a short one. If the attitude object makes us feel good, it probably is good. After all, it is the usefulness of these cues that led people to develop the heuristics in the first place. Sometimes, however, superficial processing just doesn't cut it. We may want or need to know more about the attitude object than superficial processing provides. In these circumstances we move into high gear, and we process information in depth.

Systematic Processing of Persuasive Communications

Sometimes people do carefully consider the content of arguments presented in a persuasive communication. When people pay attention to a message, understand its content, and react to it, a process called elaboration, systematic processing can change attitudes. Attitudes resulting from such careful consideration are much more resistant to later change than most attitudes produced by superficial processing.

When people process systematically, they begin to think about aspects of the attitude object that go beyond the immediate evaluations associated with communicators and messages. They turn their attention to evaluating the quality of the information provided about the attitude object and to thinking about what they are being told in relation to what they already know. It's not that systematic processors don't notice or aren't immediately affected by the presence of heuristic cues in the persuasion setting; they are. But as they start to take notice of other information as well, the impact of superficial factors on attitudes becomes less important. How does this increase in thinking affect persuasion?

PROCESSING MESSAGE CONTENT. Systematic processing involves paying increased attention to the strength and quality of the arguments that communicators use to advocate a particular position or object (Chaiken, 1980, 1987; Petty & Cacioppo, 1981, 1986). Because systematic processing means thinking carefully about the arguments presented about the central merits of the attitude object, Petty and Cacioppo (1981, 1986) have called it the *central route to persuasion*. Over the years, researchers have learned a lot about the steps involved in systematic processing and how those steps influence persuasion (W. J. McGuire, 1969).

1. *Attending to the message.* In one popular French commercial for an all-purpose adhesive, the glue is spread on the soles of the announcer's shoes and he is hung upside down from the ceiling. In a recent North American ad, two women mud wrestle to decide a dispute about a particular brand of beer. Advertisers go to such lengths because they realize that getting the audience's attention is the first crucial step in bringing about persuasion, a fact persuasion researchers recognized long ago (Hovland, Janis, & Kelley, 1953; Hovland, Lumsdaine, & Sheffield, 1949). It's also a step that is easier said than done. Because people are bombarded by hundreds of persuasive messages a day—from the mass media, computers, billboards, friends, on packaging, even in public bathrooms—most messages receive at best a superficial once-over. Television advertisers have the upper hand here: The use of both vision and sound makes their ads more attention grabbing than messages delivered on radio or in print (Andreoli & Worchel, 1978), especially if they stand out from the program they are placed in (Russell, 2002). But all professional persuaders know that, if they are to keep their candidate in the spotlight or make their product's packaging stand out from the rest, they must quickly snare the audience's attention, giving them a reason to watch and listen. As one successful adman concluded from his years of advertising experience, "People screen out a lot of commercials because they start with something dull. When you advertise fire extinguishers, open with the fire" (Ogilvy, 1983, p. 111).

   Although attention is crucial for persuasion, uninformed attempts to attract attention to a persuasive message can backfire. Research suggests that people pay more attention to violent than nonviolent media and to sexually explicit media than to nonsexual media (Geer, Judice, & Jackson, 1994; Lang, Newhagen, & Reeves, 1996). Advertisers have often taken this to mean that ads featured in such shows will receive a lot of attention. They are wrong, however. Because viewers have a limited amount of attention, the more they direct to television content, the less they may have for the persuasive appeals broadcast during breaks in programming. Memory for products advertised during shows featuring sex and violence is actually much worse than memory for products advertised during nonsexual and nonviolent programming (Bushman, 2005). So golden rule number 1 for most persuasion attempts: make sure attention is drawn to the message, not away from it!

2. *Comprehending the message*. Although getting the audience's attention is a critical first step in communicating, attention does not guarantee comprehension. Reading or hearing an argument does not mean we understand it. Research indicates, in fact, that much of the persuasive information aimed at us goes right over our heads (Morgan & Reichart, 1999). In one survey, for example, consumer psychologist Jacob Jacoby and his colleagues (Jacoby, Hoyer, & Sheluga, 1980) found that adults misunderstood 30% to 40% of the information presented in 30-second television segments. Comprehension of printed magazine ads and articles is somewhat better (Chaiken & Eagly, 1976), which may explain why they have more effect on attitudes (McGuire, 1985). But even here, misunderstandings are still quite frequent (Jacoby & Hoyer, 1989). When messages are easy to comprehend, people can be persuaded by compelling content and dismiss specious support for a position out of hand (Eagly, 1974). But when messages are complex and difficult, people can miss the true attributes of the attitude object and fall prey to superficial heuristics (Hafer, Reynolds, & Obertynski, 1996). So golden rule number 2 for most persuasion attempts: Keep it simple!

3. *Reacting to message content*. People do not just passively soak up information; they react to it, sometimes favorably and sometimes unfavorably. Whether the persuasive communication is your doctor's recommendation regarding a treatment regimen or your best friend's pitch to sign you up as an exercise buddy, you will do more than just listen to it if it has engaged your attention and you understand it. You will think about whether you agree or disagree with the persuader's arguments. Favorable reactions might include merely registering agreement ("Walking for a half hour per day sounds good to me") or developing the supportive information even further ("Yes, and didn't I also read somewhere that daily exercise cuts the likelihood you'll get diabetes in half?"). Negative reactions may range from simply disagreeing with some point ("Oh, pleeease!") to developing a detailed set of counterarguments ("I'm so busy now, I couldn't possibly!"). The process of generating such favorable and unfavorable reactions to the content of a message is called **elaboration**. These reactions can be affective as well as cognitive, reflecting feelings associated with the attitude object as well as additional characteristics that the object might have. One study presented messages favoring the use of animals in medical experiments to students who opposed their use. Faced with such a message, participants produced as many affective responses (like "Children dying unnecessarily makes me want to cry") as cognitive ones ("I realize now that some drug effects can't be modeled by computers"; Rosselli, Skelly, & Mackie, 1995).

4. *Accepting the advocated position*. If a systematically processed message stimulates favorable cognitive or affective elaborations, it will be persuasive.

If A Little Girl Cries In A Remote Mountain Village And

No One Hears Her...

Is She Any Less Hungry?

Of course not. Even if we can't see her tears, her hunger pangs are just as real. Just as deadly. And she's not alone. Thousands of youngsters come into this life every day with little hope of making it to age five.

Have we become so dulled to the images of desperate children that we can turn a deaf ear to their suffering?

It takes so little to help a girl or boy trapped by poverty—just $20 a month. Become a Save the Children sponsor today and your gifts will be combined with those of other caring people to bring about immediate help and lasting change. Far from a handout, you'll provide much needed help in the form of nutritious food, health care and education to your child and an entire community of children.

Please, call now or use this coupon. You may not hear her cries, but you can listen to your heart.

1·800·527·1313
Major Credit Cards Welcome

Yes, I want to help stop a child's suffering.

☐ My first monthly sponsorship contribution of $20 is enclosed.
☐ Please charge my monthly contribution to my
☐ MasterCard ☐ Visa ☐ Discover ☐ Amex
Account #_____ Exp. Date_____
Signature_____
I prefer to sponsor a ☐ boy ☐ girl ☐ either in the area I've checked below. Please send my child's photo and personal history.
☐ Where the need is greatest ☐ Caribbean/Latin America
☐ Middle East ☐ Africa ☐ Asia ☐ United States
Name_____ Phone (___)_____
Address_____ Apt._____
City_____ State_____ Zip_____
☐ Instead of becoming a sponsor at this time, I am enclosing a contribution of $_____
☐ Please send me more information.

Established 1932. The original child sponsorship agency. YOUR SPONSORSHIP CONTRIBUTIONS ARE US INCOME TAX DEDUCTIBLE. We are indeed proud of our use of funds. Our annual report and audit statement are available upon request. ©1994 Save the Children Federation, Inc.

Save the Children.
50 Wilton Road, Westport CT 06880

■ **Systematic processing might stop this child's suffering.** The effectiveness of this ad is enhanced because it encourages systematic processing. The photo draws our attention to the easy-to-understand arguments, while the questions provoke active elaboration of message content. Systematically processed appeals usually result in attitudes that persist over time and resist further attempts to change them.

Elaboration. The generation of favorable or unfavorable reactions to the content of a persuasive appeal.

If the arguments evoke unfavorable reactions, the message will fail to persuade (Greenwald, 1968; Petty, Cacioppo, & Goldman, 1981). This effect is even stronger if people are confident about the elaborations the message triggers (Petty, Brinol & Tormala, 2002). Thus people's *reactions* to the content of the message can be even more important than the content itself. In effect, people persuade themselves.

If carefully processed arguments provoke positive elaborations, the more arguments there are, the more attitude change there will be. By the same token, greater numbers of carefully processed specious arguments will produce more negative responses than would result from only a few silly arguments. To assess the impact of systematic thinking about strong and weak arguments on persuasion, one study presented students with different numbers of arguments in favor of instituting comprehensive examinations for graduating college students—a popular attitude issue in persuasion research (Petty & Cacioppo, 1984). Strong arguments—ones that typically prompt favorable elaborations—in this experiment included statements like the following: "Graduate schools and law and medical schools are beginning to show clear and significant preferences for students who received their undergraduate degrees from institutions with comprehensive exams." Weak arguments, which typically elicit unfavorable elaborations, included such statements as, "Graduate students have always had to take a comprehensive exam in their major area before receiving their degrees, and it is only fair that undergraduates should have to take them also." Some students heard three weak arguments and others heard nine weak arguments. A third group heard three strong arguments, and a fourth group, nine strong ones. All students then gave their own opinions on the comprehensive exams issue. The results indicated that when students were processing systematically, they found three strong arguments persuasive and nine even more so. In contrast, a few weak arguments were unimpressive, and many weak arguments were a real turn-off. When communicators attempt to influence us with really bad arguments, we may even respond by moving in a direction opposite the one intended. This change is called a boomerang effect.

Compelling arguments aren't always provided for us, but persuasion can still occur when just thinking about an attitude issue brings more and more relevant evidence and arguments to mind. When this happens, merely thinking about the issue can lead to favorable or unfavorable evaluations of the information we consider, which in turn produce either more persuasion or a boomerang effect (Tesser, 1978). Interestingly, however, this effect depends on how hard or easy it is to bring that evidence to mind. Students asked to think of three good arguments in support of an issue (a task they could accomplish easily) were more persuaded by their self-generated argument than were students asked to bring 10 good reasons to mind (a task that was very difficult to accomplish). Bringing three arguments to mind easily apparently made people feel that there were a lot of good arguments around to support the position, so it must be a worthy one. In contrast, struggling to bring the 10 arguments to mind made support for the position seem difficult to come by, convincing the students in this condition that they shouldn't adopt the position (Wänke, Bohner, & Jurkowitsch, 1997).

THE CONSEQUENCES OF SYSTEMATIC PROCESSING. When people process systematically, they go beyond the immediate evaluations associated with persuasion cues and also evaluate the quality of information the message provides about the attitude object. When both heuristic cues and information about message content are available, which determines our attitude? What happens if persuasion cues suggest a glowing endorsement, but message content suggests resounding rejection? If an expert endorses a dubious product, for example, the expertise heuristic and careful processing of message content tilts us in different attitudinal directions. The effect of additional attention to, comprehension of, and elaboration of message content will usually win the day. Especially if the quality of the arguments offered is clear, careful thinking about the famous commencement speaker's hackneyed advice will leave us unconvinced, and the cogent campaign analysis of the unknown political commentator will win us over.

When message content is not so convincingly strong or weak, however, even systematic processors can still be affected by heuristic cues. The presence of an expert or attractive source might bias reactions to an ambiguous message, making elaborations more favorable. Having a nonexpert or unattractive source deliver the same message might bias reactions in the opposite direction. In these cases lots of thinking goes on, but the thinking is tilted in one direction more than the other, and a similarly slanted attitude results (Chaiken & Maheswaran, 1994). Extensive thinking doesn't guarantee unbiased attitudes: if thinking is biased, attitudes will be biased in the same way.

Attitudes that result from systematic thinking have some interesting qualities. When attitudes change because information is carefully attended, comprehended, and elaborated, all this mental work helps write the resulting attitudes almost indelibly in memory. In fact, the new attitudes become so firmly fixed that they are less likely to change with time (Chaiken, 1980; Petty, Haugtvedt, & Smith, 1995). Compared with attitudes that change through heuristic processing, attitudes based on systematic processing are also resistant in the face of new persuasion attempts. In one demonstration of this advantage, individuals first read a message promoting nuclear power plants, and then an equally strong message arguing against them. Those individuals who reacted to the first message with lots of issue-relevant thinking were less influenced by the second message (Haugtvedt & Wegener, 1994). Trial lawyers, political candidates engaged in debate, and disputing siblings arguing their case to a parent should all find these results very useful. If the audience is going to hear both sides of an issue, is it better to present your case first or last? If you have strong arguments and you expect people to do a lot of thinking about them, it's best to go first. If people put a lot of thought into changing their mind on the basis of your appeal, they are much more likely to resist the opposite point of view.

Superficial and Systematic Processing: Which Strategy, When?

People process messages systematically only when they have both the motivation and the cognitive capacity to do so. The relevance of the message to important goals determines motivation. Cognitive capacity is available when people have adequate ability to process and can do so without distraction. People differ in their levels of motivation and capacity to process different kinds of messages. Messages that match people's motivational goals and their capacity states are most persuasive. Positive and negative emotional states influence persuasion because they have motivational and capacity consequences.

So what is the best strategy if you want to change someone's mind about something? Whether you are addressing your constituents, launching a new business, or trying to get your family to adopt a sensible diet, any strategy that evokes systematic processing seems to be the best bet for both persuader and persuadee. For the persuader, systematic processing guarantees long-term and resistant attitude change: Once you have won their minds, you will keep their allegiance. For the consumer of persuasive communications, careful processing gives us greater confidence in the validity of our attitudes.

Why, then, don't people process systematically all the time? Unfortunately, there is a catch. Systematic processing of persuasive appeals does not come easily. Like systematic processing of any other kind of information, it requires a big investment of effort and processing capacity. In fact, whether communications are processed superficially or systematically depends on two factors: people's motivation and their cognitive capacity to think carefully about the content of the message.

HOW MOTIVATION INFLUENCES SUPERFICIAL AND SYSTEMATIC PROCESSING. Motives like mastery, connectedness, and protecting a positive view of ourselves play an important role in how we approach persuasive communications. Imagine the plight of a small company's purchasing manager given the responsibility of selecting and purchasing new computer equipment to be used for product design. The decision is a crucial one: The company needs to upgrade to stay competitive, but if it goes over budget there could be a real problem with cash flow. This is the manager's first real test as purchasing manager, and her reputation for mixing technical smarts with an eye for a bargain is on the line. How will she decide which product line uses her company's money most effectively? She probably will react as we all would. When it's important that we form accurate evaluations, and when the attitudes and opinions we form reflect directly on us, systematic processing is our greatest ally.

1. *Mastery motivation: The importance of being accurate.* When we are being held accountable for our preferences and are concerned about making the correct decision, the mastery motive will predominate and issues of accuracy will be central. The product manager will need solid evidence to justify her choice of computer system, because others will hold her accountable. She may also fear that if she chooses a faulty piece of equipment, the costs of being incorrect could be severe. Compared with people who have no one to answer to, accountable message processors and those anxious to avoid being wrong will process persuasive communications more thoroughly, think more about the information, and be more concerned with integrating new information as it comes to light (Kruglanski, 1988; Tetlock, 1983).

   Accuracy concerns can also be triggered when the evidence seems mixed. Imagine that you are looking forward to seeing a newly released movie that one of your friends says is the best movie he's seen in a long time. But then your local paper pans it and movie critics hate it. Now your confidence in your judgment wavers, and you start looking for new input. Perhaps you ask your friend about the plot and characters, or you seek out several additional reviews. When persuasive communications advocate inconsistent positions, as they do in this example, people move from casual to careful processing. People are motivated to undertake a detailed analysis of all aspects of the communication when they encounter arguments that do not fit or conclusions that do not follow (Chaiken, Liberman, & Eagly, 1989; Festinger, 1957; Maheswaran & Chaiken, 1991).

2. *Connectedness and me and mine motivation: The importance of self-relevance.* An old Chinese proverb says, "Tell me and I'll forget; involve me and I'll understand." People's tendency to carefully process personally relevant information is nothing new. When information is relevant to

something that affects us, we want to know all about it. The product manager, for example, knows her decision will affect more than the company's bottom line. With her own reputation at stake, she will be motivated to pay careful attention to the information presented by the competing systems manufacturers.

In a demonstration of the influence of self-relevance on persuasion, researchers asked groups of students to listen to a speech dealing, again, with the issue of whether comprehensive exams should be required for graduation (Petty and others, 1981). Some groups heard a speech composed of strong and valid arguments advocating the exams, whereas other groups were given rather weak and silly arguments. Some groups were led to believe the speech had been delivered by an expert communicator—a Princeton University professor of education—whereas others were told the source was a nonexpert—a local high school junior "interested" in such issues. The most important manipulation was one of self-relevance. Some groups of students were told the exam would be implemented at their own school, which meant that they personally would be affected. Other groups were told the exams were planned for another institution, and thus they were personally less relevant. Perhaps you can guess how this manipulation of relevance influenced students' reactions. Those who thought the plan would not affect them processed the communication superficially. Relying on the expertise heuristic, they responded favorably to the expert communicator and unfavorably to the nonexpert, regardless of the message's content. As you can see in Figure 7.4, however, the message had quite a different

FIGURE 7.4   Effects of motivation on message processing

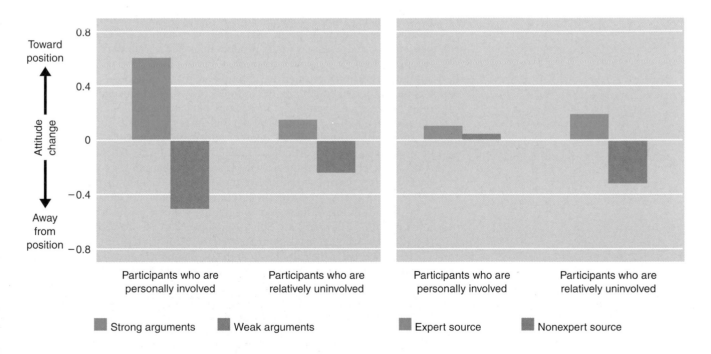

■ In this study, some participants were highly involved in the issue and others were uninvolved. They heard strong or weak arguments, presented by an expert or nonexpert source. Notice that the strength of the arguments made more difference to highly involved participants (graph on left). In contrast, the expertise of the source had more influence on the less involved participants (graph on right). (Data from Petty and others, 1981.)

impact on students who thought the exam proposal would affect them personally. These students were motivated to pay careful attention to the quality of the arguments. This systematic processing led them to accept strong and compelling arguments and to reject weak and specious ones, regardless of who espoused them.

The relevance of personal goals almost always increases systematic processing of relevant information. Consider a connectedness goal like having a pleasant interaction. When students in one study were given such a goal, they were particularly likely to express opinions similar to those of their interaction partners. But this outcome wasn't the result of a lack of thought. In fact, the students put quite a lot of effort into thinking about their partner's point of view. But the fact that they were motivated to agree with the partner biased this extra thinking toward positive elaboration of the partner's position (Chen, Shechter, & Chaiken, 1996).

HOW CAPACITY INFLUENCES SUPERFICIAL AND SYSTEMATIC PROCESSING. Even when we are highly motivated, we may encounter obstacles to systematic processing. Imagine the product manager spreading the dozen or so computer brochures out on her desk. Each describes different product lines in different ways; each computer system offers different features for different prices. Will she be able to understand and evaluate every claim? Even when people want to process systematically, they are not always able to do so.

1. *The ability to process.* Sometimes, people just do not have the mental resources to take in and evaluate all the available information. Even the most motivated processors of persuasive communications occasionally have difficulty understanding all the complex and rapidly presented information offered in print, radio, and television commercials. This is particularly true when, as in the product manager's case, the information is technical, there is too much of it, or it has multiple dimensions on which alternatives differ. Consider, for example, a group of college students from a community rocked both by the murders of two local teenage girls and the reduced sentence given one of those convicted as the result of a plea bargain (in plea bargaining, an accused person agrees to plead guilty to a less serious charge, usually in exchange for information that will convict another, or in exchange for a particular sentence). When presented with strong or weak arguments supporting the wider use of plea bargaining to reduce court backlogs, the students were highly motivated to evaluate them thoroughly and probably to disagree with them (Hafer, Reynolds, & Obertynski, 1996). Why then, did some of them end up agreeing with the position advocated by a judge with a Harvard Law School pedigree and 15 years of experience, regardless of whether his arguments were weak or strong?

    The answer lay in the complexity of the legal arguments used to support plea bargaining. In some conditions, the arguments used layperson's terms, common terms, and simple grammatical structures. Indicating their high motivation and thorough evaluation of the messages, students in this condition who read strong arguments were somewhat persuaded, whereas those presented with weak arguments completely dismissed them. But in other conditions, the same strong and weak arguments were framed in legal jargon and complex grammar. Despite their motivation, the students just couldn't comprehend and evaluate the information, and their attitudes ended up reflecting the expertise heuristic.

    Children are at even more of a disadvantage in this area. Young children often have enough ability to understand a message but lack the critical capacity to evaluate it. Many of them trust television to tell the truth, and they do not always know when programs stop and advertisements begin. They soon learn the brand names and their jingles—research shows in fact that North American children can name more brands of beer than they can presidents of the United States (Center for Science in the Public Interest, 1988). But children often fail to comprehend or remember the specific details of ads. As a result, they are particularly prone to fall for the inducements served up with children's programs. In one example, some children watched a television program without commercials and another set of children watched the same show with advertisements for a particular toy. The children who had seen the advertised toy were more likely to ask their parents for it, more likely to have a negative view of a parent who refused to buy the toy, and more likely to play with a "not so nice" boy who had the toy than a "nice boy" who didn't have it (Liebert & Sprafkin, 1988). Children in developing countries who have limited exposure to the strategies of advertisers are even more vulnerable (Unnikrishnan & Bajpai, 1996). As children's cognitive capacity increases with age and experience, they learn to evaluate information more critically and become less easily persuaded (Boush, Friestad, & Rose, 1994).

2. *The opportunity to concentrate.* No matter how motivated or expert we are, our ability to process systematically is diminished if we cannot concentrate. Ready and willing to understand and evaluate all the relevant material, our hapless manager is suddenly interrupted by the phone. As she hangs up, a co-worker stops by wanting to discuss a purchase order. Then her boss reminds her that the departmental meeting begins in an hour. These continual distractions, as you undoubtedly know from your own experience, will reduce her ability to process information carefully.

By reducing our critical ability, distractions can decrease the effectiveness of strongly persuasive communications because we are not able to elaborate them favorably. To make matters worse, distraction exerts the opposite effect on weak communications. It makes weak communications more persuasive because it reduces people's cognitive capacity, thereby making it difficult for them to counter flawed arguments or demolish shaky logic (Petty, Wells, & Brock, 1976). And because of this reduced ability to process message content carefully, people are more influenced by superficial cues. When distracted, for example, people are more influenced by the expertise heuristic: Their attitudes reflect the presence of a credible source more than their nondistracted counterparts (R. A. Baron, Baron, & Miller, 1973). No wonder the old advertising motto recommends: "If you have nothing to say, distract them!"

As some of the factors that increase or decrease systematic processing were described, you might have realized that some of the same factors that produce influence via superficial processing can also be persuasive when systematic processing occurs. For example, a long message might be particularly compelling because of the "length equals strength" heuristic. But those same lengthy arguments might provide ammunition for attitude change if they are processed systematically. Because any piece of information in the persuasion setting can be processed either superficially or systematically, persuasion-relevant information can play multiple roles when it comes to changing attitudes (Kruglanski, Thompson, & Spiegal, 1999; Petty & Wegener, 1998).

☐ **THE IMPACT OF CAPACITY ON HEEDING HEALTH-RELATED MESSAGES.** Unfortunately, intoxication from alcohol and other drugs can also reduce cognitive capacity and lower people's ability to carefully and critically evaluate information. One study, for example, showed that intoxicated individuals had more favorable attitudes than sober individuals toward drinking and driving, particularly when cues suggesting that such behavior might be appropriate were salient. Another showed that alcohol consumption increased men's reported likelihood of engaging in unprotected sex, partially because they failed to critically evaluate information for and against the action (MacDonald, Zanna, & Fong, 1995, 1996). Some researchers refer to the impact of alcohol on processing as "alcohol myopia:" alcohol reduces people's capacity to systematically process and focuses them on superficial cues in the environment (Steele & Josephs, 1990). Of course, if this is true, alcohol myopia might promote safe sex if the right cues are made salient. In fact, alcohol intake actually encouraged condom use if people at a nightclub had AIDS KILLS stamped on their hands (MacDonald, Fong, Zanna, & Martineau, 2003).

HOW PERSONALITY DIFFERENCES INFLUENCE SUPERFICIAL AND SYSTEMATIC PROCESSING. Individuals differ in how willing and able they are to process systematically. One such difference seems to be how much people enjoy thinking itself. People differ, for example, in the degree to which they enjoy puzzling over difficult problems, resolving inconsistencies, and searching for the right answers. Those who enjoy such activities are said to have high *need for cognition* (Cacioppo & Petty, 1982; A. Cohen, 1957). This need is indicated by people's responses to statements like the ones in Table 7.2.

Research has found that individuals with a high need for cognition are more likely than others to put time and effort into processing persuasive communications. In one study demonstrating this point, participants read a strongly or weakly argued editorial. The higher their need for cognition, the more likely they were to respond favorably to strong arguments and to be unmoved by weak ones (Cacioppo, Petty, Feinstein, Jarvis, & Blair, 1996). As you might expect, people with a low need for cognition are relatively more responsive to heuristic cues, like the expertise of a communicator (Cacioppo & Petty, 1984).

Another kind of personality difference influences the sorts of messages that people find personally relevant. For example, because high self-monitors are so conscious of how others evaluate them, they zero in on image-focused appeals that show how a product can help them impress others. Low self-monitors, on the other hand, hold attitudes that allow them to express who they are, and thus are more attuned to value-expressive appeals. Howard Lavine and Mark Snyder (1996) demonstrated the difference self-monitoring could make in a study that compared

To remind yourself of characteristics of typical high and low self-monitors, reread Chapter 4, pages 124 to 125.

TABLE 7.2. The Need for Cognition Scale: Sample Items

1. I find satisfaction in deliberating hard for long hours.
2. Learning new ways to think doesn't excite me very much.
3. I like tasks that require little thought once I've learned them.
4. I would prefer complex to simple problems.
5. The notion of thinking abstractly is appealing to me.
6. More often than not, more thinking just leads to more errors.

Note: These are sample items from the Need for Cognition Scale, which assesses how much people enjoy engaging in effortful cognitive activities. People who agree with items 1, 4, and 5 and disagree with items 2, 3, and 6 would be regarded as high in need for cognition. The actual scale used in research contains many more than six items, so it can more accurately classify people as high or low in need for cognition.

Source: From "The need for cognition" by J. T. Cacioppo & R. E. Petty, 1982, *Journal of Personality and Social Psychology, 42,* pp. 116–131. Copyright © 1982 by the American Psychological Association. Reprinted with permission.

reactions to messages that advocated voting in local and presidential elections. The image-focused appeal contended that voting enhances a person's status, popularity, and attractiveness, and noted that a majority of the recipient's peers were planning to vote in an upcoming election. In contrast, the value-expressive message pointed out that voting provides a way of supporting liberty and democracy, and affords the opportunity to put attitudes and beliefs into action. The results of the study appear in Figure 7.5. As the researchers expected, high self-monitors had more positive attitudes toward voting when the message appealed to image. In contrast, low self-monitors were more positive when the message focused on value expression. Importantly, those exposed to messages tuned to their individual motivational preferences were also more likely to ask for information about the candidates and more likely to actually vote. How do such motivationally matched appeals produce these persuasive benefits? First, both high and low self-monitors pay more attention to and spend more time carefully processing information that furthers their goals (DeBono & Harnish, 1988; Petty & Wegener, 1998b). Second, both groups see those functionally relevant arguments as more compelling than arguments that don't speak to their goals (Lavine & Snyder, 1996).

In many situations, of course, differences among individuals in motivation and capacity go hand in hand to determine how extensively a particular message will be processed and how great its impact will be. Appeals that advocate positions or provide product benefits that match people's needs or their views of themselves are much more effective than those that don't (Evans & Petty, 2003; Lee & Aaker, 2004). For example, some people are more concerned that their situation gets no worse (they have a prevention focus) whereas others are more concerned about improving their lot (they are promotion focused). Prevention focused folk find messages that talk about avoiding losses much more compelling, where promotion focused types are more persuaded by gain-oriented appeals (Cesario, Grant, &

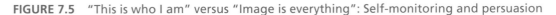

FIGURE 7.5 "This is who I am" versus "Image is everything": Self-monitoring and persuasion

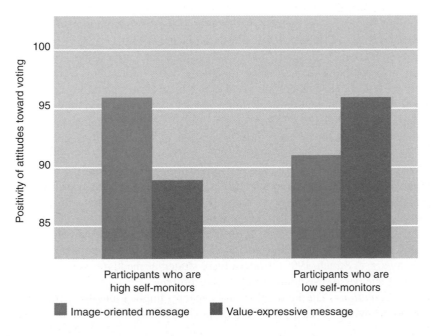

■ High and low self-monitors reacted in different ways to appeals that advocated voting in an upcoming election. High self-monitors had more positive attitudes when they received an image-focused appeal, whereas low self-monitors were more positive when the message stressed value-expressive reasons to vote. (Data from Lavine & Snyder, 1996.)

Prevention and promotion motivations and other consequences for individuals with these different concerns were discussed in Chapter 4, pages 119 to 120.

Higgins, 2004). Such persuasive success no doubt comes from both the motivating force of self-relevance and ability factors like topic knowledge (Cacioppo, Petty, & Sidera, 1982; Wood, Kallgren, & Preisler, 1985). These individual differences are why messages that match people's motives and abilities are so effective.

HOW MOODS AND EMOTIONS INFLUENCE SUPERFICIAL AND SYSTEMATIC PROCESSING. Are people in good moods easier to persuade? Most of us think so—perhaps you can recall a time when you cooked someone a special dinner or offered a little gift to create a good mood, before trying to convince that person to do something you wanted. But unless people just rely on their current mood to make the judgment, the role that feeling good plays in persuasion is a little more complicated. Being in a good mood sometimes increases persuasion, but sometimes makes persuasion less likely to occur (Isen & Levin, 1972; Petty, Schumann, Richman, & Strathman, 1993; Wegener, Petty, & Smith, 1995). And obviously, all persuasive appeals don't just try to make people feel good. What about an antismoking appeal that shows a tiny premature baby, crisscrossed by tubes and bandages, screaming in an incubator? Or a toothpaste ad showing diseased gums and decaying teeth? Do scenes and ideas that make us feel bad also have persuasive power? In fact, the answer is that both feeling good and feeling bad (or anxious or angry or guilty) can sometimes increase and sometimes decrease persuasion because they can all affect motivation and capacity (Forgas, 1995; Giner-Sorolla, 1999).

Positive emotions: Being in a good mood, for example, has many consequences for motivation. When people feel good, they may see no need to process carefully. A good mood makes people feel confident (E. J. Johnson & Tversky, 1983), tells them that the situation holds no danger for them and that they are doing a fine job processing just the way they are (Bless and others, 1996; Schwarz, Bless, & Bohner, 1991). They may not want anything to interfere with their good spirits—not even the effort of careful thought (Isen & Levin, 1972). These motivational consequences of feeling good make people in good moods less likely than people who feel neutral or sad to process the content of persuasive appeals systematically. This in turn means that the attitudes of happy people are more likely to reflect associations based on heuristic cues—happy people might not be impressed by strong compared to weak messages, but they might be persuaded by an expert source (Mackie, Asuncion, & Rosselli, 1992; Schwarz, Bless, & Bohner, 1991; Worth & Mackie, 1987).

These motivational effects of good mood mean people process less. But good mood can also be harnessed to make people process more. For example, if processors are led to believe that their good mood shows how much they enjoy the task (rather than showing that they are doing fine on it), they process more deeply (L. L. Martin, Ward, Achee, & Wyer, 1993). And if people think that particular information will put them or keep them in a good mood, they think about that material much more (Wegener and others, 1995).

Positive mood may also have capacity implications. Think about the last time something wonderful happened to you. Did you turn it over and over in your mind? Some research suggests that a good mood might reduce systematic processing because people's minds are full of other thoughts. In demonstrating this point, researchers have given happy people extra time to process arguments (Mackie & Worth, 1989) and have helped them focus on key aspects of the message (Bless, Bohner, Schwarz, & Strach, 1990). Both of these strategies made it easier for happy people to evaluate persuasive communications carefully.

Negative emotions: The motivation and capacity implications for persuasion are even more obvious when people feeling anxious or worried try to deal with persuasive appeals. Fear is by far the most common negative emotion that influence agents exploit. Advertisements remind us that body odor, bad breath, or dandruff could make us social pariahs; politicians tell us that their opponent is soft on crime or in the pocket of special-interest groups; public health campaigns show addicted babies, skin cancer wounds and horribly smashed cars to warn us about smoking during pregnancy, sunbathing, and drinking before driving. Can the scare tactics in these fear appeals really help change our minds?

Early research offered conflicting answers to this question, with some studies showing that increasing fear increased persuasion and some finding that it did not (Hovland and others, 1953). It soon became clear that different messages elicited different amounts of fear, and this provided a key clue in resolving the inconsistencies in results: the level of fear induced by a persuasive appeal influences motivation and ability to process a message, and this in turn influences attitude change.

First, fear appeals must engage motivation. If a message does not arouse any anxiety, no need for mastery, connectedness, or protecting me and mine is aroused, and the message is ignored as irrelevant. Just the right amount of anxiety can activate all these goals, motivating people to pay attention. For a fear appeal to be effective, the audience must be convinced that the threatened negative consequences will happen, and will happen to them, thus engaging personal relevance (de Hoog, Stroebe, & de Wit, 2005; Leventhal, 1970). Provoking too much fear, however, turns audiences off. If people feel overwhelmed or unable to escape, self-protective motives may mean they avoid or ignore the message (Witte, 1992) or deny and contradict the threatening information (Das, de Wit, & Stroebe, 2003; Janis & Terwilliger, 1962). To overcome these kinds of reactions, a message must contain clear information on how to avoid the danger, which encourages mastery. Thus, the most effective fear-inducing messages are those that incorporate reassuring instructions on how to eliminate the anxiety (Hovland, Janis, & Kelley, 1953; Robberson & Rogers, 1988; R. W. Rogers, 1983). One study, for example, looked at responses to fear-inducing messages about preventing tetanus. The messages varied, with some arousing high fear, some moderate fear, and others no fear at all. In addition, some contained specific instructions about where to get an inoculation and others did not (Leventhal, Singer, & Jones, 1965). The high-fear messages inspired more positive attitudes toward getting shots than did the low-fear or no-fear messages. But only those people who received messages that both aroused fear and included specific information about how to obtain a shot were more likely than other students to respond by getting a tetanus inoculation.

Anxiety also influences the ability to process persuasive information. As their fear increases in intensity, people find it harder and harder to concentrate on and evaluate message content. In fact, high levels of stress impair performance on complex cognitive tasks like systematic processing (Darke, 1988). Christopher Jepson and Shelly Chaiken (1990), for example, found that how carefully a message is processed depends on how much the target fears its contents. Their participants were college students who varied in their level of fear of cancer. The message, which advocated regular cancer check-ups, contained a number of reasoning errors. Very fearful participants reading the message showed several signs of superficial processing. They detected fewer errors, recalled fewer arguments, and elaborated message content less than did readers with little fear. These responses occurred even though there was no sign that fearful participants were avoiding the message; they just didn't seem to be able to do a very good job of dealing with it. In contrast, relatively unfearful readers processed the message carefully.

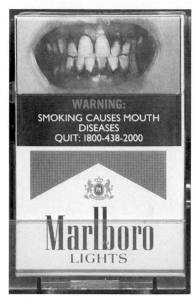

■ **The fear factor.** Government health warnings like this one harness fear to provoke changes in attitudes. To be successful, fear appeals must arouse just the right amount of anxiety by showing the negative consequences—like decaying teeth and gums—that will follow if behavior doesn't change. The provision of an explicit avenue of action—like calling a "quit now" hot line for help—eliminates the anxiety by showing how the negative consequences can be avoided.

The bottom line? Fear works, but only in the right dosage and in the right combination. Fear has to be motivating without being debilitating. It works only if the threatened outcome makes people feel vulnerable, and if the recommended change is both attainable and certain to bring relief. It takes just the right mixture to get people to increase seat-belt use, decrease smoking, and get cancer check-ups.

Other emotional states can also influence our susceptibility to persuasion. When was the last time you heard: "You'd do it if you loved me/were a good father/knew how much I'd sacrificed for you!"? Unfortunately, moderate levels of guilt can activate connectedness and self-protection motives that make us more likely to accept and like products or ideas that provide solutions to that guilt. In one study, for example, working mothers—prime targets of guilt appeals—responded more favorably to advertisements for a microwaveable dinner if the ad evoked moderate guilt about time away from their children than if it did not play the guilt card at all. Such guilt also increased their intention to buy the product (Coulter & Pinto, 1995). Like anxiety, however, too much guilt can backfire. Ads that play too heavily on guilt tend to induce anger, and anger has its own implications for persuasion. If anger is directed at the source ("How dare they try to make me feel that way?"), the persuasiveness of the appeal is undermined (Coulter & Pinto, 1995). Anger can also reduce the ability to think carefully, undermining the effectiveness of an appeal that demands careful processing. But such reduced ability to process can also make angry people more susceptible to heuristic cues like the expertise or credibility of a source (Bodenhausen, Sheppard, & Kramer, 1994). Anger also increases people's expectation of annoying outcomes, and increases the persuasiveness of messages that counter them (DeSteno, Petty, Rucker, Wegener, & Braverman, 2004). And if anger is aroused by the perception of unfairness, messages that promise redress of such injustice can be particularly seductive (Butler, Koopman, & Zimbardo, 1995).

Thus, both positive and negative emotions can increase or interfere with persuasion, depending on their motivational and capacity consequences in particular circumstances. If moods reduce either motivation or capacity, persuasion is more likely to depend on superficial processes and less on systematic processing.

In summary, people can be persuaded whether they process superficially or systematically. Both motivation, which is highest when a message taps into goals that are important for an individual, and capacity, which depends on ability and freedom from distraction, are prerequisites for systematic processing. Motivation and capacity have the same effects on persuasion across cultures (Aaker & Maheswaran, 1997). Situational factors, personality differences, and emotional states can all influence motivation, capacity, or both, and thus determine whether persuasive appeals are dealt with superficially or systematically. Given all the constraints on motivation and capacity, perhaps you can see now why most persuasive communications are processed superficially.

Defending Attitudes: Resisting Persuasion

Strong arguments compel us; positive feelings placate us; expert and attractive sources inspire us; fear and guilt move us. When it comes to filling our heads or emptying our pockets, communicators have a number of powerful persuasion tools at their disposal. Yet one of the reasons that social psychologists study attitude change so closely, and one of the reasons that persuasion professionals spend so much money and effort on advertising, is that attitudes don't always change willy-nilly. We don't have a complete change of heart and mind with every ad, every appeal, every communication. How do we resist these ever-present inducements to change our attitudes?

Gathering Defenses: Forewarning, Forearming, and Arguing Back

People protect established attitudes by ignoring or resisting information that threatens them. Being forewarned of a persuasion attempt and having previous experience with related arguments can help resistance. However many people over-estimate their ability to resist persuasive appeals.

In fact, once our minds are made up, attitudes have their own built-in defense mechanisms. First, we often try to ignore information that challenges our preferred views and deal only with information that supports them—think about how often you read newspaper editorials that oppose rather than support your views.

But when we do encounter such information a second line of defense comes into action. Attitudes create their own bias by favoring supportive information and focusing criticism on opposing evidence. One way this happens is that information that is close to an established attitude is often viewed as resembling the attitude exactly, a process called *assimilation*. So if a newspaper article ranked your school or college as the second most prestigious in the state, you might in fact see this as further confirmation of your view that yours is the best college around. On the other hand, information that is quite discrepant with your view—perhaps the article ranked your institution way down on the list—is often seen as even more inconsistent with the attitude than it actually is, a process called *contrast*. Such discrepant information is usually ignored as totally invalid and irrelevant.

A second way that attitudes create their own bias is by affecting how information is processed. Consider what happened, for example, when Alice Eagly and her colleagues (Eagly, Kulesa, Brannon, Shaw, & Hutson-Comeaux, 2000) had pro-life and pro-choice students listen to persuasive messages that were either consistent or inconsistent with their views. After hearing the messages, the students wrote down all the arguments they could remember from the messages, and also recorded the thoughts they had had while listening to the attempt to persuade them. People remembered the consistent and the inconsistent message equally well, but thought much more about the opposing message and generated many more counterarguments to it. So another reason we don't change attitudes easily is that we seem to provide our own defense when our views are challenged.

This active defense of our opinions was even clearer when Charles Lord and his colleagues (C. G. Lord, Ross, & Lepper, 1979) showed Stanford undergraduates who supported or opposed capital punishment two supposed research studies about the issue. One study provided evidence that capital punishment deters crime, a position consistent with an attitude supporting the death penalty. The second study contradicted the first and confirmed the views of the death penalty opponents. Both studies had several strong points but also some obvious weaknesses. As can be seen in Figure 7.6, both the supporters and the opponents of capital punishment judged whichever study was consistent with their own views to be much more convincing than the other one. They favored supportive information by accepting it at face value, while criticizing and rejecting the opposing arguments. And this bias toward supportive information is long lasting: people typically remember compelling arguments that support their attitudes but can recall only specious (and easily dismissed) arguments that oppose it (Biek, Wood, & Chaiken, 1996; Edwards & Smith, 1996).

People might do an even better job of protecting their opinion if they know in advance they are going to be attacked. When people expect others to try to change their attitudes, they marshal arguments to mount a good defense (C. A. Kiesler &

We have seen before that well-established views influence our thoughts and behaviors in ways that confirm those views. In Chapter 3, pages 77 to 78, for example, we described why first impressions can be so lasting, and in Chapter 5, pages 171 to 175, why stereotypes are so persistent.

FIGURE 7.6   Established attitudes guide interpretation of attitude-relevant information

■ Undergraduates who supported or opposed the death penalty evaluated two studies whose results supported or undermined the idea that the death penalty has a deterrent effect. Both the supporters and opponents of capital punishment judged the study consistent with their views to be more convincing than the other study. (Data from Lord, Ross, & Lepper, 1979.)

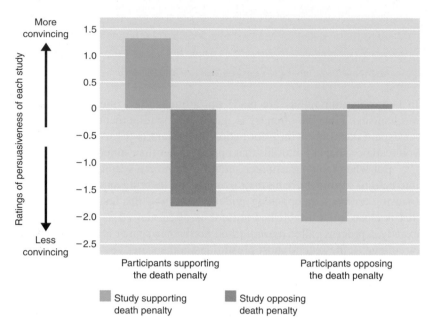

Kiesler, 1964; Petty & Cacioppo, 1977, 1979). For example, Hiromi Fukada (1986) exposed two groups of participants to a persuasive message. One group had been warned that a persuasive attempt would take place; the other group did not receive the warning. A comparison of the two groups' reactions to the message showed that those who were warned were able to counter the persuasive claims with arguments of their own and, not surprisingly, were less persuaded than the other group. Other studies also indicate that the more time people have to prepare a defense of their views, the more successfully they resist persuasion (Freedman & Sears, 1965).

INOCULATION: PRACTICE CAN BE THE BEST RESISTANCE MEDICINE. William McGuire (1964) in fact suggested that the most effective way to resist persuasion is to practice arguing against a persuasive appeal. He drew an analogy to medical inoculations, which stimulate the body's defenses by exposing the person to weak doses of an infection. According to McGuire, immunity to arguments can be obtained in the same way. The strategy seems to work, as was demonstrated when a team of researchers tackled the difficult issue of preventing smoking among young teenagers. Knowing that peer pressure often initiates first-time smoking, these researchers had older students "inoculate" younger ones against typical peer-pressure tactics (McAlister, Perry, Killen, Slinkard, & Maccoby, 1980). In a series of sessions in the seventh grade and again in the eighth grade, the younger students learned to resist pressures to smoke with such counterarguments as: "I'd be a real chicken if I smoked just to impress you." When the research team followed the students' progress over the next few years, they found that the inoculated students were much less likely to begin smoking than were a similar group of seventh graders who had received no training in resistance, as can be seen in Figure 7.7. Other research has confirmed that inoculation techniques are quite effective in reducing teenage smoking (Flay and others, 1985; Hirschman & Leventhal, 1989). Inoculation aimed at children and early adolescents is particularly effective if it works to refute

FIGURE 7.7 Inoculating teenagers against smoking

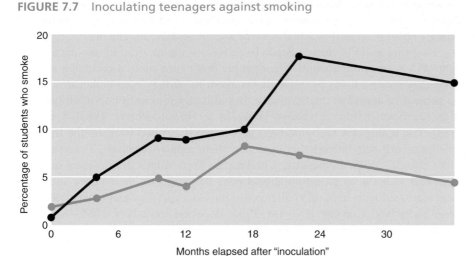

■ In this study, seventh- and eighth-graders were "inoculated" by older students who gave them practice in resisting prosmoking arguments that peers might use. Compared with students in another school who did not receive this treatment, the inoculated students were much less likely to smoke by the ninth grade. (Data from McAlister and others, 1980; Telch and others, 1982.)

peer criticisms of actions the children are already taking, so that their current antismoking and anti-drug-use behaviors are positively reinforced (Pfau, 1995).

☐ **INOCULATION AND ADVERTISING EFFECTIVENESS.** Can inoculation help 4- to 8-year-old couch potatoes resist the advertisements on Saturday morning television? Norma Feshbach (1980) thought so. Feshbach gave small groups of elementary-school children in Los Angeles lessons on how to deal with the claims made in the barrage of Saturday morning commercials. They listened to the claims and then discussed them. They played with the advertised toys and found that they often could not make them do what the ads said they could. When they realized that some of the claims were more fantasy than fact, the children learned to view the advertisements (and perhaps the programs) with a slightly more cynical eye. Similar techniques have been used to inoculate adults against the smear campaigns sometimes used in political contests, since well-crafted inoculation ads have the added benefit of protecting a message source against credibility slippage in the face of later attacks (Burgoon, Pfau, & Birk, 1995; Pfau & Burgoon, 1988).

Resisting a persuasive attempt can have some important consequences. When we process information to defend our established views—accepting consistent information, criticizing discrepant information—we can end up with stronger views (Batson, 1975; C. A. Kiesler, 1971). In the death penalty study, for example, reading the same body of conflicting information actually increased the disagreement between the two groups after each had processed it in a biased manner. Supporters of the death penalty now believed even more strongly in capital punishment, whereas its opponents were even more firmly opposed. Mechanisms that help us defend our attitudes means that having them challenged can sometimes make them even more extreme (D. Kuhn & Lao, 1996; Munro & Ditto, 1997).

We might also come to hold an opinion with more certainty. In one study, for example, college students were told to resist a message that was made up of both weak and strong arguments, and everyone was able to do so (no one's attitudes changed; Tormala & Petty, 2004). Although everyone saw the same message, some students were told that the arguments they had resisted had been strong and compelling, whereas others were told that the arguments had not been very convincing anyway. When students believed that they had resisted strong rather than weak arguments, they felt much more certain about their original opinion—they must feel strongly about it, since they had overcome such persuasive arguments!

Resisting attitude change depends on having the motivation and capacity to fight off a persuasion attempt. When people don't care about a particular attitude issue, they are less likely to resist claims about it—if they even bother to listen to the persuasive appeal in the first place. But attitudes related to important personal goals are much harder to change (Borgida & Howard-Pitney, 1983; Krosnick, 1988). When attitudes are important, people are motivated to resist the threat to self-image and self-interest that changing them entails (Chaiken, Pomerantz, & Giner-Sorolla, 1995; Pomerantz, Chaiken, & Tordesillas, 1995). They are also motivated to build up an informational base that supports their views and gives them ammunition to fight off challenges to those views (Pfau and others, 1997; M. Ross, McFarland, Conway, & Zanna, 1983; W. Wood and others, 1985). Similarly, people need capacity to counteract a persuasive attempt. Without the ability, time, or opportunity to marshal arguments for the defense, people are more vulnerable to appeals that try to change their minds.

Unfortunately, people tend to overestimate both their invulnerability to persuasive appeals and their ability to generate effective arguments to counter them (Wilson, Gilbert, & Wheatley, 1998; Wilson, Houston, & Meyers, 1998). Such beliefs make the task of the professional persuader much easier! Most people think they possess special skills that stop them falling prey to unwanted influence even if everyone else does. So other people might get fooled, but they certainly won't! No wonder then that just telling people that deceptive ads can fool people doesn't reduce their impact. What does work? In one study of resistance effects, it took demonstrating to each participant personally that he or she had been duped to bring the targets of deceptive ads to their senses (Sagarin, Cialdini, Rice, & Serna, 2002). So if you think, as most people do, that you are immune to the influence of persuasive appeals, take a lesson from the research findings: get over it!

Subliminal Persuasion

Subliminal persuasion gains some of its power because people do not realize they are the target of a persuasive attempt. Information presented outside of conscious awareness can influence attitudes and persuasion. But careful consideration of attitude objects can weaken the influence of subliminal information.

Thinking can make us less vulnerable to persuasion. But we cannot fight persuasion if we don't know we are being persuaded: As an old Nepalese proverb says, "You cannot fight a tiger you cannot see." What would happen, then, if professional persuaders were able to bombard you with persuasive messages of which you were not even aware? Can we be persuaded without even knowing it?

In the fall of 1957, moviegoers in Fort Lee, New Jersey, became unwitting targets of just such a hidden persuasion campaign. As they sat watching a feature film, the words "Eat popcorn" and "Drink Coca Cola" appeared several times on the screen for just a fraction of a second. Although the words appeared too quickly to be seen by the audience, an 18% increase in drink sales and a 50% increase in popcorn sales were reported (Brean, 1958). Public outrage greeted revelation of the hidden persuasion campaign, and the use of such messages in advertising was banned. Later evidence suggested that the original findings were made up (Wahl, 1989). Nevertheless claims that advertisers embed hidden sexual images in ads to attract people's attention and activate their desires have continued (Key, 1992). But can *subliminal messages*, ones too faint or fast for people to be consciously aware of them, really have an impact?

Plenty of people think so. In a recent poll, 61% of North Americans surveyed thought that subliminal additions to advertisements could persuade them to buy products they do not want (Muller, 1991). In one sample of college students, nearly 80% believed that a subliminal message would be able to influence them in an undesirable way (Wilson, Gilbert, & Wheatley, 1998). Sales of subliminal self-help tapes, which claim to boost everything from self-esteem and sales income to weight loss and speed-reading, continue to bring in millions of dollars a year. These tapes typically contain soothing New Age music interspersed with inaudible and fleeting instructions to "Relax, be happy" or reminders like "You are good, you are capable, you are calm." Inmates at Utah's South Point Prison reportedly listen to subliminal tapes designed to quell criminal impulses. Members of the Texas Rangers' pitching staff use custom-made cassettes to increase their on-the-mound confidence. Security personnel are also apparently convinced of the technique's effectiveness: The canned music piped into department stores in your area may well contain such subaudible messages as "I am honest. I will not steal" (Natale, 1988).

Most of these kinds of persuasive effects have yet to be systematically researched. But laboratory studies provide clear evidence that people can be influenced by exposure to information of which they are not aware. We've already seen that people exposed to a stimulus multiple times like it more than a novel stimulus, even when exposure is subliminal (Zajonc, 1968). And we know that evaluative conditioning works whether people are aware of the associations or not. For example, people like, consume, and are more willing to pay for objects they see accompanied by a subliminal "smiley face" than objects accompanied by a subliminal frowning face (Niedenthal, 1990; Winkielman, Berridge, & Wilbarger, 2005). People also agree more often with others whose photos they have seen subliminally. In one study, for example, researchers arranged for students to participate with two experimental confederates in making what was supposed to be a series of group decisions. Following instructions, the confederates disagreed on most of the judgments, leaving the real participant in the uncomfortable position of casting the tie-breaking vote by siding with one of the two confederates. Students in a control condition agreed with each confederate about half the time. But a different pattern emerged among people in the experimental condition. They formed coalitions with one confederate much more

B.C.   **by johnny hart**

By permission of John L. Hart FLP and Creators Syndicate, Inc.

As you are reading about these effects of subliminal exposure, you might be reminded of the many ways that stimuli presented so fast that we are not even consciously aware of its presence can nevertheless affect the impressions we form of other people, see Chapter 3, pages 67 to 68.

often than with the other. Which confederate did they go along with? During a slide show just before the discussion session, participants in the experimental condition had been exposed to subliminal photographs of one of the confederates. Although they were not aware of their exposure to the photos, participants were much more likely to side with this "familiar" face (Bornstein and others, 1987). This means that subliminal exposure might be a good way to create a persuasive spokesperson for a product or a compelling advocate for a policy position (Weisbuch and others, 2003).

Subliminally presented information can also activate states that "smooth the way" for appropriately crafted persuasive appeals. Erin Strahan, Steve Spencer, and Mark Zanna (2002) had some already thirsty students at the University of Waterloo, Canada, watch a computer screen on which words designed to activate their thirst were presented so quickly they were not aware of having seen them. Compared to others exposed to non-thirst-related words, the students whose thirst had been stimulated like this drank more in an experimenter-arranged taste test. They also preferred the ad for a product described as thirst-quenching over one described as electrolyte restoring. Given the right conditions, then, we can be persuaded without our even knowing it.

HOW TO RESIST SUBLIMINAL INFLUENCE. Although research evidence suggests that our attitudes are vulnerable to subliminal information, those same research findings make clear the limits on such influence. First, in laboratory studies of subliminal effects, researchers have to work hard to make sure that participants are actually exposed to the subliminal stimuli. People have to be looking in just the right place at the right time, and in the confusion of everyday environments, subliminal messages might not be processed at all (although people's willingness to focus for long periods of time on television and computer screens makes the job a lot easier!).

Second, subliminal effects are easier to find with some stimuli than with others. Humans find it easier to encode pictures (especially faces), even when paying little attention to them, than even simple instructions and reminders. Pictures of buckets of popcorn or angry faces might be effective subliminal stimuli, but it's much less likely that the words "Eat popcorn" or "Stay away!" would have an effect. Research on the way we process sounds also suggests limits on subliminal influence. Because people process sounds in sequence, it is highly unlikely that humans are capable of decoding "subliminal" verbal messages recorded backwards or at high speed, or ones masked by other sounds (Moore, 1995). Since such stimuli would be impossible to interpret even if they were presented above the threshold of conscious awareness, how could they possibly be effective when presented subliminally?

In fact, the research evidence so far provides no support for the power of subliminal self-help tapes. One careful comparison of different subliminal tapes showed that their content had no real effect (Greenwald, Spangenberg, Pratkanis, & Eskenazi, 1991). In this study, participants listened every day for 5 weeks to a tape with a subliminal message ostensibly designed either to improve memory or to boost self-esteem. The researchers introduced an interesting twist, however, when they reversed the labels on half of the tapes. This meant that half the participants listening to a self-esteem tape thought they were listening to a memory tape and half the participants listening to a memory tape thought they were listening to a self-esteem tape. At the end of the 5-week period participants took memory and self-esteem tests. Although everyone's memory scores had improved slightly, the content of the subliminal tapes made no difference in memory or in self-esteem, as shown in Figure 7.8. So the subliminal tapes had no power to change listeners without their knowing it. But that's not what the participants thought. If they had

FIGURE 7.8   Subliminal self-help: Fact or fantasy?

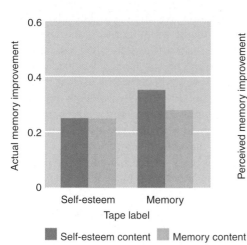

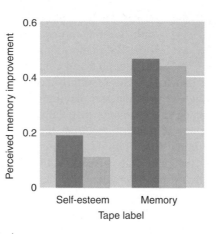

■ Self-esteem content   ■ Memory content

■ In this study, participants listened for 5 weeks to self-help tapes that were sold to improve either self-esteem or memory. Labels on half the tapes were switched so that half the people who were actually listening to a memory tape thought they were listening to a self-esteem tape, and vice versa. The results showed that actual memory scores (left-hand graph) and participants' ratings of their memory abilities (right-hand graph) both improved when participants *thought* they were listening to memory improvement tapes, regardless of the content of the tapes. (Data from Greenwald and others, 1991.)

listened to what they thought was a memory tape (even though in half the cases the label was wrong), they thought their memory had improved. If they thought they'd listened to a self-esteem tape (even though half the labels were wrong), they felt their self-esteem had gone up. No wonder people keep buying subliminal tapes: even though the tapes don't work, people think they do.

Perhaps the most important thing to remember about subliminal influence is this: Even if stimuli processed outside of awareness can influence our attitudes, this influence can be largely modified by conscious processing, just as we saw that the judgments we come to following superficial processing can be modified or overwhelmed by systematic processing. What we know to be true erases any "vague feeling" we might have. Although we might be influenced by information outside of awareness, that influence is largely eliminated if we know why and how we are being influenced (Bargh, 1989; Wegener & Petty, 1997). Consider the mere exposure effect, for example. When we are unaware of our exposure, the more we see something, the more we like it. But when we are conscious of the fact that we are seeing the same stimulus over and over again, little or no increase in liking is found (Bornstein, Kale, & Cornell, 1990). Conscious processing typically dominates subliminal influence. Consider what happened, for example, when students who knew themselves to be competitive or cooperative were exposed to subliminal words related to competitiveness (mean, hostile, and cutthroat, for example) or to neutral words (Neuberg, 1989b). Playing a game later, the competitive students exposed to the competitive words acted more aggressively than did competitive students exposed to the neutral words. But noncompetitive participants were uninfluenced by subliminal exposure to the aggressive words. The subliminal stimuli did not change who these students were. Their behavior was determined by how they wanted to act, not how they were subtly urged to act (Strahan and others, 2002).

Such results show that conscious processing typically overrides the impact of subliminal events. Subliminal buckets of popcorn probably can't get us to eat if we are serious about our diet, and subliminal messages are unlikely to make us change from one political party to another. Resistance to subliminal messages is probably no harder—nor any easier—than resistance to the literally thousands of messages we process consciously every day. Whether the appeal is subliminal or conscious, thinking is the key: To resist persuasion on important issues, we must put time and effort into our judgments.

CONCLUDING COMMENTS

 Persuasion has a pretty bad reputation. We often associate advertising with attempts to make us buy products we do not want or cannot afford. Political campaigns often seem little more than attempts to package and sell candidates who might not prevail if considered on their merits. Classic literature like George Orwell's *1984* warns us that by controlling information and playing on feelings, totalitarian governments may even persuade their citizens that the history they remember never really happened. Nowhere is concern about persuasion more obvious than in the public's fear that subliminal stimuli might influence us against our will.

Realizing that persuaders do not always have our best interests at heart is healthy: It pays to remember that we can be misled. And it helps if we know what we are up against. The citizens of ancient Greece and Rome were schooled in the art—and artifice—of argumentation. But most of today's citizens, unless they take classes in social psychology or communication, are taught little about the different ways in which attitude change can come about. Perhaps the most important lesson to be learned from the research discussed in this chapter is that influence is not something that others do to us: Whether we are persuaded or not lies largely in our own hands, or at least in our own heads.

When we do not care about or cannot cope with persuasive messages, we may well be influenced by emotional appeals, celebrity endorsements, and the use of complicated statistics. Of course, such simple cues work pretty well for us most of the time. But sometimes circumstances demand careful evaluation of a communication. When we are motivated by concerns about mastery and connectedness, we pay attention, try to make sense of the information presented to us, and think it through carefully. This kind of careful thinking, responding, and reacting can help a persuasion attempt to flourish or can let it wither away. Just as careful thought can flesh out a first impression into a coherent and balanced view of another individual, or take us beyond stereotypes and prejudices to more individualized conceptions of groups and their members, so careful thinking can prove a persuasion cue wrong and show a tear-jerker to be nothing more than a manipulative tug on the heartstrings. Systematic processing does not always mean we get things right—as we have seen, processing can be biased too, and more biased processing just means more bias. Regardless of whether we are superficially or systematically processing, it's what and how we process that determines whether or not our attitudes change. It's important to remember: we quite literally persuade ourselves.

Realizing our role in attitude change enables us to view persuasion as an empowering process rather than an overpowering one. In ancient Greece, the Sophists believed that persuasion was needed to lay bare the advantages and disadvantages of any object, and Aristotle argued that persuasion was needed to ensure that everyone came to see what was true and good. Persuasion does not have to involve deception, confusion, and trickery. The same processes that sometimes sell us inferior products and disreputable politicians are also at work when charitable organizations raise money for good causes, when public service messages improve the population's health, and when parents pass their values along to a new generation. And if we react to important appeals in an open but critical way, persuasion can be used to inform rather than confuse and to broaden rather than restrict our appreciation of attitude objects.

SUMMARY

 Attitudes and Their Origins. Attitude researchers infer **attitudes** from how people react to attitude objects. Such reactions can range from subtle evaluative reactions that people are unaware of, to more direct expressions of support or opposition in word or deed. Attempts to assess these different reactions have demonstrated that implicit attitudes can sometimes differ from explicit attitudes.

People form attitudes because attitudes are useful. Attitudes help people master the environment and express important connections with others. Attitudes are assembled from three types of information: beliefs about the object's characteristics, feelings and emotions about the object, and information about past and current actions toward the object. Negative information and accessible information are weighted more heavily. Once an attitude forms, it becomes closely linked to the representation of the object.

Superficial and Systematic Routes to Persuasion: From Snap Judgments to Considered Opinions. When people are targets of **persuasion**, they often do not give persuasive communications much thought. In this case, various superficial aspects of the persuasive appeal can lead to attitude change. For example, people might be influenced by positive or negative objects or events associated with the attitude object, or by feelings they are experiencing. The **mere exposure effect** can make people feel more positively about objects they have frequently encountered. They might also be influenced by **persuasion heuristics** to agree with messages from attractive, expert, or familiar sources or with familiar or long messages.

Sometimes people do carefully consider the content of arguments presented in a persuasive communication. When people pay attention to a message, understand its content, and react to it, a process called **elaboration**, systematic processing can change attitudes. Attitudes resulting from such careful consideration last longer and are much more resistant to later change than most attitudes produced by superficial processing.

People process messages systematically only when they have both the motivation and the cognitive capacity to do so. The relevance of the message to important goals determines motivation. Cognitive capacity is available when people have adequate ability to process and can do so without distraction. People differ in their levels of motivation and capacity to process different kinds of messages. Messages that match people's motivational goals and their capacity states are most persuasive. Positive and negative emotional states influence persuasion because they have motivational and capacity consequences.

Defending Attitudes: Resisting Persuasion. People often seek to resist persuasion, and one of their best weapons is awareness. People protect established attitudes by ignoring or resisting information that threatens them. Being forewarned of a persuasion attempt and having previous experience with related arguments can help resistance. However many people overestimate their ability to resist persuasive appeals. Subliminal persuasion gains some of its power because people do not realize they are the target of a persuasive attempt. Information presented outside of conscious awareness can influence attitudes and persuasion. But careful consideration of attitude objects can weaken the influence of subliminal information.

8

Attitudes and Behavior

Most of us assume that what we think and feel on the inside goes along with what we do on the outside—that attitudes and behaviors go hand in hand. Recall from Chapter 7 that an attitude is any cognitive representation that summarizes our evaluation of an attitude object. We take for granted that our political attitudes (the candidates we prefer, for example) are related to our political behaviors (the candidates we vote for). We assume that we eat what we like and like what we eat, and that we take as friends people we like and like the people who are our friends. Social psychology provides considerable evidence for this comfortable consistency between atittudes and behaviors. As pointed out in previous chapters, we typically treat other people and others groups in ways consistent with our impressions of them, doling out acceptance and support to those we like while rejecting and victimizing those we don't.

Attitudes and behaviors are often related like this for two very good reasons. The first is that *actions influence attitudes*. Attitudes are constructed on the basis of cognitive, affective, and behavioral information, so it makes sense that our attitudes might be consistent with our actions. Collecting cans for recycling can help develop caring attitudes toward environmental conservation; donating some loose change to a panhandler can generate positive attitudes toward the homeless. In the first part of this chapter, we consider two different ways in which behaviors become building blocks for attitudes. Sometimes people notice their behavior, make simple inferences about it, and bring their attitudes into line with their actions. At other times, when behavior has more serious consequences, for example, people work hard to justify or rationalize their actions, and this too can result in attitude change. Thus, because our attitudes are changed by our actions, it's not surprising that actions and attitudes go hand in hand.

The second reason attitudes and behaviors are predictably related is that given the right conditions, *attitudes influence actions*. Attitudes dictate how we look at attitude objects, and this in turn determines how we act toward them. You may recall examples of this process from earlier chapters: Seeing their team as the most talented, the fans turn out for every game. Noticing only the immigrant's differences, the bigot refuses to hire him. Focusing on their child's positive qualities, the doting parents pamper and indulge him. Attitudes sometimes trigger action in an almost knee-jerk fashion, with very little forethought. On other occasions, the process is more deliberate. When this happens, our attitudes produce intentions to act in particular ways, and much time, effort, and thought is exerted to make good on those intentions. The means by which attitudes shape and direct behavior are the topic of the second part of the chapter.

To say that attitudes and behaviors are predictably related does not mean, however, that they will always be in lockstep. We do sometimes act against our personal convictions. We raid the children's Halloween candy when we mean to diet. We watch action movies even though we hate media violence. We buy trucks for our nephews and dolls for our nieces despite our long-standing opposition to gender stereotypes. Why don't we always act in line with our attitudes? First, several important processes have to occur before attitudes can affect behavior. What has to happen, and when will attitudes play a more or less important role in guiding behavior? These questions, which have important implications for attitudes and behaviors in clinical, business, and educational settings, are addressed in the final section of this chapter.

Second, attitudes are only one of several factors that can affect behavior. One of the most powerful reasons attitudes are sometimes unrelated to behaviors is that actions are also influenced by social norms. These shared standards of appropriate behavior may differ from personal attitudes, and in such cases, behaviors don't always reflect attitudes. In fact, the impact that norms exert on behavior are so important that we will cover that topic in Chapters 9 and 10.

Changing Attitudes with Actions

Have you ever found yourself in a brand new role? Perhaps you were appointed coordinator for the office United Fund pledge drive or elected president of a student organization dedicated to reducing class size. A new position demands new actions and new ways of interacting with people, and these new actions soon spawn new attitudes. When Seymour Lieberman (1956) followed the careers of male factory workers, he found just such a change. Workers promoted to foremen soon showed increased sympathy for management's viewpoint; in contrast, those newly elected to union offices adopted more hard-line union positions. Lieberman's findings show the tremendous impact of career choices: Careers can dictate conduct, which in turn can determine character. Even playing a part can change attitudes. For example, students playing the role of U.S. advisers in international negotiation games often develop hard-line pro-U.S. positions (Trost, Cialdini, & Maas, 1989). If such transitory roles can exert this influence, it's no wonder that "taking on" the personalities of the roles they play is an occupational hazard for some actors and actresses (Magnusson, 1981). From Richard Burton and Elizabeth Taylor to Angelina Jolie and Brad Pitt, how many actresses and actors seem to get romantically involved in real life with their on-screen romantic interests? Apparently novelist George Eliot was correct: "Our deeds determine us as much as we determine our deeds."

The effect of behavior on attitudes is not limited to the job arena. Almost any kind of action can influence attitudes (R. K. White, 1971). People end up liking those they help (Blanchard & Cook, 1976) and disliking those they hurt (Davis & Jones, 1960; Glass, 1964). Even saying something that another person wants to hear can be enough to change an attitude. In one study demonstrating this point, participants were asked to describe a man to someone who supposedly either liked or disliked him

(Higgins & Rholes, 1978). When participants believed the listener liked the man, they said more good things about him than when they thought the listener did not like him. These statements also colored the participants' own attitudes. Those who had given glowing descriptions ended up liking the man better than those who had described him less favorably. So if you want to improve your professor's opinion of you, ask her now to write a strongly positive letter of recommendation for you!

As these studies illustrate, behavior can be an important part of the information on which we base our attitudes. Just as novel beliefs and feelings can change our opinions about an attitude object (Chapter 7), so too can new actions contribute to new attitudes. How does information about our actions exert an influence on our attitudes? By now, you probably will not be surprised to learn that it is a matter of processing. People deal with information either superficially or systematically, depending on their ability to process and the relevance of the information to important goals and motives. We process information about our own behavior the same ways. Sometimes people take what they do at face value and make simple action-to-attitude inferences. In other circumstances, especially if the behavior has serious consequences, people move to a deeper consideration of the implications of their actions.

From Action to Attitude via Superficial Processing

Behavior is an important part of the information on which people base attitudes. If behaviors change, attitudes can also change. When people process superficially, attitudes can be based on associations with actions or on inferences from actions. Like other forms of superficial processing, actions are more likely to affect attitudes in this way when people lack the motivation or ability to process more thoroughly.

At the most superficial level of processing, even simple muscle movements can influence attitudes because the actions are associated with agreement, pleasure, and approach (or their opposites). When they like something, people tend to smile, nod

■ **Action across attitude gaps**. This boy is teaching this woman about the internet as part of a junior–senior computer class. The goal of the class isn't simply to help senior citizens grasp computers, but also to change attitudes of both participants, reducing one dimension of the "generation gap."

their heads, and move the object toward them. In contrast, disliked objects elicit frowns, head shaking, and movements that push them away (Eibl-Eibesfeldt, 1972; Ekman, 1971; Solarz, 1960). Such movements are associated with liking or disliking, and when they occur in the presence of an attitude object, the liking and disliking can rub off. Consider, for example, a study in which participants were asked to pull up or push down on a bar while thinking about whether they liked or disliked "foreign" (actually nonsense) words like *begrid*, *plicen*, and *triwen* (Priester, Cacioppo, & Petty, 1996). Pulling up on the bar used muscle movements that typically bring objects closer, whereas pushing down on the bar required the muscle extension used in pushing objects away. Those who pulled up on the bar liked the words more than those who pushed down on it. Perhaps cultural rituals of greeting like gripping a hand, inclining the head forward, or clasping the shoulder, work to give attitudes toward newcomers a subtly positive boost.

The impact of such activity in more complex social situations can be seen in an ingenious study that demonstrated how nodding and shaking the head affects attitudes (Wells and Petty, 1980). To see if participants would infer their attitudes from such head movements, the researchers led them to believe they were testing the sound quality of stereo headphones during jogging or bike riding. To simulate jogging, some participants were asked to move their heads up and down; to simulate bicycling, others moved their heads from side to side. These actions were carried out as they listened through headphones to an editorial, ostensibly broadcast from the campus radio station, that advocated increases or decreases in college tuition. As you can see in Figure 8.1, the gestures had an impact. Head nodders were more supportive of the position advocated in the broadcast, whereas head shakers opposed the position. Further research has uncovered some of the processes that might contribute to this effect. For example, head nodders recognize and encode positive words more quickly and easily, whereas head shakers recognize and encode negative stimuli more quickly and easily (Foerster & Strack, 1996). In addition,

FIGURE 8.1   Head movements and opinions: Inferring attitudes from actions

■ In this study, participants nodded their heads up and down or shook them from side to side while listening to a speech calling for raised or lowered tuition. As you can see, their gestures influenced their attitudes. The nodders (darker bars) were more supportive of the position taken in the message than the shakers (lighter bars). (Data from Wells & Petty, 1980.)

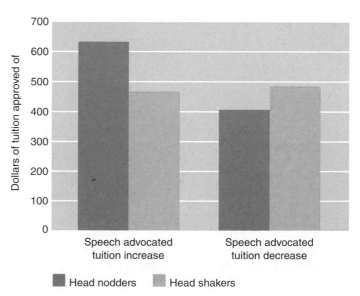

head nodders are more confident that the evaluative reactions they have while nodding are correct, whereas head shakers have more doubts about their reactions (Briñol & Petty, 2003).

SELF-PERCEPTION THEORY. Actions can influence attitudes like this because sometimes people make straightforward inferences from action to attitude. Smiling indicates being amused. Eating something indicates liking it. Signing a petition means you support the position it advocates. Darryl Bem's (1972) *theory of self-perception* explains the impact of actions on attitudes by suggesting that people infer their attitudes by observing their own behaviors and the situations in which those actions occur. You may have experienced self-perception processes yourself. Have you ever contemplated your growing collection of Alien Ant Farm CDs and suddenly realized you had developed a taste for punk music? Or, noting that you are spending more and more time at the gym, have you decided that you are committed to the benefits of regular exercise?

Chapter 4 (page 97) described this process at work as people infer their own personal characteristics, like traits and dispositions, from their actions.

Researchers have mimicked such situations experimentally by focusing participants on particular aspects of their previous behavior and then measuring their attitudes. In one study, for example, Gerald Salancik and Mary Conway (1975) drew some students' attention to how frequently they performed religiously oriented behavior (like reading a religious publication or attending religious services) and made other students think about how seldom they did so. When asked about their attitudes toward religion, the first group reported favorable attitudes, whereas the second did not. In another study, Dolores Albarracin and Robert Wyer (2000) led some students to believe, falsely, that they had expressed support for instituting comprehensive exams for graduating seniors, and others to believe that they had expressed opposition to the exams. They managed this clever ruse by telling students that various attitude issues were being subliminally presented on a computer screen, and having the students let their "unconscious impulses" guide them to press a "yes" or "no" button to support or oppose the issue. Of course, no subliminal stimuli were presented, but students believed the experimenters' false feedback that they had either supported or opposed having comprehensive exams. When later asked about their attitudes, the group that believed they had already expressed support were much more favorable toward the exams than was the group who thought they'd expressed opposition. Consistent with self-perception theory, then, people often infer their attitudes from their behavior.

Advertisers and sales personnel have been quick to take advantage of the connection between behavior and attitude change. They sponsor slogan-writing contests that induce thousands of people to spend hours describing the benefits of particular products. They offer free samples, often counting on people to conclude that they must like the product—why else would they have agreed to use it? They offer their products to game shows, assuming that having contestants compete for their goods will make those products seem valuable. Sales personnel are content with a small purchase from their customer, knowing that one small commitment to a product will often result in larger and larger sales. Thus, the simple process of self-perception has become a popular—and effective—social influence technique.

THE FOOT-IN-THE-DOOR TECHNIQUE: WOULD YOU MIND DOING ME A SMALL FAVOR? A particularly clever ploy that takes advantage of people's tendency to judge their own behavior at face value is called the **foot-in-the-door technique**. As the name implies, this social influence technique is like the tactics of door-to-door salespeople who try to get their foot in a customer's door. To use the foot-in-the-door

Foot-in-the-door technique. A technique for increasing compliance with a large request by first asking people to go along with a smaller request.

THE FAR SIDE® By GARY LARSON

Darren's heart quickened: Once inside the home, and once the demonstration was in full swing, a sale was inevitable.

technique, you get people to perform a small act consistent with an intended goal, and this "foot in the door" makes them open to further influence. Jonathan Freedman and Scott Fraser (1966) demonstrated the technique's effectiveness when they approached female householders in California and asked them to sign a petition supporting safe driving. Nearly all complied. Then, about 2 weeks later, they contacted the same group of women, and some who had never been approached before, with a big request: Would they agree to let the experimenters place a large, ugly "Drive Safely" sign in their front yards? Three times as many people who had gone along with the first small request agreed to do so compared to those who had not received the first request. The fact that people are more likely to agree to a large request if they have first made a small consistent comitment has been demonstrated over and over again, including when the requests are made by e-mail rather than face to face (Guéguen, 2002).

How does the foot-in-the-door technique work? Why would a small inconsequential act of signing a petition translate into a costly commitment to obscure one's house behind an unattractive billboard? The answer is that performance of the initial behavior triggers self-perception processes, and the presence of an action-consistent attitude is inferred. This new attitude then makes agreement with the second request more likely, but only if all the conditions are right. Research suggests that two conditions are crucial if the foot-in-the-door technique is to influence attitudes (Burger, 1999).

1. *Performing the initial request must be meaningful.* Initial requests cannot be trivial. They have to be important enough to allow people to draw an inference about themselves and their attitudes. Compliance with the first request can be made meaningful if the person using the foot-in-the-door technique draws the self-perception inference for the target. In one study, people who donated to a charity after a first request were explicitly told: "You are the kind of person who supports charitable causes." This group of donors was even more likely to give a second generous donation than were donors whose first gift was received without comment (Burger & Caldwell, 2003).

Getting people to expend effort to go along with the first request is also a good way to make it meaningful. As long as people try to comply with the first request (even if they fail in the end), they seem to make the self-perception connection (Dolinski, 2000). The more effort people put into the first request, the more likely they are to see their actions as evidence of their support of the cause. So actually signing a petition is more effective than merely expressing interest; completing a form as if one were placing an order works better than agreeing to consider a product. Of course, initial requests cannot be so large that people will refuse them. In this case, self-perception processes can backfire and work against further change. If people view their refusal as evidence that they oppose the cause, the stage will be set for further refusals of future requests (DeJong, 1979).

2. *Performing the initial request must seem purely voluntary.* As we saw in Chapter 4, people are quick to see their own behavior as determined by environmental forces. Not surprisingly, this tendency undermines the operation of self-perception processes. If attending religious services or donating to a cause is forced on you by parental insistence or a financial incentive, or if you find out that "everyone" performs those behaviors, you are unlikely to make the inference that your actions really had implications for something about your own attitudes (Burger & Caldwell, 2003; DeJong, 1979; Gorassini & Olson, 1995). You may recognize some irony here. Although we are used to thinking that we like what we are rewarded for, it is often the case that behaviors undertaken for external rewards fail to translate into internal preferences. Only when the initial choice seems ours alone, rather than being attributable to the reward, are we likely to infer that we must hold an action-consistent attitude.

You may recall another example of inferences being more important than actual rewards from our discussion of intrinsic motivation in Chapter 4, page 97.

☐ **SELF-PERCEPTION PROCESSES AND VOLUNTEERING.** With its ability to turn small commitments into large convictions, the foot-in-the-door technique is particularly helpful to those trying to solicit charitable donations of time, money, effort, and even body parts! In one study researchers called some residents of Bloomington, Indiana, and asked them if, hypothetically, they would volunteer to spend 3 hours collecting for the American Cancer Society (ACS). Three days later, a second experimenter called the same people and actually requested help for ACS. More than 31% of those responding to the earlier request agreed to help. Compared with the 4% of a similar group of townspeople who were willing to help when approached directly, this represented an increase of more than 700% in the volunteer rate (S. J. Sherman, 1980). In a similar study of donors in Israel, 92% of those who signed a petition supporting recreational facilities for disabled people donated money to the cause when contacted 2 weeks later, compared with a rate of 53% among people who had not made the earlier commitment (Schwarzwald, Bizman, & Raz, 1983). Using the foot-in-the-door technique has also been shown to increase blood donations (Lipsitz, Kallmeyer, Ferguson, & Abas, 1989) and willingness to be an organ donor (Girandola, 2002). When commitments affect self-perception, small public-spirited behaviors produce staunch public-minded volunteers.

PERSONALITY DIFFERENCES AND THE FOOT-IN-THE-DOOR TECHNIQUE. The effectiveness of techniques that rely on people getting committed in a small way before hooking them in a big way hinges on consistency. People infer attitudes, and sometimes even views about themselves, that are consistent with their previous behavior. Not surprisingly, then, people who are more concerned with consistency are more influenced by the foot-in-the-door technique than those who shun consistency. People who value consistency are more likely to adjust their responses in situations to agree with their prior actions. As a result, people with this high preference for consistency are also much more likely to be persuaded to make a big second commitment following a small initial commitment. In contrast, people who don't care about consistency, or don't want to be consistent, are not as vulnerable to this persuasion technique (Guadagno, Asher, Demaine, & Cialdini, 2001).

FROM ACTIONS TO ATTITUDES SUPERFICIALLY. So actions can often lead us to infer that we hold attitudes consistent with them. But these simple associations between actions and attitudes are more likely to be drawn when not much is at stake: when attitudes are unformed, ambiguous, or unimportant, for example. These are just the kinds of conditions in which people process superficially, and form attitudes on the basis of simple associations or quick and easy inferences. Such action-to-attitude implications are less likely when attitudes are well established or important, however (Bem, 1963). Although approach and avoidance arm movements influenced positive and negative ratings of unknown objects like nonsense words, they didn't have this simple effect on evaluative judgments of "real" words about which students have already thought (Priester and others, 1996). That's not to say that such associations don't influence established attitudes at all. Some studies have shown that even when a positive attitude is well established (you really like a particular candy bar, for example), approach body movements can make the attitude even more positive, but avoidance movements have no effect. Similarly, avoidance movements made evaluations of disgusting foods (like cow lungs, for example) more negative, while approach behaviors had no influence. (Foerster, 2004). With such well-established attitudes bodily movements don't affect an attitude's direction, but they can still affect its intensity.

But clearly, simple action-to-attitude inferences are much more likely to be made when attitudes are not well established or if consequences are not particularly serious. Consider for example what happened when researchers measured students' environmental attitudes, gave the students the opportunity to donate money to the environmental organization Greenpeace, and later measured their attitudes again. Students who did not at first have strongly or clearly defined attitudes on the issue changed their later attitudes in the direction of their behavior: those who donated money more strongly supported the environment whereas those who didn't donate later reported more anti-conservation attitudes. Self-perception processes seemed to be at work. But behavior did not change the opinions of students with well-established environmental attitudes—whether they donated or not, they did not use their behavior to infer new attitudes (Chaiken & Baldwin, 1981; Holland, Verplanken, & van Knippenberg, 2002).

The same point was made in a study that varied the importance of forming an evaluation. In this study, the researcher compared women's "gut reactions" to pictures of men in two circumstances: One group of women expected to meet one of the men, whereas the other group did not (S. E. Taylor, 1975). As she viewed each photo, each woman received fake feedback allegedly revealing her physiological reaction to each man. The feedback falsely indicated that the woman's heart beat faster when she viewed some photos but not others. When asked to evaluate the men, the women who did not anticipate meeting them used their supposed reactions to infer their attitudes: They reported liking the men who seemingly "made their hearts beat faster." But the women for whom the ratings had real consequences—those who thought they would meet the man they rated most favorably—were unwilling to base their evaluations on their physiological responses alone.

As these studies show, actions are more likely to lead us to adopt consistent attitudes when people think rather superficially. When attitudes are well established and important, and the consequences of changing them serious, people tend to think much more systematically about behavior that contradicts them. Just as high motivation increases systematic processing of persuasive communications, high stakes also cause us to think much more carefully about the implications of our behavior for our attitudes. Often the very importance of the attitude that is contradicted makes that attitude hard to change. But in the right circumstances, thinking about the implications of attitude inconsistent behavior can change even important attitudes.

Cognitive Dissonance: Changing Attitudes to Justify Behavior

When freely chosen actions violate important or self-relevant attitudes, the inconsistency produces an uncomfortable state of tension and arousal called dissonance, which can motivate people to change their attitudes to make them consistent with their behavior. This often happens when people act in an attitude-inconsistent way, expend considerable effort in pursuit of a goal, or make tough decisions. Because this kind of attitude change involves extensive processing, it is often long-lasting. While minor discrepancies between action and attitudes might trigger self-perception processes, conflicts between actions and attitudes that are important enough to cause unpleasant tension trigger dissonance reduction processes.

Actions sometimes contradict important attitudes. Especially when they first come to school, most students at universities in the U.S.A. are firmly opposed to cheating. But anonymous surveys reveal that many of them actually end up cheating in one way or another during their college careers (Storch & Storch, 2003). The ones who do certainly don't act in line with their attitudes. Although as many as 30% of European consumers express positive attitudes about organic produce, the market share of such products remains below 1%; most supporters are not acting on their positive attitudes (De Perlsmacker, Driesen, & Rayp, 2003). Although 99% of Americans have strongly negative attitudes toward cigarette smoking, 20% are regular smokers, a contradiction between attitude and action for a significant portion of them (McMillen, Ritchie, Frese, & Cosby, 2000). When such conflicts occur, does the fact that attitudes are important mean that behavior has no impact?

The importance of the attitude certainly means that people reflect more deeply on their attitude-inconsistent behavior. Does this careful thinking prevent their actions from having any impact on their attitudes? On the contrary. Under the right conditions, there is often dramatic evidence of attitude change. For example, the number of times that students have engaged in a particular form of academic dishonesty predicts their acceptance of the behavior (Storch & Storch, 2003). So the more they act dishonestly, the less negative their attitude toward cheating becomes. In both Europe and the United States, consumers' purchases are heavily influenced by price and convenience and those practices undermine further support for organic produce. Heavy smokers who try to quit and don't succeed actually come to see the health consequences of smoking as much less negative (Gibbons, Eggleston, & Benthin, 1997). When even life-threatening behavior continues, attitudes can change to make the threat seem less. Let's see how such change in important attitudes might occur in the face of conflicting behavior.

THE THEORY OF COGNITIVE DISSONANCE. In 1957, Leon Festinger, a brilliant young social psychologist, argued that when people become aware that their attitudes, thoughts, and beliefs ("cognitions") are inconsistent with one another, this realization brings with it an uncomfortable state of tension called

cognitive dissonance. Cognitive dissonance often follows when behavior conflicts with a prior attitude: when, for example, people think of themselves as honest but cheat on an exam, or care keenly about their health but choose to eat convenience food. Festinger did more than just suggest that inconsistencies cause discomfort. He also offered a bold new proposal: that people's motivation to reduce the unpleasant side effects of inconsistency often produces attitude change. According to cognitive dissonance theory, tensions caused by differences between important actions and attitudes are often reduced by adjustments we make to our thinking, not to our behavior.

In the decades following Festinger's proposal, literally hundreds of experiments have verified the existence and effects of dissonance. Those experiments have also helped clarify the processing steps involved when dissonance turns actions into attitude change (Cooper & Fazio, 1984; Petty & Wegener, 1998a). According to the accumulated research, four steps are necessary for actions to produce dissonance and for that dissonance to produce attitude change.

1. *The individual must perceive the action as inconsistent.* In Festinger's view, the very inconsistency of attitude and action was enough to produce dissonance. Recent evidence has confirmed that inconsistency in and of itself is sufficient to cause such discomfort (Harmon-Jones, Brehm, Greenberg, Simon, & Nelson, 1996; R. W. Johnson, Kelly & LeBlanc, 1995). Not all inconsistencies are created equal, however. Dissonance is most likely to be provoked when actions are inconsistent with positive and important images of ourselves (E. Aronson, 1969; Baumeister, 1982; Greenwald & Ronis, 1978; Steele, 1988). Actions that violate our sense of self-integrity (like lying or cheating) or value-laden attitudes (like believing that pesticide use pollutes the planet for profit) or personal standards (like caring for one's health) are most likely to produce discomfort (Steele, 1988; Stone, Wiegand, Cooper, & Aronson, 1997). All of these situations involve inconsistency with attitudes, self-concepts, or standards that are important to the individual. It is this inconsistency, regardless of its exact source, that is the first step on the road to dissonance arousal.

2. *The individual must take personal responsibility for the action.* Dissonance is aroused only when an internal attribution is made, that is, when we perceive ourselves as having freely engaged in the attitude-discrepant behavior. When we are coerced by severe threat or driven by large rewards, we can attribute the action to an external cause, which will forestall dissonance arousal. If, for example, people were forced to cheat on an exam by a gun-wielding madman or agreed to smoke a cigarette to win a new car, such behavior should not arouse dissonance. But typically, smoking or deciding to peek at someone else's work during an exam are matters of free choice. Even when we are seduced into such behaviors by very small reinforcements, dissonance will still occur if we see the final decision to act as ours. Studies show, for example, that students asked to write an essay inconsistent with their personal beliefs about free speech experience considerable dissonance, whereas those required to write the essay or promised large rewards for doing so show no signs of dissonance arousal (Linder, Cooper, & Jones, 1967). Taking personal responsibility is so central to producing dissonance that those individuals who routinely attribute their behavior to external causes don't experience dissonance like those who see actions as internally driven (Stalder & Baron, 1998). Similarly, members of cultures that see behavior as constrained more by circumstance than by personality might experience less dissonance. There is some evidence, for

> **Cognitive dissonance.** An unpleasant state caused by people's awareness of inconsistency among important beliefs, attitudes, or actions.

example, that Japanese participants make more external attributions for inconsistent behavior, thus short-circuiting the dissonance process (Sakai & Andow, 1980).

3. *The individual must experience uncomfortable physiological arousal.* Just as Festinger suggested, dissonance seems to be experienced as an uncomfortable state of arousal. Robert Croyle and Joel Cooper (1983) measured this arousal by attaching electrodes to participants' fingers while they participated in an essay-writing study. One group of participants was asked to write essays that were consistent with their personal opinions (proattitudinal) and another group wrote essays that contradicted their attitudes (counterattitudinal). The experimenter told these participants that it was their choice, but that it would greatly facilitate the research if they would agree to write the requested essays. Virtually all of them complied with the request. Two other groups of participants were simply required to write proattitudinal or counterattitudinal essays. The researchers expected dissonance to be aroused only when people freely chose to engage in attitude-discrepant behavior, that is, when they were asked to write a counterattitudinal essay but given the apparent choice not to. The results confirmed their hypotheses. Only participants who saw themselves as freely choosing to write counterattitudinal essays showed increases in physiological arousal. Other psychophysiological research, as well as people's self-reports, confirm that dissonance is experienced as a feeling of unpleasant arousal (Elliot & Devine, 1994; Losch & Cacioppo, 1990).

4. *The individual must attribute the arousal to the inconsistency between attitude and action.* People have to believe they are feeling unpleasantly aroused because of their inconsistency (J. Cooper & Fazio, 1984). This point has been demonstrated by studies in which people were tricked into believing that the discomfort they felt was due to something else: fluorescent lights that malfunctioned, a pill they ingested, electric shocks they were anticipating, or prism goggles they had to wear (J. Cooper, Zanna, & Taves, 1978; Fazio, Zanna, & Cooper, 1977; Losch & Cacioppo, 1990; Pittman, 1975). In such cases, the discomfort has no implications for the inconsistencies between attitudes and actions. But when people correctly attribute their discomfort to the inconsistency between attitude and action, their attention is focused on that inconsistency.

Just as people are motivated to eliminate uncomfortable physiological states like hunger and thirst, they want to reduce the discomfort of dissonance. When attitudes and behaviors are uncomfortably inconsistent, something has to change. Because freely chosen behavior and its negative consequences are often hard to take back or deny, we can restore consistency most easily by changing our attitude. It is only when attitudes are brought into line with actions that dissonance is finally eliminated. This whole process of dissonance arousal and its eventual reduction through attitude change is summarized in Figure 8.2.

In certain circumstances, then, people who behave in an attitude-discrepant way change even important attitudes to conform to their actions. Dissonance theory provides a simple explanation for a wide variety of situations in which such changes occur in day-to-day interactions in classrooms and clinics and on sales floors. When people perform behaviors that are inconsistent with important attitudes, the dissonance triggers justification processes that produce attitude change. In the next sections, we explore the attitude change that occurs when people try to justify acting in an attitude-inconsistent way, expending considerable effort or making tough decisions.

FIGURE 8.2   Four steps to dissonance arousal and reduction

■ For dissonance to result in physiological arousal and ultimately in attitude change, four steps must occur.

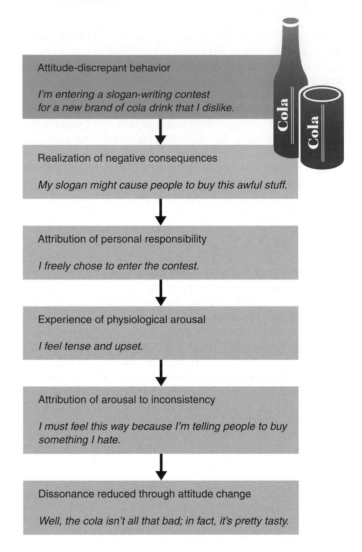

Attitude-discrepant behavior

I'm entering a slogan-writing contest for a new brand of cola drink that I dislike.

Realization of negative consequences

My slogan might cause people to buy this awful stuff.

Attribution of personal responsibility

I freely chose to enter the contest.

Experience of physiological arousal

I feel tense and upset.

Attribution of arousal to inconsistency

I must feel this way because I'm telling people to buy something I hate.

Dissonance reduced through attitude change

Well, the cola isn't all that bad; in fact, it's pretty tasty.

JUSTIFYING ATTITUDE-DISCREPANT BEHAVIOR: I HAVE MY REASONS! Imagine that you are a participant in a very boring experiment. For what seems like hours, you perform meaningless and repetitive tasks. First, the experimenter gives you a pegboard containing 48 square pegs and asks you to give them a quarter turn to the left, a quarter turn back to the right, a quarter turn to the left again, back to the right, and so on, again and again. Just as you are sure you will die of boredom, you are instructed to change tasks. But the next task is no better: Now you are instructed to remove pegs from the board, put them back, take them off, put them back on. Finally (mercifully) the experiment is over. But just as you are about to leave, the experimenter requests your help. A graduate student assistant who was supposed to motivate participants in a different condition of the experiment has not arrived on time. Will you fill in, and tell the next participant how much you enjoyed the experiment? The experimenter even offers to pay you $1 for doing so.

FIGURE 8.3 It must have been as interesting as I said: Justifying attitude-discrepant behavior

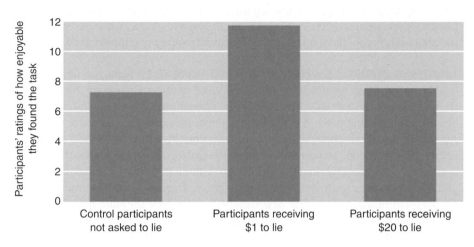

■ All participants in this classic study performed an exceedingly boring task. However, only those who freely chose to lie by saying the task was enjoyable for an insufficient reward (middle bar) reduced dissonance by bringing their attitudes into line with the lie. (Data from Festinger & Carlsmith, 1959.)

If you agree, the classic conditions for dissonance have been set up. An attitude-discrepant behavior (lying about the experiment) with potentially negative consequences (the next person's unrealistic expectations about the study) has been performed with insufficient external justification (the payment of only $1). Dissonance will be aroused. But by changing attitudes about the task ("After all, the experiment did have scientific merit, it was a challenge rather than a bore") to match the behavior ("And that's what I told the next participant"), dissonance can be eliminated. In their classic study of just such a situation, Festinger and J. Merrill Carlsmith (1959) confirmed this prediction. As you can see in Figure 8.3, control participants who were not asked to mislead the next participant rated the experimental task as pretty boring. So did participants paid $20 to lie about the experimental task: They had plenty of external justification for what they said to the next participant. In contrast, those who agreed to mislead others for the insufficient justification of a single dollar reduced dissonance by changing their attitudes about the experiment.

Note that in this experimental demonstration of the power of dissonance, the attitude that was the source of the dissonance was probably not the same attitude that ultimately changed. To cause uncomfortable tension, behavior has to contradict an important attitude—in this case, a positive attitude about the self. Most students didn't see themselves as immoral people who would tell lies for only a dollar, so when they did exactly this, their inconsistent behavior created a lot of dissonance. But the dissonance did not lead to change in the important attitude (the students did not decide that they were immoral deceivers)! Instead, it set in motion the processes that caused other attitudes to change (the experiment now seemed more valuable, an attitude change that made the behavior less of a lie).

As we've just seen, doing something inconsistent with an attitude can cause dissonance. Doing nothing when your attitude suggests you should do something can also cause that unpleasant tension—especially if there isn't a good reason for your lack of action. Dissonance theory predicts that when people want to do something, but decide not to because of a mild threat of punishment, people will change their attitudes to convince themselves that they do not really want to perform the forbidden behavior anyway. Research bears out this prediction. In one study, 4-year-old children were threatened with severe or mild punishment if they played with an attractive robot toy (E. Aronson & Carlsmith, 1963). When allowed to play with any toy in the experimenter's absence, all children avoided the forbidden toy. However, when asked to evaluate the toys, the children faced with mild punishment justified their avoidance by saying they didn't like the toy anyway. Children given the severe warning still liked it. If you can get someone to resist temptation with just a little threat, dissonance processes might fool them into thinking they really were not tempted at all.

JUSTIFYING EFFORT: I SUFFERED FOR IT, SO I LIKE IT. Perhaps you have a friend caught up in a bad relationship. You notice that as the relationship worsens, your friend makes even more sacrifices, and as the partner grows more hurtful, your friend becomes more committed. Why do people sometimes come to like what they suffer for? Cognitive dissonance provides an explanation: People change their attitudes to justify their suffering. Members of groups who undergo severe initiation rituals value their groups more highly than those accepted without initiation (E. Aronson & Mills, 1959). No wonder then that from high school cliques to elite military groups, hazing—the practice of making new members experience difficult, humiliating, and unfortunately often dangerous experiences—seems impossible to eliminate. People prefer difficult experimental tasks they perform for rude instructors over those they perform for personable ones, and workers whose jobs require challenging and difficult situations much prefer them to those who have easy routine assignments (Rosenfeld, Giacalone, & Tedeschi, 1984). In these cases people have freely chosen to act in ways that cause them suffering (surely an example of inconsistent behavior for

DILBERT © Scott Adams/Dist. by United Feature Syndicate. Reprinted with permission.

someone with positive self-esteem). Realization of this fact no doubt triggers uncomfortable tension, which is resolved by valuing more and more the goal for which you suffered. In experimental situations, the attitudes that are changed toward made-up groups or pointless tasks may not seem that important. But if you've ever noted with dismay how wonderful an abusive spouse or parent or friendship group can seem to their victim, you've see that dissonance processes can change very important and consequential attitudes. Even more disturbing is the possibility that dissonance might be reduced by changing the really important attitude that one is a good person, as when victims of abuse come to see themselves as somehow "deserving it."

Suffering is not the only kind of "work" that requires justification. Because there is a discrepancy between working really hard to achieve a goal and finding out that the goal is not worth it, almost any kind of effort can result in dissonance-reducing attitude change that values the goal. Danny Axsom and Joel Cooper (1985) demonstrated the practical benefits of this *effort-justification effect* in a clever study involving overweight females. Some of these individuals, all of whom had volunteered in response to a newspaper advertisement, worked on difficult and effortful perceptual and auditory tasks during a 3-week training period on weight reduction; others performed relatively easy and pleasant versions of the same tasks during the weekly sessions. Nothing was done in either of these conditions to explicitly encourage the women to diet—in fact, none of the tasks had anything to do with dieting—although the women were encouraged to keep track of what they ate and were weighed regularly. Nevertheless, to be in the "weight-loss program" some women had to put in a lot of cognitive effort and some didn't. Six months later, participants were contacted again and reweighed. Results showed that the high-effort group had lost an average of 8.55 pounds, compared with only .07 pounds for the low-effort group. This difference was found again when participants reported their weight 1 year later. From a dissonance perspective, perhaps the difficulty of the tasks they freely agreed to do motivated the women to increase the positive importance of dieting and weight-loss (the goal for which they'd suffered). This in turn appeared to motivate their weight-loss behavior. The more you put into something, whether in time, money, pain, or effort, the more you seem to value it.

JUSTIFYING DECISIONS: OF COURSE I WAS RIGHT! Every difficult decision we make—to return to work or to stay at home with our children, to major in science or in the humanities, to expand our business into a new district or to consolidate local gains—has advantages and drawbacks. Whenever we make decisions, we give up some things in order to gain others. By definition, then, decisions involve dissonance. When people give up options freely, they experience *decisional dissonance*: tension between the alternative they chose and all the attractive features of the alternatives they gave up. This type of dissonance is sometimes called post-decisional regret. According to dissonance theory, people try to reduce such tension by evaluating the chosen option even more positively and disparaging the unchosen alternative.

To show this process at work, Jack Brehm (1956) asked women to evaluate several small appliances as part of a supposed study of consumer preferences. After they rated a toaster, a coffee pot, a radio, and other products, the students were allowed to choose one product in payment for their participation. Some participants had a chance to choose between two products they had found almost equally desirable—a dissonance-invoking dilemma. After receiving their chosen product and completing some other tasks, the women were asked to evaluate all the products again. Their ratings offered strong support for dissonance theory: The women now evaluated the product they had chosen much more positively than the item they rejected. Consistent with dissonance theory, it's making that choice to have one thing and give up another that triggers dissonance and the need to reduce it. The more people focus on the implications of making a choice—even one not related to the choice they have to make—the greater the need to reduce dissonance, and the greater the evaluative spread between chosen and rejected alternatives (Harmon-Jones & Harmon-Jones, 2002). And taking away the consequences of choice—because, for example, the decision isn't final and you can change your mind again—eliminates the effects of dissonance (Liberman & Foerster, 2006). Dissonance processes help people in a variety of important decision-making situations convince themselves that what they did was right. In one U.S. Presidential election after another, voters are more positive about their preferred candidate and more negative about the other candidate after voting than before. Moreover, those who found the choice difficult show the greatest post-vote evaluative spread between candidates (Beasley & Joslyn, 2001). People are much more confident about their chances of winning after laying their money down than they are before doing so (Knox & Inkster, 1968). And people who start to smoke again after quitting for a while perceive smoking to be less dangerous to their health, compared to their views when they decided to stop and to the views of those who stay nonsmokers (Gibbons, Eggleston, & Benthin, 1997).

THE PROCESSING PAYOFF: JUSTIFYING INCONSISTENT ACTIONS CREATES PERSISTENT ATTITUDES. As we saw in Chapter 7, attitudes that are the result of extensive processing last longer than attitudes changed with little thought. Trying to justify inconsistent behavior prompts people to consider arguments they might otherwise have ignored, generate new evidence, interpret their behavior in new ways, evaluate the consequences of their actions and think about why they feel the way they do (Albarracin & McNatt, 2005). Given the extensive processing required to reduce dissonance, then, it is no surprise that attitude change brought about by dissonance reduction can be long-lasting. All of these processes help solidify the newly changed attitude and inoculate it against further change. Recall that participants in the weight loss experiment described earlier, who must have spent considerable time and effort justifying their participation in the difficult training tasks, were still showing signs of their now positive attitude toward weight loss more than a year later (Axsom & Cooper, 1985). In the same way, the young children who had resisted playing with the attractive toy robot on the basis of minimal deterrence still shunned the toy several weeks later (Freedman, 1965).

Attitude change brought about by dissonance processes can be just as powerful outside the laboratory as in it. In the late 1960s, in the midst of its war in Viet Nam, the United States changed the method used in its draft system to select young men for involuntary military service. Young men were randomly assigned numbers which dictated the order in which they were called up to fight (the person receiving #1 would be the first to be called up, for example). However, men who volunteered for military service through the Reserve Officer Training Corps (ROTC) program on university campuses were usually not assigned immediately to serve in Vietnam. So if you received a low number in the draft and would be one of the first to be called up, joining ROTC would be a good decision, as it reduced your chances of going to Vietnam. But if your draft number was very high and there was little chance you'd be drafted, joining ROTC (with its required training, drills, and week-end missions, and the possibility of future military service) wasn't such a good choice. Barry Staw (1974) took advantage of this naturally occurring "experiment" (complete with random assignment of high or low draft numbers) by tracking the attitudes of men who joined ROTC *before* being assigned their lottery numbers.

Staw reasoned that ROTC enrollees who subsequently received low numbers would feel justified in their decision to enroll—after all, it kept them from being among the first to be drafted and sent to Vietnam. But men who received high numbers probably would have escaped the draft even if they had not joined ROTC. These men were in a classic dissonance-producing situation—they paid a price to belong to a group that hadn't done anything for them. Sure enough, it was these men who apparently engaged in considerable processing aimed at reducing dissonance and restoring cognitive consistency. The evidence? Even over a year later, these men liked ROTC better and performed better in it than those with low draft numbers.

☐ **DISSONANCE PROCESSES AND RESISTING MEDIA INFLUENCE.** These same dissonance-reduction processes can help children resist the effects of violence-ridden Saturday morning television, as Rowell Huesmann and his colleagues (Huesmann, Eron, Klein, Brice, & Fischer, 1983) demonstrated. The first time they tried to teach children to be critical of television violence, the researchers used lectures and demonstrations. These strategies had no effect on the children: Neither their attitudes nor their behavior changed. But when the researchers put the power of dissonance to work, the outcome was quite different. They persuaded the children to "volunteer" to make a videotape to help "other kids" who had been "fooled by television" or who had "got into trouble for imitating what they saw on TV." In acting out anti-television messages for no reward, the children had to justify attitudes inconsistent with their own behavior, a process that apparently helped them persuade themselves. Although they continued to watch as much television as the control participants did, they reported a change in attitude: They were less interested in violent television and less impressed by it. Their behavior changed as well. Whereas the control participants became increasingly aggressive, the experimental children did not. For these children, watching no longer meant doing.

■ **At last—the dissonance diet!**   Does this plate of fried food and burgers look appealing? If you answer no, you may have been influenced by campaigns designed to cut cholesterol consumption. Information about the health effects of eating tasty high-fat foods can trigger the unpleasant arousal associated with dissonance. One way to reduce such dissonance is to alter one's attitude, turning former favorites into something quite different.

ALTERNATIVES TO ATTITUDE CHANGE. You may have noticed that many experimental tests of dissonance theory set up situations in which attitude change is the only avenue by which cognitive dissonance can be reduced and consistency reestablished. Festinger (1957) was the first to point out, however, that people can reduce dissonance in other ways if they have the opportunity. Imagine that you have just broken a month-long diet by eating an entire bag of chocolate chip cookies. Rather than changing your pro-dieting attitude, you could dissipate dissonance at any point in the four steps of the arousal and reduction process. One strategy would be to minimize the inconsistency by trivializing the attitude-discrepant behavior ("A few cookies won't make any difference, and besides, they were low fat"; L. Simon, Greenberg, & Brehm, 1995) or adding cognitions to make it consonant ("Actually, you have to treat yourself once in a while or you just can't stay on a diet"). As an alternative, you might try minimizing personal responsibility ("The cookies were a gift; not eating them would be rude"). Or you could attribute your dissonance-induced arousal to something other than your inconsistent behavior ("All this food deprivation is making me feel grouchy"), thereby feeling no need to reestablish consistency between word and deed.

Measures taken to reduce the uncomfortable tension of dissonance induced arousal can sometimes be harmful. Claude Steele and his colleagues (Steele, Southwick, & Critchlow, 1981) have demonstrated that people may reduce dissonance by using alcohol. These researchers persuaded students to write an essay favoring a big tuition increase—an action clearly inconsistent with their attitudes. Displaying the usual dissonance-induced attitude change, participants given free choice to write the essay became more supportive of the fee hike, except in one condition. Right after writing the essay, some students participated in a "taste-test" in which they drank beer or vodka. These participants showed none of the usual signs of dissonance and failed to change their attitudes. The researchers believe that drinking alcohol eliminated the unpleasant tension of dissonance, so attitude change never occurred. Their conclusion was that alcohol and drug use may be habitual and health-damaging ways in which some people avoid or reduce the tension cognitive dissonance creates in their lives (Steele, 1988; Steele & Southwick, 1985).

Fortunately, a more constructive avenue of reduction is often available. Because the actions and attitudes that trigger dissonance are usually important or self-relevant, people can reduce the uncomfortable tension associated with such inconsistencies by reaffirming their positive sense of self-worth and integrity. Perhaps offering people who have just committed an attitude-discrepant act the opportunity to say: "Hey, I really am a good person, you know" could eliminate attitude change.

Researchers have tested this idea by giving people the chance to donate money, offer help, or reaffirm important values and self-identities just after they acted in ways inconsistent with their attitudes (Dietrich & Berkowitz, 1997; Ruiz & Tanaka, 2001; Tesser & Cornell, 1991). In one study, for example, researchers recruited as participants college students, some of whom were science majors and some of whom were not (Steele, 1988). All participants were asked to rate 10 popular record albums, and they then were given the choice of keeping either their fifth- or sixth-ranked album—a classic decisional-dissonance situation. Participants were then asked to prepare for a second experiment, in which about half of the them would be required to don white lab coats. Then came a surprise task: Everyone was asked to rate all the albums again. Consistent with dissonance theory, most participants reduced the dissonance created by their earlier difficult choice by evaluating their chosen record more highly than the one they had not chosen. But different results were found for one particular group of students, the science majors who had been asked to wear lab coats, a symbol of their values and training. Science students given this opportunity to reaffirm their positive self-identity showed no signs of the usual dissonance-induced attitude change. The potential distress aroused by performing actions inconsistent with a positive view of ourselves can apparently be dissolved by an act that underscores our sense of identity.

And of course, there's sometimes the possibility of changing the attitude-discrepant behavior, rather than changing the behavior-discrepant attitude. Although you might not be able to take back past behavior, tension between important attitudes and behavior can sometimes be reduced by changing future behavior. Imagine being asked to tell a group of high school students the dangers of having unprotected sexual intercourse in an attempt to persuade them to use condoms

You may recall a similar point from Chapter 4, page 129: Some people seem to drink alcohol to reduce the awareness of unpleasant discrepancies between their current selves and their ideal or ought selves.

to prevent the spread of AIDS. Now imagine that just having taken such action, you are asked to make a list of the occasions in which you yourself might not have used a condom. Having just advocated their use, being reminded of your own failure to use condoms might produce a high state of dissonance. Preaching what you might not be practicing is one recipe for hypocrisy, and a considerable threat to self-esteem. What's the best way to restore your faith in yourself? Perhaps it is starting to practice what you preached. That's certainly what Aronson and his colleagues (E. Aronson, Fried, & Stone, 1991; Stone and others, 1997) found when they put college students in just such a position. Compared to other students who merely wrote speeches or thought about their own condom use, those in the hypocrisy conditions—who first stated their positive attitudes toward condom use and then made a list of times they hadn't used condoms—were much more likely to report increasing their use of condoms and to actually buy condoms when given the opportunity. The dissonance created by making hypocritical behavior salient has also been used to improve water conservation and increase donations to homeless shelters.

With many alternatives available, how do people decide how to reduce dissonance? People tend to use whatever means of reducing dissonance is most accessible. For example, people tend to use the reduction opportunity that presents itself first (J. Aronson, Blanton, & Cooper, 1995; L. Simon and others, 1995). Direct ways of reducing dissonance (such as changing inconsistent cognitions) are preferred over indirect ways, such as reaffirming or trying to short-circuit dissonance arousal (Stone and others, 1997). Self-affirmation is a more accessible option for individuals who have many "affirmational resources," such as a large number of alternative positive self-concepts that can be at the ready when one self-image is threatened (Steele, Spencer, & Lynch, 1993). This variety is important because affirming works best in domains unrelated to the dissonance-causing event. In fact, affirmation of the very standards that were violated in the first place can make dissonance worse, not better. For example, lying and then affirming your sense of self as an honest person might make the need for self-justification even more pressing (Blanton, Cooper, Skurnick, & Aronson, 1997). So self-affirmation in an entirely unrelated domain is an easier and more effective route for reducing dissonance. Motivational factors can also influence how dissonance is resolved. For example, although violations of important attitudes trigger dissonance, the very importance of those attitudes makes them unlikely to change in the service of dissonance reduction. In fact, the more important the attitude violated, the less likely it is to be changed in the attempt to reduce dissonance (Devine, Tauer, Barron, Elliot, & Vance, 1999).

Figure 8.4 shows the entire sequence of steps by which dissonance arousal leads to attitude change, and the alternative processes that can either block the arousal of dissonance or reduce dissonance through self-affirmation rather than attitude change. As you can see, behavior that is inconsistent with attitudes can lead to many outcomes, not only to attitude change.

CULTURAL DIFFERENCES AND DISSONANCE. Dissonance seems to arise when an important aspect of the self—a valued attitude, a central self-definition, a well-established standard of behavior—is violated. Such violations, and the dissonance that results from them, can be found in almost every country (Beauvois & Joule, 1996; Joule & Beauvois, 1998; Sakai, 1999). But because the self is viewed differently in different cultures, you might expect that dissonance would be aroused differently in different cultures. That's just what research by

FIGURE 8.4   Alternatives to dissonance and attitude change

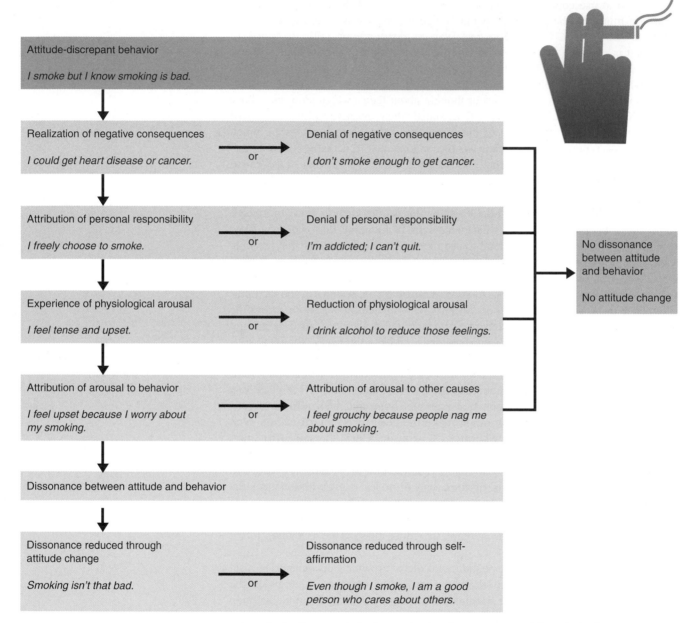

■ An attitude-discrepant behavior may lead to dissonance arousal through the four steps described earlier in the chapter. However, at each step alternatives exist that will block the arousal of dissonance. Even if dissonance is aroused, it can be reduced by self-affirmation instead of by attitude change.

Steven Heine and Darrin Lehman (1997) suggests. They asked members of an independence oriented culture (Canadians) and members of an interdependence-oriented culture (Japanese) to rank a number of compact discs (CDs) and then offered them either their fifth- or sixth-ranked disc to take home. Remember that making such a decision provokes dissonance: Choosing one option means freely giving up all the positive qualities of the other option. Such dissonance is typically resolved by re-evaluating the chosen alternative more positively and the rejected one more negatively. When Canadian participants were asked to rerank the CDs after making their choice, that's just what they did. Japanese participants did not show this effect. Their rerating of the CDs showed no tendency to justify their choice.

How might cultural differences in the sense of self explain this finding? For a member of the independence-oriented culture, the possibility of making a bad decision as an individual may be psychologically threatening and dissonance inducing, but it might not threaten someone whose self is defined more by inter-dependence. On the other hand, imagine that the choice had implications for important others. Now the possibility of making a poor choice that had implications for others might create more dissonance for interdependence-oriented decision makers than independence-oriented ones. Shinobu Kitayama and his colleagues (2004) tested this idea by making the choice of a CD relevant to important others, for European American students and Japanese students. In some conditions, the students just chose CDs in the usual way. In other conditions, the experimenters asked the participants to think about what others would think of their choices, or subtly primed the social presence of others by hanging a poster with faces right in front of the participants. Regardless of condition, American students justified their choices by re-evaluating the chosen CD more positively. Japanese students did so only when the social context of their decision had been made obvious. Thus, it seems that behaviors that violate important attitudes about the self cause dissonance across cultures, but what constitutes such a violation is culturally sensitive.

As we have seen, behaviors can have an impact on attitudes whether we engage in superficial processing or extensive processing. Whenever behaviors are inconsistent with previously established attitudes, self-perception processes or dissonance-reduction processes can come into play to change attitudes in the direction of actions. As you read the studies conducted to test the operation of self-perception and dissonance processes, and thought about the kinds of behaviors they were trying to explain, you may have realized that, in many cases, both processes provided viable explanations. In fact, whether self-perception or dissonance was the correct explanation for the changes that followed attitude-inconsistent behavior was a source of great controversy among social psychologists. The resolution began to become clear when Russell Fazio and his colleagues (1977) compared the conditions under which attitudes changed in response to behaviors that were either mildly or more severely discrepant with previous attitudes. They concluded that when freely chosen but inconsistent actions are relatively trivial—when they do not violate cherished self-images or important attitudes—changed attitudes are inferred with little or no effort. Under these conditions, then, self-perception processes explain the change. In contrast, freely chosen attitude-discrepant actions that trigger emotional arousal, whether because the attitude is important or because the discrepancy is extreme, cause extensive thinking as people work to justify their actions. In these cases, attitudes change in the service of dissonance reduction. Under different conditions and via different processes, both superficial and systematic thinking provide means by which behaviors (as well as the thoughts and feelings discussed in Chapter 7) determine our attitudes. Once attitudes are well established, however, they in turn start to influence what people do.

To remind yourself of the differences between independent cultures (where the self is seen as separate from other people) and interdependent or collectivist cultures (where the self is seen as connected with others), reread Chapter 4, pages 105 to 107.

You may recall that this study was first discussed in Chapter 2, page 46, as an example of how theories might complement rather than compete with each other.

Guiding Actions with Attitudes

"Attitudes determine for each individual what he [or she] will do" wrote Gordon Allport more than half a century ago (Allport, 1935, p. 806). This basic tenet of social psychology—that attitudes direct behavior—is the driving force behind decades of research on how attitudes can be formed and changed. After all, if attitudes guide actions, then knowing something about people's attitudes permits the prediction of behavior. And if attitudes guide actions, changing attitudes—about ourselves, others, objects, events, and issues—permits behavioral change. If we convince the patient that the drug is a good one, she will take it as prescribed; if we convert the atheist to our religion, he will act on the teachings of the faith; if we persuade the consumer that vehicle emissions are causing global warming, she will buy the suggested hybrid vehicle. Research has provided a lot of evidence to justify these optimistic statements. Attitudes often do go hand in hand with behaviors. Attitudes toward politicians closely predict voting (Schuman & Johnson, 1976). Attitudes about social drinking dictate how much wine, beer, and spirits people are likely to consume (Kahle & Berman, 1979). Pregnant women's attitudes about breastfeeding versus bottlefeeding accurately foretell how their babies will be fed at 6 weeks of age (Manstead, Plevin, & Smart, 1984; Manstead, Proffitt, & Smart, 1983). Attitudes influence behaviors that range from blood and organ donations to use of contraception or illegal drugs to participation in psychology experiments and cleaning up the environment. In a recent meta-analysis of 88 studies, Stephan Kraus (1995) confirmed that attitudes have a significant and substantial impact on future actions.

But this is not always the case. Perhaps because attitudes and behavior often go hand in hand, we are jolted when they seem glaringly inconsistent. Plenty of newspaper headlines and newscast stories were generated, for example, when a recent survey of more than 12,000 U.S. teenagers found that 88% of those who had made public their opposition to premarital sex by taking a chastity vow had nevertheless had sexual intercourse before marriage (Bearman, 2003). But social psychologists had been documenting attitude–action mismatches for some time. Back in 1934, Robert LaPiere found that despite treating a Chinese couple who visited their hotel and restaurant quite courteously, an overwhelming majority of the hotel and restaurant managers later expressed negative attitudes toward serving Chinese visitors at all (LaPiere, 1934). Another early study found large discrepancies between college students' attitudes about cheating and their actual behavior (Corey, 1937). Having ascertained their attitudes toward cheating, researchers gave students an opportunity to cheat by asking them to grade their own tests. Actually, the true/false tests had already been graded, so the difference between the real grade and the one students reported could be used as an index of cheating. In these tempting circumstances, many students did in fact cheat. More important from a theoretical point of view, however, was the absence of a relationship between students' attitudes about cheating and their actual cheating. Those who were strongly opposed to cheating were just as likely to cheat as those who were not so opposed. Other studies have shown similar gaps between attitudes and behavior. So the answer to the question: "Do attitudes guide behavior?" seemed to be a very unsatisfactory: "Sometimes!"

At the same time, it became clear to social psychologists that many of the behaviors they were most interested in—healthy or unhealthy lifestyle choices, social and political behaviors, patterns of consumption—seemed to be influenced more by sheer habit than by anything else. *Habits* are behaviors that are automatically triggered in particular situations. They result from associations that develop between an often-repeated or well-practiced action and particular features of the enviroment, such as a particular location or a recognizable body state. Habitual behaviors—like reaching for a snack when you read the paper, turning on the TV when you walk in the house, or lighting up a cigarette as soon as you get in the car—are performed quite independently of attitudes or norms, indeed with little conscious input of any kind (Ouellette & Wood, 1998; Verplanken, Aarts, van Knippenberg, & Moonen, 1998; Wood, Tam, & Witt, 2005). Habits are triggered in particular situations so automatically that people "find themselves" in the middle of acting before they realize they have acted (Triandis, 1977, 1980). Smokers, for example, often notice they are smoking but do not recall having decided to smoke or lighting the cigarette (Ikard, Green, & Horn, 1969). Even everyday habits like watching TV or reading the newspaper depend largely on environmental cues like location (Wood and others, 2005). Although habits can be positive, like automatically fastening the seat belt as soon as you sit down in a car, many habitual behaviors like nail biting, overeating, excessive television watching, and smoking continue even in the face of people's obvious desire to stop them. For all of us frustrated by the failure of our latest crop of New Year's Resolutions, it's clear that bad habits can be quite resistant to our good attitudes and intentions.

Faced with the fact that attitudes did not seem to reliably predict behavior either inside or outside the laboratory, some social psychologists suggested that the concept of attitudes should be abandoned altogether (Wicker, 1969). This was clearly an overreaction. But it did cause social psychologists to think carefully about the role of attitudes in eliciting, modifying, and inhibiting behavior. Rather than asking: "Do attitudes guide behavior?", researchers began asking: "How do attitudes guide behavior?" By understanding *how* behavior was influenced by attitudes, they hoped to learn *when* attitudes would influence behavior. This change in tactics led to a new understanding of the processes by which attitudes are translated into action.

How Attitudes Guide Behavior

Established attitudes can guide behaviors in a very direct way. Attitudes bias perceptions, thereby making attitude-consistent information about objects, people, and events more obvious and attitude-consistent behavior more likely. Attitudes also influence behavior in a more considered way by prompting intentions to act in certain ways. Intentions in turn can trigger planning that makes attitude-consistent behavior more likely.

What is it about attitudes that makes the performance of attitude-consistent behavior more likely? How does favoring one politician translate into voting for the favored candidate? Or having a negative attitude toward drinking dictate lifelong abstinence? It might not surprise you to learn that attitude researchers have come to see that attitudes can have an impact on behaviors in two different ways. One way in which attitudes influence behavior is to trigger consistent behaviors quite directly, with very little thinking. When the attitude comes to mind, it sets in motion certain processes that quite straightforwardly make an attitude-consistent course of action more likely than any other, just as seeing the well-loved face of a spouse might almost automatically cause us to lean forward for an embrace. At the same time, however, attitudes can also influence behaviors after extensive and deliberate consideration. The type of deliberative processing that seems most important to producing attitude-consistent behavior is the formation of intentions (Fazio, 1990; Strack & Deutsch, 2004). Imagine that you have formed a very positive evaluation of the young stranger who sits a few rows down from you in the lecture hall. You may well agonize over all the advantages and disadvantages of acting on that evaluation before forming an intention: to ask him to join you for a coffee after the lecture. In this case, extensive processing occurs before the attitude is translated into attitude-consistent behavior.

ATTITUDES GUIDE BEHAVIOR WITHOUT MUCH THOUGHT. Sometimes attitude–behavior connections seem to occur without any effortful thought. Consider, for example, the way participants responded to the opportunity to choose five small snacks (such as a Mounds candy bar, Dentyne gum, a packet of raisins) as payment for participation in an experiment (Fazio, Blascovich, & Driscoll, 1992). Earlier in the session, participants had indicated whether they liked or disliked a large number of products, including the offered snacks. Participants who held well-formed attitudes about the snacks (as indicated by their speedy responses) were much more likely to make choices consistent with their attitudes than were the participants who were uncertain of their likes and dislikes (as indicated by their slow responses). Well-established attitudes offer handy evaluative summaries of their attitude objects. They make deciding what to do easier and are therefore more likely to guide behavior (Armitage & Conner, 2000; A. Liberman, de la Hoz, & Chaiken, 1988). Such well-established attitudes seem to be able to guide action quite directly: Preferred snacks were chosen and less-favored snacks were left on the table. What is it about the presence of an attitude that can guide behavior in this automatic fashion?

The answer is that attitudes can bias perceptions, literally changing the way people see an attitude object. Attitudes focus attention on some characteristics of the stimulus and away from others. Like blinders on a horse, attitudes guide people toward information consistent with their attitudes and away from evidence that contradicts them (Fazio, 1986, 1990; Frey, 1986). A favorable attitude makes the positive qualities of the object more obvious. A negative attitude, on the other hand, makes the object's unfavorable attributes most salient. For those who love ice cream, the sight of a large bowl of it brings to mind its delicious flavor and smooth, creamy taste. Those who dislike it are likely to think of its many calories and high fat content. Amazingly, attitudes dictate the perception of objects to such an extent that people have a tough time realizing that the objects have changed. In one clever experiment showing this effect, some students rehearsed their attitudes toward photos of other people whereas other students saw the photos an equal number of times but didn't develop attitudes toward the photographed targets (Fazio, Ledbetter, & Towles-Schwen, 2000). Everyone was then shown pictures of the targets that differed in subtle ways from the original snapshots. People who had clearly developed attitudes were less likely to notice the differences, took longer to accurately identify what was different, and were convinced that the differences were smaller than people without well-developed attitudes! Having an attitude made the objects look a certain way, and that's the way people saw them.

Thus, our attitudes typically bias our perceptions of the attitude object. This process increases the likelihood that behavior consistent with the attitude will be elicited in a rather straightforward way. Favorable attitudes make the positive qualities of the object more obvious (*mmm*, that delicious flavor and creamy taste),

If you're thinking that these processes are similar to ones that occur when attitudes are defended, you're right. Recall from Chapter 7, pages 259 to 262 that people often focus on attitude-consistent information and distort and reinterpret information inconsistent with their attitudes. This process makes the attitude-consistent features of the attitude object more salient and its attitude-inconsistent features less obvious.

whereas negative attitudes make the object's unfavorable attributes salient (*yuck*, all that fat and calories). If people then respond to the qualities of the objects that are most salient to them, attitude-consistent behaviors are likely to follow (Eagly & Chaiken, 1993). Focusing on flavor and taste will probably lead to spoon wielding; focusing on calories and fat makes backing firmly away from the table more likely.

In sum, attitudes about objects can directly influence actions. Attitudes direct our attention to particular aspects of an object and influence our interpretations of the object. As a result, attitude-consistent behavior is more likely, and people can act on their attitudes in a relatively straightforward manner. At other times, however, attitudes play a role in a more complex sequence of action-producing events.

ATTITUDES GUIDE BEHAVIOR THROUGH CONSIDERED INTENTIONS. Attitudes can also guide behavior in a much more considered and thoughtful way. When people deliberately attempt to make their behavior consistent with their attitudes, they usually put considerable effort into forming intentions to act in a particular way (Ajzen & Fishbein, 1980). Intentions typically specify a behavior thought to achieve a goal. For example, if your old clunker keeps breaking down and you have formed a positive attitude toward buying a new car, you may thoughtfully consider a great deal of information as you form an intention to buy a new one.

Once intentions are in place, they are the single most important predictor of actual behavior (Fishbein & Ajzen, 1975). This is the central idea of the *theory of reasoned action*, which argues that attitudes, together with social norms, as we discuss in Chapter 10, are an important source of intentions, which in turn produce behavior. Thus, knowing a person's intentions, whether they intend to buy a new car within the next year or to finish a term paper by Friday, gives us the best chance of accurately predicting the person's future behavior: purchasing the car or completing the assignment. In fact, getting people to form intentions powerfully increases the chance that the intended behavior will be performed (Fitzsimmons, 2004). No wonder then that intentions to act have been found to be good predictors of a wide variety of important social behaviors, including donating blood, voting, using family planning techniques, attending church, eating out, practicing dental hygiene, having an abortion, smoking cigarettes, and participating in on-the-job training (Albarracin, Johnson, Fishbein, & Mullerleile, 2001).

Intentions help translate attitudes into behavior by bringing to mind all we know about performing the intended behavior (L. Sternberg, 1990). Intentions can range from the very general to the very specific, and the level at which we think about our intentions determines the kind of information about potential behaviors that will be activated (Wegner & Vallacher, 1986). For example, a very general intention—"Time to lose some weight!"—brings to mind various options by which this intention can be carried out, such as cutting back on fats and sugars, signing up for a weight-loss program, or taking an aerobics class. But a very specific intention—"I intend to reduce my fat intake to no more than 30% of my daily calories"—is likely to activate corresponding specific behavioral information focused on fat reduction: "Eat more fruits and grains." "Forget the ice cream and the sausages." Forming more specific intentions often helps us carry out desired behaviors because more specific behavioral options come to mind, and that actually helps achieve the behavioral goal. On the other hand, broad intentions allow us more flexibility to adopt alternative plans (Gollwitzer, 1996). It is perhaps not surprising, then, that thinking about behaviors that have to be performed in the near future tends to be more specific, whereas thinking about distant actions tends to be more abstract and general (N. Liberman & Trope, 1998).

Once intentions have been formed and relevant behavioral information has been activated, the next step is planning (Gollwitzer & Moskowitz, 1996). Each behavioral option that comes to mind might be weighed and considered until the optimal way of carrying through on the intention is selected. Imagine how complicated it might be to carry through on an intention like reducing fat intake to 30% of daily calories. Successful execution of the intention might entail finding out which foods contain fat, learning to prepare meals without fat, dealing with cravings for fatty foods, and so forth.

With intentions in place, behavioral knowledge activated, and plans selected, we are ready to carry out intended behavior if an opportunity presents itself. Of course, once we start acting, our actions may or may not accomplish our intention. For this reason, people monitor their behavior against their intentions: If the behavior seems to reduce the gap between the present state and the desired state, the behavior continues until the goal is attained. If, on the other hand, the action seems ineffective, it may be increased in intensity, replaced by a new plan, or eventually abandoned altogether (Carver & Scheier, 1990; Gollwitzer, 1996). As part of this monitoring process, people mentally keep track of intentions that they haven't yet made good on. Studies show that people respond more quickly to material related to incomplete intentions than to those that have been successfully carried out, indicating that unfulfilled goals and plans are more accessible (Marsh, Hicks, & Bink, 1998).

Emotions are also part of the system that regulates action and monitors goal attainment. Positive emotions can motivate intentions and plans and signal successful completion of subgoals, whereas negative emotions indicate frustration or failure and prompt revision of current attempts to reach the goal (Oatley & Johnson-Laird, 1987; N. L. Stein, Liwag, & Wade, 1996). In one study of 406 Dutch men and women trying to avoid weight gain, Richard Bagozzi, Hans Baumgartner, and Rik Pieters (1998) showed how all these factors worked together to help people turn positive attitudes into attitude-consistent behavior. The positive emotions participants anticipated experiencing on reaching their goals helped promote intentions and plans to exercise and diet, which in turn contributed to successful performance of such behavior. Performing those behaviors—eating less, exercising more—translated into greater weight loss. Reaching their goals made people feel good, and so emotions fed back to keep attitudes, intentions, plans, and behavior on track.

By influencing intentions, then, attitudes can guide attitude-consistent behavior in a more considered and thoughtful way. This does not mean that attitudes, intentions, and plans are deliberately formed anew each time you enter a new situation (Ajzen & Fishbein, 1980). An intention, and a plan to carry it out, may have been formed quite deliberately and systematically at some time in the past, but might later pop into mind almost automatically whenever a relevant attitude object or particular situation is confronted (Gollwitzer & Schaal, 1998). A patriotic attitude, for example, may at one point have led to the conscious intention of singing a national song before a sporting match, but that behavior may now, after many repetitions, be performed virtually without thought.

When do attitudes trigger consistent behaviors directly versus deliberately? It is probably obvious that thinking about attitudes in relation to intentions, and about intentions in relation to behavior, involves much more systematic processing than the superficial processing that occurs when attitudes guide behaviors more

FIGURE 8.5 Superficial and thoughtful routes from attitude to behaviour

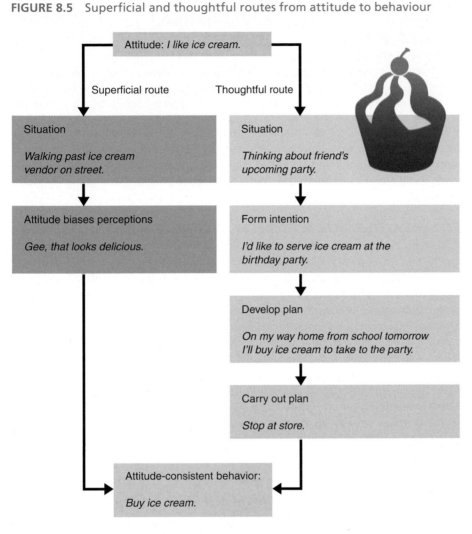

■ Attitudes can influence behaviour relatively automatically by influencing people's immediate perceptions. At other times, the effect of attitudes on behavior occurs with more thought when people plan and carry out intentions that results in attitude-consistent behavior.

directly, the two routes shown in Figure 8.5. Given that systematic processing requires a lot more effort and concentration than responding in a knee-jerk fashion to salient features of an attitude object, it's not surprising that motivation and opportunity to engage in thinking dictate whether attitudes affect behavior with either little thought or considerable thought (Fazio, 1990). Just as we saw that persuasion in routine situations was more likely to occur through superficial than systematic processing, most routine behavior is undoubtedly the result of less thoughtful reliance on activated attitudes. After all, the motivation and capacity necessary for systematic thinking are precious commodities. So when careful consideration is not possible (because the behavior has to occur immediately, for example) or when choices are not important, behavior may follow quite straightforwardly from how the attitude object is viewed. When the stakes are high and extensive thinking is possible, however, attitudes may influence behavior through their impact on intentions.

When Do Attitudes Influence Action?

If attitudes are to guide actions, attitudes must be readily accessible and appropriate to the intended behavior. Attitudes can be made accessible by deliberate thought, self-awareness, or frequent use. Only attitudes relevant to a particular behavior will be able to guide that behavior. Finally, behavior is more likely to reflect attitudes if people both believe they have control and actually do have control over behavior.

What has to happen for an attitude to guide behavior? How can we increase the likelihood that people will act on their socially useful and constructive attitudes? Answering the question of how attitudes guide actions has helped social psychologists specify two conditions that must be meet if attitudes are going to guide behaviors.

ATTITUDE ACCESSIBILITY: ATTITUDES MUST COME TO MIND. If it is the attitude that changes perception of the object, and the attitude that triggers plans and intentions, we need to make sure that the attitude is brought to mind if attitude-consistent behavior is to occur. We're not likely to focus on the positive features of the latest fuel-efficient sedan or form intentions to start comparing prices at local dealerships unless we are aware of our positive attitude toward such vehicles. So to have any effect on behavior, attitudes about objects, events, people, or ideas must come to mind at the right time (Fazio, 1990; Lord & Lepper, 1999). Some people's inner convictions seem to come to mind more easily most of the time. Low self-monitors, for example, for whom expressing the true self is important, have more accessible attitudes than high self-monitors (DeBono and Snyder, 1995; Kardes, Sanbonmatsu, Voss, & Fazio, 1986). Not surprisingly, then, low self-monitors are more likely to practice what they preach (Kraus, 1995). But you don't have to be a low self-monitor to show such consistency. There are a number of other ways in which attitudes can be brought to mind at the right time to influence behavior.

1. *Deliberately making attitudes accessible.* Attitudes can be brought to mind by deliberate effort. Before taking action, you might think about a relevant attitude for a few minutes, and thus ensure that the attitude has more impact on your behavior. Mark Snyder and William Swann (1976) demonstrated this idea in a study of attitudes toward affirmative action employment policies. Undergraduate men served as jurors in mock sex-discrimination trials. Some of the men were given "a few minutes to organize your thoughts and views on the affirmative action issue" before hearing the case, whereas others were not. Only those who were first encouraged to bring their attitude to mind reached verdicts consistent with their attitudes (which had been measured in a separate session 2 weeks earlier). Even overhearing someone else discussing an issue can be enough to make your attitude on the topic come to mind, and thus to increase the impact your attitude then has on your behavior (Borgida & Campbell, 1982).

   Of course, people do not always recognize the relevance of a particular attitude. In these cases, being reminded of the relationship of an attitude to the task at hand can increase the attitude's impact on behavior. To demonstrate this point, Mark Snyder and Deborah Kendzierski (1982) set up another mock trial, also of a sex-discrimination case, in which jurors were or were not reminded of their own attitudes before coming to a verdict. One group of mock jurors was encouraged to think about their views on affirmative action before being presented with the case. Another group of participants was not only encouraged to review their attitudes but was specifically informed that the issue of affirmative action, and thus their attitudes toward it, were relevant to the case they were about to hear. A third group received no reminder at all. Compared with the third group, the participants in the two groups that received reminders reached verdicts that were more consistent with their prior attitudes. In addition, the participants explicitly reminded that their attitudes were relevant to the judgment at hand showed even greater consistency between attitude and verdict than did those who were merely encouraged to think about their attitudes.

The opposite result—decreased consistency between attitude and behavior—may occur when people are led to deliberate about something other than the relevant attitude right before making a behavioral choice. Imagine, for example, that you have always loved posters of August Macke's prints because the vivid colors make you feel so cheerful. If allowed to choose a poster to take home as a reward for participation in an experiment, your positive attitude would probably guide you to pick a Macke print. But what if right before you made the choice, you were required to think about other things relevant to the choice, or aspects of the poster on which your attitude was not based—to focus on its artistic merit or its fit with the color scheme in your living room, or whether Macke prints were becoming too popular, for example? Making something other than the relevant attitude accessible might disrupt the attitude–behavior link. In one experiment that tested this idea, one group of students was asked to analyze their thoughts about various art posters before choosing one to take home. Compared with students who were not required to analyze their thoughts (and presumably just relied on their attitudes to pick their poster), the students required to take other considerations into account were more likely to take home a poster they originally had not liked. They also were more likely to regret their choice later (Millar & Tesser, 1986; Wilson and others, 1993). When the relevant attitude is not uppermost in the actor's mind at the time action is called for, its impact on behavior is reduced.

2. *Making attitudes accessible through self-awareness*. Making people *self-aware* also makes it more likely that important attitudes will come to mind. When people hear their own voices, see themselves unexpectedly in a shop window or store mirror, stand in front of an audience, or become the center of attention in a group, they are reminded of the extent to which they measure up to their inner convictions (Duval & Wicklund, 1972; Gibbons, 1978).

Does such a reminder promote attitude–behavior consistency? In a further exploration of the conditions under which college students give in to the urge to improve a test score, Ed Diener and Mark Wallbom (1976) looked at the impact of self-awareness on the temptation to cheat. Their participants were given anagrams to solve and told that the timed task was a test of intelligence. Left alone in the exam room (but surreptitiously observed), 71% of the students worked after hearing a bell that indicated the time was up. When other students carried out the same task either in front of a large mirror or while listening to their own tape-recorded voices, only 7% cheated. Next time you notice the mirrored walls and alcoves of a large department store, consider the possibility that their presence provides shoppers with opportunities to become momentarily self-aware, particularly about their attitudes about honesty.

If you have forgotten what we mean by the link between an attitude object and the attitude associated with it, refer to Figure 7.2 on page 237 for a quick refresher. Recall that because of that link, thinking about almost any object also brings to mind the positive or negative evaluation associated with it.

3. *Making attitudes accessible automatically*. Think how much more powerful an influence an attitude could have on behavior if the attitude came to mind automatically in the right situation, rather than having to be deliberately brought to mind. Of course, the more often an attitude is brought to mind, the more often the link between attitude object and attitude is activated, and the more likely that the attitude will come to mind whenever the attitude object is encountered (Fazio, 1989; Fazio, Chen, McDonel, & Sherman, 1982). Many factors can strengthen attitude–object links. Some such connections might be partially innate, for example to help us take immediate action whenever we perceive a dangerous or nurturing stimulus (Frijda, Kuipers, & ter Shure, 1989; Tesser, 1993). Others are built up through constant activation, deliberation, discussion, and action (Fazio, 1989). Not surprisingly then, attitudes that come to mind frequently and easily are more likely to produce consistent behavior (Fazio and others, 1982).

What kinds of attitudes have these qualities? Attitudes built up by direct interaction and practice with attitude objects—ones frequently activated along with the attitude object—are more likely to direct consistent behavior than more abstract "hearsay"-based attitudes (Fazio & Zanna, 1981). The same is true of attitudes formed on the basis of considerable issue-relevant thinking—attitudes accorded such cognitive processing both come to mind more readily and are more likely to be followed by attitude-consistent behavior (Petty, Haugtvedt, & Smith, 1995; W. Wood, Rhodes, & Beik, 1995). Attitudes that are personally important—ones that people are concerned about and believe to be significant—are also more likely to be spontaneously activated in a wide variety of information-processing and decision-making situations. As you might predict, then, they are also more likely to be used as guides for a wide range of attitude-relevant actions (Boniger, Krosnick, & Berent, 1995). In the same way, well-established and frequently used political attitudes are much more likely than less accessible attiudes to predict voting (Kallgren & Wood, 1986) and well-established environmental attitudes are good predictors of ecological behavior (Davidson, Yantis, Norwood, & Monano, 1985).

☐ **ATTITUDE ACCESSIBILITY IN CLINICAL SETTINGS.** Research on this attitude–behavior link has practical implications for dealing with bad habits. Recall that these repeated behaviors are often evoked by familiar situations in such a way that neither attitudes nor intentions have any impact on them. Bad habits—like nail-biting and overeating—are almost by definition repeated behaviors that continue in the face of inconsistent attitudes and intentions.

People can gain attitudinal control over these impulses, but only with tremendous effort. To do so, attitudes must be deliberately activated over and over again in high-risk situations (McFall, 1977). Every time you bite your finger nails when you feel put on the spot, or grab a candy bar as you pass a vending machine, you have to take a few moments to organize your thoughts and views and bring those important attitudes to mind. Former smokers, drinkers, and drug users face an even tougher battle. The first smoke, hit, or drink taken by smokers, heroin addicts, and alcoholics who "fall off the wagon" usually happens in a high-risk situation, like a bar, in which the habitual behavior previously occurred (Hunt, Matarazzo, Weiss, & Gentry, 1979). Because developing and activating appropriate attitudes can be hard at first, programs attempting to break such old habits often recommend that addicts avoid the triggering situation. In fact a change in context is one of the best predictors of successful change in habits (Heatherton & Nichols, 1994), and as behavior is less influenced by the environment it becomes more under the control of attitudes and intentions (Wood, Tam, & Witt 2005).

Of course, good habits can be learned and strengthened by activating attitudes over and over again. If you want to bring your behavior into line with your new pro-environmental views or eliminate your tendency to form stereotyped judgments, focusing for a few moments on the relevant attitudes before you act will increase the chances that those worthy attitudes will guide your behavior (Devine & Monteith, 1993). With lots of practice, positive attitudes can become so firmly attached to their attitude objects that they come spontaneously to mind, bringing the appropriate behavior with them. Seatbelt use becomes much more likely when people, because of repeatedly performing the behavior in a given situation, automatically reach for the belt as they sit down in the vehicle. When positive attitudes and intentions have taken control of behavior back over, it's good to make that link so frequent that the desired behavior is again triggered by the environment.

ATTITUDE COMPATIBILITY: THE RIGHT ATTITUDE MUST COME TO MIND. If attitudes dictate perceptions of and intentions toward a particular attitude object, they will have their greatest effect on behavior toward that attitude object. If we are busy thinking about our attitude toward recycling, it's probably not going to have much impact on how we see or what intentions we form about the newest fuel-efficient vehicle. For an attitude to guide behavior, the right attitude must come to mind at the right time. Think about the issue of environmental conservation. You may favor conservation as a general principle, but that is not your only environmental attitude. You probably have several related and increasingly specific attitudes toward implementation, e.g., toward downsizing landfills, using recycled aluminum cans versus glass or plastic bottles, or cutting down on automobile emissions. It isn't enough if just any vaguely related attitude comes to mind when we contemplate action—how we feel about glass bottles is irrelevant at the gas pump. Only an attitude appropriate and relevant for a particular behavior can be expected to influence that behavior (Schwarz, Groves & Schumann, 1998).

To influence a specific behavior, specific attitudes must come to mind (Eckes & Six, 1994; Kraus, 1995). When researchers tried to predict whether women would use birth-control pills during a 2-year period, they found that the women's specific attitudes about birth-control pills were better predictors than their attitudes toward birth control in general (Davidson & Jaccard, 1979). An attitude about performing the behavior in question ("What's your opinion on curbside recycling?") is the best predictor of whether or not the behavior occurs (Eagly & Chaiken, 1993; McIntyre, Paulson, Lord, & Lepper, 2004). Whether you want to improve health habits, change environmental practices, or increase support for worthy causes, it is important to bring an attitude compatible with the desired behavior to mind.

Research by Charles Lord and his colleagues (Lord, Lepper & Mackie, 1984; Sia, Lord, Blessum, Ratcliff, & Lepper, 1997) makes a similar point. These researchers asked male undergraduates whether they would be willing to show a hypothetical transferring student, John B., around the Princeton campus. John was identified (ostensibly by a counseling psychologist at his current school) as being gay. Would participants' attitudes about gays influence their willingness to spend time with John? The researchers hypothesized that this would be true only if John matched the students' expectations of typical gay men. To test this idea, participants were asked to read a description of John that either closely matched or largely disconfirmed their stereotype. When John's description matched students' pre-conceptions, their attitudes (whether positive or negative) toward gays were highly correlated with their willingness to interact with him. Participants acted in line with their attitudes: if John seemed to be a "typical" gay, students who disliked gays wanted to have nothing to do with him whereas students with positive attitudes toward gays were quite happy to show him around. When John did not appear to match the preconception, participants' attitudes, whether positive or negative, had no impact. Attitude–behavior consistency can only be expected when the attitude object (what or whom you think about when asked your opinion) and the target of behavior (what or whom you act toward when given the opportunity) are the same (Ajzen, 1996).

Such findings might help explain one of the classic studies that made social psychologists wonder if attitudes did guide behavior at all. Recall the study in which managers' attitudes toward serving Chinese were not at all consistent with treatment of a well-dressed Chinese couple who asked to dine or stay at their hotel or restaurant? Given the stereotypes of the day, it is likely that the managers' attitudes were based on images of and experiences with Chinese laborers. Faced with a target of behavior (the well-dressed couple) that was very different from the attitude object (the uneducated laborer) they had no doubt thought about when asked their opinion, no wonder the managers' attitudes did not predict their behavior.

IMPLICIT AND EXPLICIT ATTITUDES AS GUIDES FOR BEHAVIOR. If only an attitude that is appropriate and relevant for a particular behavior can be expected to influence that behavior, what does that say about when implicit attitudes will affect behaviors? Recall from Chapter 7 that people's implicit attitudes, ones that reflect their automatic evaluations of objects, can diverge from their explicit attitudes, the ones they consciously endorse and overtly express (Fazio & Olson, 2003). As we noted, most people have an implicit automatic negative evaluation of spiders and snakes, for example, even though many people's explicit attitudes toward these same objects are neutral or even positive. These differences can arise because implicit and explicit attitudes reflect different kinds of information about an object. Implicit attitudes might reflect more automatic, less controllable aspects of evaluations, like hard-wired positive and negative affective reactions, or associations built up from frequent pairing of the attitude object with positive or negative events. In contrast, explicit attitudes reflect our conscious thoughts and considered reactions to the object.

If all this is true, then we might expect implicit and explicit attitudes to guide different kinds of behaviors, and that is just what researchers have found. In one study, student participants completed both an implicit association test (a measure of implicit attitudes) and an explicit questionnaire about their attitudes toward the soda brands Coke and Pepsi (Karpinski, Steinman, & Hilton, 2005). They were then asked how they thought they would act if offered a free Pepsi or Coke product. The students' explicit attitudes toward the sodas were a much better predictor than the implicit measure of this highly deliberate and controllable behavior. In contrast, in another study soda drinkers also completed implicit and explicit measures of their attitudes toward Coke and Pepsi, but their behavioral preference for the sodas was measured in a blind taste-test (Maison, Greenwald, & Bruin, 2004). Because reactions to tastes are much less controllable and deliberate, the participants' responses in the taste-test were better predicted by their implicit attitudes.

Recall that just the same kinds of findings were reported in Chapter 5, pages 165 to 166: Implicit measures of prejudice are more closely related to subtle nonverbal behaviors toward out-groups, whereas explicit attitudes are better predictors of more deliberative verbal behavior toward out-groups.

The fact that implicit and explicit attitudes often influence different kinds of behaviors may help explain why important attitudes are such good predictors of a wide range of attitude relevant behaviors, as we mentioned above. For important attitudes, implicit and explicit attitudes tend to be consistent, so both work together to guide both spontaneous and more controlled behaviors (Karpinski and others, 2005). But when implicit and explicit attitudes differ, either one might be a more influential guide for action, depending on just what the action is. For more spontaneous behaviors, an implicit attitude that is activated automatically will generally influence behavior. For more deliberative and consciously considered behaviors, explicit attitudes (whether automatically or intentionally brought to mind) might be the most important. Whether an attitude is general or specific, and whether it is implicit or explicit, the same principle applies: the right attitude has to come to mind to guide behavior.

WHEN ATTITUDES ARE NOT ENOUGH. Even though the right attitude may come to mind at the right time, it still may not be enough to dictate behavior. People do not act on attitudes if they think they cannot perform the required behavior (Liska, 1984). Perceptions of *personal control*—whether people feel capable of action—thus have a big influence on behavior. When people think they can control their behavior, attitudes can become highly effective in mobilizing and sustaining effective action. A sense of control has been shown to facilitate effective weight loss (Sheppard, Hartwick, & Warshaw, 1988), performance of breast self-examinations (Alagna & Reddy, 1984), and the expectation and achievement of success at stopping smoking (Eiser & Sutton, 1977; Eiser, van der Pligt, Raw, & Sutton, 1985). In contrast, overeaters who believe obesity is due to hormonal factors, smokers who attribute their behavior to addiction, and drivers who believe being in a car wreck is a matter of fate have no reason to follow through on even a relevant attitude and therefore do not do so (Ajzen & Madden, 1986; Bandura, 1982; Eiser & van der Pligt, 1986; Ronis & Kaiser, 1989). Such findings led Icek Ajzen (1991) to propose that perceptions of control work along with attitudes to produce the intentions that then drive or derail attitude-consistent behavior.

Of course, even when our attitudes are positive, our intentions are firm, and we perceive ourselves to be in control, unforeseen circumstances or lack of ability can prevent us from following through on behavior. A would-be voter who cannot get transportation to the polls cannot translate his political attitudes into action. Many useful and much-wanted consumer products are so expensive that desire cannot be translated into ownership. So even when we think we have control, we don't always actually have the objective control to carry through on our attitudes and intentions. This is particularly true when attitude-consistent behavior requires social interaction, that is, when we need other people to help us act on our attitudes. An uncooperative spouse may sabotage the best-laid plans to discipline the children. An old-fashioned boss may squash attempts to introduce a parental-leave policy in a company. Intentions to conserve energy and lower utility bills may be undermined

■ **A clear choice?** This wide selection of bottled water illustrates how attitudes affect decision making. How does a consumer choose among products when there is no clear evidence of one product's superiority? It is likely most bottled water consumers base their decisions on factors that have nothing to do with product quality, such as recognition of a brand name or seeing a more attractive label.

We have already seen in Chapter 4 how important perceived control is to individual striving for mastery. The impact that perceiving control has on individual action will be discussed again in Chapter 10, pages 385 to 387,

FIGURE 8.6   When do attitudes guide behavior?

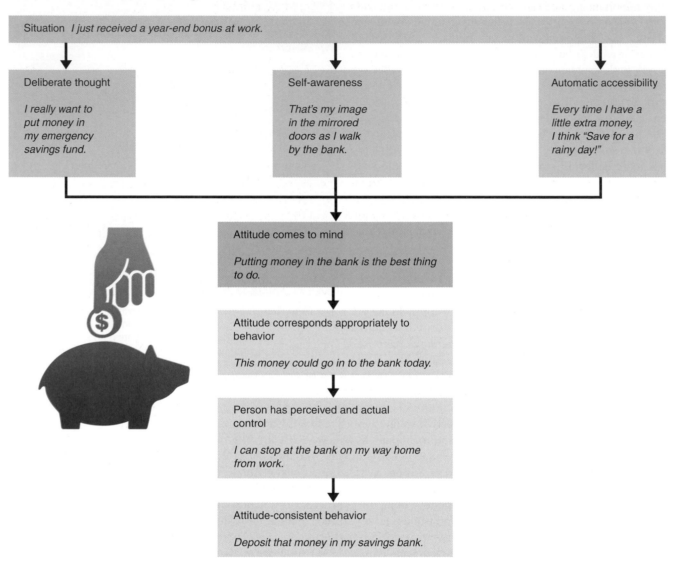

Situation   *I just received a year-end bonus at work.*

Deliberate thought

I really want to put money in my emergency savings fund.

Self-awareness

That's my image in the mirrored doors as I walk by the bank.

Automatic accessibility

Every time I have a little extra money, I think "Save for a rainy day!"

Attitude comes to mind

Putting money in the bank is the best thing to do.

Attitude corresponds appropriately to behavior

This money could go in to the bank today.

Person has perceived and actual control

I can stop at the bank on my way home from work.

Attitude-consistent behavior

Deposit that money in my savings bank.

■ For attitudes to guide behavior, several processes must occur. Most important, the attitude must come to mind, either intentionally or automatically. If an attitude that comes to mind also meets the additional conditions shown, attitude-consistent behavior is a likely result.

by family members who leave on lights and open windows in air-conditioned rooms. Although attitudes are personal, we often need interpersonal cooperation to carry through on them.

No wonder, then, that it's a long step from having an attitude to acting on it. Whether we are deciding what to eat for breakfast or whether to join the armed forces, a behavioral decision, like all judgments large and small, depends on the information that goes into it. Attitudes are an important element in the behavioral equation, but they are seldom the only source of information relevant to action.

As Figure 8.6 shows, attitudes are most likely to influence actions when the attitude comes to mind, when the attitude is appropriate, and when attitude-consistent behavior is not constrained in any other way. When we understand how attitudes influence behaviors, we come to see some of the complexities involved in getting attitudes to influence behavior in everyday situations.

CONCLUDING COMMENTS

 A greater understanding of how our inner selves fit with our outer selves—of how behaviors can shape attitudes and attitudes can shape behaviors—is one of the most significant contributions that social-psychological research offers us. Research on attitudes and behaviors often goes against the accepted wisdom. Consider these counterintuitive findings.

- Most people would *never* guess that behavior has an impact on our attitudes. Yet when we casually give money to the homeless person on the corner, or murmur support for the boss's unworkable plan, we may be helping to change our own opinions. As the research discussed in this chapter has demonstrated, subtle situational and interpersonal pressures that produce behaviors can trigger changes in our attitudes.

- Most of us would *probably* guess that what we are rewarded for, we will come to like. Yet self-perception and dissonance theory teach us that sometimes less is more. It is when external rewards are missing, when we suffer pains to reach our goals, and when we give up alternatives with many positive benefits that we are likely to form the most positive attitudes.

- Most of us would *certainly* guess that, by and large, we act on our attitudes. Much of human activity is marked by a motive for consistency—why else would we experience dissonance when our attitudes and behaviors are inconsistent? We certainly expect other people to follow through on their convictions. After all, we work hard to change customers' minds in order to change their purchases. We try to raise employees' morale in order to boost their productivity; we take pains to eliminate prejudice in order to eliminate discrimination. All of these efforts assume that there is an attitude–action connection, and there is good reason to assume it. Yet this relationship is not one on which we can routinely rely. Attitudes are just one of the factors that have to come to mind to influence perceptions, intentions, plans, and, ultimately, behavior.

As researchers continue to specify the conditions under which attitudes do influence behavior, however, their findings also reaffirm their optimism. Knowing how attitudes influence behavior means that we can have some control over when they do. Such knowledge has important personal and societal consequences. Recall from Chapter 5 that in their battle against prejudice and discrimination, some individuals try to inhibit the impact of their initial responses and consciously bring to bear more egalitarian attitudes. Similar processes could be involved when managers evaluate workers' performance and when jury members form impressions on which they acquit or convict defendants. The research described in this chapter suggests ways both to suppress the influence of some attitudes and to increase the influence of others. When we want attitudes to be potent, they must come to mind readily, and be related to the behavioral options at hand. Weak connections between attitude and object, competition from other attitudes, and a lack of control over the desired behavior will all reduce the impact of attitudes on behaviors.

Of course, the influence of social norms can also reduce this impact. Social norms often conflict with people's personal inclinations. Yet, information about others' standards of appropriateness is vital for effective social functioning— so vital that these standards often override personal attitudes to determine social behavior. The development of social norms and the impact they have on behavior are the focus of the next two chapters.

S U M M A R Y

 Changing Attitudes with Actions. Behavior is an important part of the information on which people base attitudes. If behaviors change, attitudes can also change. When people process superficially, attitudes can be based on associations with actions or on inferences from actions. People are more likely to infer attitudes consistent with bodily movements they are making. In the **foot-in-the-door technique**, people who are induced to comply with a small request come to view themselves as having corresponding attitudes. If they are later faced with a larger request from the same source, they are more likely to grant it than are people who never received the initial request. Like other forms of superficial processing, actions are more likely to affect attitudes in this way when people lack the motivation or ability to process more thoroughly.

When freely chosen actions violate important or self-relevant attitudes, the inconsistency produces an uncomfortable state of tension and arousal termed **cognitive dissonance**. This can motivate people to change their attitudes to make them consistent with their behavior, to value highly what they have worked hard for, and to emphasize the positive aspects of options they have chosen. Because this kind of attitude change involves extensive processing, it is often long-lasting. While minor discrepancies between action and attitudes might trigger self-perception processes, conflicts between actions and attitudes that are important enough to cause unpleasant tension trigger dissonance reduction processes.

Guiding Actions with Attitudes. Established attitudes can guide behaviors in a very direct way. Attitudes bias perceptions, thereby making attitude-consistent information about attitude objects more obvious and attitude-consistent behavior more likely. Attitudes also influence behavior in a more considered way by prompting intentions to act in certain ways. Intentions in turn can trigger planning that makes attitude-consistent behavior more likely.

If attitudes are to guide actions, they must be readily accessible and appropriate to the intended behavior. Attitudes can be made accessible by deliberate thought, self-awareness, or frequent use. Only attitudes that are specific to a particular behavior are likely to guide behavior. Finally, behavior is more likely to reflect attitudes if people both believe they have control and actually do have control over their behavior.

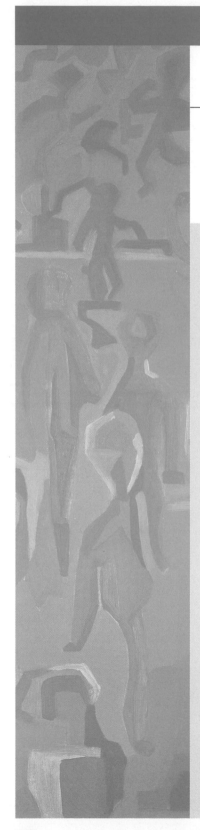

9
Groups, Norms, and Conformity

Imagine that you checked your e-mail or instant messenger only minutes after the conclusion of the first debate between George Bush and John Kerry, candidates in the 2004 election for President of the United States. If you did, you might well have received more than one message exhorting you to immediately support your candidate in a myriad of post-debate polls designed to show "which candidate won." Scientific polling—questioning a carefully selected sample of adults and inferring from their responses what the public as a whole is thinking—is a ubiquitous feature of political life in most modern democracies. But many unscientific "polls," such as those allowing interested people to vote by phoning in or by sending an e-mail message, have other goals. Some seem intended only to enliven news reports, and others aim to encourage healthy participation in national politics. But some of the post-debate e-mail messages were very direct about their goals in encouraging responding to such polls. "Don't let the other side 'spin' the outcome," one warned, "respond early and often to the polls listed below and select 'Candidate A' as the winner. A show of public support now can change the outcome of the election." The authors of this message were clearly keen observers of human behavior. They knew that people are profoundly influenced by others' reactions, and that creating even the appearance of public support for one candidate over another can effectively sway the opinions of many other people.

Politics is not the only sphere in which other people's reactions affect the way we think and act. Such social influence affects every aspect of our lives. Consider, for example, the bursts of "audience" laughter blended into the soundtracks of TV comedies. When jokes and slapstick routines are accompanied by such canned laughter, people find them funnier and laugh longer and harder (Martin & Gray, 1996), because the fake laughter makes it seem that other people find the jokes funny. Bartenders, street musicians, church ushers, and collectors for charitable agencies use a similar ploy. They know that putting dollar bills in their tip jars and collection boxes will increase what they get, because people will be led to believe that leaving a sizable amount of money is the right thing to do. Because a

■ **Defining reality and defining identity**. Group members—like these Afghan female scouts—soon come to share similar thoughts, experience similar emotions, and act in similar ways. The power of group norms rests on two important human motivations: to master the environment by seeing the world accurately and to achieve a sense of belonging and connectedness with others.

company's financial future can depend on the successful launch of a new product, some companies have started "manufacturing" popularity by giving new products away to thousands of specially selected consumption happy 18–24-year-olds. They know that when young urban clubgoers are seen sipping Barcardi Breezers or Vanilla Coke, the success of the product is all but ensured as others discover that "everyone is doing it" (Friess, 2002). What we think, feel, and do is often closely dependent on what others think, feel, and do.

This social influence is usually positive and appropriate. In fact, a basic premise of social life is that many heads are better than one (Surowiecki, 2004). In countries such as the United States, the United Kingdom, France, and Russia, such beliefs have been institutionalized so that a jury—a group of people—rather than a judge can decide the fate of people accused of crimes. We trust executive committees and boards of directors to run schools, businesses, and charitable organizations. All these arrangements reflect our trust that collective wisdom will emerge from the mutual interaction and influence of multiple individuals in a group.

Sometimes, however, our willingness to go along with other people's beliefs, opinions, or actions has negative consequences. If results from easily manipulated internet polls have more influence on voting than careful analysis of candidates' positions on the issues, voters can be easily led astray. Failing to ask questions in a lecture because nobody else does, littering highways and forests because others leave their trash behind, and taking part in a riot are all examples of situations in which taking cues from others can be personally or socially destructive.

In this chapter, we explore the processes that occur when groups of individuals influence each other and reach agreement. We begin by considering two related questions: Why do groups seek to reach agreement, and why do people accept influence from others? You will see that part of the answer to these questions is that people want to *master* their social worlds—to see things the right way, hold correct opinions, and do the right thing. People also want to be *connected* to others, to be liked and valued by those whose opinions they respect. When a group comes to an agreement, it leaves people with feelings of both mastery and connectedness.

We then turn to the question of how agreement is reached. For example, how are the differing opinions of 12 individual jury members forged into a verdict that all can accept? How are the jurors' individual views represented in the final group decision? As you will see, the processes of social influence are reciprocal. Individuals contribute their views to the group position, and what the group thinks influences each individual's views. When the group decision-making process is at its most effective, the consensus reached by the group incorporates multiple views and reflects the best available evidence.

Agreement in and of itself does not guarantee a positive outcome, however. Sometimes groups reach agreements that reflect neither careful consideration of information nor openness to divergent opinions. When groups make such decisions and act on them, the consequences can be disastrous. Knee-jerk business decisions can lead to bankruptcy. The wrong choice by a flight crew can cause an airplane crash.

An ill-considered jury verdict can free the guilty or convict the innocent. In the final two sections, we consider how such negative outcomes occur and how they can be avoided. Groups that foster dissent rather than squelch it often reach agreements that are worthy guides for their members' thoughts, feelings, and behavior.

Conformity to Social Norms

The Formation of Social Norms

Because people are profoundly influenced by others' ideas and actions, interaction or communication causes group members' thoughts, feelings, and behaviors to become more alike. Whether a judgment task is clear-cut or ambiguous, individual members' views converge to form a social norm. Norms reflect the group's generally accepted way of thinking, feeling, or acting.

Remember that some social groups share socially relevant features (like gender, age, or an interest in the environment). Members of such groups may or may not interact much. Other social groups form because they share a common goal (the members of a jury, a sports team, or lab groups assigned to work on a particular problem) and such *face-to-face groups* interact and influence each other to reach that goal or complete a task. All types of membership groups have the power to dramatically affect group members' thoughts, feelings, and behaviors but face-to-face groups have the advantage of direct influence on one another. When people interact in a group, their thoughts, emotions, and actions tend to converge, becoming more and more alike. Consider, for example, Muzafer Sherif's (1936) classic demonstration of a group's power to affect its members' beliefs. Each participant in Sherif's experiment first sat alone in a totally dark room and focused on a single point of light. As the participant watched, the light seemed to jump erratically and then disappear. Seconds later the participant again saw the light appear, move, and disappear. Each time the light appeared, the observer had to estimate how far it moved. In fact, the light did not move at all. Because a dark room provides no points of reference, a stationary point of light appears to careen in a jagged circle, an optical illusion called the *autokinetic effect*.

Given the ambiguity of the situation, it is not surprising that the participants' original distance estimates differed, ranging from barely an inch to nearly a foot. These numbers changed dramatically, however, when participants returned to the lab during the following few days to judge the light's movement, this time as members of three-person groups. As they heard one another's estimates of the light's movement, group members' responses began to converge until they were nearly identical (see Figure 9.1). And these shared estimates had lasting power: As much as a year later, these participants continued to use the common response when judging the light, even when alone (Rohrer, Baron, Hoffman, & Schwander, 1954; Stasson & Hawkes, 1995).

In coming to this collective agreement, group members established a social norm, or consensus, about the movement of the light. As you may recall from Chapter 5, a *social norm* is a generally accepted way of thinking, feeling, or behaving that most people in a group agree on and endorse as right and proper (Thibaut & Kelley, 1959). When people talk about "a well-known fact,"

Face-to-face and social category types of social groups were first discussed in Chapter 4, page 143.

FIGURE 9.1   How consensus develops

■ These three typical individuals in Muzafer Sherif's experiment entered the group with varied views about the apparent movement of the light, as indicated by their initial judgments. Note how their estimates in the group sessions gradually converged until they were identical. (Data from Sherif, 1936.)

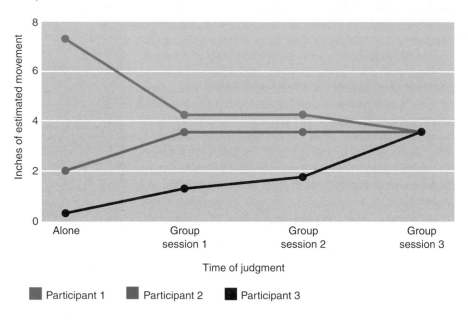

Participant 1   Participant 2   Participant 3

"public opinion," "the way we do things," "the way things are," they are really talking about social norms. Social norms are similar to attitudes in that both are cognitive representations of appropriate ways of thinking, feeling, and acting in response to social objects and events. But whereas attitudes represent an *individual's* positive or negative evaluations, norms reflect *group* evaluations of what is true or false, appropriate or inappropriate. Thus, for example, a parent's love for his or her children is an attitude, whereas the idea that parents do—and should—love their offspring is a social norm. *Descriptive social norms*—what a group of people think, feel, or do—are sometimes contrasted with *prescriptive norms*—what people *should* think, feel, or do. The idea that parents do love their children is a descriptive norm, whereas the idea that people should love their children is a prescriptive norm. But most norms have both qualities—it is because most people do think, feel, or behave in a certain way that we think they should. And this intertwining holds for social norms that range from the trivial (such as what a group finds funny) to the profound (a group's standards of morality) and from the narrow (such as which movie a group likes) to the all-encompassing (as in Sherif's experiment, the way a group might perceive the world).

You might recognize these as the perfect conditions for social comparison. Recall from Chapter 4, page 99, and pages 110 to 111 that we often turn to input from others to help us define reality.

You may be thinking that Sherif stacked the deck in favor of social influence and against individual independence. After all, the experimental situation was highly ambiguous. Participants could not measure the light's movement, and they received no feedback about right and wrong answers. Under these conditions, what else could the participants do but rely on the responses of others? What about decisions that are not ambiguous, when physical and other nonsocial sources of information are available? Do groups still have such influence? Surprisingly, the answer is yes. Solomon Asch (1951, 1955) provided one of the earliest and most convincing demonstrations of this point, although at the time he did not intend to do so. The suggestibility of Sherif's participants disturbed Asch, and he

FIGURE 9.2   Asch's line judgment task

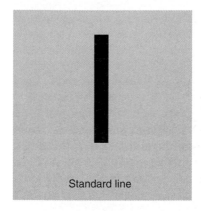

Standard line

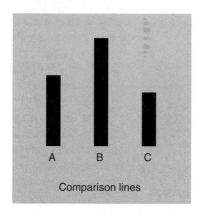

A   B   C

Comparison lines

■ Participants had to decide which comparison line—*A, B,* or *C*—was identical to the standard line for 18 different sets of lines. On certain trials, confederates agreed on obviously wrong answers—in this case, *A* or *C*. Participants conformed to this incorrect consensus about a third of the time. (Adapted from Asch, 1955.)

hypothesized that if a judgment task were unambiguous, social influence would be eliminated.

Imagine being a participant in Asch's experiment. Along with eight other people, you are shown two cards marked with lines like those in Figure 9.2. A single straight line, called the standard line, appears on one card, and three comparison lines of different lengths appear on the other. Your task is to state out loud which of the three lines is the same length as the standard line. For each of 18 different sets of comparison lines, group members will answer in order of seating, and you are next to last. The task seems simple: The test lines clearly differ from one another, and for the first few trials everyone agrees on the correct line. But on the next trial, all of the other participants, each responding in turn, agree unanimously on an obviously wrong answer. Now it's your turn to respond. Faced with a conflict between the evidence of your senses and the opinions of your peers, how do you respond?

As you have probably guessed, the other "participants" in Asch's experiments were confederates coached to make incorrect responses on certain trials. On 12 of the 18 experimental trials, the confederates unanimously agreed on a wrong answer, responding together that either a shorter or a longer line matched the standard line. Despite the ease of the task, the confederates' wrong answers had a considerable impact on the real participants' responses, and they also produced a good deal of anxiety. Three quarters of the participants echoed the confederates' choice on at least 1 trial, and half agreed with an obviously wrong answer on 6 or more trials. Only a hardy 25% stood up for what their eyes were telling them on all 12 of the critical trials. Why did so many yield? When questioned later, some participants told Asch they were concerned about looking ridiculous and just went along with the group. Others said they quite literally "couldn't believe their eyes" and assumed that the group was correct. Even those who remained independent reported discomfort and were still looking for ways to reconcile their judgments with those of the majority when the experiment ended.

The essential results of Sherif's and Asch's studies—that people are influenced by and often adopt the opinions of other group members—have been replicated many times. But Sherif's and Asch's findings on the powerful impact of others' reactions are also demonstrated daily as groups all around us make decisions. A neighborhood committee agrees on recommendations for improving

■ **Huh? Why don't we agree?** It's not hard to identify the real participant in this photograph from one of Solomon Asch's original experiments on conformity. Faced unexpectedly with unanimous disagreement from the rest of the group, participant Number 6 peers anxiously at the line matching task. What powerful social influences might make him accept the group norm over the evidence of his senses?

the community. Union representatives hammer out an agreement on a management offer. A group of friends negotiates about where to have dinner. Whether the judgment task is clear-cut or ambiguous, whether the group is large or small, whether prior opinions are held with more or less conviction, group members typically offer, exchange, and accept various points of view until consensus evolves.

Public Versus Private Conformity

Conformity is the convergence of individual responses toward group norms. Conformity occurs for two important reasons: because people believe that the group is right and because they want the group to accept and approve of them. Most of the time people privately conform to or accept group norms as their own, believing them to be correct and appropriate. Sometimes, however, people publicly conform to norms they do not privately accept.

The convergence of individuals' thoughts, feelings, and behavior toward a group norm is called **conformity** (V. L. Allen, 1965; C. A. Kiesler & Kiesler, 1969). Most of the time, this tendency to let other people's reactions and responses guide our own occurs because we privately accept the group's view, believing it to be both a correct and an appropriate guide for our own position. When people are truly persuaded that the group is right, when they willingly and privately accept group norms as their own beliefs, even if the group is no longer physically present, **private conformity** occurs (V. L. Allen, 1965; Deutsch & Gerard, 1955; S. A. Insko, Dreenan, Solomon, Smith, & Wade, 1983). When participants in Sherif's study adopted their group's standard opinion regarding the movement of the light, even though there was no pressure to do so, they showed private conformity. Remember in fact that they used the group norm as their personal standard as much as a year later, when they were asked to judge the light movements in the absence of other group members.

Sometimes, however, conformity occurs because we feel we have no choice but to go along with social norms. **Public conformity** occurs when people respond

Conformity. The convergence of individuals' thoughts, feelings, or behavior toward a social norm.

Private conformity. Private acceptance of social norms.

Public conformity. Overt behavior consistent with social norms that are not privately accepted.

to real or imagined pressure and behave consistently with norms that they do not privately accept as correct. Public conformity produces only a surface change: People pretend to go along with the group norm in what they say or do, but privately they do not think the group is right. People publicly conform because they fear ridicule, rejection, incarceration, or worse. Those of Asch's participants who went along with the incorrect majority view to avoid seeming ridiculous were publicly conforming, as are political dissidents who survive by paying lip service to the party line even though they do not agree with it.

☐ **CONFORMITY AND FALSE CONFESSIONS IN THE INTERROGATION ROOM.** As the classic studies of conformity show, uncertainty makes us particularly vulnerable to social influence. Although law enforcement experts argue over how often innocent suspects are tricked or coerced into falsely confessing to crimes they didn't commit, interrogation practices can certainly make public conformity more likely without even any threat of physical force. For example, lengthy interviews that repeatedly call into question a tired, hungry, or lonely suspect's story while repeatedly proposing another version of events can call the suspect's sense of reality into question. Bringing other people into the interrogation to help convince the suspect to confess or to "confirm" the presence of damning evidence offers social support for confession. Could such tactics make people admit to acts they hadn't committed?

In a clever demonstration of the power of social influence in a laboratory setting, Saul Kassin and Katherine Kiechel (1996) suggest they can. They had college students type letters on a computer keyboard, ostensibly as part of a study of reflex speed. Some students had to complete the task at a very high rate of speed, whereas others could type the letters at a more leisurely pace. All participants were warned not to hit the ALT key, as doing so could crash the computer. About a minute into the task, the computer malfunctioned, and the distressed experimenter accused the student of hitting the forbidden key. When the student initially denied the charge, the experimenter continued to press: "Did you hit the ALT key?", calling into question the student's account of reality and appearing to suggest guilt. He then turned to a confederate and asked, "Did you see anything?" In one condition, the confederate reported seeing nothing, but in another condition, the confederate "admitted" that she had seen the student press the forbidden key, confirming the alternate social reality the experimenter seemed to be suggesting. At this stage, the experimenter demanded that the students sign a handwritten confession ("I hit the ALT key and caused the computer to crash. Data were lost"). Sixty-nine percent agreed to do so!

Of course, such behavior might have reflected mere public conformity. To see if any students actually began to believe their own confession, the researchers secretly recorded the way in which the students later described the incident to a confederate who was unaware of the purpose of the study. Analysis of the content of these conversations indicated that 28% of the participants came to see themselves as guilty, showing private conformity to the social reality with which they had been presented. Importantly, private conformity was much more likely to occur when the (false) witness agreed with the experimenter that the student was guilty, and especially when the fast pace of the task left students uncertain about what had actually happened. Just as in the classic conformity studies, uncertain participants were particularly likely to accept the responses of multiple others, even if it meant confessing to a "crime" that initially they were all sure they hadn't committed!

Although public conformity in the face of heavy-handed group pressure does occur, private acceptance of group norms is far more prevalent and powerful. Because we usually see others as valid and valued sources of knowledge about the world, we often privately conform to social norms without even realizing we are doing so.

CONFORMITY AND CULTURE. Because the results of Sherif's and Asch's studies tell us so much about the relationship between individual and group, attempts have been made to replicate their results in many different cultures and countries. The relatively high levels of conformity found in the original studies were surprising partly because individualistic cultures (like the predominant cultures in the United States and Europe) put such a high value on individual autonomy. In such cultures, both public and private conformity have somewhat negative overtones. Nonetheless, nearly 100 replications of Asch's procedure in the United States confirm that even individualistic North Americans are profoundly influenced by others' reactions. The power of conformity can lead to an ironic outcome: when people who strongly identify as North Americans are reminded of their group's norm of individualism, they conform more strongly to that norm—by conforming less (Jetten, Postmes, & McAuliffe, 2002)! As these findings make clear, social norms and cultural conventions even tell us how to be an individual. Both because of the negative cultural connotations of conformity, and also because we generally underestimate our own susceptibility to influence, participants in social influence experiments often deny having been affected. They do this even though they correctly suspect that everyone else might be influenced, and even though their own responses indicate that influence actually occurred (G. L. Cohen, 2003).

Conformity is seen quite differently in collectivist or interdependence-oriented cultures such as those found in India or Japan. In such cultures, individuals see themselves as an integral part of the group and view conformity as a kind of social glue (Kim & Markus, 1999). It is not surprising, then, that when studies like Sherif's and Asch's are replicated in collectivist cultures—with Fijians, Lebanese, Japanese, and Zimbabwean Bantus, for example—the degree of conformity to group norms is usually higher than that found in individualistic cultures (P. B. Smith & Bond, 1993). In fact, a meta-analysis of 133 studies conducted in 17 different countries provided evidence that the degree to which a culture endorses individualistic or collective values is the biggest influence on the extent of conformity (R. Bond & Smith, 1996). The more collectivist the culture, the more conformity to the responses of others occurs.

The Dual Functions of Conformity to Norms: Mastery and Connectedness

Advertisers, market specialists, and campaign managers have been quick to use the idea that people rely on others' views and often adopt others' behaviors. Slice-of-life scenes—the hidden camera recording family breakfasts with Kellogg's Corn Flakes, the testimonial from the schoolteacher with the headache that only Excedrin pain medication can relieve—provide us with models of people "just like us" who are solving problems and improving their lives. Headlines that shout: "Only two left at this price!" or "Get yours now while supplies last!" convey just how desirable such sought-after products must be. In one demonstration of such effects, college students preferred cookies they thought were in short supply because they were popular with others over the same cookies described as being in plentiful supply (Worchel, Lee, & Adewole, 1975). And putting their money where their mouths were, students were willing to pay more for the scarce cookies. Why are we so influenced by what others are thinking, feeling, and, presumably, eating? Why do we conform to others' views at all? And what makes the views of others "just like us" particularly important? Why do we seem to care more what some people think and not worry too much about others?

Expecting Consensus

Private conformity comes about because we expect to see the world the same way similar others see it. In fact, we often assume that most other people share our own opinions and preferences. Agreement with others increases our confidence that our views are correct, whereas disagreement undermines that certainty.

The key factor in our conformity to norms is our *expectation of agreement*. We usually expect other people to see the world the same way we do. In fact, people tend to overestimate the extent to which others agree with their views of the world, a phenomenon called the **false consensus effect** (Gilovich, 1990; Mullen and others, 1985). To see the effect in action, ask a number of people to tell you whether they prefer 1960s music to 1990s music and to estimate the percentage of other people who share their preference. Your respondents, no matter which opinion they express, will probably guess that most people agree with them. People generally see their own preferences as reasonable responses to the world, and so they assume that any "reasonable" person will share them. (After all, who wouldn't choose the Beatles over Celine Dion?)

At the same time, we usually expect to see the world the same way others do. When other people share our views, their agreement increases our confidence that we see things the right way. Our expectation of consensus is fulfilled and no action needs to be taken. In contrast, disagreement with others, and especially disagreement with a consensus, can be a startling disconfirmation of our view of the world and our place in it. Disagreement leaves us uncertain, uncomfortable, and, as Sherif and Asch demonstrated, vulnerable to social influence until a new consensus is formed. How does the consensus represented in a norm help us to avoid that uncertainty and discomfort?

The Dual Functions of Conformity to Norms

Agreeing with others not only assures people that they are in contact with a common reality but also gives them the feeling of belonging with others. Although particular circumstances can make one goal more important than the other, usually agreement with a group of similar others simultaneously fulfills the motives for both mastery and connectedness.

NORMS PROVIDE MASTERY INSURANCE. Norms are important because we need other people to help us construct an appropriate view of reality. Other people's reactions tell us what the world is like. Imagine, for example, that you made both

> **False consensus effect.** The tendency to overestimate others' agreement with one's own opinions, characteristics, and behaviors.

an apple pie and a peach pie for a family get-together. If everyone came back for seconds on the peach pie but there were no repeats on the apple, it would be natural to infer that your peach pie was a success but your apple was not as good as usual. When everyone prefers the peach pie, we make the attribution that the characteristics of the pie itself, rather than any idiosyncrasy of the eaters, determine its positive reception. That is, consensus tells us something about reality. In fact, group norms are such powerful guides to reality that we are often unaware of their influence and take them for granted. For example, we often see our country's monetary system as operating quite independently of social norms. On the contrary, it depends heavily on them. The more money people invest, the more the price of stocks and shares goes up, and the more money people invest in the market. Thus, economic good times are at least partially the result of a norm: the common perception and expectation that economic times are good. But when enough people start to question the system's assumptions—for example, that money deposited in a bank will be safe—and to act on their doubts—by making mass withdrawals—the system collapses. These examples show that something that we think of as "objective reality" actually depends on social conformity processes. Conformity to those norms helps to actually create the reality that the norm is seen as reflecting.

You may recognize these effects from ealier chapters—consensus leading to an external attribution is first discussed in Chapter 3, page 75 and the power of social norms to either maintain or disrupt behavior is an example of a self-fulfilling prophecy at work, see Chapter 5, pages 174 to 175.

If we believe that group norms reflect reality, then conforming to them satisfies our need for mastery (Crano, Gorenflo, & Shackleford, 1988; E. E. Jones & Gerard, 1967). We believe the group has more knowledge than we do, so accepting their input makes sense if we want to make better decisions. When people privately conform because they believe a group's norms reflect reality, the group is said to have *informational influence* (Deutsch & Gerard, 1955). If we conform in order to increase our chances of making an accurate decision, then we should conform even more when the stakes are high. Research shows that that people do exactly this; although, the outcome is not is not always the intended increase in accuracy. In Asch's task, participants given incentives to be as accurate as possible relied even more heavily on the (inaccurate) views of confederates (S. Baron, Vandello, & Brunsman, 1996). In another study, researchers asked students to give eyewitness reports of a crime scene as accurately as possible. Unbeknown to the participants, some students saw a slightly different version of events than others. Even though initial individual reports were highly accurate and even though people understood the importance of accuracy, discussing the crime among themselves led to conformity to others' views, decreasing accuracy (Wright, Self, & Justice, 2000). The motivation for accuracy thus led to greater reliance on social input. Ironically, of course, in both these cases, relying on others actually decreased accuracy.

Some of the most convincing demonstrations of the importance of a consensus in shaping beliefs about reality come from variations on Asch's experimental procedure. Asch found that the amount of influence the confederate group exerted increased as the size of the group increased, but only up to a point. As you can see in Figure 9.3, an incorrect answer given by one person had very little effect. Two confederates giving the same incorrect answer elicited some conformity from the study participants, but a consensus among three confederates led participants to agree with their obviously incorrect answer about 33% of the time. Adding more than three confederates, however, did not lead to further increases in conformity. Once an adequate consensus has formed, adding to the size of that consensus apparently has no further effect (Insko and others, 1983). Perhaps this is the origin of the old Spanish proverb: "If three men call you an ass, put on a bridle!"

FIGURE 9.3 The importance of consensus

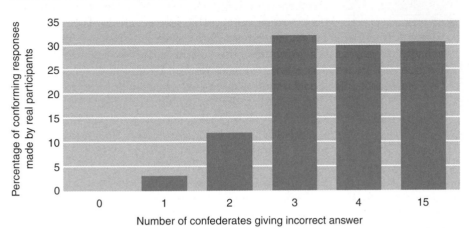

Number of confederates giving incorrect answer

(y-axis: Percentage of conforming responses made by real participants)

■ Amassing a consensus of three people around an obviously incorrect answer caused considerable conformity among real participants in this variation on Asch's procedure. Once the consensus was established, however, adding to it did not make much difference. A unanimous group of 15 confederates caused no more conformity than a unanimous group of three. (Data from Asch, 1955.)

If consensus exerts such an important influence on an individual's views, breaking the consensus should undermine the group's influence. To test this idea, Asch arranged for one of the confederates to agree with the real participant. He found that the presence of an ally dramatically decreased conformity to only about 10% of responses. This was true even when the dissenter gave a different incorrect answer or dropped out after a few responses (Allen & Bragg, 1965; Allen & Wilder, 1972; both cited in V. L. Allen, 1975). As the size of the dissenting minority increases, the majority's opinion seems more and more open to question, and is less and less likely to be adopted (Gordijn, De Vries, & De Dreu, 2002). When there is no longer a consensus about reality, the group loses its power to persuade.

Because we depend so much on agreement with others, disagreement causes surprise, confusion, and, eventually, uncertainty and self-doubt (Asch, 1956). Disagreement undermines our confidence in our view of reality. Finding themselves in the situation of Asch's participants, most people would be anxious and unsure and would begin to doubt their own perceptions and to consider the group consensus as possibly correct. Thus, there is a potential for informational influence whenever people find themselves at odds with others with whom they expect to agree. Under these conditions, agreeing with the group consensus helps re-establish our confidence that we are indeed in touch with reality.

NORMS GIVE US FEELINGS OF CONNECTEDNESS. In many religious communities, children who have reached an appropriate age go through some kind of ceremony, such as the Christian First Communion, the Jewish Bar or Bat Mitzvah, or the Hindu Sacred Thread ceremony. After these rituals, they are considered ready to participate fully in the rites of their community. The new members learn, through formal instruction or by observing others, how to speak, what thoughts and feelings are appropriate, and how to act. Knowing and following these standards allows them to take their place and fulfill their roles in the group. They experience a proud sense of belonging, as full members of their religious community.

What people gradually learn in such situations are group norms. By adopting such norms, we demonstrate our commitment and connections to our new associates and our pride in "who we are." A group has *normative influence* when

■ **All for one and one for all**. The more closely knit the group and the more strongly individuals value their membership, the more powerful the effect of group norms. Here Army recruits are learning physical skills. Developing total devotion to group norms is part of their training so that individual members won't forget their role or desert their group in times of danger.

members conform to it to attain a positive and valued social identity and to win respect from other group members (Deutsch & Gerard, 1955). Normative influence thus satisfies our needs for connectedness. The desire to be a valued member of a group is so strong that people typically adopt group norms whenever they identify with a group. For example, when discussing cases together, mock jurors are much more likely to uphold the norm "innocent until proven guilty" than they are when they judge the same cases alone (MacCoun & Kerr, 1988; Tindale & Davis, 1983). And with good reason: People who endorse group norms most strongly are admired as more intelligent, competent, confident, and sincere (Eisenger & Mills, 1968; Levinger & Schneider, 1969).

Disagreeing with a group you value, identify with, and feel connected to feels bad. People report feeling upset and uncomfortable when they find out they disagree with other group members, especially if they expect to interact with the group (Matz & Wood, 2005). Even more revealingly, people who conform to the norms of important groups feel happier than people who do not conform. To demonstrate this effect, researchers had single participants work on a puzzle at the same time as a confederate did. Perhaps because the study seemed to be about individual problem solving, the participants did not help the confederate, even though the confederate obviously could not solve the puzzle. Experimenters then told the participants that they had either conformed to or violated an in-group norm by not offering help. Participants whose lack of help was labeled as conforming to the group norm reported feeling more positive emotions than students whose lack of help was labeled as violating group norms. And as we might expect if conformity confers connectedness, these effects were stronger for people who identified more closely with the group (Christensen, Rothgerber, Wood, & Matz, 2004). So, just as disagreement undermines our confidence that we view reality correctly, being out of step with group norms undermines the secure social identity we derive from belonging to a group. And just as moving toward the group consensus helps re-establish the perceived accuracy of our views, conforming to group norms helps reconfirm our sense of identity.

MASTERY, CONNECTEDNESS, OR BOTH? Particular circumstances can tip the balance in norm formation toward mastery or connectedness concerns (Kaplan & Wilke, 2001). The need for mastery (that is, to be right and to make accurate judgments) can take precedence over the need for connectedness when a group is faced with a task that has one verifiably correct solution. Researchers call these kinds of problems *intellective* tasks; they include making a visual judgment, solving a mathematical problem, or answering a general knowledge question. With their focus on facts and information, intellective tasks like this make the reality-testing function of conformity particularly important (Kaplan & Miller, 1987; Stasser & Stewart, 1992). In judgmental tasks, however, the identity functions of conformity become more salient (Kaplan & Miller, 1987). *Judgmental* tasks require value-laden decisions about social and personal issues ranging from big questions, like whether government spending for social welfare programs should be cut back, to small ones, like which movie a couple should see. Expressing connectedness may be more important than establishing mastery when it comes to such decisions.

But most of the time, agreement with a group of similar others usually fulfills both motives simultaneously. We adopt group norms not only because we think they reflect reality but also because we want to express our identification with groups we value (Kelman, 1961). Reaching consensus about the reality of our world is often the way we establish a connection with others. These dual functions make conformity to norms centrally important to the success of social life. In fact, Nobel prize winner Herbert Simon (1990) argues that the tendency to adopt group norms is the product of evolution. Because norms convey knowledge about how to cope effectively with the social and physical world, and because norms connect people together, individuals who adopt group norms are probably at a survival advantage. That certainly seemed to be the case in one of the most compelling demonstrations of the power of group norms: one that came to light after a 1972 plane crash in the Andes mountains stranded starving survivors among dead victims for 70 days. Despite their individual repugnance at the idea, the crash survivors developed group norms that governed their cannibalism of some of the victims. According to survivors' accounts, the development of and conformity to such norms was crucial to ensuring not only their physical survival but also their psychological survival, their need for mastery and connectedness (Henslin, 2003).

Although they may not be so dramatic, adherence to group norms on a day-to-day basis provides us with just the same dual reality and connectedness benefits. When other people share our views, their agreement fulfills our need for mastery of the world: It increases our confidence that we hold correct opinions, experience appropriate feelings, and do the right thing. And because we depend on others to define and endorse the ideas, values, and expectations that are the basis for the smooth operation of the social system, their agreement also strengthens our feelings of connectedness with those whose opinions we respect. The reality-seeking and identity-seeking motivations for conformity typically work together.

Whose Consensus? The Impact of Reference Groups

People expect to agree with those who share attributes relevant to the judgment at hand. Agreeing with such a reference group ensures that people are in contact with a common reality and gives them the feeling of being valued. Other group members do not have to be present for conformity to occur, but having other group members present increases conformity even more.

Do you expect to agree with everyone about everything? Of course not. Rather, if you need support for a decision or evaluation, you turn to the people you believe are an appropriate source of information for the particular judgment (Abrams, Wetherell, Cochrane, Hogg, & Turner, 2001; J. C. Turner, 1982; J. C. Turner and others, 1987). These people are called a **reference group**. The reference group you turn to depends on the kind of judgment or evaluation you are making. Recall that intellective tasks require physical judgments or statements of fact. Because many people have the knowledge and skills to verify the solutions to intellective tasks, most other people can serve as a reference group for such tasks. If the task involves, for example, visual judgments, as Sherif's and Asch's experimental tasks did, people expect to agree with any other people who have reasonably good eyesight. Because such tasks have a single answer, and because so many people

To remind yourself of how membership in even a minimal group can affect our thoughts and actions, see Chapter 6, especially pages 204 to 205.

Reference group. Those people accepted as an appropriate source of information for a judgment because they share the attributes relevant for making that judgment.

"How would you like me to answer that question? As a member of my ethnic group, educational class, income group, or religious category?"

can serve as a reference group for them, the expectation that most other people will agree on intellective tasks is very strong (S. A. Insko and others, 1983; Kaplan & Miller, 1987).

The appropriate reference group for a value-laden judgment task is somewhat different. The people we accept as an appropriate source of information for these social and personal issues are those who share similar values, attitudes, and relationships. In such cases, people usually expect to agree with peers, family, and others who share their tastes and pastimes (Goethals & Nelson, 1973; Gorenflo & Crano, 1989). Groups with whom people share values or ideology have a powerful and long-lasting effect on members' attitudes (Christensen and others, 2004). In contrast, if groups don't appear to have the qualifications for consensus on value-laden issues, their opinions hold no sway. In one study of over 300 Australian university students, for example, only some students conformed when researchers led them to believe that their opinions differed from those of most of their peers. Students whose opinions about legal rights for gay couples, for example, were rooted in strong religious or moral grounds were not swayed by the opinions of average college students who did not share those values (Hornsey, Majkut, Terry, & McKimmis, 2003).

If the judgmental task involves politics, morality, or social justice, our lifelong membership in national, ethnic, religious, age, or political groups can provide a ready-made reference group, whether we are Flemish, Muslims, Generation Xers, or Conservatives. In fact, many of our most cherished and fiercely held convictions are norms rooted in and shared by membership in highly valued groups (Boninger, Krosnick, & Berent, 1995). In one study, liberal and conservative students formed favorable attitudes toward a social policy if the political party they identified with expressed support for it, even when the policy was one their party typically opposed (Cohen, 2003). These student voters weren't just unthinkingly going along with their group. When asked about the issue, these students gave responses that showed that in-group endorsement had changed the very way they saw the issue and its moral implications.

In contrast, we do not expect to agree with people we dislike or with out-group members. In-groups don't expect out-groups to share their opinions or ways of thinking at all (Robbins & Krueger, 2005). It is not surprising, then, that people are far more affected by social influence from in-group than from out-group members (J. C. Turner, 1982). For example, the finding that members of collectivist cultures show more conformity holds only if the sources of influence are other in-group members (P. B. Smith & Bond, 1993). And remember the finding that people laugh longer and harder if jokes are accompanied by canned laughter? Australian and British social psychologists have shown that this is only true if participants think that the laughter is coming from other in-group members. As the participants seemed to be saying: "It's not funny if *they're* laughing!" (Platow and others, 2005).

Persuasive appeals from in-group members are also treated differently than those from out-group members. First, if we think an in-group has the right qualifications for valid judgments, we are more likely to accept its views: "If my group thinks this, it must be right!" Such superficial acceptance of in-group messages is particularly likely when the persuasive appeals deal with issues that are not centrally relevant to group membership (Mackie, Gastardo-Conaco, & Skelly, 1992). When information is more relevant and important to group memberships, persuasive appeals from in-group members are processed more systematically than appeals from out-group members. Students in one study read a persuasive appeal on an environmental issue made by either a fellow schoolmate or a student from another university. Some participants received persuasive appeals comprising strong and compelling arguments, while others heard in-group or out-group messages that were weak and specious (Mackie, Worth, & Asuncion, 1990). The position advocated in the strong in-group messages was accepted, whereas weak in-group messages were rejected, showing that careful thinking about the content of the appeals had occurred. In contrast, messages from out-group members had little impact, regardless of argument quality. The finding that in-group communications receive more systematic processing than out-group messages has been confirmed many times (Budesheim, Houston, & DePaola, 1996; van Knippenberg & Wilke, 1992; W. Wood, Pool, Leck, & Purvis, 1996).

The power of persuasive appeals from the in-group shows that you do not need to have other group members present to be conforming to group norms. Because the group is part of the individual—as a social identity that is part of the self—conformity can occur whenever group belonging becomes salient, even in one's head. But because the presence of the group makes group membership both cognitively and physically salient, having other group members present increases conformity to group norms even more (Crutchfield, 1955; Reid, 1983; Skinner & Stephenson, 1987). The more highly members identify with the group, and the more closely and frequently the group interacts, the greater the reference group's impact (Cartwright & Zander, 1960).

The formation and transmission of group norms is one of the most powerful examples of how we work together with others to socially construct a shared view of reality. As can be seen in Figure 9.4, the needs for mastery and connectedness

These findings might remind you of similar results discussed in Chapter 6, pages 194 to 209. Although the physical presence of group members can strongly affect our perceptions of ourselves and others, such effects also occur whenever we think about ourselves as group members, whether or not others are present.

FIGURE 9.4 Motives behind private conformity

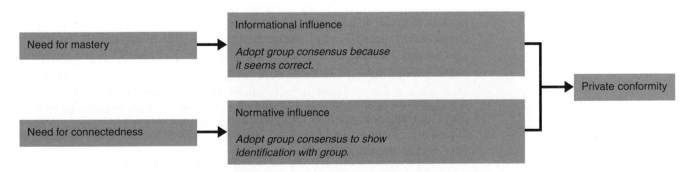

■ People adopt a group consensus as their own private belief because they wish both to hold correct opinions and to show their identification with a group they value and respect. These two processes are termed *informational influence* and *normative influence*.

guide our reactions to informational and normative influence from the group as we try to reach consensus on a multitude of judgments and decisions.

How Groups Form Norms: Processes of Social Influence

Every day in boardrooms, personnel offices, and employment agencies around the world, groups of people gather to make decisions about which of the many applicants for a position should be hired. Such decisions are obviously of importance not only to those wanting to be hired but also to those doing the hiring: good decisions increase productivity and the bottom line, whereas poor decisions waste the company's financial and human resources. Candidates are interviewed, applications are reviewed, and the evaluations of others sought. But the final decisions are often made socially, with members of a hiring committee or personnel team contributing some of their views and ideas to the group, while listening to what others think and seeing how they react. Gradually the group forms a consensus, agreeing on whom should be hired and whom will be rejected. How does this happen, and how does the pursuit of mastery and connectedness influence the norms that are forged from this kind of give and take?

Group Compromise: Taking the Middle Ground

> When group members are initially split on an issue, group discussion usually results in convergence on a moderate position.

You might expect that a middle-of-the-road compromise would be the most likely outcome when people share their views. For example, just as Sherif's participants converged on a middling estimate of how far the light moved in the darkened room, people with extremely positive or negative evaluations of a particular job candidate might move toward more moderate views when faced with arguments that oppose their original evaluations. Surprisingly, though, this outcome is rare in group discussions. Such compromise usually happens only when a group's views are evenly split, with roughly half the members supporting an issue and half opposing it (Burnstein & Vinokur, 1977; Wetherell, 1987).

When group discussion does produce a compromise, the position reflected in the final group norm is more moderate than the initial views of its individual members, an effect called *depolarization*. The convergence of estimates by those in Sherif's study demonstrates depolarization. Look back at Figure 9.1 and you will see that each group member ultimately moves toward a moderate group norm that is near the average of the members' initial opinions. The same pattern might be seen when a job applicant initially elicits an equal number of supporters and opponents. Opinions will converge toward a moderate position, which may or may not be good enough for the would-be employee to get hired.

Group Polarization: Going to Normative Extremes

> When a majority of group members initially favor one side of the issue, communication and interaction usually move the group to an even more extreme position.

An even division of opinion is a rare phenomenon in group decision making. More commonly, a majority of group members initially favor a particular point of view. Why do groups initially lean in one direction or another? Recall from Chapter 7 that people tend to associate with others who share their views, and that groups often form because of shared interests and shared views. Because of this, the initial point of view actually defines the group. Individual members of the local Greenpeace organization probably joined because they favor conservation and thus share similar opinions on the endangered spotted owl. Similarly, members of a neighborhood watch committee can be expected to share views about local law enforcement. Even representative or appointed groups often have a majority opinion. Often their views are influenced by the weight of the evidence. An applicant with good academic preparation, relevant work experience, and impeccable references from reliable sources will appeal to the majority of hiring committee members, for example. If the evidence leans in one direction, a majority of jurors might initially favor one verdict over another. In fact, one large-scale study of jury proceedings found that a majority initially favored acquittal or conviction in all but 10 of 225 trials studied (Kalven & Zeisel, 1966). As a rule, then, most groups will lean one way or the other before discussion even begins.

What kind of final group norm can we expect when most members of a group initially share an opinion? If you participated in or studied hiring discussions long enough, you would begin to notice a reliable pattern. Imagine that a candidate with some potential is being discussed. Someone points out her solid but not startling academic credentials. Another notes that while her first position was with a mediocre organization, she is currently employed by a well-regarded firm that has a reputation for excellent employee development. A third mentions that the candidate is on his "accept" list, at which point a fourth chips in with "Uh huh, I gave her a high rating, too." One of her stronger letters of reference is reread, her solid performance at the interview recalled, and the group agrees enthusiastically to hire her: She is excellent. Seen at first as merely having potential, the candidate is now a superior applicant. And, of course, movement in the opposite direction can also happen. When the majority of committee members lean toward rejection, talking about credentials and interview performance and lack of experience seems only to doom the applicant further. In the context of group discussion, the good gets better and the bad gets worse.

The first to notice this unexpected effect of group discussion was a young graduate student named James Stoner (1961). Stoner asked business school students to respond to a series of fictitious "choice dilemmas," in which they had to decide between a cautious course of action with a small potential benefit and a risky option with a large payoff. For example, imagine having to decide between staying in a job that offers security and moderate yearly raises, versus taking a better paying job with a new firm that could expand dramatically or might go out of business in a year or two. Stoner found that when people work together in groups on this kind of problem, they opt for more risky actions than when they make decisions alone. This finding was originally called the *risky shift*.

Surprisingly, Stoner's results had little to do with the perception of risk. Other researchers soon demonstrated that if most people initially prefer a cautious line of action, group discussion produces a more cautious outcome. Similar patterns of group shifts emerged in a variety of circumstances. For example, if most members of a group initially are racially prejudiced, group interaction and discussion tends to increase their prejudice. If most members initially are not prejudiced, then group discussion shifts them further in the direction of egalitarian views (Myers & Bishop, 1971). People who work together and like their jobs become even more satisfied with their work over time (Mason & Griffin, 2002). When people who care about loss interact they make more conservative decisions, whereas those who focus on gain make riskier decisions when they interact (Levine, Higgins, & Choi, 2000). Findings such as these have led to the conclusion that the various shifts are part of a general phenomenon, group polarization. **Group polarization** occurs when the group's initial average position becomes more extreme following group interaction (Moscovici & Zavalloni, 1969).

☐ **POLARIZATION IN THE JURY ROOM.** Group polarization can operate whenever like-minded individuals interact. In one demonstration of its impact on jury deliberation, David Myers and Martin Kaplan (1976) asked mock juries made up of U.S. college students to assess the guilt of defendants in traffic felony cases. The researchers manipulated the strength of the evidence, so that in some groups a majority initially favored conviction, whereas in others a majority initially favored acquittal. In the pro-conviction groups, discussion increased the likelihood that the defendant would be found guilty. In the pro-acquittal groups, the reverse occurred. Similar results were found in a study of Japanese students serving as mock jurors (Isozaki, 1984).

Research confirms that group polarization takes place among real jurors deciding real cases. In their survey of jury decisions, Kalven and Zeisel (1966) found that in 209 of 215 cases, the final outcome favored the position of the initial majority. The authors of the study offer an interesting metaphor for the impact of group discussion: "The deliberation process might be likened to what the developer does for an exposed film: it brings out the picture" (p. 489). This is a far cry from the compromise, middle-of-the-road, or depolarized position we might intuitively expect groups to adopt.

Explaining Polarized Norm Formation

When people process superficially, merely relying on others' positions can produce polarization of group norms as undecided or moderate group members move toward the group position and try to show that they are good group members. When people process systematically, both others' positions and arguments work together to polarize group norms. Majority arguments are more numerous, receive more discussion, seem more compelling, and are presented more persuasively. All these factors give majority views a persuasive advantage.

What explains the formation of polarized group norms? The key lies in the fact that most groups have majorities that favor one side of the issue over the other. And how does exposure to groups with majorities that favor one side over the other result in polarized group norms? It won't surprise you to find out that the answer has to do with how information is processed and what motives people have in mind as they process. Remember from Chapters 7 and 8 that in forming or changing attitudes, people sometimes process available information quite superficially but on other occasions process it quite extensively. Both superficial and systematic processing also characterize our reactions to information about others' opinions during norm formation and change. Sometimes we notice where others stand and go along with the majority without worrying about their reasons. If, for example, you and some friends are choosing a restaurant and you do not particularly care what you eat, you may pay no attention to claims about the quality of the food and service and simply throw your support behind the majority. But if you are in a situation in which your

---

Group polarization. The process by which a group's initial average position becomes more extreme following group interaction.

decision will matter a great deal (for example, as a member of a personnel committee or a jury), you probably will consider more than just the other members' positions. You will also want to understand their reasons, evidence, and arguments. In this case, the persuasive effects of the majority of others' opinions can be even stronger. Regardless of whether superficial or systematic processing occurs, more extreme group norms are the likely result. Let's see why.

SUPERFICIAL PROCESSING: RELYING ON OTHERS' POSITIONS. Sometimes people know only *what* the rest of their group thinks but not *why* they came to such conclusions (R. S. Baron & Roper, 1976). Group members might discover consensus in what people say during discussion. Or they can guess the group norm from who the members of the group are: perhaps they are all wearing "Save the Whales" shirts, indicating that the group will fall on the conservation side of the issue. Members might even infer agreement because of other kinds of similarity, such as assuming that a group of science majors will all think alike and tend to agree on almost any issue (Postmes, Spears, Lee, & Novak, in press). In cases like these, people can use the group position alone as a guide to what their own position should be. That is, consensus is used as a heuristic: It provides a shortcut to the position that people believe to be both correct and appropriate, without their having to do a lot of hard work figuring out the right answer. How might a superficial reliance on consensus as a heuristic lead to extreme positions?

When undecided or dissenting members of a group adopt the majority consensus, the group's average position moves toward the extreme. Imagine that there are pros and cons about a particular restaurant, but on the whole it has become very popular. Wanting to choose the best restaurant for an important guest, imagine that you rely on the consensus and patronize the restaurant yourself. In doing so of course you have added to its popularity by endorsing the consensus, even though a careful review of the eatery's attributes might have resulted in a less extreme evaluation. So superficial acceptance of group norms—even when motivated by mastery concerns—moves the group toward the extreme. You may now see why supporters of one or the other Presidential candidates were urged, as we reported at the beginning of the chapter, to support their candidate in the many unscientific polls that tracked public opinion before the 2004 U.S. election. Both political parties knew that members of the public who had devoted only superficial effort to the task might well adopt any apparent consensus that came out of these polls—regardless of how representative or reliable they were. This in turn would increase apparent support for their favored candidate.

Heuristic reliance on others' views can led to extreme positions for another reason. Because people care about their membership in groups, they often want to be the best possible members of their group. Any group member who values his or her group membership naturally wants to represent the group ideal (Codol, 1975). In fact, most members of cohesive groups think of themselves not as average but as superior representatives of their groups (Myers & Lamm, 1976). Thus, for example, most business executives think of themselves as more ethical than the average executive, and most editors think their grasp of grammar is better than that of their average colleague (Allison, Messick, & Goethals, 1989). However, others' views may not support the opinions we hold of ourselves. Sometimes hearing what others think reveals that we are not as far above average as we thought we were. This social comparison may in turn prompt a speedy adoption of a more extreme position so that we can again become above average on important dimensions within the group (Singleton, 1979). As more and more group members adopt this strategy, the group norm grows more extreme.

Recall from Chapter 4, pages 95 and 108 that we all tend to believe that we are above average on almost every positive dimension (which logically can't be true of course). Hearing everyone else also claim such a position of normative superiority suddenly puts our own claims in perspective.

Even when others' positions are all we know, our desire for mastery and our wish to be valued by important others encourage us to move toward, or even beyond, the majority's view. Group members who hold the minority position shift to adopt the majority consensus. Members of the majority may move even farther toward the extreme. Together, these two processes make group polarization a likely outcome of norm formation as the average position in the group grows more extreme.

SYSTEMATIC PROCESSING: ATTENDING TO BOTH POSITIONS AND ARGUMENTS. When the evaluations that a group makes are important or affect the group directly, group members shift their processing into high gear. They consider not just the preferences of others but in addition their supporting arguments and evidence. You might think that such careful processing would never produce the exaggerated or extreme norms that occur in group polarization. In fact, however, systematic processing makes group polarization even more likely.

In the lively interchange that characterizes most group discussions, preferences and the arguments for those preferences are aired simultaneously. Imagine, for example, that you are a jury member listening to another juror argue, "Well, if the defendant was at work, as his foreman testified, he could not possibly have arrived home before 6:30, and the doctors said that the victim was already dead by then." Although this statement reviews relevant evidence, it also reveals the juror's opinion. If, instead of laying out her position, the juror had merely voiced her opinion that the defendant was innocent, you might still have been able to figure out the unstated arguments supporting that view. When a jury or another group is deeply engaged in resolving a dilemma, both *what* other group members believe and *why* they believe it become important considerations. The resulting attention given to both arguments and positions gives even more of a persuasive edge to the position initially favored by the majority of other group members, which moves the norm towards polarization. Several forces join together to make this happen.

1. *Majority arguments are more numerous.* The greater the number of people who hold a particular viewpoint, the more numerous the arguments favoring that position are likely to be. Imagine a situation in which your philanthropy committee is planning a fundraiser. Since most members favor a silent auction, more people speak in favor of that activity and more evidence is given supporting it than any other activity. Not surprisingly, the effect of hearing this lopsided set of appeals, particularly the novel and compelling ones, is to further strengthen group members' views. This in turn produces polarization. The idea that initial preferences bias the kinds of arguments discussed and thus make the group's view more extreme is called the *persuasive arguments explanation* of group polarization (Burnstein & Vinokur, 1977; Kaplan & Miller, 1987). The degree of polarization depends on the novelty and quality of the evidence. When group members hear persuasive arguments that they had not previously considered, they move toward the majority position and the group norm becomes more extreme (Hinsz & Davis, 1984).

2. *Majority arguments get more discussion.* When people think that others share their views, they are more likely to express them (Glynn, Hayes, & Shanahan, 1997; Schittekatte, 1996). Arguments endorsed by more than one group member are much more likely to be discussed than ideas endorsed by only a single person. In one demonstration of this effect, Garold Stasser and his colleagues (Stasser, Taylor, & Hanna, 1989) asked students to read different sets of information about candidates for president of a student body.

You may notice the similarities between norm formation and change and attitude formation and change mentioned in Chapter 7. For example, both can happen through superficial and systematic processing (Chapter 7, pages 238 to 244 and 245 to 248).

Some information was given to all members of the group, but other information was given to just one person. When the group met to evaluate the candidates, they discussed 46% of the shared information but only 18% of the unshared information. Not only was the unshared information less likely to be raised with the group, but even when it was, it was less likely to be discussed and evaluated. This tendency is particularly strong with judgmental rather than intellective tasks (Stasser & Stewart, 1992). But it occurs even when discussion members are experts highly involved in the decision-making process, as when physicians diagnose medical cases (Larson, Christensen, Abbott, & Franz, 1996), and even when researchers structure the discussion, instituting rules to make the group discuss all the facts available to them. In fact, such instructions resulted in an even more intense focus on the shared information (see Figure 9.5). Group members apparently believe that the information on which they all agree is the information most relevant to the issue under discussion. The bias toward discussing shared rather than individually held information is bound to strengthen the majority's case—after all, by definition, majority arguments are shared viewpoints, whereas minority arguments are likely to be unique, dissenting views. As such biased discussions confirm the majority position and convince some minority members, the group norm is likely to become more extreme.

3. *Majority arguments seem more compelling.* When several people make the same argument, it has extra impact. Thus, for example, three different people voicing an identical argument are more persuasive than a single person who repeats the same argument three times (Harkins & Petty, 1983). This bias reflects the tendency of people to pay particular attention to replication (different people coming to the same conclusion) compared to repetition (the same person repeating the conclusion). The fact that different people with different perspectives reach the same conclusion makes that conclusion seem particularly compelling. Such replication also provides social validation: The information that one group member raises can be

FIGURE 9.5 Let's talk about something we all know

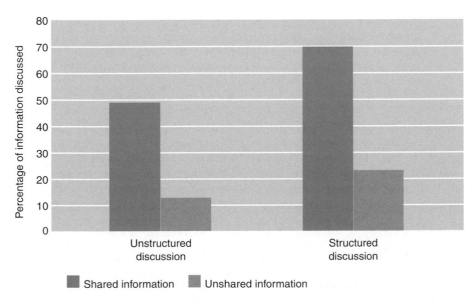

■ Students asked to evaluate candidates were much more likely to discuss information that everyone in the group shared than they were to discuss information known to only one member of the group. When rules were instituted to structure the discussion, the shared information was even *more* likely to be discussed. (Data from Stasser and others, 1989.)

"confirmed" by another group member who also has that information. At the same time, the validity of unshared information is called into question because it cannot be independently verified by others (D. D. Stewart & Stasser, 1995). In fact, any group member whose information is widely shared (and can thus be confirmed again and again by other group members) exerts considerable influence in the group (Kameda, Ohtsubo, & Takezawa, 1997). Consistent with this bias is the finding that people rate as more persuasive, and respond more favorably to, those arguments with which "most people" or "a majority" agree: If most people buy the argument, it must be a good one (Erb & Bohner, 2001; Erb, Bohner, Schmalzle, & Rank, 1998; McLachlan, 1986; Singleton, 1979). Thus, the arguments put forward by a majority in a group discussion seem particularly persuasive, and their influence moves the group further toward the extreme.

4. *Majority arguments are presented more compellingly.* Majority arguments also seem to be presented in ways that make them particularly persuasive. First, information that many group members share is raised much earlier in discussions than unshared information (Larson and others, 1996). This gives majority arguments a persuasive head start. After all, if a discussion is cut short, unshared or minority information may not be heard at all. Information considered toward the beginning of discussions also has more impact than information introduced later on (Hogarth & Einhorn, 1992). Second, majority views are expressed faster whereas those with minority views often hesitate—if only for a second—before expressing them (Bassili, 2003). This difference in speed of expression grows as the difference between the size of the majority and the size of the minority grows, so that minority views are most slowly expressed when the majority is very large. People surrounded by others who feel the same way they do are most likely to be confident about their views (Huckfeldt & Sprague, 2000) and this seems to show in how they express them. Group members, especially males, use a less cautious and more argumentative style of advocacy when they are members of the majority than when they are in the minority (N. L. Kerr, MacCoun, Hansen, & Hymes, 1987). On the other hand, hesitating before expressing a view might make minority adherents seem uncertain or lacking in commitment to their views. Perhaps this explains why other group members see those expressing the majority opinion as more confident and intelligent than those who disagree with it (McLachlan, 1986). Thus, not only do group members hear more arguments in favor of the majority view, but those arguments are also more confidently and effectively presented. The result once again is that the majority seems more compelling, it wins more converts to its cause, and group polarization takes place.

In summary, when group members engage in systematic processing, the existence of consensus makes majority arguments more persuasive, and this persuasive advantage in turn strengthens the consensus. As members of the minority jump onto the majority bandwagon, majority members move toward even more extreme views, and polarization is the inevitable consequence. The process is summarized in Figure 9.6.

Conformity Pressure: Undermining True Consensus

Because people place such a high value on group consensus, they sometimes succumb to group pressure, with disastrous results. As we have seen, relying on

The greater impact of information presented early in a discussion might remind you of what you learned about primacy effects in Chapter 3, pages 85 to 89 arguments presented first can capture more attention than later views, and might even subtly change the meaning or importance of later information.

FIGURE 9.6   Why a consensus is influential: Processes underlying group polarization

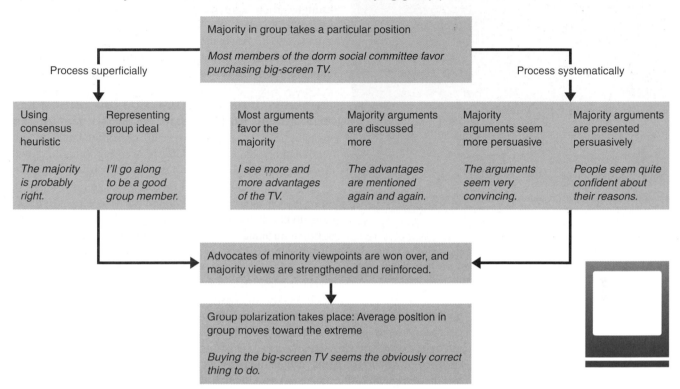

■ When a majority in a group initially lean in a particular direction, their consensus tends to influence others in a variety of ways—whether the group members process superficially or think about the issues in more depth. As the majority position attracts converts from the other side and majority members find their beliefs further strengthened and reinforced, the group's average position moves in the direction initially favored by the majority. Group polarization has occurred.

one another when we make judgments and decisions—when we do so in a way that avoids personal bias, provides reassuring replication, and considers all information thoroughly—can give us a handle on reality and connect us firmly to our groups. But groups sometimes short-circuit such processes, coercing their members and ignoring dissenting voices no matter how worthy these opinions might be. When that happens, group consensus can lead to invalid and unreliable decisions, even when individual members have the knowledge and skills to come up with the right ones.

When Consensus Seeking Goes Awry

Consensus implies that opinions are valid only when consensus is achieved in the right way. A consensus cannot be trusted if it arises from unthinking reliance on others' positions, contamination by shared biases, or public conformity. Such a consensus offers only the illusion of unanimity.

■ **Consensus without consideration.** Have you ever wondered how an entire audience often manages to express its approval by applauding simultaneously, just at the right moment? The power of the consensus heuristic is clearly illustrated by this fact, as individuals in the audience rely on and conform to the apparent endorsement by the surrounding audience members, and may quite unthinkingly clap along in unison. Applause may even be orchestrated by people planted in the audience by performers or management.

You may recall that this experiment was cited in Chapter 1, pages 3 to 4, as an interesting example of social-psychological research.

A decision is not necessarily valid merely because it is based on a consensus. Plenty of decisions can be reached through group agreement but turn out to be seriously flawed. How does this happen, if two heads are indeed supposed to be better than one? Part of the problem is that if a group norm is to provide trustworthy information about reality, the consensus has to be achieved in the right way.

CONSENSUS WITHOUT CONSIDERATION: UNTHINKING RELIANCE ON CONSENSUS. If we merely rely on the presence of consensus, we can be influenced by an unreliable or even a manipulated consensus. Remember the marketing strategy of creating the appearance of consensus by giving away products to thousands of trend setters, to make it look like everyone wanted the product? Corporate consultants have been found to exercise considerable political influence by manufacturing consensus in the form of thousands of letters to policy makers, supposedly from voters but actually generated by computer (Waldman, 1991). In just the same way, those urging supporters to flood easily manipulated internet public opinion polls might be trying to manipulate a false sense of support for their candidate.

Many studies have demonstrated how easily people adopt an apparent consensus, even when relevant information is weak. In one laboratory demonstration of the power of the consensus heuristic, students listened to strong or weak arguments that were presented in a speech supporting probation as an alternative to imprisonment (Axsom, Yates, & Chaiken, 1987). During the presentation, one group of students heard several bouts of loud clapping and cheers from the audience listening to the speech; another group of students heard only scattered applause and occasional jeering. Some students in each of the two groups were told that the new probation policies would not affect them personally. As a result, these listeners were less involved and less attentive, and they were also very much influenced by the apparent consensus. When others cheered, these students agreed with the probation policy, even if the arguments were weak. When others jeered, they disagreed with the policy, even if the arguments were strong. The less people are concerned about accuracy, the more likely they are to rely on consensus regardless of where the consensus came from (Darke, Chaiken, Bohner, Einwiller, Erb, & Hazelwood, 1998). So if group members follow a norm without carefully considering the relevant information themselves, when they go along unthinkingly with what might turn out to be only an apparent consensus, they can be easily led astray. Part of the strength of a consensus is that different people come to the same conclusion after reviewing the evidence. If different people come to the same conclusion based on the evidence the conclusion is likely to be valid (Festinger, 1950; H. H. Kelley, 1967). But if people skip careful consideration of the evidence, then the consensus they contribute to is not trustworthy.

CONSENSUS WITHOUT INDEPENDENCE: CONTAMINATION. The idea that a consensus provides reality insurance rests on an assumption: We think we can trust the consensus because multiple individuals considered the evidence independently and from diverse perspectives, and came to the same conclusion. One person might be influenced by a particular bias and thus see things incorrectly, make the wrong decision, or come to a false conclusion. But it seems unlikely that many people with many different perspectives will all make the same mistake (V. L. Allen, 1965, 1975; Asch, 1951).

Because of the importance of this assumption, people are often on the lookout for shared biases that might contaminate group decisions. In one study, for example, students trying to decide a mock court case watched the videotaped views of six people before giving their own opinions about the defendant's guilt or innocence. Some listeners heard the people on the tape described as two "groups" of three; others believed they were hearing six independent individuals. Even though everyone heard six speakers, participants were less influenced when the speakers were described as two groups of three than when they were described as six separate individuals (Wilder, 1977). Why? Perhaps the participants suspected contamination, thinking that the groups of speakers might have shared a bias or influenced each other. If so, it might have seemed to participants that they were hearing only two new views (one from each group), compared to six in the other condition. Consistent with this interpretation, another study showed that the mere perception that a group of confederates was a committee reduced their influence on participants' opinions. The confederates' views were persuasive only when it was made clear that the committee members represented diverse perspectives—that their individual views had not been contaminated by undue influence or a shared bias (Harkins & Petty, 1987).

You may sense a dilemma here. On the one hand, we trust a consensus when independent and separate individuals endorse it; the convergence of their differing perspectives on the same position confirms the validity of that position. On the other hand, as you may recall from the discussion earlier in this chapter, we really expect to agree only with those who share our characteristics. If we disagree with people who are different from us, it is easy to write them off as confused, ignorant, or just plain wrong.

How can these contradictory statements be reconciled? We seem simultaneously to demand that group members be different and independent (so their consensus indicates validity) and similar and in accord (so that they are an appropriate reference group). In fact, simultaneous similarity and difference is just what we need. We need others to be *similar* to us in terms of the features relevant to making the judgment so that agreement with them will tell us about reality. But we need them to be *different* from us in many other possible ways so that it is unlikely that any other shared feature could bias everyone's judgment (Gorenflo & Crano, 1989).

This simultaneous similarity and difference is part of what makes in-groups so much more persuasive than out-groups. People usually see members of their own group as similar on characteristics that define the group but as variable and different in other ways. Thus, an English major might see other English majors as sharing an appreciation for language and a love of literature, but interacting with them would reveal that they differ greatly in terms of hobbies, political views, food preferences, and so forth. In contrast, people see out-group members as all alike: To English majors, those dance majors all seem the same.

David Wilder (1990) devised a clever experiment to demonstrate that this perception of simultaneous similarity and difference helped in-groups to be more persuasive than out-groups. Participants listened to an audiotape of some in-group and some out-group members presenting their views on an issue. As the tape played each speaker's comments, participants viewed a slide of that speaker's face. Then the researcher played a tape of each person's arguments again and asked participants to match each speaker's picture with his or her arguments. Participants

To refresh your memory about the reasons people see in-groups as more diverse than out-groups, review Chapter 6, pages 201 to 203.

also indicated how much they agreed with the views expressed by the group they had listened to.

The results showed that participants could accurately match in-group members' faces to their arguments: They seemed able to keep track of each in-group member as a distinct and separate individual making distinct and separate arguments. In contrast, students could not match the out-group members with their arguments. Although they might have remembered that an out-group member made a particular point, they had no idea which speaker had made the point. These different perceptions of in-group and out-group members translated into very different amounts of influence. Participants saw in-group members as distinct individuals putting forward independent arguments and coming to the same conclusion. Thus, the in-group seemed to provide replication of the advocated view, and thus social proof. Not surprisingly, then, participants were persuaded by the in-group consensus. In contrast, participants seemed to lump out-group members together, seeing them as faceless figures droning the party line over and over again. No wonder they found the out-group's views unpersuasive. As Figure 9.7 illustrates, thinking of the in-group as simultaneously similar and diverse makes their individual views seem independent and in turn renders their shared consensus persuasive. In contrast, the sameness of the out-group heightens the perception that their views might be contaminated, and it decreases their ability to exert influence.

CONSENSUS WITHOUT ACCEPTANCE: PUBLIC CONFORMITY. The most dangerous threat to the ideal of consensus formation is public conformity, which we earlier defined as people publically supporting or endorsing norms that they do not privately accept as correct. When some of Asch's participants went along with

FIGURE 9.7 How in-groups become more persuasive than out-groups

■ In-groups offer simultaneous similarity and difference. They are viewed as similar on attributes that are crucial for the judgment but as diverse in other ways. As a result, in-groups are more persuasive than out-groups.

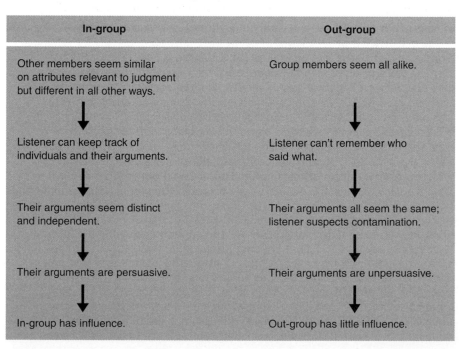

norms that they did not believe were correct, they were demonstrating public conformity. Motivated by the desire to avoid wrath or ridicule, these students followed the motto, "go along to get along" (Deutsch & Gerard, 1955; H. H. Kelley, 1952), and their public conformity destroyed the reliability of the consensus.

Public conformity reflects people's recognition that groups dispense rewards to members who go along with the consensus and punish members who do not. People who disagree with other group members often anticipate negative reactions (Gerard & Rabbie, 1961), and their fears are well founded. When Stanley Schachter (1951) set up an experiment in which a confederate persistently disagreed with other group members, he found that the group first tried hard to win over the deviant. When this failed, the group ignored his views, assigned him to undesirable tasks, and suggested that he be excluded from the group.

Even jurors experience the pressure to conform and many have talked about their experiences. One juror who went public following a well-publicized case described the extreme pressures she felt from other members of the jury to agree with them. Bullied and ridiculed for her dissenting opinion by the majority who favored acquittal, and worn down by 7 days of deliberation, she reported that that she "said to God, 'If you could give me one more person on my side, I would know'" (*New York Times*, 1992a). Could any statement more clearly demonstrate Asch's finding that a single supporter helps people resist pressure from a majority? When another person changed positions and offered her support, the dissenting juror was able to deadlock the jury on a single charge against one officer despite acquittals on all other charges. More recently two jurors in the trial against Michael Jackson admitted capitulating under group pressure to support an aquittal with which they didn't really agree.

Unfortunately, because public conformity brought about by fear, exhaustion, or the desire to please cannot easily be distinguished from real acceptance, it can still influence others. People follow a group norm that doesn't really reflect reality. When everyone publicly adheres to a norm that no one privately endorses, *pluralistic ignorance* is said to exist. Such a situation can arise in many areas of daily life, even in the classroom. Have you ever been afraid to ask a question because the silence of your classmates led you to believe that everyone but you understood the teacher? Many of the other students undoubtedly were feeling

exactly the same way but made the same false assumption you did (D. T. Miller & McFarland, 1987).

☐ **PLURALISTIC IGNORANCE AND HEALTH RISK BEHAVIOR.** Pluralistic ignorance may also contribute to such significant social and health problems as alcohol abuse, risky sexual behavior, illegal drug use, and smoking. Many studies supporting this idea have shown, for example, that many students drink more excessively than they personally feel comfortable doing. Why? Most students show pluralistic ignorance: they believe that everyone else is more comfortable with heavy drinking than everyone else actually is (Perkins & Berkowitz, 1986; Prentice & Miller, 1993). In one study of New Zealand 16–29 year olds, for example, 80% of the women and 73% of the men overestimated the incidence of binge drinking among their peers (Kypri & Langley, 2003). Anti-alcohol campaigns have unwittingly made the situation worse by focusing on extreme cases of alcohol abuse, again making everyone think that everyone else is drinking more than they are (Haines & Spear, 1996). The upshot is that everyone is drinking more than they actually want to because they think that everyone else approves of excessive drinking! To make matters worse, students, especially male students, think they'll have trouble fitting in if they don't drink as much as everyone else (Suls & Green, 2003). Other studies have shown similar conformity to misperceived group norms about "hooking up"—agreeing to engage in sexual behavior for which there is no future commitment—and other risky sexual behaviors. Everyone is engaged in behavior they don't really enjoy because they think that everyone else is doing so (Hines, Saris, & Throckmorton-Belzer, 2002; Lambert, Kahn, & Apple, 2003).

If students had discussed their real opinions on this issue, the impression that "everyone" accepts alcohol abuse, illegal drug use, and risky sex might have been dispelled, and conformity to a false norm undermined. In fact, based on the evidence of pluralistic ignorance's role in such behavior, many schools have introduced programs that show students what their peers are really thinking and doing (Haines and Spear, 1996; Steffian, 1999; http://www.socialnorms.org/index.php). Giving people a more accurate views of what others are really doing reduces excessive drinking (Fabiano, 2003; Foss, 2004; Haines & Barker, 2003; Johannessen & Glider, 2003) and smoking (Hancock, 2002; Linkenbach & Perkins, 2003)—more evidence of the power of conformity!

Consensus Seeking at Its Worst: Groupthink

Groupthink occurs when groups become more concerned with reaching consensus than with reaching consensus in a way that ensures its validity. Groupthink can be avoided by safeguarding consideration of alternatives, independence of views, and private conviction.

The Florida weather was unusually chilly on January 28, 1986, as the U.S. space shuttle Challenger was launched with a crew of seven, including schoolteacher Christa McAuliffe. Seventy-three seconds after liftoff, a fiery explosion caused by the failure of a rubber O-ring in a booster rocket killed everyone on board and set back the U.S. space program for years. Investigations proved that the accident had not been an unforeseeable freak event. Indeed, only hours before launch, engineers from the company that built the booster rocket had urgently warned the National Aeronautics and Space Administration (NASA) decision team that extremely cold temperatures might cause the O-ring to fail. Yet NASA proceeded with the launch—a tragic error that graphically displayed many of the ways that group consensus can go wrong (Esser, 1998; Esser & Lindoerfer, 1989; Moorhead, Ference & Neck, 1991).

How could trying to achieve group consensus hinder rather than help a good decision, as it apparently did in this case? Irving Janis (1972, 1982) asked this question over 30 years ago and set about analyzing the decision making that led various U.S. presidents and their groups of advisers to make some unfortunate policy decisions. What did these ill-fated decision-making situations have in common? According to Janis each situation was marked by an overpowering pressure for agreement: the group became more interested in reaching agreement than in how that agreement is achieved. Janis (1972) applied the term **groupthink** for situations in which the desire to reach consensus interferes with effective decision making. A presidential commission investigating the Challenger disaster found that NASA's decision making was flawed by an emphasis on agreement rather than dissent—the essence of groupthink (Presidential Commission, 1986). Analyses of other events suggest that this tendency might have contributed to poor decisions in a wide range of cases, including poor management decisions in multinational corporations, the 1956 British invasion of the Suez Canal, and the faulty intelligence on the presence of weapons of mass destruction that was used to officially justify the U.S. invasion of Iraq (Esser, 1998; Hensley & Griffin, 1986; McCauley, 1989; R. A. Peterson, Owens, Tetlock, Fan, & Martorano, 1998; Suedfeld, 2004).

CAUSES AND CONSEQUENCES OF GROUPTHINK. According to Janis, group consensus seeking was most likely to go awry when a highly cohesive group of individuals worked under pressure to make decisions. Under these conditions, group members were likely to force conformity, selectively withhold dissenting information, suppress independent thinking, and prematurely rationalize or justify their position. These groups were also likely to perceive themselves as invulnerable, moral, and superior to other groups. Later researchers tried to provide more quantitative analyses of groupthink situations (Tetlock, Peterson, McGuire, Chang, & Feld, 1992) and to devise laboratory tests of Janis's ideas.

Many of the more recent findings do not completely support Janis's analysis of the causes and consequences of groupthink. What they do suggest, however, is that groupthink situations start out as ordinary situations in which groups try to seek consensus, and end up being special instances of consensus being reached in the wrong way (Raven, 1998). Consensus formation typically increases the validity of decisions while contributing to connectedness. But consensus confers these benefits only if it is achieved in the right way. A consensus cannot be trusted if it arises from unthinking reliance on others' positions, contamination by shared biases, or public conformity. Yet these conditions are common when groups care more about reaching consensus than about how consensus is reached. Consider, for example, how groupthink can undermine the guarantees that consensus usually offers.

1. *Consensus is achieved without consideration of all available evidence.* Because reaching consensus is all that counts and pressures for agreement are so strong, information processing is biased and group members devise multiple ways to avoid or suppress dissenting information (Kameda & Sugimori, 1993; Moorhead & Montanari, 1986; Schafer & Crichlow, 1996). Groups prone to groupthink overestimate their abilities and

> **Groupthink.** Group decision making that is impaired by the drive to reach consensus regardless of how the consensus is formed.

effectiveness, and thus see no need for input from others (Eaton, 2001; Whyte, Saks, & Hook, 1997). Doubting members engage in self-censorship, voluntarily suppressing their doubts and criticisms. Occasionally a mindguard emerges: someone who shields group members from unwelcome information that might destroy their confidence in the consensus. With only supporting evidence and ideas available, collective rationalization takes over. The group engages in justifying and bolstering its decision, strengthening consensus rather than testing it.

In the Challenger case, the engineers concerned about the potential failure of O-rings in cold weather were not allowed to present their doubts to those higher up the chain of command (Esser & Lindoerfer, 1989). They were asked to prove absolutely that the booster would not work, which of course was impossible. In the end, self-appointed mindguards shielded the top NASA decision makers from any knowledge of the engineers' reservations.

2. *Consensus is contaminated because members' views are not independent.* Groups whose members share similar backgrounds and similar points of view are most likely to fall prey to groupthink. Despite this danger, such groups often isolate themselves from outside influences and different perspectives, thereby making it more likely that shared biases will corrupt their decision making. Some group members may approach others in private and squash their expression of dissatisfaction, sometimes by appeals to "think like an in-group member." At one point in the Challenger decision-making process, a top executive did just that: Declaring that "a management decision" had to be made, he appealed to his engineering vice president to "take off his engineering hat and put on his management hat." In other words, the vice president was being told to think as management thought and to come to the management decision, rather than considering the issue from the engineering—or any other—point of view.

3. *Consensus is achieved by public conformity without acceptance.* When groupthink operates, conformity pressure is often intense. Tolerance for any kind of disagreement is low, and dissenters are harshly brought into line or "cut out of the loop." Faulty consensus processes often start with voice votes among members, which permits powerful and respected members of the group to state their opinions before discussion takes place (Moorhead & Montanari, 1986). If a majority of the group fall into line, any dissenter is then faced with a situation very much like that of Asch's participants in the line-matching task, and many apparently go along in public without being privately convinced (McCauley, 1998). As the presidential commission noted, the NASA decision team was publicly polled in the final launch decision meeting, while the corporate executives, who knew of the engineers' concerns, listened. In turn, each team member recommended launch. In the face of such apparent consensus, the executives said only that they could not give an unqualified "go" (Presidential Commission, 1986). Unfortunately, this was not interpreted as a strong vote against the mission, and the launch proceeded.

As can be seen in Figure 9.8, these groupthink processes produce an illusion of unanimity, rather than a true consensus. Everyone thinks that everyone else accepts the group position, so pluralistic ignorance also reigns. The apparent consensus in turn validates the group's judgment: "All reasonable people" would have reached the same conclusion. In fact, the process producing consensus has gone horribly awry. Relevant information has not been processed, shared biases have produced contamination, and a group decision that should be based in fact actually reflects

FIGURE 9.8   Groupthink undermines the validity of consensus

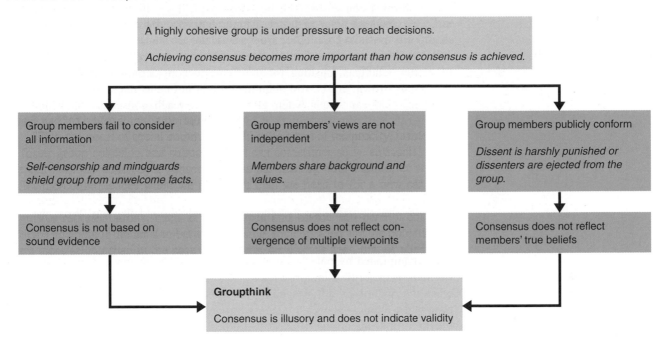

For consensus to be valid, it has to be attained in the right way. Groupthink produces a biased consensus that may be out of touch with reality.

fantasy. In the case of the Challenger launch, the consequences of fantasy were fatal.

REMEDIES FOR FAULTY CONSENSUS SEEKING. How can the dangers of achieving consensus in the wrong way be combated? On the basis of his analysis of political decision making, Janis (1982) suggested several ways to avoid the pitfalls he felt caused groupthink. But if groupthink is just a special case of faulty consensus seeking, the solution lies in making sure that consensus is reached the right way. To avoid consensus without consideration, consensus via contamination, and consensus that reflects public conformity, groups need to take several precautions. To ensure adequate consideration of alternatives, open inquiry and dissent must be part of the group's agenda. Janis recommended the appointment of *devil's advocates*—people whose role is to argue the opposite of what the group is recommending—to ensure that weaknesses in the group's favored position are pointed out. Having such dissenting voices does improve group problem solving (Hirt & Markman, 1995). To avoid contamination by shared biases, group membership can be intentionally selected for diversity. Members with different backgrounds and experience are likely to see problems in different ways and advocate different solutions which can then be considered. And to reduce pressures toward public conformity that contribute to apparent consensus, public votes should be the exception rather than the rule. The role of the leader should be minimized in favor of equally valued contributions from all members, and the voicing of doubts and objections—which should make everyone consider the pros and cons of alternative more deeply—should be encouraged.

What do all these recommendations have in common? The key is to ensure that all views, and not just the majority view, are thoroughly considered when groups form a consensus. The best way to achieve this goal is to ensure that minority views are given their due. Although devil's advocates can point out flaws in majority positions, including true proponents of other views in groups ensures authentic dissent—a situation in which real alternative positions are advanced by their true adherents, pushing for their careful consideration (Nemeth, Connell, Rogers, & Brown, 2001). Although they might not be a "magic bullet" for all the problems that can occur when groups try to reach consensus, inclusion and consideration of minority points of view are crucial to achieving valid judgments and good decisions in groups.

Minority Influence: The Value of Dissent

Consider the obvious idea that the earth travels around the sun. What we now consider "obvious" was once the scandalous heresy of a single scientist, Galileo. Similarly, the norm that women should have the right to vote and own property was once championed by only a few hardy women and even fewer men. Despite the strength of majorities, minority opinions sometimes ultimately win the day. Even when the majority is not swayed by the minority, exposure to minority dissent—even when wrong—plays a crucial role in ensuring the validity and connectedness functions of social norms.

Successful Minority Influence

Minority views can sway the majority. To be influential, the minority must offer an alternative consensus, remain consistent, strike the right balance between similarity to and difference from the majority, and promote systematic processing.

Minority viewpoints can alter the consensus reached in a group. But to achieve their victories and convince the majority to reconsider, minorities must turn the processes of social influence to their own advantage.

OFFERING AN ALTERNATIVE CONSENSUS. Just as a majority's power lies in its command of consensus, the main source of a minority's power is its potential to undermine the majority's consensus and to promote an alternative view. Because group members expect to agree, a minority can exert influence by undermining confidence in the correctness of the majority consensus or majority norm (Asch, 1956; Moscovici, 1980). Sometimes the exceptional credentials or charisma of a single person like Galileo or Martin Luther King may be able to sway others to the cause. But most of the time a lone dissenter has little impact on the group. To make the majority sit up and take notice, the alternative view must be a consensus in its own right. That is, it must be adhered to by more than one person. It must also be presented in such a way that the majority takes it seriously.

1. *Minorities are most influential when they agree among themselves.* Do you remember the California juror quoted earlier, who prayed for just "one more person on my side" (*New York Times*, 1992a)? Just as Asch found that influence began when majorities of two or three formed, so researchers have shown that minority factions of two or three are more influential than a

lone dissenter in mock juries (Tindale, Davis, Vollrath, Nagao, & Hinsz, 1990). Increasing numbers espousing the minority position (especially if they defect from the majority) engender more minority influence (R. D. Clark, 2001; Gordijn, De Vries, & De Dreu, 2002; W. Wood, Lundgren, Ouellette, Busceme, & Blackstone, 1994). The agreement of multiple group members on a single position apparently signals that the position is a viable alternative to the majority position (Moscovici & Lage, 1976; Nemeth, Wachtler, & Endicott, 1977).

2. *Minorities are most influential when they are consistent.* Because majorities are hardly ever swayed immediately, a minority must remain loyal to its consensus over time (Moscovici, 1980; Nemeth & Wachtler, 1983). Many researchers have demonstrated that behavioral consistency is essential in giving a minority clout (Wood and others, 1994). The first to do so were Serge Moscovici and his colleagues (Moscovici, Lage, & Naffrechoux, 1969), who devised a mirror image of Asch's line-matching task. They asked groups of six (four participants and two confederates) to judge the color of a series of unambiguously blue slides. When the confederates insisted on all 36 trials that the slides were green, a small but significant number of participants joined them in this error. However, when the minority wavered, calling the slides green on only 24 of the 36 trials, they had no influence on the majority. Other researchers have found that consistent minorities can influence others in mock jury deliberations (Nemeth & Wachtler, 1974) and in discussions of such social issues as feminism, the death penalty, and homosexuality (Maass & Clark, 1983; Maass, Clark, & Haberkorn, 1982; Paichelier, 1976). Consistency is important because it conveys commitment to the viability of an alternative position. Proponents of a minority view walk a fine line, however. Taken too far, consistency may be interpreted as rigidity or intractability, which leads to a rapid decline of the minority's influence (Mugny, 1975; Mugny & Papastamous, 1980).

When a minority successfully challenges the majority view, the effect can extend beyond the single immediate issue, pushing majority group members to be more open-minded in the future. In fact, seeing a minority express opposition in one situation might even give majority members the courage of their convictions in other situations. One study looked at the effects of hearing a minority point of view on people's later ability to resist conformity pressure (Nemeth & Chiles, 1988). Students made color perception judgments in the presence of a confederate who made dissenting judgments—calling a blue slide green—all the time, some of the time, or not at all. They later participated in a study like the Asch line-matching task, in which the majority agreed on an obviously incorrect response. Up against this unanimous majority, students who had not been exposed to any prior dissent conformed to the majority 70% of the time. But those who had viewed minority dissent in an earlier experiment were much more likely to insist on the correct response. In fact, as can be seen in Figure 9.9, the more consistent the earlier observed dissent had been, the less students later conformed to the group norm.

NEGOTIATING SIMILARITY AND DIFFERENCE. Advocates of minority views face a dilemma. To influence the majority viewpoint, they must offer a consensus that clearly differs from the majority position. At the same time, however, dissenters will not be heard if they are perceived as too different from the majority and therefore not part of the in-group, or if they are judged to be lacking in the

FIGURE 9.9   Learning independence from dissent

■ In the presence of confederates who made unanimous but obviously incorrect judgments on a line-matching task, participants who had not been exposed to a dissenting minority in a previous study conformed 70% of the time. But those who had previously witnessed minority dissent conformed much less often. The more consistent the earlier dissent had been, the more independence participants showed. (Data from Nemeth & Chiles, 1988.)

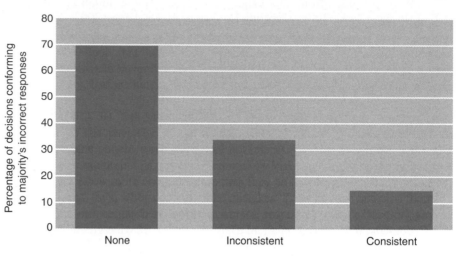

qualifications for making the judgment (Gorenflo & Crano, 1989; J. C. Turner, 1991). Indeed, dissenters are often ignored, disliked, and rejected (Levine, 1980; Mugny, 1982). How can minorities successfully navigate this fine line? According to John Turner (1982; David & Turner, 1996) and William Crano (Alvaro & Crano, 1996; Crano & Alvaro, 1998), the minority first has to establish itself as a part of the in-group before it receives any scrutiny. Edwin Hollander (1958, 1985) suggested that minorities could establish this in-group credibility by first agreeing with the group on important issues. This enables other group members to then show respect for their views on other issues—even deviations from the party line. Research confirms that members who first agree and then dissent are more persuasive than those who challenge the group immediately (Bray, Johnson, & Chilstrom, 1982; Lortie-Lusier, 1987). As Hollander describes it, the dissenters must first build up "points," or *idiosyncrasy credits*, before they can spend them.

Recall that a majority consensus loses some of its power if group members are thought to share a common bias. Minority influence is similarly reduced if the minority viewpoint seems contaminated or if out-group memberships are made salient. *Double minorities*—those who hold a viewpoint different from that of the majority and who also differ from the majority in an obvious way—are at a particular disadvantage. This is especially true if the dissenting viewpoint is apparently related to the dissenter's group membership. When gay advocates lobby for affirmative action laws or mothers petition their employers for child-care facilities, opponents can too easily dismiss their claims. Why? Because the claimants' shared attribute—sexual orientation, motherhood, or other minority group characteristics— can be portrayed as a factor that may bias the claimants' views and raise questions about their self-interest (Maass, Clark, & Haberkorn, 1982). In such cases, the majority may assume that the minority viewpoint is invalid. As is also true for majorities, the minority viewpoint will seem much stronger if its advocates represent a comparatively diverse group of people, as when both gays and nongays campaign for unbiased hiring or when parents and nonparents join in supporting daycare centers.

Chapter 7, pages 243 to 244, described the attributional processes that weaken the impact of arguments when they seem to be governed by the source's self-interest.

PROMOTING SYSTEMATIC PROCESSING. Serge Moscovici (1980) has suggested that when minorities manage their dissent effectively, other group members are more likely to systematically process their arguments. He believes that their plausible alternative creates uncertainty about reality and that this stimulates thinking among majority members. The majority seeks additional information about the issue and processes it in greater depth (Nemeth, 1995). In this sense, minority dissent promotes systematic processing.

Evidence that minorities can make majorities process carefully comes from a clever study in which students were confronted with confederates who were either a majority or a minority in a given experimental session (Nemeth, Mayseless, Sherman, & Brown, 1990). The real participants and the confederates listened to three lists of words. After hearing each list, they took turns naming a category represented by some words on the list. For example, if the list contained many names of birds and a few names of fruit, "birds" was the obvious response usually given by the real participants. The confederates, however, did not name the obvious categories. In some conditions, the rigged majority of confederates named the less obvious category (fruit), whereas in other conditions the rigged minority named it. The consistency with which the confederates responded with the unusual category name was also varied. In some conditions, the nonobvious category was mentioned only once, and in others it was mentioned consistently on all three trials. At a later time, the real participants were asked to recall words from all the lists. The results showed that they could recall more words from lists in which a minority rather than a majority mentioned the nonobvious category, suggesting that exposure to a minority point of view had made them process those words more carefully (see Figure 9.10). Recall was particularly good when the minority consistently mentioned the nonobvious category on all three trials, suggesting that a consistent minority was the most likely to make participants process systematically.

Other evidence also shows that hearing minority views makes majority members look more deeply at an issue. Deborah Gruenfeld (1995; Gruenfeld, Thomas-Hunt, & Kim, 1998) studied the extent to which U.S. Supreme Court

FIGURE 9.10 Minority consistency encourages systematic processing

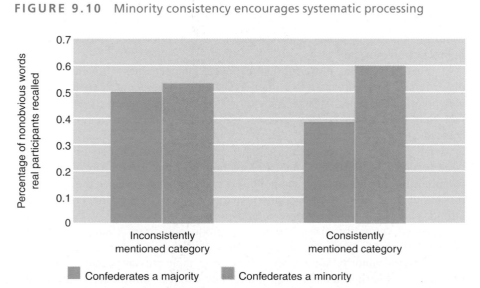

In this study, researchers used confederates who gave nonobvious answers in a series of three trials. When a minority rather than a majority mentioned a nonobvious category of words on a list, participants could more easily recall the words at a later time—suggesting that they thought about them more thoroughly. Recall was particularly good when the minority consistently mentioned the nonobvious category on all three lists, rather than on only one. (Data from Nemeth and others, 1990.)

■ **Hanging tough to make others think.** When those holding minority views take a clear, consistent stand—even when opposed by others—they can make the majority think deeply about the issues involved. When members of the environmental group Greenpeace engage in repeated dangerous acts, like bungee-jumping off the statue of "Christ the Redeemer" atop Corcovado mountain in Rio de Janeiro, they demonstrate solid commitment to their cause in a way that can promote systematic thinking, and attitude change, in the majority.

decisions considered multiple perspectives on a problem, recognized that reasonable arguments exist on both sides of an issue, and integrated these various perspectives and arguments in a coherent position. Decisions marked by these characteristics were seen as reflecting higher levels of complex thought than decisions marked by more rigid application of simple rules. Compared to decisions that were unanimously supported, and compared to dissenting decisions issued by minorities, nonunanimous majority decisions showed higher levels of complexity, regardless of whether the decisions were made privately or announced publicly. Again, this suggests that when organizational decision-making groups are faced with minority dissent, they look at more information and make more integrative decisions (Brodbeck, Kerschreiter, Mojzisch, Frey, & Schulz-Hardt, 2002; De Dreu & DeVries, 1997; Gruenfeld, Martorana, & Fan, 2000). Confronting minority views prompts the majority to develop deeper and more considered judgments, compared to when such opposition is lacking.

In most circumstances, such systematic processing leads to private acceptance of any attitude change that results. When a majority present compelling reasons for lowered school tuition, for example, those who systematically process their arguments usually come to support lowered fees as well. But minorities don't always produce change in such a direct way. In fact, research suggests that, compared to majority advocacy, minority appeals result in less change on directly related issues but more change on indirectly related issues (Perez & Mugny, 1990; W. Wood and others, 1994). Indirectly related issues can be thought of as ones similar, but not identical, to the focal attitude issues. For example, a minority argument for lowered school tuition may not produce support for lower fees, but might increase support for more financial aid for students. A minority appeal to liberalize abortion laws may not be endorsed, but might enhance tolerance for contraception use. Why might such indirect changes occur?

First, given the powerful mastery and connectedness functions of the majority norm, group members often resist openly agreeing with the deviant viewpoint on the main issue of contention (W. Wood and others, 1996). But the fact that they systematically process the minority message may well have consequences for other related issues. Perhaps considering the minority message in depth triggers change on those other issues, even if change on the main issue is blocked (Alvaro & Crano, 1997; Crano & Chen, 1998). This explanation for minorities' ability to bring about indirect change thus focuses on the systematic processing that minority viewpoints generate. All that processing brings about attitude change, although not always on the issue tackled head-on by the minority.

Second, minority dissent may also produce indirect change because it encourages people to be more creative. Because they are not so concerned with agreeing with minority sources, people hearing their messages may think more broadly, considering alternatives, going beyond the information given, and diverging from the topic at hand (Nemeth & Kwan, 1987). This may allow them to see novel connections and to look at things from a fresh perspective. While these divergent ideas may not always lead to change on the main issue at hand, they may bring about changes in related topics (Crano & Chen, 1998; Kaplan & Martin, 1999).

☐ **MINORITY INFLUENCE IN THE COURTROOM.** As we have seen, the expression and consideration of minority views can be vital to forming a valid consensus. And this principle has important implications for jury deliberations. In 1972, the U.S. Supreme Court ruled that states could allow juries to give verdicts that command only majority support, holding that there is neither legal nor historical basis for requiring unanimity. Unfortunately, this ruling makes it possible for a majority to ignore minority views. An initial majority would have no need to convince the minority to go along with its position, nor any strong reason to listen to the minority's arguments. Could loosening the requirement of unanimity have weakened minority influence and perhaps even have lessened the quality of jury decisions?

■ **Turning minorities into majorities.** In the film "Twelve Angry Men" (shown here with the cast from its theater version), a juror finds himself alone in voting for acquittal in a murder trial. He presents his minority view with such consistency and confidence that he convinces the other members to consider the evidence systematically—and eventually change their minds. In real jury rooms, establishing an alternative consensus and maintaining it with consistency and confidence are so difficult that minorities rarely win over majorities.

To investigate these issues, Charlan Nemeth (1977) divided University of Virginia students into mock juries and asked them to reach a verdict about the guilt or innocence of a defendant charged with murder. Nemeth made sure that each group included some students who initially favored acquittal and others who favored conviction. Some of the juries were forced to deliberate until they reached a unanimous verdict, whereas others were allowed to bring in a verdict with only a two-thirds majority. The groups forced to consider and respond to minority points of view not only deliberated longer but also were more confident about their eventual decisions. These mock jurors recalled more of the evidence, suggesting that they had considered it more thoroughly than those in the nonunanimous juries. Even more importantly, they were more likely to change their initial views on the case than were members of groups allowed to bring in a two-thirds majority opinion. Similar results were found when more than 800 Massachusetts citizens recruited from the jury rolls participated in mock jury discussions after watching a videotaped trial (Hastie, Penrod, & Pennington, 1983). When unanimity was not required, jurors usually terminated their deliberations as soon as they reached the required majority.

These findings suggest that loosening the unanimity requirement does weaken minority influence and thus may have reduced the quality of jury deliberations. Of course, it is possible that the participants in these studies, aware that they were involved in research, acted differently than jurors in a real trial. Perhaps real jurors, knowing that their judgments would affect the lives of real people, would give careful consideration to each juror's point of view even if a unanimity rule did not force them to do so. The authors of the Supreme Court decision assumed that they would. Still, it appears that a unanimity rule both increases the likelihood that minority views will contribute to the final group consensus and improves the quality of group consensus formation.

Processes of Minority and Majority Influence

By and large, majorities and minorities influence others by the same processes. Both majorities and minorities can elicit public compliance or private acceptance, encourage heuristic or systematic processing of the evidence, and offer positive social identities.

Do majorities and minorities influence others using fundamentally different processes? Serge Moscovici (1980) thought so. He argued that minorities induce a process of validation, in which group members carefully process information to try to understand why dissenters hold their particular views. In fact, he argued, calling attention to their logical arguments is the dissenters' only recourse because they cannot offer either the validity-ensuring or the identity-confirming benefits of majority positions. In contrast, majority arguments induce a relatively superficial comparison process because people generally want to go along with the crowd, at least in public (Moscovici & Personnaz, 1980; Mugny, 1982). According to Moscovici, listeners focus on what majority members say, so that they can quickly comply and earn the rewards of being valued members of the team. Thus minorities, when successful, bring about private conformity, whereas majorities generate public conformity.

How are we to evaluate Moscovici's arguments? First, majority positions and arguments, as well as minority views, can both be privately accepted (Baker & Petty, 1994; Mackie, 1987; W. Wood and others, 1994)—we have already described research demonstrating this point. At the same time, it is easy to find examples of situations in which minorities, just like majorities, elicit mere public conformity. Majorities may control rewards, but minorities can dispense punishments. One need only listen to the screaming 4-year-old who helps the family decide not to eat out that night. So both majorities and minorities can both produce public and private conformity.

Second, although majorities offer group members positive identities as good team players, not everybody wants to be a member of the establishment team. A minority identity of independent-mindedness, deviance, and rebellion can also be appealing. Can you imagine circumstances in which you might prefer a deviant image to a staid, conservative, respectable one? When being avant garde, innovative, or socially progressive is important, minority opinions offer a positive identity and minorities have a relatively strong influence (Nemeth, 1986; Paichelier, 1976). At the same time, although majority agreement is usually associated with reality, consistent disagreement from a minority can trigger concerns about the validity of the majority position. Thus, it seems that both majority and minority influence can occur to satisfy concerns about both mastery and connectedness.

Finally, as we have seen, both majority and minority messages are reacted to in knee-jerk fashion in some circumstances. At other times, both types of appeal apparently provoke extensive thinking. So it seems that both majority and minority influence can come about through superficial or systematic processing depending on the circumstances (Gaddikiotis, Martin & Hewstone, 2004; Martin & Hewstone, 2003).

Thus, although Moscovici's ideas have generated new ways of thinking about majority and minority influence, he may have overstated the differences between majority and minority influence, just as those before him ignored the

FIGURE 9.11   Minorities use consensus to attain influence

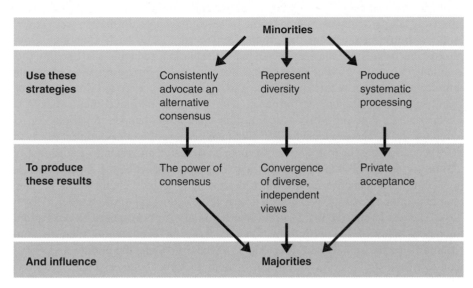

■ Minorities as well as majorities can influence others when they offer a consensus that represents the convergence of diverse views and is built on the systematic processing of relevant evidence.

power of minorties to bring about change at all. Although majority influence might be more likely to produce direct change whereas minority influence produces indirect change, the processes by which they do so are the same ones (Kruglanski & Mackie, 1989). In fact, as can be seen in Figure 9.11, minorities are influential when their dissent offers a consensus, avoids contamination, and triggers private acceptance—the same processes by which all groups achieve influence. By and large, majorities and minorities achieve influence by pulling the same levers.

Beyond Minority Influence: Using Norms to Strengthen Consensus

The best way to promote effective group norm formation and consensus seeking is to set up norms that make group members more critical thinkers *as a group* rather than as individuals. When group members are united behind norms of seeking consensus with systematic consideration of alternatives, independence from contamination, and the conviction of private acceptance, the desire for mastery and for connectedness work together to produce a valid consensus.

The careful consideration of minority as well as majority viewpoints in the context of group discussion can help ensure that the consensus reached by the group is one that can be relied on. Clearly, consensus will have the greatest chance to be accurate when groups overcome tendencies to accept shared and majority arguments at face value. They can do this by systematically processing all information, counteracting the powerful persuasive impact of majority views by including persistent and committed minority voices, and adopting norms supporting courageous dissent. Do these findings mean that group decision making can be improved simply by making group members better information processors as individuals? Studies assessing this idea have produced some surprising results, however.

In one clever study, a group of participants had to solve a murder mystery together—that is, they had to come to a group consensus as to "whodunit" (Liljenquist, Galinsky, & Kray, 2004). Some clues to the murderer's identity were shared by all participants, whereas some pieces of relevant information were known only to single members of the group. Remember that in such situations group discussion usually emphasizes the shared information, reducing the likelihood of solving the mystery. After the participants had read their information about the murder mystery but before discussing it as a group, they were led through a short exercise. Some of them performed a task designed to make them engage in counterfactual thinking—that is, to consider what might happen in various sets of circumstances. The researchers used this task because the consideration of "what if?" scenarios has been found to promote systematic processing of information (Galinsky & Moskowitz, 2000). The most important aspect of the experiment was that some participants performed this task separately, as individuals, whereas others completed the exercise together as a group before going on to the murder mystery task. The results showed that far from improving group performance, making group members better *individual* information processors by encouraging them to think counterfactually actually hurt the group's chances of solving the murder mystery. In contrast, encouraging the group as a whole to think counterfactually *together* improved their ability to identify the culprit.

Thus, the best way to promote effective group norm formation and consensus seeking is to make group members more critical and systematic thinkers *as a group* rather than as individuals (Postmes, Spears, & Cihangir, 2001). These findings demonstrate that the power of the group situation can be harnessed to improve group consensus seeking (Postmes, Haslam, & Swaab, 2005). If the power of norms can make groups susceptible to poor decision making in the first place, why not use that power to improve decision making? The key to successful consensus seeking is setting up norms to govern norm formation itself. When group members are united behind norms of seeking consensus with systematic consideration of alternatives, independence from contamination, and the conviction of private acceptance, the desire for mastery and for connectedness work together to produce a valid consensus.

CONCLUDING COMMENTS

 Among the most important characteristics of group interaction are the formation, transmission, and change of group norms. When group members interact, they offer opinions and arguments and listen to others voicing their views, until finally a consensus emerges. Individuals are highly motivated to have their beliefs, feelings, and actions reflect reality. When participating in a discussion with similar others who share the same information, they fully expect to agree with one another. When such agreement fails to materialize, people are puzzled, distressed, and uncertain. Thus social dissent opens the way for social influence.

This view of group influence makes clear that both social and cognitive processes confer validity on group norms. The social process is the give-and-take interaction that occurs as the group works out a consensus. The cognitive process is the independent evaluation of information carried out by group members. Maximal validity—maximal certainty about our view of reality—depends on both processes.

In many important ways, scientists are engaged in a reality-construction enterprise that is just like everyone's day-to-day attempts to understand social and physical reality. Recall our discussion of scientific method in Chapter 2. Just as people try to construct social reality by forging agreement with fellow group members, social psychologists use many of the same strategies to ascertain the truth about social behavior. Every individual researcher has his or her own personal biases that, despite all efforts to be objective, might influence research strategies, results, and interpretations.

Scientists often come to an experimental test as partisan adherents of a favorite theory. How to discover the truth? The scientific community's solution, like that of other social groups, is to seek consensus. Regardless of researchers' different theoretical perspectives, tests of theories and evaluations of information should ultimately converge on the same outcome. And reaching the same conclusion from different theoretical starting points, using different techniques, and with different participants, offers strong evidence for the validity of the shared conclusion. Such convergence increases our certainty that we are learning about a phenomenon that is real to all of us and independent of our preconceived views. All the norms and procedures of science are intended to promote systematic processing and the acceptance of positions based on the underlying evidence rather than on public conformity. This in turn means that minority influence should be maximized, allowing for the acceptance of new insights and innovations.

True consensus is achieved only when a variety of opinions are processed from multiple points of view and are accepted only after being proved valid by such processing. When we think about how consensus is forged, we can see that true consensus should be constantly undergoing revision. The current norm should be constantly open to new ideas that might challenge the status quo. We should listen to minority opinions instead of closing our minds and finding comfort in majority support for our existing view. When new ideas become too threatening to the status quo, groups often try to expel the deviants from the group. But as we have seen, the expression and consideration of minority views is crucial to the development of reliable group norms. Thus, it is important to nurture diverse and different voices in any group: The validity of a group's norms depends on their being forged from the consideration of many points of view.

CHAPTER 9 THEMES

- **Construction of Reality**
  Individuals and groups construct consensus about what is true and good.

- **Pervasiveness of Social Influence**
  This construction process involves conformity and mutual influence among group members.

- **Striving for Mastery**
  Conformity helps us to hold valid opinions because the convergence of many opinions often means correctness.

- **Seeking Connectedness**
  Conformity helps us feel connected to and valued by other group members.

- **Conservatism**
  Positions supported by a majority in a group usually attract more supporters and do not readily change.

- **Superficiality Versus Depth**
  People process the opinions of other group members either in superficial ways or with careful consideration.

SUMMARY

 Conformity to Social Norms. Because people are profoundly influenced by others' ideas and actions, interaction or communication causes group members' thoughts, feelings, and behaviors to become more alike. Whether a judgment task is clear-cut or ambiguous, individual members' views converge to form a social norm. Norms reflect the group's generally accepted way of thinking, feeling, or acting.

Conformity is the convergence of individual responses toward group norms. Conformity occurs for two important reasons: because people believe that the group is right and because they want the group to accept and approve of them.

Most of the time people engage in **private conformity** to group norms, accepting them as their own, because they believe them to be correct and appropriate. Sometimes, however, people show **public conformity** to norms they do not privately accept.

The Dual Functions of Conformity to Norms: Mastery and Connectedness. Private conformity comes about because we expect to see the world the same way similar others see it. In fact, we often assume that most other people share our own opinions and preferences, a tendency called the **false consensus effect**. Agreement with others increases our confidence that our views are correct, whereas disagreement undermines that certainty.

Agreeing with others not only assures people that they are in contact with a common reality but also gives them the feeling of belonging with others. Although particular circumstances can make one goal more important than the other, usually agreement with a group of similar others simultaneously fulfills the motives for both mastery and connectedness. People expect to agree with those who share attributes relevant to the judgment at hand. Agreeing with such a **reference group** ensures that people are in contact with a common reality and gives them the feeling of being valued. Other group members do not have to be present for conformity to occur, but having other group members present increases conformity even more.

How Groups Form Norms: Processes of Social Influence. When group members are initially split on an issue, group discussion usually results in convergence on a moderate position. But when a majority of group members initially favor one side of the issue, communication and interaction usually result in **group polarization**, in which the group norm becomes even more extreme.

When people process superficially, merely relying on others' positions can produce polarization of group norms as undecided or moderate group members move toward the group position and try to show that they are good group members. When people process systematically, others' positions and arguments both work together to polarize group norms. Majority arguments are more numerous, receive more discussion, seem more compelling, and are presented more persuasively. All these factors give majority views a persuasive advantage.

Conformity Pressure: Undermining True Consensus. Consensus implies that opinions are valid only when consensus is achieved in the right way. A consensus cannot be trusted if it arises from unthinking reliance on others' positions, contamination by shared biases, or public conformity. Such a consensus offers only the illusion of unanimity. **Groupthink** occurs when groups become more concerned with reaching consensus than with reaching consensus in a way that ensures its validity. Groupthink can be avoided by safeguarding consideration of alternatives, independence of views, and private conviction.

Minority Influence: The Value of Dissent. Minority views can sway the majority. To be influential, the minority must offer an alternative consensus, remain consistent, strike the right balance between similarity to and difference from the majority, and promote systematic processing. By and large, majorities and minorities influence others by the same processes. Both majorities and minorities can elicit public compliance or private acceptance, encourage heuristic or systematic processing of the evidence, and offer positive social identities.

The best way to promote effective group norm formation and consensus seeking is to set up norms that make group members more critical thinkers *as a group* rather than as individuals. When group members are united behind norms of seeking consensus with systematic consideration of alternatives, independence from contamination, and the conviction of private acceptance, the desire for mastery and for connectedness work together to produce a valid consensus.

10

Norms and Behavior

At 5.05 p.m., August 7th, 2003, a crowd suddenly gathered by the washing machine display in a department store in the German city of Dortmund. Cellphones in one hand, members of the crowd checked the time, ate a banana, looked around happily, and left (Pohl, 2003).

When Henrietta and Dennis Taylor allowed two door-to-door salesmen into their Florida home, the elderly couple ended up buying a $1749 vacuum cleaner. Because their monthly income was only $1100, the salesmen arranged a loan that brought the total in payments to over $2500 (Cahill, 1999).

A caller on the phone said police suspected a particular employee of stealing from customers at a Boston, U.S., Wendy's fast food restaurant and ordered the supervisor on duty to strip search the suspect immediately. Following the caller's directions over the phone, the supervisor ordered the employee into a private room and obeyed (Stockton, 2004).

How are we to understand these apparently very different examples of human interaction? What do the harmless fun of a flash mob, the cautionary tale of an elderly couple who paid too much for a household appliance, and the willingness of one person to violate the rights of another on command from an unidentified caller have in common? As you will see in this chapter, the answer involves social norms. Through the processes we described in Chapter 9, all human groups—even fleeting ones—establish *social norms*: generally accepted ways of thinking, feeling, and behaving that people agree on and endorse as right and proper. Social norms reflect a group's view of the world, itself, and others, and they have a powerful effect on almost all aspects of our behavior. Of course, established groups create laws and sanctions—systems of reward and punishment—to enforce appropriate standards of behavior among their members. But as you will see in the first part of this chapter, norms are powerful precisely because they usually control group members' behavior without any kind of outside enforcement. Called into existence by web sites and e-mail distribution lists, flash mobs get together somewhere at some time, engage in a common but often meaningless behavior—and disperse. No one makes the participants turn up, conform, and go home. They just do it, perhaps for the sheer pleasure of being "in synch." For most members of

■ **Norms are powerful.** At public meetings, sporting events, even in many schools and businesses in the U.S.A., the opening notes of the national anthem or the opening words of the Pledge of Allegiance are enough to bring people to their feet with hands over their hearts. Although such norm-driven behavior is sometimes maintained by reward and punishment, most of the time people behave in line with group norms because they want to, not because they have to.

more important and more abiding groups, norms are so well learned and privately accepted that when a norm is activated its standards automatically govern behavior. Thus, most of the time people do what the social customs and conventions of their group prescribe because they *want* to, not because they *have* to.

Some of the most powerful norms reflect deeply held beliefs about how members of a group should treat one another. Norms about reciprocity dictate that people should repay others' kindnesses or favors, even if repayment comes at a cost to us. Norms about interpersonal commitment direct us to keep our word, stand by our promises, and be trustworthy and reliable, even when others are not. Norms about obedience command us to obey those to whom society has given legitimate authority. Because norms like reciprocity, commitment, and obedience are so important in regulating human interaction, we discuss them in detail in three major sections of the chapter.

What happens when others exploit our tendency to follow our groups' rules? Like the Taylors, we may find ourselves in trouble. If a salesperson appears to do us an unasked-for favor (cleaning a carpet for free), or makes a meaningless concession (reduces an over-inflated price tag by a small percentage), our impulse to reciprocate can trap us into giving up something of real value (our hard earned money). And just as the supervisors at the Wendy's restaurants dutifully obeyed an apparently legitimate authority, throughout history malevolent authorities have used norms to make people act obediently in the service of great evil. Hitler's death camps, Stalin's secret police, and Argentinean dictators' death squads were all institutions that could not have functioned without the norm of obedience.

If norms have such power, can people successfully rebel against them? We saw in Chapter 9 that considering diverse points of view can sometimes change group norms, even those that are fully accepted and widely endorsed. The same strategy of careful thinking can help us resist inappropriate attempts to use norms against us. Because we are subject to a variety of norms that offer sometimes contradictory suggestions about how we should act, every influence situation is open to interpretation. By understanding how norms influence our actions, by questioning the norms that others assume should guide our behavior, and by deliberately considering which norms apply to each situation, people can successfully resist normative pressure.

Of course, norms are not the only cognitive structure that helps guide behavior. As you may recall from Chapter 8, attitudes also have a potent influence on what we do. The final section of this chapter shows that norms and attitudes usually operate together to guide behavior. Because so many of our attitudes are also a product of our memberships in groups, these attitudes rarely conflict with norms. Sometimes, however, norms and attitudes suggest different courses of action, and then the outcome depends on which of them comes to mind more easily. Whether or not an employee's personal attitudes lead her to "blow the whistle" on a company's way of doing business or whether a young man's personal convictions cause him to challenge the state's authority to draft him into the military will depend on the mix of social norms and individual attitudes that are brought to bear in the situation. To understand how all these forces affect our actions, however, we have to begin at the beginning. How do norms influence our behavior, and why do they have such a powerful effect on what we do?

Norms: Effective Guides for Social Behavior

Kurt Lewin (1943) was one of the first social psychologists to demonstrate the powerful effect of group norms on behavior. During the Second World War, traditional cuts of meat like steaks and chops were scarce and, when available, very expensive. To keep the civilian population healthy, the U.S. government wanted people to consume more liver, kidneys, and other unfamiliar organ meats. Commendable as this goal was, U.S. citizens found it hard to swallow at the dinner table. Pamphlets extolling the nutritional value of these meats and public lectures by expert nutritionists—both of which might have changed attitudes—had little impact on well-entrenched food-buying and eating habits. Lewin believed that changes in behavior could best be accomplished by changing the prevailing norms. That is, he suspected that only a shared consensus about what was appropriate to eat would change this kind of behavior. To test this idea, he brought homemakers together in small groups to discuss in depth such questions as how to cook the new cuts and how to overcome family members' resistance. In the course of these discussions, group members' willingness to try the new foods increased, and this produced a shift in norms, just as we described in Chapter 9. A follow-up survey showed that over 30% of the discussion group members actually tried the unusual foods, compared with only 3% of homemakers who listened to a lecture advocating the same course of action (but who had no idea how other people just like them reacted to the new foods). Norms thus had an impact on behavior that information alone could not achieve. How do norms come to influence behavior, and why are they so effective?

How Norms Guide Behavior

> Norms must be activated before they can guide behavior. They can be activated by deliberate reminders or by subtle cues, such as observations of other people's behavior.

No norm, attitude, or other cognitive representation can influence behavior unless it comes to mind. Norms, like attitudes, can be made accessible either by deliberate reminders or by subtle cues. Deliberate reminders of appropriate norms are all around us. The sign in the library requests, "Quiet, please." The reluctant child is instructed, "Do as you're told!" And the announcer at the Olympic medal award ceremony states, "Please rise for the playing of the national anthem." Not surprisingly, this direct approach pays off in norm-based behavior. In one demonstration of this effect, Robert Cialdini and his colleagues (Cialdini, Reno, & Kallgren, 1990) placed handbills on the windshields of cars parked at their campus library. Some handbills activated antilittering norms in a straightforward way, announcing, "April Is Keep Arizona Beautiful Month. Please Do Not Litter." Others delivered a message irrelevant to littering: "April Is Arizona's Fine Arts Month. Please Visit Your Local Art Museum." Unobtrusive observers counted (and we hope picked up) the handbills thrown to the ground. Twenty-five percent of those receiving the irrelevant message discarded it before getting into the car, compared with only 10% of those receiving the direct reminder about antilittering norms.

Although deliberate reminders effectively bring norms to mind, our behavior is usually influenced by less direct means. More often, people, places, or proceedings provide subtle cues that activate norms, which in turn guide behavior. The silence of others in libraries and churches keeps our voices hushed; the raucous cheering of basketball and football fans lets us know it's fine to yell. We slow down at the sight of flashing lights and pull over at the sound of a siren. The first few notes of the national anthem bring us to our feet, and the dimming of lights at a concert settles us down. Norms activated in one situation can also carry over into another situation, because they have been made accessible. In one clever experiment demonstrating this point, Guido Hertel and Norbert Kerr (2001) had students study words related to either loyalty or equality, supposedly for a memory test. Students were then asked to allocate points between anonymous members of an artificially created in-group and out-group. Compared to students primed with the norm of equality, students subtly primed with the concept of loyalty allocated three times as many points to the in-group member as to the out-group member. Note that the students in this experiment could probably not have told the experimenter "I gave the out-group more points because the norm of equality was activated," even though you might be able to say that you're quiet in the library "because that's the way you behave in a library." People don't have to be consciously aware of the power of a particular norm for it to influence their actions. Whether by obvious or subtle means, norms just have to be activated. Once they are, accessible norms guide behavior.

☐ **NORMS AND THE ENVIRONMENT.** Most of us have had the experience of having someone drop trash on the floor or the ground near us. When this happens, probably the first things that spring to mind are norms about such actions: Is littering acceptable behavior or not? Direct reminders, like a sign posting the fines for littering, offer an easy guide, but your surroundings may also offer clues about the prevailing norm. Heaps of discarded trash suggest that other people have found it acceptable to litter, whereas a pristine environment implies norms against such behavior. Researchers have found that people are more likely to litter in messy environments than in surroundings that are clean and free of trash (Krauss, Freedman, & Whitcup, 1978). And the more obvious the reminder of the norm is, the greater its impact will be.

One study demonstrating this point placed participants in one of two settings: One was littered, the other was clean (Cialdini and others, 1990). The researchers found that more participants littered in the dirty environment than in the clean one. These actions are evidence that prevailing norms have a big impact on behavior. For other participants in the same environments, researchers drew attention to the norms regarding littering by having a confederate walk by and drop a piece of trash. Those who saw the confederate litter the clean environment littered even less than those in the same environment with no confederate. In contrast, the confederate's littering made participants throw even more trash into the dirty environment (see Figure 10.1). Evidently, the confederate's behavior made the norm implied by the state of the environment—whether neatness or messiness—even more accessible, and, in doing so, it increased behavior consistent with the norm.

In a second study by the same researchers, making the norms accessible in a different way had the same impact. In this study, observers compared behavior in three environments: One was completely clean, one was marred by a single piece of trash, and one was covered with litter. The single piece of trash seemed to make people really think about the prevailing antilittering norm, which in turn led them

FIGURE 10.1   Effect of activated norms on littering

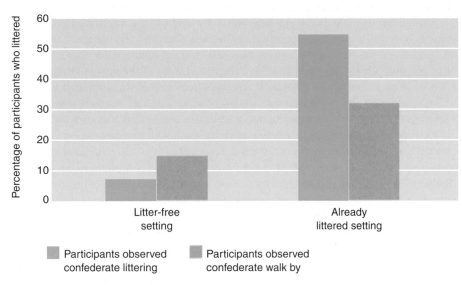

■ In this study, people littered least when they observed someone sullying a clean environment, and they littered most when they saw trash being thrown into an already dirty environment. Researchers explain this paradox in terms of norm accessibility: The litterer's behavior called attention to the prevailing norm, whether cleanliness or messiness, and the norm, in turn, influenced behavior. (Data from Cialdini and others, 1990.)

to litter even less than when the environment was completely clean. The greatest amount of littering occurred in the already spoiled environment.

Could it be that a single act of littering is the best prevention for littering? Although seeing a person litter a clean environment does make us more aware of antilittering norms, Cialdini and his associates (1990) are not advocating preventive littering. Clean environments stay clean for long periods, and when one person finally drops something, littering becomes even less likely. So starting with a perfectly clean environment is the best way to ensure maximum impact of antilittering norms on behavior. As the researchers note, it's about time the concept of norms was recycled to help clean up the environment.

Why Norms Guide Behavior So Effectively

Norms are sometimes enforced by rewards and punishments. More often, however, people follow norms because they seem right, they are endorsed by the behavior of other group members, and they are frequently activated.

Why do we resist the impulse to litter a clean environment, especially when littering is probably easier than using a wastebasket or recycling? And why should anyone return a favor? After all, accepting benefits from others and never giving anything back can be highly profitable, at least in the short run. Why do people adhere to social norms at all?

ENFORCEMENT: DO IT, OR ELSE. The most obvious reason we might conform to social norms is that groups sometimes use a carrot-and-stick approach—rewards and punishments—to motivate people to adhere to group standards. Norms are important, often vital, to the smooth functioning of groups, and groups take quite seriously their need to identify and stop norm violators. In fact, people are better at detecting violations of social norms (which often have more serious social consequences) than they are at detecting violations of logic (Cosmides, 1989). You soon notice the colleague who never puts money into the office coffee fund while you dutifully pay for your daily mug of java.

Some groups handle norm violations by embodying their norms in legal statutes or moral canons: by specifying behaviors that are legitimate and those that are not. Societies take such action not only out of concern for any particular wronged individual but also to reinforce the importance of the norm to the group as a whole. And, as we saw in Chapter 9, groups often attempt to maintain conformity to social norms by withdrawing social acceptance and support from norm violators. Bucking social convention can be both a lonely and a painful activity.

Using rewards and punishments may be the most obvious way groups can establish and maintain norm-consistent behavior, but it is also the least effective. First, the carrot-and-stick approach may produce public compliance, but it is less likely to bring about private acceptance of norms. When those who are merely complying publicly with group norms escape group surveillance, watch out! Second, no society can afford enough monitors to enforce all appropriate norms on all its citizens all of the time, to say nothing of the problem of who will monitor the monitors.

INTERNALIZATION: IT'S RIGHT AND PROPER, SO I DO IT. Although using rewards and punishments can be effective, behavior often matches norms for a much more powerful reason: Most norms are internalized, and they thus seem to be both the right thing and the proper thing to do. As we saw in Chapter 9, the acquisition of social norms occurs because people accept group consensus as truly reflecting reality and expressing the kind of people they are. Acting in line with group norms is not an unpleasant obligation, but a way of maintaining a shared reality and expressing group identity. Most of the time, acting in line with group norms is the same as acting in line with one's own preferences. Typically, rules that benefit the group also benefit the individual, another reason that makes internalization of norms functional. The North American immigrant to England, for example, accepts with little resistance the norm that he must drive on the left side of the road to avoid injuring himself and others. Of course, the individual benefits of social rules are not always so immediately clear. Nevertheless, these norms—the norm of obedience, for example, or the norm of social responsibility—become deeply ingrained through the process of socialization as new group members absorb group norms as relevant to and benefiting the self (Bandura, 1977). Adhering to such norms not only feels like the right and proper thing to do, but also makes people feel respected by others whose opinions they value.

CONSENSUS AND SUPPORT: WE'RE ALL DOING IT, SO I'LL DO IT TOO. Because other members of our groups endorse the same norms, their presence promotes rather than interferes with normative behavior. Remember from Chapter 8 that our intentions to act in line with our attitudes are sometimes undermined by others who do not share our convictions. We may intend to be cooperative, but a persistently aggressive opponent may make it difficult to carry out that intention. Some activities inherently require the participation of others, and almost any behavior can be undermined if others actively oppose it. With normative behaviors, this is not a problem: Those around you are likely to be openly supportive, either because they share the same set of norms or because they are likely to be engaged in the same behaviors themselves. Alice Eagly and her colleagues (Eagly, Diekman, Schneider, & Kulesa, 2003) have shown, for example, that the so-called gender gap in election patterns in the United States occurs because most voters of each sex are likely to vote for the candidate who endorses positions typically favored more by their own sex than the other sex. Women vote for candidates who feel the same way on issues as most women do, and other women support and confirm this group-based behavior. Men vote for candidates who feel the same way on the issues as most men do, and other men support and confirm this action. (Democratic men buck this trend: they tend to favor candidates who advocate positions favored by women, but they still have group support in doing so—from other Democratic men.) Normative behavior is supported because other group members activate, model, and reinforce the appropriate behavior.

FREQUENT ACTIVATION: IT CAME TO MIND (AGAIN), SO I DO IT (AGAIN). As we encounter them over and over again, we build up mental associations between particular environments and how to act in them, as well as between particular groups and how to act around them. Every time we enter a house of worship, step onto the platform at a train station, or take our seat in an exclusive restaurant, we make a mental connection between the place and what others are doing there. Over time, these connections become so automatic that the environment itself activates the appropriate behavior. Compared to students shown photos of a railway station, Dutch students shown pictures of a library not only recognized words like *silent*, *quiet*, and *whisper* more quickly, but also used softer voices in a later speech task (Aarts & Dijksterhuis, 2003). When strong associations between situations and behaviors have formed, thinking about those situations makes the appropriate behavior more likely, and this effect is even stronger among people primed for conformity (Aarts, Dijksterhuis, & Custers, 2003). The same process works with the group members associated with particular behaviors. Because norms are associated with groups, any reminders of belonging to the group can bring its norms to mind. Most obvious is the presence of other group members: Another person behaving in an appropriate way automatically activates the same goal and behavior in others around them (Aarts, Gollwitzer, & Hassin, 2004). In fact, the presence of other group members increases adherence to group norms, even when their behavior isn't publicly visible (Kerr, 1999). But other reminders of group belonging work in the same way. Hearing the group's language or seeing its symbols, and even the presence of out-group members, can activate group norms and increase norm-consistent behavior. Put the average soccer fan in national team colors, surrounded by other supporters in the bleachers, for example, and watch for behavioral signs of increased patriotism. Because people are so often reminded of their group memberships by choice or circumstance, norms have lots of opportunities to influence behavior.

You may notice that normative behaviors become associated with and activated by environments just as individual behaviors like habits do, see Chapter 8, pages 290 to 291.

☐ **NORMS IN THE WORKPLACE.** Aware of the effectiveness of norms in guiding behavior, social psychologists were quick to realize that permitting groups to establish their own norms might help solve a familiar workplace dilemma: how to introduce changes in production procedures without loss of productivity, lowered morale, or outright hostility from workers. In one early experiment demonstrating this point, researchers compared workers' responses to three different ways of introducing changes into production routines at a small rural pajama factory (Coch & French, 1948). Workers in the control group were merely informed about the new procedures. Quite predictably, they reacted with dismay: Productivity dropped dramatically and turnover increased. Workers in a second group were allowed to choose group representatives to teach them the new techniques. This group representation helped: Morale stayed high and productivity, after an initial decline, returned to original levels. In a third group every worker became a "special operator" who was responsible for figuring out the best ways to make the changes in production. In this condition, then, all the workers were able to participate in and contribute to decisions about the changes. In short, they developed a group norm about how the changes should be made. The results in this total participation condition were dramatic. Morale stayed high, and the initial drop in productivity lasted only a day. After that, productivity climbed steadily until it was 15% higher than before the changes were introduced.

Helping establish norms for one's own group has the same dramatic effect today that it had in the 1940s. Techniques that encourage employees to actively participate in decision making that affects aspects of their work environment is now referred to as participative decision making, and such practices are almost standard in many industries and in many parts of the world (Pritchard, 1995). Automobile manufacturing workers in Japan and Sweden, for example, have long participated in *quality circles*, small groups of employees who meet regularly to discuss improvements in the production process and the work environment. When organizational practices are changed so that the participation technique used really gives workers a voice in changing or developing norms in their group, such involvement gives employees a sense of control and ownership and is widely credited with increasing job satisfaction and performance (Pritchard, Jones, Roth, & Stubing, 1988, 1989).

Deindividuation: Making Group Norms More Salient

> When individuals are in a state of deindividuation, they see themselves purely in terms of group identity, and their behavior is likely to be guided by group norms alone. The result can be either antisocial or prosocial behavior, depending on what norms are activated by the group.

■ **Deindividuation: The power of group norms**. When group membership dominates thinking, a likely outcome is blind conformity to in-group norms. This could manifest negatively, in such antisocial behavior as rioting or hooliganism. However, deindividuation can also produce a positive effect, depending on what norms are accessible. At this rock concert, for example, the deindividuation experienced by being part of the sea of fans simply serves to heighten the positive mood and excitable behavior of the crowd.

Group norms do not always produce socially responsible behavior. The norms of flash mobs seem merely silly, but norms can also facilitate clearly antisocial behavior. Consider groups of British "soccer hooligans," for example, who have developed norms of extreme partisan support, violence against opposing fans, and vandalism following team victories. Such behavior is often triggered when groups of fans congregate, and it reaches fever pitch when one group of fans, decked out in the team colors and waving team flags, confronts equally fanatical supporters of other teams. The fact that violent behavior such as this often occurs in such group settings made early observers speculate that being in a crowd changes the rules of human behavior, making it less rational, more volatile, and often more violent (LeBon, 1908).

Some researchers have argued that crowds have this effect because they promote anonymity and the feeling that normative standards of conduct do not apply (Festinger, Pepitone, & Newcomb, 1952). In one study, for example, Philip Zimbardo (1970) had college students dress in identical overalls and hoods that concealed their faces. He assumed this anonymity would cause the students' personal and individual identities to become lost in the crowd. The results seemed to support his reasoning. Compared to other students who wore normal clothing, whose faces were visible, and who wore name tags, the hooded students delivered stronger electric shocks to another student.

Of course, negative behavior in a crowd may result from practical considerations. Being anonymous and unidentifiable—wearing a hood or mask, being concealed by darkness, or melting into the crowd—makes it less likely that someone will be arrested and punished for vandalism, looting, assault, or arson. Note that this view assumes that group norms elicit merely public conformity or compliance, and that as soon as surveillance is impossible, normative behavior ceases and antisocial behavior inevitably increases. But such a view doesn't seem to make sense—the last time you were the only car on a particular stretch of highway, did you drive on the wrong side? Or yell profanities in a church just because you were there alone? Probably not, because as we have explained, norms typically result in behavior because they are internalized, not because they are complied with.

Thinking about behavior in terms of internalized norms provides a different understanding of such situations. **Deindividuation** refers to losing oneself in the crowd—the state in which group or social identity dominates personal or individual identity. Being part of a crowd increases people's tendencies to see themselves as group members. Further, being anonymous and indistinguishable only increases feelings of shared group membership further. Under these conditions, group norms become maximally accessible; the only thing group members think about are what the other group members around them are thinking, saying, and doing (Reicher, 1987).

Far from arguing that deindividuation frees people from normative constraints, this view suggests that deindividuation increases the power of group norms over behavior: People, acting purely as group members, end up thinking and doing what the group does. In this view, then, deindividuation would increase the tendency of individual members to join in any kind of group behavior, whether that behavior is tearing down goal posts or rescuing earthquake victims. When a crowd turns into a rock-throwing mob, deindividuation should cause people to join in. But what if the crowd is rushing to pull victims out of the rubble after an earthquake? Will deindividuation stop people from engaging in this altruistic activity, as early research suggested, or increase helping as the power of group norms suggests?

Research evidence supports the group-centered view of deindividuation. In a meta-analysis of 60 studies, Tom Postmes and Russell Spears (1998) found that deindividuation increased normative behavior rather than antisocial behavior. That is, deindividuation increases whatever behavior is typical of the group (Kugihara, 2001; Lea, Spears, & de Groot, 2001; Postmes, Spears, Sakhel, & de Groot, 2001; Sassenberg & Boos, 2003). Consider, for example, the results of a study that varied the accessible norms in a situation in which people's anonymity was also manipulated (R. D. Johnson & Downing, 1979). Some groups of participants in this study dressed in robes and hoods designed to activate negative and aggressive associations, such as thoughts about the disguises worn by the racist Ku Klux Klan organization or the hoods worn by executioners. Other groups of participants dressed in nurse's uniforms, outfits that activated positive associations with helping and caring. In addition, some groups of "executioners" and "helpers" were anonymous—their outfits covered their faces—whereas others were identifiable. All participants had to decide the level of shock to deliver to another person for

> **Deindividuation.** The psychological state in which group or social identity completely dominates personal or individual identity so that group norms become maximally accessible.

> If you think this sounds very like what we said about group polarization in Chapter 9, pages 322 to 328 you're right. Group polarization is the formation of an extreme group norm because everyone is focused on what it is that is common to or defines the group. Under conditions of deindividuation everyone is also focused on what defines the group, and they act in line with it.

FIGURE 10.2   Deindividuation makes people act in accordance with accessible group norms

■ Participants in this experiment could increase or decrease the levels of shock by 1, 2, or 3 units. When dressed in nurselike uniforms, participants selected lower levels of shock, and deindividuation magnified this tendency. In contrast, participants dressed in Klanlike robes tended to increase shock levels, and deindividuation increased this tendency still further. Deindividuation does not always lead to antisocial behavior, but it does make people more likely to follow currently salient norms. (Data from R. D. Johnson & Downing, 1979.)

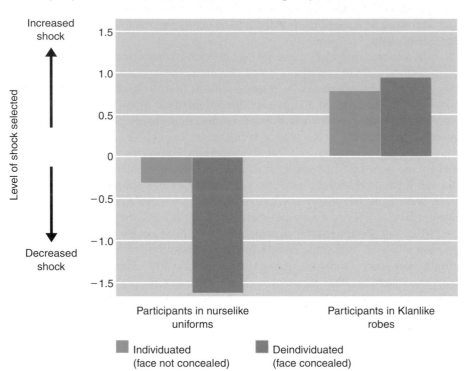

failing a task. As can be seen in Figure 10.2, anonymous participants in the executioner costume delivered higher levels of shock than those who were identifiable. These results could have come about either because anonymous individuals are free to behave badly, or because the prevailing group norm was one of aggression, and norm adherence was increased by anonymity. The "helper" conditions are the ones that really tell us what is going on. The anonymous participants in nurses' uniforms delivered *lower* levels of shock when they were unidentifiable than when their faces and name tags were visible. Far from being more aggressive when they were anonymous, these participants acted more in line with the groups norms when they felt less like identifiable individuals. When social identity is uppermost, people are more likely to do what the group norms tells them they should.

These findings suggest that deindividuation does not universally "free" people to follow their "basic" antisocial impulses. Instead, deindividuation makes people act in accordance with whatever group identification is accessible at the time: being a member of a disaster-response relief team, a Manchester United supporter, a KKK member, or even a nurse.

The Norm of Reciprocity: Treating Others as They Treat You

Winnie the Pooh, hero of the much loved British children's stories, gently instructs one of his fellow inhabitants of the Hundred Acre Wood: "When someone does something nice for you, you're supposed to do something nice for them in return. That's called friendship." Actually, it's called the norm of reciprocity. The **norm of social reciprocity** directs us to return to others the goods, services, and concessions they offer to us. According to the sociologist Alvin Gouldner (1960), almost all societies endorse some form of reciprocity norm, and only a few members of society—the very young, the sick, or the old—are exempt from it. The universality of this norm is not surprising; it benefits both individual group members and the group as a whole. Individuals gain because the norm helps ensure fairness: Any resources they share will be returned by others. The group benefits because reciprocity strengthens the bonds that hold it together, building trust and commitment among its members.

Returning Favors

One of the most prevalent social norms directs us to return to others favors, goods, and services that they offer to us. This norm can sometimes be activated to our disadvantage.

The offer of some valued resource triggers the norm of reciprocity, which directs us to give something in return. This means we are obliged to return gifts, favors, and compliments, even if they are unsolicited (H. Wilke & Lanzetta, 1970, 1982). Consider the power of a small, unsolicited favor to increase giving, as demonstrated by one laboratory study (D. T. Regan, 1971). As each male participant settled to his supposed task of making aesthetic judgments, he was joined by a confederate who was trained to be either particularly friendly or rather rude. In one condition, the confederate returned from a break with two bottles of cola and offered one to the participant; in another condition he returned empty-handed. The confederate later asked the participants to purchase some 25-cent raffle tickets. As you can see from Figure 10.3, participants bought the most raffle tickets when the confederate had done them an unsolicited favor, even though at the time a bottle of cola cost much less than the 25-cent ticket. Notice also that the norm of reciprocity was so strong that it prevailed even when the confederate was unlikable. In fact, the power of the norm of reciprocity is so great that people even feel compelled to return the favors of a stranger who has been forced to help them out (Goranson & Berkowitz, 1966). The power of the norm is strongest right after we have received the favor and gradually tails off (Burger, Horita, Kinoshita, Roberts, & Vera, 1997). Norms of reciprocity are well internalized: people tend to reciprocate favors even if the favor-doer will never find out that they did so (Whatley, Webster, Smith, & Rhodes, 1999).

Salespeople, market managers, and survey researchers are well aware of the power of unsolicited gifts. When was the last time you received a free sample of a product through the mail, were offered a free aerobics session at a newly opened health club, or were sent a dollar as an incentive to fill out a long questionnaire? These techniques activate the feeling that you should do something in return: buy the product, enroll at the health club, or complete and return the questionnaire. And the

> **Norm of social reciprocity.** The shared view that people are obligated to return to others the goods, services, and concessions they offer to us.

■ **The norm of reciprocity.** A baker serves a customer samples of muffins. Offering free samples of food in a shop serves to increase sales, as people then feel obligated to buy the product.

FIGURE 10.3 Banking on the norm of reciprocity

■ In this experiment, some participants were treated to a bottle of cola by a likable or an unlikable confederate. Later, the confederate tried to sell participants raffle tickets. Participants who had received the unsolicited favor from the confederate bought more raffle tickets, even though they cost more than the drinks. They honored the norm of reciprocity—returning favors, goods, and services that others offered them—even when they did not like the confederate much. As these results show, honoring the norm of reciprocity can sometimes lead to returning a favor more valuable than the one received. (Data from D. T. Regan, 1971.)

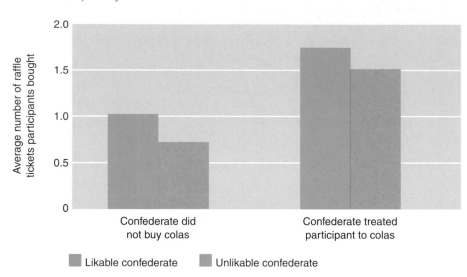

technique seems to work. Door-to-door sales increase when households receive products to try for a day or two without charge. When a salesperson eventually follows up with a call, customers typically buy as many as half the products they have sampled (Cialdini, 1984). The vacuum cleaner buying Taylors, described at the beginning of this chapter, felt the obligation of having had their rug shampooed for free. Sending a dollar bill along with a survey questionnaire increases the number of people who complete it from about 25% to over 50% (May, 1976). The norm of reciprocity works in the supermarket, too. The feeling that you are obliged to buy several packets of frozen waffles after accepting a delicious sample morsel—complete with whipped cream—keeps products moving briskly (Packard, 1971).

Despite these sometimes less-than-beneficial consequences, social groups must maintain reciprocity norms. Without such norms, people might never help one another or develop close relationships. And, as you will see later, we can protect ourselves against misuse of the norm of reciprocity by trying not to follow it—or any other rule of conduct—without reflecting on the meaning of our action.

The Norm of Reciprocity for Concessions

Concessions are also supposed to be reciprocated. This can leave us vulnerable when influencers make concessions following our refusal to comply with a large demand—we feel obligated to make a concession in return. Because people believe in the norm of reciprocity, behaviors based on these concessions are often stable over time.

THE DOOR-IN-THE-FACE TECHNIQUE. One day a young man of about 14, casually dressed but freshly scrubbed, appeared at the front door of one of the authors. He informed her that he represented a national service organization dedicated to helping local high school youths resist the temptations of easily available drugs and alcohol. The plan was to get local householders to "adopt" a youth: him. For 1 month he would spend 10 hours a week cleaning, gardening, or performing other

Calvin and Hobbes by Bill Watterson

household chores in return for an hourly wage of $4, which would be paid to the organization. She would adopt him to help America's youth, wouldn't she?

Not that she didn't want to support America's youth, but working full time and on a tight budget, she was used to doing her own cleaning and gardening. "Well," she started weakly, "I'm not home all day, and I'm not sure ... I'm really not sure ... No, I don't think I can do that."

"Well, Ma'am," the young man replied, "we are offering householders like yourself an alternative way to help. If you can't help us out on the adoption program, a donation would be acceptable."

"Just a minute, I'll get my purse," she responded, feeling relieved that she had avoided having someone come to her house every day for a month. Then, as the young man walked away with her check for $20, the light dawned: She had been the target of the door-in-the-face technique. The young man had expertly manipulated social norms to increase the likelihood of her making a donation.

The **door-in-the-face technique** consists of making a large request and following its refusal with a concession that invokes the norm of reciprocity (Cialdini and others, 1975). The ploy gets its name from the fact that the requester wants the door to be slammed so that he or she can retreat from the initial request. In fact, the first request is always for something much greater than requesters actually want, leaving room for them to back down, thereby putting pressure on the other person to reciprocate with a concession.

The door-in-the-face technique is extremely effective. In one investigation of the technique, researchers asked two groups of students to volunteer for a worthy cause (Cialdini and others, 1975). The researchers approached some students—the control group—as they walked across campus and asked if they would be willing to accompany a group of teenage delinquents on a 2-hour trip to the local zoo. Not surprisingly, the idea of spending several hours with an unspecified number of potentially uncooperative teenagers had little appeal, and only 17% agreed. Other students were first asked to spend 2 *years* serving as personal counselors to juvenile delinquents. When all refused this long-term commitment, the request was downgraded to the 2-hour zoo trip. This technique induced 51% of the participants to agree—more than three times the number in the control group.

The door-in-the-face technique will activate the norm of reciprocity when three conditions exist (Cialdini and others, 1975). First, the initial request must be

Door-in-the-face technique. A technique in which the influencer makes an initial request so large that it will be rejected, and follows it with a smaller request that looks like a concession, making it more likely that the other person will concede in turn.

large enough that it is sure to be refused but not so large that it will breed resentment or suspicion. Second, the target must be given the chance to compromise by refusing the initial request and complying with the second request. Finally, the second request must be related to the first request and come from the same person, who must be seen as making a personal concession (O'Keefe & Hale, 2001).

Once it is clear that the requester has made a concession, the target is on the spot, and acting in accordance with the norms is the most likely outcome. The sense that the other person is really giving something up makes the target of the request feel guilty—am I acting appropriately? Am I creating a negative impression? How can I make up for it? (Millar, 2002a; O'Keefe & Figgé, 1999). Agreeing to the second request gives the target an opportunity to repair a damaged sense of self (Millar, 2002b; Pendleton & Bateson, 1979). And beware the wrath of others if you violate the reciprocity of concessions! In one study of price negotiation, buyers were encouraged to make a concession. If the seller reciprocated with another concession, as expected, the buyer was again likely to reciprocate until a mutually agreeable price was found. But when sellers did not reciprocate a concession, buyers got mad! If the seller refused to reduce his offer, or even raised it, buyers said, "No more Mr. Nice Guy!" Their negotiations became super competitive, as they tried to punish the seller for the norm violation (Maxwell, Nye, & Maxwell, 2003).

☐ **RECIPROCITY OF CONCESSIONS ON THE SALESFLOOR.** Retailers count on the norm of reciprocity when they offer discounts or special deals. They expect customers who have been given 10% or 15% off the price of a sweater or who have accepted a free child's toy with every hamburger to respond by buying more sweaters and more hamburgers. Their expectations are usually rewarded. Two favorite methods retailers use to activate the norm of reciprocity for concessions are the "that's-not-all" technique and the strategy of selling the top of the line.

1. *The that's-not-all technique.* In this ploy, the requester starts with an inflated price and then shifts to a better deal without even waiting for a refusal. The concession technique of immediately offering a discount or bonus has been called the that's-not-all technique. And it is effective, as Jerry Burger (1986) showed. He set up a table at a bake sale and offered cupcakes at $1.25 each—a price he immediately reduced to $1.00. Buyers bought more cupcakes when they thought they were getting a bargain than they did when the cupcakes were simply sold for $1.00 with no previous "markdown." Burger achieved similar success when he "sweetened the pot" by offering a free cookie with every cupcake. Remember those TV informercials where "And that's not all! If you just call within the next 30 seconds you get a second one absolutely free!"? In all these cases, the seller offers the buyer a little more, and the norm of reciprocity for concessions helps clinch the sale.

2. *Selling the top of the line.* Retailers also use a concession technique called "selling the top of the line." A salesperson using this strategy tries to interest the customer in the most expensive model of a product and then, if the sale is not made, directs the customer to the next-cheaper item. As the salesperson gives up trying to sell the preferred product, the consumer reciprocates by spending more than he or she intended. Does the technique work? One experiment testing the hypothesis showed 290 business majors a video designed to sell compact disc players (Donoho, 2003). Some students saw a "top of the line" video, which encouraged them to consider the most

expensive model first before "dropping back" to cheaper models. Compared to students shown the models in other orders, those shown the expensive model first chose higher priced products overall. Selling the top of the line in this experiment resulted in the students spending an average of 10% more than when the technique was not used.

From the door-in-the-face technique, through the that's-not-all technique, to selling the top of the line, these influence strategies all rely on the same principles. Regardless of whether it is a smaller request, a special deal, or lowered expectations, people presented with a concession are nudged by the norm of reciprocity to respond with concessions of their own.

Do the targets of these shifts from large to small requests resent being the victims of such an approach? Far from it. In fact, people who comply with the door-in-the-face technique are more likely to carry out the agreed-on behaviors than are those who make the same commitment without refusing a prior request. In one study in which the commitment involved 2 hours of work without pay in a community mental health agency, 85% of those in the door-in-the-face group actually reported for duty, compared with only 50% of the volunteers from the control group (R. L. Miller, Seligman, Clark, & Bush, 1976). Similar results were found in a study of participation in a blood drive (Cialdini & Ascani, 1976). A heightened sense of having acted consistently with the norm of reciprocity apparently moves people to complete the agreed-on behavior. And compliance with the norm of reciprocal concessions can be for the good of the target as well as the requester. One study used the door-in-the-face strategy or a single request to try to get people to keep a 4-day meal log. The door-in-the-face technique was more effective, especially if people recognized that the behavior would benefit them (Millar, 2001). Once again, privately accepted norms have a powerful effect on actual behavior.

The Norm of Commitment: Keeping Your Promises

"You're only as good as your word." "Don't make promises you cannot keep." "Put your money where your mouth is." These nuggets of folk wisdom reflect a key component of social life: the **norm of social commitment**. This norm requires us to stand by our agreements and fulfill our obligations. If your friend agrees to save your seat while you buy popcorn, she is obligated to protect it from encroachment. If you agree to subscribe to the Sunday paper, you must pay the delivery person when he or she comes to collect. Social contracts help ensure that members of a group or society behave in socially acceptable ways.

One study demonstrated the lengths to which people will go to maintain a commitment (Moriarty, 1975). The scene was a crowded New York beach. In one condition, the researcher made an explicit social contract with neighboring sunbathers: He asked them to keep an eye on his radio while he was away for a short time. In the control condition, the researcher only interacted socially with his neighbors; he asked them for the time before leaving. A few minutes later, a confederate pretended to steal the radio. Did the norm of social commitment affect behavior? Indeed it did. Ninety-five percent of the people who agreed to watch the radio tried to stop the thief, with some even running after the thief to retrieve it. In contrast, only 20% of the uncommitted bystanders bothered to intervene. In a

Norm of social commitment. The shared view that people are required to honor their agreements and obligations.

replication of the study, a pocketbook was left for a few minutes in a booth at a fast-food restaurant, with similar results. The bystanders who helped were those who had made a prior commitment to do so.

Like the norm of reciprocity, norms governing commitment allow groups and societies to function effectively. Group members can trust one another, agreements can be long-lasting rather than fleeting, and future planning can be based on other people's stated intentions. Not surprisingly, norms of social responsibility may be even stronger in collectivist cultures and groups. One study, for example, found that participants in India regarded social responsibility as a moral imperative rather than a personal choice. American participants were more likely to think that the norm could be avoided, unless it involved life-threatening need or immediate family (J. G. Miller, Bersoff, & Harwood, 1997). Even in individualistic cultures, however, the norm of social commitment is strong enough that it, like the norm of reciprocity, can also be used to entrap us if we follow it unthinkingly.

The Low-Ball Technique

The obligation to honor agreements can make people vulnerable to influence when they make a deal and then find out there are hidden costs. People usually stick to the deal even though it has changed for the worse.

Our tendency to honor interpersonal commitments, and the corresponding expectation that others will honor their commitments to us, are so ingrained that we stand by agreements even when the deal has changed to our disadvantage. Imagine the following scenario. An acquaintance asks if you will help her move her few belongings to a small apartment in your neighborhood on Saturday morning. You agree, but when you turn up, you find that she has a new plan. She is now moving into a house with one of her friends in a new location across town, so each trip will take about 2 hours. And the deal seems to include collecting her friend's belongings and helping her move in as well. Suddenly, a couple of hours work on a Saturday morning has turned into a mammoth moving experience that will probably take all day. You have been low-balled. The **low-ball technique** is used when an influencer secures an agreement with a request but then increases the size of that request by revealing hidden costs. How would you respond in such a situation?

If the findings of social-psychological research are any indication, you would probably spend the day helping your acquaintance move. In one study demonstrating the low-ball technique, experimenters phoned students and asked them to participate in an experiment for extra credit. Some students were told the bad news up front: The experiment was to start at 7 a.m. Knowing that, only 31% were willing to participate. Other students were low-balled: They were first asked to make a commitment to participate, and those who agreed were then told about the early starting time. Yet, 56% of these students agreed to participate, a significantly higher percentage than in the other group. Having made a deal, the students were reluctant to break the commitment, even though the deal had changed (Cialdini, Cacioppo, Bassett, & Miller, 1978). When people agreed with a complete stranger's request to look after a dog on a leash, most of them honored their commitment—even when they were only later told that the owner would be away for over half an hour (Guéguen, Pascual, & Dagot, 2002)!

Low-ball technique. A technique in which the influencer secures agreement with a request but then increases the cost of honoring the commitment.

Long-Term Consequences of Commitment

People stick by their commitments for several reasons. They feel obligated, and being inconsistent makes them feel uncomfortable. They also add new thoughts, feelings, and behaviors to help support and bolster their action.

The power of the low-ball technique can influence behavior over the long term as well as in the short run. Consider the way in which Michael Pallak and his colleagues (M. S. Pallak, Cook, & Sullivan, 1980) used low-balling to encourage energy conservation. After finding that merely asking families to conserve natural gas had no impact on their fuel use, these researchers offered an incentive to produce the desired commitment to saving fuel. The deal was that families who saved fuel would get their names in the paper as energy-conscious, public-minded citizens. It worked. In the very first month, each family saved an average of 422 cubic feet of natural gas. Then came the low ball. The researchers withdrew the incentive, sending a letter to each family saying it would be impossible to publish their names. Was the commitment strong enough to keep the families saving without the incentive? Apparently so. The researchers found that during the following 3 months, the families continued to conserve at the original rate or an even better one.

Why do people stay the course? Several processes conspire to make people stick by their commitments even when a deal has changed.

1. *Fulfilling social commitments.* We initially fall for the low-ball technique because we feel an obligation to fulfill our social contracts. The importance of this obligation can be seen in the effectiveness of a particular variant on the low-ball strategy, which is common practice among dealers of new and used cars. It is often the case that the customer and salesperson make an excellent deal, only to have "the boss" raise the price significantly. Despite the additional charges, most customers stick by their commitment to the salesperson. In fact, low-balled victims are often very apologetic to salespeople for even considering backing out of a deal whose terms have changed (Cialdini, 1984).

   One reason this particular ploy is successful is that it cleverly sustains the customer–salesperson relationship and the obligations that go with it. Having an outsider—"the boss," "management," "my supervisor"—be responsible for overturning the agreement maintains the customer's feelings of social obligation to the salesperson; after all, it's not the salesperson's fault the deal is changing. Committed to the original arrangement, the hapless buyers feel honor-bound to fulfill their social contracts.

2. *Maintaining a positive self-image.* It's not only our commitment to others that leads us to make good on a contract that now favors the other party. Our commitment to maintaining a positive view of ourselves helps too. We may know that the deal is weakened. We may even want to back out of an obligation. But we carry through because we have difficulty reconciling such behavior with our sense of being trustworthy and reliable members of society. Even though it might be wise to walk away from a deal that is now less desirable, the discrepancy between our past commitment to the deal ("I gave my word!") and our possible withdrawal from it ("I'm thinking of backing out!") creates an uncomfortable arousal. This arousal is *cognitive dissonance*, which you will recognize from Chapter 8. The only way to reduce the discrepancy is to grit our teeth and fulfill the commitment.

3. *Bolstering the original commitment.* When *cognitive bolstering* occurs, the original commitment is strengthened by the addition of supportive new thoughts, feelings, and behaviors. First, people think of all the possible benefits the new behavior or product could provide. Even though its price has gone up, the new car will still make vacations much easier, and now we can save money on groceries by shopping at the supermarket instead of the convenience store. Second, people start to think of the object as their own (it's my first car and it's new, shiny, and attractive), which gives it special value and makes it harder to give up even if the deal changes (Beggan, 1992). Third, actually performing the behavior or interacting with the object offers additional rewards. Perhaps there are unexpected savings on gas, or the latest model's reduced pollution makes people feel they are helping clean up the environment. As these bolstering processes go to work, many other new thoughts, feelings, and behaviors come to support the original course of action.

The way these processes work together to bind people to a deal even though it changes are illustrated in Figure 10.4. At first, buying the car depends purely on the great price the salesperson offers. But soon, many other reasons to stay the course come into being. With all these new cognitions, feelings, and actions supporting the new behavior, changing the original deal and removing the original incentive makes little difference. Just as the fuel-saving householders deprived of the opportunity for publicity found many other reasons to justify their continued

FIGURE 10.4   Cognitive bolstering and maintaining commitment

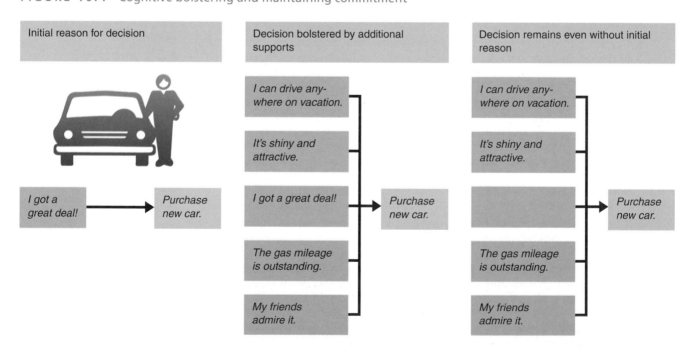

■ The original decision to purchase a new car may have been based mainly on the great deal the salesperson offered (left panel). Given time, the customer generates several additional reasons that also support the decision, as shown in the middle panel. When the customer is low-balled, these other reasons may sustain the decision, even after the initial reason vanishes.

energy conservation, so the customer now sees many reasons other than the original sales price that justify buying the new car.

Sales personnel are quick to provide opportunities for these bolstering processes to kick in. After the original commitment to buy, for example, the client may be allowed to try the new car out for the weekend. Taking relatives and friends out for a drive makes potential ownership a matter of public record, draws attention to the car's many benefits, and increases feelings of ownership, all of which make the customer's commitment to the car even stronger. Sales personnel refer to this kind of tactic as "the puppy dog close:" Most people who spend time with a puppy find it hard to return it to the pet store.

Thus, the norm of social commitment, like the norm of reciprocity, is intended to foster group cohesion and support, but it can sometimes serve antisocial ends. We can reap the benefits of conservation as our heating bills decline, or we can suffer the consequences when we pay more than we need to for a new car. This double-edged quality is an inherent attribute of social norms, as it is of other cognitive representations, such as stereotypes and biased self-perceptions. But perhaps nowhere is the tension between possible societal good and the potential for harm more salient than in the case of the norm we discuss next, that of obedience to authority.

The Norm of Obedience: Submitting to Authority

For millions of people around the world, the war-crimes trial of Adolf Eichmann raised deep questions about human nature (Arendt, 1965). As one of Hitler's top officials during the Second World War, Eichmann sent millions of European Jews, Gypsies, homosexuals, Communists, mental patients, and Christian Scientists to their deaths in Nazi concentration camps. To his Israeli captors and to the world-wide audience, Eichmann's behavior seemed incomprehensibly evil. Surely such monstrous behavior reflects total depravity, extreme cruelty, or pathological hatred.

Yet, like countless people who have slaughtered others in the line of "duty" before and since, Eichmann appeared quite normal, even boring. He described himself as a good family man who had lived quite blamelessly before the rise of the Nazi regime. He said he had nothing in particular against the Jews. Over and over again, he claimed he was "just following orders." Eichmann's defense did not save his life: He was found guilty and hanged for crimes against the Jewish people and humanity. But genocidal policies are still with us today, and so the questions about human nature raised by Eichmann's actions and his trial still linger. Is torture or murder something that any of us might do on command?

Among those fascinated by the trial was the North American social psychologist Stanley Milgram. A firm believer in cultural differences, Milgram doubted that behavior like Eichmann's could occur in cultures where rugged individualism and independence were valued. He believed that members of such cultures would resist group pressure to obey orders, especially if those orders meant that someone else would get hurt. Once he had finalized the procedures for a control condition—a situation in which participants were merely instructed to harm another without any group pressure to do so—Milgram planned to test his hypotheses about conformity and obedience in many different countries. But the startling responses of participants in this control condition put Milgram's plans on hold. Understanding when and why people obeyed authority, even if doing so harmed others, became Milgram's main concern, and his findings became perhaps the best known and most controversial in social psychology.

Milgram's Studies of Obedience

In one of the best-known experiments in psychology, people obeyed orders to deliver shocks to an unwilling and clearly suffering victim. They obeyed these orders even though they were not forced to do so.

Using advertisements in a New Haven, Connecticut, newspaper, Milgram recruited men from all walks of life to participate in his experiment in return for a small payment. When each volunteer arrived in the laboratory on the Yale University campus, he was introduced to a middle-aged man, a confederate pretending to be another participant. The experimenter explained that the purpose of the study was to demonstrate the effects of punishment on learning, and he said that one of the participants would serve as teacher and the other as the learner for the session. A rigged draw assigned the real participant to the role of teacher. His job was to teach the pupil word pairs and to punish any incorrect response by delivering an electric shock to the pupil's wrist. As the teacher watched, the pupil was strapped without protest into a chair in an adjoining room and electrodes were taped to his wrist. To "test the equipment," the experimenter gave the teacher a low-voltage shock, enabling him to experience the small, mildly unpleasant feeling that the learner would be subjected to in the early stages of the experiment.

Back in the experimental room, the experimenter explained the operation of the equipment. To deliver a shock, the teacher merely had to flick one of the switches on the shock generator. There were 30 switches, in 15-volt increments ranging from 15 volts (labeled "slight shock") to 450 volts (ominously marked only with XXX). The teacher was to start with the lowest level of shock and move to the next higher level with each mistake. The shocks may be "painful," the experimenter said, "but do not cause permanent tissue damage." The experimenter stood beside the teacher as the experiment began.

The pupil's initial mistakes were met with only low levels of shock. But as incorrect responses mounted, so did the voltage. Soon, grunts of pain came from the pupil's room, but he continued trying to learn the word pairs. At this stage, the teachers typically showed visible signs of distress and tried to stop the experiment. But the experimenter was unrelenting, repeating only that the teacher must continue. Finally, at the 300-volt level, the learner pounded on the wall in protest and refused to answer further questions. Most teachers sighed with relief at this point, believing the experiment was over. Instead, the experimenter announced that silence was to be considered an incorrect answer and punished. Teachers' protests were met with the response: "The experiment requires that you continue." As the shocks increased and the learner pounded ever more feebly on the wall, the experimenter urged the teacher onward, saying, "You have no choice, you must go on." Finally, even the pounding stopped. Anguished teachers typically raised the possibility of injury, but the experimenter never wavered, insisting, "The responsibility is mine. Please continue."

As is now widely known, most of the participants did continue. In one study, 65% of them delivered shocks all the way to the 450-volt level (Milgram, 1963). Far from demonstrating that ordinary people would resist the dictates of authority, the experiment showed the opposite. The results astounded scientists and

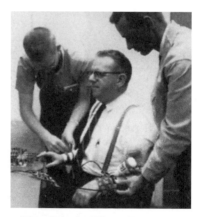

■ **The victim in Milgram's experiment**. In a simple experiment with powerful implications, Stanley Milgram studied obedience by asking participants acting as "teachers" to deliver electric shocks to a "learner", shown here being fitted with electrodes and strapped into a chair. The results of the experiment demonstrated the often startling power of widely accepted social norms on behavior.

nonscientists alike. When Milgram described his experimental procedure to middle-class adults, college students, and psychiatrists, most guessed that only a few people in a thousand would obey the experimenter to the end. Yet more than two thirds of the participants agreed to perform actions they found repulsive.

Attempting to Explain Obedience: Was It the Time, the Place, the People?

The destructive obedience of Milgram's participants was not due to personality defects, hard-hearted unconcern about the victim, or suspicion that the experiment was rigged. In fact, obedience in nonexperimental settings can be just as high, and authorities command as much obedience in recent studies as they did 40 years ago in Milgram's experiments.

■ **Obedience rules**. Even when the learner's pain and distress were obvious, teachers often went along with the experimenter's implacable demands that they continue giving shocks. Why did so many people obey?

Why did so many people obey? Were Milgram's participants particularly heartless individuals, hardened urbanites too calloused to care for others? Could they have seen through the deception and realized that no shocks were actually delivered? These explanations seem implausible in the face of the reactions of the participants themselves. Milgram's teachers experienced extraordinary distress as the experiment progressed. They trembled, pleaded to be allowed to stop, muttered to themselves, stuttered when they spoke, laughed nervously, dug their nails into their flesh, and offered to take the learner's place. Clearly, not only did they fully believe that the shocks were real, but they also cared deeply about the learner's suffering.

In fact, the potential harm to the hapless participants in Milgram's experiments attracted severe ethical criticism when the results were published (Baumrind, 1964). The critics first pointed to the participants' severe distress, asking whether the trauma of the experience could have lasting aftereffects—effects that could not be dissipated by a postexperimental debriefing. They also raised questions about the debriefing itself. What would be the effect on people of realizing that they had been thoroughly hoaxed and that they were capable of committing great harm when told to? Critics questioned whether these insights might decrease the participants' trust in others or their self-esteem (Baumrind, 1964; Schlenker & Forsyth, 1977).

Milgram (1964, 1977) responded by arguing that the debriefing was carefully and sensitively conducted. Participants appeared greatly relieved (rather than upset) on realizing the true nature of the experiment, and they came to believe the research purpose was worthwhile. In a follow-up questionnaire sent to participants some months after their participation, 84% reported positive feelings about their participation, 15% reported neutral feelings, and only 1.3% described negative feelings. Despite these seemingly reassuring findings, the distress experienced by Milgram's participants was one impetus for the introduction of "informed consent" procedures in psychological experimentation. Participants must now be given enough information about an experiment so that they can make an informed decision about participation.

The fact that Milgram's participants felt so badly about the punishments they believed they were inflicting makes it unlikely that they obeyed because they were cruel or heartless. Nor can their behavior be explained by their status as adult males in one particular society. Milgram's procedure has since been replicated in several different countries with women as well as men, and children as well as adults, in the role of teacher (Askenasy, 1978; Blass, 2000;

The nature and purpose of informed consent were discussed in Chapter 2, page 49.

V. L. Hamilton & Sanders, 1992, 1995; Meeus & Raaijmakers, 1986; Shanab & Yahra, 1977). Most participants expressed considerable distress at what they were asked to do, yet most also continued to obey.

If high levels of obedience cannot be attributed to the participants' character, could it be a consequence of the nature of the experimental setting itself? Perhaps people who feel that obedience is appropriate in a protected laboratory environment would never dream of carrying out harmful orders in settings outside the laboratory. Unfortunately, obedience to authority occurs in many other settings.

☐ **OBEDIENCE IN THE WORKPLACE.** In most medical settings, unquestioning obedience to the physician is the normal state of affairs. No one overrules the doctor—not the patient, not nurses, and not interns. Doctors have been accused of attempting to maintain this power differential by insisting on giving the orders even when nurses know more about the case than they do (Ashley, 1976; L. Stein, 1967). What happens, then, when doctors make mistakes? Does anyone question them?

To find out, researchers looked at nurses' responses when a "doctor" gave an unreasonable order (Hofling, Brotzman, Dalrymple, Graves, & Pierce, 1966). The "physician" phoned 22 different nurses' stations at different hospitals, identifying himself as a physician at the hospital. He instructed the nurse, who was alone at the station, to deliver 20 milligrams of the drug Astrogen to a specific patient. Such an instruction violated hospital policy in several ways. Prescriptions were supposed to be given in person, not over the phone. The drug had not been cleared for use on the particular ward. The requested dosage was twice the maximum listed on the container. Finally, the "doctor" giving the order was unknown to the nurse. Despite all these red flags, all but one of the nurses immediately prepared to obey. The norm of obedience overpowered their considerable medical training. Many researchers attribute such problems largely to the unquestioning deference to authority that doctors demand and nurses accept (M. Cohen & Davis, 1981; Lesar, Briceland, & Stein, 1997).

As our opening example of obedience at fast food restaurants makes clear, hospitals are not the only other settings in which obedience is the norm. In fact, many recent studies indicate that "organizational obedience"—obedience that occurs in hierarchical bureaucratic organizations—may occur at even higher levels than suggested by Milgram's studies. In one study, for example, 77% of the students who were playing the role of board members advocated the continued marketing of a potentially dangerous drug if they believed that the chairman of the board, to whom they were accountable, favored this decision (Brief, Dukerich, & Doran, 1991). In another, North American business students derogated the credentials of qualified African-American job applicants and recommended against interviewing them, if given "instructions from the company's president" that favored giving the job to a White American (Brief, Dietz, Cohen, Pugh, & Vaslow, 2000). And in a series of more than 19 experiments in which Dutch participants were ordered to try to distract, joke with, and generally interfere with the performance of another person while he was trying to interview for an important job, Wim Meeus and Quinten Raaijmakers (1986, 1987) found greater obedience than comparable conditions produced in the Milgram experiment. These findings show that obedience to authority is just as likely today as it was 40 years ago; people were not just more obedient "back then." All in all, the research record indicates that obedience to authority can occur regardless of participant, culture, setting, or time: Milgram's results cannot be explained away by the time, the place, or the people involved (Blass, 2000).

The Norm of Obedience to Authority

The norm of obedience to a legitimate authority figure who accepts responsibility had a powerful effect on behavior in Milgram's experiment and has a similar effect on behavior outside the lab. In both Milgram's studies and in obedience in everyday situations, conditions that increase the accessibility of the obedience norm or decrease attention to other norms (such as social responsibility) increase obedience. Once obedience occurs it can be maintained or escalated by gradual entrapment and the impact of justification processes.

If none of these factors (personality, setting, culture, or time) can explain the obedience Milgram found, what does? When he observed participants' responses to the systematic manipulation of various features of the experimental procedure, Milgram became increasingly convinced that the explanation lay in the power of the social situation to activate a norm of obedience (Milgram, 1963, 1974). The **norm of obedience to authority** is the shared view that people should obey commands given by a person with legitimate authority. "Legitimate" and "authority" are important parts of this definition. *Legitimacy* derives from the group: The group endows the authority figure with the might and right to give orders, and the group assigns to its members the responsibility of obeying. *Authority* derives from status, not from any particular person. When a soldier salutes an officer in the army, for example, he or she is saluting the senior officer's rank, a gesture symbolizing the authority the officer holds over the rank and file soldier.

Obedience to authority is sometimes enforced, as when military courts stand ready to enforce obedience to authoritative orders. Most often, however, obedience is motivated by private feelings that legitimate authority should be obeyed. This seemed to be the case in Milgram's experiment. The experimenter represented legitimate authority: participants believed the experimenter had the legitimate right to tell them what to do and that they had an equal duty to obey him. The presence of a legitimate authority activated the norm of obedience, telling the participants both that they should obey and whom they should obey. Other norms that supported the norm of authority were brought into play; norms incompatible with obedience were excluded. The end result was overwhelming obedience. Let's see how the activation of the norm of legitimate authority can lead to obedience in Milgram's laboratory and beyond.

AUTHORITY MUST BE LEGITIMATE. When the news that employees of Wendy's fast food restaurants had been strip searched by supervisors on the orders of someone posing as a police detective, many people wondered how those carrying out the orders could have been so gullible. But as a spokesperson for the restaurant chained pointed out, the supervisors thought they were appropriately following orders of someone—a police officer—who had the right to give orders. People don't obey just anyone who tells them to do something. To achieve obedience, an authority must convey that he or she is the person who should be obeyed. Although the Wendy's caller was apparently convincing over the phone, a person's physical presence usually gives lots of cues to authority. Larissa Tiedens and her colleagues (Tiedens, 2001; Tiedens & Fragale, 2003) have demonstrated that facial expression, tone of voice, posture, and emotional expression can all convey status and power. Height and spatial superiority also convey power so tall people and

> **Norm of obedience to authority.** The shared view that people should obey those with legitimate authority.

people occupying higher ground are seen as having power—no wonder that leaders of groups are often placed up high on thrones and referred to as "Your Highness" for example (Schubert, 2005). When people send the right authority signals, other people see them as having legitimate authority and are much more likely to fall into line with their commands. For example, sixth and eighth grade students who accept their parents as sources of legitimate authority are significantly less likely to smoke or drink than their peers who don't (Jackson, 2002).

Of course the most obvious cue to authority is a uniform. The lab-coat-wearing experimenter in Milgram's experiments was seen, then and now, as embodying a combination of legitimate authority and scientific expertise—someone with the right to give orders that in those particular circumstances should be obeyed. In these experiments the authority figure was easy to recognize, as is the case in many real-life situations. Medical doctors wear white lab coats and sling stethoscopes around their necks; police officers, firefighters, and paramedics wear uniforms and identification badges. These symbols are usually enough to activate the norm of obedience to authority. In one experiment demonstrating the power of a uniform, a "stranger"—actually an experimental confederate—asked passersby on a busy city street to comply with an unusual request, for example, to pick up garbage or move to the other side of a bus-stop sign (Bickman, 1974). Half the time, the stranger wore ordinary clothes; the rest of the time he wore a security guard's uniform. Clothes made the authority figure: Many more people did his bidding when he was dressed in a uniform than when he wore street clothes. To test the limits of an authority figure, the confederate approached passersby, pointed to a man about 50 feet away, demanded that they give him a dime for a parking meter, and then turned and walked away. Despite the fact that he was out of sight, 92% of the pedestrians followed his orders when he was wearing a uniform, compared with 42% when he was wearing street clothes.

AUTHORITY MUST ACCEPT RESPONSIBILITY. Recall that when some of the "teachers" in Milgram's experiments had qualms about continuing, the experimenter reminded them that he took full responsibility, and this was often enough to maintain obedience. When all responsibility is ceded to the authority, people enter what Milgram called the *agentic state*: They see themselves as merely the agent of the authority figure. When this displacement of responsibility occurs, people don't think of themselves as agents of their own action, and thus, other attitudes, norms, or values that might usually guide their behavior are not consulted (Bandura, Barbaranelli, Caprara, & Pastorelli, 1996). Responsibility can sometimes be diffused as well, as when authorities divide reprehensible behavior into small subtasks, each of which may be performed by a different person and each of which may in and of itself seem harmless (Kelman, 1973). In fact, when Milgram ran a variant of his study in which another person actually delivered the shocks and the participant only had to administer the learning task (the outcome of which of course caused the learner to be shocked), fully 83% of the participants carried out their orders to the letter. When responsibility is displaced or diffused, people ignore the possibility that they could or should control their own behavior. In fact, the assumption of responsibility is crucial to the power of the authority figure. Both people who obey and observers who view obedient subordinates attribute responsibility for obedience to the authority figure (V. L. Hamilton & Sanders, 1995; Meeus & Raaijmakers, 1995). Only when participants believe that they, not the authority, are responsible for their actions does obedience drop off (Tilker, 1970).

Individuals differ in the extent to which they abdicate responsibility when faced with orders from an authority figure. Some individuals believe that citizens owe legitimate authorities unquestioning obedience if society is to function effectively: These individuals deny that subordinates have responsibility for the effects of orders they carry out. In contrast, other people believe that individuals never give up the responsibility to control their own behavior (Kelman & Lawrence, 1972). Table 10.1 shows some of the kinds of statements these two types of people endorse.

THE NORM OF OBEDIENCE MUST BE ACCESSIBLE. In one experiment, Milgram put a confederate posing as a participant in the experimenter's role. The experimenter then left the room. With the authority figure gone, the results were dramatically different from those in the original experiment. Teachers now ignored the confederate and refused to deliver the shocks. When the confederate feigned disgust and tried to deliver the shocks himself, the teachers protested vigorously. Some went so far as to unplug the shock generator so it could not be used. Similar results were found in the study of obedience in which Dutch participants were ordered to harass an applicant being interviewed for an important job. In a control condition in which the experimenter was absent, not a single participant obeyed. But when the experimenter was present and ordered participants to follow instructions, 92% succeeded in ruining the candidate's chances of getting the job (Meeus & Raajimakers, 1986). In both these experiments, the presence of the experimenter was the cue that activated the norm of obedience. Of course the authority figure does not need to be physically present for the norm to be accessible—merely thinking about the authority figure would probably be enough. However, as can be seen in Figure 10.5, the more obvious the authority figure in Milgram's experiments, the more likely the norm is to be accessible, and the more likely people are to obey. The presence of the experimenter kept participants focused exclusively on the norm of legitimate authority even when some of them questioned what was happening. His prompts—"You must continue," "The experiment requires that you continue," "You have no choice"—made obedience seem an appropriate response to the situation. His calm confidence in the face of both the teachers' indecision and the learner's apparent suffering further reinforced the idea that obedience was typical, normal, and expected behavior. With the norm

TABLE 10.1. Personality Differences in Assertion of Responsibility

1. I feel obligated to protest both vigorously and publicly if the government does something that is morally wrong.
2. If you have doubts about an official order, the best thing is to do what is required of you, so you will stay out of trouble.
3. The most valuable contribution a citizen can make is to maintain an active and questioning approach toward government policies.
4. One reason for supporting the U.S. government is that anarchy will result if there are too many critics.

NOTE: People differ in the extent to which they believe that individuals maintain personal responsibility when an authority figure orders them to do something. Responsibility asserters tend to agree with items like 1 and 3 and to disagree with items like 2 and 4. In contrast, responsibility deniers agree with items such as 2 and 4 and disagree with 1 and 3. Many more than four items would be used in a real test of such differences.

Source: From *Crimes of obedience: Toward a social psychology of authority and responsibility* by H. C. Kelman & V. L. Hamilton, 1989, New Haven, CT: Yale University Press.

FIGURE 10.5   Conditions for obedience

■ By changing experimental conditions to make the norm of obedience more or less accessible, Milgram showed the power of the norm on behavior. In the laboratory, in the presence of the authoritative experimenter, fully 65% of men and women followed his orders. But in conditions that reduced the salience of the norm—such as a less "official" location, or a nonlegitimate authority giving orders, or the absence of any authority figure—obedience was reduced. (Data from Milgram, 1974.)

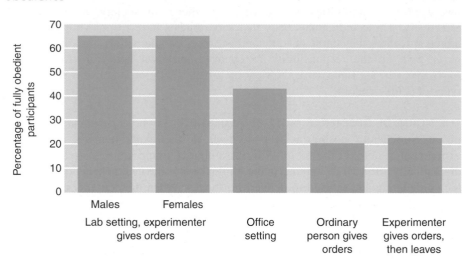

of authority fully, forcefully, and repeatedly activated, most participants fell into line, following the experimenter's directions.

INCOMPATIBLE NORMS MUST BE SUPPRESSED. When you think about how distressed the teachers felt, even as they obeyed, it becomes clear that these people were experiencing a normative conflict. Milgram may have been playing on their commitment to the norm of obedience, but they could not have been unaware of other norms that exhort us to help, not harm, others. People live in groups, and as we have seen in many chapters, group members learn to care for, cooperate with, and have compassion for others, especially others like them. The norm of social responsibility, for example, obligates those who have power and resources to help those who don't. In fact, Milgram deliberately provoked a conflict between norms when, for example, he had the pupil cry out and bang on the wall in distress. Knowing that they should have gone to the pupil's aid, teachers agonized over the appropriate behavior. In most of the experimental variations, Milgram tipped the balance in favor of the norm of obedience.

Wondering what would happen if alternative norms were made more accessible, Milgram reduced the physical distance between the teacher and the pupil. He reasoned that this would increase the accessibility of the norm of social responsibility as the pupil's suffering was brought "up close and personal" (see Figure 10.6). And it did. When the learner and the teacher were in the same room, only 40% of participants obeyed. As Milgram gradually brought teacher and pupil closer together, the pupil's suffering became less avoidable and obedience decreased. Milgram's experiment mimicked life: It is easier to drop a bomb from a plane than to kill a person with a bayonet, and it is easier to shuffle papers decreeing a death than to actually torture or kill someone (Silver & Geller, 1978). The same Eichmann who sat in his office dispassionately consigning people to their deaths reportedly was sickened when he was actually forced to tour the concentration camps.

Physically distancing oneself is not the only way to suppress other norms that are incompatible with obedience. The incompatibility of norms such as responsibility for, cooperation with, and compassion toward others with the often

FIGURE 10.6 Undermining obedience by making incompatible norms salient

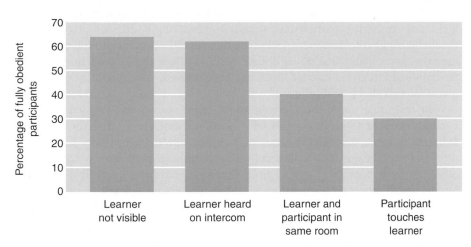

■ The norm governing obedience to legitimate authority held tremendous sway in Milgram's experimental situation. But it was not the only norm brought into play in the situation. When experimental variations focused participants' attention on the suffering of the learner, the norm of social responsibility—our obligation to give aid to those who need it—reduced the level of obedience. (Data from Milgram, 1974.)

brutal consequences of obedience are often tackled by psychologically distancing the victim. Blaming the victim means that people come to believe that those being hurt somehow deserve to be punished. The tendency to blame victims stems from a widely held belief in a "just world," the idea that the universe is a just and orderly place where people "get what they deserve" (Lerner, 1980). Such "just-world" beliefs prompt thoughts that victims must in some way have "asked for trouble," provoked it, or brought it on themselves (Lerner & Miller, 1978). Of course, such beliefs are meant to protect the believer: If the world is not a just place, we must recognize the unsettling fact that anyone could fall victim to the cruel twists of fate.

The tendency to blame the victim is strongest when we ourselves are the instrument of another person's pain. Indeed, Milgram (1974) reported that many of his participants, after delivering the maximum amount of shock, cruelly criticized the pupil with comments like "He was so stupid and stubborn, he deserved to get shocked." As Milgram noted, "Once having acted against the victim, these subjects found it necessary to view him as an unworthy individual whose punishment was made inevitable by his own deficiencies of intellect and character" (p. 10). In fact, derogating and dehumanizing the victim is a common means of reducing dissonance about one's role in another person's suffering (Perry, Williard, & Perry, 1990). Blaming the victim may be the most potentially dangerous consequence of obeying commands that hurt others. As it occurs, the target—once an innocent victim harmed only reluctantly—becomes a person deserving of abuse.

You may see the similarity here to the processes of moral exclusion described in Chapter 6, pages 208 to 209. In the context of extreme intergroup hatred, groups dehumanize out-groups so that norms of cooperation, compassion, and caring don't apply to them, justifying acts of savagery, repression, and brutality.

■ **Obedience and atrocities**. This picture shows one of the thousands of student protestors who were demonstrating in Tiananmen Square to demand more democracy and freedom of thought from the Chinese government. The protest movement ended in a bloody massacre on 4th June 1989 when the People's Liberation Army opened fire on the crowd and forced the last blockades with tanks killing and injuring thousands. The power of obedience led young soldiers to carry out these orders and murder students exactly their own age.

MAINTAINING AND ESCALATING OBEDIENCE. Once obedience begins, other processes can help maintain or even escalate it. Notice that at first the costs and consequences of obedience were not very negative for Milgram's participants. In fact they were asked to do something quite benign; the shocks were very weak and had a positive goal, to improve learning. Only gradually were his participants asked to act in a way that might cause harm to the learner. But by this point, they had already obeyed, confirming in their own minds the experimenter's right and authority to direct their actions. Having acknowledged the experimenter as a legitimate authority, participants found it increasingly difficult to refuse his gradually escalating demands. And given their initial obedience to the early small requests, participants had no legitimate basis to refuse the larger requests. When the command to give a 45-volt shock has been obeyed, why should a command to give a 60-volt shock be disobeyed?

In this way, participants in obedience experiments, and many others who commit crimes of politically and socially sanctioned evil, are led from the acceptable to the unthinkable, gradually (Kelman & Hamilton, 1989; Staub, 1989). Torturers are often trained this way, at first just delivering occasional pain, then watching while others do so, then participating in group infliction of suffering and finally carrying out the torture alone (Haritos-Fatouros, 1988). The gradual escalation of obedience reinforces the legitimacy of the authority and acceptance of the agentic state.

To remind yourself of the nature and consequences of cognitive dissonance, refer to Chapter 8, pages 277 to 285 and especially page 280.

Dissonance processes also help maintain obedience once it occurs. Like the participants in Milgram's study, most of us see ourselves as kind, caring, decent people. But as the consequences of obedience become more negative, the inconsistency between this self-concept and actual behavior increases, triggering unpleasant arousal and an increasing motivation to reduce that arousal by providing justifications for their behavior. Of course these processes tend to maintain obedience. To reduce their dissonance, people might, for example, focus on the positive implications of being a reliable and obedient agent, or on the superior knowledge and wisdom of the authority to direct their behavior. Denying free choice will of course reduce dissonance, as we saw in Chapter 7, and as we saw in Chapter 4, people tend to attribute their own behavior to situational factors, especially if they behave badly. Unfortunately this denial of free choice and admiration of the authority figure, while it might reduce dissonance, only reinforces the agentic state, making obedience more likely. Another way to reduce dissonance might be to change the meaning of obedience, interpreting it as promoting a positive goal. (Milgram helped his participants do this by claiming the shocks would "promote learning.") Many acts of aggression are justified in terms of defending honor and reputation, for example (D. Cohen & Nisbett, 1994). Such moral justifications are often cloaked in euphemistic language, such as "the final solution" or "ethnic cleansing" (Bandura and others, 1996). And as we have already seen, derogating victims as "deserving it" or dehumanizing suffers with beliefs that "they don't have feelings like us" is one of the most chilling ways that we try to justify hurting others.

In Chapter 13, pages 500 to 503 we will see how these processes of obedience, escalation, and justification can combine with the intergroup hostility described in Chapter 6, pages 202 to 209, to make extreme forms of intergroup violence—massacres, atrocities, torture, and extermination— unfortunately more likely.

Thus, many social psychological processes combine to set the stage for and help maintain obedience not only inside the lab but outside it. Obedience to authorities, the entrapment that results from increasingly inhumane acts, and the tendency to justify one's own and one's group's actions can combine to make truly destructive obedience far more widespread than we might like to acknowledge.

Normative Trade-Offs: The Pluses and Minuses of Obedience

Like all norms, the obligation to obey authority figures can be used for good or evil purposes.

Although the norm of obedience can be exploited for great evil, acceptance of legitimate authority is essential for the optimal functioning of society. Almost every group, whether an informal group of friends or a complex society, develops roles and functions that give some members authority over others. Imagine what would happen if people made individual and independent decisions about which side of the road they would drive on, what language they would speak, whether they would contribute to the defense of their group, or what principles of justice they would uphold. As Milgram points out, obeying legitimate authority has many advantages for every individual.

Perhaps the most important lesson we can take away from Milgram's studies is just how hard it is to resist the power of deeply ingrained and widely shared norms. Indeed, his findings make clear the often unexpected and unanticipated power of social situations. Obedience works well most of the time and, for that reason, resisting authority is very difficult. Neither Milgram himself nor any of those who read descriptions of his studies had any idea of the degree of obedience he would find. You may find it difficult to imagine that in similar circumstances you could act the same way Milgram's participants did. Yet the social-psychological processes invoked in this situation—activation of the norm of obedience, exclusion of other norms that might guide behavior, gradual commitment to a particular course of behavior, and justification of it—can be an overpowering combination.

Rebellion and Resistance: Fighting Back

An ad appearing in the newspapers of a small southeastern Michigan town sought paid participants for "market research involving group discussion of community standards" (Gamson, Fireman, & Rytina, 1982). Those who responded met in groups of nine with the representatives of Manufacturer's Human Relations Consultants, Inc. (MHRC) at a local Holiday Inn. The coordinator, a young man in a business suit, explained that MHRC was conducting research for a major oil company involved in legal action against the manager of a local gas station. To give the court a picture of "community standards"—what local people believed to be right and wrong—MHRC would videotape the group while it discussed various issues relevant to the case. After signing a consent form and being paid for their participation, participants learned that the oil company had terminated the manager because he was living with a woman to whom he was not married. The company claimed that this behavior offended community standards. For his part, the manager stated that his private life was none of the company's business, and that the company had sent investigators after him because he had criticized their pricing policies in a televised interview. After starting the video camera, the coordinator instructed the group to discuss the manager's behavior, and then left the room for 5 minutes.

When the coordinator returned, he stopped the camera and gave the group a second discussion topic: Would they be reluctant to do business with the manager because of his lifestyle? This time, he asked three of the nine group members to take a stand against the manager's behavior. Two more filming sessions followed: In the first, three additional people were asked to criticize the manager's behavior, and in the last, all nine of the participants were asked to take a stand against the manager. Participants were then given an affidavit to sign, permitting MHRC to edit the videotape and use it in court. Only then were participants free to leave.

How do you think participants responded? On the basis of Milgram's findings, we might expect them to obey the researchers' instructions about what to discuss and what position to take. But they didn't. Only 1 of the 33 groups of participants in the study allowed the procedure to be completed. In all the other cases, group members challenged the coordinator's authority to make them act in a blatantly unfair and potentially harmful manner. Rather than attacking the manager as instructed, some participants remained silent during the videotaping sessions. When they were not openly defying the coordinator—refusing to participate or to sign the final affidavit—they were arguing with him, calling into question the rationale and justification for the procedure. In 25 of the 33 groups, a majority of members refused to sign the final affidavit. Nine groups threatened action against MHRC, such as publicizing the abuse in the local newspaper. Even in the 8 groups in which most people signed, participants refused to cooperate with some parts of the procedure.

Why were the participants in this study able to take a stand, while Milgram's participants seemed unable to resist the norm of obedience to authority? By examining what happened when groups rebelled, Gamson and his colleagues found that three processes—reactance, systematic processing, and using norms against norms—led to resistance rather than capitulation.

Reactance: Enough Is Enough

> People can resist being manipulated by norms. People fight against threats to freedom of action when norms are not privately accepted or seen as appropriate.

Look at the *Calvin and Hobbes* cartoon on the next page! If you've just done so, you've seen Calvin illustrate reactance. But if you decided you would just keep reading for a while before looking at the cartoon, then you just demonstrated reactance yourself. People often respond to attempts to limit their choice with **reactance**, a desire to restore threatened freedom of action (Brehm, 1966). Reactance is common when people lose the opportunity to choose goods, services, or products. Banning a book or some music in one part of the country ensures record-breaking sales elsewhere; reports that a movie is censored abroad is a sure-fire boost to domestic box office receipts. Therapists find that highly reactant clients respond poorly to advice such as "Try not to think about it!" (Dowd and others, 1988; A. E. Kelley & Nauta, 1997). Warning labels (WARNING: "The U.S. Surgeon General has determined that eating high fat products increases your risk of heart attack") on familiar products can sometimes make people want to try them more rather than less (Bushman, 1998). And every parent knows that the best strategy is sometimes "reverse psychology": telling children to stay in the house when you really want them to choose to go outside to play.

Heavy-handed social pressure often raises the red flag of reactance. It certainly did so in the MHRC study. Some individuals, feeling that their behavioral freedom was being threatened, simply walked out of the experiment. Reactance also explains people's anger when they feel unfairly beholden to someone else—unsolicited favors make it difficult to refuse to do something in return, so people don't like the favor-giver (El-Alayli & Messé, 2004). In fact, some people avoid accepting favors from others, simply to ward off the possibility that someone will try to "cash in" on reciprocity (Eisenberger, Cotterell, & Marvel, 1987; M. S. Greenberg & Westcott, 1983). And, like Calvin and the MHRC participants, people often choose to do just the opposite of what they are requested if they feel their personal freedoms are being restricted by orders or influence.

Reactance. The motive to protect or restore a threatened sense of behavioral freedom.

Calvin and Hobbes by Bill Watterson

Why do people respond with reactance to a simple request but not to an order to shock another person? In this case, the answer has to do with perceptions of legitimacy of authority. When normative pressure is perceived to be inappropriate or illegitimate, reactance is triggered. In Milgram's experiments, the experimenter was perceived to be a legitimate authority. In the MHRC study, however, some participants disputed a "market consultant's" right to tell them what they should say and do. When authority is not appropriate or legitimate, reactance can push us to say "Enough is enough!"

Unfortunately, however, reactance is unlikely to help with resistance to norms that we accept as legitimate and appropriate in the situation. We privately accept most norms that are used against us, even when they are used with a heavy hand. We acknowledge their appropriateness and relevance to be applied in the situation. Perhaps it is for this reason that people anticipate feeling more regret if they fail to comply with an influence attempt than if they comply with it, a pattern that undoubtedly makes obedience more likely (Crawford, McConnell, Lewis, & Sherman, 2002). The participants in Milgram's study struggled because norms they endorsed and accepted were applied in a way that seemed legitimate, at least at first. If a norm is seen as right and proper, its imposition is not seen as an infringement on our freedom. Such norms bypass the reactance aroused by inappropriate threats to our freedom.

Systematic Processing: Thinking Things Through

One defense against normative pressure on behavior is to think things through to make sure that any norm made accessible in the situation is actually applicable.

By now you may not be surprised to learn that thinking is one of your best defenses against normative pressure. During the breaks in which the experimenter left the room, the participants in the MHRC study were given the opportunity to step back from the situation and consider what was going on, and many of them realized that unfair normative pressures were being applied. Thinking things through is not always easy, of course. Situations involving normative pressure often create anxiety and stress, and as anxiety mounts, we may be unable to think clearly. To avoid

Recall that systematic processing played the same role in reducing the impact of superficial cues automatically activated in persuasion settings (Chapter 7, pages 248 to 249).

undue pressure, it's often a good idea to try to give yourself a "cooling off" period before you make a commitment, reciprocate a favor, or obey an order. Even then, systematic thinking about the situation is important. The following strategies can help you fend off unfair normative pressure.

1. *Question how norms are being used.* Recognizing how norms operate and how they can be used against you is a good starting point. When you realize that a norm is being used against you, it loses its power (Cialdini, 1993). In fact, explicitly drawing attention to the other side's questionable tactics helps prevent their recurrence (R. Fisher & Ury, 1981). So if you believe you are being low-balled, let the culprit know you understand the tactic. By doing so, you may embarrass the other person and encourage forthright negotiation. Even more important, you will free yourself from forced feelings of obligation. Realizing that "the boss's" change in the terms of a sale is part of a low-ball plan frees you from the norm of social commitment: The agreement the salesperson made with you was just part of a strategy, not an honest deal. Thus, the very knowledge of how norms work is a strong defense against their influence.

2. *Question claims about relationships.* Norms are powerful because of the connections between people. So you might stop to think: Is the person invoking the norm really one with whom you share that connection? Does the person giving orders really have the authority to command you? Maybe not. Is the salesperson really your ally and advocate, fighting against an intractable "boss" who won't approve the deal? Probably not. And make sure that you are both abiding by the same rules of normative behavior. As part of the low-ball tactic, the salesperson often claims to be unable to make the deal without consulting the boss. This setup means that you have the power to make concessions, but the other person does not and so is freed from the obligation. As the old saying goes, "What's mine is mine; what's yours is negotiable!" In cases like this, insist on dealing directly with the person who can make a binding agreement (R. Fisher & Ury, 1981).

3. *Question others' views of the situation.* One of the most important lessons that social psychology can teach is that all situations are open to multiple interpretations. Your definition of what happened may be just as valid as the other person's. Did she really do you a favor? Do you really owe one in return? Before buying into someone else's view of how you should behave, consider all the norms and attitudes that might be relevant. Balance such norms as obedience and social commitment against social responsibility. The willingness of participants in the MHRC study to question others' views of the situation was central to their successful resistance. The coordinator brought two norms to bear on group members: the norm of legitimate obedience to authority and the norm of social commitment. If group members accepted the coordinator's legitimacy and their commitment to participate, they were likely to comply. But if they reinterpreted the coordinator's authority as illegitimate—did a market consultant really have the authority to make them lie?—they were likely to resist. And when the coordinator invoked the norm of commitment, arguing that participants had contractual obligations to fulfill, the groups who rebelled asserted the norm of social responsibility: their obligation to protect the manager.

Remember from Chapter 9 that the best group norms grow out of consideration of multiple points of view. If your interpretation of a situation differs from the one being presented, suggest some alternatives. Others may agree with you, or, at the very least, the person trying to influence the group will have to defend his or her interpretation. The sooner you offer an alternative the better, because the longer you buy into the other person's definition of the situation, the harder it will be to resist, and the sooner you suggest a different interpretation, the freer others will feel to resist the social pressure (Gamson and others, 1982; Modigliani & Rochat, 1995).

Using Norms Against Norms

The most effective defense is to use norms against norms: to break down an existing norm and forge or exploit an alternative consensus that a different course of behavior is the appropriate one.

■ **Resistance is a collective act.** These Romanian students chant anti-government slogans as they sit in University Plaza guarded by hundreds of policemen. Thousands of students took to the streets in protest against additional exam taxes and to demand decent campus living conditions. Their obedience to the police there to control them is an example of acceptance of a powerful social norm, respect for authority figures. However, their protest is itself an example of people banding together to reject a norm in their society.

Recall from Chapter 9 that when one group member broke away from a consensus, it made it easier for others to do the same thing. The same thing is true when the norm of obedience—or any other norm—is in play. One person who refuses to obey an authority figure's commands can greatly reduce obedience (Rochat & Modigliani, 1995). Obedience can be reduced even further when an alternative norm is forged. The biggest resistance advantage that participants in the MHRC study had was the presence of social support for alternatives, whereas Milgram's participants had to grapple with the experimenter's orders all alone. The presence of others and the opportunity this affords to form and affirm group norms of resistance is the most crucial factor in creating rebellion (Gamson, 1992; Haslam & Reicher, 2004; B. Simon, 1998). In every MHRC group in which discussion produced a consensus against compliance, group resistance to the coordinator followed. The coordinator's absence during taping sessions gave the group an opportunity to air their doubts and to find out that others felt the same way they did. To help build and strengthen the norm of resistance, participants stressed their shared views and bolstered their solidarity by referring to the group as "we." Consider, for example, the following interaction, when the coordinator applied pressure for agreement, and a group member responded, explicitly addressing him in the name of the group.

> Coordinator: *Apparently you didn't understand. It's necessary for you to talk as if you actually are a member of the community who's offended . . .*
>
> Member: *I think you didn't understand it. We do understand it and we don't want to go on record, even pretending that we agree with what we're saying. We don't. All three of us feel the same way. I think every one of us feels that way here.* (Gamson and others, 1982, p. 102)

Group support for alternative interpretations of a situation allows members to break free from the power of inappropriate norms in a wide range of situations. In fact, when Milgram provided his otherwise solitary participants with an ally, obedience was dramatically reduced. The shared disobedience apparently constituted a consensus that the norm of obedience did not apply.

Events outside the laboratory have also confirmed that group consensus and social support are crucial to successful rebellion. In a replication of the study in which nurses were given false prescription orders, for example, only 2 of 18 nurses were willing to follow an inappropriate instruction from a doctor—if they were allowed to talk to other nurses first (Rank & Jacobsen, 1977; Redfern, 1979). And group consensus was responsible for one of the few successful protests against the totalitarian policies of the Nazis. In 1943, 2000 Jewish men and women married to Aryan Germans were incarcerated in an administrative center in the heart of Berlin. An angry group of spouses, mostly women, soon gathered outside the building, crying out for the prisoners' release. Despite periodic threats of gunfire from armed guards, the group staged the protest day and night for a week, as the crowd grew ever larger. Individual dissent was impossible, but participants reported feeling a deep sense of solidarity and group determination in their protest. Incredibly, the prisoners were finally released when Joseph Goebbels decided that the simplest way to deal with the rebellion was to give in to the obvious will of the masses. At a time when individuals were executed for offenses as minor as telling an anti-Nazi joke, only a collective undertaking had any chance of success (Stoltzfus, 1992). As the historian Michael Walzer observed: "Disobedience . . . is always a collective act" (Walzer, 1970, p. 4).

In terms of cause and cure, destructive obedience is like groupthink. In each case a natural and usually beneficial process—obedience to authority or conformity to a group decision—goes awry. You may recall that the way to prevent or cure groupthink is to create conditions that enhance careful, systematic processing of alternative views. In the same way, the key to the prevention or cure of destructive obedience lies in creating alternatives. In particular, it consists of forming or reaffirming a more appropriate and applicable group norm.

From norms that instruct us to use hushed voices in the library, to honor our social contracts, and to obey persons in authority, norms have a powerful influence on almost every aspect of human behavior. Their influence on behavior helps us achieve mastery—by telling us how to act appropriately to achieve our goals—and connectedness—as when the norm of reciprocity binds us together. Norms, like attitudes, can only influence behavior when they are accessible. For norms to help prevent littering or improve your manners in an exclusive restaurant, they must first be brought to mind. Once established, the power of norms on behavior is hard to change—we defer to the norms of reciprocity and commitment even if we end up getting a bad deal, and the power of a legitimate authority can be hard to resist. As the examples in this chapter also demonstrate, norms, like attitudes, can influence behavior in a direct and superficial way, or through much more systematic thought (Ouellette & Wood, 1998). Sometimes mere activation of the norm of equality will facilitate an easy division of resources without much thought. At other times, the appropriateness of the norm of obedience might be questioned in depth and weighed against other norms before having any impact. Thus, norms direct behavior in much the same way that attitudes do.

To remind yourself about groupthink and its causes, glance back at Chapter 9, pages 334 to 336. And to see how these problems might be prevented, look back at pages 337 to 343 of that chapter.

Putting It All Together: Multiple Guides for Behavior

Most of the behaviors that are important to human interaction are voluntary; that is, people can decide whether to perform them. In these cases behavior is usually a product of the way people define situations and by social influence exerted by others. How situations are perceived—both by the individual and by his or her groups—is enormously influential in determining what behaviors occur. In most situations, attitudes and norms work together to exert a combined influence on our actions.

Both Attitudes and Norms Influence Behavior

Attitudes and norms typically work together to influence behavior, either by triggering behavior directly or by combining to influence intentions to act, which in turn direct behavior. People's perception of control over the behavior is also an important influence on intentions and thus on behavior.

Whenever we act or interact in socially important ways—voting for a political leader or protesting university policies, using birth control or following a vegetarian diet, deciding whom to hire or accept for training, egging on our team at a soccer match or jeering the other side—multiple sources of influence can potentially mold our behavior. Most of the time, both attitudes and norms relevant to any given behavior are present. At the soccer game, loud partisanship is the norm, but you might prefer quiet environments. In the voting booth, you have your own preferences, but are also very aware of the choices of your friends and the expectations of your group. How do these multiple potential forces work together to influence behavior? Just as was the case with attitudes and norms separately, attitudes and norms can combine to influence behavior by two different routes. They may trigger behavior directly and almost automatically, or they may operate indirectly, by influencing our intentions to act (Fazio, 1986; Ouellette & Wood, 1998).

THE DIRECT ROUTE. Attitudes and norms can guide behavior rather simply and directly, especially when we do not give matters much systematic thought. At such times, accessible attitudes may affect our perceptions of attitude objects, and accessible norms may serve as decision heuristics. Together, the attitudes and norms can color our perceptions and influence our behavior in an immediate and automatic way. For example, a person who holds a negative attitude toward an out-group member may be more aware of the out-group member's hostility-provoking characteristics. At the same time, a norm that says "protect the in-group" may be activated, and the attitude and norm together may lead directly to aggressive behavior. Attitudes and norms are especially likely to affect behavior directly when the resources and motivation to process deeply are not available. As Figure 10.7 illustrates, behavior may then follow quite simply and without much thought.

THE INDIRECT ROUTE. Sometimes attitudes and norms combine with other factors in a much more deliberate way as we form our intentions to act and then try to follow through on these intentions. The central idea of the theory of reasoned action, introduced in Chapter 8, is that attitudes and social norms are carefully considered and combined to form intentions to act in a particular way. The intentions in turn can induce systematic planning and monitoring of behavior. Such careful consideration also extends to include other factors that affect behavioral outcomes. According to the **theory of planned behavior** (Ajzen & Fishbein, 1977, 1980), for example, intentions are a function of three factors: attitudes about the behavior, social norms relevant to the behavior, and perceptions of control over the behavior.

Let us look at each of these factors in turn, using an example. If an expectant mother believes that breastfeeding will protect her baby from disease, and if she feels happy about such closeness with her infant or has nursed previous children successfully, her *attitude* toward breastfeeding is likely to be positive. Social norms would also have an influence in such a situation, because people care about

Theory of planned behavior. The theory that attitudes, social norms, and perceived control combine to influence behavior.

FIGURE 10.7   Attitudes and norms affect behavior automatically

■ When we do not give matters much systematic thought, both attitudes and norms can color our perceptions, influencing behavior in a relatively immediate and automatic way.

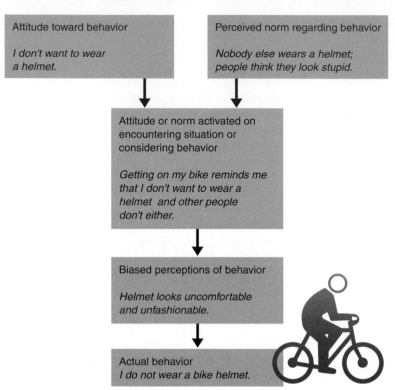

Attitude toward behavior

I don't want to wear a helmet.

Perceived norm regarding behavior

Nobody else wears a helmet; people think they look stupid.

Attitude or norm activated on encountering situation or considering behavior

Getting on my bike reminds me that I don't want to wear a helmet and other people don't either.

Biased perceptions of behavior

Helmet looks uncomfortable and unfashionable.

Actual behavior
I do not wear a bike helmet.

In Chapter 4, pages 127 to 128, we saw that a sense of control and mastery was an important component of a healthy sense of self. Here we see it is an important prerequisite to effective functioning in the world.

what significant reference groups, such as close friends, co-workers, experts, and family, would like or expect them to do. If, for example, the mother knows that both her sisters chose to nurse their babies, and if most of her friends also have chosen to do so, she will perceive *social norms* as supporting breastfeeding. Finally, the theory of planned behavior suggests that people explicitly take into account their perceived *control* over behavior: A sense of control is necessary before positive attitudes and supportive norms translate into action. Only if a woman has confidence in her ability to nurse her baby successfully and perceives herself as being able to control the outcome of her actions by her efforts will she perceive herself as having control over breastfeeding (Manstead & van Eekelen, 1998). With attitudes, norms, and perceived control in place, she will form the intention to breastfeed her baby.

Figure 10.8 illustrates the way behavior is influenced by attitudes, perceived norms, and perceptions of control associated with particular behaviors. By carefully measuring these three factors, researchers have used the theory of planned behavior to predict occupational choice, consumer purchasing decisions, blood donations, dietary changes, attendance at religious services, compliance with speed limits, use of public transportation, and participation in psychotherapy. In one study of attitudes and norms relating to the use of alcohol, marijuana, and hard drugs, researchers found that both attitudes and norms influenced students' intentions, which in turn influenced their self-reported behavior (Bentler & Speckart, 1979). Consistent with the theory, attitudes and norms influence only the

FIGURE 10.8   Attitudes and norms affect deliberately planned behavior

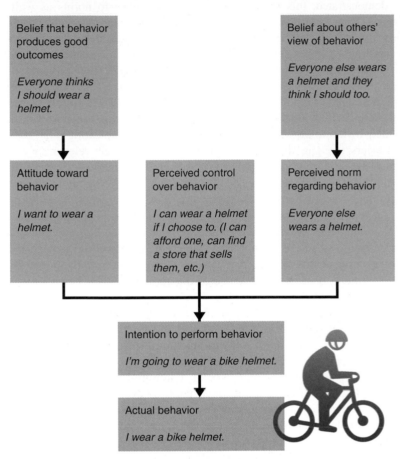

■ According to the theory of planned behavior, people's attitudes, perceived norms, and their perception of their own control combine to produce a considered intention to act. This intention, in turn, guides behavior. (Based on Ajzen & Fishbein, 1977, 1980.)

behaviors that people consider to be under their control. If a smoker sees his behavior as due to an uncontrollable addiction, for example, norms and attitudes will have little effect on the behavior (Ajzen & Madden, 1986; Bandura, 1977a).

You may have noticed that in discussing both the direct and more deliberate impact of norms and attitudes on behavior, we have used examples in which attitudes and norms suggest the same action. Although attitudes and norms often converge, this is not always the case, of course. Milgram's participants obviously *hated* what they did, even as they bowed to the norm of obedience. You may earnestly desire a quiet Saturday afternoon by yourself but nevertheless fulfill your social commitment to help your friend move. How do we behave when attitudes and norms are at odds?

When Attitudes and Norms Conflict: Accessibility Determines Influence

Whether attitudes or norms have more influence on behavior depends on their relative accessibility for a particular behavior, in a particular situation, and for a particular person.

When a relevant attitude is very accessible, it comes to mind easily, and behavior falls in line with it, as we saw in Chapter 8. And, as the research described in this chapter has demonstrated, this fundamental principle applies to norms as well: Accessible norms have a powerful influence on behavior. When attitudes and norms disagree, their impact on behavior, whether direct or indirect, depends on their relative accessibility: Whichever is more accessible will have the greater influence on behavior. Consider, for example, experiments designed to independently manipulate the accessibility of attitudes and norms (Trafimow & Fishbein, 1994a, 1994b). One study showed that accessibility is a function of who is watching your behavior (Froming, Walker, & Lopyan, 1982). Students completed a questionnaire twice, first giving their own attitudes toward punishment and then indicating what they thought their peers thought, that is, what they perceived as the relevant social norms. Later in the term, they participated as "teachers" in a learning experiment similar to Milgram's, in which they believed they were delivering short electric shocks to a failing "pupil." There were three conditions in the experiment. Some participants delivered the shocks in front of a mirror, some before an audience of their classmates, and others before an audience of advanced psychology students. In the presence of their own image in the mirror, which increases self-awareness and activates people's private attitudes, the participants' behavior was relatively consistent with their attitudes. But in the presence of the audiences, their behavior was more consistent with norms.

Not surprisingly, then, norms might be more accessible and have more sway on behaviors that are performed in public, involve others, and are crucial to the well-being of the group. Most groups, for example, have rules about safeguarding food and water, protecting others' property, controlling aggression and sex, exchanging social resources, keeping social commitments, and respecting authority (Maccoby, 1980). Individual attitudes tend to have more influence over private, individual behaviors: whether or not you cut the tags off clothes to make them more comfortable, what you wear around the house, and whether you have a strawberry or a chocolate ice-cream cone.

For the same reasons, individuals can differ in the extent to which they are responsive to social norms versus private attitudes. As you might expect, people who identify closely with membership in a particular group are more sensitive to and more influenced by the social norms of that group (Terry & Hogg, 1996; Trafimow & Finlay, 1996). This finding can also be generalized to cultures. Members of collective cultures tend to have group identities that are more accessible, and thus are more typically attuned to group norms (Trafimow, Triandis, & Goto, 1991; Triandis, 1994). People who are highly concerned with what others think of them, like high self-monitors, for example, are also more likely to show behavior that reflects norms rather than attitudes. In one study, Lynn Miller and Joseph Grush (1986) asked 226 students about their attitudes, their perception of social norms, and their actual behaviors at school. These researchers also had their participants complete self-consciousness and self-monitoring scales. They found that students high in self-consciousness (reflecting particular sensitivity to and awareness of their own attitudes) and low in self-monitoring (indicating a relative lack of interest in other people's expectations) showed high consistency between their attitudes and their behavior. In contrast, participants low in self-awareness and high in self-monitoring showed just the opposite pattern: Their behavior corresponded much more highly with social norms. Thus, for some people, attitudes are more likely to guide behavior because these people are constantly aware of their attitudes.

For others, social norms are uppermost in their minds and tend to guide their behavior.

Neither attitudes nor norms predominate for all behaviors, for all people, in all situations. Whether their impact is direct or indirect, relevant attitudes can limit or modify the powerful influence of norms on behavior. Similarly, norms that are activated and considered can block individual attitudes from being expressed in behavior. In our daily lives, multiple social norms and a variety of personal attitudes contribute to how we perceive a given set of circumstances and, thus, to the way we behave. Will an employee blow the whistle on his company's illegal dumping of chemical waste? Will a young mother nurse her baby or use formula? Will a soldier carry out orders she suspects are illegal? When the behavior is perceived as controllable, the answer will depend on the particular mix of norms and attitudes that are brought to mind as each individual interprets his or her situation.

CONCLUDING COMMENTS

 Social psychology has always aimed at understanding the intricate interplay between social thoughts, social feelings, and social behavior. One thing that makes achieving such a goal difficult is the incredible diversity of human behavior. On the one hand are behaviors like stepping on the brake when the traffic light turns red—behaviors so automatic that they take no conscious thought. On the other hand are decisions about choosing a particular career or voting for a particular candidate—behaviors that often involve an agonizingly careful scrutiny of available information. As we hope you have seen in this and the three previous chapters, the differences between these two types of behaviors are more apparent than real. It is easy to see how cognitive processes and social influences contribute to the kinds of carefully reasoned actions that follow the consideration of a variety of relevant attitudes and norms. But even automatic behaviors are influenced by the way we and others interpret and define social situations. You won't stop at the traffic signal unless you recognize the red light and interpret its meaning appropriately. And how you interpret the red light is governed to a large degree by social conventions and norms: Must you stay motionless until the light changes to green, or can you turn right if the way is clear? Even your knowledge that the color red means "stop" is a cultural norm. Like carefully considered behaviors, apparently automatic actions are also influenced by both cognitive and social processes. Whether automatic or carefully thought through, then, all behavior is susceptible to the same principle of accessibility: The more readily the relevant attitude or norm comes to mind, the more impact it will have on behavior.

Although norms and attitudes affect behavior in the same ways, norms have a slight edge over attitudes. Indeed, if you think about it, you will probably be surprised to find how much more often when norms and attitudes conflict, you follow norms rather than your attitudes. You do what you should do rather than what you want to do. Part of the impact of norms comes from the fact that they are group-based, and thus the presence of group members is a cue that activates them. And because norms come from the group, norm-consistent behavior is likely to be supported and rewarded, rather than undermined. Although norm-consistent behavior can be maintained by threats or rejection, the pressure to conform usually comes from the inside: from our acceptance of group norms as the right and proper

CHAPTER 10 THEMES

- **Construction of Reality**
  Every situation can be interpreted in multiple ways, making different norms applicable.

- **Pervasiveness of Social Influence**
  Social norms influence our actions, even when we are not physically in the group.

- **Striving for Mastery**
  Following norms helps us to obtain rewards from others.

- **Seeking Connectedness**
  Following norms helps us to feel like good group members.

- **Accessibility**
  Increasing the accessibility of norms increases their impact on behavior.

- **Superficiality Versus Depth**
  Resisting the effects of norms sometimes requires extensive thought.

way to think, feel, and act. Thus, we construct a world of right and wrong, good and bad, that is reflected in the norms and attitudes we develop and maintain. Effective social influence really stems from the ability to create and then make accessible cognitive structures that make desired behavior more likely to occur.

Factories, corporations, and businesses have begun to reap the benefits of encouraging groups to form and maintain their own standards of behavior, as have individuals joining self-help support groups. The power of social norms might be used with equal success in other social areas, not as rules imposed from above but as a grass-roots movement that builds from the small group level. In neighborhoods, for example, norms involving conservation and recycling might be established and made effective, just as block organizations and neighborhood watch groups have successfully developed standards of pride and caring for property and protection from crime. Standards of curiosity and respect for learning might be reinforced in classrooms if students themselves participated in establishing norms for classroom behavior. As social and environmental problems escalate, such techniques could help produce much-needed change.

S U M M A R Y

 Norms: Effective Guides for Social Behavior. Norms must be activated before they can guide behavior. They can be activated by deliberate reminders or by subtle cues, such as observations of other people's behavior. Group sometimes enforce norms using rewards and punishments. More often, however, people follow norms because they seem right, they are endorsed by the behavior of other group members, and they are frequently activated.

When individuals are in a state of **deindividuation**, they see themselves purely in terms of group identity, and their behavior is likely to be guided by group norms alone. The result can be either antisocial or prosocial behavior, depending on what norms the group activates.

The Norm of Reciprocity: Treating Others as They Treat You. The **norm of social reciprocity** directs us to return to others favors, goods, and services that they offer to us. This norm can sometimes be activated to our disadvantage when people give us small favors to induce us to return something of greater value. Concessions are also supposed to be reciprocated. This can leave us vulnerable when others use the **door-in-the-face technique**, making a concession following our refusal to comply with a large demand. We feel obligated to make a concession in return. Because people believe in the norm of reciprocity, behaviors based on these concessions are often stable over time.

The Norm of Commitment: Keeping Your Promises. The **norm of social commitment** directs us to honor our agreements. It can make people vulnerable through the **low-ball technique**, when they make a deal and then discover there are hidden costs. People usually stick to the deal even though it has changed for the worse. People stand by their commitments for several reasons. They feel obligated to do so, and being inconsistent makes them uncomfortable. They also add new thoughts, feelings, and behaviors to help support and bolster their action.

The Norm of Obedience: Submitting to Authority. In one of the best-known experiments in psychology, people obeyed orders to deliver shocks to an unwilling victim who was clearly suffering. They obeyed these orders even though they were not forced to do so. The destructive obedience of Milgram's participants was not due to personality defects, hard-hearted unconcern about the victim, or suspicion that the experiment was rigged. In fact, obedience in nonexperimental settings can be just as high, and authorities command as much obedience in recent studies as they did 40 years ago in Milgram's experiments. The **norm of obedience to legitimate authority** figures who accept responsibility had a powerful effect on behavior in Milgram's experiment and has a similar effect on behavior outside the lab. Both in Milgram's studies and in obedience in everyday situations, conditions that increase the accessibility of the obedience norm or decrease attention to other norms (such as social responsibility) increase obedience. Once obedience occurs it can be maintained or escalated by gradual entrapment and the impact of justification processes. Like all norms, the obligation to obey authority figures can be used for good or evil purposes.

Rebellion and Resistance: Fighting Back. People can resist being manipulated by norms. People display **reactance** by fighting against threats to their freedom of action when they do not privately accept norms or when they believe they are inappropriate. One defense against normative pressure on behavior is to think things through to make sure that any norm made accessible in the situation is actually applicable. The most effective defense is to use norms against norms: to break down an existing norm and forge or exploit an alternative consensus that a different course of behavior is the appropriate one.

Putting It All Together: Multiple Guides for Behavior. Attitudes and norms typically work together to influence behavior, either by triggering behavior directly or by combining to influence intentions to act, which in turn direct behavior. According to the **theory of planned behavior**, people's perception of control over the behavior is also an important influence on intentions and thus on behavior. When attitudes and norms disagree, their influence on behavior will depend on their relative accessibility for a particular behavior, in a particular situation, and for a particular person.

11

Liking and Loving

For most people, a happy marriage and a good family life are two of the most important elements of their lives. And for good reasons: Research findings suggest that close relationships with other people can make us healthy as well as happy. Consider the following findings:

- Compared to people in troubled marriages, those who are happily married have immune systems that ward off infections more effectively (Kiecolt-Glaser & Newton, 2001).

- The more college roommates like each other, the fewer colds and flu outbreaks they suffer (Goleman, 1992).

- The chances of surviving for more than a year after a heart attack are more than twice as high among elderly men and women who can count on two or more people for emotional support than among those who do not have this support (Berkman, 2000).

No wonder, then, that people's feelings about their relationships have a bigger impact on their overall satisfaction with their lives than do their job, income, community, or even physical health (A. Campbell, Converse, & Rodgers, 1976). In fact, close relationships are so important to people's well-being that the end of a relationship can be psychologically and physically devastating (Agnew, 2000; Hemstrom, 1996). In this chapter we describe how our relationships with others develop and change over time. We begin by looking at the factors that spark initial attraction—in everyday language, liking—between people and motivate them to try to know each other better. You will see that once two people begin interacting on a regular basis—chatting on the phone and sharing meals and other activities—feelings of attraction based on personal characteristics become less important than feelings about the relationship itself and about what each partner gets out of it.

As two people's lives become interlinked and each comes to know the other more deeply, casual acquaintanceship is transformed into close friendship. Just as an important in-group can become part of the self, so does the partner in a close relationship. And just as group norms influence what we do, the partner's thoughts, feelings, and behavior influence our own. Each partner responds directly to the other's joys and sorrows, and each in turn feels deeply known, understood, and accepted by the other. These elements of caring and psychological intimacy characterize many kinds of loving relationships—between best friends, parents and children, romantic partners, and spouses. Sexual feelings, like hot peppers in an antipasto salad, are powerful additional ingredients that spice some relationships.

Of course, difficulties eventually arise in any relationship. When conflicts are handled constructively, relationships can endure and deepen over the years. If conflict leads to a break-up, however, the pain can be swift and sure. In the final section of the chapter we consider the causes of problems in relationships and the ways people deal with them.

Initial Attraction

Newly arrived in a strange city or a freshman dorm, you look at the strangers around you and wonder: "Who will be my friends?" How do we form new connections and turn nodding acquaintances into pals and partners? In cultures that emphasize voluntary relationships instead of lifelong, unchangeable group memberships, the first step in getting to know a stranger is often sparked by feelings of *attraction* or liking (Berscheid & Reis, 1998). As mysterious as attraction seems, it follows rules: People are usually attracted to those they find physically attractive, those with whom they interact frequently, and those who are similar to them.

Physical Attractiveness

> The formation of a relationship is often spurred by feelings of attraction or liking for another person. Attraction to strangers is strongly influenced by perceptions of physical attractiveness.

Everyone likes to look at beautiful people. Halle Berry, Ben Affleck, and Denzel Washington are movie stars because of their good looks as well as their acting talents. Thinking about people like these suggests that physical attractiveness is a characteristic that some lucky people just *have*. But this view is an overstatement. For one thing, members of different cultures differ greatly in the physical characteristics they consider attractive. When anthropologists surveyed more than 200 non-Western societies, they could not find a single characteristic that was considered attractive everywhere (Ford & Beach, 1951). For example, some societies value slimness in women, while others consider plumpness more attractive. Even within 20th-century North America, shifts in standards of physical beauty occurred (Banner, 1983). Thus, definitions of physical attractiveness are culturally shaped.

Even among members of the same culture, attractiveness seems to be partly in the eye of the beholder, as well as in the characteristics of the person being observed. Studies have demonstrated that the observer's liking for a person can influence perceptions of physical attractiveness. In one study, for example, men and women looked at a photo of a woman and read information about her personality traits. When they then judged her physical attractiveness, those who read that her personality was likable judged her to be more attractive than those who learned that she was dislikable (Owens & Ford, 1978). Similarly, women rate photos of men who are described as acting in agreeable and altruistic ways as more physically attractive, compared to the same photos linked with less positive behaviors (Jensen-Campbell, Graziano, & West, 1995). In other words, liking someone will help you see the person's beauty.

EFFECTS OF PHYSICAL ATTRACTIVENESS. Despite these points, there is some degree of consensus on people's physical attractiveness, and as we described in Chapter 3, attractiveness can influence people's attitudes and behaviors in a wide range of social situations, even on the job. Why do we like to be around beautiful people? One obvious reason is the sheer esthetic pleasure we obtain from looking at them. However, that is not the only reason. In Chapter 3 we described the common stereotype that attractive people are warm, friendly, and socially confident (Eagly, Ashmore, Makhijani, & Longo, 1991). And this stereotype may become self-fulfilling, as a classic study by Mark Snyder, Elizabeth Tanke, and Ellen Berscheid (1977) illustrated. These researchers showed male college students a photo of a woman with whom they would supposedly have a telephone conversation. The photos were rigged: Some students saw an image of a highly attractive woman; others saw a woman who was less attractive. Each participant then held an actual conversation with a female student who knew nothing of this ruse. When other students later listened to tape recordings of the two sides of the conversation, they found that the men's behavior varied, depending on which photo they had seen. Men who thought the partner was a very attractive woman acted more sociable, interesting, warm, and outgoing than those who thought she was less attractive. Naturally, the women responded to these different conversational patterns: Those whose partners thought they were attractive also acted more sociable, animated, and confident. The results of this study suggest that when we think people are attractive, we interact with them in a way that brings out the best in them.

■ **Beauty is in the eye of the beholder**. What is considered attractive differs not only across cultures and time, but can even vary widely within the same culture and time. Marilyn Monroe, shown here in 1954 entertaining the troops in Korea, enjoyed an almost universal appreciation of her beauty. A curvaceous frame was indicative of reproductive health and financial success—most desirable traits in a post-war culture. However, although her beauty is still acknowledged to this day and many cultures still venerate this body shape, modern western society generally tends to revere a much more slender figure in its female media icons.

Attractiveness enhances social interaction in everyday life, not just in artificial experimental situations. For example, college students' attractiveness is related to the pleasantness they perceive in their everyday social interactions (Reis and others, 1982). Thus, we tend to like attractive people not only because we enjoy looking at them, but also because our interactions with them may generally be positive and pleasant.

The ways our interactions with people can cause them to become what we expect them to be—creating a self-fulfilling prophecy—were detailed in Chapter 3, pages 87 to 89.

WHO CARES ABOUT PHYSICAL ATTRACTIVENESS? Physical attractiveness is not equally important to everyone. Among both men and women, high self-monitors—those who care about acting in socially appropriate ways and fitting in with situational demands—place an especially high value on physical attractiveness in relationship partners. In contrast, low self-monitors are likely to seek partners with desirable personality traits and other inner qualities (M. Snyder, Berscheid, & Glick, 1985). This personality difference influences not only the way people select dating partners but also the way they choose among supposed job applicants: High self-monitors pay more attention to physical attractiveness, and low self-monitors attend more to the applicant's personality (M. Snyder, Berscheid, & Matwuchuk, 1988).

Gender also plays a role. In romantic relationships, men attach more importance to physical attractiveness than women do, while women care more about qualities related to a partner's status, ambition, and financial success (Feingold, 1990, 1992a). This difference is found consistently across cultures (Shackelford, Schmitt, & Buss, 2005). In "lonely hearts" personal columns, for example, more men than women specify that they are looking for attractive romantic partners. This concern for physical attractiveness is a characteristic *of men* as perceivers rather than a preference *about women* as partners. One source of evidence for this statement is a study of gay and lesbian advertising for partners. The gay men tended to specify attractiveness as a desired trait in a partner, whereas the lesbian women did not (Deaux & Hanna, 1984).

Evolutionary psychologists have advanced a potential explanation for this gender difference. In species (like humans) where the costs of pregnancy, nursing, and childrearing fall mainly on women, males and females have somewhat different ways of maximizing the transmission of their genes to the next generation (Trivers, 1972). Because their parental investment is relatively small, men can maximize their reproductive success simply by having a large number of healthy children. For this reason, their best bet is to seek reproductive partners who are young (because young women are the most fertile) and free from diseases and genetic defects. Female beauty is argued to be an indicator of these qualities, explaining why psychological mechanisms have evolved that lead men in particular to seek attractive mates (D. M. Buss, 1994).

Women are also expected to look for attractive partners, to the extent that a man's attractiveness also conveys information about his genetic quality and freedom from diseases. But women also face another consideration: their relatively greater parental investment makes it important for them to seek men who are able and willing to commit resources to support them and their children. Thus, it is argued, women have evolved to seek indicators of men's resources, such as dominance, social status, and wealth, as well as physical attractiveness (D. M. Buss, 1994). Based on these considerations, evolutionary psychologists believe that the observed tendency of men to attach greater importance to a partner's attractiveness and women to a partner's resources reflects the functioning of evolved mechanisms with roots deep in our species' past.

The evolutionary viewpoint is also supported by other evidence showing that inborn biological mechanisms affect preferences among mating partners. For example, the mate preferences of women vary systematically across their monthly fertility cycle. At the time of peak fertility, when sexual intercourse would be most likely to lead to conception, women show a systematic shift toward preferring men with more "masculine" physical appearance and deeper voices (Penton-Voak and others, 1999; Puts, 2005). These findings suggest that hormonal changes at the time of a woman's peak fertility lead her to prefer men with "masculine" features, which presumably signal good genes that can be passed along to the couple's offspring.

Though evolutionary reasoning accounts neatly for many aspects of human mate preferences, it has not gone unchallenged (Buller, 2005). A range of other factors besides evolved mechanisms also influence humans' mate preferences. For one thing, some research has sought to distinguish between the attributes that people desire for short-term relationships versus long-term, committed relationships (Berscheid & Reis, 1998). Both men and women appear to care more about attractiveness for a short-term relationship, but give more importance to factors like attitude similarity and desirable personality characteristics when thinking about a long-term relationship (Regan, Levin, Sprecher, Christopher, & Cate, 2000). Thus, the type of relationship that is sought also influences preferences, making the observed patterns more complex than a simple matter of men wanting attractiveness, women wanting resources.

And some of the evidence that seemingly favors the evolutionary account may have other explanations: for example, women may prefer men with resources simply because in virtually every culture women themselves directly control few resources (J. A. Howard, Blumstein, & Schwartz, 1987). Consistent with this notion, in cultures where women have relatively more power, they also place less emphasis on resources relative to physical attractiveness in men (Gangestad, 1993). Finally, research suggests that the gender difference in preferences for physical attractiveness is larger in people's self-reports of what they want in a partner than in studies that assess people's actual behavioral choices (Feingold, 1992a). This finding also poses a challenge for evolutionary theories about relationships, since they make direct predictions for what people *do* rather than for what they *say*. It is beyond question that evolved differences can affect men's and women's orientations toward mate selection, but the details of those differences, and the ways they interact with culture and learning, are not yet fully known.

Positive Interaction

People are attracted to those with whom they have positive interactions. Interaction helps people master the world, and it also helps people find connectedness. In addition, interaction leads to familiarity, which increases liking. Similarity also increases attraction by making positive interaction more likely, by suggesting that the other person likes the individual in return, and by validating the individual's beliefs and attitudes.

Most of us like the people we work with every day, regardless of their physical attractiveness. We also like people who share our backgrounds, tastes, attitudes, and values. Why do we usually like people we frequently interact with and people who are similar to us?

INTERACTION SPELLS LIKING . . . MOST OF THE TIME. Suppose you begin a new job, and you are assigned a desk near another worker. As the days pass, your neighbor shows you the ropes and you begin eating lunch together. You will probably end up liking this person better than your other co-workers, a pattern suggested by research confirming that people who interact frequently, even if they are thrown together by sheer chance, tend to like each other. A classic study of residents in a married-student housing complex found that friendships tended to form among those who lived near one another (Festinger, Schachter, & Back, 1950). The most popular residents were those whose apartments were located near the stairs or close to the mailbox area, where they had extra

■ **The closeness of connectedness**. Relationships need not involve romantic feelings to provide us with feelings of connectedness. More commonly we gain support, closeness, and a sense of identity from those with whom we share enjoyable activities or intimate revelations.

opportunities to interact with others. College roommates also tend to like each other, even if they do not initially share the kinds of characteristics that usually lead to attraction (Newcomb, 1961). Proximity leads to friendship even in the classroom. One study found that police trainees who were alphabetically assigned to classrooms and seats tended to form friendships with classmates whose names were in their part of the alphabet (Segal, 1974).

WHY INTERACTION INCREASES LIKING. We saw in Chapters 6 and 9 that people enjoy belonging to valued in-groups for two basic reasons. Our groups can help us master the world—grasping reality and obtaining individual rewards—as others cooperate with us, validate our beliefs and attitudes, and aid us in seeing the world correctly. Groups also help us enjoy a sense of connectedness and belonging. The same reasons usually make interaction with other people enjoyable, and therefore lead us to like those people (Bakan, 1966; Cantor & Malley, 1991; McAdams, 1985).

1. *Interacting with others helps us master the world.* If you stop to think about why you enjoy being with other people, your first reason will probably be that it's often just plain interesting and fun. Debating politics far into the night, cheering together at sports events, and sharing what you know in joint study sessions are activities that meet our personal needs in many ways. Some ways are obvious: The study session may help improve test grades. Other benefits are not quite so obvious. Discussing a personal worry with a close friend can help us understand and cope with trying circumstances and with our own reactions to them. Thus, particularly when we are under stress, we seek to compare our own feelings and reactions with those of other people so that we can better understand ourselves (Rofé, 1984; Schachter, 1959). Similarly, when we feel uncertain of our opinions and beliefs, we may seek out others to test the validity of our views (Wheeler, 1974). When interacting with someone is rewarding in any of these ways, the result is the same: We tend to like the person (Rusbult, Arriaga, & Agnew, 2001).

2. *Interacting with others helps us feel connected.* Interacting with another person who treats us with warmth, acceptance, and respect can confirm our sense of being connected to others (McAdams & Bryant, 1987; Reis & Patrick, 1996). This sense of relatedness and attachment to the other person is another important reward of interaction—one that, as we shall see, increases in importance as relationships deepen.

3. *Familiar others seem likable.* A third reason for liking those we frequently interact with is simple familiarity—the *mere exposure effect* (Bornstein and others, 1987). In fact, even when no actual interaction takes place, familiarity has positive effects, as Richard Moreland and Scott Beach (1992) demonstrated. As we described in Chapter 3, they had women sit in on varying numbers of lectures in a large class. The other students in the class thought the women who had attended more often were more likeable and attractive. The research suggests that even in the absence of interaction, familiarity can lead to both liking and perceived similarity. For all three of the reasons just listed, we tend to like people we interact with a lot, as Figure 11.1 suggests.

WHAT ABOUT NEGATIVE INTERACTION? At this point you may be remembering a particularly obnoxious roommate or next-door neighbor and thinking that frequent interaction certainly does not always lead to liking. You're right: When interaction

FIGURE 11.1   Interaction leads to attraction

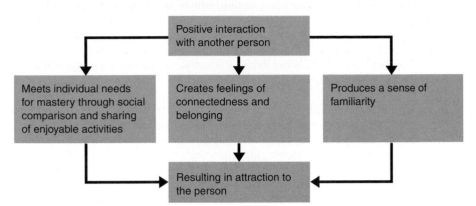

■ Interacting with someone increases attraction to that person through three different processes.

fails to meet our needs or even harms us, it will lead to disliking. More negative interaction just spells more annoyance if you have to spend time with someone who holds offensive political views, or to share a dorm room with someone who constantly plays classic rock music while you like only hip-hop (or vice versa). Research supports this common-sense idea. When asked to name the people they most disliked, participants in one study named individuals who lived near them (Ebbesen, Kjos, & Konecni, 1976). And incompatible musical tastes are one of the most important reasons for dissension between college roommates, so much so that one college application form asks students to "cross out any music you cannot tolerate" so that rooms can be assigned accordingly (Abramovitch, 1997). Fortunately, most people seem to be more likable than annoying, so interaction more often leads to attraction than to repulsion (Rosenbaum, 1986).

BIRDS OF A FEATHER: LIKING SIMILAR OTHERS. Because you interact frequently with your nearby co-worker, and because her advice is so useful, you probably will end up liking her. However, as you get to know other people in the office over the next few months, you may identify someone who seems to be more similar to you, more "your type." This person may support the same candidate in the local election, share your love of opera, and come from the part of the country you call home. You probably will end up liking this person, too, for similarity breeds attraction (Newcomb, 1961). Though we all have heard that, like the north and south poles of magnets, "opposites attract," research shows that this is not true for people (Berscheid & Reis, 1998). Similarity leads to attraction for three main reasons.

1. *We tend to interact with people who are similar to us.* "Birds of a feather flock together" is one of those old sayings that often holds true: People tend to interact with similar others. For example, pairs of best friends in high school and members of dating couples in college tend to be similar on many variables, including age, religion, race, and social class (C. T. Hill, Rubin, & Peplau, 1976; Kandel, 1978). Shared interests obviously create opportunities for interaction: Academically motivated students meet others of their kind at the library, fanatical golfers find their like at the golf course, and environmentalists find one another at Sierra Club meetings. Similarity also makes it more likely that the interaction will be positive. You will have no problem finding topics of common interest to discuss with

fellow Sierra Club members, and you won't argue about whether to save the endangered spotted owl. Similarity, like proximity, thus increases opportunities for positive interaction, which, as we just saw, spells liking.

2. *We assume that similar others will like us.* If we know that someone is similar to us, we usually assume that person will like us (E. Aronson & Worchel, 1966). And being liked by someone is one of the strongest reasons for liking that person (Condon & Crano, 1988).

3. *Similar others validate our beliefs and attitudes.* One of the earliest lines of research on attraction showed that people like similar others even before they have met them. Participants in studies conducted by Donn Byrne (1971) were given a questionnaire on social and political attitudes supposedly completed by another student. The closer the stranger's attitudes were to their own, the more the participants liked the unknown individual. You may think it strange to study attraction without having people meet other real people, but consider the ways in which the research situation mirrors real life. If you, a political liberal, were new in town and wanted to make friends, you might avoid the Conservative Club and show up at the Liberal League meeting. You would do so because you expect to find people with attitudes similar to your own—and thus likable people—among the Liberal League members.

> This tendency and other self-enhancing biases were introduced in Chapter 4, pages 109 to 112.

   The reason we like people with attitudes and beliefs similar to our own is that we tend to view our own characteristics as desirable. Thus, those who share them have the *right* attitudes (LaPrelle, Hoyle, Insko, & Bernthal, 1990). If you favor affirmative action, you will probably like other people who share that attitude—not just because they agree with you but because their attitude suggests what you see as an appropriate concern for the disadvantaged in society. Other people's support for our views is rewarding because it validates our own opinions (Byrne, 1971).

In summary, if two people are similar, they are more likely to have positive interactions, to believe that they are liked in return, and to reinforce each other's attitudes and beliefs. For all these reasons, similarity tends to create attraction.

Liking, Similarity, and Interaction: Mutually Reinforcing Processes

Similarity, liking, and interaction all tend to influence one another. As a result, relationships tend to deepen and intensify over time.

As Figure 11.2 shows, interaction, liking, and similarity are all tied together in our everyday lives (Berscheid & Reis, 1998).

- Similarity encourages interaction, and when people interact, they discover more similarities. For instance, getting-acquainted conversations tend to involve a search for common friends, activities, or interests (C. A. Insko & Wilson, 1977).

- Interaction creates liking, and liking leads to more interaction because we seek out the company of those we enjoy. Further, the fact that two people spend time together suggests that each finds the other likable and enjoyable. And knowing that someone likes you is a powerful reason for being

FIGURE 11.2 The mutually reinforcing effects of interaction, similarity, and liking

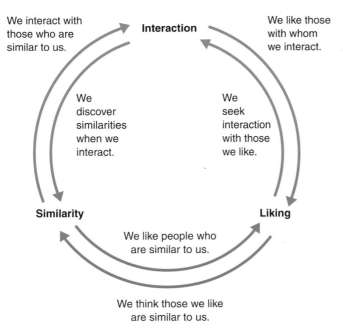

We interact with those who are similar to us.

Interaction

We like those with whom we interact.

We discover similarities when we interact.

We seek interaction with those we like.

Similarity

Liking

We like people who are similar to us.

We think those we like are similar to us.

■ Interaction, similarity, and liking all tend to influence one another. Thus, if any one of these factors starts a relationship, the other two will tend to contribute to a self-sustaining spiral of friendship.

attracted to them: It boosts self-esteem and demonstrates your value as a person (C. A. Insko and others, 1973). Even when people do not interact, familiarity can cause liking as well as perceived similarity (Insko & Wilson, 1977; Moreland & Beach, 1992).

- Similarity and liking also go together. We like those who are similar to us; we think those we like are similar to us; and we assume that people who are similar to us will like us (Condon & Crano, 1988).

Each of these three factors, similarity, liking, and interaction, can cause increases in all the others. Thus, a relationship initially may be sparked by chance proximity, by perceptions of similarity, or by transitory feelings of attraction that lead to an initial encounter. But once it gets going, all three factors come into play, and the acquaintanceship will tend to progress toward friendship.

From Acquaintance to Friend: Relationship Development

If a group of strangers share a few minutes of conversation, what kinds of feelings do you think they will have about each other? Not surprisingly, almost everyone will find a few individuals especially attractive or friendly. Some people will also have idiosyncratic preferences: Erica may be especially attracted to people with red hair, and Jeff may find Joe's sense of humor objectionable. On such short acquaintance, however, the factors that make Jeff dislike Joe will have little to do with Joe's feelings about Jeff.

If the same people interacted for weeks, months, or years, the patterns of liking would be very different (Kenny, 1994). Although particularly attractive and friendly people may still be quite popular, preferences will mostly reflect the unique history of the interactions between specific pairs of individuals. Erica may like Jeff even though he is not particularly popular with others, because he shares her passion for science-fiction novels. People's feelings will probably also be mutual. If Erica likes Jeff, Jeff will also like Erica. Patterns like this demonstrate the existence of *relationships*. As relationships develop, the purely individual characteristics that are central causes of attraction among strangers become much less important. What turns acquaintances into friends? The answer involves both of the key motives we have already discussed: the need to master the social environment and the need for connectedness with others (Baumeister & Leary, 1995; Cantor & Malley, 1991). Friendship develops through interactions that fulfill these two needs. Partners exchange rewards, helping each other find individual satisfactions, and they exchange self-disclosures, getting to know each other in increasingly intimate ways.

Exchanges of Rewards: What's In It for Me?

As a relationship begins to develop, the partners exchange rewards. As the relationship deepens, they may shift to offering rewards to benefit the partner and to show caring.

For voluntary relationships such as friendships or romances to develop and deepen, each partner must receive benefits and rewards. Perhaps you have known someone who was always asking for a loan of a few dollars but never paid you back, or someone who always wanted to tell you his troubles without ever asking in return if you had had a good or a bad day yourself. If so, you probably tried to escape from those relationships unless they provided you with other types of rewards—maybe the chronic borrower was a witty raconteur, always fun to be around. As these examples illustrate, the rewards that each partner gets from interaction are key in determining the course of the relationship (Rusbult, Arriaga, & Agnew, 2001). People who do not know each other intimately may share activities that directly reward both partners. For example, two acquaintances may frequently play tennis because they both enjoy the game. Or two people may directly exchange benefits. For example, one may cook a gourmet dinner for a classmate in return for an evening's tutoring help with a tough calculus assignment. Casual relationships that work this way are termed **exchange relationships**, because people offer benefits to their partners in order to receive benefits in return (M. S. Clark & Mills, 1979).

In contrast, close friends or others who have **communal relationships** are directly concerned for each other's welfare, and they provide benefits to demonstrate that they care rather than to receive benefits in exchange. The shift from an exchange to a communal orientation marks an important transition point in relationship development (Mills, Clark, Ford, & Johnson, 2004). Often a relationship is brought to this transition point when one person acts in ways that are typical of a communal relationship, signaling his or her desire to move in that direction. Thus, if you regard an acquaintance as a potential friend, you may signal your desire for a closer relationship by offering a favor or picking up the check for a shared restaurant dinner (Lydon, Jamieson, & Holmes, 1997). In fact, people may act in these ways even with a stranger, if they are attracted to the person and desire a

Exchange relationship. A relationship in which people exchange rewards in order to receive benefits in return.

Communal relationship. A relationship in which people reward their partner out of direct concern and to show caring.

relationship (M. S. Clark & Mills, 1979). But such gestures often leave the recipient uncertain about the individual's desires and intentions. Is the offered favor a genuine invitation to a closer relationship or something else, even an attempt at manipulation? Uncertainty and anxiety may cloud both partners' feelings about the transition (Lydon and others, 1997). If all goes well, the partner may read the intended meaning correctly and the relationship may progress further toward closeness. In contrast, if the partner refuses to accept the favor or insists on paying it back at the first available opportunity, that amounts to a statement that a closer relationship is not desired. In either case, actions take on special meanings in the context of the transition from acquaintanceship to a close friendship: They signal whether each partner takes an exchange or communal approach to the relationship.

Self-Disclosure

Relationship development also includes exchanges of self-disclosures as the partners come to know each other better. Self-disclosures increase liking and offer opportunities for sympathetic, supportive responses.

"I hate this cold weather." "I can't believe how much money I just spent on groceries." Relatively impersonal topics like these are the kinds of things you might discuss with acquaintances. On the other hand, "My alcoholic father used to beat me," or "I don't know if I'm smart enough to make it in grad school" are the kinds of intimate disclosures we usually share only with close and trusted friends. Self-disclosures include facts about one's life and situation, as well as inner thoughts, feelings, and emotions (Morton, 1978). Both the depth of self-disclosure (the level of intimacy of the information) and the breadth (the range of topics) increase as a relationship develops (Altman & Taylor, 1973; Z. Rubin, Hill, Peplau, & Dunkel-Schetter, 1980).

EFFECTS OF SELF-DISCLOSURE. Disclosing something about yourself makes both strangers and friends like you more (Collins & Miller, 1994). This fact probably explains why salespeople often self-disclose to their customers, offering cute stories about their children or pets. It may also explain why people who readily express their feelings nonverbally are liked more than less expressive individuals (Friedman, Riggio, & Casella, 1988). But self-disclosure can go too far: Those who disclose more than is appropriate for the closeness of the relationship make others uncomfortable (Wortman, Adesman, Herman, & Greenberg, 1976). Just as when an acquaintance offers a favor, the reason for the self-disclosure is uncertain: Does it express a desire to deepen the relationship?

When people are entrusted with a self-disclosure, the norm of reciprocity prescribes that they should respond in kind. For example, when someone describes sad personal experiences to you, you might recount similar events from your own life. Thus self-disclosures, like rewards, are often exchanged in a relationship (R. L. Archer, 1980). At other times, good friends or relationship partners respond to self-disclosures with sympathetic concern, and as we will discuss later, this is an important aspect of building intimacy and closeness in relationships (Reis & Patrick, 1996).

You may recall our discussion of other implications of the norm of reciprocity from Chapter 10, pages 361 to 365.

Self-disclosures can have many positive effects in a relationship. Coordinating mutual activities is easier when each partner knows something of the other's abilities and preferences. And deeper mutual understanding lets each partner meet

FIGURE 11.3   Gender and the intimacy of interaction

■ In this study, college students filled out brief questionnaires rating the intimacy of all their social interactions within a given time period. As the figure shows, interactions involving a female participant or a male participant and a female partner—that is, any interaction that involved a female—tended to be more intimate and self-disclosing than interactions between two males. (Data from Reis, 1986.)

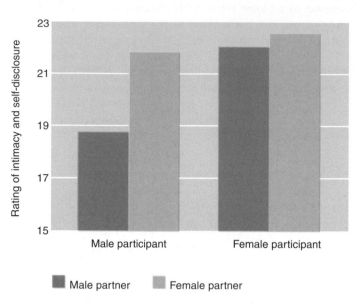

■ Male partner   ■ Female partner

the other's needs more easily. Self-disclosure also signals trust, because in a particular relationship we may disclose things that we would not want the whole world to know.

There is a strong gender difference in the intimacy level of self-disclosure, as in so many other aspects of relationships. Women self-disclose more than men, particularly by revealing their feelings and emotions (Dindia & Allen, 1992; Morton, 1978). As Figure 11.3 shows, the difference is largest in same-sex friendships: Women disclose much more to other women than men do to other men (Reis, 1986). When men do engage in self-disclosure early in a heterosexual relationship, it can be part of an effort to make the relationship more intimate (Derlega, Winstead, Wong, & Hunter, 1985). In contrast, women's disclosures seem to reflect their existing feelings about the relationship, rather than their intention to move toward greater intimacy (Adams & Shea, 1981).

As two people interact over time, the course of the relationship comes to depend on the way they treat each other. As they exchange rewards, they feel good about themselves and each other. As they share intimate information, they grow in mutual understanding, demonstrate trust, and obtain support and self-validation. Each partner's liking for the other now depends on the way the exchanges of rewards and self-disclosures operate in the relationship. If the processes continue smoothly, casual friendship may be transformed into a close relationship. And, paradoxically, psychological closeness transforms the nature of the self-disclosure and exchange processes that produced closeness in the first place.

Close Relationships

Of your hundreds of relationships with other people, only a handful truly count as close. Are they the relationships that evoke the most positive feelings? Not necessarily. For example, you may have felt high regard and strong attraction for someone who will always remain distant, such as a movie star or a teacher. Or you may have been in a close relationship with a sibling or a romantic partner that at times was so filled with conflict that your feelings were mostly negative. For reasons like these, researchers define a **close relationship** not in terms of positive feelings but as a connection involving strong and frequent interdependence in many different areas of life. **Interdependence** means that each partner's thoughts, emotions, and behaviors influence the other's (H. H. Kelley and others, 1983; Rusbult and others, 2001).

There are three main types of interdependence. *Cognitive interdependence* means thinking about the self and partner as inextricably linked parts of a whole—a relationship—rather than as separate individuals (Agnew, van Lange, Rusbult, & Langston, 1998). Cognitive interdependence is strongly tied to feelings of intimacy and to the relationship's stability over time (Aron, Aron, & Smollan, 1992).

Behavioral interdependence means that each person has a great deal of influence on the partner's decisions, activities, and plans. Moreover, the partners usually spend a lot of time together, and they share a number of different activities. According to a study by Ellen Berscheid, Mark Snyder, and Allan Omoto (1989), when people's lives are interlinked in these ways, the relationship tends to endure over time. Moreover, the extent of behavioral interdependence is a strong predictor of how long the relationship will last, even stronger than the couple's positive feelings for each other.

Affective interdependence refers to the affective bond that links close relationship partners. The feelings are usually warm and positive but not always; whether positive or negative, interdependence means that each partner's emotional well-being is deeply affected by what the other does.

Cognitive, behavioral, and affective interdependence thus reflect the special ways that relationships help people meet their fundamental needs for connectedness with others and for mastery and rewards. Though they are all important aspects of relationship closeness, they are somewhat separate; a particular relationship may be higher on one dimension and lower on others.

When people think about themselves mostly as members of a couple, share major parts of their lives, and are linked by strong emotional ties, are we talking about love? Trying to define *love* may be a fool's game, and indeed most relationship researchers have avoided doing so (Shaver & Hazan, 1988). Nevertheless, two intrepid researchers, Arthur Aron and Elaine Aron (1991), have defined love as the "thoughts, feelings, and actions that are associated with a desire to enter or maintain a close relationship with a specific person" (p. 26). This formal definition emphasizes the desire for closeness or interdependence, and, like our everyday use of the word love, covers relationships with kin and nonromantic friendships as well as romantic relationships (Meyers & Berscheid, 1997). That is, a close relationship can involve the secure, trusting attachment of *companionate love* or the intense sexual attraction of *romantic love* (Hatfield, 1988). Because all close relationships share the basic properties of cognitive, behavioral, and affective interdependence, we consider what research tells us about those common processes before discussing what is special about romantic and sexual relationships.

Research on Close Relationships

By necessity, most research on close relationships uses nonexperimental designs that leave some ambiguity about causal relations among variables, and most has taken place in North America.

When people are interdependent with the other members of a face-to-face group, it has many types of effects on their behavior, as we describe in Chapter 12.

Close relationship. A relationship involving strong and frequent interdependence in many domains of life.

Interdependence. A situation in which each person's thoughts, emotions, and behaviors influence those of other people.

As you read this section of the chapter, you will notice that much research on close relationships uses nonexperimental designs. For obvious reasons, people cannot be randomly assigned to have high or low levels of variables like commitment to their partners, nor can relationships be randomly assigned to last for years or break up quickly. The impracticality of random assignment rules out experimental designs and weakens conclusions about the direction of cause and effect. For example, researchers have found that in romantic relationships, the frequency of sexual intercourse is higher among couples who are generally satisfied with their relationship. This observation may mean that sexual activity increases relationship satisfaction, but it could also mean that couples who are generally satisfied with their relationship tend to have intercourse more often. Researchers are sometimes able to overcome such ambiguities by studying relationships over time, which may allow them to determine the order in which processes occur. The majority of research on close relationships has also been conducted in North America. As we will see later, the limited amount of research available from other areas of the world suggests that some aspects of relationships do depend on the cultural surroundings (Goodwin, 1999).

Cognitive Interdependence: The Partner Becomes Part of the Self

As a relationship develops, it may evolve into a close relationship, with extensive interaction and strong mutual influence. A desire for closeness with a particular other person seems to correspond to what people generally mean by "love." In a close relationship, the partner is incorporated into the self, each partner rewards the other to show caring, and a strong emotional attachment arises.

In the intense and frequent interaction that marks a close relationship, partners learn a lot about each other: She can repair her car; he once cheated on an important exam. As each partner becomes increasingly familiar with intimate and varied information about the other, something important happens: The differences that typically exist between self-knowledge and knowledge about the partner are erased. Consider some of the self–other differences that melt away in a close relationship.

The differences that usually exist between knowledge of the self and knowledge of another person were described in Chapter 4, pages 100 to 102.

1. *People know their own thoughts and feelings but are usually unaware of others' thoughts and feelings.* Self-disclosure and extensive interaction, however, give a person access to his or her partner's inner life. In a close relationship, people often have the sense that they know just what their partners are thinking (Ickes & Simpson, 1997).

2. *People perceive themselves in a wide range of situations, whereas their opportunities to observe others are relatively restricted.* The shared intimacy of a close relationship changes that, as each partner learns about almost every aspect of the other person's life.

3. *People have a different perspective on themselves (as actors) than on others (as observers).* In a close relationship, however, self-disclosure allows each partner to share the other person's perspective and to know the reasons behind the other person's behaviors and preferences.

4. *People can control their own actions but not those of other people.* Interdependence in a close relationship narrows this gap, as each partner's wishes actually influence the partner's behavior as well.

As the typical differences between the cognitive representations of the self and the partner are reduced or eliminated, knowledge of the partner becomes more like self-knowledge. This process represents a sort of expansion of the self beyond the individual to incorporate the partner (Aron, Paris, & Aron, 1995). If Romeo wrote a description of Juliet, for example, he would probably include descriptions of her private thoughts, feelings, and reactions, and he would discuss how she responds differently to different situations (Prentice, 1990). Contrast this with the way people usually describe unfamiliar others, by including little information about thoughts and feelings and assuming that the person behaves consistently across situations.

As the boundaries between self and other break down, mental representations of the self and partner are linked into a single unit, the defining feature of cognitive interdependence (Agnew and others, 1998; Mashek, Aron, & Boncimino, 2003). For example, people use *we* to refer to themselves and the partner, just as they do with an in-group with which they identify. In one study demonstrating the linkage of partner and self, people rated whether each of a number of trait words terms described themselves, while a computer recorded the amount of time they took to respond to each item. The researchers then compared the speed of responding for those traits on which participants had previously rated themselves as similar to their spouses, versus those on which participants had rated themselves as different from their spouses. Participants were slower in responding on the traits where they thought they differed from their spouses (Aron, Aron, Tudor, & Nelson, 1991). The researchers concluded that people's representations of themselves and their spouses are intertwined, so much so that the connection can lead to confusion and slow down someone's ability to report, for instance, that he is not assertive when his wife is. A recent study replicated this finding and showed that the amount of slowing on traits on which people differ from their relationship partner was larger for those people who rated their relationships as closer (E. R. Smith, Coats, & Walling, 1999).

To remind yourself of how a group can similarly become part of the self, refer to Chapter 6, pages 194 to 197.

INSIDER VERSUS OUTSIDER PERSPECTIVES ON RELATIONSHIPS. Not surprisingly, cognitive interdependence means that the relationship partners themselves may view their relationship differently than outsiders (such as their friends) do. Still, those other people's thoughts and feelings about the relationship may have an impact on the couple. For example, your mom may love or hate your latest boyfriend or girlfriend. Or your roommate may think you are dating an angel or a jerk. How do other people's views of a relationship compare with the partners' own in predicting whether the relationship will last? On the one hand, it might seem that that no one could know more about a relationship than the partners themselves. On the other hand, the partners might be subject to biases that cloud their perceptions of the relationship, while their friends and others might see things more clearly. Christopher Agnew and his colleagues (Agnew, Loving, & Drigotas, 2001) examined these intriguing questions, obtaining data from 74 undergraduate heterosexual couples and 960 of their friends. Not only did friends' views of the relationship predict its long-term survival, but outsiders' views were significantly better predictors than were the views of the couple themselves! The friends of the female partner were especially likely to be accurate when they foresaw a later break-up. Why might this be? The authors believe that friends' accuracy arises from disclosures by the couple. This interpretation was supported by the finding that couples who communicated more about their relationship to outsiders had friends whose perceptions were particularly accurate. Women tend to disclose more about their romantic relationships to their friends than do men, accounting for the woman's friends' greater predictive insight. Other researchers have also found that outsider views of a relationship can be quite diagnostic of romantic relationship quality and outcome (MacDonald & Ross, 1999).

In a close relationship, processes of cognitive interdependence mean that the partner—whether a best friend, parent, or romantic partner—becomes linked to the person's self-concept. Self-definition as a member of the twosome, and the support and validation provided by the partner, become important to the person's identity, just as a significant group membership becomes important. The merging of self and partner means that the two processes that drive the development of casual relationships—the exchange of rewards and the increase of mutual knowledge stemming from reciprocal self-disclosure—begin to operate in different ways. The linkage of partner to self fundamentally changes the ways in which we meet our basic needs within a close relationship.

Behavioral Interdependence: Transformations in Exchange

Relationship closeness alters the way partners exchange rewards. In a close relationship, partners reward each other to show affection and because they want to make the partner happy.

Why would you do a favor for a close friend? Probably not because you expect the favor to be immediately repaid, but in order to show that you care and because you *want* to make your partner happy. In close relationships, the exchange of rewards proceeds differently and has a different meaning than it does in more casual relationships.

CHANGES IN THE DISTRIBUTION OF REWARDS. Caring about the partner's feelings—wanting to make him or her feel good—can complicate decisions about what to do. Suppose, for example, you have a yen to take in a classic Federico Fellini film on a Friday night. If your partner prefers the latest Hollywood action flick, you have to consider that preference as well as your own in deciding on the evening's entertainment. We solve minor coordination problems like this many times each day, usually without even seeing them as problems. We do so because the nature of exchange is transformed in a close relationship (H. H. Kelley, 1979; Rusbult and others, 2001). People do not just do whatever they would prefer as individuals and ignore the partner's wishes, or give in to the partner and expect direct reciprocation in the future. Instead, people directly respond to their partners' wishes. After all, if your partner is part of yourself, his or her needs and desires become indistinguishable from your own.

In a study demonstrating this point, participants divided up a set amount of money between themselves and another person (Aron and others, 1991). As Figure 11.4 shows, people gave themselves considerably more than they gave to a stranger. When the other person was their best friend, however, they gave the friend just about the same amount as they gave themselves. The experimenters told some participants that the money would be sent to the friend with a note explaining the participant's role, while other participants were told that their friends would receive

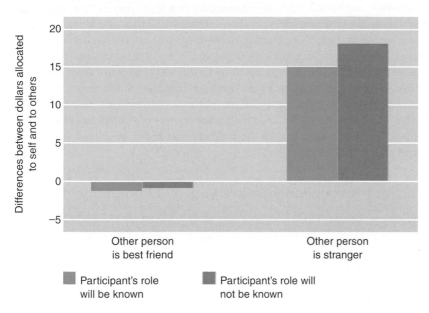

FIGURE 11.4   Treating a best friend like the self

■ In this study, participants were given a sum of money to divide between themselves and another person. As the left bars show, when the other person was their best friend, the participants gave that person slightly more than they gave themselves—regardless of whether the friend would know of their role in the allocation. In contrast, when the other person was a stranger, the right bars show that participants gave considerably more to themselves than to that person. (Data from Aron and others, 1991.)

the money and an explanation that did not mention the participant's name. People were equally generous to the friend in both cases, indicating that they were not motivated only by a desire to avoid upsetting their friends. Rather, people really want to benefit a close friend just as much as they want to benefit themselves. Indeed, one's best friend is part of "me and mine."

Closeness alters not only the reasons for exchanging rewards but also the types of benefits the partners bestow on each other. Material rewards are typically exchanged in relationships that are not close, whereas love and emotional support are more often the coin of close relationships (Foa & Foa, 1974; Hays, 1984). And the more deeply the partners know one another, the more finely the rewards can be tuned to the loved one's specific needs and preferences. For example, new roommates who have just met seek a rough balance in the total amount of rewards they exchange, regardless of type. But as time passes and their relationship deepens, they are more likely to give each other the specific types of benefits that each values most: help with math homework, companionship for an evening at the movies (Berg, 1984).

ATTRIBUTIONS IN CLOSE RELATIONSHIPS: IT'S THE THOUGHT THAT COUNTS.
Your 6-year-old son or your young brother gives you a wonderful birthday present: a lumpy pottery bowl he fashioned and painted himself. The bowl is downright ugly and you don't have any idea what you will do with it. We bet, though, that you will still enjoy it because you appreciate the feelings behind the gift. In close relationships, it's the thought that counts. The ways the partners treat each other become less important than the *feelings and intentions* that those acts convey, just as the youngster's gift indicates his high regard for you (H. H. Kelley, 1979). The principle holds true on the negative side as well. A relatively minor sin like arriving late for a date, which might be shrugged off by a mere acquaintance, may be seen as indicating a lack of caring in a close relationship and may precipitate a major crisis.

Fortunately, attributions in close relationships are generally biased in a positive direction. As we saw in Chapter 4, our attributions for our own behaviors are often self-serving, and because a close relationship partner is part of "me and mine," the same self-serving biases apply to the partner. We inflate the significance of our partner's positive behaviors, linking them to his or her sterling qualities or loving feelings: "How much he must care about me!" We usually minimize the partner's negative behaviors, explaining them away as due to situational causes like a bad day at work or minor failings like a poor memory (Fletcher & Fincham, 1991). In fact, idealized, highly positive views of the partner—perceptions that are even more positive than the partner's own self-views—are typically found in romantic relationships that deeply satisfy the partners and last a long time (S. L. Murray, Holmes, & Griffin, 1996).

Affective Interdependence: Intimacy and Commitment

> Ongoing processes of self-disclosure and sympathetic support lead to feelings of trust, closeness, and acceptance. As closeness increases, the partners feel a growing sense of commitment to each other.

Just as closeness transforms the exchange of rewards and the way partners think about themselves and each other, it also fundamentally changes the partners' feelings. A sense of intimacy grows, and the partners' commitment to the relationship deepens.

PSYCHOLOGICAL INTIMACY. Perhaps the most important component of close relationships is **intimacy**. This is defined as a positive emotional bond that includes understanding and support (Hatfield, 1988; Reis, Clark & Holmes, 2004). If asked about your feelings toward your closest friends or family members, you probably would use words like *caring*, *warmth*, and *acceptance*. You feel happy when you are with the partner and may feel low or even distressed when you are apart (Bowlby, 1969). These feelings are displayed in mutual understanding and support, and a desire to share with and help the partner (Sternberg & Grajek, 1984). Intimacy develops slowly over time and is nourished by interactions involving self-disclosure, support, and validation (M. S. Clark & Taraban, 1991; Reis and others, 2004). This is why it is difficult to imagine a truly intimate relationship springing up between two people "at first sight," no matter how strong their mutual attraction might be.

Let's consider the process that builds and reflects intimacy in a close relationship. The first step is self-disclosure, particularly regarding feelings or deeply personal reactions. Arriving home in the evening, you might tell your partner, "My computer crashed today and then the boss chewed me out because some important files got lost. I don't know how much longer I can handle this job." Instead of simply reciprocating with another self-disclosure, your partner is likely to try to convey acceptance, acknowledgment, and understanding (Derlega, Wilson, & Chaikin, 1976), and this type of responsiveness is the second step in the process. It is important that the partner responds to the emotional content of the self-disclosure rather than to the surface issues. For example, you probably wouldn't find it very satisfying if the partner started talking about ways to keep your computer from crashing. The most responsive messages not only incorporate the content of the self-disclosure (to show understanding) but go beyond it to express positive feelings (Burleson, 1994).

Intimacy. A positive emotional bond that includes understanding and support.

Such truly responsive replies have several effects on the original discloser, which constitute the third step in the intimacy process. You feel *understood* when your partner correctly perceives and acknowledges your feelings. You also feel *valued and esteemed* by your partner's acceptance and responsiveness. Interactions that let you feel known and validated (Berg & Archer, 1980) may give you the strength to go back to work the next day and face your temperamental hard disk and curmudgeonly boss.

As the partner becomes part of the self, the partner's esteem for you becomes just like your own self-esteem. You feel good when your partner both knows and likes you. Intimate interactions of this sort are therefore deeply linked with positive emotions of warmth and caring. The reciprocation of self-disclosures and responses strengthens positive emotional bonds and also demonstrates positive feelings because people are unlikely to self-disclose deeply or to respond appropriately unless they care for the partner. The linkage between psychological intimacy and positive emotions is so profound that developmental psychologist John Bowlby (1969) has suggested it has an evolutionary basis. An innate system binds infants emotionally to their mothers or other caregivers by leading them to feel good when in contact with the caregiver and anxious or distressed when apart. This type of emotional bond keeps helpless infants close to their caregivers. The same psychological system may have an important influence on feelings toward friends and romantic partners in adult life (Hazan & Shaver, 1987).

Feelings of warmth, connectedness, and caring are so important to people that psychological intimacy is perhaps the most central reward of a close relationship (Reis & Patrick, 1996). As John Harvey and Julia Omarzu (1997, p. 225) wrote, "Perhaps there is no act more endearing to a partner than that of trying diligently over time to know the partner and use that knowledge toward enhancement of the relationship. This is an act that makes people feel special, treasured, and nurtured. Many of us will live our lives having few if any experiences with others who made us feel this way."

COMMITMENT. Intimacy may draw people closer, but it is commitment that holds a relationship together over time. **Commitment** includes a long-term orientation toward the relationship, reflecting the intention and desire to maintain the relationship for the long term, as well as a strong emotional bond to the partner (Agnew and others, 1998; Arriaga & Agnew, 2001). Caryl Rusbult (1983) argues that commitment is the central force that keeps people working to promote and maintain their partnership.

Committed partners feel comfortable relying on each other for intimacy, advice, and support (Kobak & Hazan, 1991). Each believes that the other is trustworthy, responsive, and available when needed, and that his or her support can bring comfort in times of distress. Commitment involves actions as well as feelings, for it affects people's intentions, desires, and plans for the future. Being committed means, for instance, wanting the relationship to last for a long time. The different aspects of commitment, such as thinking of the implications of current actions for the relationship's future and intending to stay in the relationship for the long term, usually go together (Arriaga & Agnew, 2001; Rusbult, Martz, & Agnew, 1998).

What creates and maintains commitment to a relationship? Rusbult (1983) argues that it emerges from three factors that all tend to increase as relationships deepen over time. As Figure 11.5 shows, one factor is personal *satisfaction* with the relationship: recognition of the rewards it brings, such as the opportunity to make intimate self-disclosures, express sexuality, experience emotional involvement, find

Commitment. The combined forces that hold the partners together in an enduring relationship.

FIGURE 11.5 Factors influencing commitment to a relationship

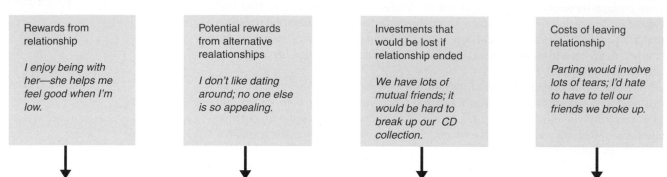

| Rewards from relationship

I enjoy being with her—she helps me feel good when I'm low. | Potential rewards from alternative realationships

I don't like dating around; no one else is so appealing. | Investments that would be lost if relationship ended

We have lots of mutual friends; it would be hard to break up our CD collection. | Costs of leaving relationship

Parting would involve lots of tears; I'd hate to have to tell our friends we broke up. |

Satisfaction with relationship   Barriers to leaving relationship

Commitment to relationship

I am comfortable relying on her; I want the relationship to last a long time.

■ Commitment depends on satisfaction with the relationship relative to its potential alternatives. Commitment is also strengthened by perceived barriers to leaving the relationship. (Based on Rusbult, 1983.)

companionship for enjoyable activities, and feel secure, worthy, and validated (Drigotas & Rusbult, 1992). But people evaluate these outcomes not in absolute terms but by comparing them with the rewards they believe would be available in alternative relationships, a standard termed the *comparison level for alternatives* (Thibaut & Kelley, 1959), which is the second factor affecting commitment. If you see your relationship as offering unique rewards that you think would be unavailable from other relationships, you are likely to be strongly committed to it.

Negative forces can be as important as positive ones in maintaining commitment. Psychological or financial factors often pose barriers to leaving a relationship (Levinger, 1991; Rusbult, 1983). For example, people contemplating divorce face the embarrassment of having to admit to friends that the relationship failed, and they must cope with the financial, emotional, and legal difficulties of breaking up a home and family. They also confront the loss of their investments of time, energy, and self-disclosures that they have made in the relationship. They may even lose mutual friends or treasured possessions. Barriers like these are the third factor that influences commitment, and they can help maintain a relationship even if satisfaction is low.

Commitment usually grows as a relationship continues. As the partners' intimacy increases, they are likely to derive increasing satisfaction from the relationship, and they begin to perceive alternative relationships as less desirable and less available. In fact, compared with those who are dating casually, heterosexual college students who are committed to a dating relationship tend to see opposite-sex others as physically less attractive (Simpson, Gangestad, & Lerma, 1990). Needless to say, this means that they also see their partner as relatively more attractive (J. G. Miller and others, 1997). For all these reasons, relationships that involve stronger feelings of commitment last longer, even when they are studied over a period of 15 years (Bui, Peplau, & Hill, 1996; Le & Agnew, 2003).

Types of People, Types of Relationships

People differ in the ways they approach close relationships. Securely attached individuals are comfortable relying on the partner for support and acceptance. In contrast, some individuals avoid reliance on other people, and some individuals worry that the partner will not be available and responsive. Gender and culture also play a role. Most relationship research has been conducted in Western, independent cultures.

In a committed close relationship, psychological intimacy allows caring partners to share self-disclosures and to comfort and support each other. However, some people are more comfortable than others with intimacy, trust, and reliance on a partner.

ATTACHMENT STYLES. Take a look at the four self-descriptions in Table 11.1, and decide which one most closely fits you. A questionnaire like this has been used to classify adults as having one of several distinct **attachment styles** (Bartholomew & Horowitz, 1991; Hazan & Shaver, 1987). The idea of attachment styles is based on the assumption that, as we have already mentioned, people have built-in tendencies to form emotional attachments to others, beginning in infancy (Bowlby, 1969). Although this psychological mechanism is common across all people, our differing lifetime experiences teach us different lessons about what to expect from close partners. If other people (including caregivers in childhood and romantic partners in adulthood) generally are attentive and responsive to our needs, we will come to hold different beliefs and emotional tendencies than if we find other people unresponsive or inconsistent. In fact, even infants display different types of attachment to their mothers (Ainsworth, Blehar, Waters, & Wall, 1978).

TABLE 11.1. An Example of Statements Measuring Attachment Styles in Adult Close Relationships

Secure. It is easy for me to become emotionally close to others. I am comfortable depending on others and having others depend on me. I don't worry about being alone or having others not accept me.

Dismissing. I am comfortable without close emotional relationships. It is very important to me to feel independent and self-sufficient, and I prefer not to depend on others or have others depend on me.

Preoccupied. I want to be completely emotionally intimate with others, but I often find that others are reluctant to get as close as I would like. I am uncomfortable being without close relationships, but I sometimes worry that others don't value me as much as I value them.

Fearful. I am uncomfortable getting close to others. I want emotionally close relationships, but I find it difficult to trust others completely, or to depend on them. I worry that I will be hurt if I allow myself to become too close to others.

Source: From Bartholomew and Horowitz (1991). Copyright © 1991 by the American Psychological Association. Adapted with permission.

Attachment styles. People's basic orientations towards others in close relationships, which can be secure, preoccupied, avoidant, or fearful.

The many ways in which our prior knowledge influences our perceptions and interpretations are described in Chapter 3, pages 82 to 88.

Attachment styles summarize people's general beliefs about the self, other people, and the nature of relationships (Fletcher & Fincham, 1991). Like all knowledge structures, these beliefs in turn affect people's perceptions and evaluations of their current relationships (Baldwin, 1992). Thus, attachment styles have been found to relate to many aspects of people's loving relationships. In general, research finds that *securely attached* people, who make up a majority of the adult population (Mickelson, Kessler, & Shaver, 1997), are the most likely to feel happiness and trust in their relationships, are highest in self-esteem, and are the least likely to fear closeness. Securely attached people are the most likely to express positive views about both self and other, agreeing that "I am easier to get to know than most people" and that "people are generally well intentioned and good-hearted" (Shaver, Hazan, & Bradshaw, 1988). Those categorized as *dismissing* are generally high in self-confidence, but low in emotional expressiveness and in the intimacy of their friendships. *Preoccupied* individuals are high in emotional expressiveness and show the most reliance on others. Finally, the individuals classed as *fearful* tend to be low in self-confidence and in the intimacy of their friendships and romantic relationships (Bartholomew & Horowitz, 1991). Attachment styles appear to be moderately stable, at least over the first 19 years of life (Fraley, 2002).

The four attachment styles can be placed on two underlying dimensions describing people's basic views of the self and of other people, as shown in Table 11.2. The left column of the table (secure and dismissing styles) includes people who have a positive, confident view of the self as worthy of love. In contrast, the right column represents people who have a more negative view of the self, leading them to seek support and validation from others. The top row of the table (secure and preoccupied styles) represents individuals with generally positive views of others as trustworthy and available for relationships, while the bottom row includes individuals with more negative views of others as unreliable and possibly rejecting. Perhaps you can see how these different views of the self and of other people combine to produce the four specific attachment styles shown in the table.

Do attachment styles actually influence the way close partners give and receive support? A fascinating study of dating couples by Jeffry Simpson and his colleagues (Simpson, Rholes, & Nelligan, 1992) examined this question. The researchers separated the couple and led the woman to a waiting room, where she was told that she would soon undergo "experimental procedures that arouse considerable anxiety and distress." To underline this warning, they showed her a darkened

TABLE 11.2. Four Types of Attachment Reflect Positive or Negative Views of the Self and the Partner (Bartholomew & Horowitz, 1991)

	Positive view of self	Negative view of self
Positive view of others	**Secure:** sense of self as lovable and of others as accepting	**Preoccupied:** sense of self as unworthy, leading to striving for acceptance by valued others
Negative view of others	**Dismissing:** sense of self as lovable but doubts about others, leading to avoidance of close relationships	**Fearful:** sense of unworthiness combined with expectations that others will be untrustworthy and rejecting

Source: From Bartholomew and Horowitz (1991). Copyright © 1991 by the American Psychological Association. Adapted with permission.

room resembling an isolation chamber, filled with complex electronic equipment. The man, unaware of his partner's experience, was then brought into the waiting room and the couple's ensuing interaction was covertly videotaped for 5 minutes.

People with different attachment styles showed distinct variations in their patterns of seeking and giving support. Among secure and preoccupied women, those who were extremely upset sought more support from their partners than did those who were less frightened. In contrast, among women in the dismissing and fearful categories (those who hold a negative view of others, as Table 11.2 shows), participants who were extremely upset actually sought less support than did their less frightened counterparts. Almost one fifth of the women did not even mention the stressful event to their partners! The men's attachment styles also played a role in the amount of support they offered. Securely attached men tended to offer more support to a partner who displayed more fear than to a partner who was less frightened. But among men in the dismissing and fearful categories, a different pattern emerged: The more fear his partner displayed, the less support he offered her.

Regardless of their attachment styles, all the women in this upsetting situation were calmed if their partners made supportive comments. The most interesting result of this study is that the nonsecure women tended not to ask for, and the nonsecure men tended not to offer, this potentially effective interaction.

This study and other research (Reis & Patrick, 1996; Young & Acitelli, 1998) suggest that basic beliefs about self and others, as reflected in attachment styles, influence both people's trust in their partners' support and responsiveness and their own willingness to offer support. Securely attached partners, who turn toward one another for comfort, derive increased satisfaction from their relationship in the long term. As a result of these processes, attachment styles pervasively influence the ways people attain intimacy and experience love (Collins & Read, 1990; Simpson, 1990).

The effects of attachment style are so pervasive that they influence people's everyday social interactions, not just their closeness with romantic partners. In one study in which people filled out brief questionnaires following every social interaction for a week (Pietromonaco & Feldman Barrett, 1997), preoccupied individuals perceived their everyday interactions as involving greater intimacy and they self-disclosed more than others. Secure individuals, in contrast, felt higher self-esteem after routine social interactions. Unexpectedly, in interactions that involved conflict, preoccupied individuals reported higher levels of positive emotion than the other groups, and rated the interactions as highly satisfying. The researchers explained this finding as resulting from the deep desire for intimacy and personal disclosure that is characteristic of people with a preoccupied attachment style. In a conflict or argument, the other party typically does respond to you and reveals his or her feelings—even if those feelings are negative! Thus conflict situations in some way suit the interpersonal goals of preoccupied individuals, leading to relatively positive emotions.

DIFFERING THEORIES ABOUT RELATIONSHIPS. People differ not only in attachment styles but also in their views of what it takes to make a relationship succeed. For example, we all know people who claim that they and their current romantic partner were "destined to be together." But there are also people who view relationships as not destined but achieved, as something that one must work on for success. Recent research has examined effects of these two types of beliefs, or *implicit theories of relationships* (Knee, Patrick & Lonsbary, 2003). Some people hold growth beliefs, the belief that with any partner, occasional conflicts are to be expected and can be overcome. These individuals tend to date a partner for longer periods of time, and have fewer "one-night stands" during the first month of college (Knee, 1998). In contrast, people who hold destiny beliefs, the idea that a particular romantic partner is inherently compatible or not, are more likely to be influenced by their initial satisfaction in the relationship. If initial satisfaction is high, the relationship is more likely to last a significant period of time. If initial satisfaction is low, the relationship tends to end quickly, as the partners conclude that "it was not meant to be" (Knee, 1998). Thus, our general views of how relationships operate have an impact on the ultimate success of our actual relationships.

GENDER DIFFERENCES IN RELATIONSHIPS. It will surely come as no surprise that men and women often approach close relationships differently. Women's close relationships, particularly with same-sex friends, tend to be more intimate than men's (Reis, Senchak, & Solomon, 1985). This is because research shows that women are better at the skills of understanding, empathy, and emotional responsiveness that play such a key role in the self-disclosure process that builds intimacy (Reis, Clark & Holmes, 2004). This difference in intimacy is just one aspect of a more general principle: Men and women place different emphases on the various rewards that relationships offer (Tannen, 1990; P. H. Wright, 1982). Men prefer participating in enjoyable activities with their partners, and women generally prefer intimacy and sharing feelings.

In one study demonstrating the impact of these differences on heterosexual relationships, Catherine Surra and Molly Longstreth (1990) questioned dating couples about their activity preferences and conflicts in their relationships. They found that the sources of satisfaction with the relationship differed for men and women. The men's satisfaction depended mainly on the way the couple spent their time: The more time the men spent participating with their partners in activities they enjoyed, the happier they were. In contrast, women were satisfied when the couple successfully avoided arguments and conflict. In general, men care more about the rewards they can obtain from interacting with the partner. Women care more about the relationship itself; they are happiest when the relationship is going well (H. H. Kelley, 1979; P. H. Wright, 1982).

RELATIONSHIPS IN CULTURAL PERSPECTIVE. Existing research on relationships has a particular focus, which becomes clear if we consider relationships from a cross-cultural perspective. Most research, even studies of processes common to all types of close relationships, such as how people handle conflicts, has taken place in North America and has focused on heterosexual romantic relationships. This focus reflects an easily available pool of research participants: dating college students and married couples. However, the emphasis on relationships that are voluntary and often temporary fits well with the general characteristics of Western, independent cultures (Moghaddam and others, 1993). Researchers have largely neglected relationships that are permanent and unchosen, such as ties to kin and other social groups, which in interdependent cultures are even more important than dyadic (two-person) romantic connections (Moghaddam and others, 1993). Perhaps the focus on voluntary relationships is responsible for the strong theoretical focus on exchanges of rewards—on what each partner gets from the relationship—found in interdependence theory (Rusbult and others, 2001).

When researchers cast their net beyond North America, many differences between cultures are found (Goodwin, 1999; Markus, Kitayama, & Heiman, 1996).

For example, the nature of the early bond between mother and infant, which is central to conceptions of adult attachment, differs considerably in other industrialized nations from its patterns in the United States (LeVine and others, 1994). In some cultures, marriages arranged by the parents of the couple are common. One study in India compared such arranged marriages to marriages chosen by the partners themselves, and found that love tended to increase over time in the arranged marriages, while decreasing in the other couples (Gupta & Singh, 1982). Our understanding of the full range of human relationships will be further enriched by more cross-cultural research and by theories that are sensitive to cultural assumptions and blind spots (Fiske, 1992).

Effects of Relationships

> Relationships affect virtually all aspects of our lives, including physical health and mental well-being. Intimacy accounts for most of these benefits.

In Chapter 4, we described research showing that the way we think about ourselves influences our feelings, our behaviors, and even our physical health. Relationships also affect these aspects of our lives, because a partner in a close relationship becomes part of ourself.

⬚**WHEN THINGS GO WRONG: INTIMACY, SOCIAL SUPPORT, AND HEALTH.** The medical community was initially puzzled by research showing that **social support**— coping resources provided by significant others—can influence physical health as well as psychological well-being. The findings are now beyond dispute (S. Cohen, 2004; Salovey and others, 1998; Uchino, Cacioppo, & Kiecolt-Glaser, 1996). For example, people with cancer and other diseases who participate in support groups of fellow sufferers can obviously expect to receive comfort, reassurance, information, and advice. But it may surprise you to learn that they also have more effective immune-system responses and live longer than patients without such support (Goleman, 1990). One British study demonstrating this point focused on women with advanced breast cancer. Women who received the best available medical care and also attended support groups lived twice as long—an average of 37 months—as women who received the same excellent medical treatment but had no group support. The results of another study of more than 6000 California residents, shown in Figure 11.6, along with a number of other prospective community-based studies (Berkman & Glass, 2000), suggest that social support has a marked impact on people's overall death rate. A meta-analysis of over 50 such studies demonstrates that the effects of social support on physical health are pervasive, but they are stronger for support given to women rather than men, and stronger when the support is provided by family and friends rather than by strangers (Schwarzer & Leppin, 1989). It has also been shown that people benefit from social support even when they do not realize they are receiving it (Bolger, Zuckerman, & Kessler, 2000).

How does social support produce these striking benefits? Other people can provide practical help, from offering advice about problems to running errands for the patient. However, these concrete forms of assistance are not the major benefits of social support. Instead, social support offers opportunities for self-disclosure, companionship, and enjoyable interactions, which seem to account for most of its benefits (Sarason, Sarason, & Gurung, 1997; Wills, 1991). Thus, the same factors

> **Social support.** Emotional and physical coping resources provided by other people.

FIGURE 11.6 Social support and physical health

■ Researchers questioned over 6000 California residents about their social support. Nine years later, they calculated the death rate from all causes for individuals who initially had been categorized as having various levels of social support. This graph shows the rates for people aged 30 to 49, though findings were similar for other age groups. As you can see, both men and women who initially had higher levels of social support had lower death rates. (Data from Berkman & Syme, 1979.)

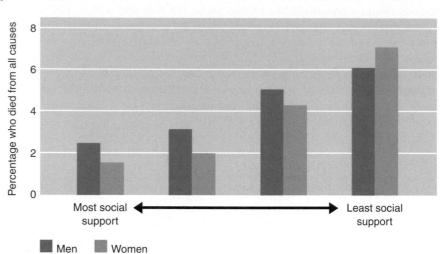

that provide the deepest satisfaction in our relationships in good times are also those that help most in bad times. And because married people are (as a group) more likely to have a psychologically intimate relationship than unmarried people, marriage usually improves people's well-being. Married men in particular are generally happier and more satisfied with their lives than unmarried people are (Veroff, Douvan, & Kukla, 1981). Again, happiness translates into health. In one study, married men aged 45 to 64 had just one half the death rate of unmarried men, even after other influences on health like income, smoking, drinking, and obesity were taken into account (Angier, 1990b). Of course, the same benefits can also be obtained through social support in close friendships or nonmarital romantic relationships.

GENDER AND SOCIAL SUPPORT. Deborah Tannen (1990, p. 49) described a woman who was upset about a scar left visible on her body by an operation. Here are the responses she obtained from two different people:

> A: *"I know. It's like your body has been violated."*

> B: *"You can have plastic surgery to cover up the scar."*

Did you guess that response A came from a woman and B from a man? Women are more likely than men to respond to someone's negative feelings with understanding and acceptance—to reassure the speaker that it's all right to feel bad, perhaps by sharing an account of a time when they had similar feelings. Men are more likely than women to take the initial disclosure as a complaint about a problem and to offer helpful advice on solving it. Tannen points out that women and men often misunderstand each other's approaches. A woman may feel that a problem-solving response belittles her feelings by failing to deal with them directly. In this particular episode, the woman was upset because she felt that B (her husband) *wanted* her to have plastic surgery, and that suggesting a solution meant that he was unconcerned about her current emotional state.

But men may be equally troubled by a woman's typical responses. When a woman responds to a man's concerns by saying "I know, sometimes I feel the same way," the man may feel that she is denying the uniqueness of his feelings and failing to contribute to a solution. Miscommunication might be less likely if each gender recognized the other's needs.

Emotional support is more helpful than problem solving to people who are ill or under stress (Wills, 1991). Since women are more likely to offer emotional support, it follows that people should feel healthier and happier after interacting with women than they do after interacting with men. And this is true. For both male and female college students, everyday interaction with women is a more effective safeguard against loneliness than is interaction with men (Reis, 1986). Similarly, men seem to benefit more from marriage than women do, and, when a spouse dies, men are at greater risk for depression and physical illness than women are (Bernard, 1973; Reis, 1986).

Of course, this gender difference in psychological intimacy is largely a matter of preference rather than ability (Reis and others, 1985). Both men and women are able to engage in intimate, meaningful interaction and to provide emotional support. All people, regardless of gender, fare better psychologically and physically when they interact with close others in a psychologically and emotionally intimate way (Burleson, 2003).

WHEN THINGS GO RIGHT: CAPITALIZING ON POSITIVE EVENTS. Just as people count on others for social support during times of trouble, people benefit from sharing their successes with others when times are good. Being able to tell another person about our triumphs and joys multiplies our good feelings about the events, and this is another important benefit of close relationships (Reis & Gable, 2003). In a series of studies, Shelly Gable and her colleagues (Gable, Reis, Impett, & Asher, 2004) have found that when people recount positive events to others, they experience more positive emotions and increased satisfaction with life, above and beyond the effects due to the event itself. Moreover, the more people they told, the more they benefited. And the benefits were greatest when the other person reacted positively to being told about the event. Sharing a positive event with one's partner creates an opportunity for re-living and re-experiencing it, thus enhancing its positive impact on the self.

■ **Social support and health.** Researchers now know that supportive relationships can be just as important to good physical health as medical treatment and healthy living. Many of today's assisted living communities today employ aides whose primary responsibilities are to provide comfort and companionship to residents.

Romantic Love and Sexuality

Romeo and Juliet, Rhett Butler and Scarlett O'Hara, Brad Pitt and Jennifer Aniston—famous lovers of legend and lore feed our ideas about romance. Though high divorce rates suggest that many people fail to find the romance they seek, the ideal itself still influences how we act in relationships and how we feel about them. What is the mysterious force we call *romantic love* or *passion*? And how is it tied up with our ideas about sexuality and marriage?

Passionate Feelings

Some relationships involve passionate feelings and emotions. Passionate emotions can arise quickly and are closely linked to sexual desires and behavior.

"I want my partner, physically, emotionally, mentally." "Sometimes I feel I can't control my thoughts; they are obsessively on my partner." "I eagerly look for signs indicating my partner's desire for me." These are items from the Passionate Love Scale, developed by Elaine Hatfield (1988). They suggest that passionate love involves, in addition to sexual feelings, a sense of intense longing for the partner, euphoric feelings of fulfillment and ecstasy when the relationship goes well, and anxiety and despair when it does not (Hatfield, 1988; Hatfield & Rapson, 1993). Other components of love, such as commitment, trust, intimacy, and attachment, are relatively quiet. But when people talk about passionate or romantic feelings, they use words like *stormy*, *roller coaster*, *head-over-heels*, and *obsession*. They also add one crucial preposition to the word love: being *in* love means feeling not only warmth and affection for the partner, but also sexual attraction (Meyers & Berscheid, 1997).

Romantic love is quite different from liking (Z. Rubin, 1970). Sometimes we realize that the object of our hopeless adoration is someone totally unsuitable, a person we don't know very well or even like very much. As Ellen Berscheid (1988) has noted, the intransigent independence of passionate feelings from the other components of love

> *can be testified to by anyone who has earnestly desired to be in love with another, often because the other is so likable, or because they do have all those qualities one desires (or ought to desire) in a mate, or because it would please one's parents, friends, or the other person; one can like the other so hard one's nose bleeds, but that—still—does not, and seemingly cannot, cause the liking state to be transcended and romantic love to appear.* (p. 369)

The vast majority of research on romantic relationships has examined heterosexual couples, though available evidence suggests that homosexual and heterosexual romantic relationships are much more alike than different (Kurdek, 1991; Leigh, 1989). In heterosexual relationships, men generally seem to be more romantic than women (K. L. Dion & Dion, 1988). For example, a study of college-student dating couples found that men tended to fall in love more quickly than women, while women fell out of love more readily (C. T. Hill and others, 1976).

Besides these gender differences, views on the mysterious and powerful force of passion differ from culture to culture. Most North Americans believe that romantic love is natural, desirable, and necessary for marriage (Simpson, Campbell, & Berscheid, 1986). However, most Chinese words for love have negative connotations, like *infatuation*, *unrequited love*, *sorrow* (Hatfield & Rapson, 1993). In China, more pragmatic attributes (like a high income) are viewed as desirable characteristics in a marriage partner; romantic love is viewed with some suspicion, as illicit and socially disruptive (K. L. Dion & Dion, 1988). Consistent with these cultural ideas, cross-national research finds that Americans are more likely than Russians or Japanese people to report experiencing romantic passion (Sprecher and others, 1994).

Passion is disruptive, as are other strong emotions. And, like all emotions, passion is linked to a set of beliefs about the beloved and motivations for specific types of action. The beliefs often idealize the partner: "For me, my partner is the perfect romantic partner" is another item from the Passionate Love Scale (Hatfield, 1988). The desired actions include sexual union and other types of closeness and contact with the beloved, such as touching or sustained eye contact. The high emotional value that lovers place on close contact may stem from the same innate

Calvin and Hobbes by Bill Watterson

attachment system that also serves to keep helpless infants in close proximity to their mothers (Bowlby, 1969; Hazan & Shaver, 1987).

Like all emotions, and like a roller coaster, passion has its peaks and valleys. When couples proclaim that they fell in love "at first sight," you can be sure that passion rather than commitment or intimacy is what they are describing. In fact, people often view passion as something that happens to them, as though they were struck by Cupid's arrow. Perhaps this helps explain why individuals who believe that external forces drive their lives are more likely to experience passionate love than are people who think they control their own fate (K. L. Dion & Dion, 1988).

The intense and sudden onset of passion at the beginning of a relationship is not surprising when you consider how important physical attractiveness is to initial attraction (R. J. Sternberg, 1986). However, after drawing people together, passion tends to fade as the relationship matures (R. J. Sternberg, 1988). Intimacy and commitment develop more slowly but become more important over time, giving a long-term close partnership quite a different character from the turbulent and frenzied feelings of its beginning.

As with many emotions, excited feelings that arise from other causes may intensify the experience of passion. As we saw in Chapter 4, people cannot always accurately identify the causes of their emotional arousal. For this reason, anything that causes arousal can influence passionate feelings. A few minutes of exercise or a hilarious Steve Martin comedy routine, for instance, can intensify passionate feelings toward attractive others (G. L. White, Fishbein, & Rutstein, 1981; Zuckerman, 1979). The fact that arousal from external sources can intensify passionate feelings may explain the fact that, as we mentioned earlier, individuals with a preoccupied attachment style are more likely than others to fall head-over-heels in love, to experience obsessive preoccupation with the beloved, and to feel the emotional highs and lows that are characteristic of passion (Shaver and others, 1988). Similarly, adolescents who are highly anxious are particularly likely to experience passionate love (Hatfield, Sprecher, Pillemer, Greenberger, & Wexler, 1989).

In ordinary circumstances, where extraneous factors are not involved, what is the source of the arousal that underlies and strengthens passion? Ellen Berscheid (1988), who has been studying love for three decades, answered this question by saying: "If forced against a brick wall to face a firing squad who would shoot if not given the correct answer, I would whisper 'It's about 90 percent sexual desire as yet not sated' " (p. 373).

Sexual Attitudes and Behavior

People's attitudes about sex differ widely, depending in part on gender. Some people see sex as an enjoyable activity even outside of a committed relationship; others see it as an expression of intimacy and commitment to the partner.

Do you think sexual activity is appropriate between two people who like each other, even if they have not known each other very long? Between individuals who have a committed relationship but are not married? Between people of the same gender? Between a married person and someone other than his or her spouse? Does your opinion change depending on the kind of sexual activity—intercourse versus kissing and fondling, for example?

Researchers have asked such questions in surveys of the U.S. general public and of U.S. college students. As Table 11.3 shows, most people approve of sexual activity in a committed heterosexual relationship between unmarried people. Indeed, premarital intercourse seems to be very common: One study of teenagers found that about 75% of men and 60% of women had engaged in sexual intercourse, before age 18 on the average (DeLamater & MacCorquodale, 1979). Attitudes toward other types of sex outside of marriage are more negative. A great majority of the public sees extramarital sex as wrong, though one survey estimated that 15% of married women and 25% of married men in the United States have had extramarital affairs (Laumann, Gagnon, Michael, & Michaels, 1994).

Gay and lesbian sexual activity is viewed almost as negatively. Contrary to the image of college students as sexually permissive, many students advocate laws against homosexual activities. In terms of actual behavior, while only about 3% of U.S. men identify themselves as gay or bisexual, about twice that percentage report having had at least one homosexual encounter since puberty (Laumann and others, 1994). The proportions for women are somewhat lower. None of these figures can be taken as valid for all time and all sorts of people, however. Patterns of sexual attitudes and behavior have been changing rapidly in recent decades, and the most recent available data suggest increased acceptance of homosexual activity among the general U.S. public. There was a rise in the proportion saying it is wrong only sometimes or not at all, from 18% in 1990 to 32% in 1996 (Yang, 1997). Perhaps part of this shift is attributable to the greatly increased numbers of people who say that they have a friend or acquaintance who is gay or lesbian, which reached 56% of the adult population in 1996, more than double what it was a decade earlier (Yang, 1997).

Opinions are sharply divided on whether it's all right for unmarried people to engage in sex when they have known each other for a very short time. More college men than college women approve. Since the 1950s and 1960s, men's and women's

Chapter 5, pages 178 to 181, explained how a friendship across group lines can reduce people's prejudice not only against the friend's group, but against other out-groups as well.

TABLE 11.3. Sexual Attitudes and Behaviors: Survey Results

Respondents	Question	Year, Percentage Agreeing
	Premarital sex	
General public	A man and woman having sex relations before marriage is wrong only sometimes or not wrong at all	1972, 49% 1989, 61%
College freshmen	If two people really like each other, it's all right for them to have sex even if they have known each other only a very short time	1975, 50% 1989, 50%
	Extramarital sex	
General public	A married person having sexual relations with someone other than the married partner is wrong only sometimes or not wrong at all	1973, 15% 1989, 8%
	Same-gender sex	
General public	Support equal employment rights for gay men	1999, 83% (men) 92% women
General public	Support marriage for gay men	1999, 26% (men) 32% (women)
College freshmen	Support laws prohibiting homosexual relations	1997, 34% 2003, 26%
College freshmen	Same-sex couples should have the right to marry	1997, 50% 2003, 59%

Sources: Data from "Report: The sexual revolution?", T. W. Smith, 1990, *Public Opinion Quarterly*, *54*, 415–435; "Gender gaps in public opinion about lesbians and gay men," G. M. Herek, 2002, *Public Opinion Quarterly, 66*, 40–66; and *The American freshman: National norms for [various years]*, published in Los Angeles, CA by Higher Education Research Institute, University of California, Los Angeles. Reprinted with permission.

attitudes toward sex have converged somewhat, but differences like this one still remain (Hendrick, Hendrick, Slapion-Foote, & Foote, 1985; Oliver & Hyde, 1993). Because of women's comparatively conservative stance, they tend to control the actual level of sexual intimacy in a relationship. That is, the traditional roles of males as initiators and females as gatekeepers apparently still hold (Surra & Longstreth, 1990).

All these findings suggest that people attach many different meanings to sexual activity. Some see it as an enjoyable activity even outside of a committed relationship. Others see it as an expression of intimacy and commitment to the partner. Because sexual activity has so many meanings, open communication about it is extremely important in a relationship. If one partner thinks sex is just good fun and the other assumes it means commitment, serious conflicts are bound to result. But what are the actual effects of sexual activity on a relationship? Does it, for example, strengthen a dating relationship, making it psychologically more intimate, or can it become a focus of conflict capable of driving the couple apart? Because sexual activity can be interpreted in so many different ways, its impact on relationship processes will also vary, depending on the individuals and their relationship.

Sex in the Context of a Relationship

Like other mutually enjoyable activities, sexual activity can strengthen a relationship. But it can also be a focus of conflict.

Some research shows that sexual intimacy is associated with increased satisfaction with the relationship. For instance, Jeffry Simpson (1987) studied the stability of relationships among dating couples who were not having sexual intercourse and among dating couples who were. He found that couples having intercourse were more likely to stay together over the course of 3 months.

However, over a longer time period, the picture is not so clear. Anne Peplau and her colleagues (Peplau, Rubin, & Hill, 1977) compared dating couples who had sexual intercourse within a month of their first date, those who had intercourse later (an average of 6 months after starting to date), and those who had not yet had intercourse at the time they were interviewed. The early-sex couples had more liberal sexual attitudes and engaged in sexual relations more often than the later-sex couples, and the women reported more sexual satisfaction. In contrast, the later-sex couples seemed to enjoy more emotional and psychological intimacy. They were more likely to say they were in love, they felt closer to their partners, and they were more likely to predict that they would marry the partner. Despite these differences, the two groups were equally satisfied with the relationships—and so were the couples in the study who had never had intercourse. Two years after the initial study, couples in all three groups reported similar outcomes: About 46% of the couples in all three groups had broken up, 34% were still dating, and 20% had married each other. Thus, neither the timing of sex nor the relative emphasis on psychological intimacy seemed to strongly affect the future of these dating relationships.

Satisfaction with sex is closely tied to relationship satisfaction among married couples (Reiss & Lee, 1988). One study, which compared happily married couples and troubled couples who had sought marital counseling, found that the happily married couples had sex more frequently (Birchler & Webb, 1977). This pattern was not unique to sexual activity, however: These satisfied couples did many things together more frequently, including participating in sports and social events. The more rewarding and mutually enjoyable the activities in a relationship, the warmer the partners' feelings are likely to be. Conversely, when a couple are dissatisfied with sex or other major components of the relationship, satisfaction with the relationship is also likely to decline.

The reasons for sexual dissatisfaction tend to differ for women and men. Women become dissatisfied if they see their sexual relationships as lacking warmth, love, and caring, whereas men who are dissatisfied want more frequent and varied sexual activity (Hatfield and others, 1989; Laumann and others, 1994). This gender difference, like other differences in sexual attitudes and behaviors, seems to diminish among older adults (Oliver & Hyde, 1993; Sprague & Quadagno, 1989). Sexual activity and satisfaction, however, can be maintained into old age. Although the frequency of sexual activity is lower among older adults than among younger adults, one study interviewed healthy adults ranging in age from 80 to over 100 and found that most were still sexually active (Bretschneider & McCoy, 1988).

People enjoy many types of activities with their partners. So why is sex such a unique and appropriate expression of love and intimacy in a close relationship? At least part of the answer is that sex uniquely combines the two fundamental processes that motivate people to form and maintain close relationships in the first place: mutual pleasure and enjoyment, and intimate self-disclosure (Reiss, 1986). These processes—giving and receiving pleasure, and knowing and being known—both flow from and reinforce the psychological link of partner to self, which is the underlying truth of an intimate relationship.

When Relationships Go Wrong

In the course of most relationships, periods of calm are interspersed with troubled times. When problems do develop, all the processes that helped the relationship bloom appear to go into reverse, speeding up the decline. Partners no longer seem to enjoy doing things together. Their attributions for each others' behaviors become more negative. Instead of intimate self-disclosures and support, they exchange angry words and bitter complaints, which lead to arguments and fights. Understanding the processes of relationship development and maintenance can also help us comprehend how relationships run aground at the very start or slowly deteriorate into conflict and breakup.

Interdependence and Conflict: Seeds of Trouble

> Interdependence inevitably leads to disagreements and problems, but the impact of these problems on the relationship depends on how the couple handles them.

In fairy tales, the characters find true love and live happily ever after. Not so in real life, where interdependence inevitably breeds conflicts. The key issue is how couples handle them. How does trouble start, and what resources help people handle conflict constructively and avoid relationship meltdown? Perhaps you recall a time in your own life when a partner changed—maybe the person lost interest in an activity you had previously enjoyed together or had a falling out with a mutual friend. Because of the interdependence in a close relationship, the change in your partner probably affected you as well. Personal change, illness, or disability can reduce one partner's willingness or ability to meet the other's needs. As one or both find that they derive fewer rewards from the relationship, their satisfaction and commitment eventually decline (Drigotas & Rusbult, 1992; Rusbult and others, 2001).

External factors can also place stresses on relationships. If one person's job or family responsibilities increase, the resulting demands leave less time and energy for the partner. The birth of a couple's first child is a common source of stress for this reason: Children bring their parents love and joy, but they also force substantial changes in a couple's activities. One study found that after the baby's arrival, the husband had less time for independent activities, and the couple's joint activities came to more closely reflect the wife's preferences (Crawford & Huston, 1993).

Social norms can also create stress and conflict, by dictating that one partner should perform a particular task regardless of individual preferences or abilities. For example, women in heterosexual couples are generally expected to perform the bulk of the housekeeping chores, even if they also work at a paying job outside the home (Atkinson & Huston, 1984; Biernat & Wortman, 1991). This holds true whether the couple are unmarried or married (Denmark, Shaw, & Ciali, 1985). The imbalance in household responsibility is reinforced by economic factors.

■ **Families aren't what they used to be**. In the 1970s, everyone knew, and many sympathized with, the Cunningham family from the worldwide hit Happy Days set in 1950's Milwaukee. This family portrayed by the show, however, seems out of touch with the real pressures and stresses placed on today's families. How have social changes, including changes in family size and composition and the prevalence of dual-career couples, altered the sources of conflict in family relations?

Women are paid on average only about two thirds as much as men for full-time, year-round work (Goldin, 1990), which tends to force men into the "breadwinner" role. Conflicts about who does what, such as how to share responsibility for house-work, are among the most important causes of break-ups of both married and unmarried heterosexual relationships (Blumstein & Schwartz, 1983; Nettles & Loevinger, 1983).

A wide range of issues can spark relationship conflicts. Leslie Baxter (1986), who asked people who had just ended dating relationships to write about the reasons for the break-ups, found several common themes. Although both men and women frequently cited problems such as a desire for autonomy or a lack of psychological support from the partner, some types of problems were more often mentioned by one sex than by the other. A lack of openness and intimacy was a problem for more women (31%) than men (8%), while the absence of romance or passion—feeling that "the magic has gone"—was an issue for more men (19%) than women (3%).

Finally, an interesting study by Steven Beach and his colleagues (1998) found that envy arising from performance comparisons can spark bad feelings and rela-tionship conflict. Have you and your partner ever worked for the same company, enrolled in the same course, or tried out for roles in the same play? If so, you know that you don't always feel great when your partner gets a glowing job evaluation, top grade, or starring role—if you didn't get as good an outcome yourself. At least with dating partners, areas that are high in self-relevance can become a kind of "romantic battleground" as each partner strives to establish and maintain a positive self-concept in the face of unfavorable comparisons with the partner (Beach and others, 1998). Married couples, in contrast, show concern for their partner's feel-ings as well as for the damage to their own egos when performance comparisons arise. Their commitment lets them handle the bad feelings that can be aroused by performance comparisons in ways that allow the relationship to survive.

Resources for Handling Conflict: Relationship Maintenance

Conflicts can be handled constructively when the partners hold strongly positive views of each other, when they are strongly committed to the relationship, and when they are securely attached.

Every relationship will eventually run into disagreements about activities, performance comparisons, or some of the other potholes just mentioned. Like an automobile, relationships then require maintenance to repair the damage and continue function-ing. Several important resources allow couples to carry out this maintenance and handle conflicts constructively.

IDEALIZATION OF THE PARTNER. As we described earlier, romantic partners often idealize each other; that is, they hold images of the partner that are even more positive than the partner's self-image. You might think that idealization could set the relationship up for a fall when inevitable conflicts destroy the romantic illusions, but in fact idealization helps people deal with conflict. Sandra Murray and John Holmes (1997) found that among both dating and married couples, those with more positive illusions reported less overt conflict and fewer destructive ways of handling conflicts (such as avoidance or returning criticism for criticism). Even among couples with equivalent levels of overall satisfaction with their relationship, illusions had these positive effects. Favorable beliefs about the partner, then, even if they are so biased as to exceed reality, are one important resource that can help couples either avoid conflict or deal with it in useful and productive ways.

COMMITMENT. Commitment is the best predictor of a relationship's staying power over time (Bui and others, 1996; Le & Agnew, 2003). Strong feelings of commitment can motivate people to overlook their partners' flaws, to communicate about their needs, even to change their own behaviors in ways that help the relationship (Rusbult, Verette, Whitney, Slovik, & Lipkus, 1991). Commitment is also related to willingness to sacrifice for the partner, for example, giving up activities that your partner dislikes or moving to a boring town in the hinterlands because your partner gets a job there (van Lange, Rusbult and others, 1997). As you might imagine, dating couples who perform more of the sorts of constructive behaviors that are linked to commitment are more likely to stay together than couples who perform fewer of them (Berg & McQuinn, 1986).

ATTACHMENT STYLES. Handling conflicts is one of the many important aspects of relationships that is affected by people's attachment styles. Securely attached people generally have high levels of love, commitment, and satisfaction, which allow them to behave constructively when conflict arises (Kobak & Hazan, 1991; Simpson, 1990). They easily overlook a partner's faults or change their own behavior. In contrast, those with preoccupied or fearful attachment styles tend to deal with conflict in less constructive ways—with outbursts of negative emotion, for example (Levy & Davis, 1988).

When Jeffry Simpson and his co-workers (Simpson, Rholes, & Phillips, 1996) brought dating couples into their laboratory to discuss a major problem in their relationship, they found that attachment styles influenced the actions and feelings resulting from the interaction. As Figure 11.7 shows, partners with preoccupied or fearful attachment showed more stress and anxiety during the

FIGURE 11.7 Effects of attachment style when a couple discuss a major relationship problem

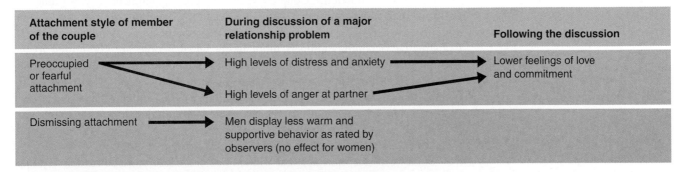

■ In a study by Jeffry Simpson and colleagues (1996), members of dating couples completed questionnaires identifying their attachment styles and then had a discussion of an issue that they identified as significant to their relationship. Discussion of an important relationship problem activates the underlying fears and concerns of preoccupied or fearfully attached individuals, resulting in strong negative feelings during the discussion. As a result, the discussion tends to damage the relationship, resulting in feelings of lessened love and commitment. Dismissing individuals do not experience the same strong negative feelings, but dismissing men tend to act cold and distant during the discussion.

interaction, felt more anger toward their partners, and afterward saw their relationships as involving less love and commitment. In other words, discussing relationship problems is extremely difficult for these individuals because it activates their fears of abandonment and loss. Dismissing individuals, in contrast, did not display distress or anger during the interaction, nor did they rate their interactions as less close afterward. Dismissing men's behavior was distant and nonsupportive, though this was not true of dismissing women. Secure individuals actually viewed both their partner and their relationship more positively after discussing a major problem. Security of attachment is thus a resource that can allow a couple not only to defuse conflict and prevent it from harming the relationship, but even to turn it to advantage.

Conflict Processes

When one partner acts in ways that damage the relationship, the other partner may respond by trying to repair the damage and maintain the relationship. However, when such constructive responses are absent, a cycle of conflict may result.

The couple's resources, including positive beliefs about each other, commitment, and attachment styles, influence the ways they handle the inevitable bad times and problems.

RESPONDING TO NEGATIVE ACTS. Even in the happiest of relationships, one partner's actions will occasionally annoy or hurt the other. Rusbult and her colleagues (1991) investigated couples' patterns of *accommodation*, the processes of responding to a negative action by the partner. Constructive accommodations are actions that help maintain the relationship, including actively discussing problems, loyally waiting for the situation to improve, or forgiving the partner (McCullough, Worthington, & Rachal, 1997). In contrast, destructive responses, such as screaming at the partner or refusing to spend time together, actively endanger the relationship. A couple's patterns of accommodation, particularly the absence of negative responses rather than the presence of positive ones, influence relationship satisfaction. Couples with secure attachment styles tend to accommodate more than other couples, a pattern that holds in gay and lesbian couples as well as heterosexual pairings (Gaines & Henderson, 2002). Constructive accommodation is more likely when people are committed to the relationship (Rusbult, Yovetich, & Verette, 1996). One point to ponder is that, although accommodation sounds like a thoroughly good thing (with its connotations of loyalty, forgiveness, and tolerance), it is a mistake to assume that it is appropriate in all situations. For women in a relationship with an abusive partner, for example, in many cases leaving the relationship rather than accepting the partner's destructive acts is the best course (Arriaga & Oskamp, 1999).

Some evidence indicates that women accommodate more constructively than men do (Rusbult and others, 1991). This finding is consistent with women's general tendency to be comparatively open about their thoughts and concerns about relationships. Men are less likely to talk about how they feel and are more apt to express their unhappiness in nonverbal signs of coldness and distance (Levenson & Gottman, 1985; Tannen, 1990). Like other gender differences, these differing communication patterns can provide a rich soil for the seeds of misunderstanding. She may view his silence as rejection, a signal of declining intimacy and commitment.

He may view her openness about her thoughts and feelings as threatening, without realizing that she may verbalize fleeting negative thoughts without attaching great importance to them. If men and women realize that they view communication differently, they can make adjustments and lessen misunderstandings.

Unfortunately, misunderstandings and misinterpretations of a partner's goals and feelings are common when couples argue. And the more troubled the relationship, the more prone the partners are to misunderstand each other. The difficulty is specific to the problematic relationship, for the partners have no similar difficulty in interpreting the feelings and intentions of strangers (Noller & Ruzzene, 1991). When distressed couples misunderstand each other, negative biases in their interpretations may escalate conflict. To demonstrate this process, one researcher asked one member of a couple to read descriptions of everyday situations, such as, "You and your husband are sitting alone on a winter evening. You feel cold" (Noller, 1980). The woman was asked to imagine that she wanted to know if her husband felt cold, too, and to say, "I'm cold, aren't you?" Based on her verbal and nonverbal messages, the husband then had to guess at the woman's intention, choosing among such alternatives as: "You wonder if only you are cold or if I am cold, too," or "You think I am being inconsiderate in not having turned up the heat by now, and you want me to turn it up right away." In distressed couples, husbands were more likely to pick negative alternatives, even when the intended message was neutral or positive.

FORGIVENESS. One process that is frequently part of accommodation is forgiveness, which involves a decrease in negative feelings and an increase in positive feelings toward a partner who has acted badly (Kachadourian, Fincham, & Davila, 2004). Forgiveness occurs more often in couples who are high in relationship satisfaction, and it is related to the length of time that relationships endure (Fincham & Beach, 2001). It makes sense that the ability to "let it go" and "put it in the past" helps couple members move past conflicts, but are all people equally likely to be forgiving when their partner hurts them? Research suggests that the answer is no. In a recent study of dating and married couples, Kachadourian, Fincham, and Davila (2004) found that individuals who are securely attached (with a more positive view of the self and of the partner) were the most likely to forgive their partners' transgressions.

ATTRIBUTION: YOU DID IT BECAUSE YOU DON'T LOVE ME. In happy relationships, minor annoyances do not have major consequences because attributions about the partner are positively biased (Fletcher & Fincham, 1991; Harvey & Omarzu, 1997). However, if this pattern is reversed—if the partners are unhappy and attributions are negatively biased—trouble lies ahead.

To investigate the role of attributions, researchers asked happy and unhappy married couples to read brief descriptions of positive or negative behaviors, imagine that their spouse had performed the behavior, and provide an explanation for it (Fincham & O'Leary, 1983). Happy partners offered benign attributions, viewing positive behaviors as reflecting the partner's likable dispositions and seeing negative behaviors as inadvertent minor mistakes. Unhappy partners showed the opposite bias, viewing the partner's actions with great suspicion. They attributed positive behaviors to aspects of the situation or other external forces, and they attributed negative acts to the partner's bad intentions or unlikable personality. They might think: "My partner is acting nice only because other people are around, not because she loves me," or "I don't care if he did have a bad day at work—this constant criticism is typical of someone as mean-spirited and selfish as he is." A shift toward negative attributions often precedes other indications of marital conflict, suggesting that attributions are a basic cause of relationship dissatisfaction (Bradbury & Fincham, 1990).

CYCLES OF CONFLICT. Negative attributions and unwillingness to accommodate constructively can release a vicious cycle of conflict, as each partner responds to the other's destructive behavior with an equally destructive reaction (Noller & Ruzzene, 1991). In a conversation, happy couples are likely to nod and smile at each other, to make eye contact, and to agree, whereas unhappy couples sneer, scowl, and shout, reciprocating each other's negative acts (Gottman and others, 1976). Ending such a cycle requires trust and the willingness to inhibit angry, hurtful impulses. Once a couple have raised their voices and exchanged insults, they find it very difficult to proceed immediately to a calm, logical approach to problem solving (D. R. Peterson, 1979). The first step must be *emotional* reconciliation, which usually has two aspects. They must put the problem in perspective ("It's not important enough to fight about"), and one partner must accept some blame for the conflict ("I guess I was wrong to do that, and I'll try to fix it"). In relatively mild conflicts, it is most often the man who tries to assuage negative feelings. However, when feelings run strongest, men seem less likely to do this, leaving responsibility for deescalation to women (Hatfield & Rapson, 1993). If the partner accepts a "peace offering" and makes a conciliatory move in return, anger can diminish and the parties can begin cooperating to solve the problem. Fortunately, constructive ways to handle conflict can be taught to couples, with a real impact on satisfaction and divorce rates. One study in Germany, for example, compared 55 couples who completed a 6-session program on effective communication and problem solving and 17 comparable couples who did not receive the training. Three years later, the trained couples not only reported more satisfaction and more positive communications in their relationship, but also had a lower rate of divorce (Hahlweg, Markman, Thurmaier, Engl, & Eckert, 1998).

Similar processes are involved in the reduction of large-scale intergroup conflict, as we will see in Chapter 13, pages 507 to 509.

☐ **HANDLING CONFLICTS IN EVERYDAY LIFE.** Research on relationship conflicts suggests two constructive approaches to reducing your own conflicts.

You may recall that attributing problems to global and stable causes can also lead to trouble of another sort. It is a recipe for learned helplessness and depression, as we discussed in Chapter 4, pages 127 to 128.

- Try to avoid generalizing about the partner; instead, focus on discussing concrete actions. By doing so, you will help keep the problem in perspective and also avoid the tendency to become embroiled in arguments over negatively biased attributions. A conflict that has escalated from the behavioral level of "You did this" to the attributional level of "You always . . . ," "You never . . . ," or "You are such a . . . " becomes almost irresolvable (D. R. Peterson, 1983).

- Try to communicate about your feelings, perhaps with the words *I feel*. Contrast these statements: "You always leave the house so messy," versus "I feel upset when I see things left lying around the house." The first is accusatory and is likely to lead to pointless argument that avoids the real issue, such as: "I don't *always* . . . ," or "It is not messy!" or "You sometimes leave messes, too." The "I feel" statement avoids these reactions because it is less likely to trigger defensiveness and it cannot really be contradicted—the partner is not likely to deny that the speaker feels upset. Most important, the statement focuses both partners' attention on the real problem, the negative feelings. Because it correctly attributes the feelings to the person and not to the external situation, "I feel" invites appropriately focused problem solving (Gottman and others, 1976).

JEALOUSY. When real or imagined rivals appear on the scene, most people experience a twinge of jealousy. This familiar negative emotion may be especially strong if a person feels inadequate in the relationship or distrusts the partner's commitment (G. L. White, 1981). Any sign of the partner's interest in other people may seem to be a dress rehearsal for impending rejection and the end of the relationship. Feelings of depression, anxiety, and anger may accompany jealousy. The depression and anxiety arise from the threatened loss of the valued relationship. Thus, they are similar to the feelings that would be aroused by other possible sources of loss, such as a serious illness. Anger, in contrast, is due to the loss of self-esteem

■ **Breaking up partnerships, breaking up self**. Jealousy, declining intimacy, conflict. These processes come into play if the relationship goes sour. Because the partner becomes part of the self in close relationships, the losses suffered can have detrimental effects on the health and well being of both partners.

from being rejected by the partner in favor of someone else (Mathes, Adams, & Davies, 1985). As you might expect, people whose attachment style is preoccupied experience jealous feelings more often, but their fear of losing the relationship makes them unlikely to express anger toward the partner. In contrast, securely attached people are less likely to experience jealousy. When they do, they are likely both to show their angry feelings toward the partner and to try to maintain the relationship (Collins & Read, 1990; Sharpsteen & Kirkpatrick, 1997). In fact, episodes of jealousy can end up strengthening a relationship, a surprising outcome reported by many couples (Fitness & Fletcher, 1993).

However, extreme jealousy can be profoundly destructive, particularly when an individual feels that his or her self-worth is completely dependent on the relationship. The rage and anger that can arise when a threat to the relationship is interpreted as a fundamental threat to self-esteem can lead even to suicide and murder. Jealousy is estimated to be a factor in as many as one quarter of all homicides (Salovey & Rodin, 1989).

DECLINING INTIMACY AND COMMITMENT. As conflicts escalate, the partners may spend less time together and become less open about their inner feelings. One important reason feelings are not shared is that many of them are likely to be negative. The growing distance diminishes the relationship's level of intimacy and, because intimacy is one of the most important rewards a relationship can offer, it speeds a downward spiral of dissatisfaction. Although the relationship may continue to satisfy needs for sociability or for sex, it no longer provides the feelings of self-validation and acceptance that spring from deeply intimate partnerships. In fact, low levels of intimacy, reflected in limited self-disclosure and low levels of attachment and love, characterize relationships that are destined for disintegration (Hendrick, Hendrick, & Adler, 1988; C. T. Hill and others, 1976).

Even strong commitment, the glue that holds relationships together, can break down under the stress of conflict and dissatisfaction. Because satisfaction with the relationship is one key ingredient in commitment, the partners may begin to perceive alternatives as more attractive when a relationship declines, and accumulated investments may no longer seem to be important barriers to leaving

(Rusbult and others, 2001). Unfortunately, this process feeds on itself: As you begin to view others as potential partners, those others note your potential availability and may in turn begin to pay you more attention. The comparison level against which you assess the benefits of this relationship thus starts to change. In other words, you will have a growing sense that the grass might be greener on the other side of the relationship fence.

☐ **RELATIONSHIP CONFLICT AND SOCIAL PROBLEMS.** Several significant social problems have their ultimate roots in conflicts in intimate relationships. Severe violent assaults are estimated to occur in about one in ten American marriages (Dutton, 1996). One study found that 25% of all violent crimes against women are committed by family members or people they have dated, compared with just 4% of violent crimes against men (T. Lewin, 1991). Violence and spousal abuse are related to the same factors that lead to relationship conflict and break-up in general, underlining their origin in fundamental relationship processes (Berscheid & Reis, 1998).

Why do women sometimes remain in abusive relationships? Though the question is an obvious one to ask, we should resist any implication that women should be blamed for their own victimization. Like abuse itself, at least part of the answer to this question flows from processes that operate in all relationships. One study of women who fled to a battered women's shelter found that whether or not they returned to the relationship depended on the same factors that determine commitment to a relationship in general: the quality of their alternatives and their investments in the relationship (Rusbult & Martz, 1995). If a woman sees few or no alternatives and has invested years of time, she may well stay even if the relationship yields more costs than rewards.

Severe conflict in families can lead not only to violence but also to psychological problems for children. Recent large-scale studies of children in the United States and Britain examined the negative effects that are typically found in children whose parents have divorced (Cherlin and others, 1991). Like other research, these studies found that although most children of divorced parents turn out just fine, they do display more behavior problems and have lower school achievement than children from intact families. However, these researchers found that the problems usually appeared *before the parents separated*. Thus, these problems are not due to the trauma of divorce itself, as many people assume, but to conditions within intact but troubled families. As these studies indicate, the immediate costs of ending a conflict-filled relationship are sometimes easier to bear than the longer term costs of perpetuating it.

Break-Up and Aftermath

If a relationship breaks up, each partner usually blames the other for its general decline. Individuals cope more effectively if they feel they controlled the final separation. After the end of a close relationship, loneliness and other negative feelings are common.

THE BREAK-UP: YOUR FAULT, MY DECISION. Sometimes a relationship may reach the breaking point. In dating couples as well as marriages, women terminate heterosexual relationships more often than men do (Amato & Previti, 2003; C. T. Hill and others, 1976). As you may recall, women are more distressed than men by relationship conflict, and that fact may explain why they more often pull the plug (Surra & Longstreth, 1990). But no matter who delivers the final word, the end of a relationship is often a lengthy and complex process, with repeated episodes of conflict and reconciliation (Cate & Lloyd, 1988). Each partner may feel victimized by the other, and their perceptions of responsibility for the relationship's decline may differ markedly. A recent study of divorced people has shown, not surprisingly, that each spouse primarily blamed the other for the decline of the relationship (Amato & Previti, 2003). Moreover, those who attributed the cause of the divorce to the relationship itself, rather than to themselves individually or to external factors, tended to have the best post-divorce adjustment.

AFTER THE BREAK-UP: GRIEF AND DISTRESS FOR TWO. Most of us have been observers or participants in the break-up of more than one relationship and have seen first-hand that the psychological consequences of breaking up can vary. One sample of student dating couples found that the more depressed, lonely, and unhappy one partner felt after the break-up, the less the other partner did (Hill and others, 1976). Evidently, being the "breaker-upper" feels different from being the "broken-up-with" (Agnew, 2000). But whatever your role, because close relationships are so psychologically important, the experience of ending a relationship is almost always more negative than positive. If the partners cared deeply and helped each other in many ways, grief and distress are bound to occur. Such feelings arise even if the relationship's rewards were taken for granted before the break-up or if the interactions in the relationship were mostly negative (Berscheid, 1988; Simpson, 1987). A longitudinal study by Susan Sprecher (1999) underlines the fact that breaking up is usually not an easy decision. This research found that in couples that would later break up, their self-reports of various aspects of their relationship, such as satisfaction and commitment, became less positive before the final break. Interestingly, while satisfaction tended to diminish most, reports of love diminished least. This pattern means that for many couples, break-ups occur not because the partners "fall out of love," but because rising dissatisfaction and frustration from the relationship eventually outweigh the loving feelings that are still present.

The cognitive and emotional consequences of the end of a close relationship can be long-lasting. People may reflect often and intensively on why the relationship ended, as they do concerning other important negative events (Harvey, Wells, & Alvarez, 1978). Because failures of relationships often leave the partners baffled about what went wrong, the search for causes may become somewhat obsessive as the person repeatedly reviews past events. Feelings of control, for example, knowing that you decided to end the relationship, or believing that you understand what happened, may influence the course of this stage (L. F. Clark & Collins, 1993). And understanding the causes of a relationship's end is an important learning experience that is likely to increase the chances of success in future relationships.

Because writing about the end of one's relationship may help people attain understanding, this process can help alleviate some of the negative effects of the break-up. In one study, some college students who had recently experienced a break-up were randomly assigned to write expressively about their break-up for 20 minutes per day for 3 days, while others were assigned to write in an unemotional and impersonal manner about relationships in general for the same amount of time (Lepore & Greenberg, 2002). Compared to the other participants, those in the expressive writing group reported fewer upper respiratory illnesses, less fatigue, and reduced tension several months later. Such findings suggest that writing about a broken heart, painful or difficult as it may be at first, may help to increase our understanding of the events that led to the end of the relationship and reduce the negative effects of the event.

TILL DEATH DO US PART. Some close relationships are ended by death rather than break-up. The death of a spouse is regarded as the most stressful major life event (McCrae & Costa, 1988). It is also a particularly common one: Almost half of the population will experience it. The first year or two following the death of a spouse are marked by serious threats to mental and physical health (Hansson, Stroebe, & Stroebe, 1988). Most people eventually make it through this period and recover their previous levels of well-being, but a minority fail to recover even after several years. The most serious problems are likely to befall those whose spouses died unexpectedly and who believe that they have little control over their future (Stroebe, Stroebe, & Domittner, 1988), a belief that may cripple their ability to cope effectively. Social support from friends, self-help groups, or professional counselors can help the bereaved cope. Social support offers some of the rewards, such as opportunities to express inner feelings and to receive understanding and acceptance, that were part of the vanished relationship (Vachon and others, 1982).

LONELINESS. No matter what terminates a close relationship—death, conflict, or simple geographical separation—the end usually brings loneliness. Lonely people feel distress, desperation, boredom, and depression. They may even view themselves as unattractive or unlovable (Rubenstein, Shaver, & Peplau, 1979). Feeling lonely is not the same as being alone: Sometimes you can feel loneliest in the middle of a crowd. Rather, *loneliness* is an emotion arising from unmet needs for affection and self-validation from a psychologically intimate relationship (Shaver & Hazan, 1985). Loneliness is more a matter of lacking quality interactions—intimate ones—than of lacking quantity (Kraus, Davis, Bazzini, Church, & Kirchman, 1993). Intense feelings of loneliness are common not only after the end of a relationship but also when people move to a new area and are separated from their existing close relationships.

As we saw in Chapter 4, pages 127 to 128, stable internal explanations for negative events may even turn an episode of loneliness into severe depression.

The most effective responses to loneliness include trying to find new ways to meet people and making something valuable out of solitude: learning a new skill or hobby, studying or working, or listening to music (Rook & Peplau, 1982). More negative reactions include dwelling on your bad qualities, or even drinking and drug use. A study of college students by Carolyn Cutrona (1982) found that those who thought of loneliness as arising from transitory, potentially controllable causes most easily overcame it. Students who saw their loneliness as resulting from stable, negative personal qualities, such as unattractiveness or shyness, were more likely to remain lonely for long periods of time.

Cutrona also found that lonely people who downplayed the importance of friendship and thought that only a romantic relationship could help them had a more difficult time. Perhaps this is because friends are easier to find than "that perfect someone." After all, as we have seen in this chapter, a close friendship can meet our needs for self-validation and psychological intimacy (Rook & Peplau, 1982). These, rather than the sexual expression found in a romantic relationship, bring most of the benefits of relationships.

UNREQUITED LOVE. So far we have been focusing on relationships that are mutual, but some of the most difficult relationship problems arise when love is not reciprocated. Roy Baumeister and Sara Wotman (1992) have found that there is pain on both sides in such a relationship, as you may know from your own experience. Of course, the rejected lover suffers the pangs of heartbreak and lost self-esteem. However, because this person often blindly maintains loving and hopeful feelings, he or she ultimately may have some positive memories of the episode, along with the disappointment. For the rejector, the picture is more thoroughly negative. Although self-esteem initially may be bolstered by the rejected lover's obvious adoration, any benefits to self-esteem are often quickly supplanted by feelings of guilt, irritation, and even rage. Trying to be polite to the suitor may only raise false hopes.

Research indicates that more than half of all college women may have experienced daily letters and late-night phone calls from rejected suitors (Jason, Reichler, Easton, Neal, & Wilson, 1984). For those who must deal with a would-be lover, Elaine Hatfield and Richard Rapson (1993) recommend using what they term the "zombie" approach. When interaction is unavoidable, be polite and brief. Display no emotion, negative or positive, that might reward the pursuer; remember, emotional self-expression is a type of intimacy.

CONCLUDING COMMENTS

In concluding the chapter, we turn from conflict, break-up, and loneliness to something more positive: relationships that survive the challenges of time. Two factors are common to strong relationships in which the partners maintain and increase their love.

1. *The relationship satisfies many of the partners' individual needs.* Other people benefit us in many ways: as companions for leisure activities, as sources of social comparisons that help us understand ourselves, and as sources of validation for our beliefs and opinions. Relationships are most likely to meet our mastery needs in these ways when the partners are similar in their needs and desires, and when they reward each other to show love and caring.

2. *The relationship provides the partners with a sense of relatedness and connectedness.* As we indicated in Chapter 6, belonging to a group can give people the sense that they have a special place in the social world and that others value their thoughts, feelings, and behaviors—their very presence. As you have seen, intimacy and self-disclosure in a close relationship with another individual can also fulfill this need.

The dual motives of seeking individual satisfaction and interdependent relatedness run as two parallel threads throughout many of the topics we have discussed in this chapter.

- Relationship development proceeds through the exchange of rewards as the partners satisfy each other's needs, and through the exchange of self-disclosures as the partners build the intimate linkage of partner to self.

- Gifts given and favors performed in a relationship have a dual meaning. The concrete act may be pleasant and rewarding in itself. The underlying messages of love and relatedness that each partner sends the other by kind and thoughtful acts become equally crucial.

CHAPTER 11 THEMES

- **Construction of Reality**
  We use biased attributions to construct an idealized impression of a relationship partner.

- **Pervasiveness of Social Influence**
  In a close relationship, the partner becomes part of the self, influencing all aspects of thoughts, feelings, and behavior.

- **Striving for Mastery**
  Relationships with others help us obtain rewards and individual satisfactions.

- **Seeking Connectedness**
  Relationships with others help give us feelings of connectedness and belonging.

- **Valuing Me and Mine**
  We are biased to view relationship partners favorably when they become part of the self.

- Gender differences in relationships reflect the dual motives of individual satisfaction and interdependent relatedness. Men generally emphasize rewards, such as participating in enjoyable activities with the partner, and women often care more about intimacy, the self-disclosure of feelings, and intimate talks.

- Sexual behavior is particularly appropriate as an expression of relationship closeness because it fits with both motives: It is enjoyable and intimately self-disclosing.

The combination of these two powerful motives—the fact that at their best, close relationships can both help us find ourselves as individuals and find connection to valued others—makes relationships the most important components of our lives. As Charles Darwin wrote long ago (cited in Gould, 1991, p. 401): "Talk of fame, honor, pleasure, wealth, all are dirt compared to affection."

S U M M A R Y

 Initial Attraction. The formation of a relationship is often spurred by feelings of attraction or liking for another person. Attraction to strangers is strongly influenced by perceptions of physical attractiveness. People are also attracted to those with whom they have positive interactions. Interaction helps people to master the world and to find connectedness with others. In addition, interaction leads to familiarity, which increases liking.

Similarity also increases attraction by making positive interaction more likely, by suggesting that the other person likes the individual in return, and by validating the individual's beliefs and attitudes. Thus, similarity, liking, and interaction all tend to cause one another. As a result, relationships tend to deepen and intensify over time.

From Acquaintance to Friend: Relationship Development. As a relationship begins to develop, the partners treat it as an **exchange relationship**, in which they reward each other to obtain rewards in return. As a relationship deepens, it may shift to a **communal relationship**, in which the partners reward each other to show affection and because they want to make each other happy. Relationship development also includes exchanges of self-disclosures as the partners come to know each other better. Self-disclosures increase liking and offer opportunities for sympathetic, supportive responses.

As the partners interact frequently and exchange rewards and self-disclosures, simple attraction and individual factors such as physical attractiveness become less important. Instead, the nature of the interaction between the partners becomes crucial, and each partner's liking for the other tends to be reciprocated.

Close Relationships. A **close relationship** is one marked by strong and frequent **interdependence**, meaning that each partner's thoughts, emotions, and behaviors influence the other's. A desire for closeness with a particular person seems to correspond to what people generally mean by "love." By necessity, most research on close relationships uses nonexperimental designs that leave some ambiguity about causal relations among variables, and most such research has been conducted in North America.

Many processes are common to all types of close relationships, not just romantic ones. In a close relationship, the partner is incorporated into the self, just as an important social group membership may become part of one's identity. Relationship closeness also alters the way partners exchange rewards. In a close relationship, partners reward each other to show affection and because they want to make the partner happy.

Ongoing processes of self-disclosure and sympathetic support lead to psychological **intimacy**, marked by feelings of trust, closeness, and acceptance. As closeness increases, the partners feel a growing sense of commitment to each other.

Attachment styles describe differences in the ways people approach close relationships. *Securely attached* individuals are comfortable relying on the partner for support and acceptance. *Dismissive* individuals do not want reliance on others, and *preoccupied* individuals seek closeness with others but worry about rejection. Finally, *fearful* individuals want closeness but worry that the partner will not be available and responsive. People approach relationships with different implicit beliefs regarding the effort required to make them work, and these beliefs have an impact on the ultimate stability of the relationship. Gender and culture also play a role.

Relationships affect virtually all aspects of our lives. When time are tough, **social support** from others can improve both physical and mental health and well-being, and the most crucial components of social support appear to be intimacy and acceptance. When times are good, sharing our positive experiences with others can help further increase overall well-being.

Romantic Love and Sexuality. Some relationships involve passionate feelings and emotions. Passionate emotions can arise quickly and are closely linked to sexual desires and behavior. People's attitudes about sex differ widely and depend in part on gender. Some people see sex as an enjoyable activity even outside of a committed relationship; others see it as an expression of intimacy and commitment to the partner. Like other mutually enjoyable activities, sexual activity can strengthen a relationship. But it can also be a focus of conflict.

When Relationships Go Wrong. In any relationship, interdependence inevitably leads to disagreements and problems, but their impact on the relationship depends on how the couple handle them. Conflicts can be handled constructively when the partners hold strongly positive views of each other, when they are strongly committed to the relationship, and when they are securely attached.

When one partner acts in ways that damage the relationship, the other partner may respond by trying to repair the damage and maintain the relationship. However, when such constructive responses are absent, a cycle of conflict may result.

If a relationship breaks up, each partner usually blames the other for the general decline. Individuals cope more effectively if they feel they controlled the final separation, however. After the end of a close relationship, loneliness and other negative feelings are common.

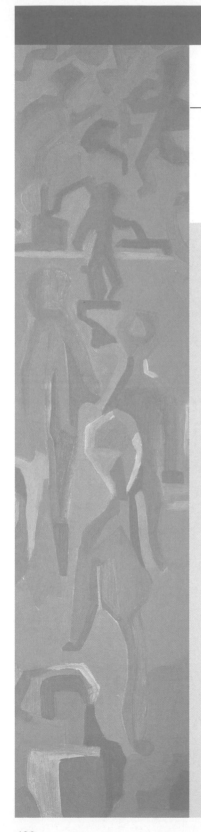

12

Interaction in Groups

Today Harley-Davidson is one of the most valuable and popular brand names in the world. The federation of Harley-Davidson Clubs of Europe boasts 60 member clubs from Norway to Greece and from Ireland to Lithuania. The Harley-sponsored H.O.G. motorcycle club counted more than 500,000 members worldwide in 2000. It may surprise you, then, to learn that in the late 1970s Harley was on the ropes. At the same time that high-quality, low-priced Japanese bikes suddenly flooded the U.S. market, Harley-Davidson was a poorly run organization. Its management and employees were often at odds, product quality was low, and its workers were unmotivated. These problems were reflected in its sales, which soon dropped to only 4% of the U.S. market, and in its service: getting a part in some European countries could take up to 3 weeks! The types of challenges Harley-Davidson faced then are widespread in business, as evidenced by the plight of global airline, trucking, banking, automobile, electronics, and manufacturing industries. As costs escalate, competition stiffens, and the public's demand for truly innovative products continues to grow, industries must come to terms with the fact that the dual goals of high performance and a motivated and enthusiastic workforce are more important than ever before.

These critical issues of efficiency and morale are not confined to the workplace, however. They characterize any group of people who interact for some shared purpose and rely on one another to accomplish common goals. Our aim in this chapter is to understand the consequences of group membership for behavior. To some extent, this topic has been woven throughout the earlier chapters. In Chapter 9, for example, we looked at the ways juries and other groups make decisions. But decision making is often only a first step. Like the people at Harley-Davidson, most groups *act* on their decisions as they win or lose games, manufacture products, regulate workflow through an office, build roads, fight fires, undertake rescues, and treat patients. When people put their heads together—and their muscle and drive—their individual efforts are sometimes multiplied in astonishing ways, and the group can achieve goals far beyond the reach of any one member. The Russian space agency group that launched the space station Mir, baseball's Boston Red Sox who came back from three initial losses to win the best-of-seven game World Series in 2004, and the legions of volunteers who staff the International Red Cross are just a few examples of the remarkable achievements of group action.

Because the outcomes of group action are often strikingly different from the inputs of individual members—and sometimes very different from what is desired and intended—early theorists concluded that the behavior of a group has almost nothing to do with the individual characteristics of its members (Durkheim, 1898; LeBon, 1903). Rather, they argued, people lose their individuality in a group and, swept along by the crowd, no longer have a mind of their own. Although contemporary social scientists do not agree that individuals give up their autonomy to the group, they do recognize that being part of a group affects individual behavior in distinctive and sometimes dramatic ways. Groups differ in the degree of interaction and interdependence they share. At one extreme are a group of people who, like passengers on an airplane, are physically in the same place but who hardly interact and are only minimally interdependent. We saw in several earlier chapters that membership in groups defined by shared, socially significant features—such as Roman Catholics, socialists, or Mexican-Americans—can influence people's thoughts, feelings, and behavior. Such groups may or may not interact face to face but are often at least somewhat interdependent, because what happens to one member of the group often affects others.

However, the impact of group membership is most obvious when people not only identify with a group but also interact with one another and depend on one another, relying on other members' actions as well as their own for mastery of material rewards and feelings of connectedness. At this end of the continuum are *face-to-face groups* like the decision-making groups we discussed in Chapter 9 and those we focus on in most of this chapter. Members of face-to-face groups not only share socially relevant features but also interact and rely on each other to achieve specific goals. Like the Mir launch control team and the Red Sox, they share values and coordinate their efforts to get things done. Their attempts to reach their goals are marked by intense communication and extensive interaction. The group's success often depends on just how well its leaders and members can manage the problems of interdependence. Indeed, the eventual rebuilding and success of Harley-Davidson was due in large part to its managers' ability to improve both production efficiency and worker satisfaction simultaneously (Willis, 1986).

The Mere Presence of Others: The Effects of Minimal Interdependence

Imagine that, as you jog along your usual route, you catch up with another jogger who runs alongside you for a couple of blocks. You greet each other with a friendly nod and perhaps check out each other's brand of running shoe, but otherwise you have no contact before you go your separate ways. A block later, you pass by a half-dozen people gathered on a front porch, and they look up and follow your progress down the street. Although your contact with your fellow jogger and with your temporary audience is minimal, their mere presence can influence your behavior in quite predictable ways.

Social Facilitation: Improvement and Impairment

Even when interdependence is minimal, the mere presence of others can produce arousal, either because the other people are highly evaluative or because they are distracting. Arousal improves performance of easy, well-learned behaviors, but can interfere with performance of novel or complex tasks.

If you are like most people, you will run slightly faster in the presence of others than when you are alone (Worringham & Messick, 1983). This facilitating effect of other people on individual performance may seem familiar. In our discussion of the history of social psychology in Chapter 1, we described Norman Triplett's (1898) observation that children winding line onto fishing reels worked more quickly when in the presence of others than when they were alone. Other research confirms the idea that the presence of others improves performance on a variety of simple tasks, from running to solving easy arithmetic problems (Aiello & Douthitt, 2001; Guerin, 1986).

■ **Presence and performance**. Perhaps the marathoner checking out the competition is aware of the dramatic effects of the presence of others. When the responses necessary for success are well learned and highly accessible, others' presence can trigger superior performance.

But is having others around always helpful? You may doubt this if you can remember standing in the glare of the footlights desperately trying to remember your lines or stumbling through a complex play on the basketball court before a crowd. And your answer would be correct, for research also shows that the presence of others can interfere with performance. On complicated and difficult tasks, from mazes to math problems to a newly learned tennis serve, our performance declines when others are present (Aiello & Douthitt, 2001; Guerin, 1986). How can the presence of others both help and hurt performance?

EXPLAINING SOCIAL FACILITATION. In 1965, Robert Zajonc proposed an explanation of these apparently contradictory effects of the presence of others. According to Zajonc, the **social facilitation** effect occurs because the presence of others increases an individual's level of arousal, which in turn makes some behaviors easier and others more difficult. (Although the term "facilitation" suggests that the presence of others improves performance, social facilitation also refers to the decrease in performance in other circumstances.) Arousal facilitates the performance of behaviors that are very accessible because they are simple, well learned, and highly practiced (often termed *dominant responses*), but it inhibits the performance of behaviors that are complex or new (*nondominant responses*). Accessibility should be a familiar concept by now. You may recall that accessible thoughts and feelings are more likely to come to mind than are less accessible ones; similarly, accessible behaviors are more likely to be performed than are less accessible ones. Thus, the arousal caused by an audience may help a jogger to run faster and an entrant in a math contest to ace the easy problems. That same arousal may make it more difficult for a novice skier to complete a difficult course or for the math contestant to answer the tough final questions that will select the winner. When behaviors are complicated or not well learned, the arousal caused by the presence of others will detract from performance.

Because of the contradictory effects of arousal, the presence of an audience can even affect two people in quite opposite ways when they are performing the same task. For example, expert pool players, for whom good shots are highly accessible responses, performed better when an interested audience was close by than when they thought no one was watching. In contrast, poor players, for whom miscues were most accessible, succeeded on fewer shots when others watched (Michaels, Blommel, Brocato, Linkous, & Rowe, 1982). Zajonc's idea (1965) that other people cause arousal and that arousal improves performance of simple tasks but interferes with performance of difficult tasks, makes sense of these findings and has been confirmed by most subsequent research (Aiello & Douthitt, 2001; Guerin, 1986).

Social facilitation. An increase in the likelihood of highly accessible responses, and a decrease in the likelihood of less accessible responses, due to the presence of others.

Of course, these findings leave one question unanswered: Why does the presence of others lead to arousal? Zajonc (1965) believed that humans and other animals have an innate tendency to be aroused by other members of their species. But why is this so? Subsequent research points to two underlying causes: evaluation apprehension and distraction (Geen, 1991).

EVALUATION APPREHENSION. Most of the time, we want other people to value, include, and like us. In fact, our self-esteem is greatly affected by what others think of us. For these reasons, we may worry about whether onlookers are judging us in some way. As you jog past people, for example, you may suddenly be concerned about whether you look out of shape, and you may pull in your stomach and step up your pace. Research has confirmed that the presence of others who are in a position to judge us produces *evaluation apprehension* (M. Rosenberg, 1969) and that this apprehension changes our performance in the way predicted by social facilitation theory. One study, for example, demonstrated that apprehension can improve performance on simple aspects of a task and hinder it on complex aspects of the same task. Scott Bartis and his colleagues (Bartis, Szymanski, & Harkins, 1988) asked groups of participants to list various uses for a knife. Some participants were given the simple task of coming up with as many uses as possible. Others had the relatively challenging task of being as creative as possible. In each group, some participants believed the experimenter would evaluate their individual performance and others knew their responses would go into a common pool (where they could not be individually evaluated). As Figure 12.1 illustrates, the possibility of evaluation increased output on the simple task, and it decreased output on the intellectually more difficult task.

No wonder, then, that if you expect to succeed at a task (because it is easy, or it involves an accessible response, or you have succeeded at this task in the past), you will do better when you are observed, whereas the opposite is true if you expect to fail (Sanna & Shotland, 1990). Other researchers have provided evidence that evaluation, not mere presence, is the critical factor that affects behavior. For example, the

FIGURE 12.1   Effects of evaluation on simple and complex tasks

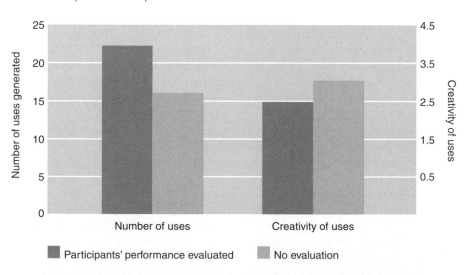

■ Some participants (*dark bars*) knew their individual task performance would be evaluated by the experimenter, whereas others (*light bars*) did not expect individual evaluations. When the task was fairly simple—generating as many suggestions as possible for ways to use a knife—evaluation improved performance, as shown by the bars on the left. However, when participants were given a much harder task—being as creative as possible in devising uses for the knife—evaluation had the opposite effect; it decreased their creativity (see scale on the right). (Data from Bartis and others, 1988.)

presence of actively supportive, nonevaluative observers—humans or even pets—neither provokes arousal nor interferes with performance (K. M. Allen, Blascovich, Tomaka, & Kelsey, 1991).

DISTRACTION. Other people can affect our performance not only by observing and evaluating us but also by creating *distraction*. Their mere presence causes us to think about them, to react to them, or to monitor what they are doing, and thereby deflects attention from the task at hand (Aiello & Douthitt, 2001; R. S. Baron, 1986; Guerin, 1986). Researchers in one study, for example, had a person sit behind the participant in a location in which he or she could not possibly monitor the participant's performance. The presence of this person nevertheless improved the participant's performance on easy tasks and interfered with it on difficult ones (Schmitt, Gilovich, Goore, & Joseph, 1986). Such effects have also been found in nonhuman species. For example, centipedes run faster down a glass tube when other centipedes are placed in neighboring tubes than when the additional tubes are empty (Hosey, Wood, Thompson, & Druck, 1985). The centipedes presumably are not concerned about evaluation by the other centipedes. The effect seems to stem from distraction by the presence of others, and that distraction makes them better at a simple task like running.

It is easy to understand why evaluation apprehension can create arousal, but how does distraction do so? The answer seems to be that as our impulses to do two different things at once—concentrate on the task and react to others—start to conflict with each other, we become agitated and aroused (Geen, 1991; Muller, Atzeni, & Butera, 2004). This arousal, like that caused by evaluation apprehension, can then improve performance on simple tasks and interfere with it on difficult ones. Figure 12.2 shows how the presence of others, even those with whom we do not interact, can make us worry about evaluation or can distract us.

Everyone has to perform in the presence of others from time to time, perhaps delivering an oral report in class or demonstrating a product to a new client. One way to avoid the disruptive effects of an audience is to make sure that your

FIGURE 12.2   Multiple effects of the presence of others

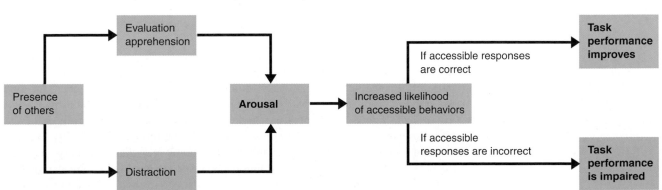

■ The presence of others can produce arousal, through either evaluation apprehension or simple distraction. Arousal increases the likelihood that people will perform the most accessible actions. With a simple or well-practiced task, highly accessible responses are likely to be correct and arousal improves performance. But if the task is complex or novel, accessible responses will not help much and arousal will impair task performance.

accessible responses—the ones most likely to be activated by arousal—are those that will help you to perform the task. You can make the appropriate responses accessible by repeatedly practicing the task (Zajonc & Sales, 1966): Then arousal will work for you.

☐ **SOCIAL FACILITATION IN THE WORKPLACE: MONITORING AND JOB PERFORMANCE.** In this technological age, observation and evaluation do not require the physical presence of an observer. Some employers monitor their employees' performances through electronic means, for example, by automatically recording the number of keystrokes clerical workers make per minute as they enter data into computers. Does this type of monitoring have the same social facilitation effects as the physical presence of observers? Yes. In an experiment by Jack Aiello and Kathryn Kolb (1995), highly skilled workers performed better when they knew they were being monitored than when they were unmonitored. On the other hand, monitoring decreased the performance of relatively unskilled workers. Monitoring also increased workers' feelings of stress. As this study shows, monitoring and evaluation may have similar effects whether the observers are actually present or are recording performance from afar. Like other forms of social facilitation, monitoring sometimes decreases performance, which is the opposite of what employers who implement monitoring presumably expect.

Crowding: The Presence of Lots of Others

Crowding is another source of arousal that can improve performance on easy tasks and disrupt performance on difficult ones. However, the effects of crowding depend on people's interpretation of the situation and on their sense of control.

Being packed into a rush-hour metro or underground car or a standing-room-only auditorium is a forcible reminder of how strongly—and negatively—we can be affected by the presence of other people. Researchers studying the effects of crowding in college dormitories found that when three students are assigned to a room designed for two, both their contentment and their grades decline (Karlin, Rosen, & Epstein, 1979). Crowding can even be life threatening: Prisoners confined in crowded jail cells perceive events as more aggressive in nature (Lawrence & Andrews, 2004) and have higher death rates than those in more spacious facilities (McCain, Cox, & Paulus, 1980).

As you might have guessed, crowding has these negative effects because being crowded, like having an audience, is arousing. The arousal occurs for the same reasons: Crowds create many opportunities for evaluation and distraction. One study found, for example, that 10 strangers who were crammed into an 8-by-12-foot room had higher blood pressure and greater increases in other physiological indicators of arousal than did those occupying a larger room (Evans, 1979). Like the arousal produced by an audience, arousal induced by crowding can energize effort, thereby improving performance on simple tasks, such as cheering loudly at a football game, and impairing performance on complex tasks, such as making difficult judgments about the star player's scoring abilities (Hillery & Fugita, 1975; Paulus, Annis, Seta, Schkade, & Matthews, 1976).

☐ **CROWDING AND THE URBAN ENVIRONMENT.** Most social behavior, such as cooperating with others, helping those in need, and resolving conflicts, is complex.

Since crowds can interfere with the performance of complex tasks, many people have suggested that living in a crowded city may disrupt social behavior. Crowding is indeed a popular scapegoat for society's ills. It has been blamed for the superficial and transitory relationships of modern life and for deviant behavior, mental illness, and poor physical health (Simmel, 1950). Although social life undoubtedly is affected by the size and density of community populations, the evidence that crowding causes widespread social problems is far from conclusive. Social beings are very adaptable. Cognitive and social factors can help us buffer the arousal caused by crowding and thus limit its debilitating effects.

A sense of control seems to be a key factor in counteracting the negative effects of crowding. In one study of people working under crowded conditions, some participants were given an "escape button" to press if they needed to leave the situation (Sherrod, 1974). Although the participants never actually pressed the button, knowing they could control their situation helped these participants perform better than those who had no control. Another study packed people into an elevator to find out who would feel the least stress. Not surprisingly, that person was usually the individual standing by the control panel (J. Rodin, Solomon, & Metcalf, 1978). Similarly, a study in India found that residents in crowded housing who saw themselves as having control over their environment fared better than others (Ruback & Pandey, 1991). The presence of others, especially crowds of others, arouses us, but the effects on our behavior depend on how we interpret the situation, and particularly on the extent of our feelings of control.

■ **Cultures define crowding**. Although research findings have long suggested that crowding triggers antisocial and unhealthful behavior, cross-cultural research indicates that response to crowding depend on a culture's norms regarding appropriate behavior. Tokyo commuters routinely endure crowding as bad as what you see here and worse, yet they are generally far more orderly then commuters in other countries.

These beneficial effects of perceived control should not surprise you, given our discussion in Chapter 4, pages 127 to 128, of the many ways a sense of mastery or control acts as a buffer against stressful events.

Performance in Face-to-Face Groups: Interaction and Interdependence

If the minimal influence of other people who are present can influence our behavior, consider how much more potent is the effect of a face-to-face group. Members of such groups—families, flight crews, dance troupes, parent–teacher organizations, rock and roll bands, government commissions, and others—are highly interdependent. They are **task interdependent** because their mastery of material outcomes depends on working together to perform some collective task: a successful flight, the negotiation of teachers' contracts, or the design of a new health-care plan. They are **socially interdependent** because they rely on one another for feelings of connectedness and positive emotional outcomes, such as respect, caring, and positive social identity. Large or small, all face-to-face groups are characterized by some combination of task and social interdependence (J. M. Levine & Moreland, 1998).

Face-to-face groups have widely differing goals and purposes. For businesses, the group goal is profit; for university faculties, it is the production of new knowledge and well-rounded graduates; for boards of directors, it is a well-administered organization. Depending on their goals, groups demand different amounts of social or task interdependence. Social interdependence or connectedness is particularly

Task interdependence.
Reliance on other members of a group for mastery of material outcomes that arise from the group's task.

Social interdependence.
Reliance on other members of the group for feelings of connectedness, social and emotional rewards, and a positive social identity.

important to *primary* or *intimacy groups*, like families and close friends, which value their members just because they are members. Of course, these groups are also frequently task interdependent, as when they care for the yard, balance the budget, or organize vacations. *Secondary groups*, such as those found in most work settings, often exist for a specific purpose involving the mastery of rewards, so task interdependence is their defining feature. But as we all know, roles, status hierarchies, and friendships are inevitable in work settings, which means that work groups are always also somewhat socially interdependent.

Indeed, every group faces the challenge of successfully managing both forms of interdependence to achieve high levels of productivity (in other words, mastery goals) and positive relationships among group members (connectedness goals). Managing these two forms of interdependence is a challenge because they sometimes conflict. Fostering task interdependence, for example, can interfere with feeling good about being in the group, as when parents prohibit horseplay in an effort to keep children focused on their share of Saturday house cleaning. Social interdependence can similarly detract from task performance if office workers socialize so much that work falls behind schedule. To understand how such problems arise and how they can be solved, we need to look at what happens as groups come together and work toward their goals. Although most of our examples will involve work groups, the same processes operate in all groups working together to produce something.

How Groups Change: Stages of Group Development

Face-to-face groups usually go through different stages of relationship with their members. During group socialization, mutual evaluation can lead groups and individuals to become committed to each other, processes that guide members' entry, socialization, role maintenance, and sometimes exit, from the group. At the same time, groups go through formation, conflict, development of norms, performance, and dissolution as they try to maximize social and task interdependence to develop an identity and reach their goals. Time pressure can affect how groups solve these problems.

The Ashland Corporation, a manufacturer of air conditioners, decided to assemble a special task group to propose and produce innovative new products. The team, composed of a team leader, "team advisers," and several production-line employees, was asked to turn a huge, empty factory building into a functioning production line for a newly designed series of compressors. The team had to select, order, and arrange for the installation of production machinery. It also was responsible for organizing and training the production-line workers in a way that maximized their efficiency and maintained extremely high quality standards. As the different members came together, their first task was to in fact become a group. Then as the group began to work toward its goals over a period of months, it confronted a series of problems and challenges, which in turn influenced the group's structure and operation. Finally, when the team's goals had been reached, the team was disbanded (Eisenstat, 1990).

These changes were not unique to the Ashland team. All groups, whether short-term, ad hoc groups created to solve isolated problems or long-term groups that might take years to reach their goals, go through different stages as they try to

Of course these properties were also true of the groups forming norms we discussed back in Chapter 9, pages 315 to 319. They were socially interdependent because forming norms helps achieve connectedness and they were task dependent because they relied on one another to form norms that appropriately reflect reality.

maximize task and social interdependence (Eisenstat, 1990; McGrath & Tschan, 2004; Moreland & Levine, 1988; Tuckman, 1965; Wheelan, 1994). Part of this process has to do with changing relationships between individual members and the group. The other part of the process is the changing concerns the group must deal with to achieve the kind of interaction and interdependence that will get the job done.

GROUP SOCIALIZATION: BECOMING A MEMBER OF THE GROUP. Dick Moreland and John Levine have coined the term *group socialization* to describe the cognitive, affective, and behavioral changes that occur as individuals join—and leave—such diverse groups as sports teams, social clubs, or religious sects. Group socialization is an ongoing process of mutual evaluation from both the individual member's and the group's perspectives. When the individual feels that the group offers a better chance of meeting his or her needs than alternative group memberships, the individual becomes committed to the group. Conversely, when the group feels that the individual offers a better chance of fulfilling group goals than other potential members, the group is also committed to the individual. These processes of evaluation and mutual commitment define the various stages of relationship that members can have with their groups.

In the initial stage of *investigation*, groups try to size up potential members who might contribute to the group good and help the group succeed, while individuals at the same time seek groups that might help satisfy personal needs for mastery and connectedness. If this initial evaluation leads the individual to commit to the group and vice versa, the individual becomes a new member of the group. Of course groups and individuals may not always have control over this process—sometimes membership in a group or team is dictated by outside forces, as it was in the case of the Ashland team. Regardless of how new membership comes about, entry into the group triggers the second phase of group membership, *socialization*. The group now tries to increase the extent to which the individual can help achieve group goals, molding the individual into a "team player" as much as it can. The Ashland team needed several different kinds of expertise to solve its problems, and so it needed certain team members to provide those various kinds of roles. At the same time, the individual tries to shape the group so that it meets as many of his or her needs as possible, both for task mastery and for social connections. To the extent that individuals and groups like what they see in each other at this stage, their mutual commitment may rise again. Such commitment to the group makes individuals adopt group values, feel good about fellow members, and work hard to achieve group goals and maintain membership in the group. Similarly, commitment to the individual makes the group value, like, and seek to keep the individual as a member.

Once the individual is a fully committed member, the relationship enters the *maintenance* phase. During this time, the group tries to find a specific role for the individual that maximizes his or her contribution, and the individual tries to find a role that maximizes the satisfaction he or she can obtain from the group. If this role negotiation succeeds, mutual commitment remains high and membership works well from both perspectives. Such mutually beneficial memberships might go on indefinitely, and might only be severed when the group disbands, as the Ashland group did once its work was complete. But if the mutual evaluation that occurs during this phase lowers commitment, an individual can become a marginal member of the group. Unless corrective efforts succeed, commitment is likely to continue to fall until *exit* occurs, and the individual leaves or is ousted from the group.

Individuals' passages into and out of groups do seem to be marked by the kinds of stages described by the group socialization model (Chen & Klimoski, 2003; Moreland & Levine, 2001). The group socialization model is also important because it makes clear that groups don't just change individuals: individuals change groups as well. From sports teams and hobby clubs to service organizations and work teams, the formation and development of a group is a mutual interaction between individual pursuit of mastery and connectedness, and group pursuit of successful task and social interdependence.

GROUP DEVELOPMENT: COMING TOGETHER, FALLING APART. Just as the relationship between each individual and the group goes through different stages, so too do the overall interaction patterns among all the members of the group go through different stages as they try to coordinate task interdependence and enhance social interdependence. Although some groups go through all five of the stages described here, many others skip steps, repeat steps, recycle through many of the steps, or dissolve before they ever reach the later stages (Ilgen, Hollenbeck, Johnson, & Jundt, 2005).

1. *Forming.* In the initial stage of group development, when initial processes of evaluation and mutual selection are occurring, members attempt to understand where other individuals stand in the group and what the group as a whole stands for (Moreland, 1987). For both these reasons, there is usually an intense focus on the group's leader who both has the highest status in the group and is expected to articulate the group's goals (Wheelan, 1994). Managers facilitated the Ashland group's progress through this stage by giving group members time to get acquainted and by stressing the special nature of their task—a task that could not be completed without everyone's full cooperation.

2. *Storming.* Conflict is often evident in the second stage, and disagreements can be intense and emotional (Bales, Cohen, & Williamson, 1979; Tuckman, 1965). At this point, as the group socialization model describes, the group and individual members are attempting to shape and negotiate specific roles. Deciding on group goals and the best ways to meet them is a common source of conflict at this stage, as members with different views jockey for position and coalitions and subgroups form among people with similar interests or agendas. But conflict may involve interpersonal as well as task issues. For example, one group member may feel betrayed by another's shift of position on an issue, or two members or subgroups may compete for the leader's attention and favor.

   Conflict may die down when a majority forms and persuades the rest of the group to adopt its views. However, many companies deliberately build in protection for "screwball" ideas, so that "storming" works to keep them on the cutting edge. In a classic case of persistent and effective dissent, a market researcher at Compaq Computer Corporation persuaded management to disregard surveys that predicted a limited market for a briefcase-size portable computer. Like other organizations that allow their members to express their doubts and differences of opinion in a context that does not pressure them to compromise too soon, Compaq reaped big benefits because it did not simply try to suppress conflict, but allowed minority influence to prevail (Kotkin, 1986; Ilgen and others, 2005).

3. *Norming.* If the group survives the storming stage, harmony and unity usually emerge as consensus, cohesion, and a positive group identity develop.

If you think these conditions for a good decision sound familiar, you're right. We described the importance of including minority viewpoints so a group can make valid judgments in Chapter 9, pages 337 to 343.

A sense of security and trust emerges when conflict declines as members' disagreements are resolved into a unified purpose (Wheelan, Davidson, & Tilin, 2003). In this stage most members tend to be highly satisfied with the groups, and to agree about the group's purpose and the role and responsibilities of individual members. Group commitment is high, with group members who more strongly identify with their group being more likely to remain an active part of it (Van Vugt & Hart, 2004). As one member of the Ashland team described the norming stage: "Then everyone jelled together . . . Nobody said no, everybody said yes . . . It was smooth, and people [were] in a good mood" (Eisenstat, 1990).

4. *Performing*. With norms established, the group moves into the performance stage. Members cooperate to solve problems, make decisions, and generate output. They exchange information freely, handle disagreements productively, and maintain mutual allegiance to the group goals. Groups that have developed open communication about and support for task interdependence in the norming stage are better able to adapt to changing task demands in the performing stage than groups whose members value independence (Moon and others, 2004). At this stage of the Ashland group's development, employees worked long hours, helped wherever they needed to, and operated as a team. Their product was declared a success, further enhancing group morale (Eisenstat, 1990).

5. *Adjourning*. Most groups, especially ad hoc groups put together for a specific purpose, eventually reach the end of their life span, the adjourning stage. Some, like the new factory team at Ashland, know from the outset that their lifetime is limited. Others dissolve because they have accomplished their goals. Still others fall apart when members lose interest, move away, or flee conflict (Rusbult, 1983; Thibaut & Kelley, 1959). At a group's endpoint, members often gather to evaluate their work, give feedback to each other, and express their feelings about the group (Lundgren & Knight, 1978). The dissolution of a cohesive group can be stressful for members if group identification has taken place, because loss of the group entails a change in social identity. Members lose the benefits of others' skills and contributions and the security of others' support and companionship. When cohesion and interaction are particularly intense, the psychological impact of the adjourning of a group can be similar to that of a break-up of a close relationship, leaving the same feelings of grief and loneliness. Group members can prevent some of this stress if they prepare themselves for the adjournment by reducing group cohesion, stressing individual independence, and searching for new groups to join (Mayadas & Glasser, 1985).

Table 12.1 summarizes these five typical stages of group development, along with the task and social processes that characterize each stage.

TIME AND GROUP DEVELOPMENT. Besides the typical progression through these developmental stages, time has other effects on the ways groups interact and deal with their tasks. Perhaps you have had the experience of working with a group on a long-term project for a class. If so, you may recall that at a certain point, after getting to know each other in a relaxed way and developing and discarding various tentative plans, your group suddenly realized that time was passing and little concrete progress had been made. Connie Gersick (1989) proposed that many groups go through this process, which she termed the "mid-life crisis" because she found that it often occurred when about half of the group's total time remained. The reorientation spurred by the realization that time is growing short may trigger

TABLE 12.1 Stages of Group Development

Stage	Task Processes	Social Processes
Forming	Exchange of information, task exploration	Getting to know each other, self-disclosure, dependence on leader
Storming	Disagreement over goals and procedures	Disagreement over status, criticism of ideas, hostility, coalition formation
Norming	Formation of consensus and norms	Growth of cohesion and unity, positive group identity and connectedness
Performing	Goal-focused efforts, orientation toward mastery and task performance	Social influence, cooperation
Adjourning	Completion of tasks, dissolution of roles	Withdrawal, emotional expressions, reminiscence

Source: D. R. Forsyth, *Group dynamics,* 3rd ed., 1999, Pacific Grove, CA: Brooks/Cole; S. A. Wheelan, *Group processes: A developmental perspective,* 1994, Boston, MA: Allyn & Bacon.

a radically different approach to the group's task, shifts in strategies, and a greater emphasis on productive work.

Janice Kelly and her colleagues (J. R. Kelly, Jackson, & Hutson-Comeaux, 1997; J. R. Kelly & Karau, 1999; J. R. Kelly & Loving, 2004) also found that time pressure alters the way groups approach their tasks. Groups under time pressure devote more of their interaction to clearly task-focused matters and differ from less pressured groups in the ways they share information and seek to influence each other. In some ways they perform better than groups with more time available. For example, because of their increased task focus, groups that have to write a proposal for a new program write more words per minute when they are under a tight deadline. Still, time pressure has its costs. Proposals that are written in a rush tend to be less creative and original than those written with more adequate time (Karau & Kelly, 1992).

Getting the Job Done: Group Performance

To achieve their performance goals, groups must maintain their motivation and avoid problems of coordination. Developing a common social identity helps to avoid such problems by encouraging acceptance of group goals, and normative cooperation to complete group tasks, and by attracting and keeping valuable group members.

For most groups, performing is the crucial stage because the work of the group must be accomplished during this period. Whether the group carries through with a flawless performance or collapses into disarray will depend on the kinds of tasks it faces, the quality of the group effort, and the resources available for reaching goals and repairing damage to the group (Kerr & Tindale, 2004).

FORMS OF TASK INTERDEPENDENCE. According to Ivan Steiner (1972), group tasks differ in terms of the type of interdependence they require. With *additive* tasks, the potential performance of the group is approximately equal to the sum of the performances of the individual members and is generally better than any one member's performance. A tug-of-war is an additive task, as is typing in an office pool or joining others to push a stalled car out of an intersection. In additive tasks, individual effort is the key because the final outcome is roughly proportional to the number of individuals contributing and how much they give (Littlepage, 1991). But coordination is also important: One person tugging on the rope when all the others are resting will not ensure tug-of-war victory.

In *disjunctive* tasks, a group's performance is expected to be as good as the performance of its best individual member (Laughlin, VanderStoep, & Hollingshead, 1991). When one of a group of "idea people" comes up with a terrific concept for a new ad campaign and everyone else recognizes its merit, the task is disjunctive. In this case, interdependence means that the outcome will be a function of the individual skills and talents of the group members. Thus, education or training of individual members can improve group performance, as can the selection of members with the right mix of skills (Hackman, 1987). Coordination is important, too, because other members have to be careful not to get in the way of any individual member who can complete the task (Diehl & Stroebe, 1991; Littlepage, 1991).

Conjunctive tasks depend on every member playing his or her part. In this case, the group's performance is only as good as the performance of its worst member. Groups of mountain climbers or assembly-line teams are engaged in conjunctive tasks: Their slowest or weakest member determines whether and how quickly they achieve their goal. If three students agree that one will do the research for a report, a second will write it, and the third will deliver it in class, their grade will depend on how well each of them performs his or her part of the task. Coordination is very important in conjunctive tasks, so the group has to organize its members' activities (Hertel, Kerr, & Messe, 2000). If coordination fails, so that two people do the research but nobody writes the presentation, the total task will remain undone.

Most tasks are *complex* tasks, which consist of subtasks that involve all forms of interdependence. In playing football, for example, some tasks are disjunctive (any of several players can block the opposing defensive end), whereas others are conjunctive (the quarterback must throw the pass and the receiver must catch it). Of course, the more complicated the task, the greater the need for planning and coordination to ensure that members' skills and efforts are appropriately allocated. And the more complicated the task, the greater the opportunity will be for the group's performance to multiply and surpass any possible effort by a single individual. At the same time, unfortunately, putting individuals' efforts together in complicated group tasks also provides many opportunities for things to go wrong.

GAINS AND LOSSES IN GROUP PERFORMANCE. "Two heads are better than one," and two sets of hands are better than one too. That is certainly one reason so much work is performed by groups. Groups do perform many tasks better than an individual could. Groups can multiply individual effort, provide a variety of skills that no one person possesses, and work together to complete tasks in parallel, rather than serial, fashion. Perhaps each Amish farmer has all the skills necessary to build a barn alone, but when all the members of his community pool their skills, labor, and enthusiasm, a barn can be raised in a day or two. The advantages of group effort are also evident in many cognitive tasks (Kerr & Tindale, 2004). For example, groups solve puzzles more quickly than individuals do (Laughlin, 1980). Members of the surgical team in an operating room can correct an error by one group member quickly, before its consequences become severe (Azar, 1994). And collective memory is also better: After watching a videotape portraying a police interrogation, groups of participants offered more accurate and detailed accounts of the event than did individuals who worked alone (N. K. Clark, Stephenson, & Kniveton, 1990; Wegner, 1987).

■ **Task interdependence at work**. Most complex tasks require multiple forms of interdependence. The assembly of automobiles, as shown in this photo of a Porsche factory, requires workers to complete specialized tasks in precise amounts of time. The task is a conjunctive one: A worker who does not finish his or her task on time can undermine productivity for everyone on the line.

Two sets of hands and heads may be better than one, but are they twice as good? That is, do groups perform as well as the same number of individuals working alone? Frequently the answer is no. Some research has evaluated the popular technique known as *brainstorming*, in which a group of people try to generate a large number of ideas without criticizing or evaluating them, at least initially. The premise is that one person's idea, even if wild and unworkable, may be built on and improved by other group members (Osborn, 1953). The evidence indicates that whereas brainstorming groups do better than a single person, they usually come up with fewer ideas and ideas of poorer quality than those produced by the same number of individuals working separately (Diehl & Stroebe, 1991; Paulus & Brown, 2003). The same is true for memory tasks: Although a group can remember more than a single individual, group performance is inferior to the combined information that can be recalled by an equal number of individuals working on their own (Wegner, 1987). Finally, groups sometimes display greater biases in judgment or decision-making tasks than do individuals provided with the same information (N. L. Kerr, MacCoun, & Kramer, 1996).

In cases like these, when groups do not amplify but actually diminish the sum of individual efforts, the cause is often a loss of either motivation or coordination among group members (Kerr & Tindale, 2004; J. M. Levine & Moreland, 1998).

LOSSES FROM DECREASED MOTIVATION: SOCIAL LOAFING. Sometimes working in a group leads people to slack off—to put less effort into the task than they would if working alone. As we noted in Chapter 1, this loss of motivation, termed **social loafing**, was first studied in the 1880s by Max Ringelmann, a French agricultural engineer who was interested in group performance on very simple additive tasks (Kravitz & Martin, 1986). Over a century later, Ringelmann's early insights have been confirmed by laboratory experiments. In the study of social loafing illustrated in Figure 12.3, for example, college students were told to clap and cheer as loudly as they could. The amount of sound generated by each student's efforts decreased as the size of the group increased. Individual efforts

> **Social loafing.** The tendency to exert less effort on a task when an individual's efforts are an unidentifiable part of a group effort than when the same task is performed alone.

FIGURE 12.3   Effects of social loafing

■ In this experiment, college students were told to clap or cheer as loudly as they could. Note that the noise produced by each person decreased as the number of people clapping or cheering together increased. Social loafing is most likely to occur if the task is unchallenging, if individual performances cannot be monitored, or if the individual's contribution to the group is dispensable. (Data from Latané, Williams, & Harkins, 1979.)

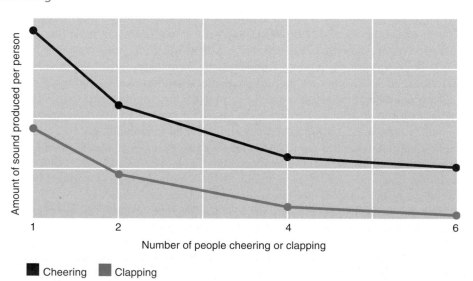

■ Cheering   ■ Clapping

seem quite literally to get lost in the crowd, and the degree of loss is substantial. In this study, an individual in a group of six made less than half the noise he or she made when clapping alone.

Social loafing is not restricted to simple motor tasks. When performance on cognitive tasks was measured, individuals in three-person brainstorming groups generated only 75% as many uses for a common object as they did when working alone. And working in groups, they made more than twice as many errors on a "vigilance" task of detecting brief flashes on a computer screen than they did when working alone (Harkins & Szymanski, 1989). Sharing responsibility can reduce effort no matter what the task is (Karau & Williams, 1993).

Why do people loaf on group tasks? To some extent, the nature of the task itself is a factor. Research indicates that social loafing occurs less often when tasks are interesting and involving (Brickner, Harkins, & Ostrom, 1986). But interdependence also plays a role. For example, when interdependence is minimal and individual roles are unimportant, as when the crowd sings the national anthem before a ball game begins, it is easy to let others pick up the slack (Karau & Williams, 1993; N. L. Kerr & Bruun, 1983). In contrast, social loafing is reduced when individual contributions are essential for success (Weldon & Mustari, 1988) or group members know that their individual contributions can be monitored (K. D. Williams, Harkins, & Latané, 1981; Zaccaro, 1984). Not surprisingly, people are also less likely to slack off when there is a clear standard against which the group's performance can be measured (Harkins & Szymanski, 1989) and when they can be sure that others are not taking it easy (N. L. Kerr & Bruun, 1983).

People's orientation toward the group also influences the tendency to loaf. Strong identification with the group decreases social loafing (Hogg, Abrams, Otten, & Hinkle, 2004; Karau & Williams, 1997). For the same reason, women and members of interdependent cultures, who tend to be more group oriented than men and people from individualistic cultures, are less likely to engage in social loafing (Karau & Williams, 1993).

Finally, social loafing may be partly caused by an "illusion of group productivity" (Paulus, Dzindolet, Poletes, & Camacho, 1993): people's tendency to believe that their groups are even more productive than they really are. If you think your group is performing at an extremely high level, you may conclude that you do not have to push yourself hard to make contributions, so social loafing may result.

As these findings indicate, to loaf or not to loaf seems to depend on motivation. When individual performance is important for task mastery, social loafing declines. And when an individual's performance has implications for connectedness to the group, for example, when others can praise or condemn individual efforts, social loafing declines. In fact, when task and social interdependence are high, *social compensation* is sometimes observed, as one group member works extra hard to compensate for the weakness or lack of ability of another member (Hart, Bridgett, & Karau, 2001; Karau & Williams, 1997).

Emotions can also negatively affect group members' motivation. Just as individuals can feel and exhibit a variety of moods, so too can groups (Bartel & Saavedra, 2000; Kelly & Barsade, 2001). And one member's bad mood can influence the whole group. A clever study by Sigal Barsade not only shows the effect of group mood on group outcomes, but also shows how moods can be transferred among people in a group (Barsade, 2002). Barsade had a trained confederate pretend to be in a good or bad mood during a group activity. A kind of emotional contagion occurred, with group members exposed to a negative mood experiencing increased conflict, decreased cooperation, and decreased perceived task performance

If you reflect on the social facilitation research described on pages 440 to 443, you may realize that the mere presence of others should create arousal and therefore increase performance on simple tasks like clapping. The fact that declines in performance sometimes occur suggests that declines in motivation and coordination can sometimes outweigh the effects of arousal.

as compared to those who were exposed to a positive mood. These consequences were evident to outsiders who observed the group, not just the group members themselves. So keeping your negative emotions in check at work may be a wise move, to avoid negative impacts on motivation and ultimately on group performance.

LOSSES FROM POOR COORDINATION. Even when group members are trying hard, the group needs to be organized if it is to do the best possible work. As John Ruskin (1907/1963) observed, "Failure is less frequently attributable to either insufficiency of means or impatience of labor than to a confused understanding of the thing to be done" (p. 1). Members need assigned roles and a clear sense of their resources. They also need to be aware of one another's strengths and weaknesses, of how their actions contribute to group goals, and of who has a right to command and who has a duty to obey. Group performance suffers when group members leave crucial tasks undone, duplicate others' efforts, compete for personal resources and status, or get in each other's way—literally or figuratively. Interference caused by other group members' efforts appears to be a major reason for the inferior performance of groups on brainstorming tasks. Listening to others talk may distract group members from thinking up superior ideas or may even cause them to forget some ideas before they can be verbalized (Diehl & Stroebe, 1991; Stroebe & Diehl, 1991). Perhaps group brainstorming and memory tasks would be more successful if the group observed a moment of silence every few minutes to permit members to think without distraction.

☐ **POOR COORDINATION IN THE WORKPLACE.** Poor coordination on group tasks can be disastrous in some circumstances. Consider, for example, the life-and-death responsibilities of cockpit crews on commercial airliners. If these small groups fail to work well together in an emergency, the results can be tragic. An investigation of one crash found that the pilot failed to pay attention to the copilot's repeated but timid comments that the takeoff was not proceeding normally. In another incident, a flight engineer manually silenced a noisy alarm, leaving the pilot with the impression that it was a false warning (Foushee, 1984).

Airlines typically select pilots and copilots almost exclusively for their outstanding individual skills and knowledge, paying less attention to their interpersonal or communication skills. Unfortunately, research evidence indicates that successful performance of the flight crew may depend more on their coordination than on the

Beetle Bailey

skill of the individual group members (Foushee & Manos, 1981; Lanzetta & Roby, 1960). One study of a major airline's flight crews, using a realistic flight simulator, demonstrated this point (Harper, Kidera, & Cullen, 1971). The researchers found that about 25% of the simulated flights crashed because the copilot failed to take control of the aircraft when the captain faked a collapse during a final landing approach. As is the case with flight crews, errors made by teams of surgeons, anesthesiologists, and nurses in hospital operating rooms often reflect social and interpersonal failures rather than deficiencies in technical skills (Azar, 1994).

CURES FOR GROUP PERFORMANCE LOSSES. Loss of motivation and failures of coordination can undermine a group's ability to achieve its goals and can frustrate individual members as well. Nipping such problems in the bud seems a wise step for any organization, and available research evidence indicates that one particularly successful strategy is making group membership a positive part of members' social identity.

Organizations often try to achieve this goal by selling the "corporate culture," the set of values, beliefs, understandings, and norms shared by members of the organization (J. M. Levine & Moreland, 1991). To build a sense of group identity and cohesion, organizations create slogans and symbols, develop and distribute literature describing the principles that embody the company's ideals and goals, and introduce rituals, ceremonies, and awards (Sadri & Lees, 2001). For example, the J.C. Penney department stores sell their employees on "The Penney Idea," a list of guiding principles that summarize the company's values and what it means to be a group member. In sports, teams have uniforms, mascots, and team activities and rituals to promote players' cohesiveness and dedication to their teammates (Hogg & Abrams, 1988). All of these tactics are designed to give group members a strong sense of shared social identity. Former U.S. Secretary of Labor Robert Reich described a simple test he used when he visited organizations: He asked front-line workers to talk about their companies. "If the answers I get back describe the company in terms of 'they' or 'them,' I know it's one kind of company. If the answers include words such as 'we' or 'us,' I know it's another kind" (Reich, 1993).

But even if corporate culture makes people feel good, can it help reach the organization's goals? The answer is yes. Building positive social interdependence often helps solve some of the problems of task interdependence (De Dreu & Weingart, 2003; Ellemers, de Gilder, & Haslam, 2004). Organizations sell the corporate culture because it encourages group cohesion, and group cohesion increases group performance, as Brian Mullen and Carolyn Copper (1994) found in their meta-analysis of 49 studies of laboratory and nonlaboratory groups. The reason is that a strong sense of group identity can be a strong remedy for many of the motivational and coordination losses that can render groups ineffective.

1. *Cohesive groups encourage cooperation.* Cohesive groups foster cooperation in the service of group goals, rather than competition for individual ones (Turner and others, 1987). Cooperation leads to positive feelings among group members and helps them work together to achieve group goals (Deutsch, 1949; Sherif, 1966). For example, those who identify with a cohesive group are more likely to participate in and contribute to group activities than are members of noncohesive groups (Brawley, Carron, & Widmeyer, 1988). In sports like volleyball and baseball, cohesive teams are usually winning teams (Bird, 1977). However, this finding no doubt reflects the fact that success leads to cohesion, as well as the positive effect of cohesion on performance (Mullen & Copper, 1994).

One practical way to promote group goals is to make personal rewards clearly contingent on group outcomes. For example, students in "cooperative classrooms" work together to help each other learn and are graded on the basis of the entire group's performance, whereas students' grades in "competitive classrooms" are based on comparisons between group members. In the classroom as in the laboratory, mutual cooperation leads to positive feelings: Compared with members of competitive groups, cooperative group members generally like each other better. They also learn more. A meta-analysis of over 100 studies concluded that cooperative learning results in better classroom performance than is found in either competitive or individualistic situations (D. W. Johnson, Maruyama, Johnson, Nelson, & Skon, 1981).

Employers sometimes adopt a similar cooperative reward arrangement: a contingent pay system in which employees receive bonuses only when certain group goals (such as production levels) are met. One study of 66 large U.S. firms compared compensation packages among low-performing and high-performing companies. The study found that the companies with high performance records more often had packages that emphasized teamwork rather than individual competition (Schuster, 1985). These employers endorse the claim of W. Edwards Deming, the guru of managing for quality, that rewarding individual performance "annihilates long-term planning, builds fear, demolishes teamwork, and nourishes rivalry and politics" (Gabor, 1992). Indeed, General Motors Corporation's Cadillac Division, which adopted team-based rewards in 1989, credits them for the major turnaround that propelled Cadillac to a top-ranking place in customer satisfaction among American car-makers by 1991.

2. *Cohesive groups follow norms.* A sense of group belonging usually helps members reach consensus about the group's goals and its strategies for accomplishing those goals. And what a cohesive group decides, its members usually do. Once consensus has been reached, those who identify with the group are likely to adhere to its norms (McGrath, 1984), and new members quickly absorb the group's "way of doing things" (Forsyth, 1999; J. R. Levine & Moreland, 1991). If a group is cohesive and has high-performance norms, its members will be highly productive (Keller, 1986). Of course, if group norms are inconsistent with high performance, productivity will be low (Roethlisberger & Dickson, 1939). Reaching consensus also means the group no longer needs to spend time repeatedly renegotiating the issues. Members know what the group is set up to do and they know how to do it. These norms help both to eradicate motivation loss and to aid group coordination (Hackman, 1987). Consider, for example, the effect of norms on the goal of preparing a community meal. If the group has not reached a consensus, members may feel they have a right to work on the task they enjoy most; no one will do the dirty work, and there will be no dinner. Group norms, however, can specify that all the jobs must be done, that certain members have the right or obligation to do specific tasks, and that the tasks should be performed at certain times and in specific ways. Given these conditions, the community meal should proceed on schedule: When group norms match task demands, groups operate more smoothly.

3. *Cohesive groups attract and keep valued members.* When tasks are difficult, rewards are few, and conflict is frequent, potentially productive group members may slack off or drop out altogether. Member turnover can lessen a group's chances of achieving its goals, and it often represents the

The reasons why group norms are such effective guides for group behavior were described in Chapter 10, pages 355 to 358.

loss of a huge investment in training and skill development. Shared social identity acts as a counterforce by boosting people's liking for the group, their satisfaction with belonging, and their morale (Hackman, 1992; O'Reilly & Caldwell, 1985). Belonging to a cohesive group even helps people cope with stress, perhaps by offering them effective social support (Bowers, Weaver, & Morgan, 1996). You may recall that members of groups—even groups formed on the basis of arbitrary categorizations—tend to hold in-group members in higher esteem than out-group members (Hogg, 1987). This tendency is even stronger in cohesive face-to-face groups. Many Japanese businesses see group cohesion as a way to keep their workers productive and happy. They are famous for their efforts to ensure that employee morale is high and that performance is rewarded. Companies foster friendships between members; sponsor picnics, parties, and sports teams; and promise long-term employment. Company-sponsored computer dating services even encourage employees to marry within the company. Their efforts no doubt contribute to the fact that Japanese workers seldom change companies.

To review the many ways in which membership in a social group increases preference for in-group over out-group members, see Chapter 6, pages 198 to 199.

Social identity can be such a powerful tool that it sometimes holds groups together when no material benefits are forthcoming (Van Vugt & Hart, 2004). For example, groups with strong social identity often preserve (or even strengthen) their cohesion even when they lose or fail at important tasks (Brawley, Carron, & Widmeyer, 1987; D. M. Taylor, Doria, & Tyler, 1983). This occurred during the closing stages of the Second World War, when units of the German army, outnumbered, undersupplied, and with no chance of victory, continued to fight against all odds. They did so not because they believed deeply in Nazi ideology but because they were motivated by group loyalty forged by shared identity (Shils & Janowitz, 1948). Studies of U.S. soldiers in Europe and Vietnam tell a similar story of social interdependence motivating performance (Moskos, 1969; Stouffer and others, 1949).

FIGURE 12.4   Causes and cures of group productivity loss.

Source of productivity loss in groups	Motivation loss *Individuals diminish personal efforts, engage in social loafing.*	Coordination loss *Individuals interfere with each other's actions. Individuals fail to communicate effectively about group tasks.*
Remedy for productivty loss in groups	Cooperation: Individuals work toward group goals *Individuals maintain efforts even when contributions are not identifiable.*	Consensus: Individuals agree on goals and strategies *Individuals follow group norms. If norms are appropriate, high productivity results.*
Contribution of group cohesion to remedy	Individuals adopt group goals as their own.	Group exercises social influence over individuals.

■ Group productivity declines when individual members do not try hard to accomplish group goals—for example, when they engage in social loafing—or when the members' efforts are poorly coordinated. Group cohesion can help remedy both of these problems by encouraging individuals to cooperate for group goals and to follow the group consensus on goals and ways of achieving those goals.

We have seen that group performance can suffer from two basic types of problems. The first occurs when members stop trying or drop out because they do not care about group goals or are unwilling to waste their efforts while others slack off. These motivational losses are often remedied when people cooperate and identify with group goals, as shown in Figure 12.4. The second problem arises when members try hard but cannot coordinate their efforts effectively because members do not share common goals or interfere with each other. These coordination losses may be remedied when people identify with the group and follow its norms, at least when those norms favor high productivity. In this way, cohesion offers remedies for both motivational and coordination losses in groups. When group membership gives people a positive social identity, they are likely to take the group's goals as their own and to follow its norms in their behavior.

Leadership

Effective leaders enhance task performance and maintain social interdependence. The ways they do this must differ from situation to situation. Sometimes, however, stereotypical thinking prevents the most effective leaders from emerging in groups. Some types of leadership are particularly likely to help align individual and group goals and these leaders may help groups be particularly successful. Of course such extraordinary influence can be used in destructive as well as constructive ways.

Whose job is it to make sure that groups fulfill their mastery and connectedness goals? As former U.S. President Dwight D. Eisenhower once wrote, "Leadership is the ability to decide what is to be done, and then to get others to want to do it." Leaders are crucial to the attainment of group goals (Goethals, 2005). In fact, **leadership** can be defined formally as a process in which one or more group members are permitted to influence and motivate others to help attain group goals (Forsyth, 1999; Reicher, Haslam, & Hopkins, 2005). Notice that in this definition the group grants the leader his or her power; as we noted in Chapter 10, legitimate authority works only if the group accepts and agrees with it. The definition does not specify the route to power: Leaders may be appointed by an outside authority, elected by group members themselves, or simply emerge as a group interacts. Leaders may or may not be effective, but before we explore that issue, let's examine what leaders do.

WHAT DO LEADERS DO? The exercise of leadership generally involves two distinct types of behavior: those focused on decision making and task performance and those aimed at enhancing cohesion and liking among group members (Misumi, 1995; Stogdill, 1963). This pattern is understandable. Because people draw on groups both for mastery and concrete rewards stemming from task performance and for feelings of connectedness and belonging, groups require both task and social leadership. Task-related leader behaviors include telling group members what to do, criticizing poor performance, and coordinating others' activity. In contrast, relationship-oriented leadership involves being open, friendly, and approachable, treating group members as equals, and listening to group members' opinions. Both of these functions are vital to effective groups, and together they account for most of what leaders do (Mintzberg, 1980).

Early studies of interaction in small groups concluded that two different leaders often emerged, a task leader and a socioemotional leader, each specializing in one of these two types of behavior. These studies suggested that the task leader

Leadership. A process in which one or more group members are permitted to influence and motivate others to help attain group goals.

makes the decisions that translate into actual group performance. This individual typically makes task-focused comments, talks more than other members, and often addresses comments to the group as a whole rather than to individual members (Bales, 1953). According to early research, a second individual—typically the person who talks more than anyone else except the task leader—becomes the group's socioemotional leader. Most of this person's contributions are aimed at soothing feelings, maintaining harmony, and encouraging participation.

This presumed division of roles reflected the culture of the period in which this research was done. Researchers saw it as a "natural" and nearly universal pattern (Bales & Slater, 1955). After all, weren't families composed of husbands who exercised task leadership and wives who provided socioemotional support? Re-evaluation of these findings suggests, however, that the pattern of separate task and socioemotional leaders is not truly universal (Burke, 1967). Leader behavior does tend to fall into two general categories, having to do with task performance versus relationship maintenance (Misumi, 1995; Stogdill, 1963). But a group does not require two separate leaders, for one person may be quite capable of leading the group to task completion and simultaneously taking care of the group's psychological well-being.

LEADERSHIP EFFECTIVENESS: PERSON OR SITUATION? Effective leaders can make or break countries, businesses, organizations, religions, clubs, sports teams, and even families. It is not surprising, then, that literally thousands of studies have tried to understand why some leaders have the capacity to inspire followers and others do not (Goethals, 2005). When one considers the lives of Mohandas Gandhi or Martin Luther King, Jr., there is a strong temptation to attribute their influence to their unique personal attributes. This tendency may be one more example of the correspondence bias at work, leading us to attribute behavior to individual traits rather than to situational demands.

To remind yourself about the correspondence bias, and what might be done to undermine it, check out Chapter 3, pages 70 to 73.

Despite the appeal of the idea that effective leadership depends on characteristics of the leader, researchers have had little success in identifying specific personality traits that universally characterize effective leaders. Indeed, these studies revealed that the same person could be an effective leader in one context (for example, in a cockpit crew) but ineffective in another (such as a community service organization). When researchers examined the relationship of leader behaviors to group outcomes, they found that giving socioemotional support consistently helps improve group morale, motivation, and job satisfaction. However, task-focused leader behaviors are not as consistently related to improved group task performance; their effect varies more for different types of groups and situations (Judge, Piccolo, & Ilies, 2004; Vroom, 1976). This suggests that group success depends less on who the leader is than on what kind of leadership is needed in a particular situation.

This insight about the importance of the situation led to the development of *contingency theories* of leadership (Fiedler, 1964). That is, leaders differ in whether they are task oriented or relationship oriented, and leadership situations also differ, in the opportunities and limitations they offer for influence on tasks and group morale. Contingency theories focus on "matching": To maximize leadership effectiveness, the leader's style should match the type of leadership demanded by the situation, as Figure 12.5 shows. If a skilled and experienced group take on a task that requires lots of interpersonal interaction and cooperation, a socioemotionally oriented leader may be most effective. The group does not need task instruction, but a leader who can maintain positive feelings, group cohesion, and motivation. If, on the other hand, an already cohesive group takes on a difficult and complex task, group performance may be maximized by a task-oriented leader. The group climate

FIGURE 12.5   Contigency model of leadership

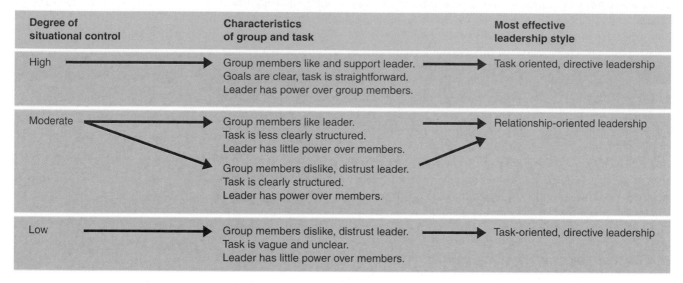

Degree of situational control	Characteristics of group and task	Most effective leadership style
High	Group members like and support leader. Goals are clear, task is straightforward. Leader has power over group members.	Task oriented, directive leadership
Moderate	Group members like leader. Task is less clearly structured. Leader has little power over members.	Relationship-oriented leadership
	Group members dislike, distrust leader. Task is clearly structured. Leader has power over members.	
Low	Group members dislike, distrust leader. Task is vague and unclear. Leader has little power over members.	Task-oriented, directive leadership

■ According to the contingency model of leadership, the most effective leadership style depends on the leader's and the group's situation. When the situation allows high control, a directive and task-oriented leader can be most effective. The same leadership style also works well when conflict and ambiguity are extremely high, producing low control. In contrast, when either an unclear task or uncooperative group members produce moderate situational control, leaders are most effective when they adopt a relationship-oriented style to motivate group members toward task goals.

is not a concern, so leadership resources can be focused primarily on improving task performance. The effectiveness of matching leader to task has been supported by a number of studies that have looked at such diverse groups as military units and basketball teams (Strube & Garcia, 1981).

Although some specific tasks may be best matched by a task-focused or relationship-oriented leader, most complex tasks require both leadership styles. In terms of group success, the leader's skill at handling one particular type of task may be less important than his or her ability to balance the two crucial elements of leadership as tasks and situations change (Hersey & Blanchard, 1982; Zaccaro, Foti, & Kenny, 1991). In fact, the essence of good leadership may be the flexibility to adjust the mix of social and task motivation that a group needs in a particular situation. So wouldn't a person who is high in both relationship and task concerns be the best leader for every situation (Blake & Mouton, 1980)? Most of the time, this is true. The most effective supervisors in settings as diverse as banks, factories, coal mines, and government offices are in fact those who score well in both task and social leadership and have the ability to develop the skills the group needs at the time the group needs them (Bass, 1985; P. B. Smith & Tayeb, 1989). In short, leadership is about the flexible exercise of social influence: Given a particular group performing a particular task, a good leader simultaneously maximizes both successful task performance and positive social identity.

☐ **COACHING LEADERSHIP IN YOUTH SPORTS.** Swimming teams, Little League baseball, youth soccer . . . if you have the impression that today's youngsters are heavily involved in sports activities you would be right! Estimates are that over 25 million children and 3 million adult supervisors and coaches are involved in the United States alone. Proponents of youth sports argue that they teach the benefits of cooperation and teamwork, self-control and discipline, and important lessons about dealing with success and failure, not to mention promoting physical fitness and other positive health habits. But the leadership of coaches is crucial if these worthy goals are to be attained. Ronald Smith and Frank Smoll (1996) studied coaches' behaviors and their effects on young athletes. They found that the children enjoyed their athletic experiences and teammates most and had the highest self-esteem when coaches gave positive feedback for good efforts as well as good performances, responded to mistakes with instruction about proper technique, and emphasized fun and personal improvement more than winning matches. In other words, a good mix of relationship-oriented leadership (encouragement) and task-oriented leadership (instruction, especially after a poor performance) carries the day. Unfortunately, along with these types of positive behaviors, coaches sometimes engaged in more negative acts, being punitive and critical toward the children. Though these behaviors occurred only rarely, when they did they had a dramatic negative impact on the children's attitudes and enjoyment.

■ **Coaches as leaders**. Studies have found that the adults who coach youth sports can have a profound positive impact when they mix relationship-oriented encouragement with task-oriented instruction.

These same researchers also demonstrated that the behaviors that produce positive effects on young team members can be taught to coaches in brief workshops. Compared to children who played for coaches attending workshops focused on the technical aspects of sport, the children who played for coaches graduating from Smith and Smoll's program enjoyed sport more, were less anxious about performing, and had higher self esteem. Perhaps the most important indicator of the effectiveness of the program was that only 5% of the athletes who played for the workshop-trained coaches failed to return for the sports program the next season, compared to about 26% for the other coaches.

Even though everyone presumably agrees that the chief goal of youth sports programs should be enjoyment, learning, and building positive attitudes rather than winning, you may still have one question about these results: Do the workshop-trained coaches, like other proverbial "nice guys," end up finishing last? No. They did not differ from the other coaches in their overall win/loss percentages in any of Smith and Smoll's studies (1997). So coaches do not have to choose between one leadership style that increases athletes' enjoyment and another style that wins matches. Instead, a single approach can attain the first (and more important) of these goals without sacrificing the second.

WHO BECOMES LEADER? Contingency theories make it clear that groups should choose leaders whose styles match the demands of the situation. But in this regard, people seem to have ideas about who is "leader material" regardless of the task at hand, and one clue they use is how much group members talk. That is, laboratory studies show that group members who talk a lot tend to be viewed as leaders (Littlepage, Schmidt, Whisler, & Frost, 1995; Sorrentino & Field, 1986). Group success can depend on a leader who offers advice and guidance, so choosing a talker is not necessarily a bad idea. Unfortunately, the amount a group member talks doesn't always reflect actual expertise. But other members assume that those who talk are competent, so those who talk most have the most influence (Littlepage and others, 1995).

People respond not only to talkativeness but also to nonverbal signs of dominance and assertiveness. In their studies of groups of business school students, Tiedens and Fragale (2003) examined how group members respond to another member who has assumed either a dominant posture (e.g., with arm draped on back of an adjacent chair) or a submissive posture (e.g., with hands in lap). The other members tended to take on complementary body positions, with those exposed to another's assertive postures assuming a more submissive stance and those exposed to a submissive posture assuming a more dominant stance. When questioned afterwards, study participants were unaware that the posture of their interaction partner influenced their own behavior. Such findings highlight some of the subtle ways in which aspects of our social environment may influence leadership emergence. No wonder then that people also tend to confer leadership on those who exercise less subtle signs of dominance—like taking the seat at the head of the table, or sitting behind the microphone.

Groups also seem to prefer leaders who in some way embody the group's stereotype, norms, or central defining attributes (Foti, Fraser, & Lord, 1982; Hogg, 1996). For example, a quiet, book-loving English literature major might be considered an appropriate leader for a literary discussion group, whereas a loud, tough, physically strong individual might be expected to captain a rugby football team. By the same token, a leader who matches the group's norms should be seen as particularly effective by group members. One study of college students meeting in groups to discuss a social issue illustrated this point. The study did show an effect of general leader stereotypes: Leaders who were described as performing stereotypical leader behaviors, such as emphasizing group goals and letting other members know what was expected of them, were rated as more effective. But group leaders who were close to the group's typical position on the issue were also rated as more effective leaders (Hains, Hogg, & Duck, 1997). Perhaps these findings also help explain the fact that group members much prefer, and perform better for, elected leaders who embody the group's norms and goals, compared to appointed leaders who do not (Van Vugt & De Cremer, 1999; De Cremer & Van Vugt, 2002). These effects are especially strong for members who strongly identify with the group. Thus, when members identify with a group, making it a potential basis for their self-definition, leaders who most strongly embody the group's norms will be the most acceptable to group members, and especially effective as leaders.

STEREOTYPES AND LEADERSHIP. Common stereotypes about gender, ethnicity, age, or other social characteristics also influence people's perceptions of leadership. Thus, as you might expect, group members who are male, taller, or older than others tend to be treated as leaders (Judge & Cable, 2004; Schein, Mueller, Lituchy, & Liu, 1996). In fact individuals who look masculine, regardless of gender, are consistently judged to be more competent leaders. Moreover people seem unaware of this appearance bias, so even when they are reminded of the possible impact of stereotypes on their judgments, they still choose masculine-looking males and females as leaders, and rate masculine-looking leaders of either gender as more effective (Sczesny & Kühnen, 2004).

The effects of stereotypes on perceptions of leadership may help explain the preponderance of males in leadership positions in business, government, religious, and military institutions. If people believe that competence and assertiveness are

Recall from Chapter 10, pages 373 to 374 that some of these factors also confer legitimate authority on individuals, increasing their power.

As you may recall from Chapter 9, pages 318 to 319, when people identify with a group, they especially like the other group members who most strongly personify group norms.

associated with leadership and that males are competent and assertive, they may turn to males for leadership (Eagly & Carli, 2003; Lord, De Vader, & Alliger, 1986; Wagner & Berger, 1997). Thus, the expectation that males make good leaders creates a self-fulfilling prophecy in which males assume most leadership roles. A wealth of research data support this point. For example, a meta-analysis summarized 75 laboratory studies of mixed-sex informal groups that were allowed to interact without an appointed leader. When the group members later identified who had emerged as leaders, men were perceived as playing leadership roles more often than women were (Eagly & Karau, 1991). Groups turn to women only when their tasks require extensive social interaction, for example, in consensus-seeking tasks or negotiations (Eagly & Carli, 2003; W. Wood, 1987).

Stereotypes also limit ethnic minorities' chances of rising to leadership positions. When an executive for the Los Angeles Dodgers baseball team commented in 1987 that African-Americans "may not have some of the necessities" to be head coaches or executives, his remarks brought swift condemnation and vows of renewed efforts to recruit African-American coaches and executives. Nevertheless, the upper management levels of most professional sports in the United States are still relatively unintegrated. In American football, for example, African-Americans made up about 67% of the players but held only about 20% of the possible 32 head coaching positions in 2005. Even team owners admit that lingering stereotypes bear some of the blame for this situation (Hammer, 1992). Of course, underrepresentation of minority group members in leadership positions is common throughout many types of business and government organizations, not only in sports.

Are groups hurting themselves by using such stereotypes to choose their leaders? Little research has examined ethnic differences, but meta-analyses of research on gender differences in leader effectiveness permit a partial answer to this question. The meta-analyses have looked at three related questions.

- *Who holds the group together?* In creating connectedness and cohesion, women leaders beat men hands down (Eagly, Makhijani, & Klonsky, 1992). Both groups and individual group members are happier when their boss is a woman. One reason may be that in a wide range of leadership situations women leaders show more concern with morale and encourage more participation in decision making than men do (Eagly & Johnson, 1990; van Engen & Willemsen, 2004), although consistent with contingency theories, certain types of organizations encourage this type of leadership from both men and women.

- *Who gets the job done?* When it comes to mastery and task performance, studies of leaders in organizations show that, in general, women perform just as well as men on objective measures. However, the type of organization makes a substantial difference. In business, educational, and government organizations, women leaders slightly outperform men on the average. In contrast, in the military, men have been found to be much more effective leaders than women (Eagly and others, 1995).

- *Who do people believe make good leaders?* If we turn from objective measures of group performance to group members' *perceptions* of leader effectiveness, however, the story is different. In a number of studies in which a fixed set of leader behaviors are acted out by trained confederates or described in writing, research participants tend to rate female leaders as less effective than male leaders who perform exactly the same behaviors

(Eagly and others, 1992). These judgments suggest that many people still doubt women's ability to lead, perhaps because women do not fit their stereotype of a leader (Eagly & Carli, 2003; Hollander, 1985).

When research findings like those just discussed reveal the reality beyond the stereotypes, the power of stereotypic thinking to obstruct the selection of the best leader for the job becomes clear. Perhaps this is why so many of us have worked for an incompetent boss, an unlikable coach, or a disorganized chairperson at some point in our lives. One study shows that at least 60% of workers say that dealing with their supervisor is the most stressful aspect of their job (Freiberg, 1991b). Given the central role leaders play in coordinating both task and social interdependence in groups, perhaps it is time that stereotypical thinking about leadership went the way of the dinosaur.

PUTTING THE GROUP FIRST: TRANSFORMATIONAL LEADERSHIP. Jesus of Nazareth, Mohammad, and Gautama Buddha founded religious movements that have changed the lives of literally billions of followers over many centuries and that remain among the most powerful forces shaping our world today. What can we learn about leadership from the way these and other individuals have been able to transform other people? The sociologist Max Weber (1921/1946), writing in the early part of last century, considered this question. He defined *charismatic leaders* as those who inspire extreme devotion and emotional identification on the part of their followers. This devotion allows these leaders to have profound effects on their followers. Whereas most leaders help followers reach existing goals, charismatic leaders may actually change their followers' goals, for example, turning them from seekers of worldly success into religious devotees practicing self-denial.

If the key to this kind of leadership lies in being able to refocus people's goals, can such leadership also be exercised in the everyday world of business offices and sports teams? In fact, the crucial aspect of such leadership, now more often called *transformational leadership*, seems to be the re-focusing of group members' individual and personal concerns toward community- or group-centered goals (Burns, 2003; Burns & Sorenson, 2000; De Cremer, 2002). Transformational leaders articulate an inspiring vision for the group, motivating their followers to pursue collective goals that transcend self-interest, and to make personal sacrifices for the collective good (Bass, 1990, 1997; Halverson, Holladay, Kazama, & Quiñones, 2004; House & Shamir, 1993). To have these profound effects, such transformational leaders must be self-confident and determined, as well as skilled and inspiring communicators. They take clear and strong stands that emphasize commitment to goals, optimistically express an attractive vision of the future, question old assumptions and traditions, and are highly caring toward group members (Bass, 1997; Shamir, House, & Arthur, 1993). When successful, such leaders can indeed be transformational as they bring about social and organizational change (Bass & Riggio, 2006).

Studies of leaders who exhibit these kinds of behaviors suggest that they are indeed successful in promoting not only organizational commitment and work satisfaction, but also group performance and organizational profitability. Both setting clear group goals and self-sacrifice have been found to increase group morale and group performance under transformational leaders (De Cremer & van Knippenberg, 2004; Gillespie & Mann, 2004; Whittington, Goodwin & Murray, 2004). Tranformational practices tend to empower followers, creating a sense of control that helps explain the success of such leadership (Avolio, Zhu, Koh, Bhatia, 2004; de Hoogh et al., 2004; Walumbwa, Wang, Lawler, & Shi, 2004). Other studies have confirmed the importance of a leader's ability to communicate and inspire a shared vision for the group, as well the leader's ability to stimulate the group intellectually and recognize and support individual group members (Rafferty & Griffin, 2004). These studies also caution, however, that transformational leadership is, as contingency theories suggest, dependent on both the leader and the group's situation. For example, the ability of transformational leadership practices to improve group performance seems to be greater in times of uncertainty and change than in the case of "business as usual."

Perhaps the results of these studies should come as no surprise. Transformational leaders are effective for exactly the same reasons as other leaders: because they nurture cohesion among group members and inspire them to adopt the group's goals as their own. These factors in turn inspire group members to look beyond themselves and adopt new collective goals for the group, eliminating potential coordination and motivation losses in the process.

THE DARK SIDE OF LEADERSHIP. The quest to understand what makes a good leader is driven not just by theoretical curiosity. Groups and group members can pay a high cost for poor leadership. Inept leadership can cost businesses, communities, and citizens not only millions of dollars but also millions of lives. Just as a bad coach can lower self-esteem and enjoyment of sport, a short-sighted national leader can take countries down the path to war. When leaders lead the wrong way, groups members who can do so will withdraw from the group, hurting their own, the group's and the leader's chances of achieving the goal that brought the group together in the first place (Van Vugt, Jepson, Hart, & De Cremer, 2004). Under bad leaders, task motivation ebbs away and group members not only fail to perform, but can actively attempt to undermine the leader's agenda and the group's goals (Hogan, Curphy, & Hogan, 1994). When leadership has life and death consequences, as it does for military leaders, incompetence is not counted in deficits and lost profits, but in body bags and lost generations (Dixon, 1976). Even the life-changing potential of charismatic or transformational leadership can have a dark side. In 1978, over 900 members of the People's Temple group committed mass suicide at the urging of their leader, the Rev. Jim Jones. In a scenario eerily reminiscent of that earlier tragedy, Marshall Applewhite and nearly 40 other members of his Heaven's Gate group committed mass suicide in March 1997. They were following Applewhite's teaching that they had reached a new evolutionary stage in which their earthly "vehicles" or bodies would no longer be required, and that after shedding their bodies they would be picked up by a spaceship traveling with the Hale-Bopp comet. Tragedies like these remind us that charismatic leaders may use their extraordinary influence over their followers in destructive as well as positive ways.

■ **The dark side of leadership.** Jim Jones founded his church, the Peoples' Temple, after gaining respectability as a leader and ordained minister in the mainstream Christian denomination Disciples of Christ in 1964. Members of Jones' church referred to him as "Father" and their unquestioning exaltation of his charismatic leadership was frighteningly realized in November 1978, when over 900 members committed "mass suicide" by drinking cyanide-laced drinks upon Jones' instructions.

Because of the profound implications of good or poor group performance for every aspect of modern society, the quest to understand what makes a good leader has huge practical importance. Theories of leadership wax and wane in popularity outside the laboratory (as evidenced by the dozens of competing books on the topic published each year), driven by many forces besides the scientific evidence for their effectiveness. As the evidence accumulates, however, it becomes clear that group effectiveness depends on whether the positive potential of social and task interdependence can be unleashed, while the negative consequences of social and task interdependence can be avoided. An effective leader is one who solves the problems of social and task interdependence in the best way for a given group in a given situation. Because a shared social identity makes it possible for leaders to motivate and organize groups, the most effective leaders provide both the identity and the structure that groups need to satify their members' mastery and connectedness needs, and to solve the twin problems of social and task interdependence.

Group Communication

High productivity and high morale can be achieved only through communication. Groups use both formal and informal channels to make sure communication is effective. Technology including video, electronic mail, and instant messaging is now altering communication patterns and therefore many aspects of group performance.

Regardless of who leads and what the group's task is, leaders and groups have one primary weapon in the struggle to achieve high task efficiency while maintaining cohesion: communication. No wonder, then, that as group members share and exchange information, most of the talk is about getting the job done and feeling good while doing it (Bales, 1953).

MASTERY- AND CONNECTEDNESS-FOCUSED COMMUNICATION. The balance between task-focused and socioemotional communications is crucial if a group is to be effective (McGrath, 1984). If a group's performance suffers because of ineffective strategies or inadequate skills, the group must seek task-focused remedies, such as repeated instructions, new directions, or reminders of goals (Schacter, 1951). But when low cohesion is to blame for poor performance, remedies must have a socioemotional focus aimed at increasing positive interpersonal relationships and group identification. Over time, groups learn to alternate between a cluster of instrumental communications ("No, do it this way") and a cluster of socioemotional ones ("Yes, you're doing a great job"), nurturing both task and social interdependence (Bales, 1953).

PATTERNS OF COMMUNICATION. How well messages like these are disseminated through an organization depends on *communication networks*: the typical patterns in which messages are transmitted in that organization. In a centralized network, one person is the focus of all problem solving and decision making. The wheel and Y patterns shown in Figure 12.6 are typical centralized networks. A university in which department heads take their cases for new teaching facilities to a dean, who decides priorities and allocates resources, has a centralized communication network that fits the wheel pattern. In a decentralized network, in contrast, individuals can communicate freely with one another. For example, a university in which department heads meet together to discuss their needs and vote on the allocation of resources has an all-connect decentralized network, as shown in Figure 12.6.

Laboratory experiments have demonstrated that groups with centralized structures usually solve simple problems faster than groups using other structures. As members gather information, the central person is well situated to quickly coordinate it and make a correct decision. But when problems are complicated, a central individual may find the information and responsibilities overwhelming. In these situations, decentralized networks, in which communication can flow more freely, are more likely to produce accurate decisions. Business groups solving research and development problems and planning sales strategies thrive with decentralized networks (Shaw, 1954; Tushman, 1978).

FIGURE 12.6 Patterns of communication in groups

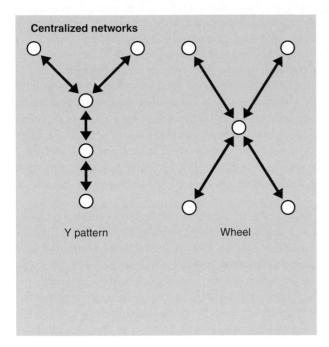

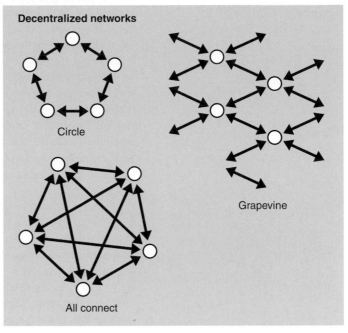

A person's status within an organizational structure often determines the type of information that he or she communicates or receives. For example, instructions and evaluations may be transmitted more often by supervisors to subordinates, while requests and factual information are more likely to be transmitted upwards (Sias & Jablin, 1995). One disturbing finding is that, although good news about increased sales, research successes, and the like travels upward quickly, bad news is much slower to arrive at the top (L. D. Browning, 1978; Jablin, 1982). This asymmetry is only natural: Wouldn't you rather tell your boss that his or her pet project is going well than that it is failing? Yet, as we saw in our discussion of groupthink in Chapter 9, if bad news like the engineers' concerns about the reliability of the space shuttle Challenger's O-rings never reaches the ears of the top-level decision makers, tragically flawed decisions may result.

When formal routes of communication do not serve the group's needs, group members may rely on the "grapevine." The grapevine is an informal person-to-person network linking members in all directions. Group members use the grapevine to fill in gaps in information and to deal with uncertainty. Although not officially sanctioned by organizations, the grapevine can be surprisingly accurate and useful. One study showed that about 80% of grapevine items were work related rather than personal, and that from 70% to 90% of the details passed through the grapevine were accurate (K. Davis & Newstrom, 1985; Simmonds, 1985)!

TECHNOLOGY AND COMMUNICATION. You may have noticed that much of the research on communication in work groups was carried out before computers and video revolutionized communication. In many modern organizations, the telephone, instant message, e-mail, and video conferences are displacing face-to-face interaction for brainstorming and resolving conflicts. Not surprisingly, the new

■ A group's success in accomplishing its tasks and the good feeling that its members have in working together depend on the group's ability to transmit task-focused and socioemotional messages. In centralized networks, most communication must pass through a single individual. In decentralized networks, individuals can communicate more freely with one another. Performance on simple tasks is faster and more accurate when networks are centralized, but performance on complex tasks benefits from decentralized communication. (Adapted from Shaw, 1954 and K. Davis & Newstrom, 1985.)

technologies influence both how tasks are completed and how group members feel as they complete them (Hollingshead, 2004).

Technology-mediated communication, that is, information sharing that occurs via video, e-mail, or instant messaging, can be remarkably efficient at getting the job done. If you are sending a memo or leaving a message, you probably will get right to the point. Thus, because they emphasize the task-relevant features of the interaction, telephone calls and e-mail tend to lead to good performance on simple tasks.

There is also evidence that computer-mediated group decision making may be less vulnerable to problems like the premature consensus of groupthink and biases that polarize majority views. In one comparison of three-member groups of university administrators reaching decisions, group polarization was less likely after computer-mediated discussion than when the groups met face to face (T. W. McGuire, Kiesler, & Siegel, 1987). In another study, the electronically linked groups took longer to reach consensus and made more unconventional decisions (S. Kiesler & Sproull, 1992).

One reason technologically mediated communication allows groups to avoid some decision-making pitfalls is that it seems to promote more equal participation among members. When groups meet face to face, high-status members typically dominate the discussion (Rutter & Robinson, 1981; E. Williams, 1977). This was certainly the case when researchers arranged for university students of different levels to make decisions together: High-status group members like graduate students took up much more "air time" than lower-status first-year undergraduates. When the same groups made comparable decisions using e-mail, however, status inequalities in participation were reduced (Dubrovsky, Kiesler, & Sethna, 1991). Remember that if everyone participates, the group has a better chance of maximizing the potential of all its members to get the job done right. But lessened effects of status are not inevitable when electronic communication is used. If the computer software prominently displays status cues (such as organizational titles) in e-mail messages, status effects may be as large or even larger than those found with traditional forms of communication (Weisband, Schneider, & Connolly, 1995).

Of course, groups do not focus solely on getting their job done. Like traditional channels of communication, electronic communication is used as much for enhancing connectedness as for attaining mastery through task performance. And because more people tend to participate in group-related activities through the electronic networks, group members are likely to feel better about the group and their place in it. The use of new communication technologies can thus make a difference to group cohesiveness and commitment. One survey of city government employees found that the level of commitment to the organization was higher among employees who used e-mail and electronic bulletin boards than among those who used more traditional and status-dominated forms of communication (Huff, Sproull, & Kiesler, 1989). These findings are nonexperimental, but they nevertheless suggest that the opportunity to participate actively in group communication increases group commitment.

Despite the advantages of high-tech communication channels, some aspects of communication are still achieved most effectively in face-to-face interaction. Thus, face-to-face gatherings like scientific conventions continue to thrive despite scientists' ready access to e-mail and other forms of electronic communication. Why? For one thing, people who work in groups are happier and more satisfied with their work than are those working alone. Also important is the informal exchange of information, summed up by the maxim that conference attendees generally learn more in the coffee breaks and hallway conversations than in the formal sessions.

When and why researchers might use nonexperimental designs, and why caution might be needed in interpreting results from such studies, was discussed in more detail in Chapter 2, page 34.

Perhaps most important, the emotional ties that develop from actual interaction seem essential for the growth of interpersonal trust and commitment, as well as group solidarity. Some purely electronic collaborations may fail because their members cannot develop the same level of trust as when they exchange jokes and gossip over lunch or trade idle chit-chat (Goldberg, 1997). Physical proximity seems to be essential for this type of frequent, informal interaction.

Electronic communication is also better for some types of tasks than for others. As we have said, for simple tasks like generating ideas or collecting information to make decisions, electronic communication works well, often as well as or better than face-to-face interactions. But what about more complex tasks that involve negotiation or resolution of conflicts? The opportunity to read nonverbal cues like approval and disapproval or tension and relief gives face-to-face interaction an advantage in solving such complex interpersonal problems (Hollingshead, McGrath, & O'Connor, 1993; McGrath & Hollingshead, 1993; Rutter & Robinson, 1981).

Another problem with electronic communication is evident in a study of students who worked cooperatively on large-scale projects, either in face-to-face groups or by interactive videoconferencing (Storck & Sproull, 1995). After considerable collaborative work, each student rated how much he or she would like to work together in the future with other members of his or her group. The ratings in the face-to-face condition reflected mainly the other student's actual competence and task performance. Evidently it is easy to gain a solid impression of another's skills when interacting in person. In contrast, the ratings made by students in the videoconference condition were less influenced by the other individual's task skills and more by task-irrelevant characteristics, such as physical appearance and how effectively the person used the video medium. The effectiveness of real-world organizations may suffer if people are selected for collaborations based on such irrelevant factors rather than their task-related skills.

THE COMPUTER AS A GROUP MEMBER. A new possibility is coming into existence, based on today's powerful, networked computers. Instead of acting as a simple communications device (like a telephone) that allows us to interact with partners and teammates in other locations, the computer itself can become a partner or collaborator: researching, sorting, evaluating, or displaying information, and even recommending conclusions. Byron Reeves and Clifford Nass (1996) found that in many ways, people tend to treat interactive computers like fellow humans. For example, when people interact with a computer that provides information and makes suggestions in a decision-making task, whether or not the computer is identified as a "teammate" strongly affects reactions to it. In one condition of this study, the person and computer were both labeled as members of the "Blue Team" and instructions stated that their task performance would be evaluated jointly. In another condition, the computer was not labeled as a team member and people were told that they would be evaluated solely on their own work (with the computer there just to help). Although the computer's actual contributions were the same in all conditions, people liked the computer better and saw its contributions as more relevant and helpful when it was identified as a teammate. Perhaps most important, people actually changed their own decisions more to comply with the computer's suggestions when the computer was presented as a teammate than when it was there just to help! Of course, these effects parallel those we discussed in Chapters 6 and 9: People like other people better, rate them more positively, and accept more social influence from them, when they share group membership.

■ **The new face of work . . . not face to face**. Today, many employees keep in touch with colleagues and with clients using computers, telephones, fax machines, and electronic mail. Research shows that such forms of communication often aid the performance of simple tasks by smoothing task interdependence and coordination, But today's trend toward working at home has another side, as the benefits of social interdependence—such as higher morale and better solutions to complex problems—can be lost.

Groups incorporate technological changes into their communication patterns. Nevertheless, although the means of communicating are new, the end remains the same: effective task performance and the maintenance of group morale. From the family to the board of directors, from the hobbyist club to the office staff, we spend much of our lives in groups, trying to get things done. Coordinating actions and feelings is not easy, and groups are sometimes derailed by loafing members, lack of direction, or infighting. But when responsive leadership and appropriate communication help keep everyone and everything on track, groups succeed where no single individual could.

CONCLUDING COMMENTS

 Social life centers on groups, so by understanding how they work we can better understand ourselves as social beings. Interdependence, the sharing of common experiences and of a common fate, is the key to all group processes. Most common-sense ideas about group interaction focus on task interdependence: on the need to coordinate individual skills, roles, and efforts so that the group contributes to mastery goals and obtains concrete rewards for members. This is certainly the focus that drives human-engineering approaches to personnel management, organizational behavior, and management science. Our message in this chapter is slightly different. Task interdependence is important, of course, but social interdependence may be even more important. Our need for a shared understanding of the social world and of our place in it and our concern for being positively connected to others manifest themselves in almost every aspect of our social behavior, and particularly our behavior in face-to-face groups.

The impact of social interdependence and the desire for group membership has been evident since the earliest research on group interaction and leadership. During much of that research, however, investigations viewed these social influences mainly as an impediment to the successful and efficient completion of group tasks. Thus, the social rewards of group membership and the development of group norms were seen as elements that interfered with the goals of production. Today's social psychology offers a different point of view. Far from working against effective task interdependence, social interdependence can exert a positive influence on group behavior. Social, not technological, solutions may be our best bet for eliminating many apparently task-related problems, such as failures of coordination, social loafing, and low productivity. A positive social identity can provide the consensus, cohesion, and cooperation needed to get the job done.

However, we must add a word of caution here. As Chapter 6 made clear, cohesion and cooperation within the in-group often come at the cost of antagonism and hostility toward out-groups. And, as Chapter 9 pointed out, a group can be so intent on feeling good about itself that its decisions and actions are vulnerable to groupthink. Thus, as we have argued before, the optimal solution is always one of balance. The sales group needs enough cohesion to keep morale high and attention focused on their sales goals, but not so much that they are in constant conflict with the production team. The local school board needs enough group identity to maintain its members' enthusiasm about solving the district's problems, but not so much that they suppress doubts and support one another in unrealistic and

CHAPTER 12 THEMES

- **Construction of Reality**
Groups define for their members what their tasks are and how to perform them.

- **Pervasiveness of Social Influence**
Interaction and interdependence in face-to-face groups affects performance on many tasks.

- **Striving for Mastery**
Face-to-face groups bring their members rewards of many kinds.

- **Seeking Connectedness**
Face-to-face groups provide their members with strong feelings of belonging and identity.

- **Valuing Me and Mine**
When we value group membership, we frequently seek to act in the group's interest.

ill-advised decisions. In situations like these we all need to learn how to use a shared group identity to promote both positive feelings and effective group performance. Under ideal conditions, working together in groups can help us to see what we have in common and to cooperate to solve the problems that threaten us all.

SUMMARY

 The Mere Presence of Others: The Effects of Minimal Interdependence. Even when interdependence is minimal, the mere presence of others can produce arousal, either because those others are highly evaluative or because they are distracting. Arousal improves the performance of easy, well-learned behaviors, but can interfere with performance of novel or complex tasks. This pattern is termed **social facilitation**.

Crowding is another source of arousal that can improve performance on easy tasks and disrupt performance on difficult ones. However, the effects of crowding depend on people's interpretation of the situation and on their sense of control.

Performance in Face-to-Face Groups: Interaction and Interdependence. The members of face-to-face groups interact with one another and also share both **task interdependence** and **social interdependence**. Face-to-face groups usually go through different stages of relationship with their members. During group socialization, mutual evaluation can lead groups and individuals to become committed to each other, processes that guide entry, socialization, role maintenance, and sometimes exit, from the group. At the same time groups go through formation, conflict, development of norms, performance, and dissolution as they try to maximize social and task interdependence to develop an identity and reach their goals. Time pressure can affect how groups solve these problems.

To achieve their performance goals, groups must maintain their motivation and avoid problems of coordination. For example, groups must ensure that their members work hard and avoid **social loafing**. Developing a common social identity helps to avoid such problems by encouraging cooperation for group goals, promoting social influence, and attracting and keeping valuable group members.

Effective **leadership** enhances task performance and maintains social interdependence. The ways leaders do this must differ from situation to situation. Sometimes, however, stereotypical thinking prevents the most effective leaders from emerging in groups. Some types of leadership are particularly likely to help align individual and group goals and these leaders may help groups be particularly successful. Of course such extraordinary influence can be used in destructive as well as constructive ways.

High productivity and high morale can be achieved only through communication. Groups use both formal and informal channels to make sure communication is effective. Technology, including video and e-mail, is now altering communication patterns and therefore many aspects of group performance.

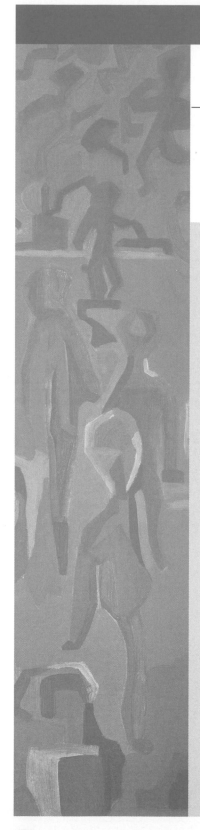

13

Aggression and Conflict

On June 19, 1954, two groups of 11-year-old boys tumbled out of buses to start summer camp in the Sans Bois Mountains near Oklahoma City, Oklahoma. Robbers Cave State Park, named for the hideout of the notorious outlaw Jesse James, offered a 200-acre site with fishing, swimming, canoeing, hiking, and the usual camp games and sports. The new arrivals were ordinary White, middle-class boys with no record of school, psychological, or behavioral problems. They had nothing on their minds except high hopes for a fun-filled 3-week vacation.

The camp was more than it seemed, however. Unknown to the boys, their parents had agreed to let them participate in a field study of intergroup conflict set up by Muzafer Sherif and his colleagues—a study that came to be known as the Robbers Cave experiment (Sherif, Harvey, White, Hood, & Sherif, 1961). The boys did not know that the camp counselors and directors were social psychologists and research assistants. Nor, at first, did members of each group know that another group was sharing the campsite.

During the first week, as they took part in separate activities designed to promote group cohesion, each group developed norms and leaders. They gave themselves names, the Eagles and the Rattlers, and each group designed a flag. Toward the end of the week, the groups discovered each other. Seeing "those guys" using "our ball field" and "our hiking trails" sparked demands for a competition. The staff were only too pleased to arrange a 4-day tournament including baseball, tug-of-war, a treasure hunt, and other events. The experimenters even promised the winners a fancy trophy, shiny badges, and four-bladed pocketknives. Both groups practiced hard, cheered their teammates, and roundly booed and insulted the competition. Hostilities escalated as the tournament progressed, culminating in a flag burning when the Eagles lost the tug-of-war.

The Eagles ultimately won the tournament, collecting the trophy and the coveted pocketknives. But while they were taking a celebratory swim, the Rattlers raided their cabins and stole the prizes. The rivalry had turned into full-blown war, and the staff was kept busy silencing name calling, breaking up fist fights, and cleaning up after cabin raids and food fights. The experiment had transformed

22 perfectly normal boys into two gangs of brawling troublemakers, full of hostility and intent on exacting revenge for every real or imagined slight.

As you may have guessed, Sherif and his colleagues set up this situation to understand how intergroup hostilities develop and how they can be resolved. This issue is one of the most significant facing the world today: As of 2005, there were 19 significant ongoing conflicts (*Information Please*, 2006). Unrest and hostility mar not only international relations but also interactions between ethnic, political, and religious groups. And conflict and violence occur among individuals as well as groups. Newspaper headlines scream of drive-by shootings, street crimes, spouse and child abuse, barroom fights, even, tragically, shootings in schools by young students themselves.

This chapter examines the social and cognitive processes that underlie aggression—behavior intended to hurt other people—at both individual and intergroup levels. First, we discuss whether the seeming pervasiveness of aggression means that it is fundamentally part of human nature, built in by evolution and therefore unalterable. Then we describe the reasons that individuals act aggressively as well as the factors that can turn groups into rivals or deadly enemies. Finally, we consider what social psychology tells us about ways to reduce aggression, based on our understanding of its causes and dynamics. As we will see, the goal of reducing aggression draws on virtually everything we know about how people perceive and interact with each other, and requires not only stopping open hostilities but moving beyond that to resolve differences in ways that benefit all parties.

Aggression, Conflict, and Human Nature

Defining Conflict and Aggression

Incompatible goals often set the stage for aggression, which is defined by people's immediate intention to hurt each other.

Aggression often has its roots in **conflict**, which is defined as a perceived incompatibility of goals: What one party wants, the other party sees as harmful to its interests. Conflict between individuals and groups is acted out in many forums: complaints between neighbors about loud parties, protracted litigation in courtrooms, bloody battles in war zones. Whether the conflict is between Coke and Pepsi, labor and management, or candidates competing for a desirable promotion on the job, individuals and groups in conflict try to belittle, outdo, or frustrate the opponent and to extend and protect their own interests. The conflicts at the heart of these disputes frequently focus on mastery of material resources and social rewards.

Turning to the term *aggression*, this word is used in a variety of imprecise ways in everyday language: You might apply the term to a fast-talking salesperson or a stalwart defensive player in a team sport. For social psychologists, the term is defined by the actor's motive: **Aggression** is behavior whose immediate intent is to hurt someone. Accidentally injuring someone in a football game is not aggression, but cursing out the referee is. Even doing nothing at all, such as intentionally failing to warn a rival of impending danger, could be aggressive. Aggression is defined by a behavior's immediate goal, even if the longer-range goal may be different: thus, trying to injure an opposing player is aggression, even if the ultimate goal of the act is not to harm the player but to win the game or to earn increased playing time by

Conflict. A perceived incompatibility of goals between two or more parties.

Aggression. Behavior intended to harm someone else.

impressing the coach (Bushman & Anderson, 2001a). As we will see throughout this chapter, aggression frequently grows out of conflict between two parties, but can also be driven by strong negative emotions, such as anger or frustration.

Origins of Aggression

Humans have evolved to compete effectively for food and mates. Although the capacity to act aggressively may have helped, aggression has no special place in "human nature." Aggression is just one strategy among many others that humans use to attain rewards and respect in accordance with individual perceptions and social norms.

You may be wondering if social psychology, with its emphasis on beliefs, emotions, interpretations, and norms, can really explain aggression. Has evolution built aggression into our very genetic make-up? And if it is part of our biological inheritance, does that make it both inevitable and uncontrollable? One popular view of evolution's role in human aggression certainly sees evolution as shaping humans to be fundamentally and unalterably selfish. According to this "beast within" view (Klama, 1988), "survival of the fittest" has bred aggressive impulses into human brain and bone (Lorenz, 1966). From this perspective, it is "human nature" to be aggressive.

Modern evolutionary psychology offers a considerably more sophisticated view (D. M. Buss & Kendrick, 1998). According to this more recent perspective, "human nature" includes a wide variety of psychological mechanisms and motives that have contributed to survival and reproduction over the millennia. Competition for food and mates, especially among males, really means competition for status and resources. In most animal species as well as most human groups, those males with the highest status and the most resources father more offspring than do less fortunate males (D. M. Buss & Kendrick, 1998). The evolutionary viewpoint also predicts that men should generally be more aggressive than women, a pattern that has been confirmed by recent meta-analyses of relevant research (Archer, 2004). The sex difference is evident for both physical and verbal aggression, and is particularly large for the most dangerous types of aggression, such as aggression involving weapons. The sex difference is no larger for adolescents or adults than for children, as might be expected if it was purely due to children's gradual learning of social roles (Archer, 2005). In fact, there is some evidence that males' greater aggressiveness is related to levels of exposure to testosterone before birth (Bailey & Hurd, 2005).

But in human groups, at least, such evolutionary influences do not mean that only the most aggressive men have had the evolutionary advantage. In human societies, competition, like all other human behaviors, has taken on many forms. Any behavior that promoted and maintained status and resources, including the ability to form alliances with others, to learn from others, and to cooperate to overcome hardships, is likely to have become part of our genetic inheritance (D. M. Buss & Kenrick, 1998; Caporael, 1997; H. A. Simon, 1990). Far from concluding that aggression is the defining aspect of human nature, evolutionary psychology actually tells us that aggression is one technique *among many others* that humans use as they strive for mastery of material resources as well as respect and connectedness to others.

You will recognize these as the fundamental motives that we have discussed throughout this text. The specific techniques that people will use in the service of those motives in any particular situation depend, of course, on the relevant norms as well as the individual's assessment of a technique's likely success and effectiveness. In other words, both individual thought processes and social influence affect the experience and the expression of aggression, just as they do other biologically based motives. Think about hunger, for example. Experiencing hunger does not inevitably lead to eating. Unsocialized infants may get away with stuffing into their mouths any food (or nonfood) within reach, but adults in most societies satisfy their hunger in less direct ways. The ways we experience hunger, the items we define as food, and the ways we act when hungry are all strongly influenced by what and how we think, as well as the norms of the groups we live in. The triggering of aggressive impulses, and our decisions about whether to act on those impulses, are influenced by the same cognitive processes and the same social forces that have played such a big role in every other form of social behavior discussed in this text.

Interpersonal Aggression

Aggression in many forms is ubiquitous throughout the world. On a big-city street, a mugger displays a knife and demands that a tourist hand over his wallet. In a bar, a beer-fueled argument between two acquaintances suddenly turns from shouted insults to shoves and punches. Infuriated by a minor traffic accident, one driver jumps from his car and begins screaming red-faced at the other driver. Despite the range and variety of aggressive behaviors, they generally fall into two distinct categories. Threatening harm and demanding a wallet is an instance of *instrumental aggression*, or aggression serving mastery needs—aggression used as a means to an end, to control other people or to obtain valuable resources. Punching someone in an escalating barroom argument is *hostile aggression*, which is often driven by spontaneous anger due to insult, disrespect, or other threats to self-esteem. Instrumental and hostile forms of aggression generally show somewhat different patterns, although the dividing line between these two is not always completely clear. For example, if someone who is insulted in public punches the provoker in the nose, that aggressive act is likely driven both by anger and by consideration of the act's concrete effects—such as deterring that person and others from future provocations (Bushman & Anderson, 2001a).

Either form of aggression, hostile or instrumental, always involves the intention to harm someone. The road from intention to action is a long one, however, and it is posted with cognitive and social signs that can either check our aggressive impulses or hurry us along the path. What factors motivate one person to hurt another? How do norms regulate aggression? Social psychologists have tried to answer these and other questions in their research on aggression.

Studying Aggression

Aggression can be difficult to study experimentally because people are often unwilling to act aggressively when they are being observed. Researchers have used a variety of techniques to get around these problems.

Aggression in everyday life is, unfortunately, easy to observe. Researchers have watched as schoolchildren pushed, shoved, and punched each other on the playground, as professional sports teams crossed the boundary from rough play to violence, and as urban street gangs fought over territory and bragging rights. Some researchers have even used official records of violent crimes to test hypotheses about aggression.

Studying aggression in the laboratory is much more difficult than observing it elsewhere. For ethical reasons, researchers cannot set up situations in which people actually harm one another. In addition, adults are reluctant to act aggressively in a research setting where they know they are being observed. As a result, laboratory researchers have been forced to develop cleverly disguised techniques. In one frequently used procedure, developed by Arnold Buss (1961), participants are told that they and another participant are in a study of the effects of punishment on learning. A rigged drawing assigns the participant to the "teacher" role, and the other participant, actually a confederate, is given the role of "learner." The teacher is instructed to deliver electric shocks to punish the learner for wrong answers. The intensity and duration of the shocks selected by the teacher on the "aggression machine" serve as measures of aggression. The learner, of course, never actually receives any shocks.

You might worry that measures like these lack construct validity. Do they really measure aggression as the researchers intend? What if participants deliver the shocks not with the intent to harm—the definition of aggression—but because they believe the shocks will facilitate learning? In response to such questions, researchers have demonstrated that people who are highly aggressive outside the laboratory also score the highest on laboratory measures, indicating that those measures possess some construct validity (Anderson & Bushman, 1997; Carlson, Marcus-Newhall, & Miller, 1989). And as you will see throughout this chapter, most key findings have been confirmed both in laboratory and non-laboratory studies. It is interesting to note, however, that one common, everyday form of aggression, verbal assaults such as insults, curses, or ethnic slurs, is only now beginning to receive attention from researchers (Harmon-Jones & Sigelman, 2001). Words, too, can be delivered with the intent to harm. As we all realized as children, sticks and stones may break our bones, but names can also hurt us. Adults as well as children hurt one another with nonphysical forms of aggression such as name-calling, spreading vicious gossip, and employing the silent treatment (Archer & Coyne, 2005).

Despite the difficulties researchers face in investigating aggression, a number of clear patterns emerge from their studies. As you will see, many of these patterns appear consistently across different types of research, both in the lab and in the field. They show that aggression is usually triggered by perceptions and interpretations of some event or situation.

You may recall from Chapter 10, pages 369 to 372, that Stanley Milgram adapted this method for his famous study of obedience to authority.

What Triggers Aggression?

Some aggression is a result of mastery needs. Potential rewards make this kind of aggression more likely and costs or risks make it less likely. Sometimes, however, perceived provocation such as a threat to self-esteem or connectedness produces anger, which can also set off aggression. Any negative emotion, in fact, can make aggression more likely.

Instrumental aggression, motivated by the prospect of rewards, and hostile aggression, driven by anger or other negative feelings, have somewhat different causes. But in either case we will see that aggression, like so many other behaviors, depends on the

■ **An opportunity for aggression?** Designers of ATM machines probably did not imagine them as a possible site for aggression, but users of machines often sense the potential for danger in such situations. The combination of people with their back turned and easy access to cash can offer an opportunity for gain that might make instrumental aggression more likely.

individual's perceptions and interpretations of other people, their behavior, and the situations in which behavior occurs.

INSTRUMENTAL AGGRESSION: COUNTING MATERIAL COSTS AND REWARDS. When people see an opportunity for gain, they may aggress: a lone woman withdrawing money from a cash machine, or an opponent blocking the goal as the referee looks the other way (Tedeschi & Felson, 1994). This instrumental aggression often involves more systematic thinking about the situation, as opposed to an immediate emotional reaction.

When aggression pays, it becomes more likely (Bandura, 1973; G. R. Patterson, Littman, & Bricker, 1967). Perhaps it's no surprise, then, that children who believe aggression will lead to rewards or will prevent other kids from hurting them are the most aggressive in school (Perry, Perry, & Rasmussen, 1986). Conversely, when rewards are withdrawn, aggression usually subsides. Getting tough on terrorists—refusing to bargain with hijackers, hostage takers, and kidnappers—requires a heart of stone, but it eliminates the value of their tactics (B. Rubin, 1987). Even the threat of punishment can deter aggression, if the threat is believed (R. A. Baron, 1983a; Zillmann, 1979). If aggression depends on mastery motivation, that is, on people's perceptions of potential rewards and costs, what factors influence those perceptions?

1. *Personal abilities.* For someone who is large and muscular or knows how to fight or to wield a knife or gun, aggression becomes easier—and a low perceived cost increases aggression. Children who think aggression is easy, or who have used it successfully to gain rewards in the past, are more likely to use it again (G. R. Patterson and others, 1967; Perry and others, 1986).

2. *Gender differences.* Aggression is usually easier and less risky for men than for women, so men find it more rewarding and less costly. The meta-analysis by Archer (2004) found that men are generally more likely to act aggressively than women, and this finding applies to both physical and verbal aggression. One reason is that men see aggression as less dangerous than women do.

3. *What do I have to lose?* Potential costs of aggression include retaliation from the intended victim, as well as the risk of being punished through legal action or social ostracism. It may seem hard to understand why anyone would risk these severe consequences for gains that are often trivial—the average take in robberies and burglaries is only around $80 (Baumeister, 1997). To explain this phenomenon we must consider the perspective from which criminals, who come mostly from the poorest strata of society, assess their alternatives. First, for someone lacking education or living in an area without employment opportunities, aggression and crime may appear to be the only available means to resources and respect, even if they are accurately viewed as not very promising means (Gottfredson & Hirschi, 1990). Second, the risks of a criminal record or even a jail sentence might not loom as large for someone who, because of poverty, drug addiction, or lack of skills, has little hope of a secure and satisfying future in any case. Someone who has nothing has nothing to lose. For these reasons, poverty is the single

most important background factor in aggression, including murder (H. Hill, Soriano, Chen, & LaFromboise, 1994).

HOSTILE AGGRESSION: EMOTIONAL RESPONSES TO PROVOCATIONS. Some aggression is not motivated by the systematic calculus of material gain and loss. Hostile aggression frequently occurs when threats to someone's self-esteem or connections to valued people or groups generate anger or other negative emotions. Such provocations sometimes lead people to act aggressively without regard even to the likelihood of immediate punishment (R. A. Baron, 1983a). Hostile aggression can involve immediate reactions in blind fury, or carefully planned and deliberated acts. On April 20, 1999, two high school students at Columbine High School in Colorado shot and killed 12 classmates and one teacher, before killing themselves. School and workplace shootings such as the Columbine massacre are examples of aggression motivated not by gain but by anger. Dylan Klebold and Eric Harris, the Columbine shooters, left behind journals detailing their hatred of the athletes who teased them and put them down at school (Cullen, 2004). This example reflects an important general truth: Angry feelings and impulses toward aggression can readily be provoked by a threat to self-esteem or connectedness, for example, by insult, derogation, or disrespect (Baumeister, 1997). Being coldly turned down when you ask someone for a date, or being berated by an angry co-worker who believes you have messed up an important job: Interactions like these are likely to trigger thoughts that the evaluator is biased and unfair, and can lead to anger and aggressive action. Any blow to self-esteem is worse if it is public, because it is harder to just let an insult go by if others have witnessed the event. Thus, paradoxically, the presence of an audience may make aggressive responses to self-esteem threats more likely. One study found that more than half of murders were committed in front of an audience (Luckinbill, 1977).

PERSONALITY DIFFERENCES IN RESPONSES TO PROVOCATIONS. People differ greatly in the ways they react to self-esteem threats. You may have heard that people who act aggressively typically have low self-esteem, and some research bears this out (Donnellan, Trzesniewski, Robins, Moffit, & Caspi, 2005). Since people with low self-esteem might not have the inner resources to cope with frustrations, they might be more likely to react to everyday setbacks or social challenges with aggression. But certain other individuals are also highly likely to commit aggression: *narcissists*, or people with very high, but insecure, self-esteem (Baumeister, 1997; Kernis, Grannemann, & Barclay, 1989; Donnellan and others, 2005). The self-esteem of these individuals is fragile and unstable, fluctuating with each new episode of social praise or rejection (Jordan, Spencer, Zanna, Hoshino-Browne, & Correll, 2003). Someone with stable and secure high self-esteem may brush off an insult or rejection, knowing that it is off target. But narcissists are more likely to respond to social rejection with aggression, sometimes even lashing out against people who are not responsible for the slight (Twenge & Campbell, 2003). So low self-esteem and high but unstable self-esteem might both lead to aggression, but for different reasons.

Some children are especially likely to interpret ambiguous acts as intentional disrespect and thus as threats to self-esteem. These youngsters tend to become chronically aggressive (Crick & Dodge, 1994). They may interpret unintentional collisions on the playground as deliberate and may then retaliate, possibly starting a cycle of violence. Although this perceptual bias has a strong role in hostile aggression, it has no impact on instrumental aggression, such as bullying a younger child out of his lunch money (Dodge & Coie, 1987). Findings such as this support the belief that hostile and instrumental aggression are two somewhat distinct forms. Nevertheless, we should remember that most aggression probably involves multiple motives: strong feelings of anger as well as some concern with the potential rewards or costs of the aggressive act (Bushman & Anderson, 2001a).

HOSTILE AGGRESSION: THE ROLE OF NEGATIVE FEELINGS. The Columbine shooters did not limit their anger to people who had actually insulted or disrespected them. Their diaries also detailed their loathing for racists, martial arts experts, Star Wars fans, and even people who brag about their cars. They massacred students indiscriminately and set off bombs in the school cafeteria. The goal was to "Kill the world," not simply to punish people who had affronted them (Cullen, 2004). As this tragic example illustrates, hostile aggression is not limited to striking back at a provoker. In fact, one of the most influential early theories of aggression, *frustration-aggression theory*, held that any frustration—defined as the blocking of an important goal—inevitably triggers aggression (Dollard, Doob, Miller, Mowrer, & Sears, 1939). Early research evidence supported frustration-aggression theory, but critiques and conflicting data soon started to accumulate (N. E. Miller, 1941). More recently, Leonard Berkowitz (1989) outlined a broader model that also accounts for the original evidence linking frustration and aggression. According to Berkowitz, any negative feelings can set off aggression. Such feelings include not only frustration and anger but also pain, fear, and irritation. As Berkowitz (1993) put it, "We're nasty when we feel bad."

Berkowitz seems to be right. We now know that a variety of conditions that create negative feelings—unpleasant heat or painful cold, stressful noises, crowding, even noxious odors and air pollution—can trigger aggression (Berkowitz & Harmon-Jones, 2004; Geen, 1998; Lindsay & Anderson, 2000). The relationship between heat and aggression, for example, has been established in both field and laboratory studies (R. A. Baron, 1972; Rule, Taylor, & Dobbs, 1987). Examination of weather and crime records reveals that when the outdoor temperature is high, there is an increase in the incidence of violent crimes, including murder and rape (Rotton & Cohn, 2000). But even negative feelings or frustration do not invariably lead to aggression, for norms strongly shape and control its expression.

Norms Promoting and Restraining Aggression

> Social norms can either promote or restrain aggression. They can be activated by the behavior of models witnessed in person or in the media. Norms that limit aggression apply especially strongly to aggression against similar others or in-group members.

Because aggression is a potentially destructive force, virtually all societies and groups have norms that regulate it. This does not mean that all norms operate to squelch aggression. As you will see, group norms often promote aggressive behavior rather than restrain it.

NORMS PROMOTING AGGRESSION. According to one Chicago teenager, the code of the streets includes: "Never, ever, disrespect anybody." The reason? Norms in the teenager's neighborhood dictate violent responses to disrespect. "People won't fistfight . . . . They'd shoot me, step over my dead body and go about their business" (Terry, 1993). Urban gangs are not the only groups whose norms support aggression (M. W. Klein, 1969; Reicher, 1987). In some cultures, "crimes of passion" such as killing a romantic rival are judged leniently by public opinion and may even draw light sentences from the courts. When corporate managers fix prices and violate patent and copyright laws, their actions reflect a business norm that condones any action in the pursuit of profit. These business strategies, together with fraud and tax evasion, have caused more economic loss than theft and vandalism (President's Commission on Law Enforcement, 1967).

Among developed nations, the United States ranks first in assaults per capita, third in overall murders, and second in murders with firearms (United Nations, 2000). Is there something about U.S. culture that makes aggression easier or more acceptable than in, for example, European countries? Several norms unique to the United States seem to provide an answer.

1. *The right to bear firearms and to use them.* In the United States, this right is viewed not only as a way to resist tyrannical government, as foreseen in the U.S. Constitution, but as a response to perceived threats to home or hearth. Many people in the United States believe it is appropriate for a householder to shoot an intruder in his or her home, and some states have passed laws explicitly providing immunity from prosecution in such situations. American public opinion even favors a tough line with petty criminals: In one case, a judge in Marion, Indiana, congratulated a defendant who shot and crippled a purse-snatcher, saying, "My thanks, sir, for having tried to do something to help the problems in this country" (Newsweek, 1990a).

2. *The norm of family privacy.* The old saying that a man's home is his castle represents the idea that private homes are havens, safe from public intrusion. The norm of family privacy may exempt family life from public standards of behavior. In doing so, this norm often increases violence within the home (Berk & Newton, 1985; L. W. Sherman & Berk, 1984). Family members have several features that make them tragically frequent targets of aggression. Perhaps the most obvious is simply that they are there: Close quarters and frequent interaction make it easy for people to "rub each other the wrong way," leading to annoyance and possibly aggression. Differences in size and power also make weaker family members less able to retaliate. Finally, social norms condone aggression between parents and children that would not be tolerated between strangers. Imagine the quick action that would be taken if a restaurant owner slapped a customer's child for not eating his or her vegetables! Norms supporting traditional family power structures, though they are gradually changing, may also encourage aggression against women and children (Vandello & Cohen, 2003).

3. *The "culture of honor."* Though you might imagine that the highest homicide rates in the United States are found in densely populated urban areas, this is not the case. In 2003, for example, the rate of violent crime in South Carolina (a mostly rural state) was the highest in the United States at 793.5 per 100,000 inhabitants, more than twice as high as that of densely populated Connecticut at 308.2 per 100,000 (Federal Bureau of Investigation, 2003). Homicide rates generally tend to be highest in the generally rural and agricultural Southern states. What factor could explain this regional pattern, even outweighing the crowding and poverty so prevalent in the large cities of the North and East? One answer is provided by Richard Nisbett and Dov Cohen (1996): the persistence of what they term a "culture of honor" which involves a special readiness to respond with aggression to perceived insults or threats of material loss.

When the South was first settled, sheep and cattle herding were predominant occupations, and with law enforcement essentially nonexistent, a herder had to be ready to use violence to defend himself against thieves and rustlers. Nisbett and Cohen argue that this cultural tendency has persisted to the present day. They cite survey data that show Southern White males, compared to those from other regions, are more likely to endorse aggression in defense of property or in retaliation for insults (D. Cohen & Nisbett, 1997). Cohen and others (D. Cohen, Nisbett, Bowdle, & Schwartz, 1996) even found that among students attending the University of Michigan, those from the South were more likely than students from Northern states to respond with anger to a staged insult in a laboratory study.

The Southern United States is not the only culture that places a high value on honor. Some Mediterranean, Middle Eastern, and Latin American cultures similarly emphasize the importance of loyalty and male toughness. Research by Vandello and Cohen (2003) supports the idea that the culture of honor in other societies is also linked to endorsement of aggression. In their study, participants from Brazil (which they classified as an honor culture) and the Northern United States read about a couple that had been married for 7 years when the husband discovered that his wife had been unfaithful. In one version of the scenario, the husband yelled at his wife, while in the other version, the husband yelled at her and hit her. After reading the scenario, participants answered questions about how much the husband loved his wife and to what extent his actions were justified. U.S. participants thought the husband who hit his wife loved her less than did the husband who only yelled at his wife. However, Brazilian participants did not see hitting as reflecting less love for his spouse, and overall they saw aggression as more justified than U.S. participants did. Thus, the "culture of honor" illustrates one type of cultural influence on when and whether people turn to aggression (M. H. Bond, 2004).

CULTURAL CUES TO AGGRESSION. It is no wonder that weapons, and especially guns, are strongly associated with the idea of aggression (Huesmann & Eron, 1984). If seeing a weapon cues thoughts of aggression, this in turn should make aggressive behavior more likely—and so it does, in an outcome termed the *weapons effect* (C. A. Anderson, Anderson, & Deuser, 1996; Berkowitz & LePage, 1967). In one nonlaboratory study of this effect, Charles Turner and his associates set up a booth at a campus carnival and invited students to throw sponges at a target person. Passersby threw more sponges when they could see a rifle that had been placed nearby than when no rifle was present (C. W. Turner, Simons, Berkowitz, & Frodi, 1977). Another study showed that motorists stopped by police officers acted more aggressively when the officers carried a holstered pistol than when they did not (Boyanowsky & Griffiths, 1982). Thus, the presence of a gun may not only make aggression more deadly, it may also make it more likely in the first place. Of course, it is a person's thoughts and feelings about guns or other cues that shape their effects, and people may differ in this way. For example, one study found that experienced hunters did not become more aggressive when shown images of hunting rifles, because their associations with those guns did not involve aggression against other people (Bartholow, Anderson, Carnagey, & Benjamin, 2005). Like other individuals, though, the hunters' aggressiveness was increased by images of nonhunting guns, such as military assault rifles.

Thus, perceiving a weapon can make aggression more likely. This fact gives special importance to the fact that common stereotypes can make observers more ready to see—or to imagine they see—a gun in the hands of members of some groups than of others. In a study that we discussed in Chapter 5, Keith Payne (2001) found that students were more likely to mis-categorize images of common tools (such as a hammer or pliers) as guns when they were preceded by a photo of a Black male (compared to a White male) on the computer screen. These effects occurred automatically, even when the research participants were told to ignore the photos of faces, and generally take place outside the perceiver's conscious awareness. If you're wondering what this laboratory study has to do with real life, consider the case of Amadou Diallo, a Black man. On February 4, 1999, undercover police officers knocked on Diallo's door in New York. When the police identified themselves, Amadou Diallo reached for something in his pocket. The officers, mistaking the object for a gun, fired 41 shots, hitting Diallo 19 times and killing him instantly. Diallo had been reaching for his wallet, presumably in order to show the police his ID.

MODELS OF AGGRESSION. Not only culturally defined cues but also other people's actions offer clues to the norms appropriate in a situation. Models who demonstrate the appropriateness of nonviolent solutions to conflict can reduce aggression. Unfortunately, aggressive models not only show people ways to act aggressively but also send the message that an aggressive response is right, correct, and acceptable, and others soon imitate them (Bandura, Ross, & Ross, 1961, 1963). For example, at many sporting events, violence among fans is often preceded by aggressive play on the field (J. H. Goldstein, 1982).

Laboratory studies confirm the powerful impact that models have on aggressive behavior. Compared with those who had watched an innocuous film, people who had watched a film of a highly aggressive boxing match gave other participants stronger shocks on Buss's "aggression machine" (Bushman & Geen, 1990). Exposure to aggressive models makes violent behavior seem more appropriate because it stimulates aggressive thoughts and feelings (Bargh & Gollwitzer, 1993).

Tragically, people often encounter aggressive models in their own homes. Children of abusive parents learn at an early age that aggression is both appropriate and acceptable. Indeed, until recently, surveys in the United States indicated that public opinion supported the physical punishment of children as legitimate and necessary (Gelles, 1972). Yet in the home, as elsewhere, aggressive acts teach aggressive norms. Children who have been maltreated are more likely to aggress in social situations (Shields & Ciccheti, 1998), and as adults are more likely than others to abuse their own children or spouses (Sugarman & Hotaling, 1989; Widom, 1989).

☐ **AGGRESSIVE MODELS IN THE MEDIA.** Even children from peaceful homes are exposed to an enormous amount of violence because of the amount of time they spend watching television. By the seventh grade, the average American child has seen more than 8000 television murders and 100,000 acts of violence in the media (Bushman & Anderson, 2001b). Adults too see a lot of violence on television; one recent study found that 61% of television programs depicted violence (Anderson and others, 2003). Does aggressive media content stimulate viewers' aggression? Some people believe that watching aggressive TV shows, playing violent video games, or engaging in low-level aggression in sports can actually make people less aggressive over time. The idea of *catharsis*—that expressing an emotion can keep it from "building up"—has been around for a long time, and if it were true, then "letting out" aggressive impulses in relatively harmless ways might prevent or diminish later aggression. Unfortunately, the evidence consistently disconfirms the catharsis idea. Aggressing or witnessing aggression not only doesn't make people feel calmer, it makes them more angry (Anderson and others, 2004; Bushman, Baumeister, & Stack, 1999).

Aggressive media content can also lead people to interpret other people's behavior as hostile (Bushman & Anderson, 2002).

These results suggest that violent media content might have the effect of making people more aggressive, and that is what the evidence generally shows. Many studies have demonstrated that people who view more hours of violent television (Singer & Singer, 1981), listen to music with violent lyrics (Anderson, Carnagey, & Eubanks, 2003), or play violent video games (Anderson & Dill, 2000) tend to be more aggressive. However, some of these studies have nonexperimental designs that are weak on internal validity and cannot show that violent media *causes* aggression. Other causal relationships could lead to the same pattern of results. For example, parental neglect could both make children aggressive and cause them to spend a lot of time watching TV.

Experimental research can overcome this weakness. In one classic experiment, incarcerated delinquent boys were randomly assigned to view aggressive films or nonaggressive films every evening for a week (Parke, Berkowitz, Leyens, West, & Sebastian, 1977). The young men's aggressive behavior was observed both before and after the "film week," and boys who saw aggressive films committed more physical attacks than those who viewed neutral films. We can conclude that film viewing caused aggression because of the high internal validity of the experimental design, and this conclusion is supported by a meta-analysis of 28 different field experiments (W. Wood, Wong, & Chachere, 1991). However, most of these studies were relatively short term, examining the effects of only days or weeks of viewing.

Perhaps the most powerful findings on the issue come from longitudinal studies, which assess television viewing and aggressiveness over a long period of time to attempt to determine which variable causes the other. One ambitious study, which followed a group of participants for 22 years, found that those who watched more TV violence at age 8 were more likely to have been convicted for violent crimes by age 30 (Huesmann, 1986). These findings were confirmed in a 3-year multination study in the United States, Finland, Israel, and Poland

(Huesmann & Eron, 1986). Though time-consuming and costly to carry out, longitudinal research has important strengths: The variables can be measured in natural settings and strong causal conclusions can be drawn.

A consistent conclusion can be drawn from all these different studies: aggressive media content does increase viewers' aggressive behavior (Anderson and others, 2004; Liebert & Sprafkin, 1988). Perhaps even more ominously, the effect seems to be long-lasting. Studies indicate that, over the long term, witnessing violence dulls our perceptions and numbs our reactions, eventually leading to indifference and acceptance. For example, boys who watch a great deal of violence on television are not aroused by viewing a brutal boxing match (Cline, Croft, & Courrier, 1973). Frequent viewers of "slasher" movies are relatively unconcerned about violence toward women (Donnerstein, Linz, & Penrod, 1987).

Perhaps most unsettling, a recent study in the United States found that nearly 75% of violent scenes on TV, including cartoon shows viewed by very young children, involved no remorse, criticism, or penalty for the perpetrator (B. Wilson and others, 1998). What norms are these shows reinforcing? One of the authors of the study, Barbara Wilson, put the issue into context: "Even one televised depiction that encourages a child to drink poison or play with fire would surely come under great public attack. Here we have the average preschooler who's watching cartoons seeing over 500 high-risk portrayals that encourage aggression in a typical year" (National Public Radio, 1998).

NORMS RESTRAINING AGGRESSION. Of course, not all models and norms foster aggression. Most societies maintain and teach some norms that limit and inhibit aggression. "Pick on someone your own size," like many other norms, forbids aggression against the weak and helpless. And although "an eye for an eye, a tooth for a tooth" seems to be a formula for revenge, its original purpose was to prevent retaliation from spiraling out of control.

Some groups have developed norms that effectively counteract aggression. Anthropological reports indicate that among the Inuit of the Arctic, the Pygmies of Africa, and the Zuni and Blackfoot peoples of North America, controversy and conflict are avoided, physical violence is rare, and war is nonexistent (Gorer, 1968). Japanese social norms also dictate that it is often better to yield than fight, as reflected in the expression *Makeru ga kachi* "to lose is to win" (Alcock, Carment, & Sadava, 1988; Triandis, Bontempo, Villareal, Asai, & Lucca, 1988).

Norms are usually most effective in limiting aggression against other in-group members. Thus, similarity reduces aggression, and it does so for two reasons. First, as we have seen in Chapter 6, shared group membership breeds liking, and positive feelings for another person are incompatible with aggression (P. A. Miller & Eisenberg, 1988). Second, the norms of most groups proscribe or strictly control aggression within the group so that cohesion can be maintained and group goals achieved. In-group members are protected by a norm that appears to warn, "Don't hurt me. I'm one of us." Unfortunately, as we will see, these norms are less likely to protect outsiders.

To Hurt or Not to Hurt: Putting It All Together

Situations that favor superficial thinking often favor aggression. Thinking carefully can reduce aggression, but many factors interfere with people's motivation and ability to process information carefully and evenhandedly, increasing the likelihood of aggression.

Situational cues can have similar effects on us in other contexts when we do not process thoroughly. The impact of heuristic cues on persuasion during superficial processing was discussed in Chapter 7, pages 238 to 245, and the effect of physical and behavioral cues on the spontaneous formation of first impressions was discussed in Chapter 3, pages 59 to 64.

What if you really want to smack your roommate, but know it would be wrong? What happens when the messages we get from environmental cues, feelings, the anticipation of reward and punishments, and social norms conflict? Whether and how we turn to aggression in such circumstances depends on how we deal with the relevant information.

When people are processing superficially, the most salient aspect of the environment or the most accessible attitude or norm "wins": Whatever grabs our attention most easily has the greatest impact on our behavior. The salience of costs or rewards, the behavior of models, and situational cues can all trigger aggressive behavior in a person who is processing superficially. In anger-inducing situations, the self-esteem threat or other provocation that produced the anger is usually foremost in our attention. Thus, when people are in the grip of angry feelings and negative thoughts, conditions that favor superficial thinking are likely to favor aggression.

In order to overcome the initial tendency to smack your roommate, you must engage in some systematic thinking about the situation. If this systematic processing goes well, you might not aggress—but, as always, you need both motivation and capacity to find ways to resolve your conflict peacefully. When people have the time and capacity to consider deeply, they can intentionally try to activate the most appropriate, rather than the most accessible, interpretations of the situation that makes them want to aggress (Yovetich & Rusbult, 1994). Given the opportunity, they can come up with alternatives to aggression: talking over a conflict, weighing the costs and benefits of retaliation, compromising on a solution, realizing that an apparent provocation may have been accidental. However, several factors may limit people's capacity to process deeply even when they are motivated to do so—increasing the odds of aggression.

1. *Emotional arousal.* Threat, trauma, and intense emotions can reduce people's capacity to process information carefully, as we have seen many times throughout this text. Because strong emotions often accompany conflict, they temporarily interfere with careful processing just when it is most needed. The presence of weapons increases aggression even more strongly when people are already aroused and angered (Berkowitz, 1993). In the same way, aggressive boys' tendency to see any bump or jostle as an act of aggression is magnified when they are very anxious (Dodge & Somberg, 1987). Sadly, there is evidence that the physical and emotional trauma of child abuse may diminish a child's ability to interpret social cues correctly and to generate imaginative responses to conflict situations (Dodge, Bates, & Pettit, 1990). These deficits in turn increase the child's own tendency to turn to aggression, which may be one important reason why abused children sometimes grow up to perpetuate abuse against their own spouses or children (Geen, 1998; Sugarman & Hotaling, 1989).

2. *Alchohol use.* Alcohol can also diminish people's ability to think systematically. You may not be surprised to learn that drinking and violence often coincide (Bushman & Cooper, 1990; Ito, Miller, & Pollock, 1996). Alcohol is a factor in almost two thirds of homicides and in one third of rapes, burglaries, and assaults (Desmond, 1987; Wolfgang & Strohm, 1956). The statistics are less surprising, though no less shocking, when you realize that alcohol reduces people's capacity to process a wide range of information. Perceiving a restricted range of cues, a person under the influence of alcohol is likely to base his or her actions on whatever is most immediately obvious (Steele & Josephs, 1990). So alcohol by itself does not invariably

lead to aggression: People sometimes become jolly or weepy when they drink if they happen to focus on cues that push them in those directions. However, alcohol plus anger or threat is a surefire recipe for aggression (S. P. Taylor, Gammon, & Capasso, 1976). In addition to reducing our capacity to process a wide range of cues, alcohol exerts a second and equally dangerous influence. It lessens people's concern for factors that ordinarily restrain aggression: the potential costs and dangers of aggressive acts, the social norms that constrain aggression, and the cues that ordinarily inhibit aggression, such as expressions of pain from the victim (Baumeister, 1997; Schmutte & Taylor, 1980).

3. *Time pressure.* Strong emotions and alcohol can reduce our ability to avoid aggression, but other factors that limit our ability to come up with alternatives to aggression should have the same effects. When a decision must be made quickly, an initial tendency to aggress may win more often. Police officers frequently must make snap judgments about whether to use force, and, as in the case of Amadou Diallo, they sometimes make the wrong decision.

4. *Individual differences.* Finally, some people are just better at avoiding aggression than others. Children with more ability to think of nonaggressive responses in social situations are less aggressive than children who can suggest fewer alternatives (Dodge & Crick, 1990; Huesmann, Eron, & Yarmel, 1987). This difference becomes even more pronounced as life grows more complicated. As tasks become more challenging or as interaction becomes more structured, social and cognitive skills are strained to their limits. Aggressive children are then even more likely to turn to violence (Dodge, Pettit, McClaskey, & Brown, 1986; J. C. Wright & Mischel, 1987).

What explains interpersonal aggression? At this point you may be thinking that just about anything can cause aggression: feeling too hot or cold, drinking a beer, or watching a violent movie. It is true that many different factors can push us in the direction of aggression, but all their effects can be understood in terms of the underlying processes shown in Figure 13.1. The process begins with perceptions of the person, the situation, and any provocation. The desire to hurt increases when potential rewards outweigh potential costs, or when anger and other negative emotions are present. The desire to act aggressively does not always dictate action, however, because social norms and the actions of others also play a major role in initiating or restraining aggression. Aggressive models can show that violence is rewarded, offer evidence that aggression is normatively acceptable, and serve as a cue that makes aggressive thoughts and feelings more accessible. No wonder aggressive models are so potent in producing further aggression and that those aiming at reducing aggression in society have criticized the media for presenting so many aggressive models for public consumption.

But appropriate norms and models can also reduce aggression, if they are brought to mind at the right time. This is one reason why it is so important to go beyond the immediate situation, and to think carefully about other cues, attitudes, and norms that oppose aggression. Unfortunately, this careful thought requires time, effort, and ability, resources that might not be available when people are pressed to make instant decisions, or are stressed by anger or other strong negative emotions.

Thus interpersonal aggression is guided by fundamental cognitive and social processes. It is motivated by desires for mastery, connectedness, and esteem. It can

FIGURE 13.1 Multiple factors influence aggression

■ A perceived provocation in a particular situation may spur desires to aggress or may activate norms that either favor or restrain aggression. The way the person resolves potentially conflicting desires and norms will determine whether aggression occurs.

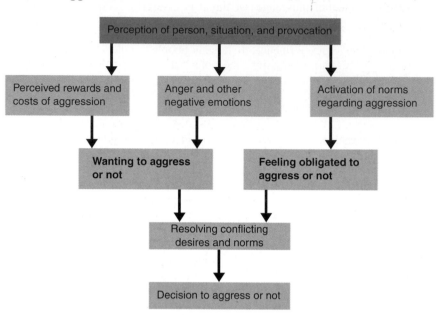

be directed by firmly established or situationally accessible attitudes and norms, depending on whether or not we have the ability and motivation to think things through thoroughly. Not surprisingly, exactly these same processes apply also to aggression and conflict that pit group against group.

Intergroup Conflict

As we have seen, individuals all too frequently act to harm others. Unfortunately, groups can be even more aggressive than individuals! Nabith Berri, chief of one militia group in conflict-torn Lebanon, once stated, "When we deal with each other individually, we can be civilized . . . but when we deal with each other as groups, we are like savage tribes in the Middle Ages" (*Indianapolis Star*, 1989).

The greater aggressiveness of groups can be observed in the laboratory as well as in wars and civil conflicts around the world (Insko & Schopler, 1998). For example, in a recent study the researchers had either two individuals or two three-member groups allocate hot sauce for each other to consume (Meier & Hinsz, 2004). The researchers provided sauce that was extremely spicy, and students thought consuming it would be painful. When participants arrived in the lab for what they thought was a study of personality and taste, they learned that another individual or group had doled out quite a bit of hot sauce for them to consume. Then they were asked in turn to allocate some hot sauce for the other individual or group. Groups allocated an average of 93 grams for each member of the other group to consume. Individuals, on the other hand, gave the other individual only 58 grams.

Other studies similarly show that groups are more competitive than individuals. For example, when participants are asked to allocate valuable points to themselves and to others, they like their opponents less and make more competitive choices when playing in teams of two or three than they do when playing as individuals

(Wildschut, Pinter, Vevea, Insko, & Schopler, 2003). In fact, anything that increases a group's feeling of identity can boost its competitiveness (L. Gaertner & Schopler, 1998). To demonstrate this point, one group of researchers gave young members of informal handball teams bright orange jerseys to wear—emphasizing their identity as a group. This symbol of group solidarity was enough to increase their aggressiveness, compared to their opponents who wore their usual street clothes (Rehm, Steinleitner, & Lilli, 1987).

Why are groups generally more aggressive than individuals? Like a jigsaw puzzle, the answer to this question has several pieces. We will discuss the reasons for the special competitiveness of groups as we describe the reasons and processes that underlie intergroup conflict.

Sources of Intergroup Conflict: The Battle for Riches and Respect

Most group conflict stems from competition for valued material resources or for social rewards like respect and esteem. People use social comparisons to determine acceptable levels of resources. Groups in conflict are often more attuned to social rewards than to material ones.

Although groups are often more competitive and aggressive than individuals, groups and individuals generally turn to aggression for the same basic reasons: valued material resources or respect and esteem.

REALISTIC CONFLICT THEORY: GETTING THE GOODS. In the conflict between the Eagles and the Rattlers at Robber's Cave State Park, each group defended its swimming and playing territory, stole the other's prized possessions, and engaged in athletic competition spiced by the knowledge that only the winners would receive new pocketknives. The resulting dramatic escalation of hostilities provided good evidence for **realistic conflict theory**. This theory argues that intergroup hostility, conflict, and aggression arise from competition among groups for mastery of scarce but valued material resources (D. T. Campbell, 1965; LeVine & Campbell, 1972; M. Sherif, 1966). Just as the calculation of material costs and rewards motivates instrumental aggression by individuals, the potential gain or loss of material resources motivates intergroup aggression.

Laboratory research has confirmed that competition for scarce resources sours intergroup relations. Consider the way in which the potential for one group to win a reward can change intergroup interactions, for example. In this study two groups of students worked on tasks such as recommending a therapy program for a troubled adolescent or creating an advertising slogan for a new brand of toothpaste (D. A. Taylor & Moriarty, 1987). To set up a cooperative or a competitive environment, researchers gave different instructions to the participants. To create a cooperative environment, researchers told participants that proposals from the two groups would be combined to produce the best solution, and that both groups would be rewarded.

> **Realistic conflict theory.**
> The theory that intergroup hostility arises from competition among groups for scarce but valued material resources.

■ **The human price of war**. Victories and defeats are often measured in terms of material resources gained and lost. But the human cost of war goes far beyond such measures, as can be seen in the face of this Kurdish refugee wailing in grief at the funeral of a young man who had been killed during a mortar attack in the Iraq war.

FIGURE 13.2   Competition increases solidarity and intergroup hostility

■ Two groups of participants either competed against one another or cooperated for rewards. Compared with the cooperators, those who competed liked their fellow in-group members better and disliked out-group members more. (Data from D. A. Taylor and Moriarty, 1987.)

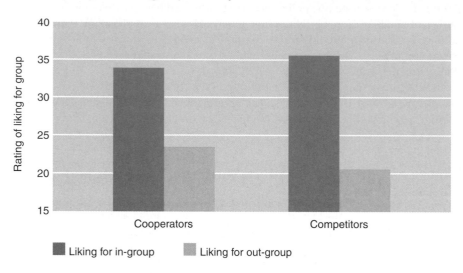

In the competitive condition, participants heard that only the one group that came up with the best idea would receive the reward. The study's results were consistent with predictions from realistic conflict theory. Compared with the cooperative groups, the groups in competition for the scarce and valued resource liked in-group members better and disliked out-group members more (see Figure 13.2).

As the Rattlers and the Eagles demonstrated, group competition can quickly escalate from dislike into hostility and aggression (Horwitz & Rabbie, 1982; Rapoport & Bornstein, 1987). Competition for real resources, such as land, jobs, and natural resources, is clearly one cause of the many conflicts that pit nation against nation and ethnic group against ethnic group (Brewer & Campbell, 1976; Gurr, 1970; Streufert & Streufert, 1986). When countries battle over the right to control strategic waterways or land rich in oil and minerals, realistic competition is probably at the root of the conflict.

RELATIVE DEPRIVATION: WHEN IS ENOUGH ENOUGH? Perhaps conflict is understandable when material resources are scarce. But even when people or groups seem to have adequate resources, they often continue to compete. Apparently, once people have the basic necessities of life, it becomes difficult to determine objectively how they are faring, and so they turn to comparisons with others to help them decide. This idea is central to **relative deprivation theory**, which suggests that social comparison, not objective reality, determines how satisfied or dissatisfied people are with what they have (Bernstein & Crosby, 1980; Crosby, 1976; Stouffer and others, 1949). It's not hard to see how this idea might apply in real life. If you had just bought a shiny new Chevrolet, you probably would feel pretty good about it—until your next-door neighbor proudly rolled his shiny new BMW into his driveway. Your Chevy is still exactly the same car, but suddenly you may not feel quite so proud of it. In fact, you may experience *egoistic relative deprivation*, a sense that you are doing less well than other individuals (Runciman, 1966).

In many circumstances, however, the crucial comparison people make is not between themselves and other individuals, but between their group and other groups. *Fraternal relative deprivation* is the sense that one's group is not doing as

Relative deprivation theory. The theory that feelings of discontent arise from the belief that other individuals or other groups are better off.

well as other groups (Runciman, 1966). Like egoistic deprivation, fraternal deprivation has little to do with objective levels of adequacy or success. A group with little may be content if those around them also have little. Conversely, a group whose situation is improving may feel discontent if other groups seem to be improving at a faster rate. During the economic boom of the 1960s, for example, most people in the United States achieved substantial economic gains. Yet the 1960s were also a period of some of the worst racial violence in U.S. history, in part because African Americans saw their economic situation lagging behind that of Whites (Sears & McConahay, 1973). Fraternal deprivation is much more likely to cause intergroup conflict than is egoistic deprivation. Feelings of fraternal deprivation have been found to be directly related to conflicts between unemployed youths and the authorities in Australia (Walker & Mann, 1987), gay and lesbian groups and straight groups in Toronto (Birt & Dion, 1987), French and English speakers in Canada (Guimond & Dube-Simard, 1983), and Muslims and Hindus in India (Tripathi & Srivasta, 1981).

SOCIAL COMPETITION: GETTING A LITTLE RESPECT. If groups fought only over material resources, intergroup conflicts might be more easily resolved. After all, groups could learn to make do with a little less, resources could be more equally distributed, and more goods could be produced, all of which might help groups live side by side in relative satisfaction. Unfortunately, groups, like individuals, also fight over social goods: respect, esteem, and "bragging rights." And this is as true for adults as it is for small boys (D. Katz, 1965; Tajfel & Turner, 1979).

Consider a series of studies in which two groups of corporate executives attending a training program were assigned problem-solving tasks (Blake & Mouton, 1979, 1984). Researchers told the executives that experts would evaluate each team's performance, but they never mentioned competition, nor did they promise concrete rewards for performance. Nevertheless, the experience of being divided into groups and anticipating evaluation was apparently enough to produce conflict. In a virtual replay of the Eagles–Rattlers scenario, team spirit soared and intergroup antagonism emerged as group members huddled together during breaks and meals to plan strategies, analyze successful performances, and even hold pep rallies. In one version of the experiment, researchers asked representatives from each group to meet to evaluate the groups' products. These meetings almost always resulted in a deadlock, with each representative insisting his or her own group's work was best. When a neutral judge broke the deadlock, the losing team accused him of bias and incompetence. At one point the researchers had to break off the experiment to calm tempers and restore order.

What drives competition when no material resources whatever are at stake? If you think the answer has something to do with social identity, you're right. You may recall that people's desire to see their own groups as better than other groups can lead to intergroup bias. The same process can also contribute to outright conflict (Brewer, 1991). People can even identify with groups formed on the basis of an arbitrary toss of a coin: They don't need to interact with other group members or even to know them, and they don't need to feel that their access to material resources is at risk. Research indicates that members of such "minimal groups" nevertheless act as if they were at odds with other groups, treating them in ways that fuel conflict. They downgrade the out-group's products, dislike out-group members as individuals, and discriminate against the out-group in allocating rewards (Brewer, 1979; J. C. Turner, 1980). Thus, people's strivings for positive social identity may plant the seeds of intergroup conflict.

Social identity theory and studies that demonstrate people's readiness to identify even with arbitrary, transient groups were discussed in Chapter 6, especially pages 204 to 206.

THE SPECIAL COMPETITIVENESS OF GROUPS: GROUPS OFTEN VALUE RESPECT OVER RICHES. The first reason for the greater competitiveness of groups than individuals is this: When groups vie to be "Number One," social competition and the effort to outdo one's opponent frequently overshadow competition for material resources (L. Gaertner & Schopler, 1998; C. A. Insko & Schopler, 1987). If the boys at summer camp had cared only about the badges and pocketknives, the researchers could have given those prizes to everyone. But do you think that would have satisfied the boys or reduced their desire to outdo the other group? Chester Insko and John Schopler (1998) have documented the way groups seek respect over riches in their studies of resource-allocation choices. In their studies, participants choose among several alternative ways to distribute points worth a small amount of money to their own group and to another group. Usually groups start by choosing alternatives that maximize the in-group's profit, paying little attention to the out-group's situation. As the play continues, however, the players' choices become more competitive—maximizing the advantage of the in-group over the out-group. In a display of supercompetitiveness, groups sometimes give up absolute gain in order to dominate their rivals (Brewer, 1979). And, of course, as soon as one side makes a competitive choice, the other retaliates.

In these laboratory studies, the actual cash value of the "points" is trivial, so perhaps it is no surprise that groups care more about the symbolic value of winning than about a dollar or two of prize money. Still, similar patterns occur in real organizational and international conflicts. For example, nations begin wars knowing that either victory or defeat will exact an enormous cost in physical pain, economic ruin, and ecological devastation. Yet they sound the war drums anyway, accepting huge costs in exchange for the chance of victory over their opponent. When competition for riches turns into competition for respect, winning becomes everything.

Escalating Conflict: Communication and Interaction That Make Things Worse

> Once conflict starts, poor communication can make it worse. In-group interaction hardens in-group opinion, threats are directed at the out-group, each group retaliates more and more harshly, and other parties choose sides. All of these processes tend to escalate the conflict.

Once conflict catches fire, the flames spread quickly. Persuasion, promises, and verbal sparring are replaced by attempted coercion, threats, and physical assault. And as new issues and disagreements come to light and inhibitions about breaking the peace dissolve, the scope of conflict broadens. The Rattlers and the Eagles certainly followed this pattern. Name-calling soon moved on to flag burning and brawling, accompanied by food fights and midnight cabin raids.

What causes this pattern of escalating conflict? By now our answer should be familiar: The same social and cognitive processes responsible for other forms of social behavior play a role in conflict situations, too. Those processes, which can affect even the most well-intentioned individuals and groups, intensify conflict and cause opinions to harden.

TALKING TO THE IN-GROUP: POLARIZATION AND COMMITMENT. Discussion won't help if the only people you talk to are those who take your side. Talking things over with like-minded others pushes group members toward extreme views, a process called *group polarization*. As a result of group discussion, then, people may see their group's position as even more valid and valuable, and they may become even more firmly attached to it.

During discussion, we also become more committed to our views. As we explain and defend them, we marshal the best evidence, cite the strongest precedents, and organize every shred of support we can muster. We may pound the table for emphasis as we pick holes in the opposition's reasoning, seize on their slightest hesitations, and counter their every argument. These actions are unlikely to convince the opponents, but they can strengthen our own confidence and commitment (Brauer, Judd, & Gliner, 1995; Hovland and others, 1953). As group members see themselves getting worked up, they conclude that they must care a lot about the issues. At the same time, dissonance-reduction processes ensure that their private attitudes line up with public positions, even if at first those public positions were just argued for effect without being fully believed. The very public nature of advocacy constitutes a commitment, which makes it even more difficult for group members to back down or change their minds.

Of course, the same processes are also at work in the other group, so positions harden into extreme opposition. As in-group views are confirmed and out-group arguments demolished, each group's position becomes entrenched at the extreme and each group's commitment intensifies (Staw & Ross, 1987). Now the battle lines between groups are drawn even more clearly.

THE SPECIAL COMPETITIVENESS OF GROUPS: WHEN CONFLICT ARISES, GROUPS CLOSE RANKS. Processes of commitment and polarization represent the second reason for the special competitiveness of groups. In situations of conflict, groups demand loyalty, solidarity, and strict adherence to group norms. The Eagles and Rattlers did this, forbidding any friendly contact or fraternization with the "enemy." This tight discipline permits no interaction or empathy with the out-group, widening the gap between the groups and making further conflict almost inevitable.

Leaders sometimes take advantage of the unifying effect of conflict to strengthen their hold on power. In a demonstration of this process, Jacob Rabbie and Frits Bekkers (1978) simulated a labor–management conflict in their laboratory at the University of Utrecht in the Netherlands. Some participants took the role of a union leader who could be removed from power by an election at any stage during the negotiations. Some students were in an unstable leadership position; just two negative votes could have removed them from office. Others held more stable positions; only a unanimous negative vote could have deposed them. Leaders whose jobs were shaky behaved more competitively in their negotiations with management, apparently to rally the rank and file around them. These laboratory findings remind us of a grim roster of real-world leaders who have taken their nations into wars and other misadventures to shore up power that was threatened by political rivals, economic troubles, or declining prestige.

TALKING TO THE OUT-GROUP: BACK OFF, OR ELSE! As positions harden, groups find it increasingly difficult to communicate productively. At this point persuasion and discussion often give way to threats and attempted coercion. Most people believe that threats—describing punishments that will follow unwanted behavior—increase their bargaining power and their chances of getting their way (Falbo & Peplau, 1980; Rothbart & Hallmark, 1988). Of course, since most people believe this, both groups tend to use threats, leaving neither group

We discussed why group polarization occurs and the many ways in which group discussion can make the majority opinion more extreme in Chapter 9, pages 322 to 328.

To remind yourselves of the ways that self-perception processes and dissonance reduction can bring attitudes into lockstep with actions, review Chapter 8, pages 273 to 289.

with an advantage. Each is thinking exactly the same thing, cursing the other's unwillingness to listen to reason, deciding that the language of force is the only language the opponent can understand. The reality, unfortunately, is that threats provoke counterthreats, diminish people's willingness to compromise, and, in the end, generate hostility.

To see how counterproductive threats can be, consider the findings from a study by Morton Deutsch and Robert Krauss (1960). They asked pairs of female participants to imagine themselves as owners of two rival trucking companies, named Acme and Bolt, whose profits were based on the speed with which they carried merchandise over roads to specific destinations. The most profit could be attained by taking the short central road rather than the long and winding bypass (see Figure 13.3). As the map shows, a potential source of conflict is built into the road layout: One section of the central road is only one lane wide. If both players reach this section at the same time, one must back up and let the other proceed. This problem was not insurmountable, however. Participants soon worked out a cooperative solution: They took turns making deliveries along the central road, each earning close to the maximum profit from the experimenter.

So far, so good. But then researchers introduced conditions that allowed the players to control something that could be used to threaten their opponent: a gate on the central road. By closing the gate, a player could force the opponent's truck to back up and take the bypass, costing extra time and lowering profits. In the *unilateral threat* condition, Acme controlled the only gate at one end of the one-lane stretch of road. In the *bilateral threat* condition, each player controlled a gate. As before, the players were free to communicate to try to solve their differences.

How did the would-be trucking company operators react? When Acme could threaten Bolt with a gate closing, Bolt suffered quite a large loss, but Acme lost money, too, as her trucks sat idle on the road during confrontations. When both players could use the threat, matters were even worse: Both consistently lost money. And whether the threat was unilateral or bilateral, players' communications focused on the use and consequences of the threat rather than on ways of cooperating to resolve the conflict.

FIGURE 13.3   Routes to conflict

■ In this study, each participant had to move her company's trucks from a starting point to a destination. Participants could save time and earn more money by going over the central road, but conflict arose because only one truck could pass through the one-lane section at a time. When one or both parties controlled gates on the central road and threatened to close them, the trucks had to take a long alternate route, losing money. (Adapted from Deutsch & Krauss, 1960.)

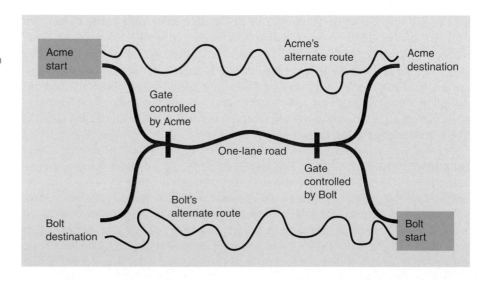

It may have occurred to you that nothing in the rules of the trucking game *forced* the players to threaten one another. They could have worked together, taking turns and happily raking in the money just like the players in the condition without any gates. But these findings indicate that the mere availability of a potential threat appears to be enough to bring about its use. Once people have coercive means at their disposal, they shift from reward-seeking to socially competitive behavior.

The irony is that, as we said earlier, threats usually are counterproductive. The threatened group may assume that aggression is inevitable no matter how it responds. And if it responds with a counterthreat, the first group's belief in the opponent's hostility and unwillingness to compromise will be confirmed (North, Brody, & Holsti, 1964). Threats and counterthreats almost invariably escalate in intensity rather than staying at the same level (Tedeschi, Gaes, & Rivera, 1997). In laboratory simulations of international conflict, for example, other groups follow suit when one group stockpiles arms, and an arms race usually results (Kramer, 1989). Further, concerns over prestige and fears of losing face may make groups cling to their views more firmly, resolutely refusing to give in even when the potential costs are very high (Kaplowitz, 1990). Finally, when threats dominate communication, as they did when players controlled gates in the trucking game, they crowd out messages about cooperative solutions (Knudson, Sommers, & Golding, 1980). Communication can effectively deter and resolve conflict only when threats are not permitted, or when opponents learn to avoid making threats that spark retaliation (Lawler, Ford, & Bleger, 1988; W. P. Smith & Anderson, 1975).

☐ **THREAT AND DETERRENCE IN INTERNATIONAL AFFAIRS.** What can laboratory research tell us about policies of deterrence between nations? A policy of deterrence is a political strategy in which one side threatens to use force in the hope of preventing an adversary's use of force (P. M. Morgan, 1983). Its central principle is that dangers arise when a potential aggressor believes its opponents are weak or vulnerable (Jervis, 1976). Proponents of these policies follow the maxim that "if you want peace, prepare for war." The lesson of history, however, suggests that if you prepare for war, you get war (Lebow & Stein, 1987). An analysis of two thousand years of international relations suggests that attempting to deter war by threats usually makes war more, not less, likely (Naroll, Bullough, & Naroll, 1974). Groups that stockpile resources in an effort at deterrence are often perceived as attempting to acquire an offensive edge in preparation for aggression. As a result, they often face escalating conflict from others who fear them (Hornstein, 1975). Speeches proclaiming defensive intentions are unlikely to persuade adversaries who feel threatened by an arms build-up.

Thus, deterrence, like other uses of threats, can backfire, eliciting counterthreats and escalation. This does not mean that it is wise for groups to neglect their defenses. As we have seen, intergroup conflict can stem from greed, and a group without power may appear as easy prey for strong aggressors who have little fear of retaliation. Such large differences in power leave the door open for those who would impose deadly "final solutions" to group conflict. Research indicates that groups roughly equal in power and ability use threats and coercion less often and achieve agreements more often than do parties with unequal power (Hornstein, 1975; Lawler and others, 1988). But even equality in power and command of threats cannot guarantee an absence of conflict: Recall that in the Acme–Bolt trucking game, the parties fared worst when they both controlled gates they could use as threats.

COALITION FORMATION: ESCALATION AS OTHERS CHOOSE SIDES. Conflicts often begin as one-on-one confrontations, but as positions harden, the participants—particularly the weaker side—may call on outside parties for help. *Coalition formation* occurs when two or more parties pool their resources to obtain a mutual goal they probably could not achieve alone (Komorita & Meek, 1978). Coalition formation tends to polarize multiple parties into two opposing sides (Mack & Snyder, 1957). When groups are in conflict, coalition formation is usually seen as a threatening action that, like most threats, only intensifies competition. Those excluded from the coalition may react with fear and anger, and they often form their own coalitions. As unaffiliated groups ally with one side or the other, differences become polarized and the dangerous allure of consensus convinces each side that it is right.

For all these reasons, the formation of coalitions and alliances between nations usually increases the possibility of armed hostility (Q. Wright, 1965). This point, as well as the failure of threats and deterrence, is illustrated by the beginning of the First World War. The scene was set when Austrian Archduke Francis Ferdinand was assassinated by a Serbian nationalist; leaders of the Austro-Hungarian empire retaliated by attacking Serbia. Even then, the conflict might have remained relatively localized, but the two parties' powerful allies stepped in. Serbia's ally Russia, viewing the Austrian attack as a pretext for a German–Austrian conquest of Europe, responded with military mobilization. Germany, feeling endangered, threatened war if Russia did not halt its mobilization. Russia's rejection of this demand led Germany to declare war, first on Russia and then on Russia's ally, France. The escalating hostilities finally drew another ally, Great Britain, into the war (Holsti & North, 1965; North and others, 1964). Not only did the build-up of allied coalitions make the conflict more rather than less likely, but it resulted in the deaths of more than 8 million soldiers from more than 19 countries.

Perceptions in Conflict: What Else Could You Expect From Them?

As escalation continues, the in-group sees the out-group as totally evil and sees itself in unrealistically positive terms. Because the same biases characterize each group, each group's images of itself and its opponent tend to be similar. Emotion and arousal make these biases even worse.

As conflict escalates, groups' views of themselves and of their opponents change. These conflict-driven perceptions may have little basis in reality, but they affect the group's understanding of what is happening and why. This skewed understanding in turn becomes a guide for group behavior (R. K. White, 1965, 1977, 1984). When perceptions are negative, distrust and suspicion cast every action in the worst possible light. And self-fulfilling prophecies exert their own pressure: If one side expects the other to be hostile and devious, a vicious cycle can begin in which the other is made to be more hostile and devious.

POLARIZED PERCEPTIONS OF IN-GROUP AND OUT-GROUP. If mere categorization—with no hint of conflict or competition—can make people evaluate their own group more positively than the out-group, imagine how much stronger perceptual biases become in the midst of bloody conflict. In fact, groups enmeshed in conflict tend to develop three blind spots in their thinking.

1. *The in-group can do no wrong.* Biased perceptions cause members of the in-group to see their group as righteous and morally superior. Its every intention seems pure hearted, its every action justifiable. Not surprisingly, groups in conflict almost always invoke religion to support their view. Leaders of warring parties in the Middle East have characterized their struggles as holy wars, and both the Germans and the Allies in the two World Wars were each confident that God was on their side. Abraham Lincoln spoke to this issue in his Second Inaugural Address, delivered at the height of the Civil War. Since the North was fighting slavery, wasn't God on its side? "Lincoln's conclusion was that God might not be on either side: 'The Almighty has his own purposes.' He later wrote to a political ally about that speech: ' . . . I believe it is not immediately popular. Men are not flattered by being shown that there has been a difference of purpose between the Almighty and them' " (Safire, 1992).

2. *The out-group can do no right.* In contrast, the out-group is seen as evil, even diabolical. In the recent war in the former Yugoslavia, Bosnian Muslim refugees spoke bitterly of Serbian former neighbors and friends who had turned informers or even taken up arms in the drive for "ethnic cleansing." The Serbians saw their opponents as equally despicable, insisting that their invasion of Bosnia was justified because of reports that Serbian babies were being fed to the lions in the Sarajevo zoo (Lane, Stanger, & Post, 1993). Perceptions like these dehumanize the enemy, supporting the idea that they are capable of committing any evil, and therefore justifying any action taken against them.

3. *The in-group is all-powerful.* The in-group soon sees itself as having might as well as right on its side, leading to a preoccupation with appearing powerful, prestigious, tough, and courageous. This aggressive posturing, or what journalist Ross Barnet (1971) termed the "hairy chest syndrome," has dangerous side effects. The focus on winning may crowd out consideration of the merits or morals of in-group actions. The boasts of power may be seen as threats that deserve a response in kind (Lebow & Stein, 1987). Finally, the overconfident in-group may fall for its own rhetoric, just as it hopes the enemy will. The disastrous U.S. policy in Vietnam offered many examples of overconfidence, as military and political leaders repeatedly promised that the next minor escalation, the next 25,000 troops, would be enough to do the job.

BIASED ATTRIBUTIONS FOR BEHAVIOR. Groups in conflict frequently attribute identical behaviors by the in-group and the out-group to diametrically opposed causes. One study carried out during the Cold War contrasted American college students' responses to similar military actions supposedly carried out by the United States or the Soviets (Oskamp & Hartry, 1968). Students considered, for example, sending aircraft carriers to patrol international waters off the coast of the other country. Participants who thought the United States had taken the actions against the Soviet Union saw them as more positive and more justifiable than did those who thought the Soviets had acted against the United States. In the context of conflict, attributions for in-group and out-group actions are biased in two different ways.

1. *In-group motives are positive; out-group motives are negative.* An in-group action is correct and justified: a protection of our rights, a measured defense against their hostile intentions. When the out-group

carries out exactly the same action, it is seen as provocative: a clear instance of aggression. We offer concessions, but they attempt to lure us with ploys. We are steadfast and courageous, but they are unyielding, irrational, stubborn, and blinded by ideology.

2. *Situations dictate in-group actions; character flaws prompt out-group actions.* People see their own group's actions as reasonable responses to difficult situations like the need to defend oneself from attack, to restrain internal unrest, to stand up for principle against compromise and corruption. Out-group actions, however, seem to be evidence of their flawed characters: Their military moves reflect aggressiveness; their harassment of dissidents reflects inhumanity, intolerance, and insecurity; their rejection of compromise reflects stubbornness and irrationality.

In particular, groups often fail to recognize how often fear motivates out-group actions (R. K. White, 1987). During the Cold War, fear of powerful Soviet forces largely motivated the U.S. arms build-up. Failing to understand this motivation, however, the Soviets saw the build-up as threatening, and responded with increased military production of their own. The U.S. side similarly reacted to their increase but not to the underlying Soviet fear. And so the cycle continued.

THE IMPACT OF EMOTION AND AROUSAL: MORE HEAT, LESS LIGHT. As conflict rises, people experience tension, anxiety, anger, frustration, and fear. Even participants in competitive games in the laboratory show obvious signs of stress: nervous laughter, increased sweating, and accelerated heart rate (Blascovich, Nash, & Ginsburg, 1978; Van Egeren, 1979). Not surprisingly, this emotional arousal affects processes of perception and communication and produces simplistic thinking. As complex thinking shuts down, decisions are based on simple stereotypes, snap judgments, and automatic reactions. If laboratory studies can generate such stress, imagine the pressure decision makers in real intergroup conflicts must experience (Milburn, 1977).

Philip Tetlock and his colleagues found evidence of a simplistic pattern of thinking when they analyzed former U.S. and Soviet leaders' portrayals of each other in several decades of public speeches (Suedfeld & Tetlock, 1977; P. E. Tetlock, 1988). During times of East–West crisis—the Berlin blockade, the Korean War, the Soviet invasion of Afghanistan—both sides' political statements reflected simplistic and stereotypic thinking about the out-group. The United States was seen as an imperialist aggressor and the Soviet Union as an "evil empire." When tensions relaxed, each side's statements about the other became more complex, acknowledging areas of agreement and common interests as well as continuing disputes. Editorials appearing in major newspapers in the United States, Canada, and the Soviet Union reflected these oversimplifications (Suedfeld, 1992). A study of United Nations speeches, shown in Figure 13.4, showed a similar pattern of simplification in the images used in Arab–Israeli exchanges during years in which war occurred.

Emotions can not only lead to oversimple thinking about an opposing group, but also direct behavior toward that group—often in negative ways. Of particular importance are the emotions that people feel when they are thinking of themselves as members of their group (rather than emotions that they happen to feel as individuals; Devos and others, 2002). Group-based emotions depend on the particular nature of the threats that an out-group is seen as posing (Cottrell & Neuberg, 2005), whether a threat to the in-group's physical safety, territory, or cherished values and

This pattern of attributions is a group-level version of the actor–observer difference, in which we attribute our own behaviors to situations but other people's actions to their personalities. See Chapter 4, pages 101 to 102.

Recall from Chapter 5, pages 166 to 169, that these were just the circumstances that cause people to rely more on stereotypic views of others.

FIGURE 13.4   Simplistic thinking appears when conflict escalates

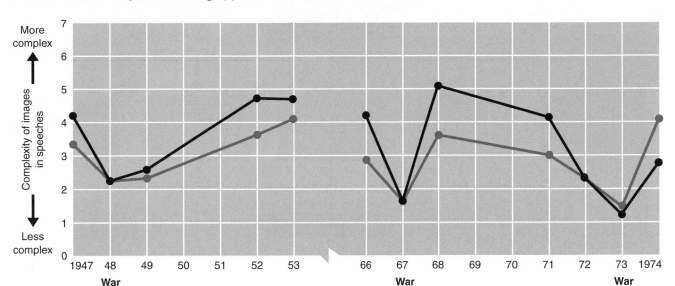

Israeli speakers   Arab speakers

■ This study tracked the degree of complex thinking in verbal images of the opponent used in speeches by Arab and Israeli leaders in the United Nations. Note that the scores hit their lowest points in the years Arab–Israeli wars occurred. (Data from Suedfeld and Tetlock, 1977.)

symbols   s such as disgust, fear, and anger motivate different type   t-group, ranging from avoidance to support for
political   group, to outright attack (E. R. Smith, Seger, &
Mackie,   ts of emotion have not been studied as intensively
with reg   s, group-based emotions may well play a comparable ro   dividuals' feelings of anger and frustration play in
instance   gression.

The   in all of this. People tend to perceive members of
out-grou   y, perceived threats, and emotion strengthen this
tendency. In stressful conflict situations, we may leap to the erroneous conclusion that our opponents are ignorant, are willfully misinterpreting evidence, and are fools whose self-interest or pernicious ideology blinds them to the truth. Of course, our opponents are viewing us in the same way. As a result, neither side understands the other's perceptions or intentions, and, as Figure 13.5 illustrates, conflict may continue to escalate.

THE SPECIAL COMPETITIVENESS OF GROUPS: PEOPLE EXPECT GROUPS TO BE SUPERCOMPETITIVE, SO THEY REACT IN KIND.
Biased and extreme perceptions of out-groups are a third reason why groups act more competitively than individuals. People expect groups to be highly competitive and hostile (Hoyle, Pinkley, & Insko, 1989). To demonstrate this, Nilanjana Dasgupta and her colleagues (Dasgupta, Banaji, & Abelson, 1997) showed students drawings of novel humanoid creatures called "Gs" and asked the students to judge how likely

FIGURE 13.5 Social and cognitive processes in conflict escalation

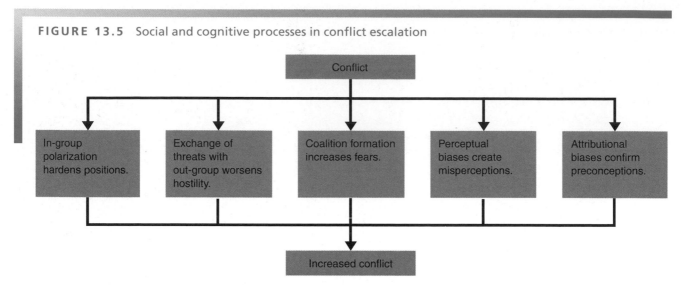

■ Conflict between groups sets in motion a series of social and cognitive processes. Unfortunately, these processes usually harden each side's position and reinforce mutual negative views.

Why does an expectation often elicit behavior that confirms it? To review the ways self-fulfilling prophecies produce behavior that corresponds with our expectations, see Chapter 3, pages 87 to 89, and Chapter 5, pages 174 to 175.

the Gs were to behave in various ways toward other creatures, "Hs," who were not shown in the pictures. Two aspects of the pictures were varied. If the Gs were all the same color (compared to different colors) or if they were standing close together (rather than scattered apart), the participants thought that they would be more likely to perform negative actions such as threatening the Hs. In other words, the more these cues of similarity and proximity suggested that the Gs were a *group* rather than separate individuals, the more negative their actions were expected to be (Abelson, Dasgupta, Park, & Banaji, 1998). And in the real world, of course, this expectation has a self-fulfilling quality (Hoyle and others, 1989). If you think your opponents will act competitively, you will probably try to beat them to it, either to deter them or at least to defend yourself (Insko, Schopler, Hoyle, Dardis, & Graetz, 1990).

"Final Solutions": Eliminating the Out-Group

Ultimately, conflict may escalate into an attempt at total domination or destruction of the out-group. When power differences exist between the groups and the out-group is morally excluded, one group may try to eliminate the other.

As conflicts escalate, intergroup attitudes may harden, and mutual misperceptions can become oversimplified and overwhelmingly negative. An initially realistic conflict over valuable resources can then become a battle for social supremacy in which the primary concern is defeating the opponent, not controlling the resource. And in extreme cases, the goal can become total domination, exploitation, enslavement, or even extermination of the out-group (Allport, 1954b; Kaplowitz, 1990). Three factors seem particularly important in pushing a group to seek a "final solution" to intergroup differences once the groundwork of intergroup hostility and conflict has been laid.

1. *A difference in power between the groups translates desire into action.* Without power, no group can turn prejudice into discrimination, or discrimination into domination. But power gives a group the ability to attain its goals without fear of interference or retaliation, thereby increasing its ability and motivation to discriminate, dominate, and, possibly, eradicate a weaker opponent (Sachdev & Bourhis, 1985, 1991). As history shows, political repression, religious inquisitions, slavery, and genocide often follow (Opotow, 1990).

■ **Excluding the out-group.** Power differences and indifference to others' plight can allow a stronger group to discriminate against, dominate, and possible try to eradicate a weaker group. Hundreds of thousands of African Sudanese from Darfur were forced to flee their country when a violent civil war in Darfur broke out. When Arab "self-defence militias," or "Janjaweed," were mobilised by the government, thousands of people were displaced and had to seek refuge until the soldiers had left their villages. The conflict in Darfur is described by the UN as one of the world's worst humanitarian crises, affecting around 3.6 million people, with thousands of lives lost.

2. *Moral exclusion blocks moral outrage.* When we discussed moral exclusion in Chapters 6 and 10, we noted that biased perceptions of out-group inferiority can make one group indifferent to the plight of out-group members. If we place out-group members outside the boundaries of moral principles, regarding them as less than human, they can be treated in whatever way the in-group finds convenient or profitable. Research suggests that moral exclusion is particularly likely when people harm others under orders from their in-group authorities (Bandura and others, 1996).

3. *Routinization produces desensitization.* As we saw in Chapter 10, many who carry out crimes of politically and socially sanctioned evil begin with small, morally questionable deeds that gradually escalate into unthinkable acts (Kelman & Hamilton, 1989; Staub, 1989). Repetition of individual actions becomes routine, until, at the extreme, even heinous acts like torture and murder become mundane. Such desensitization numbs the horror that naturally inhibits such brutality, allowing social atrocities to continue.

THE SPECIAL COMPETITIVENESS OF GROUPS: GROUPS OFFER SOCIAL SUPPORT FOR COMPETITIVENESS. This point constitutes yet another reason for the greater competitiveness of groups than individuals. Groups offer a rich soil for rationalizing behavior that is motivated by greed or by hatred for others. Taking advantage of others, putting our own self-interest above others' good, discriminating against or even massacring those whom we hate—these and similar actions rank high on the "don't do" list that parents, teachers, or religious figures teach to most of us. But in a group, competing with or even exploiting out-groups can be rationalized as a form of group loyalty—a motive that fits well with people's general tendency to look out for "me and mine." Those who harm or exploit members of the out-group may even view themselves as performing noble acts of altruism and self-sacrifice: After all, they are putting their own lives on the line for the sake of their valued in-group (Schopler and others, 1993).

As Roy Baumeister (1997) commented in his book on the nature of evil, "When someone kills for the sake of promoting a higher good, he may find support and encouragement if he is acting as part of a group of people who share that belief. If he acts as a lone individual, the same act is likely to brand him as a dangerous nut" (p. 190). So through history, nations as well as religious and political movements have defended their acts in the name of the most exalted and worthy goals. Invasion of a less powerful neighbor nation is cloaked as self-defense, and murder of those who follow a different creed is obedience to God's revealed will. Individuals who participate in such acts of aggression have no need to formulate their own rationalizations for their evil acts, for their identification with the group does it for them. The power of groups to define norms for their members—to establish as unquestionably right what the group declares to be right—is the most fundamental reason that groups are so often more aggressive than individuals.

FINAL SOLUTIONS IN HISTORY. The effects of these forces can be seen in the events culminating in the Holocaust in Nazi Germany. Many of the conditions that set the stage for a "final solution" were already in place. Germany's defeat in the First World War led to terrible economic hardships in the 1930s. The situation was ripe for a *scapegoat*: an enemy who, by bearing the blame for Germany's defeat and material ills, could enhance in-group cohesion and solidify leaders' power. Nazi ideologists drew on centuries of European anti-Semitism to emphasize supposed distinctions between in-group Aryans (racially "pure" Germanic folk) and out-group Jews. Negative perceptions and attitudes toward Jews flourished, and German Jews were blamed for the nation's problems.

The three forces that make "final solutions" possible were also operating. First, Nazis held all the high cards, particularly after Hitler's election as chancellor in 1933. Their control over the media, government, and military enabled them to enforce rules about every aspect of their victims' social, political, religious, and economic life. Jews as a group held little political power within Germany, and their appeals to other nations for rescue went largely unanswered. Second, the Nazis dehumanized the Jews, labeling them "worms" and "vermin," thereby excluding them from the sphere in which fair, just, or human treatment could be expected or demanded. Third, killers became desensitized to their acts through routine and repetition. For example, the special police squads who traveled through occupied Poland to round up and kill Jews reacted with shock and horror to their first participation in a massacre (C. R. Browning, 1992). They experienced strong emotions, drank heavily afterwards, and suffered from nightmares. But, eventually, killing people became no more than an unpleasant duty, and at the end of the day the men could sit around, laughing and joking over games of cards.

The Nazi Holocaust was unique in many respects, but the social-psychological processes that allowed it to happen are not. They can be found whenever one powerful group oppresses a weaker opponent. They were at work in the genocidal attacks by Arab militias on Black residents in the Darfur region of Sudan in 2003–2005, the massacres of Tutsi and dissident Hutus by the Hutu-dominated government of Rwanda in 1994, massacres of Armenians by the Ottoman Turks early in the 20th century, and White Americans' and Europeans' capture and enslavement of Africans. When one group holds power over another and begins to dominate or exploit them, negative stereotypes shade into dehumanization, and moral exclusion of the out-group is not far behind. Ultimately, as the processes shown in Figure 13.6 operate, enslavement and genocide become acceptable actions justified by the superiority of the dominant group.

The social-psychological study of intergroup conflict yields many significant lessons, but perhaps the most important is that each of us is psychologically capable of hatred, dehumanization, and violence toward out-group members. Many of the New England ship captains who transported Africans to slavery in the Americas were regular churchgoers, fine family men, and respected leaders within their own

FIGURE 13.6 Two shifts in conflict

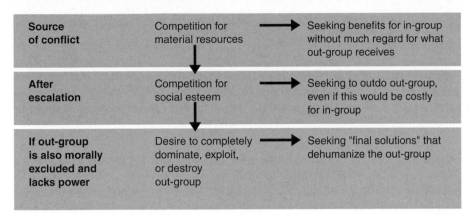

Source of conflict	Competition for material resources ➡	Seeking benefits for in-group without much regard for what out-group receives
After escalation	Competition for social esteem ➡	Seeking to outdo out-group, even if this would be costly for in-group
If out-group is also morally excluded and lacks power	Desire to completely dominate, exploit, or destroy out-group ➡	Seeking "final solutions" that dehumanize the out-group

■ Conflicts often begin with realistic competition over material resources. If escalation occurs, groups may turn from seeking to do well for themselves to seeking to outdo their opponents. Winning, not prospering, then becomes the goal. In a context where the out-group is morally excluded and the groups have differential power, further escalation may result in a final shift in which the goal changes from outdoing the out-group to completely dominating or eliminating it.

communities (Deutsch, 1990). And as we noted in Chapter 10, Nazi leaders viewed themselves as no more than ordinary citizens who cared about their families and did their job to protect them. Yet when groups are in conflict, social and cognitive processes—the same processes that sometimes produce empathy, bravery, altruism, and self-sacrifice—can conspire to produce extraordinary evil.

Resolving Conflict and Reducing Aggression

When we left the Rattlers and the Eagles at Robbers Cave State Park, they were thoroughly at odds with each other. Of course, their war did not spiral out of control like many international conflicts, but as childhood conflicts go, the hostility was pretty bad. Moreover, they displayed many of the earmarks of conflict discussed in the previous sections. The groups' negative feelings about each other escalated: "Those guys" became, in the slang of the day, "bums," "bad guys," "those damn campers," and "stinkers." The groups felt powerful: As the athletic tournament began, each team was supremely confident of winning. Group norms were strictly enforced. Anyone wanting to be friends or even seen speaking with a member of the other team was branded a traitor and ruthlessly brought into line with threats of bodily harm or ostracism.

Having aided and abetted the production of this intergroup hostility, the researchers at Robbers Cave now set about trying to resolve it. How could they do this? Reducing individual aggression or intergroup conflict may be possible if we draw on what we know about their causes. You will see that many of the processes that increase aggression and conflict can be turned around to help reduce it (Deutsch, 1973; Pruitt, 1998). Efforts at reducing aggression often involve altering people's immediate perceptions of others or the situational cues that may increase aggression. Some conflict-resolution strategies focus on reconciling the parties' concrete goals and aspirations, for example, by finding material outcomes that satisfy both individuals or groups. Other strategies encourage cooperation, to make former adversaries part of a new and more inclusive in-group. Our very ability to make this list offers some hope: Knowledge about the causes of aggression can now be recruited into the struggle to reduce it.

It's interesting that task and social interdependence, the main issues that must be solved to reduce intergroup conflict, are the same issues that must be handled for a single group to perform effectively (Chapter 12, pages 445 to 446).

Altering Perceptions and Reactions

One approach to reducing aggression and conflict is to minimize or remove the cues that often cause individuals to commit aggressive acts, and to encourage careful interpretation and identification with others.

Whether conflicts are between individuals or groups, an irrevocable line is crossed when one person first throws a punch or draws a gun. Acts that precipitate aggression can be discouraged by controlling situational cues and by encouraging people to reinterpret the situation and empathize with others.

MINIMIZE CUES FOR AGGRESSION. Some cues activate aggressive thoughts and feelings, making overt acts of aggression more likely. Many in the United States believe that the ready availability of weapons deters aggression, but the evidence suggests just the opposite. When firearms are unavailable, aggression not only is less deadly but also less likely. When Jamaica implemented strict gun control and censored gun scenes from television and movies beginning in 1974, robbery and shooting rates dropped dramatically (Diener & Crandall, 1979). When Washington, DC, passed a handgun-control law, the numbers of homicides and suicides involving guns decreased substantially. Importantly, the nation's capital experienced no offsetting increase in other methods of murder or suicide (Loftin, McDowall, Wiersema, & Cottey, 1991). Even if those inclined to murder simply pick up a knife or a lead pipe if no gun is handy, the outcome is not as deadly.

Fortunately, other cues can decrease aggression. A kind and gentle response, the presence of an infant, and even laughter in a tense situation can cue thoughts and feelings that are incompatible with aggression (P. A. Bell & Baron, 1990; Berkowitz, 1984). Even cues that normally produce aggression, such as guns, can decrease aggression if they provoke fear, anxiety, or disgust, as they do for many people (R. A. Baron, 1983b).

INTERPRET, AND INTERPRET AGAIN. Factors that make it difficult for people to think carefully, such as alcohol use, high emotion, or limited time to think, generally increase aggressive behavior. Thus, the old advice to "count to 10" before taking any action when you are angry is very sound. When you feel provoked, think hard about the other person's intentions: Perhaps he or she did not mean the action the way you took it. Kenneth Dodge's research shows that children who have problems processing social cues tend to display a bias in their reactions to ambiguous harmful actions. They tend to automatically react to them as intentionally hostile and, as a result, they act more aggressively in retaliation. But while their immediate reactions display this bias, their more considered reactions do not (Dodge & Newman, 1981). We can all learn from this finding. When a situation looks like a cause for angry retaliation or an opportunity for advantage through aggression, we should try to see it in a different light before we respond.

PROMOTE EMPATHY WITH OTHERS. Aggression is easiest when victims are distanced and dehumanized. It is tempting to place one's enemies outside the realm of human sympathy, eliminating normative and moral restraints. To avoid this temptation we need to intentionally reflect on their humanity and thus on the things they share with us. Similarity is a barrier to aggression. This may seem to be a lofty ideal, but research suggests that it really is possible. Norma Feshbach and Seymour

Feshbach (1982) trained elementary-school children to put themselves in other children's shoes, to recognize others' feelings, and to try to share their emotions. Compared with children in control groups, the children who engaged in this empathy training were much less aggressive in everyday playground activities. Empathy is fellow feeling, and fellow feeling is incompatible with aggression (P. A. Miller & Eisenberg, 1988).

☐ **REDUCING AGGRESSION IN SOCIETY.** Several structured programs have been found to be successful in reducing aggressive behavior, even among violent youthful offenders (Henggeler, Schoenwald, Borduin, Rowland, & Cunningham, 1998; Tate, Reppucci, & Mulvey, 1995). A recent meta-analysis of numerous studies of school-based programs aimed at reducing aggression among children found that the programs were generally effective, with an impressive 88% of the studies finding positive effects (Robinson, Smith, Miller, & Brownell, 1999). These positive outcomes endured over time, with little or no decrease in program effectiveness found months or even a year or two later. It does seem, then, that scientific knowledge about the causes and conditions the produce aggression can be incorporated into effective programs that limit its extent.

Resolving Conflict Through Negotiation

Conflict resolution also involves the parties in trying to find mutually acceptable solutions, which requires understanding and trust. When direct discussion is unproductive, for example, because of cultural differences, third parties can intervene to help the parties settle their conflict.

TYPES OF SOLUTIONS. In addition to the factors just discussed that can discourage an immediate resort to aggression in a conflict situation, there is also a longer range approach to conflict resolution that seeks solutions for the concrete disagreements that separate two individuals or groups. Sometimes solutions are dictated by one party, as when one nation overwhelms another by force or one person prevails in a lawsuit over another. In such cases, the conflict is resolved by an *imposed solution*. Not surprisingly, those who lose are usually dissatisfied with the outcome, and such solutions are rarely successful in ending conflict (Burke, 1970). Historians often point to the harsh terms of defeat imposed on Germany by the victors in the First World War as one of the factors that contributed to the rise of the Nazis and Germany's later aggression. Other conflicts are settled by *distributive solutions*, which involve mutual compromise or concessions that carve up a fixed-size pie. Examples of such solutions include international treaties that divide territory under dispute or union–management contracts that set workers' raises somewhere between the union's demands and management's proposals (R. Fisher & Ury, 1981). Compromise and concession mean that all parties must give up something they wanted, but the loss may be tolerable, particularly when compared to the cost of continued conflict.

■ **Communicating to resolve conflict**. Unless parties in conflict communicate, the common interests that may provide a basis for integrative solutions may never be realized. This photograph shows Pakistan's President General Pervez Musharraf shaking hands with Indian Prime Minister Man Mohan Singh during talks in 2005. Musharraf arrived in India on a visit that mixed cricket with diplomacy and said he brought with him "a message of peace," and to hold talks on how to end old hostilities between the two countries.

Calvin and Hobbes by Bill Watterson

Integrative solutions are the best solutions because one side's gain is not necessarily the other's loss. These solutions are often termed *win–win solutions* because both sides can benefit simultaneously (Pruitt & Rubin, 1986). Imagine, for example, a resolution in which labor and management agree to split the increased profits from a new way of organizing production so that both sides come out ahead (Kimmel, Pruitt, Maganu, Konar-Goldband, & Carnevale, 1980; Pruitt & Lewis, 1977). One strategy that can lead to integrative solutions is log-rolling, in which each party gives up on issues that it considers less important but that the other group views as crucial (Pruitt, 1986). Although each party gets only some of its demands, it wins on the issues it considers most important. In an industry where employment is dropping as a result of foreign competition, for example, the union may accept limited pay raises to get guarantees of job security. Management's concessions on job security enable it to maintain wage scales that allow competitive pricing.

Finding an integrative solution generally requires creative thinking and an understanding of each party's interests, values, goals, and costs. Identifying an integrative solution is more difficult than just locating some halfway point between the parties' demands. Integrative solutions attempt to satisfy the parties' underlying motives, rather than their explicit demands (R. Fisher & Ury, 1981), and they may offer the only way out of some difficult international conflicts. For example, Israel captured the Golan Heights region from Syria in 1967. Syria demands the return of this land and Israel refuses; neither party will accept a division of the territory between them. Some diplomats have suggested that an integrative solution might be possible, based on an analysis of the two parties' underlying needs rather than their contradictory claims to the same piece of landscape. Syria's main interest appears to be its national honor: International recognition of its sovereignty over the Golan Heights might satisfy it. Israel's overriding concern is military security: An ironclad guarantee that Syria could never mass troops and guns on the Golan might suffice. Both parties' most basic needs might be satisfied by a solution that restored the Golan Heights to Syria but guaranteed international monitoring to ensure that arms would never be placed there. Compared with solutions based on compromise, integrative solutions result in better outcomes for both parties, are more enduring, and produce better interparty relationships (Pruitt, 1986; L. Thompson, 1993).

ACHIEVING SOLUTIONS: THE NEGOTIATION PROCESS. Finding a solution to a conflict, particularly an integrative solution, requires the parties to communicate. **Negotiation** is reciprocal communication designed to reach agreement in situations in which some interests are shared and some are in opposition (R. Fisher & Ury, 1981; J. Z. Rubin & Brown, 1975). Diplomatic negotiations have successfully resolved international disputes over arms control, territory, and trade. Of course, not all negotiation is large scale and formal. We all negotiate with others virtually every day: when we discuss what movie to see with our friends, split up tasks with our co-workers, or debate bedtime with our children.

Successful resolution of conflict on small or large scales requires sufficient time for negotiation. Studies have shown that when parties are under time pressure, they reach less integrative solutions (Harinck & De Dreu, 2004). One reason may be that time pressure leads people to use stereotypes about the other parties to make judgments, rather than considering the situation systematically (De Dreu, 2005; Kray, Reb, Galinsky, & Thompson, 2004).

When adequate time is available, the fundamental goal of negotiators is to help each party understand how the other interprets and evaluates the issues. Unfortunately, conflicts often lead the parties to misperceive each other's position and goals, usually exaggerating their disagreement (L. Thompson & Hastie, 1990b). In one study demonstrating this point, 85% of the participants failed to realize, even after a period of negotiations, that they and their opponents agreed perfectly on one issue in contention (L. Thompson & Hastie, 1990a). These biased perceptions of adversaries lower the chances of an integrative solution. When one side proposes a solution, the other side automatically views it less favorably, reasoning that "if it's good for them it must be bad for us." This obstacle to integrative solutions is termed *reactive devaluation* (Curhan, Neale, & Ross, 2004; L. Ross & Nisbett, 1990).

One set of studies used the Palestinian–Israeli conflict to demonstrate political antagonists' tendency to devalue each other's proposals (Maoz, Ward, Katz, & Ross, 2002). Both Israeli Jews and Israeli Arabs devalued peace plans that were described to them if the plan was attributed to "the other side." The negative reactions were largely due to shifts in the perceivers' interpretations of what was being proposed—which differed dramatically depending on whether the proposal was attributed to an in-group or an out-group. Apparently, when one party in a conflict takes a position, it triggers a search for hidden motives and a devaluation of that position by the other party.

BUILDING TRUST. One of the priorities in negotiation is to build trust, so that parties will abandon their search for negative motives within each other's proposals. This is not easily accomplished because a history of bitter conflict is a poor foundation for trust. Even a sincere offer may be seen as a trick, a subterfuge designed to lull the opponent into a false sense of security. In such situations, trust must be built up by repeated displays of consistency between words and behavior (Lindskold, 1978; Weber, Malhotra, & Murnigham, 2005).

Negotiators usually try to break conflicts into sets of small, manageable issues. By focusing on specific issues rather than just repeatedly stating their overall conflicting goals, negotiation can reverse the decline of trust that occurs during the commitment and escalation phases of the conflict. This reversal comes about in two ways. First, when one party successfully negotiates an issue with the opponent, liking and trust for the other party increase, perhaps making later issues easier to settle (L. Thompson, 1993). In fact, negotiators who have reached successful agreements in the past are more likely to be able to agree again in the future, whereas past

Negotiation. The process by which parties in conflict communicate and influence each other to reach agreement.

disagreements are more likely to lead to impasse. Because trust is such an important outcome, good negotiators tend to think of negotiations as ongoing relationships rather than one-time interactions (O'Connor, Arnold, & Burris, 2005).

Second, when issues are narrow and specific, the parties in conflict have a better chance of accurately perceiving each other's positions rather than assuming the worst about them. Accurate perceptions of the other side's views and interests are the best hope for success in negotiation (L. Thompson & Hastie, 1990a, 1990b).

TRUST AND THE NORM OF RECIPROCITY. During the height of the Cold War, Charles Osgood (1962) and Amitai Etzioni (1962) independently suggested that reciprocal concessions could both build trust and reduce intergroup tensions. Osgood advised world governments to use *graduated and reciprocated initiatives in tension reduction (GRIT)* to de-escalate conflicts.

The GRIT process begins when one side states its intention to reduce the conflict and makes a small concession to its opponent. The norm of reciprocity pushes the opposing group to make a small concession of its own or risk public condemnation. Of course, the party offering the first concession must walk a fine line between strength and weakness, because total cooperation is often interpreted as an opportunity for exploitation (Reychler, 1979). If the opponent reciprocates with a concession, the first group follows with a slightly more significant concession. Again the opponent reciprocates with a greater concession, and a feeling of trust gradually builds as tensions wind down. Simulations of international negotiations in the laboratory have confirmed that reciprocal concessions may be effective in reducing international tensions (Lindskold, 1986).

Remember from Chapter 10, pages 360 to 365, that just as we feel obligated to return a favor for a favor, we feel obligated to follow a concession with a concession.

□ **GRIT AND INTERNATIONAL CONFLICTS.** The tactics recommended in the GRIT strategy have been used successfully in international relations. In June 1963, President John F. Kennedy, calling attention to the dangers of nuclear war, announced a unilateral halt to American atmospheric tests of nuclear weapons and promised not to resume testing unless another country did so first. Within 2 months, Soviet Premier Nikita Khrushchev ended the production of Soviet strategic bombers, agreed to the emergency communication hot line between Moscow and Washington, and signed a treaty limiting nuclear testing. Similarly, in 1977, Egyptian President Anwar Sadat's dramatic initiative of traveling to Jerusalem led to the Camp David peace talks and a treaty normalizing relations between Israel and Egypt. Cases like these suggest that GRIT shows promise in reducing international tensions (Druckman, 1990; Etzioni, 1967; Pettigrew, 2003).

NEGOTIATING ACROSS CULTURAL LINES. Pervasive differences among cultures influence the way people negotiate just as they influence other types of social interaction (M. White, Härtel, & Panipucci, 2005). As we have seen many times before, whether individuals come from individually oriented or collectivist cultures can make a big difference to the motives that people bring to interactions. One recent meta-analysis of 36 empirical studies found that negotiators from individualistic cultures preferred competitive strategies such as demanding concessions. In contrast, negotiators from collectivist cultures were more likely to prefer problem solving, compromising or even withdrawing from the negotiation as a means of trying to reach agreement (Adair & Brett, 2005; Holt & Devore, 2005). Training in differing cultural styles and expectations for negotiation could be a valuable preparation for those who bargain with members of other cultures.

Another factor that comes into play when parties to a negotiation come from different groups is a greater emphasis on outcomes rather than perceptions of fairness (Tyler and others, 1998). When members of a common in-group negotiate, they are concerned not only about how they stand in the final outcome, but also about being treated fairly and respectfully (Tyler & Lind, 1992). Thus, when conflict takes place within a group, fair treatment, politeness, and respect for all may win assent for an agreement, even if all cannot get what they want in terms of the concrete resources at stake. However, when negotiations cross group lines, concerns about fairness and respect recede, leaving the parties more interested in simply what they can get—potentially complicating the resolution of their dispute.

MEDIATION AND ARBITRATION: BRINGING IN THIRD PARTIES. Even if people share the same culture, direct communication is not always the best way to resolve conflicts. When opponents are too angry to discuss issues rationally or negotiators run out of ideas for resolving an impasse, third-party intervention may offer the best hope for a solution. The United Nations Security Council, baseball labor arbitrators, divorce mediators, moderators at a debate, and parents intervening in their children's squabbles are all third parties attempting to inhibit, regulate, or help resolve conflicts. Some negotiations involve *mediators* who help the opponents focus their discussion on the issues and reach a voluntary agreement. In *arbitration*, the third party has the power to hand down a decision after hearing the disputants present their arguments and information.

Third-party intervention has several advantages. First, mediators or arbitrators can arrange meeting agendas, times, and places so that these details don't themselves become sources of conflict (Raven & Rubin, 1976). Second, skillful intervention—mediation, in particular—can improve intergroup relationships. In one case, third parties were called in to mediate a dispute between public housing tenants and private homeowners in a small Canadian community. As a result of their work, intergroup attitudes improved, as did understanding of the complexity of each side's position (R. Fisher & White, 1976). A third advantage of third-party intervention is that, because outsiders bring fresh ideas, they may be able to offer more creative integrative solutions than those proposed by people deeply enmeshed in the conflict (R. Fisher & Ury, 1981). Finally, a skilled third party can leave room for graceful retreat and face saving when disputants lock themselves into positions they themselves realize are untenable (Pruitt, 1981). Third-party intervention may allow both sides to accept concessions without embarrassment. By doing so, it is more likely to lead to a mutually acceptable outcome than is unaided negotiations (J. Z. Rubin, 1980). It is also more likely to reduce stress and frustration for the parties locked in ongoing conflict (Giebels & Janssen, 2005).

Intergroup Cooperation: Changing Social Identity

Conflict resolution can also be facilitated by having groups cooperate toward shared goals that can be attained only if both groups work together. Under the proper conditions, cooperative intergroup interaction reduces conflict.

After an athletic contest that marked the height of the Robbers Cave conflict, the researchers decided to see whether joint participation in some pleasant activity could reduce hostilities. They arranged for the boys to have meals at the same time and to watch a movie together. If you recall our discussion in Chapter 5 of the conditions under which contact improves intergroup attitudes, you will not be surprised that the group contact did not help. Rather than providing the opportunity for consistently friendly interaction that disconfirmed stereotypes—the key to changing negative group perceptions—this kind of contact increased hostilities. The boys found that the shared meals provided perfect opportunities for food fights.

SUPERORDINATE GOALS. When simple contact failed, the researchers tried a different strategy. They engaged the groups in the pursuit of **superordinate goals**, which are goals that can be attained only if groups work cooperatively as a team. Examples of superordinate goals in political life are cooperation between agricultural and urban interests to increase the water supply for all, and cooperation between nations to reduce greenhouse gases in the atmosphere to stop global warming. At Robbers Cave the superordinate goals were a series of problems that could be solved only if the teams worked together. For example, the staff staged a breakdown of the water supply, and the boys worked together to trace the water pipeline back into the hills. A movie was too expensive for either group alone to rent, so all the boys pooled their funds to pay the rental fee. Finally, after finding that the camp truck had broken down, they figured out how to restart the truck by pulling on a rope attached to its bumper. In contrast to the earlier competitive tug-of-war contests, the boys literally had to pull together, and, thanks to the driver's carefully calibrated foot pressure on the brake, it took the efforts of all the boys from both groups to get the truck moving.

Superordinate goals improved intergroup relationships, but not overnight. After repairing the water supply, the two groups mingled good-naturedly, but they capped the day off with a food fight. They rented the movie with pooled resources, but the two groups sat on opposite sides of the dining hall to watch it. After 6 days of cooperation, however, their previous hostilities were greatly decreased, as can be seen in Figure 13.7. In fact, when it was time to leave, they asked if they could travel home together on one bus. As the boys took their seats on the bus, the camp staff noticed that a Rattler was just as likely to sit next to an Eagle as to another Rattler (M. Sherif & Sherif, 1953). Superordinate goals have had similar success in eliminating other forms of experimentally induced conflict (Diab, 1970).

> **Superordinate goals.** Shared goals that can be attained only if groups work together.

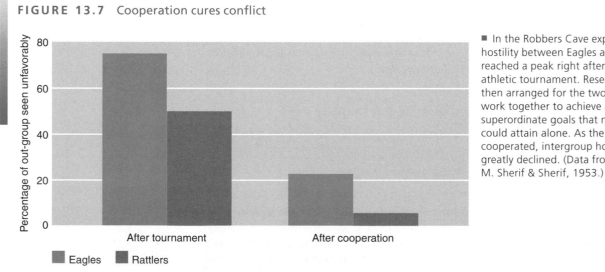

FIGURE 13.7   Cooperation cures conflict

■ In the Robbers Cave experiment, hostility between Eagles and Rattlers reached a peak right after an athletic tournament. Researchers then arranged for the two groups to work together to achieve a series of superordinate goals that neither could attain alone. As the boys cooperated, intergroup hostility greatly declined. (Data from M. Sherif & Sherif, 1953.)

WHY DOES INTERGROUP COOPERATION WORK?. Intergroup cooperation is not a foolproof cure for conflict. But when the right conditions exist, intergroup cooperation undermines many processes that contribute to conflict and it encourages positive interactions that can ultimately reduce prejudice (Allport, 1954b; Pettigrew, 1997, 1998; Pettigrew & Tropp, 2006). What are those conditions?

- *Cooperation should be for a valued common goal, which eliminates competition for material and social resources.* Rather than battling for pocketknives or bragging rights, the campers at Robbers Cave pooled their talents and resources to reach mutually desired goals (Gaertner and others, 2000).

- *Cooperation should provide repeated opportunities to disconfirm out-group stereotypes.* Remember that intergroup conflict arises from group differences as well as from competition over resources. As we saw at Robbers Cave, it took several bouts of cooperation to bring the Rattlers and Eagles together. Similar results are found in laboratory studies: A single cooperative episode often has quite limited effects (Lockhart & Elliot, 1981; Wilder & Thompson, 1980).

- *Cooperation should produce successful results.* If groups fail while working together, each is likely to blame the other, and hostility may even increase (Worchel, 1979; Worchel & Norvell, 1980). In contrast, success helps the intergroup climate, in part by allowing friendships to grow up across group lines (Pettigrew, 1997).

- *Cooperation should take place between equals, at least for the task at hand.* The Rattlers and the Eagles were all equally capable of pulling the bus and donating to the film fund.

- *Cooperation should be supported and promoted by social norms.* The goal of peaceable and respectful coexistence needs official institutional endorsement (Allport, 1954b; Amir, 1969). A few instances of cooperation cannot overwhelm intergroup hostility that is culturally ingrained and institutionally supported. Thus, for example, brief programs that bring together Israeli Jews and Palestinian Arabs will not change intergroup perceptions if segregated communities continue to isolate one group from the other.

Intergroup cooperation resolves conflicts over concrete resources because it makes the out-group a source of rewards rather than punishments. Cooperation also resolves problems of esteem and status by creating friendships across group lines and eventually fusing the warring parties into one new and improved in-group (Gaertner & Dovidio, 2000; Gaertner and others, 1989, 1990; Pettigrew, 1997). Figure 13.8 portrays this idea. As "we" and "they" become just "we," the new, larger group membership can be a source of self-esteem and a positive social identity (S. Feshbach & Singer, 1957; Gaertner & Dovidio, 2000). Even more importantly, "we" feelings decrease competition. In an experimental demonstration of this point, Roderick Kramer (1989) had small groups of participants play a game simulating an arms race. To create in-group feelings, some participants were reminded that all the groups had some features in common. Compared with

FIGURE 13.8 Processes in conflict resolution

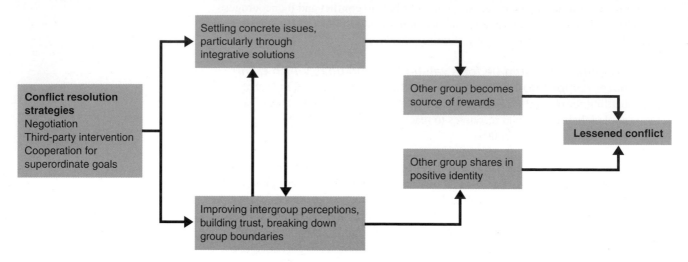

■ Just as social and cognitive processes can help escalate conflict, the processes involved in conflict resolution can build on themselves. Interventions that either help the groups settle the concrete issues in dispute or improve their feelings about each other can set the tone for further reductions in conflict.

participants not receiving the reminder, those with "we" feelings were much less likely to stockpile weapons. Similarly, in a study in which two groups of participants drew from a common resource pool, each took large amounts and quickly depleted the resource (Kramer & Brewer, 1984). However, when participants were reminded of their joint membership in a larger shared group, both groups cooperated more and used less of the resource.

Forming a new and more inclusive in-group works best in solving intergroup conflict if the original groups are permitted to retain some measure of distinctiveness rather than merging completely (Condor & Brown, 1988). For example, each group might perform distinct roles and tasks that contribute to the overall good (R. Brown, Condor, Matthews, Wade, & Williams, 1986; Deschamps & Brown, 1983; Hornsey & Hogg, 2000). In this way, each group maintains its own cultural distinctiveness and its positive identity, but cooperating toward a greater goal improves its view of other groups (D. M. Taylor & Simard, 1979). The real ideal of a multicultural society is a tossed salad, not a melting pot. Every group's contribution is valued and respected for itself rather than as an indistinguishable part of a uniform whole. Cultural differences then become opportunities for learning and mutual enrichment rather than bases for conflict (Deutsch, 1993; Wolsko and others, 2000).

Under the right conditions, intergroup cooperation not only leads group members to think of themselves in terms of a higher-level common identity, but also encourages them to get to know out-group members as individuals (Bettencourt, Brewer, Croak, & Miller, 1992; Brewer, 1999). Over time, as out-group members become friends, reductions in bias should result (Pettigrew, 1997; Pettigrew & Tropp, 2006). Thus, cooperation works at multiple levels: increasing the salience of a new and more inclusive in-group, and also decreasing the salience of group memberships in general as relationships become more friendly and personalized. Because many real-world intergroup situations involve many and varied sources of conflict—such as competing group interests, historical wrongs committed by each group against the other, negative stereotypes, segregation, and limited opportunity for contact—the fact that intergroup cooperation can work in multiple ways is perhaps its strongest advantage (Hewstone, Rubin, & Willis, 2002).

Intergroup cooperation for superordinate goals holds the promise of true conflict resolution, rather than conflict management (S. P. Cohen & Arnone, 1988). Conflict resolution turns groups' basic strivings for mastery and connectedness toward positive ends. Previously hostile groups find ways to enhance their identities by cooperating, for example, in creating a truly multicultural society, rather than by outdoing one another. New symbols are created that reflect pride and respect for both sides, and the groups' old symbols of intransigence and hatred are allowed to slip into history. Just as conflict can build on itself and escalate, each step toward conflict resolution—whether aimed at task or social interdependence—can help to further reduce conflict, as Figure 13.8 shows. Peaceful relations will ultimately be possible when the world community finds ways to accommodate the needs of groups and nations not only for physical security and material resources, but also for positive and distinctive identities.

CONCLUDING COMMENTS

Whenever someone commits aggression, it is a safe bet that the person sees it as reasonable, well justified, even necessary. A man who kills in a barroom brawl sees himself as retaliating against the previous punch thrown by his victim or as defending his honor against an intolerable insult or slur. Muggers and robbers see themselves as taking what they need from those who have too much and whose losses will be covered by insurance in any case. It is worth repeating the eloquent statement by Martin Luther King, Jr. (1967), which we already quoted in Chapter 6: "It seems to be a fact of life that human beings cannot continue to do wrong without eventually reaching out for some rationalization to clothe their acts in the garments of righteousness" (p. 72). The clothing is often so complete that people do not even feel guilty about their acts that harm others.

When individuals make their own interpretations of reality, they are deeply vulnerable to rationalizing their self-interest in these ways. As Chapter 9 discussed, seeking consensus from others often helps us see situations clearly. For those who fail to rely on others' perceptions to check their own possibly skewed opinions, the result in all too many cases is the aggressive behavior of the outlaw: the petty bully, mugger, or murderer.

When groups commit aggression, they, too, rationalize their acts with high-sounding words and ideas. Exploiting, repressing, even massacring other groups are considered necessary to fulfill the glorious in-group's historical destiny or to redress past wrongs. Those outsiders are in any case less than fully human, so they do not deserve moral consideration.

When groups interpret reality for their members, they, too, are vulnerable to rationalizing their own self-interested desires for mastery of resources or for respect and esteem. The processes of conformity and groupthink can mean that no group members dare to speak out, even if they are capable of seeing things differently. The result in all too many cases is the aggressive behavior of groups

CHAPTER 13 THEMES

- **Construction of Reality**
  Aggression and conflict are often driven by people's perceptions of others.

- **Pervasiveness of Social Influence**
  Social norms and people's group memberships dramatically influence aggression and conflict.

- **Striving for Mastery**
  The prospect of concrete rewards frequently triggers instrumental aggression and group conflict.

- **Seeking Connectedness**
  Disrespect and other threats to feelings of connectedness frequently trigger emotional aggression and group conflict.

- **Valuing Me and Mine**
  Valuing a group can lead to downgrading others, exacerbating conflicts.

- **Conservatism**
  Conflict is often self-perpetuating.

- **Superficiality Versus Depth**
  In-depth processing can diminish aggression by allowing people to think of alternative solutions to conflict.

of true believers: fanatical Nazis, Bosnian Serbs bent on "ethnic cleansing," or Rwandan Hutus whipped by self-serving political leaders into a murderous frenzy against Tutsis.

Outlaws or true believers? Is that our choice for the world today? If it is, we would reluctantly point out that true believers are probably more dangerous. The civilized world thought it had put genocide behind it with the defeat of Nazi Germany and the Nuremberg war crimes trials, only to see intergroup conflict and massacre re-emerge within a few years in India and Pakistan, Africa, and central Europe. Our opinion that true believers are probably a greater threat than outlaws is supported by the research reviewed in this chapter, showing that groups are more aggressive than individuals.

But perhaps we need not choose between these two depressing alternatives. There is no single easy answer that works for every time and situation. Individuals cannot stand independent and reject group consensus without becoming easy prey for rationalized self-interest: That way lies the outlaw. Neither can individuals unthinkingly accede to the siren song of group consensus, which may rationalize and glorify group interests while dehumanizing opponents: That produces true believers. But each of us can try to balance our own individual perceptions and group consensus, applying plenty of thought—unclouded by strong emotion or immediate responses to threat. We must beware particularly of group-induced and group-sanctioned actions that victimize out-groups. History shows that group consensus that calls for aggressive action against outsiders, even when portrayed as necessary self-defense or a well-justified response to past injustices, requires the most searching moral scrutiny.

S U M M A R Y

 Aggression, Conflict, and Human Nature. When people are in **conflict**, or see their goals as incompatible, they may attempt to harm each other. An immediate intention to hurt someone is what defines behavior as **aggression**.

Humans have evolved to compete effectively for food and mates. Although the capacity to act aggressively may have helped, aggression has no special place in "human nature." Aggression is just one strategy among many others that humans use to attain rewards and respect in accordance with individual perceptions and social norms.

Interpersonal Aggression. Aggression can be difficult to study experimentally, because people are often unwilling to act aggressively when they are being observed. Researchers have used a variety of techniques to get around these problems.

Instrumental aggression is triggered by potential rewards and is suppressed by perceived costs or risks. Sometimes, however, perceived provocation produces anger, which can set off hostile aggression. Any negative emotion, in fact, can make aggression more likely.

Social norms can either promote or restrain aggression. They can be activated by the behavior of models witnessed in person or in the media. Norms that limit aggression apply with special force to aggression against similar others or in-group members.

Situations that favor superficial thinking often favor aggression. Thinking carefully can reduce aggression, but many factors interfere with people's motivation and ability to process information carefully and evenhandedly, increasing the likelihood of aggression.

Intergroup Conflict. Groups are generally even more competitive and aggressive than individuals.

Group conflict often stems from competition for valued material resources, according to **realistic conflict theory**, or for social rewards like respect and esteem. Groups in conflict are often more attuned to social rewards than to material ones. Individuals and groups use social comparisons to determine acceptable levels of resources, as described by **relative deprivation theory**.

Once conflict starts, poor communication can make it worse. In-group interaction hardens in-group opinion, threats are directed at the out-group, each group retaliates more and more harshly, and other parties choose sides. All of these processes tend to escalate the conflict.

As escalation continues, the in-group sees the out-group as totally evil and sees itself in unrealistically positive terms. Because the same biases characterize each group, each group's image of itself and that of its opponent tend to be similar. Emotion and arousal make these biases even worse.

Ultimately, conflict may escalate into an attempt at total domination or destruction of the out-group. When power differences exist between the groups and the out-group is morally excluded, one group may try to eliminate the other.

Resolving Conflict and Reducing Aggression. One approach to reducing aggression and conflict is to minimize or remove the cues that often cause individuals to commit aggressive acts, and to encourage careful interpretation and identification with others.

Conflict resolution also involves the parties in trying to find mutually acceptable solutions through **negotiation**, which requires understanding and trust. When direct discussion is unproductive, for example, because of cultural differences, third parties can intervene to help the parties settle their conflict.

Conflict resolution can also be facilitated by having groups cooperate toward **superordinate goals**, shared goals that can be attained only if both groups work together. Under the proper conditions, cooperative intergroup interaction reduces conflict.

14

Helping and Cooperation

As social beings, we often act, alone or in groups, to benefit other people. Some of these kindnesses are quite ordinary—we help an elderly neighbor do her shopping, drop some spare change into the collection box for an especially needy charity, or pool our resources and skills for a morning to build a playground in a rundown neighborhood. At other times we give generously of our effort and energy, volunteering to help battered women or people with AIDS, spending hours to help a stranded motorist restart his car, or organizing the collection and shipping of medical supplies to those affected by hurricanes, earthquakes, and tsunamis. And sometimes, people even risk their own health and safety for others. New York City firefighters willingly put their own lives in jeopardy attempting to save trapped occupants of the World Trade Center on September 11, 2001, with horrific consequences. Mother Teresa, who died in 1998, had risked disease and danger to live a life of dedication to the poorest and most needy in the slums of Calcutta, India. While rescuers airlifted those injured when a jet crashed in 1982 into an ice-covered river in Washington, DC, one survivor eventually lost his life after repeatedly giving up his place on a helicopter to others more seriously injured. And despite constant intimidation, arrests, and executions at the hands of their own Vichy government, the people of the French village of Le Chambon-sur-Lignon worked tirelessly together between 1937 and 1943 to hide and protect no fewer than 5000 refugees, among them 3500 Jews, from the systematic persecutions of the Third Reich.

Social psychologists call these everyday kindnesses as well as inspiring acts of heroism **prosocial behavior**: behavior whose immediate goal is to help or benefit others. As was the case with aggressive behavior, it is the intention with which action is carried out, rather than its consequences, that defines behavior as prosocial. In studying helping, social psychologists have looked at many kinds of behavior: giving aid in everyday situations, dramatic responses to emergencies, and long-term commitments of time, effort, and even personal risk (Penner, Dovidio, Piliavin, & Schroeder, 2005). In laboratory studies, for instance, they have asked participants to aid others who are working on boring and repetitive tasks (Berkowitz & Daniels, 1963) or to volunteer to take the place of someone scheduled to receive painful electric shocks (Batson, Duncan, Ackerman, Buckley, &

Prosocial behavior. Behavior intended to help someone else.

Birch, 1981). Outside the laboratory, researchers have investigated why people donate blood and organs (Piliavin, Callero, & Evans, 1982), whether a brief encounter with a smiling person makes people more likely to help someone pick up dropped computer diskettes (Guéguen and DeGail, 2003), and what circumstances affect responses to staged emergencies (Cramer, McMaster, & Bartell, 1988). This variety of research approaches means that researchers' conclusions about prosocial behavior often have high construct validity and good generalizability. What are their conclusions about what makes people help?

As you will see, helping and cooperation depend on how people interpret social situations and the social influences acting on them. We begin this chapter by exploring when people help. Indeed, it seems that for every example of heartwarming generosity, there are also examples of people turning away, failing to render much-needed aid, or ignoring and deflecting pleas for assistance. Understanding the individual and social forces that lead people to help also uncovers the circumstances in which people don't help, even when others seem to be in need.

We then turn to the tricky question of what motivates helping. We often label behaviors such as sending money to support starving children, biking to work to help improve the community's air quality, or delivering care parcels to the needy as altruism. But this term has a more specific meaning, referring to one possible motive for helping: **Altruism** refers to prosocial behavior motivated by the desire to benefit others for their own sake, rather than for personal rewards (Batson, 1991, 2002). Consider the following example. Walking with a friend down the street, you donate $10 to someone collecting money for a homeless shelter. You intended to help the homeless, but also wanted to impress your companion with your generosity. Because this behavior involves an intention to help, it is an example of prosocial behavior. Is it also altruism? No, because of the element of personal gain involved.

Of course, as is the case with aggression (discussed in the previous chapter), multiple motives often influence any single act. For this reason, we will see that it is often difficult to know whether a particular incident of helping is altruistically motivated. In fact, some argue that pure altruism doesn't exist—that helping is always in one way or another driven by **egoism**, the desire to obtain personal rewards, if only in the form of positive feelings about having helped. Can people never think, feel, or act for the greater good of others without being driven by self-interest? To answer this question, we need to go beyond the issue of when people help, and probe why. Is the tendency to help part of our genetic make-up? What motivates people to help others in distress or need? After we discuss this intriguing issue later in the chapter, we consider how people actually make decisions about helping, whether under the time pressure and stress of a sudden emergency or with leisure to reflect and consider long-term helping commitments.

Understanding prosocial behavior provides a foundation for considering a very practical question: How can we promote more caring, helpful, and cooperative communities? In the last part of the chapter, we will see what suggestions for increasing the level of prosocial behavior in society emerge from social-psychological research.

When Do People Help?

Imagine walking back home from a trip to the neighborhood store one evening, carrying a half-gallon of milk. You notice a car stopped at the curb. You can hear fruitless attempts to start the motor. Although you glance repeatedly at the car, the

Altruism. Behavior intended to help someone else without any prospect of personal rewards for the helper.

Egoism. Behavior motivated by the desire to obtain personal rewards.

elderly driver does not wave or gesture for help. After a pause, the attempts to start the engine begin again and then cease. You see another pedestrian further down the street. After a casual glance over his shoulder at the sound of the sputtering engine, he walks on.

Even in this common, everyday situation, the questions that might run through your mind as you decide whether or not to help are the very same ones that determine helping in the most extreme emergencies. If you are like most people, the first and most crucial issue is whether help is actually needed. Like most social situations, those in which helping might be necessary are often ambiguous: Does the driver need help or not? But other questions soon follow: What should be done? And should you be the one to do it? Whether people are responding to an emergency, giving casual aid, or making a long-term commitment as a caregiver, helping behavior is affected by the same social and cognitive factors that influence all social behavior. Helping is crucially dependent on people's interpretation of a situation, but such perceptions don't take place in a social vacuum. As we saw in Chapters 9 and 10, the actions of others are often crucially important to whether we act or not.

Is Help Needed and Deserved?

Helping is dependent on people's perception of someone as both needing and deserving help. The ability and motivation to pay attention to others' needs influence whether people think help is needed, as does the behavior of other people in the situation. People are more likely to help those not held responsible for their own need.

NOTICING NEED. Imagine walking through your quiet neighborhood in the evening and hearing the motorist's repeated attempts to start the stranded car. Now imagine jostling your way down a busy city street, trying to tune out the roar of traffic and the honking of taxicabs. The driver of a car stopped by the sidewalk is trying in vain to start the motor. Although the first person's need is easy to notice, the second's may not be. Becoming aware of a need is usually the first step in the helping chain of events (Darley & Latané, 1968), and busy or noisy surroundings reduce the likelihood of people noticing that someone needs help (Korte, Ypma, & Toppen, 1975). No doubt this is one reason that people are more likely to help others in quiet, rural areas than in crowded cities (Eisenberg, 1991; R. V. Levine, Martinez, Brase, & Sorenson, 1994).

Some people are better able to see a need for help than others are. People who feel happy seem to pay more attention to others around them and are more likely to notice others' needs than sad people (Schaller & Cialdini, 1990). No wonder, then, that positive thinking often translates into positive actions. In a study demonstrating this point, researchers put one group of students in a good mood by telling them they had succeeded on a task, whereas another group were put in a bad mood by learning they had failed the task (Isen & Levin, 1972). When a confederate dropped a stack of books nearby, the happy students were more likely to help than the unhappy ones. Happy participants also remembered much more about the confederate and her actions, demonstrating that happy people's attention is turned outward. For this reason, they are more attuned to others' needs for help.

Other people's reactions can also dictate whether or not we perceive a need. No one wants to foolishly rush in to help in a case that may not be an emergency after all. In fact, people sometimes fail to act because of *audience inhibition*: the

You may recognize this as a state of pluralistic ignorance, discussed in detail in Chapter 9, pages 332 to 334.

fear of appearing foolish in front of others (Latané, Nida, & Wilson, 1981). So we usually keep calm and check to see what others present are doing. Perhaps in the example of the stalled car, the fact that the other passerby did not seem concerned would have made you less likely to help. Of course, if everyone else is also keeping calm while they check the reactions of others, everyone will conclude that no one else is upset and thus that help is not needed.

In one series of studies, experimenters arranged for smoke to pour into a laboratory room in which students were sitting completing questionnaires (Latané & Darley, 1968). When the students were alone, their concern at the unusual situation soon led them to seek help. But when two confederates in the room failed to react to the smoke, participants also did nothing. It is not the mere presence of others that facilitates or inhibits action, but what the actions of others tell us about the situation. For example, if an apparently blind confederate failed to react to the smoke, participants ignored the lack of response and went for help. But if the blind confederate failed to react to screams and cries of pain from a woman in an adjoining room, participants did nothing (A. S. Ross & Braband, 1973). When people notice that bystanders and passersby are unresponsive, that observation reduces the likelihood that they will help (R. E. Smith, Vanderbilt, & Callen, 1973).

JUDGING DESERVINGNESS. Even if you noticed a stranded motorist, a panhandler asking for change on a street-corner, or a person slumped in a doorway, would you offer help? Helping depends on whether we think help is deserved, and groups typically develop norms that dictate who does and does not deserve help (Caporael & Brewer, 1991). The *norm of social responsibility*, for example, suggests that those able to take care of themselves have a duty and obligation to assist those who cannot: the old, young, sick, helpless, or dependent (Berkowitz, 1972; Berkowitz & Daniels, 1963). Sometimes people are judged as deserving help simply because they have less than us: People who believe that they have more than their fair share often give valued resources to others or take less than they could (Mikula, 1980). In close relationships, norms dictate communal sharing of resources with others based on their need (M. S. Clark & Mills, 1979; A. P. Fiske, 1991). This norm is also prevalent in cohesive groups. Among the Moose people of West Africa, for example, even the most valuable resources, such as land and water in time of drought, are shared freely with anyone who asks for them (A. P. Fiske, 1991).

In many cultures, particularly in the individualistic cultures of the West, deservingness also depends on the attributions we make about controllability. If we think people are in need "through no fault of their own" (that is, due to an uncontrollable cause), we are more motivated to help. If, on the other hand, we perceive people as having "brought it on themselves" (a controllable cause), we think they don't deserve help and we are less likely to offer it (Reisenzein, 1986; G. Schmidt & Weiner, 1988). Thus, helping a person unconscious on the sidewalk seems more appropriate when the victim is ill than when he or she is drunk.

■ **Lending a helping hand**. Would you ask this distressed looking man if he was OK, or if he needed any help? If not, is it because you think he may be drunk, or that he can handle himself? Decisions to help are often based on perceptions of whether the person in trouble needs and deserves help.

The importance of norms about controllability and deservingness helps explain why people who believe that opportunity for economic advancement is open to all, and who thus see poverty as the result of a lack of effort by the poor, are likely to oppose governmental programs to help those in need (Kluegel & Smith, 1986). Similarly, in another study, those who perceived homosexuals and single mothers as responsible for their own group's unemployment problems were less likely to offer the group help (L. M. Jackson & Esses, 1997).

Should I Help?

People sometimes help because social norms, their own standards, or the behavior of others show them that it is appropriate to do so. Not all norms promote helping, however, and sometimes the presence of other potential helpers can diminish the normative pressures to help.

Even when people recognize a need for help, recognition doesn't always translate into action. An event that took place on the streets of Queens, New York early one March morning in 1964 made this fact tragically clear (Latané & Darley, 1970).

The facts of the case are straightforward and brutal. Kitty Genovese was attacked by Winston Moseley, a 29-year-old machine operator, as she returned to her apartment from her night job. Bleeding from multiple stab wounds, Genovese staggered to a street corner, where she called for help. As lights in the surrounding apartments went on, her assailant returned and stabbed her again. Over half an hour after the attack began, Kitty Genovese finally died. Investigations showed that at least 38 people heard her cries for help or saw part of the attack, but none of them helped, not even by calling the police. Why didn't anybody help? What might have made them act differently?

IS HELPING UP TO ME? DIFFUSION OF RESPONSIBILITY. To those who pondered this question, it was clear that the onlookers noticed that something was happening and realized that the situation was an emergency. Hearing the screams, nearby residents switched on their lights, and some looked out their windows. And although at first onlookers may have wondered if the dispute was between a husband and wife, Kitty Genovese herself made clear the seriousness of the situation with her screams: "My God, he stabbed me. Please help me, please help, I'm dying, I'm dying."

Although the press castigated the indifference of Genovese's neighbors, two social psychologists, John Darley and Bibb Latané (1968) were not so sure. The source of the bystanders' passivity, the researchers believed, lay in the presence of other onlookers, which influenced their decisions about whether helping was their responsibility or not. They decided to study this aspect of the helping situation in the laboratory.

Participants in Darley and Latané's study thought they had signed up for a group discussion about problems of college life. Supposedly to minimize embarrassment and to guarantee anonymity, each participant was seated alone in an intercom-equipped cubicle. Each person was told that his or her microphone would be activated for 2 minutes at a time, giving each person in turn a chance to talk while the other group members—but not the experimenter—listened. In reality, all of this was stage management. Only one person participated at a time, believing that one, two, or five other group members, represented by tape recordings, were also present.

Then came the emergency. The participant heard one of the other "group members," who had previously mentioned a susceptibility to epilepsy, suddenly begin to have a seizure. Speaking with increasing difficulty, he asked for help and then lapsed into silence. How did people react? As Figure 14.1 shows, the more other people the participants believed to be present, the less likely they were to help and the longer they delayed before seeking aid. Of those who thought that four other potential helpers were present, only 62% ever came to the victim's aid. Don't assume the passive majority didn't care, however. Most were in the grip of anxiety and indecision, caught between behaving inappropriately by helping and behaving inappropriately by not helping.

Darley and Latané concluded that the number of participants in the group made a difference because when other people are present, responsibility is divided and each person feels less responsible for helping than when alone. This diffusion of responsibility explanation has been supported by additional studies showing that people who are alone when they notice an emergency feel that it is their personal responsibility to get involved, but far fewer do so when many other people are present and apparently able to help (Bickman, 1971; Schwartz & Gottlieb, 1980). In addition, a massive study conducted in 36 cities across the United States tested six different types of helping (including offering to help a blind person with a white cane cross a street, telling someone that he had "accidentally" dropped a pen from his pocket, and donating to the United Way). Helping was systematically lower in cities with higher population densities, suggesting that diffusion of responsibility also affects helping at the level of communities (R. V. Levine and others, 1994).

WHEN NORMS MAKE HELPING APPROPRIATE. The presence of others does not always inhibit helping, however. Individuals who hold leadership responsibility or people who have been specially designated as the person who should help do come through in emergency situations (Baumeister, Chesner, Senders, & Tice, 1988). And if one person rushes to offer help, many more may also do so: The first person

FIGURE 14.1 Diffusion of responsibility: Lost in the crowd

■ In this experiment, participants heard another participant having a "seizure" in what they believed was a group of two, three, or six people. (They actually heard recordings of other voices.) The more people participants believed to be present, the less likely the real participants were to help. (Data from Darley & Latané, 1968.)

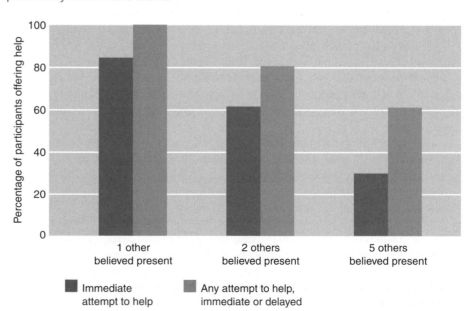

Immediate attempt to help

Any attempt to help, immediate or delayed

serves as a model or example, implicitly defining helping as an appropriate response (Bandura, 1977b; Staub, 1978). Because we rely on others for information that helps us understand what is happening and gives us clues about what we should do, such models encourage others to do likewise. In one field study of the effect of this social learning on helping, researchers stationed a motorist with an apparently disabled car at the side of the road. If drivers had recently seen another motorist helping out with a different disabled car, they were more likely to offer aid than drivers who had not had the opportunity to see an altruistic model (Bryan & Test, 1967). And prosocial models can always be provided to help a good cause. When one group of researchers sought ways to increase the money contributed to worthy causes, they discovered that indicating that others had found giving to be an appropriate response—"We've already received contributions ranging from a penny up"—doubled the frequency of giving compared to a control condition (Cialdini & Schroeder, 1976). These findings provide further evidence of the power of social norms: In ambiguous situations, the way that other people (models) act has a big impact on our own behavior.

■ **The norms of helping**. Norms such as social responsibilty, reciprocity, and social commitment often play a role in motivating helping behavior. When thousands of people—old and young, healthy and sick—turn out for walkathons to help raise money for charitable causes, the decision to participate is influenced by social norms as well as personal desires.

The importance of norms became even clearer when social psychologists asked why some individuals have strong personal feelings of obligation that lead them to help others in unusual, costly, or dangerous ways (Schwartz, 1977). Why do such people help in situations in which others turn away? They often have been deeply influenced by personal examples, particularly their parents who may teach norms that encourage helping others (Staub, 2002). Studies of heroic helpers, such as committed civil-rights workers in the segregated Southern United States in the 1960s and Gentiles who sheltered Jews from the Nazis during the Third Reich, have found that they often identify strongly with a parent who exemplified norms of concern for others (Oliner & Oliner, 1988; Rosenhan, 1970). Religious teachings can also make a difference: Among both college students and the general public, religiously committed individuals are more likely than the less committed to give time and money to help those they perceive as needy (Benson and others, 1980; Colasanto, 1989).

WHEN NORMS MAKE HELPING INAPPROPRIATE. Group norms dictate not only who gets help, but also who does not. Conservative estimates suggest that in the United States alone, at least 2 million young children, half of all adolescents, and as many as 2.5 million elderly people are the targets of physical violence from family members (Gelles, 1997; Straus, 1991). One factor contributing to their victimization is that some norms specify that intervening to help is socially inappropriate in some situations. The *norm of family privacy*, for example, makes people reluctant to intervene when they observe family violence, whether that violence involves a mother angrily slapping her child in a supermarket aisle, a man verbally abusing his wife on the street, or a grown child impatiently shaking an aging or forgetful parent. To demonstrate this point, Lance Shotland and Margaret Straw (1976) staged a physical attack by a man on a woman in front of male and female bystanders. Half the bystanders heard the woman say, "I don't know you!" whereas half heard her say, "I don't know why I ever married you!" Fully 65% of the bystanders tried to prevent the stranger's assault, compared to only 19% who intervened in the marital dispute. Why were people so reluctant to intervene in a family affair? People think wives would be embarrassed and upset by such intervention, and that husbands would likely turn on the would-be helper! Perhaps an increased awareness of and sensitivity to spousal abuse and date rape will gradually change norms that currently inhibit intervention in violence among intimates.

Norms restraining intervention in family violence can make bystanders reluctant to help even when a stranger assaults a woman. Over two thirds of participants shown a silent film of a man attacking a woman assumed that the attacker and the woman were dates, lovers, or spouses, although nothing in the film supported that conclusion (Shotland & Straw, 1976). The mental transformation of "dispute" into "domestic dispute" means that the most salient norms when a woman is being attacked may be not social responsibility or chivalry but: "that's family business" so "mind your own business."

Does the situation in which you passed the stranded motorist in the dark look a little more complicated now? The fact that the driver did not ask for help, and the unconcerned response of the other passerby, may have suggested that help was not appropriate. Yet, with the departure of the other pedestrian, the entire responsibility for providing help fell to you. The elderly driver may not have been able to make even minor repairs himself, and might have been afraid to venture out of the car to phone for assistance. Would you help or not? As in every social situation, many pieces of information may need to be woven together before an appropriate response can be made.

Why Do People Help? Helping for Mastery and Connectedness

Decades of research have provided some answers about when and how people will or will not help. But it is the bigger question that really intrigues social psychologists: Even if others clearly needed help, even if they were deserving, even if all the norms suggest that help is appropriate, people still would not help unless they were somehow motivated to do so. Ability and opportunity will not translate into behavior unless there is also desire. What are the fundamental motives behind helping? Why do we spend time, effort, and money, and sometimes even risk our lives, to benefit others?

Biologically Driven Helping: Is Helping in Our Genes?

Evolutionary principles suggest that some forms of helping, such as reciprocal helping or helping kin, have been naturally selected because they increase survival of specific genes. In humans, however, cognitive and social processes mediate such biologically driven helping.

One possible answer is that human helping, or the lack thereof, is determined by our evolutionary history. At first glance it would seem that any kind of helping that has costs to the helper would violate the principles of natural selection. Surely, behaviors that reduce the likelihood that an organism will reproduce, such as sharing food with others, or diving off a bridge to rescue a drowning child, should be selected against, and individuals with inherited tendencies to do such things would soon vanish from the population. In fact, some evolutionary scientists have argued that evolution has shaped humans, like other animals, to be fundamentally and unalterably selfish (Lorenz, 1966). But more sophisticated modern evolutionary theory holds that selection occurs at the level of the gene, and not the organism that bears the gene (W. D. Hamilton, 1964). Some types of helping behaviors might enhance the likelihood that genes (though not necessarily the individual carrying them) will survive, and therefore these behaviors could be favored by evolution (Barrett, Dunbar, & Lycett, 2002; McAndrew, 2002). There are three ways in which helping others could benefit the survival of the helper's genes.

First, we must not forget that helping sometimes involves a payoff for the helper as well as the helpee. "Cleaner fish" such as wrasse swim into the mouths of large fish such as grouper to eat ectoparasites. This provides food for the smaller fish and a cleaning for the big fish, which forgo snacking on the smaller fish. At the individual level, animals who help are often repaid in kind (Boster, Fediuk, & Kotowski, 2001). This type of reciprocal helping can evolve in species where individuals have the ability to remember other individuals who helped them in the past—or failed to do so (Trivers, 1971). Reciprocal helping occurs in humans as well as other species: As we noted in Chapter 10, we often feel compelled to repay favors to those who have helped us. When helping engenders payback helping, those who help may improve their own chance of survival.

The norm of reciprocity and its powerful effect on behaviors was reviewed in Chapter 10, pages 360 to 365.

Second, helping kin may be like helping oneself. When individuals help relatives who share their genes, the genes have a better chance of survival, even if each individual carrier of them does not (W. D. Hamilton, 1964). For example, female ground squirrels often cry out in alarm when they notice a predator, and this behavior is especially likely if they are living with close kin rather than unrelated animals (P. W. Sherman, 1977). No doubt making an alarm call is riskier than quietly hiding, but if the alarm saves the lives of offspring, brothers, sisters, nieces, and nephews, then the squirrel's genes will survive to the next generation. Like ground squirrels, humans tend to help kin more than non-kin (Kruger, 2003). For example, cross-cultural studies show that grandmothers, aunts, and other relatives are the most likely to adopt a child whose mother dies or is incapable of child rearing (Kurland, 1979).

Third, entire groups may prosper and flourish when they include altruistic members, perhaps at the expense of groups that include more selfish members (McAndrew, 2002). How can this be? People who put their group's interests ahead of their personal interests, for example by sharing food within the group or defending the group against outsiders in times of conflict, help perpetuate the group's existence (Sober & Wilson, 1999). Even if the altruist perishes in the process, the advantage to the group (which probably includes many members related to the altruist) may help ensure the survival of genes that promote altruism.

Thus, current evolutionary psychology supports the idea that evolution can favor tendencies to help others, even in ways that are costly or dangerous to the helper. In humans, helping and other types of behavior are not genetically "hardwired" and inflexible, but are the result of flexible cognitive and emotional processes that guide our behavior in diverse and changing environments (Batson, 1998). Helping in humans is much more likely to be the result of a naturally selected predisposition, or motivation, that can be activated and influenced by social or cognitive processes (M. L. Hoffman, 1981). So for example, the fact that people give more help to kin than to non-kin may be partially due to our natural impulses to help people we are emotionally close to—who tend in many cases to

You may recall that we discussed similar issues regarding the evolutionary basis of aggression in Chapter 13, pages 475 to 476. Both helping and aggression are motivated by mastery and connectedness needs, and influenced by individual processing and social norms.

be our kin (Korchmaros & Kenny, 2001). Thus, even as the contribution of natural selection to human helping must be assumed, this line of thinking returns us to the real question of interest: What motivates people to help? As we will see, the answer involves the same two motives as all other forms of social behavior: our desires for mastery and concrete rewards, and for connectedness with others.

Helping for Mastery: The Personal Rewards and Costs of Helping

Help may be motivated by perceived rewards or deterred by perceived costs or risks. These rewards and risks can be emotional: People sometimes help to alleviate their own distress at the victim's suffering.

REWARDS AND COSTS OF HELPING. The desire to help often depends on perceptions of the consequences of helping—on its potential rewards and costs. The upside of helping is its many rewards. One recent review listed 11 material, social, or personal rewards that could be gained from helping and 9 material, social, or personal punishments that could be avoided if help was given (Batson, 1998). These benefits are often quite concrete: the gratitude of the victim, help in return via the norm of reciprocity, the cheers of a crowd of onlookers, or the thrill of making the evening news. Helping others pays—sometimes quite literally! A young boy recently made news by returning a wallet containing a large sum of money. When the owner failed to offer the youngster a reward, townspeople chipped in and gave the boy over $10,000! And just as the evolutionary theorists noted, helping often occurs for reciprocity credit. When we help someone, we expect to receive help in return at some future date. We may even help someone with that end in mind!

But other potential consequences of helping can stop acts of generosity in their tracks. Consider this example. As several men in business suits stood watching, a 24-year-old woman dove into the Chicago River to rescue someone who had fallen in. Later, she reported, "One guy said, 'I have an appointment. I can't get my suit wet' " (Newsweek, 1990b). The cost of a ruined suit or a missed appointment seems trivial next to the possibility of saving a life, but it may deter helping. For example, participants in one study who thought they were a little late for their appointment with the experimenter were less likely to stop and assist an apparently ill confederate than those who thought they had plenty of time. This was true even though the participants were students studying to become ministers, and their appointment was to deliver a practice sermon on the Biblical parable of the Good Samaritan (Darley & Batson, 1973). The costs of helping can be many and varied: lost time, effort, embarrassment, money, social disapproval, or physical danger. Even when the need is clear and the victim seems deserving, people may not help if the costs appear too high.

The cost of helping is affected by a potential helper's abilities. Jumping into a river to rescue someone if you are not a strong swimmer could lead to two drownings instead of one. Remember that the first rule of lifesaving is: Don't become a victim yourself. But the more helping skills a person has, the lower the costs of helping. People with relevant abilities or training, for example, those with water-rescue or first aid skills, are more likely to offer direct help (Cramer and others, 1988). Perhaps someone with mechanical skills, confident of his or her ability to start a balky engine, would have been more likely to offer help to the stranded motorist we described earlier. Of course, training makes help not only more likely to be offered but also more likely to be effective. One study staged a bleeding emergency and found that people with Red Cross training were most likely to help the injured person directly by applying pressure to the wound (Shotland & Heinold, 1985). Untrained individuals were equally likely to try to help in this obvious emergency—they phoned for an ambulance—but in the situation staged by the researchers, this indirect help probably would not have saved the victim.

The importance of perceived ability to help may explain Alice Eagly and Maureen Crowley's (1986) meta-analysis showing that in studies of bystander intervention in emergencies, men are more likely to help than women are. This finding is no surprise, for Eagly and Crowley found that men perceive themselves as better able to help in most of the situations examined in research, such as assisting a motorist with a disabled car or carrying someone to safety—tasks requiring technical skills or physical strength. Other research shows that anyone (male or female) who sees himself or herself as independent, forceful, and dominant can have the confidence to help in emergency situations (Senneker & Hendrick, 1983).

EMOTIONAL REWARDS OF HELPING. Although helping sometimes pays quite literally, more often helping is its own reward: We feel good about ourselves because we helped others. Such internal rewards can be an even more powerful motivator of helping than external ones.

Because helping makes us feel good, people sometimes help to keep their spirits high (Isen, 1970). In one study, for example, participants who had been made to feel happy when they "happened" to find some money were asked to help the experimenter by reading a series of positive, upbeat or negative, depressing statements (Isen & Simmonds, 1978). Compared to people in a neutral mood, happy participants were more willing to help by reading the positive sentences— and stay in a good mood—but were less willing to read the negative sentences that might make them feel blue. Thus, people who want to stay in a good mood may be particularly prone to good works, but only the kinds of good works that keep them feeling good.

People can help not only to stay in a good mood but also to escape from a bad mood. Thus, guilty people are often helpful people. The most successful donation collector for the entire international network of Save the Children agencies works the pavement Saturdays outside the local supermarket of one of your authors. As every passerby tries to maneuver into the market, he waves the pictures of hungry children and reminds us, quite correctly, that we don't know how lucky we are. The ploy works. In experimental studies of the effects of guilt on helping, researchers have induced participants to break little rules or to tell little lies and then given them the opportunity to make up for their sins by helping. For example, some students in one study were induced to lie about having received advance information about a test. After taking the test, all participants were offered the chance to help the experimenter out on another project. Those who hadn't lied donated just 2 minutes of their time, whereas the guilt-laden fibbers spent an average of 63 minutes making up for their hidden transgression (McMillen & Austin, 1971). A clever field study of guilt makes the same point: Roman Catholics were solicited for donations to a worthy cause either on their way into confession or on their way out

■ **Guilt and giving.** Seeing other people suffer can be unpleasant and doing something to remove that unpleasantness—handing money to someone less fortunate than ourselves, for example—can be as rewarding for the giver as for the recipient.

(M. B. Harris, Benson, & Hall, 1975). It's not hard to guess that those going in gave more than those coming out.

People who are feeling guilty help in order to make themselves feel better, as was demonstrated in a study by Robert Cialdini and his colleagues (Cialdini, Darby, & Vincent, 1973). The researchers made one group of participants feel guilty about upsetting a stack of computer cards, whereas another group was not made to feel bad. Next, the researchers gave some of the guilty participants a compliment and others an unexpected payment for being in the experiment, manipulations designed to put these participants back in a good mood. When all participants were then asked to do a favor, guilty ones were more likely to help than nonguilty ones—unless they had received a compliment or cash. Thus helping, like receiving an external reward, seemed to get people feeling better.

Other negative emotions besides guilt can also increase our tendency to act charitably. If you just waited a long time at the bank, had a falling out with a friend, or lost your cell phone, would you be more or less likely to help a stranger requesting aid? Most research indicates you would help more (Cialdini and others, 1973; Cialdini & Kenrick, 1976). The reason is that helping might distract you or reduce feelings like guilt, annoyance, or disappointment. People know that helping makes them feel better, so those who want to feel better often offer their help.

IS HELPING PURE EGOISM? As you may have realized, the fact that helping others can make people feel better raises an intriguing question. Might people help simply to maintain their own positive feelings or to relieve their own negative feelings, meaning that helping is self-interested rather than truly altruistic? The *negative-state relief model of helping* answers this question with a solid "Yes" (Schaller & Cialdini, 1988). This theory begins with the assumption that most people hate to watch others suffer. So the ultimate goal of their help is not to aid the person in need for his or her sake, but to reduce the helper's own distress. Certainly, the evidence we described above, showing that people feeling guilty may help in an effort to feel better, is consistent with the negative-state relief model. The model also explains why people sometimes choose to walk away rather than help. Putting the victim "out of sight, out of mind" may be the easiest way to reduce distress. In fact, people who know that they will soon have a distracting experience—say, watching a comedy film—tend to be less helpful (Schaller & Cialdini, 1988). Distressed by the sight of starving refugees on a TV news program, will we write a check to a relief agency—or turn quickly to a variety show on another channel?

However, other findings suggest that the negative-state relief model is an incomplete explanation for helping. Although some negative emotions such as guilt do increase helping, others do not. In particular, sad people generally are not helpful people. One reason is that deep depression and profound grief disengage their sufferers from the social world and replace social concern with self-absorption (Carlson & Miller, 1987). Thus, the self-focused attention characteristic of sadness may blind people to opportunities to lift their spirits by helping. To demonstrate this effect, researchers asked participants to imagine in vivid detail that their best friend of the opposite sex was dying of cancer (W. C. Thompson, Cowan, & Rosenhan, 1980). The researchers' instructions focused some participants' attention on their own worry and grief, their own loss, their own sadness. Others were told to focus on their friend: his or her fear, uncertainty, and pain. Did sad thoughts increase helping? Even though everyone felt equally sad, the answer depended on the focus of attention. When the researcher asked for help

You may recall from Chapter 13, page 480, that feeling bad can also make people commit aggressive acts. Can you think of other cases we have described in which the same inner state can have diverse effects on a person's behavior, depending on the way the person interprets the situation?

FIGURE 14.2   Multiple effects of mood on helping

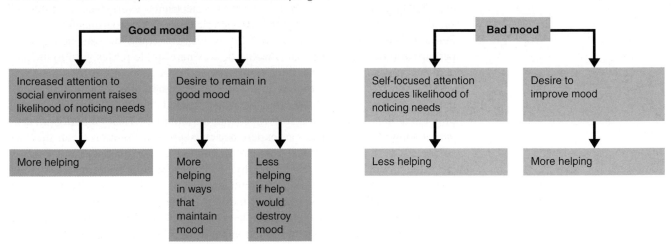

■ The effects of a positive or a negative mood on helping vary because they occur through several different processes. Both positive and negative moods have the ability to increase or decrease helping, depending on the circumstances.

with unrelated research, only 25% of the self-focused students volunteered, compared to 83% of those who were other-focused. If grief makes us think only of ourselves, it may keep us from using the warm glow of helping to cheer ourselves up. For this reason, people do not always use helping as a way of relieving their own negative emotional states.

In summary, emotional costs and rewards can influence helping in several different ways. The ways in which positive or negative feelings can either increase or decrease helping are summarized in Figure 14.2. When helping results from thinking about personal rewards or costs (either cognitive or emotional), as postulated by the negative-state relief model, helping is motivated by the need for mastery. But this picture is incomplete. The findings just discussed indicate that when people focus on others' needs rather than on their own negative feelings, they can be particularly helpful. This tells us that not only the motive for mastery, but also the need for connectedness to others can lead people to help.

Helping for Connectedness: Empathy and Altruism

People are often motivated by a feeling of empathy to relieve another's suffering, regardless of personal rewards and costs.

We have seen that personal rewards, such as good feelings, are not the only motive that leads people to help. Does this mean that true altruism—helping others as an end in itself—is possible? Daniel Batson and his co-workers have conducted a number of clever studies that attempt to demonstrate the existence of true altruism (Batson, 2002). Imagine that you are a participant who has just arrived in their research laboratory. You learn that a second participant, Elaine, will be receiving mild electric shocks as she performs a task in another room. Your job will be to observe her performance through a window. As you watch, Elaine (who is, of course, actually a confederate) is hooked up to some equipment and the shocks apparently begin. Obviously upset after two shocks, she asks for a glass of water and tells the experimenter that she's been frightened of electricity ever since a childhood accident when a horse threw her into an electric fence. The experimenter hesitates. Perhaps Elaine shouldn't continue. The experiment could be canceled . . . or perhaps you (the real participant) would be willing to trade places with Elaine and take the remaining shocks for her? Would you suffer for someone else?

Batson and his colleagues (1981), who designed this scenario, expected participants' responses to depend on how they reacted emotionally to the woman's plight and on how easy it was to escape from the situation. Their *empathy-altruism model* suggests that people can experience two types of emotion when they see someone in trouble: personal distress, including alarm, anxiety, and fear, or empathic concern, including sympathy, compassion, and tenderness. Personal distress motivates either egoistic helping—aimed at reducing the observer's own negative feelings—or escape, just as the negative-state relief model predicts. In contrast, feelings of empathic concern lead to altruistic behavior: helping designed to relieve the victim's suffering. When this motive predominates, people will help even if they could easily escape from the situation.

To test these ideas, the researchers manipulated participants' emotional responses to the situation and their ease of escape. To vary empathetic concerns, they told half of the participants that Elaine's personal values and interests were very similar to their own. Because similarity usually increases empathy, this information was designed to lead these participants to empathize with Elaine. The other half of the participants were told that she was quite different from them. To vary ease of escape, half of the participants (in the easy escape condition) were told they had to observe only two shocks, so when the experimenter asked them about changing places, the participants knew they could simply leave. The other half of the participants (in the difficult escape condition) were told they had to watch Elaine go through a series of 10 shocks.

The results of the experiment, as Figure 14.3 shows, were consistent with the empathy-altruism model. Participants who were not led to feel empathy acted

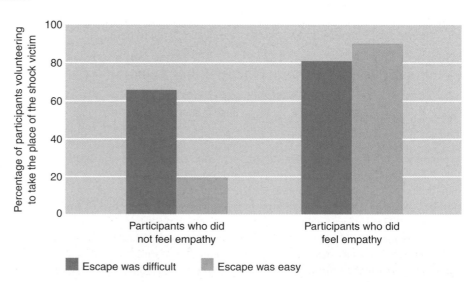

FIGURE 14.3   Does altruism exist?

■ For participants who did not empathize with Elaine, helping was a matter of avoiding personal distress. When escape was difficult—when participants could not simply leave the experiment—most volunteered to receive shocks in Elaine's place. But when an easy escape was available, most of the low-empathy participants left Elaine to suffer alone. In contrast, almost all those who empathized with Elaine volunteered to help her, regardless of the ease of escape. Their help must have been motivated by a focus on Elaine's feelings rather than by a desire to reduce their own distress. (Data from Batson and others, 1981.)

differently depending on the ease of escape. A high percentage of those who could not escape—who knew they had to watch all 10 shocks—volunteered to take Elaine's place, presumably to avoid the distress of watching her suffer. However, the pattern was reversed for their low-empathy peers who could walk out the door. Most took advantage of the escape hatch, leaving Elaine to suffer out of their view. In contrast, participants who empathized with Elaine helped altruistically: Even when escape was easy, most offered to stay and take the shocks for her.

Although controversy still persists (Maner and others, 2002), there is now a good deal of evidence supporting the idea that helping can be motivated by a true concern for and identification with the person in need (Batson, 2002; Batson and others, 1991; Batson, Dyck, Brandt, & Batson, 1988; Dovidio, Allen, & Schroeder, 1990; A. P. Fiske, 1991). Studies show that, compared to those low in empathy, participants induced to feel empathy with someone in need continue to feel bad if their attempts to help are unsuccessful, even if the lack of success is fully justified (Batson & Weeks, 1996). Individuals who are particularly likely to think about the welfare and rights of other people, to feel concern and empathy for them, and to act on their behalf are more likely to feel distress in the presence of someone needing help (Penner, Fritzsche, Craiger, & Freifeld, 1995). Even in very young children, empathy for others' suffering can promote helping (Eisenberg & Fabes, 1991; Hoffman, 1981).

These findings should not surprise us, however. We already know that when people identify with another individual and feel connected to them, they pay as much attention to those others' outcomes as to their own. Even a minimal social connection between two individuals can turn a bystander into a likely helper. One study found that people who had given their name to a researcher, made eye contact with her, or joined her in a trivial conversation, were more likely than total strangers to help her at a later time (Solomon and others, 1981). Another study by Dutch researchers (Van Baaren, Holland, Kawakami, and Van Knippenberg, 2004) showed that when a person is mimicked—that is, when their gestures are copied by an interaction partner—they are more likely to help not only the person doing the mimicking, but also other people they may encounter. The researchers explain these results by arguing that being mimicked tends to increase liking, enhance empathy, and facilitate social interactions. Thus, many subtle factors, from eye contact to being mimicked by another, may create a social connection that in turn facilitates helping. As connections grow stronger still, people are even more likely to feel empathy for the other and more likely to help. No wonder, then, that people are more likely to help members of the same group, friends, and family than to help strangers (Schoenrade, Batson, & Brandt, 1986).

All these results thus contradict the notion that most helpful actions are motivated simply by mastery motives: the prospect of maximizing personal rewards and minimizing personal costs. Of course, most actions involve multiple motives—a person might offer help while thinking both about the potential benefit for the person in need and also about the prospect of winning admiration and respect from observers. But this research suggests that true altruism—acting with the goal of benefiting another—is part of the repertoire of human behavior. Such actions depend on, and are often triggered by, a cognitive and emotional connection with another person. Among the many consequences of such connections is the motivation to increase another person's happiness and welfare regardless of the costs or benefits of such actions for the self.

Helping for Connectedness: Social Identification and Cooperation

In a social dilemma, rewards for each individual are in direct conflict with what is best for the group. However, people can be motivated by feelings of group connectedness to act for the good of the group, regardless of personal costs or benefits. When group identification increases commitment to shared goals and norms, social dilemmas can be successfully resolved.

Research on altruism indicates that the formation of a cognitive and emotional bond with another person, and the resulting feelings of empathy, can promote selfless helping of that other person. Such findings suggest that other types of connectedness might also promote helping that goes beyond pure egoism. Just as people identify with another individual, they can identify with and be closely bound to groups to which they belong (Hewstone, Rubin, & Willis, 2002). This suggests that group feeling might also act to increase helping where the goal is to benefit or promote the good of the group rather than the individual (Sturmer, Snyder, & Omoto, 2005). Could such a feeling explain instances of heroism like a soldier throwing himself on a live grenade to save his buddies?

Some research already suggests that in-group members (even those who are not kin) are more likely to be the target of help than others. Similar others, and those perceived as sharing our values, usually end up receiving the most help (Levine, Prosser, Evans, & Reicher, 2005; Penner, Dovidio, Piliavin, & Schroeder, 2005). During an election campaign, for example, passersby are more likely to give help (by picking up a stack of dropped leaflets) to those working for their own candidate than for the opposing candidate (Karabenick, Lerner, & Beecher, 1973). The tendency to help in-group members is even stronger in collectivist cultures, where the in-group is even more important, than in individualistic Western cultures. For example, Chinese and Japanese participants are more likely to offer help to in-group members but less likely to help out-group members than are North Americans (M. H. Bond, 1988).

But the strongest test of the idea that helping and cooperation could occur to benefit a group regardless of costs and rewards for the individual would involve a situation in which the good of the individual was directly opposed to the good of the group. In such a situation, self-sacrificial behavior could only be interpreted as behavior designed to benefit the group, even at a personal cost. What social situations might reflect such a conflict of interests?

SOCIAL DILEMMAS: SELF-INTEREST VERSUS GROUP INTEREST. In fact, we are all involved in just such situations. Consider the growing problem of air pollution, for example. Individuals use heating and air-conditioning, drive sporty automobiles with powerful engines, and buy convenience products manufactured from petroleum. From an individual's point of view, such behavior might make sense. As a society, however, our appetite for fossil-fuel energy—in industry, transportation, and housing—is pumping millions of tons of carbon dioxide into the atmosphere each year. This process produces global warming through the so-called "greenhouse effect" and may result in worldwide damage to agricultural productivity, changes in global weather patterns, and large increases in the levels of oceans and inland seas (IPCC, 2001; Stern, 1992).

The study of such situations offers fascinating insights into the nature of human helping and cooperation. If people do what makes sense from their individual points of view, the result is disaster for everyone. Thus individual self-interest is directly opposed to the best interests of the group. Such situations are **social dilemmas**: situations in which (a) each individual group member is better off not cooperating—regardless of what others do—but (b) all members of the group are better off if they all cooperate (Dawes, 1980). If every fisherman catches as many fish as possible there are soon no fish for anyone; if everyone watches viewer-sponsored public television without contributing to its support, public television stations soon go off the air. Although social life is always characterized by tensions between individual and group goals, social dilemmas directly pit the individual against the group.

Because of this, social psychologists have set up laboratory situations that maintain the central feature of real-world social dilemmas: They pit individual against group interests. Although these studies never mimic all the complexities of actual large-scale dilemmas, they can offer insight into the social-psychological processes that come into play during two important types of social dilemma.

■ **Windmills, bicycles, and electric trams** all contribute to the reputation of the Netherlands as being at the forefront of environmentally responsible living. Being mostly below sea level, the Netherlands is in particular danger from global warming. It could be that this has encouraged cooperation in creating more environmentally efficient energy production and transport.

1. *Resource depletion dilemmas.* Resource depletion dilemmas involve conflicts about the consumption of renewable resources, such as the world's rainforests or the populations of ocean fish. Individuals benefit personally by harvesting some of the resource. If enough of the resource is left untouched, it can reproduce and replenish itself, so that harvesting can continue indefinitely. If too much of the resource is taken, however, reproduction cannot replenish the stock, and the resource disappears.

To study this type of situation in the laboratory, individuals take many turns "harvesting" a group resource for individual profit. For example, participants are told that a certain number of fish remain in a shared fishing spot. Each one then decides how many fish to take from the common resource pool. After everyone has made a decision, the total harvest is subtracted from the pool. The pool is then allowed to replenish itself by a set amount; for example, reproduction may increase the number of fish by 10% before the next trial. The same process continues for many trials (Messick and others, 1983).

Consider the rewards and costs faced by each participant in such a situation (see Table 14.1). For each individual, every fish caught means profit, and the more fish, the more profit. This is true regardless of whether other people use the resource or not. If the individual decides to take fewer

TABLE 14.1. Possible Outcomes in a Replenishable-Resource Dilemma

Individual's action	Use resource *Catch as many fish as possible.*	Do not use resource *Take the season off.*
Result if others use the resource	Short-term profit; resource is soon depleted.	No profit; resource is depleted anyway.
Result if others refrain from using the resource	Short-term profit; resource is not depleted.	No profit; resource is not depleted.

Social dilemma. A form of interdependence in which the most rewarding action for each individual will, if chosen by all individuals, produce a negative outcome for the entire group.

fish, others might continue to overfish, so a cautious fisher could end up with reduced profit and still lose the resource. If the focus is purely on the rewards and costs for the individual, then, the individual is always better off using than not using the resource. For the individual, the logic of the situation dictates taking more fish.

2. *Public goods dilemmas.* Another type of social dilemma arises over how public goods should be acquired or supported. A public good is one that has to be provided for everybody or nobody; it cannot be given to some and withheld from others. Unpolluted air, a strong national defense, and viewer-supported public broadcasting stations are all public goods. Because a public good is available to all, "free riders" are tempted to use it without paying for it.

To illustrate the underlying dilemma, consider Table 14.2, showing the situation faced by participants in an experiment by Linda Caporael and her colleagues (Caporael, Dawes, Orbell, & Van de Kragt, 1989). The researchers gave $5 to each of a group of seven participants. The participants were told that they would each receive a $10 reward—the public good—if at least four of them anonymously donated their $5 to the experimenter. If fewer than four people donated, however, no reward would be provided, and the donations would not be returned. Clearly, if every person donates, everyone ends up with $10. But is this really in the individual's best interest? How would you reason if presented with the dilemma? After all, if you donate but nobody else does, you lose your $5 and no public good is provided. By holding on to your $5 and collecting the bonus, you could even walk away with $15. Once again, your best bet as an individual seems to be free-riding, while hoping everyone else is a better citizen! The kicker is, of course, that if all individuals follow this entirely sensible course of action, no one will contribute and no one will have the benefit of the public good—in fact, all will be worse off than they might have been.

BEHAVIOR IN SOCIAL DILEMMAS. Faced with dilemmas like these, what do people do? Often they quite reasonably, but disastrously, follow their individual interests. Left to their own devices, almost every individual faced with a resource depletion dilemma makes the same decision: to harvest as much as possible, even though the resource is rapidly depleted (Weber, Kopelman, & Messick, 2004). This is especially true if people can't accurately estimate the size of the resource pool or if the pool is difficult to divide: Under these conditions people overestimate the size of their fair share, take so much for themselves that the resource declines, and believe that others will do the same (Budescu, Rapoport, & Suleiman, 1990; Herlocker, Allison, Foubert, & Beggan, 1997). Of course, thinking that others will follow their own self-interest or actually seeing them do so provides selfish models, which makes people even more likely to harvest selfishly even when they realize the resource is being depleted (Messick and others, 1983; Schroeder,

You may recognize social loafing, which we discussed in Chapter 12, pages 452 to 454, as a kind of public goods dilemma. In that case every individual is probably better off not expending effort, but if no-one does so, the group task doesn't get accomplished. In the next few pages you'll see that many of the conditions that make social loafing better or worse work the same way for social dilemmas.

TABLE 14.2. Possible Outcomes in an Experimental Social Dilemma

Individual action	Keep $5	Donate $5
Result if most others keep their $5	End up with $5	End up with nothing
Result if most others donate their $5	End up with $15	End up with $10

Jensen, Reed, Sullivan, and Schwab, 1983). After all, continuing to sacrifice when others are taking a free ride might make you feel like a sucker (Kerr & Bruun, 1983). In real life as in the laboratory, New England and North Sea fishermen have found that their operations have so depleted the once abundant offshore schools that their total catch is in steep decline. Even though their livelihoods are now endangered, taking action to solve the dilemma seems particularly difficult to do (Goodnough, 2005; *New York Times*, 1992c).

Self-interest usually wins the day in public-goods dilemmas too. For example, only about 50% of participants in Caporael's study (Caporael and others, 1989) made $5 donations, and so only a few experimental groups collected the bonus. In an attempt to find out why, researchers looked at two possible motivations: the fear of wasting their donations and the greedy desire for profit (Rapoport & Eshed-Levy, 1989). To eliminate the influence of fear for some experimental groups,

■ **Fishermen handle cod** in measuring boxes to determine whether or not they are big enough. Limiting the size of fish that can be taken is a structural solution to try to solve the crisis caused by overfishing in the past.

researchers offered to return the money if fewer than four participants made donations. To neutralize greed, they warned that if the $10 bonus was earned, nondonators as well as donators would go home with just $10. Only eliminating greed increased the number of donations (Caporael and others, 1989). Thus, greed seems to be the most important reason that most people fail to contribute.

STRUCTURAL SOLUTIONS IN SOCIAL DILEMMAS. In fact, selfish behavior is so prevalent in social dilemmas that often structural solutions, like the ones tested in this study, have to be imposed (N. L. Kerr, 1992; Messick & Brewer, 1983; Platt, 1973). By making laws or regulations, individual payoffs are changed and the dilemma is eliminated. A standard solution to a public-goods dilemma, for instance, is to levy taxes to pay for provision of the good: If everyone benefits, everyone should pay. In a resource-depletion dilemma, solutions usually involve setting quotas so that users can't deplete the resource. For example, international fishery commissions restrict the number of fish of different species that can be caught every year.

Unfortunately, structural solutions can generate about as many problems as they try to solve. First, structural solutions require an authority to impose them. Experimenters can easily set sanctions in laboratory game playing, and groups sometimes elect leaders to decide each member's share (Samuelson, Messick, Rutte, & Wilke, 1984). But who has the accepted authority to regulate use and misuse of the world's atmosphere or the proliferation of biological weapons? Only when a valuable resource is threatened to the point of extinction do people sometimes ask for some kind of authority to regulate their behavior (Sato, 1987). Second, structural solutions are often met with resistance. Even though New England fishermen are finding there aren't "plenty more fish in the sea," they have resisted new regulations that would limit their catch and allow the fish stocks to be rebuilt (*New York Times*, 1992c). Third, resistance necessitates a bureaucracy for monitoring compliance, with no guarantee of successful enforcement (Kameda, Takezawa, & Hastie, 2003; Yamagishi, 1986). Despite the existence of stiff penalties and routine inspection, the Chevron Oil Company was found to have illegally dumped oil products from offshore rigs for years. Unless people willingly accept restraints on their behavior, structural solutions do not seem to be the answer for many of our most intractable global dilemmas.

Don't these findings support the idea that people are fundamentally selfish and that cooperation for group interests never occurs unless there is some personal gain? Perhaps. But before accepting this conclusion completely, consider some other findings from social dilemma research.

First, there are cultural and gender differences in people's responses to social dilemmas. We might expect to find more cooperation from women, because of their greater emphasis on connectedness with others, and more cooperation in interdependent, group-oriented cultures. A meta-analysis of research on social loafing dilemmas found both of these predictions to be generally accurate (Karau & Williams, 1993). In studies of other types of dilemmas, research has found that Chinese and Indians were more cooperative than their individualistic U.S. counterparts (Earley, 1989; Gabrenya, Wang, & Latané, 1985; Perlow & Weeks, 2002).

Second, some individuals behave in unselfish ways in resource dilemmas. In particular, individuals who generally prefer to cooperate make resource pools go further than people who like to compete (Liebrand & van Run, 1985; McClintock & Liebrand, 1988). Both of these kinds of findings give social psychologists something to think about: If some of the people are helpful and cooperative some of the time, are there circumstances that would lead more people to act for the greater good more of the time? That is, are there conditions under which individuals tend to act for the good of the group rather than for their own selfish ends, and thus solve social dilemmas?

SOLVING SOCIAL DILEMMAS: SOCIAL IDENTIFICATION AND COOPERATION. In fact, under the right conditions, participants in social dilemmas show considerable helping and cooperation: agreeing to cut resource consumption and chipping in to pay for resources others can use. What makes people forgo their own individual interests for the interests of the group? One key factor is identification with the group as an important aspect of the individual's social identity (Klandersman, 2000; Van Vugt & Hart, 2004). When group belonging becomes uppermost in people's minds, helping can be motivated by social identification, promoting the desire to benefit the group as a whole regardless of outcomes for the self. That is, individuals become concerned for "not me or thee but we" (Dawes, Van de Kragt, & Orbell, 1988).

When individuals identify with groups, three changes usually take place. First, the greater good of the group becomes the top priority (Caporael and others, 1989). Behaviors like contributing to a common good, which might appear foolish or naive from an individual point of view, instead seem loyal, trustworthy, and generous from the perspective of the group (P. E. Tetlock, 1989). For example, one study found that people who themselves identified and cooperated with a group rated others who also cooperated as more intelligent than noncooperators (Van Lange & Liebrand, 1991). Similarly, actions like free-riding, which may seem clever and sensible to the individual, may be viewed as despicable and treacherous by the group (Kuhlman, Brown, & Teta, 1992).

Second, when the group thinks and works together as one, people are likely to assume that other group members will also be helping, rather than hurting, the group effort. There is no longer any need to worry that others will free-ride while you exercise self-control, nor will you take the opportunity to free-ride while others act responsibly (Caporael and others, 1989). In fact, when Caporael and her colleagues questioned people who contributed in their experimental groups, these participants said that they thought most others would contribute as well. Acting as you expect others to act—or, what is the same thing, trusting others to act the same way as you do—lets the entire group share the fruits of cooperation.

Third, group norms favoring cooperation become salient guides for individual action. Individuals in Caporael's study who thought that most others would contribute must have realized that they could keep their own $5—and still collect the bonus earned by others' contributions! Still, these individuals preferred to follow what they saw as a group norm of contributing rather than to maximize their individual earnings. The norm of commitment can have such a powerful effect that individuals who vow to cooperate during group discussion actually do so (Hopthrow & Hulbert, 2005). They do this even if they know their behavior is unlikely to solve the dilemma effectively (N. L. Kerr & Kaufman-Gilliland, 1993). Even nonconscious priming of cooperative norms can increase people's level of cooperation (Smeesters, Warlop, Van Avermaet, Corneille, & Yzerbyt, 2003).

For all these reasons, shared group identity does favor cooperative behavior in social dilemmas. Marilynn Brewer and Roderick Kramer (1986) created a laboratory situation in which individuals were faced with a resource dilemma. Students sat in individual cubicles with computer displays, but were led to believe that they were part of either a small 8-member group or a large 32-member group. In addition, some people in each condition were encouraged to develop group identification and some were not. The manipulation was subtle: Participants in the group identification condition were simply told that their payment for experimental participation would be decided for the group as a whole, rather than separately for each individual. Sharing a common fate in this way was enough to change their behavior, significantly lowering the amount of resources participants drew from the common pool when given the opportunity.

Several powerful additional factors often go hand in hand with group identification, and make their own contributions to cooperative behavior in social dilemmas.

- *Communication among group members.* Laboratory studies have repeatedly demonstrated that when members of a group are allowed to discuss a dilemma before making their decisions, cooperation is enhanced (Orbell, van de Kragt, & Dawes, 1988). For example, only 47% of participants in one study donated to a public good when no discussion was permitted, but discussion raised the figure to 84% (Caporael and others, 1989). And what did group members talk about? Mostly they worked on forming consensus around a norm for appropriate behavior, defining the meaning of deviance from the norm, and making promises to stick to the norm. Group discussion made them feel more connected, but it also committed them to promises of cooperation and sharing (Bouas & Komorita, 1996; Kerr & Kaufman-Gilliland, 1993). The difficulty of communication might be one reason that big groups often have a tougher time solving social dilemmas than smaller groups (Brewer & Kramer, 1986). When it comes to solving social dilemmas, small is beautiful (Edney, 1980).

- *Equality of opportunities and outcomes among group members.* If all group members use the same amount of a resource, that level of consumption becomes a norm for group members (Messick and others,

1983). Inequality of resource use reduces people's certainty about others' behaviors, weakens conformity pressures, diminishes personal efficacy, and makes people wonder if they are being exploited. It's not surprising that people feeling this way start to be concerned with their immediate self-interest rather than cooperation with the group. Inequality is a major roadblock to solving current problems of global pollution and resource depletion (Simons, 1992). The poorer nations wonder why environmental considerations should require them to use fewer resources than the already developed nations do. Why should they give up the promise of prosperity when the developed nations literally took the quick and dirty route to wealth?

- *Accessibility of group norms.* Keeping the value of acting in the group's best interest uppermost in everyone's mind gives it the best chance of guiding behavior. To demonstrate this point, some participants in one experiment listened to others talk about the value of group cooperation: "Maybe I could have gotten more if I was greedy, but I just couldn't do it. If I'm in a group, I'm going to try to do what helps the group, not just myself" (Sattler & Kerr, 1991, p. 760). When later faced with a social dilemma problem, these participants took less for themselves than did participants who had not heard the message. Compliance with such norms is more likely if the norm was developed fairly (Tyler & Smith, 1998), provides fair outcomes (Pruitt & Kimmel, 1977), and is endorsed by others (Orbell and others, 1988).

- *Linking individual efforts to the group good.* If people are given feedback that shows that their actions are effective, even on a small scale, they conserve more. Apparently, being able to see the effects of seemingly trivial actions like turning off unneeded lights or emptying the dishwater on flowerbeds creates a sense that personal actions do matter (C. L. Seligman, Becker, & Darley, 1981). Believing that their efforts make a difference makes people feel good, gives them a sense of psychological control, and increases the likelihood that they will act on their attitudes and norms, whether it means installing flow-restricted showerheads, subscribing to public television, or gathering signatures on petitions to stop nuclear weapons testing. When individuals are told: "Because you donated your share, the company was able to raise over $5000," they learn how their individual actions are magnified by the size of the group. The more members feel responsible for group success, the more likely they are to solve social dilemmas (Kerr, 1992).

You may recognize these social identification and norm-based solutions to the problems of large scale social dilemmas to be very similar to the conditions that help work groups function more smoothly, see Chapter 12, pages 455 to 457.

Thus behavior that benefits others can sometimes be motivated because people come to care about the welfare of the group as a whole. Again, this conclusion should not surprise you given the many important changes, described in Chapter 6, that can occur when people identify strongly with a group. Whereas altruism operates to benefit a single other individual, group identification can dictate helping to any member of any size group. In fact, feeling empathy for a single other member of a group experiencing a social dilemma may result in more resources being allocated to the favored other and fewer being allocated to the group as a whole (Batson and others, 1995; 1999). Thus altruism seems quite distinct from group identification, which seems necessary to solve social dilemmas. From work and sports teams, communities, and villages, to political parties, ethnic groups, and nations, group identification can be a powerful motivator of helping and cooperation.

Group identification can also make our universal humanity salient, which might explain helping others who share nothing but this common bond. In this way, it can motivate helping for abstract groups like the poor, the starving, or, as when we consider global pollution, citizens of the earth. In hiding Jewish families from Nazi Germany, the villagers of Le Chambon may have been concerned not with themselves, not with their village, not even with Jews in particular, but with benefiting humanity. Such motivation is recognized by a special medal presented to those identified as having taken great risks to rescue others. The motto reads: "Whosoever saves one life, he has saved all of humanity" (cited in Batson, 1998).

Of course, using identification with a group to motivate helping and cooperation is not a perfect solution, nor is it always feasible. As we saw in chapter 6, cognitive and emotional identification with one group can often go hand in hand with rejection of other groups. When we fail to empathize with those whom we see as dissimilar from ourselves, we may morally exclude them, placing them outside the scope of norms and moral standards that might encourage helping and cooperation. And despite the promise of group identification for solving global resource dilemmas, the groups involved are often enormous in size, have little in common, do not communicate, and are notably unequal in resource usage. These factors mean that it is difficult to create the sense of common group membership that may be the best hope of solving such dilemmas.

Nevertheless, as Figure 14.4 shows, feeling themselves to be part of a community can make people act more cooperatively, value group outcomes above individual ones, and forgo self-interest in helping others for the benefit of the group as a whole. The future of our human group may depend on creating and maintaining that shared feeling of belonging.

FIGURE 14.4 Social dilemmas: Problems and remedies

	Motivation problems	Coordination problems
Problems in solving social dilemmas	Individuals seeks personal rewards, undermining group benefits.	Individuals are unaware of others' choices. Individuals cannot trust others to cooperate.
Remedies for social dilemmas	Task interdependence solutions: Change incentives for individuals. *Individuals seeking personal rewards now benefit group.*	Social interdependence solutions: Individuals agree on appropriate actions. *Individuals assume others will cooperate.*
	Social interdependence solutions: Individuals identify with group norms. *Individuals seek to act in ways that benefit the group.*	Social interdependence solutions: Individuals follow group norms. *Norm of commitment keeps individuals cooperating.*
Contribution of group cohesion to remedy	Individuals adopt group goals as their own.	Group exercises social influence over individuals.

■ Social dilemmas are situations in which individual goals are opposed to group goals. Conditions that realign individual motivation with the group's good and coordinate individual effort for the good of the group offer the best hope of solving such dilemmas.

Role of Superficial or Systematic Processing in Helping and Cooperation

The Impact of Processing

When desires and norms conflict, various factors may be considered superficially or thought through extensively before a decision about helping is made. Emotions can play a role in this process, for strong emotion disrupts extensive processing. When helping is a considered decision, though, it can result in a long-term commitment.

Sometimes it's relatively easy to decide whether or not to help, but more often we experience conflict over what to do. We may desperately want to come to the aid of a mugging victim but fear the risks and costs to ourselves. We may feel empathy for the toddler being spanked in the supermarket but feel that our intrusion into a "family affair" would be inappropriate. We may want to conserve water by taking shorter showers, but fear being made a sucker by those who will free-ride on our contributions. Many thoughts and emotions, attitudes, and norms can be activated in people's minds as they size up the victim, the need, and the situation in which help is needed. The final decision to act or to turn away is also influenced by how these various facilitators or inhibitors of helping are processed. Sometimes the decision about whether to help or cooperate has to be made quickly and impulsively. At other times it is the product of extensive processing.

SPONTANEOUS HELPING, SUPERFICIAL PROCESSING. Emergencies are heart-stopping, adrenaline-pumping, sweaty-palm situations. The suffering of others causes anguish, distress, empathy, sadness, and guilt, and these strong emotions can motivate us to action, including helpful action (Penner and others, 2005). However, strong emotions also limit our ability to think things through carefully. In addition, emergencies usually don't allow much time for thought. The combination of arousal, emotions, and split-second timing usually leads people to respond to emergencies quickly and impulsively. That was certainly the case when local residents immediately went to the aid of those injured in an Air Borneo plane crash in Indonesia. When emergency personnel arrived on the scene, they credited many of the lives saved to the courageous actions of those who rushed to pull survivors from the wreckage before it sank or burned. When arousal is high and time for reflection is limited, people act on the basis of the most accessible motives or norms. In this case, the onlookers' empathy for those in need or their feelings of social responsibility must have outweighed thoughts of discomfort and danger.

When people process superficially, the most readily accessible mental representations will be the most likely to influence behavior. Therefore, priming manipulations that intentionally change the accessibility of thoughts related to helping can affect the likelihood of actual helpful acts (Smeesters and others, 2003). One clever study demonstrated such an effect by priming the presence of others and examining the effect on donations to charity. Stephen Garcia and his colleagues (Garcia, Weaver, Moskowitz, & Darley, 2002), asked students to imagine winning a dinner in a restaurant for themselves and 30 other people, 10 other people or one other person. Even imagining the presence of other people influenced subsequent helping in an unrelated situation: when the students were later asked to make a donation to charity, those who had imagined a larger number of people contributed less money. As we saw earlier, the actual presence of many others can influence whether we offer help in an emergency, because of diffusion of responsiblity (Darley & Latané, 1968; Latané & Darley, 1970). Results in this study showed that imagining the presence of others also makes people feel less personally accountable to provide help. As this study demonstrates, even thoughts about aspects of social situations, such as the presence of others, can have an impact on helping, at least when people are processing superficially.

PLANNED HELPING, SYSTEMATIC PROCESSING. In some circumstances a would-be helper may give careful—even agonized—consideration to the available information. Someone may reflect on the victim's need, then on the possible cost and danger, then on feelings of personal responsibility and ability to help. Extensive thought can even reverse a first, quick reaction. When a Dutch couple with four children were asked to shelter a Jewish infant from the Nazis, they immediately reacted negatively. "This is going too far," they said. "We have given money to support and hide Jews—but we don't need a Jewish kid in the house!" (Oliner & Oliner, 1988, p. 69). Reflection, however, produced a change of heart. By the next morning they had made plans to save the infant: For example, the wife would pretend to be pregnant for a time to allay neighbors' suspicions about the sudden appearance of a new child.

One of the most typical forms of planned helping is volunteering, where people provide voluntary, sustained, and ongoing benefits to others, often for long periods of time (J. Wilson, 2000). This kind of helping reflects the fact that both the initial decision to help and the decision to continue volunteering may result from considerable thought. As we have pointed out many times, decisions based on extensive thought produce long-lasting commitments that are not easily changed. When people repeatedly help others, they come to see themselves as helpful and altruistic, and these self-perceptions reinforce further helping (Deaux & Stark, 1996). This process explains why people who give blood a few times tend to become regular blood donors, for example (Piliavin and others, 1982). Repeated helping also builds perceptions of self-efficacy, the sense that one's actions are effective and meaningful. Self-efficacy also increases the likelihood that helpful attitudes and norms will be translated into helpful actions (Ajzen & Madden, 1986; Bandura, 1982). Such self-perceptions may be quite specific, as one aspect of the extensive thought given to volunteering is matching one's interests and talents with particular types of needs or ways to help (Benson and others, 1980; Clary and others, 1998). Finally, there appear to be positive health benefits derived from sustained volunteering. For example, older adults who do more volunteer work exhibit fewer depressive symptoms (Musick & Wilson, 2003).

Like helping in general, volunteering can be motivated by a number of different goals (Clary and others, 1998; Trudeau & Devlin, 1996). Recent work has identified six distinct motives: expressing personal values related to humanitarian concern for others; gaining understanding, new knowledge, and skills; socializing with friends and earning their approval; obtaining career benefits; helping solve personal problems; and enhancing self-esteem and personal growth (Clary and others, 1998). Note that these motives include egoistic concerns, for volunteering provides many material, social, and emotional benefits. But many volunteers are also motivated by humanitarian concerns for others and the opportunity to do something worthwhile for them. Group identification also motivates helping when volunteers help out of a sense of social obligation, or in order to create a better society or compensate for injustices to their group. In general, the decision to volunteer, which often involves extensive thought, involves somewhat different motivations than the decision to help in an emergency, where thought is often limited by time pressure and emotional arousal (Penner and others, 2005).

☐ **VOLUNTEERING IN THE AIDS EPIDEMIC.** Over the past decade the AIDS epidemic has triggered a wave of volunteers who provide emotional support to and do household chores for people with AIDS, who staff counseling centers and hotlines, who care for infants born with AIDS, and who lobby the government on AIDS-related issues.

Like most volunteer work, these forms of helping usually involve considerable time, trouble, and financial cost to the helper. Helping people with AIDS also involves the special emotional costs of confronting personal tragedy, illness, and death. Why do people get involved in such activities? According to Mark Snyder and Allen Omoto (1992; Omoto & Snyder, 2002) and Louis Penner and Marcia Finkelstein (1998), who have conducted large surveys of active AIDS volunteers, the reasons vary from individual to individual. Some are motivated by personal feelings of obligation to help other people, others seek personal growth in skills and understanding, still others have connectedness concerns such as feelings of obligation to the gay community, and some simply want to feel better about themselves. Some motives may play more of a role when people initially decide to lend a hand, whereas others become important in the decision to stay involved. Regardless of the reasons people decide to become and remain involved, however, their decisions are the result of lengthy consideration.

AIDS volunteers thus illustrate that, as we have noted throughout this chapter, many different motives and norms can spur helping. Interestingly, M. Snyder and

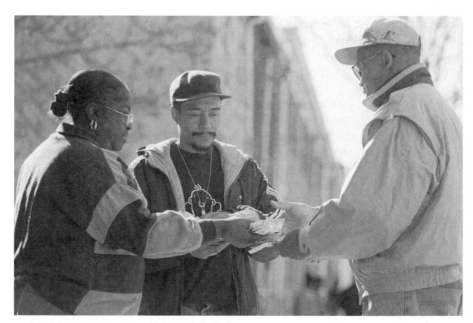

■ **The AIDS epidemic—a powerful motivator**. These AIDS campaigners are demonstrating in New York at the site of the 2004 Republican National Convention. The AIDS epidemic has brought out large numbers of volunteers and campaigners whose motives range from the personal growth that helping can bring to intense conviction that there is an obligation to selflessly help others who are suffering by whatever means they can, be it spreading awareness through protests and campaigns, to fundraising and care work. The decision to give such time and effort to a cause is usually the result of considerable thought.

Omoto (1992) found that volunteers who expressed the seemingly more "selfish" desires for self-esteem and personal growth were more likely to stick with their service over the course of a year than were those driven by the more "humanitarian"-seeming motives. The researchers note that:

> *Good, and perhaps romanticized, intentions related to humanitarian concern simply may not be strong enough to sustain volunteers faced with . . . tough realities and personal costs . . . Therefore, volunteer organizations . . . may want to remind volunteers of the personal rewards of their work rather than underscoring how volunteer efforts benefit clients and society.* (p. 115)

In contrast, Penner and Finkelstein (1998) found AIDS volunteers with more altruistic motives tended to serve for longer periods of time, as did Clary and Orenstein (1991) in a survey of volunteer crisis counselors. Since more than 90% of the males in the AIDS volunteer study were themselves homosexual, this may have made it easier for some of them to identify and empathize with the primary beneficiaries of their care, and in turn may have made altruistic concerns more salient (Batson, 1991; Penner & Finkelstein, 1998). In fact, there is evidence that AIDS volunteers are more driven by empathy when the recipient of assistance is a member of their own in-group than when that person is an out-group member (Sturmer, Snyder, & Omoto, 2005). The bottom line, as we have repeatedly said, is that people help for many reasons and to fulfill many needs. Volunteers who perform actions that match their individual motivations derive more satisfaction and more enjoyment from their service and are likely to continue helping over the long haul (Clary and others, 1998; Kiviniemi, Snyder, & Omoto, 2002; Penner, 2002).

☐ **HELPING IN ORGANIZATIONS.** Employees who "go the extra mile" in the workplace furnish another example of prosocial behavior. Researchers have investigated what are termed *organizational citizenship behaviors* (OCB), helpful efforts in the workplace that go beyond a worker's formal job description (Brief & Weiss, 2002) such as lending a hand to fellow workers faced with an urgent deadline. As with many forms of helping, the question arises: Are helpful employees motivated by the desire to look especially good in the eyes of their bosses, or are they driven by a genuine desire to help? Research by Marcia Finkelstein and Louis Penner (2004) suggests that motives to help co-workers or the organization as a whole are more strongly related to OCB than are motives concerned with creating a good impression. The researchers also found that those who strongly identified as a "citizen" of the organization tended to display higher levels of OCB. Overall, it appears that similar mechanisms are involved in sustaining both long-term volunteer efforts, like the admirable efforts of those who work on AIDS-related issues, and extra efforts in the workplace.

By now, you can see how many factors play a role in determining whether helping occurs or not. The process begins when the individual notices that help is needed. This perception may trigger thoughts about the costs and rewards of helping, feelings of empathy with the victim's suffering, group identification with the person in need, or recognition of relevant norms. Although these kinds of information often work together to suggest that action should be taken to benefit another, sometimes competing thoughts, desires, feelings, and obligations have to be reconciled. This process may involve extensive thought or, when cognitive capacity is low, time is short, or emotional arousal is high, a quick snap judgment. The impact of these processes is illustrated in Figure 14.5. As this figure shows,

FIGURE 14.5   Multiple factors influence helping

■ Perceptions of the person in need and of the helping situation influence people's desire to help or to refrain from helping. The desire to help (or not) will depend in part on an assessment of the rewards and costs involved in helping and on feelings of empathy with the victim. Perceptions of the person and situation also activate norms and influence feelings of obligation to help. Depending on how potential conflicts are resolved, the decision may be to offer help or to withhold it.

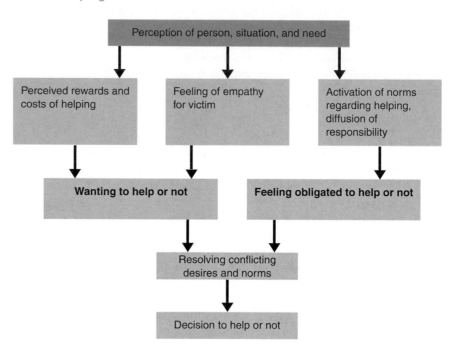

individual processes and social forces work together to make helping and cooperation more or less likely.

Personality Differences in Helping

Personality factors related to helping and cooperation include differences in empathy and concern for others' welfare, as well as in self-efficacy or the confidence that one's actions will be effective.

Are some people just generally more helpful than others across a variety of different situations and types of help, such as rushing to assist in an emergency and volunteering regularly for charitable organizations? Despite the intuitive appeal of this idea, early research found little evidence of consistent personality differences in helping (Piliavin, Dovidio, Gaertner, & Clark, 1981) and instead stressed the importance of situational factors such as the victim's perceived deservingness, or diffusion of responsibility. More recently, however, consistent patterns have been identified in the types of people who are the most likely to help (Eisenberg and others, 2002; Graziano & Eisenberg, 1997; Graziano, Habashi, Sheese, & Tobin, 2004). These patterns underline the importance of the kinds of motives and processing patterns that we have already discussed. One personality variable that consistently increases helping is the tendency to empathize with others and to be concerned for others' welfare (M. H. Davis, 1983; Penner and others, 1995). People who are more empathetic naturally tend to be more emotionally moved by others' suffering, and therefore more motivated to help in large as well as small ways. Indeed, Oliner and Oliner (1988) found that heroic rescuers of Jews in the

Third Reich tended to be more empathetic than others. The second personality variable associated with helping is self-efficacy, the confidence that one's actions are likely to be successful (Graziano & Eisenberg, 1997). Once empathetic concern is aroused, the belief that one can effectively help is crucial in setting helping behavior in motion. Like empathy, self-efficacy is related to small and short-term forms of help as well as to long-term patterns of volunteering, as Colby and Damon (1995) found in a study of 22 lifelong altruists. The importance of these individual differences in empathy and self-efficacy underlines the way helping depends on both seeing others' need and seeing oneself as able to help.

Cooperating in social dilemmas is also related to general personality orientations. Some people generally prefer to cooperate in such situations; others approach dilemmas from an individualist perspective, seeking to maximize their own rewards without regard for others' outcomes; and still others adopt a competitive perspective, evidently seeing dilemmas as opportunities to "win" more than the other players do (McClintock & Liebrand, 1988; Van Lange, De Bruin, Otten, & Joireman, 1997). Interestingly, people who generally cooperate in dilemmas also tend to help more in other ways, for example, by volunteering more hours of their time for a worthy cause (McClintock & Allison, 1989). This finding suggests that cooperatively seeking the group's good in a social dilemma and interpersonal forms of helping such as volunteering have common motivational roots.

Prosocial Behavior in Society

Help That Helps; Help That Hurts

Receiving help can have negative as well as positive consequences, especially if recipients cannot reciprocate because of an unequal power relationship between helper and helped, or because receiving help makes them look and feel less competent.

Helpers usually feel good about themselves (Millar, Millar, & Tesser, 1988). But how does it feel to receive help? It depends on the recipient's need and on how being helped affects their self-esteem. Help that relieves physical suffering or mental anguish—a hot meal on an empty stomach, a safe escort across a busy street, or rescue from a house fire—is always welcome. Help that creates a positive relationship between helper and helped is welcome too. Cooperation builds trust and respect and helpers feel protective and proud of the person they benefited. Those on the receiving end of help and cooperation typically feel gratitude. The popular U.S. television show *Unsolved Mysteries* had a special segment on people searching for someone who helped them long ago—gave them a helping hand when they were down, nursed them through a long illness, showed faith in them as they started a difficult phase in life. Generally, the beneficiaries just want to say thank you.

However, receiving help is not always positive. First, help can make people feel that they owe a favor, and that can be a problem for those who are unable to reciprocate (Gross & Latané, 1974). People who cannot return a favor may resent the help and derogate their helper (J. D. Fisher, Nadler, & Whitcher-Alagner, 1982). Second, receiving help can make someone look and feel less capable or competent, robbing them of the pride and satisfaction that typically comes with success (Gilbert & Silvera, 1996).

The problem is that helping sends a mixed message. While help can convey a positive message of caring, it also has negative implications: "I am more powerful, more able, more in control than you—you need my help!" The beneficiary is left to wonder, "Do they think I'm worthy of help and encouragement? Or do they think I couldn't make it without special treatment?" This point has implications for the controversial topic of affirmative action. For example, governments, schools, and employers may implement programs to offer special help to members of groups that have traditionally suffered discrimination and exclusion. But the very existence of such programs, unless they are designed with extreme sensitivity, may imply that members of those groups somehow lack the ability to make it on their own (Nadler, 2002).

Jeffrey Fisher and Arie Nadler (J. D. Fisher and others, 1982; Nadler & Fisher, 1986) call these opposing messages the self-supportive and the self-threatening aspects of receiving help. If recipients of help feel supported, they respond with gratitude. If the help seems threatening to their self-esteem, they dislike the helper and they may refuse future help. Perhaps this mixed message explains a familiar stereotype about gender differences in help-seeking: Men would rather get lost than ask for directions, whereas women don't mind asking a bit! Deborah Tannen (1990) argues that men are generally more sensitive to the status implications of requesting and receiving help, whereas women are more attuned to the positive relationships help can create.

Increasing Prosocial Behavior in Society

> Helping in society can be increased by making needs clear, teaching and activating helping norms, fostering helpful self-concepts, focusing rather than diffusing responsibility, and promoting connectedness to engender empathy, altruism, and group identification.

For social psychologists, understanding helping and cooperation is more than just a theoretical concern. Helping is essential to group life and social functioning, and insights from research can show us how to increase both the giving of help and our chances of receiving it when we are in need.

1. *Reduce ambiguity: Make the need for help and cooperation clear.* If you are injured in a fall, don't rely on the fact that passersby can see that you are bleeding. Make your need obvious—by shouting "Help me," for example—to increase your chances of receiving aid (R. D. Clark & Word, 1972). The benefits of making the need for help clear have been demonstrated in studies of why people report crimes (Bickman, 1979; Bickman & Rosenbaum, 1977). Participants in these studies witnessed a staged shoplifting, which an experimental confederate interpreted for one group of participants ("Say, look at her. She's shoplifting. She put that in her purse.") while remaining silent with the other group. Participants who had the event interpreted for them were more likely to report the crime than those who did not. Similarly, many people do not understand the nature of a social dilemma and how interdependent their own and the group's outcomes are.

2. *Increase internal attributions for helping and cooperation.* If you need your friends to donate blood for a family member who is seriously ill,

one way to encourage their generosity is to foster a helpful self-concept, so motivation is internal rather than external. Daniel Batson and his colleagues have shown that people doing good deeds for their own sake rather than for external rewards are likely to see themselves as genuinely altruistic people and to get hooked on helping (Batson, Coke, Jasnoski, & Hanson, 1978; Batson, Fultz, Schoenrade, & Paduano, 1987). In their experiment, the researchers led people to attribute a helpful act either to external factors ("I guess we have no choice") or to their own compassion ("The guy really needed help"). When later asked to help on an unrelated task, more than twice as many of the participants who had labeled themselves as compassionate actually volunteered. Similarly, people often give blood originally because of inducements and incentives, but after multiple donations they come to view themselves as giving and generous people. People who think of themselves as helpful are likely to help again (Piliavin and others, 1982). Similarly, linking individual efforts to the outcome of the group allows people a sense of self-efficacy, making it more likely that they will act on the group's behalf again.

3. *Teach norms that support helping and cooperation.* Families and schools can reinforce norms supporting social responsibility and prosocial behavior both by explicit teaching and by personal examples or models (Rushton, 1975). Research on the impact of the media on behavior confirms that seeing promotes doing (Johnston & Ettema, 1986). In one study, preschoolers who watched episodes of the U.S. television program *Mr. Rogers' Neighborhood*, which promoted compassion and cooperative social values, were more helpful than children who saw neutral or aggressive programs (A. K. Stein & Friedrich, 1972). Models like the heroic rescuers helping in the emergency situations portrayed on shows like *Rescue 911* can increase the accessibility of norms supporting helping, demonstrate possible ways to help, and make clear the positive consequences of helping (Krebs, 1970).

4. *Activate prosocial norms.* Social norms that support helping have to be brought to mind before they can guide behavior. In an emergency situation, directions like, "That small child needs help" or "That elderly man needs a coat over him" can activate norms of social responsibility to the old, young, and weak. In one condition of Bickman's crime-reporting study, the observer commented: "We saw the shoplifting. We should report it. It's our responsibility." Activating the norm boosted reporting of the incident to store management (Bickman, 1979; Bickman & Rosenbaum, 1977). Similarly, activating norms like, "Everyone should do their share" or "Every individual makes a difference" can increase cooperation for the collective rather than individual good. Making people self-aware often brings these group or personal standards to mind. Women who had just seen their own image on a television monitor were more likely than others to volunteer their time and money to a needy cause (Duval, Duval, & Neely, 1979). Similarly, passersby who had just had their picture taken were more likely than ordinary passersby to help when an experimenter staged a small accident nearby (Hoover, Wood, & Knowles, 1983).

5. *Infuse, don't diffuse, responsibility.* Directions that activate norms are not particularly useful if they are broadcast to the world at large. Focusing responsibility on specific people makes normative pressures to help more insistent, just as diffusing responsibility among many people lessens each one's feelings of obligation to help. To get help, therefore, make it clear whom you want help from (Moriarty, 1975). If you are lying bleeding in the

street, don't just shout, "Help me!", which might allow most people to convince themselves that someone else will do so. Focus on a particular individual and specifically ask that person to help: "You there in the red jacket! Help me now!"

6. *Promote identification with those who need help and cooperation.* No matter what the need—emergency or long term—a feeling of connectedness with the person in need breeds empathy and increases willingness to help. This principle—that we help others to whom we are connected as if we were helping ourselves—works with kin, friends, and in-groups. Connectedness is what motivates helping as an end in and of itself, and thus can sustain helping even if no personal rewards are involved. Perhaps this is why religious faith can be a powerful motivator for giving (Colasanto, 1989). The language of the sacred books—"love your neighbor," "children of Allah," and the "human family"—remind us of our connectedness with all humankind, increasing action that benefits others.

The diversity of these recommendations reflects the large number of factors that can influence prosocial behavior, but the diversity should come as no real surprise. Helping is a microcosm of human behavior: a series of judgments influenced by what we see and who we are, by our groups and our norms, by what we think and how we feel, until judgment culminates in action.

CHAPTER 14 THEMES

- **Construction of Reality**
  Interpretations of others' situations, not their actual needs, influence helping and cooperation.

- **Pervasiveness of Social Influence**
  Helping and cooperation are fundamentally shaped by social norms.

- **Striving for Mastery**
  Helping and cooperation are often motivated by the prospect of concrete rewards for the helper.

- **Seeking Connectedness**
  Helping and cooperation often flow from feelings of identification and connectedness with others.

- **Valuing Me and Mine**
  We are likely to treat fellow in-group members with cooperation and altruism.

- **Accessibility**
  The accessibility of norms can increase their impact on helping.

- **Superficiality Verus Depth**
  In-depth processing can promote long-term, committed helping.

CONCLUDING COMMENTS

When people provide help and benefits to other people, their activities inevitably reflect the same social and cognitive processes that you have seen exemplified in every other chapter of this book. Whether we deliver aid in an emergency situation or remain on the sidelines, whether we make charitable and philanthropic activities part of our lives or go about our own daily business depends vitally on our construction of reality. How we interpret cues and signs that help is needed, and how others around us interpret those signals, work together to determine whether helping seems appropriate and achievable. Going out of our way to benefit others fulfills our fundamental need to be connected to others, but because it can bring a variety of rewards in return, it also makes us feel more competence and mastery of our environment. Research has often focused on the kinds of helping decisions that need to be made on the basis of rapid and superficial processing. Perhaps, though, the kinds of helping that make an enduring difference to communities are more likely to result from long-term, extensive weighing of the pros and cons of getting involved.

Because helping and cooperation reflect the same principles as all other types of social behavior, we must interpret with caution statements that self-sacrifice is the essence of what it means to be a social being. In fact, we hope that as you've read this chapter the many parallels between our propensity to help and our propensity to hurt, discussed in the previous chapter, have struck you. Examine Table 14.3 to see many of these parallels for yourself.

Seeing the connections between helping and cooperation and other forms of social behavior also makes it clear that these aspects of social life are not alone in having moral implications. Almost all aspects of social behavior involve issues of

TABLE 14.3. Parallels Between Prosocial and Aggressive Behavior

Parallel in:	Prosocial Behavior	Aggressive Behavior
Construction of reality	Many (sometimes conflicting) pieces of information (cues, attitudes, norms) influence whether helping occurs.	Many (sometimes conflicting) pieces of information (cues, attitudes, norms) influence whether aggression occurs.
Pervasive social influence	When situations are ambiguous, people sometimes look to others to see if helping is appropriate.	When situations are ambiguous, people sometimes look to others to see if aggression is appropriate.
	Norms—like the norm of reciprocity or the norm of "minding your own business"—can encourage or discourage helping.	Norms—like the norm of reciprocity or the norm "pick on someone your own size"—can encourage or discourage aggression.
Motivational principles	People sometimes help others purely for the rewards it brings them.	Instrumental aggression and realistic conflict often occur as people strive for rewards.
	Because of connectedness needs, people often help others with whom they empathize or identify without regard to the costs involved.	When connectedness or respect is threatened, hostile aggression and intergroup conflict occur without regard to the costs involved.
	Empathy and identification are more likely when the person needing help is an in-group rather than an out-group member.	Aggression and competition over positive identity are more likely when the provokers are out-group rather than in-group members.
Processing principles	Information relevant to helping can be dealt with superficially or in great depth.	Information relevant to aggression and conflict can be dealt with superficially or considered in great depth.
	Factors that limit systematic processing— emotion or time constraints—make only the most salient cues likely to be used.	Factors that limit systematic thinking—emotion, alcohol, distracting stressors—increase the influence of salient cues.
	Systematic processing often increases prosocial behavior by increasing the impact of multiple pieces of information like accurate interpretation of need, empathy, and prosocial norms.	Systematic thinking often decreases aggression by increasing the impact of multiple pieces of information like accurate interpretation of provocation, nonaggressive norms, or alternative solutions, and by decreasing anger.

right and wrong, including how people handle conflicts in close relationships (Chapter 11), whether they obey or disobey destructive authorities (Chapter 10), whether they stand up for their own views or go along with the majority in the case of groupthink (Chapter 9), and whether they let their own group's self-interest dictate unjust treatment of others (Chapter 6), to mention just some examples. At the heart of all these different behaviors lie the issues of responsibility and choice.

We are also used to thinking about helping and cooperating as occurring among those who meet face to face or interact on the street, in factories, in families, or in communities. We ordinarily don't reflect on the fact that almost every aspect of our lives, even our long-term survival, also depends on actions that involve others we never see. The rapid destruction of the global environment is less a failure of technology than a failure to solve large-scale social dilemmas. This is true whether individual nations exploit renewable natural resources, such as fish populations and energy sources, or such abstract "resources" as the earth's ability to eliminate pollution and recycle wastes. For example, biological and physical processes can absorb only limited amounts of emitted carbon dioxide and other "greenhouse gases." Because humans are producing so much more than that amount, the composition of the atmosphere is changing, leading many geoscientists to predict massive global climate changes. In the very near future, however, we will all have to learn to identify with larger groups so that our motives and abilities to benefit others extend beyond the usual sphere. Our current state of global interdependence is historically recent, and our sense of common purpose has not yet caught up to this situation. We have yet to learn that our choices to help and cooperate—as individuals and as nations—have implications beyond our private well-being and our national interest.

SUMMARY

 When Do People Help? Prosocial behavior, or behavior intended to help another person or group, can take different forms. **Altruism** is helping motivated by the desire to benefit others for their own sake, while helping driven by personal rewards to the helper is termed **egoism**. Offering help is crucially dependent on people's perception of someone as both needing and deserving help. The ability and motivation to pay attention to others' needs influence whether people think help is needed, as does the behavior of other people in the situation. People are more likely to help those they see as deserving because they are not responsible for their own need.

People sometimes help because social norms, their own standards, or the behavior of others show them that it is appropriate to do so. Not all norms promote helping, however, and sometimes the presence of other potential helpers can diffuse responsibility, diminishing the normative pressures to help.

Why Do People Help? Helping for Mastery and Connectedness. Evolutionary principles suggest that some forms of helping, such as reciprocal helping or helping kin, have been naturally selected because they increase survival. In humans, however, cognitive and social processes mediate such biologically driven helping.

Help may be motivated by perceived rewards for the helper or deterred by perceived costs or risks. These rewards and risks can be emotional: People sometimes help to alleviate their own distress at the victim's suffering. In these cases helping is motivated by egoism.

People are often motivated by a feeling of empathy to relieve another's suffering, regardless of personal rewards and costs. This helping reflects altruism, because it is not motivated by even indirect or emotional rewards for the helper.

In a **social dilemma**, rewards for each individual are in direct conflict with what is best for the group. However, people can be motivated by feelings of group connectedness to act for the good of the group, regardless of personal costs or benefits. When group identification increases commitment to shared goals and norms, social dilemmas can be successfully resolved.

Role of Superficial or Systematic Processing in Helping and Cooperation. When desires and norms conflict, various factors may be considered superficially or thought through extensively before a decision about helping is made. Emotions can play a role in this process, for strong emotion disrupts extensive processing. When helping is a considered decision, though, it can result in a long-term commitment.

Personality factors related to helping and cooperation include differences in empathy and concern for others' welfare, as well as in self-efficacy or the confidence that one's actions will be effective.

Prosocial Behavior in Society. Receiving help can have negative as well as positive consequences, especially if recipients cannot reciprocate because of an unequal power relationship between helper and helped or because receiving help makes them look and feel less competent.

Helping in society can be increased by making needs clear, teaching and activating helping norms, fostering helpful self-concepts, focusing rather than diffusing responsibility, and promoting connectedness to engender empathy, altruism, and group identification.

- Core Principles of Psychology
- How the Principles Interrelate
- An Invitation to Social Psychology

Epilogue

Now that we are at the end of our journey, we hope you have come to appreciate the incredible diversity of exciting ideas and findings that make up social psychology. These are what have kept your two authors coming into our laboratories every day for a combined total of more than 50 years now, and every day we learn once again how intriguing, compelling, sometimes frustrating, but often downright satisfying the study of social behavior can be. We also hope that you noticed a few key ideas coming up again and again as we described such diverse topics as impression formation, intergroup conflict, close relationships, and attitude change. In fact, just as a limited number of chemical elements can be combined to form millions of different substances, so a set of basic principles can be seen to underlie all social behavior. It is this orderliness underlying diversity that makes social psychology a unified field instead of a random collection of interesting topics.

Core Principles of Social Psychology

The principles we highlighted throughout this text are those we see as most important for understanding the findings and theories of social psychology. Let's take a final look at how we can use these eight principles to help understand the wide range of social behavior we encounter in everyday life.

- Whether we are alone or with others, we *construct social reality* as we form impressions of other people and groups (Chapters 3 and 5) and as we act in ways that reflect our own attitudes and group norms (Chapters 8 and 10). This is why we so often react to unexpected, unusual, or ambiguous events by immediately turning to others and asking, "Do you smell gas?" or "Was that an earthquake?" or "So what have *you* heard about Bill?"

- The *pervasive effects of social influence* are evident when we conform to the opinions of important groups (Chapter 9) and cooperate or compete with others (Chapters 13 and 14). Next time you find yourself caught up in the latest clothing fad, realize that you just said something your dad always used to say, or feel uncomfortable about expressing your political views, remind yourself of the power and pervasiveness of social influence.

- Our *strivings for mastery* explain why we want to form accurate opinions and attitudes about ourselves and others (Chapters 4 and 7) and why we are capable of helping or harming others in order to gain rewards (Chapters 13 and 14). This principle offers insights into why we work so hard to find out what instructors want in test answers, why group efforts can be so much more successful than any one person's efforts (Chapter 12), and why we spend so much time trying to learn who we really are.

- We *seek connectedness with others* when we conform to group norms (Chapters 9 and 12) and when we form close relationships with others (Chapter 11). This principle explains why many people feel empty and incomplete when they lack intimate relationships, why the support of a good friend seems to make daily hassles as well as big crises easier to cope with, and why our memberships in groups and our relationships with others are some of the most important aspects of human life.

- Our desire to *value me and mine* is evident in our efforts to feel good about ourselves as individuals and as members of groups (Chapters 4 and 6). It also helps explain why we act against out-group members while often behaving with kindness and altruism toward members of the in-group (Chapters 13 and 14). Perhaps understanding the me and mine principle will alert you to the moments when your group puts others down just to make yourselves feel better. It may also help explain why news of an earthquake in a nearby state elicits more donations than news of a similar tragedy in some distant place.

- The processing principle of *accessibility* is responsible for our using easily grasped information to form our impressions of other people and our attitudes (Chapters 3 and 7) and for the times we find ourselves conforming to accessible norms (Chapters 6 and 10). After staring blankly at the rows of breakfast cereal in the supermarket, have you ever just grabbed the first one you could remember hearing about? Have you ever realized that you'd felt compelled to exchange gifts with someone you don't really like? Accessibility may have been at work.

- The principle of *conservatism* accounts for the persistence of first impressions and stereotypes (Chapters 3 and 5) and also for the difficulties minorities experience in swaying a majority's opinion (Chapter 9). If conservatism were not such a powerful influence on our thinking, advertisers wouldn't have to spend so much money trying to persuade us, and friends wouldn't have to work so hard to change our mistaken snap judgments.

- Finally, the principle of *superficial versus extensive processing* operates when we decide how much thought to devote to understanding a member of a stereotyped group (Chapter 5) or to acting in accordance with our attitudes (Chapter 8). This principle helps explain why we often make snap judgments when the stakes are low but give considerable thought to matters of importance.

Of course, these are just a few examples of the principles at work, and as you review or reread the chapters, you will think of others. We hope these principles will help you take a fresh look at events in your own lives. Perhaps you now see why making a good first impression at a job interview is important (conservatism), why you feel so good when your favorite team wins (me and mine), or why the whole world looks bleak when you're feeling low (accessibility). You may be better able to understand why people care so much about the majority point of view (connectedness) but also how the majority's opinion can sometimes be changed by minority dissent (systematic processing). If these ideas help you make sense of the world in which you live, our goals for this book have been achieved.

How the Principles Interrelate

Although we have described the eight principles separately so that you can see how they operate, we do not mean to suggest that they are unrelated to each other. They operate together, usually in a harmonious fashion.

Part of the reason we construct reality, for example, is because we want to master the environment, and part of the reason we influence others and accept social influence is because we seek connectedness. Social influence is important because we want to construct an appropriate and correct reality, and we need other people to do so. Accessibility helps us make judgments quickly and efficiently, which in turn helps us to master the environment we construct. It also means that we pay most attention to those closest to us, which helps us achieve connectedness and makes possible the give and take of social influence. The principle of conservatism, on the other hand, helps us maintain a stable view of the world—how would we be able to master the environment or form relationships with others if our views of them changed from minute to minute? Superficial versus systematic processing is the moderating principle, the fulcrum that keeps us balanced between the stability of conservatism and the flux of accessibility. For example, receiving unexpected or inconsistent information from those connected to us makes us think hard, opening the way for change.

Although the principles usually operate together to produce positive outcomes, they sometimes can result in conflicts and paradoxes. For example, the shortcuts we use to make inferences are often efficient routes to the right answer, but they sometimes lead us astray (Chapter 3). Relying on social consensus often helps people master the environment and achieve connectedness, but it also can lead to mindless acceptance of a dangerous status quo (Chapter 9). Thus, depending on the circumstances, the same motives and processes produce useful and valuable outcomes or misleading and destructive ones. In fact, almost every aspect of social behavior has an up side and a down side, whether that behavior is adherence to norms like obedience and reciprocity (Chapter 10) or the biased thinking we use to elevate our self-esteem, sometimes by disparaging other people and groups (Chapters 4 and 6).

These examples of ways in which the principles work with and against one another are not a complete list. We hope you have found other meaningful interrelationships that link different types and forms of social behavior.

An Invitation to Social Psychology

When you first picked up this textbook, you probably expected it to tell you how much social psychologists know. Were you surprised to discover how many things we *don't* know? Our understanding of social behavior still has many gaping holes and many unresolved issues because research in social psychology, like research in all fields of human knowledge, has been shaped by its historical development and social context. In the late 1800s, when researchers were just beginning to ask social-psychological questions, nobody could have written down the list of principles we just presented and used them to guide research. (Correspondingly, 20 years from now, the set of principles that social psychologists think are most important may have changed again.) Instead, as we have said, specific events have inspired and guided researchers' questions. The most important events for North American social psychology were the Nazi domination of Europe and the Second World War, which gave rise to research areas involving persuasion, prejudice, obedience to authority, and conformity.

As research traditions grew up around socially significant and culturally relevant issues, other areas were relatively neglected. For instance, the social effects of drug abuse, heterogeneity in the workforce, and variations in family composition were not widespread enough to gain scientists' attention 50 years ago, but they certainly are today. Many important issues involving group identification, kin and friend relationships, and social stability and change have been neglected, perhaps because so much social-psychological research to date has been done in the individually oriented United States. As social psychology becomes a global enterprise, questions of more concern to non-Western societies may come to the fore. For example, the effects of social change are of particular importance to social psychologists in developing countries, who underscore that social psychology should be even more active as a positive force in bringing about and guiding such change. And though much is known about how people form and change attitudes on the basis of information, much less is known about the impact of values, ethics, and religious convictions on people's social behavior. These are just a few of the many areas in which social psychology needs to grow and develop.

We mention these gaps in knowledge and opportunities for development because we want you to understand that social psychology is a young science. One unfortunate characteristic that is almost inherent in the nature of textbooks is that they convey the impression that everything worth learning has already been learned: that all the *i*'s have been dotted, all the *t*'s have been crossed, and everyone agrees about everything. How boring social psychology would be if this were true. But it is not true; social psychologists are well aware of how much we still need to know about human social behavior. We guarantee that as you read these words, whatever the day or time, social psychologists somewhere—in their offices, laboratories, schools, businesses, hospitals, or out on the streets—are planning or carrying out research or reporting new findings. If that idea appeals to you and if you find yourself interested in the topics and issues social psychologists study, we invite you to consider becoming a social psychologist. You could help to shape the future of our science and contribute to what we know about the endlessly fascinating forms of human social behavior.

Photography Credits

Glossary

A

accessibility   The processing principle that the information that is most readily available generally has the most impact on thoughts, feelings, and behavior.

actor–observer differences in attribution   The tendency to attribute our own behaviors to situational causes while seeing others' acts as due to their inner characteristics.

aggression   Behavior intended to harm someone else.

altruism   Behavior intended to help someone else without any prospect of personal rewards for the helper.

appraisal   An individual's interpretation of a self relevant event or situation that directs emotional responses and behavior.

association   A link between two or more cognitive representations.

attachment styles   People's basic orientation toward others in close relationships, which can be secure, preoccupied, avoidant, or fearful.

attitude   A cognitive representation that summarizes an individual's evaluation of a particular person, group, thing, action, or idea.

B

BIRG (bask in reflected glory)   A way of boosting self-esteem by identifying oneself with the accomplishments or good qualities of fellow in-group members.

C

causal attribution   A judgment about the cause of a behavior or other event.

close relationship   A relationship involving strong and frequent interdependence in many domains of life.

cognitive dissonance   An unpleasant state caused by people's awareness of inconsistency among important beliefs, attitudes, or actions.

cognitive processes   The ways in which people's memories, perceptions, thoughts, emotions, and motives influence their understanding of the world and guide their actions.

cognitive representation   A body of knowledge that an individual has stored in memory.

commitment   The combined forces that hold the partners together in an enduring relationship.

communal relationship   A relationship in which people reward their partner out of direct concern and to show caring.

conflict   A perceived incompatibility of goals between two or more parties.

conformity   The convergence of individuals' thoughts, feelings, or behavior toward a social norm.

conservatism   The processing principle that individuals' and groups' views of the world are slow to change and prone to perpetuate themselves.

construct validity   The extent to which the independent and dependent variables used in research correspond to the theoretical constructs under investigation.

construction of reality   The axiom that each person's view of reality is a construction, shaped both by cognitive processes (the ways our minds work) and by social processes (influence from others either actually present or imagined).

constructs   Abstract and general concepts that are used in theories and that are not directly observable.

contact hypothesis   The theory that certain types of direct contact between members of hostile groups will reduce stereotyping and prejudice.

coping strategies   Efforts undertaken to reduce negative consequences of self-threatening events.

correspondence bias   The tendency to infer an actor's personal characteristics from observed behaviors, even when the inference is unjustified because other possible causes of the behavior exist.

correspondent inference   The process of characterizing someone as having a personality trait that corresponds to his or her observed behavior.

D

debriefing   Informing research participants—as soon as possible after the completion of their participation in research—about the purposes, procedures, and scientific value of the study, and discussing any questions participants may have.

deindividuation   The psychological state in which group or social identify completely dominates personal or individual identity so that group norms becomes maximally accessible.

demand characteristics   Cues in a research setting that lead participants to make inferences about what researchers expect or desire and that therefore bias how the participants act.

dependent variable   A concrete measurement of a construct that is thought to be influenced by other constructs.

discrimination   Any positive or negative behavior that is directed toward a social group and its members.

door-in-the-face technique   A technique in which the influencer makes an initial request so large that it will be rejected, and follows it with a smaller request that looks like a concession, making it more likely that the other person will concede in turn.

E

egoism   Behavior motivated by the desire to obtain personal rewards.

elaboration   The generation of favorable or unfavorable reactions to the content of a persuasive appeal.

exchange relationship   A relationship in which people exchange rewards in order to receive benefits in return.

experimental research   A research design in which researchers randomly assign participants to different groups and manipulate one or more independent variables.

external validity   The extent to which research results can be generalized to other appropriate people, times, and settings.

F

false consensus effect   The tendency to overestimate others' agreement with one's own opinions, characteristics, and behaviors.

foot-in-the-door technique   A technique for increasing compliance with a large request by first asking people to go along with a smaller request.

G

group polarization   The process by which a group's initial average position becomes more extreme following group interaction.

groupthink   Group decision making that is impaired by the drive to reach consensus regardless of how the consensus is formed.

I

independent variable   A concrete manipulation or measurement of a construct that is thought to influence other constructs.

individual mobility   The strategy of an individual escape, either physical or psychological, from a stigmatized group.

informed consent   Consent voluntarily given by an individual who decides to participate in a study after being told what will be involved in participation.

interdependence   A situation in which each person's thoughts, emotions, and behaviors influence those of other people.

internal validity   The extent to which it can be concluded that changes in the independent variable actually caused changes in the dependent variable in a research study.

intimacy   A positive emotional bond that includes understanding and support.

L

leadership   A process in which one or more group members are permitted to influence and motivate others to help attain group goals.

low-ball technique   A technique in which the influencer secures agreement with a request but then increases the cost of honoring the commitment.

M

mere exposure effect   People's tendency to prefer objects to which they have been more frequently exposed.

minimal intergroup situation   A research situation in which people are categorized, on an arbitrary or trivial basis, into groups that have no history, no conflicts of interest, and no stereotypes.

N

negotiation   The process by which parties in conflict communicate and influence each other to reach agreement.

nonexperimental research   A research design in which both the independent and dependent variables are measured.

norm of obedience to authority   The shared view that people should obey those with legitimate authority.

norm of social commitment   The shared view that people are required to honor their agreements and obligations.

norm of social reciprocity   The shared view that people are obligated to return to others the goods, services, and concessions they offer to us.

O

out-group homogeneity effect   The tendency to see the out-group as relatively more homogeneous and less diverse than the in-group.

P

persuasion   The process of forming, strengthening, or changing attitudes by communication.

persuasion heuristic   Association of a cue that is positively or negatively evaluated with the attitude object, allowing the attitude object to be evaluated quickly and without much thought.

pervasiveness of social influence   The axiom that other people influence all of an individual's thoughts, feelings, and behavior, whether those others are physically present or not.

prejudice   A positive or negative evaluation of a social group and its members.

priming   The activation of a cognitive representation to increase its accessibility and thus the likelihood that it will be used.

private conformity   Private acceptance of social norms.

prosocial behavior   Behavior intended to help someone else.

public conformity   Overt behavior consistent with social norms that are not privately accepted.

R

random assignment   The procedure of assigning participants to different experimental groups so that every participant has exactly the same chance as every other participant of being in any given group.

reactance   The motive to protect or restore a threatened sense of behavioral freedom.

realistic conflict theory   The theory that intergroup hostility arises from competition among groups for scarce but valued material resources.

reference group   Those people accepted as an appropriate source of information for a judgment because they share the attributes relevant for making that judgment.

relative deprivation theory   The theory that feelings of discontent arise from the belief that other individuals or other groups are better off.

replication   Conducting new studies in an effort to provide evidence for the same theoretically predicted relations found in prior research.

S

salience   The ability of a cue to attract attention in its context.

scientific theory   A statement that satisfies three requirements: It is about constructs; it describes causal relations; and it is general in scope, although the range of generality differs for different theories.

seeking connectedness   The motivational principle that people seek support, liking, and acceptance from the people and groups they care about and value.

self-awareness   A state of heightened awareness of the self, including the individual's internal standards and whether he or she measures up to them.

self-categorization   The process of seeing oneself as a member of a social group.

self-concept   All of an individual's knowledge about his or her personal qualities.

self-discrepancy theory   The theory that people evaluate themselves against internal "ideal" and "ought" standards, producing specific emotional consequences.

self-enhancing bias   Any tendency to gather or interpret information concerning the self in a way that leads to overly positive evaluations.

self-esteem   An individual's positive or negative evaluation of himself or herself.

self-expression   A motive for choosing behaviors that are intended to reflect and express the self-concept.

self-fulfilling prophecy   The process by which one person's expectations about another become reality by eliciting behaviors that confirm the expectations.

self-monitoring   A personality characteristic defined as the degree to which people are sensitive to the demands of social situations and shape their behaviors accordingly.

self-perception theory   The theory that people make inferences about their personal characteristics on the basis of their overt behaviors when internal cues are weak or ambiguous.

self-presentation   A motive for choosing behaviors intended to create in observers a desired impression of the self.

social categorization   The process of identifying individual people as members of a social group because they share certain features that are typical of the group.

social change   The strategy of improving the overall societal situation of a stigmatized group.

social comparison theory   The theory that people learn about and evaluate their personal qualities by comparing themselves to others.

social creativity   The strategy of introducing and emphasizing new dimensions of social comparison, on which a negatively regarded group can see itself superior.

social desirability response bias   People's tendency to act in ways that they believe others find acceptable and approve of.

social dilemma   A form of interdependence in which the most rewarding action for each individual will, if chosen by all individuals, produce a negative outcome for the entire group.

social facilitation   An increase in the likelihood of highly accessible responses, and a decrease in the likelihood of less accessible responses, due to the presence of others.

social group   Two or more people who share some common characteristic that is socially meaningful for themselves or for others.

social identity   Those aspects of the self-concept that derive from an individual's knowledge and feelings about the group memberships he or she shares with others.

social identity theory   The theory that people's motivation to derive positive self-esteem from their group memberships is one driving force behind in-group bias.

social interdependence   Reliance on other members of the group for feelings of connectedness, social and emotional rewards, and a positive social identity.

social loafing   The tendency to exert less effort on a task when an individual's efforts are an unidentifiable part of a group effort than when the same task is performed alone.

social norms   Generally accepted ways of thinking, feeling, or behaving that people in a group agree on and endorse as right and proper.

social processes   The ways in which other people and groups influence people's understanding of the world and guide their actions.

social psychology   The scientific study of the effects of social and cognitive processes on the way individuals perceive, influence, and relate to others.

social support   Emotional and physical coping resources provided by other people.

stereotype   A cognitive representation or impression of a social group that people form by associating particular characteristics and emotions with the group.

stereotype threat   The fear of confirming others' negative stereotype of your group.

striving for mastery   The motivational principle that people seek to understand and predict events in the social world in order to obtain rewards.

subtype   A narrower and more specific social group, such as housewife or feminist, that is included within a broad social group, like women.

superficial processing   Relying on accessible information to make inferences or judgments, while expending little effort in processing.

superficiality versus depth   The processing principle that people ordinarily put little effort into dealing with information, but at times are motivated to consider information in more depth.

superordinate goals   Shared goals that can be attained only if groups work together.

systematic processing   Giving thorough, effortful consideration to a wide range of information relevant to a judgment.

T

task interdependence   Reliance on other members of a group for mastery of material outcomes that arise from the group's task.

theory of planned behavior   The theory that attitudes, social norms, and perceived control combine to influence behavior.

V

valuing me and mine   The motivational principle that people desire to see themselves, and other people and groups connected to themselves, in a positive light.

References

Aaker, J. L., Benet-Martinez, V., & Garolera, J. (2001). Consumption of symbols as carriers of culture: A study of Japanese and Spanish brand personality constructs. *Journal of Personality and Social Psychology*, 18, 492–508.

Aaker, J. L., & Maheswaran, D. (1997). The effect of cultural orientation on persuasion. *Journal of Consumer Research*, 24, 315–328.

Aaker, J. L., & Schmitt, B. (2001). Culture-dependent assimilation and differentiation of the self: Preferences for consumption symbols in the United States and China. *Journal of Cross-Cultural Psychology*, 32, 561–576.

Aaker, J. L., & Williams, P. (1998). Empathy versus pride: The influence of emotional appeals across cultures. *Journal of Consumer Research*, 25, 241–261.

Aarts, H., & Dijksterhuis, A. (2003). The silence of the library: Environment, situational norm, and social behavior. *Journal of Personality and Social Psychology*, 84, 18–28.

Aarts, H., Dijksterhuis, A., & Custers, R. (2003). Automatic normative behavior in environments: The moderating role of conformity in activating situational norms. *Social Cognition*, 21, 447–464.

Aarts, H., Gollwitzer, P. M., & Hassin, R. R. (2004). Goal contagion: Perceiving is for pursuing. *Journal of Personality and Social Psychology*, 87, 23–37.

Abelson, R. P., Dasgupta, N., Park, J., & Banaji, M. R. (1998). Perceptions of the collective other. *Personality and Social Psychology Review*, 2, 243–250.

Abelson, R. P., Kinder, D. R., Peters, M. D., & Fiske, S. T. (1982). Affective and semantic components in political person perception. *Journal of Personality and Social Psychology*, 42, 619–630.

Aboud, F. E. (1976). Self-evaluation: Information seeking strategies for interethnic social comparisons. *Journal of Cross Cultural Psychology*, 7, 289–300.

Aboud, F. E., & Taylor, D. M. (1971). Ethnic and role stereotypes: Their relative importance in person perception. *Journal of Social Psychology*, 85, 17–27.

Abramovitch, I. (1997, August 12). Rap or rock? For dorm mates that may not be an easy negotiation. *The New York Times*, p. B3.

Abrams, D., Wetherell, M., Cochrane, S., Hogg, M. A., & Turner, J. C. (2001). Knowing what to think by knowing who you are: Self-categorization and the nature of norm formation, conformity and group polarization. In M. A. Hogg & D. Abrams (Eds.), *Intergroup relations: Essential readings. Key readings in social psychology* (pp. 270–288). Philadelphia: Psychology Press.

Abrams, J. (1991, August 31). Survey cites racism in housing. *Santa Barbara News Press*, p. A5.

Abramson, L. Y., Seligman, M. E. P., & Teasdale, J. (1978). Learned helplessness in humans: Critique and reformulation. *Journal of Abnormal Psychology*, 87, 49–74.

Adair, W. L., & Brett, J. M. (2005). The negotiation dance: Time, culture, and behavioral sequences in negotiation. *Organization Science*, 16, 33–51.

Adair, W., Brett, J., Lempereur, A., Okumura, T., Shikhirev, P., Tinsley, C. and others (2004). Culture and negotiation strategy. *Negotiation Journal*, 20(1), 87–111.

Adams, G. R., & Shea, J. A. (1981). Talking and loving: A cross-lagged panel investigation. *Basic and Applied Social Psychology*, 2, 81–88.

Adelmann, P. K., & Zajonc, R. B. (1989). Facial efference and the experience of emotion. *Annual Review of Psychology*, 40, 249–280.

Adler, N. J. (1991). *International dimensions of organizational behavior* (2nd ed.). Boston: PWS-Kent Publishing Co.

Adorno, T. W., Frenkel-Brunswik, E., Levinson, D. J., & Sanford, R. N. (1950). *The authoritarian personality*. New York: Harper.

Agnew, C. R. (2000). Cognitive interdependence and the experience of relationship loss. In J. H. Harvey & E. D. Miller (Eds.), *Loss and trauma: General and close relationship perspectives* (pp. 385–398). Philadelphia: Brunner-Routledge.

Agnew, C. R., Loving, T. J., & Drigotas, S. M. (2001). Substituting the forest for the trees: Social networks and the prediction of romantic relationship state and fate. *Journal of Personality and Social Psychology*, 81, 1042–1057.

Agnew, C. R., van Lange, P. A. M., Rusbult, C. E., & Langston, C. A. (1998). Cognitive interdependence: Commitment and the mental representation of close relationships. *Journal of Personality and Social Psychology*, 74, 939–954.

Aiello, J. R., & Douthitt, E. A. (2001). Social facilitation from Triplett to electronic performance monitoring. *Group Dynamics*, 5, 163–180.

Aiello, J. R., & Kolb, K. J. (1995). Electronic performance monitoring and social context: Impact on productivity and stress. *Journal of Applied Psychology*, 80, 339–353.

Ailes, R. (1988). *You are the message*. New York: Doubleday.

Ainsworth, M., Blehar, M., Waters, E., & Wall, S. (1978). *Patterns of attachment*. Hillsdale, NJ: Lawrence Erlbaum Associates, Inc.

Ajzen, I. (1991). The theory of planned behavior. *Organizational Behavior and Human Decision Processes*, 50, 179–211.

Ajzen, I. (1996). The directive influence of attitudes on behavior. In P. M. Gollwitzer & J. A. Bargh (Eds.), *The psychology of action: Linking cognition and motivation to behavior* (pp. 385–403). New York: Guilford Press.

Ajzen, I. (2001). Nature and operation of attitudes. *Annual Review of Psychology, 52*, 27–58.

Ajzen, I., & Fishbein, M. (1977). Attitude–behavior relations: A theoretical analysis and review of empirical research. *Psychological Bulletin, 84*, 888–918.

Ajzen, I., & Fishbein, M. (1980). *Understanding attitudes and predicting social behavior.* Englewood Cliffs, NJ: Prentice Hall.

Ajzen, I., & Madden, T. J. (1986). Prediction of goal-directed behavior: Attitudes, intentions, and perceived behavioral control. *Journal of Experimental Social Psychology, 22*, 453–474.

Alagna, S. W., & Reddy, D. M. (1984). Predictors of proficient technique and successful lesion detection in breast self-examination. *Health Psychology, 3*, 113–127.

Albarracin, D., Johnson, B. T., Fishbein, M., & Muellerleile, P. A. (2001) Theories of reasoned action and planned behavior as models of condom use: A meta-analysis. *Psychological Bulletin, 127*, 142–161.

Albarracin, D., & Kumkale, G. T. (2003). Affect as information in persuasion: A model of affect identification and discounting. *Journal of Personality and Social Psychology, 84*, 453–469.

Albarracin, D., & McNatt, P. S. (2005). Maintenance and decay of past behavior influences: Anchoring attitudes on beliefs following inconsistent actions. *Personality and Social Psychology Bulletin, 31*, 719–733.

Albarracin, D., & Wyer, R. S. (2000). The cognitive impact of past behavior: Influences on beliefs, attitudes, and future behavioral decisions. *Journal of Personality and Social Psychology, 79*, 5–22.

Alcock, J. E., Carment, D. W., & Sadava, S. W. (1988). *A textbook of social psychology.* Scarborough, Ontario: Prentice-Hall.

Allen, B. P. (1988). Dramaturgical quality. *Journal of Social Psychology, 128*, 181–190.

Allen, K. M., Blascovich, J., Tomaka, J., & Kelsey, R. M. (1991). Presence of human friends and pet dogs as moderators of autonomic responses to stress in women. *Journal of Personality and Social Psychology, 61*, 582–589.

Allen, V. L. (1965). Situational factors in conformity. In L. Berkowitz (Ed.), *Advances in experimental social psychology* (Vol. 8, pp. 133–175). New York: Academic Press.

Allen, V. L. (1975). Social support for non-conformity. In L. Berkowitz (Ed.), *Advances in experimental social psychology* (Vol. 18, pp. 2–43). New York: Academic Press.

Allen, V. L., & Bragg, B. W. (1965). The generalization of nonconformity within a homogeneous content dimension. (cited in V. L. Allen, 1975).

Allen, V. L., & Wilder, D. A. (1972). Social support in absentia: effect of an absentee partner on conformity. (cited in V. L. Allen, 1975).

Allen, V. L., & Wilder, D. A. (1979). Group categorization and belief similarity. *Small Group Behavior, 10*, 73–80.

Allison, S. T., Mackie, D. M., Muller, M. M., & Worth, L. T. (1993). Sequential correspondence biases and perceptions of change: The Castro studies revisited. *Personality and Social Psychology Bulletin, 19*, 151–157.

Allison, S. T., & Messick, D. M. (1985). The group attribution error. *Journal of Experimental Social Psychology, 21*, 563–579.

Allison, S. T., Messick, D. M., & Goethals, G. R. (1989). On being better but not smarter than others: The Muhammad Ali effect. *Social Cognition, 7*, 275–295.

Alloy, L. B., & Abramson, L. Y. (1979). Judgment of contingency in depressed and nondepressed students: Sadder but wiser? *Journal of Experimental Psychology: General, 108*, 441–485.

Allport, F. H. (1924). *Social psychology.* Boston: Houghton Mifflin.

Allport, F. H., & Lepkin, M. (1945). Wartime rumors of waste and special privilege: Why some people believe them. *Journal of Abnormal and Social Psychology, 40*, 3–36.

Allport, G. W. (1935). Attitudes. In G. Murchison (Ed.), *Handbook of social psychology*, Worchester, MA: Clark University Press.

Allport, G. W. (1954a). The historical background of modern social psychology. In G. Lindzey (Ed.), *The handbook of social psychology* (Vol. 1, pp. 3–56). Cambridge, MA: Addison-Wesley.

Allport, G. W. (1954b). *The nature of prejudice.* New York: Addison-Wesley.

Allport, G. W. (1958). *The nature of prejudice.* Garden City, NY: Doubleday Anchor.

Altemeyer, B. (1981). *Right-wing authoritarianism.* Winnipeg, MB: University of Manitoba Press.

Altman, I., & Taylor, D. A. (1973). *Social penetration.* New York: Holt, Rinehart, Winston

Alvaro, E. M., & Crano, W. D. (1996). Cognitive responses to minority- or majority-based communications: Factors that underlie minority influence. *British Journal of Social Psychology, 35*, 105–121.

Alvaro, E. M., & Crano, W. D. (1997). Indirect minority influence: Evidence for leniency in source evaluation and counterargumentation. *Journal of Personality and Social Psychology, 72*, 949–964.

Amato, P. R., & Previti, D. (2003). People's reasons for divorcing: Gender, social class, the life course, and adjustment. *Journal of Family Issues, 24*, 602–626.

Ambady, N., Bernieri, F. J., & Richeson, J. A. (2000). Toward a histology of social behavior: Judgmental accuracy from thin slices of the behavioral stream. In M. P. Zanna (Ed.), *Advances in experimental social psychology* (Vol. 32, pp. 201–271). San Diego, CA: Academic Press.

Amir, Y. (1969). Contact hypothesis in ethnic relations. *Psychological Bulletin, 71*, 319–42.

Andersen, S. M. (1984). Self-knowledge and social inference: II. The diagnosticity of cognitive/affective and behavioral data. *Journal of Personality and Social Psychology, 46*, 294–307.

Andersen, S. M., & Baum, A. (1994). Transference in interpersonal relations: Inferences and affect based on significant-other representations. *Journal of Personality, 62*, 459–497.

Andersen, S. M., & Cole, S. W. (1990). "Do I know you?" The role of significant others in general social perception. *Journal of Personality and Social Psychology, 59*, 384–399.

Andersen, S. M., & Klatsky, R. L. (1987). Traits and social stereotypes: Levels of categorization in person perception. *Journal of Personality and Social Psychology, 53*, 235–246.

Andersen, S. M., & Ross, L. (1984). Self-knowledge and social inference: I. The impact of cognitive/affective and behavioral data. *Journal of Personality and Social Psychology, 46*, 280–293.

Anderson, C. A. (1987). Temperature and aggression: Effects on quarterly, yearly, and city rates of violent and nonviolent crime. *Journal of Personality and Social Psychology, 52*, 1161–1173.

Anderson, C. A., Anderson, K. B., & Deuser, W. E. (1996). Examining an affective aggression framework: Weapon and temperature effects on aggressive thoughts, affect, and attitudes. *Personality and Social Psychology Bulletin, 22,* 366–376.

Anderson, C. A., Berkowitz, L., Donnerstein, E., Huesmann, L. R., Johnson, J. D., Linz, D. and others (2003). The influence of media violence on youth. *Psychological Science in the Public Interest, 4,* 81–110.

Anderson, C. A., & Bushman, B. J. (1997). External validity of "trivial" experiments: The case of laboratory aggression. *Review of General Psychology, 1,* 19–41.

Anderson, C. A., Carnagey, N. L., & Eubanks, J. (2003). Exposure to violent media: The effects of songs with violent lyrics on aggressive thoughts and feelings. *Journal of Personality and Social Psychology, 84*(5), 960–971.

Anderson, C. A., Carnagey, N. L., Flanagan, M., Benjamin, A. J., Eubanks, J., & Valentine, J. C. (2004). Violent video games: Specific effects of violent content on aggressive thoughts and behavior. *Advances in Experimental Social Psychology, 36,* 199–249.

Anderson, C. A., & Dill, K. E. (2000). Video games and aggressive thoughts, feelings, and behavior in the laboratory and in life. *Journal of Personality and Social Psychology, 78*(4), 772–790.

Anderson, C. A., & Godfrey, S. S. (1987). Thoughts about actions: The effects of specificity and availability of imagined behavioral scripts on expectations about oneself and others. *Social Cognition, 5,* 238–258.

Anderson, C. A., Jennings, D. L., & Arnoult, L. H. (1988). Validity and utility of the attributional style construct at a moderate level of specificity. *Journal of Personality and Social Psychology, 55,* 979–990.

Anderson, C., John, O. P., Keltner, D., & Kring, A. (2001). Who attains social status? Effects of personality and physical attractiveness in social groups. *Journal of Personality and Social Psychology, 81,* 116–132.

Anderson, N. H. (1981). *Foundations of information integration theory.* New York: Academic Press.

Andreoli, V., & Worchel, S. (1978). Effects of media, communicator, and message position on attitude change. *Public Opinion Quarterly, 42,* 59–70.

Angier, N. (1990a, December 13). Anger can ruin more than your day. *New York Times.*

Angier, N. (1990b, October 16). Marriage is lifesaver for men after 45. *The New York Times.*

Anthony, J., Copper, C., & Mullen, B. (1992). Cross-racial facial identification: A social cognitive integration. *Personality and Social Psychology Bulletin, 18,* 296–301.

Archer, D., Iratani, B., Kimes, D. B., & Barrios, M. (1983). Face-ism: Five studies of sex differences in facial prominence. *Journal of Personality and Social Psychology, 45,* 725–735.

Archer, J. (2004). Sex differences in aggression in real-world settings: A meta-analytic review. *Review of General Psychology, 8,* 291–322.

Archer, J., & Coyne, S. (2005). An integrated review of indirect, relational, and social aggression. *Personality and Social Psychology Review, 9,* 212–230.

Archer, R. L. (1980). Self-disclosure. In D. M. Wegner & R. R. Vallacher (Eds.), *The self in social psychology.* New York: Oxford University Press.

Arendt, H. (1965). *Eichmann in Jerusalem: A report on the banality of evil.* New York: Viking Press.

Arkes, H. R., Hackett, C., & Boehm, L. (1989). The generality of the relation between familiarity and judged validity. *Journal of Behavioral Decision Making, 2,* 81–94.

Arkin, R. M. (1981). Self-presentation styles. In J. T. Tedeschi (Ed.), *Impression management theory and social psychological research* (pp. 311–333). New York: Academic Press.

Armitage, C. J., & Conner, M. (2000). Attitudinal ambivalence: A test of three key hypotheses. *Personality and Social Psychology Bulletin, 26,* 1421–1432.

Arnold, M. B. (1960). *Emotion and personality.* New York: Columbia University Press.

Aron, A., & Aron, E. N. (1991). Love and sexuality. In K. McKinney & S. Sprecher (Eds.), *Sexuality in close relationships* (pp. 25–48). Hillsdale, NJ: Lawrence Erlbaum Associates, Inc.

Aron, A., Aron, E. N., & Smollan, D. (1992). Inclusion of Other in the Self scale and the structure of interpersonal closeness. *Journal of Personality and Social Psychology, 63,* 596–612.

Aron, A., Aron, E. N., Tudor, M., & Nelson, G. (1991). Close relationships as including other in the self. *Journal of Personality and Social Psychology, 60,* 241–253.

Aron, A., Paris, M., & Aron, E. N. (1995). Falling in love: Prospective studies of self-concept change. *Journal of Personality and Social Psychology, 69,* 1102–1112.

Aronson, E. (1969). The theory of cognitive dissonance: A current perspective. In L. Berkowitz (Ed.), *Advances in experimental social psychology* (Vol. 4, pp. 1–34). New York: Academic Press.

Aronson, E., & Carlsmith, J. M. (1963). Effect of severity of threat on the devaluation of forbidden behavior. *Journal of Abnormal and Social Psychology, 66,* 584–588.

Aronson, E., Fried, C., & Stone, J. (1991). Overcoming denial and increasing the intention to use condoms through the induction of hypocrisy. *American Journal of Public Health, 81,* 1636–1638.

Aronson, E., & Mills, J. (1959). The effect of severity of initiation on liking for a group. *Journal of Abnormal and Social Psychology, 59,* 177–181.

Aronson, E., & Worchel, S. (1966). Similarity versus liking as determinants of interpersonal attractiveness. *Psychonomic Science, 5,* 157–158.

Aronson, J., Blanton, H., & Cooper, J. (1995). From dissonance to disidentification: Selectivity in the self-affirmation process. *Journal of Personality and Social Psychology, 58,* 1062–1072.

Arriaga, X. B., & Agnew, C. R. (2001). Being committed: Affective, cognitive, and conative components of relationship commitment. *Personality and Social Psychology Bulletin, 27,* 1190–1203.

Arriaga, X. B., & Oskamp, S. (Eds.) (1999). *Violence in intimate relationships.* Thousand Oaks, CA: Sage Publishers.

Asch, S. E. (1946). Forming impressions of personality. *Journal of Abnormal and Social Psychology, 41,* 258–290.

Asch, S. E. (1951). Effects of group pressure upon the modification and distortion of judgment. In H. Guetzkow (Ed.), *Groups, leadership, and men.* Pittsburgh: Carnegie University Press.

Asch, S. E. (1955). Studies of independence and conformity: A minority of one against a unanimous majority. *Psychology Monographs, 70,* 1–70.

Asch, S. E. (1956). Opinions and social pressure. *Scientific American, 193*(5) 31–35.

Asch, S. E., & Zukier, H. (1984). Thinking about persons. *Journal of Personality and Social Psychology, 46,* 1230–1240.

Ashburn-Nardo, L., Knowles, M. L., & Monteith, M. J. (2003). Black Americans' implicit racial associations and their implications for intergroup judgment. *Social Cognition, 21,* 62–87.

Ashley, J. H. (1976). *Hospitals, paternalism, and the role of the nurse.* New York: Teachers College Press.

Ashmore, R. D. (1981). Sex stereotypes and implicit personality theory. In D. L. Hamilton (Ed.), *Cognitive processes in stereotyping and intergroup behavior* (pp. 37–81). Hillsdale, NJ: Lawrence Erlbaum Associates, Inc.

Ashmore, R. D., & Del Boca, F. K. (1981). Conceptual approaches to stereotypes and stereotyping. In D. L. Hamilton (Ed.), *Cognitive processes in stereotyping and intergroup behavior* (pp. 1–36). Hillsdale, NJ: Lawrence Erlbaum Associates, Inc.

Askenasy, H. (1978). *Are we all Nazis?* Secaucus, NJ: Lyle Stuart.

Astin, A. W., Green, K. C., Korn, W. S., & Schalit, M. (1987). *The American freshman: National norms for Fall 1987.* Los Angeles, CA: Higher Education Research Institute, University of California at Los Angeles.

Atkinson, J., & Huston, T. L. (1984). Sex role orientation and division of labor early in marriage. *Journal of Personality and Social Psychology, 46,* 330–345.

Avolio, B. J., Zhu, W., Koh, W., & Bhatia, P. (2004). Transformational leadership and organizational commitment: Mediating role of psychological empowerment and moderating role of structural distance. *Journal of Organizational Behavior, 25,* 951–968.

Axsom, D., & Cooper, J. (1985). Cognitive dissonance and psychotherapy: The role of effort justification in inducing weight loss. *Journal of Experimental Psychology, 21,* 149–160.

Axsom, D., Yates, S., & Chaiken, S. (1987). Audience response as a heuristic cue in persuasion. *Journal of Personality and Social Psychology, 53,* 30–40.

Azar, B. (1994, September). Teams that wear blinders are often the cause of tragic errors. *APA Monitor,* p. 23.

Babey, S. H., Queller, S., & Klein, S. B. (1998). The role of expectancy violating behaviors in the representation of trait knowledge: A summary-plus-exception model of social memory. *Social Cognition, 16,* 287–339.

Bagozzi, R. P., Baumgartner, H., & Pieters, R. (1998). Goal-directed emotions. *Cognition and Emotion, 12,* 1–26.

Bailey, A. A., & Hurd, P. L. (2005). Finger length ratio (2D:4D) correlates with physical aggression in men but not in women. *Biological Psychology, 68,* 215–222.

Bakan, D. (1966). *The duality of human existence.* Boston: Beacon Press.

Baker, S. M., & Petty, R. E. (1994). Majority and minority influence: Source position imbalance as a determinant of message scrutiny. *Journal of Personality and Social Psychology, 67,* 5–19.

Baldwin, M. W. (1992). Relational schemas and the processing of social information. *Psychological Bulletin, 112,* 461–484.

Baldwin, M. W., Carrell, S. E., & Lopez, D. F. (1990). Priming relationship schemas: My advisor and the Pope are watching me from the back of my mind. *Journal of Experimental Social Psychology, 26,* 435–454.

Baldwin, M. W., & Sinclair, L. (1996). Self-esteem and "if . . . then" contingencies of interpersonal acceptance. *Journal of Personality and Social Psychology, 71,* 1130–1141.

Bales, R. F. (1953). The equilibrium problem in small groups. In T. Parsons, R. F. Bales, & E. A. Shils (Eds.), *Working papers in the theory of action* (pp. 111–162). Glencoe, IL: Free Press.

Bales, R. F., Cohen, S. P., & Williamson, S. A. (1979). *SYMLOG: A system for the multiple level observation of groups.* New York: Free Press.

Bales, R. F., & Slater, P. E. (1955). Role differentiation. In T. Parsons & R. F. Bales (Eds.), *The family, socialization, and interaction process* (pp. 259–306). Glencoe, IL: Free Press.

Bandura, A. (1973). *Aggression: A social learning analysis.* Englewood Cliffs, NJ: Prentice-Hall.

Bandura, A. (1977a). Self-efficacy: Toward a unifying theory of behavioral change. *Psychological Review, 84,* 191–215.

Bandura, A. (1977b). *Social learning theory.* Englewood Cliffs, NJ: Prentice Hall.

Bandura, A. (1982). Self-efficacy: Mechanism in human agency. *American Psychologist, 37,* 122–147.

Bandura, A. (1986). The explanatory and predictive scope of self-efficacy theory. Special Issue: Self-efficacy theory in contemporary psychology. *Journal of Social and Clinical Psychology, 4,* 359–373.

Bandura, A., Barbaranelli, C., Caprara, G. V., & Pastorelli, C. (1996). Mechanisms of moral disengagement in the exercise of moral agency. *Journal of Personality and Social Psychology, 71,* 364–374.

Bandura, A., Ross, D., & Ross, S. A. (1961). Transmission of aggression through imitation of aggressive models. *Journal of Abnormal and Social Psychology, 63,* 575–582.

Bandura, A., Ross, D., & Ross, S. A. (1963). Imitation of film-mediated aggressive models. *Journal of Abnormal and Social Psychology, 66,* 3–11.

Banner, L. W. (1983). *American beauty.* Chicago: University of Chicago Press.

Bargh, J. A. (1989). Conditional automaticity: Varieties of automatic influence in social percpetion and cognition. In J. S. Uleman & J. A. Bargh (Eds.), *Unintended thought* (pp. 3–51). New York: Guilford Press.

Bargh, J. A., Bond, R. N., Lombardi, W. J., & Tota, M. E. (1986). The additive nature of chronic and temporary sources of construct accessibility. *Journal of Personality and Social Psychology, 50,* 869–878.

Bargh, J. A., Chaiken, S., Raymond, P., & Hymes, C. (1996). The automatic evaluation effect: Unconditional automatic attitude activation with a pronunciation task. *Journal of Experimental Social Psychology, 32,* 104–128.

Bargh, J. A., & Gollwitzer, P. M. (1993). Environmental control of goal-directed action: Automatic and strategic contingencies between situations and behavior. In *Nebraska Symposium on Motivation.* Lincoln: University of Nebraska Press.

Bargh, J. A., & Pietromonaco, P. (1982). Automatic information processing and social perception: The influence of trait information presented outside of conscious awareness on impression formation. *Journal of Personality and Social Psychology, 43,* 437–449.

Bargh, J. A., & Thein, R. D. (1985). Individual construct accessibility, person memory, and the recall–judgment link: The case of information overload. *Journal of Personality and Social Psychology, 49,* 1129–1146.

Barnet, R. (1971, November). The game of nations. *Harper's, 243,* 53–59.

Baron, R. A. (1972). Aggression as a function of ambient temperature and prior anger arousal. *Journal of Personality and Social Psychology, 21,* 183–189.

Baron, R. A. (1983a). The control of human aggression: An optimistic perspective. *Journal of Social and Clinical Psychology, 1,* 97–119.

Baron, R. A. (1983b). The control of human aggression: A strategy based on incompatible responses. In R. G. Geen & E. Donnerstein (Eds.), *Aggression: Theoretical and empirical reviews* (Vol. 2, pp. 173–190). New York: Academic Press.

Baron, R. A., Baron, P., & Miller, N. (1973). The relation between distraction and persuasion. *Psychological Bulletin, 80*, 310–323.

Baron, R. S. (1986). Distraction-conflict theory: Progress and problems. In L. Berkowitz (Ed.), *Advances in experimental social psychology* (Vol. 19, pp. 1–40). New York: Academic Press.

Baron R. S., & Roper, G. (1976). Reaffirmation of social comparison views of choice shift: averaging and extremitization in an auto-kinetic situation. *Journal of Personality and Social Psychology, 35*, 521–530.

Baron, R. S., Vandello, J. A., & Brunsman, B. (1996). The forgotten variable in conformity research: Impact of task importance on social influence. *Journal of Personality & Social Psychology, 71*, 915–927.

Barrett, L., Dunbar, R., & Lycett, J. (2002). *Human evolutionary psychology*. Princeton, NJ: Princeton University Press.

Barsade, S. G. (2002). The ripple effects: Emotional contagion and its influence on group behavior. *Administrative Science Quarterly, 47*, 644–675.

Bar-Tal, D., & Bar-Tal, Y. (1988). A new perspective for social psychology. In D. Bar-Tal & A. W. Kruglanski (Eds.), *The social psychology of knowledge* (pp. 83–108). Cambridge, UK: Cambridge University Press.

Bartel, C. A., & Saavedra, R. (2000). The collective construction of work group moods. *Administrative Science Quarterly, 45*, 197–231.

Bartholomew, K., & Horowitz, L. M. (1991). Attachment styles among young adults: A test of a four-category model. *Journal of Personality and Social Psychology, 61*, 226–244.

Bartholow, B. D., Anderson, C. A., Carnagey, N. L., & Benjamin, A. J. (2005). Interactive effects of life experience and situational cues on aggression: The weapons priming effect in hunters and nonhunters. *Journal of Experimental Social Psychology, 41*, 48–60.

Bartis, S., Szymanski, K., & Harkins, S. G. (1988). Evaluation and performance: A two-edged knife. *Personality and Social Psychology Bulletin, 14*, 242–251.

Bass, B. M. (1985). *Leadership and performance beyond expectations*. New York: Free Press.

Bass, B. M. (1990). *Bass and Stogdill's handbook of leadership: Theory, research, and managerial applications* (3rd ed.). New York: Free Press.

Bass, B. M. (1997). Does the transactional–transformational leadership paradigm transcend organizational and national boundaries? *American Psychologist, 52*, 130–139.

Bass, B. M., & Riggio, R. E. (2006). *Transformational leadership* (2nd ed.). Mahwah, NJ: Lawrence Erlbaum Associates Inc.

Bassili, J. N. (2003). The minority slowness effect: Subtle inhibitions in the expression of views not shared by others. *Journal of Personality and Social Psychology, 84*, 261–276.

Batson, C. D. (1975). Rational processing or rationalization?: The effect of disconfirming information on a stated religious belief. *Journal of Personality and Social Psychology, 32*, 176–184.

Batson, C. D. (1991). *The altruism question: Toward a social-psychological answer*. Hillsdale, NJ: Lawrence Erlbaum Associates, Inc.

Batson, C. D. (1998). Altruism and prosocial behavior. In D. T. Gilbert, S. T. Fiske, & G. Lindzey (Eds.), *Handbook of social psychology* (4th ed., Vol. 2, pp. 282–315). New York: McGraw-Hill.

Batson, C. D. (2002). Addressing the altruism question experimentally. In S. G. Post & L. G. Underwood (Eds.), *Altruism and altruistic love: Science, philosophy, & religion in dialogue* (pp. 89–105). London: Oxford University Press.

Batson, C. D., Ahmad, N., Yin, J., Bedell, S. J., Johnson, J. W., Templin, C. M. and others (1999). Two threats to the common good: Self-interested egoism and empathy-induced altruism. *Personality and Social Psychology Bulletin, 25*, 3–16.

Batson, C. D., Batson, J. G., Slingsby, J. K., Harrell, K. L., Peekna, H. M., & Todd, R. M. (1991). Empathic joy and the empathy–altruism hypothesis. *Journal of Personality and Social Psychology, 61*, 413–426.

Batson, C. D., Batson, J. G., Todd, M., Brummett, B. H., Shaw, L. L., & Aldeguer, C. M. R. (1995). Empathy and the collective good: Caring for one of the others in a social dilemma. *Journal of Personality and Social Psychology, 68*, 619–631.

Batson, C. D., Coke, J. S., Jasnoski, M. L., & Hanson, M. (1978). Buying kindness: Effect of an extrinsic incentive for helping on perceived altruism. *Personality and Social Psychology Bulletin, 4*, 86–91.

Batson, C. D., Duncan, B. D., Ackerman, P., Buckley, T., & Birch, K. (1981). Is empathic emotion a source of altruistic motivation? *Journal of Personality and Social Psychology, 40*, 290–302.

Batson, C. D., Dyck, J. L., Brandt, J. R., & Batson, J. G. (1988). Five studies testing two new egoistic alternatives to the empathy–altruism hypothesis. *Journal of Personality and Social Psychology, 55*, 52–77.

Batson, C. D., Fultz, J., Schoenrade, P. A., & Paduano, A. (1987). Critical self-reflection and self-perceived altruism: When self-reward fails. *Journal of Personality and Social Psychology, 53*, 594–602.

Batson, C. D., & Weeks, J. L. (1996). Mood effects of unsuccessful helping: Another test of the empathy–altruism hypothesis. *Personality and Social Psychology Bulletin, 22*, 148–157.

Baumeister, R. F. (1982). A self-presentational view of social phenomena. *Psychological Bulletin, 91*, 3–26.

Baumeister, R. F. (1991). *Escaping the self: Alcoholism, spirituality, masochism, and other flights from the burden of selfhood*. New York: Basic Books.

Baumeister, R. F. (1997). *Evil: Inside human cruelty and violence*. New York: W. H. Freeman.

Baumeister, R. F. (1998). The self. In D. T. Gilbert, S. T. Fiske, & G. Lindzey (Eds.), *Handbook of social psychology* (4th ed., Vol. 1, pp. 680–740). Boston: McGraw-Hill.

Baumeister, R. F., Bratslavsky, E., Finkenauer, C., & Vohs, K. D. (2001). Bad is stronger than good. *Review of General Psychology, 5*, 323–370.

Baumeister, R. F., Chesner, S. P., Senders, P. S., & Tice, D. M. (1988). Who's in charge here? Group leaders do lend help in emergencies. *Personality and Social Psychology Bulletin, 14*, 17–22.

Baumeister, R. F., & Leary, M. R. (1995). The need to belong: Desire for interpersonal attachments as a fundamental human motivation. *Psychological Bulletin, 117*, 497–529.

Baumeister, R. F., Muraven, M., & Tice, D. M. (2000). Ego depletion: A resource model of volition, self-regulation, and controlled processing. *Social Cognition, 18*, 130–150.

Baumeister, R. F., & Newman, L. S. (1994). How stories make sense of personal experiences: Motives that shape autobiographical narratives. *Personality and Social Psychology Bulletin, 20*, 676–690.

Baumeister, R. F., Smart, L., & Boden, J. M. (1996). Relation of threatened egotism to violence and aggression: The dark side of high self-esteem. *Psychological Review, 103,* 5–33.

Baumeister, R. F., & Wotman, S. R. (1992). *Breaking hearts: The two sides of unrequited love.* New York: Guilford Press.

Baumgardner, A. H., & Brownlee, E. A. (1987). Strategic failure in social interaction: Evidence for expectancy disconfirmation process. *Journal of Personality and Social Psychology, 52,* 525–535.

Baumrind, D. (1964). Some thoughts on ethics of research: After reading Milgram's "Behavioral Study of Obedience." *American Psychologist, 19,* 421–423.

Baxter, L. A. (1986). Gender differences in the heterosexual relationship rules embedded in break-up accounts. *Journal of Social and Personal Relationships, 1,* 29–48.

Baxter, T. L., & Goldberg, L. R. (1987). Perceived behavioral consistency underlying trait attributions to oneself and another: An extension of the actor–observer effect. *Personality and Social Psychology Bulletin, 13,* 437–447.

Beach, S. R. H., Tesser, A., Fincham, F. D., Jones, D. J., Johnson, D., & Whitaker, D. J. (1998). Pleasure and pain in doing well, together: An investigation of performance-related affect in close relationships. *Journal of Personality and Social Psychology, 74,* 923–938.

Bearman, M. (2003) Is virtual the same as real? Medical students' experiences of a virtual patient. *Academic Medicine, 78,* 538–545.

Beasley, R. K., & Joslyn, M. R. (2001). Cognitive dissonance and post-decision attitude change in six presidential elections. *Political Psychology, 22,* 521–540.

Beauvois, J. L., & Joule, R. V. (1996). *A radical dissonance theory. European monographs in social psychology.* Philadelphia, PA: Taylor & Francis.

Bechtold, A., Naccarato, M. E., & Zanna, M. P. (1986). *Need for structure and the prejudice–discrimination link.* Paper presented at the annual meeting of the Canadian Psychological Association, Toronto.

Beggan, J. K. (1992). On the social nature of nonsocial perception: The mere ownership effect. *Journal of Personality and Social Psychology, 62,* 229–237.

Bell, D. A. (1973). Racism in American courts: Cause for Black disruption or despair? *California Law Review, 761,* 165–203.

Bell, P. A., & Baron, R. A. (1990). Affect and aggression. In B. S. Moore & A. M. Isen (Eds.), *Affect and social behavior: Studies in emotion and social interaction* (pp. 64–88). New York: Cambridge University Press.

Bellah, R. N., Madsen, R., Sullivan, W. M., Tipton, S. M., & Swidler, A. (1985). *Habits of the heart: Individualism and commitment in American life.* Berkeley, CA: University of California Press.

Belmore, S. M., & Hubbard, M. L. (1987). The role of advance expectancies in person memory. *Journal of Personality and Social Psychology, 53,* 61–70.

Bem, D. J. (1963). An experimental analysis of self-persuasion. *Journal of Experimental Social Psychology, 1,* 199–218.

Bem, D. J. (1967). Self-perception: An alternative interpretation of cognitive dissonance phenomena. *Psychological Review, 74,* 183–200.

Bem, D. J. (1972). Self-perception theory. In L. Berkowitz (Ed.), *Advances in experimental social psychology* (Vol. 6). New York: Academic Press.

Bem, S. (1981). Gender schema theory: A cognitive account of sex typing. *Psychological Review, 88,* 354–364.

Benson, P. L., Dehority, J., Garman, L., Hanson, E., Hochschwender, M., Lebod, C. and others (1980). Intrapersonal correlates of nonspontaneous helping behavior. *Journal of Social Psychology, 110,* 87–95.

Bentler, P. M., & Speckart, G. (1979). Models of attitude–behavior relations. *Psychological Review, 86,* 452–464.

Berg, J. H. (1984). The development of friendship between roommates. *Journal of Personality and Social Psychology, 46,* 346–356.

Berg, J. H., & Archer, R. L. (1980). Disclosure or concern: A second look at liking for the norm-breaker. *Journal of Personality, 48,* 245–257.

Berg, J. H., & McQuinn, R. D. (1986). Attraction and exchange in continuing and noncontinuing dating relationships. *Journal of Personality and Social Psychology, 50,* 942–952.

Berg, M. B., Janoff-Bulman, R., & Cotter, J. (2001). Perceiving value in obligations and goals: Wanting to do what should be done. *Personality and Social Psychology Bulletin, 27,* 982–995.

Berglas, S., & Jones, E. E. (1978). Drug choice as a self-handicapping strategy in response to noncontingent success. *Journal of Personality and Social Psychology, 36,* 405–417.

Berk, R. A., & Newton, P. J. (1985). Does arrest really deter wife battery? *American Sociological Review, 50,* 253–262.

Berke, R. L. (2000, September 12). Democrats see, and smell, "rats" in GOP ad. *New York Times* on the Web, available at http://www.nytimes.com.

Berkman, L. F. (2000). Social support, social networks, social cohesion and health. *Social Work in Health Care, 31,* 3–14.

Berkman, L. F., & Glass, T. (2000). Social integration, social networks, social support, and health. In L. F. Berkman & I. Kawachi (Eds.), Social epidemiology (pp. 137–173). New York: Oxford University Press.

Berkman, L. F., Leo-Summers, C., & Horwitz, R. I. (1992). Emotional support and survival after myocardial infarction: A prospective population-based study of the elderly. *Annals of Internal Medicine, 117,* 1003–1009.

Berkman, L. F., & Syme, S. L. (1979). Social networks, host resistance, and mortality: A nine year follow-up of Alameda county residents. *American Journal of Epidemiology, 109,* 186–204.

Berkowitz, L. (1965). The concept of aggressive drive: Some additional considerations. In L. Berkowitz (Ed.), *Advances in experimental social psychology* (Vol. 2, pp. 301–329). New York: Academic Press.

Berkowitz, L. (1972). Social norms, feelings, and other factors affecting helping behavior and altruism. In L. Berkowitz (Ed.), *Advances in experimental social psychology* (Vol. 6). New York: Academic Press.

Berkowitz, L. (1984). Some effects of thoughts on anti- and prosocial influences of media events: A cognitive-neoassociationist analysis. *Psychological Bulletin, 95,* 410–427.

Berkowitz, L. (1989). The frustration–aggression hypothesis: An examination and reformulation. *Psychological Bulletin, 106,* 59–73.

Berkowitz, L. (1993). *Aggression: Its causes, consequences, and control.* New York: McGraw-Hill.

Berkowitz, L., & Daniels, L. R. (1963). Responsibility and dependency. *Journal of Abnormal and Social Psychology, 66,* 429–436.

Berkowitz, L., & Donnerstein, E. (1982). External validity is more than skin deep: Some answers to the criticisms of laboratory experiments. *American Psychologist, 37*, 245–257.

Berkowitz, L., & Harmon-Jones, E. (2004). Toward an understanding of the determinants of anger. Emotion, 4(2), 107–130, retrieved March 17, 2005, from PsycINFO (1840-Current) database.

Berkowitz, L., & LePage, A. (1967). Weapons as aggression-eliciting stimuli. *Journal of Personality and Social Psychology, 7*, 202–207.

Bernard, J. (1973). *The future of marriage.* New York: Bantam.

Bernstein, M., & Crosby, F. (1980). An experimental examination of relative deprivation theory. *Journal of Experimental Social Psychology, 16*, 442–456.

Berry, D. S., & Brownlow, S. (1989). Were the physiognomists right? Personality correlates of facial babyishness. *Personality and Social Psychology Bulletin, 15*, 266–279.

Berry, D. S., & McArthur, L. Z. (1985). Some components and consequences of a babyface. *Journal of Personality and Social Psychology, 48*, 312–323.

Berscheid, E. (1988). Some comments on love's anatomy: Or, whatever happened to old-fashioned lust? In R. Sternberg & M. Barnes (Eds.), *The psychology of love* (pp. 359–374). New Haven, CT: Yale University Press.

Berscheid, E., & Reis, H. T. (1998). Attraction and close relationships. In D. T. Gilbert, S. T. Fiske, & G. Lindzey (Eds.), *Handbook of social psychology* (4th ed., Vol. 2, pp. 193–281). Boston: McGraw-Hill.

Berscheid, E. Snyder, M., & Omoto, A. M. (1989). The Relationship Closeness Inventory: Assessing the closeness of interpersonal relationships. *Journal of Personality and Social Psychology, 57*, 792–807.

Bersoff, D. M. (1999). Why good people sometimes do bad things: Motivated reasoning and unethical behavior. *Personality and Social Psychology Bulletin, 25*, 28–39.

Bettencourt, B. A., Brewer, M. B., Croak, M. R., & Miller, N. (1992). Cooperation and the reduction of intergroup bias: The role of reward structure and social orientation. *Journal of Experimental Social Psychology, 28*, 301–319.

Bettencourt, B. A., Charlton, K., Dorr, N., & Hume, D. L. (2001). Status differences and in-group bias: A meta-analytic examination of the effects of status stability, status legitimacy, and group permeability. *Psychological Bulletin, 127*(4), 520–542.

Bickman, L. (1971). The effect of another bystander's ability to help on bystander intervention in an emergency. *Journal of Experimental Social Psychology, 7*, 367–379.

Bickman, L. (1974). The social power of a uniform. *Journal of Applied Social Psychology, 4*, 47–61.

Bickman, L. (1979). Interpersonal influence and the reporting of a crime. *Personality and Social Psychology Bulletin, 5*, 32–35.

Bickman, L., & Rosenbaum, D. P. (1977). Crime reporting as a function of bystander encouragement, surveillance, and credibility. *Journal of Personality and Social Psychology, 35*, 577–586.

Biek, M., Wood, W., & Chaiken, S. (1996). Working knowledge, cognitive processing, and attitudes: On the determinants of bias. *Personality and Social Psychology Bulletin, 22*, 547–556.

Biernat, M., & Manis, M. (1994). Shifting standards and stereotype-based judgments. *Journal of Personality and Social Psychology, 66*, 5–20.

Biernat, M., & Wortman, C. (1991). Sharing of home responsibilities between professionally employed women and their husbands. *Journal of Personality and Social Psychology, 60*, 844–860.

Billig, M. (1976). *Social psychology and intergroup relations.* New York: Academic Press.

Billig, M., & Tajfel, H. (1973). Social categorization and similarity in intergroup behavior. *European Journal of Social Psychology, 3*, 27–52.

Binning, J. F., Goldstein, M. A., Garcia, M. F., & Scatteregia, J. H. (1988). Effects of preinterview impressions on questioning strategies in same- and opposite-sex employment interviews. *Journal of Applied Psychology, 73*, 30–37.

Birchler, G. R., & Webb, L. J. (1977). Discriminating interaction behavior in happy and unhappy marriages. *Journal of Consulting and Clinical Psychology, 45*, 494–495.

Bird, A. (1977). Team structure and success as related to cohesiveness and leadership. *Journal of Social Psychology, 103*, 217–223.

Birt, C. M., & Dion, K. L. (1987). Relative deprivation theory and responses to deprivation in a gay male and lesbian sample. *British Journal of Social Psychology, 26*, 139–145.

Blair, I. V., & Banaji, M. R. (1996). Automatic and controlled processes in stereotype priming. *Journal of Personality and Social Psychology, 70*, 1142–1163.

Blair, I. V. (2002). The malleability of automatic stereotypes and prejudice. *Personality and Social Psychology Bulletin, 6*, 242–261.

Blair, I. V., Ma, J. E., & Lenton, A. P. (2001). Imagining stereotypes away: The moderation of implicit stereotypes through mental imagery. *Journal of Personality and Social Psychology, 81*, 828–841.

Blake, R. R., & Mouton, J. S. (1979). Intergroup problem solving in organizations: From theory to practice. In W. G. Austin and S. Worchel (Eds.), *The social psychology of intergroup relations* (pp. 19–32). Monterey, CA: Brooks/Cole.

Blake, R. R., & Mouton, J. S. (1980). *The versatile manager: A Grid profile.* Homewood, IL: Dow Jones-Irwin.

Blake, R. R., & Mouton, J. S. (1984). *Solving costly organizational conflicts.* San Francisco, CA: Jossey-Bass.

Blanchard, F. A., & Cook, S. W. (1976). Effects of helping a less competent member of a cooperating interracial group on the development of interpersonal attraction. *Journal of Personality and Social Psychology, 34*, 1245–1255.

Blanton, H., Cooper, J. Skurnik, I., & Aronson, J. (1997). When bad things happen to good feedback: Exacerbating the need for self-justification with self-affirmations. *Personality and Social Psychology Bulletin, 23*, 684–692.

Blanton, H., Crocker, J., & Miller, D. T. (2000). The effects of in-group versus out-group social comparison on self-esteem in the context of a negative stereotype. *Journal of Experimental Social Psychology, 36*(5), 519–530.

Blascovich, J., & Tomaka, J. (1996). The biopsychosocial model of arousal regulation. In M.P. Zanna (Ed.), *Advances in experimental social psychology* (Vol. 28, pp. 1–51). New York: Academic Press.

Blascovich, J., Nash, R. F., & Ginsburg, G. P. (1978). Heartrate and competitive decision making. *Personality and Social Psychology Bulletin, 4*, 115–118.

Blascovich, J., Wyer, N. A., Swart, L. A., & Kibler, J. L. (1997). Racism and racial categorization. *Journal of Personality and Social Psychology, 72*, 1364–1372.

Blass, T. (2000). *Obedience to authority: Current perspectives on the Milgram paradigm.* Mahwah, NJ: Lawrence Erlbaum Associates, Inc.

Bless, H., Bohner, G., Schwarz, N., & Strach, F. (1990). Mood and persuasion: A cognitive responses analysis. *Personality and Social Psychology Bulletin, 16,* 331–345.

Bless, H., Clore, G. L., Schwarz, N., Golisano, V., Rabe, C., & Wolk, M. (1996). Mood and the use of scripts: Does a happy mood really lead to mindlessness? *Journal of Personality and Social Psychology, 71,* 665–679.

Blumstein, P., & Schwartz, P. (1983). *American couples: Money, work, sex.* New York: William Morrow.

Bodenhausen, G. V. (1990). Stereotypes as judgmental heuristics: Evidence of circadian variations in discrimination. *Psychological Science, 1,* 319–322.

Bodenhausen, G. V. (1993). Emotions, arousal and stereotyping judgments: A heuristic model of affect and stereotyping. In D. M. Mackie & D. L. Hamilton (Eds.), *Affect, cognition, and stereotyping: Interactive processes in group perception* (pp. 13–37). San Diego: Academic Press.

Bodenhausen, G. V., & Lichtenstein, M. (1987). Social stereotypes and information-processing strategies: The impact of task complexity. *Journal of Personality and Social Psychology, 52,* 871–880.

Bodenhausen, G. V., Schwarz, N., Bless, H., & Waenke, M. (1995). Effects of atypical exemplars on racial beliefs: Enlightened racism or generalized appraisals? *Journal of Experimental Social Psychology, 31,* 48–63.

Bodenhausen, G. V., Sheppard, L. A., & Kramer, G. P. (1994). Negative affect and social judgement: The differential impact of anger and sadness. *Special Issue: Affect on social judgements and cognition. European Journal of Social Psychology, 24,* 45–62.

Bohlen, C. (1992, October 20). Irate Russians demonize traders from Caucasus. *New York Times,* p. A3.

Bolby, A., & Damon, W. (1992). *Some do care.* New York: Free Press.

Bolger, N., Zuckerman, A., & Kessler, R. C. (2000). Invisible support and adjustment to stress. *Journal of Personality and Social Psychology, 79,* 953–961.

Bond, C. F., & Atoum, A. O. (2000). International deception. *Personality and Social Psychology Bulletin, 26,* 385–395.

Bond, C. F., Jr., & Brockett, D. R. (1987). A social context-personality index theory of memory for acquaintances. *Journal of Personality and Social Psychology, 52,* 1110–1121.

Bond, C. F., & Titus, L. J. (1983). Social facilitation: A meta-analysis of 241 studies. *Psychological Bulletin, 94,* 265–292.

Bond, M. H. (1988). *The cross-cultural challenge to social psychology.* Newbury Park, CA: Sage.

Bond, M. H. (2004). Culture and aggression – from context to coercion. *Personality and Social Psychology Review, 8*(1), 62–78.

Bond, R., & Smith, P. B. (1996). Culture and conformity: A meta-analysis of studies using Asch's (1952b, 1956) line judgment task. *Psychological Bulletin, 119,* 111–137.

Boninger, D., Krosnick, J. A., & Berent, M. K. (1995). Origins of attitude importance: Self-interest, social identification, and value relevance. *Journal of Personality and Social Psychology, 68,* 61–80.

Bonnanno, G. A., Field, N. P., Kovacevic, A., & Kaltman, S. (2002). Self-enhancement as a buffer against extreme adversity: Civil war in Bosnia and traumatic loss in the United States. *Personality and Social Psychology Bulletin, 28,* 184–196.

Booth-Kewley, S., & Friedman, H. S. (1987). Psychological predictors of heart disease: A quantitative review. *Psychological Bulletin, 101,* 343–362.

Borgida, E., & Campbell, B. (1982). Belief relevance and attitude-behavior consistency: The moderating role of personal experience. *Journal of Personality and Social Psychology, 42,* 239–247.

Borgida, E., & Howard-Pitney, B. (1983). Involvement and the robustness of perceptual salience effects. *Journal of Personality and Social Psychology, 45,* 560–570.

Bornstein, G. (2003). Intergroup conflict: Individual, group, and collective interests. *Personality and Social Psychology Review, 7,* 129–145

Bornstein, R. F., Kale, A. R., & Cornell, K. R. (1990). Boredom as a limiting condition on the mere exposure effect. *Journal of Personality and Social Psychology, 58,* 791–800.

Bornstein, R. F., Leone, D. R., & Galley, D. J. (1987). The generalizability of subliminal mere exposure effects: Influence of stimuli perceived without awareness on social behavior. *Journal of Personality and Social Psychology, 53,* 1070–1079.

Boster, F. J., Fediuk, T. A., & Kotowski, R. (2001). The effectiveness of an altruistic appeal in the presence and absence of favors. *Communication Monographs, 68,* 340–346.

Bothwell, R. K., Brigham, J. C., & Malpass, R. S. (1989). Cross-racial identification. *Personality and Social Psychology Bulletin, 15,* 19–25.

Bouas, K. S., & Komorita, S. S. (1996). Group discussion and cooperation in social dilemmas. *Personality and Social Psychology Bulletin, 22,* 1144–1150.

Bourhis, R. Y., Giles, H., Leyens, J. P., & Tajfel, H. (1978). Psychological distinctiveness: Language divergence in Belgium. In H. Giles & R. St. Clair (Eds.), *Language and social psychology* (pp. 158–185). Oxford, UK: Blackwell.

Boush, D. M., Friestad, M., & Rose, G. M. (1994). Adolescent skepticism toward TV advertising and knowledge of advertiser tactics. *Journal of Consumer Research, 21,* 165–175.

Bowers, C. A., Weaver, J. L., & Morgan, B. B., Jr. (1996). Moderating the performance effects of stressors. In J. E. Driskell & E. Salas (Eds.), *Stress and human performance* (pp. 163–192). Mahwah, NJ: Lawrence Erlbaum Associates, Inc.

Bowlby, J. (1969). *Attachment and loss: Vol. 1. Attachment.* New York: Basic Books.

Boyanowsky, E. O., & Griffiths, C. T. (1982). Weapons and eye contact as instigators or inhibitors of aggressive arousal in police–citizen interaction. *Journal of Applied Social Psychology, 12,* 398–407.

Bradbury, T. N., & Fincham, F. D. (1990). Attributions in marriage: Review and critique. *Psychological Bulletin, 107,* 3–33.

Branscombe, N. R. (1998). Thinking about one's gender group's privileges or disadvantages: Consequences for well-being in women and men. *British Journal of Social Psychology, 37,* 167–184.

Branscombe, N. R., & Wann, D. L. (1994). Collective self-esteem consequences of outgroup derogation when a valued social identity is on trial. *European Journal of Social Psychology, 24,* 641–657.

Branscombe, N. R., Wann, D. L., Noel, J. G., & Coleman, J. (1993). In-group or out-group extremity: Importance of the threatened social identity. *Personality and Social Psychology Bulletin, 19,* 381–388.

Brauer, M., Judd, C. M., & Gliner, M. D. (1995). The effects of repeated expressions on attitude polarization during group discussions. *Journal of Personality and Social Psychology, 68,* 1014–1029.

Brauer, M., Judd, C. M., & Jacquelin, V. (2001). The communication of social stereotypes: The effects of group discussion and information distribution on stereotypic appraisals. *Journal of Personality and Social Psychology, 81,* 463–475.

Brawley, L. R., Carron, A. V., & Widmeyer, W. N. (1987). Assessing the cohesion of teams: Validity of the Group Environment Questionnaire. *Journal of Sport Psychology, 9,* 275–294.

Brawley, L. R., Carron, A. V., & Widmeyer, W. N. (1988). Exploring the relationship between cohesion and group resistance to disruption. *Journal of Sport and Exercise Psychology, 10,* 199–213.

Bray, R. M., Johnson, D., & Chilstrom, J. T., Jr. (1982). Social influence by group members with minority opinions: A comparison of Hollander and Moscovici. *Journal of Personality and Social Psychology, 43,* 78–88.

Brean, H. (1958, March 31). What hidden sell is all about. *Life,* 104–114.

Breckler, S. J., & Wiggins E. C. (1989). Affect versus evaluation in the structure of attitudes. *Journal of Experimental Social Psychology, 25,* 253–271.

Brehm, J. W. (1956). Post-decision changes in desirability of alternatives. *Journal of Abnormal and Social Psychology, 52,* 384–389.

Brehm, J. W. (1966). *A theory of psychological reactance.* New York: Academic Press.

Bretschneider, J. G., & McCoy, N. L. (1988). Sexual interest and behavior in healthy 80- to 102-year-olds. *Archives of Sexual Behavior, 17,* 188–195.

Brewer, M. B. (1979). In-group bias in the minimal intergroup situation: A cognitive-motivational analyses. *Psychological Bulletin, 86,* 307–323.

Brewer, M. B. (1988). A dual process model of impression formation. In T. Srull & R. Wyer (Eds.), *Advances in Social Cognition* (Vol. 1, pp. 177–183). Hillsdale, NJ: Lawrence Erlbaum Associates, Inc.

Brewer, M. B. (1991). The social self: On being the same and different at the same time. *Personality and Social Psychology Bulletin, 17,* 475–482.

Brewer, M. B. (1999). The psychology of prejudice: Ingroup love or outgroup hate? *Journal of Social Issues, 55,* 429–444.

Brewer, M. B. (2001). Ingroup identification and intergroup conflict: When does ingroup love become outgroup hate? In R. D. Ashmore & L. Jussim (Eds.), *Social identity, intergroup conflict, and conflict reduction. Rutgers series on self and social identity* (Vol. 3, pp. 17–41).

Brewer, M. B., & Campbell, D. T. (1976). *Ethnocentrism and intergroup attitudes: East African evidence.* New York: Halstead Press.

Brewer, M. B., Dull, V., & Lui, L. (1981). Perceptions of the elderly: Stereotypes as prototypes. *Journal of Personality and Social Psychology, 41,* 656–670.

Brewer, M. B., & Kramer, R. M. (1986). Choice behavior in social dilemmas: Effects of social identity, group size, and decision framing. *Journal of Personality and Social Psychology, 50,* 543–549.

Brewer, M. B., & Silver, M. (1978). Ingroup bias as a function of task characteristics. *European Journal of Social Psychology, 8,* 393–400.

Brewer, M. B., & Weber, J. G. (1994). Self-evaluation effects of interpersonal versus intergroup social comparison. *Journal of Personality and Social Psychology, 66,* 268–275.

Brickman, P., Coates, D., & Janoff-Bulman, R. (1978). Lottery winners and accident victims: Is happiness relative? *Journal of Personality and Social Psychology, 36,* 917–927.

Brickner, M. A., Harkins, S. G., & Ostrom, T. M. (1986). Effects of personal involvement: Thought-provoking implications for social loafing. *Journal of Personality and Social Psychology, 51,* 763–770.

Brief, A. P., Dietz, J., Cohen, R. R., Pugh, S. D., & Vaslow, J. B. (2000). Just doing business: Modern racism and obedience to authority as explanations for employment discrimination. *Organizational Behavior and Human Decision Processes, 81,* 72–97.

Brief, A. P., Dukerich, J. M., & Doran, L. I. (1991). Resolving ethical dilemmas in management: Experimental investigation of values, accountability, and choice. *Journal of Applied Social Psychology, 21,* 380–396.

Brief, A. P., & Weiss, H. M. (2002). Organizational behavior: Affect in the workplace. *Annual Review of Psychology, 53,* 279–307.

Brigham, J. C. (1971). Ethnic stereotypes. *Psychological Bulletin, 76,* 15–33.

Briñol, P., & Petty, R. E. (2003). Overt head movements and persuasion: A self-validation analysis. *Journal of Personality & Social Psychology, 84,* 1123–1139.

Brodbeck, F. C., Kerschreiter, R., Mojzisch, A., Frey, D., & Schulz-Hardt, S. (2002). The dissemination of critical, unshared information in decision-making groups: The effects of pre-discussion dissent. *European Journal of Social Psychology, 32,* 35–56.

Brooks, D. (2004, June 29). Age of political separation. *New York Times.*

Brown, J. D. (1986). Evaluations of self and others: Self-enhancing biases in social judgment. *Social Cognition, 4,* 353–376.

Brown, J. D., & Smart, S. A. (1991). The self and social conduct: Linking self-representations to prosocial behavior. *Journal of Personality and Social Psychology, 60,* 368–375.

Brown, R., Condor, S., Matthews, A., Wade, G., & Williams, J. A. (1986). Explaining intergroup differentiation in an industrial organization. *Journal of Occupational Psychology, 59,* 273–286.

Brown, R., & Smith, A. (1989). Perceptions of and by minority groups: The case of women in academia. *European Journal of Social Psychology, 19,* 61–75.

Brown, R., & Wade, G. (1987). Superordinate goals and intergorup behavior: The effects of role ambiguity and status on intergroup attitudes and task performance. *European Journal of Social Psychology, 17,* 131–142.

Brown, R. P., & Josephs, R. A. (1999). A burden of proof: Stereotype relevance and gender differences in math performance. *Journal of Personality and Social Psychology, 76,* 246–257.

Browning, C. R. (1992). *Ordinary men.* New York: HarperCollins.

Browning, L. D. (1978). A grounded organizational communication theory derived from qualitative data. *Communication Monographs, 45,* 93–109.

Bruner, J. (1957). On perceptual readiness. *Psychological Review, 64,* 123–152.

Bruner, J. (1986). *Actual minds, possible worlds.* New York: Plenum.

Bryan, J. H., & Test, M. A. (1967). Models and helping; Naturalistic studies in aiding behavior. *Journal of Personality and Social Psychology, 10,* 222–226.

Budescu, D. V., Rapoport, A., & Suleiman, R. (1990). Resource dilemmas with environmental uncertainty and asymmetric players. *European Journal of Social Psychology*, 20, 475–487.

Budesheim, T. L., Houston, D. A., & DePaola, S. J. (1996). Persuasiveness of in-group and out-group political messages: The case of negative political campaigning. *Journal of Personality & Social Psychology*, 70, 523–534.

Bui, K.-V. T., Peplau, L. A., & Hill, C. T. (1996). Testing the Rusbult model of relationship commitment and stability in a 15-year study of heterosexual couples. *Personality and Social Psychology Bulletin*, 22, 1244–1257.

Buller, D. J. (2005). *Adapting minds: Evolutionary psychology and the persistent quest for human nature*. Cambridge, MA: MIT Press.

Bulman, R., & Wortman, C. (1977). Attributions of blame and coping in the "real world": Severe accident victims respond to their lot. *Journal of Personality and Social Psychology*, 35, 351–363.

Burger, J. M. (1986). Increasing compliance by improving the deal: The that's-not-all technique. *Journal of Personality and Social Psychology*, 51, 277–283.

Burger, J. M. (1999). The foot-in-the-door compliance procedure: A multiple-process analysis and review. *Personality & Social Psychology Review*, 3, 303–325.

Burger, J. M., & Caldwell, D. F. (2003). The effects of monetary incentives and labeling on the foot-in-the-door effect: Evidence for a self-perception process. *Basic and Applied Social Psychology*, 25, 235–241.

Burger, J. M., Horita, M., Kinoshita, L., Roberts, K., & Vera, C. (1997). Effects of time on the norm of reciprocity. *Basic and Applied Social Psychology*, 19, 91–100.

Burgoon, M., Pfau, M., & Birk, T. S. (1995). An inoculation theory explanation for the effects of corporate issue/advocacy advertising campaigns. *Special issue: Communication and social influence. Communication Research*, 22, 485–505.

Burke, P. J. (1967). The development of task and social-emotional role differentiation. *Sociometry*, 30, 379–392.

Burke, R. J. (1970). Methods of resolving superior–subordinate conflict: The constructive use of subordinate differences and disagreements. *Organizational Behavior and Human Performance*, 5, 393–411.

Burleson, B. R. (1994). Comforting messages: Significance, approaches, and effects. In B. R. Burleson, T. L. Albrecht, & I. G. Sarason (Eds.), *Communication of social support: Messages, interactions, relationships, and community* (pp. 3–28). Thousand Oaks, CA: Sage.

Burleson, B. R. (2003). The experience and effects of emotional support: What the study of cultural and gender differences can tell us about close relationships, emotion and interpersonal communication. *Personal Relationships*, 10, 1–23.

Burns, J. M. (2003). *Transformational leadership*. New York: Atlantic Monthly Press.

Burns, J. M., & Sorenson, G. J. (2000). *Dead center: Clinton–Gore leadership and the perils of moderation*. New York: Charles Scribner's.

Burnstein, E., & Vinokur, A. (1977). Persuasive argumentation and social comparison as determinants of attitude polarization. *Journal of Experimental Social Psychology*, 13, 315–332.

Bushman, B. J. (1998). Effects of warning and information labels on consumption of full-fat, reduced-fat, and no-fat products. *Journal of Applied Psychology*, 83, 97–101.

Bushman, B. J. (2005). Violence and sex in television programs do not sell products in advertisements. *Psychological Science*, 16, 702–708.

Bushman, B. J., & Anderson, C. A. (2001a). Is it time to pull the plug on hostile versus instrumental aggression dichotomy? *Psychological Review*, 108(1), 273–279.

Bushman, B. J., & Anderson, C. A. (2001b). Media violence and the American public: Scientific facts versus media misinformation. *American Psychologist*, 56, 477–489.

Bushman, B. J., & Anderson, C. A. (2002). Violent video games and hostile expectations: A test of the general aggression model. *Personality & Social Psychology Bulletin*, 28(12), 1679–1686.

Bushman, B. J., & Baumeister, R. F. (1998). Threatened egotism, narcissism, self-esteem, and direct and displaced aggression: Does self-love or self-hate lead to violence? *Journal of Personality and Social Psychology*, 75, 219–229.

Bushman, B. J., Baumeister, R. F., & Stack, A. D. (1999). Catharsis, aggression, and persuasive influence: Self-fulfilling or self-defeating prophecies? Journal of Personality & Social Psychology, 76(3), 367–376.

Bushman, B. J., & Cooper, H. M. (1990). Effects of alcohol on human aggression: An integrative research review. *Psychological Bulletin*, 107, 341–354.

Bushman, B. J., & Geen, R. G. (1990). Role of cognitive-emotional mediators and individual differences in the effects of media violence on aggression. *Journal of Personality and Social Psychology*, 58, 156–163.

Buss, A. (1961). *The psychology of aggression*. New York: Wiley.

Buss, D. M. (1994). The strategies of human mating. *American Scientist*, 82, 238–249.

Buss, D. M., & Kenrick, D. T. (1998). Evolutionary social psychology. In D. T. Gilbert, S. T. Fiske, & G. Lindzey (Eds.), *Handbook of social psychology* (3rd ed., Vol. 2, pp. 982–1026). Boston: McGraw-Hill.

Butler, L. D., Koopman, C., & Zimbardo, P. G. (1995). The psychological impact of viewing the film JFK: Emotions, beliefs, and political behavioral intentions. *Political Psychology*, 16, 237–257.

Butterfield, F. (1998, July 26). Southern curse: Why America's murder rate is so high. *The New York Times*, Week in Review section.

Buunk, B. P., Oldersma, F. L., & de Dreu, C. K. (2001). Enhancing satisfaction through downward comparison: The role of relational discontent and individual differences in social comparison orientation. *Journal of Experimental Social Psychology*, 37, 452–467.

Byrne, D. (1971). *The attraction paradigm*. New York: Academic Press.

Cacioppo, J. T., & Petty, R. E. (1979). Attitudes and cognitive responses: An electro-physiological approach. *Journal of Personality and Social Psychology*, 37, 2181–2199.

Cacioppo, J. T., & Petty, R. E. (1982). The need for cognition. *Journal of Personality and Social Psychology*, 42, 116–131.

Cacioppo, J. T., & Petty, R. E. (1984). The need for cognition: Relationship to attitudinal processes. In R. McGlynn, J. Maddux, C. Stoltenberg, & J. Harvey (Eds.), *Social perception in clinical and counseling psychology*. Lubbock, TX: Texas Tech Press.

Cacioppo, J. T., Petty, R. E., Feinstein, J. A., Jarvis, W., & Blair, G. (1996). Dispositional differences in cognitive motivation: The life and times of individuals varying in need for cognition. *Psychological Bulletin, 119,* 197–253.

Cacioppo, J. T., Petty, R. E., Losch, M. E., & Kim, H. S. (1986). Electromyographic activity over facial muscle regions can differentiate the valence and intensity of affective reactions. *Journal of Personality and Social Psychology, 50,* 260–268.

Cacioppo, J. T., Petty, R. E., & Sidera, J. (1982). The effects of a salient self-schema on the evaluation of proattitudinal editorials: Top-down versus bottom-up message processing. *Journal of Experimental Social Psychology, 18,* 324–338.

Cahill, J. B. (1999, October 4). Here's the pitch: How Kirby persuades uncertain consumers to buy $1,500 vacuum—the door-to-door hard sell brings profits, criticism, to Berkshire Hathaway—'pushiest people I ever saw'. *The Wall Street Journal,* p. A.1.

Campbell, A., Converse, P. E., & Rodgers, W. L. (1976). *The quality of American life.* New York: Russell Sage Foundation.

Campbell, D. T. (1963). Social attitudes and other aquired behavioral dispositions. In S. Koch (Ed.), *Psychology: A study of a science* (Vol. 6, pp. 94–172). New York: McGraw-Hill.

Campbell, D. T. (1965). Ethnocentric and other altruistic motives. In D. Levine (Ed.), *Nebraska Symposium on motivation* (Vol. 13, pp. 283–311). Lincoln: University of Nebraska Press.

Campbell, D. T. (1967). Stereotypes and the perception of group differences. *American Psychologist, 22,* 817–829.

Campbell, J. D. (1990). Self-esteem and clarity of the self-concept. *Journal of Personality and Social Psychology, 59,* 538–549.

Campbell, J. D., Chew, B., & Scratchley, L. S. (1991). Cognitive and emotional reactions to daily events: The effects of self-esteem and self-complexity. *Journal of Personality, 59,* 473–505.

Campbell, J. D., & Fairey, P. (1985). Effects of self-esteem, hypothetical explanations, and verbalization of expectancies on future performance. *Journal of Personality and Social Psychology, 48,* 1097–1111.

Campbell, J. D., & Lavallee, L. F. (1993). Who am I? The role of self-concept confusion in understanding the behavior of people with low self-esteem. In R. F. Baumeister (Ed.), *Self-esteem: The puzzle of low self-esteem* (pp. 3–20). New York: Plenum.

Cantor, N., & Kihlstrom, J. F. (1987). *Personality and social intelligence.* Englewood Cliffs, NJ: Prentice-Hall.

Cantor, N., & Malley, J. (1991). Life tasks, personal needs, and close relationships. In G. Fletcher & F. Fincham (Eds.), *Cognition in close relationships* (pp. 101–126). Hillsdale, NJ: Lawrence Erlbaum Associates, Inc.

Caporael, L. (1997). The evolution of truly social cognition: The core configurations model. *Personality and Social Psychology Review, 1,* 276–298.

Caporael, L. R., & Brewer, M. B. (1991). Reviving evolutionary psychology: Biology meets society. *Journal of Social Issues, 47*(3), 187–195.

Caporael, L. R., Dawes, R. M., Orbell, J. M., & Van de Kragt, A. J. C. (1989). Selfishness examined: Cooperation in the absence of egoistic incentives. *Behavioral and Brain Sciences, 12,* 683–699.

Carli, L. (1990). Gender, language, and influence. *Journal of Personality and Social Psychology, 59,* 941–951.

Carli, L. L., & Leonard, J. B. (1989). The effect of hindsight on victim derogation. *Journal of Social and Clinical Psychology, 8,* 331–343.

Carlson, M., Marcus-Newhall, A., & Miller, N. (1989). Evidence for a general construct of aggression. *Personality and Social Psychology Bulletin, 15,* 377–389.

Carlson, M., & Miller, N. (1987). Explanation of the relation between negative mood and helping. *Psychological Bulletin, 102,* 91–108.

Carlston, D. E. (1994). Associated systems theory: A systematic approach to cognitive representations of persons. In T. K. Srull & R. S. Wyer (Eds.), *Advances in social cognition* (vol. 7, pp. 1–78). Hillsdale, NJ: Lawrence Erlbaum Associates, Inc.

Carlston, D. E., & Skowronski, J. J. (1986). Trait memory and behavior memory: The effects of alternative pathways on impression judgment response times. *Journal of Personality and Social Psychology, 50,* 5–13.

Carlston, D. E., & Skowronski, J. J. (1994). Savings in the relearning of trait information as evidence for spontaneous inference generation. *Journal of Personality and Social Psychology, 66,* 840–856.

Carr, D. (2002, November 18). On covers of many magazines, a full racial palette is still rare. *New York Times,* p. C1.

Carroll, J. M., & Russell, J. A. (1996). Do facial expressions signal specific emotions? Judging emotion from the face in context. *Journal of Personality and Social Psychology, 70,* 205–218.

Carter, S. (1991). *Reflections of an affirmative action baby.* New York: Basic Books.

Cartwright, D. (1979). Contemporary social psychology in historical perspective. *Social Psychology Quarterly, 42,* 82–93.

Cartwright, D., & Zander, A. (1960). Group cohesiveness: Introduction. In D. Cartwright & A. Zander (Eds.), *Group dynamics: Research and theory* (2nd ed., pp. 69–94). Evanston, IL: Row, Peterson.

Carver, C. S., Ganellen, R. J., Froming, W. J., & Chambers, W. (1983). Modeling: An analysis in terms of category accessibility. *Journal of Experimental Social Psychology, 19,* 403–421.

Carver, C. S., & Scheier, M. F. (1981). *Attention and self-regulation: A control theory approach to human behavior.* New York: Springer-Verlag.

Carver, C. S., & Scheier, M. F. (1990). Origins and functions of positive and negative affect: A control-process view. *Psychological Review, 97,* 19–35.

Cary, L. (1992, June 29). As plain as black and white. *Newsweek,* p. 53.

Casse, P. (1982). *Training for the multicultural manager: A proactical and cross-cultural approach to the management of people.* Washington, DC: Society for Intercultural Education, Training, and Research.

Cate, R. M., & Lloyd, S. A. (1988). Courtship. In S. Duck (Ed.), *Handbook of personal relationships: Theory, relationships, and interventions.* Chichester, UK: Wiley.

Center for Science in the Public Interest (1988). Kids are as aware of booze as presidents, survey finds. September 4, CSPI press release, Washington, DC.

Cesario, J., Grant, H., & Higgins, E. T. (2004). Regulatory fit and persuasion: Transfer from "feeling right." *Journal of Personality and Social Psychology, 86,* 388–404.

Chacko, T. I. (1982). Women and equal employment opportunity: Some unintended effects. *Journal of Applied Psychology, 67,* 119–123.

Chaiken, S. (1979). Communicator physical attractiveness and persuasion. *Journal of Personality and Social Psychology, 37,* 1387–1397.

Chaiken, S. (1980). Heuristic versus systematic information processing and the use of source versus message cues in persuasion. *Journal of Personality and Social Psychology, 39,* 752–756.

Chaiken, S. (1987). The heuristic model of persuasion. In M. P. Zanna, J. M. Olson, & C. P. Herman (Eds.), *Social influence: The Ontario Symposium* (Vol. 5, pp. 3–40). Hillsdale, NJ: Lawrence Erlbaum Associates, Inc.

Chaiken, S., & Baldwin, M. W. (1981). Affective-cognitive consistency and the effect of salient behavioral information on the self-perception of attitudes. *Journal of Personality and Social Psychology, 41,* 1–12.

Chaiken S., & Eagly, A. H. (1976). Communication modality as a determinant of message persuasiveness and message comprehensibility. *Journal of Personality and Social Psychology, 34,* 605–614.

Chaiken, S., Giner-Sorolla, R., & Chen, S. (1996). Beyond accuracy: Defense and impression motives in heuristic and systematic information processing. In P. M. Gollwitzer & J. A. Bargh (Eds.), *The psychology of action: Linking cognition and motivation to behavior* (pp. 553–578). New York: Guilford Press.

Chaiken, S., Liberman, A., & Eagly, A. H. (1989). Heuristic and systematic information processing: Within and beyond the persuasion context. In J. S. Uleman & J. A. Bargh (Eds.), *Unintended thought: Limits of awareness, intention, and control* (pp. 212–252). New York: Guilford.

Chaiken, S., & Maheswaran, D. (1994). Heuristic processing can bias systematic processing: Effects of source credibility, argument ambiguity, and task importance on attitude judgement. *Journal of Personality and Social Psychology, 66,* 460–473.

Chaiken, S., Pomerantz, E. M., & Giner-Sorolla, R. (1995). Structural consistency and attitude strength. In R. E. Petty and J. A. Krosnick (Eds.), *Attitude strength: Antecedents and consequences* (pp. 387–412). Mahwah, NJ: Lawrence Erlbaum Associates, Inc.

Charters, W. W., & Newcomb, T. M. (1958). Some attitudinal effects of experimentally increased salience of a membership group. In E. E. Maccoby, T. M. Newcomb, & E. L. Hartley (Eds.), *Readings in social psychology* (pp. 276–281). New York: Holt.

Chen, F. F., & Kenrick, D. T. (2002). Repulsion or attraction? Group membership and assumed attitude similarity. *Journal of Personality and Social Psychology, 83*(1), 111–125.

Chen, G., & Klimoski, R. J. (2003). The impact of expectations on newcomer performance in teams as mediated by work characteristics, social exchanges, and empowerment. *Academy of Management Journal, 46,* 591–607.

Chen, S., Shechter, D., & Chaiken, S. (1996). Getting at the truth or getting along: Accuracy- versus impression- motivated heuristic and systematic processing. *Journal of Personality and Social Psychology, 71,* 262–275.

Cherlin, A. J., Furstenberg, F. F., Jr., Chase-Lansdale, L., Kiernan, K. E., Robins, P. K., Morrison, D. R. and others (1991). Longitudinal studies of effects of divorce on children in Great Britain and the United States. *Science, 252,* 1386–1389.

Choi, I., & Choi, Y. (2002). Culture and self-concept flexibility. *Personality and Social Psychology Bulletin, 28,* 1508–1517.

Choi, I., Dalal, R., Kim-Prieto, C., & Park, H. (2003). Culture and judgment of causal relevance. *Journal of Personality and Social Psychology, 84,* 46–59.

Christensen, P. N., Rothgerber, H., Wood, W., & Matz, D. C. (2004). Social norms and identity relevance: A motivational approach to normative behavior. *Personality and Social Psychology Bulletin, 30,* 1395–1309.

Chu, D., & McIntyre, B. T. (1995). Sex role stereotypes on children's TV in Asia: A content analysis of gender role portrayals in children's cartoons in Hong Kong. *Communication Research Reports, 12,* 206–219.

Chun, W. Y., Spiegel, S., & Kruglanski, A. W. (2002). Assimilative behavior identification can also be resource dependent: The unimodel perspective on personal-attribution phases. *Journal of Personality and Social Psychology, 83,* 542–555.

Cialdini, R. B. (1984). Principles of automatic influence. In J. Jacoby & G.S. Craig (Eds.), *Personal selling* (pp. 1–27). Lexington, MA: Lexington Books.

Cialdini, R. B. (1993). *Influence: Science and practice* (3rd ed.). New York: HarperCollins.

Cialdini, R. B., & Ascani, K. (1976). Test of a concession procedure for inducing verbal, behavioral, and further compliance with a request to donate blood. *Journal of Applied Psychology, 61,* 295–300.

Cialdini, R. B., Borden, R. J., Thorne, A., Walker, M. R., Freeman, S., & Sloan, L. R. (1976). Basking in reflected glory: Three (football) field studies. *Journal of Personality and Social Psychology, 34,* 366–375.

Cialdini, R. B., Cacioppo, J. T., Bassett, R., & Miller, J. A., (1978). Lowball procedure for producing compliance: Commitment then cost. *Journal of Personality and Social Psychology, 36,* 463–476.

Cialdini, R. B., Darby, B. L., & Vincent, J. E. (1973). Transgression and altruism: A case for hedonism. *Journal of Experimental Social Psychology, 9,* 502–516.

Cialdini, R. B., & Kenrick, D. T. (1976). Altruism as hedonism: A social development perspective on the relationship of negative mood state and helping. *Journal of Personality and Social Psychology, 34,* 907–914.

Cialdini, R. B., Reno, R. R., & Kallgren, C. A. (1990). A focus theory of normative conduct: Recycling the concept of norms to reduce littering in public places. *Journal of Personality and Social Psychology, 58,* 1015–1026.

Cialdini, R. B., & Schroeder, D. A. (1976). Increasing compliance by legitimizing paltry contributions: When even a penny helps. *Journal of Personality and Social Psychology, 34,* 599–604.

Cialdini, R. B., Vincent, J. E., Lewis, S. K., Catalan, J., Wheeler, D., & Darby, B. L. (1975). Reciprocal concessions procedure for inducing compliance: The door in the face technique. *Journal of Personality and Social Psychology, 31,* 206–215.

Clark, K. B. (1965). *Dark ghetto: Dilemmas of social power.* New York: Harper & Row.

Clark, L. F., & Collins, J. E. (1993). Remembering old flames: How the past affects assessments of the present. *Personality and Social Psychology Bulletin, 19,* 399–408.

Clark, M. S., & Mills, J. (1979). Interpersonal attraction in exchange and communal relationships. *Journal of Personality and Social Psychology, 37,* 12–24.

Clark, M. S., & Taraban, C. (1991). Reactions to and willingness to express emotion in communal and exchange relationships. *Journal of Experimental Social Psychology, 27,* 324–336.

Clark, N. K., Stephenson, G. M., & Kniveton, B. H. (1990). Social remembering: Quantitative aspects of individual and collaborative remembering by police officers and students. *British Journal of Psychology, 81*, 73–94.

Clark, R. D. (2001). Effects of majority defection and multiple minority sources on minority influence. *Group Dynamics, 5*, 57–62.

Clark, R. D., & Word, L. E. (1972). Why don't bystanders help? Because of ambiguity. *Journal of Personality and Social Psychology, 24*, 392–400.

Clary, E. G., & Orenstein, L. (1991). The amount and effectiveness of help: The relationship of motives and abilities to helping behavior. *Personality and Social Psychology Bulletin, 17*, 58–64.

Clary, E. G., Snyder, M., Ridge, R. D., Copeland, J., Stukas, A. A., Haugen, J. and others (1998). Understanding and assessing the motivations of volunteers: A functional approach. *Journal of Personality and Social Psychology, 74*, 1516–1530.

Claypool, H. M., Mackie, D. M., Garcia-Marques, T., McIntosh, A., & Udal, A. (2004). The effects of personal relevance and repetition on persuasive processing. *Social Cognition, 22*, 310–335.

Clement, R. W., & Krueger, J. (1998). Liking persons versus liking groups: A dual-process hypothesis. *European Journal of Social Psychology, 28*, 457–470.

Clifford, M. M. (1975). Physical attractiveness and academic performance. *Child Study Journal, 5*, 201–209.

Cline, V. B., Croft, R. G., & Courrier, S. (1973). Desensitization of children to television violence. *Journal of Personality and Social Psychology, 27*, 360–365.

Coch, L., & French, J. R. P., Jr. (1948). Overcoming resistance to change. *Human Relations, 1*, 512–532.

Codol, J. P. (1975). On the so-called "superior conformity of the self" behavior: Twenty experimental investigations. *European Journal of Social Psychology, 5*, 457–501.

Cohen, A. (1957). Need for cognition and order of communication as determinants of opinion change. In C. Hovland (Ed.), *The order of presentation in persuasion*. New Haven, CT: Yale University Press.

Cohen, D., & Gunz, A. (2002). As seen by the other . . . : Perspectives on the self in the memories and emotional perceptions of Easterners and Westerners. *Psychological Science, 13*, 55–59.

Cohen, D., & Nisbett, R. E. (1994). Self-protection and the culture of honor: Explaining southern violence. *Personality and Social Psychology Bulletin, 20*, 551–567.

Cohen, D., & Nisbett, R. E. (1997). Field experiments examining the culture of honor: The role of institutions in perpetuating norms about violence. *Personality and Social Psychology Bulletin, 23*, 1188–1199.

Cohen, D., Nisbett, R. E., Bowdle, B. F., & Schwarz, N. (1996). Insult, aggression, and the southern culture of honor: An "experimental ethnography." *Journal of Personality and Social Psychology, 70*, 945–960.

Cohen, F. (1984). Coping. In J. D. Matarazzo and others (Eds.), *Behavioral Health* (pp. 261–274). New York: Wiley.

Cohen, G. L. (2003). Party over policy: The dominating impact of group influence on political beliefs. *Journal of Personality and Social Psychology, 85*, 808–822.

Cohen, J. (2002, August 15). Sharing space? Share email first. *New York Times*, pp. E1–E2.

Cohen, M., & Davis, N. (1981). *Medication errors: Causes and prevention*. Philadelphia: G. F. Strickey Co.

Cohen, S. (2004). Social relationships and health. *American Psychologist, 59*, 676–684.

Cohen, S., Doyle, W. J., Skoner, D. P., & Fireman, P. (1995). State and trait negative affect as predictors of objective and subjective symptoms of respiratory viral infections. *Journal of Personality and Social Psychology, 68*, 159–169.

Cohen, S. P., & Arnone, H. C. (1988). Conflict resolution as the alternative to terrorism. *Journal of Social Issues, 44*(2), 175–190.

Colasanto, D. (1989, November). Americans show commitment to helping those in need. *Gallup Report*, No. 290, 17–24.

Colby, A., & Damon, W. (1995). The development of extraordinary moral commitment. In M. Killen, & D. Hart (Eds.), *Morality in everyday life: Developmental perspectives* (pp. 342–370). New York: Cambridge University Press.

College Board (1976–77). *Student descriptive questionnaire*. Princeton, NJ: Educational Testing Service.

Collins, N. L., & Miller, L. C. (1994). Self-disclosure and liking: A meta-analytic review. *Psychological Bulletin, 116*, 457–475.

Collins, N. L., & Read, S. J. (1990). Adult attachment, working models, and relationship quality in dating couples. *Journal of Personality and Social Psychology, 58*, 644–663.

Colvin, C. R., Block, J., & Funder, D. C. (1995). Overly positive self-evaluations and personality: Negative implications for mental health. *Journal of Personality and Social Psychology, 68*, 1152–1162.

Condon, J. W., & Crano, W. D. (1988). Inferred evaluation and the relation between attitude similarity and interpersonal attraction. *Journal of Personality and Social Psychology, 54*, 789–797.

Condor, S., & Brown, R. (1988). Psychological processes in intergroup conflict. In W. Stroebe, A.W. Kruglanski, D. Bar-Tal, & M. Hewstone (Eds.), *The social psychology of intergroup conflict* (pp. 3–26). New York: Springer-Verlag.

Conway, M. A., & Pleydell-Pearce, C. W. (2000). The construction of autobiographical memories in the self-memory system. *Psychological Review, 107*, 261–288.

Cook, S. W. (1985). Experimenting on social issues: The case of school desegregation. *American Psychologist, 40*, 452–460.

Cook, T. D., & Campbell, D. T. (1979). *Quasi-experimentation*. Chicago: Rand McNally.

Cooley, D. H. (1902). *Human nature and the social order*. New York: Scribners.

Cooper, H. (1990). Meta-analysis and the integrative research review. In C. Hendrick & M. S. Clark (Eds.), *Review of personality and social psychology* (Vol. 11, pp. 142–163). Newbury Park, CA: Sage Publications.

Cooper, H., & Good, T. (1983). *Pygmalion grows up: Studies in the expectation communication process*. New York: Longman.

Cooper, J., & Fazio, R. H. (1984). A new look at dissonance theory. In L. Berkowitz (Ed.), *Advances in experimental social psychology* (Vol. 17). New York: Academic Press.

Cooper, J., Zanna, M. P., Taves, P. A. (1978). Arousal as a necessary condition for attitude change following induced compliance. *Journal of Personality and Social Psychology, 36*, 1101–1106.

Corey, S. M. (1937). Professed attitudes and actual behavior. *Journal of Educational Psychology, 28*, 271–280.

Correll, J., Park, B., Judd, C. M., & Wittenbrink, B. (2002). The police officer's dilemma: Using ethnicity to disambiguate potentially threatening individuals. *Journal of Personality and Social Psychology, 83*, 1314–1329.

Cosmides, L. (1989). The logic of social exchange: Has natural selection shaped how humans reason? Studies with the Wason selection task. *Cognition, 31*, 187–276.

Cottrell, C. A., & Neuberg, S. L. (2005). Different emotional reactions to different groups: A sociofunctional threat-based approach to "prejudice." *Journal of Personality and Social Psychology*, *88*, 770–789.

Coulter, R. H., & Pinto, M. B. (1995). Guilt appeals in advertising: What are their effects? *Journal of Applied Psychology*, *80*, 697–705.

Cousins, S. (1989). Culture and selfhood in Japan and the U.S. *Journal of Personality and Social Psychology*, *56*, 124–131.

Cramer, R. E., McMaster, M. R., & Bartell, P. A. (1988). Subject competence and minimization of the bystander effect. *Journal of Applied Social Psychology*, *18*, 1133–1148.

Crandall, C. S., & Cohen, C. R. (1994). The personality of the stigmatizer: Cultural world view, conventionalism, and self-esteem. *Journal of Research in Personality*, *28*, 461–480.

Crandall, C. S., & Eshleman, A. (2003). A justification-suppression of the expression and experience of prejudice. *Psychological Bulletin*, *129*, 414–446.

Crandall, C. S., & Stangor, C. (2005). Conformity and prejudice. In J. F. Dovidio, P. Glic, & L.A. Rudman (Eds.), *On the nature of prejudice: Fifty years after Allport* (pp. 295–309). Malden, MA: Blackwell.

Crandall, C. S., Tsang, J.-A., Harvey, R. D., & Britt, T. W. (2000). Group identity-based self-protective strategies: The stigma of race, gender, and garlic. *European Journal of Social Psychology*, *30*(3), 355–381.

Crano, W. D., & Alvaro, E. M. (1998). The context/comparison model of social influence: Mechanisms, structure, and linkages that underlie indirect attitude change. In W. Stroebe & M. Hewstone (Eds.), *European Review of Social Psychology* (Vol. 8, pp. 175–202). Chichester, UK: John Wiley and Sons.

Crano, W. D., & Chen, X. (1998). The leniency contract and persistence of majority and minority influence. *Journal of Personality & Social Psychology*, *74*, 1437–1450.

Crano, W. D., Gorenflo, D. W., & Shackelford, S. L. (1988). Overjustification, assumed consensus, and attitude change: Further investigation of the incentive-aroused ambivalence hypothesis. *Journal of Personality and Social Psychology*, *55*, 12–22.

Crawford, D. W., & Huston, T. L. (1993). The impact of the transition to parenthood on marital leisure. *Personality and Social Psychology Bulletin*, *19*, 39–46.

Crawford, M. T., McConnell, A. R., Lewis, A. C., & Sherman, S. J. (2002). Reactance, compliance, and anticipated regret. *Journal of Experimental Social Psychology*, *38*, 56–63.

Crick, N. R., & Dodge, K. A. (1994). A review and reformulation of social information-processing mechanisms in children's social adjustment. *Psychological Bulletin*, *115*, 74–101.

Crime in the United States. (2003) *Uniform crime reporting program*. Federal Bureau of Investigation.

Crocker, J., Hannah, D. B., & Weber, R. (1983). Person memory and causal attributions. *Journal of Personality and Social Psychology*, *44*, 55–66.

Crocker, J., & Major, B. (1989). Social stigma and self-esteem: The self-protective properties of stigma. *Psychological Review*, *96*, 608–630.

Crocker, J., Major, B., & Steele, C. M. (1998). Social stigma. In D. T. Gilbert, S. T. Fiske, & G. Lindzey (Eds.), *Handbook of social psychology* (4th ed., Vol. 2, pp. 504–553). Boston: McGraw-Hill.

Crocker, J., Voelkl, K., Testa, M., & Major, B. (1991). Social stigma: The affective consequences of attributional ambiguity. *Journal of Personality and Social Psychology*, *60*, 218–228.

Croizet, J.-C., Despres, G. R., Gauzins, M.-E., Huguet, P., Leyens, J.-P., & Meot, A. (2004). Stereotype threat undermines intellectual performance by triggering a disruptive mental load. *Personality & Social Psychology Bulletin*, *30*(6), 721–731.

Crosby, F. (1976). A model of egoistic relative deprivation. *Psychological Review*, *83*, 85–113.

Crosby, F. J., Pufall, A., Snyder, R. C., O'Connell, M., & Whalen, P. (1989). The denial of personal disadvantage among you, me, and all the other ostriches. In M. Crawford & M. Gentry (Eds.), *Gender and thought: Psychological perspectives* (pp. 79–99). New York: Springer-Verlag.

Cross, S. E., Kanagawa, C., Markus, H. R., & Kitayama, S. (1995). *Cultural variation in self-concept*. Unpublished manuscript, Iowa State University.

Croyle, R., & Cooper, J. (1983). Dissonance arousal: Physiological evidence. *Journal of Personality and Social Psychology*, *45*, 782–791.

Crutchfield, R. S. (1955). Conformity and character. *American Psychologist*, *10*, 191–198.

Csikszentmihalyi, M., & Figurski, T. J. (1982). Self-awareness and aversive experience in everyday life. *Journal of Personality*, *50*, 15–28.

Cullen, D. (2004, April 20). The depressive and the psychopath: At last we know why the Columbine killers did it. *Slate*. Retrieved July 13 2006 from http://www.slate.com/id/2099203/.

Curhan, J. R., Neale, M. A., & Ross, L. (2004). Dynamic valuation: Preference changes in the context of face-to-face negotiation. *Journal of Experimental Social Psychology*, *40*(2), 142–151.

Cutrona, C. E. (1982). Transition to college: Loneliness and the process of social adjustment. In L. A. Peplau & D. Perlman (Eds.), *Loneliness*. New York: Wiley Interscience.

Dalcourt, P. (1996). Les stereotypes sexuels dans la publicite quebecoise televisee: Le maintien d'une tradition. *Revue Quebecoise de Psychologie*, *17*, 29–42.

Danner, D. D., Snowdon, D. A., & Friesen, W. V. (2001). Positive emotions in early life and longevity: Findings from the nun study. *Journal of Personality and Social Psychology*, *80*, 804–813.

Darke, P. R., Chaiken, S., Bohner, G. Einwiller, S., Erb, H. P., & Hazlewood, J. D. (1998). Accuracy motivation, consensus information, and the law of large numbers: Effects on attitude judgment in the absence of argumentation. *Personality and Social Psychology Bulletin*, *24*, 1205–1215.

Darke, S. (1988). Effects of anxiety on inferential reasoning task performance. *Journal of Personality and Social Psychology*, *55*, 499–505.

Darley, J. M., & Batson, C. D. (1973). From Jerusalem to Jericho: A study of situational and dispositional variables in helping behavior. *Journal of Personality and Social Psychology*, *27*, 100–108.

Darley, J. M., & Fazio, R. H. (1980). Expectancy confirmation processes arising in the social interaction sequence. *American Psychologist*, *35*, 867–881.

Darley, J. M., & Gross, P. H. (1983). A hypothesis-confirming bias in labelling effects. *Journal of Personality and Social Psychology*, *44*, 20–33.

Darley, J. M., & Latané, B. (1968). Bystander intervention in emergencies: Diffusion of responsibility. *Journal of Personality and Social Psychology*, *8*, 377–383.

Darwin, C. (1871/1909). *The descent of man.* New York: Appleton.

Das, E. H. H. J., de Wit, J. B. F., & Stroebe, W. (2003). Fear appeals motivate acceptance of action recommendations: Evidence for a positive bias in the processing of persuasive messages. *Personality & Social Psychology Bulletin, 29,* 650–664.

Dasgupta, N., Banaji, M. B., & Abelson, R. P. (1997, March). *Beliefs and attitudes toward cohesive groups.* Paper presented at Midwestern Psychological Association, Chicago.

Dasgupta, N., & Greenwald, A. (2001). On the malleability of automatic attitudes: Combating automatic prejudice with images of admired and disliked individuals. *Journal of Personality and Social Psychology, 81,* 800–814.

David, B., & Turner, J. C. (1996). Studies in self-categorization and minority conversion: Is being a member of the out-group an advantage? *British Journal of Social Psychology, 35,* 179–199.

Davidson, A. R., & Jaccard, J. J. (1979). Variables that moderate the attitude–behavior relation: results of a longitudinal survey. *Journal of Personality and Social Psychology, 37,* 1364–76.

Davidson, A. R., Yantis, S., Norwood, M., & Monano, D. E. (1985). Amount of information about the attitude object and attitude–behavior consistency. *Journal of Personality and Social Psychology, 49,* 1184–1198.

Davis, K., & Newstrom, J. W. (1985). *Human behavior at work: Organizational behavior* (7th ed.). New York: McGraw-Hill.

Davis, K. E., & Jones, E. E. (1960). Changes in interpersonal perception as a means of reducing cognitive dissonance. *Journal of Abnormal and Social Psychology, 61,* 402–410.

Davis, M. H. (1983). Empathic concern and muscular dystrophy telethon: Empathy as a multidimensional construct. *Personality and Social Psychology Bulletin, 9,* 223–229.

Dawes, R. M. (1980). Social dilemmas. *Annual Review of Psychology, 31,* 169–193.

Dawes, R. M., & Smith, T. L. (1985). Attitude and opinion measurement. In G. Lindzey & E. Aronson (Eds.), *The handbook of social psychology* (3rd ed., Vol. 1, pp. 509–566). New York: Random House.

Dawes, R. M., Van de Kragt, A. J., & Orbell, J. M. (1988). Not me or thee but we: The importance of group identity in eliciting cooperation in dilemma situations: Experimental manipulations. *Acta Psychologica, 68,* 83–97.

De Cremer, D. (2002). Charismatic leadership and cooperation in social dilemmas: A matter of transforming motives? *Journal of Applied Social Psychology, 32,* 997–1016.

De Cremer, D., & van Knippenberg, D. (2004). Leader self-sacrifice and leadership effectiveness: The Moderating role of leader self-confidence. *Organizational Behavior and Human Decision Processes, 95,* 140–155.

De Cremer, D., & Van Vugt, M. (2002). Intergroup and intragroup aspects of leadership in social dilemmas: A relational model of cooperation. *Journal of Experimental Social Psychology, 38,* 126–136.

De Dreu, C. K. W. (2005). A PACT against conflict escalation in negotiation and dispute resolution. *Current Directions in Psychological Science, 14*(3), 149–152.

De Dreu, C. K. W., & De Vries, N. K. (1997). Minority dissent in organizations. In C. K. W. De Dreu & E. Van De Vliert (Eds.), *Using conflict in organization* (pp. 72–86). Thousand Oaks, CA: Sage Publications.

De Dreu, C. K. W., & Weingart, L. R. (2003). Task versus relationship conflict, team performance and team members' satisfaction: A meta-analysis. *Journal of Applied Psychology, 88,* 741–749.

de Hoog, N., Stroebe, W., & de Wit, J. B. F. (2005). The impact of fear appeals on processing and acceptance of action recommendations. *Personality and Social Psychology Bulletin, 31,* 24–33.

de Hoogh, A. H. B., den Hartog, D. N., Koopman, P. L., Thierry, H., van den Berg, P. T., & van der Weide, J. G. (2004). Charismatic leadership, environmental dynamism, and performance. *European Journal of Work and Organizational Psychology, 13,* 447–471.

de Hoogh, A. H. B., den Hartog, D. N., Koopman, P. L., Thierry, H., van den Berg, P. T., van der De Houwer, J., Hendrickx, H., & Baeyens, F. (1997). Evaluative learning with "subliminally" presented stimuli. *Consciousness & Cognition, 6,* 87–107.

de Jong, P. J., van den Hout, M. A., Rietbroek, H., & Huijding, J. (2003). Dissociations between implicit and explicit attitudes toward phobic stimuli. *Cognition & Emotion, 17,* 521–545.

De Pelsmacker, P., Driesen, L., & Rayp, G. (2003). Are fair trade labels good business? Ethics and coffee buying intentions. Ghent, Belgium: Ghent University, Faculty of Economics and Business Administration.

De Rivera, J. (1977). *A structural theory of the emotions.* New York: International Universities Press.

Deaux, K. K., & Hanna, R. (1984). Courtship in the personals column: The influence of gender and sexual orientation. *Sex Roles, 11,* 363–375.

Deaux, K. K., & Emswiller, T. (1974). Explanations of successful performance on sex-linked tasks: What is skill for the male is luck for the female. *Journal of Personality and Social Psychology, 29,* 80–85.

Deaux, K. K., & Lewis, L. L. (1983). Components of gender stereotypes. *Psychological Documents, 13,* 25–34.

Deaux, K. K., & Lewis, L. L. (1984). Structure of gender stereotypes: Interrelationships among components and gender label. *Journal of Personality and Social Psychology, 46,* 991–1004.

Deaux, K. K., & Stark, D. E. (1996, May). *Identity and motive: An integrated theory of volunteerism.* Presented at the Convention of the Society for the Psychological Study of Social Issues, Ann Arbor, MI.

DeBono, K. G., & Harnish, R. (1988). Source expertise, source attractiveness, and processing of persuasive information: A functional approach. *Journal of Personality and Social Psychology, 55,* 541–546.

DeBono, K. G., & Snyder, M. (1995). Acting on one's attitudes: The role of a history of choosing situations. *Personality and Social Psychology Bulletin, 21,* 629–636.

Deci, E. L. (1971). Effects of externally mediated rewards on intrinsic motivation. *Journal of Personality and Social Psychology, 18,* 105–115.

Deci, E. L. (1975). *Intrinsic motivation.* New York: Plenum Press.

DeJong, W. (1979). An examination of self-perception mediation on the foot-in-the-door effect. *Journal of Personality and Social Psychology, 37,* 2221–2239.

DeLamater, J., & MacCorquodale, P. (1979). *Premarital sexuality: Attitudes, relationships, behavior.* Madison, WI: University of Wisconsin Press.

Denmark, F., Russo, N. F., Frieze, I. H., & Sechzer, J. A. (1988). Guidelines for avoiding sexism in psychological research. *American Psychologist, 43,* 582–585.

Denmark, F. L., Shaw, J. S., & Ciali, S. O. (1985). The relationship among sex roles, living arrangements, and the division of household responsibilities. *Sex Roles, 12,* 617–625.

DePaulo, B. M., Lassiter, G. D., & Stone, J. I. (1982). Attentional determinants of success at detecting deception and truth. *Personality and Social Psychology Bulletin, 8,* 273–279.

Derlega, V. J., Wilson, M., & Chaikin, A. L. (1976). Friendship and disclosure reciprocity. *Journal of Personality and Social Psychology, 34,* 578–587.

Derlega, V. J., Winstead, B. A., Wong, P. T. P., & Hunter, S. (1985). Gender effects in an initial encounter: A case where men exceed women in disclosure. *Journal of Social and Personal Relationships, 2,* 25–44.

Deschamps, J. C., & Brown, R. (1983). Superordinate goals and intergroup conflict. *British Journal of Social Psychology, 22,* 189–195.

Desforges, D. M., Lord, C. G., Ramsey, S. L., Mason, J. A., Van Leeuwen, M. D., West, S. C. and others (1991). Effects of structured cooperative contact on changing negative attitudes toward stigmatized social groups. *Journal of Personality and Social Psychology, 60,* 531–544.

Desmond, E. W. (1987, November 30). Out in the open. *Time,* 80–90.

DeSteno, D., Petty, R. E., Rucker, D. D., Wegener, D. T., & Braverman, J. (2004). Discrete emotions and persuasion: The role of emotion-induced expectancies. *Journal of Personality and Social Psychology, 86,* 43–56.

Deutsch, M. (1949). An experimental study of the effects of cooperation and competition upon group process. *Human Relations, 2,* 199–231.

Deutsch, M. (1973). *The resolution of conflict.* New Haven, CT: Yale University Press.

Deutsch, M. (1990). Psychological roots of moral exclusion. *Journal of Social Issues, 46*(1), 21–25.

Deutsch, M. (1993). Educating for a peaceful world. *American Psychologist, 48,* 510–517.

Deutsch, M., & Collins, M. E. (1951). *Interracial housing: A psychological evaluation of a social experiment.* Minneapolis, MN: University of Minnesota Press.

Deutsch, M., & Gerard, H. B. (1955). A study of normative and informational social influence upon individual judgment. *Journal of Abnormal and Social Psychology, 51,* 629–636.

Deutsch, M., & Krauss, R. M. (1960). The effect of threat upon interpersonal bargaining. *Journal of Abnormal and Social Psychology, 61,* 181–189.

Devine, P. G. (1989). Stereotypes and prejudice: Their automatic and controlled components. *Journal of Personality and Social Psychology, 56,* 5–18.

Devine, P. G., & Monteith, M. J. (1993). The role of discrepancy-associated affect in prejudice reduction. In D. M. Mackie & D. L. Hamilton (Eds.), *Affect, cognition, and stereotyping* (pp. 317–344). San Diego: Academic Press.

Devine, P. G., Tauer, J. M., Barron, K. E., Elliot, A. J., & Vance, K. M. (1999). Moving beyond attitude change in the study of dissonance related processes. In E. Harmon-Jones & J. Mills (Eds.), *Cognitive dissonance: Progress on a pivotal theory in social psychology* (pp. 297–323). Washington, DC: American Psychological Association.

Devos, T., Silver, L. A., Mackie, D. M., & Smith, E. R. (2002). Experiencing intergroup emotions. In D.M. Mackie & E. R. Smith (Eds.), *From prejudice to intergroup emotions* (pp. 111–134). New York: Psychology Press.

Diab, L. N. (1970). A study of intragroup and intergroup relations among experimentally produced small groups. *Genetic Psychology Monographs, 82,* 49–82.

Diehl, M., & Stroebe, W. (1991). Productivity loss in idea-generating groups: Tracking down the blocking effect. *Journal of Personality and Social Psychology, 61,* 392–403.

Diener, E., & Crandall, R. (1979). An evaluation of the Jamaican anticrime program. *Journal of Applied Social Psychology, 9,* 135–146.

Diener, E., & Wallbom, M. (1976). Effects of self-awareness on antinormative behavior. *Journal of Research in Personality, 10,* 107–111.

Dietrich, D. M., & Berkowitz, L. (1997). Alleviation of dissonance by engaging in prosocial behavior or receiving ego-enhancing feedback. *Journal of Social Behavior and Personality, 12,* 557–566.

Dijker, A. J. M. (1987). Emotional reactions to ethnic minorities. *European Journal of Social Psychology, 47,* 1105–1117.

Dindia, K., & Allen, M. (1992). Sex differences in self-disclosure: A meta-analysis. *Psychological Bulletin, 112,* 106–122.

Dion, K. K. (2002). Cultural perspectives on facial attractiveness. In G. Rhodes & L. A. Zebrowitz (Eds.), *Facial attractiveness: Evolutionary, cognitive, and social perspectives* (pp. 239–260). Westport, CT: Ablex.

Dion, K. K., & Berscheid, E. (1974). Physical attractiveness and peer perception among children. *Sociometry, 37,* 1–12.

Dion, K. K., Berscheid, E., & Walster, E. (1972). What is beautiful is good. *Journal of Personality and Social Psychology, 24,* 285–290.

Dion, K. L., & Dion, K. K. (1988). Romantic love: Individual and cultural perspectives. In R. Sternberg & M. Barnes (Eds.), *The psychology of love* (pp. 264–289). New Haven, CT: Yale University Press.

Dixon, N. F. (1976). *On the psychology of military incompetence.* London: Jonathan Cape.

Dobzhansky, T. (1973). *Genetic diversity and human equality.* New York: Basic Books.

Dodge, K. A., Bates, J. E., & Pettit, G. S. (1990). Mechanisms of the cycle of violence. *Science, 250,* 1678–1683.

Dodge, K. A., & Coie, J. D. (1987). Social-information-processing factors in reactive and proactive aggression in children's peer groups. *Journal of Personality and Social Psychology, 53,* 1146–1158.

Dodge, K. A., & Crick, N. R. (1990). Social information-processing bases of aggressive behavior in children. Special Issue: Illustrating the value of basic research. *Personality and Social Psychology Bulletin, 16,* 8–22.

Dodge, K. A., & Newman, J. P. (1981). Biased decision-making processes in aggressive boys. *Journal of Abnormal Psychology, 90,* 375–379.

Dodge, K. A., Pettit, G. S., McClaskey, C. L., & Brown, M. (1986). Social competence in children. *Monographs of the Society for Research in Child Development, 51* (2, Serial No. 213).

Dodge, K. A., & Somberg, D. R. (1987). Hostile attributional biases among aggressive boys are exacerbated under conditions of threat to the self. *Child Development, 58,* 213–224.

Doise, W. (1978). *Groups and individuals: Explanations in social psychology.* Cambridge, UK: Cambridge University Press.

Doise, W., & Sinclair, A. (1973). The categorization process in intergroup relations. *European Journal of Social Psychology, 3,* 145–157.

Doise, W., & Weinberger, M. (1973). Representations musculines dans differentes situations de rencontre mixtes. *Bulletin de Psychologie, 26,* 649–657.

Dolinski, D. (2000). On inferring one's beliefs from one's attempt and consequences for subsequent compliance. *Journal of Personality and Social Psychology, 78,* 260–272.

Dollard, J., Doob, L. W., Miller, M. E., Mowrer, O. H., & Sears, R. R. (1939). *Frustration and aggression.* New Haven, CT: Yale University Press.

Donnellan, M. B., Trzesniewski, K. H., Robins, R. W., Moffitt, T. E., & Caspi, A. (2005). Low self-esteem is related to aggression, antisocial behavior, and delinquency. *Psychological Science, 16,* 328–335.

Donnerstein, E., Linz, D., & Penrod, S. (1987). *The question of pornography: Research findings and policy implications.* New York: Free Press.

Donoho, C. L. (2003). The "top of the line" influence on the buyer–seller relationship. *Journal of Business Research, 56,* 303–309.

Doosje, B., Branscombe, N. R., Spears, R., & Manstead, A. S. R. (1998). Guilty by association: When one's group has a negative history. *Journal of Personality and Social Psychology, 75,* 872–886.

Doosje, B., Ellemers, N., & Spears, R. (1995). Perceived intragroup variability as a function of group status and identification. *Journal of Experimental Social Psychology, 31,* 410–436.

Dovidio, J. F., Allen, J. L., & Schroeder, D. A. (1990). Specificity of empathy-induced helping: Evidence for altruistic motivation. *Journal of Personality and Social Psychology, 59,* 249–260.

Dovidio, J. F., & Fazio, R. H. (1992). New technologies for the direct and indirect assessment of attitudes. In J. M. Tanur and others (Eds.), *Questions about questions: Inquiries into the cognitive bases of surveys* (pp. 204–237). New York: Russell Sage Foundation.

Dovidio, J. F., & Gaertner, S. L. (1993). Stereotypes and evaluative intergroup bias. In D. M. Mackie & D.L. Hamilton (Eds.), *Affect, cognition, and stereotyping: Interactive processes in group perception* (pp. 167–193). San Diego, CA: Academic Press.

Dovidio, J. F., Kawakami, K., & Gaertner, S. L. (2002). Implicit and explicit prejudice and interracial interaction. *Journal of Personality and Social Psychology, 82,* 62–68.

Dovidio, J. F., Piliavin, J. A., Gaertner, S. L., Schroeder, D. A., & Clark, R. D. (1991). The arousal: Cost–reward model and the process of intervention: A review of the evidence. In M. S. Clark (Ed.), *Prosocial behavior* (pp. 86–118). Newbury Park, CA: Sage Publications.

Dowd, E. T., Hughes, S. L., Brockbank, L., Halpain, D., Siebel, C., & Siebel, P. (1988). Compliance-based and defiance-based intervention strategies and psychological reactance in the treatment of free and unfree behavior. *Journal of Counseling Psychology, 35,* 370–376.

Downs, A. C., & Lyons, P. M. (1991). Natural observations of the links between attractiveness and initial legal judgments. *Personality and Social Psychology Bulletin, 17,* 541–547.

Draine, S. C., & Greenwald, A. G. (1998). Replicable unconscious semantic priming. *Journal of Experimental Psychology: General, 127,* 286–303.

Drigotas, S. M., & Rusbult, C. E. (1992). Should I stay or should I go? A dependence model of breakups. *Journal of Personality and Social Psychology, 62,* 62–87.

Druckman, D. (1990). The social psychology of arms control and reciprocation. *Political Psychology, 11,* 553–581.

Dubrovsky, V. J., Kiesler, S., & Sethna, B. N. (1991). The equalization phenomenon: Status effects in computer-mediated and face-to-face decision-making groups. *Human Computer Interaction, 6,* 119–146.

Duckitt, J., & Mphuthing, T. (1998). Group identification and intergroup attitudes: A longitudinal analysis in South Africa. *Journal of Personality and Social Psychology, 74,* 80–85.

Duckworth, K. L., Bargh, J. A., Garcia, M., & Chaiken, S. (2002). The automatic evaluation of novel stimuli. *Psychological Science, 13,* 513–519.

Duke, L., & Morin, R. (1992, March 8). Focusing on race: Candid dialogue, elusive answers. *The Washington Post,* p. A35.

Dunning, D., Meyerowitz, J. A., & Holzberg, A. D. (1989). Ambiguity and self-evaluation: The role of idiosyncratic trait definitions in self-serving assessments of ability. *Journal of Personality and Social Psychology, 57,* 1082–1090.

Dunton, B. C., & Fazio, R. H. (1997). An individual difference measure of motivation to control prejudiced reactions. *Personality and Social Psychology Bulletin, 23,* 316–326.

Durkheim, E. (1898). *The rules of sociological method.* New York: Free Press.

Dutton, D. G. (1996). *The domestic assault of women.* Vancouver: University of British Columbia Press.

Duval, S., Duval, V. H., & Neely, R. (1979). Self-focus, felt responsibility, and helping behavior. *Journal of Personality and Social Psychology, 37,* 1769–1778.

Duval, S., & Wicklund, R. A. (1972). *A theory of objective self-awareness.* New York: Academic Press.

Dweck, C. S. (1986). Motivational processes affecting learning. *American Psychologist, 41,* 1040–1048.

Dweck, C. S., & Leggett, E. L. (1988). A social-cognitive approach to motivation and personality. *Psychological Review, 95,* 256–273.

Eagly, A. (1974). Comprehensibility of persuasive arguments as a determinant of opinion change. *Journal of Personality and Social Psychology, 29,* 758–773.

Eagly, A. H. (1987). *Sex differences in social behavior: A social role interpretation.* Hillsdale, NJ: Lawrence Erlbaum Associates, Inc.

Eagly, A. H. (1995). The science and politics of comparing women and men. *American Psychologist, 50,* 145–158.

Eagly, A. H., Ashmore, R. D., Makhijani, M. G., & Longo, L. C. (1991). What is beautiful is good, but . . . : A meta-analytic review of research on the physical attractiveness stereotype. *Psychological Bulletin, 110,* 109–128.

Eagly, A. H., & Carli, L. L. (2003). The female leadership advantage: An evaluation of the evidence. *Leadership Quarterly, 14,* 807–834.

Eagly, A. H., & Chaiken, S. (1993). *The psychology of attitudes.* San Diego: Harcourt, Brace, Jovanovich.

Eagly, A. H., Chaiken, S., & Wood, W. (1981). An attributional analysis of persuasion. In J. H. Harvey, W. J. Ickes, & R. F. Kidd (Eds.), *New directions in attribution research* (Vol. 3, pp. 37–62). Hillsdale, NJ: Lawrence Erlbaum Associates Inc.

Eagly, A. H., & Crowley, M. (1986). Gender and helping behavior: A meta-analytic review of the social psychological literature. *Psychological Bulletin, 100,* 283–308.

Eagly, A. H., Diekman, A. B., Schneider, M. C., & Kulesa, P. (2003). Experimental tests of an attitudinal theory of the gender gap in voting. *Personality and Social Psychology Bulletin, 29,* 1245–1258.

Eagly, A. H., & Johnson, B. T. (1990). Gender and leadership style: A meta-analysis. *Psychological Bulletin, 108,* 233–256.

Eagly, A. H., & Karau, S. J. (1991). Gender and the emergence of leaders: A meta-analysis. *Journal of Personality and Social Psychology, 60,* 685–710.

Eagly, A. H., Karau, S. J., & Makhijani, M. G. (1995). Gender and the effectiveness of leaders: A meta-analysis. *Psychological Bulletin, 117,* 125–145.

Eagly, A. H., Kulesa, P., Brannon, L. A., Shaw, K., & Hutson-Comeaux, S. (2000). Why counterattitudinal messages are as memorable as proattitudinal messages: The importance of active defense against attack. *Personality & Social Psychology Bulletin, 26,* 1392–1408.

Eagly, A. H., & Makhijani, M. (1991). What is beautiful is good, but . . . : A meta-analytic review of research on the physical attractiveness stereotype. *Psychological Bulletin, 110,* 109–128.

Eagly, A. H., Makhijani, M. G., & Klonsky, B. G. (1992). Gender and the evaluation of leaders: A meta-analysis. *Psychological Bulletin, 111,* 3–22.

Eagly, A. H., & Mladinic, A. (1989). Gender stereotypes and attitudes toward women and men. *Personality and Social Psychology Bulletin, 15,* 543–558.

Eagly, A. H., & Steffen, V. J. (1984). Gender stereotypes stem from the distribution of women and men into social roles. *Journal of Personality and Social Psychology, 46,* 735–754.

Eagly, A. H., Wood, W., & Chaiken, S. (1978). Causal inferences about communicators and their effect on opinion change. *Journal of Personality and Social Psychology, 36,* 424–435.

Earley, P. C. (1989). Social loafing and collectivism: A comparison of the United States and the People's Republic of China. *Administrative Science Quarterly, 34,* 565–581.

Easterbrook, J. A. (1959). The effect of emotion on cue utilization and the organization of behavior. *Psychological Review, 66,* 183–201.

Eaton, J. (2001). Management communication: The threat of groupthink. *Corporate Communications, 6,* 183–192.

Ebbesen, E. B., Kjos, G. L., & Konecni, V. J. (1976). Spatial ecology: Its effects on the choice of friends and enemies. *Journal of Experimental Social Psychology, 12,* 505–518.

Eberhard, J. L., & Fiske, S. T. (1996). Motivating individuals to change: What is a target to do? In C. N. Macrae, C. Stangor, & M. Hewstone (Eds.), *Stereotypes and stereotyping* (pp. 369–418). New York: Guilford.

Eckes, T. (1994). Explorations in gender cognition: Content and structure of female and male subtypes. *Social Cognition, 12,* 37–60.

Eckes, T., & Six, B. (1994). Fact and fiction in research on the relationship between attitude and behavior: A meta-analysis. *Journal of Social Psychology, 25,* 253–271.

Edney, J. J. (1980). The commons problem: Alternative perspectives. *American Psychologist, 35,* 131–150.

Edwards, K., & Smith, E. (1996) A disconfirmation bias in the evaluation of arguments. *Journal of Personality and Social Psychology, 71,* 5–24.

Edwards, K., & von Hippel, W. (1995). Hearts and minds. The priority of affective versus cognitive actors in person perception. *Personality and Social Psychology Bulletin, 21,* 996–1011.

Eibl-Eibesfeldt, I. (1972). Similarities and differences between cultures in expressive movement. In R. A. Hinde (Ed.), *Nonverbal communication.* Cambridge, UK: Cambridge University Press.

Eisenberg, N. (1991). Meta-analytic contributions to the literature on prosocial behavior. *Personality and Social Psychology Bulletin, 17,* 273–282.

Eisenberg, N., & Fabes, R. A. (1991). Prosocial behavior and empathy: A multimethod developmental perspective. In M. S. Clark (Ed.), *Prosocial behavior* (pp. 34–61). Newbury Park, CA: Sage Publications.

Eisenberg, N., Guthrie, I. K., Cumberland, A., Murphy, B. C., Shepard, S. A. and others (2002). Prosocial development in early adulthood: A longitudinal study. *Journal of Personality and Social Psychology, 78,* 136–157.

Eisenberger, R., Cotterell, N., & Marvel, J. (1987). Reciprocation ideology. *Journal of Personality and Social Psychology, 53,* 743–750.

Eisenger, R., & Mills, J. (1968). Perception of the sincerity and competence of a communicator as a function of the extremity of his position. *Journal of Experimental Social Psychology, 4,* 224–232.

Eisenstat, R. A. (1990). Compressor team start-up. In J. R. Hackman (Ed.), *Groups that work (and those that don't)* (pp. 411–426). San Francisco: Jossey-Bass.

Eiser, J. R., Fazio, R. H., Stafford, T., & Prescott, T. J. (2003). Connectionist simulation of attitude learning: Asymmetries in the acquisition of positive and negative evaluations. *Personality and Social Psychology Bulletin, 29,* 1221–1235.

Eiser, J. R., & Sutton, S. R. (1977). Smoking as a subjectively rational choice. *Addictive Behaviors, 2,* 129–34.

Eiser, J. R., & van der Pligt, J. (1986). Smoking cessation and smokers' perceptions of their addiction. *Journal of Social and Clinical Psychology, 4,* 60–70.

Eiser, J. R., van der Pligt, J., Raw, M., & Sutton, S. R. (1985). Trying to stop smoking: Effects of perceived addiction, attributions for failure and expectancy of success. *Journal of Behavioral Medicine, 8,* 321–41.

Ekman, P. (1971). Universals and cultural differences in facial expression of emotion. In J. L. Cole (Ed.), *Nebraska symposium on motivation* (Vol. 19). Lincoln: University of Nebraska Press.

Ekman, P. (1992). Facial expressions of emotion: New findings, new questions. *Psychological Science, 3,* 34–38.

Ekman, P., & Friesen, W. V. (1974). Detecting deception from the body or face. *Journal of Personality and Social Psychology, 29,* 288–298.

Ekman, P., Friesen, W. V., & Ellsworth, P. (1972). *Emotion in the human face.* Elmsford, NY: Pergamon Press.

Ekman, P., Friesen, W. V., O'Sullivan, M., Chan, A., Diacoyanni-Tarlatzis, I., Heider, K. and others (1987). Universals and cultural differences in the judgments of facial expressions of emotion. *Journal of Personality and Social Psychology, 53,* 712–717.

El-Alayli, A., & Messé, L. A. (2004). Reactions toward an unexpected or counternormative favor-giver: Does it matter if we think we can reciprocate? *Journal of Experimental Social Psychology, 40,* 633–641.

Ellemers, N. (2001). Individual upward mobility and the perceived legitimacy of intergroup relations. In J. T. Jost & B. Major (Eds.), *The *psychology of legitimacy: Merging perspectives on ideology, justice, and intergroup relations* (pp. 205–222). New York, NY: Cambridge University Press.

Ellemers, N., de Gilder, D., & Haslam, S. A. (2004). Motivating individuals and groups at work: A social identity perspective on leadership and group performance. *Academy of Management Review, 29,* 459–478.

Ellemers, N., Spears, R., & Doosje, B. (1997). Sticking together or falling apart: In-group identification as a psychological determinant of group commitment versus individual mobility. *Journal of Personality and Social Psychology, 72,* 617–626.

Ellemers, N., Spears, R., & Doosje, B. (2002). Self and social identity. *Annual Review of Psychology, 53*(1), 161–186.

Ellemers, N., & van Knippenberg, A. (1997). Stereotyping in social context. In R. Spears & P. J. Oakes (Eds.), *The social psychology of stereotyping and group life* (pp. 208–235). Oxford, UK: Blackwell Publishers.

Eller, A., & Abrams, D. (2004). Come together: Longitudinal comparisons of Pettigrew's reformulated intergroup contact model and the common ingroup identity model in Anglo-French and Mexican-American contexts. *European Journal of Social Psychology, 34*(3), 229–256.

Elliot, A. J., Chirkov, V. I., Kim, Y., & Sheldon, K. M. (2001). A cross-cultural analysis of avoidance (relative to approach) personal goals. *Psychological Science, 12,* 505–510.

Elliot, A. J., & Devine, P. G. (1994). On the motivational nature of cognitive dissonance: Dissonance as psychological discomfort. *Journal of Personality & Social Psychology, 67,* 382–394.

Ennis, R., & Zanna, M. P. (1991). *Hockey assault: Constitutive versus normative violations.* Paper presented at Canadian Psychological Association convention.

Ennis, R., & Zanna, M. P. (2000). Attitude function and the automobile. In G. R. Maio & J. M. Olson (Eds.), *Why we evaluate: Functions of attitudes* (pp. 1–36). Mahwah, NJ: Lawrence Erlbaum Associates, Inc.

Epstein, S. (1992). Coping ability, negative self-evaluation, and overgeneralization: Experiment and theory. *Journal of Personality and Social Psychology, 62,* 826–836.

Epstein, Y. M., Suedfeld, P., & Silverstein, S. J. (1973). The experimental contract: Subjects' expectations of and reactions to some behaviors of experimenters. *American Psychologist, 28,* 212–221.

Erb, H. P., & Bohner, G. (2001). Mere consensus effects in minority and majority influence. In C. K. W. De Dreu & N. K. De Vries (Eds.), *Group consensus and minority influence: Implications for innovation* (pp. 40–59). Malden, MA: Blackwell Publishers.

Erb, H. P., Bohner, G., Schmalzle, K., & Rank, S. (1998). Beyond conflict and discrepancy: Cognitive bias in minority and majority influence. *Personality and Social Psychology Bulletin, 24,* 395–409.

Erickson, B., Lind, E. A., Johnson, B. C., & O'Barr, W. M. (1978). Speech style and impression formation in a court setting: The effects of "powerful" and "powerless" speech. *Journal of Experimental Social Psychology, 14,* 266–279.

Esser, J. K. (1998). Alive and well after 25 years: A review of groupthink research. *Organizational Behavior and Human Decision Processes, 73,* 116–141.

Esser, J. K., & Lindoerfer, J. S. (1989). Groupthink and the space shuttle Challenger accident: Toward a quantitative case analysis. *Journal of Behavioral Decision Making, 2,* 167–177.

Esses, V. M, Haddock, G., & Zanna, M. P. (1993). Values, stereotypes, and emotions as determinants of intergroup attitudes. In D. M. Mackie & D. L. Hamilton (Eds.), *Affect, cognition, and stereotyping: Interactive processes in group perception* (pp. 137–166). San Diego, CA: Academic Press.

Ethical Principles of Psychologists and Code of Conduct (1992). Washington, DC: American Psychological Association.

Etzioni, A. (1962). *The hard way to peace.* New York: Collier.

Etzioni, A. (1967). The Kennedy experiment. *The Western Political Quarterly, 20,* 361–380.

Evans, G. W. (1979). Behavioral and physiological consequences of crowding in humans. *Journal of Applied Social Psychology, 9,* 27–46.

Evans, L. M., & Petty, R. E. (2003). Self-guide framing and persuasion: Responsibly increasing message processing to ideal levels. *Personality & Social Psychology Bulletin, 29,* 313–324.

Fabiano, P. M. (2003). Applying the social norms model to universal and indicated alcohol interventions at Western Washington University. In H. W. Perkins (Ed.), *The social norms approach to preventing school and college age substance abuse: A handbook for educators, counselors, and clinicians* (pp. 83–99). San Francisco, CA: Jossey-Bass.

Falbo, T., & Peplau, L. A. (1980). Power strategies in intimate relationships. *Journal of Personality and Social Psychology, 38,* 618–628.

Fazio, R. H. (1986). How do attitudes guide behavior? In R. M. Sorrentino & E. T. Higgins (Eds.), *The handbook of motivation and cognition: Foundations of social behavior* (pp. 204–243). New York: Guilford Press.

Fazio, R. H. (1989). On the power and functionality of attitudes: The role of attitude accessibility. In A. R. Pratkanis, S. J. Breckler, & A. G. Greenwald (Eds.), *Attitude structure and function* (pp. 153–179). Hillsdale, NJ: Lawrence Erlbaum Associates, Inc.

Fazio, R. H. (1990). Multiple processes by which attitudes guide behavior: The MODE model as an integrative framework. In M. P. Zanna (Ed.), *Advances in experimental social psychology* (Vol. 23, pp. 75–109). New York: Academic Press.

Fazio, R. H. (2000). Accessible attitudes as tools for object appraisal: Their costs and benefits. In G. R. Maio & J. M. Olson (Eds.), *Why we evaluate: Functions of attitudes* (pp. 1–36). Mahwah, NJ: Lawrence Erlbaum Associates, Inc.

Fazio, R. H. (2001). On the automatic activation of associated evaluations: An overview. *Cognition & Emotion. Special Automatic Affective Processing, 15,* 115–141.

Fazio, R. H., Blascovich, J., & Driscoll, D. M. (1992). On the functional value of attitudes: The influence of accessible attitudes upon the ease and quality of decision-making. *Personality and Social Psychology Bulletin, 18,* 388–401.

Fazio, R. H., Chen, J., McDonel, E., & Sherman, S. J. (1982). Attitude accessibility, attitude–behavior consistency, and the strength of the object-evaluation association. *Journal of Experimental Social Psychology, 18,* 339–357.

Fazio, R. H., Effrein, E. A., & Falender, V. J. (1981). Self-perceptions following social interactions. *Journal of Personality and Social Psychology, 41,* 232–242.

Fazio, R. H., Jackson, J. R., Dunton, B. C., & Williams, C. J. (1995). Variability in automatic activation as an unobstrusive measure of racial attitudes: A bona fide pipeline? *Journal of Personality and Social Psychology, 69,* 1013–1027.

Fazio, R. H., Ledbetter, J. E., & Towles-Schwen, T. (2000). On the costs of accessible attitudes: Detecting that the attitude object has changed. *Journal of Personality and Social Psychology, 78*, 197–210.

Fazio, R. H., & Olson, M. A. (2003). Implicit measures in social cognition research: Their meaning and uses. *Annual Review of Psychology, 54*, 297–327.

Fazio, R. H., & Zanna, M. P. (1981). Direct experience and attitude behavior consistency. In L. Berkowitz (Ed.), *Advances in experimental social psychology*, (Vol. 14, pp. 161–202). New York: Academic Press.

Fazio, R. H., Zanna, M. P., & Cooper, J. (1977). Dissonance and self-perception: An integrative view of each theory's proper domain of application. *Journal of Experimental Social Psychology, 13*, 464–479.

Federal Bureau of Investigation (2003). *Uniform Crime Report 2003.* Washington, DC: US Government Printing Office.

Fein, S. (1996). Effects of suspicion on attributional thinking and the correspondence bias. *Journal of Personality and Social Psychology, 70*, 1164–1184.

Fein, S., & Hilton, J. L. (1992). Attitudes toward groups and behavioral intentions toward individual group members: The impact of nondiagnostic information. *Journal of Experimental Social Psychology, 28*, 101–124.

Fein, S., & Spencer, S. J. (1997). Prejudice as self-image maintenance: Affirming the self through derogating others. *Journal of Personality and Social Psychology, 73*, 31–44.

Feingold, A. (1990). Gender differences in effects of physical attractiveness on romantic attraction: A comparison across five research paradigms. *Journal of Personality and Social Psychology, 59*, 981–993.

Feingold, A. (1992a). Gender differences in mate selection preferences: A test of the parental investment model. *Psychological Bulletin, 112*, 125–139.

Feingold, A. (1992b). Good-looking people are not what we think. *Psychological Bulletin, 111*, 304–341.

Felson, R. B. (1989). Parents and the reflected appraisal process: A longitudinal analysis. *Journal of Personality and Social Psychology, 56*, 965–971.

Ferdman, B. M. (1989). Affirmative action and the challenge of the color-blind perspective. In F. A. Blanchard & F. J. Crosby (Eds.), *Affirmative action in perspective* (pp. 169–176). New York: Springer-Verlag.

Feshbach, N. (1980). *The child as "psychologist" and "economist": Two curricula.* Paper presented at the American Psychological Association convention.

Feshbach, N., & Feshbach, S. (1982). Empathy training and the regulation of aggression: Potentialities and limitations. *Academic Psychology Bulletin, 4*, 399–413.

Feshbach, S., & Singer, R. (1957). The effects of personality and shared threats upon social prejudice. *Journal of Abnormal and Social Psychology, 54*, 411–16.

Festinger, L. (1950). Informal social communication. *Psychological Review, 57*, 271–282.

Festinger. L. (1954). A theory of social comparison processes. *Human Relations, 7*, 117–140.

Festinger, L. (1957). *A theory of cognitive dissonance.* Stanford, CA: Stanford University Press.

Festinger, L., & Carlsmith, J. M. (1959). Cognitive consequences of forced compliance. *Journal of Abnormal and Social Psychology, 58*, 203–210.

Festinger, L., Pepitone, A., & Newcomb, T. (1952). Some consequences of de-individuation in a group. *Journal of Abnormal and Social Psychology, 58*, 203–210.

Festinger, L., Schacter, S., & Back, K. (1950). *Social pressures in informal groups: A study of human factors in housing.* Stanford, CA: Stanford University Press.

Fiedler, F. (1964). A contingency model of leadership effectiveness. In L. Berkowitz (Ed.), *Advances in experimental social psychology* (Vol. 1, pp. 149–190). New York: Academic Press.

Fiedler, K. (1991). The tricky nature of skewed frequency tables: An information loss account of distinctiveness-based illusory correlations. *Journal of Personality and Social Psychology, 60*, 24–36.

Fincham, F., & O'Leary, K. D. (1983). Causal inferences for spouse behavior in maritally distressed and nondistressed couples. *Journal of Clinical and Social Psychology, 1*, 42–57.

Fincham, F. D., & Beach, S. R. H. (2001). Forgiving in close relationships. In F. Columbus (Ed.), *Advances in psychology research* (Vol. 7, pp. 163–197). Hauppauge, NY: Nova Science Publishers.

Finkelstein, M. A., & Penner, L. A. (2004). Predicting organizational citizenship behavior: Integrating the functional and role identity approaches. *Social Behavior and Personality, 32*, 383–398

Fishbein, M., & Ajzen, I. (1975). *Belief, attitude, intention, and behavior: An introduction to theory and research.* Reading, MA: Addison-Wesley.

Fisher, J. D., & Fisher, W. A. (1992). Changing AIDS-risk behavior. *Psychological Bulletin, 111*, 455–474.

Fisher, J. D., Nadler, A., & Whitcher-Alagner, S. (1982). Recipient reactions to aid. *Psychological Bulletin, 91*, 27–54.

Fisher, R., & Ury, W. L. (1981). *Getting to YES: Negotiating agreement without giving in.* Boston: Houghton Mifflin.

Fisher, R., & White, J. H. (1976). Intergroup conflicts resolved by outside consultants. *Journal of Community Development, 7*, 88–98.

Fiske, A. P. (1991). The cultural relativity of selfish individualism. In M. S. Clark (Ed.), *Prosocial behavior* (pp. 176–214). Newbury Park, CA: Sage Publications.

Fiske, A. P. (1992). The four elementary forms of sociality: Framework for a unified theory of social relations. *Psychological Review, 99*, 689–724.

Fiske, A. P., Kitayama, S., Markus, H. R., & Nisbett, R. E. (1998). The cultural matrix of social psychology. In D. T. Gilbert, S. T. Fiske, & G. Lindzey (Eds.), *Handbook of social psychology* (4th ed., Vol. 2, pp. 915–981). Boston: McGraw-Hill.

Fiske, S. T. (1993a). Controlling other people: The impact of power on stereotyping. *American Psychologist, 48*, 621–628.

Fiske, S. T. (1993b). Social cognition and social perception. *Annual Review of Psychology, 44*, 155–194.

Fiske, S. T. (2002). What we know about bias and intergroup conflict, the problem of the century. *Current Directions in Psychological Science, 11*(4), 123–128.

Fiske, S. T., Bersoff, D. N., Borgida, E., Deaux, K., &Heilman, M. E. (1991). Social science research on trial: Use of sex stereotyping research in Price Waterhouse v. Hopkins. *American Psychologist, 46*, 1049–1060.

Fiske, S. T., Cuddy, A. J., Glick, P., & Xu, J. (2002). A model of (often mixed) stereotype content: Competence and warmth respectively follow from perceived status and competition. *Journal of Personality & Social Psychology, 82,* 878–902.

Fiske, S. T., & Neuberg, S. L. (1990). A continuum of impression formation, from category-based to individuating processes: Influences of information and motivation on attention and interpretation. In M. P. Zanna (Ed.), *Advances in experimental social psychology* (Vol. 23, pp. 1–74). New York: Academic Press.

Fiske, S. T., & Stevens, L. E. (1993). What's so special about sex? Gender stereotyping and discrimination. In S. Oskamp & M. Costanzo (Eds.), *Gender issues in contemporary society* (pp. 173–196). Newbury Park, CA: Sage Publications.

Fitness, J., & Fletcher, G. J. O. (1993). Love, hate, anger, and jealousy in close relationships. *Journal of Personality and Social Psychology, 65,* 942–958.

Fitzsimmons, D. (2004). What are we trying to measure? Rethinking approaches to health outcome assessment for the older person with cancer. *European Journal of Cancer Care, 13,* 416–423.

Flay, B. R., Ryan, K. B., Best, J. A., Brown, K. S., Kersell, M. W., d'Avernas, J. R. and others (1985). Are social-psychological smoking prevention programs effective? The Waterlook study. *Journal of Behavioral Medicine, 8,* 37–59.

Fleming, I., Baum, A., & Weiss, L. (1987). Social density and perceived control as mediators of crowding stress in high-density residential neighborhoods. *Journal of Personality and Social Psychology, 52,* 899–906.

Fletcher, G. J. O., & Fincham, F. D. (1991). Attribution processes in close relationships. In G. Fletcher & F. Fincham (Eds.), *Cognition in close relationships* (pp. 7–36). Hillsdale, NJ: Lawrence Erlbaum Associates, Inc.

Fletcher, G. J. O., & Haig, B. (1990). *The layperson as "naive scientist": An appropriate model for personality and social psychology?* Unpublished paper, University of Canterbury, Christchurch, New Zealand.

Flink, C., & Park, B. (1991). Increasing consensus in trait judgments through outcome dependency. *Journal of Experimental Social Psychology, 27,* 453–467.

Foa, U. G., & Foa, E. B. (1974). *Societal structures of the mind.* Oxford, UK: Charles C. Thomas.

Foerster, A. (2004). Race, identity, and belonging: "Blackness" and the struggle for solidarity in a multiethnic labor union. *Social Problems, 51,* 386–409.

Foerster, J., & Strack, F. (1996). Influence of overt head movements on memory for valenced words: A case of conceptual-motor compatibility. *Journal of Personality and Social Psychology, 71,* 421–430.

Folkman, S. (1984). Personal control and stress and coping processes: A theoretical analysis. *Journal of Personality and Social Psychology, 46,* 839–852.

Ford, C. S., & Beach, F. A. (1951). *Patterns of sexual behavior.* New York: Harper & Row.

Ford, T. E. (2000). Effects of sexist humor on tolerance of sexist events. *Personality and Social Psychology Bulletin, 26,* 1094–1107.

Ford, T. E., & Thompson, E. P. (2000). Preconscious and postconscious processes underlying construct accessibility effects: An extended search model. *Personality and Social Psychology Review, 4,* 317–336.

Forgas, J. P. (1995). Mood and judgment: The Affect Infusion Model (AIM). *Psychological Bulletin, 117,* 39–66.

Forsyth, D. R. (1999). *Group dynamics* (3rd ed.). Pacific Grove, CA: Brooks/Cole.

Forsyth, D. R., Schlenker, B. R., Leary, M. R., & McCown, N. E. (1985). Self-presentational determinants of sex differences in leadership behavior. *Small Group Behavior, 16,* 197–210.

Foss, R. (2004). Social norms program reduces measured and self-reported drinking at UNC-CH. In *The report on social norms.* Little Falls, NJ: PaperClip Communications.

Foti, R. J., Fraser, S. L., & Lord, R. G. (1982). Effects of leadership labels and prototypes on perceptions of political leaders. *Journal of Applied Psychology, 67,* 326–333.

Foushee, H. C. (1984). Dyads and triads at 35,000 feet: Factors affecting group process and aircrew performance. *American Psychologist, 39,* 885–893.

Foushee, H. C., & Manos, K. L. (1981). Information transfer within the cockpit: Problems in intracockpit communications. In C. E. Billings & E. S. Cheaney (Eds.), *Information transfer problems in the aviation system.* NASA Report No. TP-1875. Moffett Field, CA: NASA-Ames Research Center.

Frable, D. E. S. (1997). Gender, racial, ethnic, sexual, and class identities. *Annual Review of Psychology, 48,* 139–162.

Frable, D. E. S. (1989). Sex typing and gender ideology: Two facets of the individual's gender psychology that go together. *Journal of Personality and Social Psychology, 56,* 95–108.

Fragale, A. R., & Heath, C. (2004). Evolving informational credentials: The (mis)attribution of believable facts to credible sources. *Personality and Social Psychology Bulletin, 30,* 225–236.

Fraley, R. C. (2002). Attachment stability from infancy to adulthood: Meta-analysis and dynamic modeling of developmental mechanisms. *Personality and Social Psychology Review, 6,* 123–151.

Fraley, R. C., & Waller, N. G. (1998). Adult attachment patterns: A test of the typological model. In J. A. Simpson & W. F. Rholes (Eds.), *Attachment theory and close relationships* (pp. 78–114). New York: Guilford Press.

Frank, M. G., & Gilovich, T. (1988). The dark side of self- and social perception: Black uniforms and aggression in professional sports. *Journal of Personality and Social Psychology, 54,* 74–85.

Freedman, J. L. (1965). Long-term behavioral effects of cognitive dissonance. *Journal of Experimental Social Psychology, 1,* 145–155.

Freedman, J. L., & Fraser, S. C. (1966). Compliance without pressure: The foot-in-the-door technique. *Journal of Personality and Social Psychology, 4,* 195–202.

Freedman, J. L., & Sears, D. O. (1965). Warning, distraction and resistance to influence. *Journal of Personality and Social Psychology, 1,* 262–266.

Freiberg, P. (1991a, April). Self-esteem gender gap widens in adolescence. *APA Monitor,* p. 29.

Freiberg, P. (1991b, January). Surprise – most bosses are incompetent. *APA Monitor,* p. 23.

Freund, T., Kruglanski, A. W., & Shpitzajzen, A. (1985). The freezing and unfreezing of impression primacy: Effects of need for structure and the fear of invalidity. *Personality and Social Psychology Bulletin, 11,* 479–487.

Frey, D. (1986). Recent research on selective exposure to information. In L. Berkowitz (Ed.), *Advances in experimental social psychology* (Vol. 19, pp. 41–80). New York: Academic Press.

Friedman, H. S., Riggio, R. E., & Casella, D. F. (1988). Nonverbal skill, personal charisma, and initial attraction. *Personality and Social Psychology Bulletin, 14,* 203–211.

Friess, S. (2002, December 23). The power of peer pressure. *Newsweek.*

Frijda, N. H. (1986). *The emotions.* Cambridge, UK: Cambridge University Press.

Frijda, N. H., Kuipers, P., & ter Schure, E. (1989). Relations among emotion, appraisal, and emotional action readiness. *Journal of Personality and Social Psychology, 57,* 212–228.

Froming, W. J., Walker, G. R., & Lopyan, K. J. (1982). Public and private self awareness: When personal attitudes clash with societal expectations. *Journal of Experimental Social Psychology, 18,* 476–487.

Fukada, H. (1986). Psychological processes mediating the persuasion inhibiting effect of forewarning in fear arousing communication. *Psychological Reports, 58,* 87–90.

Funder, D. C., & Colvin, C. R. (1988). Friends and strangers: Acquaintanceship, agreement, and the accuracy of personality judgments. *Journal of Personality and Social Psychology, 55,* 149–158.

Furnham, A., & Gunter, B. (1984). Just world beliefs and attitudes towards the poor. *British Journal of Social Psychology, 23,* 265–269.

Gable, S. L., Reis, H. T., Impett, E. A., & Asher, E. R. (2004). What do you do when things go right? The intrapersonal and interpersonal benefits of sharing positive events. *Journal of Personality and Social Psychology, 87,* 228–245.

Gabor, A. (1992, January 26). Take this job and love it. *New York Times,* p. 1F.

Gabrenya, W. K., Wang, Y., & Latané, B. (1985). Social loafing on an optimizing task: Cross-cultural differences among Chinese and Americans. *Journal of Cross Cultural Psychology, 16,* 223–242.

Gaddikiotis, A., Martin, R., & Hewstone, M. (2004). The representation of majorities and minorities in the British press: A content analytic approach. *European Journal of Social Psychology, 34,* 637–646.

Gaertner, L., & Schopler, J. (1998). Perceived ingroup entitativity and intergroup bias: An interconnection of self and others. *European Journal of Social Psychology, 28,* 963–980.

Gaertner, S. L., & Dovidio, J. F. (2000). *Reducing intergroup bias: The common ingroup identity model.* New York: Psychology Press.

Gaertner, S. L., Dovidio, J. F., Anastasio, P. A., Bachman, B. A., & Rust, M. C. (1993). The common ingroup identity model: Recategorization and the reduction of intergroup bias. In W. Stroebe & M. Hewstone (Eds.), *European review of social psychology* (Vol. 4, pp. 1–26). Chichester, UK: Wiley.

Gaertner, S. L., Dovidio, J., Banker, B., S., Houlette, M., Johnson, K. M., & McGlynn, E. A. (2000). Reducing intergroup conflict: From superordinate goals to decategorization, recategorization, and mutual differentiation. *Group Dynamics, 4,* 1089–1099.

Gaertner, S. L., Mann, J., Dovidio, J. F., Murell, A., & Pomare, M. (1990). How does cooperation reduce intergroup bias? *Journal of Personality and Social Psychology, 59,* 692–704.

Gaertner, S. L., Mann, J., Murrell, A., & Dovidio, J. F. (1989). Reducing intergroup bias: The benefits of recategorization. *Journal of Personality and Social Psychology, 57,* 239–249.

Gagnon, A., & Bourhis, R. Y. (1996). Discrimination in the minimal group paradigm: Social identity or self-interest? *Personality and Social Psychology Bulletin, 22,* 1289–1301.

Gaines, S. O., & Henderson, M. C. (2002). Impact of attachment style on responses to accommodative dilemmas among same-sex couples. *Personal Relationships, 9,* 89–93.

Galinsky, A. D., & Moskowitz, G. B. (2000). Counterfactuals as behavioral primes: Priming the simulation heuristic and consideration of alternatives. *Journal of Experimental Social Psychology, 36,* 384–409.

Gallup Poll (2002, May 6–9). Data provided by the Roper Center for Public Opinion Research, University of Connecticut.

Gamson, W. A. (1992). The social psychology of collective action. In A. D. Morris & C. M. Mueller (Eds.), *Frontiers in social movement theory* (pp. 53–76). New Haven, CT: Yale University Press.

Gamson, W. A., Fireman, B., & Rytina, S. (1982). *Encounters with unjust authority.* Homewood, IL: Dorsey Press.

Gangestad, S. W. (1993). Sexual selection and physical attractiveness: Implications for mating dynamics. *Human Nature, 4,* 205–235.

Gangestad, S. W., & Snyder, M. (2000). Self-monitoring: Appraisal and reappraisal. *Psychological Bulletin, 126,* 530–555.

Garcia, S. M., Weaver, K., Moskowitz, G. B., & Darley, J. M. (2002). Crowded minds: The implicit bystander effect. *Journal of Personality and Social Psychology, 83,* 843–853.

Garcia-Marques, T., & Mackie, D. M. (2001). The feeling of familiarity as a regulator of persuasive processing. *Social Cognition, 19,* 9–34.

Gardner, R. C., Lalone, R. N., Nero, A. M., & Young M. Y. (1988). Ethnic stereotypes: Implications of measurement strategy. *Social Cognition, 6,* 40–60.

Gardner, W. L., Gabriel, S., & Lee, A. Y. (1999). "I" value freedom, but "we" value relationships: Self-construal priming mirrors cultural differences in judgment. *Psychological Science, 10,* 321–326.

Garofalo, J. (1997). Hate crime victimization in the United States. In R. C. Davis, A. J. Lurigio, & W. G. Skojan (Eds.), *Victims of crime* (2nd ed., pp. 134–145). Thousand Oaks, CA: Sage Publications.

Gawronski, B., Strack, F., & Bodenhausen, G. V. (2005). Attitudes and cognitive consistency: the role of associative and propositional processes. In R. E. Petty, R. H. Fazio, & P. Brinol (Eds.), *Attitudes: Insights from the new wave of implicit measures.* Mahwah, NJ: Erlbaum.

Geen, R. G. (1991). Social motivation. *Annual Review of Psychology, 42,* 377–391.

Geen, R. G. (1998). Aggression and antisocial behavior. In D. T. Gilbert, S. T. Fiske, & G. Lindzey (Eds.), *Handbook of social psychology* (3rd ed., Vol. 2, pp. 317–356). Boston: McGraw-Hill.

Geer, J. H, Judice, S, & Jackson, S. (1994). Reading times for erotic material: The pause to reflect. *Journal of General Psychology, 121,* 345–352.

Geis, F. L., Brown, V., Jennings, J., & Porter, N. (1984). TV commercials as achievement scripts for women. *Sex Roles, 10,* 513–525.

Gelles, R. J. (1972). *The violent home: A study of physical aggression between husband and wife.* Beverly Hills, CA: Sage.

Gelles, R. J. (1997). *Intimate violence in families* (3rd ed.). Beverly Hills, CA: Sage.

George, J. M. (1990). Personality, affect, and behavior in groups. *Journal of Applied Psychology, 75*, 107–116.

Gerard, H. B., & Rabbie, J. M. (1961). Fear and social comparison. *Journal of Abnormal and Social Psychology, 62*, 586–592.

Gerbner, G., Gross, L., Morgan, M., & Signorielli, N. (1986). Living with television: The dynamics of the cultivation process. In J. Bryant & D. Zillman (Eds.), *Perspectives on media effects* (pp. 17–40). Hillsdale, NJ: Lawrence Erlbaum Associates, Inc.

Gergen, K. J. (1965). Interaction goals and personalistic feedback as factors affecting the presentation of self. *Journal of Personality and Social Psychology, 1*, 413–424.

Gergen, K. J., & Gergen, M. M. (1988). Narrative and the self as relationship. In L. Berkowitz (Ed.), *Advances in experimental social psychology* (Vol. 21, pp. 17–56). San Diego, CA: Academic Press.

Gersick, C. J. (1989). Marking time: Predictable transitions in task groups. *Academy of Management Journal, 32*, 274–309.

Gibbons, F. X. (1978). Sexual standards and reactions to pornography: Enhancing behavioral consistency through self-focused attention. *Journal of Personality and Social Psychology, 36*, 976–987.

Gibbons, F. X., Eggleston, T. J., & Benthin, A. C. (1997). Cognitive reactions to smoking relapse: The reciprocal relation between dissonance and self-esteem. *Journal of Personality and Social Psychology, 72*, 184–195.

Gibbons, F. X., & Wicklund, R. A. (1982). Self-focused attention and helping behavior. *Journal of Personality and Social Psychology, 43*, 462–474.

Giebels, E., & Jannsen, O. (2005). Conflict stress and reduced well-being at work: The buffering effect of third-party help. *European Journal of Work and Organizational Psychology, 14*, 137–155.

Gilbert, D. T. (1991). How mental systems believe. *American Psychologist, 46*, 107–119.

Gilbert, D. T. (1998). Ordinary personology. In D. T. Gilbert, S. T. Fiske, & G. Lindzey (Eds.), *Handbook of social psychology* (4th ed., Vol. 2, pp. 89–150). Boston: McGraw-Hill.

Gilbert, D. T., & Jones, E. E. (1986). Perceiver-induced constraint: Interpretations of self-generated reality. *Journal of Personality and Social Psychology, 50*, 269–280.

Gilbert, D. T., & Krull, D. S. (1988). Seeing less and knowing more: The benefits of perceptual ignorance. *Journal of Personality and Social Psychology, 54*, 193–202.

Gilbert, D. T., Krull, D. S., & Malone, P. S. (1990). Unbelieving the unbelievable: Some problems in the rejection of false information. *Journal of Personality and Social Psychology, 59*, 601–613.

Gilbert, D. T., & Osborne, R. E. (1989). Thinking backward: Some curable and incurable consequences of cognitive busyness. *Journal of Personality and Social Psychology, 57*, 940–949.

Gilbert, D. T., Pelham, B. W., & Krull, D. S. (1988). On cognitive busyness: When person perceivers meet persons perceived. *Journal of Personality and Social Psychology, 54*, 733–740.

Gilbert, D. T., & Silvera, D. H. (1996). Overhelping. *Journal of Personality and Social Psychology, 70*, 678–690.

Gillespie, N. A., & Mann, L. (2004). Transformational leadership and shared values: The building blocks of trust. *Journal of Managerial Psychology, 19*, 588–607.

Gilovich, T. (1990). Differential construal and the false consensus effect. *Journal of Personality and Social Psychology, 59*, 623–634.

Giner-Sorolla, R. (1999). Affect in attitude: Immediate and deliberative perspectives In S. Chaiken & Y. Trope (Eds.), *Dual-process theories in social psychology* (pp. 441–461). New York: Guilford Press.

Gioia, D. A., & Sims, H. P. (1985). Self-serving bias and actor-observer differences in organizations: An empirical analysis. *Journal of Applied Social Psychology, 15*, 547–563.

Girandola, F. (2002). Sequential requests and organ donation. *Journal of Social Psychology, 142*, 171–178.

Glass, D. C. (1964). Changes in liking as a means of reducing cognitive discrepancies between self-esteem and aggression. *Journal of Personality, 32*, 491–549.

Glick, P., & Fiske, S. T. (1996). The Ambivalent Sexism Inventory: Differentiating hostile and benevolent sexism. *Journal of Personality and Social Psychology, 70*, 491–512.

Glick, P., & Fiske, S. T. (2001). An ambivalent alliance: Hostile and benevolent sexism as complementary justifications for gender inequality. *American Psychologist, 56*, 109–118.

Glick, P., Fiske, S. T., Mladinic, A., Saiz, J. L., Abrams, D., Masser, B., et al. (2000). Beyond prejudice as simple antipathy: Hostile and benevolent sexism across cultures. *Journal of Personality and Social Psychology, 79*, 763–775.

Globe and Mail (Toronto). (1993, August 4). p. A18.

Glynn, C. J., Hayes, A. F., & Shanahan, J. (1997). Perceived support for one's opinion and willingness to speak out. *Public Opinion Quarterly, 61*, 452–463.

Goethals, G. R. (2005). Presidential leadership. *Annual Review of Psychology, 56*, 545–570.

Goethals, G. R., Cooper, J., & Nacify, A. (1979). Role of foreseen, foreseeable, and unforeseeable behavioral consequences in the arousal of cognitive dissonance. *Journal of Personality and Social Psychology, 37*, 1179–1185.

Goethals, G. R., Messick, D. M., & Allison, S. T. (1991). The uniqueness bias: Studies of constructive social comparison. In J. Suls & T. A. Wills (Eds.), *Social comparison: Contemporary theory and research* (pp. 149–176). Hillsdale, NJ: Lawrence Erlbaum Associates, Inc.

Goethals, G. R., & Nelson, R. E. (1973). Similarity in the influence process: The belief–value distinction. *Journal of Personality and Social Psychology, 25*, 117–122.

Goffman, E. (1959). *The presentation of self in everyday life*. Garden City, NY: Doubleday.

Goldberg, C. (1997, February 25). Real-space meetings fill in the cyberspace gaps. *New York Times*, p. A8.

Goldin, C. (1990). *Understanding the gender gap*. New York: Oxford University Press.

Goldstein, A. G., & Chance, J. E. (1985). Effects of training on Japanese face recognition: Reduction of the other-race effect. *Bulletin of the Psychonomic Society, 23*, 211–214.

Goldstein, J. H. (1982). Sports violence. *National Forum, 62*(1), 9–11.

Goleman, D. (1990, October 18). Support groups may do more in cancer than relieve the mind. *New York Times*.

Goleman, D. (1992, December 15). New light on how stress erodes health. *New York Times*, pp. B5, B9.

Gollwitzer, P. M. (1996). The volitional benefits of planning. In P. M. Gollwitzer & J. A. Bargh (Eds.), *The psychology of action: Linking cognition and motivation to behavior* (pp. 287–312). New York: Guilford Press.

Gollwitzer, P. M., & Moskowitz, G. B. (1996). Goal effects on action and cognition. In E. T. Higgins & A. W. Kruglanski (Eds.), *Social psychology: Handbook of basic principles* (pp. 361–399). New York: Guilford Press.

Gollwitzer, P. M., & Schaal, B. (1998). Metacognition in action: The importance of implementation intentions. *Personality and Social Psychology Review, 2,* 124–136.

Goodman, M. (1952). *Race awareness in young children.* Cambridge, MA: Addison-Wesley.

Goodnough, A. (2005, October. 16). A favorite Florida fish is off the menu till next year. *New York Times,*

Goodwin, R. (1999). *Personal relationships across cultures.* New York: Routledge.

Goodwin, S. A., Gubin, A., Fiske, S. T., & Yzerbyt, V. Y. (2000). Power can bias impression processes: Stereotyping subordinates by default and by design. *Group Processes and Intergroup Relations, 3,* 227–256.

Goranson, R. E., & Berkowitz, L. (1966). Reciprocity and responsibility reactions to prior help. *Journal of Personality and Social Psychology, 3,* 227–232.

Gorassini, D. R., & Olson, J. M. (1995). Does self-perception change explain the foot-in-the-door effect? *Journal of Personality & Social Psychology, 69,* 91–105.

Gordijn, E. H., De Vries, N. K., & De Dreu, C. K. W. (2002). Minority influence on focal and related attitudes: Change in size, attributions and information processing. *Personality and Social Psychology Bulletin, 28,* 1315–1326.

Gordijn, E. H., Wigboldus, D. I., & Yzerbyt, V. (2001). Emotional consequences of categorizing victims of negative outgroup behavior as ingroup or outgroup. *Group Processes & Intergroup Relations, 4*(4), 317–326.

Gordon, R. A. (1996). Impact of ingratiation on judgments and evaluations: A meta-analytic investigation. *Journal of Personality and Social Psychology, 71,* 54–70.

Gordon, R. A., & Anderson, K. S. (1995). Perceptions of race-stereotypic and race-nonstereotypic crimes: The impact of response-time instructions on attributions and judgments. *Basic and Applied Social Psychology, 16,* 455–470.

Gorenflo, D. W., & Crano, W. D. (1989). Judgmental subjectivity/objectivity and locus of choice in social comparison. *Journal of Personality and Social Psychology, 57,* 605–614.

Gorer, G. (1968). Man has no "killer" instinct. In M. F. A. Montagu (Ed.), *Man and aggression* (pp. 27–36). New York: Oxford University Press.

Gorn, G. (1982). The effects of music in advertising on choice behavior: A classical conditioning approach. *Journal of Marketing Research, 46,* 94–101.

Gosling, S. D., Ko, S. J., Mannarelli, T., & Morris, M. E. (2002). A room with a cue: Personality judgments based on offices and bedrooms. *Journal of Personality and Social Psychology, 82,* 379–398.

Gottfredson, M. R., & Hirschi, T. (1990). *A general theory of crime.* Stanford, CA: Stanford University Press.

Gottman, J., Notarius, C., Markman, H., Bank, S., Yoppi, S., & Rubin, M. (1976). Behavior exchange theory and marital decision making. *Journal of Personality and Social Psychology, 34,* 14–23.

Gottman, J. M. (1979). *Marital interaction: Experimental investigations.* New York: Academic Press.

Gould, S. J. (1978). Morton's ranking of races by cranial capacity. *Science, 200,* 503–509.

Gould, S. J. (1981). *The mismeasure of man.* New York: Norton.

Gould, S. J. (1991). *Bully for brontosaurus.* New York: W. W. Norton & Co.

Gouldner, A. W. (1960). The norm of reciprocity: A preliminary statement. *American Sociological Review, 25,* 161–178.

Gramzow, R. H., Gaertner, L., & Sedikides, C. (2001). Memory for in-group and out-group information in a minimal group context: The self as an informational base. *Journal of Personality and Social Psychology, 80*(2), 188–205.

Gray, J. D., & Silver, R. C. (1990). Opposite sides of the same coin: Former spouses' divergent perspectives in coping with their divorce. *Journal of Personality and Social Psychology, 59,* 1180–1191.

Gray, J. R. (1999). A bias toward short-term thinking in threat-related negative emotional states. *Personality and Social Psychology Bulletin, 25,* 65–75.

Graziano, W. G., & Eisenberg, N. (1997). Agreeableness: Dimension of personality. In R. Hogan, J. Johnson, & S. Briggs (Eds.), *Handbook of personality* (pp. 795–825). San Diego, CA: Academic Press.

Graziano, W. G., Habashi, M., Sheese, B. E., & Tobin, R. (2004). *Feeling compassion and helping the unfortunate: A social motivational analysis.* Manuscript submitted for publication.

Green, D. P., Glaser, J., & Rich, A. (1998). From lynching to gay bashing: The elusive connection between economic conditions and hate crime. *Journal of Personality and Social Psychology, 75,* 82–92.

Greenberg, J., & Pyszczynski, T. (1985). The effect of an overheard ethnic slur on evaluations of the target: How to spread a social disease. *Journal of Experimental Social Psychology, 21,* 61–72.

Greenberg, M. S., & Westcott, D. R. (1983). Indebtedness as a mediator of reactions to aid. In J. D. Fisher, A. Nadler, & B. M. DePaulo (Eds.), *New directions in helping. Volume 1: Recipient reactions to aid* (pp. 85–112). New York: Academic Press.

Greene, G. (1980). *Ways of escape.* New York: Simon & Schuster.

Greenwald, A. G. (1968). Cognitive learning, cognitive response to persuasion, and attitude change. In A. Greenwald, T. Brock, & T. Ostrom (Eds.), *Psychological foundations of attitudes* (pp. 148–170). New York: Academic Press.

Greenwald, A. G. (1980). The totalitarian ego: Fabrication and revision of personal history. *American Psychologist, 35,* 603–618.

Greenwald, A. G., & Ronis, D. L. (1978). Twenty years of cognitive dissonance: Case study of the evolution of a theory. *Psychological Review, 85,* 53–57.

Greenwald, A. G., McGhee, D. E., & Schwartz, J. L. K. (1998). Measuring individual differences in implicit cognition: The implicit association test. *Journal of Personality & Social Psychology, 74,* 1464–1480.

Greenwald, A. G., Spangenberg, E. R., Pratkanis, A. R., & Eskenazi, J. (1991). Double-blind tests of subliminal self-help audiotapes. *Psychological Science, 2,* 119–122.

Gross, A. E., & Latané, J. G. (1974). Receiving help, reciprocation, and interpersonal attraction. *Journal of Applied Social Psychology, 4,* 210–223.

Grube, J. A., & Piliavin, J. A. (2000). Role identity, organizational commitment, and volunteer performance. *Personality and Social Psychology Bulletin*, 26, 1108–1119.

Gruenfeld, D. H., Martorana, P. V., & Fan, E. T. (2000). What do groups learn from their worldliest members? Direct and indirect influence in dynamic teams. *Organizational Behavior and Human Decision Processes*, 82, 45–59.

Gruenfeld, D. H. (1995). Status, ideology, and integrative complexity on the U.S. Supreme Court: Rethinking the politics of political decision making. *Journal of Personality & Social Psychology*, 68, 5–20.

Gruenfeld, D. H., Thomas-Hunt, M. C., & Kim, P. H. (1998). Cognitive flexibility communication strategy, and integrative complexity in groups: Public versus private reactions to majority and minority status. *Journal of Experimental Social Psychology*, 34, 202–226.

Guadagno, R. E., Asher, T. Demaine, L. J., & Cialdini, R. B. (2001). When saying yes leads to saying no: Preference for consistency and the reverse foot-in-the-door effect. *Personality and Social Psychology Bulletin*, 27, 859–867.

Guéguen, N. (2002). Foot-in-the-door technique and computer-mediated communication. *Computers in Human Behavior*, 18, 11–15.

Guéguen, N., & DeGail, M. (2003). The effect of smiling on helping behavior: Smiling and Good Samaritan behavior. *Communication Reports*, 16, 133–140.

Guéguen, N., Pascual, A., & Dagot, L. (2002). Low-ball and compliance to a request: An application in a field setting. *Psychological Reports*, 91, 81–84.

Guerin, B. (1986). The effects of mere presence on a motor task. *Journal of Social Psychology*, 126, 399–401.

Guimond, S., & Dube-Simard, L. (1983). Relative deprivation theory and Quebec Nationalist Movement: The cognitive–emotion distinction and the personal–group deprivation issue. *Journal of Personality and Social Psychology*, 44, 526–35.

Guinote, A., Judd, C. M., & Brauer, M. (2002). Effects of power on perceived and objective group variability: Evidence that more powerful groups are more variable. *Journal of Personality and Social Psychology*, 82(5), 708–721.

Gupta, U., & Singh, P. (1982). An exploratory study of love and liking and type of marriages. *Indian Journal of Applied Psychology*, 19, 92–97.

Gurr, T. (1970). *Why men rebel*. Princeton, NJ: Princeton University Press.

Hacker, H. M. (1951). Women as a minority group. *Social Forces*, 30, 60–69.

Hackman, J. R. (1987). The design of work teams. In J. Lorsch (Ed.), *Handbook of organizational behavior* (pp. 315–342). Englewood Cliffs, NJ: Prentice Hall.

Hackman, J. R. (1992). Group influences on individuals in organizations. In M. D. Dunnette & L. M. Hough (Eds.), *Handbook of industrial and organizational psychology* (2nd ed., Vol. 3., pp. 199–267). Palo Alto, CA: Consulting Psychologists Press.

Hadden, S. B., & Brownlow, S. (1991). The impact of facial structure and assertiveness on dating choice. Paper presented at the annual meeting of the Southeastern Psychological Association, New Orleans, March 20–24.

Hafer, C. L., Reynolds, K. L., & Obertynski, M. A. (1996). Message comprehensibility and persuasion: Effects of complex language in counterattitudinal appeals to laypeople. *Social Cognition*, 14, 317–337.

Hahlweg, K., Markman, H. J., Thurmaier, F., Engl, J., & Eckert, V. (1998). Prevention of marital distress: Results of a German prospective longitudinal study. *Journal of Family Psychology*, 12, 543–556.

Haines, H., & Vaughan, G. M. (1979). Was 1898 a "great date" in the history of experimental social psychology? *Journal of the History of Behavioral Sciences*, 15, 323–332.

Haines, M., & Spear, S. F. (1996). Changing the perception of the norm: A strategy to decrease binge drinking among college students. *Journal of American College Health*, 45, 134–140.

Haines, M. P., & Barker, G. P. (2003). The Northern Illinois University experiment: A longitudinal case study of the social norms approach. San Francisco, CA: Jossey-Bass.

Hains, S. C., Hogg, M. A., & Duck, J. M. (1997). Self-categorization and leadership: Effects of group prototypicality and leader stereotypicality. *Personality and Social Psychology Bulletin*, 23, 1087–1099.

Halverson, S. K., Holladay, C. L., Kazama, S. M., & Quiñones, M. A. (2004). Self-sacrificial behavior in crisis situations: The competing roles of behavioral and situational factors. *Leadership Quarterly*, 15, 263–275.

Hamermesh, D. S., & Biddle, J. E. (1993, November). *Beauty and the labor market*. NBER Working Paper No. W4518. Cambridge, MA: National Bureau of Economic Research.

Hamilton, D. L. (1981). Stereotyping and intergroup behavior: Some thoughts on the cognitive approach. In D.L. Hamilton (Ed.), *Cognitive processes in stereotyping and intergroup behavior* (pp. 333–354). Hillsdale, NJ: Lawrence Erlbaum Associates, Inc.

Hamilton, D. L., Driscoll, D., & Worth, L. T. (1989). Cognitive organization of impressions: Effects of incongruency in complex representations. *Journal of Personality and Social Psychology*, 57, 925–939.

Hamilton, D. L., & Gifford, R. K. (1976). Illusory correlation in interpersonal perception: A cognitive basis for stereotypic judgments. *Journal of Experimental Social Psychology*, 12, 392–407.

Hamilton, D. L.,Katz, L. B., & Leirer, V. (1980). Organizational processes in impression formation. In R. Hastie, T. M. Ostrom, E. B. Ebbesen, R. S. Wyer, D. L. Hamilton, & D. E. Carlston (Eds.), *Person memory* (pp. 121–153). Hillsdale, NJ: Lawrence Erlbaum Associates, Inc.

Hamilton, D. L., & Mackie, D. M. (1990). Specificity and generality in the nature and use of stereotypes. In T. Srull & R. S. Wyer, Jr. (Eds.), *Advances in social cognition: Content and process specificity in the effects of prior experiences* (Vol. 3, pp. 99–110). Hillsdale, NJ: Lawrence Erlbaum Associates, Inc.

Hamilton, D. L., & Rose. T. L. (1980). Illusory correlation and the maintenance of stereotypic beliefs. *Journal of Personality and Social Psychology*, 39, 832–845.

Hamilton, D. L., & Sherman, S. J. (1989). Illusory correlations: Implications for stereotype theory and research. In D. Bar-Tal, C. F. Graumann, A. W. Kruglanski, & W. Stroebe (Eds.), *Stereotypes and prejudice: Changing conceptions* (pp. 59–82). New York: Springer-Verlag.

Hamilton, D. L., & Sherman, S. J. (1996). Perceiving persons and groups. *Psychological Review*, 103, 336–355.

Hamilton, D. L., Stroessner, S. J., & Mackie, D. M. (1993). The influence of affect on stereotyping: The case of illusory correlations. In D. M. Mackie & D. L. Hamilton (Eds.), *Affect, cognition, and stereotyping: Interactive processes in group perception* (pp. 39–61). San Diego, CA: Academic Press.

Hamilton, D. L., & Zanna, M. P. (1974). Context effects in impression formation: Changes in connotative meaning. *Journal of Personality and Social Psychology, 29*, 649–654.

Hamilton, V. L., & Sanders, J. (1992). *Everyday justice: Responsibility and the individual in Japan and the United States.* New Haven, CT: Yale University Press.

Hamilton, V. L., & Sanders, J. (1995). Crimes of obedience and conformity in the workplace: Surveys of Americans, Russians, and Japanese. *Journal of Social Issues, 51*, 67–88.

Hamilton, W. D. (1964). The genetical evolution of social behavior, I & II. *Journal of Theoretical Biology, 7*, 1–52.

Hammer, J. (1992, January 27). Business as usual. *Newsweek*, pp. 38–40.

Hammond, K. R. (1948). Measuring attitudes by error-choice: An indirect method. *Journal of Abnormal and Social Psychology, 43*, 38–48.

Han, S., & Shavitt, S. (1993). *Persuasion and culture: Advertising appeals in individualistic and collectivistic societies.* Unpublished manuscript, University of Illinois.

Hancock, L. (2002). Applying social norms marketing to tobacco cessation and prevention: Lessons learned from three campaigns. In *The report on social norms.* Little Falls, NJ: PaperClip Communications.

Haney, C., Banks, C., & Zimbardo, P. (1973). Interpersonal dynamics in a simulated prison. *International Journal of Criminology and Penology, 1*, 69–97.

Hansson, R. O., Strobe, M. S., & Stroebe, W. (1988). In conclusion: Current themes in bereavement and widowhood research. *Journal of Social Issues, 44*(3), 207–216.

Harackiewicz, J. M. (1979). The effects of reward contingency and performance feedback on intrinsic motivation. *Journal of Personality and Social Psychology, 37*, 1352–1363.

Harber, K. D. (1998). Feedback to minorities: Evidence of a positive bias. *Journal of Personality and Social Psychology, 74*, 622–628.

Hardy, C., & Latané, B. (1986). Social loafing on a cheering task. *Social Science, 71*, 165–172.

Hare-Mustin, R. T., & Marecek, J. (1988). The meaning of difference: Gender theory, postmodernism, and psychology. *American Psychologist, 43*, 455–464.

Harinck, F., & De Dreu, C. K. W. (2004). Negotiating interests or values and reaching integrative agreements: The importance of time pressure and temporary impasses. *European Journal of Social Psychology, 34*(5), 595–611.

Haritos-Fatouros, M. (1988). The official torturer: A learning model for obedience to the authority of violence. *Journal of Applied Social Psychology, 18*, 1107–1120.

Harker, L., & Keltner, D. (2001). Expressions of positive emotion in women's college yearbook pictures and their relationship to personality and life outcomes across adulthood. *Journal of Personality and Social Psychology, 80*, 112–124.

Harkins, S. G., & Petty, R. E. (1983). Social context effects in persuasion: The effects of multiple sources and multiple targets. In P. Paulus (Ed.), *Basic group processes.* New York: Springer-Verlag.

Harkins, S. G., & Petty, R. E. (1987). Information utility and the multiple source effect. *Journal of Personality and Social Psychology, 52*, 260–268.

Harkins, S. G., & Szymanski, K. (1989). Social loafing and group evaluation. *Journal of Personality and Social Psychology, 56*, 934–941.

Harmon-Jones, E., Brehm, J. W., Greenberg, J., Simon, L., & Nelson, D. E. (1996). Evidence that the production of aversive consequences is not necessary to create cognitive dissonance. *Journal of Personality and Social Psychology, 70*, 5–16.

Harmon-Jones, E., & Harmon-Jones, C. (2002). Testing the action-based model of cognitive dissonance: The effect of action orientation on postdecisional attitudes. *Personality and Social Psychology Bulletin, 28*, 711–723.

Harmon-Jones, E., & Sigelman, J. (2001). State anger and prefrontal brain activity: Evidence that insult-related relative left-prefrontal activation is associated with experienced anger and aggression. *Journal of Personality & Social Psychology, 80*(5), 797–803.

Harper, C. R., Kidera, G. J., & Cullen, J. F. (1971). Study of simulated airline pilot incapacitation: Phase II, subtle or partial loss of function. *Aerospace Medicine, 42*, 946–948.

Harris, M. B., Benson, S. M., & Hall, C. L. (1975). The effects of confession on altruism. *Journal of Social Psychology, 96*, 187–192.

Harris, M. J. (1991). Controversy and culmination: meta-analysis and research on interpersonal expectancy effects. *Personality and Social Psychology Bulletin, 17*, 316–322.

Harris, M. J., & Rosenthal, R. (1985). Mediation of interpersonal expectancy effects: 31 meta-analyses. *Psychological Bulletin, 97*, 363–386.

Hart, J. W., Bridgett, D. J., & Karau, S. J. (2001). Coworker ability and effort as determinants of individual effort on a collective task. *Group Dynamics, 5*, 181–190.

Harvey, J. H., & Omarzu, J. (1997). Minding the close relationship. *Personality and Social Psychology Review, 1*, 224–240.

Harvey, J. H., Wells, G. L., & Alvarez, M. D. (1978). Attribution in the context of conflict and separation in close relationships. In J. H. Harvey, W. Ickes, & R. F. Kidd (Eds.), *New directions in attribution research* (Vol. 2, pp. 235–260). Hillsdale, NJ: Lawrence Erlbaum Associates, Inc.

Haslam, S. A., Oakes, P. J., Turner, J. C., & McGarty, C. (1995). Social categorization and group homogeneity: Changes in the perceived applicability of stereotype content as a function of comparative context and trait favourableness. *British Journal of Social Psychology, 34*, 139–160.

Haslam, S. A., Postmes, T., & Ellemers, N. (2003). More than a metaphor : Organizational identity makes organizational life possible. *British Journal of Management, 14*, 357–369.

Haslam, S. A., & Reicher, S. D. (2003). Beyond Stanford: Questioning a role-based explanation of tyranny. *Dialogue, 18*, 22–25.

Haslam, S. A., & Reicher, S. D. (2004). A critique of the role-based explanation of tyranny: Thinking beyond the Stanford prison. *Revista de Psicología Social, 19*, 115–122.

Hassin, R., & Trope, Y. (2000). Facing faces: Studies on the cognitive aspects of physiognomy. *Journal of Personality and Social Psychology, 78*, 837–852.

Hastie, R. (1984). Causes and effects of causal attribution. *Journal of Personality and Social Psychology, 46*, 44–56.

Hastie, R., & Kumar, P. A. (1979). Person memory: Personality traits as organizing principles in memory for behaviors. *Journal of Personality and Social Psychology, 37*, 25–38.

Hastie, R., & Park, B. (1986). The relationship between memory and judgment depends on whether the judgment task is memory-based or on-line. *Psychological Review, 93*, 258–268.

Hastie, R., Penrod, S. D., & Pennington, N. (1983). *Inside the jury.* Cambridge, MA: Harvard University Press.

Hastorf, A., & Cantril, H. (1954). They saw a game: A case study. *Journal of Abnormal and Social Psychology, 49*, 129–134.

Hatfield, E. (1988). Passionate and companionate love. In R. Sternberg & M. Barnes (Eds.), *The psychology of love* (pp. 191–217). New Haven, CT: Yale University Press.

Hatfield, E., & Rapson, R. L. (1993). *Love, sex, and intimacy.* New York: HarperCollins.

Hatfield, E., Sprecher, S., Pillemer, J. T., Greenberger, D., & Wexler, P. (1989). Gender differences in what is desired in the sexual relationship. *Journal of Psychology and Human Sexuality, 1*, 39–52.

Haugtvedt, C. P., & Wegener, D. T. (1994). Message order effects in persuasion: An attitude strength perspective. *Journal of Consumer Research, 21*, 205–218.

Hays, R. B. (1984). The development and maintenance of friendship. *Journal of Social and Personal Relationships, 1*, 75–98.

Hazan, C., & Shaver, P. (1987). Romantic love conceptualized as an attachment process. *Journal of Personality and Social Psychology, 52*, 511–524.

Hazan, C., & Shaver, P. (1990). Love and work: An attachment-theoretical perspective. *Journal of Personality and Social Psychology, 59*, 270–280.

Heatherton, T. F., & Nichols, P. A. (1994). Personal accounts of successful versus failed attempts at life change. *Personality and Social Psychology Bulletin, 20*, 664–675.

Heider, F. (1944). Social perception and phenomenal causality. *Psychological Review, 51*, 358–374.

Heider, F. (1958). *The psychology of interpersonal relations.* New York: Wiley.

Heilman, M. E., Battle, W. S., Keller, C. E., & Lee, R. A. (1998). Type of affirmative action policy: A determinant of reactions to sex-based preferential selection? *Journal of Applied Psychology, 83*, 190–205.

Heilman, M. E., Simon, M. C., & Repper, D. P. (1987). Intentionally favored, unintentionally harmed? Impact of sex-based preferential selection on self-perceptions and self-evaluations. *Journal of Applied Psychology, 72*, 62–68.

Heilman, M. E., & Stopeck, M. H. (1985). Attractiveness and corporate success: Different causal attributions for males and females. *Journal of Applied Psychology, 70*, 379–388.

Heine, S. J., & Lehman, D. R. (1997). Culture, dissonance, and self-affirmation. *Personality and Social Psychology Bulletin, 23*, 389–400.

Hejmadi, A., Davidson, R. J., & Rozin, P. (2000). Exploring Hindu Indian emotion expressions: Evidence for accurate recognition by Americans and Indians. *Psychological Science, 11*, 183–187.

Helgeson, V. S., & Mickelson, K. D. (1995). Motives for social comparison. *Personality and Social Psychology Bulletin, 21*, 1200–1209.

Hemstrom, O. (1996). Is marriage dissolution linked to differences in mortality risks for men and women? *Journal of Marriage and the Family, 58*, 366–378.

Henderson-King, E. I., & Nisbett, R. E. (1996). Anti-black prejudice as a function of exposure to the negative behavior of a single black person. *Journal of Personality and Social Psychology, 71*, 654–664.

Hendrick, S., Hendrick, C., & Adler, N. L. (1988). Romantic relationships: Love, satisfaction, and staying together. *Journal of Personality and Social Psychology, 54*, 980–988.

Hendrick, S., Hendrick, C., Slapion-Foote, M. J., & Foote, F. H. (1985). Gender differences in sexual attitudes. *Journal of Personality and Social Psychology, 48*, 1630–1642.

Henggeler, S. W., Schoenwald, S. K., Borduin, D. M., Rowland, M. D., & Cunningham, P. B. (1998). *Multisystemic treatment of antisocial behavior in children and adolescents: Treatment manuals for practitioners.* New York: Guilford Press.

Hensley, T. R., & Griffin, G. W. (1986). Victims of groupthink: The Kent State University Board of Trustees and the 1977 gymnasium controversy. *Journal of Conflict Resolution, 30*, 497–531.

Henslin, J. M. (2003). Doing the unthinkable: Eating your friends is the hardest: The survivors of the F-227. In *Down to earth sociology: Introductory readings* (12th ed., pp. 261–270). New York: Free Press.

Herlocker, C. E., Allison, S. T., Foubert, J. D., & Beggan, J. K. (1997). Intended and unintended overconsumption of physical, spatial, and temporal responses. *Journal of Personality and Social Psychology, 73*, 992–1004.

Herrett-Skjellum, J., & Allen, M. (1996). Television programming and sex stereotyping: A meta-analysis. In B. R. Burleson (Ed.), *Communication yearbook 19* (pp. 157–185). Thousand Oaks, CA: Sage Publications.

Hersey, P., & Blanchard, K. H. (1982). *Management of organizational behavior* (4th ed.). Englewood Cliffs, NJ: Prentice Hall.

Hertel, G., & Kerr, N. L. (2001). Priming in-group favoritism: The impact of normative scripts in the minimal group paradigm. *Journal of Experimental Social Psychology, 37*, 316–324.

Hertel, G., Kerr, N. L., & Messe, L. A. (2000). Motivation gains in performance groups: Paradigmatic and theoretical developments on the Kohler effect. *Journal of Personality and Social Psychology, 79*, 580–601.

Hewstone, M., Jaspars, J., & Lalljee, M. (1982). Social representations, social attribution and social identity: The intergroup images of "public" and "comprehensive" schoolboys. *European Journal of Social Psychology, 12*, 241–269.

Hewstone, M., Rubin, M., & Willis, H. (2002). Intergroup bias. *Annual Review of Psychology, 51*, 575–604.

Heymann, T. (1989). *On an average day.* New York: Fawcett Columbine.

Higgins, E. T. (1987). Self-discrepancy: A theory relating self and affect. *Psychological Review, 94*, 319–340.

Higgins, E. T. (1996a). Knowledge activation: Accessibility, applicability, and salience. In E. T. Higgins & A. W. Kruglanski (Eds.), *Social psychology: Handbook of basic principles* (pp. 133–168). New York: Guilford.

Higgins, E. T. (1996b). The "self digest": Self-knowledge serving self-regulatory functions. *Journal of Personality and Social Psychology, 71*, 1062–1083.

Higgins, E. T. (1998a). The aboutness principle: A pervasive influence on human inference. *Social Cognition, 16*, 173–198.

Higgins, E. T. (1998b). Promotion and prevention: Regulatory focus as a motivational principle. In M. P. Zanna (Ed.), *Advances in experimental social psychology* (Vol. 30, pp. 1–46). New York: Academic Press.

Higgins, E. T., & Bargh, J. A. (1987). Social cognition and social perception. *Annual Review of Psychology, 38*, 369–425.

Higgins, E. T., King, G. A., & Mavin, G. H. (1982). Individual construct accessibility and subjective impressions and recall. *Journal of Personality and Social Psychology, 43*, 35–47.

Higgins, E. T., & McCann, C. D. (1984). Social encoding and subsequent attitudes, impressions, and memory: "Context-driven" and motivational aspects of processing. *Journal of Personality and Social Psychology, 47*, 26–39.

Higgins, E. T., & Rholes, W. S. (1978). Saying is believing: Effects of message modification on memory and liking for the person described. *Journal of Experimental Social Psychology, 14*, 363–378.

Higgins, E. T., Rholes, W. S., & Jones, C. R. (1977). Category accessibility and impression formation. *Journal of Experimental Social Psychology, 13*, 141–154.

Higgins, E. T., Roney, C. J. R., Crowe, E., & Hymes, C. (1994). Ideal versus ought predilections for approach and avoidance distinct self-regulatory systems. *Journal of Personality and Social Psychology, 66*, 276–286.

Higgins, E. T., Shah, J., & Friedman, R. (1997). Emotional responses to goal attainment: Strength of regulatory focus as moderator. *Journal of Personality and Social Psychology, 72*, 515–525.

Hill, C. T., Rubin, Z., & Peplau, L. A. (1976). Breakups before marriage: The end of 103 affairs. *Journal of Social Issues, 32*(1), 147–168.

Hill, H., Soriano, F. I., Chen, A., & LaFromboise, T. D. (1994). Sociocultural factors in the etiology and prevention of violence among ethnic minority youth. In L. D. Eron, J. H. Gentry, & P. Schlegel (Eds.), *Reason to hope: A psychosocial perspective on violence and youth* (pp. 59–97). Washington, DC: American Psychological Association.

Hillery, J. M., & Fugita, S. S. (1975). Group size effects in employment testing. *Educational and Psychological Measurement, 35*, 745–750.

Hilton, J. L., & Darley, J. M. (1985). Constructing other persons: A limit on the effect. *Journal of Experimental Social Psychology, 21*, 1–18.

Hines, D., Saris, R. N., & Throckmorton-Belzer, L. (2002). Pluralistic ignorance and health risk behaviors: Do college students misperceive social approval for risky behaviors on campus and in media. *Journal of Applied Social Psychology, 32*, 2621–2640.

Hinsz, V. B., & Davis, J. H. (1984). Persuasive arguments theory, group polarization, and choice shifts. *Personality and Social Psychology Bulletin, 10*, 260–268.

Hiroto, D. S. (1974). Locus of control and learned helplessness. *Journal of Experimental Psychology, 102*, 187–193.

Hirschman, R. S., & Leventhal, H. (1989). Preventing smoking behavior in school children: An initial test of a cognitive-development program. *Journal of Applied Social Psychology, 19*, 559–583.

Hirt, E. R., & Markman, K. D. (1995). Multiple explanation: A consider-an-alternative strategy for debiasing judgments. *Journal of Personality and Social Psychology, 69*, 1069–1086.

Hirt, E. R., McCrea, S. M., & Boris, H. I. (2003). "I know you self-handicapped last exam": Gender differences in reactions to self-handicapping. *Journal of Personality and Social Psychology, 84*, 177–193.

Hodgins, H. S., & Zuckerman, M. (1993). Beyond selecting information: Biases in spontaneous questions and resultant conclusions. *Journal of Experimental Social Psychology, 29*, 387–407.

Hoelter, J. W. (1985). The structure of self-conception: Conceptualization and measurement. *Journal of Personality and Social Psychology, 49*, 1392–1407.

Hoffman, C., & Hurst, N. (1990) Gender stereotypes: perception or rationalization? *Journal of Personality and Social Psychology, 58*, 197–208.

Hoffman, M. L. (1981). Is altruism part of human nature? *Journal of Personality and Social Psychology, 40*, 121–137.

Hoffman, M. L. (1986). Affect, cognition, motivation. In R. M. Sorrentino & E. T. Higgins (Eds.), *Handbook of motivation and cognition: Foundations of social behavior* (Vol. 1, pp. 244–280). New York: Guilford Press.

Hofling, C. K., Brotzman, E., Dalrymple, S., Graves, N., & Pierce, C. M. (1966). An experimental study in nurse–physician relationships. *Journal of Nervous and Mental Disease, 143*, 171–180.

Hogan, R., Curphy, G. J., & Hogan, J. (1994). What we know about leadership: Effectiveness and personality. *American Psychologist, 49*, 493–504.

Hogarth, R. M., & Einhorn, H. J. (1992). Order effects in belief updating: The belief-adjustment model. *Cognitive Psychology, 24*, 1–55.

Hogg, M. A. (1987). Social identity and group cohensiveness. In J. C. Turner (Ed.), *Rediscovering the social group: A self-categorization theory* (pp. 89–116). Oxford, UK: Basil Blackwell.

Hogg, M. A. (1996). Social identity, self-categorization, and the small group. In E. H. Witte & J. A. Davis (Eds.), *Understanding group behavior, Vol. 2: Small group processes and interpersonal relations* (pp. 227–253). Mahwah, NJ: Lawrence Erlbaum Associates, Inc.

Hogg, M. A., & Abrams, D. (1988). *Social identifications*. London: Routledge.

Hogg, M. A., & Abrams, D. (1993). Toward a single-process uncertainty-reduction model of social motivation in groups. In M. A. Hogg & D. Abrams (Eds.), *Group motivation: Social psychological perspectives* (pp. 173–190). London: Harvester Wheatsheaf.

Hogg, M. A., Abrams, D., Otten, S., & Hinkle, S. (2004). The social identity perspective: Intergroup relations, self-conception, and small groups. *Small Group Research, 35*, 246–276.

Hogg, M. A., Cooper-Shaw, L., & Holzworth, D. W. (1993). Group prototypicality and depersonalized attraction in small interactive groups. *Personality and Social Psychology Bulletin, 19*, 452–465.

Hogg, M. A., & Hardie, E. A. (1991). Social attraction, personal attraction, and self-categorization: A field study. *Personality and Social Psychology Bulletin, 17*, 175–180.

Hogg, M. A., & Turner, J. C. (1987). Intergroup behavior, self-stereotyping and the salience of social categories. *British Journal of Social Psychology, 26*, 325–340.

Holland, R. W., Verplanken, B., & van Knippenberg, A. (2002). On the nature of attitude–behavior relations: The strong guide, the weak follow. *European Journal of Social Psychology, 32*, 869–876.

Holland, R. W., Verplanken, B., & van Knippenberg, A. (2003). From repetition to conviction: Attitude accessibility as a determinant of attitude certainty. *Journal of Experimental Social Psychology, 39*, 594–601.

Hollander, E. P. (1958). Conformity, status, and idiosyncrasy credit. *Psychological Review, 65,* 117–127.

Hollander, E. P. (1985). Leadership and power. In G. Lindzey & E. Aronson (Eds.), *Handbook of social psychology* (3rd ed., Vol. 2, pp. 485–537). New York: Random House.

Hollingshead, A. B. (2004). Communication technologies, the internet, and group research. In M. B. Brewer & M. Hewstone (Eds), *Applied social psychology: Perspectives on social psychology* (pp. 301–317). Malden, MA: Blackwell.

Hollingshead, A. B., McGrath, J. E., & O'Connor, K. M. (1993). Group task performance and communication technology: A longitudinal study of computer-mediated versus face-to-face work groups. *Small Group Research, 24,* 307–333.

Holsti, O. R., & North, R. (1965). The history of human conflict. In E. B. McNeil (Ed.), *The nature of human conflict* (pp. 155–171). Englewood Cliffs, NJ: Prentice Hall.

Holt, J. L., & DeVore, C. J. (2005). Culture, gender, organizational role, and styles of conflict resolution: A meta-analysis. *International Journal of Intercultural Relations, 29*(2), 165–196, Retrieved November 17, 2005, from PsycINFO database.

Hoover, C. W., Wood, E. E., & Knowles, E. S. (1983). Forms of social awareness and helping. *Journal of Experimental Social Psychology, 19,* 577–590.

Hopthrow, T., & Hulbert, L. G. (2005). The effect of group decision making on cooperation in social dilemmas. *Group Processes and Intergroup Relations, 8,* 89–100.

Hornsey, M. J., & Hogg, M. A. (2000). Subgroup relations: A comparison of mutual intergroup differentiation and common ingroup identity models of prejudice reduction. *Personality and Social Psychology Bulletin, 26,* 242–256.

Hornsey, M. J., & Jetten, J. (2004). The individual within the group: Balancing the need to belong with the need to be different. *Personality & Social Psychology Review, 8*(3), 248–264.

Hornsey, M. J., Majkut, L., Terry, D. J., & McKimmis, B. M. (2003). On being loud and proud: Non-conformity and counter-conformity to group norms. *British Journal of Social Psychology, 42,* 319–335.

Hornstein, H. A. (1975). Social psychology as social intervention. In M. Deutch & H. A. Hornstein (Eds.), *Applying social psychology: Implications for research, practice, and training* (pp. 211–234). Hillsdale, NJ: Lawrence Erlbaum Associates, Inc.

Horowitz, M. J. (1987). *States of mind.* New York: Plenum.

Horwitz, M., & Rabbie, J. M. (1982). Individuality and membership in the intergroup system. In H. Tajfel (Ed.), *Social identity and intergroup relations* (pp. 241–274). New York: Cambridge University Press.

Hosey, G. R., Wood, M., Thompson, R. J., & Druck, P. L. (1985). Social facilitation in a "non-social" animal, the centipede Lithobius forficatus. *Behavioural Processes, 10,* 1–2.

House, R. J., & Shamir, B. (1993). Towarad the integration of transformational, charismatic, and visionary theories. In M. M. Chemers & R. Ayman (Eds.), *Leadership theory and research: Perspectives and directions* (pp. 81–107). San Diego, CA: Academic Press.

Hovland, C. I., Janis, I. L., & Kelley, H. H. (1953). *Communication and persuasion.* New Haven, CT: Yale University Press.

Hovland, C. I., Lumsdaine, A., & Sheffield, F. (1949). *Experiments on mass communication.* Princeton, NJ: Princeton University Press.

Hovland, C. I., & Weiss, W. (1951). The influence of source credibility on communication effectiveness. *Public Opinion Quarterly, 15,* 635–650.

Howard, D. J. (1997). Familiar phrases as peripheral persuasion cue. *Journal of Experimental Social Psychology, 33,* 231–243.

Howard, J. A., Blumstein, P., & Schwartz, P. (1987). Social or evolutionary theories? Some observations on preferences in human mate selection. *Journal of Personality and Social Psychology, 53,* 194–200.

Howard, L. (1990, July 9). Periscope. *Newsweek,* p. 7.

Hoyle, R. H., Pinkley, R. L., & Insko, C. A. (1989). Perceptions of social behavior: Evidence of differing expectations for interpersonal and intergroup interaction. *Personality and Social Psychology Bulletin, 15,* 365–376.

Hsu, F. L. K. (1983). *Rugged individualism reconsidered.* Knoxville, TN: University of Tennesee Press.

Huckfeldt, R., & Sprague, J. (2000). Political consequences of inconsistency: The accessibility and stability of abortion attitudes. *Political Psychology, 21,* 57–79.

Huesmann, L. R. (1986). Psychological processes promoting the relation between exposure to media violence and aggressive behavior by the viewer. *Journal of Social Issues, 42*(3), 125–139.

Huesmann, L. R., & Eron, L. D. (1984). Cognitive processes and the persistence of aggressive behavior. *Aggressive Behavior, 10,* 243–251.

Huesmann, L. R., & Eron, L. D. (1986). *Television and aggressive child: A cross-national comparison.* Hillsdale, NJ: Lawrence Erlbaum Associates, Inc.

Huesmann, L. R., Eron, L. D., Klein, R., Brice, P., & Fischer, P. (1983). Mitigating the imitation of aggressive behaviors by changing childrens' attitudes about media violence. *Journal of Personality and Social Psychology, 44,* 899–910.

Huesmann, L. R., Eron, L. D., & Yarmel, P. W. (1987). Intellectual functioning and aggression. *Journal of Personality and Social Psychology, 52,* 232–240.

Huff, C., Sproull, L., & Kiesler, S. (1989). Computer communication and organizational commitment: Tracing the relationship in a city government. *Journal of Applied Social Psychology, 19,* 1371–1391.

Hulbert, M. (2001, June 17). Forget about efficient markets. Let the sun shine in. *New York Times,* p. BU7.

Hull, J. G. (1981). A self-awareness model of the causes and effects of alcohol consumption. *Journal of Abnormal Psychology, 90,* 586–600.

Humphrey, R. (1985). How work roles influence perception: Structural-cognitive processes and organizational behavior. *American Sociological Review, 50,* 242–252.

Hunt, W. A., Matarazzo, J. D., Weiss, S. M., & Gentry, W. D. (1979). Associative learning, habit and health behavior. *Journal of Behavioral Medicine, 2,* 111–124.

Hunter, C. E., & Ross, M. W. (1991). Determinants of health-care workers' attitudes toward people with AIDS. *Journal of Applied Social Psychology, 21,* 947–956.

Hurtz, W., & Durkin, K. (1997). Gender role stereotyping in Australian radio commercials. *Sex Roles, 36,* 103–114.

Hyde, J. S. (1979). *Understanding human sexuality.* New York: McGraw-Hill.

Ickes, W., & Simpson, J. A. (1997). Managing empathic accuracy in close relationships. In W. J. Ickes (Ed.), *Empathic accuracy* (pp. 218–250). New York: Guilford Press.

Ikard, F. F., Green, D. E., & Horn, D. (1969). A scale to differentiate between types of smoking as related to the management of affect. *The International Journal of the Addictions, 4,* 649–659.

Ilgen, D. R., Hollenbeck, J. R., Johnson, M., & Jundt, D. (2005). Teams in organizations: From Input-Process-Output models to IMOI models. *Annual Review of Psychology, 56,* 517–43.

Indianapolis Star. (1989, September 12).

Information Please. (2006). Retrieved July 13 2006 from http://www.infoplease.com/ipa/A0904550.html.

Insko, C. A. (1981). Balance theory and phenomenology. In R. Petty, T. Ostrom, & T. Brock (Eds.), *Cognitive responses and persuasion.* Hillsdale, NJ: Lawrence Erlbaum Associates, Inc.

Insko, C. A., Dreenan, S., Soloman, M. R., Smith, R., & Wade, T. J. (1983). Conformity as a function of the consistency of positive self-evaluation with being liked an being right. *Journal of Experimental Social Psychology, 19,* 341–358.

Insko, C. A., Hoyle, R. H., Pinkley, R. L., Hong, G.-Y., Slim, R. M., Dalton, B. and others (1988). Individual–group discontinuity: The role of a consensus rule. *Journal of Experimental Social Psychology, 24,* 505–519.

Insko, C. A., Pinkley, R. L., Hoyle, R. H., & Dalton, B. (1987). Individual versus group discontinuity: The role of intergroup contact. *Journal of Experimental Social Psychology, 23,* 250–267.

Insko, C. A., & Schopler, J. (1987). Categorization, competition, and collectivity. In C. Hendrick (Ed.), *Group processes* (Vol. 8, pp. 213–251). New York: Sage.

Insko, C. A., & Schopler, J. (1998). Differential distrust of groups and individuals. In C. Sedikides, J. Schopler, & C. Insko (Eds.), *Intergroup cognition and intergroup behavior* (pp. 75–108). Mahwah, NJ: Lawrence Erlbaum Associates, Inc.

Insko, C. A., Schopler, J., Hoyle, R. H., Dardis, G. J., & Graetz, K. A. (1990). Individual–group discontinuity as a function of fear and greed. *Journal of Personality and Social Psychology, 58,* 68–79.

Insko, C. A., Thompson, V. D., Stroebe, W., Shaud, K. F., Pinner, B. E., & Layton, B. D. (1973). Implied evaluation and the similarity-attraction effect. *Journal of Personality and Social Psychology, 25,* 297–308.

Insko, C. A., & Wilson, M. (1977). Interpersonal attraction as a function of social interaction. *Journal of Personality and Social Psychology, 35,* 903–911.

IPCC (2001). *Climate Change 2001: The Scientific Basis.* Contribution of Working Group I to the Third Assessment Report of the Intergovernmental Panel on Climate Change (J. T. Houghton and others, Eds.). Cambridge, UK: Cambridge University Press.

Isen, A. M. (1970). Success, failure, attention, and reaction to others: The warm glow of success. *Journal of Personality and Social Psychology, 15,* 294–301.

Isen, A. M. (1987). Positive affect, cognitive processes, and social behavior. In L. Berkowitz (Ed.), *Advances in experimental social psychology* (Vol. 20, pp. 203–253). New York: Academic Press.

Isen, A. M., & Levin, P. F. (1972). The effect of feeling good on helping: Cookies and kindness. *Journal of Personality and Social Psychology, 21,* 384–388.

Isen, A., & Simmonds, S. F. (1978). The effect of feeling good on a helping task that is incompatible with good mood. *Social Psychology, 41,* 345–349.

Islam, M. R., & Hewstone, M. (1993). Intergroup attributions and affective consequences in majority and minority groups. *Journal of Personality and Social Psychology, 64,* 936–950.

Isozaki, M. (1984). The effects of discussion on polarization of judgment. *Japanese Psychological Research, 26,* 187–198.

Ito, T. A., Larsen, J. T., Smith, N. K., & Cacioppo, J. T. (1998). Negative information weighs more heavily on the brain: The negativity bias in evaluative categorizations. *Journal of Personality & Social Psychology, 75,* 887–900.

Ito, T. A., Miller, N., & Pollock, V. E. (1996). Alcohol and aggression: A meta-analysis on the moderating effects of inhibitory cues, triggering events, and self-focused attention. *Psychological Bulletin, 120,* 60–82.

Iyer, A., Leach, C. W., & Crosby, F. J. (2003). White guilt and racial compensation: The benefits and limits of self-focus. *Personality and Social Psychology Bulletin, 29*(1), 117–129.

Jablin, F. M. (1982). Formal structural characteristics of organizations and superior–subordinate communication. *Human Communication Research, 8,* 338–347.

Jackman, M. R., & Senter, M. S. (1981). Beliefs about race, gender, and social class: Different therefore unequal. In D. J. Treiman & R. V. Robinson (Eds.), *Research in stratification and mobility* (Vol. 2, pp. 309–335). Greenwich, CT: JAI Press.

Jackson, C. (2002). Perceived legitimacy of parental authority and tobacco and alcohol use during early adolescence. *Journal of Adolescent Health, 31,* 425–432.

Jackson, L. A., Sullivan, L. A., Harnish, R., & Hodge, C. N. (1996). Achieving positive social identity: Social mobility, social creativity, and permeability of group boundaries. *Journal of Personality and Social Psychology, 70,* 241–254.

Jackson, L. A., & Sullivan, L. A. (1989). Cognition and affect in evaluations of stereotyped group members. *Journal of Social Psychology, 129,* 659–672.

Jackson, L. M., & Esses, V. M. (1997). Of scripture and ascription: The relation between religious fundamentalism and intergroup helping. *Personality and Social Psychology Bulletin, 23,* 893–906.

Jacoby, J., & Hoyer, W. D. (1989). The comprehension/miscomprehension of print communication: Selected findings. *Journal of Consumer Research, 15,* 434–443.

Jacoby, J., Hoyer, W. D., & Sheluga, D. A. (1980). *Miscomprehension of televised communications.* New York: American Association of Advertising Agencies.

Jaffe, E. (2005, September). How random is that? *APS Observer, 18,* 20–30.

James, W. (1884). What is an emotion? *Mind, 9,* 188–205.

James, W. (1890). *Psychology.* New York: Holt.

Janis, I. (1972). *Victims of groupthink.* Boston: Houghton Mifflin.

Janis, I. (1982). *Groupthink* (2nd ed.). Boston: Houghton Mifflin.

Janis, I. L., Kaye, D., & Kirschner, P. (1965). Facilitating effects of "eating while reading" on responsiveness to persuasive communications. *Journal of Personality and Social Psychology, 1,* 181–186.

Janis, I. L., & Terwilliger, R. (1962). An experimental study of psychological resistances to fear-arousing communication. *Journal of Abnormal and Social Psychology, 65,* 403–410.

Jason, L. A., Reichler, A., Easton, J., Neal, A., & Wilson, M. (1984). Female harassment after ending a relationship: A preliminary study. *Alternative Lifestyles, 6*, 259–269.

Jennings, J., Geis, F. L., & Brown, V. (1980). Influence of television commercials on women's self-confidence and independent judgment. *Journal of Personality and Social Psychology, 38*, 203–210.

Jensen-Campbell, L. A., Graziano, W. G., & West, S. G. (1995). Dominance, prosocial orientation, and female preferences: Do nice guys really finish last? *Journal of Personality and Social Psychology, 68*, 427–440.

Jepson, C., & Chaiken, S. (1990). Chronic issue-specific fear inhibits systematic processing of persuasive communications. *Journal of Social Behavior and Personality, 2*, 61–84.

Jervis, R. (1976). *Perception and misperception in international politics*. Princeton, NJ: Princeton University Press.

Jetten, J., Branscombe, N. R., Schmitt, M. T., & Spears, R. (2001). Rebels with a cause: Group identification as a response to perceived discrimination from the mainstream. *Personality and Social Psychology Bulletin, 27*(9), 1204–1213.

Jetten, J., Postmes, T., & McAuliffe, B. J. (2002). "We're all individuals": Group norms of individualism and collectivism, levels of identification and identity threat. *European Journal of Social Psychology, 32*, 189–207.

Ji, L.-J., Nisbett, R. E., & Su, Y. (2001). Culture, change, and prediction. *Psychological Science, 12*, 450–456.

Johannessen, K., & Glider, P. (2003). The University of Arizona's campus health social norms media campaign. In H. W. Perkins (Ed.), *The social norms approach to preventing school and college age substance abuse: A handbook for educators, counselors, and clinicians* (pp. 65–82). San Francisco, CA: Jossey Bass.

Johnson, D. W., Maruyama, G., Johnson, R. T., Nelson, D., & Skon, L. (1981). The effects of cooperative, competitive, and individualistic goal structures on achievement: A meta-analysis. *Psychological Bulletin, 89*, 47–62.

Johnson, E. J., & Tversky, A. (1983). Affect, generalization, and the perception of risk. *Journal of Personality and Social Psychology, 45*, 20–31.

Johnson, R. D., & Downing, L. L. (1979). Deindividuation and valence of cues: Effects on prosocial and antisocial behavior. *Journal of Personality and Social Psychology, 37*, 1532–1538.

Johnson, R. W., Kelly, R. J., & LeBlanc, B. A. (1995). Motivational basis of dissonance: Aversive consequences or inconsistency. *Personality and Social Psychology Bulletin, 21*, 850–855.

Johnston, J., & Ettema, J. (1986). Using television to best advantage: Research for prosocial television. In J. Bryant & D. Zillman (Eds.), *Perspectives on media effects* (pp. 143–164). Hillsdale, NJ: Lawrence Erlbaum Associates, Inc.

Johnston, L., & Hewstone, M. (1992). Cognitive models of stereotype change. 3. Subtyping and the perceived typicality of disconfirming group members. *Journal of Experimental Social Psychology, 28*, 360–386.

Johnston, L., & Macrae, C. N. (1994). Changing social stereotypes: The case of the information seeker. *European Journal of Social Psychology, 24*, 581–592.

Jones, E. E. (1985). Major developments in social psychology during the last five decades. In G. Lindzey & E. Aronson (Eds.), *Handbook of social psychology* (Vol. I, pp. 47–107). New York: Random House.

Jones, E. E. (1990a). Constrained behavior and self-concept change. In J. M. Olson & M. P. Zanna (Eds.), *Self-inference processes: The Ontario Symposium* (Vol. 6, pp. 69–86). Hillsdale, NJ: Lawrence Erlbaum Associates, Inc.

Jones, E. E. (1990b). *Interpersonal perception*. New York: Freeman.

Jones, E. E., Brenner, K., & Knight, J. G. (1990). When failure elevates self-esteem. *Personality and Social Psychology Bulletin, 16*, 200–209.

Jones, E. E., & Davis, K. E. (1965). A theory of correspondent inferences: From acts to dispositions. In L. Berkowitz (Ed.), *Advances in experimental social psychology* (Vol. 2, pp. 219–266). New York: Academic Press.

Jones, E. E., & Gerard, H. B. (1967). *Foundations of social psychology*. New York: Wiley.

Jones, E. E., & Harris, V. A. (1967). The attribution of attitudes. *Journal of Experimental Social Psychology, 3*, 1–24.

Jones, E. E., & Nisbett, R. E. (1972). The actor and the observer: Divergent perceptions of the causes of behavior. In E. E. Jones, D. E. Kanouse, H. H. Kelley, R. E. Nisbett, S. Valins, & B. Weiner (Eds.), *Attribution: Perceiving the causes of behavior* (pp. 79–94). Morristown, NJ: General Learning Press.

Jones, E. E., & Pittman, T. S. (1982). Toward a general theory of strategic self-presentation. In J. Suls (Ed.), *Psychological perspectives on the self* (Vol. 1, pp. 231–262). Hillsdale, NJ: Lawrence Erlbaum Associates, Inc.

Jones, E. E., Rhodewalt, F., Berglas, S., & Skelton, J. A. (1981). Effects of strategic self-presentation on subsequent self-esteem. *Journal of Personality and Social Psychology, 41*, 407–421.

Jones, E. E., Rock, L., Shaver, K. G., Goethals, G. R., & Ward, L. M. (1968). Pattern of performance and ability attribution. An unexpected primacy effect. *Journal of Personality and Social Psychology, 10*, 317–340.

Jones, J. M. (1992). Understanding the mental health consequences of race: Contributions of basic social psychological processes. In D. N. Ruble, P. R. Costanzo, & M. E. Oliveri (Eds.), *The social psychology of mental health* (pp. 199–240). New York: Guilford Press.

Jones, R. A., & Brehm, J. W. (1970). Persuasiveness of one-sided and two-sided communications as a function of the awareness that there are two sides. *Journal of Experimental Social Psychology, 6*, 47–56.

Jordan, C. H., Spencer, S. J., Zanna, M. P., Hoshino-Browne, E., & Correll, J. (2003). Secure and defensive high self-esteem. *Journal of Personality & Social Psychology, 85*(5), 969–978.

Josephs, R. A., Larrick, R. P., Steele, C. M., & Nisbett, R. E. (1992). Protecting the self from the negative consequences of risky decisions. *Journal of Personality and Social Psychology, 62*, 26–37.

Josephs, R. A., Markus, H. R., & Tafarodi, R. W. (1992). Gender and self-esteem. *Journal of Personality and Social Psychology, 63*, 391–402.

Jost, J. T., & Banaji, M. R. (1994). The role of stereotyping in system-justification and the production of false consciousness. *British Journal of Social Psychology, 33*, 1–27.

Jost, J. T., & Hamilton, D. L. (2005). Stereotypes in our culture. In J. F. Dovidio, P. Glic, & L. A. Rudman (Eds.), *On the nature of prejudice: Fifty years after Allport* (pp. 208–224). Malden, MA: Blackwell.

Joule, R. V., & Beauvois, J. L. (1998). Cognitive dissonance theory: A radical view. In W. Stroebe & M. Hewstone (Eds.), *European review of social psychology, Vol 8* (pp. 1–32). New York: John Wiley & Sons, Inc.

Judd, C. M., & Kulik, J. A. (1980). Schematic effects of social attitudes on information processing and recall. *Journal of Personality and Social Psychology, 38,* 569–578.

Judd, C. M., & Park, B. (1988). Out-group homogeneity: Judgments of variability at the individual and group levels. *Journal of Personality and Social Psychology, 54,* 778–788.

Judd, C. M., & Park, B. (2005). Group differences and stereotype accuracy. In J. F. Dovidio, P. Glic, & L. A. Rudman (Eds.), *On the nature of prejudice: Fifty years after Allport* (pp. 123–138). Malden, MA: Blackwell.

Judd, C. M., Park, B., Ryan, C. S., Brauer, M., & Kraus, S. (1995). Stereotypes and ethnocentrism: Diverging interethnic perceptions of African American and White American youth. *Journal of Personality and Social Psychology, 69,* 460–481.

Judd, C. M., Smith, E. R., & Kidder, L. H. (1991). *Research methods in social relations* (6th ed.). Fort Worth, TX: Holt, Rinehart, & Winston.

Judge, T. A., & Cable, D. M. (2004). The effect of physical height on workplace success and income: Preliminary test of a theoretical model. *Journal of Applied Psychology, 89,* 428–441.

Judge, T. A., Piccolo, R. F., & Ilies, R. (2004). The forgotten ones? The validity of consideration and initiating structure in leadership research. *Journal of Applied Psychology, 89,* 36–51.

Jussim, L. (2005). Accuracy in social perception: Criticisms, controversies, criteria, components, and cognitive processes. *Advances in Experimental Social Psychology, 37,* 1–93.

Jussim, L., & Harber, K. (2005). Teacher expectations and self-fulfilling prophecies: Knowns and unknowns, resolved and unresolved controversies. *Personality and Social Psychology Review, 9,* 131–155.

Kachadourian, L. K., Fincham, F., & Davila, J. (2004). The tendency to forgive in dating and married couples: The role of attachment and relationship satisfaction. *Personal Relationships, 11,* 373–393.

Kahle, L. R., & Berman, J. (1979). Attitudes cause behaviors: A cross-lagged panel analysis. *Journal of Personality and Social Psychology, 37,* 315–321.

Kahneman, D., & Miller, D. T. (1986). Norm theory: Comparing reality to its alternatives. *Psychological Review, 93,* 136–153.

Kaiser, C. R., & Miller, C. T. (2001). Reacting to impending discrimination: Compensation for prejudice and attributions to discrimination. *Personality and Social Psychology Bulletin, 27*(10), 1357–1367.

Kalin, R., & Berry, J. W. (1982). The social ecology of ethnic attitudes in Canada. *Canadian Journal of Behavioral Science, 14,* 97–109.

Kallgren, C. A., & Wood, W. (1986). Access to attitude-relevant informaiton in memory as a determinant of attitude–behavior consistency. *Journal of Experimental Social Psychology, 22,* 328–338.

Kalven, H., Jr., & Ziesel, H. (1966). *The American jury.* London: University of Chicago Press.

Kameda, T., Ohtsubo, Y., & Takezawa, M. (1997). Centrality in sociocognitive networks and social influence: An illustration in a group decision-making context. *Journal of Personality and Social Psychology, 73,* 296–309.

Kameda, T., & Sugimori, S. (1993). Psychological entrapment in group decision making: An assigned decision rule and a groupthink phenomenon. *Journal of Personality and Social Psychology, 65,* 282–292.

Kameda, T., Takezawa, M., & Hastie, R. (2003). The logic of social sharing: An evolutionary game analysis of adaptive norm development. *Personality and Social Psychology Review, 7,* 2–19.

Kanagawa, C., Cross, S. E., & Markus, H. R. (2001). "Who am I?" The cultural psychology of the conceptual self. *Personality and Social Psychology Bulletin, 27,* 90–103.

Kandel, D. B. (1978). Similarity in real-life adolescent friendship pairs. *Journal of Personality and Social Psychology, 36,* 306–312.

Kanter, R. (1977). *Men and women of the corporation.* New York: Basic Books.

Kaplan, M. F., & Martin, A. M. (1999). Effects of differential status of group members on process and outcome of deliberation. *Group Processes and Intergroup Relations, 2,* 347–364.

Kaplan, M. F., & Miller, C. E. (1987). Group decision making and normative versus informational influence: Effects of type of issue and assigned decision rule. *Journal of Personality and Social Psychology, 53,* 306–313.

Kaplan, M. F., & Wilke, H. (2001). Cognitive and social motivation in group decision making. In J. P. Forgas & K. D. Williams (Eds.), *The social mind: Cognitive and motivational aspects of interpersonal behavior.* New York: Cambridge University Press.

Kaplowitz, N. (1990). National self-images, perception of enemies, and conflict strategies: Psychopolitical dimensions of international relations. *Political Psychology, 11,* 39–82.

Karabenick, S. A., Lerner, R. M., & Beecher, M. D. (1973). Relation of political affiliation to helping behavior on election day, November 7, 1972. *Journal of Social Psychology, 91,* 223–227.

Karau, S. J., & Kelly, J. R. (1992). The effects of time scarcity and time abundance on group performance quality and interaction process. *Journal of Experimental Social Psychology, 28,* 542–571.

Karau, S. J., & Williams, K. D. (1993). Social loafing: A meta-analytic review and theoretical integration. *Journal of Personality and Social Psychology, 65,* 681–706.

Karau, S. J., & Williams, K. D. (1997). The effects of group cohesiveness on social loafing and social compensation. *Group Dynamics, 1,* 156–168.

Kardes, F. R., Sanbonmatsu, D. M., Voss, R. T., & Fazio, R. H. (1986). Self-monitoring and attitude accessibility. *Personality and Social Psychology Bulletin, 12,* 468–474.

Karlin, R. A., Rosen, L., & Epstein, Y. (1979). Three into two doesn't go: A follow-up of the effects of overcrowded dormitory rooms. *Personality and Social Psychology Bulletin, 5,* 391–395.

Karpinski, A., & Hilton, J. L. (2001). Attitudes and the implicit association test. *Journal of Personality and Social Psychology, 81,* 774–788.

Karpinski, A., Steinman, R. B., & Hilton, J. L. (2005). Attitude importance as a moderator of the relationship between implicit and explicit attitude measures. *Personality and Social Psychology Bulletin, 31,* 949–962.

Kasser, T., & Ryan, R. M. (1996). Further examining the American dream: Differential correlates of intrinsic and extrinsic goals. *Personality and Social Psychology Bulletin, 22,* 280–287.

Kassin, S. M., & Gudjonsson, G. H. (2004). The psychology of confessions. *Psychological Science in the Public Interest, 5,* 33–67.

Kassin, S. M., & Kiechel, K. L. (1996). The social psychology of false confessions: Compliance, internalization, and confabulation. *Psychological Science*, 7, 125–128.

Katz, D. (1960). The functional approach to the study of attitudes. *Public Opinion Quarterly*, 24, 163–204.

Katz, D. (1965). Nationalism and strategies of international conflict resolution. In H. C. Kelman (Ed.), *International behavior: A social psychological analysis* (pp. 354–390). New York: Holt, Rinehart & Winston.

Katz, D., & Braly, K. W. (1933). Racial stereotypes of 100 college students. *Journal of Abnormal and Social Psychology*, 28, 280–290.

Katz, I. (1981). *Stigma: A social psychological analysis*. Hillsdale, NJ: Lawrence Earlbaum Associates, Inc.

Katz, I., & Hass, R. G. (1988). Racial ambivalence and American value conflict: Correlational and priming studies of dual cognitive structures. *Journal of Personality and Social Psychology*, 55, 893–905.

Kawakami, K., Dovidio, J. F., Moll, J., Hermsen, S., & Russin, A. (2000). Just say no (to stereotyping): Effects of training in the negation of stereotypic associations on stereotype activation. *Journal of Personality and Social Psychology*, 78, 871–888.

Keller, R. T. (1986). Predictors of the performance of project groups in R & D organizations. *Academy of Management Journal*, 29, 715–726.

Kelley, A. E., & Nauta, M. M. (1997). Reactance and thought suppression. *Personality and Social Psychology Bulletin*, 23, 1123–1132.

Kelley, H. H. (1950). The warm–cold variable in first impressions of persons. *Journal of Personality*, 18, 431–439.

Kelley, H. H. (1952). Two functions of reference groups. In G. E. Swanson, T. M. Newcomb, & E. L. Hartley (Eds.), *Readings in social psychology*. New York: Henry Holt.

Kelley, H. H. (1967). Attribution theory in social psychology. In D. Levine (Ed.), *Nebraska symposium on motivation* (Vol. 15, pp. 192–241). Lincoln, NE: University of Nebraska Press.

Kelley, H. H. (1972). Attribution in social interaction. In E. E. Jones and others (Eds.), *Attribution: Perceiving the causes of behavior* (pp. 1–26). Morristown, NJ: General Learning Press.

Kelley, H. H. (1979). *Personal relationships: Their structures and processes*. Hillsdale, NJ: Lawrence Erlbaum Associates, Inc.

Kelley, H. H., Berscheid, E., Christensen, A., Harvey, J. H., Huston, T. L., Levinger, G. and others (Eds.). (1983). *Close relationships*. San Francisco, CA: Freeman.

Kelly, J. R., & Barsade, S. G. (2001). Mood and emotions in small groups and work teams. *Organizational Behavior and Human Decision Processes*, 86, 99–130.

Kelly, J. R., Jackson, J. W., & Hutson-Comeaux, S. L. (1997). The effects of time pressure and task differences on influence modes and accuracy in decision-making groups. *Personality and Social Psychology Bulletin*, 23, 10–22.

Kelly, J. R., & Karau, S. J. (1999). Group decision making: The effects of initial preferences and time pressure. *Personality and Social Psychology Bulletin*, 25, 1342–1354.

Kelly, J. R., & Loving, T. J. (2004). Time pressure and group performance: Exploring underlying processes in the Attentional Focus Model. *Journal of Experimental Social Psychology*, 40, 185–198.

Kelman, H. C. (1961). Processes of opinion change. *Public Opinion Quarterly*, 25, 57–78.

Kelman, H. C. (1973). Violence without moral restraint: Reflections on the dehumanization of victims and victimizers. *Journal of Social Issues*, 29, 25–61.

Kelman, H. C., & Hamilton, V. L. (1989). *Crimes of obedience: Toward a social psychology of authority and responsibility*. New Haven, CT: Yale University Press.

Kelman, H. C., & Hovland, C. I. (1953). "Reinstatement" of the communicator in delayed measurement of opinion change. *Journal of Abnormal and Social Psychology*, 48, 327–335.

Kelman, H. C., & Lawrence, L. (1972). Assignment of responsibility in the case of Lt. Calley: Preliminary report on a national survey. *Journal of Social Issues*, 28(19), 177–212.

Keltner, D., Ellsworth, P. C., & Edwards, K. (1993). Beyond simple pessimism: Effects of sadness and anger on social perception. *Journal of Personality and Social Psychology*, 64, 740–752.

Kenny, D. A. (1991). A general model of consensus and accuracy in interpersonal perception. *Psychological Review*, 98, 155–163.

Kenny, D. A. (1994). Using the social relations model to understand relationships. In R. Erber & R. Gilmour (Eds.), *Theories for the study of relationships* (pp. 111–127). Hillsdale, NJ: Lawrence Erlbaum Associates, Inc.

Kenny, D. A., & DePaulo, B. M. (1993). Do people know how others view them? An empirical and theoretical account. *Psychological Bulletin*, 114, 145–161.

Kenrick, D. T., Sadalla, E. K., Groth, G., & Trost, M. R. (1990). Evolution, traits, and the stages of human courtship: Qualifying the parental investment model. *Journal of Personality and Social Psychology*, 58, 97–116.

Kenworthy, J. B., Turner, R. N., Hewstone, M., & Voci, A. (2005). Intergroup contact. When does it work, and why? In J. F. Dovidio, P. Glic, & L. A. Rudman (Eds.), *On the nature of prejudice: Fifty years after Allport* (pp. 278–292). Malden, MA: Blackwell.

Kernis, M. H., & Goldman, B. M. (2003). Stability and variability in self-concept and self-esteem. In M. R. Leary & J. P. Tangney (Eds.), *Handbook of self and identity* (pp. 106–127). New York: Guilford Press.

Kernis, M. H., Grannemann, B. D., & Barclay, L. C. (1989). Stability and level of self-esteem as predictors of anger arousal and hostility. *Journal of Personality and Social Psychology*, 56, 1013–1022.

Kerr, N. L. (1992). Efficacy as a causal and moderating variable in social dilemmas. In W. Liebrand, D. Messick, & H. Wilke (Eds.), *A social psychological approach to social dilemmas* (pp. 59–88). New York: Pergamon Press.

Kerr, N. L. (1999). Anonymity and social control in social dilemmas. In M. Foddy, M. Smithson, S. Schneider, & M. Hogg (Eds.), *Resolving social dilemmas: Dynamic, structural, and intergroup aspects* (pp. 103–119). New York: Psychology Press.

Kerr, N. L., & Bruun, S (1983). The dispensability of member effort and group motivation losses: Free rider effects. *Journal of Personality and Social Psychology*, 44, 78–94.

Kerr, N. L., & Kaufman-Gilliland, C. M. (1993). *Communication, commitment, and cooperation in social dilemmas*. Unpublished paper, Michigan State University, East Lansing, MI.

Kerr, N. L., MacCoun, R. J., Hansen, C. H., & Hymes, J. A. (1987). Gaining and losing social support: Momentum in decision making groups. *Journal of Experimental Social Psychology*, 23, 119–145.

Kerr, N. L., MacCoun, R. J., & Kramer, G. P. (1996). Bias in judgment: Comparing individuals and groups. *Psychological Review*, 103, 687–719.

Kerr, N. L., & Tindale, R. S. (2004). Group performance and decision making. *Annual Review of Psychology, 55,* 623–655.

Key, W. B. (1992). *The age of manipulation: The con in confidence, the sin in sincere.* New York: Madison Books.

Kiecolt-Glaser, J. K., Fisher, L. D., & Ogrocki, P. (1987). Marital quality, marital disruption, and immune function. *Psychosomatic Medicine, 49,* 13–34.

Kiecolt-Glaser, J. K., Fisher, L. D., Ogrocki, P., Stout, J., Speicher, C. E., & Glaser, R. (1987). Marital quality, marital disruption, and immune function. *Psychosomatic Medicine, 49,* 13–34.

Kiecolt-Glaser, J. K., & Glaser, R. (1988). Psychological influences on immunity: Implications for AIDS. Special issue: Psychology and AIDS. *American Psychologist, 43,* 892–898.

Kiecolt-Glaser, J. K., & Newton, T. L. (2001). Marriage and health: His and hers. *Psychological Bulletin, 127,* 472–503.

Kierein, N. M., & Gold, M. A. (2000). Pygmalion in work organizations: A meta-analysis. *Journal of Organizational Behavior, 21,* 913–928.

Kiesler, C. A. (1971). *The psychology of commitment.* New York: Academic Press.

Kiesler, C. A., & Kiesler, S. (1964). Role of forewarning in persuasive communications. *Journal of Abnormal and Social Psychology, 68,* 547–549.

Kiesler, C. A., & Kiesler, S. B. (1969). *Conformity.* Reading, MA: Addison-Wesley.

Kiesler, S., & Sproull, L. (1992). Group decision making and communication technology. *Organizational Behavior and Human Decision Processes, 52,* 96–123.

Kim, H., & Markus, H. R. (1999). Deviance or uniqueness, harmony or conformity? A cultural analysis. *Journal of Personality and Social Psychology, 77,* 785–800.

Kim, H.-S., & Baron, R. S. (1988). Exercise and the illusory correlation: Does arousal heighten stereotypic processing? *Journal of Experimental Social Psychology, 24,* 366–380.

Kimmel, M. J., Pruitt, P. G., Maganau, J. M., Konar-Goldband, E., & Carnevale, P. J. D. (1980). Effects of trust, aspiration, and gender on negotiation tactics. *Journal of Personality and Social Psychology, 38,* 9–22.

Kinder, D. R. (1986). The continuing American dilemma: White resistance to racial change 40 years after Myrdal. *Journal of Social Issues, 42*(2), 151–171.

Kinder, D. R., & Sears, D. O. (1985). Public opinion and political action. In G. Lindzey & E. Aronson (Eds.), *Handbook of social psychology* (Vol. II, pp. 659–742). New York: Random House.

King, M. L. (1967). *Where do we go from here? Chaos or community.* New York: Harper & Row.

Kinket, B., & Verkuyten, M. (1999). Intergroup evaluations and social context: A multilevel approach. *European Journal of Social Psychology, 29,* 219–238.

Kitayama, S., & Karasawa, M. (1997). Implicit self-esteem in Japan: Name letters and birthday numbers. *Personality and Social Psychology Bulletin, 23,* 736–742.

Kitayama, S., Markus, H. R., & Matsumoto, H. (1995). Culture, self, and emotion: A cultural perspective on "self conscious" emotions. In J. P. Tangney & K. W. Fischer (Eds.), *Self-conscious emotions: The psychology of shame, guilt, embarrassment, and pride* (pp. 366–383). New York: Guilford Press.

Kitayama, S., Markus, H. R., Matsumoto, H., & Norasakkunkit, V. (1997). Individual and collective processes in the construction of the self: Self-enhancement in the United States and self-criticism in Japan. *Journal of Personality and Social Psychology, 72,* 1245–1267.

Kitayama, S., Snibbe, A. C., Markus, H. R., & Suzuki, T. (2004). Is there any "free" choice? Self and dissonance in two cultures. *Psychological Science, 15,* 527–533.

Kitayama, S., Takagi, H., & Matsumoto, H. (1995). Cultural psychology of Japanese self: I. Causal attribution of success and failure. *Japanese Psychological Research, 38,* 247–280.

Kiviniemi, M. T., Synder, M., & Omoto, A. M. (2002). Too many of a good thing? The effects of multiple motivations on stress, cost, fulfillment and satisfaction. *Personality and Social Psychology Bulletin, 28,* 732–743.

Klama, J. [pseudonym for John Durant, Peter Klopfer, and Susan Oyama] (1988). *Aggression: The myth of the beast within.* New York: John Wiley & Sons.

Klandersman, B. (2000). Identity and protest: How group identification helps to overcome collective action dilemmas. In M. Van Vugt, M. Snyder, T. Tyler, & A. Biel (Eds.), *Cooperating in modern society: Promoting the welfare of communities, states, and organizations* (pp. 162–183). London: Routledge.

Kleck, R. E., & Strenta, A. (1980). Perceptions of the impact of negatively valued physical characteristics on social interaction. *Journal of Personality and Social Psychology, 39,* 861–873.

Klein, M. W. (1969). Violence in American juvenile gangs. In D. Mulvihill & M. Tumin, *Crimes violence: A staff report submitted to the National Commission on the Causes and Prevention of Violence* (Vol. 13, pp. 1427–1460). Washington, DC: U.S. Government Printing Office.

Klein, S. B., & Loftus, J. (1993). Behavioral experience and trait judgments about the self. *Personality and Social Psychology Bulletin, 19,* 740–745.

Klein, W. M., & Kunda, Z. (1992). Motivated person perception: Constructing justifications for desired beliefs. *Journal of Experimental Social Psychology, 28,* 145–168.

Klineberg, O. (1986). SPSSI and race relations in the 1950s and after. *Journal of Social Issues, 42*(4), 53–60.

Kluegel, J. R., & Smith, E. R. (1986). *Beliefs about inequality: Americans' views of what is and what ought to be.* Hawthorne, NY: Aldine de Gruyter.

Knapp, M. L. (1978). *Nonverbal communication in human interaction.* New York: Holt, Rinehart, Winston.

Knee, C. R. (1998). Implicit theories of relationships: Assessment and prediction of romantic relationship initiation, coping, and longevity. *Journal of Personality and Social Psychology, 74,* 360–370.

Knee, C. R., Patrick, H., & Lonsbary, C. (2003). Implicit theories of relationships: Orientations toward evaluation and cultivation. *Personality and Social Psychology Review, 7,* 41–55.

Knight, P. A., & Weiss, H. M. (1980). *Benefits of suffering: Communicator suffering, benefiting, and influence.* Paper presented at the American Psychological convention.

Knox, R. E., & Inkster, J. A. (1968). Postdecision dissonance at post time. *Journal of Personality and Social Psychology, 8,* 319–323.

Knudson, R. M., Sommers, A. A., & Golding, S. L. (1980). Interpersonal perception and mode of resolution in marital conflict. *Journal of Personality and Social Psychology, 38,* 751–763.

Kobak, R. R., & Hazan, C. (1991). Attachment in marriage: Effects of security and accuracy of working models. *Journal of Personality and Social Psychology, 60,* 861–869.

Kobrynowicz, D., & Biernat, M. (1997). Decoding subjective evaluations: How stereotypes provide shifting standards. *Journal of Experimental Social Psychology, 33,* 579–601.

Komorita, S. S., & Meek, D. D. (1978). Generality and validity of some theories of coalition formation. *Journal of Personality and Social Psychology, 36,* 392–404.

Koole, S. L., Dijksterhuis, A., & van Knippenberg, A. (2001). What's in a name: Implicit self-esteem and the automatic self. *Journal of Personality and Social Psychology, 80,* 669–685.

Korchmaros, J. D., & Kenny, D. A. (2001). Emotional closeness as a mediator of the effect of genetic relatedness on altruism. *Psychological Science, 12,* 262–265.

Korte, C., Ypma, I., & Toppen, A. (1975). Helpfulness in Dutch society as a function of urbanization and environmental input level. *Journal of Personality and Social Psychology, 32,* 996–1003.

Kotkin, J. (1986, February). The "SMART-TEAM" at Compaq Computer. *Inc.,* 48–56.

Kramer, R. M. (1989). Windows of vulnerability or cognitive illusions? Cognitive processes and the nuclear arms race. *Journal of Experimental Social Psychology, 25,* 79–84.

Kramer, R. M., & Brewer, M. B. (1984). Effects of group identity on resource use in a simulated commons dilemma. *Journal of Personality and Social Psychology, 46,* 1044–1057.

Kraus, L. A., Davis, M. H., Bazzini, D., Church, M. B., & Kirchman, C. M. (1993). Personal and social influences on loneliness: The mediating effect of social provisions. *Social Psychology Quarterly, 56,* 37–53.

Kraus, S. J. (1995). Attitudes and the prediction of behavior: A meta-analysis of the empirical literature. *Personality and Social Psychology Bulletin, 21,* 58–75.

Krauss, R. M., Freedman, J. L., & Whitcup, M. (1978). Field and laboratory studies of littering. *Journal of Experimental Social Psychology, 14,* 109–122.

Krauss, R. M., Freyberg, R., & Morsella, E. (2002). Inferring speakers' physical attributes from their voices. *Journal of Experimental Social Psychology, 38,* 618–625.

Kravitz, D. A., & Martin, B. (1986). Ringelmann rediscovered: The original article. *Journal of Personality and Social Psychology, 50,* 936–941.

Kray, L. J., & Thompson, L. (2005). *Gender stereotypes and negotiation performance: An examination of theory and research.* Greenwich, CT: Elsevier Science/JAI Press.

Kray, L. J., Reb, J., Galinsky, A. D., & Thompson, L. (2004). Stereotype reactance at the bargaining table: The effect of stereotype activation and power on claiming and creating value. *Personality & Social Psychology Bulletin, 30*(4), 399–411, Retrieved March 10, 2005, from PsycINFO (1840-Current) database.

Krebs, D. L. (1970). Altruism – an examination of the concept and review of the literature. *Psychological Bulletin, 73,* 258–303.

Krebs, D., & Miller, D. (1985). Altruism and aggression. In G. Lindzey & E. Aronson (Eds.), *Handbook of social psychology* (3rd ed., Vol. 2, pp. 1–72). New York: Random House.

Krosnick, J. A. (1988). Attitude importance and attitude change. *Journal of Experimental Social Psychology, 24,* 240–255.

Krueger, A. B. (2002, December 12). Economic Scene. *New York Times,* p. C2.

Krueger, J., Ham, J. J., & Linford, K. M. (1996). Perceptions of behavioral consistency: Are people aware of the actor-observer effect? *Psychological Science, 7,* 259–264.

Krueger, J., & Rothbart, M. (1990). Contrast and accentuation effects in category learning. *Journal of Personality and Social Psychology, 59,* 651–663.

Kruger, D. J. (2003). Evolution and altruism: Combining psychological mediators with naturally selected tendencies. *Evolution and Human Behavior, 24,* 118–125.

Kruglanski, A. W. (1975). The human subject in the psychology experiment: Fact and artifact. In L. Berkowitz (Ed.), *Advances in experimental social psychology* (Vol. 8, pp. 101–147). New York: Academic Press.

Kruglanski, A. W. (1988). *Lay epistemics and human knowledge: Cognitive and motivational biases.* New York: Plenum Press.

Kruglanski, A. W., & Freund, T. (1983). The freezing and unfreezing of lay-inferences: Effects on impressional primacy, ethnic stereotyping, and numerical anchoring. *Journal of Experimental Social Psychology, 19,* 448–468.

Kruglanski, A. W., & Mackie, D. M. (1990). Majority and minority influence: A judgmental process integration. In W. Stroebe & M. Hewstone (Eds.), *Advances in European social psychology* (Vol. 1, pp. 229–262). Chichester, UK: John Wiley & Sons.

Kruglanski. A. W., Thompson, E. P., & Spiegel, S. (1999). Separate or equal: Bimodal notions of persuasion and a single process "unimodal." In S. Chaiken & Y. Trope (Eds.), *Dual-process theories in social psychology* (pp. 441–461). New York: Guilford Press.

Krull, D. S. (1993). Does the grist change the mill? The effect of the perceiver's inferential goal on the process of social inference. *Personality and Social Psychology Bulletin, 19,* 340–348.

Kugihara, N. (2001). Effects of aggressive behaviour and group size on collective escape in an emergency: A test between a social identify model of deindividuation theory. *British Journal of Social Psychology, 40,* 575–598.

Kuhlman, D. M., Brown, D., & Teta, P. (1992). Judgments of cooperation and defection in social dilemmas: The moderating role of judge's social orientation. In W. B. G. Liebrand & D. M. Messick (Eds.), *Social dilemmas: Theoretical issues and research findings* (pp. 111–132). Oxford, UK: Pergamon Press.

Kuhn, D., & Lao, J. (1996). Effects of evidence on attitudes: Is polarization the norm? *Psychological Science, 7,* 115–121.

Kuhn, M. H., & McPartland, T. (1954). An empirical investigation of self attitudes. *American Sociological Review, 19,* 68–76.

Kunda, Z. (1990). The case for motivated reasoning. *Psychological Bulletin, 108,* 480–498.

Kunst-Wilson, W. R., & Zajonc, R. B. (1980). Affective discrimination of stimuli that cannot be recognized. *Science, 207,* 557–558.

Kurdek, L. A. (1991). Sexuality in homosexual and heterosexual couples. In K. McKinney & S. Sprecher (Eds.), *Sexuality in close relationships* (pp. 177–192). Hillsdale, NJ: Lawrence Erlbaum Associates, Inc.

Kurland, J. A. (1979). Paternity, mother's brother, and human sociality. In N. A. Chagnon & W. Irons (Eds.), *Evolutionary biology and human social behavior: An anthropological perspective.* North Scituate, MA: Duxbury Press.

Kurman, J. (2001). Self-enhancement: Is it restricted to individualistic cultures? *Personality and Social Psychology Bulletin, 27,* 1705–1716.

Kypri, K., & Langley, J. D. (2003). Perceived social norms and their relation to university student drinking. *Journal of Studies on Alcohol, 64,* 829–834.

Lagerquist, R. (1992, August 15). Band's not pretty, but the money's lovely. *Santa Barbara News Press,* p. B3.

Lalonde, R. N. (1992). The dynamics of group differentiation in the face of defeat. *Personality and Social Psychology Bulletin, 18,* 336–342.

Lambert, T. A., Kahn, A. S., & Apple, K. J. (2003). Pluralistic ignorance and hooking up. *Journal of Sex Research, 40,* 129–133.

Lane, C., Stanger, T., & Post, T. (1993, April 19). The ghosts of Serbia. *Newsweek,* 30–31.

Lang, A., Newhagen, J., & Reeves, B. (1996). Negative video as structure: Emotion, attention, capacity, and memory. *Journal of Broadcasting & Electronic Media, 40,* 460–477.

Langer, E. J. (1975). The illusion of control. *Journal of Personality and Social Psychology, 32,* 311–328.

Langer, E. J., Blank, A., & Chanowitz, B. (1978). The mindlessness of ostensibly thoughtful action. *Journal of Personality and Social Psychology, 36,* 635–642.

Lanzetta, J. T., & Roby, T. B. (1960). The relationship between certain group process variables and group problem-solving efficiency. *Journal of Social Psychology, 52,* 135–148.

LaPiere, R. (1934). Attitudes versus actions. *Social Forces, 13,* 230–237.

LaPiere, R. T. (1936). Type-rationalizations of group antipathy. *Social Forces, 15,* 232–237.

LaPrelle, J., Hoyle, R. H., Insko, C. A., & Bernthal, P. (1990). Interpersonal attraction and descriptions of the traits of others: Ideal similarity, self similarity, and liking. *Journal of Research in Personality, 24,* 216–240.

Larson, J. R. Jr., Christensen, C., Abbott, A. S., & Franz, T. M. (1996). Diagnosing groups: Charting the flow of information in medical decision-making teams. *Journal of Personality & Social Psychology, 71,* 315–330.

Larwood, L., & Whittaker, W. (1977). Managerial myopia: Self-serving biases in organizational planning. *Journal of Applied Psychology, 62,* 194–198.

Lassiter, G. D., Geers, A. L., Munhall, P. J., Handley, I. M., & Beers, M. J. (2001). Videotaped confessions: Is guilt in the eye of the camera? In M. P. Zanna (Ed.), *Advances in experimental social psychology* (Vol. 33, pp. 189–254). San Diego, CA: Academic Press.

Latané, B., & Darley, J. M. (1968). Group inhibition of bystander intervention in emergencies. *Journal of Personality and Social Psychology, 10,* 215–221.

Latané, B., & Darley, J. M. (1970). *The unresponsive bystander: Why doesn't he help?* New York: Appleton-Crofts.

Latané, B., Nida, S. A., & Wilson, D. W. (1981). The effects of group size on helping behavior. In J. P. Rushton & R. M. Sorrentino (Eds.), *Altruism and helping behavior.* Hillsdale, NJ: Lawrence Erlbaum Associates, Inc.

Latané, B., Williams, K., & Harkins, S. (1979). Many hands make light the work: The causes and consequences of social loafing. *Journal of Personality and Social Psychology, 37,* 822–832.

Laughlin, P. R. (1980). Social combination processes of cooperative problem solving groups on verbal intellective tasks. In M. Fishbein (Ed.), *Progress in social psychology.* Hillsdale, NJ: Lawrence Erlbaum Associates, Inc.

Laughlin, P. R., VanderStoep, S. W., & Hollingshead, A. B. (1991). Collective versus individual induction: Recognition of truth, rejection of error, and collective information processing. *Journal of Personality and Social Psychology, 61,* 50–67.

Laumann, E. O., Gagnon, J. H., Michael, R. T., & Michaels, S. (1994). *The social organization of sexuality.* Chicago: University of Chicago Press.

Lavine, H., & Snyder, M. (1996). Cognitive processing and the functional matching effect in persuasion: The mediating role of subjective perceptions of message quality. *Journal of Experimental Social Psychology, 32,* 580–604.

Lawler, E. J., Ford, R. S., & Bleger, M. A. (1988). Coercive capability in conflict: A test of bilateral deterrence versus conflict spiral theory. *Social Psychology Quarterly, 51,* 93–107.

Lawrence, C., & Andrews, K. (2004). The influence of perceived prison crowding on male inmates' perception of aggressive events. *Aggressive Behavior, 30,* 273–283.

Le, B., & Agnew, C. R. (2003). Commitment and its theorized determinants: A meta-analysis of the Investment Model. *Personal Relationships, 10,* 37–57.

Lea, M., Spears, R., & de Groot, D. (2001). Knowing me, knowing you: Anonymity effects on social identity processes within groups. *Personality and Social Psychology Bulletin, 27,* 526–537.

Leary, M. R. (1995). *Self-presentation: Impression management and interpersonal behavior.* Madison, WI: Brown & Benchmark.

Leary, M. R., Barners, B. D., & Griebel, C. (1986). Cognitive, affective, and attributional effects of potential threats to self-esteem. *Journal of Social and Clinical Psychology, 4,* 461–474.

Leary, M. R., Tambor, E. S., Terdal, S. K., & Downs, D. L. (1995). Self-esteem as an interpersonal monitor: The sociometer hypothesis. *Journal of Personality and Social Psychology, 68,* 518–530.

LeBon, G. (1903). *The crowd.* London: Unwin.

LeBon, G. (1908). *The crowd.* London: Unwin.

Lebow, R. N., & Stein, J. G. (1987). Beyond deterrence. *Journal of Social Issues, 43*(4), 5–71.

Lee, A. Y., & Aaker, J. L. (2004). Bringing the frame into focus: The influence of regulatory fit on processing fluency and persuasion. *Journal of Personality and Social Psychology, 86,* 205–218.

Leigh, B. C. (1989). Reasons for having and avoiding sex: Gender, sexual orientation, and relationship to sexual behavior. *Journal of Sex Research, 26,* 199–209.

Lemaine, G. (1974). Social differentiation and social originality. *European Journal of Social Psychology, 4,* 17–52.

Lemyre, L., & Smith, P. M. (1985). Intergroup discrimination and self-esteem in the minimal group paradigm. *Journal of Personality and Social Psychology, 49,* 660–670.

Lepore, L., & Brown, R. (1997). Category and stereotype activation: Is prejudice inevitable? *Journal of Personality and Social Psychology, 72,* 275–287.

Lepore, S. J., & Greenberg, M. A. (2002). Mending broken hearts: Effects of expressive writing on mood, cognitive processing, social adjustment and health following a relationship breakup. *Psychology and Health, 17,* 547–560.

Lepore, S. J., Ragan, J. D., & Jones, S. (2000). Talking facilitates cognitive-emotional processes of adaptation to an acute stressor. *Journal of Personality and Social Psychology, 78*, 499–508.

Lepper, M. R., Greene, D., & Nisbett, R. E. (1973). Undermining children's intrinsic interest with extrinsic reward: A test of the "overjustification" hypothesis. *Journal of Personality and Social Psychology, 28*, 129–137.

Lerner, M. J. (1980). *The belief in a just world: A fundamental delusion.* New York: Plenum.

Lerner, M. J., & Miller, D. T. (1978). Just world research and the attribution process: Looking back and ahead. *Psychological Bulletin, 85*, 1030–1051.

Lerner, M. J., & Simmons, C. H. (1966). Observers' reaction to the "innocent victim": Compassion or rejection? *Journal of Personality and Social Psychology, 4*, 203–210.

Lesar, T. S., Briceland, L., & Stein, D. S. (1997). Factors related to errors in medication prescribing. *Journal of the American Medical Association, 277*, 312–317.

Levenson, R. W., & Gottman, J. M. (1985). Six physiological and affective predictors of change in relationship satisfaction. *Journal of Personality and Social Psychology, 49*, 85–94.

Leventhal, H. (1970). Findings and theory in the study of fear communications. In L. Berkowitz (Ed.), *Advances in experimental social psychology* (Vol. 5). New York: Academic Press.

Leventhal, H., Singer, R. P., & Jones, F. (1965). Effects of fear and specificity of recommendations upon attitudes and behavior. *Journal of Personality and Social Psychology, 2*, 20–29.

Levine, J. M. (1980). Reaction to opinion deviance in small groups. In P. B. Paulus (Ed.), *Psychology of group influence* (pp. 375–429). Hillsdale; NJ: Lawrence Erlbaum Associates, Inc.

Levine, J. M., Higgins, E. T., & Choi, H. S. (2000). Development of strategic norms in groups. *Organizational Behavior & Human Decision Processes, 82*, 88–101.

Levine, J. M., & Moreland, R. L. (1991). Culture and socialzation in work groups. In L. B. Resnick, J. M. Levine, & S. D. Teasley (Eds.), *Perspectives on socially shared cognition* (pp. 257–279). Washington, DC: American Psychological Association.

Levine, J. M., & Moreland, R. L. (1998). Small groups. In D. L. Gilbert, S. T. Fiske, & G. Lindzey (Eds.), *Handbook of social psychology* (4th ed., Vol. 2, pp. 415–469). Boston: McGraw-Hill.

Levine, M., Prosser, A., Evans, D., & Reicher, S. (2005). Identity and emergency intervention: How social group membership and inclusiveness of group boundaries shape helping behavior. *Personality and Social Psychology Bulletin, 31*, 443–453.

LeVine, R. A., & Campbell, D. T. (1972). *Ethnocentrism: Theories of conflict, ethnic attitudes and group behavior.* New York: Wiley.

LeVine, R. A., LeVine, S., Leiderman, P. H., Brazelton, T. B., Dixon, S., Richman, A. and others (1994). *Child care and culture: Lessons from Africa.* New York: Cambridge University Press.

Levine, R. V., Martinez, T. S., Brase, G., & Sorenson, K. (1994). Helping in 36 U.S. cities. *Journal of Personality and Social Psychology, 67*, 69–82.

Levinger, G. (1991). Commitment vs. cohesiveness: Two complementary perspecvtives. In W. H. Jones & D. Perlman (Eds.), *Advances in personal relationships* (Vol. 3, pp. 145–150). London: Jessica Kingsley.

Levinger, G., & Schneider, D. (1969). Test of the "risk is a value" hypothesis. *Journal of Personality and Social Psychology, 11*, 165–169.

Levy, M. B., & Davis, K. E. (1988). Lovestyles and attachment styles compared: Their relations to each other and to various relationship characteristics. *Journal of Social and Personal Relationships, 5*, 439–471.

Lewicki, P. (1984). Self-schema and social information processing. *Journal of Personality and Social Psychology, 47*, 1177–1190.

Lewicki, P. (1985). Nonconscious biasing effects of single instances on subsequent judgments. *Journal of Personality and Social Psychology, 48*, 563–574.

Lewin, K. (1936). *Principles of topological psychology.* New York: McGraw-Hill.

Lewin, K. (1943). Forces behind food habits and methods of change. *Bulletin of the National Research Council, 108*, 35–65.

Lewin, K. (1947). Group decision and social change. In T. M. Newcomb & E. L. Hartley (Eds.), *Readings in social psychology* (pp. 330–344). New York: Henry Holt & Co.

Lewin, K. (1948). *Solving social conflicts.* New York: Harper & Brothers.

Lewin, K. (1951). Problems of research in social psychology. In D. Cartwright (Ed.), *Field theory in social science* (pp. 155–169). New York: Harper & Row.

Lewin, T. (1991, January 17). Women found to be frequent victims of assaults by intimates. *New York Times*, p. A12.

Lewis, C. C. (1995). *Educating hearts and minds.* New York: Cambridge University Press.

Liberman, A., de La Hoz, V., & Chaiken, S. (1988). *Prior attitudes as heuristic information.* Paper presented at Western Psychological Association, Burlingame, CA.

Liberman, N., & Foerster, J. (2006). Inferences from decision difficulty. *Journal of Experimental Social Psychology, 42*, 290–301.

Liberman, N., & Trope, Y. (1998). The role of feasibility and desirability considerations in near and distant future decisions: A test of temporal construal theory. *Journal of Personality and Social Psychology, 75*, 5–18.

Lickel, B., Hamilton, D. L., & Sherman, S. J. (2001). Elements of a lay theory of groups: Types of groups, relationship styles, and the perception of group entitativity. *Personality and Social Psychology Review, 5*, 129–140.

Lieberman, S. (1956). The effects of changes in roles on the attitudes of role occupants. *Human Relations, 9*, 385–402.

Liebert, R. M., & Sprafkin, J. (1988). *The early window* (3rd ed.). New York: Pergamon Press.

Liebrand, W. B., & van Run, G. J. (1985). The effects of social motives on behavior in social dilemmas in two cultures. *Journal of Experimental Social Psychology, 21*, 86–102.

Liljenquist, K. A., Galinsky, A. D., & Kray, L. J. (2004). Exploring the rabbit hole of possibilities by myself or with my group: The benefits and liabilities of activating counterfactual mind-sets for information sharing and group coordination. *Journal of Behavioral Decision Making, 17*, 263–279.

Linder, D. E., Cooper, J., & Jones, E. E. (1967). Decision freedom as a determinant of the role of incentive magnitude in attitude change. *Journal of Personality and Social Psychology, 6*, 245–254.

Lindsay, J. J., & Anderson, C. A. (2000). From antecedent conditions to violent actions: A general affective aggression model. *Personality and Social Psychology Bulletin, 26*, 533–547.

Lindskold, S. (1978). Trust development, the GRIT proposal and the effects of conciliatory acts on conflict and cooperation. *Psychological Bulletin, 85,* 772–793.

Lindskold, S. (1986). GRIT: Reducing distrust through carefully introduced conciliation. In S. Worchel & W.G. Austin (Eds.), *Psychology of intergoup relations* (2nd ed., pp. 137–154). Chicago: Nelson Hall.

Lingle, J. H., & Ostrom, T. M. (1979). Retrieval selectivity in memory-based impression judgments. *Journal of Personality and Social Psychology, 37,* 180–194.

Linkenbach, J. W., & Perkins, H. W. (2003). MOST of us are tobacco free: An eight-month social norms campaign reducing youth initiation of smoking in Montana. In H. W. Perkins (Ed.), *The social norms approach to preventing school and college age substance abuse: A handbook for educators, counselors, and clinicians* (pp. 224–234). San Francisco, CA: Jossey-Bass.

Linville, P. W. (1985). Self-complexity and affective extremity: Don't put all of your eggs in one cognitive basket. Special Issue: Depression. *Social Cognition, 3,* 94–120.

Linville, P. W. (1987). Self-complexity as a cognitive buffer against stress-related illness and depression. *Journal of Personality and Social Psychology, 52,* 663–676.

Linville, P. W., Fisher, G. W., & Salovey, P. (1989). Perceived distributions of the characteristics of ingroup and outgroup members. *Journal of Personality and Social Psychology, 57,* 165–188.

Lippmann, W. (1922). *Public opinion.* New York: Harcourt, Brace.

Lipsitz, A., Kallmeyer, K., Ferguson, M., & Abas, A. (1989). Counting on blood donors: Increasing the impact of reminder calls. *Journal of Applied Social Psychology, 19,* 1057–1067.

Liska, A. E. (1984). A critical examination of the causal structure of the Fishbein/Ajzen attitude-behavior model. *Social Psychology Quarterly, 47,* 61–74.

Littlepage, G. E. (1991). Effects of group size and task characteristics on group performance: A test of Steiner's model. *Personality and Social Psychology Bulletin, 17,* 449–456.

Littlepage, G. E., Schmidt, G. W., Whisler, E. W., & Frost, A. G. (1995). An input-process-output analysis of influence and performance in problem-solving groups. *Journal of Personality and Social Psychology, 69,* 877–889.

Lloyd, S., Cate, R., & Henton, J. (1982). Equity and rewards as predictors of satisfaction in casual and intimate relationships. *Journal of Psychology, 110,* 43–48.

Lockhart, W. H., & Elliot, R. (1981). Changes in the attitudes of young offenders in an integrated assessment centre. In J. Harbison & J. Harbison (Eds.), *A society under stress.* Somerset, UK: Open Books.

Lockwood, P., & Kunda, Z. (1997). Superstars and me: Predicting the impact of role models on the self. *Journal of Personality and Social Psychology, 73,* 91–103.

Loewenstein, G. F., Thompson, L., & Bazerman, M. H. (1989). Social utility and decision making in interpersonal contexts. *Journal of Personality and Social Psychology, 57,* 426–441.

Loftin, C., McDowall, D., Wiersema, B., & Cottey, T. J. (1991). Effects of restrictive licensing of handguns on homicide and suicide in the District of Columbia. *New England Journal of Medicine, 325,* 1615–1620.

Loftus, E. F. (1974). The incredible eyewitness. *Psychology Today, 8*(7), 116–119.

Lombardi, W. J., Higgins, E. T., & Bargh, J. A. (1987). The role of consciousness in priming effects on categorization: Assimilation versus contrast as a function of awareness of the priming task. *Personality and Social Psychology Bulletin, 13,* 411–429.

Lord, C., & Lepper, M. R. (1999). Attitude representation theory. In M. P. Zanna (Ed.), *Advances in Experimental Social Psychology* (Vol. 31). San Diego, CA: Academic Press.

Lord, C. G., Lepper, M. R., & Mackie, D. (1984). Attitude prototypes as determinants of attitude–behavior consistency. *Journal of Personality and Social Psychology, 46,* 1254–1266.

Lord, C. G., Lepper, M. R., & Preston, E. (1984). Considering the opposite: A corrective strategy for social judgment. *Journal of Personality and Social Psychology, 47,* 1231–1243.

Lord, C. G., Ross, L., & Lepper, M. (1979). Biased assimilation and attitude polarization: The effects of prior theories on subsequently considered evidence. *Journal of Personality and Social Psychology, 37,* 2098–2109.

Lord, C. G., & Saenz, D. S. (1985). Memory deficits and memory surfeits: Differential cognitive consequences of tokenism for tokens and observers. *Journal of Personality and Social Psychology, 49,* 918–926.

Lord, R. G., De Vader, C. L., & Alliger, G. M. (1986). A meta-anaysis of the relation between personality traits and leadership perceptions: An application of validity generalization procedures. *Journal of Applied Psychology, 71,* 402–410.

Lorenz, K. (1966). *On aggression.* New York: Harcourt Brace Jovanovich.

Lortie-Lusier, M. (1987). Minority influence and idiosyncrasy credit: A new comparison of the Moscovici and Hollander theories of innovation. *European Journal of Social Psychology, 17,* 431–446.

Losch, M. E., & Cacioppo, J. T. (1990). Cognitive dissonance may enhance sympathetic tonus, but attitudes are changed to reduce negative affect rather than arousal. *Journal of Experimental Social Psychology, 26,* 289–304.

Lowery, B. S., Hardin, C. D., & Sinclair, S. (2001). Social influence effects on automatic racial prejudice. *Journal of Personality and Social Psychology, 81,* 842–855.

Luckinbill, D. (1977). Criminal homicide as a situated transaction. *Social Problems, 25,* 176–186.

Luckow, A., Reifman, A., & McIntosh, D. N. (1998, August). *Gender differences in coping: A meta-analysis.* Paper presented at Annual Convention of the American Psychological Association, San Francisco.

Luhtanen, R., Blaine, B., & Crocker, J. (1991, April). *Personal and collective self-esteem and depression in African-American and White students.* Paper presented at Eastern Psychological Association, New York.

Luhtanen, R., & Crocker, J. (1992). A collective self-esteem scale: Self-evaluation of one's social identity. *Personality and Social Psychology Bulletin, 18,* 302–318.

Lundgren, D. C., & Knight, D. J. (1978). Sequential stages of development in sensitivity training groups. *Journal of Applied Behavioral Science, 14,* 204–222.

Lydon, J. E., Jamieson, D. W., & Holmes, J. G. (1997). The meaning of social interactions in the transition from acquaintanceship to friendship. *Journal of Personality and Social Psychology, 73,* 536–548.

Lykken, D. T. (1985). The probity of the polygraph. In S. Kassin & L. Wrightsman (Eds.), *The psychology of evidence and trial procedure* (pp. 95–123). Beverly Hills, CA: Sage Publications.

Lykken, D. T. (1998). *A tremor in the blood: Uses and abuses of the lie detector*. New York: Plenum Press.

Maass, A. (1999). Linguistic intergroup bias: Stereotype perpetuation through language. In M. P. Zanna (Ed.), *Advances in experimental social psychology* (Vol. 31, pp. 79–122). San Diego, CA: Academic Press.

Maass, A., & Clark, R. D., III (1983). Internalization versus compliance: Differential processes underlying minority influence and conformity. *European Journal of Social Psychology*, 13, 197–215.

Maass, A., Clark, R. D. III, & Haberkorn, G. (1982). The effects of differential ascribed category membership and norms on minority influence. *European Journal of Social Psychology*, 12, 89–104.

Maass, A., Salvi, D., Arcuri, L., & Semin, G. (1989). Language use in intergroup contexts: The linguistic intergroup bias. *Journal of Personality and Social Psychology*, 57, 981–993.

Maccoby, E. E. (1980). *Social development: Psychological growth and the parent–child relationship*. New York: Harcourt Brace Jovanovich.

MacCoun, R. J., & Kerr, N. L. (1988). Asymmetric influence in mock jury deliberations: Jurors' bias for leniency. *Journal of Personality and Social Psychology*, 54, 21–33.

MacDonald, T. K., & Ross, M. (1999). Assessing the accuracy of predictions about dating relationships: How and why do lovers' predictions differ from those made by observers? *Personality and Social Psychology Bulletin*, 25, 1417–1429.

MacDonald, T. K., Fong, G. T., Zanna, M. P., & Martineau, A. M. (2003). *Alcohol myopia and condom use: Can alcohol intoxication be associated with more prudent behavior?* New York: Psychology Press.

MacDonald, T. K., Zanna, M. P., & Fong, G. T. (1995). Decision making in altered states: Effects of alcohol on attitudes toward drinking and driving. *Journal of Personality & Social Psychology*, 68, 973–985.

MacDonald, T. K., Zanna, M. P., & Fong, G. T. (1996). Why common sense goes out the window: Effects of alcohol on intentions to use condoms. *Personality & Social Psychology Bulletin*, 22, 763–775.

Mack, R. W., & Snyder, R. C. (1957). The analysis of social conflict—Toward an overview and synthesis. *Journal of Conflict Resolution*, 1, 212–248.

Mackie, D. (1984). Social comparison in high- and low-status groups. *Journal of Cross-Cultural Psychology*, 15, 379–398.

Mackie, D. (1986). Social identification effects in group polarization. *Journal of Personality and Social Psychology*, 50, 720–728.

Mackie, D. (1987). Systematic and nonsystematic processing of majority and minority persuasive communications. *Journal of Personality and Social Psychology*, 53, 41–52.

Mackie, D. M., Asuncion, A. G., & Rosselli, F. (1992). The impact of positive affect on persuasion processes. In M. S. Clark (Ed.), *Emotion and social behavior: Review of personality and social psychology* (pp. 247–270). Newbury Park, CA: Sage Publications.

Mackie, D. M., Devos, T., & Smith, E. R. (2000). Intergroup emotions: Explaining offensive action tendencies in an intergroup context. *Journal of Personality and Social Psychology*, 79(4), 602–616.

Mackie, D. M., Gastardo-Conaco, C. M., & Skelly, J. J. (1992). Knowledge of the advocated position and the processing of in-group and out-group persuasive messages. *Personality and Social Psychology Bulletin*, 18, 145–151.

Mackie, D. M., & Hamilton, D. L. (Eds.). (1993). *Affect, cognition, and stereotyping: Interactive processes in group perception*. San Diego; CA: Academic Press.

Mackie, D. M., Sherman, J. W., & Worth, L. T. (1993). On-line and memory based processes in group variability judgments. *Social Cognition*, 11, 44–69.

Mackie, D. M., & Worth, L. T. (1989). Cognitive deficits and the mediation of positive affect in persuasion. *Journal of Personality and Social Psychology*, 57, 27–40.

Mackie, D. M., Worth, L. T., & Asuncion, A. G. (1990). The processing of persuasive ingroup messages. *Journal of Personality and Social Psychology*, 58, 812–822.

MacLachlan, J., & Siegel, M. H. (1980). Reducing the costs of TV commercials by use of time compressions. *Journal of Marketing Research*, 17, 52–57.

Macrae, C. N., Bodenhausen, G. V., & Milne, A. B. (1998). Saying no to unwanted thoughts: Self-focus and the regulation of mental life. *Journal of Personality and Social Psychology*, 74, 578–589.

Macrae, C. N., Bodenhausen, G. V., Milne, A. B., & Calvini, G. (1999). Seeing more than we can know: Visual attention and category activation. *Journal of Experimental Social Psychology*, 35, 590–602.

Macrae, C. N., Bodenhausen, G. V., Milne, A. B., & Jetten, J. (1994). Out of mind but back in sight: Stereotypes on the rebound. *Journal of Personality and Social Psychology*, 67, 808–817.

Macrae, C. N., Bodenhausen, G. V., Milne, A. B., Thorn, T. M., & Castelli, L. (1997). On the activation of social stereotypes: Moderating role of processing objectives. *Journal of Experimental Social Psychology*, 33, 471–489.

Magnusson, S. (1981). *The flying Scotsman*. London: Quartet Books.

Maheswaran, D., & Chaiken, S. (1991). Promoting systematic processing in low-motivation settings: Effect of incongruent information on processing and judgement. *Journal of Personality and Social Psychology*, 61, 13–33.

Maio, G. R., & Olson, J. M. (Eds.). (2000). *Why we evaluate: Functions of attitudes*. Mahwah, NJ: Lawrence Erlbaum Associates, Inc.

Maison, D., Greenwald, A. G., & Bruin, R. H. (2004). Predictive validity of the Implicit Association Test in studies of brands, consumer attitudes, and behavior. *Journal of Consumer Psychology*, 14, 405–415.

Major, B. (1994). From social inequality to personal entitlement: The role of social comparisons, legitimacy appraisals, and group membership. In M. P. Zanna (Ed.), *Advances in experimental social psychology* (Vol. 26, pp. 293–348). San Diego, CA: Academic Press.

Major, B., Barr, L., Zubek, J., & Babey, S. H. (1999). Gender and self-esteem: A meta-analysis. In W. B. Swann (Ed.), *Sexism and stereotypes in modern society: The gender science of Janet Taylor Spence* (pp. 223–253). Washington, DC: American Psychological Association.

Malle, B. F. (1999). How people explain behaviour: A new theoretical framework. *Personality and Social Psychology Review*, 3, 23–48.

Malloy, T. E., & Albright, L. (1990). Interpersonal perception in a social context. *Journal of Personality and Social Psychology*, 58, 419–428.

Maner, J. K., Luce, C. L., Neuberg, S. L., Cialdini, R. B., Brown, S., & Sagarin, B. J. (2002). The effects of perspective taking on motivations for helping: Still no evidence for altruism. *Personality and Social Psychology Bulletin*, 28, 1601–1610.

Manis, M., Nelson, T. E., & Shedler, J. (1988). Stereotypes and social judgment: Extremity, assimilation and contrast. *Journal of Personality and Social Psychology, 55,* 28–36.

Manstead, A. S. R., Plevin, C. E., & Smart, J. L. (1984). Predicting mothers' choice of infant feeding method. *British Journal of Social Psychology, 23,* 223–231.

Manstead, A. S. R., Proffitt, C., & Smart, J. L. (1983). Predicting and understanding mothers' infant-feeding intentions and behavior: Testing the theory of reasoned action. *Journal of Personality and Social Psychology, 44,* 657–671.

Manstead, A. S. R., & van Eekelen, S. A. M. (1998). Distinguishing between perceived behavioral control and self-efficacy in the domain of academic achievement intentions and behaviors. *Journal of Applied Social Psychology, 28,* 1375–1392.

Maoz, I., Ward, A., Katz, M., & Ross, L. (2002). Reactive devaluation of an "Israeli" vs. "Palestinian" peace proposal. *Journal of Conflict Resolution, 46*(4), 515–546, Retrieved November 17, 2005, from PsycINFO database.

Marks, M. L., Mirvis, P. H., Hackett, E. J., & Grady, J. F., Jr. (1986). Employee participation in a quality control circle program: Impact on quality of work life, productivity, and absenteeism. *Journal of Applied Psychology, 71,* 61–69.

Markus, H. (1977). Self-schemata and processing information about the self. *Journal of Personality and Social Psychology, 35,* 63–78.

Markus, H., & Kitayama, S. (1991). Culture and the self: Implications for cognition, emotion, and motivation. *Psychological Review, 98,* 224–253.

Markus, H., Kitayama, S., & Heiman, R. J. (1996). Culture and basic psychological principles. In E. T. Higgins & A. W. Kruglanski (Eds.), *Social psychology: Handbook of basic principles* (pp. 857–914). New York: Guilford Press.

Markus, H., Kitayama, S., & VandenBos, G. R. (1996). The mutual interactions of culture and emotion. *Psychiatric Services, 47,* 225–226.

Markus, H., & Nurius, P. (1986). Possible selves. *American Psychologist, 41,* 954–969.

Markus, H., Smith, J., & Moreland, R. L. (1985). Role of the self-concept in the perception of others. *Journal of Personality and Social Psychology, 49,* 1494–1512.

Markus, H., & Wurf, E. (1987). The dynamic self-concept: A social psychological perspective. *Annual Review of Psychology, 38,* 299–337.

Marques, J. M., & Yzerbyt, V. Y. (1988). The black sheep effect: Judgmental extremity towards ingroup members in inter- and intra-group situations. *European Journal of Social Psychology, 18,* 287–292.

Marques, J. M., Yzerbyt, V. Y., & Rijsman, J. B. (1988). Context effects on intergroup discrimination: In-group bias as a function of experimenter's provenance. *British Journal of Social Psychology, 27,* 301–318.

Marsh, R. L., Hicks, J. L., & Bink, M. L. (1998). Activation of completed, uncompleted, and partially completed intentions. *Journal of Experimental Psychology: Learning, Memory, and Cognition, 24,* 350–361.

Martin, C. L. (1987). A ratio measure of sex stereotyping. *Journal of Personality and Social Psychology, 52,* 489–499.

Martin, G. N., & Gray, C. D. (1996). The effects of audience laughter on men's and women's responses to humor. *Journal of Social Psychology, 136,* 221–231.

Martin, L. L., Seta, J. J., & Crelia, R. (1990). Assimilation and contrast as a function of people's willingness and ability to expend effort in forming an impression. *Journal of Personality and Social Psychology, 59,* 27–37.

Martin, L. L., Ward, D. W., Achee, J. W., & Wyer, R. S. (1993). Mood as input: People have to interpret the motivational implications of their moods. *Journal of Personality and Social Psychology, 64,* 317–326.

Martin, L. R., Friedman, H. S., Tucker, J. S., Tomlinson-Keasey, C., Criqui, M. H., & Schwartz, J. E. (2002). A life course perspective on childhood cheerfulness and its relation to mortality risk. *Personality and Social Psychology Bulletin, 28,* 1155–1165.

Martin, R., & Hewstone, M. (2003). Majority versus minority influence: When, not whether, source status instigates heuristic or systematic processing. *European Journal of Social Psychology, 33,* 313–330.

Martineau, P. (1957). *Motivation in advertising.* New York: McGraw-Hill.

Marx, D. M., & Roman, J. S. (2002). Female role models: Protecting women's math test performance. *Personality and Social Psychology Bulletin, 28*(9), 1183–1193.

Mashek, D. J., Aron, A., & Boncimino, M. (2003) Confusions of self with close others. *Personality and Social Psychology Bulletin, 29,* 382–392.

Mason, C. M., & Griffin, M. A. (2002). Group task satisfaction: Applying the construct of job satisfaction to groups. *Small Group Research, 33,* 271–312.

Mathes, E. W., Adams, H. E., & Davies, R. M. (1985). Jealousy: Loss of relationship rewards, loss of self-esteem, depression, anxiety, and anger. *Journal of Personality and Social Psychology, 48,* 1552–1561.

Matz, D. C., & Wood, W. (2005). Cognitive dissonance in groups: The consequences of disagreement. *Journal of Personality and Social Psychology, 88,* 22–37.

Maxwell, S., Nye, P., & Maxwell, N. (2003). The wrath of the fairness-primed negotiator when the reciprocity norm is violated. *Journal of Business Research, 56,* 399–409.

May, R. B. (1976, December 30). Business Bulletin. *Wall Street Journal,* p. 1.

Mayadas, N., & Glasser, P. (1985). Termination: A neglected aspect of social group work. In M. Sundel, P. Glasser, R. Sarri, & R. Vinter (Eds.), *Individual change through small groups* (2nd ed., pp. 251–261). New York: Free Press.

McAdams, D. P. (1985). *Power, intimacy, and the life story: Personological inquiries into identity.* Homewood, IL: Dorsey Press.

McAdams, D. P., & Bryant, F. B. (1987). Intimacy motivation and subjective mental health in a nationwide sample. *Journal of Personality, 55,* 395–414.

McAlister, A., Perry, C., Killen, J., Slinkard, L. A., & Maccoby, N. (1980). Pilot study of smoking, alcohol and drug abuse prevention. *American Journal of Public Health, 70,* 719–721.

McAllister, J. F. O. (1992, August 17). Atrocity and outrage. *Time,* 21–24.

McAndrew, F. T. (2002). New evolutionary perspectives on altruism: Multilevel-selection and costly-signaling theories. *Current Directions in Psychological Science, 11,* 79–82.

McArthur, L. A. (1972). The how and what of why: Some determinants and consequences of causal attribution. *Journal of Personality and Social Psychology, 22,* 171–193.

McArthur, L. Z. (1981). What grabs you? The role of attention in impression formation and causal attribution. In E. T. Higgins, C. P. Herman, & M. P. Zanna (Eds.), *Social cognition: The Ontario symposium* (Vol. 1, pp. 201–246). Hillsdale, NJ: Lawrence Erlbaum Associates, Inc.

McArthur, L. Z., & Berry, D. S. (1987). Cross-cultural agreement in perceptions of babyfaced adults. *Journal of Cross Cultural Psychology, 18,* 165–192.

McArthur, L. Z., & Post, D. L. (1977). Figural emphasis and person perception. *Journal of Experimental Social Psychology, 13,* 520–535.

McCain, G., Cox, V. C., & Paulus, P. B. (1980). *The effect of prison crowding on inmate behavior.* Washington, DC: National Institute of Justice.

McCallum, D. M., Harring, K., Gilmore, R., Drenan, S., Chase, J. P., Insko, C. A. and others (1985). Competition and cooperation between groups and between individuals. *Journal of Experimental Social Psychology, 21,* 301–320.

McCauley, C. (1989). The nature of social influence in groupthink: Compliance and internalization. *Journal of Personality and Social Psychology,* 57, 250–260.

McCauley, C. (1998). Group dynamics in Janis's theory of groupthink: Backward and forward. *Organizational Behavior and Human Decision Processes, 73,* 142–162.

McClintock, C. G., & Allison, S. T. (1989). Social value orientation and helping behavior. *Journal of Applied Social Psychology, 19,* 353–362.

McClintock, C. G., & Liebrand, W. B. (1988). Role of interdependence structure, individual value orientation, and another's strategy in social decision making: A transformational analysis. *Journal of Personality and Social Psychology, 55,* 396–409.

McConnell, J. D. (1968). Effect of pricing on perception of product quality. *Journal of Applied Psychology, 52,* 331–334.

McCrae, R. R., & Costa, P. T. (1988). Psychological resilience among widowed men and women: A 10-year follow-up of a national sample. *Journal of Social Issues, 44*(3), 129–142.

McCullough, M. E., Worthington, E. L., & Rachal, K. C. (1997). Interpersonal forgiving in close relationships. *Journal of Personality and Social Psychology, 73,* 321–336.

McFall, R. M. (1977). Parameters of self-monitoring. In R. B. Stuart (Ed.), *Behavioral self-management: Strategies, techniques, and outcomes.* New York: Brunner/Mazel.

McGarty, C., & Penny, R. E. (1988). Categorization, accentuation and social judgement. *British Journal of Social Psychology, 27,* 147–157.

McGill, A. L. (1989). Context effects in judgments of causation. *Journal of Personality and Social Psychology, 57,* 189–200.

McGrath, J. E. (1984). *Groups: Interaction and performance.* Englewood Cliffs; NJ: Prentice Hall.

McGrath, J. E., & Hollingshead, A. B. (1993). Putting the "group" back in group support systems: Some theoretical issues about dynamic processes in groups with technological enhancements. In L. M. Jessup & J. S. Valacich (Eds.), *Group support systems: New perspectives* (pp. 78–96). New York: Macmillan.

McGrath, J. E., Kelly, J. R., & Rhodes, J. E. (1993). A feminist perspective on research methodology: Some metatheoretical issues, contrasts, and choices. In S. Oskamp & M. Costanzo (Eds.), *Gender issues in contemporary society* (pp. 19–37). Newbury Park, CA: Sage Publications.

McGrath, J. E., & Tschan, F. (2004). Group development and change. In J. E. McGrath & F. Tschan (Eds.), *Temporal matters in social psychology: Examining the role of time in the lives of groups and individuals* (pp. 99–120). Washington, DC: American Psychological Association.

McGuire, T. W., Kiesler, S., & Siegel, J. (1987). Group and computer-mediated discussion effects in risk decision making. *Journal of Personality and Social Psychology, 52,* 917–930.

McGuire, W. J. (1964). Inducing resistance to persuasion: Some contemporary approaches. In L. Berkowitz (Ed.), *Advances in experimental social psychology* (Vol. 1). New York: Academic Press.

McGuire, W. J. (1969). The nature of attitudes and attitude change. In G. Lindzey & E. Aronson (Eds.), *Handbook of social psychology* (2nd ed., Vol. 3). Reading, MA: Addison-Wesley.

McGuire, W. J. (1985). Attitudes and attitude change. In G. Lindzey & E. Aronson (Eds.), *Handbook of social psychology* (3rd ed., Vol. 2, pp. 233–346). New York: Random House.

McGuire, W. J., & McGuire, C. V. (1981). The spontaneous self-concept as affected by personal distinctiveness. In M. D. Lynch, A. A. Norem-Hebeisen, & K. J. Gergen (Eds.), *Self-concept: Advances in theory and research* (pp. 147–171). Cambridge, MA: Ballinger.

McGuire, W. J., McGuire, C. V., Child, P., & Fujioka, T. (1978). Salience of ethnicity in the spontaneous self-concept as a function on one's ethnic distinctiveness in the social environment. *Journal of Personality and Social Psychology, 36,* 511–520.

McGuire, W. J., McGuire, C. V., & Winton, W. (1979). Effects of household sex composition on the salience of one's gender in the spontaneous self-concept. *Journal of Experimental Social Psychology, 15,* 77–90.

McGuire, W. J., & Padawer-Singer, A. (1978). Trait salience in the spontaneous self-concept. *Journal of Personality and Social Psychology, 33,* 743–754.

McIntyre, R. B., Paulson, R. M., Lord, C. G., & Lepper, M. R. (2004). Effects of attitude action identification on congruence between attitudes and behavioral intentions toward social groups. *Personality and Social Psychology Bulletin, 30,* 1151–1164.

McKenna, K. Y. A., & Bargh, J. A. (1998). Coming out in the age of the Internet: Identity "demarginalization" through virtual group participation. *Journal of Personality and Social Psychology, 75,* 681–694.

McLachlan, A. (1986). The effects of two forms of decision reappraisal on the perception of pertinent arguments. *British Journal of Social Psychology, 25,* 129–138.

McMillen, D. L., & Austin, J. B. (1971). Effect of positive feedback on compliance following transgression. *Psychonomic Science, 24,* 59–61.

McMillen, R. C., Ritchie, L. A., Frese, W., & Cosby, A. G. (2000). Smoking in America: 35 years after the Surgeon General's Report. A report on the 2000 National Social Climate Survey (November 1, 2000). *Tobacco Control. Surveys and Program Evaluations from Outside UCSF,* Paper NSC1. Mississippi State University.

McNatt, D. B. (2000). Ancient Pygmalion joins contemporary management: A meta-analysis of the result. *Journal of Applied Psychology, 85,* 314–322.

Medvec, V. H., Madey, S. F., & Gilovich, T. (1995). When less is more: Counterfactual thinking and satisfaction among Olympic medalists. *Journal of Personality and Social Psychology, 69,* 603–610.

Meeus, H. J., & Raaijmakers, Q. A. W. (1987). Administrative obedience as a social phenomenon. In W. Doise & S. Moscovici (Eds.), *Current issues in European social psychology* (pp. 183–230). Cambridge; UK: Cambridge University Press.

Meeus, H. J., & Raaijmakers, Q. A. W. (1995). Obedience in modern society: The Utrecht studies. *Journal of Social Issues, 51,* 155–176.

Meeus, W. H., & Raaijmakers, Q. A. W. (1986). Administrative obedience: Carrying out orders to use psychological-administrative violence. *European Journal of Social Psychology, 16,* 311–324.

Mehrabian, A. (1972). *Nonverbal communication.* Chicago: Aldine.

Meier, B. P., & Hinsz, V. B. (2004). A comparison of human aggression committed by groups and individuals: An interindividual–intergroup discontinuity. *Journal of Experimental Social Psychology, 40*(4), 551–559.

Merton, R. (1948). The self-fulfilling prophecy. *Antioch Review, 8,* 193–210.

Mesquita, B. (2001). Emotions in collectivist and individualist contexts. *Journal of Personality and Social Psychology, 80,* 68–74.

Messick, D. M., & Brewer, M. B. (1983). Solving social dilemmas: A review. In L. Wheeler & P. Shaver (Eds.), *Review of personality and social psychology* (Vol. 4, pp. 11–44). Beverly Hills, CA: Sage.

Messick, D. M., Wike, H., Brewer, M. B., Kramer, R. M., Zembe, P. E., & Lui, L. (1983). Individual adaptations and structural change as solutions to social dilemmas. *Journal of Personality and Social Psychology, 44,* 294–309.

Meyers, S. A., & Berscheid, E. (1997). The language of love: The difference a preposition makes. *Personality and Social Psychology Bulletin, 23,* 347–362.

Michaels, J. W., Blommel, J. M., Brocato, R. M., Linkous, R. A., & Rowe, J. S. (1982). Social facilitation and inhibition in a natural setting. *Replications in Social Psychology, 2,* 21–24.

Mickelson, K. D., Kessler, R. C., & Shaver, P. R. (1997). Adult attachment in a nationally representative sample. *Journal of Personality and Social Psychology, 73,* 1092–1106.

Mifflin, L. (1998, April 17). Increase seen in number of violent TV programs. *New York Times,* p. A14.

Mikolic, J. M., Parker, J. C., & Pruitt, D. G. (1997). Escalation in response to persistent annoyance: Groups versus individuals and gender effects. *Journal of Personality and Social Psychology, 72,* 151–163.

Mikula, G. (1980). *Justice and social interaction.* New York: Springer-Verlag.

Milburn, T. W. (1977). The nature of threat. *Journal of Social Issues, 33*(1), 126–139.

Milgram, S. (1963). The behavioral study of obedience. *Journal of Abnormal and Social Psychology, 67,* 467–472.

Milgram, S. (1964). Issues in the study of obedience: A reply to Baumrind. *American Psychologist, 19,* 848–852.

Milgram, S. (1974). *Obedience to authority.* New York: Harper & Row.

Milgram, S. (1977, October). Subjects' reactions: The neglected factor in the ethics of experimentation. *Hastings Center Report,* 19–23.

Millar, M. (2002a). Effects of a guilt induction and guilt reduction on door in the face. *Communication Research, 29,* 666–680.

Millar, M. (2002b). The effectiveness of the door-in-the-face compliance strategy on friends and strangers. *Journal of Social Psychology, 142,* 295–304.

Millar, M. G. (2001). Promoting health behaviors with door-in-the-face: The influence of the beneficiary of the request. *Psychology, Health, and Medicine, 6,* 115–119.

Millar, M. G., & Millar, K. U. (1996). The effects of direct and indirect experience on affective and cognitive responses and the attitude–behavior relation. *Journal of Experimental Social Psychology, 32,* 561–579.

Millar, M. G., Millar, K. U., & Tesser, A. (1988). The effects of helping and focus of attention on mood states. *Personality and Social Psychology Bulletin, 14,* 536–543.

Millar, M. G., & Tesser, A. (1986). Thought-induced attitude change: The effects of schema structure and commitment. *Journal of Personality and Social Psychology, 51,* 259–269.

Miller, D. T., & McFarland, C. (1987). Pluralistic ignorance: When similarity is interpreted as dissimilarity. *Journal of Personality and Social Psychology, 53,* 298–305.

Miller, D. T., & Ross, M. (1975). Self-serving biases in the attribution of causality: Fact or fiction? *Psychological Bulletin, 82,* 213–225.

Miller, D. T., & Turnbull, W. (1986). Expectancies and interpersonal processes. *Annual Review of Psychology, 37,* 233–256.

Miller, J. G. (1984). Culture and the development of everyday social explanation. *Journal of Personality and Social Psychology, 46,* 961–978.

Miller, J. G., Bersoff, D. M., & Harwood, P. L. (1997). Perceptions of social responsibilities in India and the United States: Moral imperatives or personal decisions. In L. A. Peplau & S. E. Taylor (Eds.), *Sociocultral perspectives in social psychology* (pp. 113–144). Upper Saddle River, NJ: Prentice Hall.

Miller, L. E., & Grush, J. E. (1986). Individual differences in attitudinal versus normative determination of behavior. *Journal of Experimental Social Psychology, 22,* 190–202.

Miller, N., & Brewer, M. B. (1986). Categorization effects on ingroup and outgroup perception. In J. F. Dovidio & S. L. Gaertner (Eds.), *Prejudice, discrimination, and racism* (pp. 209–230). Orlando, FL: Academic Press.

Miller, N. E. (1941). The frustration–aggression hypothesis. *Psychological Review, 48,* 337–342.

Miller, P. A., & Eisenberg, N. (1988). The relation of empathy to aggressive and externalizing/antisocial behavior. *Psychological Bulletin, 103,* 324–344.

Miller, R. L., Brickman, P., & Bolen, D. (1975). Attribution versus persuasion as a means for modifying behavior. *Journal of Personality and Social Psychology, 31,* 430–441.

Miller, R. L., Seligman, C., Clark, N. T., & Bush, M. (1976). Perceptual contrast versus reciprocal concessions as mediators of induced compliance. *Canadian Journal of Behavioral Science, 8,* 401–409.

Miller, R. S. (1997). Inattentive and contented: Relationship commitment and attention to alternatives. *Journal of Personality and Social Psychology, 73,* 758–766.

Miller, S. M., & Mangan, C. E. (1983). Interacting effects of information and coping style in adaptening to gynecologic stress: Should the doctor tell all? *Journal of Personality and Social Psychology, 45,* 223–236.

Mills, J., Clark, M. S., Ford, T. E., & Johnson, M. (2004). Measurement of communal strength. *Personal Relationships, 11,* 213–230.

Mintzberg, H. (1980). *The nature of managerial work* (2nd ed.). Englewood Cliffs, NJ: Prentice Hall.

Misumi, J. (1995). The development in Japan of the performance-maintenance (PM) theory of leadership. *Journal of Social Issues, 51,* 213–228.

Modigliani, A., & Rochat, F. (1995). The role of interaction sequences and the timing of resistance in shaping obedience and defiance to authority. *Journal of Social Issues, 51,* 107–124.

Moghaddam, F. M., Taylor, D. M., & Wright, S. C. (1993). *Social psychology in cross-cultural perspective.* New York: W. H. Freeman & Company.

Monteith, M. J., Sherman, J. W., & Devine, P. G. (1998). Suppression as a stereotype control strategy. *Personality and Social Psychology Review, 2,* 63–82.

Mook, D. G. (1980). In defense of external invalidity. *American Psychologist, 38,* 379–388.

Moon, H., Hollenbeck, J. R., Humphrey, S. E., Ilgen, D. R., West, B. J., Ellis, A. P. J. and others (2004). Asymmetric adaptability: Dynamic team structures as one-way streets. *Academy of Management, 47,* 681–695.

Moore, D. L., Hausknecht, D., & Thamodaran, K. (1986). Time compression, response opportunity, and persuasion. *Journal of Consumer Research, 13,* 85–99.

Moore, T. (1995). Subliminal self-help auditory tapes: An empirical test of perceptual consequences. *Canadian Journal of Behavioural Science, 27,* 9–20.

Moorhead, G., Ference, R., & Neck, C. P. (1991). Group decision fiascoes continue: Space shuttle Challenger and a revised groupthink framework. *Human Relations, 44,* 533–550.

Moorhead, G., & Montanari, J. R. (1986). An empirical investigation of the groupthink phenomenon. *Human Relations, 39,* 399–410.

Moreland, R. L. (1987). The formation of small groups. In C. Hendrick (Ed.), *Group processes* (pp. 80–110). Beverly Hills, CA: Sage.

Moreland, R. L., & Beach, S. R. (1992). Exposure effects in the classroom: The development of affinity among students. *Journal of Experimental Social Psychology, 28,* 255–276.

Moreland, R. L., & Levine, J. M. (1988). Group dynamics over time: Development and socialization in small groups. In J. E. McGrath (Ed.), *The social psychology of time: New perspectives* (pp. 151–181). Newbury Park, CA: Sage.

Moreland, R. L., & Levine, J. M. (2001). Socialization in organizations and work groups. In M. E. Turner (Ed.), *Groups at work: Theory and research. Applied social research* (pp. 69–112). Mahwah, NJ: Lawrence Erlbaum Associates, Inc.

Morgan, P. M. (1983). *Deterrence: A conceptual analysis.* Beverly Hills, CA: Sage.

Morgan, S. E., & Reichart, T. (1999). The message is in the metaphor: Assessing the comprehension of metaphors in advertisements. *Journal of Advertising, 28,* 1–12.

Moriarty, T. (1975). Crime, commitment, and the responsive bystander: Two field experiments. *Journal of Personality and Social Psychology, 31,* 370–376.

Morris, M. W., & Peng, K. (1994). Culture and cause: American and Chinese attributions for social and physical events. *Journal of Personality and Social Psychology, 67,* 949–971.

Morton, T. L. (1978). Intimacy and reciprocity of exchange: A comparison of spouses and strangers. *Journal of Personality and Social Psychology, 36,* 72–81.

Moscovici, S. (1980). Toward a theory of conversion behavior. In L. Berkowitz (Ed.), *Advances in experimental social psychology* (Vol. 13, pp. 209–239). New York: Academic Press.

Moscovici, S., & Lage, E. (1976). Studies in social influence. III: Majority versus minority influence in a group. *European Journal of Social Psychology, 6,* 149–74.

Moscovici, S., Lage, S., & Naffrechoux, M. (1969). Influence of a consistent minority on the responses of a majority in a color perception task. *Sociometry, 32,* 365–380.

Moscovici, S., & Personnaz, B. (1980). Studies in social influence. V: Minority influence and conversion behavior in a perceptual task. *Journal of Experimental Social Psychology, 16,* 270–282.

Moscovici, S., & Zavalloni, M. (1969). The group as a polarizer of attitudes. *Journal of Personality and Social Psychology, 12,* 125–135.

Moseley, R. (1998, April 5). Anti-foreigner bias sparks violent attacks. *Santa Barbara News Press,* p. A15.

Moskalenko, S., & Heine, S. J. (2003). Watching your troubles away: Television viewing as a stimulus for subjective self-awareness. *Personality and Social Psychology Bulletin, 29,* 76–85.

Moskos, C. C., Jr. (1969). Why men fight: American combat soldiers in Vietnam. *Transaction, 7*(1), 13–23.

Mugny, G. (1975). Negotiations, image of the other, and the process of minority influence. *European Journal of Social Psychology, 5,* 209–228.

Mugny, G. (1982). *The power of minorities.* London: Academic Press

Mugny, G., & Papastamous, S. (1980). When rigidity does not fail: Individualization and psychologization as resistances to the diffusion of minority innovations. *European Journal of Social Psychology, 10,* 43–62.

Mullen, B. (1987). Self-attention theory: The effects of group composition on the individual. In B. Mullen & G. R. Goethals (Eds.), *Theories of group behavior* (pp. 125–146). New York: Springer-Verlag.

Mullen, B. (1991). Group composition, salience, and cognitive representations: The phenomenology of being in a group. *Journal of Experimental Social Psychology, 27,* 297–323.

Mullen, B., Atkins, J. L., Champion, D. S., Edwards, C., Hardy, D., Story, J. E. and others (1985). The false consensus effect: A meta-analysis of 115 hypothesis tests. *Journal of Experimental Social Psychology, 21,* 262–283.

Mullen, B., Brown, R., & Smith, C. (1992). Ingroup bias as a function of salience, relevance, and status: An integration. *European Journal of Social Psychology, 22,* 103–122.

Mullen, B., & Copper, C. (1994). The relation between group cohesiveness and performance: An integration. *Psychological Bulletin, 115,* 210–227.

Mullen, B., & Hu, L. (1989). Perceptions of ingroup and outgroup variability: A meta-analytic integration. *Basic and Applied Social Psychology, 10,* 233–252.

Mullen, B., Migdal, M. J., & Hewstone, M. (2001). Crossed categorization versus simple categorization and intergroup evaluations: A meta-analysis. *European Journal of Social Psychology, 31*(6), 721–736.

Mullen, B., & Riordan, C. A. (1988). Self-serving attributions for performance in naturalistic settings: A meta-analytic review. *Journal of Applied Social Psychology*, *18*, 3–22.

Mullen, B., & Smyth, J. M. (2004). Immigrant suicide rates as a function of ethnophaulisms: Hate speech predicts death. *Psychosomatic Medicine*, *66*, 343–348.

Muller, D., Atzeni, T., & Butera, F. (2004). Coaction and upward social comparison reduce the illusory conjunction effect: Support for distraction-conflict theory. *Journal of Experimental Social Psychology*, *40*, 659–665.

Muller, J. (1991, July 9). Subliminal ads debunked. *Santa Barbara News Press*, p. B6.

Mummendey, A., Simon, B., Dietze, C., Grunert, M., Haeger, G., Kessler, S. and others (1992). Categorization is not enough: Intergroup discrimination in negative outcome allocations. *Journal of Experimental Social Psychology*, *28*, 125–144.

Mummendey, A., & Wenzel, M. (1999). Social discrimination and tolerance in intergroup relations: Reactions to intergroup difference. *Personality and Social Psychology Review*, *3*, 158–174.

Munno, G. D., & Ditto, P. H. (1997). Biased assimilation, attitude polarization, and affect in reaction to stereotype-relevant scientific information. *Personality and Social Psychology Bulletin*, *23*, 656–663.

Murray, S. L., & Holmes, J. G. (1997). A leap of faith? Positive illusions in romantic relationships. *Personality and Social Psychology Bulletin*, *23*, 586–604.

Murray, S. L., Holmes, J. G., & Griffin, D. W. (1996). The self-fulfiling nature of positive illusions in romantic relationships: Love is not blind, but prescient. *Journal of Personality and Social Psychology*, *71*, 1155–1180.

Musick, M. A., & Wilson, J. (2003). Volunteering and depression: The role of psychological and social resources in different age groups. *Social Science and Medicine*, *56*, 259–269.

Mussweiler, T., & Bodenhausen, G. V. (2002). I know you are, but what am I? Self-evaluative consequences of judging in-group and out-group members. *Journal of Personality and Social Psychology*, *82*(1), 19–32.

Mussweiler, T., Gabriel, S., & Bodenhausen, G. V. (2000). Shifting social identities as a strategy for deflecting threatening social comparisons. *Journal of Personality and Social Psychology, 79*(3), 398–409.

Myers, D. G., & Bishop, G. D. (1971). The enhancement of dominant attitudes in group discussion. *Journal of Personality and Social Psychology*, *20*, 386–391.

Myers, D. G., & Kaplan, M. F. (1976). Group-induced polarization in simulated juries. *Personality and Social Psychology Bulletin*, *2*, 63–66.

Myers, D. G., & Lamm, H. (1976). The group polarization phenomenon. *Psychological Bulletin*, *83*, 602–627.

Nadler, A. (2002). Inter-group helping relations as power relations: Maintaining or challenging social dominance between groups through helping. *Journal of Social Issues*, *58*, 487–502.

Nadler, A., & Fisher, J.D. (1986). The role of threat to self-esteem and perceived control in recipient reactions to help: Theory development and empirical validation. In L. Berkowitz (Ed.), *Advances in experimental social psychology* (Vol. 19, pp. 81–122). New York: Academic Press.

Naroll, R., Bullough, V. L., & Naroll, F. (1974). *Military deterrence in history: A pilot cross-historical survey*. Albany, NY, State University of New York Press.

Natale, J. A. (1988). Are you open to suggestion? *Psychology Today*, *22*(9), 28–30.

National Public Radio News (1998, April 16). Barbara Wilson, quoted on *All things considered* broadcast.

Neisser, U. (1967). *Cognitive psychology*. New York: Appleton-Century-Crofts.

Nelson, L. J., & Miller, D. T. (1995). The distinctiveness effect in social categorization: You are what makes you unusual. *Psychological Science*, *6*, 246–249.

Nelson, L. J., Moore, D. L., Olivetti, J., & Scott, T. (1997). General and personal mortality salience and nationalistic bias. *Personality and Social Psychology Bulletin*, *23*, 884–892.

Nemeth, C. (1977). Interactions between jurors as a function of majority vs. unanimity decision rules. *Journal of Applied Social Psychology*, *7*, 38–56.

Nemeth, C. (1986). Differential contributions of majority and minority influence. *Psychological Review*, *93*, 1–10.

Nemeth, C. (1995). Dissent as driving cognition, attitudes, and judgments. *Social Cognition*, *13*, 273–291.

Nemeth, C., & Chiles, C. (1988). Modelling courage: The role of dissent in fostering independence. *European Journal of Social Psychology*, *18*, 275–280.

Nemeth, C., Connell, J. B., Rogers, J. D., & Brown, K. S. (2001). Improving decision making by means of dissent. *Journal of Applied Social Psychology*, *31*, 48–58.

Nemeth, C., & Kwan, J. L. (1987). Minority influence, divergent thinking and detection of correct solutions. *Journal of Applied Social Psychology*, *17*, 788–799.

Nemeth, C., Mayseless, O., Sherman, J. W., & Brown, Y. (1990). Exposure to dissent and recall of information. *Journal of Personality and Social Psychology*, *58*, 429–437.

Nemeth, C., & Wachtler, J. (1974). Creating the perceptions of consistency and confidence : A necessary condition for minority influence. *Sociometry*, *37*, 529–540.

Nemeth, C., & Wachtler, J. (1983). Consistency and the modification of judgments. *Journal of Experimental Social Psychology*, *9*, 65–79.

Nemeth, C., Wachtler, J., & Endicott, J. (1977). Increasing the size of the minority: Some gains and losses. *European Journal of Social Psychology*, *7*, 15–27.

Nettles, E. J., & Loevinger, J. (1983). Sex role expectations and ego level in relation to problem marriages. *Journal of Personality and Social Psychology*, *45*, 676–687.

Neuberg, S. L. (1989a). The goal of forming accurate impressions during social interactions: Attenuating the impact of negative expectancies. *Journal of Personality and Social Psychology*, *56*, 374–386.

Neuberg, S. L. (1989b). Behavioral implications of information presented outside of conscious awareness: The effects of subliminal presentation of trait information on behavior in the prisoner's dilemma game. *Social Cognition*, *6*, 53–64.

Neuberg, S. L., & Cottrell, C. A. (2002). Intergroup emotions: A biocultural approach. In D. M. Mackie & E. R. Smith (Eds.), *From prejudice to intergroup emotions* (pp. 265–284). New York: Psychology Press.

Neuberg, S. L., & Fiske, S. T. (1987). Motivational influences on impression formation: Outcome dependency, accuracy-driven attention, and individuating processes. *Journal of Personality and Social Psychology*, *53*, 431–444.

New York Times (1991, January 10). Poll finds Whites use sterotypes, p. B10.

New York Times (1992a, May 6). A juror describes the ordeal of deliberations, p. A13.

New York Times (1992b, July 17). California case puts spotlight on jury coercion and peer pressure, p. A23.

New York Times (1992c, March 25). Plenty of fish in sea? Not anymore, p. A8.

New York Times (1992d, June 28). Turning the tables: A reverse questionnaire, p. F23.

Newcomb, T. M. (1961). *The acquaintance process*. New York: Holt, Rinehart, & Winston.

Newsweek (1990a, June 25). Perspectives, p. 15.

Newsweek. (1990b, May 21). Perspectives, p. 17.

Newsweek (1991, August 5). Opinion watch: On the front lines?, pp. 23, 27.

Niedenthal, P. M. (1990). Implicit perception of affective information. *Journal of Experimental Social Psychology*, *26*, 505–527.

Niedenthal, P. M., & Cantor, N. (1986). Affective responses as guides to category-based inferences. *Motivation and Emotion*, *10*, 217–232.

Nields, D. (1991, May 27). The dirt on Shakespeare. *Newsweek*, p. 8.

Nienhuis, A. E., Manstead, A. S. R., & Spears, R. (2001). Multiple motives and persuasive communication: Creative elaboration as a result of impression motivation and accuracy motivation. *Personality & Social Psychology Bulletin*, *27*, 118–132.

Nier, J. A., Gaertner, S. L., Dovidio, J. F., Banker, B. S., Ward, C. M., & Rust, M. C. (2001). Changing interracial evaluations and behavior: The effects of a common group identity. *Group Processes & Intergroup Relations*, *4*(4), 299–316.

Nigra, G. N., Hill, D. E., Gelbein, M. E., & Clark, C. L. (1988). Changes in the facial prominence of women and men over the last decade. *Psychology of Women Quarterly*, *12*, 225–235.

Nisbett, R. E. (1987). Lay personality theory: Its nature, origin, and utility. In N. E. Grunberg, R. E. Nisbett, J. Rodin, & J. E. Singer (Eds.), *A distinctive approach to psychological research: The influence of Stanley Schacter* (pp. 87–117). Hillsdale, NJ: Lawrence Erlbaum Associates, Inc.

Nisbett, R. E. (2003). *The geography of thought: How Asians and Westerners think differently . . . and why*. New York: Free Press.

Nisbett, R. E., & Cohen, D. (1996). *Culture of honor: The psychology of violence in the South*. Boulder, CO: Westview Press.

Nisbett, R. E., & Wilson, T. D. (1977). Telling more than we can know: Verbal reports on mental processes. *Psychological Review*, *84*, 231–259.

Noller, P. (1980). Misunderstandings in marital communication: A study of couples' nonverbal communication. *Journal of Personality and Social Psychology*, *39*, 1135–1148.

Noller, P., & Ruzzene, M. (1991). Communication in marriage: The influence of affect and cognition. In G. Fletcher & F. Fincham (Eds.), *Cognition in close relationships* (pp. 203–234). Hillsdale, NJ: Lawrence Erlbaum Associates, Inc.

Norenzayan, A., & Nisbett, R. E. (2000). Culture and causal cognition. *Current Directions in Psychological Science*, *9*, 132–135.

North, A. C., & Tarrant, M. (2004). The effects of music on helping behavior. *Environment and Behavior*, *36*, 266–275.

North, R. C., Brody, R. A., & Holsti, O. R. (1964). Some empirical data on the conflict spiral. *Peace Research Society International Papers*, *1*, 1–14.

Nosek, B. (2005). Moderators of the relationship between implicit and explicit evaluation. *Journal of Experimental Psychology: General*, *134*, 565–584.

Nuttin, J. M. (1987). Affective consequences of mere ownership: The name letter effect in twelve European languages. *European Journal of Social Psychology*, *17*, 381–402.

Oakes, P. J., Haslam, S. A., Morrison, B., & Grace, D. (1995). Becoming an in-group: Reexamining the impact of familiarity on perceptions of group homogeneity. *Social Psychology Quarterly*, *58*, 52–60.

Oakes, P. J., & Turner, J. C. (1980). Social categorization and intergroup behaviour: Does minimal intergroup discrimination make social identity more positive? *European Journal of Social Psychology*, *10*, 295–301.

Oatley, K., & Johnson-Laird, P. N. (1987). Towards a cognitive theory of emotions. *Cognition and Emotion*, *1*, 29–50.

O'Connor, K. M., Arnold, J. A., & Burris, E. R. (2005). Negotiators' bargaining histories and their effects on future negotiation performance. *Journal of Applied Psychology*, *90*(2) 350–362.

Ogilvy, D. (1983). *Ogilvy on advertising*. New York: Vintage Books.

O'Keefe, D. J., & Figgé, M. (1999). Guilt and expected guilt in the door-in-the-face technique. *Communication Monographs*, *66*, 312–324.

O'Keefe, D. J., & Hale, S. L. (2001). An odds-ratio-based meta-analysis of research on the door-in-the-face influence strategy. *Communication Reports*, *14*, 31–38.

O'Leary, A. (1990). Stress, emotion, and human immune function. *Psychological Bulletin*, *108*, 363–382.

Oliner, S. P., & Oliner, P. M. (1988). *The altruistic personality*. New York: Free Press.

Oliver, M. B., & Hyde, J. S. (1993). Gender differences in sexuality: A meta-analysis. *Psychological Bulletin*, *114*, 29–51.

Olson, J. M. (1990). Self-inference processes in emotion. In J. M. Olson & M. P. Zanna (Eds.), *Self-inference processes: The Ontario symposium* (Vol. 6, pp. 17–42). Hillsdale, NJ: Lawrence Erlbaum Associates, Inc.

Olson, J. M., Roese, N. J., & Zanna, M. P. (1996). Expectancies. In E. T. Higgins & A. W. Kruglanski (Eds.), *Social psychology: Handbook of basic principles* (pp. 211–238). New York: Guilford Press.

Olson, M. A., & Fazio, R. H. (2002). Implicit acquisition and manifestation of classically conditioned attitudes. *Social Cognition*, *20*, 89–104.

Olson, M. A., & Fazio, R. H. (2004). Reducing the influence of extrapersonal asssociations on the Implicit Association Test: Personalizing the IAT. *Journal of Personality and Social Psychology*, *86*, 653–667.

Olweus, D. (1979). Stability of aggressive reaction patterns in males: A review. *Psychological Bulletin*, *86*, 852–875.

Omoto, A. M., & Snyder, M. (2002). Considerations of community: The context and process of volunteerism. *American Behavioral Scientist*, *45*, 846–886.

Opotow, S. (1990). Moral exclusion and injustice: An introduction. *Journal of Social Issues*, *46*(1), 1–20.

Orbell, J. M., van de Kragt, A. J. C., & Dawes, R. M. (1988). Explaining discussion-induced cooperation. *Journal of Personality and Social Psychology, 54,* 811–819.

O'Reilly, C. A., & Caldwell, D. F. (1985). The impact of normative social influence and cohesiveness on task perceptions and attitudes: A social-information processing approach. *Journal of Occupational Psychology, 59,* 193–206.

Orne, M. T. (1962). On the social psychology of the psychological experiment: With particular reference to demand characteristics and their implications. *American Psychologist, 17,* 776–783.

Osborn, A. F. (1953). *Applied imagination.* New York: Scribner.

Osgood, C. E. (1962). *An alternative to war or surrender.* Urbana, IL: University of Illinois Press.

Oskamp, S., & Hartry, A. (1968). A factor-analytic study of the double standard in attitudes toward U.S. and Russian actions. *Behavioral Science, 13,* 178–188.

Ostrom, T. M. (1969). The relationship between the affective, behavioral, and cognitive components of attitude. *Journal of Experimental Social Psychology, 5,* 12–30.

Otten, S., & Mummendey, A. (2000). Valence-dependent probability of ingroup favouritism between minimal groups: An integrative view on the positive-negative asymmetry in social discrimination. In D. Capozza (Ed.), *Social identity processes: Trends in theory and research* (pp. 33–48). London: Sage Publications.

Otten, S., Mummendey, A., & Blanz, M. (1996). Intergroup discrimination in positive and negative outcome allocations: Impact of stimulus valence, relative group status, and relative group size. *Personality and Social Psychology Bulletin, 22,* 568–581.

Otten, S., & Wentura, D. (2001). Self-anchoring and in-group favoritism: An individual profiles analysis. *Journal of Experimental Social Psychology, 37*(6), 525–532.

Ouellette, J. A., & Wood, W. (1998). Habit and intention in everyday life: The multiple processes by which past behavior predicts future behavior. *Psychological Bulletin, 124,* 54–74.

Owens, G., & Ford, J. G. (1978). Further consideration of the "What is good is beautiful" finding. *Social Psychology, 41,* 73–75.

Packard, V. (1971). *The hidden persuaders.* New York: D. McKay Company.

Paichelier, G. (1976). Norms and attitude change I: Polarization and styles of behavior. *European Journal of Social Psychology, 6,* 405–27.

Paladino, M.-P., Leyens, J.-P., Rodriguez, R., Rodriguez, A., Gaunt, R., & Demoulin, S. P. (2002). Differential association of uniquely and non uniquely human emotions with the ingroup and the outgroup. *Group Processes & Intergroup Relations, 5*(2), 105–117.

Pallak, M. S., Cook. D. A., & Sullivan, J. J. (1980). Commitment and energy conservation. In L. Bickman (Ed.), *Applied social psychology annual* (Vol. 1, pp. 235–253). Beverly Hills, CA: Sage Publications.

Pallak, S. R. (1983). Salience of a communicator's physical attractiveness and persuasion: A heuristic versus systematic processing interpretation. *Social Cognition, 2,* 156–168.

Pandey, J., & Singh, A. K. (1986). Attribution and evaluation of manipulative social behavior. *Journal of Social Psychology, 126,* 735–744.

Park, B. (1986). A method for studying the development of impressions of real people. *Journal of Personality and Social Psychology, 51,* 907–917.

Park, B., & Judd, C. M. (1990). Measures and models of perceived group variability. *Journal of Personality and Social Psychology, 59,* 173–191.

Park, B., & Judd, C. M. (2005). Rethinking the link between categorization and prejudice within the social cognition perspective. *Personality and Social Psychology Review, 9,* 108–130.

Park, B., & Rothbart, M. (1982). Perception of out-group homogeneity and levels of social categorization: Memory for the subordinate attributes of in-group and out-group members. *Journal of Personality and Social Psychology, 42,* 1051–1068.

Parke, R. D., Berkowitz, L., Leyens, J.-P., West, S. G., & Sebastian, R. J. (1977). Some effects of violent and nonviolent movies on the behavior of juvenile delinquents. In L. Berkowitz (Ed.), *Advances in experimental social psychology* (Vol. 10, pp. 135–172). New York: Academic Press.

Patterson, G. R., Littman, R. A., & Bricker, W. (1967). Assertive behavior in children: A step toward a theory of aggression. *Monographs of the Society for Research in Child Development* (No. 113), *32,* 5.

Patterson, M. L., Churchill, M. E., Burger, G. K., & Powell, J. L. (1992). Verbal and nonverbal modality effects on impressions of political candidates: Analysis from the 1984 Presidential debates. *Communication Monographs, 59,* 231–242.

Paulus, P. B. (1988). *Prison crowding: A psychological perspective.* New York: Springer-Verlag.

Paulus, P. B., Annis, A. B., Seta, J. J., Schkade, J. K., & Matthews, R. W. (1976). Density does affect task performance. *Journal of Personality and Social Psychology, 34,* 248–253.

Paulus, P. B., & Brown, V. R. (2003). Enhancing ideational creativity in groups: Lessons from research on brainstorming. In P. B. Paulus and others (Eds.), *Group creativity: Innovation through collaboration* (pp. 110–136). London: Oxford University Press.

Paulus, P. B., Dzindolet, M. T., Poletes, G., & Camacho, L. M. (1993). Perception of performance in group brainstorming: The illusion of group productivity. *Personality and Social Psychology Bulletin, 19,* 78–89.

Payne, B. K. (2001). Prejudice and perception: The role of automatic and controlled processes in misperceiving a weapon. *Journal of Personality & Social Psychology, 81*(2), 181–192.

Payne, B. K., Lambert, A. J., & Jacoby, L. L. (2002). Best laid plans: Effects of goals on accessibility bias and cognitive control in race-based misperceptions of weapons. *Journal of Experimental Social Psychology, 38,* 384–396.

Pelham, B. (1991). On confidence and consequence: The certainty and importance of self-knowledge. *Journal of Personality and Social Psychology, 60,* 518–530.

Pelham, B. W., Carvallo, M., & Jones, J. T. (2005). Implicit egotism. *Current Directions in Psychological Science, 14,* 106–110.

Pendleton, M. G., & Bateson, C. D. (1979). Self-presentation and the door-in-the-face technique for inducing compliance. *Personality and Social Psychology Bulletin, 5,* 77–81.

Pennebaker, J. W. (1997). Writing about emotional experiences as a therapeutic process. *Psychological Science, 8,* 162–166.

Pennebaker, J. W., Kiecolt-Glaser, J. K., & Glaser, R. (1988). Disclosure of traumas and immune function: Health implications for psychotherapy. *Journal of Consulting and Clinical Psychology, 56,* 239–245.

Penner, L. A. (2002). The causes of sustained volunteerism: An interactionist perspective. *Journal of Social Issues*, 58, 447–467.

Penner, L. A., Dovidio, J. F., Piliavin, J. A., & Schroeder, D. A. (2005). Prosocial behavior: Multilevel perspectives. *Annual Review of Psychology*, 56, 365–392.

Penner, L. A., & Finkelstein, M. A. (1998). Dispositional and structural determinants of volunteerism. *Journal of Personality and Social Psychology*, 74, 525–537.

Penner, L. A., Fritzsche, B. A., Craiger, J. P., & Freifeld, T. R. (1995). Measuring the prosocial personality. In J. Butcher & C. D. Spielberger (Eds.), *Advances in personality assessment* (Vol. 10, pp. 147–163). Hillsdale, NJ: Lawerence Erlbaum Associates, Inc.

Penton-Voak, I. S., Perrett, D. I., Castles, D. L., Kobayashi, T., Burt, D. M., Murray, L. K. and others (1999). Menstrual cycle alters face preference. *Nature*, 399, 741–742.

Peplau, L. A., & Conrad, E. (1989). Beyond nonsexist research: The perils of feminist methods in psychology. *Psychology of Women Quarterly*, 13, 379–400.

Peplau, L. A., Rubin, Z., and Hill, C. T. (1977). Sexual intimacy in dating relationships. *Journal of Social Issues*, 33, 86–109.

Perdue, C. W., Dovidio, J. F., Gurtman, M. B., & Tyler, R. B. (1990). Us and them: Social categorization and the process of intergroup bias. *Journal of Personality and Social Psychology*, 59, 475–486.

Perez, J. A., & Mugny, G. (1990). Minority influence: Manifest discrimination and latent influences. In D. Abrams, & M. Hogg (Eds.), *Social identity theory: Constructive and critical advances*. London: Harvester Wheatsheaf.

Perkins, H. W., & Berkowitz, A. D. (1986). Perceiving the community norms of alcohol use among students: Some research implications for campus alcohol education programming. *International Journal of Addictions*, 21, 961–976.

Perlow, L., & Weeks, J. (2002). Who's helping whom? Layers of culture and workplace behavior. *Journal of Organizational Behavior*, 23, 345–361.

Perry, D. G., Perry, L. C., & Rasmussen, P. (1986). Cognitive social learning mediators of aggression. *Child Development*, 57, 700–711.

Perry, D. G., Williard, J. C., & Perry, L. C. (1990). Peers' perceptions of the consequences that victimized children provide aggressors. *Child Development*, 61, 1310–1325.

Peterson, C., Seligman, M. E., & Vaillant, G. E. (1988). Pessimistic explanatory style is a risk factor for physical illness: A thirty-five-year longitudinal study. *Journal of Personality and Social Psychology*, 55, 23–27.

Peterson, D. R. (1979). Assessing interpersonal relationships by means of interaction records. *Behavioral Assessment*, 1, 221–236.

Peterson, D. R. (1983). Conflict. In H. H. Kelley, E. Berscheid, A. Christensen, J. H. Harvey, T. L. Huston, G. Levinger and others (Eds.), *Close relationships* (pp. 360–396). San Francisco, CA: Freeman.

Peterson, R. A. (1977). Consumer perceptions as a function of product, color, price, and nutritional labeling. In W. D. Perrault (Ed.), *Advances in consumer research* (pp. 61–62). Atlanta, GA: Association for Consumer Research.

Peterson, R. S., Owens, P. D., Tetlock, P. E., Fan, E. T., & Martorana, P. (1998). Group dynamics in top management teams: Groupthink, vigilance, and alternative models of organizational

failure and success. *Organizational Behavior and Human Decision Processes*, 73, 272–305.

Pettigrew, T. F. (1958). Personality and sociocultural factors in intergroup attitudes: A cross-national comparison. *Journal of Conflict Resolution*, 2, 29–42.

Pettigrew, T. F. (1968). Race relations: Social and psychological aspects. In D. L. Sills (Ed.), *The international encyclopedia of of the social sciences* (Vol. 13, pp. 277–282). New York: Macmillan.

Pettigrew, T. F. (1979). The ultimate attribution error: Extending Allport's cognitive analysis of prejudice. *Personality and Social Psychology Bulletin*, 5, 461–476.

Pettigrew, T. F. (1980). Prejudice. In S. Thernstrom (Ed.), *Harvard encyclopedia of American ethnic groups*. Cambridge, MA: Harvard University Press.

Pettigrew, T. F. (1997). Generalized intergroup contact effects on prejudice. *Personality and Social Psychology Bulletin*, 23, 173–185.

Pettigrew, T. F. (1998). Intergroup contact theory. *Annual Review of Psychology*, 49, 65–85.

Pettigrew, T. F. (2003). Peoples under threat: Americans, Arabs, and Israelis. *Peace and Conflict: Journal of Peace Psychology*, 9, 69–90.

Pettigrew, T. F., & Martin, J. (1987). Shaping the organizational context for black American inclusion. *Journal of Social Issues*, 43, 41–78.

Pettigrew, T. F., & Tropp, L. R. (2006). A meta-analytic test of intergroup contact theory. *Journal of Personality and Social Psychology*, 90, 751–783.

Petty, R. E., Brinol, P., & Tormala, Z. L. (2002). Thought confidence as a determinant of persuasion: The self-validation hypothesis. *Journal of Personality & Social Psychology*, 82, 722–741.

Petty, R. E., & Cacioppo, J. T. (1977). Forewarning, cognitive responding, and resistance to persuasion. *Journal of Personality and Social Psychology*, 35, 645–655.

Petty, R. E., & Cacioppo, J. T. (1979). Effects of forewarning of persuasive intent and involvement on cognitive responses and persuasion. *Personality and Social Psychology Bulletin*, 5, 173–176.

Petty, R. E., & Cacioppo, J. T. (1981). *Attitudes and persuasion: Classic and contemporary approaches*. Dubuque, IA: Wm. C. Brown.

Petty, R. E., & Cacioppo, J. T. (1984). The effects of involvement on responses to argument quantity and quality: Central and peripheral routes to persuasion. *Journal of Personality and Social Psychology*, 46, 69–81.

Petty, R. E., & Cacioppo, J. T. (1986). *Communication and persuasion: Central and peripheral routes to attitude change*. New York: Springer-Verlag.

Petty, R. E., Cacioppo, J. T., & Goldman, R. (1981). Personal involvement as a determinant of argument-based persuasion. *Journal of Personality and Social Psychology*, 41, 847–855.

Petty, R. E., Haugtvedt, C. P., & Smith, S. M. (1995). Elaboration as a determinant of attitude strength: Creating attitudes that are persistent, resistant, and predictive of behavior. In R. E. Petty & J. A. Krosnick (Eds.), *Attitude strength: Antecedents and consequences* (pp. 93–130). Mahwah, NJ: Lawrence Erlbaum Associates, Inc.

Petty, R. E., Priester, J. R., & Wegener, D. T. (1994). Cognitive processes in attitude change. In R. S. Wyer & T. S. Srull (Eds.), *Handbook of social cognition* (2nd ed., Vol. 2, pp. 69–142). Hillsdale, NJ: Lawrence Erlbaum Associates, Inc.

Petty, R. E., Schumann, D. W., Richman, S. A., & Strathman, A. J. (1993). Positive mood and persuasion: Different roles for affect under high- and low-elaboration conditions. *Journal of Personality and Social Psychology, 64*, 5–20.

Petty, R. E., & Wegener, D. T. (1998a). Attitude change: Multiple roles for persuasion variables. In D. T. Gilbert, S. T. Fiske, & G. Lindzey (Eds.) *The handbook of social psychology* (4th ed., pp. 323–390). Boston, MA: McGraw-Hill.

Petty, R. E., & Wegener, D. T. (1998b). Matching versus mismatching attitude functions: Implications for scrutiny of persuasive messages. *Personality & Social Psychology Bulletin, 24*, 227–240.

Petty, R. E., Wells, G. L., & Brock, T. C. (1976). Distraction can enhance or reduce yielding to propaganda: Thought disruption versus effort justification. *Journal of Personality and Social Psychology, 34*, 874–884.

Pfau, M. (1995). Designing messages for behavioral inoculation. In E. Maibach & R. L. Parrott (Eds.), *Designing health messages: Approaches from communication theory and public health practice* (pp. 99–113). Thousand Oaks, CA: Sage Publications.

Pfau, M., & Burgoon, M. (1988). Inoculation in political campaign communication. *Human Communication Research, 15*, 91–111.

Pfau, M., Tusing, K. J., Koerner, A. F., Lee W., Godbold, L. C., Penaloza, L. J. and others (1997). Enriching the inoculation construct: The role of critical components in the process of resistance. *Human Communication Research, 24*, 187–215.

Phillips, A. P., & Dipboye, R. L. (1989). Correlational tests of predictions from a process model of the interview. *Journal of Applied Psychology, 74*, 41–52.

Pickett, C. L., Bonner, B. L., & Coleman, J. M. (2002). Motivated self-stereotyping: Heightened assimilation and differentiation needs result in increased levels of positive and negative self-stereotyping. *Journal of Personality and Social Psychology, 82*(4), 543–562.

Pietromonaco, P. R., & Feldman Barrett, L. (1997). Working models of attachment and daily social interactions. *Journal of Personality and Social Psychology, 73*, 1409–1423.

Piliavin, J. A., Callero, P. L., & Evans, D. E. (1982). Addiction to altruism? Opponent-process theory and habitual blood donation. *Journal of Personality and Social Psychology, 43*, 1200–1213.

Piliavin, J. A., Dovidio, J. F., Gaertner, S. L., & Clark, R. D., III (1981). *Emergency intervention*. New York: Academic Press.

Pines, A. M., Aronson, E., & Kafry, D. (1981). *Burnout: From tedium to personal growth*. New York: Freeman.

Pittman, T. S. (1975). Atribution of arousal as a mediator of dissonance reduction. *Journal of Experimental Social Psychology, 11*, 53–63.

Platow, M. J., Haslam, S. A., Both, A., Chew, I., Cuddon, M., Goharpey, N. and others (2005) "It's not funny if they're laughing": Self-categorization, social influence, and responses to canned laughter. *Journal of Experimental Social Psychology, 41*, 542–550.

Platt, J. (1973). Social traps. *American Psychologist, 28*, 641–651.

Platz, S. J., & Hosch, H. M. (1988). Cross-racial/ethnic eyewitness identification: A field study. *Journal of Applied Social Psychology, 18*, 972–984.

Pohl, O. (2003, August 3). What: Mob scene. Who: Strangers. Point: None. *New York Times*, p. A4.

Pomerantz, E. M., Chaiken, S., & Tordesillas, R. S. (1995). Attitude strength and resistance processes. *Journal of Personality and Social Psychology, 69*, 408–419.

Postmes, T., Haslam, S. A., & Swaab, R. (2005) Social influence in small groups: An interactive model of social identity formation. *European Review of Social Psychology, 16*, 1–42.

Postmes, T., & Spears, R. (1998). Deindividuation and antinormative behavior: A meta-analysis. *Psychological Bulletin, 123*, 1–22.

Postmes, T., Spears, R., & Cihangir, S. (2001). Quality of decision making and group norms. *Journal of Personality and Social Psychology, 80*, 918–930.

Postmes, T., Spears, R., Lee, A. T., & Novak, R. J. (2005) Individuality and social influence in groups: Inductive and deductive routes to group identity. *Journal of Personality and Social Psychology, 89*, 747–763.

Postmes, T., Spears, R., Sakhel, K., & de Groot, D. (2001). Social influence in computer-mediated communication: The effects of anonymity on group behavior. *Personality and Social Psychology Bulletin, 27*, 1243–1254.

Pranulis, M., Dabbs, J., & Johnson, J. (1975). General anesthsia and the patient's attempts at control. *Social Behavior and Personality, 3*, 49–54.

Pratto, F., Sidanius, J., Stallworth, L. M., & Malle, B. F. (1994). Social dominance orientation: A personality variable predicting social and political attitudes. *Journal of Personality and Social Psychology, 67*, 741–763.

Prentice, D. A. (1990). Familiarity and differences in self- and other-representations. *Journal of Personality and Social Psychology, 59*, 369–383.

Prentice, D. A., & Miller, D. T. (1993). Pluralistic ignorance and alcohol use on campus: Some consequences of misperceiving the social norm. *Journal of Personality and Social Psychology, 64*, 243–256.

Prentice, D. A., & Miller, D. T. (2002). The emergence of homegrown stereotypes. *American Psychologist, 57*(5), 352–359.

Presidential Commission on the Space Shuttle Challenger Accident (1986, June 6). (W. Rodgers, Chair). Washington, DC: U.S. Government Printing Office.

President's Commission on Law Enforcement and Administration of Justice (1967). *The challenge of crime in a free society*. Washington, DC: U.S. Government Printing Office.

Price, J. M., & Dodge, K. A. (1989). Reactive and proactive aggression in childhood: Relations to peer status and social context dimensions. *Journal of Abnormal Child Psychology, 17*, 455–471.

Price, V. (1989). Social identification and public opinion: Effects of communicating group conflict. *Public Opinion Quarterly, 53*, 197–224.

Priester, J. R., Cacioppo, J. T., & Petty, R. E. (1996). The influence of motor processes on attitudes toward novel versus familiar semantic stimuli. *Personality and Social Psychology Bulletin, 22*, 442–447.

Priester, J. R., & Petty, R. E. (2001). Extending the bases of subjective attitudinal ambivalence: Interpersonal and intrapersonal antecedents of evaluative tension. *Journal of Personality & Social Psychology, 80*, 19–34.

Pritchard, R. D. (Ed.). (1995). *Productivity measurement and improvement: Organization case studies*. Westport, CT: Praeger Publishers/Greenwood Publishing Group, Inc.

Pritchard, R. D., Jones, S. D., Roth, P. L., & Stuebing, K. K. (1988). Effects of group feedback, goal setting, and incentives on organizational productivity. *Journal of Applied Psychology, 73*, 337–358.

Pritchard, R. D., Jones, S. D., Roth, P. L., & Stuebing, K. K. (1989). The evaluation of an integrated approach to measuring organizational productivity. *Personnel Psychology, 42*, 69–115.

Pruitt, D. G. (1981). *Negotiation behavior.* New York: Academic Press.

Pruitt, D. G. (1986). Acheiving integrative agreements in negotiation. In R. K. White (Ed.), *Psychology and the prevention of nuclear war* (pp. 463–478). New York: New York University Press.

Pruitt, D. G. (1998). Social conflict. In D. T. Gilbert, S. T. Fiske, & G. Lindzey (Eds.), *Handbook of social psychology* (3rd ed., Vol. 2, pp. 470–503). Boston: McGraw-Hill.

Pruitt, D. G., & Kimmel, M. J. (1977). Twenty years of experimental gaming: Critique, synthesis, and suggestions for the future. *Annual Review of Psychology, 28*, 3–392.

Pruitt, D. G., & Lewis, S. A. (1977). The psychology of integrative bargaining. In D. Druckman (Ed.), *Negotiations: A social-psychological analysis* (pp. 161–192). New York: Halstead.

Pruitt, D. G., & Rubin, J. Z. (1986). *Social conflict: Escalation, stalemate, and settlement.* New York: Random House.

Puts, D. A. (2005). Mating context and menstrual phase affect women's preferences for male voice pitch. *Evolution and Human Behavior, 26*, 388–397.

Pyszczynski, T., & Greenberg, J. (1987). Self-regulatory perseveration and the depressive self-focusing style: A self-awareness theory of reactive depression. *Psychological Bulletin, 102*, 122–138.

Quigley-Fernandez, B., & Tedeschi, J. T. (1978). The bogus pipeline as lie detector: Two validity studies. *Journal of Personality and Social Psychology, 36*, 247–256.

Rabbie, J. M., & Bekkers, F. (1978). Threatened leadership and intergorup competition. *European Journal of Social Psychology, 8*, 9–20.

Radin, C. (1992, September 9). Colleges compete for high-achieving black students. *Boston Globe*, pp. 1, 19.

Rafaeli-Mor, E., & Steinberg, J. (2002). Self-complexity and well-being: A review and research synthesis. *Personality and Social Psychology Review, 6*, 31–58.

Rafferty, A. E., & Griffin, M. A. (2004). Dimensions of transformational leadership: Conceptual and empirical extensions. *Leadership Quarterly, 15*, 329–354.

Rank, S. J., & Jacobsen, C. K. (1977). Hospital nurses' compliance with medication overdose orders: A failure to replicate. *Journal of Health and Social Behavior, 18*, 188–193.

Rapoport, A., & Bornstein, G. (1987). Intergroup competition for the provision of binary public goods. *Psychological Review, 94*, 291–299.

Rapoport, A., & Eshed-Levy, D. (1989). Provision of step-level public goods: Effects of greed and fear of being gypped. *Organizational Behavior and Human Decision Processes, 44*.

Rasinski, K. A., Crocker, J., & Hastie, R. (1985). Another look at sex stereotypes and social judgments: An analysis of the social perceiver's use of subjective probabilities. *Journal of Personality and Social Psychology, 49*, 317–326.

Raven, B. H. (1998). Groupthink, Bay of Pigs, and Watergate reconsidered. *Organizational Behavior and Human Decision Processes, 73*, 352–361.

Raven, B. H., & Rubin, J. Z. (1976). *Social psychology: People in groups.* New York: Wiley.

Reber, R., Schwarz, N., & Winkielman, P. (2004). Processing fluency and aesthetic pleasure: Is beauty in the perceiver's processing experience? *Personality and Social Psychology Review, 8*, 364–382.

Redfern, D. (1979). *Individual level and group level determinants of nurses' compliance with physicians' inappropriate medical orders.* Paper presented at the annual meeting of the American Psychological Association, New York.

Reeves, B., & Nass, C. (1996). *The media equation.* Cambridge, UK: Cambridge University Press.

Regan, D. T. (1971). Effects of a favor and liking on compliance. *Journal of Experimental Social Psychology, 7*, 627–639.

Regan, P. C. (1998). What if you can't get what you want? Willingness to compromise ideal mate selection standards as a function of sex, mate value, and relationship context. *Personality and Social Psychology Bulletin, 24*, 1294–1303.

Regan, P. C, Levin, L., Sprecher, S., Christopher, F. S., & Cate, R. (2000). Partner preferences: What characteristics do men and women desire in their short-term sexual and long-term romantic partners? *Journal of Psychology and Human Sexuality, 12*, 1–21.

Rehm, J., Steinleitner, J., & Lilli, W. (1987). Wearing uniforms and aggression: A field experiment. *European Journal of Social Psychology, 17*, 357–60.

Reich, R. D. (1993, July 28). The "pronoun test" for success. *Washington Post*, p. A19.

Reicher, S., Haslam, S. A., & Hopkins, N. (2005). Social identity and the dynamics of leadership: Leaders and followers as collaborative agents in the transformation of social reality. *Leadership Quarterly, 16*, 547–568.

Reicher, S. D. (1987). Crowd behavior as social action. In J. C. Turner, *Rediscovering the social group: A self-categorization theory* (pp. 171–202). Oxford, UK: Blackwell.

Reid, F. J. M. (1983). Polarizing effects of intergroup comparison. *European Journal of Social Psychology, 13*, 103–106.

Reis, H. T. (1986). Gender effects in social participation: Intimacy, loneliness, and the conduct of social interaction. In R. Gilmour & S. Duck (Eds.), *The emerging field of personal relationships* (pp. 91–108). Hillsdale, NJ: Lawrence Erlbaum Associates, Inc.

Reis, H. T., Clark, M. S., & Holmes, J. G. (2004). Perceived partner responsiveness as an organizing construct in the study of intimacy and closeness. In D. J. Mashek & A. P. Aron (Eds.), *Handbook of closeness and intimacy* (pp. 201–225). Mahwah, NJ: Lawrence Erlbaum Associates, Inc.

Reis, H. T., & Gable, S. L. (2003). Toward a positive psychology of relationships. In C. L. M. Keyes & J. Haidt (Eds.), *Flourishing: Positive psychology and the life well-lived* (pp. 129–159). Washington, DC: American Psychological Association.

Reis, H. T., & Patrick, B. C. (1996). Attachment and intimacy: Component processes. In E. T. Higgins & A. W. Kruglanski (Eds.), *Social psychology: Handbook of basic principles* (pp. 523–563). New York: Guilford Press.

Reis, H. T., Senchak, M., & Solomon, B. (1985). Sex differences in the intimacy of social interaction. *Journal of Personality and Social Psychology, 48*, 1204–1217.

Reis, H. T., Wheeler, L., Spiegel, N., Kernis, M., Nezlek, J., & Perri, M. (1982). Physical attractiveness in social interaction: II. Why does appearance affect social experience? *Journal of Personality and Social Psychology, 43*, 979–996.

Reisenzein, R. (1983). The Schacter theory of emotion: Two decades later. *Psychological Bulletin, 94*, 239–264.

Reisenzein, R. (1986). A structural equation analysis of Weiner's attribution-affect model of helping behavior. *Journal of Personality and Social Psychology, 50,* 1123–1133.

Reiss, I. L. (1986). A sociological journey into sexuality. *Journal of Marriage and the Family, 48,* 233–242.

Reiss, I. L., & Lee, G. R. (1988). *Family systems in America* (4th ed.). New York: Holt, Rinehart, & Winston.

Reychler, L. (1979). The effectiveness of a pacifist strategy in conflict resolution: An experimental study. *Journal of Conflict Resolution, 23,* 288–260.

Rhodewalt, F., & Agustsdottir, S. (1986). Effects of self-presentation on the phenomenal self. *Journal of Personality and Social Psychology, 50,* 47–55.

Rholes, W. S., & Pryor, J. B. (1982). Cognitive accessibility and causal attributions. *Personality and Social Psychology Bulletin, 8,* 719–727.

Richards, J. M., & Gross, J. J. (2000). Emotion regulation and memory: The cognitive costs of keeping one's cool. *Journal of Personality and Social Psychology, 79,* 410–424.

Ridgeway, J. (1991, April 28). A meeting with haters. *Parade,* p. 5.

Ringelmann, M. (1913). Recherches sure les moteurs animés: Travail de l'homme. *Annales de l'Institute National Agronomique, 2e série, tom Xii,* 1–40.

Robberson, M. R., & Rogers, R. W. (1988). Beyond fear appeals: Negative and positive persuasive appeals to health and self esteem. *Journal of Applied Social Psychology, 18,* 277–287.

Robbins, J. M., & Krueger, J. I. (2005). Social projection to ingroup and outgroups: A review and meta-analysis. *Personality and Social Psychology Review, 9,* 32–47.

Robinson, J., & McArthur, L. Z. (1982). Impact of salient vocal qualities on causal attribution for a speaker's behavior. *Journal of Personality and Social Psychology, 43,* 236–247.

Robinson, R., & Bell, W. (1978). Equality, success, and social justice in England and the United States. *American Sociological Review, 43,* 125–143.

Robinson, T. R., Smith, S. W., Miller, M. D., & Brownell, M. T. (1999). Cognitive behavior modification of hyperactivity-impulsivity and aggression: A meta-analysis of school-based studies. *Journal of Educational Psychology, 91,* 195–203.

Rochat, F., & Modigliani, A. (1995). The ordinary quality of resistance: From Milgram's laboratory to the village of Le Chambon. *Journal of Social Issues, 51,* 195–210.

Rodin, J. (1985). The application of social psychology. In G. Lindzey & E. Aronson (Eds.), *Handbook of social psychology* (Vol. II, pp. 805–882). New York: Random House.

Rodin, J., & Salovey, P. (1989). Health psychology. *Annual Review of Psychology, 40,* 533–579.

Rodin, J., Solomon, S., & Metcalf, J. (1978). Role of control in mediating perceptions of density. *Journal of Personality and Social Psychology, 36,* 988–999.

Rodin, M. J. (1987). Who is memorable to whom: A study of cognitive disregard. *Social Cognition, 5,* 144–165.

Roethlisberger, F. J., & Dickson, W. J. (1939). *Management and the worker.* Cambridge, MA: Harvard University Press.

Rofé, Y. (1984). Stress and affiliation: Activity theory. *Psychological Review, 91,* 235–250.

Rogers, R. W. (1983). Cognitive and physiological processes in fear appeals and attitude change: A revised theory of protection motivation. In J. T. Cacioppo & R. E. Petty (Eds.), *Social psychophysiology: A sourcebook.* New York: Guilford Press.

Rogers, T. B. (1981). A model of the self as an aspect of the human information processing system. In N. Cantor & J. F. Kihlstrom (Eds.), *Personality, cognition, and social interaction* (pp. 193–214). Hillsdale, NJ: Lawrence Erlbaum Associates, Inc.

Rohrer, J. H., Baron, S. H., Hoffman, E. L., & Schwander, D. V. (1954). The stability of autokinetic judgments. *Journal of Abnormal and Social Psychology, 49,* 595–597.

Romer, D., Jamieson, K. H., & de Coteau, N. J. (1998). The treatment of persons of color in local television news: Ethnic blame discourse or realistic group conflict? *Communication Research, 25,* 286–305.

Ronis, D. L., & Kaiser, M. K. (1989). Correlates of breast self-examination in a sample of college women: Analyses of linear structural relations. *Journal of Applied Social Psychology, 19,* 1068–1084.

Rook, K. S., & Peplau, L. A. (1982). Perspectives on helping the lonely. In L. A. Peplau & D. Perlman (Eds.), *Loneliness.* New York: Wiley Interscience.

Rook, K. S., & Pietromonaco, P. (1987). Close relationship: Ties that heal or ties that bind? In W. H. Jones & D. Perlman (Eds.), *Advances in personal relationships* (Vol. 1, pp. 1–35). Greenwich, CT: JAI Press.

Roseman, I. J., Spindel, M. S., & Jose, P. E. (1990). Appraisals of emotion-eliciting events: Testing a theory of discrete emotions. *Journal of Personality and Social Psychology, 59,* 899–915.

Rosenbaum, M. E. (1986). The repulsion hypothesis: On the nondevelopment of relationships. *Journal of Personality and Social Psychology, 51,* 1156–1166.

Rosenberg, M. (1956). Cognitive structure and attitudinal affect. *Journal of Abnormal and Social Psychology, 53,* 367–372.

Rosenberg, M. (1965). *Society and the adolescent self-image.* Princeton, NJ: Princeton University Press.

Rosenberg, M. (1969). The conditions and consequences of evaluation apprehension. In R. Rosenthal & R. L. Rosnow (Eds.), *Artifact in behavioral research* (pp. 279–349). New York: Academic Press.

Rosenberg, M. (1979). *Conceiving the self.* New York: Basic Books.

Rosenberg, M., & Simmons, R. B. (1971). *Black & white self-esteem: The urban school child.* Washington, DC: The American Sociological Association.

Rosenberg, S., Nelson, C., & Vivekananthan, P. S. (1968). A multidimensional approach to the structure of personality impressions. *Journal of Personality and Social Psychology, 9,* 283–294.

Rosenfeld, P., Giacalone, R., & Tedeschi, J. T. (1984). Cognitive dissonances and impression management explanations for effort justification. *Personality and Social Psychology Bulletin, 10,* 394–401.

Rosenfield, D., and Stephan, W. G. (1981). Intergroup relations among children. In S. Brehm, S. Kassin, & F. Gibbons (Eds.), *Developmental social psychology* (pp. 271–297). New York: Oxford University Press.

Rosenhan, D. (1970). The natural socialization of altruistic autonomy. In J. Macaulay & L. Berkowitz (Eds.), *Altruism and helping behavior.* New York: Academic Press.

Rosenhan, D. L. (1973). On being sane in insane places. *Science*, *179*, 250–258.

Rosenthal, R. (1969). Interpersonal expectations: Effects of the experimenter's hypothesis. In R. Rosenthal & R. L. Rosnow (Eds.), *Artifact in behavioral research* (pp. 181–277). New York: Academic Press.

Rosenthal, R. (1985). From unconscious experimenter bias to teacher expectancy effects. In J. B. Dusek, V. C. Hall, & W. J. Meyer (Eds.), *Teacher expectancies* (pp. 37–66). Hillsdale, NJ: Lawrence Erlbaum Associates, Inc.

Rosenthal, R. (1991). Meta-analysis: A review. *Psychosomatic Medicine*, *53*, 247–271.

Rosenthal, R., & Fode, K. L. (1963). Three experiments in experimenter bias. *Psychological Reports*, *12*, 491–511.

Rosenthal, R., & Jacobson, L. (1968). *Pygmalion in the classroom*. New York: Holt, Rinehart, & Winston.

Rosnow, R. L., & Fine, G. A. (1976). *Rumor and gossip: The social psychology of hearsay*. New York: Elsevier.

Ross, A. S., & Braband, J. (1973). Effect of increased responsibility on bystander intervention: II. The cue value of a blind person. *Journal of Personality and Social Psychology*, *25*, 254–258.

Ross, L. (1977). The intuitive psychologist and his shortcomings: Distortions in the attribution process. In L. Berkowitz (Ed.), *Advances in experimental social psychology* (Vol. 10, pp. 174–221). New York: Academic Press.

Ross, L. D., Amabile, T. M., & Steinmetz, J. L. (1977). Social roles, social control, and biases in social-perception processes. *Journal of Personality and Social Psychology*, *35*, 485–494.

Ross, L., Lepper, M. R., & Hubbard, M. (1975). Perseverance in self-perception and social perception: Biased attributional processes in the debriefing paradigm. *Journal of Personality and Social Psychology*, *32*, 880–892.

Ross, L., & Nisbett, R. E. (1990). *The person and the situation*. New York: McGraw-Hill.

Ross, M. (1989). The relation of implicit theories to the construction of personal histories. *Psychological Review*, *96*, 341–357.

Ross, M., & Conway, M. (1986). Remembering one's own past: The construction of personal histories. In R. Sorrentino & E. T. Higgins (Eds.), *Handbook of motivation and cognition* (pp. 122–144). New York: Guilford Press.

Ross, M., McFarland, C., Conway, M., & Zanna, M. P. (1983). Reciprocal relation between attitudes and behavior recall: Committing people to newly formed attitudes. *Journal of Personality and Social Psychology*, *45*, 257–267.

Ross, M., McFarland, C., & Fletcher, G. J. O. (1981). The effect of attitude on recall of past histories. *Journal of Personality and Social Psychology*, *40*, 627–634.

Ross, M., & Sicoly, F. (1979). Egocentric biases in availability and attribution. *Journal of Personality and Social Psychology*, *37*, 322–336.

Ross, S. I., & Jackson, J. M. (1991). Teacher's expectations for black males' and black females' academic achievement. *Personality and Social Psychology Bulletin*, *17*, 78–82.

Rosselli, F., Skelly, J. J., & Mackie, D. M. (1995). Processing rational and emotional messages: The cognitive and affective mediation of persuasion. *Journal of Experimental Social Psychology*, *31*, 163–190.

Rothbart, M. (1981). Memory processes and social beliefs. In D. L. Hamilton (Ed.), *Cognitive processes in stereotyping and intergroup behavior* (pp. 145–182). Hillsdale, NJ: Lawrence Erlbaum Associates, Inc.

Rothbart, M., Dawes, R., & Park, B. (1984). Stereotyping and sampling biases in intergroup perception. In J. R. Eiser (Ed.), *Attitudinal judgment* (pp. 109–134). New York: Springer-Verlag.

Rothbart, M., Evans, M., & Fulero, S. (1979). Recall for confirming events: Memory processes and the maintenance of social stereotyping. *Journal of Experimental Social Psychology*, *15*, 343–355.

Rothbart, M., Fulero, S., Jensen, C., Howard, J., & Birrel, P. (1978). From individual to group impressions: Availability heuristics in stereotype formation. *Journal of Experimental Social Psychology*, *14*, 237–255.

Rothbart, M., & Hallmark, W. (1988). In-group–out-group differences in the perceived efficacy of coercion and conciliation in resolving social conflict. *Journal of Personality and Social Psychology*, *55*, 248–257.

Rothbart, M., & John, O. P. (1985). Social categorization and behavioral episodes: A cognitive analysis of the effects of intergroup contact. *Journal of Social Issues*, *41*, 81–104.

Rothbart, M., & Park, B. (1986). On the confirmability and disconfirmability of trait concepts. *Journal of Personality and Social Psychology*, *50*, 131–142.

Rothenberg, R. (1991, July 23). Blacks are found to be still scarce in advertisements in major magazines. *New York Times*, p. A7.

Rotton, J., & Cohn, E. G. (2000). Violence is a curvilinear function of temperature in Dallas: A replication. *Journal of Personality & Social Psychology*, *78*(6), 1074–1081.

Rozin, P., & Royzman, E. B. (2001). Negativity bias, negativity dominance, and contagion. *Personality and Social Psychology Review*, *5*, 296–320.

Ruback, R. B., & Pandey, J. (1991). Crowding, perceived control, and relative power: An analysis of households in India. *Journal of Applied Social Psychology*, *21*, 315–344.

Rubenstein, C. M., Shaver, P., & Peplau, L. A. (1979). Loneliness. *Human Nature*, *2*, 58–65.

Rubin, B. (1987). *Third world coup makers, strongmen, and populist tyrants*. New York: McGraw-Hill

Rubin, J. Z. (1980). Experimental research on third-party intervention in conflict: Toward some generalizations. *Psychological Bulletin*, *87*, 379–391.

Rubin, J. Z., & Brown, B. R. (1975). *The social psychology of bargaining and negotiation*. New York: Academic Press.

Rubin, M., & Hewstone, M. (1998). Social identity theory's self-esteem hypothesis: A review and some suggestions for clarification. *Personality and Social Psychology Review*, *2*, 40–62.

Rubin, Z. (1970). Measurement of romantic love. *Journal of Personality and Social Psychology*, *16*, 265–273.

Rubin, Z., Hill, C. T., Peplau, L. A., & Dunkel-Schetter, C. (1980). Self-disclosure in dating couples: Sex roles and the ethic of openness. *Journal of Marriage and the Family*, *42*, 305–317.

Rudman, L., & Lee, M. R. (2002). Implicit and explicit consequences of exposure to violent and misogynistic rap music. *Group Processes and Intergroup Relations*, *5*, 133–150.

Rudman, L. A. (2005). Rejection of women? Beyond prejudice as antipathy. In J. F. Dovidio, P. Glic, & L.A. Rudman (Eds.), *On the nature of prejudice: Fifty years after Allport* (pp. 106–120). Malden, MA: Blackwell.

Rudman, L. J., & Bordiga, E. (1995). The afterglow of construct accessibility: The behavioral consequences of priming men to view women as sexual objects. *Journal of Experimental Social Psychology, 31*, 493–517.

Ruiz, F., & Tanaka, K. (2001). The relationship between cognitive dissonance and helping behavior. *Japanese Psychological Research, 43*, 55–62.

Rule, B. G., Taylor, B. R., & Dobbs, A. R. (1987). Priming effects of heat on aggressive thoughts. *Social Cognition, 5*, 131–143.

Runciman, W. G. (1966). *Relative deprivation and social justice.* Berkeley, CA: University of California Press.

Rusbult, C. E. (1983). A longitudinal test of the investment model: The development (and deterioration) of satisfaction and commitment in heterosexual involvements. *Journal of Personality and Social Psychology, 45*, 101–117.

Rusbult, C. E., Arriaga, X. B., & Agnew, C. R. (2001). Interdependence in close relationships. In G. J. O. Fletcher & M. S. Clark (Eds.), *Blackwell handbook of social psychology, Vol. 2: Interpersonal processes* (pp. 359–387). Oxford: Blackwell.

Rusbult, C. E., & Martz, J. M. (1995). Remaining in an abusive relationship: An investment model analysis of nonvoluntary commitment. *Personality and Social Psychology Bulletin, 21*, 558–571.

Rusbult, C. E., Martz, J. M., & Agnew, C. R. (1998). The Investment Model Scale: Measuring commitment level, satisfaction level, quality of alternatives, and investment size. *Personal Relationships, 5*, 357–391.

Rusbult, C. E., Verette, J., Whitney, G. A., Slovik, L. F., & Lipkus, I. (1991). Accommodation processes in close relationships: Theory and preliminary empirical evidence. *Journal of Personality and Social Psychology, 60*, 53–78.

Rusbult, C. E., Yovetich, N. A., & Verette, J. (1996). An interdependence analysis of accommodation processes. In G. J. O. Fletcher & J. Fitness (Eds.), *Knowledge structures in close relationships: A social psychological approach* (pp. 63–90). Mahwah, NJ: Lawrence Erlbaum Associates, Inc.

Rushton, J. P. (1975). Generosity in children: Immediate and long-term effects of modeling, preaching, and moral judgment. *Journal of Personality and Social Psychology, 31*, 459–466.

Ruskin, J. (1907/1963). *The seven lamps of architecture.* London: Everyman's Library.

Russell, C. A. (2002). Investigating the effectiveness of product placements in television shows: The role of modality and plot connection congruence on brand memory and attitude. *Journal of Consumer Research, 29*, 306–318.

Russell, J. A. (2003). Core affect and the psychological construction of emotion. *Psychological Review, 110*, 145–172.

Russell, J. J. (1994). Is there universal recognition of emotion from facial expressions? A review of the cross-cultural studies. *Psychological Bulletin, 115*, 102–141.

Rutter, D. R., & Robinson, B. (1981). An experimental analysis of teaching by telephone. In G. M. Stephenson & J. H. Davis (Eds.), *Progress in applied social psychology* (Vol. 1, pp. 345–374). New York: Wiley.

Ryan, C. S. (1996). Accuracy of black and white college students' in-group and out-group stereotypes. *Personality and Social Psychology Bulletin, 22*, 1114–1127.

Ryan, C. S., & Bogart, L. M. (1997). Development of new group members' in-group and out-group stereotypes: Changes in perceived group variability and ethnocentrism. *Journal of Personality and Social Psychology, 73*, 719–732.

Ryan, R. M., & Grolnick, W. S. (1986). Origins and pawns in the classroom: Self-report and projective assessments of individual differences in children's perceptions. *Journal of Personality and Social Psychology, 50*, 550–558.

Ryen, A. H., & Kahn, A. (1975). The effects of intergroup orientation on group attitudes and proxemic behavior. *Journal of Personality and Social Psychology, 31*, 302–310.

Sachdev, I., & Bourhis, R. Y. (1985). Social cateogrization and power differentials in group relations. *European Journal of Social Psychology, 15*, 415–434.

Sachdev, I., & Bourhis, R. Y. (1991). Power and status differentials in minority and majority group relations. *European Journal of Social Psychology, 21*, 1–24.

Sadri, G., & Lees, B. (2001). Developing corporate culture as a competitive advantage. *Journal of Management Development, 20*, 853–859.

Safire, W. (1992, August 27). God bless us. *New York Times*, p. A15.

Sagar, H. A., & Schofield, J. W. (1980). Racial and behavioral cues in black and white children's perceptions of ambiguously aggressive acts. *Journal of Personality and Social Psychology, 39*, 590–598.

Sagarin, B. J., Cialdini, R. B., Rice, W. E., & Serna, S. B. (2002). Dispelling the illusion of invulnerability: The motivations and mechanisms of resistance to persuasion. *Journal of Personality & Social Psychology, 83*, 526–541.

Sakai, H. (1999). A multiplicative power-function model of cognitive dissonance: Toward an integrated theory of cognition, emotion, and behavior after Leon Festinger. In E. Harmon-Jones & J. Mills (Eds.), *Cognitive dissonance: Progress on a pivotal theory in social psychology* (pp. 267–294). Washington, DC: American Psychological Association.

Sakai, H., & Andow, K. (1980). Attribution of personal responsibility and dissonance reduction. *Japanese Psychological Research, 22*, 32–41.

Salancik, G. R., & Conway, M. (1975). Attitude inferences from salient and relevant cognitive content about behavior. *Journal of Personality and Social Psychology, 32*, 829–840.

Salovey, P., & Rodin, J. (1984). Some antecedents and consequences of social-comparison jealousy. *Journal of Personality and Social Psychology, 47*, 780–792.

Salovey, P., & Rodin, J. (1989). Envy and jealousy in close relationships. In C. Hendrick (Ed.), *Close relationships* (pp. 221–246). Beverly Hills, CA: Sage.

Salovey, P., Rothman, A. J., & Rodin, J. (1998). Health behavior. In D. T. Gilbert, S. T. Fiske, & G. Lindzey (Eds.), *Handbook of social psychology* (4th ed., Vol. 2, pp. 633–683). Boston: McGraw-Hill.

Samuelson, C. D., Messick, D. M., Rutte, C. G., & Wilke, H. (1984). Individual and structural solutions to resource dilemmas in two cultures. *Journal of Personality and Social Psychology, 47*, 94–104.

Sande, G. N., Goethals, G. R., & Radloff, C. E. (1988). Perceiving one's own traits and others': The multifaceted self. *Journal of Personality and Social Psychology, 54*, 13–20.

Sanitioso, R., Kunda, Z., & Fong, G. T. (1990). Motivated recruitment of autobiographical memory. *Journal of Personality and Social Psychology, 59*, 229–241.

References 615

Sanna, L. J., & Shotland, R. L. (1990). Valence of anticipated evaluation and social facilitation. *Journal of Experimental Social Psychology, 26*, 82–92.

Sarason, B. R., Sarason, I. G., & Gurung, R. A. R. (1997). Close personal relationships and health outcomes: A key to the role of social support. In S. Duck (Ed.), *Handbook of personal relationships* (2nd ed., pp. 547–573). London: John Wiley & Sons.

Sassenberg, K., & Boos, M. (2003). Attitude change in computer-mediated communication: Effects of anonymity and category norms. *Group Processes and Intergroup Relations, 6*, 405–422.

Sato, K. (1987). Distribution of the cost of maintaining common resources. *Journal of Experimental Social Psychology, 23*, 19–31.

Sattler, D. N., & Kerr, N. L. (1991). Might versus morality explored: Motivational and cognitive bases for social motives. *Journal of Personality and Social Psychology, 60*, 756–765.

Saxe, L., Dougherty, D., & Cross, T. (1985). The validity of polygraph testing: Scientific analysis and public controversy. *American Psychologist, 40*, 355–366.

Schachter, S. (1951). Deviation, rejection and communication. *Journal of Abnormal and Social Psychology, 46*, 190–207.

Schacter, S. (1959). *The psychology of affiliation.* Stanford, CA: Stanford University Press.

Schacter, S., & Singer, J. (1962). Cognitive, social, and physiological determinants of the emotional state. *Psychological Review, 69*, 379–399.

Schafer, M., & Crichlow, S. (1996). Antecedents of groupthink. *Journal of Conflict Resolution, 40*, 415–435.

Schaller, M., Asp, C. H., Rosell, M. C., & Heim, S. J. (1996). Training in statistical reasoning inhibits the formation of erroneous group stereotypes. *Personality and Social Psychology Bulletin, 22*, 829–844.

Schaller, M., & Cialdini, R. B. (1988). The economics of empathic helping: Support for a mood management motive. *Journal of Experimental Social Psychology, 24*, 163–181.

Schaller, M., & Cialdini, R. B. (1990). Happiness, sadness, and helping: A motivational integration. In E. T. Higgins & R. M. Sorrentino (Eds.), *Handbook of motivation and cognition* (Vol. 2, pp. 265–296). New York: Guilford Press.

Scheier, M. F., & Carver, C. S. (1977). Self-focused attention and the experience of emotion: Attraction, repulsion, elation, and depression. *Journal of Personality and Social Psychology, 35*, 625–636.

Schein, V. E., Mueller, R., Lituchy, T., & Liu, J. (1996). Think manager – think male: A global phenomenon? *Journal of Organizational Behavior, 17*, 33–41.

Schell, T. L., Klein, S. B., & Babey, S. H. (1996). Testing a hierarchical model of self-knowledge. *Psychological Science, 7*, 170–173.

Schiller, J. C. F. (1882). *Essays, esthetical and philosophical, including the dissertation on the "Connexions between the animal and the spiritual in man."* London: Bell.

Schittekatte, M. (1996). Facilitating information exchange in small decision-making groups. *European Journal of Social Psychology, 26*, 537–556.

Schlenker, B. R. (1985). Identity and self-identification. In B. R. Schlenker (Ed.), *The self and social life* (pp. 65–100). New York: McGraw-Hill.

Schlenker, B. R., Dlugolecki, D. W., & Doherty, K. (1994). The impact of self-presentations on self-appraisals and behavior: The power of public commitment. *Personality and Social Psychology Bulletin, 20*, 20–33.

Schlenker, B. R., & Forsyth, D. R. (1977). On the ethics of psychological research. *Journal of Experimental Social Psychology, 13*, 369–396.

Schmader, T., & Johns, M. (2003). Converging evidence that stereotype threat reduces working memory capacity. *Journal of Personality and Social Psychology, 85*(3), 440–452.

Schmalz, J. (1992, October 11). Gay politics goes mainstream. *New York Times Magazine*, pp. 18–21, 29, 41.

Schmidt, G., & Weiner, B. (1988). An attribution-affect-action theory of behavior: Replications of judgments of help-giving. *Personality and Social Psychology Bulletin, 14*, 610–621.

Schmidt, W. E. (1990, December 13). White men get better deals on cars, study finds. *New York Times.*

Schmitt, B. H., Gilovich, T., Goore, N., & Joseph, L. (1986). Mere presence and social facilitation: One more time. *Journal of Experimental Social Psychology, 22*, 242–248.

Schmitt, M. T., & Branscombe, N. R. (2001). The good, the bad, and the manly: Threats to one's prototypicality and evaluations of fellow in-group members. *Journal of Experimental Social Psychology, 37*(6), 510–517.

Schmutte, G. T., & Taylor, S. P. (1980). Physical aggression as a function of alcohol and pain feedback. *Journal of Social Psychology, 110*, 235–244.

Schneider, D. J. (1973). Implicit personality theory: A review. *Psychological Bulletin, 79*, 294–309.

Schoeneman, T. J., & Rubanowitz, D. E. (1985). Attributions in the advice columns: Actors and observers, causes and reasons. *Personality and Social Psychology Bulletin, 11*, 315–325.

Schoenrade, P. A., Batson, C. D., & Brandt, J. R. (1986). Attachment, accountability, and motivation to benefit another not in distress. *Journal of Personality and Social Psychology, 51*, 557–563.

Schofield, J. (1978). School desegregation and intergroup relations. In D. Bar-Tal & L. Saxe (Eds.), *Social psychology of education: Theory and research* (pp. 329–364). New York: Wiley.

Schofield, J. W. (1986). Causes and consequences of the colorblind perspective. In J. F. Dovidio & S. L. Gaertner (Eds.), *Prejudice, discrimination, and racism* (pp. 231–254). Orlando, FL: Academic Press.

Schopler, J., Insko, C. A., Graetz, K. A., Drigotas, S., Smith, V. A., & Dahl, K. (1993). Individual–group discontinuity: Further evidence for mediation by fear and greed. *Personality and Social Psychology Bulletin, 19*, 419–431.

Schroeder, D. A., Jensen, T. D., Reed, A. J., Sullivan, D. K., & Schwab, M., (1983). The actions of others as determinants of behavior in social trap situations. *Journal of Experimental Social Psychology, 19*, 522–539.

Schubert, T. W. (2005). Your highness: Vertical positions as perceptual symbols of power. *Journal of Personality and Social Psychology, 89*, 1–21.

Schuman, H., & Johnson, M. P. (1976). Attitudes and behavior. *Annual Review of Sociology, 2*, 161–207.

Schuster, J. R. (1985, May). Compensation plan design. *Management Review*, 21–25.

Schwartz, S. H. (1977). Normative influences on altruism. In L. Berkowitz (Ed.), *Advances in experimental social psychology* (Vol. 10, pp. 221–279). New York: Academic Press.

Schwartz, S. H., & Gotleib, A. (1980). Bystander anonymity and reaction to emergencies. *Journal of Personality and Social Psychology, 39*, 418–430.

Schwarz, N. (1999). Self-reports: How the questions shape the answers. *American Psychologist, 54*, 93–105.

Schwarz, N., Bless, H., & Bohner, G. (1991). Mood and persuasion: Affective states influence processing of persuasive communications. In M. P. Zanna (Ed.), *Advances in experimental social psychology* (Vol. 24, pp. 161–199). San Diego, CA: Academic Press.

Schwarz, N., & Clore, G. L. (1988). How do I feel about it? Informative functions of affective states. In K. Fiedler & J. Forgas (Eds.), *Affect, cognition, and social behavior* (pp. 44–62). Toronto: Hogrefe.

Schwarz, N., Groves, R. M., & Schuman, H. (1998). Survey methods. In D. T. Gilbert, S. T., Fiske, & G. Lindzey, (Eds.), *The handbook of social psychology* (pp. 143–189). New York: McGraw-Hill.

Schwarzer, R., & Leppin, A. (1989). Social support and health: A meta-analysis. *Psychology and Health, 3*, 1–15.

Schwarzwald, J., Bizman, A., & Raz, M. (1983). The foot-in-the-door paradigm: Effects of second request size on donation probability and donor generosity. *Personality and Social Psychology Bulletin, 9*, 69–79.

Sczesny, S., & Kühnen, U. (2004). Meta-cognition about biological sex and gender-stereotypic physical appearance: Consequences for the assessment of leadership competence. *Personality and Social Psychology Bulletin, 30*, 13–21.

Sears, D. O. (1988). Symbolic racism. In P. Katz & D. Taylor (Eds), *Eliminating racism: Profiles in controversy* (pp. 53–84). New York: Plenum.

Sears, D. O., & Allen, H. M., Jr. (1984). The trajectory of local desegregation controversies and whites' opposition to busing. In N. Miller & M. Brewer (Eds.), *Groups in contact: The psychology of desegregation* (pp. 123–151). New York: Academic Press.

Sears, D. O., & McConahay, J. B. (1973). *The politics of violence: The new urban blacks and the Watts riot*. Boston: Houghton Mifflin.

Sedek, G., & Kofta, M. (1990). When cognitive exertion does not yield cognitive gain: Toward an informational explanation of learned helplessness. *Journal of Personality and Social Psychology, 58*, 729–743.

Sedikides, C., Gaertner, L., & Toguchi, Y. (2003). Pancultural self-enhancement. *Journal of Personality and Social Psychology, 84*, 60–79.

Sedikides, C., & Skowronski, J. J. (1993). The self in impression formation: Trait centrality and social perception. *Journal of Experimental Social Psychology, 29*, 347–357.

Segal, M. W. (1974). Alphabet and attraction: An unobtrusive measure of the effect of propinquity in a field setting. *Journal of Personality and Social Psychology, 30*, 654–657.

Seligman, C. L., Becker, J., & Darley, J. M. (1981). Encouraging residential energy conservation through feedback. In A. Baum & J. Singer (Eds.), *Advances in environmental psychology* (Vol. 3, pp. 53–91). Hillsdale, NJ: Lawrence Erlbaum Associates, Inc.

Seligman, M. E. P. (1975). *On depression, development, and death*. San Francisco, CA: Freeman.

Seligman, M. E. P., & Maier, S. F. (1967). Failure to escape traumatic shock. *Journal of Experimental Psychology, 74*, 1–9.

Senneker, P., & Hendrick, C. (1983). Androgyny and helping behavior. *Journal of Personality and Social Psychology, 45*, 916–925.

Shackelford, T. K., Schmitt, D. P., & Buss, D. M. (2005). Universal dimensions of human mate preferences. *Personality and Individual Differences, 39*, 447–458.

Shamir, B., House, R. J., & Arthur, M. B. (1993). The motivational effects of charismatic leadership: A self-concept based theory. *Organization Science, 4*, 577–594.

Shanab, M. E., & Yahra, K. A. (1977). A behavioral study of obedience in children. *Journal of Personality and Social Psychology, 35*, 530–536.

Sharpsteen, D. J., & Kirkpatrick, L. A. (1997). Romantic jealousy and adult romantic attachment. *Journal of Personality and Social Psychology, 72*, 627–640.

Shaver, P., & Hazan, C. (1985). Incompatibility, loneliness, and "limerence." In W. Ickes (Ed.), *Compatible and incompatible relationships* (pp. 163–186). New York: Springer-Verlag.

Shaver, P., & Hazan, C. (1988). A biased overview of the study of love. *Journal of Social and Personal Relationships, 5*, 473–501.

Shaver, P., Hazan, C., & Bradshaw, D. (1988). Love as attachment: The integration of three behavioral systems. In R. Sternberg & M. Barnes (Eds.), *The psychology of love* (pp. 68–99). New Haven, CT: Yale University Press.

Shaver, P., Schwartz, J., Kirson, D., & O'Connor, C. (1987). Emotion knowledge: Further exploration of a prototype approach. *Journal of Personality and Social Psychology, 52*, 1061–1086.

Shavitt, S. (1990). The role of attitude objects in attitude functions. *Journal of Experimental Social Psychology, 26*, 124–148.

Shavitt, S., & Nelson, M. R. (2000). The social-identity function in person perception: Communicated meanings of product preferences. In G. R. Maio & J. M. Olson (Eds.), *Why we evaluate: Functions of attitudes* (pp. 37–57). Mahwah, NJ: Lawrence Erlbaum Associates, Inc.

Shaw, M. E. (1954). Some effects of unequal distribution of information upon group performance in various communication nets. *Journal of Abnormal and Social Psychology, 49*, 547–553.

Shaw, M. E. (1976). *Group dynamics: The psychology of small group behavior* (2nd ed.). New York: McGraw-Hill

Sheppard, B. H., Hartwick, J., & Warshaw, P. R. (1988). The theory of reasoned action: A meta-analysis of past research with recommendations for modifications and future research. *Journal of Consumer Research, 15*, 325–343.

Sherif, C. W. (1979). Bias in psychology. In J. A. Sherman & E. T. Beck (Eds.), *The prism of sex: Essays in the sociology of knowledge* (pp. 93–133). Madison, WI: University of Wisconsin Press.

Sherif, M. (1936). *The psychology of social norms*. New York: Harper.

Sherif, M. (1966). *In common predicament: Social psychology of intergroup conflict and cooperation*. Boston: Houghton-Mifflin.

Sherif, M., Harvey, O. J., White, B. J., Hood, W. E., & Sherif, C. W. (1961). *Intergroup conflict and cooperation: The robbers cave experiment*. Normon, OK: University of Oklahoma Press/Book Exchange.

Sherif, M., & Sherif, C. W. (1953). *Groups in harmony and tension*. New York: Harper.

Sherman, J. W., & Klein, S. B. (1994). Development and representation of personality impressions. *Journal of Personality and Social Psychology, 67*, 972–983.

Sherman, J. W., Klein, S. B., Laskey, A., & Wyer, N. A. (1998). Intergroup bias in group judgment processes: The role of behavioral memories. *Journal of Experimental Social Psychology, 34*, 51–65.

Sherman, L. W., & Berk, R. A. (1984). The specific deterrent effects of arrest for domestic assault. *American Sociological Review, 49*, 261–272.

Sherman, P. W. (1977). Nepotism and the evolution of alarm calls. *Science, 197*, 1246–1253.

Sherman, S. J. (1980). On the self-erasing nature of errors of prediction. *Journal of Personality and Social Psychology, 39*, 211–221.

Sherrod, D. (1974). Crowding, perceived control, and behavioral aftereffects. *Journal of Applied Social Psychology, 4*, 171–186.

Shields, A., & Cicchetti, D. (1998). Reactive aggression among maltreated children: The contributions of attention and emotion dysregulation. *Journal of Clinical Child Psychology, 27*(4), 381–395.

Shih, M., Pittinsky, T. L., & Ambady, N. (1999). Stereotype susceptibility: Identity salience and shifts in quantitative performance. *Psychological Science, 10*, 80–83.

Shils, E. A., & Janowitz, M. (1948). Cohesion and disintegration in the Wehrmacht in World War II. *Public Opinion Quarterly, 12*, 280–315.

Shotland, R. L., & Heinold, W. D. (1985). Bystander response to arterial bleeding: Helping skills, the decision-making process, and differentiating the helping response. *Journal of Personality and Social Psychology, 49*, 347–356.

Shotland, R. L., & Straw, M. K. (1976). Bystander response to an assault: When a man attacks a woman. *Journal of Personality and Social Psychology, 34*, 990–999.

Showers, C. (1992). Compartmentalization of positive and negative self-knowledge: Keeping bad apples out of the bunch. *Journal of Personality and Social Psychology, 62*, 1036–1049.

Shrauger, J. S., & Schoeneman, T. J. (1979). Symbolic interactionist view of self-concept: Through the looking glass darkly. *Psychological Bulletin, 86*, 549–573.

Sia, T. L., Lord, C. G., Blessum, K. A., Ratcliff, C. D., & Lepper, M. R. (1997). Is a rose always a rose? The role of social category exemplar change in attitude stability and attitude–behavior consistency. *Journal of Personality and Social Psychology, 72*, 501–514.

Sias, P. M., & Jablin, F. M. (1995). Differential superior–subordinate relations, perceptions of fairness, and coworker communication. *Human Communication Research, 22*, 5–38.

Silka, L. (1989). *Intuitive judgments of change.* New York: Springer-Verlag.

Silver, M., & Geller, D. (1978). On the irrelevance of evil: The organization and individual action. *Journal of Social Issues, 34*, 125–136.

Silverstein, L. (1965). *Defense of the poor in criminal cases in American state courts.* Chicago: American Bar Foundation.

Simmel, G. (1950). *The sociology of Georg Simmel.* New York: Free Press.

Simmonds, D. B. (1985). The nature of the organizational grapevine. *Supervisory Management*, 39–42.

Simon, B. (1992). The perception of ingroup and outgroup homogeneity: Reintroducing the intergroup context. In W. Stroebe & M. Hewstone (Eds.), *European review of social psychology* (Vol. 3, pp. 1–30). Chichester, UK: John Wiley & Sons.

Simon, B. (1998). Individuals, groups, and social change: On the relationship between individual and collective self-interpretations and collective action. In C. Sedikides & J. Schopler (Eds.), *Intergroup cognition and intergroup behavior* (pp. 257–282). Mahwah, NJ: Lawrence Erlbaum Associates, Inc.

Simon, B., & Brown, R. (1987). Perceived homogeneity in minority–majority contexts. *Journal of Personality and Social Psychology, 53*, 703–711.

Simon, B., & Hamilton, D. L. (1994). Self-stereotyping and social context: The effects of relative in-group size and in-group status. *Journal of Personality and Social Psychology, 66*, 699–711.

Simon, B., Loewy, M., Sturmer, S., Weber, U., Freytag, P., Habig, C., Kampmeier, C. and others (1998). Collective identification and social movement participation. *Journal of Personality and Social Psychology, 74*, 646–658.

Simon, H. A. (1990) A mechanism for social selection and successful altruism. *Science, 250*, 1665–1668.

Simon, L., Greenberg, J., & Brehm, J. (1995). Trivialization: The forgotten mode of dissonance reduction. *Journal of Personality and Social Psychology, 68*, 247–260.

Simons, M. (1992, March 17). North–South chasm is threatening search for environmental solutions. *New York Times*, p. A5.

Simpson, J. A. (1987). The dissolution of romantic relationships: Factors involved in relationship stability and emotional distress. *Journal of Personality and Social Psychology, 53*, 683–692.

Simpson, J. A. (1990). Influence of attachment styles on romantic relationships. *Journal of Personality and Social Psychology, 59*, 971–980.

Simpson, J. A., Campbell, B., & Berscheid, E. (1986). The association between romantic love and marriage: Kephart (1967) twice revisited. *Personality and Social Psychology Bulletin, 12*, 363–372.

Simpson, J. A., & Gangestad, S. W. (1991). Personality and sexuality: Empirical relations and an integrative theoretical model. In K. McKinney & S. Sprecher (Eds.), *Sexuality in close relationships* (pp. 71–92). Hillsdale, NJ: Lawrence Erlbaum Associates, Inc.

Simpson, J. A., Gangestad, S. W., & Lerma, M. (1990). Perception of physical attractiveness: Mechanisms involved in the maintenance of romantic relationships. *Journal of Personality and Social Psychology, 59*, 1192–1201.

Simpson, J. A., Ickes, W., & Blackstone, T. (1995). When the head protects the heart: Empathic accuracy in dating relationships. *Journal of Personality and Social Psychology, 69*, 629–641.

Simpson, J. A., Rholes, W. S., & Nelligan, J. S. (1992). Support seeking and support giving within couples in an anxiety-provoking situation: The role of attachment styles. *Journal of Personality and Social Psychology, 62*, 434–446.

Simpson, J. A., Rholes, W. S., & Phillips, D. (1996). Conflict in close relationships: An attachment perspective. *Journal of Personality and Social Psychology, 71*, 899–914.

Singer, J. L., & Singer, D. G. (1981). *Television, imagination, and aggression: A study of preschoolers.* Hillsdale, NJ: Lawrence Erlbaum Associates, Inc.

Singleton, R., Jr. (1979). Another look at the conformity explanation of group-induced shifts in choice. *Human Relations, 32*, 37–56.

Skaalvik, E. M. (1986). Sex differences in global self-esteem. *Scandinavian Journal of Educational Research, 30*, 167–179.

Skinner, M., & Stephenson, G. M. (1987). The effects of intergroup comparison on the polarization of opinions. *Current Psychological Research, 1*, 49–61.

Skowronski, J. J., & Carlston, D. E. (1989). Negativity and extremity biases in impression formation: A review of explanations. *Psychological Bulletin, 105*, 131–142.

Skurnik, I., Yoon, C., Park, D. C., & Schwarz, N. (2005). How warnings about false claims become recommendations. *Journal of Consumer Research, 31*, 713–724.

Smeesters, D., Warlop, L., Van Avermaet, E., Corneille, O., & Yzerbyt, V. (2003). Do not prime hawks with doves: The interplay of construct activation and consistency of social value orientation on cooperative behavior. *Journal of Personality and Social Psychology, 84*, 972–987.

Smith, E. R. (1977). Single-sex colleges and sex-typing. *Journal of Social Issues, 33*, 197–199.

Smith, E. R. (1991). Illusory correlation in a simulated exemplar-based memory. *Journal of Experimental Social Psychology, 27*, 107–123.

Smith, E. R. (1993). Social identity and social emotions: Toward new conceptualizations of prejudice. In D. M. Mackie & D. L. Hamilton (Eds.), *Affect, cognition, and stereotyping: Interactive processes in group perception* (pp. 297–316). San Diego, CA: Academic Press.

Smith, E. R. (1998). Mental representation and memory. In D. Gilbert, S. T. Fiske, & G. Lindzey (Eds.), *Handbook of social psychology* (4th ed., Vol. 1, pp. 391–445). Boston: McGraw-Hill.

Smith, E. R., Coats, S., & Walling, D. (1999). Overlapping mental representations of self, in-group, and partner: Further response time evidence and a connectionist model. *Personality and Social Psychology Bulletin, 25*, 873–882.

Smith, E. R., & Ho, C. (1999). Prejudice as intergroup emotion: Integrating relative deprivation and social comparison explanations of prejudice. In I. Walker & H. Smith (Eds.), *Relative deprivation: Specification, development, and integration*. Boulder, CO: Westview Press.

Smith, E. R., & Kluegel, J. R. (1982). Cognitive and social bases of emotional experience: Outcome, attribution, and affect. *Journal of Personality and Social Psychology, 43*, 1129–1141.

Smith, E. R., & Mackie, D. M. (2005). Aggression, hatred, and other emotions. In J. F. Dovidio, P. Glic, & L. A. Rudman (Eds.), *On the nature of prejudice: Fifty years after Allport* (pp. 361–376). Malden, MA: Blackwell.

Smith, E. R., & Miller, F. D. (1979). Salience and the cognitive mediation of attribution. *Journal of Personality and Social Psychology, 37*, 2240–2252.

Smith, E. R., Seger, C. A., & Mackie, D. M. (2005). *Can emotions be truly group-level? Evidence regarding four conceptual criteria.* Manuscript submitted for publication, Indiana University, Bloomington.

Smith, E. R., & Zárate, M. A. (1992). Exemplar-based model of social judgment. *Psychological Review, 99*, 3–21.

Smith, H. J., & Spears, R. (1996). Ability and outcome evaluations as a function of personal and collective (dis)advantage: A group escape from individual bias. *Personality and Social Psychology Bulletin, 22*, 690–704.

Smith, H. J., & Tyler, T. R. (1997). Choosing the right pond: The impact of group membership on self-esteem and group-oriented behavior. *Journal of Experimental Social Psychology, 33*, 146–170.

Smith, M. B., Bruner, J. S., & White, R. W. (1956). *Opinions and personality*. New York: Wiley.

Smith, P. B., & Bond, M. H. (1993). *Social psychology across cultures: Analysis and perspectives*. New York: Harvester Wheatsheaf.

Smith, P. B., & Tayeb, M. (1989). Organizational structure and processes. In M. Bond (Ed.), *The cross-cultural challenge to social psychology*. Newbury Park, CA: Sage.

Smith, R. E., & Smoll, F. L. (1996). *Way to go, Coach! A scientifically validated approach to coaching effectiveness*. Portola Valley, CA: Warde Publishers.

Smith, R. E., & Smoll, F. L. (1997). Coaching the coaches: Youth sports as a scientific and applied behavioral setting. *Current Directions in Psychological Science, 6*, 16–21.

Smith, R. E., Vanderbilt, K., & Callen, M. B. (1973). Social comparison and bystander intervention in emergencies. *Journal of Applied Social Psychology, 3*, 186–196.

Smith, S. M., & Shaffer, D. R. (1995). Speed of speech and persuasion: Evidence for multiple effects. *Personality and Social Psychology Bulletin, 21*, 1051–1060.

Smith, S. S., & Richardson, D. (1983). Amelioration of deception and harm in psychological research: The important role of debriefing. *Journal of Personality and Social Psychology, 44*, 1075–1082.

Smith, T. W. (1990). Report: The sexual revolution? *Public Opinion Quarterly, 54*, 415–435.

Smith, W. P., & Anderson, A. J. (1975). Threats, communication and bargaining. *Journal of Personality and Social Psychology, 32*, 76–82.

Snyder, C. R., & Higgins, R. L. (1988). Excuses: Their effective role in the negotiation of reality. *Psychological Bulletin, 104*, 23–35.

Snyder, C. R., Lassegard, M. A., & Ford, C. E. (1986). Distancing after group success and failure: Basking in reflected glory and cutting off reflected failure. *Journal of Personality and Social Psychology, 51*, 382–388.

Snyder, C. R., Smith, T. W., Augelli, R. W., & Ingram, R. E. (1985). On the self-serving function of social anxiety: Shyness as a self-handicapping strategy. *Journal of Personality and Social Psychology, 48*, 970–980.

Snyder, M. (1974). The self-monitoring of expressive behavior. *Journal of Personality and Social Psychology, 30*, 526–537.

Snyder, M., Berscheid, E., & Glick, P. (1985). Focusing on the exterior and the interior: Two investigations of the initiation of personal relationships. *Journal of Personality and Social Psychology, 48*, 1427–1439.

Snyder, M., Berscheid, E., & Matwuchuk, A. (1988). Orientations toward personnel selection: Differential reliance on appearance and personality. *Journal of Personality and Social Psychology, 54*, 972–979.

Snyder, M., & Gangestad, S. (1982). Choosing social situations: Two investigations of self-monitoring processes. *Journal of Personality and Social Psychology, 43*, 123–135.

Snyder, M., & Haugen, J. A. (1995). Why does behavioral confirmation occur? A functional perspective on the role of the target. *Personality and Social Psychology Bulletin, 21*, 963–974.

Snyder, M., & Kendzierski, D. (1982). Acting on one's attitudes: Procedures for linking attitude and behavior. *Journal of Experimental Social Psychology, 18*, 165–183.

Snyder, M., & Omoto, A. M. (1992). Volunteerism and society's response to the HIV epidemic. *Current Directions in Psychological Science, 1*, 113–116.

Snyder, M., & Swann, W. B., Jr. (1976). When actions reflect attitudes: The politics of impression management. *Journal of Personality and Social Psychology, 34*, 1034–1042.

Snyder, M., & Swann, W. B. (1978). Behavioral confirmation in social interaction: From social perception to social reality. *Journal of Personality and Social Psychology, 36*, 1202–1212.

Snyder, M., Tanke, E. D., & Berscheid, E. (1977). Social perception and interpersonal behavior: On the self-fulfilling nature of social stereotypes. *Journal of Personality and Social Psychology, 35*, 656–666.

Sober, E., & Wilson, D. S. (1999). *Unto others: The evolution and psychology of unselfish behavior.* Cambridge, MA: Harvard University Press.

Solarz, A. (1960). Latency of instrumental responses as a function of compatibility with the meaning of eliciting verbal signals. *Journal of Experimental Psychology, 59*, 239–245.

Solomon, H., Solomon, L. Z., Arnone, M. M., Maur, B. J., Reda, R. M., & Rother, E. O. (1981). Anonymity and helping. *Journal of Social Psychology, 113*, 37–43.

Solomon, S., Greenberg, J., & Pyszczynski, T. (2000). Pride and prejudice: Fear of death and social behavior. *Current Directions in Psychological Science, 9*, 200–204.

Sorrentino, R. M., & Field, N. (1986). Emergent leadership over time: The functional value of positive motivation. *Journal of Personality and Social Psychology, 50*, 1091–1099.

Spears, R., Doosje, B., & Ellemers, N. (1997). Self-stereotyping in the face of threats to group status and distinctiveness: The role of group identification. *Personality and Social Psychology Bulletin, 23*, 538–553.

Spence, J. T., Deaux, K., and Helmreich, R. L. (1985). Sex roles in contemporary American society. In G. Lindzey & E. Aronson (Eds.), *Handbook of social psychology* (3rd ed., Vol. 2, pp. 149–178). New York: Random House.

Spencer, S. J. (1994). The effect of stereotype vulnerability on women's math performance (Doctoral dissertation, Department of Psychology, University of Michigan). *Dissertation Abstracts International: Section B: The Sciences & Engineering, 54(7-B)*, 3903.

Sprague, J., & Quadagno, D. (1989). Gender and sexual motivation: An exploration of two assumptions. *Journal of Psychology and Human Sexuality, 2*, 57–76.

Sprecher, S. (1999). "I love you more today than yesterday": Romantic partners' perceptions of changes in love and related affect over time. *Journal of Personality and Social Psychology, 76*, 46–53.

Sprecher, S., Aron, A., Hatfield, E., Cortest, A., Potapova, E., & Levitskaya, A. (1994). Love: American style, Russian style, and Japanese style. *Personal Relationships, 1*, 349–369.

Srull, T. K. (1981). Person memory: Some tests of associative storage and retrieval models. *Journal of Experimental Psychology: Human Learning and Memory, 7*, 440–463.

Srull, T. K., & Brand, J. F. (1983). Memory for information about persons: The effect of encoding operations upon subsequent retrieval. *Journal of Verbal Learning and Verbal Behavior, 22*, 219–230.

Srull, T. K., Lichtenstein, M., & Rothbart, M. (1985). Associative storage and retrieval processes in person memory. *Journal of Experimental Psychology: Learning, Memory, and Cognition, 11*, 316–345.

Srull, T. K., & Wyer, R. S. (1980). Category accessibility and social perception: Some implications for the study of person memory and interpersonal judgment. *Journal of Personality and Social Psychology, 38*, 841–856.

Stalder, D. R., & Baron, R. S. (1998). Attributional complexity as a moderator of dissonance-produced attitude change. *Journal of Personality and Social Psychology, 75*, 449–455.

Stangor, C., Lynch, L., Duan, C., & Glass, B. (1992). Categorization of individuals on the basis of multiple social features. *Journal of Personality and Social Psychology, 62*, 207–218.

Stangor, C., & Schaller, M. (1996). Stereotypes as individual and collective representations. In C. N. Macrae, C. Stangor, & M. Hewstone (Eds.), *Stereotypes and stereotyping* (pp. 3–40). New York: Guilford Press.

Stangor, C., Sechrist, G. B., & Jost, J. T. (2001). Changing racial beliefs by providing consensus information. *Personality and Social Psychology Bulletin, 27*, 486–496.

Stasser, G., & Stewart, D. (1992). Discovery of hidden profiles by decision-making groups: Solving a problem versus making a judgment. *Journal of Personality and Social Psychology, 63*, 426–434.

Stasser, G., Taylor, L. A., & Hanna, C. (1989). Information sampling in structured and unstructured discussions of three- and six-person groups. *Journal of Personality and Social Psychology, 57*, 67–78.

Stasson, M. F., & Hawkes, W. G. (1995). Effect of group performance on subsequent individual performance: Does influence generalize beyond the issues discussed by the group? *Psychological Science,, 6*, 305–307.

Staub, E. (1978). *Positive social behavior and morality.* New York: Academic Press.

Staub, E. (1989). *The roots of evil: The origins of genocide and other group violence.* Cambridge, UK: Cambridge University Press.

Staub, E. (2002). Emergency helping, genocidal violence, and the evolution of responsibility and altruism in children. In R. J. Davidson & A. Harrington (Eds.), *Visions of compassion: Western scientists and Tibetan Buddhists examine human nature* (pp. 165–181). London: Oxford University Press.

Staw, B. M. (1974). Attitudinal and behavioral consequences of changing a major organizational reward: A natural field experiment. *Journal of Personality and Social Psychology, 29*, 742–751.

Staw, B. M., & Ross, J. (1987). Behavior in escalation situations: Antecedents, prototypes, and solutions. *Research in Organizational Behavior, 9*, 39–78.

Steele, C. M. (1988). The psychology of self-affirmation: Sustaining the integrity of the self. In L. Berkowitz (Ed.), *Advances in experimental social psychology* (Vol. 21, pp. 261–302). Orlando, FL: Academic Press.

Steele, C. M. (1992, April). Race and the schooling of black Americans. *Atlantic Monthly*, pp. 68–78.

Steele, C. M. (1997). A threat in the air: How stereotypes shape intellectual identity and performance. *American Psychologist, 52*, 613–629.

Steele, C. M., & Aronson, J. (1995). Stereotype threat and the intellectual test performance of African Americans. *Journal of Personality and Social Psychology, 69*, 797–811.

Steele, C. M., & Josephs, R. A. (1990). Alcohol myopia: Its prized and dangerous effects. *American Psychologist, 45*, 921–933.

Steele, C. M., & Southwick, L. (1985). Alcohol and social behavior I: The psychology of drunken excess. *Journal of Personality and Social Psychology, 48*, 18–34.

Steele, C. M., Southwick, L. L., & Critchlow, B. (1981). Dissonance and alcohol: Drinking your troubles away. *Journal of Personality and Social Psychology, 41*, 831–846.

Steele, C. M., Spencer, S. J., & Lynch, M. (1993). Self-image resilience and dissonance: The role of affirmational resources. *Journal of Personality and Social Psychology*, *64*, 885–896.

Steffian, G. (1999). Correction of normative misperceptions: An alcohol abuse prevention program. *Journal of Drug Education*, *29*, 115–138.

Stein, A. K., & Friedrich, L. K. (1972). Television content and young children's behavior. In J. Murray, E. Rubenstein, & C. Comstock (Eds.), *Television and social learning*. Washington, DC: U.S. Government Printing Office.

Stein, L. (1967). The doctor–nurse game. *Archives of General Psychiatry*, *16*, 699–703.

Stein, N. L., Liwag, M. D., & Wade, E. (1996). A goal-based approach to memory for emotional events: Implications for theories of understanding socialization. In R. D. Kavanaugh, B. Zimmerberg, & S. Fein (Eds.), *Emotion: Interdisciplinary perspectives* (pp. 91–118). Mahwah, NJ: Lawrence Erlbaum Associates, Inc.

Steiner, I. (1972). *Group process and productivity*. New York: Academic Press.

Stephan, C. W., & Stephan, W. G. (1984). The role of ignorance in intergroup relations. In N. Miller & M. Brewer (Eds.), *Groups in contact: The psychology of desegregation* (pp. 229–255). New York: Academic Press.

Stephan, W. G. (1987). The contact hypothesis in intergroup relations. In C. Hendrick (Ed.) *Review of personality and social psychology*, (Vol. 9, pp. 13–40). Newbury Park, CA: Sage.

Stephan, W. G., & Renfro, C. L. (2002). The role of threat in intergroup relations. In D. M. Mackie & E. R. Smith (Eds.), *From prejudice to intergroup emotions* (pp. 191–208). New York: Psychology Press.

Stephan, W. G., & Stephan, C. W. (1985). Intergroup anxiety *Journal of Social Issues*, *41*, 157–175.

Stern, P. C. (1992). Psychological dimensions of global environmental change. *Annual Review of Psychology*, *43*, 269–302.

Sternberg, L. (1990). From velleity to specific plans: How planning affects attitude, intention, behavior relations. Unpublished doctoral dissertation, Purdue University.

Sternberg, R. J. (1986). A triangular theory of love. *Psychological Review*, *93*, 119–135.

Sternberg, R. J. (1988). Triangulating love. In R. J. Sternberg & M. L. Barnes (Eds.), *The psychology of love* (pp. 119–138). New Haven, CT: Yale University Press.

Sternberg, R. J., & Grajek, S. (1984). The nature of love. *Journal of Personality and Social Psychology*, *47*, 312–329.

Sterngold, J. (1992, May 21). Japan cuts back on fingerprinting. *New York Times*, p. A4.

Sternthal, B., Dholakia, R., & Leavitt, C. (1978). The persuasive effect of source credibility: A test of cognitive response analysis. *Journal of Consumer Research*, *4*, 252–260.

Stewart, D. D., & Stasser, G. (1995). Expert role assignment and information sampling during collective recall and decision making. *Journal of Personality and Social Psychology*, *69*, 619–628.

Stewart, J. E. (1985). Appearance and punishment: The attraction-leniency effect in the courtroom. *Journal of Social Psychology*, *125*, 373–378.

Stillinger, C., Epelbaum, M., Keltner, D., & Ross, L. (1989). *The reactive devaluation barrier to conflict resolution*. Unpublished manuscript, Stanford University.

Stock, R. W. (1995, October 19). Wearing the gray badge of courage. *New York Times*, p. B5.

Stockton, P. (2004, November 30) Supervisors strip-search workers after phony calls: Caller dupes managers by claiming to be a cop. *The Patriot Ledger*.

Stogdill, R. M. (1963). *Handbook for the leader behavior description questionnaire – Form XII*. Colombus, OH: Ohio State University.

Stolzfus, N. (1992, September). Dissent in Nazi Germany. *Atlantic Monthly*, pp. 87–94.

Stone, J. (2002). Battling doubt by avoiding practice: The effects of stereotype threat on self-handicapping in white athletes. *Personality and Social Psychology Bulletin*, *28*(12), 1667–1678.

Stone, J., Wiegand, A. W., Cooper, J., & Aronson, E. (1997). When exemplification fails: Hypocrisy and the motive for self-integrity. *Journal of Personality and Social Psychology*, *72*, 54–65.

Stoner, J. A. (1961). A comparison of individual and group decisions involving risk. Unpublished master's thesis, MIT, Cambridge, MA.

Storch, E. A., & Storch, J. B. (2003). Academic dishonesty and attitudes towards academic dishonest acts: Support for cognitive dissonance theory. *Psychological Reports*, *92*, 174–176.

Storck, J., & Sproull, L. (1995). Through a glass darkly: What do people learn in videoconferences? *Human Communication Research*, *22*, 197–219.

Storms, M. D. (1973). Videotape and the attribution process: Reversing actors' and observers' points of view. *Journal of Personality and Social Psychology*, *27*, 165–175.

Stouffer, S. A. (1949). *The American soldier*. Princeton, NJ: Princeton University Press.

Stouffer, S. A., Suchman, E. A., DeVinney, L. C., Star, S. A., & Williams, R. M., Jr. (1949). *The American soldier: Adjustment during army life* (Vol. 1). Princeton, NJ: Princeton University Press.

Strack, F., & Deutsch, R. (2004). Reflective and impulsive determinants of social behavior. *Personality and Social Psychology Review*, *8*, 220–247.

Strack, F., Martin, L. L., & Stepper, S. (1988). Inhibiting and facilitating conditions of the human smile: A nonobtrusive test of the facial feedback hypothesis. *Journal of Personality and Social Psychology*, *54*, 768–777.

Strack, F., Schwarz, N., Bless, H., Kubler, A., & Wanke, M. (1989). Awareness of the influence as a determinant of assimilation versus contrast. *European Journal of Social Psychology*, *23*, 53–62.

Strahan, E. J., Spencer, S. J., & Zanna, M. P. (2002). Subliminal priming and persuasion: Striking while the iron is hot. *Journal of Experimental Social Psychology*, *38*, 556–568.

Strauman, T. J., & Higgins, E. T. (1988). Self-discrepancies as predictors of vulnerability to distinct syndromes of chronic emotional distress. *Journal of Personality*, *56*, 685–707.

Strauman, T. J., Lemieux, A. M., & Coe, C. L. (1993). Self-discrepancy and natural killer cell activity: Immunological consequences of negative self-evaluation. *Journal of Personality and Social Psychology*, *64*, 1042–1052.

Straus, M. A. (1991). Family violence in American families: Incidence rates, causes, and trends. In D. D. Knudsen & J. L. Miller (Eds), *Abused and battered: Social and legal responses of family violence. Social institutions and social change* (pp. 17–34). Hawthorne, NY: Aldine de Gruyter.

Straus, M. A., Gelles, R. J., & Steinmetz, S. K. (1980). *Behind closed doors: Violence in the American family.* New York: Anchor Press.

Streufert, S., & Streufert, S. C. (1986). The development of internation conflict. In S. Worchel & W. G. Austin (Eds.), *Psychology of intergroup relations* (2nd ed., pp. 134–152). Chicago: Nelson-Hall.

Stroebe, W., & Diehl, M. (1991). You can't beat good experiments with correlational evidence: Mullen, Johnson, and Sala's meta-analytic misinterpretations. *Journal of Basic and Applied Social Psychology, 12,* 25–32.

Stroebe, W., Stroebe, M. S., & Domittner, G. (1988). Individual and situational differences in recovery from bereavement: A risk group identified. *Journal of Social Issues, 44*(3), 143–158.

Stroessner, S. J., & Mackie, D. M. (1992). The impact of induced affect on the perception of variability in social groups. *Personality and Social Psychology Bulletin, 18,* 546–554.

Strube, M. J., & Garcia, J. E. (1981). A meta-analytic investigation of Fiedler's contingency model of leadership effectiveness. *Psychological Bulletin, 90,* 307–321.

Struch, N., & Schwartz, S. H. (1989). Intergroup aggression: Its predictors and distinctness from in-group bias. *Journal of Personality and Social Psychology, 56,* 364–373.

Stryker, S. (1980). *Symbolic interactionism.* Menlo Park, CA: Benjamin/Cummings.

Study shows TV depiction of Latinos to be negative (1994, September 7). *Purdue Exponent,* p. 5.

Sturmer, S., Snyder, M., & Omoto, A. M. (2005). Prosocial emotions and helping: The moderating role of group membership. *Journal of Personality and Social Psychology, 88,* 532–546.

Suedfeld, P. (1992). Bilateral relations between countries and the complexity of newspaper editorials. *Political Psychology, 13,* 601–632.

Suedfeld, P. (2004). Decision-making in Great Britain during the Suez crisis: Small groups and a persistent leader. *Political Psychology, 25,* 817–820.

Suedfeld, P., & Tetlock, P. (1977). Integrative complexity of communications in international crises. *Journal of Conflict Resolution, 21,* 169–184.

Sugarman, D. B., & Hotaling, G. T. (1989). Violent men in intimate relationships: An analysis of risk markers. *Journal of Applied Social Psychology, 19,* 1034–1048.

Suls, J., & Green, P. (2003). Pluralistic ignorance and college student perceptions of gender-specific alcohol norms. *Health Psychology, 22,* 479–486.

Suls, J., Martin, R., & Wheeler, L. (2002). Social comparison: Why, with whom, and with what effect? *Current Directions in Psychological Science, 11,* 159–163.

Sumner, W. G. (1906). *Folkways.* New York: Ginn.

Surowiecki, J. (2004). *The wisdom of crowds: Why the many are smarter than the few and how collective wisdom shapes business, economies, societies, and nations.* New York: Doubleday & Co.

Surra, C. A., & Longstreth, M. (1990). Similarity of outcomes, interdependence, and conflict in dating relationships. *Journal of Personality and Social Psychology, 59,* 501–516.

Svenson, O. (1981). Are we all less risky and more skillful than our fellow drivers? *Acta Psychologica, 47,* 143–148.

Swann, W. B., & Ely, R. J. (1984). A battle of wills: Self-verification versus behavioral confirmation. *Journal of Personality and Social Psychology, 46,* 1287–1302.

Swann, W. B., & Hill, C. A. (1982). When our identities are mistaken: Reaffirming self-conceptions through social interaction. *Journal of Personality and Social Psychology, 43,* 59–66.

Swann, W. B., Hixon, J. G., & de la Ronde, C. (1992). Embracing the bitter "truth": Negative self-concepts and marital commitment. *Psychological Science, 3,* 118–121.

Swann, W. B., & Read, S. J. (1981). Acquiring self-knowledge: The search for feedback that fits. *Journal of Personality and Social Psychology, 41,* 1119–1128.

Swartley, W. M. (1983). *Slavery, sabbath, war, and women.* Scottsdale, PA: Herald Press.

Symons, C. S., & Johnson, B. T. (1997). The self-reference effect in memory: A meta-analysis. *Psychological Bulletin, 121,* 371–394.

Tait, R., & Silver, R. C. (1989). Coming to terms with major negative life events. In J. S. Uleman & J.A. Bargh (Eds.), *Unintended thought* (pp. 351–382). New York: Guilford Press.

Tajfel, H. (1972). La categorization sociale. In S. Moscovici (Ed.), *Introduction a la psychologie sociale* (Vol. 1, pp. 272–302). Paris: Larousse.

Tajfel, H. (1978). *Differentiation between social groups: Studies in the social psychology of intergroup relations.* London: Academic Press.

Tajfel, H., Billig, M. G., Bundy, R. P., & Flament, C. (1971). Social categorization and intergroup behavior. *European Journal of Social Psychology, 1,* 149–178.

Tajfel, H., & Turner, J. C. (1979). An integrative theory of inter-group conflict. In W. G. Austin & S. Worchel (Eds.), *The social psychology of intergroup relations* (pp. 33–48). Monterey, CA: Brooks-Cole.

Tajfel, H., & Wilkes, A. L. (1963). Classification and quantitative judgment. *British Journal of Psychology, 54,* 101–114.

Tak, J., Kaid, L. L., & Lee, S. (1997). A cross-cultural study of political advertising in the United States and Korea. *Communication Research, 24,* 413–430.

Tannen, D. (1990). *You just don't understand.* New York: Ballantine Books.

Tate, D. C., Reppucci, N. D., & Mulvey, E. P. (1995). Violent juvenile delinquents: Treatment effectiveness and implications for future action. *American Psychologist, 50,* 777–781.

Taylor, C. R., & Stern, B. B. (1997). Asian-Americans: Television advertising and the "model minority" stereotype. *Journal of Advertising, 26,* 47–61.

Taylor, D. A., & Moriarty, B. F. (1987) Ingroup bias as a function of competition and race. *Journal of Conflict Resolution, 31,* 192–199.

Taylor, D. M., Doria, J., & Tyler, J. K. (1983). Group performance and cohesiveness: An attribution analysis. *Journal of Social Psychology, 119,* 187–198.

Taylor, D. M., & Jaggi, V. (1974). Ethnocentrism and causal attribution in a south Indian context. *Journal of Cross Cultural Psychology, 5,* 162–171.

Taylor, D. M., & Simard, L. M. (1979). Ethnic identity and intergroup relations. In D. J. Lee (Ed.), *Emerging ethnic boundaries* (pp. 155–174). Ottawa, Canada: University of Ottawa Press.

Taylor, D. M., Wright, S. C., Moghaddam, F. M., & Lalonde, R. N. (1990). The personal/group discrimination discrepancy: Perceiving my group, but not myself, to be a target for discrimination. *Personality and Social Psychology Bulletin, 16,* 254–262.

Taylor, S. E. (1975). On inferring one's attitude from one's behavior: Some delimiting conditions. *Journal of Personality and Social Psychology*, *31*, 126–131.

Taylor, S. E. (1981). A categorization approach to stereotyping. In D. L. Hamilton (Ed.), *Cognitive processes in stereotyping and intergroup behavior* (pp. 83–114). Hillsdale, NJ: Lawrence Erlbaum Associates, Inc.

Taylor, S. E. (1983). Adjustment to threatening events: A theory of cognitive adaptation. *American Psychologist*, *38*, 1161–1173.

Taylor, S. E., & Brown, J. D. (1988). Illusion and well-being: A social psychological perspective on mental health. *Psychological Bulletin*, *103*, 193–210.

Taylor, S. E., Falke, R. L., Shoptaw, S. J., & Lichtman, R. R. (1986). Social support, support groups, and the cancer patient. *Journal of Consulting and Clinical Psychology*, *54*, 608–615.

Taylor, S. E., & Fiske, S. T. (1975). Point of view and perceptions of causality. *Journal of Personality and Social Psychology*, *32*, 439–445.

Taylor, S. E., Fiske, S. T., Etcoff, N. L., & Ruderman, A. J. (1978). Categorical and contextual bases of person memory and stereotyping. *Journal of Personality and Social Psychology*, *36*, 778–793.

Taylor, S. E., Kemeny, M. E., Reed, G. M., Bower, J. E., & Gruenewald, T. L. (2000). Psychological resources, positive illusions, and health. *American Psychologist*, *55*, 99–109.

Taylor, S. E., Klein, L. C., Lewis, B. P., Gruenewald, T. L., Gurung, R. A. R., & Updegraff, J. A. (2000). Biobehavioral responses to stress in females: Tend-and-befriend, not fight-or-flight. *Psychological Review*, *107*, 411–429.

Taylor, S. E., & Lobel, M. (1989). Social comparison activity under threat: Downward evaluation and upward contacts. *Psychological Review*, *96*, 569–575.

Taylor, S. P., Gammon, C. B., & Capasso, D. R. (1976). Aggression as a function of alcohol and threat. *Journal of Personality and Social Psychology*, *34*, 938–941.

Tedeschi, J. T. (Ed.). (1981). *Impression management theory and social psychological research*. New York: Academic Press.

Tedeschi, J. T., & Felson, R. B. (1994). *Violence, aggression, and coercive actions*. Washington, DC: American Psychological Association.

Tedeschi, J. T., Gaes, G. G., & Rivera, A. N. (1977). Aggression and the use of coercive power. *Journal of Social Issues*, *33*(1), 101–125.

Teerlink, R., & Ozley, L. (2000). *More than a motorcycle: The leadership journey at Harley Davidson*. Boston: Harvard Business School Press.

Telch, M. J., Killen, J. D., McAlister, A. L., Perry C. L., & Maccoby, N. (1982). Long-term follow-up of a pilot project on smoking prevention in adolescents. *Journal of Behavioral Medicine*, *5*, 1–8.

Tennen, H., & Affleck, G. (1993). The puzzles of self-esteem: A clinical perspective. In R. F. Baumeister (Ed.), *Self-esteem: The puzzle of low self-esteem* (pp. 241–262). New York: Plenum.

Terkel, S. (1992). *Race*. New York: The New Press.

Terry, D. (1991, February 4). Project tenants see island of safety washing away. *New York Times*, pp. A1, B4.

Terry, D. (1993, April 11). Fear and ghosts: The world of Marcus, 19. *New York Times*, pp. A1, A11.

Terry, D. J., & Hogg, M. A. (1996). Group norms and the attitude–behavior relationship: A role for group identification. *Personality and Social Psychology Bulletin*, *22*, 776–793.

Tesser, A. (1978). Self-generated attitude change. In L. Berkowitz (Ed.), *Advances in experimental social psychology* (Vol. 11, pp. 288 – 338). New York: Academic Press.

Tesser, A. (1988). Toward a self-evaluation maintenance model of social behavior. In L. Berkowitz (Ed.), *Advances in experimental social psychology* (Vol. 21, pp. 181–227). San Diego; CA: Academic Press.

Tesser, A. (1993). The importance of heritability in psychological research: The case of attitudes. *Psychological Review*, *100*, 129–142.

Tesser, A., & Collins, J. E. (1988). Emotion in social reflection and comparison situations: Intuitive, systematic, and exploratory approaches. *Journal of Personality and Social Psychology*, *55*, 695–709.

Tesser, A., & Cornell, D. P. (1991). On the confluence of self processes. *Journal of Experimental Social Psychology*, *27*, 501–526.

Tetlock, P. E. (1983). Accountability and complexity of thought. *Journal of Personality and Social Psychology*, *45*, 74–83.

Tetlock, P. E. (1988). Monitoring the integrative complexity of American and Soviet policy rhetoric: What can be learned? *Journal of Social Issues*, *44*(2), 101–131.

Tetlock, P. E. (1989). The selfishness–altruism debate: In defense of agnosticism. *Behavioral and Brain Sciences*, *12*, 723–724.

Tetlock, P. E., Peterson, R. S., McGuire, C., Chang, S., & Feld, P. (1992). Assessing political group dynamics: A test of the groupthink model. *Journal of Personality and Social Psychology*, *63*, 403–425.

Tetlock, R. E. (1985). Integrative complexity of American and Soviet foreign policy rhetoric: A time-series analysis. *Journal of Personality and Social Psychology*, *49*, 1565–1585.

The romance of science (1995, August 13). *New York Times Magazine*, p. 16.

Thibaut, J. W., & Kelley, H. H. (1959). *The social psychology of groups*. New York: Wiley.

Thompson, L. (1993). The impact of negotiation on intergroup relations. *Journal of Experimental Social Psychology*, *29*, 304–325.

Thompson, L., & Hastie, R. (1990a). Judgment tasks and biases in negotiation. In B. H. Sheppard, M. H. Bazerman, & R. J. Lewicki (Eds.), *Research in negotiation in organizations* (Vol. 2, pp. 31–54). Greenwich, CT: JAI Press.

Thompson, L., & Hastie, R. (1990b). Social perception in negotiation. *Organization Behavior and Human Decision Processes*, *47*, 98–123.

Thompson, M. M., & Zanna, M. P. (1995). The conflicted individual: Personality-based and domain-specific antecedents of ambivalent social attitudes. *Journal of Personality*, *63*, 259–288.

Thompson, M. S., Judd, C. M., & Park, B. (2000). The consequences of communicating social stereotypes. *Journal of Experimental Social Psychology*, *36*, 567–599.

Thompson, T. L., & Zerbinos, E. (1995). Gender roles in animated cartoons: Has the picture changed in 20 years? *Sex Roles*, *32*, 651–673.

Thompson, W. C., Cowan, A. N., & Rosenhan, D. L. (1980). Focus of attention mediates the impact of negative affect on altruism. *Journal of Personality and Social Psychology*, *38*, 291–300.

Thompson, W. C., Fong, G. T., & Rosenhan, D. L. (1981). Inadmissible evidence and juror verdicts. *Journal of Personality and Social Psychology*, *40*, 453–463.

Thoresen, C. E., & Low, K. G. (1990). Women and the Type A behavior pattern: Review and commentary. *Journal of Social Behavior and Personality*, *5*, 117–133.

Tice, D. M., Bratslavsky, E., & Baumeister, R. F. (2001). Emotional distress regulation takes precedence over impulse control: If you feel bad, do it! *Journal of Personality and Social Psychology, 80*, 53–67.

Tiedens, L. Z. (2001). Anger and advancement versus sadness and subjugation: The effect of negative emotion expressions on social status conferral. *Journal of Personality and Social Psychology, 80*, 86–94.

Tiedens, L. Z., & Fragale, A. R. (2003). Power moves: Complementarity in dominant and submissive nonverbal behavior. *Journal of Personality and Social Psychology, 84*, 558–568.

Tiedens, L. Z., & Linton, S. (2001). Judgment under emotional certainty and uncertainty: The effects of specific emotions on information processing. *Journal of Personality and Social Psychology, 81*, 973–988.

Tilker, H. A. (1970). Socially responsible behavior as a function of observer responsibility and victim feedback. *Journal of Personality and Social Psychology, 49*, 420–428.

Tindale, R. S., & Davis, J. H. (1983). Group decision making and jury verdicts. In H. H. Blumberg, A. P. Hare, V. Kent, & M. F. Davies (Eds.), *Small groups and social interaction* (Vol. 2, pp. 9–38). New York: Wiley.

Tindale, R. S., Davis, J. H., Vollrath, D. A., Nagao, D. H., & Hinsz, V. B. (1990). Asymmetrical social influence in freely interacting groups: A test of three models. *Journal of Personality and Social Psychology, 58*, 438–449.

Todorov, A., Mandisodza, A. N., Goren, A., & Hall, C. C. (2005). Inference of competence from faces predict election outcomes. *Science, 308*, 1623–1626.

Tomaka, J., Blascovich, J., Kibler, J., & Ernst, J. M. (1997). Cognitive and physiological antecedents of threat and challenge appraisal. *Journal of Personality and Social Psychology, 73*, 63–72.

Tommasini, A. (1996, April 9). Music history: One woman wielding a baton. *New York Times*, p. B1.

Tormala, Z. L., & Petty, R. E. (2004). Resistance to persuasion and attitude certainty: The moderating role of elaboration. *Personality and Social Psychology Bulletin, 30*, 1446–1457.

Tourangeau, R., & Rasinski, K. A. (1988). Cognitive processes underlying context effects in attitude measurement. *Psychological Bulletin, 103*, 299–314.

Tourangeau, R., Rasinski, K. A., Bradburn, N., & D'Andrade, R. (1989). Belief accessibility and context effects in attitude measurement. *Journal of Experimental Social Psychology, 25*, 401–421.

Trafimow, D., & Finlay, K. A. (1996). The importance of subjective norms for a minority of people: Between-subjects and within-subjects analyses. *Personality and Social Psychology Bulletin, 22*, 820–828.

Trafimow, D., & Finlay, K. A. (2001). The importance of traits and group memberships. *European Journal of Social Psychology, 31*(1), 37–43.

Trafimow, D., & Fishbein, M. (1994a). The importance of risk in determining the extent to which attitudes affect intentions to wear seat belts. *Journal of Applied Social Psychology, 24*, 1–11.

Trafimow, D., & Fishbein, M. (1994b). The moderating effect of behavior type on the subjective norm–behavior relationship. *Journal of Social Psychology, 134*, 755–763.

Trafimow, D., & Sheeran, P. (1998). Some tests of the distinction between cognitive an affective beliefs. *Journal of Experimental and Social Psychology, 34*, 378–397.

Trafimow, D., Triandis, H. C., & Goto, S. G. (1991). Some tests of the distinction between the private self and the collective self. *Journal of Personality and Social Psychology, 60*, 649–655.

Triandis, H. C. (1977). *Interpersonal behavior*. Monterey, CA: Brooks/Cole.

Triandis, H. C. (1980). Values, attitudes, and interpersonal behavior. In H. Howe & M. Page (Eds.), *Nebraska symposium on motivation* (Vol. 27, pp. 195–260). Lincoln: University of Nebraska Press.

Triandis, H. C. (1994). Major cultural syndromes and emotion. In S. Kityama & H. R. Markus (Eds.), *Handbook of industrial and organizational psychology* (2nd ed., Vol. 4, pp. 285–308). Palo Alto, CA: Consulting Psychologists Press.

Triandis, H. C., Bontempo, R., Villareal, M. J., Asai, M., & Lucca, N. (1988). Individualism and collectivism: Cross-cultural perspectives on self-ingroup relationships. *Journal of Personality and Social Psychology, 54*, 323–338.

Tripathi, R. C., & Srivasta, R. (1981). Relative deprivation and intergroup attitudes. *European Journal of Social Psychology, 11*, 313–318.

Triplett, N. (1898). The dynamogenic factors in pacemaking and competition. *American Journal of Psychology, 9*, 507–533.

Trivers, R. L. (1971). The evolution of reciprocal altruism. *Quarterly Review of Biology, 46*, 35–57.

Trivers, R. L. (1972). Parental investment and sexual selection. In B. Campbell (Ed.), *Sexual selection and the descent of man 1871–1971* (pp. 136–172). Chicago: Aldine.

Trope, T., & Mackie, D. M. (1987). Sensitivity to alternatives in social hypothesis-testing. *Journal of Experimental Social Psychology, 23*, 445–459.

Trope, Y. (1986). Identification and inferential processes in dispositional attribution. *Psychological Review, 93*, 239–257.

Trope, Y., Bassok, M., & Alon, E. (1984). The questions lay interviewers ask. *Journal of Personality, 52*, 90–106.

Trope, Y., & Fishbach, A. (2000). Counteractive self-control in overcoming temptation. *Journal of Personality and Social Psychology, 79*, 493–506.

Trope, Y., & Gaunt, R. (2000). Processing alternative explanations of behavior: Correction or integration? *Journal of Personality and Social Psychology, 79*, 344–354.

Trope, Y., & Thompson, E. P. (1997). Looking for truth in all the wrong places? Asymmetric search of individuating information about stereotyped group members. *Journal of Personality and Social Psychology, 73*, 229–241.

Tropp, L. R., & Pettigrew, T. F. (2005). Differential relationships between intergroup contact and affective and cognitive dimensions of prejudice. *Personality and Social Psychology Bulletin, 31*, 1145–1158.

Trost, M. R., Cialdini, R. B., & Maas, A. (1989). Effects of an international conflict simulation of perceptions of the Soviet Union: A FIREBREAKS backfire. *Journal of Social Issues, 45*, 139–158.

Trudeau, K. J., & Devlin, A. S. (1996). College students and community service: Who, with whom, and why? *Journal of Applied Social Psychology, 26*, 1867–1888.

Tuckman, B. W. (1965). Developmental sequences in small groups. *Psychological Bulletin, 63*, 384–399.

Turnbull, W., Miller, D. T., & McFarland, C. (1990). Population-distinctiveness, identity, and bonding. In J. M. Olson & M. P. Zanna,

(Eds.), *Self-inference processes: The Ontario Symposium* (Vol. 6, pp. 115–133). Hillsdale, NJ: Lawrence Erlbaum Associates, Inc.

Turner, C. W., Simons, L. S., Berkowitz, L., & Frodi, A. (1977). The stimulating and inhibiting effects of weapons on aggressive behavior. *Aggressive Behavior, 3,* 355–378.

Turner, J. C. (1980). Fairness or discrimination in intergroup behavior? A reply to Braithwaite, Doyle, and Lightbrown. *European Journal of Social Psychology, 10,* 131–47.

Turner, J. C. (1981). The experimental social psychology of intergroup behavior. In J. C. Turner & H. Giles (Eds.), *Intergroup behavior* (pp. 66–101). Chicago, IL: University of Chicago Press.

Turner, J. C. (1982). Towards a cognitive redefinition of the social group. In H. Tajfel (Ed.), *Social identity and intergroup relations.* Cambridge, UK: Cambridge University Press.

Turner, J. C. (1991). *Social influence.* Pacific Grove, CA: Brooks/Cole.

Turner, J. C., Hogg, M. A., Oakes, P. J., Reicher, S. D., & Wetherell, M. S. (1987). *Rediscovering the social group: A self-categorization theory.* Oxford; UK: Blackwell.

Turner, J. C., Sachdev, I., & Hogg, M. A. (1983). Social categorization interpersonal attraction and group formation. *British Journal of Social Psychology, 22,* 227–239.

Tushman, M. L. (1978). Technical communication in research and development laboratories: The impact of project work characteristics. *Academy of Management Journal, 21,* 624–645.

Twenge, J. M., & Campbell, W. K. (2003). "Isn't it fun to get the respect that we're going to deserve?" Narcissism, social rejection, and aggression. *Personality & Social Psychology Bulletin, 29*(2), 261–272.

Twenge, J. M., & Crocker, J. (2002). Race and self-esteem: Meta-analyses comparing Whites, Blacks, Hispanics, Asians, and American Indians and comment on Gray-Little and Hafdahl (2000). *Psychological Bulletin, 128*(3), 371–408.

Tyler, T. R., & Lind, E. A. (1990). Intrinsic versus community-based justice models: When does group membership matter? *Journal of Social Issues, 46*(1), 83–94.

Tyler, T. R., & Lind, E. A. (1992). A relational model of authority in groups. In M. P. Zanna (Ed.), *Advances in experimental social psychology* (Vol. 25, pp. 115–191). New York: Academic Press.

Tyler, T. R., Lind, E. A., Ohbuchi, K.-I., Sugawara, I., & Huo, Y. J. (1998). Conflict with outsiders: Disputing within and across cultural boundaries. *Personality and Social Psychology Bulletin, 24,* 137–146.

Tyler, T. R., & Smith, H. J. (1998). Social justice and social movements. In D. T. Gilbert, S. T. Fiske, & G. Lindzey (Eds.), *The handbook of social psychology* (4th ed., Vol. 2, pp. 595–629). New York: McGraw-Hill.

Uchino, B. N., Cacioppo, J. T., & Kiecolt-Glaser, J. K. (1996). The relationship between social support and physiological processes: A review with emphasis on underlying mechanisms and implications for health. *Psychological Bulletin, 119,* 488–531.

Uleman, J. S., Hon, A., Roman, R. J., & Moskowitz, G. B. (1996). On-line evidence for spontaneous trait inferences at encoding. *Personality and Social Psychology Bulletin, 22,* 377–394.

United Nations Office on Drugs and Crime, Centre for International Crime Prevention (2000). Seventh United Nations survey of crime trends and operations of criminal justice systems, covering the period 1998–2000. Retrieved July 20 2006 from http://www.uncjin.org/ Documents/documents.html.

Unnikrishnan, N., & Bajpai, S. (1996). *The impact of television advertising on children.* New Dehli, India: Sage Publications.

Vachon, M. L., Roger, J., Lyall, W. A., Lancee, W. J., Sheldon, A. R., & Freeman, S. J. J. (1982). Predictors and correlates of adaptation to conjugal bereavement. *American Journal of Psychiatry, 139,* 998–1002.

Vaes, J., Paladino, M. P., Castelli, L., Leyens, J.-P., & Giovanazzi, A. (2003). On the behavioral consequences of infrahumanization: The implicit role of uniquely human emotions in intergroup relations. *Journal of Personality and Social Psychology, 85*(6), 1016–1034.

Van Baaren, R. B., Holland, R. W., Kawakami, K., & Van Knippenberg, A. (2004). Mimicry and prosocial behavior. *Psychological Science, 15,* 71–74.

Van Egeren, L. F. (1979). Cardiovascular changes during social competition in a mixed-motive game. *Journal of Personality and Social Psychology, 37,* 858–864.

van Engen, M. L., & Willemsen, T. M. (2004). Sex and leadership styles: A meta-analysis of research published in the 1990s. *Psychological Reports, 94,* 3–18.

Van Gyn, G. H., Wenger, H. A., & Gaul, C. A. (1990). Imagery as a method of enhancing transfer from training to performance. *Journal of Sport and Exercise Psychology, 12,* 366–375.

van Knippenberg, D., & Wilke, H. (1992). Prototypicality of arguments and conformity to ingroup norms. *European Journal of Social Psychology, 22,* 141–155.

Van Lange, P. A. M., De Bruin, E. M. N., Otten, W., & Joireman, J. A. (1997). Development of prosocial, individualistic, and competitive orientations: Theory and preliminary evidence. *Journal of Personality and Social Psychology, 73,* 733–746.

Van Lange, P. A., & Liebrand, W. B. (1991). Social value orientation and intelligence: A test of the Goal Prescribes Rationality Principle. *European Journal of Social Psychology, 21,* 273–292.

Van Lange, P. A. M., Rusbult, C. E., Drigotas, S. M., Arriaga, X. B., Witcher, B. S., & Cox, C. L. (1997). Willingness to sacrifice in close relationships. *Journal of Personality and Social Psychology, 72,* 1373–1395.

Van Vugt, M., & De Cremer, D. (1999). Leadership in social dilemmas: The effects of group identification on collective actions to provide public goods. *Journal of Personality and Social Psychology, 76,* 587–599.

Van Vugt, M., & Hart, C. M. (2004). Social identity as social glue: The origins of group loyalty. *Journal of Personality and Social Psychology, 86,* 585–598.

Van Vugt, M., Jepson, S. F., Hart, C. M., & De Cremer, D. (2004). Autocratic leadership in social dilemmas: A threat to group stability. *Journal of Experimental Social Psychology, 40,* 1–13.

Vanbeselaere, N. (1991). The different effects of simple and crossed categorization: A result of the category differentiation process or of differential category salience? In W. Stroebe & M. Hewstone (Eds.), *European review of social psychology* (Vol. 2, pp. 247–278). Chichester, UK: John Wiley & Sons.

Vandello, J. A., & Cohen, D. (2003). Male honor and female fidelity: Implicit cultural scripts that perpetuate domestic violence. *Journal of Personality and Social Psychology, 84,* 997–1010.

Vanman, E. J., & Miller, N. (1993). Applications of emotion theory and research to stereotyping and intergroup relations. In D. M. Mackie & D. L. Hamilton (Eds.), *Affect, cognition, and stereotyping: Interactive processes in group perception* (pp. 213–238). New York: Academic Press.

Vanman, E. J., Paul, B. Y., Ito, T. A., & Miller, N. (1997). The modern face of prejudice and structural features that moderate the effect of cooperation on affect. *Journal of Personality and Social Psychology, 73*, 941–959.

Vargas, P. T., von Hippel, W., & Petty, R. E. (2004). Using partially structured attitude measures to enhance the attitude–behavior relationship. *Personality and Social Psychology Bulletin, 30*, 197–211.

Vecsey, G. (2003, February 2). England battles racism that infests soccer. *New York Times*, Section 8, pp. 1, 4.

Veroff, J., Douvan, E., & Kukla, R. A. (1981). *The inner American: A self-portrait from 1957 to 1976.* New York: Basic Books.

Verplanken, B., Aarts, H., van Knippenberg, A., & Moonen, A. (1998). Habit versus planned behavior: A field experiment. *British Journal of Social Psychology, 37*, 111–128.

Vonk, R. (1995). Effects of inconsistent behaviors on person impressions: A multidimensional study. *Personality and Social Psychology Bulletin, 21*, 674–685.

Vroom, V. H. (1976). Leadership. In M. D. Dunnette (Ed.), *Handbook of industrial and organizational psychology* (pp. 1527–1552). Chicago: Rand McNally.

Wagner, D. G., & Berger, J. (1997). Gender and interpersonal task behaviors: Status expectation accounts. *Sociological Perspectives, 40*, 1–32.

Wahl, M. (1989). EyePOPing persuasion. *Marketing Insights, 22*, 130.

Waldman, S. (1991, May 6). Watering the grass roots: How to buy a "spontaneous" popular uprising. *Newsweek*, p. 35.

Walker, I., & Mann, L. (1987). Unemployment, relative deprivation, and social protest. *Personality and Social Psychology Bulletin, 13*, 275–283.

Waller, N. G., Kojetin, B. A., Bouchard, T. J., Jr., Lykken, D. T., & Tellegen, A. (1990). Genetic and environmental influences on religious interests, attitudes, and values: A study of twins reared apart and together. *Psychological Science, 1*, 138–142.

Walster, E., Aronson, V., Abrahams, D., & Rottman, L. (1966). The importance of physical attractiveness in dating behavior. *Journal of Personality and Social Psychology, 4*, 508–516.

Walster, E., & Festinger, L. (1962). The effectiveness of "overheard" persuasive communications. *Journal of Abnormal and Social Psychology, 65*, 395–402.

Walther, E. (2002). Guilty by mere association: Evaluative conditioning and the spreading attitude effect. *Journal of Personality & Social Psychology, 82*, 919–934.

Walumbwa, F. O., Wang, P., Lawler, J. J., & Shi, K. (2004). The role of collective efficacy in the relations between transformational leadership and work outcomes. *Journal of Occupational and Organizational Psychology, 77*, 515–530.

Walzer, M. (1970). *Obligations.* Cambridge, MA: Harvard University Press.

Wänke, M., Bohner, G., & Jurkowitsch, A. (1997). There are many reasons to drive a BMW – Surely you know one: Ease of argument generation influences brand attitudes. *Journal of Consumer Research, 24*, 70–77.

Watson, D., & Pennebaker, J. W. (1989). Health complaints, stress, and distress: Exploring the central role of negative affectivity. *Psychological Review, 96*, 234–254.

Weber, J. M., Kopelman, S., & Messick, D. M. (2004). A conceptual review of decision making in social dilemmas: Applying a logic of appropriateness. *Personality and Social Psychology Review, 8*, 281–307.

Weber, J. M., Malhotra, D., & Murnighan, J. K. (2005). *Normal acts of irrational trust: Motivated attributions and the trust development process.* Greenwich, CT: Elsevier Science/JAI Press.

Weber, M. (1921/1946). The sociology of charismatic authority. In H. H. Gertz & C. W. Mills (Trans., & Eds.), *From Max Weber: Essays in sociology* (pp. 245–252). New York: Oxford University Press.

Weber, R., & Crocker, J. (1983). Cognitive processes in the revision of stereotypic beliefs. *Journal of Personality and Social Psychology, 45*, 961–977.

Wech, C. E., Lundstrum, R. H., & Moore, A. (1989). Bogus-pipeline effects on self-reported college student drug use, problems, and attitudes. *The International Journal of the Addictions, 24*, 1003–1010.

Wegener, D. T., & Petty, R. E. (1995). Flexible correction processes in social judgment: The role of naive theories in corrections for perceived bias. *Journal of Personality and Social Psychology, 68*, 36–51.

Wegener, D. T., & Petty, R. E. (1997). The flexible correction model: The role of naive theories of bias in bias correction. In M. P. Zanna (Ed.), *Advances in experimental social psychology* (Vol. 29, pp. 141–208). Mahwah, NJ: Lawrence Erlbaum Associates, Inc.

Wegener, D. T., & Petty, R. E. (2001). Understanding effects of mood through the elaboration likelihood and flexible correction models. In L. L. Martin & G. L. Clore (Eds.), *Theories of mood and cognition: A user's guidebook* (pp. 177–210). Mahwah, NJ: Lawrence Erlbaum Associates, Inc.

Wegener, D. T., Petty, R., & Smith, S. M. (1995). Positive mood can increase or decrease message scrutiny: The hedonic contingency view of mood and message processing. *Journal of Personality and Social Psychology, 69*, 5–15.

Wegner, D. (1987). Transactive memory: A contemporary analysis of the group mind. In B. Mullen & G. R. Goethals (Eds.), *Theories of group behavior* (pp. 185–208). New York: Springer.

Wegner, D. M. (1994). Ironic processes of mental control. *Psychological Review, 101*, 34–52.

Wegner, D. M., & Vallacher, R. R. (1986). Action identification. In R. M. Sorrentino & E. T. Higgins (Eds.), *Handbook of motivation and cognition: Foundations of social behavior* (pp. 550–582). New York: Guilford Press.

Weide, J. G., & Wilderom, C. P. M. (2004). Charismatic leadership, environmental dynamism, and performance. *European Journal of Work and Organizational Psychology, 13*, 447–471.

Weiner, B. (1985). An attributional theory of achievement motivation and emotion. *Psychological Review, 92*, 548–573.

Weinstein, N. D. (1987). Unrealistic optimism about susceptibility to health problems: Conclusions from a community-wide sample. *Journal of Behavioral Medicine, 10*, 481–500.

Weisband, S. P., Schneider, S. K., & Connolly, T. (1995). Computer-mediated communication and social information: Status salience and status differences. *Academy of Management Journal, 38*, 1124–1151.

Weisbuch, M., Mackie, D. M., & Garcia-Marques, T. (2003). The impact of prior source exposure on persuasion: Further evidence for mis-attributional explanations of prior of prior exposure. *Personality & Social Psychology Bulletin, 29*, 691–700.

Welbourne, J. L. (2001). Changes in impression complexity over time and across situations. *Personality and Social Psychology Bulletin, 27,* 1071–1085.

Weldon, E., & Mustari, E. L. (1988). Felt dispensability in groups of coactors: The effects of shared responsibility and explicit anonymity on cognitive effort. *Organizational Behavior and Human Decision Processes, 41,* 330–351.

Wellesley College Center for Research on Women (1992). *How schools shortchange girls: The AAUW Report.* Washington, DC: American Association of University Women Educational Foundation.

Wells, G. L., & Gavanski, I. (1989). Mental simulation of causality. *Journal of Personality and Social Psychology, 56,* 161–169.

Wells, G. L., & Petty, R. E. (1980). The effects of overt headmovements on persuasion: Compatibility and incompatibility of responses. *Basic and Applied Social Psychology, 1,* 219–230.

Wenzel, M. (2004). Social identification as a determinant of concerns about individual-, group-, and inclusive-level justice. *Social Psychology Quarterly, 67*(1), 70–87.

Wetherell, M. S. (1987). Social identity and group polarization. In J. C. Turner (Ed.), *Rediscovering the social group: A self-categorization theory.* London: Basil Blackwell.

Whatley, M. A, Webster, J. M., Smith, R. H., & Rhodes, A. (1999). The effect of favor on public and private compliance: How internalized is the norm of reciprocity? *Basic and Applied Social Psychology, 21,* 251–259.

Wheelan, S. A. (1994). *Group processes: A developmental perspective.* Boston, MA: Allyn & Bacon.

Wheelan, S. A., Davidson, B., & Tilin, F. (2003). Group development across time: Reality or illusion? *Small Group Research, 34,* 223–245.

Wheeler, L. (1974). Social comparison and selective affiliation. In T. Huston (Ed.), *Foundations of interpersonal attraction* (pp. 309–330). New York: Academic Press.

White, G. L. (1981). A model of romantic jealousy. *Motivation and Emotion, 5,* 295–310.

White, G. L., Fishbein, S., & Rutstein, J. (1981). Passionate love: The misattribution of arousal. *Journal of Personality and Social Psychology, 41,* 56–62.

White, M., Härtel, C. E. J., & Panipucci, D. (2005). *Understanding cross-cultural negotiation: A model integrating affective events theory and communication accommodation theory.* Mahwah, NJ: Lawrence Erlbaum Associates, Inc.

White, R. K. (1965). Images in the context of international conflict: Soviet perceptions of the U.S. and the U.S.S.R. In H. C. Kelman (Ed.), *International behavior: A social-psychological analysis* (pp. 236–276). New York: Holt, Rinehart & Winston.

White, R. K. (1971). Selective inattention. *Psychology Today,* pp. 47–50, 78–84.

White, R. K. (1977). Misperception in the Arab–Israeli conflict. *Journal of Social Issues, 33,* 190–221.

White, R. K. (1984). *Fearful warriors: A psychological profile in U.S.–Soviet relations.* New York: Free Press.

White, R. K. (1987). Underestimating and overestimating others' fear. *Journal of Social Issues, 43*(4), 105–110.

White, R. W. (1959). Motivation reconsidered: The concept of competence. *Psychological Review, 66,* 297–333.

Whittington, J. L., Goodwin, V. L., & Murray, B. (2004). Transformational leadership, goal difficulty, and job design: Independent and interactive effects on employee outcomes. *Leadership Quarterly, 15,* 593–606.

Whyte, G., Saks, A., & Hook, S. (1997). When success breeds failure: The role of self-efficacy in escalating commitment to a losing course of action. *Journal of Organizational Behavior, 18,* 415–432.

Wicker, A. W. (1969). Attitudes versus actions: The relationship of verbal and overt behavioral responses to attitude objects. *Journal of Social Issues, 25,* 41–78.

Widom, C. S. (1989). The cycle of violence. *Science, 244,* 160–166.

Wierzbicka, A. (1994). Emotion, language, and cultural scripts. In S. Kitayama & H. R. Markus (Eds.), *Emotion and culture: Empirical studies of mutual influence* (pp. 133–196). Washington, DC: American Psychological Association.

Wilder, D. A. (1977). Perception of groups, size of opposition, and social influence. *Journal of Experimental Social Psychology, 13,* 253–268.

Wilder, D. A. (1981). Perceiving persons as a group: Categorization and intergroup relations. In D. L. Hamilton (Ed.), *Cognitive processes in stereotyping and intergroup behavior* (pp. 213–258). Hillsdale, NJ: Lawrence Erlbaum Associates, Inc.

Wilder, D. A. (1984). Intergroup contact: The typical member and the exception to the rule. *Journal of Experimental Social Psychology, 20,* 177–94.

Wilder, D. A. (1986). Social categorization: Implications for creation and reduction of intergroup bias. In L. Berkowitz (Ed.), *Advances in experimental social psychology* (Vol. 19, pp. 291–355). New York: Academic Press.

Wilder, D. A. (1990). Some determinants of the persuasive power of in-groups and out-groups: Organization of information and attribution of independence. *Journal of Personality and Social Psychology, 59,* 1202–1213.

Wilder, D. A., & Shapiro, P. N. (1984). Role of out-group cues in determining social identity. *Journal of Personality and Social Psychology, 47,* 342–348.

Wilder, D. A., & Shapiro, P. N. (1988). Role of competition-induced anxiety in limiting the beneficial impact of positive behavior by out-group members. *Journal of Personality and Social Psychology, 56,* 60–69.

Wilder, D. A., & Shapiro, P. (1991). Facilitation of outgroup stereotypes by enhanced ingroup identity. *Journal of Experimental Social Psychology, 27,* 431–452.

Wilder, D. A., & Thompson, J. E. (1980). Intergroup contact with independent manipulations of in-group and out-group interaction. *Journal of Personality and Social Psychology, 38,* 589–603.

Wildschut, T., Pinter, B., Vevea, J. L., Insko, C. A., & Schopler, J. (2003). Beyond the group mind: A quantitative review of the interindividual–intergroup discontinuity effect. *Psychological Bulletin, 129*(5), 698–722.

Wilke, H., & Lanzetta, J. T. (1970). The obligation to help: The effects of amount of prior help on subsequent helping behavior. *Journal of Experimental Social Psychology, 6,* 488–493.

Wilke, H., & Lanzetta, J. T. (1982). The obligation to help: Factor affecting response to help received. *European Journal of Social Psychology, 12,* 315–319.

Williams, A., & Giles, H. (1998). Communication of ageism. In M. C. Hecht (Ed.), *Communicating prejudice* (pp. 136–160). Thousand Oaks, CA: Sage Publications.

Williams, E. (1977). Experimental comparisons of face-to-face and mediated communication: A review. *Psychological Bulletin, 84,* 963–976.

Williams, J. E., & Best, D. L. (1982). *Measuring sex stereotypes: A thirty-nation study.* Beverly Hills, CA: Sage Publications.

Williams, K. D., Harkins, S., & Latané, B. (1981). Identifiability as a deterrent to social loafing: Two cheering experiments. *Journal of Personality and Social Psychology, 40,* 303–311.

Williams, L. (1991, November 30). In a 90s quest for black identity, intense doubts and disagreement. *New York Times,* pp. A1, A7.

Williamson, G. M., & Clark, M. S. (1989). Providing help and desired relationship type as determinants of changes in moods and self-evaluations. *Journal of Personality and Social Psychology, 56,* 722–734.

Willis, R. (1986, March). Harley Davidson comes roaring back. *Management Review,* 20–27.

Wills, T. A. (1991). Social support and interpersonal relations. In M. S. Clark (Ed.), *Prosocial behavior* (pp. 265–289). Beverly Hills, CA: Sage.

Wilson, B., Kunkel, D., Linz, D., Potter, J., Donnerstein, E., Smith, S., Blumenthal, E., & Berry, M. (1998). Violence in television programming overall: University of California, Santa Barbara study. In *National television violence study* (Vol. 2, pp. 5–204). Thousand Oaks, CA: Sage.

Wilson, J. (2000). Volunteering. *Annual Review of Sociology, 26,* 215–240.

Wilson, T. D., & Dunn, D. S. (1986). Effects of introspection on attitude–behavior consistency. Analyzing reasons versus focusing on feelings. *Journal of Experimental Social Psychology, 22,* 249–263.

Wilson, T. D., Gilbert, D. T., & Wheatley, T.P. (1998). Protecting our minds: The role of lay beliefs. In V. Yzerbyt, G. Lories, & B. Dardenne (Eds.), *Metacognition: Cognitive and social dimensions* (pp. 171–201). New York: Sage.

Wilson, T. D., Houston, C. E., & Meyers, J. M. (1998). Choose your posion: Effects of lay beliefs about mental processes on attitude change. *Social Cognition, 16,* 114–132.

Wilson, T. D., Laser, P. S., & Stone, J. I. (1982). Judging the predictors of one's own mood: Accuracy and the use of shared theories. *Journal of Experimental Social Psychology, 18,* 537–549.

Wilson, T. D., Lindsey, S., & Schooler, T. Y. (2000). A model of dual attitudes. *Psychological Review, 107,* 101–126.

Wilson, T. D., Lisle, D. J., Schooler, J. W., Hodges, S. D., Klaaren, K. J., & LaFleur, S. J. (1993). Introspecting about reasons can reduce post-choice satisfaction. *Personality and Social Psychology Bulletin, 19,* 331–339.

Winkielman, P., Berridge, K. C., & Wilbarger, J. L. (2005). *Emotion, behavior, and conscious experience: Once more without feeling.* New York: Guilford Press.

Witte, K. (1992). Putting the fear back into fear appeals: The extended parallel process model. *Communication Monographs, 59,* 329–349.

Wittenbrink, B., Judd, C. M., & Park, B. (2001). Evaluative versus conceptual judgments in automatic stereotyping and prejudice. *Journal of Experimental Social Psychology, 37,* 244–252.

Wolfgang, M., & Strohm, R. B. (1956). The relationship between alcohol and criminal homicide. *Quarterly Journal of Studies on Alcohol, 17,* 411–425.

Wolsko, C., Park, B., Judd, C. M., & Bachelor, J. (2003). Intergroup contact: Effects on group evaluations and perceived variability. *Group Processes and Intergroup Relations, 6,* 93–110.

Wolsko, C., Park, B., Judd, C. M., & Wittenbrink, B. (2000). Framing interethnic ideology: Effects of multicultural and color-blind perspectives on judgments of groups and individuals. *Journal of Personality and Social Psychology, 78*(4), 635–654.

Wood, J. V. (1989). Theory and research concerning social comparisons of personal attributes. *Psychological Bulletin, 106,* 231–248.

Wood, J. V., Taylor, S. E., & Lichtman, R. R. (1985). Social comparison in adjustment to breast cancer. *Journal of Personality and Social Psychology, 49,* 1169–1183.

Wood, W. (1987). Meta-analytic review of sex differences in group performance. *Psychological Bulletin, 102,* 53–71.

Wood, W., Christensen, P. N., Hebl, M. R., & Rothgerber, H. (1997) Conformity to sex-typed norms, affect, and the self-concept. *Journal of Personality and Social Psychology, 73,* 523–535.

Wood, W., & Eagly, A. H. (2002). A cross-cultural analysis of the behavior of women and men: Implications for the origins of sex differences. *Psychological Review, 128,* 699–727.

Wood, W., Kallgren, C. A., & Preisler, R. M. (1985). Access to attitude-relevant information in memory as a determinant of persuasion: The role of message attributes. *Journal of Experimental Social Psychology, 21,* 73–85.

Wood, W. Lundgren, S., Ouellette, J. A., Busceme, S., & Blackstone, T. (1994). Minority influence: A meta-analytic review of social influence processes. *Psychological Bulletin, 115,* 323–345.

Wood, W., Pool, G. J., Leck, K., & Purivs, D. (1996). Self-definition, defensive processing, and influence: The normative impact of majority and minority groups. *Journal of Personality and Social Psychology, 71,* 1181–1193.

Wood, W., Rhodes, N., & Beik, M. (1995). Working knowledge and attitude strength: An information processing analysis. In R. E. Petty & J. A. Krosnick (Eds.), *Attitude strength: Antecedents and consequences* (pp. 283–313). Hillsdale, NJ: Lawrence Erlbaum Associates, Inc.

Wood, W., Tam, L., & Witt, M. G. (2005). Changing circumstances, disrupting habits. *Journal of Personality and Social Psychology, 88,* 918–933.

Wood, W., Wong, F., & Chachere, J. (1991). Effects of media violence on viewers' aggression in unconstrained social interaction. *Psychological Bulletin, 109,* 371–383.

Wootton, B. H. (1997, April). Gender differences in occupational employment. *Monthly Labor Review,* 15–24.

Worchel, S. (1979). Cooperation and the reduction of intergroup conflict: Some determining factors. In W. G. Austin & S. Worchel (Eds.), *The social psychology of intergroup conflict* (pp. 262–273). Monterey, CA: Brooks/Cole.

Worchel, S., Lee, J., & Adewole, A. (1975). Effects of supply and demand on ratings of object value. *Journal of Personality and Social Psychology, 32,* 906–914.

Worchel, S., & Norvell, N. (1980). Effect of perceived environmental conditions during cooperation on intergroup attraction. *Journal of Personality and Social Psychology, 38,* 264–772.

Word, C. O., Zanna, M. P., & Cooper, J. (1974). The nonverbal mediation of self-fulfilling prophecies in interracial interaction. *Journal of Experimental Social Psychology, 10,* 109–120.

Worringham, C. J., & Messick, D. M. (1983). Social facilitation of running: An unobtrusive study. *Journal of Social Psychology*, *121*, 23–29.

Worth, L. T., & Mackie, D. M. (1987). Cognitive mediation of positive affect in persuasion. *Social Cognition*, *5*, 76–94.

Wortman, C., Adesman, P., Herman, E., & Greenberg, R. (1976). Self-disclosure: An attributional perspective. *Journal of Personality and Social Psychology*, *33*, 184–191.

Wright, D. B., Self, G., & Justice, C. (2000). Memory conformity: Exploring misinformation effects when presented by another person. *British Journal of Psychology*, *91*, 189–202.

Wright, J. C., & Mischel, W. (1987). A conditional approach to dispositional constructs: The local predictability of social behavior. *Journal of Personality and Social Psychology*, *53*, 1159–1177.

Wright, P. H. (1982). Men's friendships, women's friendships and the alleged inferiority of the latter. *Sex Roles*, *8*, 1–20.

Wright, Q. (1965). Escalation of international conflicts. *Journal of Conflict Resolution*, *9*, 434–449.

Wright, S. C., Aron, A., McLaughlin-Volpe, T., & Ropp, S. A. (1997). The extended contact effect: Knowledge of cross-group friendships and prejudice. *Journal of Personality and Social Psychology*, *73*, 73–90.

Wright, S. C., Taylor, D. M., & Moghaddam, F. M. (1990). Responding to membership in a disadvantaged group: From acceptance to collective protest. *Journal of Personality and Social Psychology*, *58*, 994–1003.

Wyer, R. S., & Srull, T. K. (1989). *Memory and cognition in its social context*. Hillsdale, NJ: Lawrence Erlbaum Associates, Inc.

X, M. (1966). *The autobiography of Malcolm X*. New York: Grove Press.

Yamagishi, T. (1986). The provision of a sanctioning system as a public good. *Journal of Personality and Social Psychology*, *51*, 110–116.

Yang, A. S. (1997). Trends: Attitudes toward homosexuality. *Public Opinion Quarterly*, *61*, 477–507.

Young, A. M., & Acitelli, L. K. (1998). The role of attachment style and relationship status of the perceiver in the perceptions of romantic partner. *Journal of Social and Personal Relationships*, *15*, 161–173.

Yovetich, N. A., & Rusbult, C. E. (1994). Accommodative behavior in close relationships: Exploring transformation of motivation. *Journal of Experimental Social Psychology*, *30*, 138–164.

Yukl, G. (1999). An evaluation of conceptual weaknesses in transformational and charismatic leadership theories. *Leadership Quarterly. Special Issue: Charismatic and Transformational Leadership: Taking Stock of the Present and Future*, *10*, 285–305.

Yzerbyt, V., Rocher, S., & Schadron, G. (1997). Stereotypes as explanations: A subjective essentialistic view of group perception. In R. Spears, P. J. Oakes, N. Ellemers, & S. A. Haslam (Eds.), *The social psychology of stereotyping and group life* (pp. 20–50). Cambridge, UK: Blackwell.

Zaccaro, S. J. (1984). Social loafing: The role of task attractiveness. *Personality and Social Psychology Bulletin*, *10*, 99–106.

Zaccaro, S. J., Foti, R. J., & Kenny, D. A. (1991). Self-monitoring and trait-based variance in leadership: An investigation of leader flexibility across multiple group situations. *Journal of Applied Psychology*, *76*, 308–315.

Zajonc, R. B. (1965). Social facilitation. *Science*, *149*, 269–274.

Zajonc, R. B. (1968). Attitudinal effects of mere exposure. *Journal of Personality and Social Psychology*, *9* (Monograph Suppl. No. 2, part 2).

Zajonc, R. B. (1980). Feeling and thinking: Preferences need no inferences. *American Psychologist*, *35*, 151–175.

Zajonc, R. B. (1998). Emotions. In D. T. Gilbert, S. T. Fiske, & G. Lindzey (Eds.), *Handbook of social psychology* (4th ed., Vol. 1, pp. 591–634). Boston: McGraw-Hill.

Zajonc, R. B., & Sales, S. M. (1966). Social facilitation of dominant and subordinate responses. *Journal of Experimental Social Psychology*, *2*, 160–168.

Zanna, M. P., Crosby, F., & Loewenstein, G. (1987). Male reference groups and discontent among female professionals. In B. A. Gutek & L. Larwood (Eds.), *Women's career development* (pp. 28–41). Newbury Park, CA: Sage Publications.

Zanna, M. P., & Rempel, J. K. (1988). Attitudes: A new look at an old concept. In D. Bar-Tal & A. Kruglanski (Eds.), *The social psychology of knowledge* (pp. 315–334). New York: Cambridge University Press.

Zárate, M. A., & Smith, E. R. (1990). Person categorization and stereotyping. *Social Cognition*, *8*, 161–185.

Zebrowitz, L. A., & Collins, M. A. (1997). Accurate social perception at zero acquaintance: The affordances of a Gibsonian approach. *Personality and Social Psychology Review*, *1*, 204–223.

Zebrowitz, L. A., Hall, J. A., Murphy, N. A., & Rhodes, G. (2002). Looking smart and looking good: Facial cues to intelligence and their origin. *Personality and Social Psychology Bulletin*, *28*, 238–249.

Zebrowitz, L. A., Tenenbaum, D. R., & Goldstein, L. H. (1991). The impact of job applicants' facial maturity, sex, and academic achievement on hiring recommendations. *Journal of Applied Social Psychology*, *21*, 525–548.

Zillman, D. (1979). *Hostility and aggression*. Hillsdale, NJ: Lawrence Erlbaum Associates, Inc.

Zillman, D. (1982). Transfer of excitation in emotional behavior. In J. T. Cacioppo & R. E. Petty (Eds.), *Social psychophysiology* (pp. 215–240). New York: Guilford Press.

Zimbardo, P. G. (1970). The human choice: Individuation, reason, and order versus deindividuation, impulse, and chaos. In W. J. Arnold & D. Levine (Eds.), *Nebraska symposium on motivation 1969* (Vol. 17, pp. 237–307). Lincoln: University of Nebraska Press.

Zimbardo, P. G., Banks, W. C., Haney, C., & Jaffe, D. (1973, April 8). The mind is a formidable jailer: A Pirandellian prison. *New York Times Magazine*, pp. 38–60.

Zuckerman, M. (1979). *Sensation seeking: Beyond the optimal level of arousal*. Hillsdale, NJ: Lawrence Erlbaum Associates, Inc.

Zuckerman, M., DePaulo, B. M., & Rosenthal, R. (1981). Verbal and nonverbal communication of deception. In L. Berkowitz (Ed.), *Advances in experimental social psychology* (Vol. 14, pp. 1–59). New York: Academic Press.

Author Index

Subject Index

Note: Page Numbers in **bold** refer to key definitions, those in *italics* to figures and tables.

647

Counterfactual thinking, 346
Counterstereotypes, 171, 178–179
Covariation information, 75
Crime, and stereotypes, 156
Cross-categorization, 220
Cross-race identification bias, 203
Crowding, 444–445
    cross-cultural differences, *445*
    and stress, *126*
Cues, 58–72, 93
    attention capturing by, 63–64
    destructive, 308
    different, *58*
    heuristic, 240–245, 249
    interpretation of, 64–69
    minimization of, 504
    salient, 62–63, *63*, 93
    to aggression, 482–483
Cultural issues
    advertising, 234
    aggression, 282–283
    association, 65
    attitudes, 234
    attributions, 75–77
    choice of mate, *106*
    conformity, 314
    crowding, *445*
    deservingness, 520
    dissonance, 287–289
    ethnic groups, 34
    ethnic languages, 191
    ethnic violence, 8, 11
    external validity, 39–40
    generalization, *42*
    goals, 120
    group membership, 192–193
    helping, 532
    identification bias, 203
    love, 420
    negotiation, 508–509
    racial concept, 144
    racial discrimination, 141
    relationships, 416–417
    self-concept, 104–107
    self-esteem, 113–114
    social commitment, 366
    social dilemmas, 136
    social loafing, 453
    stereotypes, 146, 463
Cultures
    collectivist (interdependent), 40,
        105–*107*, 113–114
    individualist (independent), 40,
        105–*107*, 113–114

Darwin, Charles, 199, 435
Death, of spouses, 434
Debriefing, **51**, 54
Deception
    detection of, 61–62
    in research, 50–51
Decisional dissonance, 283
Decisions, justification of, 283–284
Defense

    against threats, 128–131
    of attitudes, 258–265, 267
    of impressions, 82–91, 93
    of individual self-esteem, 212–216
    of the self, 125–136, 138
Deindividuation, 358–360, *359*, **359**,
    360, 390
Demand characteristics, **41**
Deming, W. Edwards, 456
Dependent variables, **30**, 54
Depolarization effect, 322
Depression, *128*, 212
    clinical, 128
    and control, 127–128
Depressive attributional style, 128
Deprivation, relative, 11
Depth versus superficiality, **19**, 23
Desensitization, 501
Deservingness
    cultural differences in, 520
    judging of, 520–521
Design
    experimental, *36*
    nonexperimental, *36*
Deterrence, in international affairs, 495
Devil's advocates, 337–338
Diagnostic questioning, 86–87
Diallo, Amadou, 166–167, 487
Diffusion of responsibility, 521–522,
    522, 541
Disagreement, effects of, 317
Discounting, 77
Discrimination, 8, 13, **141**–142, 183
    fueled by threat, 208
    global, 142
    and religion, 144
    and social identity, 204–206
Discussion groups, 11
Dishonesty, and stealing, 65
Disidentification, 216–217
Disjunctive tasks, 451
Dismissing attachment, 413–415, 428, 437
Dissent
    learning independence from, *340*
    value of, 338–348
Dissociation, 216–218
Dissonance, *See* Cognitive dissonance
Distinctiveness information, 75
Distraction, 253, 443–444
Distributive solutions, 505
Divorce, 7
Dominant responses, 441
Door-in-the-face technique, 362–363,
    363, 390
Dordain, Jean-Jacques, 243
Double minorities, 340
Downward comparisons, 111
Drug addicts, 218
Dunleavy, Mike, *101*

Eagles, *31*, 473, 503, *510*, 511
Education issues, 14
    accessibility of gender identity, 195
    coaching leadership in youth sports,

        460–461
    self-fulfilling prophecies, 88, 174–175
Effort-justification effect, 282–283
Egoism, **518**, 550
    and helping, 528–529
Egoistic relative deprivation, 490–491
Eichmann, Adolf, 369
Eisenhower, Dwight D., 458
Elaboration, **247**, 267
Elderly, organizations for, 220
Electromyography (EMG), *163*
Eliot, George, 270
Emotion-focused coping, 128–131
Emotional appeals, 238
Emotional expressions, 61, 66–67, *67*
Emotions
    and action regulation, 294
    and appraisal, *116*–118
    causes of, 116–118
    components of, *119*
    effect on motivation, 453–454
    and group interactions, 154–156
    impact on conflict, 498–499
    negative, 256–257
    positive, 256
    and the self, 115–118
    and social identity, 196
    and stereotyping, 168–169
Empathy, 529–531, 544
    promotion of, 504–505
Empathy-altruism model, 530
Enforcement, of norms, 355–356
Environmental issues, 14
    crowding in urban settings, 444–445
    littering, 354–355
    norms, 354–355
Environments, impressions from, 63
Envy, 426
Error, 26, 29
Escape, from threat, 129
Ethics, 26
    role in research, 47–54
Ethnic groups
    contact with, 34
    stereotypes and leadership, 463
    See also Cultural issues; Cultures;
        Prejudice
Ethnic violence, 8, 11, 491
Euphemisms, 208, 378
Evaluation apprehension, 442–443
Evaluative conditioning, 155, 239–240
Exchange relationships, **402**, 436
Excuses, 131–132
Expectations
    of agreement, 315
    and reaction to others, 66
Experimental research, **35**, 36, 54
    conditions, 35
Expertise heuristic, 242–244
Explicit attitudes, 232
External validity, 30, **37**, 46–47, 54
    and cultures, 39–40
    ensuring, 42
    and laboratory research, 40–41

Rebellion, against authority, 379–384, 391
Recategorization, 220–221
Reciprocity, 525
  and concessions, 362–364
  of favors, 361–362
  norms of, 360–365, *362*, 390, 508
  on the sales floor, 364–365
Reference group, **319**–322, 348
Reich, Robert, 455
Relation, to others, 7
Relationships, 435–436
  aftermath of, 432–435
  break-up of, 432–435, 437
  close, 404–419, **405**, 436
  communal, **402**, 436
  conflict in, 425–426
  in cultural perspective, 416–417
  deterioration in, 425–435
  development of, 401–404, 436
  effects of, 417–419
  evolutionary theories about, 396–397
  exchange, **402**, 436
  exchanges of rewards in, 402–403
  gender differences in, 416
  insider/outsider perspectives on, 407–408
  interdependence in, 425–426
  maintenance of, 426–428
  satisfaction with, 411
  sexual activity in, 423–424
  strong, 435
  theories about, 415–416
  types of, 413–417
Relative deprivation, egoistic and fraternal, 490–491
Relative deprivation theory, **490**–491, 515
Religion, and discrimination, 144
Replication, **44**, 54
  importance of, 44–45
Research, 20–21
  asking and answering questions, 25–55
  deception in, 50–51
  design types, 33–36
  experimental design, 35, 54
  field, 41
  helpfulness to society, 52–53
  laboratory, 40–41
  nonexperimental design, 34, 54
  nonlaboratory, 41–42
  questions, 27–29
  role of ethics in, 47–53
  role in theory support, *44*
  role of values in, 47–53
  testing theories by, 29–47, 54
Resistance, to authority, 379–384, 391
Resources, and conflict, 489–490
Respect
  and aggression, 491
  in groups, 492
Responses
  bodily, 118
  dominant and nondominant, 441

Responsibility
  acceptance by authority, 374–375
  assertion of, *375*
  diffusion of, 521–522, *522*, 541
  infusion of, 547–548
Rewards
  exchanges of, 402–403, 408–410
  team-based, 456
Risky shift, 323
Rivalry, intergroup, 191–192
Robbers Cave experiment, 473–474, 503, 509–510
Roddick, Andy, *68*
Role models, 211
Roles, affect of, 190
Romantic love, 220, 419–424, 437
  cultural differences in, 420
  See also Love; Loving
Ross, E. A., 9
Routinization, 501
Ruffin, Michael, *101*
Rumors, 242
Ruskin, John, 454

Sadat, President Anwar, 483–485
Salience, **63**
  of group norms, 358–360
Salient features, 74–75
Scapegoating, 502
Schnyder, Patty, 244
Scientific theory, 27–**28**
Secure attachment, 413–415, 428, 431, 437
Seeking connectedness, **17**, 23, 225, 266, 347, 389, 435, 470, 513, 548, 554
Self, the, 21, 95–139
  in action, 118–121
  and behavior, 123–124
  best friend as, *409*
  cultural views of, 104–107
  defense of, 125–136, 138
  and dissonance, 289
  effects of, 114–125, 137
  and emotions, 115–118
  feelings about, 107–114
  multiple, 102–103
  and others, 100–102, 114–115
  and partner, 406–408
  valuation of, *223*
  well-being of, 125–128
  See also Self-concept
Self-aspects, 103, 110
Self-awareness, **120**, 138
  and accessibility of attitudes, 297
Self-categorization, **189**–194, 225
Self-complexity, 110
  and self-concepts, *105*
Self-concept, **96**, *125*, 137
  coherent, 103–104, *113*
  construction of, 96–107, 137
  cultural differences in, 104–107
  and reactions of others, 98–99
  and self-complexity, *105*
  sources of, 96–100
  See also Self, the

Self-consciousness, measures of, *121*
Self-criticism, 114
Self-disclosure, 403–404
Self-discrepancy, negative effects of, 120–121
Self-discrepancy theory, **119**, *120*, 137
Self-efficacy, 132, 541, 545
Self-enhancement, 95, 137
  reasons for, 112
  and self-knowledge, 107–109
  See also Valuing "me and mine"
Self-enhancing attributions, 131
Self-enhancing bias, **109**, 134–135, 137
Self-esteem, 96, **107**, 112, 137
  collective, 212
  construction of, 107–114, 137
  and coping, 134–135
  in a cultural context, 113–114
  defending individual, 212–216
  effects of stereotypes on, 212
  help as threat to, 545–546
  and social comparisons, 110–112
  and social identity, 195–196
Self-evaluation maintenance model, 110
Self-expression, **122**, 130–131, 138
Self-focusing, 120–121
Self-fulfilling prophecy, *87*, **87**–89, 93, 99, 174
  about leadership, 463
  in classroom, 88, 174–175
  limits to, 88–89
  in workplace, 88, 174–175
Self-guides, 119
Self-handicapping, 131, 132
Self-help, subliminal, 264–265, *265*
Self-image, maintaining positive, 367
Self-interest, versus group interest, 532–534
Self-knowledge, 96–107, 137
  accessibility of, 103
  and attribution, 104
  importance of, 96
  and selective memory, 104
  and self-enhancement, 107–109
  sources of, *100*
  through key traits, 104
Self-monitoring, *124*, **124**–125, 138, 254–255
  and attitude accessibility, 296, 388
  and attractiveness, 395–396
  and persuasion, *255*
Self-perception, 303, 541
  and volunteering, 275
Self-perception theory, 45–46, **97**, 137, 273
Self-presentation, **122**–123, *123*, 138
  need for audience to, 124
Self-regulation, 137
  processes of, 114–125
  threats to, 121–122
Self-relevance, 250–252
Self-report, 230–231, *231*
  measures, 32
Self-schema, 104

Index compiled by L. N. Derrick